THE HANDBOOK OF

# THE POLITICAL ECONOMY OF FINANCIAL CRISES

THE HANDBOOK OF

# THE POLITICAL ECONOMY OF FINANCIAL CRISES

*Edited by*

MARTIN H. WOLFSON

*and*

GERALD A. EPSTEIN

OXFORD
UNIVERSITY PRESS

OXFORD
UNIVERSITY PRESS

Oxford University Press is a department of the University of Oxford.
It furthers the University's objective of excellence in research, scholarship,
and education by publishing worldwide.

Oxford New York
Auckland Cape Town Dar es Salaam Hong Kong Karachi
Kuala Lumpur Madrid Melbourne Mexico City Nairobi
New Delhi Shanghai Taipei Toronto

With offices in
Argentina Austria Brazil Chile Czech Republic France Greece
Guatemala Hungary Italy Japan Poland Portugal Singapore
South Korea Switzerland Thailand Turkey Ukraine Vietnam



Published in the United States of America by
Oxford University Press
198 Madison Avenue, New York, NY 10016



First issued as an Oxford University Press paperback, 2015.



Library of Congress Cataloging-in-Publication Data
The handbook of the political economy of financial crises / edited by
Martin H. Wolfson and Gerald A. Epstein.
p. cm.
Includes bibliographical references and index.
ISBN 978-0-19-975723-7 (cloth : alk. paper); 978-0-19-024093-6 (paper : alk. paper)
1. Global Financial Crisis, 2008-2009. 2. Business cycles—United States—History—21st century
3. Monetary policy—United States— History—21st century. 4. United States—Economic policy—
21st century. 5. United States— Politics and government—21st century.
I. Wolfson, Martin H. II. Epstein, Gerald A. III. Title: Handbook of the political economy of financial crises.
HB37172008-2009 .O94 2013
332.0973—dc23
2012016693

# Contents

# CONTRIBUTORS

**Dean Baker** is a codirector of the Center for Economic and Policy Research in Washington, DC.

**Josh Bivens** is Acting Research and Policy Director at the Economic Policy Institute in Washington, DC.

**Zuzana Brixiová** is Economic Advisor at the United Nations Development Programme in Swaziland.

**C. P. Chandrasekhar** is Professor of Economics at the Centre for Economic Studies and Planning in the School of Social Sciences at Jawaharlal Nehru University in New Delhi, India.

**James Crotty** is Professor Emeritus in the Department of Economics at the University of Massachusetts at Amherst and a Research Associate at the Political Economy Research Institute at the University of Massachusetts at Amherst.

**Mario Damill** is a researcher at Centro de Estudios de Estado y Sociedad and the National Council for Scientific and Technical Research in Buenos Aires, Argentina.

**Jane D'Arista** writes and lectures on economics and finance and is a research associate at the Political Economy Research Institute at the University of Massachusetts at Amherst.

**Rachel B. Drew** is a Ph.D. student in the Public Policy program at the McCormack School of Policy and Global Affairs at the University of Massachusetts at Boston.

**Gary Dymski** is Professor of Economics at the University of California, Riverside.

**Gerald A. Epstein** is Professor of Economics and a codirector of the Political Economy Research Institute at the University of Massachusetts at Amherst.

**Korkut Erturk** is Professor of Economics at the University of Utah in Salt Lake City.

**Duncan K. Foley** is the Leo Model Professor of Economics at the New School for Social Research in New York City and External Professor at the Santa Fe Institute.

**Roberto Frenkel** is Principal Research Associate at Centro de Estudios de Estado y Sociedad and Professor at Buenos Aires University in Buenos Aires, Argentina.

**Teresa Ghilarducci** is Professor of Economics, and Director of the Schwartz Center for Economic Policy Analysis at the New School for Social Research in New York.

**Jayati Ghosh** is Professor of Economics at the Centre for Economic Studies and Planning in the School of Social Sciences at Jawaharlal Nehru University in New Delhi, India.

**Ilene Grabel** is Professor of International Finance and codirector of the Masters in Global Finance, Trade and Economic Integration Program at the Josef Korbel School of International Studies at the University of Denver, Colorado.

**Michael Greenberger** is the founder and director of the Center for Health and Homeland Security and a Professor at the University of Maryland School of Law in Baltimore, Maryland.

**Robert Guttmann** is Professor of Economics at Hofstra University in Hempstead, New York.

**Pierre Habbard** is Senior Policy Advisor to the Trade Union Advisory Committee to the Organisation for Economic Co-operation and Development in Paris, France.

**Dorene Isenberg** is Professor of Economics at the University of Redlands, California.

**Marc Jarsulic** is the chief economist for Better Markets, Inc., in Washington, DC.

**Arjun Jayadev** is Assistant Professor of Economics at the University of Massachusetts at Boston.

**David M. Kotz** is Professor of Economics at the University of Massachusetts at Amherst.

**Jan Kregel** is a senior scholar at the Levy Economics Institute of Bard College and director of the Monetary Policy and Financial Structure Program. He currently holds the positions of Distinguished Research Professor at the Center for Full Employment and Price Stability of the University of Missouri in Kansas City and Professor of Development Finance at the Tallinn University of Technology.

**Costas Lapavitsas** is Professor of Economics at the School of Oriental and African Studies in London.

**William Lazonick** is Professor and Director of the UMass Center for Industrial Competitiveness, and President of the Academic-Industry Research Network.

**Minqi Li** is Associate Professor of Economics at the University of Utah, Salt Lake City.

**Robert N. McCauley** is a senior advisor in the Monetary and Economic Department of the Bank for International Settlements in Basel.

**Fred Moseley** is Professor of Economics at Mount Holyoke College.

**Léonce Ndikumana** is the Andrew Glyn Professor of Economics, and Director of the African Policy Program at the Political Economy Research Institute at the University of Massachusetts at Amherst.

**José Antonio Ocampo** is Professor and Director of the Economic and Political Development Program in the School of International and Public Affairs, and Fellow of the Committee on Global Thought at Columbia University.

**Thomas I. Palley** holds a Ph.D. in Economics from Yale University and is Senior Economic Policy Adviser to the AFL-CIO.

**José Gabriel Palma** is University Senior Lecturer in the Faculty of Economics at Cambridge University and a coeditor of the *Cambridge Journal of Economics*.

**Dominique Plihon** is Professor of Economics at the University of Paris XIII, France.

**Martin Rapetti** is a researcher at Centro de Estudios de Estado y Sociedad and Professor at Buenos Aires University in Argentina.

**Christopher Rude** holds a Ph.D. in Economics from the New School for Social Research, and writes and lectures on economics and political economy in New York.

**Heidi Shierholz** is an economist at the Economic Policy Institute in Washington, DC.

**Damon Silvers** is the Director of Policy and Special Counsel for the AFL-CIO. He serves on a pro bono basis as a Special Assistant Attorney General for the state of New York and is also a member of the Public Company Accounting Oversight Board's Standing Advisory Group and Investor Advisory Group.

**Ajit Singh** is Professor Emeritus of Economics at the University of Cambridge.

**Engelbert Stockhammer** is Professor of Economics at Kingston University, London.

**William K. Tabb** is the author of *The Restructuring of Capitalism in Our Time* (Columbia University Press, 2012).

**Jennifer S. Taub** is Associate Professor of Law at the Vermont Law School in South Royalton.

**Christian E. Weller** is Professor of Public Policy and Public Affairs at the McCormack Graduate School at the University of Massachusetts at Boston, and a senior fellow at the Center for American Progress in Washington, DC.

**Martin H. Wolfson** teaches economics and is the Director of the Higgins Labor Studies Program at the University of Notre Dame, Indiana.

**L. Randall Wray** is Professor of Economics at the University of Missouri in Kansas City, and Senior Scholar at the Levy Economics Institute of Bard College, New York.

THE HANDBOOK OF

# THE POLITICAL ECONOMY OF FINANCIAL CRISES

## CHAPTER 1

# INTRODUCTION

# THE POLITICAL ECONOMY OF FINANCIAL CRISES

GERALD A. EPSTEIN
AND MARTIN H. WOLFSON

THE world financial crisis that began to develop in 2007 has proven to be longer lasting, more complex, and more devastating than even some of the strongest critics had expected. By the end of 2011, at least four years from the start of the crisis, the spread of the crisis to the eurozone threatened to break apart the euro area and, according to some observers, transform the Great Recession into a genuine Great Depression on a global scale (Buiter, 2011). The costs of the financial crisis, which has transformed into a major economic crisis that spans several continents, have already taken a massive toll on people's livelihoods and on the balance sheets of households, corporations, banks, and nations. Andrew Haldane (2010) of the Bank of England has estimated that these costs could ultimately amount to between $60 trillion and $200 trillion (that's right: trillion).

What caused this financial meltdown? Why has it been so severe? What kind of theoretical framework can we use to help us understand its nature and dynamics? Who has been hurt and helped by this crisis?

Because the crisis is a global one, what is the global context within which this is occurring? For example, is the crisis manifesting itself differently in different places depending on their financial structures, political structures, and nature of their integration into the global economy? What are the regional variations that we must take into account in developing our understanding of the crisis?

What solutions have been tried and with what effects? Are they sufficient to prevent future crises? Throughout, we ask what political economy forces of power and politics have shaped the causes, dynamics, and responses to the recent crisis? Finally, do our economies need to move beyond capitalism to truly solve this crisis and create a period of sustainable development for the world economy?

This book addresses these and related questions, with a focus on financial aspects of the crisis. Of course, financial crises are not new. Indeed, they are endemic to capitalism as Charles Kindleberger (1978) so well reminded us, and as Reinhart and Rogoff (2008) have recently detailed. But crises can vary quite dramatically over time and across space. It is precisely this variation, as well as the common features of financial crises, that this book tries to capture.

We recognize that financial crises are not caused by finance alone and certainly have impacts that go way beyond finance. The chapters in this book attempt to take this into account by setting the financial causes and impacts of the economic troubles we are facing into the broader context of shifts in the underlying relations of the world economy. The shifts include, for example, the integration of China, India, and other developing countries into the world economy, and the resultant "global imbalances"—the huge current account surpluses of China and other developing countries and some developed countries such as Germany, and the large deficits of the United States in particular. They also include the rise of the neoliberal global economy, which has led to a reduction in labor's bargaining power and an increase in inequality and stagnation of wage incomes in many parts of the world.

But this book focuses on other equally profound, broad, and important shifts that have emanated from the financial sector: the rise of financialization, the deregulation of finance, the transformation of banking from relational banking to speculative and trading banking, the rise of a "parallel" or "shadow" banking system that is poorly understood and virtually unregulated, and the globalization of finance that has generated massive but still obscure interconnections among financial institutions and markets.

At the same time, to gain a hold on this brave new world of finance, many of the chapters in this book draw on the insights of economists who wrote decades ago: Karl Marx, John Maynard Keynes, and Hyman Minsky. As a number of the chapters make clear, the finance and macroeconomic paths of the economics profession made a serious wrong turn when they abandoned the insights of these economists and adopted the neoclassical ideas of Milton Friedman, Robert Lucas, Eugene Fama, and Thomas Sargent. These ideas, of efficient markets, shareholder value, and an inherently stable full-employment macroeconomy contributed to the abandonment of financial regulation, countercyclical macroeconomic policy, and the broad public orientation toward socially productive finance and investment that had been envisaged, for example, by both Keynes and Minsky.

Building on this common foundation, the authors of the chapters of this book develop some common themes. One theme stems from the title of the volume itself: the "political economy" of financial crises. In general, the term "political economy" implies a broad approach to analyzing financial crises, one that is interdisciplinary, theoretically diverse, and methodologically broad. In particular, the term reflects the "capture" of the political and regulatory system and parts of the economics profession (a type of "cognitive capture") by the financial sector. Without this capture, the financial deregulation that was such a major factor in causing the crisis, and the inadequate response that followed and has now allowed the crisis to lengthen and spread, could not have occurred.

Second, as mentioned earlier, the economic frameworks needed to understand the origins of the crisis and to develop cures and preventions can be found by building on the works of Marx, Keynes, and Minsky, as well as institutionalist economists like Thorstein Veblen, Wesley Clair Mitchell, and Karl Polanyi. These authors understood the inherently unstable forces of capitalism. They recognized the need for not only regulations to keep these forces at bay, but also more profound institutional and structural changes to address the sources of instability.

Third, the crisis has become a global crisis because of the relatively unregulated and globalized nature of finance and the massive degrees of uncontrolled capital mobility and global financial trading. Hence, future regulation of finance and capital mobility must involve global cooperation that might itself require supranational mechanisms of global financial management. A nation-state, even one as large as the United States, will not be able to manage this system alone.

Fourth, to solve these problems and to reduce financial capture, there needs to be a democratization of financial policy making. This means a significant shift of political power away from financial elites in the United States and elsewhere, and the democratization, and in some cases, nationalization, of key financial institutions. Such a shift would include more democratic control over central banks and more public control over the private financial system itself.

In what follows we will briefly elaborate on these themes as developed in the chapters in this book. We start with what some have called the Great Financial Crisis. We believe that a concrete examination of that phenomenon, in many respects the most severe crisis since the Great Depression, is an excellent vantage point from which to understand the general and specific features of financial crises.

## The Great Financial Crisis

Marc Jarsulic lays out the basic dimensions of the crisis that began in the United States in 2007. He explains clearly how it was precipitated by a housing bubble. Dean Baker describes in detail how this bubble formed and how it is one example of a number of bubbles that have plagued the global economy in recent decades. Baker also analyzes the logic of speculation, discusses how to recognize and defuse bubbles, and looks at how the collapse of the housing bubble was responsible for the economic difficulties we are now experiencing.

Importantly, Jarsulic adds that the housing bubble could not have been sustained, nor would it have been so destructive, had it not been fed by what he calls a "credit bubble." The credit bubble was fed by the largest financial conglomerates in the United States, along with an entire chain of lenders and support companies that facilitated the provision of credit to homebuyers. These mortgages were combined into mortgage-backed securities, which were then used to form the basis for collateralized debt obligations (CDOs). The CDOs were marketed and sold by investment banks with the help of credit ratings agencies that were being paid by the very same investment banks trying to sell the securities. The CDOs were also intertwined with credit default swaps (CDS) that were used to insure and also to speculate against the securities. The CDS, though, were not backed with sufficient capital to pay off the insurance when the CDO values collapsed. As Jarsulic describes in detail, all of these risky and fraudulent practices were allowed to take place because of regulatory gaps and because of the financial deregulation that had been successfully pushed by financial elites. The collapse of the housing and credit bubbles was followed by taxpayer-funded bailouts. The bailouts at least temporarily saved most of the large financial firms, but in such a way that preserved their political power and enabled them to fight against significant financial reform in the future.

Josh Bivens and Heidi Shierholz thoroughly document the major toll that the crisis has taken on the livelihoods of American workers. They present detailed statistics on developments in employment, wages, and incomes. They also carefully demonstrate, moreover, as in the Keynesian argument, that unemployment in the United States is due to lack of aggregate demand, rather than a structural mismatch between labor demand and supply.

Arjun Jayadev's research on the link between inequality and crises reinforces the conclusions of Bivens and Shierholz. After reviewing much evidence, Jayadev concludes that financial crises, though they can hurt the wealthiest members of society, often end up leading to a redistribution from the mass of society to the wealthy elite. More work needs to be done on the channels, but they seem to include the mechanism of government rescues of the financial sector, a factor that is certainly operative in the current crisis.

Rachel Drew and Christian Weller show how the crisis has harmed the ability of Americans to benefit from their most important asset: their homes. They describe the distress caused by the dramatically high rate of foreclosures, and they also note the strong connection between a decline in housing investment and mortgage-repayment difficulties. Both of these chapters, by Drew and Weller, and also by Bivens and Shierholz, seem consistent with the argument by Jayadev that financial crises harm those in the middle and the poor more than the wealthy.

## Theoretical Understandings

Political capture by financial elites goes a long way toward explaining the financial deregulation and regulatory gaps analyzed by Marc Jarsulic. But cognitive capture of the economics profession by profoundly incorrect analyses of financial markets also bears some of the blame for the disastrous financial collapse. James Crotty argues that the neoclassical theory of "efficient financial markets" played an important role in helping to justify the radical financial deregulation that contributed to the crisis in the United States and abroad. Crotty describes this theory as a fairy tale based on grossly unrealistic assumptions. Such a theory gained credence in the economics profession because of flawed methodological arguments claiming that the lack of realism of assumptions did not matter as long as the theory was empirically verified. Yet, as Crotty shows, the theory of efficient markets was not and cannot be empirically validated, for various reasons. One of the most important of these reasons is that the central hypothesis of rational expectations cannot be verified in a world in which, as Keynes demonstrated, the future is inherently uncertain. Crotty concludes that it is far better to base our analysis on the Keynes/Minsky approach—which itself has roots in Marx—which argues that economic theories must be based on realistic assumptions about the way financial markets work. The conclusion that follows from the realistic assumption of fundamental uncertainty is that financial markets are inherently unstable and inefficient.

Jan Kregel also discusses these themes by focusing on the work of Hyman Minsky. As Kregel demonstrates, Minsky challenged the conventional interpretation of Keynesian economics by analyzing the importance of the banking and financial systems in the development of a capitalist economy. Minsky showed how the behavior of modern capitalism was crucially affected by the ways in which the owners of capital assets financed those assets through borrowing, and by the role of profits in validating those debts. This focus on liabilities, and the need to service them with cash out of the profits generated in the accumulation process, ties the evolution of capitalism to an inherently risky and unstable system that is underwritten in the modern world by the ability and willingness of the Federal Reserve, the lender of last resort, to provide cash for ultimate payment. The willingness of the Federal Reserve to do this during the financial crisis of 2008, and the reluctance thus far of the European Central Bank to do so, helps us to understand key dynamics driving the current financial crisis.

As Kregel notes, Minsky saw modern capitalism as inherently unstable. So the crisis we are currently experiencing is a manifestation of a deep instability in the accumulation process of a capitalist system, one that is exacerbated by a lack of financial regulation. As Kregel explains, "Following Schumpeter, Minsky placed the banking system at the center of the process of financing capital accumulation, and thus at the center of the explanation of economic growth and its fluctuations. But, different from Schumpeter, Minsky was not a believer in periodic cycles, but rather of cumulative destabilizing tendencies such as those outlined by Marx, Veblen, Myrdal, and Kaldor."

But the nature of these destabilizing tendencies and the way they manifest themselves will differ depending on the specific institutional and historical context. Martin H. Wolfson's chapter demonstrates how an understanding of financial crises encompasses two aspects: the basic dynamics of a financial crisis due to the characteristics of modern capitalism, and variations in the behavior of financial crises that appear as a result of changes in the institutional structure of financial systems over time. Based on a generalization of financial crises, he argues that the basic dynamics of a financial crisis can be understood by incorporating the following aspects: the cyclical and credit-market context, fundamental uncertainty, the endogenous development of expectations, speculation, financial fragility, the development of financial difficulties, panic and the drying up of credit, the danger of debt deflation, and an intervention by a lender of last resort.

Yet a financial crisis in the US experience has varied dramatically, from the destructive banking collapse during the Great Depression to the disappearance of crises following World War II, to their reappearance with increasing frequency and severity since the 1960s, and now to the current crisis. Wolfson explains these differences by using the concept of a system of financial regulation. This framework describes the institutional structure of the financial system. Systems of financial regulation are usually created during crises and are based on concrete conditions, relative power, and ideology.

The tranquility of the post–World War II period was based on the ability of the environment of the postwar system of financial regulation to constrain the inherent tendency toward financial crises within a capitalist economy. However, dynamic economic growth and the development of postwar capitalism undermined the functionality of the relatively fixed institutional structure of the postwar system. Financial elites pushed to eliminate regulations, and the result was what could be described as the neoliberal system of financial regulation. That system is characterized by deregulation, lax regulation, a shadow banking system, securitization, short-termism, globalization, and financialization. (Many of these developments are described in the chapters that follow.) Under the neoliberal system, financial crises have reemerged with greater frequency and severity.

Duncan K. Foley also notes that the current global financial system is inherently prone to instabilities. He describes some of these in terms of "externalities" that financial actors impose on others. These make the system, which Foley describes as "at heart a network of promises and expectations," prone to a misallocation of resources and instabilities unless this network is managed through appropriate principles and regulations. When this network collapses, it can lead to a "bad equilibrium," which is difficult to move away from.

This theoretical conceptualization, based on "networks" and good and bad equilibria, is a different framework from the nonequilibrium characterizations of Minsky and Keynes developed by Crotty, Kregel, and Wolfson, but it yields interesting insights. For example, Foley presses for the need to develop redundant, diversified structures to reduce vulnerability, even if these imply less strictly "efficient" outcomes according to strict neoclassical criteria. Foley's chapter explicitly confronts the role of "global imbalances." He argues that such global imbalances, which were underlying the financial crisis, were connected to the foreign production strategies of multinational corporations. These strategies were based on externalities since they did not take into account the domestic wealth—human, real, and community—that was made obsolete by the movement of production abroad. He argues that there needs to be a revitalization of domestic production that may entail limits on capital mobility, if some of the real imbalances that result in a financial crisis are not to repeat themselves.

The Minsky and Keynes processes of financial evolution turn out to underlie, implicitly or explicitly, much of the analysis in the chapters of this book. As we will see in more detail, these chapters suggest the need for vigilant financial regulation that is able to be flexible and updated, not subject to financial capture, and that spans across nation-states just as financial markets span nation-states. Also, financial flows and financial position taking must be regulated. This relies on active central banks that can serve as lenders of last resort. But these interventions need to be buttressed by others to limit wage inequalities, which lead to excessive household debt accumulation, unstable investment by private companies, and excess and unstable lending by financial firms.

## Global Aspects of the Financial Crisis

As mentioned earlier, the financial markets have become globalized. Unsurprisingly, when the financial crisis hit, it quickly became a global financial crisis. Ajit Singh notes that the US crisis soon spread to most countries, rich as well as poor. In the context of a liberalized and interconnected global financial system, securitization and leverage increased risk, contrary to the predictions of orthodox economic analysis. Singh describes the result: contagion, a vicious circle of circular and cumulative causation that spread the US crisis throughout the globe.

Following the Lehman bankruptcy, some of the contagion was limited by the coordinated liquidity actions of the central bank and the coordinated fiscal efforts orchestrated by the G20 with the support of the International Monetary Fund (IMF). Indeed, Singh highlights the importance of international cooperation in achieving the potential of global economic growth. But as the crisis has dragged on and centered more and more on the euro, it is once again spreading.

The other chapters in this part of the book describe various global aspects of financial crises, from several different perspectives. Jane D'Arista and Korkut Erturk look at the role of global imbalances. They argue that "the trouble was not with global imbalances per se, but the unsustainable way they were being recycled and what they were used to finance." Rather than contributing to genuine development in the developing countries or the United States, they were used to support the US housing bubble and helped to finance US government spending at low interest rates. D'Arista and Erturk argue that a big part of this problem stems from the role of the US dollar as the reserve currency. It allows financial developments in the United States, through fiscal and monetary policy as well as financial excess, to lead to capital booms and busts throughout the liberalized global markets. As a result, other countries must adjust to US policy. Either countries have to wait until they get into trouble and are forced to go to the IMF, where they face strict conditionalities, or they must accumulate large amounts of reserves without using them for domestic purposes.

José Gabriel Palma shows how this capital mobility has led to financial crises in Latin America, no matter how Latin American countries have tried to manage these flows. Mario Damill, Roberto Frenkel, and Martin Rapetti describe the Frenkel cycle, where capital inflows lead to an overvalued exchange rate, a brief burst of economic expansion as imported goods are cheap and asset prices go up, but eventually a depletion of reserves as the economy becomes less competitive and an exchange-rate crisis and crash. In the meantime, exports and import-competing domestic production are decimated because of the overvalued exchange rate.

It should be pointed out, as Singh notes, that these impacts of global finance are a far cry from the roles that many mainstream economists had predicted. Far from financing growth and development and helping with risk reduction, the global financial system promoted large amounts of reserve accumulation (lending by developing countries to the United States and other wealthy countries) and hot flows of money in and out. These led to bouts of overvaluation and undervaluation of currencies. C. P. Chandrasekhar and Jayati Ghosh further argue that these capital inflows, and the changes in foreign ownership that they imply, amount to a type of colonial control that destroys national economies and that creates instabilities and crises.

Gerald Epstein and Pierre Habbard elaborate on how the finance and banking structures that are still in place, despite the pledges to reform the system following the onset of the crisis, are continuing to result in financial instability and the misallocation of financial resources. They utilize the concept of "speculation"– short-term directional bets based on expectations of what other investors will do—to shed light on these practices. Building on Keynes's beauty-contest analogy, they discuss new modes of speculation—high-frequency trading, exchange-traded funds, and new uses of exotic derivatives—as mechanisms for making bets on and undermining the real economy. Epstein and Habbard show how this type of speculation, including naked credit default swaps, has contributed to a vicious cycle that is undermining sovereign debt in the eurozone. Like other contributors here, they point out that, despite the promises of financial reform, the reform agenda is being blocked on both sides of the Atlantic by governments influenced by the forces of the financial sector.

Indeed, as we write this during the summer of 2012, the eurozone has become the epicenter of the crisis. Although the crisis spread outward from the United States, now, with the threatened breakup of the euro, it will possibly reverberate with even greater force back to the United States and beyond. Robert Guttmann and Dominique Plihon attribute the crisis in the eurozone to problems in its initial structure, including the attempt to turn it into a neoliberal zone of financial liberalization and free capital mobility. They also point to insufficient risk sharing among regions subject to asymmetric shocks and to the promotion of mercantilist policies by the larger countries, especially Germany. These policies have created financial and political imbalances in the zone.

Costas Lapavitsas shares some of this analysis, but he adds a more general dimension: Marx's concept of "world money." He argues that, from a Marxist perspective, world money is a mechanism for exerting imperial domination over an economic sphere and that the euro (in its current configuration) represents the attempt by Germany within the eurozone to wield this power to achieve special advantages. As with the analysis by Guttmann and Plihon, the implication of this mercantilist policy has been imbalances that threaten to explode the zone and bring crises beyond its confines. For Guttmann and Plihon, the solution is a more Keynesian and egalitarian reconfiguration of the eurozone rules, while for Lapavitsas it is more likely that a breakup of the zone can allow freedom for development among the "peripheral countries."

## The Role of Institutional and Structural Change in the Development of Financial Crises

A number of contributors point out the institutional and structural changes over the last several decades that have led to the problems discussed above. David Kotz traces the historical evolution that brought about the neoliberal stage of capitalism, and he specifies the financial/real interactions that contribute to financial crises in the neoliberal era. He points out that wage suppression, a result of the drive to sustain capitalist profit, led to overproduction, which could be temporarily addressed only by credit and housing bubbles. But these bubbles, as we have seen, were not sustainable and had to eventually collapse. Kotz argues that a wage-led expansion would be more sustainable than a debt-led expansion, but that, too, could be undermined by the profit requirements of an inherently unstable capitalism.

Gary Dymski also digs into the institutional changes that led to the current crisis. He identifies three important developments that contributed to problems in the subprime mortgage market: "the strategic transformation of US banking in the 1980s and 1990s, the financial exclusion experienced by racial/ethnic minorities, and the structure of global imbalances that emerged in the neoliberal era." He also analyzes why most economists writing about the subprime lending issue have been unwilling to recognize the historical and institutional roots of the problem. He criticizes the narrow, market-oriented focus of economists who view the history of racial and ethnic discrimination in housing markets as outside the province of their discipline.

Damon Silvers also uses historical and institutional analysis to investigate the ways in which the current unregulated neoliberal system was created and how the current system has become more conducive to financial crises. He describes in detail the New Deal financial regulatory structure, which was dismantled piece by piece by financial lobbyists and their political allies.

Silvers argues that the New Deal regulatory system reduced the incidence of financial crises and also directed savings toward productive investment and away from speculative activity. Reinhart and Rogoff (2008) illustrate this point. They show that the weighted average of the share of countries undergoing a banking crisis fluctuates up and down with the exception of one historical period: the period following World War II, when there were both highly regulated and limited international capital mobility and highly regulated financial institutions.

The system that replaced the New Deal regime, though, was quite different. Silvers shows that banks became more and more dependent on short-term financing and more oriented toward organizing transactions, servicing customers and trading for their own accounts. As a result, they fostered more dangerous speculative finance and were less able to provide the patient capital the economy needs to develop. Silvers argues that the United States set the pace in the globalized march to financial deregulation.

Jennifer Taub notes the special role of shadow banks in building up out of the sight of regulators these dangerous financial positions. She describes shadow banks generally as those financial intermediaries, other than traditional banks, that stand between savers at one end and borrowers at the other. Examples include investment banks, money market mutual funds, and hedge funds.

Taub emphasizes the role of the shadow banking system in providing the short-term, wholesale financing for the banking system as a whole. As Taub notes, it was the run on the shadow banks that escalated the subprime mortgage crisis into a full-blown global financial crisis. All of these factors were facilitated by a radical deregulation of the financial system and the refusal of the regulators to regulate where they still had the power to do so, as well as the refusal to regulate new dangerous areas as they were developing.

These episodes of financial deregulation eliminated the remaining barriers to banking consolidation. By 2000, deregulation had proceeded sufficiently to allow the reappearance of universal national megabanks in the United States. As Silvers notes, after that point, it took only seven years for the whole system to virtually crash.

Michael Greenberger elaborates on the implications of deregulation in the specific case of derivatives. He shows how over-the-counter derivatives, that is, derivatives traded bilaterally between banks and their customers (which include other banks), were at the heart of the financial crisis. These derivatives were used to disguise leverage and risks, to bet against investments sold to bank customers, and to write insurance without an adequate capital cushion. Most important, derivatives created dangerous interconnections among banks that regulators, investors, and even the banks themselves, could not trace.

As Greenberger shows, these instruments avoided regulation because of the relentless interventions of major financial institutions, many of which have now been rescued with taxpayer money. The Dodd-Frank financial reform legislation made significant initial strides to regulate these instruments, largely because of the efforts by Greenberger and the grassroots efforts of Americans for Financial Reform and others. However, the financial lobbies and their allies in Congress have been trying to roll back these reforms. As Epstein and Habbard show, there have been insufficient regulatory reforms in Europe as well.

Among key changes in the institutions and ideology of finance has been the rise of "shareholder value" as a principle driving the governance of corporations. William Lazonick presents a scathing critique of this ideology. He dissects it logically and also critiques its impacts on investment, employment, and productivity growth in the United States and elsewhere. The shareholder value revolution of the 1980s argued that shareholders are the residual claimants of firms; because shareholders supposedly put capital at risk without a guaranteed return, they should be carefully incentivized to make sure their scarce resource is efficiently allocated. This idea led to the idea of giving CEOs and other managers stock options to align their interests with those of shareholders and to maximize shareholder value. In the process, though, the interests of all other stakeholders were ignored.

In the end, the focus on stock options led CEOs to undertake all kinds of tricks, including stock buybacks to raise the short-term value of equities, rather than to invest in the long-run health of the company and its workers. Lazonick argues that, in fact, other stakeholders, such as workers and taxpayers, invest scarce resources into firms and do not have guaranteed returns. They are residual claimants as well. Public policy must reorient firms away from a narrow focus on shareholder value and toward a broader stakeholder culture if long-term investments in people and innovation are to occur.

Another important institutional development affecting financial crises has been the increasing role of the financial sector. Englebert Stockhammer uses the term "financialization" as an organizing principle for analyzing the evolution of the financial sector in recent years and for identifying the dynamics that created the financial crisis. Though the term has been increasingly used in academic and popular discourse, there is no single definition for it. (See Epstein [2006] for one set of definitions and a range of papers that discuss financialization.)

Stockhammer argues that financialization means a "finance-dominated" accumulation regime, and he uses the term to describe how various types of financial domination have evolved in recent years. Focusing mostly on developed countries, he presents data that square with the popular perception that finance has grown much more than real activity and arguably dominates the dynamics of the overall economy. Stockhammer attributes the rise of financialization at least partly to radical liberalization of financial markets. Importantly, Stockhammer argues that the financialization of households has been just as dramatic as the financialization of nonfinancial firms.

Extending the concept to the global arena, Stockhammer links financialization to exchange-rate and debt crises and to the leverage and speculative bubbles that are created. An important innovation in Stockhammer's chapter is his argument that the finance-dominated accumulation regime has given rise to two distinct growth models: a credit-financed, consumption-driven growth model (mostly in Anglo-Saxon countries such as the US and the UK) and an export-driven growth model (in Germany, Japan, and, possibly, China). Both growth models suffer from a structural demand deficiency due to wage suppression, but each tries to overcome this by different means (credit-financed consumption or export promotion). These distinct but problematic paths both lead to financial crisis.

William K. Tabb also uses "financialization" to help us understand the political economy of financial crises, especially on the global level. Tabb defines the term in the following way: "Financialization denotes the dominance of the financial sector in the totality of economic activity such that financial markets dictate nonfinancial company behavior and significantly shape the overall economy."

While some might argue that the term "dictate" in this definition is a bit strong, there is no doubt that the power and influence of the financial sector over the overall economy has grown substantially and that, indeed, the massive recent financial crisis is precisely a measure of that power. As Tabb notes, "When the financial sector moves beyond lubricating the wheels of commerce to dominate the 'real' economy, problems develop."

Tabb argues that this is not an inevitable market phenomenon of today's epoch but is partly due to choices made by the government. In any event, financialization means that speculation dominates real production and undermines the economic and social fabric of society. Tabb argues that when financialization takes a globalized form, leading to footloose capital and a lack of significant job-creating investment in developed countries, labor becomes a major loser. Citizens of the developing world are also hurt, because footloose capital buffets them around like row boats on a tumultuous sea, and bailouts help only the wealthy elites. Tabb's discussion of the class implications of financialization recall the Occupy movement's references to the 99 percent and the 1 percent, and he suggests that a broad-based overturning of this financialized, globalized capitalism may be the only way forward for the bulk of the world's population.

## Policy and Institutional Change to Limit Financial Crises

In this book authors offer four, not mutually exclusive, policy solutions to address the havoc that financial crises can cause in the global economy. First, Ocampo proposes greater use of capital controls and more broadly based capital management techniques, or capital flow regulations. Grabel notes that the IMF has reluctantly changed its tune on its evaluation of capital controls, now agreeing that inflow controls, particularly in some circumstances, can be part of the policy toolkit.

Second, Damill, Frenkel, and Rapetti argue that more sensible macroeconomic management to discourage capital inflows, including capital controls, must be pursued. Especially important are actions that should be taken to limit overvalued exchange rates. Third, Ocampo argues for more regional cooperation to help insulate national economies from the vagaries of the international financial instability emanating from the major financial centers.

Finally, the ability of the major financial centers, especially the United States, to create havoc abroad should be limited. Also, and more important, institutional innovations are needed to create more use of special drawing rights, while moving toward the creation of a global central bank to issue them (see Ocampo's and D'Arista and Erturk's chapters for variations on this theme). Palma remains skeptical that capital and macroeconomic management can work in a highly globalized financial system; he suggests, with Keynes, that finance should remain a national issue.

The chapter by McCauley on Japan suggests that keeping finance national by itself will not always work, and he stresses the need for careful domestic financial regulation. Domestic institutional structure matters in the propagation and prevention of financial cycles: the devil is in the details.

McCauley describes the process by which bank equity investments contributed to the Japanese real-estate crisis of the 1980s. When the real-estate bubble started to inflate, the value of bank equities increased as well, due to bank holdings of property-company stock. As a result—in a positive feedback loop—the Japanese banks could lend more, driving up real-estate prices, which further increased the value of their capital and also their capacity to lend. The important lesson that McCauley draws attention to in this process is that that the institutional structure of the financial system can affect how well capital requirements for banks will work.

McCauley also notes that from the time the bubble peaked ten years had passed before Japanese authorities injected capital on a significant basis into their banks. This policy contrasted sharply with what was done during the Nordic banking crisis: "fairly early recognition of the problem of widespread distress among bank borrowers, rigorous supervisory challenge of bank valuations, removal of bad loans from banks, and parliamentary appropriation of public funds to recapitalize the banks, including nationalization where necessary, and restructuring of banks to reduce capacity." The resulting disaster in Japan is now well known as the "lost decade," with the country's economy suffering from stagnation.

Chris Rude describes the different Federal Reserve roles following the recent financial crisis in the United States. As he shows, the Federal Reserve played a highly active role after the Lehman bankruptcy and "created order out of chaos." The Fed did this by taking highly unorthodox policies. In particular, it made many direct loans, including loans to support the housing market. Ironically, though, as Rude and others have noted, in the process the Federal Reserve "reestablished the political power of US financial capital." As a result, US financial capital intervened strongly in the political process to prevent fundamental structural changes in the financial system following the crisis.

Tom Palley argues that, to restore the proper role for monetary policy, one has to change its mandate: the Federal Reserve should contribute to the achievement of the "American Dream." The Fed should focus on full employment, reduce its obsession with fighting inflation, and broaden its toolkit to allow it to play a bigger role in allocating credit. This would include expanding the role of margin requirements or asset-based reserve requirements. To make this happen, the Federal Reserve should be restructured to be more democratic to avoid financial capture of the type that Chris Rude discussed. Also, it should support a wider variety of economic research, in order to broaden the scope of economic ideas it listens to and to reduce cognitive capture by the flawed neoclassical analysis described earlier.

Fred Moseley describes the rationale for the US government's bank bailouts and the problems these bailouts have created. His analysis reinforces that of Chris Rude by confirming the ways in which the bailouts only served to reinforce the banks' powers. He argues that a more nationalized banking system, at least in part, would be a better way forward in terms of stabilizing the financial system and helping to direct credit to the needs of the population.

Dorene Isenberg discusses in detail an earlier episode that presaged the current crisis: the US savings and loan crisis in the 1980s. Her discussion draws an interesting lesson from the way in which this crisis was resolved. Isenberg shows that, once the Resolution Trust Corporation (RTC) was created, it acted swiftly to close failing institutions and remove toxic assets from the banking system.

Although the RTC was not without problems, its example of forceful action was unfortunately not one that was copied in the aftermath of the recent crisis.

Teresa Ghilarducci discusses policy issues for another major player in the financial system: pension funds. She shows that, even though pension funds get massive tax breaks, they do not serve the public well. They are covering less and less of what is needed for retirement. As they shift more and more to defined contribution plans, they become more pro-cyclical. Ghilarducci argues that there should be a guaranteed retirement account for all citizens that would supplement Social Security. This not only would provide more adequate resources for retirement, but also would help stabilize the overall financial system by creating a countercyclical role for pension funds.

Randall Wray draws on Minsky's analysis (Minsky, 1982; Minsky, 1986) to discuss additional financial policies and structures that could help serve the needs of true economic development. He argues for raising incomes at the bottom by promoting full employment through an employment guarantee system. Having a central bank committed to full employment is another important component of reform. Financing a network of cooperative banks is another idea derived from Minsky's writings.

The chapter by Zuzana Brixiova and Léonce Ndikumana also shows how public policy can improve public welfare. Using Africa as an example, the authors describe how, in the wake of the global financial crisis, African governments initiated policy responses to support domestic demand and boost key sectors of the economy. Activist central banks, as in the case of Nigeria, limited the damage from the crisis; also, financial regulations that some African countries had implemented in the wake of previous crises helped limit the damage of this one. Institutional differences can matter.

Skepticism remains as to whether the capitalist system, which has led to so much inequality and is mired in widespread financial crisis, can be reformed. At the same time, as Minqi Li points out, the problems facing global capitalism go way beyond the financial crises we are experiencing. Most menacing is the environmental crisis from air and water pollution and the danger of massive social and ecological destruction that could be wrought by climate change. It seems clear that a commitment to more of the same neoliberal approach to capitalism will only exacerbate these problems further.

Many of the authors of this book seem to suggest that a more managed capitalism of the type envisaged by Keynes and Minsky, adopted on a global scale, is minimally required to support sustainable increases in living standards. Even though this is a much more radical vision than many politicians are currently willing to embrace, Li challenges us to think beyond it. He argues that we should move beyond even a highly interventionist and managed capitalism and that we must draw more inspiration from Marx. As the global financial crisis continues and possibly deepens, it may be that we will have to think more radically and creatively to find ways to create a world capable of affirming human dignity.

## Acknowledgments

The editors would like to thank Matt Denny, Joao Paulo de Souza, and Jessica Carrick-Hagenbarth for excellent research assistance. They also appreciate the quality of scholarship and cooperation of the contributing authors of this book.

## References

Buiter, Willem. (2011). "The Terrible Consequences of a Eurozone Collapse." *Financial Times*, December 7, 2011. http://www.ft.com/cms/s/0/6cf8ce18-2042-11e1-9878-00144feabdc0.html.

Epstein, Gerald, ed. (2006). *Financialization and the World Economy.* Cheltenham, UK: Edward Elgar.

Haldane, Andrew. (2010). "The $100 Billion Question." http://www.bis.org/review/r100406d.pdf.

Kindleberger, Charles. (1978). *Manias, Panics and Crashes: A History of Financial Crises.* New York: Basic Books.

Minsky, Hyman. (1982). *Can "It" Happen Again*? Armonk, NY: M. E. Sharpe.

Minsky, Hyman. (1986). *Stabilizing an Unstable Economy.* New Haven: Yale University Press.

Reinhart, Carmen, and Kenneth Rogoff. (2008). *This Time Is Different: Eight Centuries of Financial Folly.* Princeton: Princeton University Press.

# PART I

# THE GREAT FINANCIAL CRISIS

# *US Dynamics And Effects*

CHAPTER 2

# THE ORIGINS OF THE US FINANCIAL CRISIS OF 2007

## HOW A HOUSE-PRICE BUBBLE, A CREDIT BUBBLE, AND REGULATORY FAILURE CAUSED THE GREATEST ECONOMIC DISASTER SINCE THE GREAT DEPRESSION

MARC JARSULIC

## 1. Introduction

The US financial crisis, which began in the middle of 2007, had its origins in economic events that began a decade earlier. Starting around 1997, house prices in many parts of the United States began a historically unprecedented run-up that accelerated remarkably in 2002 and did not end until the middle of 2006. This house price bubble could not have developed without the continuous support of large, sophisticated financial intermediaries. Most households need mortgage loans to purchase houses, so the creation of the house price bubble required a credit bubble to sustain it.

Had mortgage lending remained unchanged as the house price bubble expanded—with most mortgage originators maintaining reasonably strict underwriting criteria designed to limit the probability of default—the inevitable collapse of the bubble still would have produced significant damage to financial institutions and the real economy. When households take out mortgage loans they are making highly leveraged investments in illiquid assets. So when the price of houses declines sharply, those who bought at bubble prices can easily find themselves with "negative equity," rendering them unable to repay their mortgage loans by selling their homes. Hence the collapse of the house price bubble would have raised the rate of mortgage defaults, caused losses for financial firms and other entities exposed to mortgage-related assets, dramatically reduced aggregate household wealth, and caused significant disruption to the real economy.

Unfortunately the house price bubble enabled, and was in part supported by, a dramatic transformation in mortgage lending practices. As the bubble inflated, an increasing share of mortgage loans were of the high-risk "nonprime" variety. Collectively these "subprime" and "Alt-A" loans were made to borrowers who had characteristics such as low credit scores and high debt-to-income ratios, who lacked verifiable sources of income, or who had other characteristics that indicated that they were likely to have difficulty repaying their loans. Lenders often supported extraordinarily leveraged borrowing, sometimes requiring little or no down payment.

So long as house prices continued to inflate, the risk associated with these loans was masked. The continuous creation of house equity allowed weak borrowers to sell their homes or refinance their loans when they got into financial difficulty. When the house price bubble burst, homeowners lost their ability to escape their mortgage debt without damage. And when high-risk mortgage borrowers lost their financial protection, so did everyone who was connected to such mortgage loans.

Finance for nonprime lending flowed through distinct financial-market channels. Independent mortgage banks, and the lightly regulated mortgage bank subsidiaries of bank holding companies, borrowed short-term funds directly and set up "conduits" that issued asset-backed commercial paper secured by mortgages. These funds allowed mortgage banks to originate loans, which subsequently were pooled and used as collateral for residential mortgage-backed securities (RMBS). Investment banks, and the investment bank divisions of bank holding companies, created significant demand for RMBS by using them as collateral for the "structured" securities issued by collateralized debt obligations (CDOs) and structured investment vehicles (SIVs).

Securitization and structured finance were widely touted as devices for spreading mortgage risk, a process that was believed to increase financial stability. However, these financial innovations instead produced significant concentrations of nonprime assets in a host of financial intermediaries. In the private sector, certain commercial banks, mortgage banks, investment banks, SIVs, and conduits were laden with nonprime exposure. The two government-sponsored entities (GSEs), Fannie Mae and Freddie Mac, were also exposed through nonprime RMBS that they had purchased as investments and through nonprime mortgages included in RMBS that they guaranteed.

In mid-2007, well after the price bubble burst, came the first widespread recognition that those with exposure to nonprime assets would experience significant losses. It was less clear exactly where those losses were concentrated and how large they would be. But because some of the entities thought to be holding part of the subprime bag were highly leveraged and dependent on short-term borrowing, it was obvious that the situation was potentially explosive. High leverage means that small declines in asset prices can lead to big reductions in net capital. This in turn can expose firms to creditor runs, force fire sales of assets, and produce insolvency.

The damage from nonprime losses was at first confined to relatively smaller "shadow banking" entities such as mortgage banks, SIVs, and conduits.[1] These entities were highly leveraged and dependent on short-term funding, and they lacked deposit insurance or borrowing rights at the central bank.[2] They were highly vulnerable to debt-holder runs, which caused the failure of the largest independent mortgage banks, and this forced the collapse or rescue of SIVs and conduits with nonprime exposure.

While the damage at first appeared to be manageable, the collapses of Bears Stearns and Lehman Brothers, two very large shadow banks, made it clear that the entire financial system was at risk. Authorities were forced to staunch a run on money market funds, save some of the largest US bank holding companies, rescue AIG, and place the GSEs into an expensive conservatorship. The steps required to prevent a financial crash demonstrated the fragile structure of nominally well-regulated bank holding companies, as well as the potentially destabilizing role that shadow banks can play in the financial system.

## 2. Nonprime Lending Exploded during 2001–2006, Supported by the House Price and Credit Bubbles

High-risk mortgage lending existed long before the financial crisis brought this part of the credit market into the collective consciousness. Indeed, "subprime" and "Alt-A" are long-standing mortgage industry categories. They denote types of loans that are known to be riskier than the much more common "prime" loans. While the criteria for inclusion in either category are not universal, mortgage lenders know them when they see them. Compared to prime borrowers, subprime borrowers generally have a higher-than-average risk of defaulting on their loans. In general, these borrowers have lower FICO credit scores, higher debt-to-income ratios, and other characteristics that serve as markers of increased default probability. These borrowers are typically more highly leveraged, reflected in their higher loan-to-value ratios. Subprime borrowers pay substantially higher interest rates than prime borrowers, and their loans are more likely to include costly prepayment penalties that raise the cost of refinancing. Alt-A mortgages go to nonprime borrowers who typically have good credit scores but are unable to document their income or assets, or they may have some other attribute that disqualifies them for prime loans. These borrowers also pay higher interest rates on their loans (Mortgage Bankers Association, 2007).

Before 2001 nonprime mortgage loans were niche products in the United States. From 1998 to 2001 they accounted for 10 to 15 percent of annual mortgage originations. This is not terribly surprising, because borrowers prefer lower-cost loans, and lenders generally have a limited appetite for high-risk/high-return assets. Beginning in 2001, however, nonprime lending took on dramatic new importance in the mortgage market. By 2006 nonprime loans accounted for more than a third of all mortgage originations. During 2001–2006 more than $4 trillion in nonprime loans were originated (Inside Mortgage Finance, 2008a, 4).

As the volume and share of nonprime lending surged, the underwriting standards for nonprime loans deteriorated significantly. Historically mortgage lenders paid close attention both to borrowers and to the property that secures their loans. They asked borrowers to document their employment, income, assets, and debt. They looked to third-party evaluations of borrower credit scores. They sought third-party appraisals of home values. And they insured against moral hazard by requiring down payments that put borrowers in a first loss position should they default.

Between 2001 and 2006, however, the underwriting standards of subprime lenders plummeted. For example, the share of subprime loans with incomplete documentation of basic information such as borrower income or debt increased from 20 percent to 35 percent. Absent documentation meant increased risk of fraud. It also served as a way around state predatory lending statutes, because lenders could claim they had relied on borrowers' "stated income" and other data when originating the loans. During this period lenders allowed increasing amounts of borrower leverage. The share of loans that originated with a loan-to-value ratio greater than 90 percent or with a second lien reached a peak of 30 percent by 2006. Second liens often meant that the borrower had obtained a loan to cover the down payment (Gerardi et al., 2008).

The explosion of increasingly risky mortgage lending depended crucially on the historically anomalous behavior of house prices. (See figure 2.1.) This house price bubble created equity for mortgage borrowers, a development with

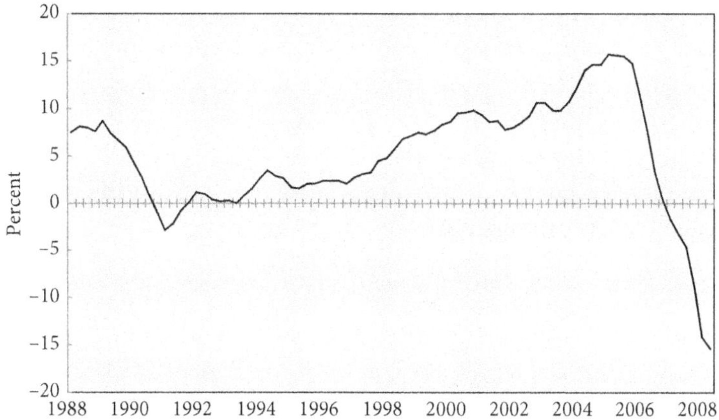


**Figure 2.1** Case-Shiller national home price index, four-quarter percent change.
*Source*: Standard & Poor's

salutary effects on borrower defaults. When a mortgage borrower is unable to pay his loan, the presence of positive equity gives him the option to sell his home to repay the loan, or to refinance the loan and use the realized equity to support the new loan. So even though nonprime loan quality was declining, the performance of these loans (as measured by foreclosure rates) actually improved during 2002–2006.

The house price bubble led to significant changes in household expectations. In 2003, for example, survey results in several large cities indicated that households expected the real rate of house price appreciation to continue indefinitely (Case and Shiller, 2003). These expectations were implausible. In 2003 the rate of real house price appreciation was 6.8 percent. Had house prices continued to increase at that rate, the real cost of houses would have doubled every 10 years, rapidly putting houses beyond the reach of almost everyone. These expectations, however poorly grounded, also help to explain why people willingly purchased increasingly expensive houses.

By increasing home equity, bubble prices also provided support for household consumption in a period when median household income was stagnant. A Federal Reserve study showed that mortgage equity withdrawals accounted for an increasing share of household consumption over the course of the bubble. During 1991–2000, the free cash flow from home sales accounted for 1.1 percent of personal consumption expenditure. During 2001–2005 free cash flow accounted for 2.9 percent of consumption (Greenspan and Kennedy, 2005). Household dependence on realized equity may help explain the widespread willingness to believe that house prices would continue to rise at rapid rates.

Of course the house price bubble could not have inflated without the aid of financial intermediaries. Most households cannot afford to buy homes without mortgage credit. Therefore, sustained support for rising house prices required sustained lending. Absent that support, house prices would have ceased to rise well before the bubble burst in 2006. While feeding the house price bubble, financial intermediaries were also feeding a credit bubble. That is to say they made loans and created mortgage-related assets, and the values of both depended on the willingness of other financial firms to continue lending and continue buying mortgage-related assets. A slowdown in credit creation threatened the house price bubble, which threatened the value of the previously created mortgage credit instruments.

## 3. Banks and Shadow Banks Combined to Finance the Bubbles

The rapid expansion of nonprime lending was funded to a significant extent through a distinct, lightly regulated channel of financial intermediaries. The majority of subprime borrowers found their mortgages through independent mortgage brokers. These brokers arrange loans through business relationships with lenders, but they do not themselves fund the loans. In 2006, 63.3 percent of all subprime loans were initiated through brokers, while for the mortgage market in total, the broker share was 29.4 percent (Inside Mortgage Finance, 2008a, 5). Mortgage brokers are lightly supervised. Under state law they are not fiduciaries, and unlike securities brokers they are not obligated to sell borrowers financial products that are suitable for the borrowers' budgets.

Most subprime loans were originated by companies that specialized in mortgage lending, which are also lightly supervised. It has been estimated that subsidiaries of commercial banks or thrifts, which are less closely supervised than their parent companies, made about 30 percent of all subprime loans in 2004. Independent mortgage companies, which are supervised by the states, made about 50 percent of subprime loans (Gramlich, 2007, 7). Lending was highly concentrated within the independent mortgage companies. Another study found that "905 lenders specialized in higher priced [subprime] lending, meaning that higher-priced loans accounted for more than 50 percent of their overall lending activity in 2004. Of these, 17 large independent mortgage companies collectively originated 506 thousand loans, or 39 percent of all higher-priced loans originated that year" (Apgar et al., 2007, iii).

Although independent mortgage banks played a very large role in subprime originations, many large and important financial institutions were deeply involved. A glance at the top ten subprime originators for 2006 illustrates this point. (See figure 2.2.) The independent mortgage banks—New Century, Fremont, Ameriquest, Option One—are represented. But so are the subsidiaries of major bank and thrift holding companies, including HSBC, Countrywide, Citigroup, and Wells Fargo. First Franklin was a subsidiary of Merrill Lynch,

| | | 2006 | |
|---|---|---|---|
| Rank | Lender | Volume ($ billions) | Market Share (%) |
| 1 | HSBC | 52.8 | 8.8 |
| 2 | New Century Financial | 51.6 | 8.6 |
| 3 | Countrywide | 40.6 | 6.8 |
| 4 | Citigroup | 38 | 6.3 |
| 5 | WMC Mortgage | 33.2 | 5.5 |
| 6 | Fremont | 32.3 | 5.4 |
| 7 | Ameriquest Mortgage | 29.5 | 4.9 |
| 8 | Option One | 28.8 | 4.8 |
| 9 | Wells Fargo | 27.9 | 4.7 |
| 10 | First Franklin | 27.7 | 4.6 |
| | Top 10 | 362.4 | 60.4 |
| | Total | 600 | 100.0 |

**Figure 2.2** Top subprime mortgage originators.
*Source*: Jarsulic (2010)

and WMC was a subsidiary of General Electric, so investment banks and finance companies were also part of the process. The concentration of firms originating subprimes is also apparent from these data. The ten largest originators made more than 60 percent of the subprime loans in 2006.

Once nonprime mortgages were originated, a large proportion were pooled and used as collateral for RMBS. In 2001 the securitization rate for nonprime loans was 45.8 percent, rising to 81.4 percent by 2006 (Inside Mortgage Finance, 2008b, 3). These securities were known in the trade as "private label," reflecting the fact that they were issued by free-standing special-purpose vehicles, without any guarantee by the mortgage GSEs.

These RMBS were purchased by a wide variety of investors, but one important source of demand, especially in the later years of the nonprime credit boom, were the issuers of collateralized debt obligations. CDO securities are synthesized from other securities: issuers take a collection of debt instruments, pool them, and use them as the basis for a new set of securities. Those CDOs that use previously structured products—such as RMBS, commercial mortgage-backed securities, or credit default swaps—as collateral are called "structured finance" CDOs.

Structured finance CDOs provided a remarkable share of the demand for subprime RMBS during the bubble. For example, 45 percent of collateral in the CDOs rated by Moody's in 2006 consisted of subprime RMBS securities. Assuming that the Moody's data are representative, then 2006 vintage CDOs contained subprime RMBS equal to 23 percent of all subprime RMBS issued that year (Jarsulic, 2010, 28).

Demand for nonprime RMBS was also created by SIVs. These shadow banking entities—sponsored by commercial banks or hedge funds—were special-purpose vehicles set up to make leveraged purchases of long-term assets using short-term borrowing. Large investors provided equity, banks provided partial liquidity guarantees, and the majority of finance was obtained by issuing asset-backed commercial paper and medium-term notes.[3]

It was widely believed that mortgage securitization and the creation of structured securities collateralized by RMBS would spread mortgage risk widely throughout the economy and to entities that were best suited to bear it. Unfortunately, many financial actors who helped to create the credit bubble retained large exposures to nonprime assets. Mortgage banks such as New Century, which warehoused nonprime loans before securitization, had large inventories in conduits or on their balance sheets. The affiliates of commercial banks and thrifts, such as HSBC, Citigroup, Washington Mutual, and Countrywide, and of investment banks, such as Lehman Brothers and Bear Stearns, were engaged in the origination of nonprime mortgages, and they had similar exposures.

Involvement in structured finance also left some banks and investment banks with large concentrations of nonprime assets. It was standard practice for CDO issuers to fund much of the senior securities (or "tranches") from their own balance sheets and from the creation of conduits. It has been estimated that during 2006 and 2007, 68 percent of the AAA tranches of CDOs issued were funded by conduits or by banks (Bank of America, 2007, 13). Hence when they originated CDOs with subprime collateral, banks often retained a large amount of the senior tranches, or the banks stood behind them via liquidity guarantees to the conduits that purchased them.

Although as SIV sponsors banks had limited liability, they had far more de facto exposure to the subprime assets held by SIVs that they sponsored. That de facto exposure derived from a need to preserve their reputations as reliable financial counterparties. Allowing substantial SIV failures, when senior note holders anticipated little risk to their investment, would have opened the possibility of legal claims and would likely threaten future SIV business and perhaps other business relationships.

The mortgage GSEs also accumulated large exposures to nonprime assets. They did so through purchases of nonprime assets and through guarantees of the nonprime assets that they securitized. By mid-2008 Fannie Mae and Freddie Mac collectively held $114.3 billion in subprime RMBS that had been issued by others.[4] They purchased these securities because they wanted to get in on a good thing and make money for their shareholders. They created additional exposure by guaranteeing subprime mortgages that they securitized and holding subprime mortgages in their portfolios. An upper bound estimate of the total unpaid balance on these mortgages was $204.1 billion, or about 28 percent of the outstanding unpaid balance of all subprime mortgages.[5]

Fannie and Freddie also had large exposures to Alt-A assets. Together they held $77.5 billion in Alt-A RMBS, and the estimated total unpaid balance of the Alt-A loans they held or guaranteed was $500 billion. Since the total unpaid balance of outstanding Alt-A mortgages was approximately $807 billion in August 2008, the two GSEs were exposed to losses on about 72 percent of the outstanding pool of Alt-A mortgages.

## 4. The Collapse of the House Price Bubble Triggered a Foreclosure Wave

The end to the house price bubble was caused by trends in economic fundamentals. By 2006 there was a truly remarkable excess supply of single-family houses. Inventories of vacant homes for sale, both new and existing, were rising. The number of buyers willing to bet on continued house-price increases proved insufficient to absorb the inventories. And so price increases ceased.

Well before house prices reached their peak in mid-2006, several measures of the inventory of unsold houses began to rise to historically high levels. The spikes in these measures can be illustrated graphically. Figure 2.3 traces the stock of new single-family homes for sale since 1963. These values fluctuate substantially over time, usually declining after a recession and then recovering. However, for the two decades prior to 2006, the inventory levels stayed within a relatively restricted range. Between 1980 and 2005, the average number of new homes for sale was 320,000. However, around 2003 the inventory began to rise, reaching a peak value of 570,000 in 2006. The fraction of all homes vacant and for sale (including apartments as well as single-family homes) also began to rise in 2005 (US Bureau of the Census, 2011).

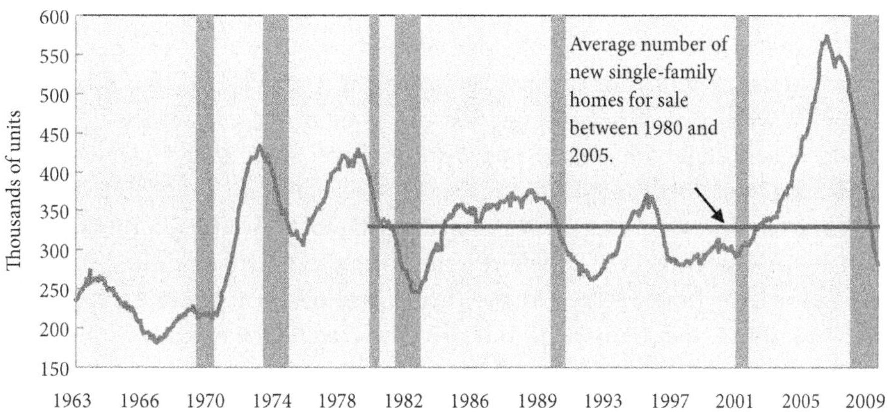


Note: The gray areas indicate periods of recession as defined by the National Bureau of Economic Research.

**Figure 2.3** New single-family homes for sale.
*Source*: U. S. Department of Commerce and National Bureau of Economic Research

As inventories grew, the dynamics of the housing market changed. Even during a speculative boom, when households generally expect house prices to continue rising, increasing numbers of vacant and unsold houses reduce the bidding competition among buyers. Sellers find that unless they adjust their asking prices they have to pay greater carrying costs for their properties. Therefore, by mid-2006 house prices ceased rising.

The end to rapid home-price appreciation created the conditions for a wave of subprime and Alt-A foreclosures. During the price run-up between 1997 and 2006, weak nonprime borrowers who would otherwise have defaulted on their loans were rescued by rising prices that created home equity where there had been none. That equity allowed them to pay off their mortgages or to refinance into new ones. However, once price increases came to an end, equity creation ceased and foreclosure rates among nonprime borrowers rose.

The wave of foreclosures began in earnest in 2006 for subprime borrowers with adjustable rate mortgages (ARMs), which went to the weakest borrowers and included the most onerous financial terms. By 2008, 23.3 percent of subprime ARM borrowers were in foreclosure. Foreclosure rates for fixed-rate subprime borrowers were not as high, and began to rise at a later date, but they also increased from their lows in 2006. Subsequently foreclosure rates for other categories of borrowers began to rise, as declining prices left millions of mortgage borrowers with "negative equity."

## 5. The Collapse of the Credit Bubble Triggered the Financial Panic

The collapse of the house price bubble meant large losses for any entity with big exposures to nonprime assets. The locations and scale of the losses were not known with precision. However, because some of the entities thought to be in danger were highly leveraged and dependent on short-term borrowing, the situation was potentially explosive.

While the use of leverage can bring the delights of arbitrage profits, it also brings the risk of runs by debtholders and other short-term creditors. If suppliers of short-term funds perceived significant declines in the market value of a borrower's assets, they refused to roll over the credit they extended. Of course if the borrower is actually insolvent it will fail. But even if the borrower is not insolvent, a run can provoke a liquidity crisis, in which the firm loses access to funding and can only obtain fire-sale prices for its assets. Either outcome can produce a failure.

Debtholder runs can also have spillover effects on other financial firms. Fire sales by weak firms can reduce asset values for entities previously judged to be solvent. These price declines can then provoke new debtholder runs, forcing additional asset sales and more asset-price reductions. Runs can also produce a general sense of panic, making it difficult for sound firms to obtain needed finance.

As the scale of nonprime losses became evident, runs by debtholders materialized with increasing frequency and scale. Starting first in relatively small shadow banking entities, runs spread to large bank holding companies and to the mortgage GSEs. The process was interrupted only by large-scale government intervention.

Among the first institutions to be demolished by subprime losses were mortgage banks specializing in subprime lending. Mortgage banks originate mortgages, sell them to others, and pool them in special-purpose vehicles that are funded through the issue of RMBS. Funding for originations is typically through "warehouse" lines and "master repurchase" agreements. Warehouse lines are revolving loans extended by banks or investment banks. These loans are used to originate mortgages and are secured by those mortgages. Master repurchase agreements allow the mortgage bank to transfer mortgages to a lender in exchange for funds. These funds are then available to the bank to originate additional mortgages. Mortgage banks also obtain short-term funding by issuing asset-backed commercial paper through conduits that contain mortgages and mortgage securities.

Lenders and investors advancing credit to mortgage banks include conditions to reduce their risk of loss. Under warehouse and master repurchase arrangements, the lender usually has the right to mark the value of the loans to market periodically, and it can issue margin calls if the value of the collateral falls below the value of the loans (Stang et al., 2007). When mortgage banks securitize pools of mortgages and sell RMBS to investors, or when they sell pools of mortgages to other financial institutions, they are typically obligated to repurchase or replace loans that violate "representations or warranties," related to such matters as early defaults by the mortgage borrower or inadequate supporting documentation for the loan.

Beginning in late 2006, in response to conditions in the subprime lending market, lenders began to issue margin calls to mortgage banks and to cancel their warehouse and master repurchase arrangements. These actions quickly demonstrated the insolvency of many of these firms, and this led to a cascade of bankruptcies and takeovers. By June 2007 dozens of mortgage banks were in bankruptcy or had been acquired by other firms (Bloomberg.com, 2007).

As it became very obvious that losses on subprime assets were unavoidable and likely to be substantial, the credit-rating agencies began to downgrade first subprime RMBS, and then CDOs that contained subprime securities or derivatives that referenced them. In mid-July 2007, Moody's, Standard & Poor's, and Fitch all reduced ratings on tranches of subprime RMBS. Downgrades of CDOs followed quickly (Moody's Investor Services, 2008). Credit-rating agency downgrades, and the continuing downward march of housing prices, had a rapid negative effect on the value and liquidity of outstanding subprime mortgages, RMBS, and structured finance CDOs exposed to subprime mortgages.

The impact of nonprime losses was next felt in conduits and SIVs. Because these vehicles had no public reporting requirements, information about the assets they purchased was proprietary and available to investors only. There are, however, estimates of the aggregate size and composition of these entities. In 2007 there were an estimated $1.4 trillion in conduit securities and about $400 billion in SIV securities outstanding (International Monetary Fund, 2007, 70–71). Although the financial world is very large, this amounts to real money. Total assets of the US commercial banking system were about $10 trillion in 2007, so the conduit/SIV sector was about 20 percent of the size of US banks. These branches of the shadow banking system may have been hard to see but they were important.

In the aggregate, only a small fraction of the assets funded through conduits were related to mortgages of any kind. However, that was not true for certain individual conduits. On July 30, 2007, the IKB Deutsche Industriebank, which provided liquidity facilities for a conduit with subprime exposure, had to be bailed out by another bank that was a major shareholder. The $1.6 billion Broadhollow Funding conduit, set up by American Home Mortgage, a mortgage bank, to fund its subprime lending, announced on August 6 that it was unable to redeem outstanding asset-backed commercial paper and would instead extend the maturity of its notes. On the same day American Home Mortgage declared bankruptcy. Other conduits quickly began to have difficulty rolling over their short-term debt.

Funding difficulties soon extended to SIVs with subprime exposure. These vehicles had lower liquidity support than conduits, and in the aggregate had greater subprime exposure (International Monetary Fund, 2007, 70–71). A firm providing liquidity to an SIV usually had an obligation to support only a fraction of the outstanding securities that it issued. However, several banks, including Citibank, HSBC, Societe Generale SA, and WestLB AG decided to assume the liabilities of the SIVs they had set up, in order to avoid damage to their reputations.

The difficulties at conduits and SIVs created a run on these shadow banking entities, and the asset-backed commercial paper market contracted dramatically. Outstanding borrowing contracted from a peak value of $1.2 trillion on August 6, 2007, to less than $800 billion by mid-December. (See figure 2.4.) In doing so the outstanding value returned, approximately, to its 2001–2005 level. The contraction of this market meant that a significant source of credit, used to fund a wide variety of loans, had been damaged. Subprime losses had thus extended beyond the housing market to other credit markets.

There was another profound impact of this contraction, felt by commercial banks around the world. As the asset-backed commercial paper market began to shrink, commercial banks became less willing to make short-term uncollateralized loans to each other. This unwillingness is reflected in the statistics such as the "TED spread."[6]

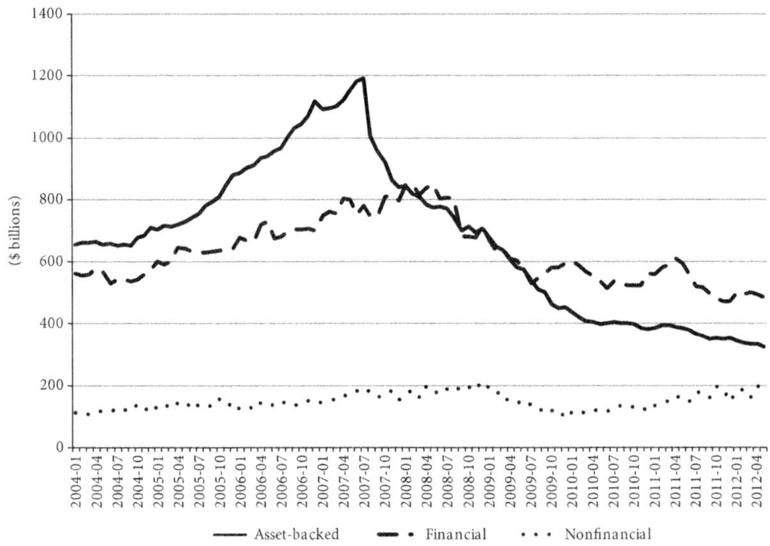


**Figure 2.4** Commercial paper outstanding ($ billions).
*Source*: Federal Reserve

The next shadow banking entities to fail were large investment banks. Investment banks are highly leveraged intermediaries involved in a wide variety of high-risk activities. They trade and underwrite equities and fixed-income securities and derivatives; act as broker-dealers and prime brokers; facilitate mergers and acquisitions; and act as investment advisers. They were active in creating, making markets in, and trading structured financial products such as CDOs. They were heavily involved in originating or securitizing subprime mortgages and in creating CDOs based on those securities.

Bear Stearns was the first to go. In public filings in 2008, the bank had described itself as "a market leader in mortgage-backed securitization and other structured finance arrangements" and noted that it was "an active market maker in mortgage-backed securities and therefore may retain interests in assets it securitizes, predominantly highly rated or government agency-backed securities."

Bear's self-characterization was excessively sanguine. In reality, the bank was very heavily exposed to declining subprime assets. The first indication of this exposure came in July 2007. About a year earlier Bear had created two highly leveraged hedge funds—High-Grade Structured Credit Strategies Fund and High-Grade Structured Credit Strategies Enhanced Leverage Fund—that had purchased CDOs based on subprime assets. As the subprime assets cratered, the lenders that had extended about $6 billion in loans to the funds had seized the fund assets, which had been pledged as collateral. The failure of the funds damaged trading in CDOs, and this shook investor confidence in Bear. The bank's stock price began a long period of decline.

The reason for the stock price decline went well beyond the hedge fund losses. An examination of Bear's public disclosures made it clear that the bank would probably experience significant additional losses because of its subprime exposure. This was evident, for example, in the bank's disclosures about the "fair value" of its assets.

When a US company discloses the value of its financial assets, accounting rules require that it allocate these values into one of three categories (Financial Accounting Standards Board, 2007). Level 1 assets are those for which there are quoted market prices for identical assets; Level 2 assets are valued according to observed market-based inputs or unobservable inputs that are corroborated by market data; and Level 3 assets are valued using unobservable inputs that are not corroborated by market data. The higher the level, the more subjective the valuation. Level 2 assets are likely to be thinly traded, and trade in Level 3 assets is likely to have ceased or is routinely based on projections from mathematical models.

The Bear Stearns holdings of Level 3 assets alone suggested that the bank had high levels of subprime exposure. In a February 2008 report, Bear disclosed $22.2 billion in Level 3 mortgages and mortgage-backed and asset-backed securities. Because trade in subprime mortgages and RMBS had ceased in February, it was a reasonable guess that some portion of the $22 billion consisted of toxic assets. Bear also disclosed $6 billion in Level 3 derivatives holdings, and it was also reasonable to guess that this figure included nontradable subprime CDO tranches. Moreover, given the subjectivity involved in allocating assets between levels, it was impossible for an outside observer to know whether Level 2 assets really belonged in Level 3.

Bear's total equity in February was $11.9 billion, and these public disclosures suggested that Bear might be insolvent: after all, the firm admitted to having $28 billion in suspect assets, and there could well have been more. Moreover, since Bear's leverage ratio was 33.5, and because it depended very heavily on short-term repo financing, it was very vulnerable to a debtholder run (Board of Governors of the Federal Reserve, 2008b).

A collapse materialized quickly, as Bear's stockholders, creditors, customers, and counterparties concluded that the firm might fail. The stock price plunged, prime brokerage clients pulled their assets from the bank, trading partners withdrew as counterparties, and creditors declined to roll over lending agreements. Ultimately the bank could no longer obtain the cash it needed to conduct daily operations (*Wall Street Journal*, 2008). On March 6, before the debtholder run, Bear had $20 billion in cash and highly liquid assets on hand to run its business. By March 13 it was down to $2 billion in cash and could find no lenders, even on a short-term, secured basis (US Securities and Exchange Commission, 2008).

The Federal Reserve and the Treasury stepped in and arranged for the acquisition of Bear by JPMorgan Chase on March 16. As part of that transaction, the Federal Reserve agreed to fund a special-purpose vehicle called Maiden Lane, to hold $30 billion in Bear assets. The first $1.1 billion in losses were borne by JPMorgan, and the rest by the Federal Reserve.

Although Christopher Cox, the chairman at the time of the Securities and Exchange Commission (SEC), insisted that the failure of Bear was a "liquidity crisis" and did not reflect insolvency, JPMorgan apparently did not agree: it required that the Federal Reserve effectively insure it against losses on $30 billion of illiquid Bear assets before it would assume responsibility for Bear's liabilities.[7] Note that the amount of insured securities is close to the $28 billion in Level 3 securities reported by Bear.

Lehman Brothers was the next investment bank to fail. Like Bear Stearns, it was highly dependent on borrowed funds—its leverage ratio was 24.3. Its holdings of suspect assets were large relative to its equity—the total value of the bank's Level 3 mortgage securities plus derivatives was $25.6 billion, and its equity was $26.3 billion (Lehman Brothers 10-Q form, May 31, 2008, 29). Like Bear, Lehman experienced a dramatic decline in its stock market price, followed by a debtholder run that cut off short-term funding. However, the Federal Reserve and the Treasury were unable to find a private-sector firm that was willing and able to take over Lehman. On September 15 Lehman filed for bankruptcy protection.

The Lehman bankruptcy provoked a new level of disorder and panic in financial markets. The reason for the strong reaction was probably fear that regulators would not or could not prevent the failure of large institutions with significant outstanding debt. This made commercial paper, asset-backed commercial paper, bonds, and other bank debt appear riskier, no matter how sound the issuer appeared to be.

The new level of fear was first reflected in a run on money market mutual funds, also part of the shadow banking system. The Reserve Prime Money Market Fund held $785 million in Lehman commercial paper. Because of the losses it had sustained, Reserve Prime shareholders withdrew more than $40 billion from the fund in two days (Standard & Poor's, 2008). The fund elected to freeze redemptions, because of losses that would have accompanied a forced liquidation of its assets.

These events provoked a widespread run on other prime money market funds, leading to $500 billion in withdrawals within two weeks (Bernanke, 2008). It is likely that many of these withdrawals originated with banks and securities firms, which had routinely deposited overnight sweep accounts in money market funds. Money market funds in turn began to exit the commercial paper market, which briefly contracted. The run on the funds was ended by Treasury and Federal Reserve action.[8]

On the day Lehman failed, Merrill Lynch, another large investment bank, was acquired by Bank of America. Prior to the acquisition Merrill had the characteristics of Bear and Lehman: a leverage ratio of 24.4 and plenty of subprime exposure. On July 28 Merrill had agreed to sell $30.6 billion of senior ABS CDO tranches to Lone Star Funds for $6.7 billion (i.e., for a mere 22 percent of their face value). Yet even after this transaction Merrill still retained significant "sizeable exposure to the market through securities, derivatives, loans and loan commitments" (according to Merrill Lynch's Form 10-Q, for the period ending September 26, 2008, 39). With its stock price under pressure, Merrill decided to merge with Bank of America.

On the weekend of September 20 the two remaining investment banks, Goldman Sachs and Morgan Stanley, announced their applications to become bank holding companies supervised by the Federal Reserve. Although federal regulation meant that the two banks needed to reduce leverage ratios and meet other standards, bank charters give them access to the new sources of liquidity through the Federal Reserve and the Treasury.

On September 16, one day after Lehman failed, the Federal Reserve and the Treasury effectively nationalized the American International Group (AIG), a large financial conglomerate. The immediate cause of AIG's problem was a short-term debtholder run, which had created a liquidity crisis. This crisis was, in turn, a result of two leveraged investment strategies pursued by AIG subsidiaries.[9]

The first strategy was executed through AIG's securities lending program. AIG's insurance subsidiaries operate a securities lending business that pools the highly rated fixed-income securities owned by the insurance companies and lends them in exchange for cash. Cash from securities lending is usually invested in liquid, short-term securities. AIG, however, used the collateral from its securities lending to fund the purchase of $56.5 billion in subprime RMBS. The rate of return on these assets was much higher than the company could have earned on Treasury securities or other safe investments. But it also exposed AIG to losses on RMBS.

The second strategy, deceptively profitable in the short term, was to write CDS on senior tranches of asset-backed CDOs, some of which contained subprime and Alt-A mortgage assets. As of June 2008 the AIG Financial Products group (AIGFP), which was funded with substantial borrowing, had written CDS guaranteeing $441 billion of these securities. Of this total, about $307 billion were held by banks. Hence AIGFP CDS contracts were crucial to the credit ratings of bank-held assets, and by extension to the capital position of these banks.

Some of AIGFP's borrowing agreements, and many of the CDS contracts it wrote, required AIGFP to post additional collateral should AIG's long-term debt rating be downgraded. APGFP also was required to post more collateral if the value of the CDO securities insured by its CDS contracts declined. When the contracts were initially written, the CDOs looked like good investments, which meant low levels of collateral relative to the losses insured, as well as a steady stream of premiums. But as subprime and Alt-A assets deteriorated, collateral calls increased, and AIG needed additional credit to cover its liquidity needs. Banks and credit markets were unwilling to provide the needed cash.

At the moment that its RMBS and CDS contracts were deteriorating, AIG's credit rating was under review by the major credit-rating agencies. A downgrade was likely, and the resulting increase in collateral calls was likely to force it to default on some of its borrowings. In the view of the Federal Reserve and the Treasury, this could have produced dangerous systemic shocks. The principal risk to the financial system came from AIG's role in guaranteeing the ratings of financial assets held by banks. The fear was that an AIG ratings downgrade would lead to downgrades of the CDOs guaranteed by AIG CDS. The CDO downgrades, in turn, would have forced the commercial banks holding the CDOs to write down their value, at a moment when losses were already mounting (Board of Governors of the Federal Reserve, 2008e, 3).

Just before Lehman failed, the federal government had been forced to rescue Fannie Mae and Freddie Mac, the two mortgage GSEs. At the beginning of July 2007, shares in both GSEs had traded above $60. A year later shares in both firms had fallen by more than two-thirds. In the second week of July the share price of each firm declined sharply, by some 60 percent. The July 2008 equity price decline was a response to the possibility of a debtholder run and a possible default by the GSEs. In early July Freddie Mac experienced difficulty auctioning short-term debt, an unprecedented event. News of Freddie Mac's problems with creditors alarmed equity traders.

A default by Fannie and Freddie would have produced very negative consequences for them, for mortgage and financial markets, and for the federal government. By 2008, investors were not buying RMBS unless they were issued by Fannie or Freddie. If the GSEs were unable to function, mortgage finance would have become almost unavailable. Moreover, given the trillions in outstanding RMBS guaranteed by the GSEs, questions about their ability to meet their guarantees would have reduced the value of these assets and added to the financial crisis. In addition, because GSE debt was treated as nearly equivalent to Treasury debt, and considerable amounts were held by foreign central banks, there was a possibility that contagion would harm the ability of the federal government to borrow.

Congress responded by passing the Housing and Economic Recovery Act of 2008, giving the Treasury authority to place the two GSEs in conservatorship. The Treasury did so on September 7, thereby making the government the guarantor of GSE debt explicit in all but name (Congressional Research Service, 2008).

Several commercial bank holding companies, although regulated by the Federal Reserve, also required rescuing because of their exposure to nonprime assets. The first major commercial bank to suffer from its exposure to nonprime assets was Wachovia, then the fourth largest bank in the country. Wachovia's difficulties were due to its 2006 acquisition of Golden West, a California-based thrift that specialized in nonprime mortgage lending. Wachovia had bought the Golden West portfolio at the height of the house price bubble. By September 2008 the losses on the Golden West loan portfolio were so large that Wachovia was about to fail. On September 16, the same day that the AIG rescue began, the Federal Reserve, Treasury, and Federal Deposit Insurance Corporation announced a program of open bank assistance to help Citigroup acquire it. That deal was not consummated, and Wells Fargo ultimately acquired Wachovia.

Citigroup, a leading multinational bank with over $2 trillion in assets, was itself soon in trouble. Part of the damage to Citigroup came from its role as a large issuer of CDOs based on subprime mortgages (Credit Sights, 2007). As part of its CDO business, Citigroup retained senior tranches from many of the securities it issued. Citigroup also held an inventory of subprime loans, used as inputs to the securities. In September 2007 Citigroup listed its total exposure to these assets as $53.4 billion. By the third quarter of 2008, cumulative write-downs on these assets had reached $33.2 billion.

Citigroup's exposure to subprime losses did not stop there. According to its 2006 10-K, at the end of 2006, Citigroup had involvement in "variable interest entities" (VIEs) valued at $388.3 billion. This sum included conduits, CDOs, and SIVs valued at $182.5 billion.[10] Although Citigroup did not say so explicitly, it was likely that the underlying collateral in these entities included nonprime mortgage assets.

Citigroup's acknowledged losses—together with uncertainty about the scale of additional losses—raised questions about the bank's solvency. The price of credit default swaps written on Citigroup, already significantly higher than those for JPMorgan Chase and Bank of America, began to move sharply upward on November 18. Counterparties became less willing to extend short-term funding in the form of overnight "federal funds" loans or even secured loans. Citigroup shares—which had traded at $28.92 at the beginning of 2008 and had declined to slightly more than $8 on November 18—began to plummet, reaching $3.77 on November 21. That same day corporations in the United States and Europe began a run, withdrawing their uninsured deposits and threatening Citigroup's ability to operate (SIGTARP, 2011, 8–12).

The Federal Reserve, the Treasury, and the Federal Deposit Insurance Corporation responded on November 23 with a set of measures intended to end the depositor run and preserve Citigroup's access to short-term funding. These included an injection of $20 billion in capital via the purchase of preferred shares under the Troubled Asset Relief Program (TARP) (bringing Citigroup's total to $45 billion) as well as an agreement to guarantee the value of $301 billion in Citibank assets.

Both before and after the November 23 rescue package, Citigroup required substantial additional help to replace sources of short-term funding that were drying up. Some of this help came from the Federal Reserve's Primary Dealer Credit Facility (PDCF), which was designed to help large securities dealers obtain the secured overnight loans that they normally got through the repo market. Citigroup began borrowing from the PDCF in March 2008 and continued to do so through April 2009. It was the second largest PDCF borrower, taking out loans amounting to nearly 23 percent of the $8.95 trillion in loans made through the facility.[11]

Citigroup also increased its access to short-term funding by using the Federal Reserve's Term Securities Lending Facility (TSLF). The TSLF allowed primary dealers to swap eligible securities for Treasuries for a period of a month. These swaps allowed Citigroup and other TSLF users to trade illiquid assets for completely liquid ones, which in turn could be used to raise needed short-term cash.

Citigroup was the second largest user of the TSLF, borrowing a total of $330 billion in Treasuries, or about 9 percent of the aggregate securities lent by the facility. Citigroup also sold $32.7 billion of commercial paper and asset-backed commercial paper to the Federal Reserve's Commercial Paper Funding Facility, approximately 4 percent of the more than $600 billion purchased by the facility.

The scale and variety of Citigroup's reliance on Federal Reserve emergency debt financing are clear illustrations of its connections with, and dependence on, the shadow banking system.

Bank of America, then the country's largest bank holding company, was the next to require a rescue. By the beginning of 2009 losses associated with the acquisitions of Merrill Lynch and Countrywide had put the bank into a precarious condition. Its stock market value declined and the price of insuring its debt via CDS spiked. Because it was the largest US bank holding company by assets, threats to the bank were viewed as a threat to financial stability. On January 19 the Federal Reserve and the FDIC announced that they would guarantee a pool of $118 billion of Bank of America assets, which included loans, RMBS, and commercial real-estate loans. The Treasury also purchased an additional $20 billion in preferred shares under the TARP program (Board of Governors of the Federal Reserve, 2009).

The scale and scope of the government rescue measures—which provided banks and others with capital, asset guarantees, debt guarantees, loans with maturities from one day to several months, Treasury securities swaps, and commercial paper funding—ultimately succeeded in ending the panic.[12] Use of Federal Reserve liquidity facilities, which were the source of loans and swaps, began to decline from a peak at the end of 2008. Other indices of funding distress—such as the TED spread—also reflected a reduction in panic from the end of 2008 (Bloomberg.com, 2010).

The financial rescue, however, did nothing to reverse the damage to the real US economy. The recession that began in December 2007 was the most severe since the Great Depression. Real GDP declined, and it currently remains below capacity; more than eight million jobs were lost during 2008–2009. Fiscal stimulus measures, widely recognized to be inadequate when enacted in 2009, reduced the depth of the real contraction but were insufficient to produce the sustained growth necessary for rapid employment growth.

## 6. Regulatory Failure and Regulatory Gaps Enabled the Crisis

Although US financial regulators helped to interrupt the financial crisis once it started, there is compelling evidence that several of them failed to exercise regulatory authority that could have limited it. The list of these failures is long and appalling (Jarsulic, 2010, 109–123). However, it is useful to review a few of them to show how important they were.

Among the more important is the Federal Reserve's long-standing refusal to define acceptable rules for nonprime lending. In 1994 Congress passed the Home Ownership and Equity Protection Act (HOPEA). According to the Federal Reserve's own analysis, HOPEA and the Truth in Lending Act gave the bank regulator very broad authority to create mortgage-related regulations (Board of Governors of the Federal Reserve, 2008a, 2008c). It could have prohibited asset-based lending that ignores the borrower's ability to repay, insisted on income and asset verification, prohibited prepayment penalties, required creditors to establish escrow accounts for property taxes and homeowners' insurance, and prohibited lenders and mortgage brokers from coercing real-estate appraisers to misstate a home's value. We know that the Federal Reserve could have made these rules because in July 2008 it did so, amending its own "Regulation Z."

Had these changes been made in a timely fashion, they would have eliminated many nonprime loans because borrowers would have been disqualified, loans would have been less profitable to lenders, the real costs of homeownership would have been more apparent to borrowers, and lender and broker fraud would have been more difficult. The fact that the Federal Reserve chose not to do so, even after the house price bubble was under way, and reports of shoddy nonprime lending were widespread, indicates willful blindness.

It is also evident that regulatory capital requirements for bank holding companies, also the province of the Federal Reserve, failed to constrain a rapid expansion of holding company leverage during the run-up to the crisis. To see this, consider the behavior of leverage ratios for the ten largest bank holding companies, depicted in figure 2.5.[13] Between 2001 and 2007 these ratios jump remarkably. Although investment banks are thought of as higher-risk enterprises, by 2007 there was very little difference between their leverage ratios and those of the large bank holding companies. For the five large investment banks the average leverage ratio was 36.3, and for the ten largest bank holding companies it was 33.7.

The parallel evolution of holding company and investment bank leverage reflects the fact that the nondepository subsidiaries of large bank holding companies—think Citigroup here—engage in many of the high-risk activities associated with investment banking and are similarly dependent on access to short-term borrowing through the shadow banking system to fund their operations. As events have demonstrated, while leverage helped these holding companies become huge and reap large profits during boom times, it also made them vulnerable in financial-market downturns and created huge threats to financial stability.

It must also be recognized that gaps in the financial regulatory system contributed to crisis. There was, for example, no regulator with the responsibility to oversee the asset-backed commercial paper market. The run in this market,

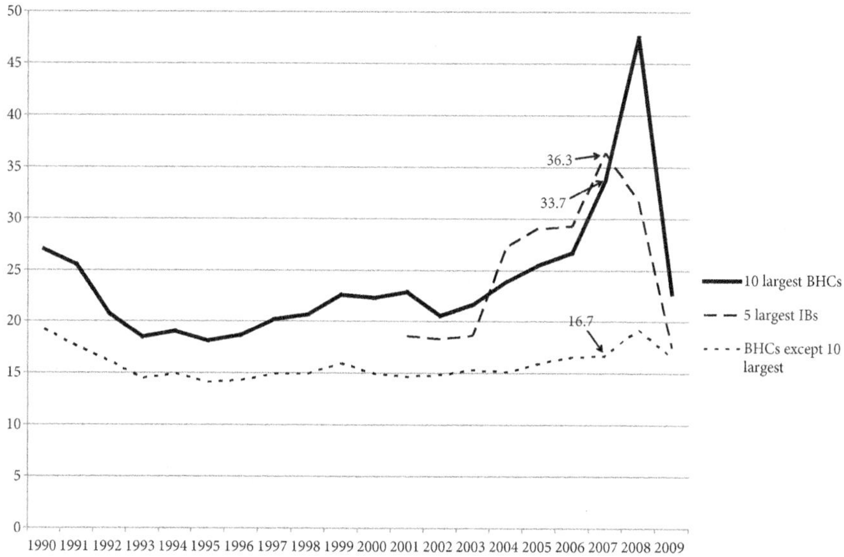


**Figure 2.5** Leverage ratios for bank holding companies, the five largest investment banks (leverage ratio = tangible assets/tangible common equity).
*Source*: end of year data from FR Y-9C and SEC 10-K and 10-Q.
*Note*: The population of investment banks in 2008 and 2009 is three because of the failure of Bear Stearns and Lehman.

which began in the latter third of 2007, reduced the overall availability of credit, threatened the operation of money market mutual funds, and weakened bank holding companies. AIGFP was able to write credit default swaps on billions in nonprime CDOs without reserving any capital to cover potential losses, because no regulator was tasked with setting capital standards for derivatives dealers (Jarsulic, 2010, 114–123).

## 7. Conclusion

Although the financial crisis appeared to come out of nowhere and occur with shocking speed, the ingredients of disaster had been assembled over the course of a decade. The house price bubble, which was widely recognized as it inflated, was essential. But the bubble—and the nonprime mortgage lending that it supported—could not have existed without the financial support of sophisticated financial intermediaries. A wide variety of banks and shadow banks provided funding to credulous homebuyers. As they did so they simultaneously created a credit bubble.

The willingness of financial intermediaries to participate in the credit bubble is easy enough to understand. The immediate profits were simply too good to pass up. Attempts to excuse their reckless behavior by arguing that these sophisticated intermediaries were unaware of what they were doing, or of the extraordinary risks created by the market conditions in which they operated, are not credible. The evidence for this conclusion is compelling and has been set out in detail elsewhere (Jarsulic, 2010, 91–109).

Because regulators declined to fully use their authority, and because regulation did not reach important financial entities and markets, there was no one to curb the enthusiasm of financial intermediaries before the damage was done. Explaining why regulation was so constrained is no simple matter, but those who have done so do not paint a pretty picture (Johnson and Kwak, 2010).

Whether recent efforts at financial-market reform will limit the frequency or intensity of financial crises remains to be seen. But it seems very clear that the potential for a disastrous crisis will remain, so long as there are significant, highly leveraged intermediaries dependent on short-term borrowing to operate their businesses.

## Notes

1. "Shadow banks" are financial intermediaries that engage in some or all of the activities traditionally performed by banks, but they do not observe the regulatory capital requirements, deposit insurance, or access to central bank lending that are part of commercial banking. Entities such as investment banks, conduits, SIVs, and other SPVs issuing asset-backed securities are included in this definition. For a recent pioneering attempt to map the shadow banking system, see Z. Poszsar et al. (2010).
2. Both conduits and SIVs are special-purpose entities set up to fund long-term assets using short-term debt that is sold in the asset-backed commercial paper markets. They are designed to make profit on the arbitrage between short- and long-interest rates. Conduits include liquidity support agreements, provided either by the sponsor or by some third party. These agreements guarantee the buyers of the conduit's commercial paper that these debts will be redeemed, even if the conduit is unable to roll over its borrowing when it comes due.

   SIVs have partial liquidity support and a capital cushion raised from third parties in the form of senior securities. SIVs also have trigger mechanisms built into their structures. These triggers require, for example, that the market value of the SIV assets can redeem the senior securities. If this requirement cannot be met, then the SIV assets must be sold and the results distributed to the senior note holders. Both conduits and SIVs require continued access to short-term borrowing. When that borrowing is disrupted, the entity can fail.

   Sponsors set up conduits or SIVs for several reasons. Aside from the fees that sponsors can earn from setting up and operating the vehicles, they can be used to provide funding for the sponsor's other businesses. For example, if a bank wants to finance tranches of the CDOs it has created, or fund the pools of credit-card receivables it owns, these vehicles can provide the needed cash. Because these vehicles are funded using short-term borrowing, they provide a relatively cheap source of finance. They also allow banks to increase their use of leverage. Regulations require banks to reserve less capital against a liquidity guarantee for a conduit than they require for direct ownership of the same assets.

4. Data from Fannie Mae are for the period ending in the first quarter of 2008; those for Freddie Mac are for the period ending in the second quarter of 2008. The value of the total outstanding subprime and Alt-A mortgage balances was estimated by using data on average unpaid balances of outstanding *owner-occupied* properties collateralizing MBS in August 2008. More comprehensive data for all mortgages are not available. Fannie Mae data were obtained from Fannie Mae (2008), and Freddie Mac data from Freddie Mac (2008). Outstanding subprime and Alt-A unpaid balances were estimated from August 2008 data found in Federal Reserve Bank of New York (2009).
5. The unpaid balance of subprime mortgages guaranteed by the GSEs was estimated by assuming that any loan made to a borrower with a FICO score of 620 or less was subprime. Because the performance of a loan is actually a function of a vector of characteristics such as the loan-to-value ratio and the debt-to-income ratio of the borrower, as well as the FICO score of the borrower, this estimate very likely overstates the amount of subprime mortgages guaranteed by the GSEs. Given the data available about the GSEs' guarantees, this is the best that can be done.
6. The "TED spread" is the difference between the rate of interest on US Treasury securities and the London Interbank Offer Rate on unsecured lending. The acronym reflects the fact that the interest rate spread reflects a Treasury/Europe differential. Data are available at Bloomberg.com (2010).
7. "In accordance with customary industry practice, Bear Stearns relied each day on its ability to obtain short-term financing through borrowing on a secured basis. Beginning late Monday, March 10, and increasingly through the week, rumors spread about liquidity problems at Bear Stearns, which eroded investor confidence in the firm. Notwithstanding that Bear Stearns continued to have high-quality collateral to provide as security for borrowings, market counterparties became less willing to enter into collateralized funding arrangements with Bear Stearns. This resulted in a crisis of confidence late in the week. In particular, counterparties to Bear Stearns were unwilling to make secured funding available to Bear Stearns on customary terms.

   This unwillingness to fund on a secured basis placed enormous stress on the liquidity of the firm. On Tuesday, March 11, the holding company liquidity pool declined from $18.1 billion to $11.5 billion. This improved on Wednesday, March 12, when Bear Stearns's liquidity pool increased by $900 million to a total of $12.4 billion. On Thursday, March 13, however, Bear Stearns's liquidity pool fell sharply and continued to fall on Friday. The market rumors about Bear Stearns liquidity problems became self-fulfilling. On Sunday, March 16, Bear Stearns entered into the transaction with JP Morgan Chase. These events illustrate just how critical not just capital, but also liquidity is to the viability of financial firms and how the evaporation of market confidence can lead to liquidity being impaired." US Securities and Exchange Commission (2008).
8. The run on money market funds and the contraction of the commercial paper market were stopped by a temporary Treasury program that allowed the funds to insure investor assets and by the establishment of two Federal Reserve facilities—the

Money Market Investor Funding Facility, which bought highly rated commercial paper, certificates of deposit, commercial paper, and bank notes from money market funds, and the Asset-Backed Commercial Paper Money Market Fund Liquidity Facility, which lent to banks purchasing eligible ABCP from money market funds.

9. This section relies on information from Board of Governors of the Federal Reserve (2008d) and (2008e).
10. Citigroup noted that "an entity is referred to as a variable interest entity (VIE) if it meets the criteria outlined in FASB Interpretation No. 46-R,'Consolidation of Variable Interest Entities (revised December 2003)' (FIN 46-R), which are: (1) the entity has equity that is insufficient to permit the entity to finance its activities without additional subordinated financial support from other parties, or (2) the entity has equity investors that cannot make significant decisions about the entity's operations or that do not absorb the expected losses or receive the expected returns of the entity.

    In addition, as specified in FIN 46-R, a VIE must be consolidated by the Company if it is deemed to be the primary beneficiary of the VIE, which is the party involved with the VIE that has a majority of the expected losses or a majority of the expected residual returns or both.

    Along with the VIEs that are consolidated in accordance with these guidelines, the Company has significant variable interests in other VIEs that are not consolidated because the Company is not the primary beneficiary. These include multi-seller finance companies, collateralized debt obligations (CDOs), many structured finance transactions, and various investment funds. All other entities not deemed to be VIEs, with which the Company has involvement, are evaluated for consolidation under Accounting Research Bulletin (ARB) No. 51, 'Consolidated Financial Statements,' and SFAS. 94, 'Consolidation of All Majority-Owned Subsidiaries' (SFAS 94)." This is according to Citigroup's 10-K form for the period ending December 31, 2006, 109.
11. Data on usage of the PDCF and other liquidity facilities are available from the Board of Governors of the Federal Reserve (2010a).
12. Data on capital injections for banks and other measures taken under TARP can be found at US Treasury (2010) and at Board of Governors of the Federal Reserve (2010b).
13. The leverage ratio shown in figure 2.5 is calculated as the ratio of tangible assets to tangible common equity. Tangible assets are not risk-weighted and do not include goodwill or other intangibles, and tangible common equity does not include perpetual preferred stock, goodwill, and other intangibles. A leverage ratio using the measures of risk-weighted assets and Tier 1 capital that are part of US statutory capital requirements would show lower levels of leverage than those depicted. However, tangible common equity is a better measure of a firm's capacity to absorb losses, especially during a crisis, and therefore a leverage ratio with tangible common equity as the denominator more closely reflects a firm's vulnerability to asset price declines. The population of investment banks in 2008 and 2009 is reduced to three because of the failure of Bear Stearns and Lehman Brothers.

## References

Apgar, W., et al. (2007). "Mortgage Market Channels and Fair Lending." Joint Center for Housing Studies, Harvard University, iii, available at http://www.jchs.harvard.edu/sites/jchs.harvard.edu/files/mm07-2_mortgage_market_channels.pdf

Bank of America. (2007). "Credit Market Strategist." August 13.
Bernanke, B. (2008). "Troubled Asset Relief Program and the Federal Reserve's Liquidity Facilities." Testimony before the Committee on Financial Services, US House of Representatives.
Bloomberg.com. (2007). "Lehman Shuts Unit; Toll of Lenders Tops 100: Subprime Scorecard." August 23.
Bloomberg.com. (2010). TED Spread, available at http://www.bloomberg.com/apps/quote?ticker=.TEDSP:IND.
Board of Governors of the Federal Reserve. (2008a). "Truth in Lending; Proposed Rule." Federal Register, Volume 73, No. 6, January 9.
Board of Governors of the Federal Reserve. (2008b). "Report Pursuant to Section 129 of the Emergency Economic Stabilization Act of 2008: Loan to Facilitate the Acquisition of The Bear Stearns Companies, Inc. by JPMorgan Chase & Co.", available at http://www.federalreserve.gov/monetarypolicy/files/129bearstearnsacquisitionloan.pdf
Board of Governors of the Federal Reserve. (2008c). Press release, July 14, available at www.federalreserve.gov/newsevents/press/bcreg/20080714a.htm.
Board of Governors of the Federal Reserve. (2008d). "Report Pursuant to Section 129 of the Emergency Economic Stabilization Act of 2008: Secured Credit Facility Authorized for American International Group, Inc. on September 16, 2008" available at http://www.federalreserve.gov/monetarypolicy/files/129aigseccreditfacility.pdf.
Board of Governors of the Federal Reserve. (2008e). "Report Pursuant to Section 129 of the Emergency Economic Stabilization Act of 2008: Restructuring of the Government's Financial Support to American International Group, Inc., on November 10, 2008" available at http://www.federalreserve.gov/monetarypolicy/files/129aigrestructure.pdf.
Board of Governors of the Federal Reserve, Federal Deposit Insurance Corporation, and US Department of the Treasury. (2009). Joint press release, available at http://www.federalreserve.gov/newsevents/press/bcreg/20090116a.htm.
Board of Governors of the Federal Reserve (2010a). Usage of Federal Reserve Credit and Liquidity Facilities, http://www.federalreserve.gov/newsevents/reform_transaction.htm.
Board of Governors of the Federal Reserve. (2010b). "Credit and Liquidity Programs and the Balance Sheet," at http://www.federalreserve.gov/monetarypolicy/bst_recenttrends.htm.
Case, K. and Shiller, R. (2003). Is There a Bubble in the Housing Market? Brookings Papers on Economic Activity, Issue 2, 299–322.
Congressional Research Service. (2008). "Fannie Mae and Freddie Mac in Conservatorship." September 15.
Credit Sights. (2007). "US Banks/Brokers—CDOs Top the Hit Parade; Where's the Bottom?" November 5.
Fannie Mae. (2008). Fannie Mae 2008 Q2 10-Q Investor Summary, August 8. Federal Reserve Bank of New York. (2009). Credit Conditions in the United States, at www.newyorkfed.org/regional/subprime.html.
Financial Accounting Standards Board. (2007). Statement No. 157, "Fair Value Measurements," at http://www.fasb.org/summary/stsum157.shtml.
Freddie Mac (2008). Freddie Mac Update, August.
Gerardi, K., et al. (2008). "Making Sense of the Subprime Crisis." Federal Reserve Bank of Boston, Public Policy Discussion Paper No. 09-01.

Gramlich, E. (2007). *Subprime Mortgages, America's Latest Boom and Bust.* Washington, DC: Urban Institute Press.
Greenspan, A., and J. Kennedy. (2005). "Estimates of Home Mortgage Originations, Repayments, and Debt on One-to-Four Family Residences." Federal Reserve Finance and Economics Discussion Series, Working Paper 2005–41.
Inside Mortgage Finance (2008a). *The 2008 Mortgage Market Statistical Annual, Volume I.* Bethesda, MD: Inside Mortgage Finance.
Inside Mortgage Finance (2008b). *The 2008 Mortgage Market Statistical Annual, Volume II.* Bethesda, MD: Inside Mortgage Finance.
International Monetary Fund (2007). "World Economic Outlook, Washington, D.C. International Monetary Fund."
Jarsulic, M. (2010). *Anatomy of a Financial Crisis.* New York: Palgrave Macmillan.
Johnson, S., and J. Kwak. (2010). *Thirteen Bankers.* New York: Pantheon.
Moody's Investor Services. (2008). "Structured Finance Ratings Transitions: 1983–2007." February.
Mortgage Bankers Association. (2007). "MBA Data Notes, Characteristics of Outstanding Residential Mortgage Debt: 2006." January, at http://mortgagebankers.org/files/Bulletin/InternalResource/47210_DataNoteCharacteristicsofOuttandingResidentialMortgageDebtfor2006.pdf.
Poszsar, Z., et al. (2010). "Shadow Banking. Federal Reserve Bank of New York Staff Report, No. 458." July.
Special Inspector General for the Troubled Assets Relief Program (SIGTARP). (2011). "Extraordinary Financial Assistance Provided to Citigroup, Inc.", available at http://www.sigtarp.gov/Audit%20Reports/Extraordinary%20Financial%20Assistance%20Provided%20to%20Citigroup,%20Inc.pdf.
Standard & Poor's (2008). "How Are Events in the Financial Markets Affecting Money-market Funds?" September 30.
Stang, J., et al. (2007). "The Subprime Lending Industry: A Look at the Restructuring of a Market in Turmoil." American Bar Association Annual Meeting, Section of Business Law, August 11, panel presentation.
US Bureau of the Census. (2011). "Quarterly Homeowner Vacancy Rates: 1956 to Present," at http://www.census.gov/hhes/www/housing/hvs/historic/index.html.
US Securities and Exchange Commission. (2008). "Chairman Cox Letter to Basel Committee in Support of New Guidance on Liquidity Management," at www.sec.gov.
US Treasury. (2010). "TARP Transactions," at http://www.treasury.gov/initiatives/financial-stability/briefing-room/reports/tarptransactions/Pages/default.aspx.
*Wall Street Journal.* (2008). "The Fall of Bear Stearns." May 27–29.

# CHAPTER 3

# SPECULATION AND ASSET BUBBLES

DEAN BAKER

ASSET bubbles in the form of the stock market bubble and the housing bubble largely drove the US economy in the 1990s and the 2000s. In both cases they created a powerful source of demand that might have otherwise been absent. However, much of the growth spurred by these bubbles was wasteful, leading to the diversion of capital to useless Internet retailers or to the overbuilding of new developments in many parts of the country. The collapse of both bubbles led to recessions, with the second one clearly much more severe than the first. In spite of the extraordinarily negative consequences of the puncturing of these bubbles, there has been remarkably little acknowledgment of the dangers posed by asset bubbles and of the measures that can be taken to prevent them.

This chapter assesses the logic of speculation, which is a necessary part of any asset bubble. It then describes the circumstances that led to the growth first of the stock bubble and then the housing bubble, describing how each bubble became central to the growth of the economy by the point it reached its peak. It then discusses how bubbles can be recognized and the sorts of measures that can be taken to prevent them from growing large enough to pose a threat to the economy.

## THE LOGIC OF SPECULATION

Speculation is an inevitable part of financial markets. While there is no perfect and universally accepted definition of speculation, the most useful way to characterize it is as trading that is based on anticipating the behavior of other actors in the market rather than trading that is based on the underlying fundamentals of the market.

Speculation is likely to be destabilizing because it can amplify departures from fundamental values. This is likely to be the case as speculators are not bringing new information to the market. Instead they are acting based on the information given by other market participants. If this information happens to be wrong, for example, by being overly optimistic, then speculators are likely to further inflate the market beyond where it would be driven by fundamental traders alone.

This contrast is worth noting because, in principle, the more fundamental traders there are in a market, the more stable it should be. If these traders arrive at an independent assessment of the fundamentals of the market, then their opinions should tend to converge on the trend value since the errors would in general be offsetting. However, if traders are not acting based on an assessment of the fundamentals but rather are just following the behavior of other traders, then it is easy to construct models in which more traders lead to greater divergences from the values that are justified by the income flows for the asset (e.g., profits and rents). Keynes first discussed this logic in *The General Theory*, but it has more recently been formalized in a number of works (e.g., DeLong et al., 1990).

The logic is that speculators seize on movements in the market and act based on the anticipation that these movements will continue to go forward. For example, if the price of a particular asset—stock, commodity, or currency—is rising, then speculators invest on the assumption that it will continue to rise. Speculators may make this assessment based on their appraisal of attitudes of other traders, not an evaluation of market fundamentals. This can cause any run-up in prices to be carried far beyond the levels that would be justified by market fundamentals.

Speculation is often associated with short-term trading, although speculation need not be short-term, and not all short-term trading is speculative. The rationale for the connection between short-term trading and speculation is that a speculator is likely to be less concerned about the fundamentals reversing the course of a market in a short period than over a longer period of time. In other words, if a stock or commodity has been moving far out of line with the price that would be predicted based on the fundamentals of the market, the fundamentals are less likely to reassert themselves over the short term than the long term.

The reason for this is straightforward. Typically, there will be a time lag before a price that is out of line with fundamentals can bring about a corrective supply and/or a demand response. For example, if speculation drives oil prices to a level that is far above what would be supported by the fundamentals of the market, it will take a period of time before consumers adjust to this higher price and consume less oil. Similarly, the full supply response, in the form of more oil being pumped out of existing wells and more exploration for new wells, can take many years. A speculator betting on the price of oil over the next month, week, or day need not be very concerned about these potential corrective dynamics.

On the other hand, the decision to hold oil over a period of years, without paying attention to the fundamentals of the market, would be an extremely risky strategy. In that time, the supply-and-demand responses to an excessive price could easily overwhelm the impact of speculative buying, leading to large losses for speculators. Obviously the actual turning point in a speculative run-up, where the fundamentals reassert themselves, will come in some short period. In other words, there will be some particular day or week where prices turn. This adjustment can also be a rapid process if a change in prices leads to a change in expectations, effectively reversing the direction of speculation.

However, the probability that a speculator will still be holding the asset at a turning point increases the longer the period is in which he holds the asset. For this reason, speculators tend to be interested in shorter-term holdings and rapid turnover. This also suggests why some items might be more suitable for speculative price movements than others. A manufactured product, like steel, will not generally provide much basis for speculation, because output can generally be increased quickly in response to an increase in demand. This is less likely to be the case with most natural resources and agricultural crops, which require at least a growing season.

Short-term trading can also be stabilizing. Arbitrage trading of various types is by definition short-term. In this case traders seek out small divergences from fundamentals, for example, differences in interest-rate spreads between comparable assets. They buy or sell to take advantage of these divergences, usually with the effect of reducing or eliminating them.

There are also trading patterns that can be both short-term and stabilizing. For example, there is considerable evidence that stock price movements are mean-reverting, which means that sharp movements in one direction are likely to be at least partially reversed (Poterba and Summers, 1988; Fama and French, 1988). To take advantage of this pattern, several hedge funds employed a trading strategy in which they shorted the stocks that had the biggest gains the previous day, while buying shares in the stocks that had the largest losses. In this case, the effect of this short-term trading pattern should be to move stock prices more quickly back to their trend values.

There is some clear value to the short-term trading that is stabilizing. In principle, financial markets are providing signals to market actors. If prices are out of line with fundamentals, then markets are giving the wrong signal. For example, when oil is trading substantially above a price dictated by the fundamentals then it will lead to overinvestment in oil equipment and exploration. If arbitragers or other short-term traders bring the price back in line with the fundamentals more quickly then it will minimize the misinvestment caused by an excessive price.

On the other hand it is important to recognize that the potential harm from short-term fluctuations from fundamental values is likely to be rather limited, and therefore the benefits from these short-term stabilizing trades are also likely to be rather limited. If the price of oil is above its fundamental level by a fraction of a percent for one to two days, it is not likely to lead to any major flows of investment in oil exploration. Similarly, if stock prices deviate from fundamental levels by small amounts for short periods of time it is likely to have little consequence for the allocation of capital.

In short, the speculative run-ups in price that form the basis for any asset bubble must be in large part driven by short-term trading. While not all short-term trading is speculative, and it may actually be a stabilizing force in financial markets, the economic benefits of quicker movements back to trend values are likely to be limited. They certainly would be small compared with the costs associated with an out-of-control asset bubble. Insofar as short-term speculation is a major factor leading to the growth of asset bubbles, the gains from stabilizing arbitrage trading can hardly be viewed as offsetting.

# The Dynamics of the Stock Bubble

In the six decades following the stock market crash in 1929, the ratio of aggregate stock prices to trend corporate earnings always remained under 20 to 1.[1] This relatively low price-to-earnings ratio allowed for a substantial equity premium in the range of four percentage points relative to risk-free government bonds. While there has been a long-standing debate about the rationale for an equity premium of this size, the difference in returns between stock and Treasury bonds reflected at least in part the risk attributed to holding stock (Mehra and Prescott, 1985).

As long as price-to-earning ratios were in the range of their long-term average of 14.5 to 1, it was possible to maintain the historic equity premium. A price-to-earning ratio of 14.5 implies that earnings are just below 7.0 percent of the stock price. If firms pay out 60 percent of their profits as either dividends or as share buybacks (these are logically equivalent from the standpoint of the shareholder), then the amount directly paid out to shareholders from corporate profits is equal to just over 4 percent of the share price.

The other portion of the return is the capital gain. If the price-to-earnings ratio remains constant and the profit share of output also stays constant over time (but not over the business cycle), then stock prices will grow at the same rate as the economy. Over the post-World War II era, economic growth has averaged just below 3 percent. This growth, coupled with the 4 percent annual dividend/share buyback payout translated into a 7 percent real return. This is approximately 4 percentage points above the 3 percent average real interest rate on long-term government debt over the postwar period.

However, in the 1990s, stock prices rose to levels that were inconsistent with sustaining the historic equity premium. The price-to-earnings ratio first exceeded 20 in 1991. At this level, simple arithmetic shows that only a 3 percentage point equity premium is possible. If firms pay out 60 percent of their earnings as dividends or share buybacks, but their earnings are just 5 percent of the share price, then the dividend yield would be 3 percent. If this is coupled with a 3 percent real capital gain then it implies a 6 percent real return for stock, not the historic 7 percent average.

While the higher-than-normal price-to-earnings ratios already present in the early 1990s implied that future returns would be lower than they had been in the past, there was virtually no appreciation of this fact among investors or even economists. The run-up in prices was taken as evidence that stocks could provide extraordinary returns. There was an expectation that because stock prices had been rising rapidly—far faster than either GDP or corporate profits—that they would continue to rise rapidly in the future. This attitude continued through the 1990s and in fact drew in more investors as the market continually hit new highs over the course of the decade (Shiller, 2000).

There were two important factors that helped to amplify the run-up in stock prices. First, the replacement of traditional defined-benefit pensions with defined-contribution pensions meant that ownership of stock was much more widely spread than it had been in the past. For the first time, tens of millions of middle-class families saw themselves having a direct stake in the stock market, as the value of their retirement accounts came to depend on it (Aizcorbe et al., 2003, Table 6). This sort of mass involvement in the market created an environment in which enthusiasm over rising stock prices could spread more widely.

The other factor that amplified the upward trend in the stock market was the acceleration in the rate of productivity growth that began in 1995. This uptick in productivity growth, which is generally attributed to the impact of computerization, reversed more than two decades of relatively slow growth. With productivity growth averaging 2.5 percent annually in the period since 1995, it was suddenly possible for the economy to sustain a considerably more rapid pace of growth. Official projections had shown growth slowing to a rate of close to 2 percent, as a result of weaker labor force growth coupled with slow productivity growth (Congressional Budget Office, 1995: Table 1-4). The uptick in productivity growth meant that the economy's near-term rate of sustainable growth would still be close to 3 percent.

However, the run-up in stock prices over the course of the decade far exceeded even the levels that might have been justified by this uptick in productivity growth. By the end of the decade, the price-to-earnings ratio for the market as a whole was above 30. This meant that profits were just over 3 percent of share prices. A 60 percent dividend payout implied a yield of just 1.8 percent. If this was coupled with a capital gain of 3 percent, it provided a total return of 4.8 percent, less than 2 percentage points above the return on government bonds. Even this return would have been more optimistic than was justified by the projections at the time. These projections showed corporate profits declining in real terms over the decade from 2000 to 2010 (Congressional Budget Office, 2000; Table 2-1), from what were viewed (correctly) as levels that were cyclical peaks. This meant that if the ratio of stock prices to corporate earnings remained constant over the course of the decade, stockholders would see no capital gains. Their only return would be their 1.8 percent dividend yield.

Remarkably, almost no one in the financial industry and very few people in the economics profession bothered to do this simple analysis. Discussions of the stock market were removed from any basis in reality. Proponents of the "new economy" would make outlandish predictions for GDP growth that not only assumed that the recent uptick in productivity growth would continue but also that productivity growth would actually accelerate. The Federal Reserve Board chairman, Alan Greenspan himself, contributed to this strange worldview when he backed away from his famous "irrational exuberance" comment, suggesting that stock prices could be justified if "profit margins will continue to increase" ("Irrational Exuberance," *New York Times*, April 21, 1997).

At the peak of the bubble some professional analysts actually proclaimed that price-to-earnings ratios no longer mattered. They could find some basis for this claim as many Internet startups had initial public offerings (IPOs) that raised hundreds of millions or even billions of dollars. Almost none of the startups were making a profit and many did not have even business plans that showed how they could make a profit. Clearly in such cases, earnings had little relevance to the share price.

This sort of run-up in stock prices could not continue indefinitely. If any new startup, no matter how ill conceived it might be as a profitable business, could raise hundreds of millions through an IPO, then it was inevitable that there would be a huge number of IPOs. This is exactly what happened in 1999 and 2000, with a peak issuance of $69.1 billion (0.7 percent of GDP) in 1999 ("In Both Price and Volume, IPOs End 1999 with a Bang," *Los Angeles Times*, December 27, 1999). Eventually, there were not enough people prepared to pay exorbitant prices for shares in companies that had no obvious value.

In March 2000, the NASDAQ (the exchange that hosted most of the startups) peaked at 5060. It hit a midsummer low of less than 3,600. It would continue to fall through most of the next two years until it finally bottomed at less than 1,200. The larger stock market plunged as well. While the bubble was largest in the tech sector, it affected the entire market. The S&P 500 peaked at 1552 in March 2000. It hit bottom at 776 in July 2002, a decline of 50 percent.

The stock bubble was not just about twentysomethings getting rich with crazy or not-so-crazy Internet schemes. It was large enough that it was actually driving the economy through the second half of the 1990s. It drove the economy through two channels. First, the run-up in the stock market generated an enormous amount of wealth, at least on paper.

Historically, the size of the effect of stock wealth on consumption has been estimated in the range of 3–4 percent, meaning that an additional dollar of stock wealth will increase annual consumption by between 3–4 cents. At the market's peak, the bubble had created roughly $10 trillion in additional wealth compared to a scenario in which stock prices had remained at their historic level. This implied between $300 billion to $400 billion in additional consumption each year, an amount that was between 3–4 percent of GDP at the time. Consistent with this prediction, the saving rate fell to 2 percent in 2000. This is down from a postwar average of more than 8 percent.

Second, another way in which the stock bubble drove the economy at the end of the 1990s was through its effect on investment. Ordinarily, stock prices have little impact on investment because the overwhelming majority of investment is financed through retained earnings. Even when firms rely on external funds for investment, they often turn to bond issues or bank loans than to equity issues.

Usually the stock market is primarily a mechanism through which early investors cash out their holdings, not a major source of funding for new investment. However, this changed in the bubble years. With even new companies able to raise large amounts of capital through IPOs, stock issues were an important source of funding at the end of the 1990s. The investment share of GDP rose by 0.8 percentage points in 1999–2000, compared with its average during the prior two years.

When the market collapsed in 2000–2002, this surge meant that investment fell off in addition to the decline in consumption due to the loss of stock market wealth. While the official dating of the 2001 recession, from March 2001 to November 2001, implied that it was a short and mild recession, the economy actually did not begin to create jobs again until September 2003. At the time, this was the longest jobless stretch of the postwar era.

It was more difficult for the economy to recover from this downturn than a traditional recession because the dynamic from a recession brought on by a collapsed asset bubble is very different. A typical recession is brought on when the Fed raises interest rates to rein in inflation. Higher interest rates slow car purchases and homebuying. When the Fed reverses course and starts lowering interest rates, there is pent-up demand for cars and housing. Lower interest rates spark this demand, leading to sharp surges in these sectors, which provide the initial boost to have a self-sustaining recovery.

The 2001 recession was not brought on by a plunge in demand for cars and housing; the demand for both remained reasonably strong throughout the recession. This meant that demand could not surge in response to the Fed's lowering of interest rates. When the economy finally did begin to create jobs it was on the back of a recovery that was led by the growth of the housing bubble.

## The Dynamics of the Housing Bubble

House prices first began to diverge from their long-term trend in the middle of the 1990s, coinciding with the growth of the stock bubble. The obvious logic for this dynamic is that the stock bubble led to increased demand for consumption goods generally, including increased demand for housing. At least in the short term the supply of housing is relatively fixed. This meant that as investors with large gains in the stock market sought to buy bigger or better homes, there was a limited supply of available housing. As a result, house prices began to rise. By the end of the decade, house prices had risen by 12 percent nationwide in excess of the rate of inflation. This followed a century in which house prices had just kept even with the overall rate of inflation.

Just as it was easy to recognize the stock bubble through the divergence between the traditional premium demanded by stock investors and the sustainable rate of return at the bubble peaks, it was also easy to see a sharp divergence between bubble-inflated house prices and the fundamentals of the housing market. The fact that a century of data showed nationwide house prices just staying even with the overall rate of inflation should have suggested that only a major shift in the fundamentals of the housing market could justify a substantial increase in house prices. It was easy to determine that there was no such shift during this period.

On the demand side, neither the trends in income growth nor population growth would have supported a large rise in house prices. Income growth had been healthy through the late 1990s, but it was no more rapid than the growth rate sustained for the quarter century following World War II, a period in which there was no real increase in house prices. Population growth was not especially rapid in this period. The baby boom cohort had been forming their own households in the 1970s and the 1980s. By the 1990s, the vast majority of baby boomers who would be homeowners had already bought homes. Many in fact were already downsizing as their children had grown and moved away. There was clearly nothing on the demand side of the market that would have justified the sharp increase in prices over this period.

Similarly, it was easy to determine that no special supply constraints could justify the run-up in house prices. Insofar as regulations restricted the supply of housing, the constraints were likely to be less binding at a time when governments at the federal, state, and local levels were mostly controlled by pro-business politicians. This is demonstrated by the near record rates of construction in 2002–2005. Clearly, supply constraints could not explain the unprecedented run-up in house prices.

Another check of the fundamentals was the trend in rents. In the long run it is reasonable to expect that house sale prices and rents will follow roughly the same pattern because people will always have the choice to be either renters or owners. If the prices become out of line then people would switch over time to renting from owning until prices are bought back in line.

Rental prices in this period showed no unusual increases. Nationwide, the owner equivalent rent component of the consumer price index rose slightly more rapidly than the overall rate of inflation from 1996 to 2000, but it remained even or slightly behind inflation in the years until the bubble began to collapse.[2]

A last basis for assessing the fundamentals of the housing market is the vacancy rate. If the run-up in house prices is being driven by the fundamentals of the housing market then the vacancy rate should be very low, indicating a shortage of housing. Instead the data showed the opposite. As early as 2002, the Commerce Department's data already showed a record level of vacancies. While the record was on the rental side of the market rather than in ownership units, this makes little difference. A record rental vacancy rate would be expected to exert downward pressure on rental prices, which would eventually put downward pressure on sales prices.

Furthermore, landlords can turn rental units into ownership units, if there is enough profit to be gained from such a conversion. During this period there were many apartment buildings that were converted to condominiums. But in a large number of cases, such conversion is not necessary. Roughly 30 percent of rental units are single-family homes. There would be little effort required to convert most of these units to ownership units. Therefore, the record vacancy rates coming at a time of an unprecedented and unexplained run-up in house prices should have been a very clear warning sign that this was an unsustainable bubble.

The bad financial practices, and occasional outright fraud, associated with subprime and other nonstandard mortgages and their securitization allowed the housing bubble to grow much longer and larger than otherwise would have been possible. However, it should have been easy to see that the fundamentals of the market would not support the rise in house prices in this period and that it was in fact a bubble.

## Mechanisms for Countering Bubbles

Because the collapse of a bubble can lead to enormous damage to the economy and society, it would be very desirable to prevent bubbles from growing to a size where they present dangers to the economy. There are three methods that government regulators can use to rein in asset bubbles:

1. Provide financial markets and the general public with the information that allows them to recognize the run-up in prices as an unsustainable bubble.

2. Use regulatory measures that limit the flow of capital to the bubble.
3. Raise interest rates.

These will be discussed in turn.

If the logic of a bubble is that it is an irrational run-up in prices, then government regulators can help to slow the run-up by calling attention to the fact that prices have gotten out of line with the fundamentals in the market. This is not simply a question of expressing an opinion, as Alan Greenspan famously did in December 1996 when he warned of "irrational exuberance" in the stock market. It is a question of supplying actors in financial markets with the evidence that prices in a particular market have grown out of line with fundamentals.

In effect, this would be an effort to inject rationality into a market that has become irrational. Government agencies, like central banks, are uniquely situated to play this role, because they have a considerable amount of authority in financial circles. Actors in financial markets may well opt to disagree with the arguments presented by government authorities, but it is unlikely that they would ignore them. Shareholders and corporate boards may have little influence over the daily operations of banks and other financial institutions, but they would likely look to hold top executives to account if their recklessness led to the bankruptcies that followed the collapse of the housing bubble. If executives were to claim that they did not pay attention to the warnings of the central bank and other regulators (i.e., that they ignored the warnings, not that they disagreed with them), this could even be grounds for making them personally liable for shareholder losses.

In effect, the information provided by central banks and other regulatory agencies can have an enormous influence on the nature of the debate among actors in financial markets. In the stock and housing bubbles, it is difficult to believe that the exuberance could have withstood a serious debate. In neither case was the evidence a close call for a fundamentals-based explanation for the run-up in prices. In the case of the stock bubble, a fundamentals-based explanation required believing either that the equity premium had disappeared and that stockholders were essentially expecting the same return as they would get holding government bonds, or that the economy would be growing far faster than almost any forecaster predicted for the indefinite future. Neither of these arguments seemed very plausible at the time. It seems unlikely that many investors would really want to cling to either position if they were forced to say that this was the basis for their confidence in the stock market.

In the case of the housing bubble, investors would have had to explain why they felt that house prices had diverged sharply from a 100-year-long trend. They also would have to explain why the factors that were leading to sharply higher house prices were not also pushing up rents. There was one somewhat plausible explanation for the run-up in prices and the divergence between sales prices and rents—low interest rates—that was both suggested at the time and in retrospect. However, a more careful examination shows this explanation really should not have given anyone confidence that high house prices would persist.

Mortgage interest rates had fallen to 50-year lows in 2002–2003 as Greenspan lowered the federal funds rate to 1 percent in an effort to boost the economy. The first problem with low interest rates as an explanation for high house prices is that house prices had never been very responsive to interest rates in the past. There had been large changes in both real and nominal interest rates over the prior three decades with limited effect on house prices.

The more important problem with the interest-rate explanation was that no one expected interest rates to stay at such historically low levels. Virtually all projections showed interest rates rising back to more normal levels once the economy recovered. This meant that if low interest rates explained the run-up in house prices, then this run-up would be temporary, because higher interest rates would push prices back down to their trend levels. In other words, if low interest rates explained the run-up in house prices, then investors should have expected the market to soon plummet just the same as did those who thought the run-up was an irrational bubble.

In short, there were no plausible ways to reconcile the sharp divergence between house prices and rents except as a temporary phenomenon. Nor would it have been easy to explain why the record rate of construction, which had already led to a record vacancy rate, would not eventually lead to an oversupply of housing, which would create substantial downward pressure on prices.

In the case of both the stock and housing bubbles, it is reasonable to believe that if the Federal Reserve Board and other regulatory agencies had committed themselves to publicizing the evidence for bubbles in these markets, it would have had an impact on investor behavior. Offhand remarks from top officials have often led to sharp short-term movements in financial markets. It is difficult to believe that a sustained barrage of data and arguments would have no effect.

The second mechanism for stemming the growth of bubbles is the regulatory controls available to the central bank and other regulatory agencies. The exact nature of these controls will vary depending on the market. In the case of the stock market, the most obvious level is the Federal Reserve Board's control over the margin requirement—the percentage of borrowed stock that an investor must put down up front. If the Fed were to raise the margin requirement, it would limit the amount of stock that could be purchased with borrowed money.

As a practical matter, raising the margin requirement would likely have little direct impact in the current market environment. Margin borrowing has been relatively limited in recent decades. Even at the peak of the bubble in 2000, margin borrowing accounted for just 1.5 percent of the value of the stock market.[3] Even this limited borrowing could in many cases have been replaced with other sources of borrowing, such as credit-card debt or mortgage loans.

However, an increase in the margin requirement would have been an unambiguous statement from the Fed that it viewed the market as being overvalued. This would likely have a large impact on investors, especially if they thought that the Fed was prepared to take additional measures to bring prices down.

In the case of the housing bubble, regulators had many more effective levers for slowing or reversing the growth in house prices. The first and most simple lever was producing the guidelines for banks to follow in issuing mortgages. The Fed was supposed to produce such guidelines from the mid-1990s but put off developing them until 2009. While many of the items in the guidelines that were eventually produced were painfully obvious as good business practice (for example, one guideline said that in the case of adjustable rate mortgages, banks should evaluate a borrower's ability to pay based on the reset rates, not the initial rate), they were not being followed in the frenzy of the bubble.

Other regulations went in exactly the wrong direction as the bubble expanded. For example, in 2004 the Securities and Exchange Commission substantially relaxed the leverage restrictions for investment banks, allowing them to have an asset-to-capital ratio of 40 to 1, instead of the prior 10 to 1. This relaxation allowed the investment banks to get far more overextended in the issuance of mortgage-backed securities and derivative instruments than would have otherwise been possible.

Given the widespread abuses in the issuance and securitization of mortgages during the peak years of the housing bubble, it is difficult to believe that a concerted effort by regulators could not have put an end to many of the practices that fueled the growth of the bubble. These regulatory measures could have pushed prices back to trend levels before the bubble grew to such dangerous levels.

The third route for deflating a bubble is raising interest rates. Higher interest rates increase the risk associated with betting on a bubble. It means that speculators must forgo more money for an investment that does not directly pay a return, or at least not a high one. At a high-enough interest rate any bubble will eventually burst. The raising of interest rates can be especially effective if the central bank explicitly ties the higher interest rate to the goal of popping the bubble. If the central bank effectively sets a target for lower prices in the bubble-inflated market, and this target is credible in the sense that the markets believe the bank will raise rates enough to reach the target, then the bubble is likely to burst quickly in response to a rise in interest rates.

Higher interest rates have a negative side effect in that they will also slow economic activity in areas other than the bubble-inflated market, thereby leading to lower growth and higher unemployment. For this reason, higher interest rates are a much less desirable path than either providing information to the market or using regulatory authority. However, if these first two routes are tried and fail to stem the growth of a bubble, it is necessary to weigh the potential harm from the unchecked growth of a bubble with the short-term costs of higher unemployment due to higher interest rates. Certainly in the case of the housing bubble, a short period of higher unemployment induced by a rise in interest rates would have been preferable to the prolonged downturn the United States is now experiencing.

## Conclusion

Asset bubbles can pose enormous economic risks. Price bubbles in most items will have little macroeconomic impact, although they can seriously distort production and consumption in the affected markets. However, a bubble in large markets, like the stock and housing market, can have large macroeconomic effects. In the United States the bubbles largely determined the pattern of growth in both the late 1990s and the 2000s.

There is no easy path to reverse a pattern of growth created by an asset bubble. In the short term the demand created by an asset bubble can only be replaced by the government. While the economy may eventually adjust and get set on a different growth path, unless the government sustains demand in the interim, countries with burst bubbles are likely to experience a prolonged period of high unemployment and slow growth.

For this reason, central banks should make combating asset bubbles a key part of their mission. This means taking steps to prevent bubbles from growing so large that they present a danger to the economy. This will require central banks to first recognize bubbles and then to take the actions necessary to bring them under control. The failure to do so can be enormously costly.

## Notes

1. Economic Report of the President, 2010, Table B-95, Washington, D.C.: U.S. Government Printing Office.
2. The owner equivalent rent index provides better basis for comparison with house sale prices than the rent proper index because the latter also includes many utilities, such as heating and electricity, that are often included in the rent that is charged to tenants.
3. This calculation uses the estimate ($235.1 billion) for security credit issued by primary broker deals in 2000 (Board of Governors of the Federal Reserve System, (2012), Table L.130, Line 11), divided by the value ($17,566 billion) of the shares traded in the United States ( Board of Governors of the Federal Reserve System, (2012), Table L.213, Line 5).

## References

Aizcorbe, A., A. Kennickell, and K. Moore. (2003). "Recent Changes in US Family Finances: Evidence from the 1998 and 2001 Survey of Consumer Finances." *Federal Reserve Bulletin* 89 (January 2003): 1–32.

Board of Governors of the Federal Reserve System, (2012). "Flow of Funds Accounts of the United States." *Federal Reserve Statistical Release Z.1. http://www.federalreserve.gov/releases/z1/*

Congressional Budget Office. (1995). *Budget and Economic Outlook: 1996–2000.* Washington, DC: Congressional Budget Office.

Congressional Budget Office. (2000). *Budget and Economic Outlook: 2001–2010.* Washington, DC: Congressional Budget Office.

DeLong, J. B., A. Shleifer, L. Summers, and R. Waldmann. (1990). "Noise Trader Risk in Financial Markets." *Journal of Political Economy* 98: 4 (August 1990): 703–738.

Economic Report, of the President, 2010. Washington, D.C.: U.S. Government Printing Office.

Fama, E., and K. French. (1988). "Permanent and Temporary Components of Stock Prices." *Journal of Political Economy* 96:2 (April 1988): 246–273.

Mehra, R., and E. Prescott. (1985). "The Equity Premium: A Puzzle." *Journal of Monetary Economics* 15:2 (March 1985): 145–161.

Poterba, J., and L. Summers. (1988). "Mean Reversion in Stock Prices: Evidence and Implications." *Journal of Financial Economics* 22:1 (October 1988): 27–59.

Shiller, R. (2000). *Irrational Exuberance.* Princeton, NJ: Princeton University Press.

CHAPTER 4

# THE GREAT RECESSION'S IMPACT ON JOBS, WAGES, AND INCOMES

JOSH BIVENS AND HEIDI SHIERHOLZ

THE roots of the Great Recession and the financial crisis of 2007–2009 are already some of the most-analyzed and commented-upon economic events of recent decades. While much about these events remains contested, in terms of their impact on the nonfinancial side of the economy they are surprisingly easy to understand: the bursting of the housing bubble provided a large, negative shock to aggregate demand and the economy has been struggling to recover ever since. The large reductions in output led directly to large reductions in employment and rising rates of unemployment and underemployment. The shock to employment prospects then contributed directly to sharply decelerating nominal wage growth, and the lower wages, combined with greatly reduced hours of work, led to sharply falling family incomes.

In this chapter we present descriptive statistics on developments in employment, wages, and incomes since the Great Recession began and also demonstrate that these trends are consistent with this strictly Keynesian view of labor-market distress caused by deficient aggregate demand and are *not* consistent with the view that the labor-market distress of recent years can be ascribed to "structural" factors.

We argue further that the largest policy intervention into the labor market during these years—the very large increase in spending on and duration of unemployment insurance benefits (UI)—has clearly resulted in higher employment levels and has likely led to lower unemployment rates as well.

We then examine the empirical evidence on the effects of prolonged unemployment on growth in labor earnings and family incomes to project what is the likely outcome for these labor-market indicators given projected unemployment rates through 2015. The evidence suggests that very large drops in both labor earnings and family incomes for the lower parts of these respective distributions are likely in coming years, as most forecasters do not have prerecession unemployment rates reached until nearly 2015. These large projected falls seem plausible—between 2001 and 2007, a business cycle that saw unemployment rise from 4 percent to 6 percent and then fall back to 4.6 percent, family incomes for the lowest quintile *fell* by 8 percent from peak to trough, and remained 5 percent below their 1999 peak in 2007—the highest point in the expansion. Given that unemployment rose from 4.6 percent to 9.6 percent between 2007 and 2010 and that projections are that several years will pass before the prerecession level is reached again, one imagines that family income declines will be much greater for this group as a result of the current recession than what was seen in previous ones.

## Descriptive Statistics about Jobs, Wages, and Incomes during the Great Recession

### Jobs

Various versions of figure 4.1 have achieved near-iconic status in recent years, showing job losses during the Great Recession relative to other post-World War II recessions. In this version, we center the graph on the employment trough. The Great Recession is labeled, and the gray lines represent the ten other recessions since World War II. This highlights that not only was the Great Recession's trough much deeper than previous recessions but also that it was a long time in coming and is looking much more persistent than most previous labor-market slumps as well.

The 6.3 percent decline in payroll employment at the trough of the Great Recession is the largest by far of any postwar recession. This very large loss in jobs led to the unemployment rate rising further from the previous business cycle peak than in any other postwar recession, along with a record spike in the underemployment rate. Figure 4.2 shows the rise in the unemployment and underemployment rates over the Great Recession.

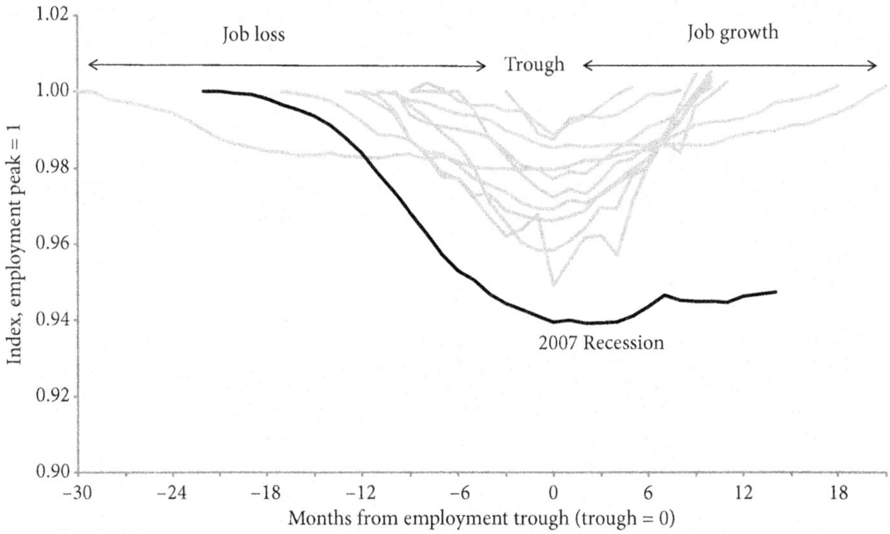


**Figure 4.1** Payroll employment over postwar business cycles.
*Note*: The 2007 recession is labeled; the gray lines represent the ten other recessions since World War II.
*Source*: EPI analysis of Bureau of Labor Statistics data.

**Figure 4.2** Unemployment and underemployment rates, 2000–2010.
*Note*: Shaded areas denote recession. The underemployment rate is the U-6 measure of labor underutilization.
*Source*: Current Population Survey.

This large increase in reported unemployment and underemployment occurred even as there was a rapid decline in the labor-force participation rate (LFPR), which should have led to a lower unemployment rate, ceteris paribus. In the little over three years between December 2007 and January 2011, a period during which the economy was in recession in the first half and in official recovery in the second, the LFPR fell from 66.0 percent to 64.2 percent. If the LFPR had remained stable at its 2007 level there would have been 4.9 million more workers in the labor force in January 2011 than there actually were. If just *half* of these workers had been in the labor force in January 2011 and were unemployed, the unemployment rate would have been 10.5 percent instead of 9.0 percent. One imagines that in coming years, if there is significant improvement in the labor market, the LFPR will indeed begin rising back to its prerecession level. This influx of workers into the job market will keep upward pressure on the unemployment rate for possibly years to come.

One can combine data on job losses as well as the jobs that would have been needed to absorb new workers had the labor-force participation rate remained unchanged over the Great Recession to get a measure of the "jobs shortfall" that has accumulated in recent years—this shortfall tells us roughly how many payroll jobs would need to be created to push the unemployment rate back to its immediate prerecession level (5 percent in December 2007). As shown in figure 4.3, in January 2011, the labor market was 7.7 million payroll jobs below where it was at the start of the recession in December 2007. However, to keep the payroll-jobs-to-working-age-population ratio constant, the number of payroll jobs should have *increased* by 3.7 million over this period. The punch line of this calculation is that as of January 2011 11.4 million jobs were needed to return the unemployment rate to its prerecession level. It is important to note that this implies around 100,000 jobs need to be created each month just to keep the unemployment rate from rising unless the labor-force participation rate begins falling. Needing 11.4 million jobs before prerecession unemployment rates are reached is daunting. To close the jobs gap in five years would require roughly 285,000 jobs to be created per month, or nearly three times as many jobs as were created in an average month during the business cycle expansion from 2002 to 2007. To close it in three years would require around 412,000 jobs to be created each month, or over twice the average monthly job gain of the much more job-intensive expansion of the 1990s.

## Wages

A large literature (discussed more extensively below) has argued that rising rates of unemployment and growing labor-market slack lead to reduced wage growth, albeit often with a lag. Due to compositional effects (i.e., the stylized fact that lower-paid workers tend to be more likely to lose their jobs during recessions), this relationship can be hard to pick up in simple cuts of the data, but this pattern is

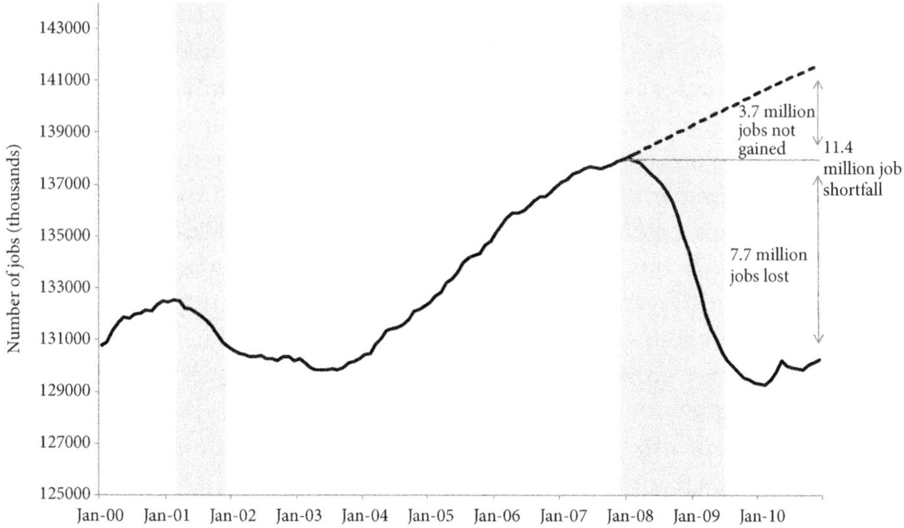


**Figure 4.3** Job shortfall—actual payroll employment and employment needed to return to prerecession unemployment rate (5.0 percent in December 2007).
*Note*: Shaded areas denote a recession.
*Source*: EPI analysis of Bureau of Labor Statistics data.

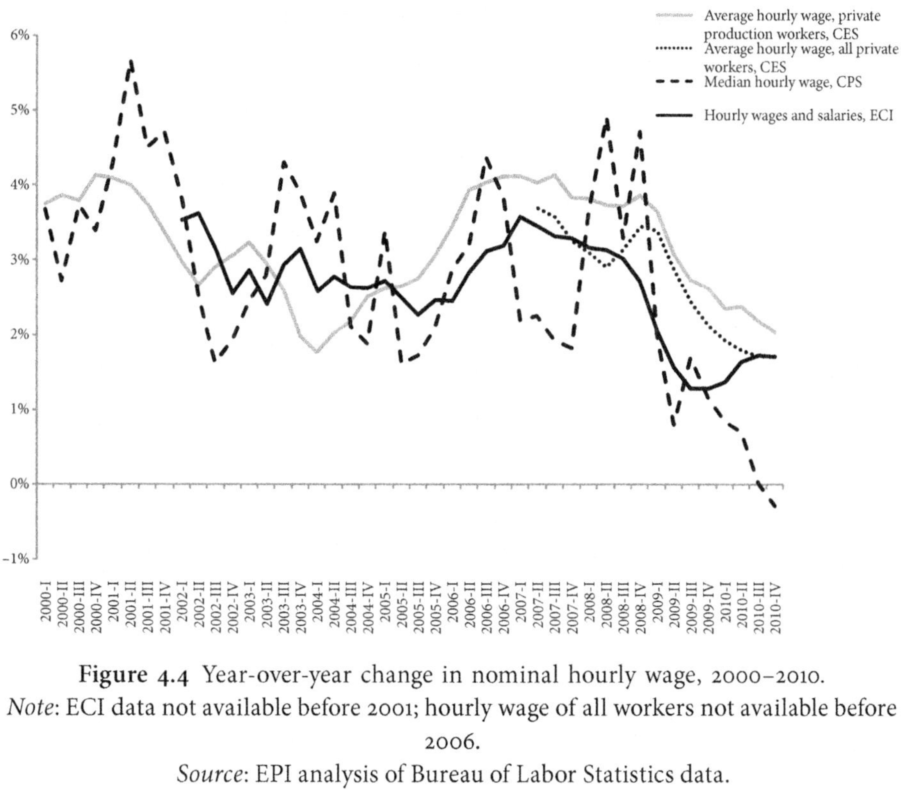


**Figure 4.4** Year-over-year change in nominal hourly wage, 2000–2010.
*Note*: ECI data not available before 2001; hourly wage of all workers not available before 2006.
*Source*: EPI analysis of Bureau of Labor Statistics data.

clear in the evolution of unemployment and nominal wage growth since the Great Recession began. Figure 4.4 shows how nominal wages have fared since 2000. In addition to the average hourly wage of all workers and of production workers, both from the Current Establishment Survey (CES), and the median hourly wage from the Current Population Survey (CPS), figure 4.4 also shows wage and salary growth from the Employment Cost Index (ECI), a fixed-weight measure of wages that, to some extent, controls for the problem of composition bias.

While obviously much besides changing unemployment rates affects the growth of nominal wages (changes in the rate of inflation, in particular), this figure provides preliminary evidence that high and rising unemployment has taken a toll on wage growth over the course of the Great Recession. Later sections in this chapter provide some econometric findings on what prolonged high unemployment has already meant for wage growth and what is likely to mean for future wage growth.

### Incomes

The Great Recession generated very large declines in family and household incomes. Average family income fell by 3.7 percent between 2007 and 2009 while median incomes fell by 5.3 percent. This decline was actually ameliorated a bit by the fact that households over 65 actually saw income gains, shown in figure 4.5. Working-age households (aged 25–54) saw the largest declines in median income, 4.6 percent.

This loss in working-age household median income is the largest two-year decline since 1994 (the first year this measure was tracked) and has actually pushed this metric below the level that prevailed in 1997. Given that 2010 has ended with unemployment slightly higher than what prevailed over 2009, it is virtually certain that household and family incomes fell again in 2010.

This income fall led, unsurprisingly, to significant increases in the poverty rate. The overall rate rose from 12.5 percent in 2007 to 14.3 percent in 2009. Again, however, this rise was ameliorated by stability in the elderly poverty rate. The rise in poverty among working-age households in 2009 tied the largest single-year increase on record (rising 1.2 percentage points just since 2008)—hitting 12.9 percent of this population, up 2.0 percentage points since 2007, shown in figure 4.6.

## The US Experience with the Great Recession in an International Context

A noteworthy aspect of the Great Recession, and one that makes it particularly difficult to escape from, is its global reach. Virtually the entire developed world

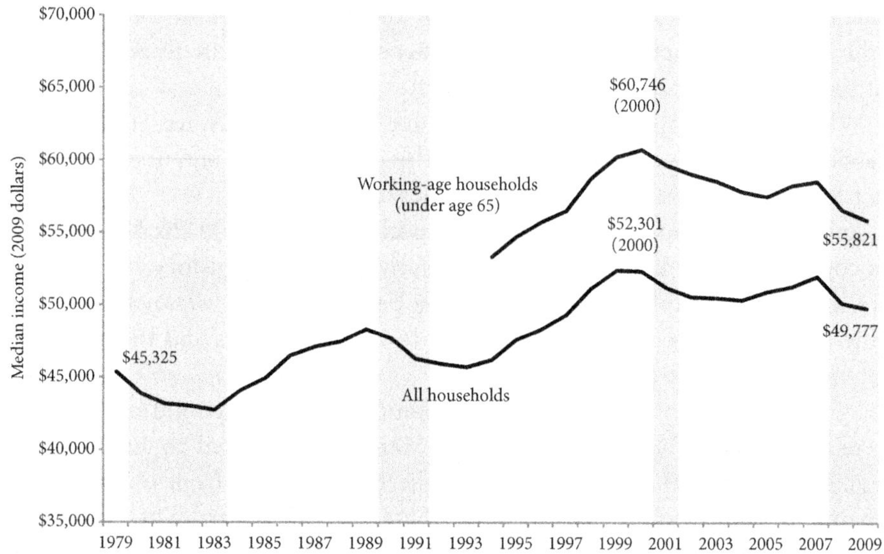


**Figure 4.5** Real median household income for working-age and total population, 1979–2009.
*Note*: Shaded areas denote recessions. Median income for workers below 65 starts in 1994.
*Source*: EPI analysis of US Census Bureau data.

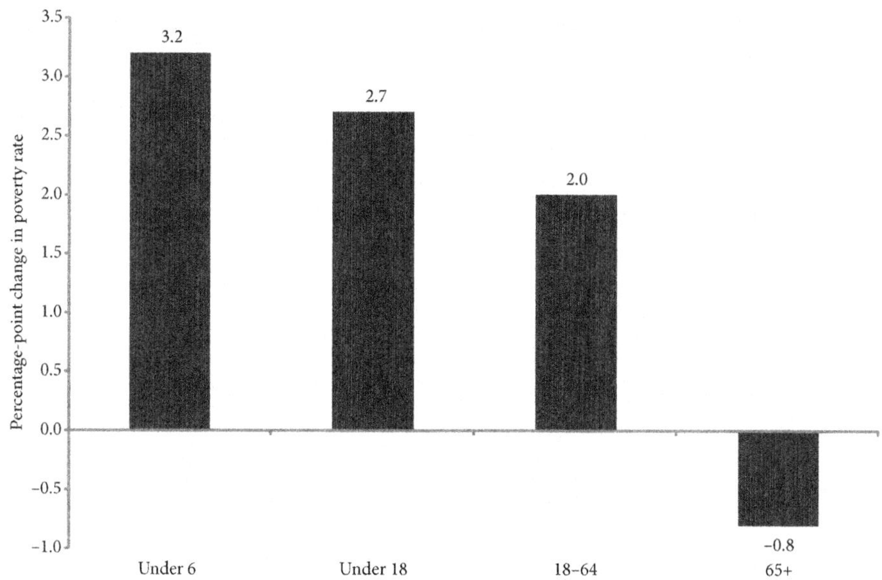


**Figure 4.6** Percentage-point change in poverty rates, by age, 2007–2009.
*Source*: US Census Bureau, Historical Poverty Tables.

entered recession between 2007 and 2009, and growth rates in the developing world decelerated rapidly—2009 was in fact the first year in recorded history that saw an outright decline in *global* GDP.

While virtually all of the advanced global peers of the United States entered recession, there were clear differences in the magnitude of output and employment losses and some very unexpected ones at that.

For example, relative to Germany the decline in output in the United States was comparatively mild (still very large relative to its own history, but mild relative to what was experienced by its global peers). Yet, the *employment* decline in the US economy was very large relative to its global peers and the rise in the unemployment rate was similarly severe.

What explains this strange US combination of relatively mild output losses yet relatively severe employment losses? Many have pointed to European (in particular) policies that aim to cushion the labor market from output shocks as being a prime explanation for why these countries were better able than the United States to blunt the rise in unemployment stemming from the Great Recession. Work sharing is often singled out as a particularly effective policy in this regard.

While work sharing is, in our view, a very useful policy that has substantial power to de-link output and employment declines, it remains the case that average hours worked per week in the United States actually fell far faster than virtually all of its global peers. Given this, it seems that work-sharing policies cannot explain much of why US employment performance has been so poor relative to its output performance over the course of the recession.

Arithmetically, of course, given that hours of work declined faster in the United States than in most other countries, the only remaining explanation for the slower output yet faster employment declines is simple: productivity grew much faster in the United States throughout the recession compared to most other advanced countries (see column 3 in table 4.1).

It seems possible that part of this productivity "advantage" registered by the US economy over the course of the recession is an artifact of sectoral shifts. It is likely that the US economy, having seen a more pronounced housing bubble, lost more construction jobs—which are relatively low-productivity jobs, especially those in the residential construction sector—than other countries.

However, this pattern of rapid productivity growth all the way through a recession also characterized the US recession of the early 2000s, one that was not centered disproportionately on the housing sector. Even the recession of the early 1990s saw productivity that was far less pro-cyclical than the norm displayed during previous business cycles. Figure 4.7 shows the average trajectory of productivity during the nine recessions between 1948 and 1990 as well as the average trajectory that has characterized the recessions of the early and late 2000s. The figure shows that previous recessions saw clearly pro-cyclical productivity behavior—actually falling during recessions and accelerating in the

**Table 4.1** Economic indicators over the Great Recession

| Country | GDP | Total hours | Productivity | Average weekly hours | Employment | Unemployment rate |
|---|---|---|---|---|---|---|
| *United States* | −2.1% | −5.8% | 4.0% | −2.0% | −3.9% | 4.7 |
| *Japan* | −6.1% | −6.5% | 0.5% | −3.5% | −3.1% | – |
| *Germany* | −4.0% | −1.5% | −2.5% | −2.8% | 1.3% | −0.9 |
| *United Kingdom* | −4.1% | −3.3% | −0.9% | −2.0% | −1.3% | 2.3 |
| *France* | −1.9% | −2.6% | 0.7% | −1.4% | −1.2% | 1.1 |
| *Italy* | −5.8% | −2.2% | −3.6% | −1.4% | −0.8% | 1.7 |
| *Canada* | −2.7% | −1.9% | −0.9% | −1.8% | −0.1% | – |
| *Australia* | 2.9% | 0.1% | 2.7% | −2.0% | 2.2% | – |
| *Austria* | −2.6% | −1.2% | −1.5% | −1.4% | 0.3% | 0.4 |
| *Belgium* | −2.1% | 0.8% | −2.8% | −0.2% | 1.0% | 0.5 |
| *Denmark* | −5.5% | −2.3% | −3.3% | −0.5% | −1.8% | 2.3 |
| *Finland* | −5.9% | −3.0% | −3.0% | −1.7% | −1.3% | 1.5 |
| *Greece* | 0.9% | −1.0% | 1.9% | −0.2% | −0.8% | 1.2 |
| *Ireland* | −10.2% | −9.9% | −0.3% | −1.5% | −8.6% | 7.4 |
| *Netherlands* | −2.5% | 0.4% | −2.9% | −0.5% | 0.9% | 0.2 |
| *New Zealand* | −1.9% | 0.1% | −2.0% | −1.2% | 1.3% | – |
| *Norway* | 0.4% | 2.1% | −1.7% | 0.8% | 1.3% | 0.7 |
| *Spain* | −2.8% | −7.8% | 5.4% | −0.6% | −7.2% | 9.8 |
| *Sweden* | −4.8% | −2.0% | −2.9% | −0.7% | −1.3% | 2.3 |
| *Switzerland* | −1.1% | 1.9% | −3.0% | 0.1% | 1.8% | 0.5 |
| *Average excluding US* | −3.2% | −2.1% | −1.1% | −1.2% | −0.9% | 2.1 |

Changes in GDP, total hours, productivity, average weekly hours, employment, and the unemployment rate 2007–2009.
*Source*: The Conference Board and Groningen Growth and Development (2010), Eurostat, and Bureau of Labor Statistics Current Population Survey.

early phase of recovery—while the last two recessions show no pro-cyclicality at all.

DeLong and Waldmann (1997) interpret the (previous) pro-cyclicality of productivity as evidence that American employers "hoarded" labor during downturns. Because it was hard to find skilled workers that were well matched

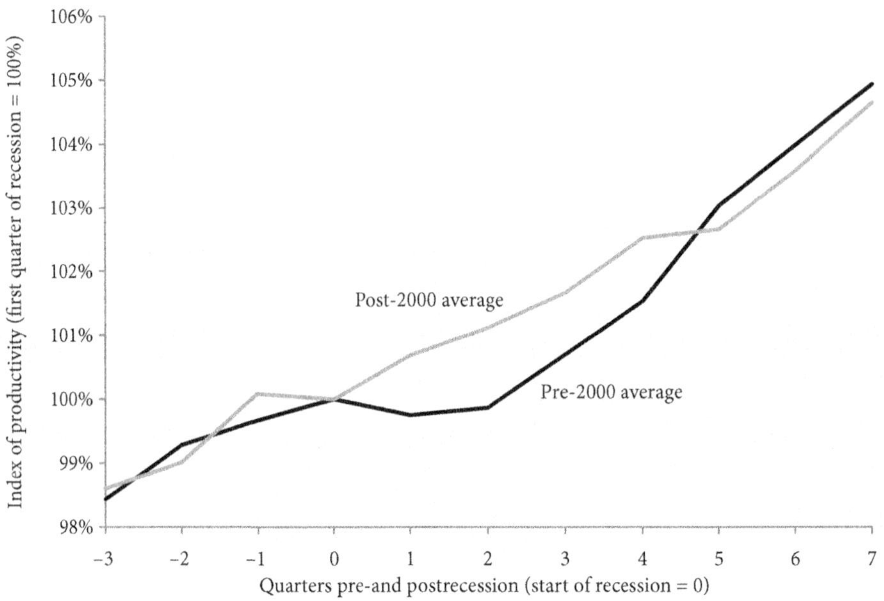


**Figure 4.7** Productivity growth no longer pro-cyclical? Productivity pre- and postrecessions.

to the jobs provided by particular firms, employers were reluctant to shed these workers at the first sign of a downturn in sales—in short, employment changes were blunted because employers "valued the match" they had made with their employees.

If this is the real explanation for pro-cyclical productivity (and we think it is a plausible one), American employers over the past decade (at least) seem to have placed much less value on the match they have made with workers, as evidenced by the conspicuous failure to hoard labor when sales turned down in the last two recessions.

Gordon (2010) notes that a decline in the value that employers place on incumbent employees is consistent with other (noncyclical) evidence that American workers have seen a marked decline in bargaining power in recent decades. The claim that American workers have suffered declines in bargaining power is one most often made (convincingly, in our view) in arguments about the secular increase in wage and income inequality over the past three decades—the richest 10 percent of tax-filing units, for example, can account for roughly 91 percent of the rise in average incomes between the business-cycle peaks of 1979 and 2007. However, this traditional measurement of incomes between business-cycle peaks has perhaps obscured the possibility that reduced bargaining power can manifest in different ways besides inequality, with the vastly increased probability of job loss (conditional on output declines) being but one example.

## Labor-Market Controversies during the Great Recession

The Great Recession has sparked a number of debates about the underlying causes of and the most promising remedies for the extended period of high unemployment and underemployment. We'll examine two here. The first concerns the classification of unemployment: specifically whether or not it is usefully classified as "Keynesian" and stemming from deficient aggregate demand, or whether it is "structural" and stemming from a mismatch between the skills or geographical locations of American workers and the demands of potential employers. The second (and related) concerns the effect of extending the period of eligibility for receipt of unemployment benefits on the measured unemployment rate.

## Unemployment: Keynesian or Structural?

The case for a *Keynesian* diagnosis is pretty straightforward; a wealth of macroeconomic indicators indicates that the US economy is operating well below potential. Figures 4.8 and 4.9 show the estimate of potential and actual GDP calculated by the Congressional Budget Office (CBO) as well as the rate of core inflation. The CBO has estimated that actual GDP has been a cumulative 14 percentage points below potential since the start of the Great Recession (representing roughly $2 trillion of lost output). Over this same time, the prediction regarding core inflation stemming from very large output gaps has held true as there has been a rapid deceleration in the rate of core inflation and the possibility of outright deflation in the future is far from unthinkable.

The case for a *structural* diagnosis of unemployment remains thin—probably the most-cited piece of evidence is a blog post by David Altig, the research director at the Federal Reserve Bank of Atlanta (Altig, 2010a).

In it, Altig notes that there is a roughly linear relationship between the number of unemployed workers and the number of posted job openings (from the Job Openings and Labor Turnover Survey, or JOLTS) for the period from 2000 and 2008. As might be expected, high levels of unemployment tend to coexist with low levels of posted job openings. The data for 2009 and 2010, however, deviate from the seemingly well-behaved linear relationship, as high levels of unemployment are accompanied by higher levels of job openings than the relationship between these series that held between 2000 and 2008 would lead one to expect.

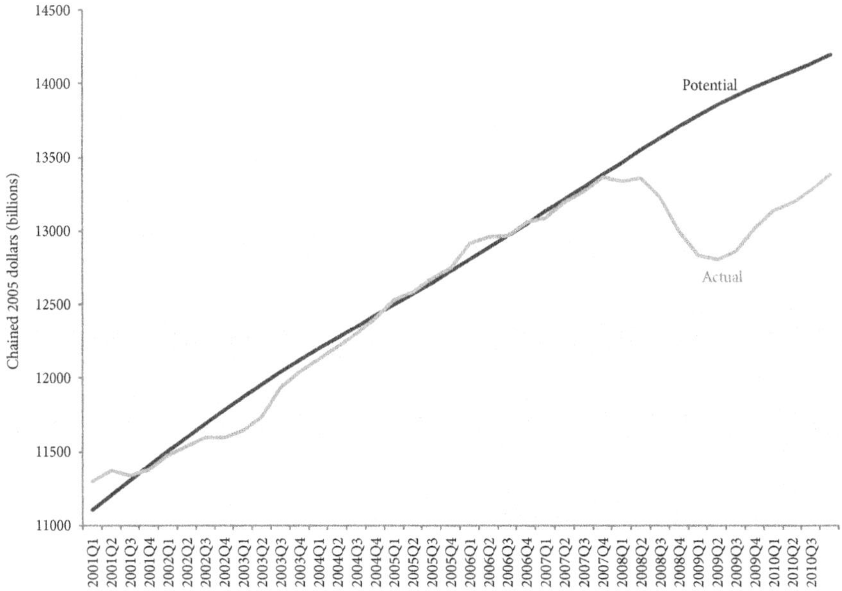


**Figure 4.8** Potential GDP and actual GDP, real dollars, 2001Q1—2010Q3.
*Source*: Congressional Budget Office and Bureau of Economic Analysis.

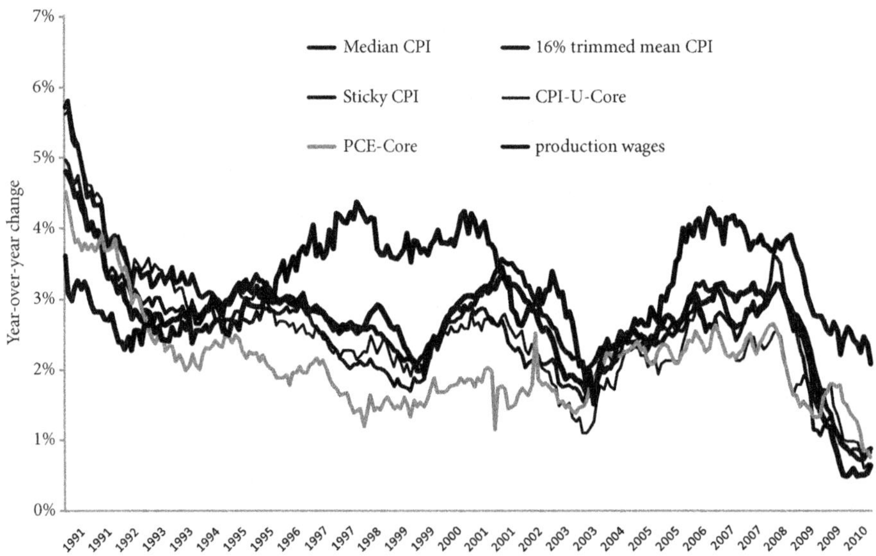


**Figure 4.9** Various measures of core inflation.
*Source*: Atlanta Federal Reserve Bank, Clevel and Federal Reserve Bank, BLS and BEA.

Altig goes on to write that "the most tempting explanation for the seeming shift in the Beveridge curve relationship (to me, anyway) is a problem with the mismatch between skills required in the jobs that are available and skills possessed by the pool of workers available to take those jobs."

However, Tasci and Lindner (2010) point out that these data do not cover most of the post-World War II period. Using more data to obtain a longer time frame (going back to 1951) they find that the recent dynamics are common in the recovery phase of business cycles, especially recoveries following very deep recessions. They write that "during and after recessions in the postwar period, the Beveridge curve has generally followed a pattern of shifting to the right during a recovery...the path of the curve going forward looks poised to follow in the footsteps of previous recessionary periods." In other words, the current relationship between unemployment and job openings is not anomalous: instead it is what would be expected based on past evidence. This can be seen for the last ten years in figure 4.10.

Perhaps the most influential proponent of the structural diagnosis of current unemployment is the president of the Minneapolis Federal Reserve Bank (and now-voting member of the Federal Open Market Committee), Narayana Kocherlakota. Kocherlakota (2010) wrote:

> Firms have jobs, but can't find appropriate workers. The workers want to work, but can't find appropriate jobs. There are many possible sources of mismatch—geography, skills, demography—and they are probably all at work. Whatever the source, though, it is hard to see how the Fed can do much to cure this problem. Monetary stimulus has provided conditions so that

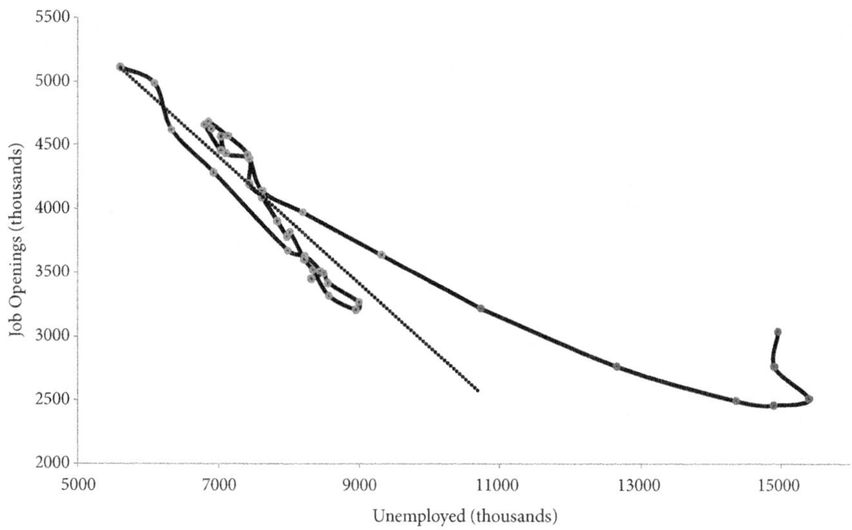


**Figure 4.10** Beveridge curve: 2000q4—2010q2.
*Note*: Trendline is shown with dotted line and represents the relationship between 2000q4—2008q4.
*Source*: Current Population Survey and Job Openings and Labor Turnover Survey.

> manufacturing plants want to hire new workers. But the Fed does not have a means to transform construction workers into manufacturing workers.

This provides a useful and clear statement of the structural unemployment diagnosis. Taken literally, however, it's clearly wrong. The commonly heard claim that the continuing labor-market distress following the Great Recession is driven by the need to move workers out of construction and into other sectors (where perhaps they do not have the appropriate skills) is belied by the fact that construction job losses accounted for less than a quarter of all jobs lost in the Great Recession. Most unfortunately for Kocherlakota's example is that more jobs were lost in manufacturing than in construction during the Great Recession. In 2010, unemployed construction workers made up only 12.1 percent of the unemployed, up less than 3.0 percentage points from the peak of construction employment in 2006, when construction's unemployment share was 9.6 percent. Of course, construction is a particularly pro-cyclical industry and its unemployment share tends to rise during downturns. To take an unrealistic but useful example: if the construction share of unemployment had not risen at all during the Great Recession and, holding everything else constant, those construction workers that made up the difference were employed instead of unemployed, there would have been 380,000 fewer unemployed construction workers in 2010. With that many fewer unemployed workers, the overall unemployment rate in 2010 would be 9.4 percent instead of 9.6 percent. In other words, even in this unrealistic example, unemployed construction workers are not the reason for the persistent high unemployment. Unemployment today is spread across all industries.

Figure 4.11 illustrates this further, showing the number of unemployed workers and the number of job openings in 2010 by industry. For structural unemployment to be a major part of overall unemployment, you would expect to find labor shortages in some areas, as employers with job openings could not find suitable workers. But there are no major sectors where that is happening—unemployed workers dramatically outnumber job openings in every sector. It is not that the economy is lacking the right workers: it is instead, across the board, lacking jobs.

## A Geographic Mismatch?

There is a large amount of variation in unemployment by geographic area. In 2010 in Arlington County, Virginia, the unemployment rate averaged 4.2 percent, whereas in Wayne County, Michigan, it was 15.5 percent. Some claim that the Great Recession's high unemployment is due in large part to immobility—in particular that because the decline in housing prices over the past several years has left many homeowners owing more on their mortgages than their houses are worth, workers are more tied to their homes than in prior recessions and in

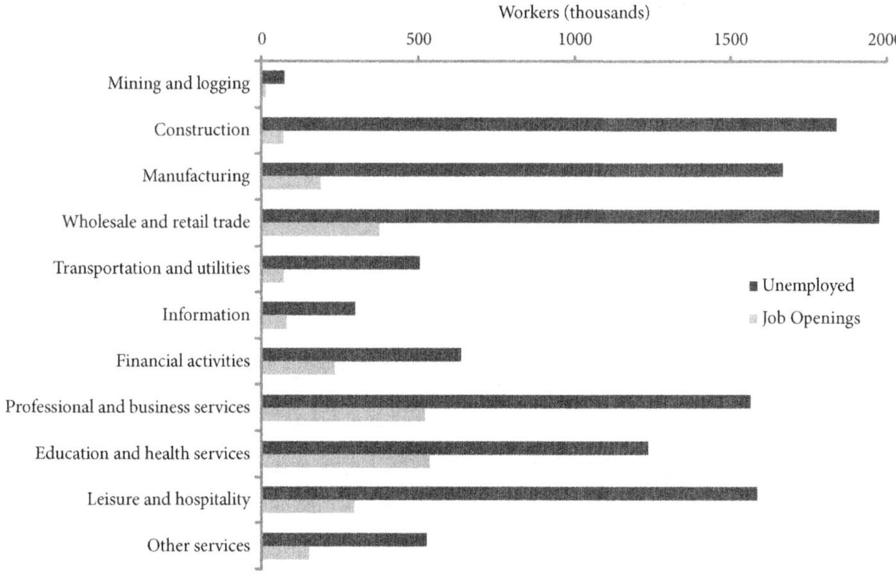


**Figure 4.11** Job openings and number of unemployed workers by industry, in thousands.
*Source*: EPI analysis of Bureau of Labor Statistics data, 12-month averages (Nov 2009–Oct 2010).

the event of a job loss they are less able to move to places where there are jobs. Could immobility account for a significant portion of the Great Recession's unemployment? Theoretical predictions about the effect of negative home equity on mobility are ambiguous, so whether being underwater increases or reduces mobility is an empirical question. Schulhofer-Wohl (2011)—after correcting for problems with the coding of "movers" by Ferreira and colleagues (2010)—finds that homeowners with negative equity are slightly *more* likely to move than homeowners with positive equity. Engelhardt (2003) finds that low equity due to house-price declines does not reduce mobility. On the other hand, Chan (2001) finds that homeowners with negative equity are less mobile.

A straightforward way to investigate the possibility that immobility could be keeping unemployment high is to determine whether it is possible that a significant portion of today's unemployed workers could move and be readily absorbed elsewhere. In 2010, only 786 of the 3,218 counties in the United States had an unemployment rate of less than 7 percent.[1] Of these, only 652 had faced an increase in their unemployment rate of less than 3 percentage points since 2007. While having an unemployment rate that is less than 7 percent and that has not increased by 3 percentage points or more over the last three years is a rather generous definition of labor-market health, these 652 counties are nevertheless the set of counties that could plausibly absorb unemployed workers from the outside. But not only are there relatively few of them, they are also relatively rural—over half of these counties are in Nebraska, Kansas, North Dakota, South Dakota, and

Iowa. These 652 counties account for only 9 percent of the country's employment. For these counties to absorb the unemployed workers from the other 2,566 counties in the United States, the number of jobs in the "receiving" counties would have to more than double. The failure to relocate cannot be a key part of high unemployment unless there are places where a significant portion of unemployed workers could go and be readily absorbed, which there are not.

# The Effect of Extended Unemployment Benefits on the Unemployment Rate

As part of the response to the Great Recession, the normal period of eligibility for receipt of unemployment benefits has been repeatedly extended. In high-unemployment states (those with unemployment rates exceeding 8.5 percent), as of December 2010 the maximum duration for receipt of these benefits stood at 99 weeks, up from a prerecession maximum of 26 weeks. The extended benefits were set to continue through 2011.

These are, by far, the longest periods of unemployment eligibility in American history and have accordingly attracted much attention.

Some have worried, based on microeconomic analyses of labor markets, that the disincentive effect provided by extended unemployment benefits have kept some workers from conducting an aggressive job search. In short, the worry is that unemployment benefits change the relative price of leisure (making it cheaper) and hence encourage potential workers to consume more of it than they would, absent the policy change.

Others have noted that unemployment benefits are uniquely good macroeconomic "automatic stabilizers"—transfer programs that are automatically triggered by countercyclical movements in the labor market. Besides the good timing of unemployment benefits, they are also by definition targeted—they transfer money to households that are very likely to be cash-constrained and that would otherwise likely sharply curtail their consumption spending, providing further downward pressure on aggregate demand.

## Microeconomic Effects of Extended Unemployment Benefits

The most careful estimates of the effect of today's extended unemployment benefits on the measured unemployment rate come from Valletta and Kuang (2010a). They use the fact that not all unemployed individuals are eligible to receive unemployment insurance benefits—the program is meant to provide benefits to only those unemployed "through no fault of their own"; workers fired for poor performance or those who have voluntarily quit a job would be ineligible for benefits. Further, workers must have worked enough in the period immediately prior to a job loss to have passed a (relatively modest) earnings test. While many laid-off workers will pass this test, it does effectively make unemployment benefits completely unavailable to new labor-market entrants.

Valletta and Kuang find that while unemployment *durations* during the Great Recession have risen substantially, this has been true generally for both workers eligible for and those ineligible for receipt of unemployment insurance benefits. They look specifically at the increase in unemployment duration observed as unemployment benefits were extended in 2008 and 2009. They argue that the gap in duration rates between eligible and noneligible workers that has opened since the extension of unemployment benefits is a good measure of the effect of this policy shift on unemployment durations of eligible workers. As of the last quarter of 2009, the average duration of unemployment for UI-eligible workers was 18.7 weeks while the duration for UI-ineligibles was just 17.1. They conclude that this 1.6-week gap, multiplied by the number of UI-eligible workers, suggests that extended benefits had increased the measured unemployment rate by roughly 0.4 percentage points. In an update to this first work they provide a range of the effect of extended benefits on the measured unemployment rate, bracketing it between 0.4 and 0.8 weeks. Given that the overall unemployment rate rose by 5.2 percentage points (from 4.8 percent to 10 percent) between the fourth quarter of 2007 and the fourth quarter of 2009, 0.6 percentage points (the midpoint of the Valletta and Kuang [2010b] estimates) represents less than 12 percent of the total increase seen over this time.

There are three other issues to note about microeconomic estimates of the effect of extended unemployment durations on the measured unemployment rate. First, as pointed out by Chetty (2008), much of the increase in unemployment durations spurred by unemployment insurance is actually welfare-improving and not due to simple disincentive effects (choosing subsidized leisure over work) but instead are due to the consumption-smoothing benefits provided by unemployment benefits to liquidity-constrained households.

For example, households with no income (including unemployment benefits) and no liquid savings may well make inefficient choices simply to meet daily living requirements (feeding and clothing their kids, for example). They may spend less time with their kids than they'd otherwise choose or even undertake illegal activities that they would otherwise not choose. If unemployment benefits are introduced (or extended), these same parents may well decide to increase the duration of unemployment, but this will not be an inefficiency generated by changing the relative price of leisure. Instead it will be efficiency-generating through its effect on releasing a binding liquidity constraint. Further, as Chetty (2008) as well as Acemoglu and Shimer (1999) have emphasized, by increasing potential unemployment durations unemployment benefits may well allow workers to be choosier and find better matches with employers, leading to longer-lasting and more productive employment spells.

Furthermore, while Valletta and Kuang (2010a) showed that UI-eligible unemployed workers saw an increase in unemployment duration of 1.6 weeks more than did ineligible unemployed workers, it is far from clear that the elimination of the extensions would have led to a lower unemployment rate. Job opportunities plummeted in the Great Recession—in 2009 there were 44.1 percent fewer job openings than in 2007, while there were 22.5 percent more layoffs. In other words, there were many *more* job seekers competing for far *fewer* available jobs. Shorter UI benefits would not have made job openings more plentiful. The extensions likely affected the *mix* of the unemployed, with a higher percentage of UI recipients composing the pool of the unemployed than would have been the case in the absence of extensions, as UI recipients had more room than nonrecipients to take time to try to find jobs that matched their skills and experience. But given the severe lack of job openings, it is a substantial leap from increased duration for UI eligibles to the conclusion that fewer workers overall would have been unemployed in the absence of extensions.

However, if we take Valletta and Kuang's (2010a, 2010b) assertion that extended benefits increased the measured unemployment rate as given, it is important to note that these results are consistent with the possibility that the increased relative duration of UI-eligible workers actually reflects *increased* job search. That is, because active job search is a precondition for the receipt of UI benefits, it would not be surprising if many workers who otherwise would have given up looking and therefore dropped out of the labor force entirely continue to actively seek work in order to qualify for extended UI benefits. To say it another way, assuming it is the case that 0.6 percent of the labor force would no longer be classified as unemployed if UI benefits had not been extended over the course of the Great Recession, it is by no means clear that this would translate into those (roughly) 900,000 workers actually being employed. A portion (perhaps even a substantial portion) of them could well instead have been jobless but classified as not in the labor force at all, if the incentive created by extended UI benefits to actively seek work despite the severe lack of job openings had not been in effect.

## Macroeconomic Effects of Extended Unemployment Benefits

Unemployment benefits are often pointed to as near-ideal "automatic stabilizers"—transfer payments to households that rise sharply as private spending falls and economies enter recessions. Besides being timely, UI benefits are well targeted as an economic stimulus, going to households that are (almost by definition) otherwise income-constrained and hence likely to have a high marginal propensity to spend their UI benefits. In the Great Recession, with the US economy stuck at the "zero-bound" on short-term policy interest rates and traditional monetary policy hence largely ineffective, direct government spending of this sort is particularly useful in combatting recessions. Estimates of the macroeconomic multiplier effect of unemployment benefits generally run from 1.7 to over 2—that is, each $1 spent on unemployment benefits by the government generates $1.70 to $2.00 in additional economic output.[2]

Given these estimated multipliers and the amount of money allocated for UI benefit extensions since the Great Recession began, Mishel and Shierholz (2010) estimate that the Keynesian benefit of these extensions added roughly $244 billion in cumulative GDP (or 1.7 percent of starting-year GDP) that supported 1.1 million jobs, shown in table 4.2.

All else being equal, these 1.1 million jobs would lower the measured unemployment rate by 0.8 percent, and the entirety of this decrease in unemployment would reflect employed workers, not possibly those that had chosen to drop out of the labor force.

**Table 4.2** Output and employment impact of unemployment compensation system in 2010

| | *Regular unemployment benefits* | **Unemployment compensation provisions in Recovery Act** | | | | |
|---|---|---|---|---|---|---|
| | | *Extended weeks** | *Additional weekly benefits ($25)* | *COBRA* | *Total* | *Total unemployment compensation* |
| **Spending ($ billions, annualized)** | | | | | | |
| *2007 4th qtr* | $31.6 | $0.0 | $0.0 | $0.0 | $0.0 | $31.6 |
| *2010 1st qtr* | 74.5 | 82.2 | 13.7 | 12.2 | 109.1 | 183.6 |
| *Change* | 42.9 | 82.2 | 13.7 | 12.2 | 109.1 | 152.1 |
| **Impact on GDP** | | | | | | |
| *Dollars* | $69.1 | $132.3 | $22.1 | $21.3 | $175.7 | $244.8 |
| *as % GDP* | 0.5% | 0.9% | 0.2% | 0.1% | 1.2% | 1.7% |
| **Impact on employment (thousands)** | | | | | | |
| *Payroll count* | 325 | 622 | 104 | 100 | 826 | 1151 |
| *Full-time equivalents* | 482 | 923 | 154 | 148 | 1225 | 1707 |

*Extended weeks include spending under both the Emergency Unemployment Compensation and the Extended Benefits programs.
*Source*: Mishel and Shierholz (2010), table 1.

## Putting the Micro- and the Macroestimates Together

The most basic thing to note about this quick review is that even the high-end estimates of how much the microeconomic disincentive effects of extended UI benefits *increased* measured unemployment do not overcome the macroeconomic estimates of how much these benefits *reduced* measured unemployment through their Keynesian demand effects. At worst, extended UI benefits had no effect at all on keeping unemployment high.

Further, given that much of any extended duration stemming from the microeconomic effects of extended benefits may well have been welfare-improving and that at least some of the increase in measured unemployment was probably a classification effect, it seems clear that these extended UI benefits were welfare-improving.

# Jobs, Wages, and Incomes Going Forward

As of January 2011, the Great Recession had been officially over for 19 months, yet there was precious little improvement in the labor market: the unemployment rate of 9.0 percent was lower than the 9.5 percent rate that prevailed at the recession's official trough, but that improvement was entirely due to the decline in labor-force participation—the employment-to-population ratio was 1.0 percent *lower* than at the recession's trough, and payroll employment was down another 228,000 jobs.

This failure of the labor market to rebound quickly following the official recovery looks drearily familiar—payroll employment recovered its prerecession peak only at 23 months after the official end of the 1990s recession and at 38 months after the end of the 2001 recession.

It's important to note that sputtering labor-market recoveries were *not* the historic norm in the United States before the early 1990s recession. As figure 4.1 made clear, before 1990 every single post-World War II recession saw a complete recovery of payroll employment within 13 months of the recession's end. This change in the business cycle behavior of labor markets begs the question: what about the last three recessions has caused the labor-market recovery to lag so far behind other business cycle dating measures?

While this question has inspired much commentary and research, the most basic answer is simply that output growth following the official trough of each of these recessions has been slow relative to historic averages. Table 4.3 shows GDP growth, productivity growth, average hours growth, and employment growth in the first two years of recovery following the trough of the last four recessions.

**Table 4.3** Output, productivity, and employment in recoveries

| | | **Recession:** ***Total peak-to-trough changes*** | **Recovery*:** ***Average annualized change*** |
|---|---|---|---|
| GDP | 1981 (5**) | −2.7% | 6.7% |
| | 1990 (2) | −1.4% | 3.0% |
| | 2001 (3) | 0.4% | 2.9% |
| | 2007 (6) | −3.7% | 3.0% |
| Productivity | 1981 | **−1.7%** | 2.4% |
| | 1990 | **−0.3%** | 2.5% |
| | 2001 | 2.3% | 3.2% |
| | 2007 | 2.2% | 2.9% |
| Total hours | 1981 | −4.3% | 5.3% |
| | 1990 | −1.6% | 0.9% |
| | 2001 | −2.9% | −0.9% |
| | 2007 | −7.4% | 0.9% |
| Total employment | 1981 | −2.7% | 4.6% |
| | 1990 | −0.9% | 0.4% |
| | 2001 | −1.7% | −0.4% |
| | 2007 | −5.3% | −0.1% |

* First two years of recovery for 1981, 1990, and 2001 recessions. First 18 months of recovery for 2007 recession, except productivity, which is the first 15 months of recovery.

** Length of recession in quarters.

*Note*: The rates shown are the average of annualized growth rates during and also 24 months following the end of a recession. The total hours are for production and nonsupervisory workers.

*Source*: EPI analysis of Current Establishment Survey and Bureau of Economic Analysis data.

Figures 4.12 and 4.13 provide further evidence that this slow-output growth explains most of the poor labor-market performance in these recoveries, showing the two-year change in GDP and the unemployment rate for two time periods, 1948–1984 and 1985–2010. These scatter plots are essentially a crude estimate of Okun's law—the empirical regularity that relates changes in GDP growth to changes in the unemployment rate. There is no significant change in the Okun coefficient in this time period; in fact the unemployment rate is, if anything, *more* responsive to output growth in the latter period than previously.

Given that little has changed in recent business cycles *besides* the expected growth rate of output, it is useful to examine what the latest research tells us to

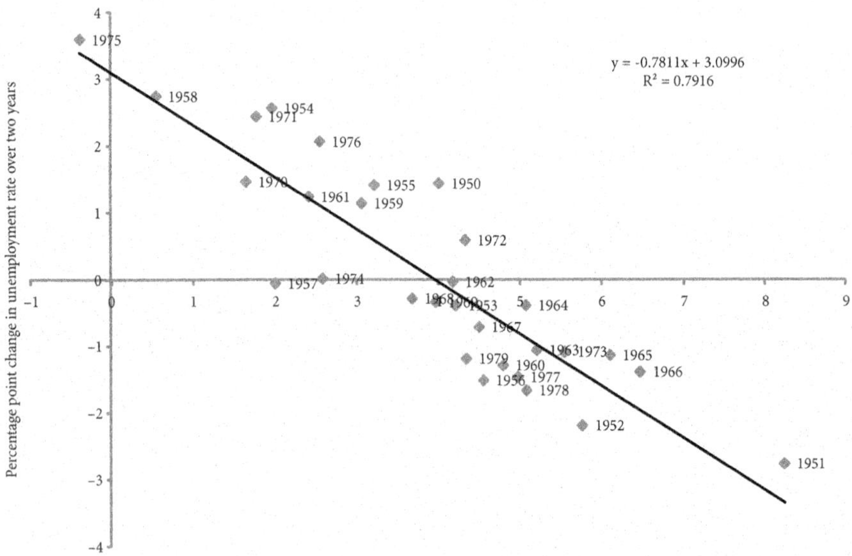


**Figure 4.12** Two-year change in GDP and unemployment, 1950–1979.
*Source*: EPI analysis of Bureau of Economic Analysis, National Income Product Accounts and Bureau of Labor Statistics, Current Population Survey.

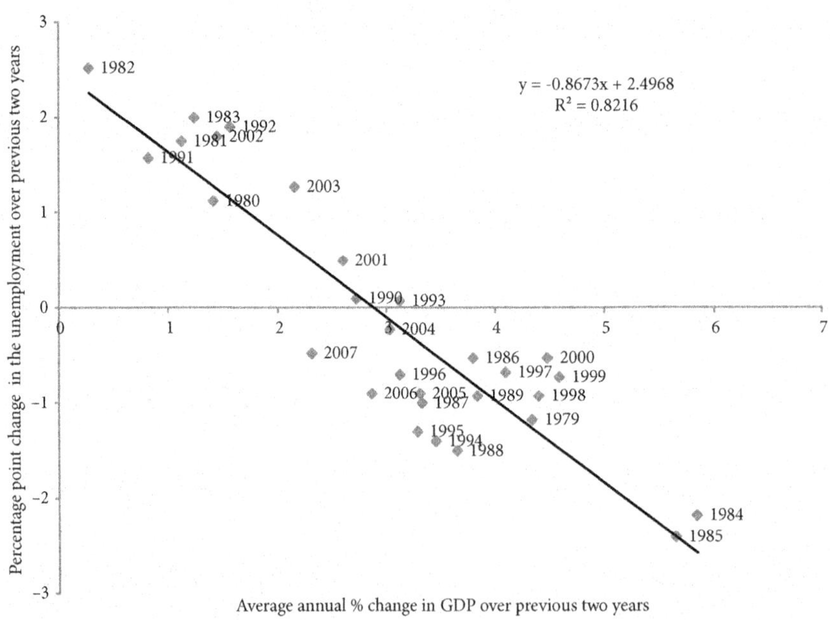


**Figure 4.13** Two-year change in GDP and unemployment, 1979–2007.
*Source*: EPI analysis of Bureau of Economic Analysis, National Income Product Accounts and Bureau of Labor Statistics, Current Population Survey.

expect for output growth in coming years. In 2009 the International Monetary Fund (Terrones et al., 2009) examined recessions and recoveries in advanced economies that have been associated with (a) financial crises and (b) globally synchronous downturns, shown in table 4.4.

Unsurprisingly it found that recovery from recessions has been much slower following *either* a financial crisis or a globally synchronous downturn, and recessions and recoveries associated with *both* are deeper, last longer, and inflict more damage on growth even after the prerecession output peak is reached. So far, the US economy has been following this script for countries recovering from both financial crises and globally synchronous recessions very closely. Further, forecasts for the next two to three years show that output growth will remain slow relative to historical recoveries. While it is probably well known that it takes longer to reach the prerecession peak following recessions associated with both financial crises and synchronous downturns, it may be surprising that the IMF study shows that growth rates are much slower even *after* prerecession output levels are reached following these events: 2.9 percent annualized growth rates as compared to growth rates of just under 3.4 percent following other recessions.

Given this slow projected output recovery, the implications for jobs and unemployment are dire. Most forecasters (both private and public-sector) do not see a return to prerecession unemployment rates until 2015 or 2016—and applying our crude Okun estimates from figures 4.12 and 4.13 suggests that output growth in the expansion that tracks the IMF projections would take

**Table 4.4** US Great Recession as compared to other recessions associated with financial crises and global downturns

| | **Duration** | | **Amplitude** | | |
|---|---|---|---|---|---|
| | ***Recession**** | ***Recovery***** | ***Recession****** | ***Recovery******* | ***Expansion******** |
| IMF average for recessions associated with financial crises and global downturns | 7.3 | 6.8 | −4.8 | 2.8 | 2.9 |
| US Great Recession | 6.0 | 6.0 | −4.1 | 3.0 | ? |

* Length of recession, in quarters
** Length until prerecession output level is reached, in quarters
*** Output loss from peak to trough
**** Output growth in the year following the trough
***** Output growth after prerecession peak is reached

literally decades to spur an unemployment rate as low as the prerecession peak.

While the IMF data are based largely on an international comparison of economies emerging from recessions associated with financial crises and global downturns, figure 4.14 uses historical US data to reinforce the point that a return to 2007 unemployment rates could take an extraordinarily long time. The figure shows projected recoveries in payroll employment corresponding to the employment recoveries following the recessions of 1981 (a recession that saw a very quick bounceback of both output and employment), 1991, and 2001 (two recessions that saw very slow output and employment recoveries).

Nineteen months into the current recovery, the employment path is most closely following the 2001 trajectory. This is bad news—at these rates of recovery, payroll employment will hit prerecession levels by the middle of 2013, and if labor-force participation rates rebound to make up even half of their decline between December 2007 and December 2010 this would imply an unemployment rate of 7.7 percent in that year.

## The Effect of Prolonged High Unemployment on Wage and Income Growth

A slow recovery in jobs and unemployment will almost surely translate into a slow recovery of wages and salaries as well. A long economics literature has argued that high rates of unemployment are bad for incumbent workers' wages.

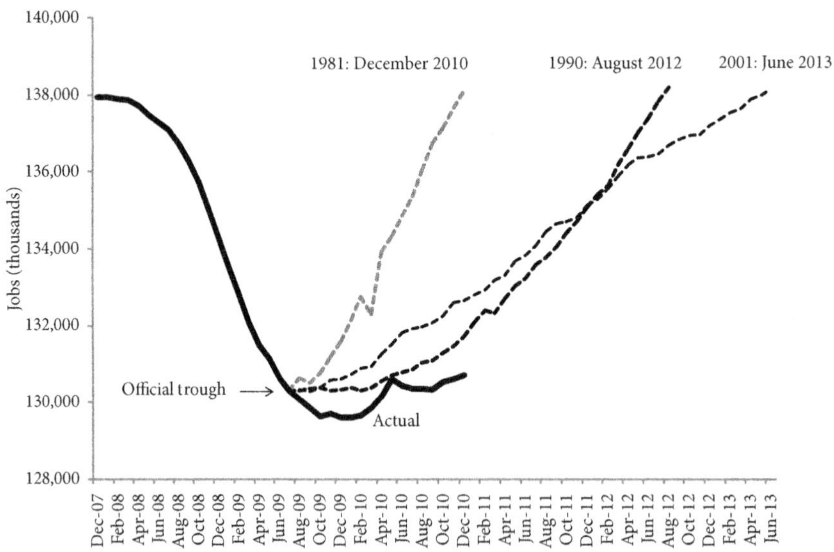


**Figure 4.14** Projected month of labor-market recovery from 2007 recession based on recoveries from three prior recessions (1981, 1990, and 2001).

*Source*: EPI analysis of Bureau of Labor Statistics, Current Establishment Survey.

Classical economists framed this in terms of a "reserve army of labor" that provided employers a ready substitute for their current labor force if incumbent workers' wage demands rose. Modern empirical studies have provided several pieces of evidence that are consistent with the general proposition that high and rising unemployment suppresses wage growth, regardless of the theoretical channel.

A literature starting with Dunlop (1938) and Tarshis (1939) has documented the pro-cyclicality of real wages—wages that rise faster during economic expansions and more slowly during recessions. Card (1995) provides a summary of a number of these studies that use microeconomic data to track individuals' wages over the business cycle.

Besides this literature based largely on microdata, Blanchard and Katz (1999) write that "U.S. macroeconometric evidence shows a negative relation between the rate of change of wages and the unemployment rate.... This Phillips [wage] curve can be interpreted as a negative relation between the expected rate of change of the real wage and unemployment" (page 69). Tavani and colleagues (2010) similarly use macroeconomic aggregates to document that at both high and low rates of capacity utilization, a higher unemployment rate corresponds to a lower wage share in output.[3]

Katz and Krueger (1999) and Bernstein and Baker (2003) examine the relationships among unemployment rates, prices, and wages *at different points in the wage distribution*. In essence, these authors estimate percentile-specific Phillips wage curves to see if the responsiveness of wages to changing unemployment rates differs by wage level. They find that the wage elasticity of unemployment is significantly higher for low- and middle-wage workers than for workers at the top of the wage distribution, and this is true for both men and women.

Table 4.5 summarizes findings from a sampling of the literature relating unemployment changes to changes in labor compensation—it reports the effects of a 1 percentage point rise in the unemployment rate on various measures of labor compensation based on a review of the Phillips wage-curve literature.

In the projections that follow, we attempt to construct likely paths for growth in labor compensation based on projections (provided by Mark Zandi of Moody's Analytics and Economy.com) of the aggregate unemployment rate in coming years.

For our wage measures, we use total compensation of all civilian workers from the Employment Cost Index of the Bureau of Labor Statistics (BLS). A common concern with examining the link between rising unemployment rates and many measures of labor compensation is the degree of *composition bias* of the workforce at different points in the business cycle. If, for example, the first workers to lose their jobs during a downturn are disproportionately lower paid, then average *measured* compensation may actually rise (or at least not fall much) during downturns. The ECI largely side-steps this problem because it is a fixed-weight index—it follows the same jobs (not workers) over

**Table 4.5** Effect of a 1 percentage-point rise in unemployment on wage growth

| | | **% change in wages** |
|---|---|---|
| Bernstein and Baker (2002) | CPS, estimate is of responsiveness of median wage. | 1.5 |
| | Average of male and female responsiveness. 1979–2001. | |
| Blanchard and Katz (1997) | Average of several different wage measures they used: weekly UI record measures, CES industry earnings, CPS ORG wages, CPS March, Annual wages from CPS March. 1980–1991, including variation across US states | 0.7 |
| Bils (1985) | NLS measure of young white male wages. 1966–1980 | 1.9 |
| Blank (1990) | PSID, hourly wages for white males. 1969–1982 | 1.7 |
| Katz and Krueger (1999) | Average of four wage measures: NIPA overall compensation per hour, ECI total compensation and wages, CPS hourly wages. 1973–1968 | 1.8 |
| Solon, Barsky, and Parker (1994) | PSID, hourly wages for white males. 1967–1987 | 1.1 |
| Tavani, Flaschel, and Taylor (2010) | NIPA compensation per hour. 1960–2009 | 0.6 |

the course of the business cycle (and fixes their weights in the index) so it should be relatively free of composition bias.

Katz and Krueger (1999) and Blanchard and Katz (1997) test various measures of compensation (including the ECI) to see if significant differences exist between them and their relationship to the unemployment rate—both papers find that *all* compensation measures respond negatively to higher unemployment rates and the magnitudes of responsiveness are quite close. Given this, our choice of the ECI seems to present no problems in terms of comparability with the wider literature.

One problem that arises from examining real-wage dynamics right around the Great Recession is the large spike in energy prices that began in 2008 (cutting real wages in that year) but that reversed nearly as sharply in 2009 (and boosted wages right during the recession's trough). Because energy price spikes can be likely thought of as exogenous to the labor-market dynamics we're examining here, we deflate the ECI using the core personal consumption expenditures deflator (excluding food and energy prices) from the Bureau of Economic Analysis (BEA).

In the first projection, shown in figure 4.15, we show two possible paths for compensation growth between 2007 and 2015—one is based on the trend growth of wages between 2001 and 2006 while one is based on the average of the Phillips curve-based estimates incorporating the impact of higher unemployment on wage growth. In essence, the first compensation path is the (heroic) counterfactual answering what likely would have happened to compensation in the absence of the Great Recession while the other incorporates the high unemployment rates seen (and projected) as the recession's result. The last line in the graph is the *actual* ECI data through 2010.

Total compensation growth in the six years before the Great Recession was averaging roughly 1.7 percent—although it is important to note that wage growth was rising significantly more slowly than total compensation growth, as the rising cost of employer-provided health care was providing substantial upward pressure on the ECI. The top line in this figure extends this trend growth through 2015 to provide the assumed compensation growth that would have occurred in the absence of the Great Recession. The bottom line shows this trend growth with the effect of high unemployment rates removed.

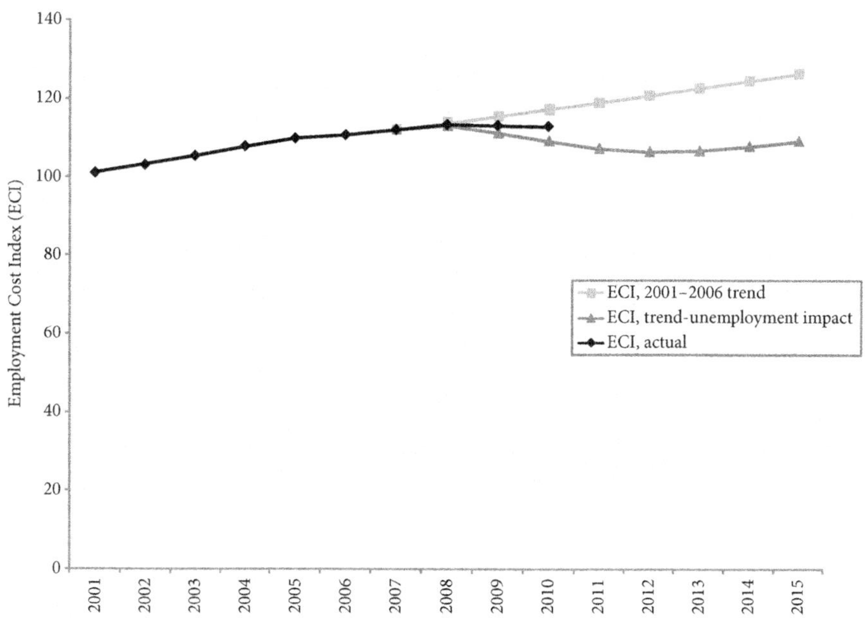


**Figure 4.15** Nominal compensation growth with and without the unemployment impact of the 2007 recession using the Employment Cost Index (ECI).
*Source*: EPI analysis of ECI data. See the text for further explanation.

This figure shows that the likely effect of the Great Recession on compensation growth is large. By the (likely) unemployment peak of 2010, high unemployment was, according to our Phillips wage-curve estimates, subtracting 3.5 percent from total compensation growth in that year. By 2015, the cumulative effect of prolonged higher-than-trend unemployment is likely to result in real total compensation that is 13 percent lower than would have been the case in a world without the Great Recession.

It is important to note that these compensation losses affect even those workers that remain employed during the Great Recession. Furthermore, the costs of compensation not earned due to job losses are not accounted for here. That said, it is equally important to note that the compensation declines caused by prolonged high unemployment do not necessarily represent dead-weight costs to the overall economy—these declines in compensation are likely to show up as increases in corporate profits or other forms of income (realized capital gains, etc.).

## Percentile-Specific Phillips Wage Estimates

Further, while these *overall* effects are large, they are likely not evenly borne across the distribution of compensation. Table 4.6 displays estimates based on Bernstein and Baker (2003) and Katz and Krueger (1999) that show the impact of prolonged high unemployment on wage growth by various deciles of the wage distribution. Both papers' results show that the largest wage declines occurring due to extended high (overall) unemployment accrue to workers in the low and middle deciles.[4]

We use these results to look at the effect of unemployment on the likely path for compensation growth for workers at the 30th, 50th, and 90th percentiles, as demonstrated in figure 4.16. Because the ECI does not allow us to know the 2001–2006 trend in compensation for each of these different groups, we assume that the trend in compensation growth is the same for each group. We then subtract the (differential) impact of high unemployment on compensation growth for each.[5] The compensation-depressing effects of high unemployment are essentially twice as large for workers at the 30th percentile relative to those at the 90th percentile. By 2015, these projections show compensation for the 30th percentile worker that is a full 22 percent lower than it is in the absence of the Great Recession.

## High Unemployment and Family Income Growth

Given the importance of wages to overall household and family incomes (which remains well over half of total gross domestic income), we replicate some of the above analysis with family income as the dependent variable

**Table 4.6** Phillips wage-curve estimates by wage decile

| | Bernstein and Baker (2002) | Katz and Krueger (1999) |
|---|---|---|
| 30th | 1.9 | 1.5 |
| 50th | 1.4 | 0.9 |
| 90th | 1.0 | 0.4 |
| Ratio of 90th/30th elasticity | 54.1% | 26.9% |

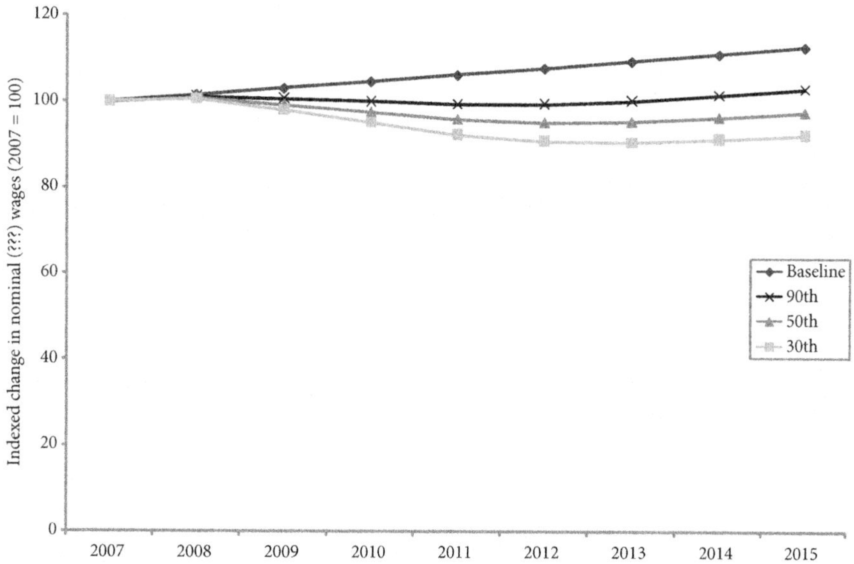


**Figure 4.16** Impact of prolonged unemployment on wage growth, trend (baseline), and wages at the 20th, 50th, and 90th percentiles.
*Source*: EPI analysis of ECI data. See the text for further explanation.

rather than hourly wages. Given that total family income will capture the effect of *both* falling hours of work and pressure on hourly compensation, one might see even larger effects of rising unemployment on these measures. Additionally, the data on family incomes allow us to see *both* long-run trends in income growth and sensitivity to high unemployment that differs by quintile.

Figure 4.17 shows that the relationship between the overall unemployment rate and family income growth is generally statistically significant and economically meaningful—for example an increase in the unemployment rate from 5 percent to 6 percent (a 20 percent increase) is associated with a 0.88 percent decline in the *average* family income.

This figure also, following the lead of Bernstein and Baker (2003) and Katz and Krueger (1999), examines the link between the overall unemployment rate

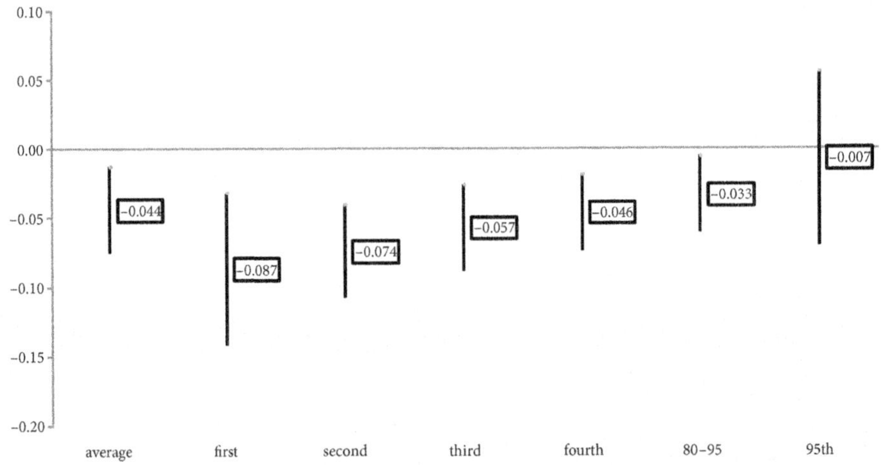


**Figure 4.17** Elasticity of family income growth with respect to unemployment rate, by income percentile, 1950–2007.

*Note*: Regression coefficient from log-log regression of real annual family income growth on overall unemployment rate. Lines show the point estimate plus and minus two standard deviations. Each estimate except for the 80–95th and 95th percentile is significant at the 99 percent level. Estimate for 80th-95th percentile is significant at the 95 percent level.

*Source*: EPI analysis of US Census Bureau and Bureau of Labor Statistics data.

and family income by income quintiles and for the 95th family income percentile. Just as with the wage distribution, lower family incomes seem more responsive to changes in the unemployment rate. In fact, the effect of unemployment on family income growth is monotonically decreasing as one moves to higher-income percentiles. In the extreme, family income growth for the top 5 percent of the family income distribution does *not* show any statistically significant sensitivity to the unemployment rate.

Figure 4.18 shows trend growth for the first and third quintiles of the family income distribution as well as the top 5 percent of the distribution, based on long-run (1950 to 2007) annual income growth. It also shows trend growth minus the effect of projected high unemployment through 2015 as well as *actual* income growth through 2009. The implied income declines for the first and third quintiles are very large—coming in at nearly 30 percent and 20 percent below trend growth by 2015, respectively.

These large falls strike us as plausible, however. Incomes for the first quintile have actually fallen by over 8 percent *already* between 2007 and 2009. The average unemployment rate for 2010 is even higher than 2009, meaning that incomes almost surely fell again in this year. Further, this quintile actually saw incomes fall over the last business cycle, which saw unemployment at the cycle's peak (4.6 percent in 2007) never quite reach the low of the previous cycle's peak (4 percent in 2000). This says to us that very low rates of unemployment

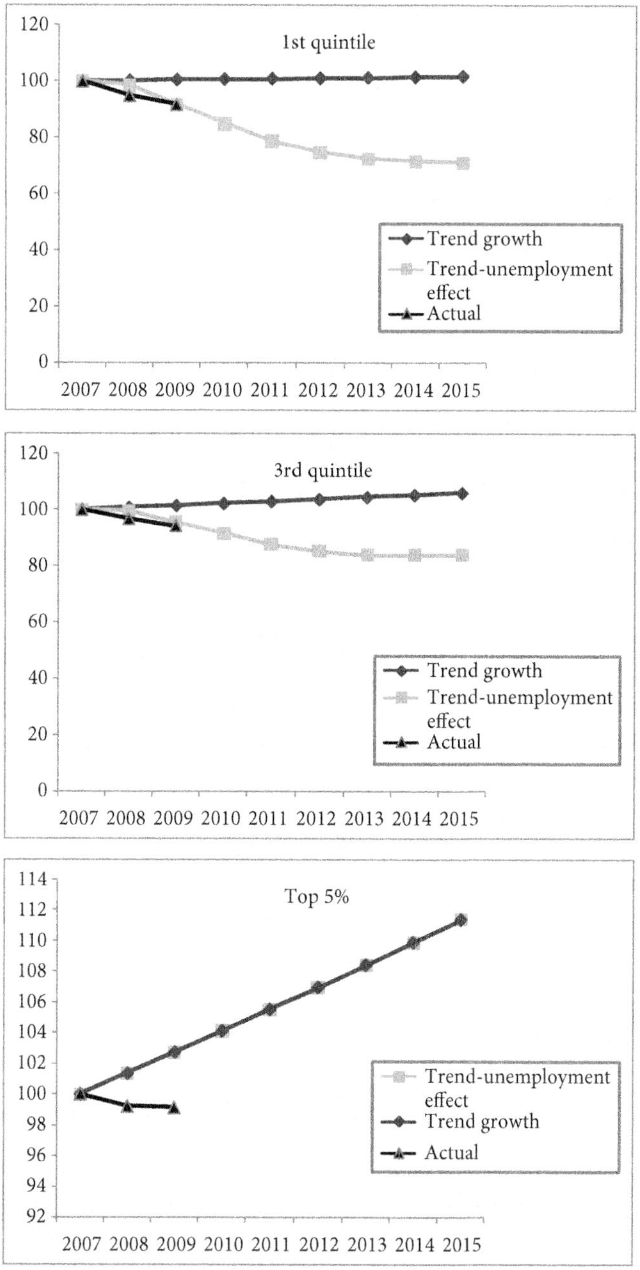


**Figure 4.18** Family income growth: Trend, simulated impact of unemployment, and actual at 1st quintile, 3rd quintile, and top 5 percent.
*Source*: EPI analysis of ECI data. See the text for further explanation.

indeed are necessary to spur outright income growth for the bottom quintile, and low rates like this seem nowhere on the horizon in the wake of the Great Recession.[6]

## Summing Up the Likely Outlook for Wages and Incomes

The projections in this section are pretty clear—absent a much more rapid recovery to prerecession unemployment rates, wages, and incomes look to end 2015 not appreciably higher than they were *more than 15 years in the past*—a lost decade and a half for the most important sources of living standards' growth for most American families. And the loss of wages and incomes experienced by low- and middle-income workers and their families will be the largest.

Just as clear as this grim diagnosis is that the precise degree of wage and income repression is largely amenable to macroeconomic policy—Terrones and colleagues (2009), for example, show clearly that aggressive fiscal and monetary policy can shorten recessions and boost recoveries (even over the medium term—up to 10 years) *especially* in the case of recessions associated with both financial crises and globally synchronous downturns. Once one factors in the wage income likely to be foregone unless more aggressive policy actions are undertaken to boost growth in coming years, any potential cost of this kind of aggressive policy action radically shrinks. However, the hope for more aggressive policy action appears increasingly politically unrealistic. The second decade of the 2000s, in short, looks poised to mirror the wage and income trends that characterized the 1980s and early 1990s, a time period that Richard Freeman (1995) characterized as an "economic disaster" for a large swath of the overall labor force.[7]

## Notes

1. In this paragraph, "2010" refers to the average of December 2009-November 2010, the latest data available as of this writing.
2. See the Congressional Budget Office (2011).
3. In the intermediate range of capacity utilization, they find no relation between nominal wage growth and unemployment.
4. Katz and Krueger (1999) confirm the result that low- and middle-wage workers see larger wage declines as a result of rising unemployment.
5. Given the large and relentless rise in both earnings and benefits inequality in recent decades, the assumption is clearly wrong. However, given that in this section we are more concerned about the differential impact of high unemployment, the effect of unemployment on trend growth is the same regardless of what one thinks the underlying trend is.

6. Katz and Krueger (1999) estimate the unemployment rate necessary to achieve zero wage growth across wage percentiles. They estimate that workers at the 30th percentile in the wage distribution needed unemployment rates under 6 percent in order to achieve positive real-wage growth. Most forecasts of the coming years do not project unemployment rates this low until 2014.
7. Freeman (1995) specifically referred to male workers without college degrees.

## References


Acemoglu, Daron, and Robert Shimer. (1999). "Efficient Unemployment Insurance." *Journal of Political Economy* 107(5): 893–928.

Altig, David. (2010a). "A Curious Unemployment Picture Gets More Curious." *Macroblog*, the Federal Reserve Bank of Atlanta, July 16, 2010. http://macroblog.typepad.com/macroblog/2010/07/a-curious-unemploymen t-picture-gets-more-curious.html.

Blanchard, Oliver and Richard Katz. (1999). "Wage Dynamics: Reconciling Theory and Evidence." *American Economic Review Papers and Proceedings* 89(3): 69–74.

Bernstein, Jared, and Dean Baker. (2003). *The Benefits of Full Employment: When Markets Work for People*. Washington, DC: Economic Policy Institute.

Bils, Mark. (1985). "Real Wages over the Business Cycle: Evidence from Panel Data." *Journal of Political Economy* 93(4): 666–689.

Blanchard, Olivier, and Lawrence Katz. (1997). "What We Know and Do Not Know about the Natural Rate of Unemployment." *Journal of Economic Perspectives* 11(1): 15–51.

Blank, Rebecca. (1990). "Why are Wages Cyclical in the 1970s?" *Journal of Labor Economics* 8(1): 16–47.

Card, David. (1995). "*The Wage Curve*: A Review." *Journal of Economic Literature* 33(6): 785–799.

Chan, Sewin. (2001). "Spatial Lock-in: Do Falling House Prices Constrain Residential Mobility?" *Journal of Urban Economics* 49(3): 567–586.

Chetty, Raj. (2008). "Moral Hazard vs. Liquidity and Optimal Unemployment Insurance." *Journal of Political Economy* 116(2): 173–234.

Congressional Budget Office. (2011). "Estimated Impact of the American Recovery and Reinvestment Act on Employment and Economic Output from July 2010 through September 2010." Available at: http://www.cbo.gov/sites/default/files/cbofiles/ftpdocs/119xx/doc11975/11-24-arra.pdf

DeLong, J. Bradford, and Robert J. Waldmann. (1997). "Interpreting Procyclical Productivity: Evidence for a Cross-Nation Cross-Industry Panel." *Federal Reserve Bank of San Francisco Economic Review* (1): 33–52.

Dunlop, John T. (1938). "The Movement of Real and Money Wage Rates." *Economic Journal* 48: 413–434.

Engelhardt, Gary V. (2003). "Nominal Loss Aversion, Housing Equity Constraints, and Household Mobility: Evidence from the United States." *Journal of Urban Economics* 53(1): 171–195.

Ferreira, Fernando, Gyourko, Joseph and Joseph Tracy. (2010). "Housing Busts and Household Mobility." *Journal of Urban Economics* 68(1): 34–45.

Freeman, Richard. (1995). "Are Your Wages Set in Beijing?" *Journal of Economic Perspectives* 9(3): 15–52.

Gordon, Robert J. (2010). "Okun's Law, Productivity Innovations, and Conundrums in Business Cycle Dating." *Papers and Proceedings of the American Economic Review* 100(2): 1–9.

Katz, Lawrence, and Alan B. Krueger. (1999). "The High-pressure US Labor Market of the 1990s." Working Paper #416. Princeton, NJ: Princeton University.

Kocherlakota, Narayana. (2010). "Inside the FOMC." Speech given at Marquette, Michigan, August 17, 2010. http://www.minneapolisfed.org/news_Events/pres/speech_ display.cfm?id=4525.

Mishel, Lawrence, and Heidi Shierholz. (2010). "Two for the Price of One: Providing Unemployment Insurance Both Assists the Unemployed and Generates Jobs." Economic Policy Institute.

Schulhofer-Wohl, Sam. (2011). "Negative Equity Does Not Reduce Homeowners' Mobility." National Bureau of Economic Research, Working Paper No. 16701. Cambridge, MA: NBER.

Solon, Gary, Robert Barsky, and Jonathan Parker. (1994). "Measuring the Cyclicality of Real Wages: How Important in Composition Bias?" *The Quarterly Journal of Economics* 109(1): 1–25.

Tarshis, Lorie. (1939). "Changes in Real and Money Wages." *Economic Journal* 49: 150–154.

Tasci, Murat, and John Lindner. (2010). "Has the Beveridge Curve Shifted?" *Economic Trends*, Federal Reserve Bank of Cleveland, August 10, 2010. http://www.clevelandfed.org/research/trends/2010/0810/02labmar.cfm.

Tavani, Daniele, Peter Flaschel, and Lance Taylor. (2010). "Estimated Non-linearities and Multiple Equilibria in a Model of Distributive-Demand Cycles." Schwartz Center for Economic Policy Analysis, Working Paper #2010-6. New York: SCEPA.

Terrones, Marco E., Alasdair Scott, and Prakesh Kannan. (2009). "Chapter 3: From Recession to Recovery: How Soon and How Strong?" *World Economic Outlook*. International Monetary Fund, World Economic Outlook.

Valletta, Rob, and Katherine Kuang. (2010a). "Extended Unemployment and UI Benefits." *Economic Letter*, Federal Reserve Bank of San Francisco, April 25, 2010. http://www.frbsf.org/publications/economics/letter/2010/el2010-12.html.

Valletta, Rob, and Katherine Kuang. (2010b). "Is Structural Unemployment on the Rise?" *Economic Letter*, Federal Reserve Bank of San Francisco, November 8, 2010. http://www.frbsf.org/publications/economics/letter/2010/el2010-34.html.

# CHAPTER 5

# DISTRIBUTION AND CRISIS

## REVIEWING SOME OF THE LINKAGES

ARJUN JAYADEV

## Introduction: Distribution and Crisis—A Deep Connection?

In the last 100 years the United States has undergone two protracted financial crises: the Great Depression of 1929–1933 and the Great Recession beginning in late 2007. What initially manifested as financial crises ultimately resulted in sharp contractions in output, very high levels of unemployment, and, in the case of the Great Depression, a fundamental reconfiguration of the US economy. Economists have expended enormous effort trying to identify and understand the myriad reasons that led to these events, and new causal mechanisms and narratives continue to be generated. Figure 5.1 provides a striking and suggestive image in this vein. Both of these monumental crises were immediately preceded by the most unequal years in the period as measured by a commonly used metric of inequality. In 1929, the top 10 percent of the US population enjoyed nearly 48 percent of the income generated in that year. In 2007, the same proportion garnered nearly 50 percent of the income generated in the year. Indeed, as noted by numerous scholars, the years preceding the Great Recession were marked by rising levels of inequality in a large number

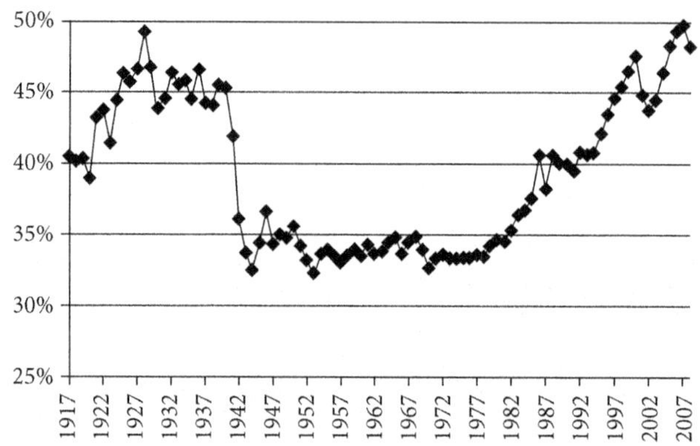


**Figure 5.1** Share of total income going to the top 10 percent.
*Source*: Pikkety and Saez (2010).

of OECD countries. A perhaps even more striking picture is provided by Moss (2010) in figure 5.2, which displays a similarly intriguing correlation between the share of income of the top 10 percent and banking failures in the United States over the same time frame.

Is this correlation merely a coincidence or is it indicative of a deep underlying relationship between income and/or wealth distribution on the one hand and the stability of economic activity on the other? Mainstream economists have begun to scrutinize this hypothesis as a consequence of the Great

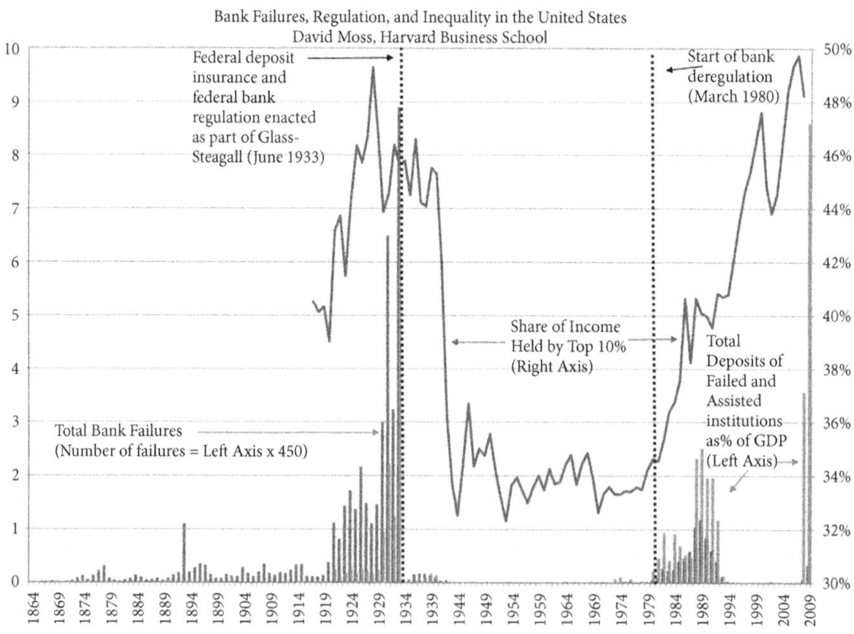


**Figure 5.2** Inequality and banking failures.

Recession.[1] Can high or increasing levels of inequality contribute to or be seen as an important cause of this (and other) financial crises? At first glance, this may appear as a somewhat strange claim, because most accounts of the current crisis as well as the Great Depression focus on other factors: deregulation, excessive credit expansion, asset bubbles, new forms of financial products, mistaken monetary policy, insufficient or too much government guarantees, and so on. Having noted this, the idea that growing income disparities may have been a particularly potent contributor to the current financial crisis both directly and indirectly has been given recent popular attention by such researchers as Stiglitz (2009) and Rajan (2010),[2] and plausible linkages have been made in academic and policy-making circles in this regard.

Crises are by their nature few and far between; as such, methodical examinations of the relationship between inequality and crises have been relatively rare. There have been virtually no papers that have identifed systematic statistical regularities regarding the pattern of inequality before the numerous financial crises observed over the last century.[3] Where such a relationship has been examined, typically in the context of case studies, there is little or no compelling relationship that has been found. Perhaps not surprisingly, there is a larger empirical literature on the *effect* of financial crises on distribution, often in the context of studies of the social impact of crises in Latin America, East Asia, and more recently in the industrialized world. Part of the advantage that the crisis = inequality literature has is a much clearer set of ideas as to the causal channels. The weight of the evidence here quite strongly favors the hypothesis that crises (in particular, currency crises) make economies more unequal. Even here, as a later section will show, there are some important caveats.

Both inequality and crisis are complex concepts, and identifying relationships between them typically involves some intuitions about growing disparities between *particular* sections of the income or wealth distribution (or, in the case of Marxian and Kaleckian models, between returns to different factors of production) and tendencies toward crisis as a result. As an example, Acemoglu (2011) suggests that the relevant inequality for this crisis was the rising gap between the incomes of the top 1 percent of the distribution—those with financial-market interests and the ability to suborn the political order to their interests, thereby exacerbating inequality as well as increasing the propensity for a crisis—and that of others. An empirical examination of the correlation between rising inequality and subsequent financial crises conceived of in this very particular manner would be different in nature than one that looked at other broader measures of inequality. Heterodox models concerning the relationship between income distribution and macroeconomic stability focus on the apportioning of income between capital and labor—the functional or factor distribution of income is the relevant income disparity.While this may be correlated with interpersonal income disparities, there is not necessarily a close mapping. Given these facts, while establishing correlations between changes in interpersonal inequality and crisis may be helpful, understanding the causal logic of the relationship between types of rising income disparities and the potential for crisis is key to advancing our knowledge about such links. Similarly, identifying the impacts of financial crises on the income or wealth distribution also requires some clarification of the main channels by which this can occur. For example, one may assume that financial crises have the most signficant impact on the poor relative to the rest of the population, which would necessitate a close analysis of the divergence of the poor from the rest. On the other hand, one might expect that the financial crisis might hurt the relatively rich if they own the assets that lose value in the crisis.

This chapter seeks to provide a brief review of the state of understanding thus far on the relationship between inequality and financial crises. The focus will be on systemic *financial* crises and not either on localized dislocations in financial intermediation of other forms of downturns that arise from the real sector. As we will see in the empirical sections, there is no clear definition about what constitutes a systemic financial crisis and how to identify it empirically, in addition to numerous other conceptual and operational challenges in identifying the relevant causal effects running from inequality to crisis and from crisis to inequality. The agenda in the next section is to set out and describe the various theoretical linkages that have been made, suggesting a causal connection between rising inequality and crisis; particularly with respect to the US crisis of 2007–2009 in the context of which many of these hypotheses have been made. The section that follows the next reviews the sparse and disparate empirical literature on this causation. The distributional consequences of financial crises represents a more established body of research and the penultimate section reviews some of the key theoretical channels identified and looks at some of the more relevant empirical examinations. The final section concludes and points out the myriad open avenues for future research.

## Income Distribution as a Cause of Crisis: Theoretical Approaches

Theoretical accounts of the causal relationship between inequality and crisis can be broadly classified into those that posit a relatively direct and deep cause—for example, rising inequality leading to an increased propensity for risk taking among those falling behind, and those that point to more indirect causes (e.g., inequality leading to insufficient aggregate demand in the real economy and a propensity to crisis, or inequality promoting financial elites who in turn promote deregulation and exacerbate the potential for crisis). For the most part, it is the second set of explantions—those that rely on a political economy narrative that have gotten the most attention and focus. Depending on the explanation, as noted, different sections of the income distribution are implicated.

At the outset, it is important to note that Marxian and Kaleckian models of the macroeconomy have always maintained that income distribution and in particular factor distribution constitutes a critical determinant of macroeconomic stability. The Kaleckian distribution cycle (Kalecki, 1939, 1943) was a seminal contribution to business cycle theories in which investment, effective demand, profitability, and hence the business cycle itself depended, among other things, on the distribution of income between capitalists and workers. Several later contributions, including Goodwin (1967), Bhaduri and Marglin (1990), and Bowles and Boyer (1988), all maintain this factor as being key to generating patterns of aggreate demand, business cycles, and crises. More recent work identifies the importance of including a third class of rentiers whose income is generated at the expense of returns to the other two classes, capitalists and workers into the analytics (see Dutt [1992] as an early example and Hein and van Treeck [2007] for a review).[4]

Researchers from such traditions have only recently begun to develop models that link factor distribution and the development of financial fragility and bubbles.[5] There have been numerous less formalized accounts of the genesis of this particular financial crisis by authors drawing from such insights. Typically, these accounts focus on the case of the United States as the paradigmatic example and the key player in the global crisis. The major points of interest can be summarized as follows. The crisis was, in part, caused by a change in the social structure of accumulation in capitalism after around 1970 following which the global core moved toward what has been termed a "finance-dominated accumulation regime" (Stockhammer, 2008). The pattern of growth embodied in the three decades of postwar prosperity meant that a serious problem of capitalism in the core economies arose in the early 1970s, in which it was difficult to maintain growth under conditions of full employment and assertive labor, because this led to rates of profits that were low, especially for rentiers. As such, finance was released from its regulatory shackles and made the driving force of the economy in a new pattern of growth. This involved a fundamental transfer of power, influence, and economic advantage to capital at the expense of labor and especially an increase in the power and returns to the financial sector.[6]

Several studies have shown a declining labor share of income in many OECD countries over the period (Jayadev and Rodriguez, 2010; Harrison, 2004), a finding that certainly is consistent with the idea of labor losing political and economic power over the period. Epstein and Jayadev (2007) provide additional empirical buttressing for the idea that the distributional gains were won by the financial sector. They show that in all the OECD countries they study, the rentier fraction of GDP has increased sharply during this period. Onaran, Stockhammer and Grafl(2011) show that aggregate demand in the United States was driven by wealth effects arising from a rise in the rentier share and that in the absence of this, redistribution of income to rentiers would have resulted in lower growth.

The consequences for increasing financial fragility are two-fold: first, there is a fall in effective demand arising from the decline in labor incomes, and second, there is a tendency for financial actors to increase risky activities, often called "financial innovation" by market players to maintain the high rates of growth of income within the sector (Stockhammer, 2009; Crotty,(2007). Brenner (2007) suggests that the financial crisis was delayed and simultaneouly exarcebated by the process of "asset price Keynesianism" whereby declining real wages and lower labor shares led to falls in purchasing power that were offset by increasing indebtedness and borrowing by the household sector. As he puts it:

> Governments, led by the US, have underwritten ever greater volumes of debt, through ever more baroque channels, to subsidise purchasing power...since the mid-90s they have had to resort to more powerful and risky forms of stimulus to counter the tendency to stagnation, replacing the public deficits of traditional Keynesianism with the private deficits and asset inflation of what might be called asset-price Keynesianism—or, with equal accuracy, bubblenomics.

Authors such as Wisman and Baker (2009) and Bibow (2010) provide additional empirical support for this argument. In particular they show clear patterns of falling or stagnant average real wages, a collapse in personal savings rates and a rise in indebtedness over the last three decades in the United States.

Other explanations that have sought to link the rise in inequality to household debt and the US housing bubble and financial crisis discuss similar processes but without alluding to them in the class terms favored by heterodox approaches. Instead, therefore, they examine the linkages between interpersonal inequality and the financial crisis of 2008. A large literature has documented sharp increases in income and earnings inequality in the United States (see Katz and Autor, 1999; Cutler and Katz, 1992; Gottschalk and Danziger, 2005; Piketty and Saez, 2003; Krueger and Perri, 2006;, 2008; contra these, see Gordon, 2009). Given that class conflict and factor distribution is typically ignored as a lens with which to view distributional conflicts, these explanations turn instead to viewing the crisis on a result of policy interventions or reactions by individual households to rising inequality. The closest mainstream perspective to the hypotheses favored by the heterodox analyses mentioned above is provided by Stiglitz (2009). He provides a close rendering of the insufficient effective demand thesis by suggesting that growing inequality in most countries of the world has meant that lower-income households were unable to spend as income growth slowed down, while higher-income households used their high levels of income to engage in speculation. A more extended version of this idea is provided by Fitoussi and Saraceno (2010), who claim that stagnating real incomes led households in the lower part of the distribution to borrow to maintain living standards, while richer households leveraged their assets and surplus income in a search for ever-increasing returns.

Such a contention has also been provided some support in the context of a standard Dynamic Stochastic General Equilibrium framework by Kumhof and Rancière (2010). For them, however, the emphasis is not on effective demand but on the development of a particular mode of financial intermediation.

Specifically, they contend that increased savings needs at the top end of the distribution and increased borrowing needs at the lower ends resulted in a large and rapidly growing financial sector that sought to fulfill these needs. Thus, the financial sector worked to recycle the additional income obtained by high-income households by way of loans to allow the latter to sustain consumption—a suggestion that has at least some empirical merit because consumption inequality rose much more slowly than income inequality during these periods (Krueger and Perri, 2006).

A variant of the inequality-interacting-with politics argument is associated with the work of Raghuram Rajan (2010). For Rajan, the housing bubble was the result of a political response to rising inequality, particularly by lowering restrictions to lending to low-income households. While the first argument suggests a longer-term pattern of promoting indebtedness, Rajan focuses specifically on the implicit public guarantee of Freddie Mac and Fannie Mae, which encouraged the population to gamble on the housing market and led thereby to instability and crisis.

Acemoglu (2011) points to some difficulties with the Rajan narrative. In particular, the timing of the alleged reaction to inequality does not fit the data. According to Acemoglu, the growth in inequality at the lower end was mostly felt in the 1980s while the housing bubble took place in the late 1990s and 2000s. Instead, he also sees inequality as being causal and political economy reasons—specifically regulatory capture—as driving the bubble. From this point of view, inequality at the top end led to calls for deregulation of finance that further increased incomes at the top and hence caused greater financial fragility. The fact that the major rise in inequality was driven by the growth of incomes of those in the financial sector provides some potential support for the narrative (Kaplan and Ruah, 2010; Phillipon and Reshef, 2008). Equally important, as Gordon (2009) points out, inequality among the bottom 90 percent of the distribution has been relatively stable in the period leading up to the crisis, suggesting that it is the divergence of the top from everyone else that needs explanation. Cahuc and Challe (2009) draw from Phillipon and Reshef's (2008) paper, which suggested a model for the formation of rational bubbles in which inequality and asset bubbles coevolve due to occupational choices of skilled and unskilled labor in such a dynamic.

Brescia (2010) suggests another indirect causal narrative: income and racial inequality in the United States created larger gaps in social distance, which in turn allowed for much greater predatory conduct on the part of the mortgage lenders. He finds that the greater the income inequality in a state, on average, the greater the delinquency rate in that state.

A more direct link between rising interpersonal inequality and the crisis is provided by Shleifer and Vishny (2010), who provide a model in which a change in which the introduction of securitization leads to an increase in risk taking that in turn increases with higher levels of inequality. Other scholars have pointed to behavioral arguments that do not rely on political economy but on microeconomic explanations of the link between increased consumer debt and rising inequality. A particularly relevant paper in this regard is that by Levine and colleagues (2010), who argue that inequality leads to a Veblen effect whereby individuals and households whose income does not rise as fast as others increase their borrowing to maintain consumption growing at similar rates. Such an explanation is consistent with some of the arguments provided above, and it is an extension of an older set of arguments about the importance of relative income rather than absolute income as an explanation of household behavior (Duesenberry, 1949). An alternative hypothesis again grounded in microeconomic theory about increased consumer debt is provided by Iacoviello (2008), who argues that the inequality can explain a significant amount of the rise in consumer debt in 1963–2003, with debt being used as an insurance mechanism against consumption volatility that arose from increased income volatility in this period.

## Inequality as a Predictor of Crisis: Empirical Issues

Given the multiple causal linkages that can be drawn between inequality and the incidence of financial crises and the many arguments as to why they have been linked to this crisis in particular, it may be that a large empirical literature exists on the subject. In fact, such a literature is sparse at best and in some cases only very recent. Heterodox economists have begun linking changes in the functional distribution to financial fragility and the potential for crises, but the empirical examinations are relatively few. Furthermore, they are almost always located in examinations of dynamics of advanced industrialized economies (thereby not considering the many crises that have occurred in, for example, Latin America and Asia), focus most often on real sector dislocations, and typically have paid little attention to the formation of asset bubbles and their consequences.

Nor is such an empirical project very far advanced with regard to the investigation of interpersonal inequality and its linkages to financial crises by other approaches. There are several operational and conceptual reasons for this. Perhaps most important, it is hard to conceive of a convincing manner in which to effectively identify causal relationships between increasing disparities and financial crises. Even if one were to find a strong correlation in which increasing inequality predicted financial crises, there would be little to suggest causality because several processes (financialization, liberal reforms, global integration) could be causing both outcomes simultaneously. Second, systemic financial crises occur relatively rarely (although by some accounts, they have increased in frequency in the liberal era (see Kaminksy and Reinhart, 1999) and studying the role of interpersonal inequality in a consistent and empirically compelling manner therefore requires the gathering of cross-country data over extensive periods of time. This has only become very recently possible with the collation of a large and long time series on inequality (see Atkinson and Piketty, 2010); but this again is skewed toward developed countries where the data are more easily available. Third, it is still an open question as to what kind of inequality is causally relevant. Income has been stressed in some of the accounts we have noted in the preceding section, but wealth/net worth may be the more critical variable, especially when financial crises are driven by asset bubbles. Data on wealth are less easily available and typically are not collected with the frequency that would allow for systematic explorations of the issue (see Davies 2008, for a review of studies of wealth inequality). Fourth, there is not an immediate agreement as to what constitutes a financial crisis. Crises may manifest in different ways as banking crises, currency crises, and stock market crashes, and classifications as to what constitutes a crisis differ widely. In developing countries, a financial crisis often manifests as a currency crisis or a stock market crisis, but not always as a banking crisis. Furthermore, the channels by which inequality could affect each of these sorts of crises might vary. Another problem with attempting to identify empirical regularities is that focusing simply on the actual incidence of crisis (however defined) and examining patterns of inequality in the buildup to the crissis as opposed to looking at an increased potential for crisis (say through increased leverage on private-sector balance sheets) may miss an important and existing link. Finally, it is not clear as to what measure of inequality is appropriate and it is not always possible to obtain accurate data on the relevant section of the income parade.

These difficulties noted, and taking into account the lack of theoretical guidance, it would be surprising to find a robust correlation between such complex aggregate patterns as rising levels of inequality and the incidence of financial crises. Perhaps the most explicit effort thus far in trying to examine the link between inequality and crisis is the work of Atkinson and Morelli (2010). They identify 66 systemic banking crises (as opposed to financial crises more generally) and examine 25 of these for which they have adequate distributional data. They find at best weak evidence supporting the contention that inequality rises prior to a crisis. In the bare majority of the cases this pattern is evident and is more pronounced in crises that have occurred after 1980.

Other evidence on the patterns of inequality preceding the crisis tends to be drawn from case studies. Birdsall and Haggard (2000), reviewing the Asian financial crisis, find that inequality was rising in Thailand, Indonesia, and South Korea in the years preceding the crisis. Conversely, in Malaysia and the Phillipines income inequality was relatively constant if also higher in level. The Russian financial crisis of 1998 was preceded by sharply rising inequality (Gorodnichenko et al., 2010), primarily as a result of the movement toward a more liberal economy and the concomitant collapse of livelihoods at the bottom of the distribution. Finally, as many have noted, Latin America is a region that has both high levels of inequality and a greater propensity to currency crises and macroeconomic instability. This noted, there has been no systematic study that has shown a consistent pattern of rising interpersonal inequality preceding financial crises in the region. As a whole then, there is at best very scant evidence that rising interpersonal inequality can serve as a reliable lead variable for predicting a financial crisis.

## Patterns of Inequality Following a Financial Crisis: Theoretical and Empirical Relationships

Policy makers and researchers are often interested in the social impacts of financial crises: in particular, the impact on poverty and inequality. As such, there is certainly a more substantial empirical literature examining the distributional consequences of financial crises, especially because data availability on such outcomes has improved over the last three decades. These papers have tended to focus on the major regional crises of the last two decades: the Latin American financial crises, the East Asian financial crisis, the Tequlila crisis, and so on. Here, once again, the causal linkages are potentially complex and the expected impacts are thus ambiguous. Researchers have pointed to multiple channels to consider (see, e.g., Fiorio and Saget, 2010; Ferreira et al., 1999; and Baldaci, De Mello, and Inchauste, 2002, for reviews of the main channels). One might expect inequality to fall if the rich held a disproportionately larger share of assets that lost value (Blejer and Guerrero, 1990).[7] If they work in nontradeable sectors that are most affected by reductions in labor demand (e.g., the financial sector), one might expect that inequality might fall as labor earnings of the relatively rich fall sharply. Conversely, because financial crises often lead to generalized downturns and reductions in income, it could be the poor and middle-class who are the most hurt, as they lack the resources and means to hedge against such shocks. Labor-market conditions can be further exacerbated for the poor as informal-sector workers face increased competition from newly unemployed formal-sector workers that can serve to reduce wages. When financial crises manifest as sharp currency depreciations, one might expect that the poor are worse off when necessities such as food or oil are imported at higher costs. To the extent that a financial crisis leads to reductions in fiscal capacity and a reduction in public services, this can serve to hurt the relatively poor and increase inequality. Finally, as Halac and Schmulker (2004) argue, the response of the state in terms of bailouts can have the effect of increasing inequality as they involve a transfer from taxpayers to the relatively rich. Once again, the relative importance of these and other channels can only be gauged empirically.

Perhaps the most robust finding, not surprisingly, is a rise in the poverty rate following a crisis. Lustig (2000) focuses on 20 Latin American crises and finds that all were followed by an increase in poverty. This is the general conclusion of Baldaci, De Mello, and Inchauste (2002) as well, who study 65 financial crises in developing and transition economies over the last three decades. More detailed case studies of the East Asian financial crisis also bear out similar trends. Bourguignon, Robilliard, and Robinson (2001) and Friedman and Levinsohn (2002) examine the case of Indonesia and find a sharp rise in the incidence of poverty from 1996 to 1999. Similarly, poverty also rose in South Korea, Thailand, and Malaysia (Zin, 2001; Ragayah, 2008). Studies of other crises such as the Russian crisis yield the same pattern: Lokshin and Ravallion (2000) find that poverty rose by almost 50 percent in the immediate aftermath.

Another consistent finding in the literature on distributional consequences of financial crises is a sharp reduction in labor's share of income. Diwan (2002) finds an average drop in the labor share of around five percentage points of GDP per crisis, with some catchup thereafter. This finding has been confirmed by Harrison (2004), Jayadev (2007), and Onaran (2009). Following the onset of the US financial crisis in 2007, Atkinson and Morelli (2010) note that the labor share of income in the United States has fallen by two percentage points in the two following years. Distributional changes may be a part of the resolution of the financial crisis, with labor incomes falling relative to capital incomes. This is perhaps because labor is relatively immobile and so bears a higher proportion of the overall losses.

The impact of a crisis on interpersonal inequality is more ambiguous, although the weight of evidence suggests that the most recent crises preceding the Great Recession have tended to be followed by increasing inequality. For example, of the 20 crises examined by Lustig (2000), in three-fourths of the cases the countries experienced a consequent rise in the Gini coefficient. Similarly, Baldaci, De Mello, and Inchauste (2002) note that the Gini coefficient percentage points rises by about 0.6 percent relative to the precrisis year on average. They also find that there are declines in income for the bottom two quintiles, with the second lowest quintile experiencing the sharpest declines.

There are nevertheless a few interesting cases in which this has not been the case. In the Mexican crisis, for example, Lopez-Acevedo and Salinas (2000) find that although poverty increased between 1994 and 1996, the richest decile lost the largest amount and inequality fell as a result. This is confirmed by using similar techniques by Baldacci, De Mello, and Inchauste (2002) as well. A similar pattern is found in the current crisis in Brazil, where the rich and the middle class were disproportionately hurt by declines in stock values and financial assets (Fundaçao Getulio Vargas, 2009). Similarly, Roine, Vlachos, and Waldenstrom (2009) find that of the 16 banking crises they examine using the top income data, the general tendency is for the incomes of the rich to fall more. Halac and Shmuckler (2004) address what they term the financial channel and examine transfers associated with crisis resolution in several Latin American countries. They find that the resolution often involved large-scale transfers from poor nonparticipants to wealthier and more informed depositors, thereby increasing inequality. Atkinson and Morelli (2010) report similarly indefinite results in their examination of the aftermath of 25 banking crises. They find that there is virtually no systematic pattern in inequality in the years following the banking crisis, with 10 out of the 25 cases seeing higher inequality, 9 out of the 25 seeing lower inequality, and 6 seeing no change. One possibility for these somewhat contradictory findings may be that the types of financial crises that are being studied vary (many of the cases are currency crises while Atkinson and Morelli and Roine, Vlachos, and Waldenstrom are concerned solely with banking crises) and the time periods being considered also matter for the results. In particular, earlier crises may have had more equalizing effects on the postcrisis distribution because wealth was more strongly concentrated in societies before World War II and shocks to wealth hurt the rich relatively more.[8]

Given the fact that these effects vary substantially across regions and times, it is important to identify factors that can ameliorate or conversely exacerbate the negative social impacts of crises. Galbraith and Lu (1999) identify some variables in this regard. In their study of 34 financial crises they find that the negative impact on manufacturing wage inequality following a crisis was worse in developing regions (in Latin America and in Asia to be specific) than in developed countries. In Nordic countries, the impact on inequality from financial crisis was negligible. They take this as indicative of the importance of strong labor-market institutions and social safety nets to mitigate the impact of financial crises on distribution. Easterly (2003) examines the role of IMF and World Bank programs for stabilization and finds that such programs moderated increases in poverty following a crisis. A third related literature is associated with the impact of "good institutions" (usually a composite of such indices as corruption, democratic accountability, law and order, and bureaucratic quality) on mitigating the impact of financial crises. Mandel (2010) finds that the presence of such institutions dampens the effect of financial crises on worsening the income distribution. Additionally, several case studies examine the impacts of numerous ad hoc postcrisis policies that attempt to reduce poverty rates. These are too numerous to detail, and perhaps the one broad conclusion for such studies is that the overall impact of the financial crisis on income distribution can be quite significantly altered and moderated. As such, while financial crises on average in the recent period have tended to make the income distribution more unequal, such an outcome is not predetermined.

## Conclusion

A review of such a complex literature often leads to as many questions as there are answers. The literature on the impacts of financial crises on distribution is more clearly defined, and a fairly vigorous research program has been established. Thus noted, there are still several open topics. How do financial crises impact other relevant distributions, for example, the distribution of wealth? How do currency crises, banking crises, and stock market crises differ in their impact? How and in what ways does the financialization of advanced economies serve to shift the distributional burden of crises? Can one trace distributional impacts more effectively when financial crises spill over borders? And so on. If there is a serious lacuna, however, it is the lack of theoretical clarity about the other direction of causality: in what ways does income distribution affect macroeconomic outcomes in general, and financial markets and the formation of asset bubbles in particular? While newer post-Keynesian models offer some hope in this regard, the work of Kumhof and Rancière (2010) serves to suggest that such considerations may become part of more mainstream models. Future models may help provide a clearer lens through which to view these relationships, and supplement the more historical and narratival approaches that have thus far been adopted. A tentative answer to the question posed in the first section—whether there is a deep connection between inequality and crisis—can nevertheless be proferred. While it is not always the case that inequality leads to crisis (at least in the narrow sense of a financial crisis), there is certainly strong and compelling evidence that for the current US financial crisis, inequality may have played a meaningful albeit complex causal role. Rising inequality and consequently lower aggregate demand may have led to excessive debt on the one hand, while concentrated income and the political power associated with it may have led to regulatory capture on the other. Such an answer, of course, is contingent on political and institutional features and cannot be used to generalize a relationship between the two. Until there is more clarity as to what types of variables are relevant and what data can be used to illuminate these relationships, empirical research on this topic will necessarily seem to be groping in the dark. This noted, it would be foolhardy to expect, even then, hard and fast answers. The effect of distribution on financial fragility is probably highly contingent on such factors as the degree to which the economy is geared toward financial activities, the political balance between labor and capital, the international context, and so on. As such, there will always be a need for a more considered political economy approach to these questions.

## Notes

1. I emphasize "mainstream" because the relationship between unequal distribution in general and the aptitude of capitalist economies to suffer periodic mass upheavals is one that has had a much longer tradition—notably in the Marxian and post-Keynesian frameworks, partly because income distribution is a key variable in the macroeconomic dynamics examined by these models. For researchers coming from such traditions, there is a self-evident and plausible link between increasing

inequality and the potential for crisis (through either the real or the financial sector).

2. This is not an altogether new hypothesis. Eccles (1951) and Galbraith (1954) also point to high levels of income inequality as a key contributor to the Great Depression.
3. In this regard, the work of Atkinson and Morelli (2010), who examine banking crises, constitutes a pioneering attempt.
4. Some recent examples of distribution and growth models integrating issues of "financialization" include Mouakil (2008), Lavoie (2008), and Skott and Ryoo (2008a, 2008b).
5. See, for example, Dos Santos and Silva (2009), who try and combine a model in the Marglin-Bhaduri framework with Minskian insights.
6. This process has been central to the idea of financialization that has become widely accepted in this literature. Epstein (2005) defines financialization to be "the increasing role of financial motives, financial markets, financial actors and financial institutions in the operation of the domestic and international economies."
7. In terms of the functional distribution, this might manifest as a fall in the rentier share.
8. In this regard, the US crisis of 1929 is a classic example, with income inequality falling sharply from its high preceding the crisis.

## References

Acemoglu, D. (2011). "Thoughts on Inequality and the Financial Crisis." Presentation at the AEA meeting in Denver, January 8, 2011. Available at econ-www.mit.edu/files/634 (last accessed May 6, 2011).

Atkinson, A. B., and S. Morelli. (2010). "Inequality and Banking Crises: A First Look." Working Paper, available at isites.harvard.edu/fs/docs/icb.topic457678.files/ATKINSON%20paper.pdf (last accessed May 6, 2011).

Atkinson, A. B., and T. Piketty, eds. (2010). *Top Incomes: A Global Perspective*. Oxford: Oxford University Press.

Baldacci, E., L. de Melo, and G. Inchauste. (2002). "Financial Crises, Poverty, and Income Distribution." Working Paper 02/04. Washington, DC: International Monetary Fund.

Bhaduri, A., and S. Marglin. (1990). "Unemployment and the Real Wage: The Economic Basis for Contesting Political Ideologies." *Cambridge Journal of Economics* 14(4): 375–393.

Bibow, J. (2010). "Financialization of the US Household Sector: The 'Subprime Mortgage Crisis.' In *US and Global Perspective*." IMK Working Paper.

Birdsall, Nancy and Stephan Haggard. 2000. *After the Crisis: The Social Contract and the Middle Class in East Asia*. Washington, D.C.: Carnegie Endowment for International Peace.

Blejer, M. and I. Guerrero. (1990). "The Impact of Macroeconomic Policies on Income Distribution: An Empirical Study of the Philippines", *Review of Economics and Statistics* 72: 414–423.

Bourguignon, F., A. S. Robilliard, and S. Robinson. (2001). "Crisis and Income Distribution: A Micro-Macro Model for Indonesia." Washington, DC: World Bank. Mimeograph.

Bowles, Samuel, and Robert Boyer. (1988). "Labor Discipline and Aggregate Demand: A Macroeconomic Model." *American Economic Review* 78(2): 395–400.

Brenner, R. (2007). "That Hissing? It's the Sound of Bubblenomics Deflating." *Guardian*, September 26, http://www.guardian.co.uk/commentisfree/2007/sep/26/comment.business.

Brescia, Raymond H. (2010). "The Cost of Inequality: Social Distance, Predatory Conduct, and the Financial Crisis." August 19, 2010, NYU Annual Survey of American Law, Albany Law School Research Paper No. 10–20. Available at SSRN: http://ssrn.com/abstract=1661746.

Cahuc, P., and E. Challe. (2009). "Produce or Speculate? Asset Bubbles, Occupational Choice and Efficiency," IZA Discussion Paper 4630.

Crotty, James. (2007). "If Financial Market Competition Is So Intense, Why Are Financial Firm Profits So High? Reflections on the Current 'Golden Age' of Finance." Working Paper wp134, Political Economy Research Institute, University of Massachusetts at Amherst.

Cutler, D. M., and L. F. Katz, (1992). "Rising Inequality? Changes in the Distribution of Income and Consumption in the 1980s." *American Economic Review* 82: 546–551.

Davies, J. B., ed. (2008). *Personal Wealth from a Global Perspective*. Oxford: Oxford University Press.

Diwan, Ishac. (2002). "Debt as Sweat: Labor, Financial Crises, and the Globalization of Capital." Washington, DC: World Bank. Mimeograph.

Dos Santos, C., and A. E. Silva. (2009). "Revisiting (and Connecting) Marglin-Bhaduri and Minsky: An SFC Look at Financialization and Profit-led Growth." Levy Institute Working Paper No. 567.

Duesenberry, J. (1949). *Income, Saving and the Theory of Consumer Behaviour*. Cambridge, MA: Harvard University Press.

Dutt, A. K. (1992). "Rentiers in Post Keynesian Models." In P. Arestis and V. Chick, eds., *Recent Developments in Post-Keynesian Economics*, 95–122. Aldershot, UK: Edward Elgar, 1992.

Easterly, W. (2003). "IMF and World Bank Structural Adjustment Programs and Poverty." In Michael P. Dooley and Jeffrey A. Frankel, ed., *Managing Currency Crises in Emerging Markets*, 361–392. Conference Report, Boston, MA: National Bureau of Economic Research.

Eccles, M. S. (1951). *Beckoning Frontiers: Public and Personal Recollections*. New York: Knopf.

Epstein, G., ed. (2005). *Financialization and the World Economy*. Northampton, MA: Edward Elgar.

Epstein, G., and A. Jayadev. (2007). "The Correlates of Rentier Returns in OECD Countries." Available at: http://works.bepress.com/gerald_epstein/139.

Ferreira, Francisco, Giovanna Prennushi, and Martin Ravallion. (1999). "Protecting the Poor from Macroeconomic Shocks: An Agenda for Action in a Crisis and Beyond." Working Paper 2160. Washington, DC: World Bank.

Fiorio, C., and C. Saget. (2010). "Reducing or Aggravating Inequality? Preliminary Findings from the 2008 Financial Crisis." ILO Working Paper.

Fitoussi, J.P and F. Saraceno (2010). "Inequality and Macroeconomic Performance OFCE/POLHIA". Working Paper no 2010-13. Available at http://www.ofce.sciences-po.fr/pdf/dtravail/WP2010–13.pdf

Friedman, Jed, and James Levinsohn. (2002). "The Distributional Impacts of Indonesia's Crisis on Household Welfare: A 'Rapid Response' Methodology." *World Bank Economic Review* 16(3): 397–423.

Fundaçao Getulio Vargas (FGV). (2009). "Chronicle of the Crisis." Mimeograph.

Galbraith, J.K (1954). *The Great Crash, 1929*. Houghton Mifflin.

Galbraith, J., and Q. Lu. (1999). "Inequality and Financial Crises: Some Early Findings." UTIP Working Paper No. 9. http://utip.gov.utexas.edu/papers/utip_09enc.pdf.

Goodwin, R. M. (1967). "A Growth Cycle." In Feinstein, C.H ed., *Socialism, Capitalism and Economic Growth*, Cambridge, UK: Cambridge University Press.

Gordon, Robert J. (2009). "Has the Rise in American Inequality Been Exaggerated?" *Challenge* 52(3): 92–120.

Gorodnichenko Yuriy, Klara Sabirianova Peter, and Dmitriy Stolyarov. (2010). "Inequality and Volatility Moderation in Russia: Evidence from Micro-Level Panel Data on Consumption and Income." *Review of Economic Dynamics*, 13(1): 209–237.

Gottschalk, Peter, and Sheldon Danziger. (2005). "Inequality of Wage Rates, Earnings and Family Income in the United States, 1975–2002." *Review of Income and Wealth*, 51(2): 231–254.

Halac, Marina, and Sergio L. Schmukler. (2004). "Distributional Effects of Crises: The Financial Channel." *Economía* 5(1): 1–67.

Harrison, Ann E. (2004). "Has Globalization Eroded Labors Share of Income?" University of California, Berkeley. Mimeograph.

Hein, Eckhard, and Till van Treeck. (2007). "Financialisation." In *Kaleckian/Post-Kaleckian Models of Distribution and Growth*, No 07-2007, IMK Working Paper, IMK at the Hans Boeckler Foundation, Macroeconomic Policy Institute, http://econpapers.repec.org/RePEc:imk:wpaper:07-2007.

Iacoviello, M. (2008). "Household Debt and Income Inequality, 1963–2003." *Journal of Money, Credit and Banking* 40: 929–965.

Jayadev, A. (2007). "Capital Account Openness and the Labour Share of Income." *Cambridge Journal of Economics* 31(3): 423–443.

Jayadev, A., and Francisco Rodriguez. (2010). "The Declining Labor Share of Income." Human Development Report Working Paper. Available at http://hdr.undp.org/en/reports/global/hdr2010/papers/HDRP_2010_36.pdf.

Kalecki, M. (1939). *Essays in the Theory of Economic Fluctuations*. London: George Allen & Unwin.

Kalecki, M. (1943). "Political Aspects of Full Employment." *Political Quarterly*, Vol. 14. No. 4.

Kaminsky, Graciela L., and Carmen M. Reinhart. (1999). "The Twin Crises: The Causes of Banking and Balance-of-Payments Problems." American Economic Review, 89(3): 473–500.

Kaplan, S., and J. Ruah (2010). "Wall Street and Main Street: What Contributes to the Rise in the Highest Incomes?" *Review of Financial Studies*, 23(3): 1004–1050.

Katz, Lawrence F., and David H. Autor. (1999). "Changes in the Wage Structure and Earnings Inequality." In O. Ashenfelter and D. Card, eds., *Handbook of Labor Economics*, 1463–1555. Amsterdam: Elsevier.

Krueger, D., and F. Perri. (2006). "Does Income Inequality Lead to Consumption Inequality? Evidence and Theory." *Review of Economic Studies* 73: 163–193.

Kumhof, M., and R. Rancière. (2010). "Inequality, Leverage and Crises." International Monetary Fund Working Paper.

Lavoie, Marc. (2008). "Financialisation Issues in a Post-Keynesian Stock-flow Consistent Model." *Intervention. European Journal of Economics and Economic Policies* 5(2): 331–356.
Lemieux, T. (2008). "The Changing Nature of *Wage Inequality*." *Journal of Population Economics* 21(1): 21–48.
Levine, Adam Seth, Robert H. Frank, and Oege Dijk. (2010). "Expenditure Cascades." Available at SSRN: http://ssrn.com/abstract=1690612.
Lokshin, Michael, and Martin Ravallion. (2000). "Welfare Impacts of the 1998 Financial Crisis in Russia and the Response of the Public Safety Net." *Economics of Transition* 8(2): 269–295.
Lopez-Acevedo, Gladys, and Angel Salinas. (2000). "How Mexico's Financial Crisis Affected Income Distribution." Policy Research Working Paper 2406. Washington, DC: World Bank.
Lustig, Nora. (2000). "Crises and the Poor: Socially Responsible Macroeconomics." *Economía* 1(1): 1–30.
Mandel, B. (2010). "Dependencia Revisited: Financial Liberalization and Inequality in Latin America." *Michigan Journal of Business* 3(2): 57–96.
Moss, David. (2010). "Bank Failures, Regulation, and Inequality in the United States." Mimeograph.
Mouakil, T. (2008). "Financial Keynesianism Counterattacks: A Minsky Crisis in a Tobin-Kalecki Model." Centre for Financial Analysis and Policy, Judge Business School, University of Cambridge.
Ozlem, Onaran. (2009). "Wage Share, Globalization and Crisis: The Case of the Manufacturing Industry in Korea, Mexico, and Turkey." *International Review of Applied Economics* 23(2): 113–134.
Onaran, O., E. Stockhammet and L. Grafl. (2011). "The Finance-dominated Growth Regime, Distribution, and Aggregate Demand in the US." *Cambridge Journal of Economics*, Oxford University Press, 35(4): 637–661.
Philippon, T., and A. Reshef. (2008). "Wages and Human Capital in the US Financial Industry: 1909–2006." New York University Working Papers. Available at: http://pages.stern.nyu.edu/~tphilipp/papers/pr_rev15.pdf
Piketty, T., and E. Saez (2003). "Income Inequality in the United States, 1913–1998." *Quarterly Journal of Economics* 118: 1–39.
Piketty, T., and E. Saez (2010). "Income Inequality in the United States, 1913–1998: Data Appendix." Data extended till 2007.
Ragayah, H. M. Z. (2008). "Income Inequality in Malaysia." *Asian Economic Policy Review* 3: 114–132.
Rajan, R. G. (2010). *Fault Lines: How Hidden Fractures Still Threaten the World Economy*. Princeton: Princeton University Press.
Roine, J., J. Vlachos, and D. Waldenström. (2009). "The Long-run Determinants of Inequality: What Can We Learn from Top Income Data?" *Journal of Public Economics* 93: 974–988.
Shleifer, A., and R. W. Vishny. (2010). "Unstable Banking." *Journal of Financial Economics* 97: 306–318.
Skott, P., and S. Ryoo. (2008a). "Financialisation in Kaleckian Economics with and without Labor Constraints." Working Paper 2008-05. Amherst, University of Massachusetts.
Skott, P., and S. Ryoo. (2008b). "Macroeconomic Implications of Financialisation." *Cambridge Journal of Economics* 32: 827–862.

Stiglitz, J. E. (2009). "Joseph Stiglitz and Why Inequality Is at the Root of the Recession." http://www.nextleft.org/2009/01/joseph-stiglitz-and-why-inequality-is.html.

Stockhammer, E. (2008). "Some Stylized Facts on the Finance-dominated Accumulation Regime." *Competition & Change* 12: 184–202.

Stockhammer, E. (2009). "The Finance-dominated Accumulation Regime, Income Distribution and Present Crisis." Working Paper Series No. 127. Department of Economics, Vienna University of Economics.

Wisman J., and Barton Baker. (2009). "Increasing Inequality, Status Insecurity, Ideology, and the Financial Crisis of 2008." Working Papers 2009-14, American University, Department of Economics.

Zin, Ragayaj Haji Mat. (2001). "Improving Quality of Life after the Crisis: New Dilemmas." *Malaysian Journal of Economic Studies*. XXXVIII(1 & 2), June/December, 25–40.

# CHAPTER 6

# HOUSING MARKETS AND FORECLOSURES

RACHEL B. DREW AND
CHRISTIAN E. WELLER

## I. Introduction

The world economy drove into a deep ditch in 2008 and only emerged very slowly from the most severe recession and financial crisis since the Great Depression. The onset of the crisis was marked by the US housing crash starting as early as 2006. House prices dropped dramatically, sales of new homes shrank rapidly, mortgage foreclosures soared to record highs, and mortgage bank failures foreshadowed what was to come for the entire US financial system. The link between the US housing market crash and a severe global recession and financial crisis is particularly remarkable because spending on new residential real estate has never surpassed 7.4 percent of gross domestic product (GDP) and on average amounts to a little over 4 percent of GDP.[1]

The outsized contribution of housing investment to the recession and the crisis is not an aberration but the norm. Housing investment tends to be more volatile than other components of the economy, thus contributing more to swings in the overall economy. Fluctuations in housing investment in fact tend to precede GDP fluctuations and financial instability. A big part of this regularity is the feedback loop between housing investment and mortgages. When housing fails, so do mortgages, creating a spillover effect from the real economy to the financial sector. And more failing mortgages erode banks' capital, lowering the amount available for loans, slowing economic growth, completing a vicious reinforcing cycle between the real economy and the financial sector. Importantly, leverage has risen over time as US financial markets have become increasingly deregulated. The link between the real and financial sectors has thus only become stronger over time, contributing to rising economic and financial instability.

Housing policy further contributes to these cycles. US policy affecting housing serves as an illustrative example of this potential pro-cyclical homeownership bias. Homeowners receive a subsidy from the tax deductibility of mortgage interest payments, and public insurance mechanisms for many mortgages tend to reduce mortgage interest rates by reducing the risk exposure of the original lenders. Both policies provide a stronger incentive to become a homeowner during a boom, when prices are high, than during a recession, when prices are low. The economic value of the tax incentives, for instance, rises with the price of a home, which tends to go up with incomes during an economic boom. The opposite is true during a recession, when house prices fall and the economic value of homeownership incentives declines as well.

Public supports for renting, meanwhile, exhibit a countercyclical bias, which reinforces the pro-cyclical bias of homeownership policies and the pro-cyclicality of leverage because renters do not have to borrow to rent a house, as homeowners often do. Often only a fixed total amount of rent subsidies are available and qualification for the subsidy depends mainly on income levels. Fewer families qualify for rental subsidies during boom years due to rising incomes that make many people ineligible for rental subsidies. The opposite is true during a recession, when families more easily qualify for rental subsidies and rents may be somewhat lower. Rental demand thus declines in a boom and increases in a bust, reinforcing the movements of homeownership.

This chapter will present the evidence and emerging research questions that could ultimately lead to a reconsideration of existing pro-cyclical housing policies with the goal to reduce the cyclicality of housing investment. We summarize the role of housing investment during business cycles in section II, followed by a discussion of the role of leverage in section III. Our elaboration of the role of existing housing policies in business cycle swings is shown in section IV. We sketch the parameters for alternative housing and rental policies and highlight the research necessary to support a more balanced, less pro-cyclical housing policy in section V.

## II. Housing Investment and Business Cycles

Housing investment on residential real estate is typically a comparatively small part of the overall economy. Spending on new houses and renovations explains on average 3.6 percent of the growth rate during past business cycles after

World War II.[2] Construction employment, including for residential and commercial construction, accounted for 5.4 percent of total employment during the business cycle from March 2001 to December 2007,[3] when the housing sector had boomed.

The housing sector, though, plays a disproportionate role with respect to business cycle fluctuations. Housing investment plays a particularly large role during the initial stages of a recovery and just before a recession (Coulson and Kim, 2000; Miles, 2009). Growth in US housing investment, for example, explains on average 16.0 percent of US economic growth during the first year of a recovery. During the last year of an economic expansion, just before the onset of a recession, US housing investment lowers US economic growth by 17.4 percent below where it would have been otherwise.[4] Housing investment clearly provides an extra boost to economic growth in a recovery, but then it applies the brakes once the economy has expanded for some time. Evidence shows that these fluctuations in fact precede upturns and downturns in GDP (Green, 1997; Barbosa-Filho et al., 2008).

The contributions of housing to business cycles result primarily from five economic factors. First, housing investment is intricately linked to personal income, which fluctuates with the business cycle. Second, housing is a long-term proposition and thus depends crucially on households' and businesses' future expectations of house price changes. Housing investment thus can fall prey to boom-and-bust cycles as expectations oscillate between euphoria and depression (Shiller, 2007). Third, rising housing investment translates into more construction and related hiring domestically, thus boosting incomes and increasing demand for more housing (Case and Quigley, 2008). Fourth, fluctuations in housing investment lead to fluctuations in house prices and thus in household wealth. Personal consumption spending will consequently fluctuate as well due to the wealth effect (Case and Quigley, 2008; Miles, 2009). Fifth, housing investment is highly leveraged and thus its fluctuations are augmented by financial-market swings (Case and Quigley, 2008; Case, Quigley, and Shiller, 2003). When housing does well, so do bank assets as foreclosures and mortgage delinquencies decline, leading banks to lend more, fueling an economic and financial boom. And on the opposite end, when the economy fails, foreclosures and delinquencies rise, resulting in less bank capital and contributing to credit constraints.

Housing investment depends on people's economic situations and outlook. In the simplest terms, the rise in employment and household incomes that frequently accompanies a growing economy increases the purchasing power of renter households that could not previously afford to buy a home, while also making it easier for such households to qualify for home mortgage financing (Ortalo-Magne and Rady, 1998; Belsky and Duda, 2002). Higher incomes will also aid new household formations, thus raising housing demand, house prices, and potential rental incomes on investment properties.

Potential homeowners will also purchase in expectation of rising prices. The late 1990s, for instance, experienced increases in US household incomes and US house prices (US Census Bureau, 2009; FHFA, 2010), while the period from 2000 to 2006 saw both falling incomes (US Census Bureau, 2009) and rising house prices (FHFA, 2010). Yet both periods were marked by increasing homeownership rates (US Census Bureau, 2010).[5] Higher incomes make it easier for homeowners to service their mortgages, whereas rising home prices provide homeowners with more equity and thus a larger financial cushion in the event that the homeowner can no longer service the mortgage. Mortgages thus become more available during periods of rising prices. The fixed supply of housing in the short term, however, places upward pressure on house prices when demand rises, prompting more households to enter the homeowning market to lock in fixed mortgage costs before house prices become unaffordable (Green and Malpezzi, 2003). Often, a mob mentality takes over, fueled by media reports of rising prices and increased homebuying, which encourages still more households to buy during booms, simply because they see others doing it (Case and Shiller, 1988). Households and businesses thus become more willing to invest more of their money in housing, when they believe that incomes and house prices will go up, setting a housing boom cycle in motion.

The first spillover effect of housing investment onto the business cycle occurs through increased hiring in construction. Increased construction employment boosts incomes and domestic demand, thus supporting additional housing demand, while a downturn in construction employment goes along with weakness in housing investment and can precede overall labor-market weaknesses (Case and Quigley, 2008). US construction employment, for example, peaked in April 2006, while total nonfarm employment peaked in December 2007 during the most recent boom (BLS, 2010).

There is another spillover effect from housing to other consumption through the wealth effect. More demand for housing will result in rising values for non-transacting homes as well, which increases household wealth. Unexpected increases in household wealth, due, for instance, to a housing boom, give households the impression that they can more easily reach their savings goals than they had thought. Households will feel that they have to save less and that they can spend more when wealth unexpectedly increases. During the last housing boom this factor was further exacerbated by the fact that households could easily access the equity in their homes due to the ready availability of second mortgages. A housing boom thus can contribute to an expansion of total consumption spending and a decrease in personal saving rates, more so than changes in other forms of household wealth (Poterba, 2000; Congressional Budget Office, 2007).

The initial housing investment decisions are further augmented because they are highly leveraged. Debt provides added fuel to a housing expansion, but it also poses a burden on housing investment and the economy during a downturn (Case and Quigley, 2008; Mian and Sufi, 2010).

The link between housing and business cycle fluctuations is further strengthened by lenders' expectations. Lenders will feel more confident of mortgage repayment when incomes and house prices rise. Both will result in lower foreclosures and better credit quality. Rising incomes mean easier mortgage repayments, and higher house prices mean more collateral, even if a borrower defaults. Lenders will extend credit due to rising credit quality. Increased availability of mortgages hence meets a growing demand for mortgages, which in turn contributes to a surge in leveraged housing investment.

Leverage, though, also puts a disproportionate burden from the housing sector on the economy and the financial sector, when income growth and house prices falter. The explanation is that lenders initially extend credit and borrowers increase their leverage in anticipation of continued income and house-price increases. If these increases do not materialize, repaying a mortgage becomes a larger burden than expected and the chance of a mortgage being under water—the house being worth less than the outstanding mortgage—increases. Rising debt burdens and owing more than a house is worth are disincentives for homeowners to repay their mortgages, particularly if they believe that house prices will continue to fall or remain low. A vicious cycle of rising foreclosures and falling mortgages then ensues. The share of US mortgages in foreclosure started to increase from its low of 1.0 percent in the middle of 2006 to 1.4 percent in June 2007 and 2.0 percent in December 2007 (Mortgage Bankers Association, 2010). The sharp rise in foreclosures ultimately contributed to an unprecedented decrease in total mortgage debt relative to after-tax income, from 100.0 percent in March 2008 to 92.3 percent in March 2010,[6] as lenders became increasingly reluctant to extend credit (Federal Reserve Board, 2010b). This spillover from a recessionary economy to financial instability has recurred in earlier recessions, most notably in the late 1980s, when the failure of many small mortgage lenders during the savings and loan crisis precipitated a severe recession.

Leverage is an important factor that augments the initial housing investment decision's impact on the economy. The relevance of leverage in driving the economy up or down has risen over time (Miles, 2009). The ratio of home equity to total house values stayed relatively stable between 62 percent and 70 percent from 1961 to 2000 (Federal Reserve Board, 2010a). The onset of the recession in March 2001, however, coincided with an almost continuous decline in this ratio, falling to 58.3 percent by June 2007, before house values started to decline (Federal Reserve Board, 2010a). The growing leverage reflected the increasing home equity cashouts, whereby mortgages rose continuously faster than home values, from June 2000 to June 2007.[7] The combination of a recession and a financial crisis, following the housing boom of the 2000s, was thus presaged by decades-long trends that brought business cycles and financial instability closer together.

## III. Policy and Housing Investment

The link between housing and business cycle fluctuations occurs against the backdrop of several large public-policy changes. These changes primarily make up financial-market deregulation and a deliberate policy to emphasize homeownership in the United States over renting. A trend toward more homeowner leverage has followed financial-market deregulation, while the implementation of policies to encourage homeownership has exacerbated the cyclicality and financial instability contribution of housing investment.

## Financial Deregulation

The rising leverage was partially the result of the increased availability of mortgage debt due to legislative and regulatory changes from the late 1970s to the 1990s. Financial deregulation in the United States started in the late 1970s (Spong, 2000). Additional regulatory changes in the 1990s led to greater financial sector consolidation, with larger and more complex financial institutions that offered a much wider array of products and services.

Mortgage supply increased, particularly from new lenders, with new products, and from less regulated institutions (Goodhart et al., 2006). Deregulation freed banks to diversify their lending activities and invited new players (e.g., non-deposit-taking institutions) into financial markets. These lenders favored the relatively standardized (thanks to FHA requirements established in the 1940s) and stable home-purchase market over the more idiosyncratic commercial and multifamily investor-owned real-estate markets, and they channeled more supply into single-family home loans (Schwartz, 2006). This lending became increasingly financed with mortgage-backed securities (MBS) issued by government-sponsored enterprises (GSEs), including privately held but federally regulated Fannie Mae and Freddie Mac (Green and Malpezzi, 2003; Schwartz, 2006; Stone, 2006). Meanwhile, the special relationship between the GSEs and the federal government provided an implicit government guarantee of GSE securities, making them even more attractive to risk-averse investors. These factors contributed to the growth of less-regulated financial institutions, such as hedge funds. Much of the recent mortgage boom, for instance, was fueled by hedge funds, which channeled funds into the market for collateralized debt obligations (CDOs). It was estimated that in 2006 about $1.9 trillion, or 76 percent of all new mortgages, were securitized. Securitization was larger in the subprime-mortgage sector, which accounted for an estimated 20 percent of mortgage originations and 25 percent of securitizations (Kornfeld, 2007). With increasing securitization, lenders faced fewer risks and a growing share of the mortgage market was handled by less-regulated entities; hedge fund investments alone grew from $211 billion in 1999 to $1.2 trillion in late 2006 (Dodd, 2006).

The result of this combination of rising demand and growing supply of mortgages was a secular increase in homeowners' leverage, particularly in the 2000s, as we discussed before. The effect was a trend toward a stronger link between housing investment and economic fluctuations.

## US Housing Policies

Housing policy is the other policy lever that has contributed to a tighter connection between housing investment and business cycles. US housing policy has increasingly emphasized homeownership over renting and has done so with pro-cyclical incentives, as we discuss in the next section.

Initially, federal economic policies to stimulate the construction and finance industries introduced the policy preference for homeownership over renting, although that was not the intended goal (Carliner, 1998). The subsidized and insured home purchase loans, for instance, offered in the 1940s and 1950s through the Federal Housing Administration (FHA) and later through the Veterans Administration (VA) as part of the GI Bill, were developed to encourage lending by banks and to create jobs in the homebuilding industry for returning servicemen (Jackson, 1985; Carliner, 1998). The federal government also directed Fannie Mae, then under government control and not yet privatized, to purchase FHA/VA mortgages, providing the liquidity that banks needed to finance the expansion in home-purchase lending (Carliner, 1998; Schwartz, 2006). The private lending market quickly followed suit, adopting the standards and practices of both the FHA and Fannie Mae, and it offered home mortgages to millions of households. The United States quickly transitioned from being a nation of mostly renters to one of mostly homeowners, as the national homeownership rate increased from 43.6 percent in 1940 to 62.1 percent in 1960 (Hughes, 1996).

Most US housing policy following World War II, meanwhile, was initially focused on improving the quality of the housing stock, assisting low-income households facing housing affordability challenges, or redressing prejudices in private housing markets prior to the mid-1980s (Carliner, 1998; Schwartz, 2006).

The policy-aided growth in homeownership continued largely unabated through the 1960s and 1970s, as early baby boomers began to enter the housing market and thereby fuel new demand for owned housing. However, the combination of an economic recession and emerging problems in the private residential lending market made home financing more expensive in the late 1970s, thus causing the national homeownership rate to stagnate and eventually peak in 1980 at 65.6 percent (Hughes, 1996). When the homeownership rate began to decline in the 1980s, policy makers responded in three ways. First, there was the deregulation of financial markets, which expanded the residential lending industry and made home mortgages more attractive investments relative to other loans, as discussed in the previous section. Second, the Tax Reform Act of 1986 phased out the deductibility of most nonmortgage interest, leading to a shift of loans to mortgages and home equity lines (Carliner, 1998; Stango, 1999; Dunsky and Follain, 2000; Green and Malpezzi, 2003).[8]

The third policy intervention into housing markets in the 1980s was a remaking of housing policy itself to emphasize homeownership, particularly for low-income and minority buyers traditionally underserved or shut out of residential lending markets (Schwartz, 2006; Stone, 2006; Shlay, 2007). The economic and social disparity between homeowners (mostly white, middle-income suburbanites) and renters (mostly minority, low-income urban dwellers) convinced some policy makers that homeownership was key to antipoverty efforts, allowing low-income households to invest and build wealth while reaping the benefits of better communities and the pride of ownership (Apgar, 2004; Shlay, 2007). Housing policy thus followed this logic, introducing a series of programs and laws to promote low-income homeownership. Among these was the Community Reinvestment Act, passed in 1977 but not greatly enforced until deregulation prompted a rash of financial company mergers in the late 1980s, which required banks to lend in communities where they took deposits, including urban areas long ignored by the financial industry (Green and Malpezzi, 2003; Schwartz, 2006). Congress established affordable lending goals for Freddie Mac and Fannie Mae in 1992, who in turn placed pressure on the lenders they financed to increase low-income mortgages (Stone, 2006; Shlay, 2007). Some of the increased funding being channeled into home-purchase lending was applied to these policy requirements, though many moderate and higher-income homeowners benefited as well. Indeed, some policy analysts argue that the net effect of many of these policies was actually to make housing less affordable to low-income households (Glaeser and Gyourko, 2008). The result of the sum of these policy changes was increased demand for owner-occupied housing and mortgages that went along with an increased mortgage supply, starting in the 1990s.

The national homeownership rate did not rebound until the late 1980s, and it remained largely stagnant through the early 1990s as another recession prompted job losses and income declines (Hughes, 1996). It was not until the economic expansion of the late 1990s and early 2000s that the policy prescriptions of the 1980s began to bear fruit, with homeownership rate increases for minorities and low-income households outpacing those for whites and higher-income households (Belsky and Duda, 2002; Herbert and Belsky, 2008).

The increased demand for homeownership, however, also drove up prices beyond the reach of some low-income households, requiring three new kinds of policy interventions to meet affordable housing goals. These policy interventions put the emphasis on homeownership and showed a growing neglect of affordable rental options. The first policy option was a more accommodative monetary policy that lowered mortgage interest rates (Green and Malpezzi, 2003; Stone, 2006). The second policy included new housing programs that provided down-payment subsidies to qualified borrowers, at the expense of assistance programs for low-income renters (Schwartz, 2006; Herbert and Belsky, 2008). The third policy approach was further deregulation of the expanding residential lending market. Mortgage brokers, which are not subject to the same regulatory standards as deposit-taking banks, increased their lending to low-income households by developing innovative mortgage products that deferred some or all of the initial principal payments on a loan, offered a low introductory interest rate that would rise a few months or years into the loan, and/or required only a low down payment and no income verification to qualify for a mortgage (Calem et al., 2009). The secondary mortgage market adapted to these new loan products, creating securities reflecting the higher risk that such loans carried, but the loans were still implicitly guaranteed by Fannie Mae and Freddie Mac (Schwartz, 2006; Stone, 2006). Yet regulatory oversight of these loans and the securities derived from them was minimal, in spite of abuses and occasionally fraudulent uses of these loans to finance home purchases, and increasingly home refinances, by low-income households (Stone, 2006).

The consequence of the growing mortgage supply through less regulated institutions and secured through less regulated instruments ultimately exposed borrowers and the financial system to massive default risks, increasing the likelihood of a major financial crisis along with the probability of a severe recession. The wave of foreclosures that characterized the recession from 2007 to 2009 was the clearest manifestation of this default risk. The share of mortgages in foreclosure rose from a low of 1.0 percent in 2006, before the crisis went into full effect, to an unprecedented high of 4.6 percent in the first half of 2010 (Mortgage Bankers Association, 2010).

The crisis, though, did not materially alter the policy framework with respect to housing. Initial efforts by the Obama administration to stabilize housing markets concentrated on helping households avoid foreclosure and stay in homes, with limited success, or offering incentives for new households to buy through tax credits (Immergluck, 2009). Efforts to support renting, for which demand soared during the recession, meanwhile remained limited and slow in comparison (US Department of Housing and Urban Development, 2010). The prioritization of homeownership over renting in US housing policy has continued.

## The Pro-cyclicality of Housing Policies

Housing policies during an economic expansion in the United States generally addressed the symptoms of rising house prices and increased affordability challenges for homebuyers, rather than looking at the forces contributing to the pro-cyclicality of housing markets and the residential lending industry. Many of the federal policy efforts, housing and otherwise, that promoted homeownership over the last 65 years have in fact increased the incentives to homebuyers to purchase homes during times of economic growth and despite rising house prices.[9]

Not all housing will be subject to fluctuations with economic cycles (Arnott, 1987; Case and Shiller, 1988). On the demand side, households that do not move during booms and busts will likely see little impact on their housing behavior, provided that their incomes and other resources allow them to maintain a constant level of housing consumption (Ball, 1983). And housing investment decisions are based on more than just economic conditions and income because homeownership is often regarded as part of a natural life cycle of housing consumption that will occur regardless of external forces (Ortalo-Magne and Rady, 1998). On the supply side, mortgages are often fixed for long periods and the transaction costs of buying and selling a home are substantial, providing owners with incentives to stay, particularly during economic downturns (Arnott, 1987; Belsky and Duda, 2002). The timing of homeownership, however, is greatly influenced by both micro- and macroeconomic conditions (Case and Shiller, 1988). The pro-cyclicality of homeownership incentives is thus only relevant to a small subset of homebuyers during any given period of economic expansion, but the aggregate effects from the housing decisions of this fraction of households are still significant (Arnott, 1987; Case and Shiller, 1988).

The existing US tax policy to support homeownership serves to further bolster the incentives to buy in a growing economy. The main policy tool to promote homeownership is the tax benefit derived from the mortgage-interest deduction. These incentives dwarf federal expenditures on all other forms of housing assistance (Glaeser and Gyourko, 2008). Their pro-cyclicality arises because the value of the benefit is greater for households with higher incomes and for purchasers of more costly homes, both of which are more common in growing versus contracting economies (Arnott, 1987; Carliner, 1998; Glaeser and Gyourko, 2008; Green and Malpezzi, 2003). The tax benefit is also substantially greater for owners than for renters, such that higher-income homeowners may receive as much as three times the benefit that lower-income renter households receive (Glaeser and Gyourko, 2008), which again incentivizes homeownership during an economic expansion.

Another pro-cyclical housing policy channel exists through the political process. As an economic expansion continues to elevate house prices, policy makers will feel pressured to intervene, particularly in a policy environment that prioritizes homeownership, in order to offer additional assistance to homebuyers. Policy makers will try to help low- and moderate-income households afford homeownership through subsidy programs, affordability block grants to state and local governments, and the loosening of lending standards for federally insured mortgage programs (Ball, 1983; Green and Malpezzi, 2003). During a recession, policy makers will feel pressured to increase support for renting, accelerating the downturn in housing investment, as we discuss below.

An additional pro-cyclical, albeit asymmetric, incentive for housing investment decisions arises from limited support measures for homeowners to remain in their homes during an economic downturn. People who buy homes during economic booms, when house prices are rising, will face higher fixed housing costs for the duration of ownership (Apgar, 2004; Shlay, 2007). Many households will buy even when their personal and financial circumstances might prescribe otherwise, regardless of economic conditions because of the social and psychological ideal of homeownership (Pelletiere et al., 2005). Deteriorating economic conditions can quickly result in rising foreclosures for many homeowners, especially those who are already financially strapped and who have few assets outside of the home (Weller and Sabatini, 2008). Yet policy-based remedies to these consequences are scarce and generally not applicable to many failed homeowners (Immergluk, 2009). The result is larger foreclosures and downward pressures during an economic downturn than would otherwise be the case.

The pro-cyclical US incentives for homeownership are further augmented by countercyclical rental policies. Renters can adjust their housing consumption more easily than owners when employment and income fall, creating more turnover in the rental stock and more demand for affordable rental units during periods of economic decline (Apgar, 2004). Some homeowners will also transition to renting in a recession, either because they can no longer afford their owned homes or when making a move in search of better job prospects, adding to rental demand (Apgar, 2004; Pelletiere et al., 2005). Rents, which are less fixed in the long term than house prices, can rise when demand grows. Demand-side subsidies increase in down economies when incomes fall relative to housing costs (Green and Malpezzi, 2003). Rental demand thus declines in a boom and increases in a bust, reinforcing the cyclical demand for homeownership.

## International Comparisons

The United States is not the only developed country to show pro-cyclicality in its housing markets and its policies that influence housing decisions. Recent research by the International Monetary Fund (IMF) demonstrates a high degree of correlation between house prices and real business activity within 20 Western countries, though some variations do exist as to the timing and duration of these cycles (Igan et al., 2009). Countries such as Denmark, Finland, and Spain also saw significant house-price swings prior to the current financial crisis, while the relationships between housing prices and economic cycles in Germany and Austria were less clear. The authors of the IMF study attribute this variation to differences in domestic financial structures and mortgage-lending behaviors, specifically noting faster transmission of housing market changes to the broader economy in countries that experience higher rates of mortgage refinancing and equity cashouts, directly impacting household cash flows and consumption, confirming the findings of Leamer (2007). Regulations and financial-market mechanisms also influence the magnitude of correlations, particularly in countries with sophisticated mortgage securitization systems such as the United States.

The IMF (Igan et al., 2009) makes two additional points on the cyclicality of housing. First, housing and economic cycles not only are correlated within countries but also are increasingly influenced cross-nationally as financial markets have become more internationally integrated and economic shocks are felt globally. US cycles in particular lead those of other developed countries. Second, longer-term changes in housing markets are less impacted by economic factors and more influenced by other factors, including demographic, social, and policy trends that occur over years and decades. Nonetheless, the clear relationships between not just domestic housing and business cycles but also international effects of pro-cyclical policies only strengthen the need for revisiting existing housing-policy structures.

## IV. Considerations for Developing Policy Alternatives

It is worth considering alternative housing-policy regimes that could counteract this pro-cyclicality of homeownership. One starting point for an alternative policy approach is the realization that homeownership may not be appropriate for all people at all times. Encouraging people into homeownership prematurely increases the risks that they will fail at keeping their homes. Apgar (2004), for example, concludes that findings of the benefits of homeownership often rest on the fact that homeowners tend to live in one place longer than renters (i.e., the characteristics of homeowners may not systematically differ from those of renters who live in their units for extended periods). Policies that encourage homeownership alter the populations, though, of homeowners and renters. There will consequently be a number of homeowners who should be renters, given their characteristics, but who became homeowners as a result of a policy prioritization of homeownership. These homeowners may not have been well prepared for the challenges of homeownership and may face increased default risks when the economy turns sour.

Some advocates and scholars have begun calls for a set of housing policies that do not favor one form of tenure over the other but rather promote a range of housing options that allow households to find and afford the housing that is appropriate for their circumstances (Apgar, 2004; Pelletiere et al., 2005; Shlay, 2007). A balanced housing-policy regime will devote less attention to the means and more to the ends of housing-policy objectives, by offering households a range of options available to meet their diverse housing needs in the short term while helping them prepare for longer-term housing solutions, including possible homeownership (Apgar, 2004; Shlay, 2007). Balanced policies still recognize that homeownership is a worthy goal, but they place more emphasis on policy prescriptions that seek to sustain homeownership, through long-term commitments to low-income homeowners, more funding for housing counseling programs, and more options for households that do fall behind on mortgage payments (Calem et al., 2009). Finally, a balanced housing policy means more support for the private rental housing market, so it can provide attractive housing options with the same benefits of economic security and a social advantage on par with homeownership (Shlay, 2007; Glaeser and Gyourko, 2008). A more balanced housing-policy approach could thus result in less pro-cyclicality of housing investment because it deemphasizes homeownership and increases incentives for renting, compared to the current US housing-policy approach.

A more balanced approach would lead to a redesign of existing US incentives for homeownership and renting. For example, the mortgage-interest deduction may be replaced with a flat mortgage-interest tax credit (Green and Malpezzi, 2003), which would lower the incentive for homeownership when incomes and housing prices go up compared to the current US practice of tax deductibility. A cap on the amount of mortgage interest that can be deducted (Glaeser and Gyourko, 2008) may have a similar impact. Likewise, a balanced housing policy would offer fewer subsidies to potential homebuyers, at the expense of rental assistance programs, during economic booms. A third set of policy proposals would tighten oversight of crucial parts of the US mortgage market, particularly over mortgage brokers, who originated the vast majority of new mortgages during the boom that preceded the housing crush after 2007 (Glaser and Gyourko, 2008). Such policy changes can facilitate better labor mobility as economic conditions change and vary from market to market, evening out economic cycles somewhat (Glaser and Gyourko, 2008).

These policy suggestions, however, are based mostly on presumptions of how a balanced housing policy would work in the abstract. More research is needed to test the application of specific balanced policy elements—whether changes to the tax code, tighter regulations on nonbank mortgage brokers and secondary market securities dealers, or increased commitment to spending on affordable rental housing and other tenure forms—to assure policy makers of the new policies' advantages over the pro-homeownership regime that has been the norm for more than 60 years. Furthermore, in spite of the overwhelming evidence showing the negative consequences of overextending credit to borrowers unsuited for long-term homeownership, more attention must still be placed on addressing the social and political constructs around homeownership as the preferred tenure option for all households. Without more acceptance of the idea that homeownership does not in and of itself demonstrate successful achievement of the American Dream, and a belief that strong communities and beneficial socioeconomic outcomes are possible from a variety of tenures, a truly balanced housing policy will not be able to gain the political and popular traction necessary for its success.

## V. Conclusion

Housing investments play an integral role in the generation and promotion of business cycles and a financial crisis. The ability of housing investments to speed up recoveries and slow the economy into recession, in addition to creating financial instabilities, is much larger than average spending shares of housing investments out of GDP would suggest. This disproportionate contribution of housing to business cycle fluctuations can be explained in part by the basic economic feedback effects between housing investment, personal incomes, credit availability, and interest rates. Yet these pro-cyclicality effects can be exacerbated or muted by housing-policy decisions. Tax deductions, implicit mortgage subsidies, and limited public support for rental options all provide incentives for more homeownership during good times and less homeownership during economic downturns.

An alternative housing-policy approach that could lead to more economic and financial stability will have to include three separate components. First, policy makers will have to show a clear commitment to end the prioritization of one form of housing tenure over others. Second, research will have to demonstrate the effectiveness of alternative policies in lowering the pro-cyclicality of housing investments. Third, policy makers will have to show the willingness to implement alternative policies that could prove effective.

## Notes

1. Authors' calculations based on BEA (2010).
2. We calculated the average growth contribution of residential real estate during each of the past business cycles before 2008 and then we calculated an average from these averages. Calculations based on BEA (2010).
3. Calculations based on BLS (2010).
4. We calculate the average growth contribution of residential real estate during the first year of each of the past recoveries before 2008 and during the year just before a recession starts, and then we calculated the average from these averages. Calculations based on BEA (2010).
5. Homeownership rates leveled off in 2005 and 2006, but they started to decline in 2007 (US Census Bureau, 2010).
6. Calculations based on Federal Reserve Board (2010b).
7. Calculations based on Federal Reserve Board (2010a).
8. Tax policies also exempted the proceeds on the sale of an owned home from capital gain taxes when used toward the purchase of a new home, which encourages homeowners to remain homeowners (Carliner, 1998). It is unclear, however, how much impact these tax benefits directly have on homeownership, because high-income homeowners that gain the most from them would be likely to own in their absence, while lower-income homeowners derive little benefit from these deductions (Glaeser and Gyourko, 2008).
9. It should be noted that monetary policy also contributes to the pro-cyclicality of housing investment. Interest rates tend to be low at the start of a recovery and high just before a recession. Interest rates, though, tend to be a strong incentive for housing investment (Case and Shiller, 1988; Case, Quigley, and Shiller, 2003), thereby further augmenting other pro-cyclical housing investment incentives.

## References


Apgar, W. (2004). Rethinking rental housing: Expanding the ability of rental housing to serve as a pathway to economic and social opportunity. *Joint Center for Housing Studies Working Paper Series, W04-11*. Cambridge, MA: Harvard University, Joint Center for Housing Studies.

Arnott, R. (1987). "Economic Theory and Housing." In E. S. Mills, ed., *Handbook of Regional and Urban Economics*, vol. 2, 959–988. Amsterdam: Elsevier.

Ball, M. (1983). *Housing Policy and Economic Power: The Political Economy of Owner Occupation*. London: Methuen & Co. Ltd.

Barbosa-Filho, N. H., von Arnim, C. R., Taylor, L., and Zamparelli, L. (2008). "Cycles and Trends in US Net Borrowing Flows." *Journal of Post-Keynesian Economics* 30(4): 623–647.

Belsky, E. S., and Duda, M. (2002). "Anatomy of the Low-Income Homeownership Boom in the 1990s." In N. P. Retisnas and E. S. Belsky, eds., *Low-Income Homeownership: Examining the Unexamined Goal*, 15–63. Washington, DC: Brookings Institution Press.

Bureau of Economic Analysis. (2010). "National Income and Product Accounts." Washington, DC: BEA.

Bureau of Labor Statistics. (2010). "Current Population Statistics." Washington, DC: BLS.

Calem, P. S., Courchane, M. J., and Wachter, S. M. (2009). "Sustainable Homeownership." Paper presented at Housing After the Fall: Reassessing the Future of the American Dream, March 19, 2009, Washington, DC.

Carliner, M. (1998). "Development of Federal Homeownership 'Policy.'" *Housing Policy Debate* 9(2): 299–321.

Case, K. E., and Quigley, J. M. (2008). "How Housing Booms Unwind: Income Effects, Wealth Effects, and Feedbacks through Financial Markets." *European Journal of Housing Policy* 8(2): 161–180.

Case, K. E., Quigley, J., and Shiller, R. J. (2003). "Home-Buyers, Housing, and the Macroeconomy." In A. Richards and T. Robinson, eds., *Asset Prices and Monetary Policy*, 149–188. Sydney: Reserve Bank of Australia.

Case, K. E., and Shiller, R. J. (1988). "The Behavior of Home Buyers in Boom and Post-Boom Markets." *New England Economic Review* (Nov/Dec): 29–46.

Congressional Budget Office. (2007). "Housing Wealth and Consumer Spending." Washington, DC: Congressional Budget Office.

Coulson, E., and Kim, M. (2000). "Residential Investment, Nonresidential Investment, and GDP." *Real Estate Economics* 28: 233–248.

Dodd, R. (2006). "Hedge Funds Again: A Response to Deregulation, Financial Policy Forum Special Policy Brief No. 30." Washington, DC: Financial Policy Forum.

Dunsky, R., and Follain, J. (2000). "Tax-induced Portfolio Reshuffling: The Case of the Mortgage Interest Deduction." *Real Estate Economics* 28 (4): 683–718.

Federal Housing Finance Agency. (2010). "House Price Index." Washington, DC: FHFA.

Federal Reserve Board. (2010a). "Release Z.1 Flow of Funds Accounts of the United States." Washington, DC: Board of Governors, Federal Reserve System.

Federal Reserve Board. (2010b). "Senior Loan Officer Opinion Survey on Bank Lending Practices." Washington, DC: Board of Governors, Federal Reserve System.

Glaeser, E. L., and Gyourko, J. (2008). *Rethinking Federal Housing Policy: How to Make Housing Plentiful and Affordable*. Washington, DC: American Enterprise Institute.

Goodhart, C., Hofmann, B., and Segoviano, M. (2006). "Bank Regulation and Macroeconomic Fluctuations." *Seoul Journal of Economics* 19(1): 3–41.

Green, R. K. (1997). "Follow the Leader: How Changes in Residential and Non-Residential Investment Predict Changes in GDP." *Real Estate Economics* 25(2): 253–270.

Green, R. K., and Malpezzi, S. (2003). *A Primer on US Housing Markets and Housing Policy*. Washington, DC: Urban Institute Press.

Herbert, C. E., and Belsky, E. S. (2008). "The Homeownership Experience of Low-Income and Minority Households: A Review and Synthesis of the Literature." *Cityscape: A Journal of Policy Development and Research* 10(2): 5–60.

Hughes, J. W. (1996). "Economic Shifts and the Changing Homeownership Trajectory." *Housing Policy Debate* 7(2): 293–325.

Igan, D., Kabundi, A., Nadal De Simone, F., Pinheiro, M., and Tamirisa, N. (2009). "Three Cycles: Housing, Credit, and Real Activity." IMF Working Paper 09-231. Washington, DC: IMF.

Immergluck, D. (2009). "The Foreclosure Crisis, Foreclosed Properties, and Federal Policy." *Journal of the American Planning Association* 75(4): 406–423.

Jackson, K. T. (1985). *Crabgrass frontier: The suburbanization of the United States*. New York: Oxford University Press.

Kornfeld, W. (2007). Testimony before the Hearing on the "Role of Securitization in Subprime Mortgage Market Turmoil" by the Subcommittee on Securities, Insurance, and Investment, United States Senate, April 17.

Leamer, E. E. (2007). "Housing Is the Business Cycle." NBER Working Paper Series No. 13428. Cambridge, MA: National Bureau of Economic Research.

Mian, A. R., and Sufi, A. (2010). "Household Leverage and the Recession of 2007 to 2009." NBER Working Paper No. 15896. Cambridge, MA: National Bureau of Economic Research.

Miles, W. (2009). "Housing Investment and the US Economy: How Have the Relationships Changed?" *Journal of Real Estate Research* 31(3): 329–349.

Mortgage Bankers Association. (2010). "National Delinquency Survey." Washington, DC: Mortgage Bankers Association.

Ortalo-Magne, F., and Rady, S. (1998). "Housing Market Fluctuations in a Life-Cycle Economy with Credit Constraints." Stanford University GSB Research Paper 1501, Palo Alto, CA.

Pelletiere, D., Hockett, D., McElwee, P., Schwartz, D., and Treskon, M. (2005). *The Crisis in America's Housing: Confronting Myths and Promoting a Balanced Housing Policy*. Washington, DC: Center for Economic and Policy Research. http://www.cepr.net/documents/publications/housing_book_2005_01.pdf (accessed July 8, 2010).

Poterba, J. M. (2000). "Stock Market Wealth and Consumption." *Journal of Economic Perspectives* 14(2): 99–118.

Schwartz, A. F. (2006). *Housing Policy in the United States: An Introduction*. New York: Routledge.

Shiller, R. (2007). "Understanding Recent Trends in House Prices and Homeownership." Cowles Foundation Discussion Papers No. 1630. New Haven, CT: Cowles Foundation, Yale University.

Shlay, A. B. (2007). "Low-income Homeownership: American Dream or Delusion?" *Urban Studies* 43(3): 511–531.

Spong, K. (2000). "Banking Regulation: Its Purposes, Implementation, and Effects." Federal Reserve Bank of Kansas City.

Stango, V. (1999). "The Tax Reform Act of 1986 and the Composition of Consumer Debt." *National Tax Journal* 52: 717–739.

Stone, M. E. (2006). "The Pernicious Problems of Housing Finance." In R. G. Bratt, M. E. Stone, and C. A. Hartman, eds., *A Right to Housing: Foundation for a New Social Agenda*, 82–104. Philadelphia: Temple University Press.

US Census Bureau. (2009). "Income, Poverty, and Health Insurance Coverage in the United States: 2008." Washington, DC: US Census Bureau.

US Census Bureau. (2010). "Housing Vacancies and Homeownership, Historical Tables." Washington, DC: US Census Bureau. http://www.census.gov/hhes/www/housing/hvs/historic/index.html (accessed August 25, 2010).

US Department of Housing and Urban Development. (2010). "Transforming Rental Assistance (TRA): A Presentation on the Future of HUD's Rental Assistance Programs." Washington, DC: Department of Housing and Urban Development. http://portal.hud.gov/portal/page/portal/HUD/fy2011budget/signature_initiatives/transforming_rental_assistance/documents/TRAPowerpointFINAL5-23.pdf (accessed July 13, 2010).

Weller, C., and Sabatini, K. (2008). "From Boom to Bust: Did the Financial Fragility of Homeowners Increase in an Era of Greater Financial Deregulation?" *Journal of Economic Issues* 42(3): 607–632.

PART II

# THEORETICAL APPROACHES FOR UNDERSTANDING FINANCIAL CRISES

CHAPTER 7

# THE REALISM OF ASSUMPTIONS DOES MATTER

## WHY KEYNES-MINSKY THEORY MUST REPLACE EFFICIENT MARKET THEORY AS THE GUIDE TO FINANCIAL REGULATION POLICY

JAMES CROTTY

## 1. Introduction

In the aftermath of the financial collapse in the United States that began in 1929, it was almost universally believed that unregulated financial markets are inherently unstable, vulnerable to fraud and manipulation by insiders, and capable of triggering deep economic crises and political and social unrest. These economic and political events were compatible with the theories of endogenous financial instability created by John Maynard Keynes and augmented by Hyman Minsky. To protect the country from financial instability, the US government created a strict regulatory system that worked effectively through the 1960s. Economic and financial turbulence in the 1970s and early 1980s led to both a paradigm and a policy regime shift. The neoclassical theory of "efficient" or "perfect" financial markets and new classical macro theory (which assumes that markets always generate full employment) replaced the theoretical visions of Keynes and Minsky.[1] The government, influenced by the belief that efficient financial-market theory was sanctioned by economic "science," radically deregulated US financial markets after 1980.

Most financial economists argue that lightly regulated financial markets allow individual and institutional investors to achieve the maximum return for a given risk level and to choose the amount of risk that is optimal for them. Such markets also allocate scarce resources to their most productive uses, making the real sector of the economy itself more efficient. It would have been much harder to enact radical deregulation if the core of the economics profession had opposed efficient market theory and supported tight regulation, as they did in the 1950s and 1960s.[2] In the words of Nobel Laureate Joseph Stiglitz:

> The economics profession bears more than a little culpability [for the global financial and economic crisis]. It provided the models that gave comfort to regulators that markets could be self-regulated; that they were efficient and self-correcting. The efficient markets hypothesis—the notion that market prices fully revealed all the relevant information—ruled the day. Today, not only is our economy in a shambles but so too is the economic paradigm that predominated in the years before the crisis—or at least it should be.[3]

Francis Fukuyama, an advisor to Ronald Reagan and the second George Bush, commented on the symbiotic relation between large financial firms and financial economists that he believes contributed to the professions' support of the efficient financial-market hypothesis:

> Wall Street seduced the economics profession not through overt corruption, but by aligning the incentives of economists with its own. It was very easy for academic economists to move from universities to central banks to hedge funds—a tightly knit world in which everyone shared the same views about the self-regulating and beneficial effects of open capital markets. The alliance was enormously profitable for everyone: the academics got big consulting fees, and Wall Street got legitimacy. And it has kept the system going despite the enormous policy failures it has generated, not to exclude the recent crisis. (quoted in Skomarovsky, 2011)[4]

Efficient market theory was not universally supported by the profession's elite. There *were* respected financial economists whose criticism of mainstream theory appeared in first-rank economics journals. Some used assumptions of principal-agent conflict, asymmetric information, and incomplete contracts to undermine to some unspecified degree the conclusion of market efficiency. Others relied on behavioral financial theory to demonstrate that various forms of psychologically grounded investor "irrationality" can help explain disappointing empirical tests of market efficiency. But these theories are not intended to be substitutes for the vision incorporated in neoclassical financial theory. Rather, they are meant to be amendments to it that do not challenge its dominant position in the profession. "The behavioral finance literature... simply adopts the neoclassical view with biases added (e.g., overshooting, undershooting, framing, etc.)" (Findlay and Williams, 2008–2009, 224). Camerer and Lowenstein insist that behavioral finance does not seek "a wholesale rejection of the neoclassical approach to economics based on utility maximization, equilibrium *and efficiency*" (2004, 1, emphasis added). Matthew Rabin, a star in the behaviorist camp, argues that the behaviorists' research program is "not only built on the premise that mainstream economic *methods* are great, but also that most mainstream economic *assumptions* are great" (2002, 658, emphasis in original). However, neither politicians nor the general public were aware of these arcane theoretical disputes. Thus, their existence did not erode the widespread and correct belief that the profession strongly supported deregulation.

The theory of efficient and optimal financial markets appears to nonbelievers to be a rather absurd theory because it is based on a long list of grossly unrealistic assumptions that bear little relationship to the real-world financial system. Moreover, empirical tests of the theory are disappointing. This raises two interesting questions: How could a theory built on an assumption set that bears no resemblance to real-world markets and has very weak empirical support become so widely accepted by financial economists? And why do financial economists reject the much more realistic theories associated with Keynes and Minsky that can explain events such as the recent crisis?

An important part of the answer to such questions resides in the peculiar methodology used by most of the economics profession—the theory of positivism as explained and defended by Milton Friedman in his famous 1953 essay "The Methodology of Positive Economics."[5] This methodology is examined in section 2, where its claim that the realism of assumptions has no relevance in judging the validity of a theory is assessed and is found wanting. Section 3 critically evaluates empirical tests used to defend the theory of optimal financial markets. Section 4 compares the canonical neoclassical capital asset-pricing model with the theory of financial markets associated with Keynes and Minsky (KM), and it argues that KM theory is a superior theory and therefore a much better guide to regulation policy precisely because it is based on realistic assumptions. Section 5 presents three examples of how the unrealistic assumptions of mainstream theory misled regulators and investors in the recent crisis. The last section offers concluding observations.

## 2. Friedman's Positivism and the Dominance of the Theory of Optimal Financial Markets

The theory of ideal financial markets has two component parts. The first is the assumption that financial markets have perfect *informational* efficiency: this is the "efficient market" hypothesis (EMH). The second is the assumption that market prices are optimal equilibrium prices set by rational utility-maximizing agents who have perfect information about the cash flows associated with all securities.

The EMH asserts that all information relevant to the correct pricing of securities is utilized in the pricing process. As Eugene Fama, one of the creators of the EMH, put it: "I take the market efficiency hypothesis to be the simple statement that security prices fully reflect all available information" (1991, 1575). Fama observed that "models of market equilibrium start with the *presumption* that markets are efficient" (Federal Reserve Bank of Minneapolis, 2007, emphasis added). Thus, efficiency is neither a derived nor an observable nor a directly testable property of financial markets. It is an assumption required to construct optimal asset-pricing models that conclude that risk and return are appropriately priced by financial markets.

The EMH raises two important questions: What is the "relevant" information set that is available to investors? What does it mean to say that this information is "fully reflected" in security prices? With respect to the first question, neoclassical financial markets theory assumes that the information set available to investors consists of the correct expectation of the distribution of future cash flows associated with each security. In other words, the theory is built on the assumption that investors, through some miraculous but unspecified process, gain perfect knowledge of the future.[6] Through a peculiar twist in language, these expectations are called "rational" expectations, even though it would seem to be the height of irrationality to assume that that anyone can know the future. However, as discussed below, the assumption that all relevant information is used to price securities is not uniquely associated with neoclassical theory. In a Keynesian world in which no one can know the future, sensible agents would also use all information they deemed relevant to form their expectations, though they would have no reason to believe that their expectations were assuredly correct.

An answer to the second question requires the specification of a pricing model or theory that can be used to convert cash-flow expectations into security prices. Mainstream financial-market theory posits that all agents use "rational" expectations as input into one of the canonical models of optimal security pricing, such as the capital asset-pricing model (CAPM) or the options-pricing model. The models use rational expectations to generate prices that are optimal in that they accurately reflect the risk and return associated with all securities. The perfect financial markets paradigm that has sustained the deregulation movement thus consists of the joint hypothesis that the EMH and a canonical theory of optimal pricing together explain how markets generate security prices.

There are two serious problems with the mainstream theory of optimal financial security pricing. The first is methodological and deals with the relation between assumptions and conclusions or derived hypotheses. The second relates to the empirical evidence used to support the theory.

Few economists think about methodology, but the methodological foundation of neoclassical economics is Milton Friedman's (1953) version of "positivism." Positivism asserts two important theses. First, in evaluating the validity or usefulness of a theory, neither the extent to which the assumption set of a theory incorporates all the core elements of the phenomenon under investigation, nor the institutional or behavioral or empirical *realism* of the assumptions adopted matter. The "relation between the significance of a theory and the 'realism' of its 'assumptions' is almost the opposite of that suggested by [critics of positivism]. Truly important and significant hypotheses will be found to have 'assumptions' that are wildly inaccurate descriptive representations of 'reality'" (Friedman, 1953, 14). Second, it is impossible to determine whether one assumption is more realistic than another. A theory "cannot be tested by comparing its 'assumptions' directly with 'reality.' Indeed, there is no meaningful way in which this can be done" (41). The only legitimate test of a theory, then, is whether its derived hypotheses can be used to make predictions that are consistent with relevant data: "The only relevant test of the validity of a hypothesis is comparison of its predictions with experience" (Friedman, 1953, 9). Because prediction testing of necessity involves ceteris paribus assumptions, in practice the profession relies on econometric hypothesis testing with past data.

Why would an academic profession sanction the use of theories based on crassly unrealistic assumptions? It is not an intuitively attractive idea. One suspects that the underlying reason is that economists are, in the main, committed to the defense of propositions that cannot be generated by models based on realistic assumptions. For example, a long string of unrealistic assumptions is necessary to generate the desired conclusion that unregulated financial markets perform optimally. Consider the comment by William Sharpe in a seminal article on the CAPM that helped win him the Nobel Prize:

> Needless to say, [the assumptions of the model] are highly restrictive and undoubtedly unrealistic assumptions. However, since the proper test of a theory is not the realism of its assumptions, but *the acceptability of its implications*, and since these assumptions imply equilibrium conditions which form a major part of classical financial doctrine, it is far from clear that this formulation should be rejected. (1964, 434, emphasis added)

Of course, classical financial doctrine insists that competitive financial markets are efficient.

In 1970 Sharpe acknowledged that if just one of the many unrealistic assumptions used to create the CAPM—that agents could borrow without limit at the risk-free interest rate—is rejected, "the theory is in shambles." He argued that the inclusion of "such aspects of reality are likely to be disastrous in terms of the usefulness of the resulting theory" (quoted in Smith, 2010, 82–83). The method used here clearly is to adopt whatever assumptions set is required to generate the desired efficient-market conclusion.

Milton Friedman was not only an economist; he was also an energetic conservative political activist. His positivist methodology made it possible for conservative economists to use an absurd set of assumptions that no one would accept as a reasonable description of real-world capitalism to generate widespread acceptance of the proposition that unregulated capitalism is an ideal economic system. Realistic assumptions lead to theories that show both the strengths but also the myriad dangers and failures of unregulated capitalism contained in the historical record. But positivism made possible a "scientific" defense of the proposition that capitalism has no dangers and failures. In other words, Friedman's positivism insulates flawed theories of capitalism that cannot explain or predict the actual behavior of capitalism from effective criticism.

There are numerous problems with Friedman's methodology, which has little support outside the economics profession.[7] We mention two. First, if very unrealistic or patently false assumptions are adopted, as they often are, and impeccable logic is applied to deduce hypotheses from them, these hypotheses cannot—*as a matter of logic*—be an accurate reflection of reality. It was quite an accomplishment for positivism to triumph in spite of its denial of this proposition.

Second, by insisting that the only way to evaluate the extent to which a theory corresponds with reality is through econometric tests of its derived hypotheses, positivism places a stronger burden on the use of econometrics than it can possibly bear. Consider just two problems. The first is that, in the age of high-powered computers, one can literally run millions of econometrics tests on a hypothesis until some of these tests deliver an acceptable result. Statistical tests of significance used to assess the realism of derived hypotheses have little meaning in this environment and opportunities for "data mining" are unlimited. Virtually any hypothesis will be found to be statistically significant if enough regressions are run to test it.

Another problem is that all hypothesis tests combine theoretical propositions with empirical proxies for unobservable variables. Neoclassical theory per se has no testable propositions. It essentially argues that, in whatever context, agents will optimize. The properties of all general functions—production functions, utility functions, and so forth—must be specified in order to generate testable propositions. These properties are not an inherent part of the theory. Take the case of hypotheses in which unobservable expectations are important. A proxy for expectations must be selected before appropriate econometric tests can be conducted. The econometrics test is thus a joint hypothesis combining elements of theory with ad hoc assumptions about expectation formation not specified in or related to the theory. If the joint hypothesis is rejected, this does not mean the theory is "wrong"—and conversely. It could be that the theory is "right," but the ad hoc assumptions are not—and conversely. In the philosophy of science this is referred to as the Duhem–Quine thesis, which says that it is impossible to adequately test a theoretical proposition in isolation from assumptions not specified within the theory.

Because of these and other problems, it is extremely difficult to demonstrate solely on the basis of econometric tests that one theory is consistent with reality while another is not. This is a fatal flaw in Friedman's methodology because it rejects all tests of validity other than "prediction." It also helps explain why conflicting theories can coexist. It is therefore of the utmost importance that economists use all relevant information in theory testing, including not only econometrics but especially the degree of realism and completeness of the theory's assumption set and the ability of the theory to explain historical dynamic processes—such as the recent global crisis—endogenously.

The proposition that crudely unrealistic assumptions are not inferior to realistic assumptions in theory construction must be distinguished from the more reasonable proposition that some degree of abstraction—or approximation of reality—is necessary in theory building. The methodological debate, therefore, is not about whether some degree of abstraction is necessary, but rather whether or not we should favor theories whose assumptions are not excessively and unnecessarily at odds with the reality we wish to theorize.

Positivists claim that it is not possible to distinguish realistic from unrealistic assumptions, but this is not persuasive. Consider the assumption of "rational" expectations—the belief by rational agents that they have true knowledge of the future. This is clearly absurd.[8] No sane economist believes anyone can know with certainty the "true" stochastic distribution of future cash flows. Yet the "rationality" of expectations is widely accepted because positivism sanctions the use of unrealistic assumptions. Economists *can* assess the realism of the assumption set through institutional and historical studies, survey research, experiments, insights from psychology and sociology, and basic fact checking. This idea is hardly new or original. Robert Solow stated that "we have no choice but to take seriously our own direct observations of the way economic institutions work" (1988, 311). Tony Lawson argued for devoting "more resources into learning about the institutional behaviours, norms, conventions—or, more generally, rule systems—that are produced and reproduced by people in the various spheres of activity" (1985, 925). Robert Shiller suggested that "we must base further modeling efforts on observation and human behavior and on the popular models that inform that behavior" (1992, 435). Keynes insisted that "our conclusions must be based upon the actual observation of markets and business psychology" (1973, 149).

There is a superior method available to analyze the nature of financial markets and other important theoretical issues. Rather than searching for an assumption set that can demonstrate that financial markets are efficient, economists should construct a set of realistic assumptions about financial markets and then ask what hypotheses about the behavior of financial markets can be derived from these assumptions. This theory could then be evaluated by using all feasible methods, from historical studies to econometrics. This is the method associated with work by Keynes and Minsky.

When it comes to methodology, Keynes is the anti-Friedman. Keynes argued that useful theories can only be generated by realistic assumptions. Indeed, his most important methodological criticism of orthodox macro theory was that it is based on unrealistic assumptions and therefore *must* come to unrealistic conclusions. In the concluding chapter of *The General Theory*, he wrote

> our criticism of the accepted classical theory of economics has consisted not so much in finding logical flaws in its analysis as in pointing out that *its tacit assumptions are seldom or never satisfied, with the result that it cannot solve the economic problems of the actual world.* (1973, 378, emphasis added)

In the preface to *The General Theory*, Keynes said that the objective of the book is to persuade economists to "to re-examine critically certain of their basic assumptions" (1973, xxi). The conclusions of classical theory are wrong, he said, because "the postulates of the classical theory are applicable to a special case only" and "the characteristics of the special case assumed by classical theory happen not to be those of the economic society in which we actually live" (1973, 3). His clear message is that the realism of assumptions does matter: conclusions generated from unrealistic assumptions cannot possibly be correct.

Perhaps the clearest example of this message is his powerful attack, in *The General Theory* and in his 1937 defense of that book in the *Quarterly Journal of Economics*, on the mainstream assumption that agents know the correct probability distribution of future states of the economy. This assumption is a necessary condition for the construction of theories of perfect markets. He argued to the contrary that the future is unknowable or uncertain: "there is no scientific basis on which to form any calculable probability whatever.... We simply do not know" (1937, 214). The replacement of the assumption of "risk" with the assumption of "uncertainty" revolutionized our understanding of the nature of financial markets.

## 3. Testing the Theory of Optimal Unregulated Financial Markets: Friedman's Positivism in Action

There is a large and conflicted literature on econometrics tests of the EMH itself. The main problem here is that tests require both the assumption of EMH and the specification of a model of equilibrium asset pricing. This makes it impossible to test the EMH by itself. It "is not empirically testable unless some equilibrium model of security returns is specified" (Beaver, 1981, 28). As Fama put it:

> We can only test whether information is properly reflected in prices in the context of a pricing model that defines the meaning of "properly." As a result, when we find anomalous evidence on the behavior of returns, the way it should be split between market inefficiency or a bad model of market equilibrium is

> ambiguous.... It is a disappointing fact that, because of the joint-hypothesis problem, *precise inferences about the market efficiency are likely to remain impossible*. (1991, 1576, emphasis added)

The CAPM is a canonical neoclassical theory in which agents trading in perfectly competitive markets use the complete and correct information contained in rational expectations of future cash flows to determine equilibrium security prices. It assumes the EMH is correct. The assumptions that are used lead inevitably to the conclusion that security prices are optimal because they were chosen to do just that. The CAPM demonstrates that all investors will hold the same portfolio of securities—the "market portfolio"—that includes all risky securities available plus a risk-free security. It is optimal because asset diversification takes advantage of imperfect covariance among security cash flows to minimize risk at a given return. Less risk-averse investors hold proportionately less of the risk-free security and borrow to increase their holdings of the market portfolio, raising expected return while increasing portfolio risk.

It is important to understand that the CAPM is a theory of optimal *relative* price determination. It has nothing to say about the behavior of security price *levels*, which are the focus of concern in theories of financial-market instability and in regulation debates. The key question for those trying to understand the behavior of financial markets is not whether GM's stock price is correctly in line with GE's but why security prices move in boom-bust patterns. Larry Summers famously ridiculed the much-ballyhooed main finding of the CAPM: "They have shown that two-quart bottles of ketchup [risk-adjusted return] invariably sell for twice as much as one-quart bottles of ketchup" (Summers, 1985, 634).

It is not difficult to test the derived hypotheses of the CAPM because it has a specific assumption about the way in which risk affects the relative prices of securities, and a clear definition of risk—the covariance of a security with the market portfolio.[9] However, empirical tests of the CAPM have, for the most part, been disappointing to supporters of neoclassical theory. Econometrics tests thus raise serious questions about whether financial markets get even relative security prices "right." In a widely discussed survey of empirical tests of hypotheses derived from the CAPM, Fama and French (2004) come to a stunning conclusion: "Despite its seductive simplicity, the CAPM's empirical problems probably invalidate its use in applications" (44). The tenets of positivism suggest that economists should not accept the CAPM because its derived hypotheses do not have convincing econometric confirmation.

However, rather than accept this conclusion, neoclassical financial economists instead argued that the CAPM must have failed econometric tests because it defined risk too narrowly. This led to a wealth of econometric studies of "arbitrage pricing models" that add numerous and sundry additional variables to the risk measure of the CAPM. Because, in contrast to the CAPM, arbitrage pricing theory does not define what these other risk factors should be, the entire effort appears to be data mining—searching for any plausible variables that might lead to acceptable econometric results. There is, in principle, no limit to the extent of this search.

There are other widely discussed tests of the theory of optimal financial markets. "Event studies" are designed to show that when new information about a company's profit prospects appears in the press, its stock price quickly moves in the appropriate direction. These tests are much less impressive than proponents suggest.[10] First, there is selection bias in deciding what kinds of new information to use in the tests. Events whose effect on stock prices is inconsistent with the desired conclusion may be excluded from testing. Second, event studies do not test for the *size* of price movements, only their direction. They therefore cannot be used as evidence that stock prices are in equilibrium as required by canonical neoclassical models. Third, virtually any theory of financial markets would pass these event tests. For example, KM theory also predicts that new information showing that profits were higher than expected would cause stock prices to rise. Event tests may provide evidence that market prices react quickly to news, but they are not evidence that the neoclassical theory of security pricing is correct. This is a general weakness of all econometric tests of canonical models such as the CAPM. *They never test whether these theories are superior or inferior to alternative theories.* In a review of the methodology of modern financial-market theory, Findley and Williams argued that "in an empirical-positivist sense, at best [the neoclassical financial-market theory's] implications could not be rejected by the available evidence—a test which many opposing models could also pass" (1985, 1).

Another important test is whether or not professional investors generally outperform financial markets, which is presumed to be equivalent to asking whether they outperform individual investors. Canonical models assume that everyone has the same information and uses the same model to translate that information into security prices. Most empirical studies do find that professionals cannot generate greater returns (at the same risk) than amateurs, which is taken as confirmation that these assumptions are correct. Important financial economists seem to rely on this test more than anything else in their defense of market efficiency. Burton Malkiel stated: "For me, the strongest evidence suggesting that markets are generally quite efficient is that professionals do not beat the market" (2005, 2).[11]

However, even if the pros don't beat the market, it would not necessarily mean that everyone had access to the same information at the same time and used it in the same model. In the current era, professional investors *are* the market, at least to a first approximation. They hold most of the securities and do almost all the trading. So it would be hard for them to outperform themselves.[12] Moreover, tens of millions of individuals pay professional investors large sums of money to manage their portfolios. If professionals cannot manage portfolios better than these individuals do, then this army of individual investors must be irrational. But irrational agents are prohibited by assumption in canonical neoclassical financial theory; it is a rational-agent-based theory. So the finding that pros don't beat the market implies that a fundamental assumption of neoclassical financial theory is incorrect.

All these tests reflect the assumption that markets are always in equilibrium. The canonical models contain a "no arbitrage" assumption; you can't find arbitrage opportunities in equilibrium pricing models. But the narrative in which the model is embedded contains an explanation of *why* prices remain in equilibrium. If there are excess profits to be made without increasing risk because markets are not in equilibrium, professional arbitrageurs will take advantage of this opportunity, thereby quickly eliminating out-of-equilibrium profit. For example, hedge funds are supposed to excel at relative-price arbitrage. So the justification of the "no arbitrage" assumption of the CAPM is a posited belief in quick and efficient arbitrage when prices are out of equilibrium. This raises the question of why out-of-equilibrium dynamics are not incorporated in the CAPM. The answer is that modeling disequilibrium processes can destroy the desired conclusion that security prices are always optimal, as can be seen in debates over "noise trading" and "rational bubbles." Ironically, the ubiquitous arbitrage story also implies that many professionals do outperform the market.[13]

Given that mainstream methodology rejects the use of the realism of assumptions as an acceptable criterion for testing the validity of a theory, *econometric tests must carry the entire burden of defense of optimal financial-market theory.* Because the assumptions used to construct the theory and derive its hypotheses are strikingly unrealistic, one would assume that empirical tests would have to pass with flying colors in order to sustain support for the theory and its general vision of financial markets. Yet, as in the case of the CAPM, mediocre to disappointing empirical tests have not led to rejection of its underlying theoretical vision—which is essential to the defense of radical deregulation—as it should have under the positivist method, but rather to ever-changing models of market efficiency. It would seem that the vision captured by the CAPM is deeply anchored in an ideological commitment to free markets rather than in disinterested scientific study, and that the profession's commitment to positivism in practice is only skin deep.

Finally, it is interesting to understand what some important professional defenders of financial-market efficiency and optimality think about the relation between their theory and the nature of real-world security price *levels.* Burton Malkiel said the following:

> What I do not argue is that market pricing is always perfect. After the fact, we know that markets have made *egregious mistakes*, as I think occurred during the recent internet "bubble." Nor do I deny that psychological factors influence security prices. But I am convinced that Benjamin Graham was correct in suggesting that while the stock market in the short run may be a voting machine, *in the long run* it is a weighing mechanism. True value will win in the end. (2003, 5–6, emphasis added)

This is an astounding statement. In Malkiel's opinion, markets generate "egregious" pricing errors much of the time, and psychological factors strongly influence stock prices, something ruled out by assumption in mainstream models. If markets badly misprice securities much of the time, real-sector resources are badly allocated much of the time. How inefficient! Nevertheless, he tells us we should be comforted by the belief that, in the long run, security prices will be forced into proper balance with the ability of firms to generate profits. In this context, the term "long-run" can only mean at brief periods between booms and busts. Ironically, this belief is also embedded in the financial-market theories of Keynes, Minsky, and Marx. These theorists argue that security prices are inherently prone to substantial cyclical and secular volatility. Self-reinforcing bubbles inevitably occur from time to time; it is crises and panics that bring security prices back into temporary equilibrium with cash flows. Busts are the markets' "long-run" equilibrator. Of course, this balance is soon broken by the next bubble or crash. This is a vision in fundamental conflict with efficient market theory, which implies that security prices are always in harmony with cash flows, yet Malkiel seems to agree with its conclusion.

Fischer Black, who helped create the options pricing model, made the following observation about absolute pricing efficiency in real-world financial markets.

> We might define an efficient market as one in which price is within a factor of 2 of value, that is, the price is more than half of the value and less than twice the value. By this definition, I think almost all markets efficient almost all the time. 'Almost all' means at least 90 percent. (quoted in Mehrling, 2005, 236)

It is curious, to say the least, that such prominent supporters of the neoclassical theory of optimal financial markets believe that real-world security price levels are likely to be much higher or much lower than their "correct" values much of the time and that booms and busts are common. Given this belief, they should have been opponents of radical deregulation.

## 4. The Realism of Assumptions Does Matter: Why the Keynes-Minsky Theory of Financial Markets Is Superior to Mainstream Theories of Perfect Markets

Consider the following assumptions used to construct the CAPM. Note that assumptions 2 and 3 reflect the fact that this is a model of static equilibrium with no dynamic processes and, therefore, no endogenous source of movement.

1. Agents are risk-averse.
2. The degree of risk-aversion embodied in the utility function is exogenous to the model; agents do not become less risk-averse in the boom

and more risk-averse in a panic because the theory only considers equilibria.

3. Expectations are exogenous. Agents do not become more optimistic in a boom and more pessimistic in a collapse.
4. Expectations are homogeneous—there is no disagreement about future cash flows among agents.
5. Because this is an equilibrium model with identical information sets, there is no trading in the model.
6. Expectations are correct or "rational"—the statistical distributions of future cash flows are known with certainty.[14]
7. The expected cash flows from the real sector are exogenous: nothing that happens within financial markets affects real-sector cash flows in the model.[15]
8. Future cash-flow expectations are embodied in normal or Gaussian statistical distributions.
9. Because prices are always in equilibrium, liquidity is perfect; securities can always be sold (without cost) at their equilibrium value.
10. There is a risk-free security—like a Treasury Bill.
11. Agents can borrow or lend without limit at the risk-free rate of interest.
12. No one can default.
13. There are no financial institutions in the model, only agents holding nonintermediated portfolios.

With the possible exception of the assumptions that investors are risk-averse and that the shortest-term Treasury Bills are relatively riskless, *this assumption set is a severe distortion of, rather than an approximation to, reality.* These assumptions were chosen because they are necessary and sufficient conditions for the conclusion that unregulated financial markets are optimal. A profession working with a reasonable methodology and a different ideology would have concluded that since the hypothesis that markets are optimal cannot be generated except by an absurdly unrealistic assumption set, the hypothesis is quite likely to be wrong.

Consider the following assumptions typically used in KM financial theory. Though they are abstractions from reality, they are reasonable approximations to it. This theory emphasizes endogenous dynamic processes. Assumption 1, the assertion that the future is inherently unknowable or uncertain, is a cornerstone of Keynes's macro theory as well as of his theory of financial markets. This assumption set generates a realistic theory of financial-market dynamics as described in the rest of this section.

1. The future is inherently unknowable. The world is characterized by uncertainty rather than calculable risk.
2. Expectations are endogenous and pro-cyclical. They become more optimistic in booms, more pessimistic in downturns, and wildly unstable in panics.

3. The degree of agent risk-aversion is endogenous. Agents become less risk-averse in a bubble and more risk-averse in a downturn.
4. Agents are heterogeneous: they have different objectives, different degrees of risk-aversion, and different expectations. Agent heterogeneity is the main reason why there is massive daily and hourly trading on security markets.[16]
5. Financial-market decisions affect real-sector outcomes and conversely in an interactive, dynamic, and path-dependent process. Future cash flows are changed by agents' current financial decisions.
6. There is no stable financial-market equilibrium, though there are periods of relative stasis. Financial-market centers of gravity are always being altered by endogenous change in expectations and risk-aversion, as well as by the creation and spread of real and financial innovations.
7. The degree of liquidity changes over time. There is excessive liquidity in the boom that pushes security prices to unsustainable levels, but liquidity evaporates in a crisis, making the crisis worse.
8. Agents cannot borrow without limit at a risk-free interest rate. Credit is cheap and widely available in a bubble, which accelerates the speed of security price appreciation. However, when the bubble ends, credit evaporates and interest rates spike.
9. Defaults (and therefore counter party risks) exist and are important. Defaults are highly countercyclical. The fear of default is a major source of downward price pressure in a collapse.
10. Financial institutions strongly affect the performance of financial markets. They are complex agents whose incentives, information sets, objectives, and constraints differ from individual agents.[17]

The economic outcomes we observe over time are generated by a system of ever-changing agents, agent preferences, expectations, risk-aversion, innovations, and economic, political, and social institutions. Thus, the mechanisms that generate future outcomes cannot possibly be known in the present. Consider financial innovation. It has qualitatively changed the nature of financial markets in recent decades, but future innovations by their very nature cannot be known today. Indeed, some future changes are not only unknowable but unimaginable. Thus, real-world agents must make decisions today, such as the capital investment decision and the portfolio composition decision, whose outcomes depend on future states of the economy that they cannot possibly know. The best that agents can do is base their decisions on fallible expectations of some kind. These fallible expectations guide agent choices today and thereby influence the future trajectory of the economy. "What is imagined for a coming period must, in an ultimate sense, help to shape what will, ex *post*, emerge as the ultimate facts of that period" (Shackle, 1972, 440).

The assumption of uncertainty raises the interesting question of what it means for agents to be "rational." In neoclassical theory, agents are provided with complete and correct information about the future, which they can use to make assuredly optimal decisions. This is the definition of rationality in neoclassical theory—given complete and correct information, agents do the optimization math correctly. But what if agents at best have information about the future they know to be incorrect and incomplete? (Strictly speaking, there can be no "knowledge" of the future.) How can they make "rational decisions"? Neoclassical theory has nothing to say about this question because it has assumed it out of existence. *However, the main challenge facing economists is not to understand why fully informed agents act irrationally (though they may do so), but rather to understand how sensible agents make decisions under conditions of fundamental uncertainty.* Crotty (1994) provides a detailed Keynesian answer to the question of "sensible" agent choice in uncertain conditions.

Because agents are aware that they do not know the future, they can never have complete *confidence* that their expectations will be correct. This means that their decisions will be affected both by their forecasts and by the degree of confidence they have in the usefulness or validity or reliability or truth content of these forecasts—"on how highly we rate the likelihood of our best forecast turning out quite wrong" (Keynes, 1973, 148). "Confidence" is a psychological and potentially unstable variable.

In KM theory both expectation and confidence formation are endogenous, changing with economic conditions. Agents have no choice but to use heuristics or conventions to forecast the future path of security prices and estimate their potential volatility or riskiness. Security price expectations are formed through extrapolation from the relevant past—unless there are strong reasons not to do so. Amromin and Sharpe analyze data on consumer financial-market expectations to demonstrate that the description of the Keynesian process of conventional expectation and confidence formation is the way investors in fact behave. "In forming expectations of future returns, household investors appear to extrapolate from recent-years' realized returns.... [E]xpected returns appear to be procyclical" (2009, 28).

The longer conventionally determined expectations lead to decisions that generate satisfactory outcomes, as they do in booms, the greater the confidence that agents place in them. When a financial boom lasts for some time, agents begin to project its continuance. Given optimistic expectations of future prices, buying securities previously seen as risky will seem like a reasonable decision. As the boom proceeds and optimistic expectations are shown to be justified, buying securities with borrowed money will also seem reasonable. This drives the financial boom forward, raising leverage while raining capital gains on investors. The heaviest rain falls on the most aggressive investors, which leads most agents to believe either that risk is objectively low or that risk taking brings much higher rewards than it used to. Risk assessment and risk preference are thus endogenous. When risky behavior is being highly rewarded, fear of risk declines and conversely.

Because agents are heterogeneous, trading is active. In the early stages of a boom, expectations may differ widely among agents. Bulls will buy securities from bears. But as optimism and confidence spread in the boom, bears turn bullish, and the optimistic begin to sell to the super-optimistic or least risk-averse.

Liquidity rises endogenously in a boom; eventually almost anyone can sell securities for more than they paid for them. Leverage rises as well because both borrowers and lenders come to believe that leverage is not as risky as it used to be. In recent cycles, the perverse compensation system used by key financial institutions rationally induced agents to use excessive leverage to boost their bonuses. Interest rates remain low through much of the boom, and credit is available even to individuals and institutions previously considered to be bad credit risks.

There is a crucial feedback loop joining the real and financial sectors missing in efficient financial-market theories. Rising security prices in the boom increase the value of individual and institutional agents' assets and net worth. This increases the amount of debt they believe they can "safely" hold and also increases financial institutions willingness to lend as conventional definitions of adequate safety margins become less stringent. The rising use of credit to buy securities leads to yet higher prices, which in turn lead to more optimistic expectations held with increasing confidence and to higher wealth that can be used as collateral in leveraged security purchases. Meanwhile, rising consumer and business wealth and easy and cheap credit lead to increased consumption and investment spending. This raises aggregate demand, income, employment, and profit, which all lead to higher actual and expected future cash flows that raise security prices.

Because every long-term financial boom is accompanied by the widespread belief that we have entered a "new era" in which the forces that ended all previous booms are no longer operative, the current boom eventually comes to be seen as permanent. A near-universal belief develops that high yields previously achievable only by accepting high risk can now be gained safely.[18]

As Keynes and Minsky stress, market ebullience cannot go on forever. As a boom matures, the economy becomes, in Minsky's famous phrase, "financially fragile." At some point, the economy becomes unable to generate the cash flows needed to sustain euphoria-inflated financial asset prices. Profits eventually decline and household income growth slows, leading to falling investment and sluggish consumption. As aggregate demand growth slows and unemployment rises, agents discover that their expectations were too optimistic and that security prices are too high relative to expected future cash flows. Expectations will be revised downward, confidence in the accuracy of forecasts will ebb, and security prices will begin to fall. Falling asset prices will cause a reverse wealth effect on consumption spending. In a typical downturn, falling home prices play an important role in the decline of household wealth. In the recent crisis, they were the central force in the process.

As financial institutions retrench in the face of rising risk, interest rates rise and defaults—assumed out of existence in the CAPM—jump. Fear of higher default rates will cause interest rates to rise further, and credit for riskier agents will be eliminated. Risk-aversion will increase. The rising leverage that drove the boom will then be reversed. As the price of at-risk securities falls, collateral calls from lenders will be issued to all who bought now-shaky securities on credit. This will lead to the "forced sale" of these securities, which will accelerate their rate of price decline. As the market for suspect securities collapses, borrowers will be forced to sell "sound" securities, which will spread the crisis across markets. The CAPM assumes that liquidity is perfect and costless, but in a financial downturn few agents want to buy suspect financial assets, so they can only be sold at fire-sale prices as liquidity evaporates. Watching their own asset values and their capital shrink, financial institutions will be less willing to loan to corporations, to households, or to each other. In the mid-2000s, intra-financial-market debt was bloated and bank balance sheets and off-balance-sheet entities were loaded with excessively risky and nontransparent mortgage-related loans. This caused frightened banks to stop lending to each other when the boom ended, which helped turn the financial downturn into a panic.

Both the causes of the recent financial boom and the destructive downward dynamics of the subsequent collapse can be explained by KM theory because its assumption set adequately reflects the forces that drive financial markets. On the other hand, the assumption set used to construct canonical neoclassical financial and macro models makes such endogenous instability impossible. If the economics profession had rejected Friedman's positivism and built its core financial models on the realistic assumptions used in KM theory, it would have been much harder for supporters of radical deregulation to have achieved their objective.

## 5. Three Examples of How the Assumption Set Used in the Neoclassical Model Profoundly Misrepresented the Dangers in Financial Markets to Regulators and Market Participants[19]

### a. The Assumption That the Future Is Characterized by Knowable "Risk" Rather Than Keynesian "Uncertainty" Allowed Banks to Become Dangerously Risky with Their Regulators' Blessing

Mainstream financial theory assumes that financial products and institutions are perfectly transparent. This is a precondition for efficient pricing. In fact, deregulation and financial innovation made the portfolios of the giant bank conglomerates that are at the center of the global financial system so complex that it became impossible for *anyone* to make a reliable estimate of their risk. In 1998 the Bank for International Settlements sanctioned the idea that regulators, who were now incapable of assessing the riskiness of large banks, should shift responsibility for setting limits on the giant banks' risk to the banks themselves, who might be better informed. Banks were allowed to manage their own risk through a statistical exercise known as Value at Risk (VAR). They were, in effect, permitted to set their own capital requirements. Not surprisingly, they used this freedom to minimize them.

VAR is an estimate of the highest possible loss in the value of a portfolio of financial assets and liabilities over a fixed time interval with a specific statistical confidence level. Mimicking the CAPM and options-pricing models, VAR models assume that the probability distribution of future security prices is predetermined and knowable—they are characterized by risk rather than uncertainty. They also assume that expectations can be adequately represented by a "normal" distribution. "All the models in the financial economics edifice assume a normal distribution" (Smith, 2010, 79).

There are three fundamental flaws in this mode of risk assessment. First, a VAR calculation uses historical data to forecast future financial-market performance, typically data from the past year or less. If this calculation is done in the midst of a boom, the data will reflect the "perfect calm" of the period—corporate profits will be high as will capital gains on securities, while interest rates, defaults, and asset-price volatility will be low. The possibility of the outbreak of crisis will not be considered because there are no crises in the database. VAR analysis implicitly assumes this ideal environment is permanent. Thus, the risk associated with boom-induced high leverage and excessively optimistic expectations will be severely underestimated. VAR's rosy risk estimates allowed banks to hold dangerously low capital cushions and therefore enabled them to use extra leverage to continue to add risky securities to their portfolios. However, even if the data were extended to cover crises in past decades, growth and innovation would have changed the system so substantially that there would be little likelihood that the future would mimic the past.

Second, while VAR models assume that security price movements conform to the normal distribution used in canonical financial models, in fact they follow a distribution in which the preponderance of observations are "normal," but on occasion observations very far from the mean appear—the well-known "fat tail" phenomenon. The standard exercise calculates VAR under negative conditions likely to occur only 5 percent of the time. In a normal distribution the likelihood that an observation ten or twenty standard deviations or more beyond a 95 percent confidence interval will occur is infinitesimal.[20] Yet such tail events inevitably occur from time to time. *The use of normal distributions allowed banks to assume that serious future crises were impossible.* Thus, VAR risk estimates led banks to minimize required capital and to maximize leverage and lending capacity. This maximized profits and bonuses in the boom even as it sowed the seeds of a future crisis.

Third, the asset-price correlation matrix is a key determinant of measured VAR. The lower the correlation among security prices, the lower the portfolio's risk. VAR models assume that asset prices are jointly normally distributed and that future asset-price correlations will be identical to those of the recent past. However, in crises most prices fall together as all investors run for liquidity and safety, creating a high positive correlation and dangerously high risk that is unaccounted for in VAR calculations.

## b. Core Neoclassical Models Assume That Leverage Is Not Dangerous: Belief in These Models Contributed to a Cavalier Attitude toward Debt

The canonical models of optimal financial markets assume that leverage is never dangerous because fully informed agents rationally choose an optimal debt position. In fact, under radical deregulation debt had risen to systemically dangerous levels by 2007.

From the mid-1990s until the onset of the crisis, economic growth was largely driven by rising household borrowing and the stimulus to consumption provided first by a booming stock market and, later, by an enormous increase in housing prices augmented by an explosion in home equity loans. In 1981 household debt was 48 percent of GDP, while in 2007 it was 100 percent. This meant that if job or wage growth slowed, the ability of households to sustain heavy debt loads would be compromised. It also meant that if interest rates rose or credit tightened, or if stock or housing prices declined, consumption spending and aggregate demand would decelerate, threatening job and wage growth. The economy had become extremely financially fragile.

Financial firms were also excessively indebted; financial-sector debt rose from 22 percent of GDP in 1981 to 117 percent in late 2008. The spectacular leverage and financial fragility of key financial sectors along with the gross overvaluation of the securities they held made a severe financial crisis almost inevitable. Excessive household debt and boom-augmented household wealth ensured that the real-sector fallout from a financial-sector crisis would be severe, but this threat was hidden by neoclassical fairy tales about market efficiency.

It is estimated that half of the spectacular rise in investment banking return on equity in the four years ending in mid-2007 was attributable not to clever investment strategies or even to super-heated boom conditions, but simply to higher leverage with higher risk.[21] Moreover, about half the debt of the big investment banks consisted of overnight borrowing that would evaporate in a crisis. Commercial banks appeared to be adequately capitalized during the boom, but only because a high percentage of their assets—for some, more than half—was kept off-balance-sheet, and the prices of all their assets were inflated by the bubble. In fact, banks were dangerously leveraged. When the crisis hit, the value of these assets, and therefore of bank capital, plummeted, causing a frantic global search for new capital, a spike in interest rates, and a tightening of credit standards. The initial decline in security prices triggered a deleveraging process in financial markets in which liquidity disappeared. Asset-price declines led to margin calls, which led to forced asset sales and more margin calls in a dangerous downward spiral.

The shrinking availability and rising cost of credit brought on by the crisis, a strong negative wealth effect on consumption, and a declining construction industry in the United States led to a slowdown in economic growth and a rise in unemployment. This in turn led to lower profits and wages, which triggered rising defaults on both business and household loans, especially residential mortgages. Real- and financial-sector problems were mutually infectious.

Excessive leverage, rising defaults, deteriorating expectations, evaporating liquidity, and a destructive interaction between the real and financial sectors drove the downturn. These phenomena are integral components of the KM theory of financial-market dynamics but are invisible in the mainstream financial-market narrative about why radical deregulation is the best policy.

## c. Everyone Acted as If the Theory of Optimal Financial Markets Applied to all Major Financial Products, but It Could not Possibly Apply to the Inherently Nontransparent Securities at the Center of the Recent Boom and Bust

Financial innovation has proceeded to the point where important financial products such as mortgage-backed securities (MBSs) and collateralized debt obligations (CDOs) are so complex and so opaque that they are *inherently* nontransparent. As such, they cannot be traded on standard competitive financial markets but are sold instead through negotiation between the originating investment bank and a buyer—"over the counter." It has been estimated that half of all securities are privately traded. *Nontransparent securities traded privately cannot possibly generate "optimal" prices as defined in mainstream theory.*[22] For this reason alone, no one should have put any credence in efficient market theory as a guide to regulatory policy.

According to the Securities Industry and Financial Markets Association (SIFMA 2009), there was $7.4 trillion worth of MBSs outstanding in the first quarter of 2008, more than double the amount outstanding in 2001. Over $500 billion in CDOs were issued in both 2006 and 2007, up from $157 billion as recently as 2004 (SIFMA 2009 website). The explosion of complex MBSs and derivative products created large profits and bonuses at giant banks and other financial institutions, but it also destroyed the transparency necessary for any semblance of market efficiency. Because these securities were nontransparent, so were the institutions that held them.

Exchange-traded securities are sold in highly competitive and transparent markets with low profit margins accruing to the market-making institution. Thus, banks had a strong incentive to create products so complex that they could not be sold on exchanges at all. By the mid-2000s, 80 percent of derivatives were sold over-the-counter in private deals. Such agreements are characterized by oligopoly pricing power, asymmetric information, and unequal bargaining power that allowed banks to generate high profit margins.

Consider CDOs. A mortgage-backed CDO converts the cash flows from the mortgages in its domain into tranches or slices with different risk characteristics. Several thousand mortgages may go into a single MBS and as many as 150 MBSs can be packaged into a single CDO.

A textbook on credit derivatives explains that

> even with a mathematical approach to handling correlation, the complexity of calculating the expected default payment, which is what is needed to arrive at a CDO price, grows exponentially with an increasing number of reference assets [the original mortgages]....As it turns out, it is hard to derive a generalized model or formula that handles this complex calculation while still being practical to use. (Chacko, Sjoman, Motohashi, and Dessain, 2006, 226)

The risk associated with mortgage-backed CDOs cannot possibly be priced correctly. Ratings agencies and the investment banks that create these securities rely on simulation models to assess their risk, but these models are unreliable and easily manipulated, and these institutions have strong incentives to produce unrealistically high ratings. The models are "black boxes": data are fed in, and millions of lines of computer code spit out a rating. It should come as no surprise that market operatives referred to the process through which investment banks and ratings agencies priced or marked CDOs as marking to "magic" or to "myth."

The fact that neoclassical financial theory obviously cannot generate its signature optimality conclusion when no one knows the properties of a security somehow never came up in the deregulation debate.

## 6. Concluding Thoughts

Many factors contributed to the recent financial crisis. Instability is built into capitalist financial markets, a historical fact incorporated in the financial-market theories of Keynes, Minsky, Marx, and others.[23] In recent decades, financial innovation, perverse bonus-driven compensation systems, rising leverage, and global integration led to reckless financial-market expansion and excessive risk taking that generated a series of dangerous financial crises. Government intervention to shorten and limit the depth of these crises in turn created a moral hazard that induced even greater risk taking that accelerated the long-term financial explosion. Nevertheless, there is no doubt that radical financial-market deregulation was a necessary condition for the generation of a secular financial expansion this long and this strong, as well as for the creation of a global crisis as severe as the one we are still living through.

So many powerful forces demanded deregulation in this period that it might have taken place even if the economics profession had adopted KM theory and spoken out forcefully against it. But had this happened, the deregulation process would have been much more difficult and the current crisis might have been much less destructive. The economics profession does bear some responsibility for the severity of the current crisis and the human suffering associated with it. In this chapter I have argued that the profession's support for deregulation is based on a misleading theory of financial markets constructed on obviously unrealistic assumptions. This theory has little empirical support. As the world recently observed, predictions based on efficient financial-market theory turned out to be catastrophically wrong. To take this theory seriously, one must accept Friedman's positivist methodology because it asserts, against logic and common sense, that the realism of assumptions has no bearing on the validity of a theory, and that it is impossible to distinguish between realistic and nonrealistic assumptions. Because neither of these propositions is true, economists should accept Keynes's method, which asserts that realistic theories cannot be founded on crudely unrealistic assumptions and which rejects *all* theories of perfect markets. As Harvard's Dani Rodrik (2011) put it, "The idea that markets are self-correcting received a mortal blow in the recent financial crisis and should be buried once and for all." Until the profession rejects Friedman's positivism and adopts some variant of the Keynes-Minsky approach to theories of financial markets, policy makers should pay no attention to advice from the economics profession on matters of financial-market regulation.

## Acknowledgments

I am grateful to Jerry Epstein and Jennifer Taub for comments on a previous draft, and especially to Tom Bernardin, who provided valuable research assistance and helpful advice. I would like to thank the University of Massachusetts Economics Department for research support through its Sheridan Scholar program.

## Notes

1. As explained below, there is a distinction in theory between financial-market efficiency and optimality. In ordinary discourse, the term "efficiency" often embodies both properties.
2. Government officials also supported deregulation because they received huge campaign contributions from Wall Street firms. Moreover, politicians and top staff members who supported Wall Street's agenda frequently were rewarded with high-paying lobbyist jobs or employment by large financial institutions.
3. Joseph Stiglitz, "Needed: A New Economic Paradigm," *Financial Times*, August 19, 2010).
4. A softer version of Fukuyama's thesis can be found in Epstein and Carrick-Hagenbarth (2010). They argue that many top financial economists had close and highly remunerative ties to Wall Street firms, and this may have affected their public support of radical financial markets deregulation.
5. In this chapter, the term "positivism" refers specifically to Friedman's interpretation of the concept.
6. The theory acknowledges that unforeseen changes in the economy might alter cash-flow distributions. However, because agents are assumed to act as if they were positive that the current expected cash-flow distributions were permanent, this is a distinction without a difference.
7. For a critical evaluation of positivism, see Caldwell (1994).
8. This assumption involves a logical contradiction. If agents did assume they knew the future, they could not be rational agents because there is no logical foundation for this belief. See Crotty (1994) for a defense of this assertion.
9. There is the challenge of finding an empirical proxy for the expected covariance of a security. In practice, the past covariance is used as the proxy, which may introduce serious error into the econometric tests. This is an example of the Duhem-Quine problem at work.
10. See Glickman (1994) for a general discussion of this problem.
11. Malkiel's presumption is that professionals can't beat the market because security prices always properly incorporate complete and correct information about future cash flows. However, if the future is uncertain and unknowable as Keynes insisted, it might still be impossible to beat the market on a consistent basis. Even if pros cannot beat the market, this does not imply that markets are efficient.
12. Shiller offered a related criticism: "Individual investors get advice from professional investors, and they can easily observe (albeit with some time lag) what professional investors are doing. So there may be no significant difference between the success of professional investors and the market as a whole, even if their analysis is valuable to others" (2005, 180).
13. Shiller also provided a widely accepted critique of the CAPM by testing whether the behavior of stock-price indices is consistent with their assumed determination by the present value of future market profits. He finds that it is not: "Stock price indices are far more volatile than the corporate profits that are assumed to determine their value" (2005, 185).
14. Perfect knowledge implies perfect transparency. This means all agents have perfect information about financial products, an assumption badly violated in important financial markets recently.

15. Connecting real and financial sectors is a separate task left to macroeconomics, but in "modern" macro theory, the financial sector is usually represented by only an interest rate.
16. In 2008, the annual turnover on the New York Stock Exchange was 138 percent. On average, the entire value of all the firms listed on the exchange was sold 1.4 times in 2009.
17. See Crotty (2010) for an explanation of how perverse compensation incentives in financial institutions contributed to the recent financial crisis.
18. The importance of the "new era" syndrome in the generation of recurrent financial crises is stressed in Reinhart and Rogoff (2009).
19. These examples as well as other structural flaws in financial markets prior to the crisis are discussed in depth in Crotty (2009).
20. Taleb states that the assumption that security prices are normally distributed implies that "an episode such as the [1987] crash (more than twenty standard deviations) would take place every several billion lifetimes of the universe" (2007, 274).
21. "Worst Period for Investment Banking in 30 Years," *Financial Times*, April 2, 2008.
22. A *Financial Times* article noted that most of the $600 trillion dollars worth of private or over-the-counter derivatives contracts "are rarely if ever traded." It cited a regulator who said there was one day in 2008 when just two trades in credit default swaps caused worldwide market panic ("Raising the Curtain on the Private Nature of Derivatives," September 17, 2010).
23. See Crotty (1985) for a defense of the thesis that Marx's theory of financial markets is similar to those of Keynes and Minsky.

## References

Amromin, G., and S. Sharpe. (2009). "Expectations of Risk and Return among Household Investors." Federal Reserve Board of Governors, Finance and Economics Discussion Series, No. 17.

Beaver, W. (1981). "Market Efficiency." *Accounting Review* 56(1): 23–37.

Caldwell, B. (1994). *Beyond Positivism*. London: Routledge.

Camerer, C., and G. Lowenstein. (2004). "Behavioral Economics: Past, Present, and Future." In C. Camerer, G. Lowenstein and M. Rabin, eds., *Advances in Behavioral Economics*, 105–147. Princeton: Princeton University Press.

Chacko, G., A. Sjoman, H. Motohashi, and V. Dessain. (2006). *Credit Derivatives*. Philadelphia: Wharton School.

Crotty, J. (1985). "The Centrality of Money, Credit and Financial Intermediation in Marx's Crisis Theory." In S. Resnick and R. Wolff, eds., *Rethinking Marxism: Essays in Honor of Harry Magdoff and Paul Sweezy*, 45–82. New York: Autonomedia.

Crotty, J. (1994). "Are Keynesian Uncertainty and Macrotheory Incompatible? Conventional Decision Making, Institutional Structures and Conditional Stability in Keynesian Macromodels." In G. Dymski and R. Pollin, eds., *New Perspectives in Monetary Macroeconomics: Explorations in the Tradition of Hyman Minsky*, 105–142. Ann Arbor: University of Michigan Press.

Crotty, J. (2009). "Structural Causes of the Global Financial Crisis: A Critical Assessment of the 'New Financial Architecture.' " *Cambridge Journal of Economics* 33(4): 563–580.

Crotty, J. (2010). "The Bonus-Driven Rainmaker Financial Firms: How These Firms Enrich Top Employees, Destroy Shareholder Value and Create Systemic Financial Instability." Political Economy Research Institute, University of Massachusetts, Amherst, Working Paper 209. Available at http://www.peri.umass.edu/fileadmin/pdf/working_papers/working_papers_201-250/WP209_revised2.pdf.

Epstein, G., and J. Carrick-Hagenbarth. (2010). "Financial Economists, Financial Interests and Dark Corners of the Meltdown: It's Time to Set Ethical Standards for the Economics Profession." Political Economy Research Institute Working Paper Series, No. 239. Available at http://www.peri.umass.edu/fileadmin/pdf/working_papers/working_papers_201-250/WP239_revised.pdf.

Fama, E. (1991). "Efficient Capital Markets: II." *Journal of Finance* 46(5): 1575–1617.

Fama, E., and K. French. (2004). "The CAPM: Theory and Evidence." *Journal of Economic Perspectives* 18(3): 25–46.

Federal Reserve Bank of Minneapolis. (2007). "Interview with Eugene Fama." *The Region*, December. Available at http://www.minneapolisfed.org/publications_papers/pub_display.cfm?id=1134.

Findley, M., and E. Williams. (1985). "A Post Keynesian View of Modern Financial Economics: In Search of Alternative Paradigms." *Journal of Business Finance and Accounting* 12(1): 1–18.

Findley, M., and E. Williams. (2008–2009). "Financial Economics at 50: An Oxymoronic Tautology." *Journal of Post Keynesian Economics* 31(2): 213–226.

Friedman, Milton. (1953). *Essays in Positive Economics*. Chicago: University of Chicago Press.

Glickman, M. (1994). "The Concept of Information, Intractable Uncertainty, and the Current State of the 'Efficient' Markets Theory: A Post Keynesian View." *Journal of Post Keynesian Economics* 16(3): 325–349.

Keynes, J. M. (1937). "The General Theory of Employment." *Quarterly Journal of Economics* 51: 209–223.

Keynes, J. M. (1973). *The General Theory of Employment, Interest and Money*. London: Macmillan.

Lawson, T. (1985). "Uncertainty and Economic Analysis." *Economic Journal* 95(380): 909–927.

Malkiel, B. (2003). "The Efficient Market Hypothesis and Its Critics," *The Journal of Economic Perspectives*, Vol. 17, No 1, Winter, 59–82.

Malkiel, B. (2005). "Reflections on the Efficient Market Hypothesis: 30 Years Later," *The Financial Review*, 40, 1–9.

Mehrling, P. (2005). *Fischer Black and the Revolutionary Idea of Finance*. Hoboken, N.J.: John Wiley.

Rabin, M. (2002). "A Perspective on Psychology and Economics." *European Economics Review* 46: 657–685.

Reinhart, C., and K. Rogoff. (2009). *This Time Is Different: Eight Centuries of Financial Folly*. Princeton: Princeton University Press.

Rodrik, D. (2011). "New Rules for the Global Economy." Available at http://www.project-syndicate.org/commentary/rodrik52/English.

Securities Industry and Financial Markets Association (2009). Available at http://www.sifma.org/about/.

Shackle, G. L. S. (1992). *Epistemics and Economics*. London: Transaction.
Sharpe, W. (1964). "Capital Asset Prices: A Theory of Market Equilibrium under Conditions of Risk." *Journal of Finance* 19(3): 425–442.
Shiller, R. (1992). *Market Volatility*. Boston: MIT Press.
Shiller, R. (2005). *Irrational Exuberance*. New York: Broadway.
Skomarovsky, M. (2011). "Evidence of an American Plutocracy: The Larry Summers Story." *Truthout*, January 10. Available at http://www.truth-out.org/evidence-american-plutocracy-the-larry-summers-story67007.
Smith, Y. (2010). *Econned*. New York: Palgrave Macmillan.
Solow, R. (1988). "Growth Theory and After." *American Economic Review* 78: 307–317.
Summers, L. (1985). "On Economics and Finance." *Journal of Finance* 40(3): 633–635.
Taleb, N. (2007). *The Black Swan: The Theory of the Highly Improbable*. New York: Random House.

CHAPTER 8

# POLITICAL ECONOMY APPROACHES TO FINANCIAL CRISIS

## HYMAN MINSKY'S FINANCIAL FRAGILITY HYPOTHESIS

JAN KREGEL

HYMAN Minsky is best known for his financial instability hypothesis.[1] However, his work presented a complete reformulation of Keynesian economics through the introduction of the explicit analysis of banking and the financial system in the determination of the evolution of a capitalist economy. Indeed, he followed a number of dissident economists such as Marx, Veblen, and Schumpeter in insisting on capitalism as a peculiar and evolving form of economic organization. His work is thus also close to the traditions of evolutionary and institutional economics. He eschewed association with the post-Keynesian extensions of Keynes's work built on models of steady growth and distribution, and instead he preferred to place his work in the realm of what might be called financial macroeconomics.

## The Simple Principles of the Financial Instability Hypothesis

Minsky's economics of financial fragility was built on some simple characteristics of a capitalist economy.[2] The first was the existence of private property and, in particular, private ownership of the means of production. The second was that the dynamism that characterizes capitalism is due to its dynamic, evolving financial structure. This was reflected in his dictum that capitalism was like Heinz pickles—it came in at least 57 different varieties. It was the economist's task to keep abreast of these changes.

Minsky identified an initial stage of "commercial" capitalism in which external finance was mainly for trade. He also recognized a subsequent period of "finance" capitalism in which the single entrepreneur built up a dominant position through investment of profit or monopoly advantage. This stage evolved into a more modern form of what Chandler called managerial capitalism, where financiers such as J. P. Morgan provided the financing for the consolidation of small innovative firms into corporations of increasingly large size that required fixed income financing from third parties, or "industrial capitalism" dominated by the reliance on external funds to finance capital accumulation. The Great Depression led to New Deal regulatory reforms that sharply constrained such activity and produced what he called "paternalistic" capitalism. The modern economy is represented by "money manager" capitalism that reflects the changes brought about by greater contractual saving in the form of insurance, private pensions, and other investment institutions in shifting the locus of the investment decision to the hired portfolio managers. This introduces a new layer of intermediation into the financial structure because the objective aim of money managers—and the sole criterion by which they are judged—is the maximization of the total return on assets. A consequence is that business leaders become increasingly sensitive to the stock-market valuation of their firms; rather than looking to the overall performance of the firm, management concentrates on shareholder value. The consequences may be seen in the scandals of the 1990s such as Enron's use of accounting deception to influence its share price and the behavior of the management of large banks in undertaking increasing risks in order to raise share prices and increase their incomes composed increasingly of options to buy their company stock.

For Minsky the main proposition of modern forms of capitalism was that the ownership and control of capital assets was achieved by borrowing, that is, by issuing liabilities that generated commitments to pay cash to lenders that had to be serviced by the production of profits from the means of production they financed. The role of profits was thus of primary importance in the validation of the debts incurred by capitalists and held by the financial system and the public. The behavior of modern capitalism could only be understood by reference to the nature of the liabilities that were issued to support the process of capital accumulation. The composition of firm balance sheets and the nature of the assets and the liabilities issued to procure them provided crucial information on the system's evolution. For Minsky the capitalist financial system is a complex of money-in/money-out transactions. Financial fragility arises because of the necessity to meet the payment commitments on debt in cash. But investors cannot themselves create cash, so the only way that they can meet these cash commitments is through the receipts from the sale of the output or services generated by the capital goods, or from the income from the ownership of financial contracts, from cash on hand, from the sale of assets or financial contracts, or by borrowing cash from the financial system. While debt commitments are fixed, the cash receipts from the assets they finance are variable, and the other sources of cash have finite limits; thus, there may eventually come a time when cash commitments on debt cannot be met. Financial fragility then becomes financial instability.

## Modern Finance and the Interconnected Complex of Financial Flows

In eighteenth-century capitalism, capitalists owned their own firms and often provided financing for their brethren but did not use external financing. Modern capitalism on the other hand depended on the financial system to provide the financing for the ownership of capital. J. P. Morgan and other private banks initiated this process, but they were quickly displaced by commercial and trust banks as the ultimate providers of liquidity for the financial system, using in Brandeis's terms "other people's money," that is, bank deposits, to provide the financing for firms' acquisitions of capital assets. Facing recurrent liquidity crises in the form of deposit runs on commercial banks, the United States finally created a central bank with the power to create money and to provide the needed liquidity in times of crisis. Thus, Minsky identifies the complex of money-in/money-out transactions as an interconnected chain in which investment banks provide the services of underwriting and placement of securities that allow capitalists to obtain ownership of the means of production. It is the commercial banks that provide the source of the liquidity to the investment banks, through call loans to brokers that allow secondary trading of securities and short-term lending to finance holdings of securities. But financial institutions, just like firms, cannot create cash; it is thus the central bank that provides the ultimate source of liquidity in the system because it is the only entity in the system capable of creating cash without constraint or, as Chairman Bernanke has recently reminded the public, with the simple stroke of a computer key.

In this interconnected financing chain, the liabilities issued by the firms that show up as assets of the investment banks are financed by the issue of liabilities sold to other financial institutions and by the sale of securities to the general public through primary offerings in capital markets. The commercial banks have the liabilities of firms and investment banks as their investment assets and deposits from the public as their liabilities.

## The Source of Uncertainty in the Complex Maze of Financial Contracts Financing Investment

Because the financial commitments made by firms to finance the acquisition of capital assets can only be met if the investments in fact produce expected profits, Minsky notes that expectations and realizations will be a crucial part of the stability of the system. Any investment will require earnings over its life, and other capitalists will compete with it: therefore, the ability to meet commitments will be highly uncertain. Thus, for Minsky, uncertainty is not a fact of nature but is the result of the capitalist process of production in which capital ownership has to be financed. This also means that financial institutions will frequently find that their borrowers cannot meet the service commitments on their debts.

The stability of the system thus depends on the ability of firms' capital assets to produce a sufficient cash flow to service the securities issued and the loans from the investment and commercial banks and for the investment banks to meet their exposure to commercial banks. Shortfalls in these income flows compromise the ability to meet financial servicing costs and create the potential for a liquidity crisis that can only be met by the central bank, the only institution that does not depend on cash inflows to validate its liabilities. The recognition of the interlocking nature of the balance sheets of firms and financial institutions highlights the importance of earnings of the productive sector in the validation of financial assets and thus on the stability of the financial system as well as the importance of the banking system in providing liquidity when cash flows from investments are deficient.

## The Central Role of Banks in the Financial System

Following Schumpeter, Minsky placed the banking system at the center of the process of financing capital accumulation and, thus, at the center of the explanation of economic growth and its fluctuations. But, different from Schumpeter, Minsky was not a believer in periodic cycles; instead, he believed in cumulative destabilizing tendencies such as those outlined by Marx, Veblen, Myrdal, and Kaldor. He clearly rejected the possibility of any stabilizing tendency of the capitalist system toward equilibrium; at best he considered capitalism as an evolution of real financial constellations, each producing its own specific conditions for expansion and a natural evolution that led to economic breakdown.

Minsky noted that deposit-taking commercial banks played the crucial role in this process because they were the initial creators of system liquidity. He considered "the fundamental banking activity is accepting, that is, guaranteeing that some party is creditworthy,...A bank loan is equivalent to a bank's buying a note that it has accepted. Banks make financing commitments because they can operate in financial markets to acquire funds as needed; to so operate they hold assets that are negotiable in markets and hold credit lines at other banks" (Minsky, 1986, 256).

Thus, the role of the banking system was to convert idiosyncratic illiquid liabilities of business firms into liquid means of payment; this involved banks taking the firms' liabilities onto the bank's balance sheet and issuing the firm a liquid deposit account. This provided the firms with the possibility of acquiring real assets that they could combine to initiate a series of investments that produced the cash flows required to repay the loans. Banks could do this "because of the private knowledge involved in bank lending" that is the due diligence undertaken by the bank loan officer in investigating the ability of the borrower to repay the loan. Minsky thus concluded that banks' "loans are presumably not transferable without the bank's accepting a contingent liability" (1986, 257). It is interesting that this is precisely what the financial system attempted to do in the securitization of banks' consumer, automobile, and other loans and eventually mortgages. As was eventually discovered, the special investment vehicles that were part of this process did in fact contain invisible contingent liabilities in the form of "liquidity puts." The residential mortgage-backed securities and the collateralized mortgage obligations that bundled these securities did not retain any formal contingent bank liabilities from banks but rather relied on overcollateralization and guarantees from other financial institutions in the form of monoline insurers' guarantees or credit default swaps. But, through the interconnection of balance sheets, these guarantees were also supported by deposit-taking banks. When banks refuse, or are unable to provide the necessary liquidity, because they are suffering from losses on their holdings of firms' liabilities, the system may be subject to a liquidity crisis that quickly converts into insolvency and generalized crisis.

## Why Doesn't Financial Fragility Produce Endemic Financial Instability?

What is the antidote to financial fragility that produces financial instability? First, as Minsky notes there is one actor in the system that is not constrained to raise cash because it can produce it—the government. The government is thus always in a position to prevent a financial crisis if it acts to provide cash to those institutions who need it to meet their debt commitments. This highlights the importance of the central bank as the only institution capable of offsetting a shortfall in earnings and providing liquidity through discount window lending to provide the validation of assets that will prevent a financial crisis.

The only substitute for central bank liquidity is in the composition of firms' and financial institutions' assets. Minsky follows Ben Graham and highlights the importance of a "cushion of safety" to protect against volatility in the cash flows from firms' assets and repayment of loans to banks. This cushion of safety takes the form of a margin between the cash flows expected from assets held and the cash-flow commitments of interest and amortization attached to the liabilities of the assets issued to obtain them. In addition, highly liquid assets may also provide a buffer to the potential shortfall of cash inflows from continuing operations. It is in the changes in these cushions of safety and their decreasing ability to compensate for unforeseen variations in cash inflows as the economy progresses that Minsky locates the source of potential financial instability.

Thus, it is not in external shocks or entrepreneurial errors that Minsky locates financial instability but rather in the progressive decline in the ability of the system to absorb external shocks as the economy undergoes sustained expansion. Increasing financial fragility is thus seen as an endogenous process that accompanies periods of stable economic expansion, an inevitable accoutrement of the capitalist system. Here, Minsky clearly follows Marx, but it is not a realization crisis that is the outcome of this process but rather a validation crisis in which the commitments on financial liabilities can no longer be met from current income. Cushions of safety are insufficient and further financing cannot be obtained, and this leads to a chain reaction of defaults and the need to sell assets, or as Minsky would say, "sell position to make position," which leads to sales of capital assets and falling prices.[3] The end result is a process in which the attempt to reduce debt simply increases it in a Fisherian debt-deflation process that produces the downward spiral of default and depression.

Many have classified, and thus dismissed, Minsky's characterization of the endogenous evolution of financial fragility and its conversion into instability as depending on irrational euphoria on the part of bankers and businessmen, or irrational exuberance, or simply excessive optimism on the part of entrepreneurs. Yet Minsky was always aware that the process of financing a loan or funding a liability was one that took place between an entrepreneur and a commercial or investment bank lender. While it was the natural role of the borrower to be overly optimistic (recall Keynes's comments about animal spirits driving the investment decision), it was the natural role of the banker to be skeptical, to continually ask the question, how am I going to get my money back from this loan? The banker should thus provide a natural break on excessive optimism.

Instead Minsky appealed to a rather different explanation of the decline in the cushions of safety . It relied on what came to be called "learning by doing." In a credit system, credit can only be built up on the basis of continued evidence of the ability to repay debt. As an expansion continues, more and more entrepreneurs find their expectations of cash flows on investment projects confirmed, and thus their ability to validate the debt underlying the investment. The universe of creditworthy borrowers grows at the same time as the entrepreneurs' confidence in their ability to forecast earnings and meet debt commitments. As Keynes noted, the investor who is in the market during a boom considers himself a genius, rather than simply being lucky enough to be on the right side of history. Nonetheless, the increasing confidence feeds upon itself in a form of a cumulative loop, for more confidence means more lending and more investment means higher incomes available to meet the cash flows. The result is a natural tendency for cushions of safety to be considered to be excessive for they are never needed. They can thus be safely reduced.

In statistical terms, if entrepreneurs and bankers have a mean expected result in mind and require a two standard deviation cushion of safety around the mean to make the loan, as results continue to accumulate at the mean value, the absolute value of the two standard deviation cushion of safety will continuously decline. But neither the banker nor the entrepreneur will consider that risk is increased because the cushion of safety is still two standard deviations on the expected result. Thus, as long as the economy continues to expand the cushion of safety will continue to be reduced without any conscious decision to take on more risk. A random event that produces a shortfall in cash flow and a possibility of nonpayment and default need not be a five-hundred-year event. A quite average change in any variable affecting cash flows—a drought or currency turmoil affecting financing conditions or a decision to increase interest rates to fend off a threat of inflation—may be sufficient to create financial instability. If there is no central bank intervention, it may quickly lead to a rush for liquidity to meet commitments, exhausting the cushion of safety and leading to the liquidation of capital assets and a debt-deflation process, leading to a great depression.

## The Endogenous Evolution of Financial Fragility

Minsky formalized this insight in what has become known as the core of the financial instability hypothesis, the classification of three financing scenarios based on the degree of risk as measured by the cushion of safety of cash inflows over cash commitments on liabilities. If a firm engages in "hedge" financing, cash inflows are more than sufficient to cover any variation in cash inflows from those initially expected at the planning stage of the investment or in the possible variation in financing conditions due to changes in interest rates or other conditions. The cushion may include what Minsky called a "cash kicker," that is, the holding of some highly liquid assets available to meet financing costs. Thus, in every future period there is virtually no risk that the firm will be unable to pay all its creditors. Such firms would be characterized by an extremely low degree of leverage, with the lower risk reducing potential returns. Their credit ratings would be A or above.

A firm engaging in speculative finance has a reasonable expectation that in some future periods its cash inflows will be below its financing costs. This will be true of investments with large start-up costs in which initial gross revenue may be low or zero and net revenue negative. Many dot-com start-up firms were launched on this basis. These firms receive financing because the future income flows are expected to be more than sufficient to cover the initial losses. The same is true for a firm that experiences what is expected to be a temporary downturn in sales at some point over the life of the investment, but that subsequent performance will return to normal. As a formal condition for these firms, the present value of net income must be equal or greater than the present value of the expected financing costs. Here, the ability of the firm to access bank credit to fund the early period of low income or a period of negative earnings over the life of the project is crucial to its survival. Commercial banks become important in ensuring the survival of the investment and the possibility of achieving the repayment of all of the prior existing debt. If the firm cannot obtain interim financing to carry it through a temporary downturn it will have to truncate the project or it may default and reorganize. These firms will have credit ratings above BBB-, that is, they will be investment grade, but there is a positive probability that some of them will not be able to make full repayment on their debts.

Finally, the most well known of the Minsky scenarios is Ponzi finance, most recently made famous by the classification of the mortgage market crisis as representing an example of Ponzi finance and its collapse as a "Minsky moment." When an external event or a change in domestic policy conditions causes even anticipated cash flows to fall below the commitments to pay interest and amortization, the only way the firm can continue to operate is by borrowing to meet the carry cost of its debt. Thus, outstanding debt continues to accumulate. As long as the firm can convince lenders of the possibility of recovery so that they are willing to finance an increasing payment of interest on an increasing amount of indebtedness, the firm remains in business, even though it is technically insolvent and has a negative net present value. This is denominated a Ponzi financing scheme because it is equivalent to a successful pyramid scheme devised by Charles Ponzi and employed more recently by

Bernard Madoff. In technical terms the rate of increase in the firm's outstanding debt through new borrowing has to equal or exceed the rate of interest payable on the debt. In simple terms, new debt is required simply to pay the interest on existing debt. Eventually, the size of debt becomes so large or lenders become dubious, and a simple decline in the rate of the increase in lending is sufficient to cause a suspension of payments and default.

Thus, in a state of sustained expansion, there would be a natural progression of firms from hedge financing profiles to speculative profiles as cushions of safety were cut back in the presence of continued success in meeting debt service on an increasing amount of debt and an increase in leverage. This would produce an economy exhibiting increasing financial fragility, that is, an economy less and less capable of absorbing the normal variations in income or monetary policy that accompany an economic expansion. Such conditions need not produce a financial crisis, in the sense of acute financial instability, as long as the expansion continues. Such conditions appeared to be the case in the 1960s with the success of Keynesian "fine-tuning" policies to keep the economy growing at near full employment with stable prices. It was also the case of the more recent experience denominated the "great moderation." Both of these periods were characterized by the stability of real variables.

## The Genesis of Economic Instability

Given his view of the evolution of financial fragility, Minsky became an agnostic in the 1960s environment of the Keynesian neoclassical synthesis that relied on fine-tuning to stabilize the real economy.[4] Against the prevailing wisdom of the time, he argued that even if fiscal and monetary policy might succeed in producing stable real growth at stable prices, the financial system would continue to provide the risk of financial instability. Indeed, he argued that the very stability of the real sector would produce an evolution of the financial system that would create instability and crisis. This prediction, made in the early 1960s, was verified in the 1966 credit crunch, which nearly brought primary government securities dealers and commercial banks to insolvency. Although Minsky did not live to see the "Great Moderation," his theory would also have predicted the eventual collapse of the financial system that occurred in 2007–2008.

Financial instability could emerge from any of a number of factors. A simple downturn in the expansion might be enough to push enough firms from speculative to Ponzi and then for banks to withdraw additional funding, leading to a failure to meet payment commitments. Alternatively, and for Minsky more probably, the continued expansion would lead to tightness in labor and product markets that would cause the monetary authority to increase interest rates. This would not only raise borrowing costs for firms, but it would also lead banks to call in some existing lending, leading to firms cutting down on investment and a generalized search for liquidity to pay down the current level of debt. Given the interconnected nature of the real and financial system, this would lead to a fall in the value of firms' outstanding liabilities. Because these liabilities are assets on the balance sheets of banks and the private sector, this would lead to a reduction in financial accommodation and a further fall in cash flows available to validate debt. This would eventually lead to the need to liquidate not only those assets held as cushions of safety but also longer-term assets with little market liquidity, producing steep falls in prices, or even the absence of transactions. In the limit, firms would be forced to suspend current investment plans or even sell existing capital goods in order to raise the funds required to pay down debt. This may sound extreme, but it did in fact occur in Korea after the Asian crisis, as Korean chaebol packaged up heavy capital equipment for shipment to foreign buyers at fire-sale prices.

The important aspect of this kind of "debt deflation" crisis is that it is not self-correcting. The more firms sell assets to pay off debts, the lower the prices of their assets and the lower is aggregate investment which reduces the firms' cash flow; falling prices may thus increase the real value of debt not yet sold, leaving firm with no option but to sell even more assets to repay debt. Here, the value of the asset side of the balance sheet falls more rapidly than the liability side even with accelerated sales of assets, leaving the firm in conditions of technical insolvency no matter how much liquidity is raised from the sale of assets. And the same thing will be true of banks, whose assets are the liabilities of the firms. The result is a situation in which the normal operation of supply and demand in flow markets is offset by changes in the values of the stock of existing liabilities. This concept has been recently recovered in Richard Koo's explanation of the continuing weakness of the Japanese economy after the collapse of the stock and real-estate markets in 1989 as a balance sheet recession.

Minsky was always clear that the buildup of financial fragility only laid the groundwork for a full scale debt-deflation crisis similar to the Great Depression. He considered two basic characteristics of the postwar US economy as important in preventing a full-scale crisis despite the buildup of fragility and continuous financial disruption in the period. The first factor was "Big Government," the expansion of the government's role in economic activity that effectively placed a floor under national income. While private-sector expenditure would be influenced by fragility and eventually the default and contraction of financing, the government was not subject to any such financing constraint and as such it acted as a stabilizer on the overall performance of the system. The second was the "Big Bank," the Federal Reserve, which, after the Banking Act of 1935, gained full power to lend to the private-sector financial and nonfinancial system to avoid default. This action, if exercised expeditiously, could stop a debt deflation in its tracks. Although the original discount function of the central bank was limited to member commercial banks, Minsky's observation that these banks were the effective suppliers of liquidity to the entire financial system led to the conclusion that if the Fed was providing emergency liquidity to its members, this was equivalent to providing support to every other financial institution that had balance-sheet interlocks with member banks. It was thus more efficient for the central bank to open the discount window to all financial and nonfinancial institutions at the outbreak of instability. This is what was proposed in the 1933 Emergency Banking Act and eventually became part of Section 13 of the Federal Reserve's Statutes. Minsky thus argued that the Fed keep the window open to all on a permanent basis.

It is interesting to note that in the current crisis the Fed was eventually led to provide such support to both financial and nonfinancial institutions, but it did so only in response to the declared insolvency of different classes of institution, that is, after the fact. Minsky would have argued that, had the support been provided fully before each different class of institution had to declare default on payment, much of the contagion of the crisis might have been avoided. It is also interesting that the crisis emerged after the clear increase in the fragility of the dot-com stock-market boom and after the US fiscal balance went into sustained surplus for the first time in the postwar period.

While these measures to support liquidity and to prevent the precipitous decline in asset prices may prevent a fragile economy from experiencing full-scale financial instability they come at a cost. If the central bank is financing bank assets that have a negative net present value because the firms they have lent to do not have the cash flows to service them, then there will be an increasing accumulation of bad assets in the economy. They must either be liquidated with the associated capital losses and the negative impact on spending and employment, or the cash flows must be restored to initial levels to make them viable. This may involve an increase in prices and inflation (a policy that was advocated by Fisher in the 1930s and by many economists today for resolving the debt deflation in the Japanese economy). This would place the central bank in a self-contradictory policy position of acting to support financial asset prices at the cost of inflation, which they would have to take action to control, thereby recreating instability. As a result Minsky considered the policy objectives of financial stability and price stability to be incompatible and recommended that the central bank concentrate on financial stability and leave price stability to overall fiscal policy. This is precisely the opposite of what is proposed in the recent reform of the US financial system in which the Federal Reserve maintains regulatory authority and economic policy prerogative.

But Minsky believed that there were some procedural and structural changes that could be introduced to resolve some of these contradictions. He recommended a revised approach to bank supervision and examination based on banks' cash flow structures (Minsky, 1975b).

Because Minsky considered the issue of liabilities to finance of investment and capital asset ownership to be the major destabilizing influence in the economy he proposed the substitution of higher levels of employment for higher levels of investment as the proximate objective of economic policy. He argued that a full-employment economy is bound to expand, whereas an economy that aims at accelerating growth through capital-intensive private investment not only may not grow, but also may be increasingly inequitable in its income distribution, inefficient in its choices of techniques, and unstable in its overall growth performance. Thus, increased stability in an inherently unstable economy could be attained through a direct government employment guarantee program in which the government offers employment to all those willing and able to work at a wage near the prevailing minimum wage. In this way the cash flows that validate assets would be created through actual sales rather than through increased borrowing or increasing prices. This would imply the application of Lerner's concept of functional finance in which the direct objective of government budget policy should be employment, rather than balance. Indeed, it was always something of a puzzle that economists could recommend a policy target that was endogenous and had no direct instrument of control. Minsky, Keynes, and Lerner all agreed that it would be more effective to target employment.

When faced with the current crisis, largely driven by consumption spending, Minsky would certainly have replied that much of the crisis would have been avoided if consumption had been financed by wages increasing in step with productivity rather than being transferred to the financial sector. Banks' fragility would have been lower if banks had transferred their higher earnings to their capital reserves rather than paying large bonuses to their star traders; their capital structure could have easily resisted the losses incurred in the crisis. For Minsky the inequitable distribution of income was a major factor in creating financial instability. Thus, Minsky would have much preferred that the recent increase in budget expenditures would have been directed first to households facing reduced incomes and an impaired ability to meet their mortgage commitments than directly to the banks to remove the impaired mortgages from their balance sheets. But this simple policy reflects his basic belief that both the government and the financial system exist to serve the private citizen rather than vice versa.

## Notes

1. Minsky spent most of his life outlining and refining the financial instability hypothesis. Its nucleus is already present in Minsky (1964) and Minsky (1972). The nomenclature emerges in the early 1970s as Minsky worked on his book *John Maynard Keynes* (published in Minsky 1975a), initiated during a sabbatical in Cambridge in 1970. A useful summary is found in Minsky 1976.
2. These characteristics are already present in Minsky (1964).
3. This phrase is one of Minsky's best known but is not always fully understood. He defined "position" as those assets owned that could not be used to generate cash.

Making position was defined as the borrowing required to finance the essential income-earning assets defined as "position-making" assets. Thus, selling position to make position involved the sale of illiquid assets to raise funding to repay existing financing. Minsky (1986, 78 ff.).

4. This is the leitmotif of Minsky (1964).

## References

Minsky, H. P. (1964). "Financial Crisis, Financial Systems, and the Performance of the Economy." In *Private Capital Markets*, 173–380. Englewood Cliffs, NJ: Prentice-Hall.

Minsky, H. P. (1972). "Financial Instability Revisited: The Economics of Disaster." In Board of Governors, ed., *Reappraisal of the Federal Reserve Discount Mechanism*, vol. 3: 95–136. Washington, DC: Board of Governors.

Minsky, H. P. (1975a). *John Maynard Keynes*. New York: Columbia University Press, reprinted by McGraw-Hill, 2008.

Minsky, H. P. (1975b). "Suggestions for a Cash Flow–oriented Bank Examination." In Federal Reserve Bank of Chicago, ed., *Proceedings of a Conference on Bank Structure and Competition*, 150–184. Chicago: Federal Reserve Bank of Chicago.

Minsky, H. P. (1976). "Banking and a Fragile Financial Environment." Paper presented at the American Economic Association annual meeting, Atlantic City, NJ, September 16.

Minsky, H. P. (1986). *Stabilizing an Unstable Economy*. New Haven, CT: Yale University Press.

CHAPTER 9

# AN INSTITUTIONAL THEORY OF FINANCIAL CRISES

MARTIN H. WOLFSON

THE history of financial crises in the United States demonstrates both remarkable similarities and striking differences. The similarities appear in the dynamics of the crises as they develop, reach a breaking point, and are resolved. The differences appear in the timing, severity, and frequency of crises in different time periods. For example, after the collapse of the banking system in the Great Depression, financial crises disappeared from the US economy for 20 years in the post-World War II period. But then mild crises eventually reappeared, becoming more severe and culminating in 2008 in the dramatic threat to the stability of the global financial system.

It is the thesis of this chapter that an understanding of financial crises encompasses two aspects: basic dynamics of a financial crisis due to the characteristics of modern capitalism, and variations in the behavior of financial crises that appear as a result of changes in the institutional structure of the financial system over time.[1] So an institutional theory of financial crises has to specify the particular institutional environment and how that environment affects the behavior of financial crises. Theories that limit themselves to abstract "first principles" are unable to explain the differences in the behavior of financial crises. In fact, a comprehensive theory would also include an analysis of the historical changes that bring about the transformation of institutional structures, and thus changes in financial crises over time.

The next section of this chapter will discuss the basic dynamics of financial crises in a capitalist economy, in particular the capitalist economy of the United

States in the twentieth and twenty-first centuries. The section after that will describe the changes in the behavior of financial crises that have taken place in the United States since the Great Depression. The remainder of the chapter will analyze how a changing institutional structure affected the behavior of financial crises and also why the institutional structure changed over time.

## The Dynamics of a Financial Crisis

What follows are the similarities in the experience of financial crises in the United States. That experience is complex and varied, but there are reliable generalizations that can be drawn.

### The Cyclical Context

There is a cyclical component to financial crises, in the sense that there are processes that develop over the course of an economic expansion that lead to a financial crisis. Often these processes coincide with a conventionally defined business cycle, but this is not always the case. Interestingly, as discussed below, during 1966–1982 in the United States, financial crises appeared regularly at the peak of the business cycle and did not appear at other times. After 1982 this precise regularity has not been maintained.

### The Credit-Market Context

Financial crises typically involve the use of credit or, from the perspective of the borrower, debt. The dynamics of a financial crisis often have to do with the extension of credit in the expansion, the inability of borrowers to repay debt as the crisis develops, and the desperate search for credit as the crisis unfolds. Defaults on debt obligations can lead to bankruptcies, and the magnitude of crises is generally correlated with the degree to which debt has been used.

### Fundamental Uncertainty

The concept of fundamental uncertainty, central to the analysis of John Maynard Keynes, is a key component of the analysis of financial crises. As Keynes (1937, 214) explained, about events that extend far into the future, "We simply do not know." But this does not have to lead to chaos or irrationality. Keynes (1936) described a decision-making process in which financial-market participants rely upon conventions and try to figure out what average opinion thinks about the future, or even what average opinion thinks average opinion will be.

Given conditions of uncertainty, it is not necessarily irrational to use this decision-making process rather than relying on "fundamentals," because, as Keynes (1936, 155) noted, "It is not sensible to pay 25 for an investment of which you believe the prospective yield to justify a value of 30, if you also believe that the market will value it at 20 three months hence." And given methods of rewarding professional investors, it is difficult for an individual to be out of step from the crowd: "Worldly wisdom teaches that it is better for reputation to fail conventionally than to succeed unconventionally" (Keynes, 1936, 158).

## The Endogenous Development of Expectations

However, the reliance on conventions, which are simply collective guesses about an uncertain future, can result in waves of optimism and pessimism. As an expansion proceeds, employment, profits, and asset prices typically increase. Confidence increases, and as it does, expectations about the future become more optimistic. Lenders become more willing to lend and investors more willing to take risks. As the loans and risks turn out to be profitable, confidence again increases and the conventional wisdom about the future becomes more and more optimistic. (The same endogenous process of expectations formation and convention setting can work in the downward direction as well.)

## Speculation

Speculation often goes hand in hand with the increase in optimistic expectations and conventions about the future. In an expansion, speculative investors buy assets on the expectation that the price of the asset will increase. This is of course to be expected when optimistic expectations predominate. As lenders also are caught up in this environment, it becomes easier to finance speculative asset purchases with debt.

## Financial Fragility

The debt that is extended in the context of ever-increasing optimistic expectations about the future results in a financial structure that becomes increasingly fragile. Credit is extended on the assumption that profits and asset prices will continue to increase. Both lenders and borrowers revise their estimates of prudent lending limits, debt-to-asset ratios, sufficient liquidity buffers, and so on. As a result, not only does debt increase, but short-term debt also typically increases and liquidity declines. As Minsky notes, financial fragility is a typical attribute of an expanding economy: "*Systemic fragility* means that the development of a fragile financial structure results from the normal functioning of our economy" (Minsky, 1977, 140; emphasis in original).

## The Development of Financial Difficulties

At some point in the expansion, the fragile financial structure can no longer be sustained. The optimistic expectations enshrined in conventions about the future can no longer be achieved. Borrowers have increasing difficulty in repaying the debt that was extended on the basis of the optimistic expectations. Typically, the speculative bubble bursts, or company profits decline, or interest rates increase. Often all three developments occur. Defaults on debt repayments increase and bankruptcies escalate. Banks and other financial institutions suffer increasing losses on outstanding loans.

## Panic, the Drying Up of Credit, and the Flight to Quality

Because the optimistic expectations of the expansion were based on conventions, not knowledge of the future, they are quick to change. As debt defaults, bankruptcies, and loan losses escalate, optimism changes quickly to pessimism. Attitudes about prudent lending limits, debt-to-asset ratios, and liquidity buffers become much more conservative. Lenders that were quick to extend loans in the expansion are now gripped by fear and refuse to lend, especially to any firms or banks that are experiencing financial difficulties.

Borrowers sell assets in order to obtain cash for debt repayment commitments. Lenders sell assets in order to obtain cash, and they rush to invest in super-safe assets like US Treasury securities. But the sale of assets of course reduces the prices of those assets, thereby eroding the collateral pledged for loans, exacerbating pessimistic expectations, and generally worsening an already difficult situation.

## The Danger of Debt Deflation

In the 1930s, in the context of falling prices during the Great Depression, Irving Fisher (1933) analyzed a debt-deflation process. Falling prices increased the real value of debt, which made debt repayment more difficult and increased defaults and bankruptcies. Failing businesses worsened the economic situation and led to higher unemployment, a worsening economy, and lower prices. These lower prices further increased the real value of debt, and the whole process continued in a worsening downward spiral.

In today's economy, falling prices are not the norm, but economists have recently raised the dangers of a return to price deflation (Bernanke, 2002). Also, it is possible for falling asset prices, because of their effects on the value of collateral, the willingness to lend, and the ability to repay debt, to set off an interactive process similar to Fisher's debt-deflation process (Wolfson, 1996; Minsky, 1982). In the international context, falling currency prices can play a similar role (Wolfson, 2000, 373–374).

### The Lender of Last Resort

In recent financial crises, the Federal Reserve has intervened as a lender of last resort to prevent the worsening of the financial crisis and the possible development of a debt-deflation process. As Minsky (1986) has pointed out, the effect of a large government sector on maintaining demand and profits has also helped contain the financial crisis.

As the name implies, the traditional role of a lender of last resort is to provide emergency funds to a bank that is having difficulties funding itself from usual sources. The concept is usually associated with Walter Bagehot (1895), who advocated lending at a penalty rate to illiquid but solvent banks with adequate and acceptable collateral.[2]

As financial crises in the United States have increased in severity and complexity, the Federal Reserve has expanded its activities as a lender of last resort almost beyond recognition. In the recent crisis in 2008, the Federal Reserve lent to banks that were considered by many people to be insolvent, not just illiquid; it lent not only to banks but also to other financial institutions; it lent indirectly to nonfinancial corporations by means of its support of the commercial paper market; and it expanded the collateral it accepted far beyond the usual US Treasury securities to include even the "toxic assets" generated by Wall Street investment banks.

## The Variety of Financial Crisis Experience

We come now to the differences. Although the discussion above is reasonable enough as a generalization of the financial crisis experience in the United States, the actual occurrence of financial crises has shown marked differences.

### The Great Crash and the Collapse of the Banking System in the 1930s

In the 1930s the stock-market crash in 1929 and the gathering Depression led to a collapse of the banking system. Banks suffering financial difficulties were besieged by depositors eager to withdraw their money. Banks suspected of financial difficulties were also subject to depositor runs. Eventually the contagion became so widespread that President Roosevelt declared a bank "holiday" upon taking office in 1933. The "holiday" was not a day of celebration; instead, all banks were closed. Eventually banks were reopened after receiving a certification of good health, and Congress passed federal deposit insurance as well as a series of other financial reform measures.

## The Disappearance of Financial Crises in the 1940s–1960s

The passage of the financial reform legislation, especially the federal insurance of bank deposits, did much to calm fears about bank safety. Bank failures dropped sharply and remained quite low through most of the early post-World War II period. And financial crises disappeared! There were no financial crises recorded until 1966, when a very mild "credit crunch" appeared and caused some brief disruption to the tax-exempt municipal securities market. For 20 years after World War II, it appeared that financial crises had become a quaint historical oddity, something that used to happen to financial markets in the United States but that no longer did.

## The Reemergence of Financial Crises in the 1960s–1980s

But such tranquillity was short-lived. After the 1966 credit crunch, a financial crisis developed in the commercial paper market in 1970, following the failure of Penn Central Railroad. In 1974, the failure of Franklin National Bank set off a financial crisis that affected the domestic market for large negotiable certificates of deposit and international foreign-exchange and Eurodollar markets. In 1980, the site of the crisis was the speculative market for silver and silver futures contracts, accompanied by the attempt by the Hunt Brothers to manipulate the markets and control silver. In 1982 there were several financial disturbances that centered around the nation's banks: financial manipulations by a small government securities dealer, Drysdale Securities, Inc., caused losses at Chase Manhattan Bank and disruption to the government securities market; the failure of a small Oklahoma bank, Penn Square Bank, caused losses at Continental Illinois and 43 other banks that had lent money with the help of Penn Square (through loan participations); and the threat of default by Mexico on loans to large US multinational banks resulted in an intervention and rescue package from the United States and the Bank for International Settlements.[3]

These crises are interesting in that they all appeared in quite regular fashion at the peak of the business cycle, just after the beginning of the recession demarcated by the National Bureau of Economic Research's Business Cycle Dating Committee. Also, although they were more severe than the nonexistent financial crises of the 1940s–1960s period, they were less severe than the financial crises that followed.

## The Increasing Severity and Frequency of Financial Crises Since the 1980s

After 1982, the regularity of the appearance of the financial crisis at the business-cycle peak broke down. A crisis appeared a year and a half into the new expansion, as the nation's eleventh-largest bank holding company, Continental Illinois National Bank, failed and was effectively taken over by the US government. Problems at thrift institutions (savings and loan associations and savings banks) intensified during the 1980s and led to depositor runs on state-insured thrifts in Ohio, Maryland, and Rhode Island and the bailout of the thrift industry in 1989. The collapse of speculative lending and investment in commercial real estate, the oil industry, and junk-bond-financed hostile takeovers led to escalating commercial bank failures, the loss of independence of all Texas bank holding companies, the bankruptcy of the junk-bond firm Drexel Burnham Lambert, and a depositor run—despite federal deposit insurance—at the Bank of New England. A sharp crash of the stock market on October 19, 1987, jolted financial markets.

Crises continued apace in the 1990s. A more globalized financial system witnessed a currency crisis in the European Monetary System (the prelude to the euro) in 1992 and the Asian financial crisis in 1997. The Asian crisis, which began in Thailand, again involved the collapse of speculative lending and investment. The run on the Thai currency quickly escalated into a panicked withdrawal from the currencies of other Asian countries and a slowdown in economic activity throughout the region.

In 1998, there was the collapse of Long-Term Capital Management (LTCM), a speculative hedge fund created by John Meriwether, the former vice chairman and head of bond trading at Salomon Brothers. LTCM's Board of Directors included Myron Scholes and Robert C. Merton, the winners of the 1997 Nobel Prize in Economics. Although as a hedge fund, LTCM was technically outside the "ring of protection" of the Federal Reserve's lender-of-last-resort operations, the Federal Reserve Bank of New York convened an extraordinary meeting of the nation's largest banks and encouraged the banks to rescue LTCM in order to prevent severe repercussions in the global financial system.

Soon after the LTCM fiasco, the speculative run-up of tech stocks on the NASDAQ market came to an end in 2000, followed by a crash of the broader stock market in 2001. But speculative activity and risky behavior simply moved on to another area of the financial system. A bubble in housing prices developed, fueled by subprime lending, securitization of home mortgages, and exotic derivatives contracts created by Wall Street investment banks and financed by hedge funds and other financial institutions looking for outsized returns. As we now know, all this activity collapsed and led to the Financial Crisis of 2008 and the Great Recession. It was clearly the worst financial calamity since the Great Depression.

So how was it possible for the US financial system to go from a banking crisis that shut all the nation's banks, to an extended period in which no financial crisis appeared, to the reappearance of financial crises on a scale that rivals the problems of the Great Depression? The basic thesis is that the forces identified above, in the section on the dynamics of a financial crisis, operate in economic expansions, but the actual behavior of financial crises is determined by specific institutional conditions at any point in time.

But to fully understand the experience of financial crises in the United States, it is necessary not only to have an institutional analysis of how particular conditions affect the behavior of financial crises, but also to develop a historical analysis of how these institutional conditions change over time. In the remainder of this chapter, we will apply these concepts to explain the history of financial crises since the Great Depression in the United States.

## The Postwar System of Financial Regulation

Out of the turmoil of the Great Depression, a new institutional structure for the financial system was created. A useful term for this integrated institutional structure is a *system of financial regulation* (Wolfson, 1994, 219–232). It is similar to the concept of a social structure of accumulation (Gordon, Edwards, and Reich, 1982), which refers to economy-wide institutions, but the system of financial regulation is focused specifically on the financial system.

The system of financial regulation that was created in the wake of the financial difficulties of the Great Depression was based on two principles: the restriction of competition and government protection. In exchange for government protection, financial institutions accepted a prudential limitation on the kinds of activities they could undertake and the degree of risk that they could accept. The underlying assumption was that, if the government were to promise to backstop the nation's banks and thrifts, then it had the right to try to limit the potential difficulties that those institutions could get into.

The restriction of competition took the form of the prohibition of payment of interest on bank demand deposits and the power given to the Federal Reserve to regulate the maximum amount of interest to be paid on time deposits (as specified in the Federal Reserve's Regulation Q). This restriction enabled the banks to avoid unprofitable bidding wars for deposits.

A second form of restriction of competition was the continuation and extension of the "compartmentalization" of financial institutions. The Glass-Steagall Act of 1933 separated commercial from investment banking.[4] It thus added to the specialization of financial institutions, in particular the focus of commercial banks on business lending, thrift institutions on home mortgages, and credit unions on consumer finance. Also, competition was restricted by the ban on interstate banking.

The most important form of government protection for financial institutions was the introduction of federal deposit insurance in 1933. The Glass-Steagall Act created the Federal Deposit Insurance Corporation and provided government payment to depositors who lost money in a FDIC-insured bank.[5] Deposit insurance was instrumental in drastically reducing the depositor runs on banks that had decimated the banking system in the early 1930s.

A second form of government protection was the strengthening of the ability of the Federal Reserve to act as a lender of last resort. The Banking Act of 1935 centralized power in the Federal Reserve Board, coordinated control over open market operations, and liberalized the collateral that the Federal Reserve would accept for lending through the discount window.

Economic and financial conditions during the Great Depression and World War II both encouraged the creation of the new institutional structure and enhanced its success. During the Depression, many companies failed. Debt was wiped out. Economic conditions, of course, were stagnant, which led to limited private debt creation and falling prices. On the other hand, during World War II, government debt expanded dramatically. Private economic activity and debt creation were limited by the need to focus economic activity toward the war. The Federal Reserve kept interest rates low in order to limit government borrowing costs, and it kept interest rates pegged until the Federal Reserve-Treasury Accord of 1951. The government securities, which had a broad and deep market, enhanced the liquidity of bank and corporate portfolios.

In the environment of low debt, prices, and interest rates, and high liquidity, the compartmentalized financial system worked well. Banks and thrifts could confidently take in deposits at low interest rates and lend them out at stable spreads. Borrowers were less likely to have trouble repaying loans because of the generally low level of debt and high liquidity. And federal deposit insurance further increased confidence in the banks' financial integrity. So it was not a surprise that financial crises seemed to disappear during the postwar period.

## The Creation of Systems of Financial Regulation

In the creation of the postwar system of financial regulation, and in the creation of systems of financial regulation in general, there are three concepts to take into account: the concrete conditions, power, and ideology.

## The Concrete Conditions

New institutional structures can be created at crisis points in history, but they cannot be created at will. They need to be based on the concrete conditions that exist at the time. So a compartmentalized financial system made sense in the context of depository financial institutions that had little competition for depositor funds. Also, the profitability of depositories was enhanced by a low-inflation environment that made possible a stable spread between borrowing and lending rates. And the low debt levels and high liquidity helped to create the environment in which financial crises seemed to disappear.

## Power

In the 1930s, workers were successful in organizing and in creating unions. They increased their power in relationship to business interests, although the 1930s and 1940s saw a relative balance of power between labor and capital rather than the dominance of either one. Workers were able to influence government and use the power of government to promote their interests—to encourage the formation of unions, to create a social safety net, and, most relevant for our purposes here, to restrain the destructive competitive tendencies of an unrestrained market and to provide government support for depositors through deposit insurance.

But there are also important power relationships within classes, between nonfinancial and financial capital, for instance. In the 1930s important power was wielded by the thousands of small banks that blanketed the geographical and political landscape. In 1934, even after the failures of many banks in the early 1930s, there were 14,146 banks in the United States (FDIC, 2011). The existence of such a large number of banks, many of them small, was a situation that was quite unusual, compared to the number of banks in other countries. By pushing for an institutional structure that limited competition, the small banks were able to maintain their existence and avoid being swallowed up by the larger banks.

## Ideology

As the previous discussion implies, ideology—especially an ideological view of the proper role of government and markets—can play an important role in the creation of a system of financial regulation. With power comes the ability to shape policy and also the ability to influence the ideological agenda. Workers in the 1930s used their relative power to push the government into supporting unions and in expanding the social safety net. Small banks used their relative power to promote the views that a limitation of the free market was helpful in the banking industry and that it was appropriate for the government to subsidize banks by providing insurance for bank deposits.[6]

# The Crisis of the Postwar System of Financial Regulation

An institutional structure that is created in conformity to specific concrete economic and financial conditions can run into trouble if those conditions change. And although institutional configurations are relatively stable, economic and financial conditions are more subject to change. Indeed, the postwar system of financial regulation ran into trouble when the conditions upon which it was based began to change.

## The Increase in Financial Fragility

As the postwar period progressed, the unusual and, in fact, unique financial conditions that characterized the financial system at the end of World War II began to change. Debt levels increased as opportunities for private investment and consumption began to emerge. As memories of the Great Depression faded, businesses and consumers became more willing to incur debt. Also, government war financing no longer dominated credit markets with the end of the war. As government securities therefore fell in bank, corporate, and individual portfolios, the unusually high levels of liquidity did as well.

## Changing Economic Conditions

Economic conditions, too, began to change, especially in the 1960s and 1970s. Spending for an unpopular war in Vietnam, which wasn't funded by tax increases, led to an overheated economy in the context of an already strongly growing economy in the late 1960s. Profits fell and inflation increased. Oil price increases in the 1970s led to a wage-price spiral, as both labor and business attempted to maintain their relative income in the face of a decline in overall real income due to the oil-price increases. The wage-price spiral added to the inflationary pressures in the economy.

The new inflationary environment led to problems for depository institutions. Higher prices led to higher interest rates, as lenders demanded an inflationary premium to protect themselves from the loss of income. But higher interest rates wreaked havoc with ceiling interest rates on deposits. For thrift institutions, this meant that deposit interest rates were no longer competitive with interest rates on comparable investments. The thrifts were faced with a loss of deposits, or disintermediation.

The commercial banks, on the other hand, had a slightly different problem. The banks, or at least the large banks, had been issuing large negotiable certificates of deposit since 1961. These paid competitive rates of interest, so the problem for the banks was more an increase in the cost of deposits rather than the loss of deposits.

## Financial Innovation

The changing economic and financial conditions also led to financial innovations, which generally aggravated the problems of the banks and thrifts. The most important of these innovations was the introduction of money market mutual funds (MMMFs).

Although the general level of interest rates rose above depository ceiling interest rates, most small depositors could not take advantage of the higher rates because the purchase of instruments that paid these higher rates, such as Treasury Bills and commercial paper, required relatively large investments. MMMFs stepped into this breach and enabled small investors to obtain these market rates of interest. By pooling the savings of many small investors and investing them in money-market instruments that paid higher interest rates, MMMFs brought the benefits of higher interest-rate returns to a much larger segment of the population. As a consequence, they significantly worsened the depositories' disintermediation problems.

## The Erosion of Restricted Competition

Under the changed economic and financial conditions of the 1960s and 1970s, the barriers to competition that had surrounded the banks and thrifts were difficult to maintain. The challenge of the MMMFs clearly eroded the depositories' monopoly on deposits. Although shares in MMMFs are not technically deposits and are not subject to federal deposit insurance, money invested in MMMFs has almost always maintained its value. MMMF shares are functionally, if not legally, the same as deposits.

In addition, the banks faced heightened competition on the asset side of their balance sheets. Banks had traditionally had a monopoly on business lending, but here, too, the MMMFs posed a competitive challenge. MMMFs, by purchasing commercial paper from business borrowers (directly from nonfinancial corporations and also from finance companies often owned by nonfinancial corporations), effectively took away some of the market for business lending that had previously been the sole province of the commercial banks.

Also eroding the banks' traditional monopoly on business lending was the increasing importance of the use of securities markets to finance credit needs. Although the general process of securitization and the role of institutional investors as purchasers of securities would grow rapidly in importance and become a central feature of the 2008 financial crisis, they were already in the 1970s contributing to the erosion of the banks' monopoly on business lending.

# The Neoliberal System of Financial Regulation

By the late 1970s the basis for the postwar system of financial regulation was disappearing. Higher debt levels, increasing financial fragility, inflation, and the erosion of the barriers to competition that had protected the depository intermediaries, were causing significant problems. The institutional arrangements that had formed the basis for the postwar system of financial regulation, which had conformed to the economic and financial conditions of the 1930s and 1940s, were beginning to break down. The balance that had existed between government regulations to restrict competition and government protection to protect depository intermediaries no longer existed. While government protection continued, and in fact even increased, government regulation was rapidly eroding.

Financial policy faced a decision point. It could attempt to restore the balance by devising new government regulations to protect depository intermediaries from destructive competition.[7] But the large financial institutions that dominated the policy process ultimately saw their interests aligned with deregulation and the elimination of remaining barriers to competition. They used the ideology of the "free market" to rationalize their policy objectives.[8] The result was a new institutional structure for the financial system, what we could call the neoliberal system of financial regulation,[9] which is characterized by the following.

## Deregulation

The dismantling of the postwar regulatory structure began in earnest in the early 1980s with two laws: the Depository Institutions Deregulation and Monetary Control Act of 1980 and the Garn-St. Germain Depository Institutions Act of 1982. These two laws began a process of completely phasing out Regulation Q ceiling interest rates and authorized depository institutions to offer interest-bearing checking accounts. However, the trouble with this "solution," in an environment of rising interest rates, was that the short-term interest rates on deposits repriced faster than did long-term mortgage rates. So thrift institutions, with traditional mortgage concentrations, often found themselves paying more for deposits than they were receiving on mortgage loans.

But the two laws also allowed thrift institutions the freedom to expand beyond their traditional mortgage lending and make business and other types of loans, while at the same time suspending state usury ceilings that limited the amount of interest that could be charged on loans. Unfortunately, many savings and loan associations that jumped into these new and unfamiliar areas of lending saw loan losses increase, which contributed to the problems that led to the thrift bailout in 1989 (see the chapter by Dorene Isenberg in this book).

The Reigle-Neale Interstate Banking and Branching Act of 1994 repealed the decades-old ban on interstate banking. The last vestige of the postwar regulatory structure, the separation of commercial and investment banking enacted by the Glass-Steagall Act of 1933, was overturned by the Gramm-Leach-Bliley Act in 1999.[10]

At the same time that one pillar of the postwar regulatory system, the regulatory restrictions to limit destructive competition, was being dismantled, the other pillar, federal protection for financial institutions, was expanding. In 1980 Congress raised the amount of deposits insured by the federal government to $100,000 per account, from $40,000. In the Dodd-Frank Wall Street Reform and Consumer Protection Act of 2010, this limit was raised to $250,000. And a guarantee of the deposit insurance funds by the full faith and credit of the US government was made explicit in the Financial Institutions Reform, Recovery, and Enforcement Act of 1989 (the thrift bailout legislation).

Of course, the bailout of thrift institutions was a prime example of the way in which the government had expanded its protective blanket to cover financial institutions. Also, the Federal Reserve drastically expanded its actions as a lender of last resort (see the chapter by Chris Rude in this book), including its unprecedented actions to rescue financial institutions during the financial crisis of 2008 (see the chapter by Fred Moseley in this book).

## Lax Regulation

In addition to legislation that eliminated competitive barriers and restrictions, the liberalization of financial markets and institutions was also accomplished by a lax attitude on the part of regulatory authorities. Some of this was mandated by legislation, such as the Commodities Futures Modernization Act of 2000, which essentially told regulators not to regulate derivatives (see the chapter by Michael Greenberger in this book). But regulators also took the attitude that it was best if the financial system was left relatively free to innovate without government interference. This attitude became more prominent in 1987, when Alan Greenspan replaced Paul Volcker as the chairman of the Federal Reserve Board of Governors. Volcker, an old-school regulator, took a dim view of the deregulatory winds blowing through the financial system, but Greenspan embraced them.[11] He implemented his free-market philosophy during his tenure at the Federal Reserve, until he retired in 2006. Greenspan also took no action to limit speculation in the stock market in the 1990s and the housing market in the 2000s (except for a brief comment about "irrational exuberance" in 1996).

## The Shadow Banking System

Another characteristic of the neoliberal system of financial regulation is the shadow banking system. Although there are various definitions of the shadow banking system, it is generally considered to be "those financial intermediaries, *other than* traditional banks, that stand between savers at one end and borrowers at the other" (see Jennifer Taub's chapter in this book, emphasis in the original; also see D'Arista and Schlesinger, 1993). These financial intermediaries, in the most general definition, could include investment banks, hedge funds, MMMFs, finance companies, off-balance-sheet entities, mortgage companies, predatory lenders like check-cashing operations, and even perhaps government-sponsored enterprises like Fannie Mae and Freddie Mac and traditional institutional investors like insurance companies and pension funds.

Clearly the breakdown of the barriers to competition that had protected traditional banks and thrifts from competition has led to the rise of the shadow banking system. For the most part, these shadow banking institutions fund their lending and investment by borrowing in credit markets, and they are not subject to federal deposit insurance. Because they are generally outside the orbit of banking regulation, there are fewer requirements for prudential behavior on such issues as appropriate leverage ratios. As we know, many of these institutions, like investment banks, were leveraged at 30 or 40 to one. This use of debt increased the overall fragility of the financial system and played a major role in leading to the financial crisis of 2008.

## Securitization

In line with the increasing role of the shadow banking system has gone an increase in the process of securitization. Securitization refers in general to the increased use of securities markets for the extension of credit and in particular to the specific procedure of dedicating the interest and principal payments from a specific pool of loans to the issuance of securities. Accompanying the securitization process has been an explosion in the use of complex and esoteric derivative products. Investment banks used securitization to package subprime loans into opaque derivative products that were then sold to financial institutions in the shadow banking system—again setting the stage for the financial crisis of 2008.

## Short-termism

Another implication of the increasing role of securities markets and the shadow banking system is the rise of short-termism. Unlike traditional banking, which used to base loan decisions on a knowledge of the borrower and a long-term relationship, lending by the shadow banking system emphasizes a hands-off relationship and short-term results. In addition, banks and shadow banking financial institutions have increasingly emphasized fee income and trading profits as opposed to lending. Sophisticated mathematical models not only devise derivative products, but also develop computerized trading strategies that have dramatically increased volatility in financial markets.

This short-term orientation has had a profound effect on equity markets and corporate behavior. Traders who demand immediate results put enormous pressure on corporate executives to boost the stock price. The increased importance of shareholder value ideology and efficient markets theory (see the chapters by William Lazonick and James Crotty in this book) has reinforced this orientation. Executives will sacrifice long-term growth and development in favor of strategies to buy back shares and pay cash out as dividends in order to boost stock prices.

Executives try to increase stock prices not only to please short-term investors, but also to boost their own compensation. Executive pay is increasingly dependent on bonuses and stock options, which rise or fall in accordance with short-term profits and the price of the company's stock. In addition, financial executives and traders have adopted this short-term orientation as well. As analyzed by James Crotty (2009), "rainmakers" in financial firms took excessive risk and employed excessive leverage in order to boost short-term profits and increase their compensation. Obviously, this kind of behavior contributed directly to bringing about the financial crisis of 2008.

## Globalization

The breakdown of traditional banking has expanded not only the kinds of activities in which financial institutions engage, but also the geographical area in which they participate. And just as deregulation has opened up new opportunities for financial institutions in the US economy, so deregulation in the global economy, especially the liberalization of capital flows and the rollback of capital controls, has provided financial institutions the opportunity to lend and invest on a global scale. Most large financial institutions are now global players.

So financial crises, even if they start in one country, are not confined to that country; they spread quickly because of the interconnectedness of the global financial system. For example, the Asian financial crisis in 1997, which started in Thailand, quickly spread to other Asian nations like Taiwan and Korea, but it then also had implications for Russia, Brazil, and the United States, even contributing to the financial difficulties at LTCM in 1998 (Friedman, 1999, ix-xiii).

## Financialization

Most of the developments discussed above, which have increased the power, influence, and importance of financial institutions in the global economy, can be summarized under the general term of financialization (Epstein, 2006).

Financialization refers to changes in the relationship between the financial and real sectors "which give greater weight than heretofore to financial actors or motives" (see Stockhammer in this book). It also "denotes the dominance of the financial sector in the totality of economic activity such that financial markets dictate nonfinancial company behavior and significantly shape the overall economy" (see Tabb in this book). Is it any wonder that financial crises have increased in severity and frequency in the neoliberal system of financial regulation?

## Conclusion

This chapter has hopefully made it clear why institutional conditions matter. An understanding of institutional realities is essential to a theory of financial crises. The particular institutional conditions created in the context of the postwar system of financial regulation led to a tranquil period in the United States after World War II in which financial crises seemed to disappear. Yet, as the basis for the postwar system—the economic and financial conditions, power relations, and ideology—began to erode, the postwar system faced a crisis and eventually collapsed.

The replacement of the postwar system of financial regulation with the neoliberal system, however, has ushered in a period of increasing financial turbulence and financial crises. If we are to reduce the impact of financial crises on our lives, it will be necessary to devise a new system of financial regulation that can limit the destructive impact of an unrestrained capitalist financial system.

## Notes

1. In reality, even the basic dynamics of a financial crisis are a function of the institutional environment. Capitalism is a particular institutional structure and there are varieties of capitalism that differ over time and place. In a fascinating investigation, James Crotty (1990) notes that even Keynes's *General Theory* (1936) was specific to the institutional structure of the financial system as it existed in Great Britain in the early twentieth century. Crotty contrasts Keynes's analysis of speculation and financial instability in the *General Theory* to his analysis of the more stable "invest-for-life" attitude of nineteenth-century British capitalism. Also, variations in the behavior of financial crises are affected by changes in the nonfinancial system as well. Although these changes are beyond the scope of this chapter, it should be noted that the dramatic increase in income and wealth inequality in the United States in the last 30 years has played an important role in creating the conditions for financial crisis. For a discussion of these issues, see MacEwan and Miller (2011) and the chapter by Arjun Jayadev in this book.

2. An illiquid but solvent bank has total assets that exceed its total liabilities but is unable to convert enough assets to cash in time to meet current liabilities.
3. See Wolfson (1994) for a discussion and analysis of all these crises.
4. For further detail on legislation during the New Deal and its impact on bank stability, see the chapter by Damon Silvers in this book.
5. In addition to its responsibilities with regard to deposit insurance, the FDIC also was given a role in supervising and regulating the nation's commercial banks, thus reinforcing the restrictions on bank risk taking that federal protection required.
6. For an important analysis that uses the concepts of power, ideology, and inequality, see MacEwan and Miller (2011).
7. For one proposal along these lines, see Wolfson (1993).
8. This perspective dovetailed well with the efforts of large nonfinancial corporations to reduce barriers to capital mobility; to undermine workplace, labor, and environmental regulations; to erode the social safety net; and to shift the burden of taxation away from the wealthy. For an analysis of these institutional changes in the context of the theory of a social structure of accumulation, see Wolfson (2003) and Wolfson and Kotz (2010). See also the chapter by David Kotz in this book.
9. The word "neoliberal" here refers to a recent version of the classical liberal philosophy of unregulated markets.
10. The legislation in 1999 was encouraged by the merger of the bank holding company Citicorp and the insurance conglomerate The Travelers Group in 1998, in clear violation of Glass-Steagall.
11. The contrast between the philosophies of these two chairmen was evident when I was an economist at the Federal Reserve Board from 1983 to 1989.

## References


Bagehot, Walter. (1895). *Lombard Street: A Description of the Money Market*. New York: Scribner's.

Bernanke, Ben S. (2002). "Deflation: Making Sure 'It' Doesn't Happen Here." Speech at the National Economists Club, Washington, DC, November 21.

Crotty, James. (1990). "Keynes on the Stages of Development of the Capitalist Economy: The Institutionalist Foundation of Keynes's Methodology." *Journal of Economic Issues* 24(3): 761–780.

Crotty, James. (2009). "The Bonus-Driven 'Rainmaker' Financial Firm: How These Firms Enrich Top Employees, Destroy Shareholder Value and Create Systemic Financial Instability." Available at http://works.bepress.com/james_crotty/9.

D'Arista, Jane, and Tom Schlesinger. (1993). "The Parallel Banking System." In Gary Dymski, Gerald Epstein, and Robert Pollin, eds., *Transforming the U.S. Financial System: Equity and Efficiency for the 21st Century*, 157–199. Armonk, NY: M. E. Sharpe.

Epstein, Gerald A. (2006). *Financialization and the World Economy*. Northampton, MA: Edward Elgar.

Federal Deposit Insurance Corporation. (2011). "Historical Statistics on Banking, Table CB01, Number of Institutions, Branches and Total Offices, FDIC-Insured Commercial Banks, United States and Other Areas, Balances at Year End, 1934–2010." Available at http://www2.fdic.gov/hsob/hsobRpt.asp.

Fisher, Irving. (1933). "The Debt-Deflation Theory of Great Depressions." *Econometrica* 1: 337–357.

Friedman, Thomas L. (1999). *The Lexus and the Olive Tree*. New York: Farrar Straus, and Giroux.

Gordon, David M., Richard Edwards, and Michael Reich. (1982). *Segmented Work, Divided Workers: The Historical Transformation of Labor in the United States*. Cambridge, England: Cambridge University Press.

Keynes, John Maynard. (1936). *The General Theory of Employment, Interest, and Money*. New York: Harcourt, Brace, and World.

Keynes, John Maynard. (1937). "The General Theory of Employment." *Quarterly Journal of Economics* 51(2): 209–223.

MacEwan, Arthur, and John Miller. (2011). *Economic Collapse, Economic Change: Getting to the Roots of the Crisis*. Armonk, NY: M. E. Sharpe.

Minsky, Hyman P. (1977). "A Theory of Systemic Fragility." In Edward I. Altman and Arnold W. Sametz, eds., *Financial Crises: Institutions and Markets in a Fragile Environment*, 138–152. New York: John Wiley.

Minsky, Hyman P. (1982). "Debt Deflation Processes in Today's Institutional Environment." *Banco Nazionale del Lavoro Quarterly Review* 143: 377–393.

Minsky, Hyman P. (1986). *Stabilizing an Unstable Economy*. New Haven: Yale University Press.

Wolfson, Martin H. (1993). "The Evolution of the Financial System and the Possibilities for Reform." In Gary Dymski, Gerald Epstein, and Robert Pollin, eds., *Transforming the U.S. Financial System: Equity and Efficiency for the 21st Century*, 133–155. Armonk, NY: M. E. Sharpe.

Wolfson, Martin H. (1994). *Financial Crises: Understanding the Postwar U.S. Experience*. 2nd ed. Armonk, NY: M. E. Sharpe.

Wolfson, Martin H. (1996). "Irving Fisher's Debt-Deflation Theory: Its Relevance to Current Conditions." *Cambridge Journal of Economics* 20: 315–333.

Wolfson, Martin H. (2000). "Neoliberalism and International Financial Instability." *Review of Radical Political Economics* 32(3): 369–378.

Wolfson, Martin H. (2003). "Neoliberalism and the Social Structure of Accumulation." *Review of Radical Political Economics* 35(3): 255–262.

Wolfson, Martin H., and David M. Kotz. (2010). "A Re-conceptualization of Social Structure of Accumulation Theory." In Terrence McDonough, David M. Kotz, and Michael Reich, eds., *Understanding Contemporary Capitalism: Social Structure of Accumulation Theory for the Twenty First Century*, 72–92. Cambridge, England: Cambridge University Press.

CHAPTER 10

# THE ANATOMY OF FINANCIAL AND ECONOMIC CRISIS

DUNCAN K. FOLEY

## 1. The Market Giveth and the Market Taketh Away

Economic life at the national and increasingly at the international level has become organized along the lines that Adam Smith (1937) foresaw and Karl Marx (1976) criticized. We produce our daily bread (and our daily clothing, shelter, medical care, transportation, information, and pretty much everything else we consume) through a complex division of labor largely organized through the exchange of products on markets (which Marx called the "commodity form" of production). Capitalist commodity production is based on money and money capital, and so we also depend on an equally complex set of financial institutions and transactions to finance the production and circulation of goods and services. Thus, our economic security and well-being are intimately connected with the functioning and malfunctioning of markets, as the current financial crisis reminds us so forcibly (see Foley, 2006, chapter 3).

As the economic advocates of laissez-faire market organization of production who dominate the economic profession in the United States and increasingly in the world (though thankfully not at Barnard College) tirelessly remind us, this capitalist commodity system of the organization of production through markets has many good things to offer. Markets, when they are competitive and reasonably transparent, can aggregate information from many dispersed individuals to guide production and investment toward the approximate satisfaction of human needs. The capitalist form of productive organization puts primary control of technological innovation in the hands of successful entrepreneurs, thus encouraging a technologically dynamic and progressive pattern of economic development. We also know from long historical experience that this system has some less attractive features. It tends to distribute the fruits of economic effort very unequally. It also creates a great deal of individual risk and insecurity through the turbulence and instability of market fluctuations.

Economists have spent great effort in understanding the limitations of markets (though they tend as a rule to place the discussion of the advantages of market organization at the beginning and of the disadvantages at the end of the curriculum). Ideally, markets work best when the economic decisions of individuals are independent of each other. When the decisions of individuals have consequences for other individuals, or depend on each other in ways that are not completely captured by the market transactions themselves, various market pathologies result. Economists call these extra-market dependencies externalities (see Bowles, 2004, chapters 1, 5, and 6).

We experience externalities all the time in real life, though we may not always use economic terminology to label them. Traffic congestion, for example, is a vivid constant reminder of external effects. I am just minding my own business, for example, going to work, but at the same time I can get in your way and slow down your effort to mind your own business. Some externalities come to our attention indirectly, such as the impact of the burning of fossil fuels on global climate change. In fact, when we examine almost any economic interaction closely, we find that externalities are involved. In some cases they may be relatively small in relation to the market-mediated aspects of commodity transactions, but in other cases they are extremely important and have impacts on human welfare on the same scale as the gains from commodity production itself.

When individual economic behavior affects others in ways not encompassed by the market interactions, markets can reach stable equilibrium but will fail to allocate resources efficiently. If there is a real economic cost in the form of global climate change to burning fossil fuels, individual decisions guided by prices that do not reflect these costs will be inefficient (burning too much carbon-emitting fuel, for example). In these cases some social-political intervention is necessary to correct the externality. This may take the form of an extension of the commodity relations to include the externality (e.g., creating property rights in climate through a cap-and-trade system of a restriction of carbon dioxide emissions), or it might take the form of the regulation or restriction of commodity transactions (e.g., direct regulation of emissions or the imposition of a tax on emissions).

Market interactions become even more complex and vulnerable to malfunction when there is a feedback from the decisions of other individuals onto the decisions of any particular individual. For example, individual stock traders might act completely independently in buying and selling stocks, each forming his or her own opinion as to the long-run profitability of the companies by looking at "fundamental information." In this case the market would act according to ideal theory as an aggregator of the information that all the various individual traders bring to it. But if traders, as they surely often do in reality, take into account the decisions of others, through, for example, looking at what is happening to average stock prices in making their decisions about buying and selling, a potentially destabilizing feedback enters into the picture. If rising stock prices predispose individual traders to buy stocks at higher prices, a self-reinforcing "bubble" in prices can result. (There can also be negative bubbles in which stock prices are driven down by self-fulfilling prophecies of decline.) In these situations externalities can compromise the stability of markets as well as lead to the misallocation of resources. The external interactions may make drastically different levels of prices consistent with market equilibrium. These different levels of market equilibrium may have very different consequences for important human issues, such as levels of production, employment, risk, and the like (see Keynes, 1936).

The dramatic events of the last year in the world economy and financial system can be understood in terms of the externality problem. This crisis is, in fact, nothing particularly new in the history of capitalist economics (Kindleberger, 1989). Capitalist economies repeatedly experience financial crises of more or less serious degree, and often, though not always, these financial crises spill over into the production system and disrupt employment and output. In the course of this discussion I will look more closely at the specific types of external interactions that lie behind the financial and economic crises we are experiencing. A better understanding of these market pathologies can illuminate the policy issues involved in coping with crises.

Before embarking on this examination, however, I'd like to underline the larger point, which is that the advantages of capitalist-commodity organization of production through markets are inextricably combined with its pathologies and dysfunctions. Any particular pathology can be addressed by some combination of institutional reform or regulation, but the idea of completely purifying the market of externalities is a will-o-the-wisp.

## 2. Equilibrium with Externalities

We can roughly visualize a market with externalities as the intersection of two geometric loci, as in figures 10.1–10.4.

Suppose a "representative" individual agent, which might be a financial institution or a household, controls some variable $x$ (lending standards or spending),

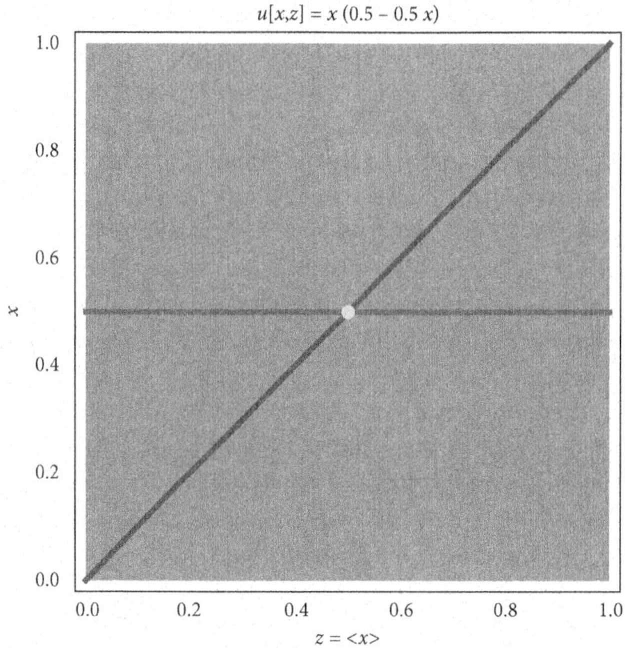


**Figure 10.1** When there is no externality, equilibrium at the intersection of the representative agent's best response (the horizontal line) and the $x = z$ locus (the upward-sloping line) is Pareto-optimal.

and we represent the social average level of the choice as $z = \langle x \rangle$. (Physicists use the notation $\langle x \rangle$ to represent an average of some variable over a system.) Then the utility of the representative agent is $u[x, z] = u[x, \langle x \rangle]$. The individual Smithian self-regarding agent takes the social average as given, and she then maximizes her utility by choosing $x[z]$ as a function of $z$. Economists call this the agent's "Cournot-Nash" best-response function.[1] The best-response function will maximize the utility function over $x$ given $z$, and hence will satisfy $\partial u[x[z],z]/\partial x = 0$. Because we assume that the agents are identical, the equilibria of this system are points where $x[z] = \langle x[z] \rangle = z$. As figure 10.1 shows, the equilibria can be visualized as the intersection of the $x[z]$ function with the $x = z$ locus.

What if the representative agent were not Smithian but saw herself as deciding for the society as a whole? In that case she would "internalize the externality," assuming that when she changed her own $x$, everyone else would do so as well. Like a social planner she would choose $x$ to maximize $u[x, x]$, not taking the level of $z = \langle x \rangle$ as given but would assume that she could control it by controlling her own decision. Another way to look at this type of behavior is that the representative agent would decide not selfishly but as if she were deciding for the whole society, taking the whole society's interest into account. This "Pareto-optimal" or *efficient* level of $x$ would satisfy $\partial u[x, x]/\partial x + \partial u[x, x]/\partial z = 0$. In terms of the graph, the efficient allocation is where the $x = z$ locus is tangent to the indifference curves of the representative agent.

When $\partial u/\partial z = 0$, the social average has no influence on the individual; there is no externality, and the social equilibrium arising from everyone consulting only his or her own self-interest is efficient. This is the invisible-hand game in Samuel Bowles's terminology (2004, chapter 1).

When $\partial u/\partial z \neq 0$, however, the social equilibrium is not efficient, as we know from economic textbook examples. When $\partial u/\partial z > 0$, there is a positive externality and the social equilibrium leads to a level of $z$ that is lower than optimal; with a negative externality the equilibrium level of $z$ is too high, as figure 10.2 illustrates.

Externalities can also affect the number and stability of the social equilibria. In figure 10.3 the nonlinear best-response schedule $x[z]$ crosses the $x = z$ locus three times. It is natural to view the outer equilibria where $x[z]$ crosses $x = z$ from above as stable, because a perturbation of $z$ upward from equilibrium gives individual incentives to reduce $x$, and conversely for perturbations of $z$ downward. If we interpret $x$ as the willingness of financial institutions to lend freely, for example, we can see how a rise in interest rates or a fall in housing prices leading to increased default rates on mortgages might shift the $x[z]$ schedule downward, as in figure 10.4, in which the "good" equilibrium of high financial efficiency disappears, and the system is forced toward the "bad" equilibrium of credit crisis (see Zeeman, 1977, for a more detailed discussion).

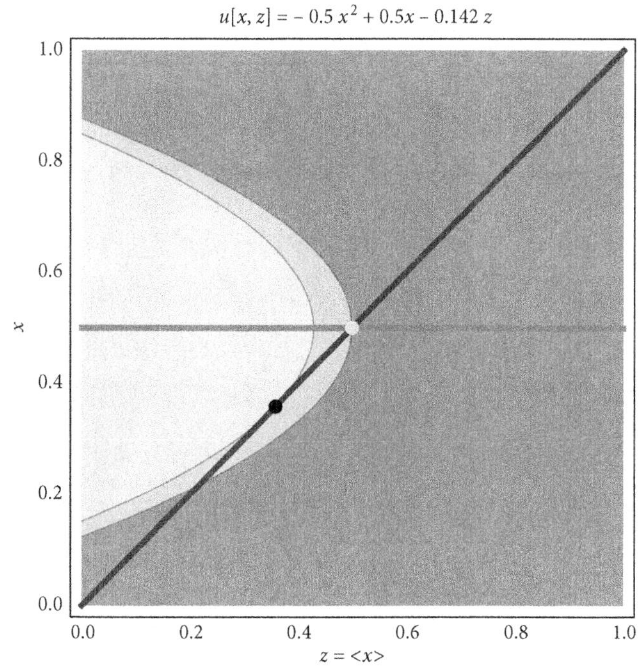


**Figure 10.2** With a negative externality, the equilibrium (at the intersection of the best-response and $x = z$ schedules) is not Pareto-optimal; the equilibrium level of $z$ is higher than the efficient level (where the $x = z$ locus is tangent to an indifference curve).

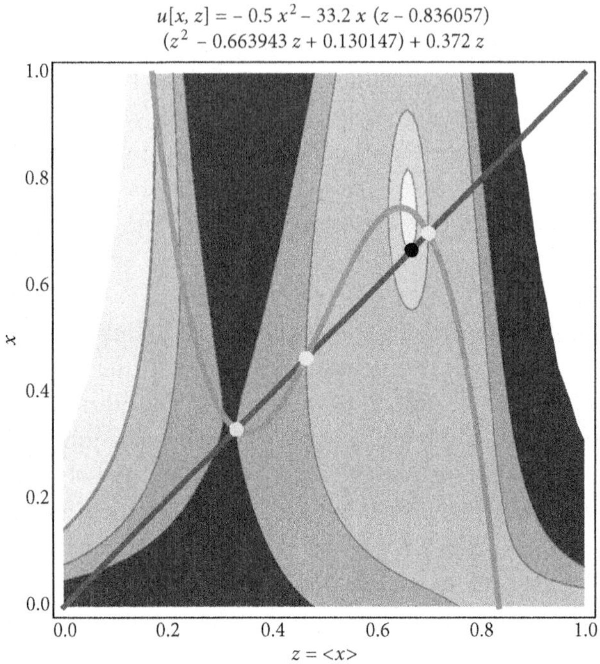


**Figure 10.3** With a nonlinear best-response function for the representative agent, there can be multiple equilibria, in this case three. The outer equilibria are stable and the inner one is unstable. None of the equilibria are Pareto-optimal.

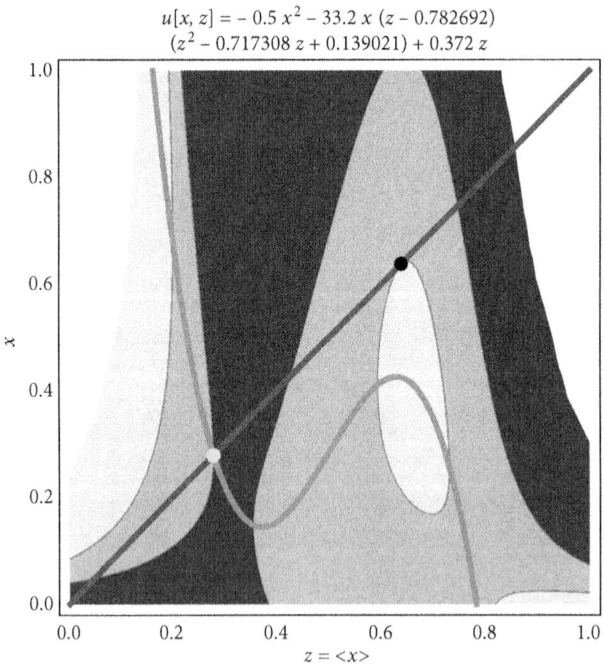


**Figure 10.4** The economic environment may change so as to lower the best-response function. In this case the result is the disappearance of the high-level stable equilibrium so that the system is forced to the low-level stable equilibrium.

The sudden collapse of lending in the credit system and the very rapid decline in spending levels in the world and US economies suggest that the loss of "good" equilibria due to gradual changes in underlying factors (such as interest-rate policies, housing prices, and the willingness of financial institutions and households to take risks) led to a catastrophic change in systemwide behavior.

The immediate policy goal in a situation of sudden collapse is usually to try to restore the status quo ante equilibrium by moving the best-response schedule (e.g., by lowering interest rates, flooding the system with liquidity, or raising spending through deficit-financed government spending). Two problems can make this difficult. First, the new low-level equilibrium is stable, and it thus inherently resists changes in policy. Second, the old high-level equilibrium may simply not exist, due to changes in underlying contextual factors. The best case is where the good equilibrium still exists but has drifted to a lower position. In this case policy may have a good chance to preserve the equilibrium and improve its social performance. The worst case is where the good equilibrium has completely disappeared. In this case policy has to re-shape the context in which individual financial institutions, firms, and households make their best-response decisions with the aim of restoring the high-level equilibrium.

## 3. The Financial Confidence Game

The defining feature of the modern debt contract is that it is impossible for the lender to compel the borrower to pay what the borrower promises (Bowles, 2004, chapter 9). (Bodily punishment as a sanction for nonpayment is available only to lenders such as the mob, who operate outside the law; the debtors' prison has thankfully been abolished.) Bankruptcy law does prevent selective default on debt: a borrower cannot pick and choose which creditors' demands to meet out of limited cash flow. This feature of debt contracts builds into the financial system the potential for an unstable chain reaction of bankruptcies. Because financial institutions are both borrowers and lenders on a large scale, the failure of one borrower to meet its obligations can compromise the ability of its creditors to meet their obligations. This is a fundamental externality of credit markets: borrowers in considering bankruptcy do not take into account the impact of their decisions on the solvency of their creditors and hence on the credit system as a whole.

Given this peculiarity of the debt contract, there are two ways to lend money. One is to require the borrower to put up some valuable asset (such as a house, a car, or stock) as collateral against the debt. The owner of such a "collateralized debt obligation" then can seize the collateral in case of the borrower's default and in theory could realize the value of the debt promise by selling the collateral asset. Among financial institutions themselves, however, collateral debt contracts have a great disadvantage in that the assets pledged as collateral against one loan cannot be used for any other purpose. Thus, a financial system that operated solely by using collateralized obligations would require an enormous amount of capital, that is, assets actually owned directly by the financial institutions, in order to supply the necessary collateral.

In every phase of capitalist development, financial institutions have devised means of avoiding the costs of collateral in lending among themselves. Large, well-known financial institutions begin to lend among themselves without collateral security, depending on the reputation and stability of the borrower as a guarantee of the debt rather than requiring borrowers to post collateral. Typically this unsecured lending is restricted to a circle of institutions regarded as "names" in the credit markets. Outsiders either must post collateral or need to get the guarantee of such names on their debt obligations in order to acquire unsecured loans. The system of unsecured loans greatly economizes the capital required to operate the financial system but creates another layer of feedback in the system. When all the other financial institutions are lending freely among each other without collateral, it is much more profitable for any given institution to follow suit; but if a significant fraction of the institutions lose confidence in the system and begin to demand collateral, the entire edifice of intertwined lending among the large institutions can implode. Other borrowers, such as productive firms and households, who depend on the unsecured borrowing system to finance their expenditures are cut off from finance in such an implosion.

In 2007 Northern Rock, a British mortgage banking institution, experienced this type of problem. It had evolved a business model based on short-term unsecured borrowing in the commercial paper market (through which mutual funds and pension funds make short-term loans directly to borrowers without the intervention of a bank) in order to finance the initiation of long-term mortgages from household borrowers. Because the cost of short-term funds in the commercial paper market was low, Northern Rock could compete very effectively in offering low rates and other advantages to potential borrowers. In 2007, however, the willingness of lenders to buy unsecured commercial paper dried up on several occasions. During these periods, Northern Rock, faced with the need to roll over its short-term debt position, became illiquid, and it required direct lending from the UK government to avoid bankruptcy. After several worsening episodes of this type, the British government nationalized the company.

Hyman Minsky, an American economist who also served as a bank director, devoted much of his professional attention to the problem of financial instability or, as he called it, "financial fragility" (Minsky, 1982; Foley, 2001, 2003). Minsky's thesis was that, in periods of robust capitalist growth, financial institutions become more and more willing to make unsecured loans. This willingness can increase the availability of finance, which encourages further growth in business and household spending but also increases the vulnerability of the financial system to an implosion if there is a faltering in the willingness of the financial institutions to expand unsecured borrowing. Minsky's analysis is based on the distinction among "hedged" financial units, whose cash flow is large enough to pay their debt-service obligations with something left over; "speculative" financial units, whose cash flow is large enough to pay the interest on their debts but that need to borrow to finance the payment of principal and the acquisition of new assets; and "Ponzi" financial units, who must borrow in order to pay the interest on their existing debts. (Minsky adopted the name "Ponzi" for this financial regime from the notorious Boston swindler-financier Charles Ponzi, who offered high "guaranteed" rates of return to his clients that actually were paid from the inflow of new money into his business.)

Households, businesses, and other borrowers do not, of course, only use borrowed funds to finance investment or to shift consumption from one part of their life cycle to another. They also use borrowed funds to speculate in assets such as real estate. Thus the expansion of credit as a result of increased financial fragility can finance speculative bubbles in asset prices. This is another externality built into the financial capitalist system.

Since the 1980s the US government has aggressively pursued an international policy of promoting free capital movements (Duménil and Lévy, 2004, 2011). This policy, enforced in many cases as "conditionalities" of International Monetary Fund loans to distressed national borrowers, requires national governments and central banks to remove regulatory obstacles to the free purchase and sale of capital assets across national boundaries. While a few large economies, notably India and China, were able to resist these pressures, many other important economies, including Russia, Brazil, Argentina, Indonesia, South Korea, and Mexico, adopted this system of financial liberalization. Each of these countries experienced a similar type of financial crisis as a result. In the initial stages the liberalizing economy experiences a large inflow of foreign capital, which supplies a lot of funds to its financial system. Typically this inflow of funds results in a rise in the economy's exchange rate (which is "floating" or market-determined under the liberal regime), which makes it difficult for its industries to export and leads to a deindustrialization of the economy, combined with a consumption binge as imported foreign goods become cheaper. In these episodes, the external capital flows finance not only a consumption binge but also a bubble in local assets such as real estate. When this bubble pops, the financial system of the country experiences a severe crisis, with a chain reaction of bankruptcies and defaults, and the real economy experiences a severe downturn with negative rates of growth of GDP and sharply rising unemployment. In the case of the economies I just mentioned, the crisis culminates in a sharp fall in the value of the national currency in relation to the rest of the world. These experiences seem to indicate that the regime of international financial liberalization based on freely floating exchange rates determined in speculative markets greatly amplifies the financial fragility inherent in financial capitalism.

In 2008 the US financial system experienced its worst crisis since the 1930s. The broad patterns of this crisis were strikingly similar to those experienced by other smaller economies over the years of international financial liberalization. The United States experienced a large, continuing capital inflow especially from oil-producing countries and China, which tended to hasten the deindustrialization of the US economy, making traditional manufacturing sectors like automobiles less competitive. This inflow also financed a huge consumption binge, in which US national saving plunged to record low levels; to a large degree this financed the bubble in US housing prices. When this bubble began to burst, partly due to the delayed response of the Federal Reserve by raising interest rates to reduce the incentives to buy homes at inflated prices with mortgages, it caught the financial system in a classic posture of financial fragility and vulnerability to crisis.

Every financial crisis is different in its details. In 2008 the weakest link in the US (and, as we have learned, the developed world's) financial network was the widespread purchase of mortgage-backed securities by large financial institutions. The decline in housing prices predictably set off a rise in defaults on mortgages, lowering the value of these assets and threatening the institutions with insolvency. The situation of the big financial institutions, which had loaded their balance sheets with these securities, was made more perilous by their reliance on mathematical models rather than market transactions to value the exotic and opaque bundles of assets they owned. The resulting financial crisis remains.

It would be a mistake, however, to suppose that this financial crisis was solely caused by the mistaken investment decisions of the large financial institutions in buying mortgage-backed securities, or in the ill judgment or corruption involved in issuing these mortgages in the first place. A certain degree of corruption, manipulation, and opportunism is built in to financial capitalism. When the whole economy prospers and grows, and prices in general continue to rise, much of the potential systemwide damage is avoided. A financial crisis, on the other hand, not only reveals the borderline and criminal transactions that have taken place but also compromises the quality of transactions that would have passed muster in "normal" times.

It seems to me (especially with the clarity of post-crisis hindsight) more reasonable to suppose that the financial system was in so fragile a state that any one of a number of disturbances could have precipitated this crisis. If the rise in mortgage defaults as a consequence of falling housing prices had somehow not devalued mortgage-backed securities, then some other factor, such as defaults on credit-card debt or even on commercial loans, would have been the trigger.

The reason that the 2008 financial crisis had its epoch-making consequences was that it was so severe and generalized that banks and other "named" financial institutions stopped being willing to lend freely to each other without collateral. As a result the flow of credit on which the real economy depends to finance production, including purchases of inputs and payment of wages to workers, largely ceased. In other historical episodes of financial stringency credit has become expensive and harder to qualify for, which has led to more or less severe downturns in business spending and more or less serious recessions. But generally the core interinstitutional lending at the heart of the system survived these episodes. In 2008 this core lending did not survive, and in fact it appears that many of the financial institutions will not survive. The damage to the financing of real production will be correspondingly more devastating and the business downturn longer-lasting.

When an equilibrium such as the practice of collateral-free lending among financial institutions breaks down, typically a new stable equilibrium emerges at a much lower level of lending and with much less efficient use of scarce capital funds. Efforts of policy makers to restore the "old" equilibrium face two formidable obstacles. First, key factors, such as the rapid growth of the world economy that supported the old equilibrium, may no longer exist, so the old equilibrium itself may just have evaporated. Second, the low-level equilibrium of low borrowing and extremely tight credit availability may be stable, so that individual incentives of financial institutions tend to restore it, making policy ineffective or self-defeating.

In my view this is the reason the financial "bailout" policies pursued by both the Bush and Obama administrations are highly uncertain to work and risk incurring large amounts of federal debt, because money was transferred to private firms and managers without actually solving the underlying problem.

What is particularly disturbing about this sequence of events is that the crisis arose from the internal evolution of the institutions of finance and credit themselves, not from any external stress put on them by outside factors. As policy makers struggle with the wreckage of the private financial system, they must also consider what fundamental changes will be necessary to minimize future fragility of the system.

## 4. Global Stagnation

As John Maynard Keynes emphasized in his revolutionary work in the 1930s on macroeconomic stability, market-based capitalism faces another fundamental destabilizing externality because of the inherently monetary character of market transactions (Keynes, 1936). David Ricardo (1951) based his analysis of capitalist growth on the assumption that "money is a veil," that there is no motive to sell except to buy, and hence that Jean Baptiste Say's "law" that supply creates its own demand holds, except perhaps in the very short run. Under these assumptions all commodities are equally liquid, and the only constraint on household and firm spending is their long-run real resources. In this Ricardian world a temporary decline in incomes will have little impact on spending.

Keynes insisted by contrast that in real-world monetary economies many households and firms are "liquidity-constrained," that is, unable to finance spending beyond their immediate cash inflows by borrowing. In this more realistic world, spending itself has an important externality. Each household or firm that spends money not only accomplishes its own ends (consumption or production), but also relieves the liquidity constraint of other spending units. This is a potentially important externality for the market capitalist system. When liquidity constraints are pervasive, the total level of spending in the system (which Keynes called "effective demand") will tend to be too low, with the consequence of low or negative growth of output and incomes, and the emergence of widespread unemployment of labor and capital. Like the low-level financial equilibrium I described above, the resulting low-level spending equilibrium may be stable and difficult for policy to change.

In times of vigorous capitalist economic growth, and when the financial system is operating smoothly, the proportion of firms and households that are liquidity-constrained will be relatively small. The Federal Reserve can manage to balance the system at a high equilibrium in the face of external fluctuations by relatively small adjustments in the supply of money to the system. This is the regime, more or less, in which the US and world economies have been operating since the late 1970s. While this regime deviates in important ways from the Ricardo-Say assumptions, it is close enough that policy makers and economists can plausibly base their analyses on Ricardian principles. The Keynesian spending externality, however, is lurking below the surface of this "classical" world; the veil of money is potentially an entrapping web.

By an ironic turn of intellectual history, "mainstream" macroeconomics in the United States, and increasingly in other parts of the world eager to imitate the success of US economics, has little to say about financial instability or liquidity-constrained economies. Under the influence of the critique of Keynesian economics (which departed in important respects from the "economics of Keynes" himself) put forward by Robert Lucas and Thomas Sargent (see Sargent, 2008, for a summary) in the 1970s, the study of theories that rule out financial instability and liquidity constraints in their assumptions has come to dominate contemporary macroeconomic research and teaching. Furthermore, the tendency of economic journal editors and departments to exclude points of view at variance with current dominant fashion has prevented dissenting analyses from participating in the intellectual debate over macroeconomics or diluting the orthodox content of macroeconomic education. The result of these developments is that mainstream economists find themselves deprived of the concepts and intellectual resources necessary to diagnose and effectively address the current crisis. Their models tell them that the kind of disruption of market-directed economies we are observing can never happen, or will be reliably and rapidly reversed by spontaneous decentralized reactions to it. This kind of conventional economics offers us little improvement as a basis for macroeconomic policy over the "Treasury view" that hamstrung British and American policy in the 1930s (see Cooper and John, 1988; Diamond, 1982, for alternative mainstream views).

The globalization boom of the 1990s and 2000s led to the generation of enormous profit flows in some developing economies, particularly China, and in energy-exporting economies such as Russia, Saudi Arabia, and Iran. None of these economies, however, are thoroughly capitalist in their structure or behavior, and all of them came to depend more on a high level of world spending (effective demand) than on the generation of their own internal spending equilibrium through reinvestment of these profit incomes. This globalization had a distinctive and, as we now see, unstable pattern in terms of world spending. Global profits were generated from the exploitation of labor in China and other emerging economies, and were realized largely in high energy prices. Global effective demand depended, however, on the financial system borrowing these profits and re-lending them in developed countries, particularly the United States. But US industry during this period showed no great appetite for funds to finance domestic investment. Over time, the maintenance of adequate levels of global effective demand came to depend on the spending of middle- and lower-middle-income US households financed by one-shot increases in the availability of credit. Once again, with the benefit of post-crisis hindsight it is not hard to see that this arrangement was unsustainable.

One symptom of this underlying world imbalance in spending patterns was the increasing difficulty the Federal Reserve experienced in finding a sustainable monetary policy that met the needs both of the global economy and of the US economy. The Federal Reserve found itself manipulating interest rates in an increasingly extreme alternation of excessive ease (which promoted bubbles in stock and real-estate prices) and ineffectual restraint (in which it found its ability to influence long-term interest rates compromised by the enormous flows of funds in the global economy).

As in the case of the broken financial system, this sequence of events raises some troubling fundamental questions. The global effective demand imbalances, like financial fragility, arose as the systematic effects of the pattern of world economic development. If we are not to re-create the situation that led to the current disaster, either we must alter the patterns of world economic development in a more sustainable direction or we must alter the institutions that regulate global effective demand to be more balanced or responsive or, preferably, both.

It is worth reflecting that Keynes himself foresaw these problems. At the 1944 Bretton Woods meetings devoted to negotiating a world financial-economic framework for the post–World War II era, Keynes proposed the creation of a world central bank, which could flexibly supply liquidity to the world economy in the same way that national central banks such as the Federal Reserve can regulate the liquidity of national monetary systems. Keynes's proposal foundered on a political issue, which was the unwillingness of the United States to give up its financial sovereignty to an international central bank governed in some kind of "multipolar" fashion (see Ahamed, 2009, for one account). Are we any better positioned to resolve these issues today than we were 65 years ago?

The trouble is that the "flat-earth" globalization we have been pursuing over the last 25 years in the world economy rests primarily on investments to cut costs by moving productive activities to lower-wage regions of the world rather than increasing productivity. These cost-cutting investments can promise very large private returns, but it is doubtful that the social returns are commensurate. While the private investor who relocates production to reduce costs reaps the full increase in profitability, a side effect of this investment is the economic obsolescence of abandoned productive facilities and capacities in high-wage regions. Furthermore, the incentives to invest under flat-earth policies have not proved to be particularly strong; the "world savings glut" Ben Bernanke and others have identified is a sign that growth in real investment spending has tended to fall short of the enormous growth of profits that globalization has fostered. This structural imbalance induced the flood of capital into the US economy that overwhelmed its capacity to find profitable investment outlets, and this ultimately destabilized our financial system.

## 5. All the King's Horses and All the King's Men

So what is to be done? There are several dimensions to this question. What can we do to hasten recovery of the functioning of the world financial system? What can we do to limit the depth and duration of the world depression that is upon us? In a longer-term perspective, what can we do to fashion a global economic-financial system that is more robust and less vulnerable to catastrophic crisis? These questions are all interlinked, and connected to even larger ones, which we face, crisis or no, including the management of the relation between the world environment and the world economy, reducing the vast gulf in income between rich and poor nations, and adapting to an unprecedented age distribution of the world population as population stabilizes in total numbers.

From some perspectives financial disaster ought to be the easiest aspect of the crisis to deal with, because the financial system is at its heart a network of promises and expectations. Legal, legislative, and judicial processes can alter the framework of promise making, promise breaking, and promise enforcement without large real resource costs. The consequences of intervention in this system are large, but they have to do with the distribution of wealth, not with the creation or destruction of wealth. This is one reason to doubt the necessity for the financial bailout policies I discussed earlier. The classic method for addressing financial dislocation is reorganization through the Federal Deposit Insurance Corporation (or some extension of it devised for particular emergencies, such as the Resolution Trust Corporation, which was set up to deal with the savings and loan crisis). Rather than trying to keep insolvent institutions afloat through a constant infusion of government money, reorganizations preserve the assets of the institutions and recapitalize them by wiping out the interests of stockholders and risky bondholders altogether, rendering the institutions solvent and available to new management.

The framework I outlined earlier showed that the interaction of markets and externalities is helpful in thinking about these problems. For the sake of concreteness, suppose that in the pre-crisis period there are two equilibria in the financial markets: a "good" equilibrium in which the big financial institutions lend freely to each other and to firms and households, and a "bad" equilibrium in which lending is restricted to a much lower volume of fully collateralized transactions. Each of these equilibria is stable against small disturbances and tends to reassert itself but it is possible that a large disturbance will shift the system from the good equilibrium to the bad equilibrium, with dire results for the financial system itself and the real economy. A financial crisis takes the form of a disturbance of the good equilibrium. The first recourse of policy makers when faced with a financial crisis is to try to restore the good equilibrium or at least to prevent the disturbance from tipping the system to the bad equilibrium. Concretely this type of policy means ensuring the liquidity of the participants in the system by massive lending from the central bank, and the orderly liquidation of institutions that are revealed to be insolvent even under the assumptions of the good equilibrium. This kind of policy works when the good equilibrium remains attainable, and the system is disturbed from it by some kind of "external" shock, such as a big change in energy prices, or a war. But our present financial crisis seems to have developed out of the logic of the system itself, not as a reaction to an external shock. This suggests that the problem is not that the financial system has moved away from the good equilibrium but that the good equilibrium has disappeared due to the evolution of the behavior of the system. If this is indeed what has happened, as appears increasingly to be the case, traditional policy measures may be ineffectual and even counterproductive.

The problem is that, as it plunges toward the remaining bad equilibrium state, the whole system dooms a large proportion of the institutions that would have remained solvent anywhere near the good equilibrium. If the financial system is going to operate for some time near the bad equilibrium, some type of liquidation or bankruptcy or nationalization of these institutions is unavoidable. Money lent by the Fed or the Treasury to these institutions cannot be recovered, and continued attempts to keep them doing business hampers the adjustment of the system to the new environment. We are familiar with the recourses necessary in this type of situation from many past financial crises in individual countries and in sectors of the US financial system, such as the savings and loan debacle. Some government entity takes over the assets and liabilities of the failed institutions and manages them outside the normal processes of financial business, using judicial and administrative measures to allocate the remaining wealth to the claimants, and guaranteeing the claims of the most vulnerable creditors, such as depositors. Once this massive process of removal of the troubled promises of the past from the system has taken place, financial institutions seeking private profit can at least operate at the smaller scale of the bad equilibrium, which, though it is far from the high-flying performance of the pre-crisis era, at least does represent a viable, ongoing, and functioning financial process. This is the kernel of good sense in the much-vilified advice of Herbert Hoover's Secretary of the Treasury, Andrew Mellon, to "liquidate" labor, capital, and finance. The trick is to do this in a way that shortens the time to the restored functioning of the system and that minimizes the unnecessary damage the financial wreckage imposes on production and employment.

The great obstacle to the execution of such a policy is the power of the financial oligarchy, which prospered so mightily in material terms, even more mightily in political terms in the era of global liberalization (Ferguson and Johnson, 2009a, 2009b). This dominant class, to use Marxist terminology, has an enormous amount to lose and will predictably fight in every way it can to preserve its special privileges in the US and world political economy. The crisis creates a situation in which the interests of this financial super-elite are in direct conflict with the interests of the great majority of the population, including industrial capitalists, in hastening the recovery of employment and production. So far the financial elite have prevailed despite sharp political divisions over "bailout" measures, with the predictable effect of lengthening and worsening the real economic distress that afflicts the world economy.

As I have explained, the global Depression in output and employment that has disrupted so many people's lives and imposed so much real hardship and damage can also be seen as a collapse from a good to a bad equilibrium in world effective demand. The same logic applies: attempts to restore the pre-crisis equilibrium are futile if that equilibrium no longer exists as a viable option. There is good reason to think that this is the case, because the pre-crisis equilibrium of demand in the global economy depended so much on the expansion of the financial-credit system that is now in collapse. As I argued, the deeper vulnerability of this configuration of the world economy was the asymmetric role assigned to the United States as the regulator of global effective demand. Keynesian attempts to reflate US effective demand through deficit-financed fiscal measures are likely to have limited impact under the system of floating exchange rates, free capital movements, and "free" but subsidized trade the United States has so enthusiastically pushed on the rest of the world over the last 25 years. Even unimaginably large "stimulus" measures represent a very small part of the world gap in effective demand; much of whatever increased spending these measures induce will leak out to the rest of the world in imports, particularly because foreign central banks will not permit the devaluation of the dollar, which would be required to reinforce the stimulus measures domestically.

The philosophy of "flat-earth" globalization pursues the realization of a world division of labor in which every tiny piece of every productive process is outsourced or reallocated to the very lowest-cost producers. If we look at this process from the point of view of national or regional economies, its logical consequence is a high degree of specialization of each region in a small part of the spectrum of social production. Every economy depends on the whole world economy, and each is vulnerable, as we are experiencing now, to its disruptions. The study of complex systems of many kinds suggests that this pattern of economic development is not robust. This means that it is vulnerable to the catastrophic spread of small failures. The reasons for this lack of robustness are not hard to understand. Cost-minimizing allocation of global production leads to a situation in which there is only one supplier at each critical stage of production, and in which the failure of that one supplier to function for whatever reason, whether a natural or a human-created financial disaster, disrupts all the other links in the productive chain. Regional and national economies share this vulnerability due to the disappearance of redundancy and backup systems. A country whose connection to the rest of the world is for any reason interrupted finds itself unable to supply basic needs to its people.

Flat-earth globalization creates its own characteristic incentives for investment. The main driver of investment is the temptation to move productive activities in order to have the work performed at lower costs. A large part of the economics profession has promoted this pattern as "export-led growth," without questioning much where the demand for the resulting exports might come from. The social returns to globalizing investment may be quite low, when the effect is to destroy the usefulness of existing productive facilities and human skills in return for a small reduction in private costs of production. To revive global and US aggregate demand I believe that the incentives for investment, both public and private, will have to be reoriented to more traditional patterns of diversification and the deepening of national and regional economies. Until the credibility and long-run profitability of such investment is established, it is unlikely that attempts to reflate global effective demand by one or another form of credit expansion (including government borrowing to finance deficit spending) will foster a sustained world economic expansion.

Such a change in the orientation of global investment implies some fundamental changes in world financial and economic policies and institutions. The fostering of a system of prosperous, robust, diversified national and regional economies will require a return to a system of fixed exchange rates in order to limit the disruptive effect of financial stabilization on individual economies and on the profitability of investment. Stabilizing exchange rates in turn will require at least the occasional use of direct controls on short-term capital movements (as is envisioned in the International Monetary Fund charter). Carrying out coherent regional development planning implies government control over key prices, including interest rates, exchange rates, energy prices, and wages and profits through income policies, and in some cases even direct intervention in trade through the imposition of tariffs.

Economists have elaborated the ways in which these policies impose "real social costs," and in the static, idealized world of traditional economic modeling there is little rationale for these measures. Enthusiasm for flat-earth globalization has been driven by the chimerical hope that maximizing absolute economic efficiency will somehow provide the resources to deal with global poverty. As we have seen, the reality is that globalization reproduces the global divide between rich and poor, even as it maximizes indices of economic efficiency, such as profit rates and gross products. We also now are learning the hard way that the single-minded pursuit of economic efficiency imposes higher and higher degrees of economic insecurity. (At the purely financial level this trade-off appears as the choice between risk and return.) To achieve more economic security, for example, by creating a world system of robust, redundant, and diversified regional economies, we are going to have to give up some theoretical economic efficiency.

Human beings notoriously do not like change, and they rarely, if ever, change fundamental institutions just because a better idea comes along. Change when it comes tends more often to succeed because the old ways of doing things simply do not work anymore. If this crisis provides an opportunity to restructure the global economy and address some of its real and serious problems, including climate change, energy availability, and inequality, it will be because we come to realize that recovery is possible only through a change of institutions. We today are responsible to future generations: we must think through what kind of social and economic world we want them to inherit.

## Acknowledgments

This chapter originated as the Gildersleeve Lecture at Barnard College, April 17, 2009. I'd like to thank Barnard College, the Gildersleeve Fund, the Barnard Economics Department, and David Weiman for inviting me as Gildersleeve Lecturer. This version of the lecture has been edited only for style, not for substance, so that the reader can see my views on the crisis at that time without revision with the benefit of hindsight

## Note

1. In setting up the problem this way, we are implicitly assuming that the representative agent is a "free rider" because she ignores the impact of her own decision on the social average. This assumption is often defended on the ground that when the number of agents in the system is very large, the impact of any one agent's decision on the outcome is negligible.

## References

Ahamed, L. (2009). *Lords of finance: the bankers who broke the world.* New York: Penguin.

Bowles, S. (2004). *Microeconomics: Behavior, Institutions, and Evolution.* Princeton, NJ: Princeton University Press.

Cooper, R., and John, A. (1988). "Coordinating Coordination Failures in Keynesian Models." *Quarterly Journal of Economics* 103(3): 441–463.

Diamond, P. A. (1982). "Aggregate Demand Management in Search Equilibrium." *Journal of Political Economy* 90(5): 881–894.

Duménil, G., and Lévy, D. (2004). *Capital Resurgent.* Cambridge, MA: Harvard University Press.

Duménil, G., and Lévy, D. (2011). *The Crisis of Neoliberalism.* Cambridge, MA: Harvard University Press.

Ferguson, T., and Johnson, R. (2009a). "Too Big to Bail: The 'Paulson Put,' Presidential Politics, and the Global Financial Meltdown." *International Journal of Political Economy* 38(1): 3–34.

Ferguson, T., and Johnson, R. (2009b). "Too Big to Bail: The 'Paulson Put,' Presidential Politics, and the Global Financial Meltdown." *International Journal of Political Economy*, 38(2): 5–45.

Foley, D. K. (2001). "Hyman Minsky and the Dilemmas of Contemporary Economic Method." In R. Bellofiore and P. Ferri, eds., *Financial Fragility and Investment in the Capitalist Economy: The Economic Legacy of Hyman Minsky*, vol. I. Cheltenham, England: Edward Elgar.

Foley, D. K. (2003). "Financial Fragility in Developing Economies." In A. Dutt and J. Ros, eds., *Development Economics and Structuralist Macroeconomics: Essays in Honor of Lance Taylor.* Aldershot, England: Edward Elgar.

Foley, D. K. (2006). *Adam's Fallacy: A Guide to Economic Theology.* Cambridge, MA: Harvard University Press.

Keynes, J. M. (1936). *The General Theory of Employment, Interest, and Money.* London: Macmillan.

Kindleberger, C. P. (1989). *Manias, Panics, and Crashes: A History of Financial Crises.* New York: Basic Books.

Marx, K. (1976). *Capital.* Vol. 1. New York: Penguin [1867].

Minsky, H. P. (1982). Can "*It*" Happen Again? Essays on Instability and Finance." Armonk, NY: M. E. Sharpe

Ricardo, D. (1951). *On the Principles of Political Economy and Taxation.* Cambridge, UK: Cambridge University Press [1817].

Sargent, T. J. (2008). "Evolution and Intelligent Design." *American Economic Review* 98(1): 3–37.

Smith, A. (1937). *An Inquiry into the Nature and Causes of the Wealth of Nations.* New York: Random House [1776].

Zeeman, E. C. (1977). *Catastrophe Theory: Selected Papers, 1972–1977.* Reading, MA: Addison-Wesley.

PART III

# THE GLOBAL DIMENSIONS OF FINANCIAL CRISES

CHAPTER 11

# THE ECONOMIC AND FINANCIAL CRISIS OF 2008–2010

## THE INTERNATIONAL DIMENSION

AJIT SINGH

## 1. Introduction

My remit in this chapter is to examine specifically the international dimensions of the current economic and financial crisis in order to help understand its dynamics. This crisis has been truly international and has affected countries around the globe. It might have started as a relatively minor disturbance in the US property and financial markets (the bursting of the subprime mortgage bubble), but it soon spread to most countries, rich as well as poor. One purpose of this chapter is to analyze this process of the globalization of the crisis, which, as will be explained below, is closely linked to financial globalization. These matters will be taken up in section 2.

Although it is too soon after the event for there to be a consensus among economists concerning the causes of the crisis, a widely held theory is that the crisis was caused mainly by growing financial imbalances between nation-states in the world economy. This, as we shall see, is not a view held by all economists.

There is a sizeable body of opinion, which does not regard the financial imbalances to have been the primary cause of the crisis. These scholars suggest that the crisis was not accompanied by other relevant events such as volatile movements in major currencies or interruption in the use of the reserve currency, namely the US dollar. Financial imbalances are therefore unlikely to be a major source of the crisis, and so the argument goes. This debate will be reviewed in section 3.

A further important question raised by the current crisis is why the world slump of 2008–2010 has been so mild compared to the apocalyptic scenarios set out by the vast majority of mainstream economists in the wake of the fall of Lehman Brothers in September 2008. These forecasts often suggested that the current US economic downturn might be of a similar order of magnitude to that which afflicted that country's economy in the 1930s. Although in 2009 the meltdown of the financial system was prevented at a huge expense by governments around the world, the real economy did not suffer an overall decline comparable to the 1930s Depression. These issues will be discussed in section 4 together with the role of the international factors in the economic outcomes in the two crisis periods (the current downturn and the 1930s). Sections 5 and 6 will report on simulations based on a UN world econometric model about different scenarios concerning the world economy. This discussion will further emphasize the role of international factors in determining the likely course of the current crisis and what will be the optimal policy framework for ensuring fast and sustainable growth of the world economy in different countries and regions.

Not surprisingly, there exists by now a large literature on the 2008–2010 crisis and its causes and its policy implications among other aspects. This chapter contributes by departing from existing literature in the following ways. First, I consider all issues squarely from the perspective of emerging countries; my main objective is to analyze the options for these countries faced with the current global crisis and the implied slowdown in world trade and growth. Second, I depart from both mainstream as well as many heterodox economists by suggesting that the pre-crisis financial system had some tangible merits, which should not be overlooked in the reform process. A balanced picture of the entire financial system is important if correct policy conclusions are to be drawn from it. Third, taking India and China as models of developing countries and the United States as the representative of industrial countries, I ask how changes in the pattern and speed of growth in the two most populous developing countries in the world would affect economic variables in the United States and other countries. This question is asked both in the context of long-term evolution of the world economy as well as in terms of the experience during the current downturn. The main purpose of these investigations is to see whether fast growth in India and China as desired by the governments of those countries is compatible with the objective of full employment growth in the United States. This analysis, although necessarily brief, will hopefully shed light on the nature of the possible north/south conflict.

An important result of this analysis and simulations is that even if China and India were to abandon their policies of export-led growth (which is more applicable to China than to India in any case) and shift toward internal income distribution and domestic demand-oriented policy, this would not be sufficient to correct global imbalances in either developed or developing countries.[1] The world economy is so complex and already so integrated that a much deeper role of the government is required to coordinate policy in the management of income distribution as well as to reduce instability of exchange rates and commodity markets. Far greater cooperation between nation-states, rich as well as poor countries, is necessary in order for them to achieve their full productive potential and sustainable growth, reduce poverty, and increase the living standards of the people. Without such a high degree of cooperation there is a danger that the world economy may plunge into a cascade of sovereign debt defaults, double-dip economic downturns, and, worse still, a prolonged recession or a fully fledged depression. I will argue that what is required today is developmental globalization rather than free-market globalization. These issues will be taken up in sections 5 and 6.

## 2. Sub-prime Mortgages and the Crisis of the Global Economy

Although there are still a few economists who do not regard the subprime mortgages and the associated economic events in the United States as the trigger for the current US crisis as well as downturn of the world economy, this view is not widely shared. Most scholars accept these problems as the proximate cause of the crisis. Baker (2010), however, argues that subprime mortgages played only a minor role in causing the crisis. For other views, consisting of both the mainstream and heterodox contributions on the crisis see the following: Aiginger (2009), Arestis and Singh (2010), *Cambridge Journal of Economics* (2009 and 2010), IMF (2008a, 2008b, 2009a, 2009b, 2009c, 2010a, 2010b), Krugman (2008, 2010), Ormerod (2010), Solow (2009), UNCTAD (2008, 2009, 2010), UNDESA (2008, 2009, 2010), and the US Council of Economic Advisers (2010).

Complex financial instruments that incorporated subprime house mortgages lost their value as the housing bubble burst following ten years of continuous price rises based on expectations of a continuation of such increases. This housing bubble occurred despite the fact that during the previous two decades the supply of housing had increased appreciably (Solow, 2009). In brief, house prices had risen because interest rates were low and credit was easily available, and prices were expected to continue to increase, much as in the case of the classic tulip mania and bubble in the early seventeenth century when, at its peak, the price of a tulip bulb in Holland was equivalent to that of a three-story townhouse.

There is, however, an apparent puzzle here. It was not the first time in US economic history that there had been a bursting of the housing bubble. This did not invariably lead to a depression in the US economy, let alone in the whole world. Moreover, the initial losses from the subprime bubble were relatively small, about $250 billion (Blanchard, 2009). He also estimated that within a year the decrease in world stock-market capitalization amounted to more than $2.5 trillion, a figure that was a hundred times larger. The consequential reductions in world GDP during the period of 2008 to 2015 were estimated by Blanchard to be of the order of $5 trillion. Robert Solow (2009) noted that the combined result of the housing and the stock-market shocks was a fall in US household wealth from US$64.4 trillion in mid-2007 (before the crisis) to US$51.5 trillion at the end of 2008. Thus $13 trillion of household wealth disappeared in the space of about one year. Solow rightly observed that nothing very much had changed; people had not lost their skills, and the machines were still working and were capable of producing the same goods and services. However, the public had 20 percent less wealth at the end of 2008 than they had 12 months earlier.

Equally interesting is the spread of the economic and financial decline from the United States to the rest of the world. This was entirely due to "financial globalization" in the previous two decades when the world's financial markets began to integrate as a result of liberalization of regulations[2] on the operations of the financial institutions. The following facts are revealing:

1) The McKinsey Global Institute data indicate that the ratio of global financial assets to annual world output increased from 109 percent in 1980 to 316 percent in 2005. This increase in financial depth has been particularly marked in rich countries: in the eurozone the ratio of financial assets to gross domestic product grew from 180 percent in 1995 to 303 percent in 2005. In the same period this variable rose from 278 percent to 359 percent, in the United Kingdom, and from 303 percent to 403 percent, in the United States.
2) Wolf (2007) also notes that the nature of financing has changed. In 1980 bank deposits made up 42 percent of all financial securities. By 2005 this had fallen to 27 percent.
3) The capital markets increasingly perform the intermediation functions of the banking system.
4) There has been widespread financial innovation, which has brought to the market derivatives, options futures, and swaps, among other devices.
5) As a consequence of financial globalization the interconnectedness between banks and other financial institutions in different countries greatly increased. At an early stage, observers noted, for example, the

> surprisingly large exposure of regional German banks to US subprime loans. More rigorous data bearing on this point are provided by the IMF: foreign claims by banks from five major advanced countries rose from \$6.3 trillion in 2000 to \$22 trillion in June 2008.

The financial globalization above is not an accident but a project backed by financial interests, banks, insurance companies, the stock markets in the US and in other advanced countries. One of the major triumphs of globalization was the repeal in 1999 of the US Glass-Steagall Act, which had limited the size and scope of financial institutions.

It was not just the financial lobbies' pressure that led to liberalization of global finance. There was strong ideological conviction at the highest levels of US government that financial innovation is good for the economy and the best way to promote it is to regulate it lightly, if at all. This was the view strongly held by Alan Greenspan and leading Wall Street executives. In a speech, Greenspan (2005) outlined how innovation had brought about a multitude of new products, speaking approvingly of how such "improvements" had led to a rapid growth in subprime mortgage lending.

The *New York Times*, reporting on Greenspan's evidence before a 2008 US Congressional Committee, wrote, "Mr. Greenspan conceded error on regulation, stating that he had 'put too much faith' in the self-correcting powers of free markets... refused to accept blame for the crisis but acknowledged that his belief in deregulation had been shaken" (Andrews 2008). In testifying before the 2010 US Congress Financial Crisis Inquiry Committee (established to investigate the subprime mortgage crisis), Greenspan defended himself against the dual charge that he was responsible for (a) the housing bubble due to his low interest-rate policy and for (b) not puncturing the bubble before it reached a level that would cause serious systemic difficulties. Greenspan suggested that his critics had short memories as many of them had earlier applauded subprime mortgages as being of tremendous benefit to low-income Americans. Furthermore, he suggested that at the time many people would have questioned whether there was indeed a housing bubble and asked how, in any case, the Federal Reserve would know the answer to this question better than the market. He also told the committee that regulators were helpless to stop the economic meltdown and the subprime mortgage crisis (Greenspan, 2010).

The net result of this mind-set was the evolution of a largely unregulated parallel banking system performing the functions of banks but without being subject to banking regulations (Krugman, 2008).

Robust responses to Greenspan's arguments have been made by James Galbraith (2010), Paul Krugman (2010), and Robert Solow (2009), among others. They suggest that the securitization of subprime mortgages through their marketing as a combined financial product was little understood by the market. This, together with complex credit default swaps, as well as several other financial innovations, should be regarded as a fraudulent practice that should have been tightly regulated. Krugman (2010) suggests that, had the wide-ranging reforms currently under discussion in the US Congress been in place earlier, "a handful of lavishly-paid leaders of the financial industry would not have been able to mislead and exploit consumers and investors."

How the crisis arose is now well understood, and the process is succinctly summarized by Blanchard. He describes how the initial conditions on the eve of the crisis transformed the relatively small subprime mortgage losses from the fall in housing prices in the United States into much bigger losses through the fall in share prices on the US stock market. Moreover, because of financial interconnectedness between countries these losses were further increased by declining share prices all over the world. Blanchard (2008, 2009) argues that, for this sequence of events to occur, it was necessary to have four initial conditions with respect to the rules of the game and two amplifying factors as outlined below.

1) Assets were created, sold, and bought, which appeared much less risky than they truly were. Blanchard offers a Minskyan explanation for this condition to prevail. He writes that "history teaches that benign economic environments often lead to credit booms and to the creation of marginal assets and the issuance of marginal loans."
2) Securitization led to complex and hard-to-value assets on the balance sheets of financial institutions. It was supposed to lead to more efficient allocation of risk and thereby reduced risk overall. In practice, however, the opposite happened. Blanchard admits that he himself believed that the US economy would withstand a fall in house prices better than most—the shock will be absorbed by a larger set of investors because of securitization. However, because of the complexity and opacity of the process this expectation was not fulfilled.
3) Securitization was also supposed to spread risk between countries and thereby lead to a safer environment overall. Again the opposite happened in practice. This is a phenomenon that is difficult to comprehend within the orthodox framework of analysis. Why should increasing the number of countries increase risk, and not lower it? This paradox, which is empirically much observed in practice, has recently been analyzed by Stiglitz (2010) in a pathbreaking contribution. He argues that, in some circumstances, adding countries to the existing international financial system may make it unsafe for everybody just as adding a bad egg in a basket endangers all the other eggs. A simple economic example would probably be one where a country with higher leverage joins up with countries with lower leverage to reduce the risk of default. However, depending on particular conditions it is possible to suggest that the high-leverage country may increase the risk of default for all countries in the group. Stiglitz (2010) presents a rigorous theoretical analysis of this issue.

4) Leverage increased within the financial system. Blanchard notes that financial institutions finance their portfolios with less and less capital, thus increasing the rate of return on capital. Because of globalization and liberalization, the world economy was subject to much more intense competition than before, in product markets, in capital markets, in the markets for managers, in fact in most markets. This compelled fund managers to seek the highest returns in whatever way they could. The banks were assisted by the authorities who made several regulatory concessions. As indicated by Blanchard, banks, for instance, were allowed to reduce their capital requirements by moving assets off their balance sheets. In 2006 the value of the off-balance assets of Citigroup were $2.1 trillion compared with a value of assets on the balance sheet of $1.8 trillion. The all-around increase in leverage in the economy made the institutions and individuals much more subject to the danger of insolvency.

To sum up, the above analysis indicates how the international dimension (specifically financial globalization) produced a vicious cycle of circular and cumulative causation, leading to the worldwide spread of the contagion from the failure of the market in the subprime mortgages in the United States.

## 3. Comparative Economic Performance: The Current Crisis and the Great Depression

Having noted one of the important ways in which the international dimension has harmed the US as well as the world economy, it may be useful at this stage to bring in the positive side of international dimension associated with the present crisis. It is illustrated here in this section by exploring the analytical issue of why the economies of the United States and the world performed apparently so much better than they did during the Great Depression of the 1930s. It will be recalled that in September 2008, following the demise of Lehman Brothers, a Wall Street icon, many leading commentators both from the academic world and the media argued that the current crisis is likely to be as bad as that of the 1930s. In contrast the economy in the recent period has shown remarkable resilience and there has been an apparent v-shaped recovery: a short downturn followed by a quick economic upturn. This is not to deny that the current recovery is lopsided in which the emerging countries are on the whole doing well, while the industrial countries are doing not so well. The economic performance of developing countries has been vigorous and has continued at much the same trend as before while that of advanced countries has been rather tepid and these nations could easily slip back into a double-dip recession.

Nevertheless, the present downturn compares very favorably with the economic situation in the 1930s. Despite the uncertain nature of the present recovery, the record is reasonably clear. The reasons for such diverse outcomes in the two periods are interesting to analyze because these embody a distinct international dimension. The following facts make this point clear.[3] In the current downturn, falls in GDP in the US, Europe and world economies have been of a much lower order than during the Depression years. Although the numbers of unemployed, underemployed, and discouraged workers have increased during the current crisis, the rise has been far less than during the 1930s Depression.[4]

In 2009, for the first time in 50 years, world GDP shrank, but it was only by 2 percent, and had returned to positive growth in 2010 (UNDESA, 2010). Whether or not this growth is sustained and leads to resumption of the pre-crisis growth path is as yet an open question. It will depend on a number of factors, including the debt and solvency crises in Greece, Spain, and Ireland.

Although the decline in GDP for individual advanced countries has been greater than that for the world as a whole, none of these have reached the proportions of the 1930s Depression. The maximum reduction in GDP growth in 2009 in advanced countries has ranged between 2 percent and 6 percent. Furthermore, IMF data and projections indicate that most countries will have positive growth by 2010.

The comparison with the performance during the Great Depression could not be more striking. The largest fall in US GDP in a 12-month period during the Depression was of the order of 30 percent. In the same 12-month period employment fell by 25 percent.

These comparative data raise the prior question of whether the relatively good performance of the US and world economies in the current period is better than that for the 1920s and 1930s due to the fact that the shocks to the economy in the earlier period were much more severe. Many students of the subject argue that the shocks that hit the US economy in the autumn of 2008 were at least as large as those experienced in 1929. A salient shock in both crises was the fall in household wealth: this fell by 17 percent between December 2007 and December 2008 in the United States. This was more than five times the decrease in 1929.

An important negative feature of the current crisis compared with that of the 1930s is the role and nature of banks and the collapse of interbank relations and that of trade credit for big and small businesses. Banks have refused to lend to other banks or to nonbank financial institutions. Similarly, asset-price volatility in the United States has been greater in the current crisis than in the past. A great deal of research indicates that such volatility has an adverse effect on the level of investment.

What explains the seeming ability of the world economy in the current period to avert a depression as serious as that of the 1930s? Evidence and analysis suggest three main reasons. The first is the outstanding record of India, China, and other emerging countries both before and during the crisis. As Wolf (2008) suggests, "Emerging economies had been an engine of growth for the past five years. China accounted for a quarter, Brazil, Russia, and India for another quarter, and all emerging and developing countries together for about two thirds. World growth is measured here in PPP exchange rates." Despite the crisis these countries, particularly India and China, have been able to continue on their fast long-term growth path. They may therefore be expected to remain as long-term positive factors in the evolution of the world economy: fast growth in these countries helps the United States and other countries by maintaining high levels of world demand.

The second major factor explaining the relatively good performance of the world economy during the present downturn has been the unexpected and welcome degree of cooperation between countries, symbolized by their adoption of coordinated global measures through the creation of the G20. This grouping includes all leading advanced countries and a number of emerging nations that together constitute about 85 percent of world production and about two-thirds of the world population. In 2009 the G20 agreed to a huge international stimulus even when many of them already had fiscal deficits. It was also agreed to cut interest rates and to strengthen the IMF and World Bank in order to help developing countries. This high degree of cooperation stands in striking contrast to the lack of cooperation and beggar-thy-neighbor policies that characterized nation-states' behavior in the 1930s.[5] (See further Felix, 2002; Nurkse, 1944; and Maddison, 1985).

As mentioned above, a striking feature of the response to the current crisis has been an aggregate coordinated fiscal stimulus amounting in 2008–2009 to an enormous US$2.6 trillion, equivalent to 3.4 percent of world GDP.[6] As a proportion of their GDP, developing countries in general have had a greater stimulus than developed countries.

There is evidence that the stimulus has been successful in the sense that, in general, the greater the stimulus received, the greater was the countries' economic growth (US Council of Economic Advisers, 2010). Nevertheless, alongside this positive effect of the stimulus, the stimulus created fiscal difficulties for governments, leading to calls for the stimulus to be withdrawn or diminished in size. This would, however, be a serious mistake as a premature withdrawal of the stimulus when the world economy has not yet achieved reasonable economic growth (let alone reverted to its long-term growth rate) may push economies further into recession or even into full-scale depression if there are negative effects on expectations. It is, therefore, all the more important that the cooperation achieved so far in the G20 arrangement should continue so that there is a coordinated and well-organized withdrawal of the fiscal stimulus at the appropriate time. The US experience between 1937 and 1940 (Romer, 2009) and that of Japan more recently should be a warning to present-day policy makers in this respect.

The third positive factor that has also helped improve the performance of world economy in relation to the present crisis can be described as an issue of governance. It so happened that economic leadership in the United States in this period of crisis was held by an intellectually and politically close group of economists. These were conventional US Keynesian economists who defined the essential problem facing the world economy as being that of a shortage of aggregate demand. Unlike the Chicago economists, they also believed that government-induced stimuli could correct the demand deficits and thereby could help the real economy. The cohesive economic outlook of this team of economic advisors helped ensure clarity of purpose in the stimulus program and its implementation.

Not only were these economists well versed in economic theory, but also, equally importantly, some of them, including Ben Bernanke (the chairman of the Federal Reserve) and Christina Romer (the chairwoman of the US Council of Economic Advisers), were serious students of the history of the Great Depression and were determined not to repeat the serious policy mistakes made during that period.

To sum up, three factors—namely continuing fast growth in India, China, and other developing countries; unprecedented cooperation between countries symbolized by the G20; and governance by like-minded people of a corrective economic policy program—have made positive differences in the recent evolution of the world economy. Hopefully, these factors will continue to operate in this direction, even if certain other developments present obstacles to widespread resumption of reasonable growth rates.

## 4. Global Financial Imbalances

Having seen in the previous two sections how under different circumstances the international dimension has both harmed and helped the US and the world economies, we now come to the pivotal role of these and certain other international factors in determining the course that the world economy has taken in recent years and one it may take in the foreseeable future. The main reason for the prominence of international interactions in such analyses is financial globalization so, unless the latter is reversed, as happened in the 1930s, international factors will continue to be at the heart of the economic processes at work in the world and national economies. This is particularly true of the so-called international financial imbalances, which, as we have seen, have characterized the world economy in the recent period. These have further interacted with certain national imbalances, leading to adverse outcomes in some countries and regions and good outcomes in others. The rest of this section focuses on the nature and significance of international financial imbalances. The following section will take up the questions of international and interregional differential performances.

Even those who do not see the international financial imbalances as a prime cause of the 2008–2010 economic crisis would concede that these do lead to fragility in the world economy, which in turn could degenerate into the crisis of the kind we have recently experienced. Keynes (1980) was extremely concerned about the processes of the adjustment of balance of payments between nation-states:

> The problem of maintaining equilibrium in the balance of payments between countries has never been solved...the failure to solve this problem has been a major cause of impoverishment and social discontent and even wars and revolutions...to suppose that there exists some smoothly functioning automatic mechanism of adjustment which preserves equilibrium if only we trust to matters of *laissez faire* is a doctrinaire delusion which disregards the lessons of historical experience without having behind it the support of sound theory. (Keynes, 1980, 21–22)

Keynes's 1941 plan of an international clearing union was designed to overcome the problem of global imbalances of that time. Ironically, the United States was the offending country then. It thwarted the adjustment of payment balances by a tendency to accumulate gold reserves, which imposed deflation on the rest of the world (Skidelsky, 2011). Keynes further cautioned about the asymmetries of adjustment between creditor and debtor countries. He noted in 1941 that

> the process of adjustment is compulsory for the debtor and voluntary for the creditor. If the creditor does not choose to make, or allow, his share of the adjustment, he suffers no inconveniences. For a whilst a country's reserve cannot fall below zero, there is no ceiling which sets an upper limit. The same is true if international loans are to be the means of adjustment. The debtor must borrow; the creditor is under no...compulsion [to lend]. (Keynes, 1980, 28)

In the present context, Skidelsky argues that the increased desire to save by the Chinese has subjected the US economy to deflation, which in turn was offset by the Chinese purchase of US Treasury Bills, which enabled the Federal Reserve to keep US interest rates low. This did not, however, lead to higher investment levels in the United States but rather to a consumption-led boom that ultimately led to the crises as outlined earlier.

Mayer (2010) notes that, in examining international financial imbalances, most economists use the following accounting identities:

$$CA = X - M + NFI = S^N - I = \Delta NFA,$$

where $CA$ is the current-account balance, $X$ and $M$ are exports and imports of goods and services, $NFI$ is the balance on income (net foreign incomes from abroad), $S^N$ is national saving, $I$ is national investment, and $\Delta NFA$ are changes in net foreign assets.

Different writers stress different parts of these identities, with some concentrating on the balance of payments and on savings and investment, while others emphasize the trade balance and capital flows. However, here I follow an analysis of the global economy and global imbalances set out in two recent papers: Cripps, Izurieta, and Singh (2011), and Izurieta and Singh (2010). These papers examined the global imbalances in more rigorous terms with the help of the UN global econometric model.

The three authors use a stock-flow methodology, different to that of conventional analysis, by allowing for holding gains and losses due to changes in the price level and in share prices to be taken into account. The key equation in the analysis is that of the net acquisition of financial assets, which in their model is the outcome of three factors:

$$NA_{j_t} = \left(Y_{j_t} - Y^e_{j_t}\right) + \rho_j.\left(W^*_{j_t} - K^e_{j_t} - A_{j_{t-1}}\right)$$

where

1) unanticipated changes in income $Y - Y^e$

2) the gap between the wealth target $W^*$ and the expected value of real capital $K^e$

3) whether the wealth gap (ii) exceeds or falls short of the inherited financial position $A_{-1}$.

Cripps, Izurieta, and Singh (2011) use this logical framework outlined above to provide a comprehensive analysis of the world economy under different scenarios. Most of that discussion is beyond the scope of this chapter. However, what is most relevant for the current paper is that the results that the three authors obtained from the model simulations were because of some specific assumptions.

## 5. Empirical Results under Alternative Assumptions

Cripps, Izurieta, and Singh (2011) first considered a baseline scenario, which is predicated on the continuation of the current observed relationships between the relevant variables. This scenario essentially showed a slowdown in the growth of demand in the main developed countries but no decline in global financial imbalances. In addition the analysis suggested that the United States would become over time a very large debtor with net liabilities rising to 100 percent of GDP.

The second scenario has similar assumptions to that of the first, except that China and India would be constrained to have a growth rate of 8 percent each. This is accompanied by a change in the basic development strategy of the two countries

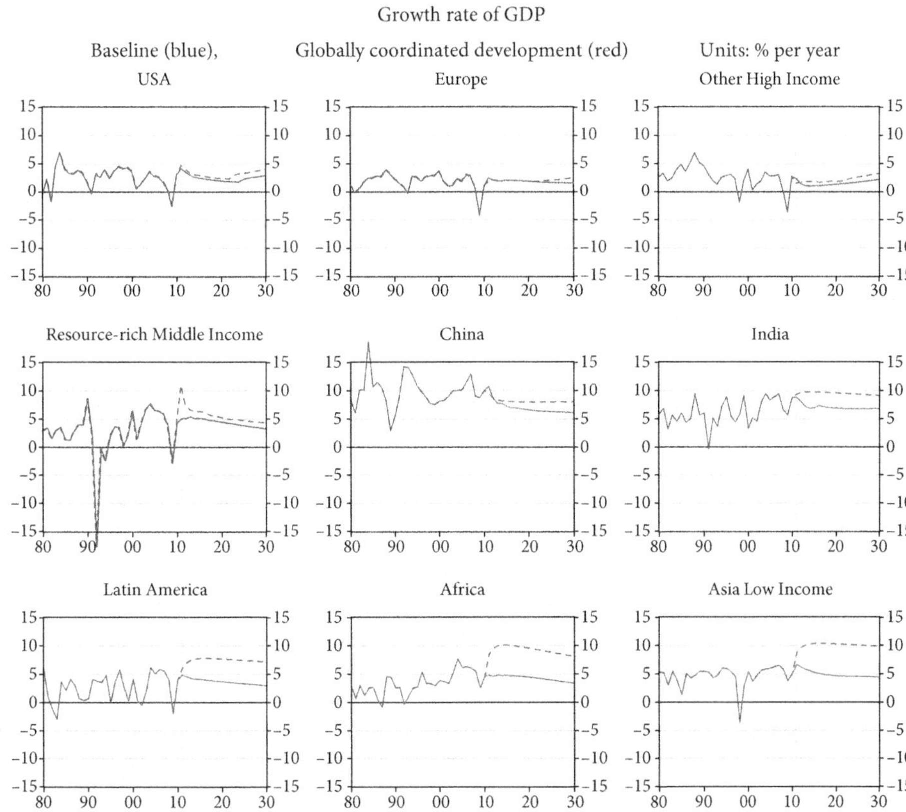


**Figure 11.1** Convergence of growth rates without sacrifices.
**Note:** The original diagram was created with blue and red graph lines. Seen in black and white print form, these are seen as a solid and dotted line, respectively.
*Source:* Cripps, Izurieta and Singh (2011).

from an export-led growth strategy (which was particularly true in the case of China) toward internal income redistribution and domestic demand-oriented strategies. However, the results indicate that this would not be sufficient to correct global imbalances or to induce faster growth in other developing regions.

A third scenario, the global development scenario, is defined by the three authors in terms of a combination of the following:

- Targets for government expenditure and public and private investments that supposedly facilitate a more equitable distribution of employment and income.
- Stable real exchange rates and greater efforts toward formation of regional trade areas in developing regions.
- Selective incentives and support for exports of commodities, manufactures, and services by countries that lack a sufficient export base.

- Cooperation in management of energy resources and markets to maintain incentives for producers and users of energy to invest in green technologies and reduce the long-run dependence on fossil fuels (27)

Cripps, Izurieta, and Singh's (2011) simulations on the UN global model indicate that the cooperative solution, with far-reaching detailed government interventions, does yield helpful results. As figure 11.1 shows, all groups of countries help to reduce global inequality without a reduction in growth rates in high-income countries. There is thus a high potential for raising the economic performance of poor countries to converge toward higher incomes of richer countries but this requires a degree of policy coordination that has not been achieved or even attempted in the past.

## 6. Conclusion

To sum up, in terms of economic policy, the international dimension in the form of international cooperation acquires new significance in relation not only to resolving the problem of financial imbalances but also to thinking about the future development of the world economy. This would require building new institutions to enhance international policy coordination and international cooperation in general. As Keynes has taught us, the world economy represents a highly complex phenomenon of which we understand very little. It is important to carefully study the reasons for the current crisis, where the fault lines lay and significantly whether there was anything positive to be said for the pre-crisis organization of the economy. The data indicate that, significantly, the real world economy did extremely well in the pre-crisis years 2000–2007. It achieved a faster rate of growth than ever before. Developing countries expanded at twice the rate of the developed countries. For the first time the number of people in absolute poverty declined to less than a billion.

The truth of the matter is that globalization helped some countries and not others. Among developing countries, India and China, the world's most populous and hitherto very poor countries were the stellar performers. The United States was the star performer in terms of GDP and productivity growth among the rich countries. Just as millions of people in the third world escaped absolute poverty, so were the subprime mortgages helpful in bringing housing to millions of poor Americans. Although the whole experiment ended in failure, leading to diverse international financial imbalances, the positive side should not be totally forgotten. What was achieved in the pre-crisis period was fast growth but at the expense of stability. It will be ironic if stability were now to eclipse growth altogether. The billion people in absolute poverty and the millions in rich countries facing high unemployment need a faster rate of growth of the world economy.

Although the growth path for the world economy for the period 2000–2007 was ultimately unsustainable, it is certainly arguable that it took the global economy a long way forward. This exercise certainly established that the world economic potential is much bigger than previously considered. To achieve that potential, international cooperation at a detailed level, in the sense outlined above, will be essential.

## Notes

1. These simulations are reported in two recent papers: Cripps, Izurieta, and Singh (2011), and Izurieta and Singh (2010). These results, to the extent that they are relevant to this chapter, are explained in the following sections.
2. The following facts are based on Wolf (2007).
3. This is documented in IMF (2010), UNCTAD (2010), and UNDESA (2010).
4. The only OECD country to reach the unemployment level experienced by the United States in the 1930s is Spain, with a current unemployment rate of 19 percent (Cripps, Izurieta, and Singh [2011]).
5. However, it can be argued that the G20 is far from an ideal vehicle for international cooperation because it excludes more than 150 countries. Nevertheless, some argue that a group bigger than the G20 may not be a practical device for agreeing and implementing decisive measures to cope with the crisis.
6. The source of these figures is UNDESA (2010, table 4, page 12).

## References


Aiginger, K. (2009). "The Current Economic Crisis: Causes, Cures and Consequences." WIFO Working Papers No. 431, August, Osterrreichisches Institut fur Wirtshaftschung.

Andrews, E. L. (2008). "Greenspan Concedes Error on Regulation." *New York Times*, October 23.

Arestis, P., and A. Singh. (2010). "Financial Globalisation and Crisis, Institutional Transformation and Equity." *Cambridge Journal of Economics* 34(2): 225–238.

Baker, D. (2010). *False Profits: Recovering from the Bubble Economy*. Sausalito, CA: Polipointpress.

Blanchard, O. (2008). *The Crisis: Basic Mechanisms and Appropriate Policies*. Munich: Center for Economic Studies.

Blanchard, O. (2009). "The Perfect Storm." *Finance & Development*, June.

Cambridge Journal of Economic (2009). Special Issue: The Global Financial Crisis, Volume 33 Issue 4, July, pp 531–869.

Cambridge Journal of Economics (2010). Special Focus: Globalisation, Institutional Transformation and Equity, Volume 34 Issue 2, March, pp 255–411.

Cripps, F., A. Izurieta, and A. Singh. (2011). "Global Imbalances, Under-consumption and Over-borrowing: The State of the World Economy and Future Policies." Development and Change, Volume 42 Issue 1, January, pp 228–261.

Felix, D. (2002). "The Economic Case against Free Mobility." In Leslie Elliott Armijo, ed., *Debating the Global Financial Architecture*. Albany: State University of New York Press.
Galbraith, J. (2010). "In Defense of Deficits." *The Nation*, March 4.
Greenspan, A. (2005). "Consumer Finance." Speech given at the Federal Reserve System's Fourth Annual Community Affairs Research Conference, April 8, Federal Reserve Board, Washington, DC.
Greenspan, A. (2010). Evidence given to the US Congress Financial Crisis Inquiry Committee (established to investigate the subprime mortgage crisis), Washington, DC.
IMF (International Monetary Fund). (2008a). *World Economic Outlook. Housing and the Business Cycle*. February. Washington, DC: IMF.
IMF (International Monetary Fund). (2008b). *World Economic Outlook—Financial Stress, Downturns and Recovery*. October 2008. Washington, DC: IMF.
IMF (International Monetary Fund). (2009a). *World Economic Outlook Update. Contractionary Forces Receding but Weak Recovery Ahead*. July 8. Washington, DC: IMF.
IMF (International Monetary Fund). (2009b). *World Economic Outlook—Crisis and Recovery*, April. Washington, DC: IMF.
IMF (International Monetary Fund). (2009c). *World Economic Outlook. Sustaining the Recovery*. October 15. Washington, DC: IMF.
IMF (International Monetary Fund). (2010a). *World Economic Outlook. A Policy-Driven, Multispeed Recovery*. January 26. Washington, DC: IMF.
IMF (International Monetary Fund). (2010b). *World Economic Outlook, Rebalancing Growth*. April 21. Washington, DC: IMF.
Izurieta, A., and A. Singh. (2010). "Does Fast Growth in India and China Help or Harm US Workers?" *Journal of Human Development and Capabilities* 11(1): 115–142.
Keynes, J. M. (1980). *The Collected Writings of John Maynard Keynes*. Vol. 25. Cambridge, England: Cambridge University Press.
Krugman, P. (2008). "The Big Meltdown." *New York Times*, March 2.
Krugman, P. (2010). "Goldman Sachs, Salaried Looters." *The Indian Express, Chandigarh*, April 24.
Maddison, A. (1985). *Two Crises: Latin America and Asia, 1929–1938 and 1973–1983*. Paris: OECB.
Mayer, J. (2010). "Global Rebalancing: Effects on Trade Flows and Employment." UNCTAD Discussion Paper No. 200, September.
Nurkse, R. (1944). *International Currency Experience: Lessons of the Interwar Period*. Princeton: League of Nations.
Ormerod, P. (2010). "The Current Crisis and the Culpability of Macroeconomic Theory." *21st Century Society, Journal of the Academy of Social Sciences* 5(1): 5–18.
Romer, C. (2009). "Back from the Brink." Address given on September 24 at the Federal Reserve Bank of Chicago, Illinois.
Skidelsky, R. (2011). "The Relevance of Keynes." *Cambridge Journal of Economics* 35: 1–13.
Solow, R. (2009). "How to Understand the Disaster." *New York Review of Books*, May 14.
Stiglitz, J. E. (2010). "Contagion, Liberalization and the Optimal Structure of Globalization." *Journal of Globalization and Development* 1(2): 1–45.
UNCTAD (United Nations Conference on Trade and Development). (2008). *Trade and Development Report*. Geneva: United Nations.
UNCTAD (United Nations Conference on Trade and Development). (2009). *Trade and Development Report*. Geneva: United Nations.

UNCTAD (United Nations Conference on Trade and Development). (2010). *Trade and Development Report*. Geneva: United Nations.

UNDESA (United Nations Department of Economic and Social Affairs). (2008). *Global Economic Outlook, May*. New York: United Nations.

UNDESA (United Nations Department of Economic and Social Affairs). (2009). Global Economic Outlook, May. New York: United Nations.

UNDESA (United Nations Department of Economic and Social Affairs). (2010). Global Economic Outlook, May. New York: United Nations.

US Council of Economic Advisers. (2010). *Annual Report of the Council of Economic Advisers*. Washington, DC: US Government Printing Office,.

Wolf, M. (2007). "Unfettered Finance Is Fast Reshaping the Global Economy." *Financial Times*, June 18.

Wolf, M. (2008). "The World Wakes from the Wish-dream of Decoupling." *Financial Times*, October 22.

# CHAPTER 12

# GLOBAL IMBALANCES AND THE INTERNATIONAL MONETARY SYSTEM

## PROBLEMS AND PROPOSALS

JANE D'ARISTA AND KORKUT ERTURK

THE US trade deficit rose steadily from the 1980s until the financial crisis in 2007 except for a brief dip during the recession that followed the dot-com stock-market collapse in 2001. But US trade deficits resumed their upward trend with the resumption of growth in 2003, helping to create a period of rapid economic expansion worldwide that pushed up asset prices and unprecedented increases in debt. In the United States, the debt of both the household and financial sectors rose to historically high levels—largely driven by rising home prices—and savings plummeted. When excessive debt slowed the ongoing rise in house prices, a financial crisis erupted as major international financial institutions could no longer fund inflated positions with collateral (mortgage-backed securities) that was fast eroding in value. The downward spiral that followed reached into the real economy, affecting aggregate demand through the loss of jobs, income, and wealth and, in the global economy, it brought about a collapse in trade greater than that experienced in the early years of the Great Depression.[1]

The rising US trade deficit prompted much discussion of the sustainability of global imbalances, focusing mainly on three questions: its causes, whether it should be a cause for concern, and what, if anything, should be done about it. In Eichengreen's (2006) memorable metaphor of the story of the blind men describing the elephant, the contributors to this debate often only recognized one aspect of a complex reality, all the while believing it to be the whole picture. The cause of the imbalances was attributed either to US residents saving too little or to foreigners, especially Asians, saving too much. Those who thought the low US savings rate was the culprit often blamed the government for its yawning budget deficits, though, over time, it was clear that personal savings had periodically fallen even more than public savings. Those who thought foreigners were saving too much based their arguments variously on demographic patterns, the Asian culture, policy exchange rates, and the excessive buildup of international reserves within China and other export-oriented countries.

There was not much agreement on whether global imbalances were or should be a source for concern. If markets always worked efficiently, as most economists accepted as an article of faith before the crisis, there had to be a rational explanation as to why imbalances were—if not a blessing in disguise—at least innocuous. It was assumed that capital was flowing into the United States from the rest of the world for a reason. Perhaps foreigners were taking advantage of the deep, highly liquid, and efficient US financial markets or investing in the future of the United States because of its superior productivity growth. Some even argued that the imbalances were an illusion created by poor accounting and resulting from the failure to capture the true value of the financial services the United States was "exporting" to the rest of the world. In the view of these optimists, little if anything had to be done.

The pessimists, on the other hand, doubted that the imbalances could be sustained for long, and they warned of an eventual hard landing if policies were not adopted to bring them into balance. Some feared that foreign demand for US financial assets would sooner or later fall short of the rapidly growing amount needed to finance the US current account deficit. Views differed about how immanent the danger might be. And while there was no clear idea about the shape or form a hard landing might take, a run on the dollar and prohibitively high US interest rates were invariably the opening acts in a list of undesirable scenarios. There was, however, broad agreement that sooner or later the United States would need to save more and foreigners less, with differing views on who should do more of the adjusting.

Unsurprisingly, the terms of the debate shifted over time. After the dot-com debacle, it became harder to argue that the US stock-market boom in the late 1990s reflected rapid productivity growth and thus rational expectations about a higher level of future income. It also became more difficult to argue that capital inflows into the United States reflected private-market decisions when purchases of US assets by foreign central banks became an increasingly important part of the net capital inflow into the United States. Still, denial that a housing bubble was underway in the early 2000s ended only after the bubble had burst.

The financial crisis raised similar problems because it was not triggered by a run on the dollar caused by a disorderly unraveling of global imbalances as pessimists had feared. Instead, it was caused by problems having to do with the collapse of confidence and the availability of funding within the financial sector itself. Nevertheless, the pessimists' basic understanding of global imbalances appears to have survived the crisis intact to become the conventional wisdom. In a nutshell, it amounts to a few basic propositions: (1) imbalances were the ultimate cause of the crisis; (2) they were the result of overspending—mainly in the United States—exacerbated by the undervalued currencies of East Asian surplus countries; (3) spending had to fall in deficit countries and rise in surplus countries, and (4) taking steps to enhance exchange-rate flexibility would help achieve that end.

While none of these arguments are new, one new emphasis has been on the importance of financial regulation. Before the crisis, overspending was blamed on mistakes of macroeconomic policy but, afterward, blame began to shift to the failure of financial regulation to detect and prevent the excessive credit growth that led to overspending and the fall in household savings. Following the passing of legislation that dealt with at least some of the regulatory problems, the US policy focus appears to have shifted to more flexible exchange rates and placing limits on current account surpluses and deficits relative to GDP. In the meantime, surplus countries continued to blame global imbalances on the profligacy of deficit countries.

The difficulty of having the eradication of global imbalances as the main policy objective is that it would require cutting spending in the United States and other deficit countries when they were in a deep slump. Recognizing how counterproductive this would be, many policy prescriptions make short-run/long-run distinctions: revive growth with additional spending in the short run but cut back when growth is restored in the long run. But there is no assurance that this will address the problem of anemic recovery. For example, global imbalances were drastically reduced with the steep contraction in world trade at the beginning of the crisis and they began to widen again with the revival of trade. Does it follow, then, that the world was closer to a solution to its structural ills at the bottom of its slump than it is today? It is unclear what appropriate policy guidance the prevailing conventional wisdom offers for a robust global recovery today.

It is possible to argue that the conventional view fails at a deeper level also. Such a view assumes a world that no longer exists. It implicitly presupposes an *inter*national economy consisting of distinct national economies with their own separate systems of financial intermediation that are tied to each other mainly through trade—a world where financial assets are traded to move goods, where central banks are in control of credit growth within their borders, and where current account transactions are the main determining factor in moving capital flows and exchange rates. Such a view is inconsistent with the increasingly *trans*national world that has come into being as a result of the rapid acceleration of financial globalization over the last two decades. The expansion of cross-border financial transactions, already beginning to outstrip the expansion of trade in goods as early as the 1970s, has increased at a spectacular pace since the 1990s and has spread—though faster in some groups of countries than others—worldwide. In this new world, it is misleading to assume that trade in assets is still the same as trade in goods. The notion of a unified and globally integrated process of financial intermediation today is far from an empty supposition.

It might thus be more sensible to look at global imbalances from the capital account side—a perspective that gives a very different understanding of the nature of the problem. Think of Ben Bernanke's "savings glut" thesis—and ignore for a second his Pollyanna-ish use of it. His thesis basically says that the US credit boom that led to overconsumption and ballooning trade deficits was caused by capital flowing into the United States from the rest of the world through its capital account. In other words, it was ultimately the capital inflow that fueled the credit expansion and brought long-term interest rates down, making it possible for US households to overspend and thereby be the engine of world growth. Note that in this view what needs to be done to restore world growth is not as obvious as in the conventional view. Here, the overspending in the United States, along with the trade deficit it gave rise to, appears as a "solution" to a deeper problem involving excessive savings in the global economy. One could thus say that the US real-estate boom was perversely functional in creating a source of demand that forestalled the deflationary effect of excess savings for as long as that could last. This implies that the trouble was not with global imbalances per se but the unsustainable way they were being recycled and what they were used to finance.

As US households and banks continued to face an ongoing threat of insolvency since the crisis, personal savings predictably began to rise and the adverse effect on aggregate demand was partially offset by a sharp increase in public dis-saving. With recovery supposedly under way, the conventional view called for cutting public spending so that the US trade deficit could be reduced (Blanchard and Milesi-Feretti, 2009). That, in our view, will only deepen the slump and help push the world toward what it was before globalization had transformed it—an objective unlikely to be achieved without slogging through a global slump comparable only to the Great Depression in length and depth. But if returning to the status quo via US private consumption-led growth is problematic in the short run and unsustainable over time, the question is whether there is a way out other than deglobalization, however painful and treacherous that might be.

We believe another way forward might be to ask what can take the place of US overspending in offseting the deflationary effect of global excess savings. If one poses the question in that way, it becomes clear that the real policy challenge is to figure out what to do with the huge dollar reserves that have been accumulated and how to use them to finance sustainable development in poor countries rather than speculation and overconsumption in the rich while benefiting both. That, we argue, might be the only sound way to revive global intermediation.[2] By contrast, pushing with the conventional policy prescription to *rebalance*, we are afraid, will cause the world to drift toward deglobalization, which implies a prolonged period of stagnation at best.

The following discussion is organized in two parts. The first gives a historical analysis of the rise of and eventual crisis within the emergent global system of intermediation. The second focuses on proposed reforms.

## Part 1: From Bretton Woods to Recurrent Crises

To avoid getting trapped in a deflationary spiral similar to that which occurred during the interwar years, it was generally agreed that what the world needed first and foremost was an elastic money supply. That in turn required a balance-of-payments mechanism that did not put the onus of adjustment on countries that ran trade deficits. Addressing both concerns, Keynes's well-known International Clearing Union (ICU) proposals for the post–World War II period envisioned a system that would favor expansion, not contraction, and one that would not restrain domestic policy. In addition, the ICU was structured to avoid creating a system that relied on one or more dominant currencies as reserve assets to minimize governmental influence and prevent a repetition of the collapse of foreign exchange reserves that had occurred in the period 1928–1932. It was to be a multilateral system with automatic overdrafts based on the relative size of a country's trade. Purchases and sales of currencies would take place only through central bank accounts with the ICU, denominated in "bancor," which were to constitute the reserves of the system. Private-capital movements across countries were restricted. Creditor countries would make deposits of current account surpluses that they did not wish to spend and thus create an additional supply of funds for debtor countries to borrow, while both would be required to pay interest on their accounts to equalize the burden of adjustment. Thus, the ICU was designed as a system that could recycle trade imbalances as they emerged in the world economy without forcing deficit countries into deflation.[3]

The original US proposal offered by Harry Dexter White also envisioned a fund that could play an active rather than passive role in the system. Its main idea was to have subscriptions to the fund made in transferable securities rather than currencies that would allow it to conduct open-market operations in member country markets and engage in countercyclical policy interventions.

The problem is that neither of these plans was adopted in the final structure of the new system. Compared with the outcome, the International Monetary

Fund (IMF), which was overly reliant on US dollar contributions and limited in its ability to lend, a system such as the ICU would have made it possible to use the resources contributed by all surplus country depositors as well as the contributions to its capital base. In addition, White's proposal for subscriptions of transferable securities would have provided the framework for global countercyclical open-market operations. And, more important, in either proposal there would be a true global lender of last resort rather than, as now with the IMF, a lender that depends on taxpayer funding.

What all this means is that the Bretton Woods system was not particularly successful in providing an effective mechanism of recycling trade surpluses that did not put the onus of adjustment on deficit countries alone. However, the potentially deflationary effect of trade imbalances could still be forestalled at least for some time as long as the restrictions on private-capital flows remained in place. But the lack of an effective mechanism to deal with trade imbalances eventually undermined the system's ability to provide flexible monetary reserves and to simultaneously safeguard its integrity.

For the world to have an elastic money supply, its dollar holdings had to increase steadily to meet that need. However, that required the world to run a trade surplus with the United States, and the United States had to continue to run ever-larger trade deficits to enable the size of these dollar holdings to expand.[4] But that arrangement raised doubts about the sustainability of the dollar-gold parity and undermined confidence in the monetary standard. This is what came to be called the "Triffin dilemma" (Triffin 1960). The prerequisite expansion of monetary reserves on which world growth depended undermined the monetary standard that was the backbone of those reserves. Fine-tuning the US policy mix could, at best, strike a balance between opposing scales and help buy time but not solve the problem—or not until the *strong dollar policy* of the 1980s gave the dollar a second lease on life under much altered conditions, as discussed below.

As the unsustainability of the dollar-gold exchange-rate system became increasingly obvious in the 1960s, Triffin led the way in calling for a new post–Bretton Woods system. He believed the creation of new reserve assets such as special drawing rights (SDRs) by the IMF to strengthen the balance-of-payments adjustment mechanism was a first step in the right direction—but only a first step. He warned that it would not constitute a viable reform effort if it failed to take a more comprehensive approach in assigning roles to all three components of reserves—gold, foreign exchange, and collectively created assets—especially because gold would certainly be demonetized internationally as it had been nationally since the 1930s.

In Triffin's view, "The alternative to the gold standard is not a dollar standard unilaterally run and managed by the United States alone, but a true international standard, calling for concerted decisions and management by all participating countries (Triffin, 1968, 187)." The reserve asset Triffin called for was similar to the one Keynes called "bancor" in his 1940s proposal. Unlike

Keynes, however, Triffin linked the distribution of collectively created assets to development finance. But the major industrial countries with the majority of votes in the IMF linked the distribution of SDRs to the size of existing quotas. This was, as Triffin complained, "as indefensible economically as it [was] morally" (1968, 187)—especially because two of the world's richest countries (the United States and the United Kingdom) were assigned about one-third of the total. Meanwhile, what Triffin tried to prevent is exactly what emerged after the fall of the Bretton Woods system: a dollar standard unilaterally run by the United States, which in turn became the foundation on which financial globalization forged a privatized system of global intermediation. As we shall see, the very fault lines that Triffin warned against are now exposed anew by the crisis.

The critical issue in reconstituting the unilateral dollar standard was how to deal with the US trade deficits that a dollar-based system required, given that these deficits also undermined its strength. In the 1980s, however, the dollar strengthened in the wake of sharp interest-rate increases and its strength was not undercut by ballooning current account deficits that facilitated reserve accumulation in the rest of the world even after the interest rates fell in the later period. What made this possible was a shift in the US political regime.

## The Unilateral Dollar Standard

Two general themes are often emphasized to explain why efforts to return to a reconstituted Bretton Woods system failed. One is the incompatibility of fixed exchange rates and international capital flows that were becoming increasingly liberalized. The other is the Europeans' frustration with being forced to accommodate the turns and twists in US macroeconomic policy as well as their complaint about the inflationary impact of the weak dollar.[5] In the aftermath of the Bretton Woods collapse, there was widespread recognition that disciplining a superpower such as the United States by requiring that it anchor the dollar to gold was impossible. For many, the real source of inflation was the growing political strength of labor that gave rise to a wage-price spiral throughout the advanced capitalist countries. This meant that the threat of inflation could be much better contained if the United States led Europe in abrogating the post–World War II social compact that made it hard to discipline labor.

The monetary tightening that started under Federal Reserve Chairman Paul Volcker at the end of the Carter administration and the growing fiscal deficit caused by the Reagan stimulus resulted in higher real interest rates, a much stronger dollar, and ballooning trade deficits. But in this new configuration, US trade deficits were no longer a threat to confidence in the dollar. The trade deficits and shift in manufacturing offshore in response to the strong dollar began the process of breaking the back of labor unions and provided the backing the dollar needed as the increased threat of unemployment proved a much more convincing anchor than gold for wealth owners around the world. Although the recession at the end of the 1980s slowed the emergence of the new unilateral dollar standard, advancing globalization, the triumphalism that ensued after the fall of the Berlin Wall and the return of the strong dollar and trade deficits in the mid-1990s clinched the trend and made it clear that there was no going back.

US trade deficits were now the key to world economic growth while posing no threat to confidence in the dollar. The majority of reserves were being accumulated by a few successful exporters—first Japan and Germany, then China, the oil exporters, and a few others—who ran increasing trade surpluses with the United States, which were then recycled to the rest of the world through the US financial system, shaping the structure of global intermediation for years to come.[6] Trade imbalances were no longer deflationary for the world economy or for the United States or other deficit countries that could attract capital. Less successful exporters in the periphery could choose between deflation and making themselves hospitable to foreign capital and, more often than not, the hope of expansion on borrowed money won over the prospect of deflation.

It was as though a privatized version of Keynes's ICU was put in place, recycling trade imbalances that obviated the need of deficit countries to deflate. However, this was an inherently unstable system, for it relied on pro-cyclical private-capital flows whose destabilizing effect was hard to counter. Shrinking domestic policy space made countercyclical policy exceedingly difficult in individual countries, while the type of global countercyclical intervention that White had envisioned was simply not an option. When crises hit, especially in the periphery, there was no lender of last resort to speak of.

It is true that deficit countries no longer had to deflate to the extent they could attract foreign capital, but when that happened they invariably suffered from credit booms that often ended in a crisis when the capital flow reversed itself. Thus, the threat of deflation and exchange-rate volatility was replaced by capital-flow volatility, leading to capital-account-driven boom-and-bust cycles that culminated in one currency crisis after another in the emerging economies throughout the 1990s. Similar tremors caused by the same fault lines are now being felt in the center of the world economy since the financial crisis.

## A Privatized System of Intermediation

Two distinct forms of intermediation at the global level can be distinguished in the early post–World War II era. One involves long-term US investment abroad with foreign borrowers owing debts directly or indirectly to US banks whose liabilities are held by US-based creditors—the holders of bank deposits who would normally want to stay in dollars. US short-term borrowing throughout the same period is the second form of intermediation. Here the roles are reversed between foreigners and US entities. Debts were still denominated in dollars and banks received dollar payments but now creditors were foreigners who needed inducements to keep their holdings in dollars since they had no specific reason to do so. While the first form of intermediation was larger and more important than the latter during the early part of this era, the latter acquired an importance comparable to the former by the 1980s, turning the currency mismatch in the banking system into a potential problem.

In the 1990s these two forms of intermediation became intertwined as short-term borrowing increasingly became the source of funds to finance a rising portion of US long-term investment in other countries. At that point, the United States became truly the world's banker, issuing short-term liabilities to foreigners and making long-term investments in the rest of the world. At the same time, the US current income account deteriorated as US entities began to get an ever-smaller share of interest income from total dollar-denominated debts worldwide. Although the US net asset position had turned negative at the beginning of the 1990s, its net income flow in the current account remained positive and actually began to rise more recently—an outcome consistent with its role as the world's banker, making long-term investments with higher yields than interest costs on the short-term liabilities it issues. Other countries' need for dollars did not diminish as a result of these changes. On the contrary, the rest of the world now needed dollars to make investments as well as to trade and service debt.

The following hallmarks characterized this emergent privatized system of global financial intermediation. First and foremost, bank liabilities that financed dollar-denominated long-term investment in developing economies were now increasingly held by foreign entities that had no special preference for dollars. Thus, currency mismatch, only a potential problem in the 1980s, became pervasive by the 1990s. Second, financial liberalization and innovation around the world turned variable-price assets into the main conduit for capital flows. Compared to the fixed-price bank loans of the 1980s, variable-price assets blurred the distinction between borrowing and the sale of equity, making long-term investment much easier to reverse and speculation less costly. Finally, both the scale of capital flows and rising investment in variable-price assets caused central banks to lose control over credit expansion. This was true not only in the periphery but in the United States as well—though countries that resisted capital account liberalization fared better than others.

This means that what finally emerged was a fragile system that was especially sensitive to currency fluctuations and speculative shifts in capital flows and was basically impervious to policy intervention. Throughout the 1990s, the inherent instability in the system showed up primarily (though not exclusively) in the periphery—emerging economies were plagued by currency mismatch, sudden stops, and abrupt capital-flow reversals without the benefit of countercyclical policy or a lender of last resort—and these issues are making themselves increasingly felt in the center.

In retrospect, the Asian crisis marked an important turning point. In its aftermath, the "savings glut" discussed by Bernanke became real, caused by the collapse of investment in Asia, which resulted from both growing competition from China and the crisis itself. Foreign exchange reserves of emerging economies steadily increased as many of them began to run large current account surpluses and, wary of the anticompetitive effects of consumption booms, chose to invest their earnings abroad rather than at home. Even countries that continued to run deficits began to accumulate reserves as net spending remained below the capital inflow. As it progressively became harder to recycle global funds through the United States after the dot-com crisis, intermediation could only be revived in a lopsided way by absorbing much of the incoming funds within the United States, and that is what the US housing bubble made possible. But that in turn eventually wrecked the balance sheets of US households and banks, putting global intermediation in jeopardy again. The short-term fix not only wore off but ended up compounding the underlying problem by seriously injuring confidence in the reserve asset as well.

## Part II: Addressing the Crisis in Global Intermediation

As discussed above, the debt-financed US real-estate boom was perversely functional in creating a source of demand for as long as that could last. Now, in the aftermath of the crisis and the global recession that followed, the task is to restore the system of global financial intermediation—to replace US overspending as the solution to offsetting the deflationary effect of global excess saving and to find ways to use the large accumulation of dollar reserves to finance development in poor countries for the benefit of the global economy as a whole. The following sections discuss proposals to address these issues.

As is the case in a typical national currency system, the issuer of the international reserve asset must have the authority to create credit and must use some form of backing for the asset that can channel credit to recipients. Unlike the IMF, which functions more like a Treasury operation that recycles taxpayer funds, such an institution must be a monetary agency. If structured as a monetary agency, it could, as Eichengreen (2009) has suggested, have the potential to evolve over time into a global central bank and issue liabilities in sufficient amounts and with sufficient credibility to be used by both public and private sectors in international transactions. But it could also lead to the adoption of a single currency for the global economy, which, as recent experience with the euro underscores, may create rather than solve balance-of-payments and exchange-rate problems in the absence of agreements to consolidate other sovereign powers of member-states. Obtaining such agreements among a majority of the world's countries is unlikely but there are frequent calls to set up such arrangements for developing countries on a regional basis.

The following sections outline a set of alternative proposals that we believe can move the international monetary system beyond the current reliance on assets denominated in national currencies. The first two focus on new ways to create and distribute international reserve assets by public international institutions. The last addresses the need for institutional arrangements that will permit all currencies to be used in international transactions as a more democratic alternative to the current strong-currency system or proposals for global or regional currencies.

An important call for reform, the 2009 *Report of the United Nations Commission of Experts on Reforms of the International Monetary and Financial System*, argues that using assets denominated in national currencies as international reserves is a system that creates global payment imbalances and inequities by channeling capital flows away from developing countries to rich countries that issue strong currencies in highly liquid financial markets. Despite the evident inequity of this arrangement, some doubt that there is sufficient political will to support meaningful reform, and others believe the current system will endure for some time or possibly evolve into a multicurrency system (Mateos y Lago et al., 2009). While there is strong opposition to a multicurrency system (Greenwald and Stiglitz, 2008; Ocampo, 2009), it is the most likely outcome in the absence of a coordinated approach to reform but one that, as demonstrated in the 1930s, can greatly magnify deflation if assets in which international reserves are invested lose value in a downturn (D'Arista, 2009).

Most reform proposals to date have focused on expanding the role of SDRs as a replacement for dollar assets in international reserve holdings.[7] Some believe that shifting to SDRs as the reserve asset while continuing to use the dollar in international payments is the necessary and sufficient direction for reform (Ocampo, 2009). Others (Eichengreen, 2009; Greenwald and Stiglitz, 2008) see the need for a link between the reserve asset and the means of payment and argue that SDRs must be made more liquid through their use in both private- and public-sector transactions if they are to be credible as a reserve asset. Despite these and other differences in views on the direction and depth of reform proposals, most of the recent proposals—including those of the UN Commission of Experts (2009)—suggest some of the elements needed to make a non-national currency reserve asset effective.

## A Modified SDR Proposal

The institutional and instrumental framework for using SDRs as international reserves already exists and, as a result of a G-20 decision, a substantial new issue in mid-2009 raised the share of SDRs in nongold reserves from 0.5 to 5.0 percent (Helleiner, 2009). For many SDR proponents, the absence of a need to change the instrument or the way it is issued argues strongly for proceeding down the SDR path. Nevertheless, some SDR proposals (including those offered by the 2009 UN Commission Report) recognize the limitations of the instrument and issuing arrangements and include reforms that would require additional international agreements. The following outline of our modified SDR-type plan draws on elements in those more ambitious proposals and would also need multinational agreement at the level of the G-20 and the IMF. The plan would be structured as follows:

- The international agency would issue a reserve asset to central banks of member countries in exchange for securities issued by their governments. Those securities would serve as backing for the reserve asset.
- The value of the reserve asset would reflect the aggregate market value of all members' currencies. The amount of reserves issued to a given country would be determined by its shares of global population, trade, and output. The governance of the international agency issuing the asset should reflect those same weights.
- The international agency could provide liquidity to member countries by exchanging its holdings of government securities with central banks of other member countries for their currencies or selling them to private or public investors.
- For example, the agency could sell the government securities of country A to investors in exchange for the currency of country A or that of any other country at its discretion. It could then exchange the currency acquired with the government or central bank of country B in exchange for that country's reserve assets.
- In such transactions, country A's reserve balance would be unaffected and the agency's holdings of country B's securities would remain unaffected. However, the agency would now have a loan to country B on the asset side of its balance sheet and a liability to country A for the securities sold. When the loan by country B is repaid (in country A's currency), the proceeds would be used to reconstitute the agency's holdings of country A's securities. Thus, there would be no change in the agency's balance sheet and no expansion of global liquidity.
- New issues of reserve assets would, however, expand credit in member countries and expand global liquidity. Redemptions of countries' holdings of reserve assets by the international agency in exchange for their government securities would contract credit. Thus, the international agency would have countercyclical powers to issue and redeem reserve assets.

This modified system would moderate the intrusion on national sovereignty of a new regional or global currency while providing a number of benefits to member countries. One benefit is that it can supply the means of payment for international transactions to countries that do not issue widely tradable currencies. Countries would still use their own national currencies at home but would be able to acquire international reserves without borrowing from private financial institutions or earning reserves by promoting export-led growth at the expense of domestic demand. Thus, they would not be compelled to shape their economies to ensure that they can earn or borrow dollars to conduct external trade and investment transactions. Yet another benefit is that it fosters development by absorbing government debt in exchange for reserve assets that can back credit expansion in the domestic economy of the member country. This enables countries that have not been able to engage in fiscal stimulus to do so, and, equally important, it provides an effective lender of last resort in currency crises.

For instance, consider the current fiscal crisis in Greece. In this modified SDR proposal, to provide assistance to Greece the international agency could sell some of its holdings of the government debt of one or more member countries (China, the United States, Germany, Japan, etc.) for any one or several of the currencies favored by investors (euros, dollars, yen, rinminbi, etc.) and exchange the currency or currencies for some of the international reserves it has issued to Greece—in effect, monetizing the reserves. The Greek central bank could then use the currency received to replace the international reserves it returned to the international agency with domestic assets, buying new issues of government debt from the Greek Treasury and providing funds for the Treasury to repurchase outstanding debt from domestic and foreign investors.

In other words, this essentially involves a lender-of-last-resort strategy that can transfer a share of outstanding public debt from private investors to a public agency quickly without involving taxpayer funding from other countries. It could thereby prevent a debt deflation spiral by restoring confidence in the Greek economy and its public and private financial assets, making it possible to restructure the maturity and interest rate on Greece's government debt in more manageable terms.

## Creating an International Investment Fund

While the SDR proposals have the benefit of building on a known organizational and asset base, there are other institutional and instrumental structures possible and they, too, should be explored. The following proposal grows out of the need to improve the economic benefits of holding reserves and create a channel for using reserves to support development goals. Currently, the investment of emerging economies' current account surpluses in the United States and other major national and international financial markets ensures not only that these poorer countries will be financing the rich but also that some portion of the funds will be recycled back to those same creditor countries in the form of foreign acquisition and ownership of their financial assets and productive facilities.[8]

The primary channel for flows to emerging economies is foreign portfolio investment and this reflects the shift toward a dominant role for institutional investors in global financial markets. More often than not, however, portfolio investment has tended to change prices and exacerbate volatility in secondary markets rather than provide long-term financing for economic expansion, while outflows often trigger and intensify currency crises. Moreover, many developing countries that need long-term financing for infrastructure and other basic components of development strategies do not have markets that can absorb foreign portfolio investment flows or the credit standing to attract them. What is needed is a new channel for portfolio investment to provide flows that are stable, in amounts appropriate to the size of a country's economy and directed toward the goals of development rather than solely toward the short-term profits of investors.

Creating one or more closed-end funds for emerging market investment through a separate institution under the Bretton Woods umbrella could constitute an important step toward accomplishing those goals.[9] These new funds would issue their own liabilities in national currencies in markets where there is strong demand for portfolio investment from pension funds and other institutional investors and would buy stocks and bonds of private enterprises and public agencies (including development banks) denominated in local currencies in emerging and developing economies. Marketed to both private institutional investors and official investors, shares in the funds would qualify as international reserve holdings with a guarantee from the multinational agency that issues them and its member countries. Such a channel would enable emerging and developing economies to redirect their external savings back into their own economies rather than into the financial markets of strong currency countries. In addition, their closed-end structure would allow the new agency to make long-term investments and ensure that sales of the fund's liabilities would not disrupt development projects.

In addition to creating a stable channel for financing development, these funds would create a new international reserve asset that, in time, would expand sufficiently to bring about an incremental shift away from reserve holdings based on the financial assets of the wealthier, strong-currency countries. Their status as reserve assets would be enhanced by their multilateral (rather than bilateral) backing by both advanced and emerging economies.

## Reforming the International Payments System

The above proposal for an international investment fund addresses one critical flaw in the current international monetary system but, as our brief overview of the debate on reform suggests, continuing a system that uses one or a few national currencies for international payments will perpetuate the imbalances that are now constraining effective international financial intermediation. As long as the dollar or another strong currency remains the means of payment for cross-border transactions, countries will be compelled to rely on promoting exports and to adopt economic policies that ensure they can earn or borrow key currencies to engage in external trade and investment. It also means that key currency countries must import more than they export to meet the demand for their currencies and accept the resulting current-account deficits and buildup in debt. In short, the development of payment imbalances is embedded in the structure of the system.

Ideally, the international payments system should be one in which every country could engage in trade and borrow and invest in its own currency. This was a core assumption in Keynes's Bretton Woods proposal to create an ICU and it is one we believe should be revived by creating an institutional structure that can accommodate such a system. Keynes's clearinghouse platform would be a key element in this structure. For example, an international clearing agency (ICA) could clear cross-border transactions in members' own currencies by crediting and debiting their clearing accounts.[10] These clearing accounts would, in fact, constitute the international reserves of the system, held by the ICA and valued by using a trade-weighted basket of all members' currencies. Thus, the clearing process would change the ownership of reserves and reinstate the original intent of the Bretton Woods agreement to maintain public control of international payments. It would preserve the valid role of market forces in determining exchange rates while ensuring that speculators would no longer dominate the process.

A revised clearinghouse structure could also reintroduce former US Undersecretary of the Treasury Harry Dexter White's Bretton Woods proposal to authorize the IMF to engage in open-market operations (Boughton, 2006), and it would permit the ICA to acquire government securities of its member countries as backing for their reserve holdings.[11] This instrumental structure would give the ICA means and authority to conduct open-market operations at the international level, enabling it to help national authorities correct imbalances, carry out exchange-rate adjustments, and promote stability by altering holdings of international reserves relative to national central bank reserves invested in domestic assets. Equally important, it would allow the ICA to act as a true lender of last resort, supplying liquidity by buying government securities of member countries and augmenting their international reserves.

The ICA's ability to create and extinguish international reserves would give it authority to expand or contract liquidity at the international level. The need for that authority has become increasingly evident throughout the post-Bretton Woods era as crisis after crisis has damaged the global economy. Establishing an international monetary authority to conduct countercyclical operations was never needed more than now.

# Conclusion

During the interwar years, the collapse of confidence and competitive devaluations eviscerated monetary reserves around the world, deepening the worldwide slump. Bretton Woods sought to design a monetary standard that could withstand these potential pitfalls with mixed success at best. Its ability to furnish the world economy with a flexible money supply eventually foundered when growing US trade deficits began to undermine confidence in the dollar, contributing to rising inflation in the 1970s. In the unilateral dollar system that emerged gradually after the 1980s, ballooning US trade deficits no longer posed a threat to confidence in the dollar and liberalized private-capital flows could recycle global imbalances through the US financial system to the rest of the world. However, the system of global intermediation that emerged was highly unstable, mainly because the private-capital flows it relied on were strongly pro-cyclical and no lender of last resort existed, which meant that capital-flow reversals gave rise to full-blown currency crises. With the growing difficulty of recycling funds to emerging economies after the Asian crisis and the dot-com crisis, a growing portion of global imbalances had to be absorbed within the United States. But that meant that the center of the debt buildup shifted onto the United States, eventually wrecking the balance sheets of households and banks and culminating in the financial crisis that now threatens global disintermediation.

Thus, the policy challenge today is how to revive global intermediation on a sound footing, which involves two related but separate problems. One is figuring out how to recycle global imbalances in a way that they finance development investment in the developing world. The other is to enable all countries to engage in global trade and investment without having to amass someone else's currency—a requirement that forces all but those with strong currencies to overborrow or promote exports at the expense of other policy objectives.

A win-win situation would require deepening international cooperation and new institutions that would make many of the reform proposals discussed above politically viable. But inertia and short-sighted policy decisions on the part of the rich and powerful nations, especially the United States, might push the global system toward an outcome inferior to one that could provide greater benefits for all. Even so, the increased economic power of emerging economies and their financial clout means that they might be able to have much greater influence than has ever been possible before, provided they act in tandem though global or regional fora to redirect global intermediation in ways that encourage development. Indeed, any change in financial intermediation that channels investment toward development globally—or at least regionally—could increase the potential for reform by strengthening the economies of a wider group of nations and giving them greater voice in managing the global system.

## Notes

1. For data and sources supporting the analysis in this section, see D'Arista and Erturk (2010).
2. That, however, might also require an international currency reform: see D'Arista and Erturk (2010).
3. The historical material in this section is drawn from D'Arista (2009).
4. The story of how the severe dollar shortage of the early post-World War II era quickly turned into rising US trade deficits and the accumulation of excess dollars by European central banks by the 1960s is too well known to recount here. It was inevitable that the dollar would become the key reserve currency, given the reality of US economic and political power at the end of World War II. It did, however, require the United States to subordinate fiscal and monetary policy to the objective of ensuring exchange-rate stability—an objective the United States (or any other country) could not meet over time.
5. The common European currency, it is often remarked, largely owes its inception to this sense of frustration. Nevertheless, Europe's own contributions to the massive increase in global liquidity that resulted from intervention in foreign exchange markets are often ignored.
6. The fact that exports became the sole, safe source of demand stimulus helped contain the exchange-rate volatility of the earlier decade. The appreciation of any currency against the dollar was self-limiting because any country whose currency appreciated was liable to experience falling exports and succumb to economic stagnation, which then curtailed the demand for its currency.
7. For historical discussions of the SDR, see IMF (1987). For details of current proposals promoting its use, see D'Arista and Erturk (2010).
8. For a discussion of the spillover effects of these patterns of capital flows, see D'Arista and Griffith-Jones (2006).
9. For a discussion of the benefits of closed-end funds and other details of their structure, see D'Arista (2000).
10. For details of the ICA proposal, see D'Arista (2000).
11. This proposal is also incorporated in the modified SDR plan described above.

## References

Blanchard, O., and G. M. Milesi-Feretti. (2009). *Global Imbalances: In Midstream?* Staff Position Note No. 09/29. Washington, DC: IMF.

Boughton, J. M. (2006). "American in the Shadows: Harry Dexter White and the Design of the International Monetary Fund." Working Paper No. 06/6. Washington, DC: IMF.

D'Arista, J. (2000). "Reforming the Privatized International Monetary and Financial Architecture." *Challenge* 43(3), 44–82.

D'Arista, J. (2009). "The Evolution of the International Monetary System." *Cambridge Journal of Economics* 33(4), 633–52.

D'Arista, J., and K. Erturk. (2010). "Reforming the International Monetary System." Background Paper for the 2010 World Economic and Social Survey. New York: United Nations.

D'Arista, J. and S. Griffith-Jones. (2006). "The Dilemmas and Dangers of the Build-up of US Debt." In J. J. Teunissen and A. Akkerman, eds., *Global Imbalances and the US Debt Problem: Should Developing Countries Support the US Dollar?* The Hague: Forum on Debt and Development (FONDAD).

Eichengreen, B. (2006). "The Blind Men and the Elephant." *Issues in Economic Policy,* No. 1, January. Washington, DC: The Brookings Institution.

Eichengreen, B. (2009). "Out of the Box Thoughts about the International Financial Architecture." Working Paper No. 09/116. Washington, DC: IMF.

Greenwald, B., and J. Stiglitz. (2008). "A Modest Proposal for International Monetary Reform." Paper prepared for the International Economic Association Meeting, Istanbul, June.

Helleiner, E. (2009). "The IMF and the SDR: What to Make of China's Proposals?" The Center for International Governance Innovation, http://www.cigionline.org.

International Monetary Fund. (1987). *The Role of the SDR in the International Monetary System.* Staff Study. Washington, DC: IMF.

Mateos y Lago, I., R. Duttagupta, and R. Goyal. (2009). "The Debate on the International Monetary System." Staff Position Note No. 09/26. Washington, DC: IMF.

Ocampo, J. A. (2009). "Special Drawing Rights and the Reform of the Global Reserve System." In K. S. Jomo, ed., *Reforming the International Financial System for Development.* Washington, DC: G24.

Triffin, R. (1960). *Gold and the Dollar Crisis: The Future of Convertibility.* New Haven: Yale University Press.

Triffin, R. (1968). *Our International Monetary System: Yesterday, Today and Tomorrow.* New York: Random House.

United Nations. (2009). *Report of the Commission of Experts of the President of the United Nations General Assembly on Reforms of the International Monetary and Financial System.* New York: United Nations.

CHAPTER 13

# HOW THE FULL OPENING OF THE CAPITAL ACCOUNT TO HIGHLY LIQUID AND UNSTABLE FINANCIAL MARKETS LED LATIN AMERICA TO TWO AND A HALF CYCLES OF 'MANIA, PANIC AND CRASH'

JOSÉ GABRIEL PALMA

The problem is that [...] the theories embedded in general equilibrium dynamics [...] don't let us think about [issues such as ...] financial crises and their real consequences in Asian and Latin America [...]. Robert Lucas

"Swollen" financial markets tend to produce socially useless products and innovations. Chair, Financial Service Authority

I can [understand and] calculate the motions of the heavenly bodies, but not the madness of [the South Sea Bubble] people. Isaac Newton

Globalization opened up opportunities to find new people to exploit their ignorance. And we found them. Joseph Stiglitz

When you combine ignorance and leverage, you get some pretty interesting results. Warren Buffett

[...] and, above all, let finance be primarily national. John Maynard Keynes

# 1. Introduction

Latin America (LA) has experienced three cycles of capital inflows since the mid-1970s, the first two ending in major financial crises. The first cycle took place between the oil-price increase that followed the 1973 "Yom Kippur" war and the 1982 debt crisis, with Chile (the only country that had fully opened up its capital account) being the most affected—with a 20 percent drop in GDP between the third quarters of 1981 and 1983.[1] The second cycle took place between the 1989 "Brady bonds" agreement (and the beginning of the economic reforms and financial liberalization that followed) and the 2001-2002 Argentinian crisis, and it ended up with four major crises (as well as the 1997 one in East Asia): one in Mexico (1994), one in Brazil (1999), and two in Argentina (1995, the "Tequila-crisis," and in 2001–2002). Finally, the third inflow cycle began in 2003 as soon as international financial markets felt reassured by the surprisingly neoliberal orientation of President Lula da Silva's government (see Palma, 2012). This cycle intensified in 2004 with the beginning of a commodity-price boom, and actually strengthened after a brief interlude following the 2008 global financial crash—and at the time of writing this cycle is still unfolding, but it is already showing considerable signs of distress.[2]

The main aim of this chapter is to analyze the dynamics of the second cycle—from the 1989 "Brady bonds" to the 2001-2002 Argentinian crisis (and 9/11). Two common characteristics of the financial crises resulting from this second cycle—in both LA and East Asia (EA)—are that the countries involved had recently opened up their capital accounts, and they had done so at a time of high liquidity in international financial markets and slow growth in most OECD economies. That is, at a time when ever more liquid, volatile, and progressively unregulated international financial markets were anxiously seeking new high-yield investment opportunities—hopefully also uncorrelated with their existing portfolio.

I will attempt to show that no matter how diversely these newly financially liberalized developing countries (DCs) in both LA and EA tried to deal with the absorption problem created by the subsequent inflow surges (and they did follow different routes), they invariably ended up in a major financial crisis. I shall identify three different ways in which these DCs tried to deal with massive surges of inflow, and conclude that each of them led to a financial crisis via a different path. These are best illustrated by the Mexican 1988–1994 experience—henceforth "route 1" (the "try to keep public finances in balance, and let markets resolve the resulting private imbalances by themselves" route), with Chile and Argentina (at least until its "Tequila crisis" of 1994-1995) following the same route;[3] by the Brazilian 1994–1999 path—"route 2"—characterized by a country that tried to avoid becoming another "route-1-Mexico" via an aggressive sterilization and tough monetary policy; and by the Korean 1988–1997 one—"route 3"—where most inflows were used to finance private investment, in a scenario of falling corporate profitability; this route also included Malaysia and Thailand.

This chapter further attempts to show that all three "routes" led to financial crises in ways that have little to do with the financial processes described in the most popular mainstream models of financial crises—in particular "second"- and "third-generation" ones—especially with their supposed *unpredictable* and *undeserved* nature.[4] That is, the key proposition of this chapter is that the common feature of all three routes to financial crises during the second cycle is that the resulting crises were both (fairly) predictable and (certainly) deserved. Basically, they were the outcomes of economies opting to integrate fully (and indiscriminately) into international capital markets via an open capital account, and then being unable to absorb the subsequent surge of inflows (no matter how hard they tried to deal with them). The experiences of China, India, and Taiwan during the same period (as well as those of Chile and Colombia in the 1990s, when they implemented "price-based" capital controls) show that a more *selective* path of participation in international capital markets is a far more effective way of avoiding the pro-cyclical dynamics of unrestricted capital flows—or the huge costs of sterilization (Ocampo and Palma, 2008). They also help avoid the massive costs in the alternate phase of the cycle, associated with stampedes by intrinsically restless (and often underinformed) fund managers who are prone to oscillating between manias and panics.

# 2. The Three Main Stylized Facts of Capital Flows into Middle-Income DCs since the Liberalization of Their Capital Accounts

## 2.1. Opening Up to a World of Financial "Virtual Realities"

Following Kindleberger, my main contention is that the most likely source of a financial crisis is a sudden surge of liquidity—i.e., when too much liquidity begins to chase too few "prime" financial assets. The financial crises studied here are no exception. So, the starting point of the analysis has to be the "when, how, and why" there was this increase in liquidity. The next question, of course, is how did financial markets manage to "clear" the extra liquidity? My central point here is a complete heresy from the point of view of mainstream economics: from my point of view, the main problem with financial markets is that they are always able to "clear"—no matter how liquid they have become, and how much 'prime' financial assets end up in short supply. However, when they become "over-liquid" the clearing process inevitably leads to unsustainable leverages, asset-price bubbles dodgy financial engineering (to cover-up the inevitable decline in the quality of financial assets, old and new), an increase in fraud, and by the opening up of new and increasingly risky "liquidity outlets." The 'rediscovery' of DCs and the 'sub-prime' mortgage-market in the lead up to the 2008 global financial crisis are clear examples of the latter. For example, the US financial markets not only issued nearly half a trillion dollars in 'sub-prime' mortgages, but, according to the WSJ, in 2007 alone the number of new credit-card solicitations mailed to sub-prime borrowers reached more than 1.3 million.[5]

In fact, my preferred definition of "over-liquidity" is when "toxic" assets can be sold with ease. That is, (first) when financial markets need to create "sub-prime" assets in order to "clear", and (second) when money managers have no difficulties in selling them (i.e., there always be a "greater fool" down the line). This is essentially why over-liquid and under-regulated financial markets become 'self-destructive': they begin to be driven by agents who can take little notice of underlying values—by investors who have incentives to interpret information in a biased fashion in a *systematic* way. In this scenario financial markets can be seriously wrong *as a whole*. One way of looking at how liquid international financial markets had become is that between 1980 and 2007 (i.e., between the beginning of financial deregulation with Thatcher and Reagan, and the year before the current crisis), the four components of the *stock* of global financial assets (equity, public and private bonds, and bank assets) jumped *nine-fold* in real terms (to US$241 trillion). As a result, as a multiple of world output, the stock of financial assets increased from 1.1 to 4.4 (see Palma, 2009a). In turn, the outstanding amounts of over-the-counter derivative contracts soared from 2.4 to 11 times the size of global output. And the gross market value of these "financial weapons of mass destruction" grew eight times faster than world output. In fact, just those involving commodities increased 59-fold during the same decade (BIS, 2011; excludes gold). This frantic speculation is certainly more important than China or India in explaining the post-2003 boom in commodity prices. Also, total assets of hedge funds whose primary focus were DCs grew 4.5-fold in only the three years before 2008—with emerging market equity managers becoming the best niche group in the hedge fund industry (returning on average 37 percent; HFR, 2007).

That is, despite the fact that financial markets had become so liquid, and 'prime' financial assets so scarce, they managed to find (ever more imaginative) ways to unload that liquidity. In fact, under these excess liquidity conditions financial markets failed so badly that it came to the point in which almost any financial asset could be sold with ease—no matter how toxic it was. In other words, the remarkable capacity of financial markets to "clear" any amount of liquidity became its own self-destructive force—if only financial markets, as labor markets, would end up stuck with some 'unemployment' (i.e., with some liquidity that they are unable to "clear")! Had this been the case, maybe this (welcome) 'market failure' could have saved us from many financial crises. In fact, the real 'market failure' is that they can always "clear", not the other way round!

Two of the many problems emerging from these post-1980 increasingly liquid and unregulated international financial markets were the increased *volatility* and *correlation* of returns on financial assets. In fact, now shockwaves are transmitted—and amplified—to such an extent that a simple way of looking at the onset of the 2007-2008 financial crisis would be to say that (long-delayed) concerns over US$500 billion of "subprime" mortgage lending led to the disappearance of more than US$40 trillion in global asset markets. In fact, it used to be that when the United States sneezed, the rest of the world caught a cold; now it is enough for Greece to sneeze, and the rest of the world will catch pneumonia. And these are the international financial markets which LA and EA chose to open their capital accounts fully. As Lawrence Summers once famously said, for DCs to open capital accounts without capital controls has proved to be like building a nuclear plant without safety valves.

Figure 13.1 shows the massive "financial deepening" that took place in the five years between 9/11 and the 2007–2008 crisis.

Basically, in only five years the above countries increased the values of their stock of financial assets by an amount larger than a whole GDP: Ireland by 3.6 GDPs; Spain, 2.3; Asia, 1.8; and Greece (of all countries), by 1.3. That this happened in countries with dynamic growth, could plausibly have some justification. But that it took place in Portugal (0.9 percent growth per annum (p.a.) for GDP, and 15 percent for financial assets—both in real terms), Greece (4.3 percent and 24 percent), or Spain (3.5 percent and 27 percent) can only be labeled as surreal. The outcome of "self-regulation" in financial markets becoming the freedom to run amok, and "market discipline" becoming a joke. In fact, cheap finance was so plentiful that during the five years before the crisis, the value of the stock of financial assets was growing in Spain and Greece twice as fast than in Germany; and the capitalization of the stock market was growing in Greece, Spain and Portugal twice as fast than in the UK (doubling every three years). Something similar happened in LA (4.8 percent and 27 percent), Africa (5.7 percent and 30 percent), or Eastern Europe (5.6 percent and 45 percent).

These asymmetries between the real and the financial economy are *precisely* what FDR tried to avoid with the "New Deal" type financial regulation, and Keynes with Bretton Woods. Also, they are not exactly what the "efficient-market hypothesis" had in mind when they asserted that in liberalized financial markets "prices at all times fully reflect all available information—public and private" (Fama, 1976). That is, financial markets are assumed to be "informationally efficient"; i.e., no one can consistently achieve returns in excess of average market returns (on a risk-adjusted basis). In essence, according to this theory there cannot be an *endogenous* gap between prices in the financial market and fundamentals—let alone a bubble. That is, asset prices deserve a pedestal, and stock options are therefore the most efficient reward for good performance.

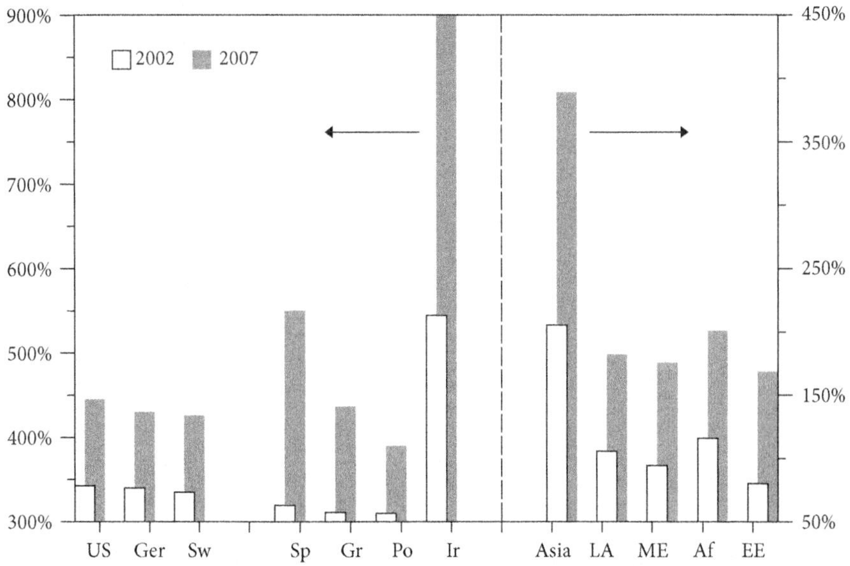


**Figure 13.1** "Financial deepening": ratio of financial assets to GDP, 2002–2007.
*Note*: Ger = Germany; Sw = Sweden; Sp = Spain; Gr = Greece; Po = Portugal; Ir = Ireland; LA = Latin America; ME = Middle East; Af = Africa; EE = Eastern Europe.
*Source:* IMF (2011a). The four components of the stock of financial assets are the capitalization of stock markets, public bonds, private bonds, and bank assets. The source does not report data for Iceland (according to a senior IMF official, what one has to understand now is that "Iceland is no longer a country—it is a hedge fund"; quoted in Lewis, 2009). On Iceland, see Wade and Sigurgeirsdottir (2010).

## 2.2. The First Stylized Fact of Post-1990 Inflows into (Newly Financially Liberalized) DCs: A Massive Surge of Highly Volatile Capital Flows

Figure 13.2 shows the first and crucial stylized fact of post-1990 inflows into these middle-income DCs: the sudden surge, the high volumes, and the huge instability of these inflows.

According to mainstream economic theory (and the Washington Con-sensus discourse), full integration into international capital markets should be highly beneficial to DCs with "sound fundamentals" for a number of reasons, but especially because the integration should pool risk and provide countercyclical access to finance. Well, there's little evidence of that. In fact, since 1990 almost all LA countries have had (what in the narrow sense of the Washington Consensus is understood as) "sound fundamentals" as well as remarkably easy access to international finance. However, the outcome of this has been rather different from the prediction of mainstream economists and neoliberal politicians (of all political persuasions).

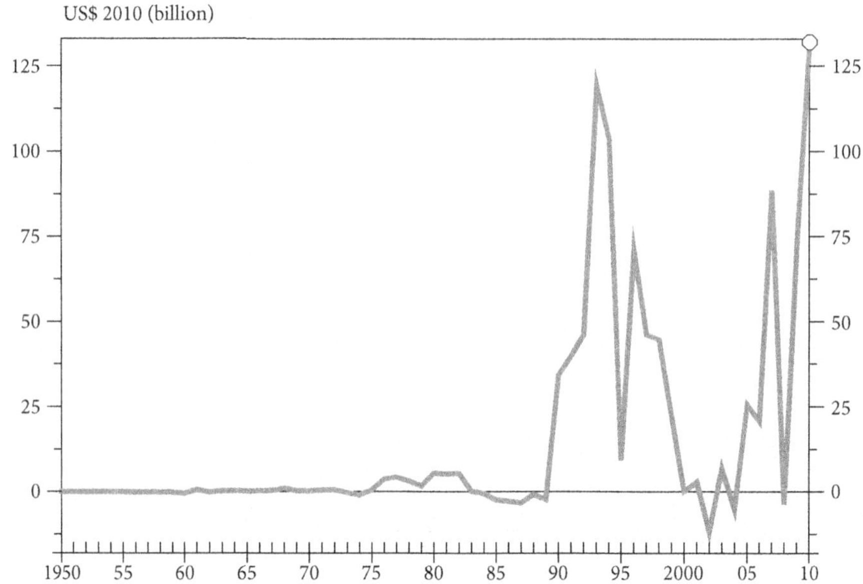


**Figure 13.2** Latin America: Portfolio inflows, 1950–2010.
*Source*: ECLAC (2011; gross portfolio inflows).

As figure 13.2 indicates, this has been one of damaging surges of inflows, *pro-cyclical* finance, and hugely increased financial fragility—and augmented *uncertainty*. In particular, as will become clear below, the key characteristic of "route 1" countries in LA was the *intensity* of the pro-cyclical nature of the surge in inflows when these were dealt with following the credo of the "efficient-capital-market" theory, and the first law of welfare economics (that is, try to keep public finances in balance and leave markets to resolve the resulting private imbalances by themselves).

Looking at LA's overall scenario since 1990, if I was asked to put forward the argument for capital controls as an effective mechanism for dealing with the problem of the volatility of inflows *at source*, figure 13.2 would be my "exhibit A."

## 2.3. The Second Stylized Fact: At Least in LA, the Tsunami of Inflows Has Had Little or No Positive Impact on the Real Economy

Figure 13.3 indicates that it would be rather difficult to argue that the opening up of the capital account circa 1990 has had an unambiguous positive impact on LA's real economy—this is true even for foreign direct investment (FDI)!

As the left-hand panel of figure 13.3 indicates, before 1980, when inflows averaged less than US$20 billion per year (in 2010 US$), productivity growth reached 2.6 percent p.a. (3.8 percent for Brazil). But when inflows increased by more than three times (1990–2010), productivity growth only reached half the pre-1980 rate (1.2 percent p.a.; 1.3 percent for Brazil). Of course the disappointing post-1990 performance in "liberalized" LA has many roots (see Palma, 2011a), but there is little doubt that the negative effects of the massive surge of (volatile) inflows is part of that narrative. For example, huge inflows led to a chronic deficiency of effective demand for noncommodity tradable activates, especially manufacturing; this was the outcome of the "deadly triad" of overvalued exchange rates (that switched aggregate demand toward foreign markets); high interest rates (due to "tough" monetary policies to deal with these inflows); and remarkably low levels of public investment by "sterilized" governments (of about 3 percent of GDP; these were necessary to balance public finances in a context of low taxation, as part of the "sound fundamentals" shop-window part of the open-capital account story).[6]

One aspect of inflows that is truly remarkable is shown in the right-hand panel of figure 13.3: a significant surge of inflows of FDI after the "Brady-bonds" agreement and the beginning of economic reform—reaching an average of US$75 billion a year between 1988 and 2010 (in 2010 US$; ECLAC, 2011)—has been associated with a remarkably poor rate of investment (as a share of GDP). In fact, despite the growth acceleration in many countries after the post-2003 commodity-price boom and the new surge in inflows, as well as the rapid recovery after the 2008 crisis, by 2010 the average investment share of the region was

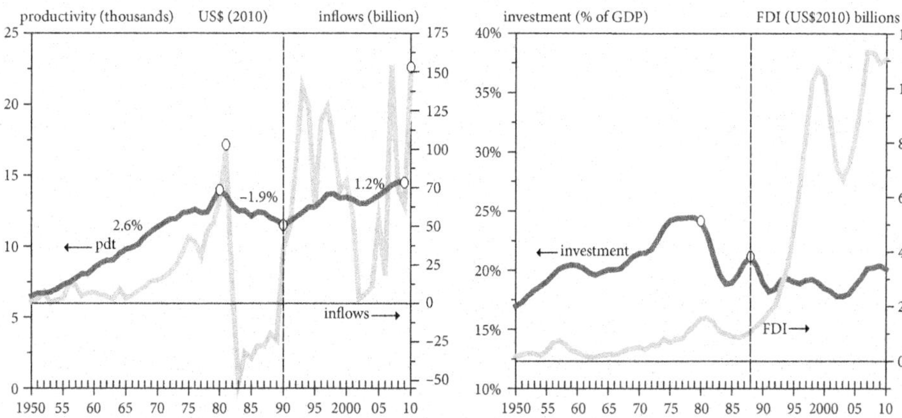


**Figure 13.3** Latin America: Labor productivity and net private capital inflows, 1950–2010. Investment as % of GDP and FDI inflows, 1950–2010.

*Note*: pdt = labor productivity. The percentages in the left-hand panel are average rates of productivity growth for respective periods (1950–1980, 1980–1990, and 1990–2010). In the right-hand panel, investment and FDI are three-year moving averages.

*Sources:* Productivity, World Bank (2011; for output), and GGDC (2011; for employment); investment, ECLAC (2011; current prices); net private inflows, ECLAC (2011; for 1950–1970), and IMF (2011b; for 1970–2010); and FDI, ECLAC (2011).

still below its (already disappointing) starting point. Among the main countries, Brazil and Venezuela, although for different reasons, lagged behind. In other words, as figure 13.3 clearly indicates, in LA, inflows of FDI equivalent to *US$1.5 trillion* (1988–2010; 2010 US$) have been associated with a rate of accumulation that is poor even from the perspective of its inadequate historical record—on average just 19 percent of GDP (17.6 percent for Brazil; ECLAC, 2011; WDI, 2012; see also Palma, 2011a).[7]

So, again, there is not much support here for the mainstream proposition that DCs are full of investment opportunities, just waiting for the availability of finance (which, supposedly, can only come from rich countries and not from the high proportion of the national income appropriated by their elites). And there is significant support for the Keynesian proposition that the mere availability of cheap finance does not lead to higher investment.

In fact, perhaps the most striking political-economy difference between LA and Asia is found in their contrasting relationships between income distribution and investment (see figure 13.4).

While in LA private investment (which usually hovers around 15 percent of GDP) accounts for only one-third of the income share of the top decile (about 45 percent of national income), in most of Asia this ratio jumps to more than twice that level—with Korea's even above 1.[8] In other words, while LA's top deciles appropriate *twice* as much as those of Korea and Taiwan, LA's share of private investment in GDP reaches *half* their levels. From my own perspective, this is *the* most crucial characteristic of the (subprime) nature of LA's capitalism: what I like to call the "two-times-half-style capitalism" (i.e., how to create an institutional environment in which one can get twice as much, with half the effort).[9] And FDI, instead of making a positive impact on that asymmetry, has been more than happy to adjust to the *modus operandi* of these markets "flowing with milk and honey."[10]

Oddly enough, in South Africa (in this respect, LA's honorary middle-income country in Africa), and in the Philippines (the honorary one in Asia) similar low ratios for this statistic as those of LA indicate that their capitalist elites have the same Latin preference for having their cake and eating it too.

Keith Griffin (1970) once wrote that foreign aid may well end up simply *substituting* domestic savings; post-reform LA seems to indicate that in DCs FDI also could have a strong substituting effect on national private investment—except, of course, in Asia. It is fairly obvious that LA's capitalist elite preferred both sumptuous consumption and accumulation via mobile assets (financial ones and capital flight) rather than via "fixed" capital formation.[11] And neoliberal reforms—despite all the efforts toward defining and enforcing property rights, and all the other "market-friendly" policies aimed at incentivizing investment—have had little impact on that (in spite of all the resources and foreign exchange provided by inflows, and the particularly favorable terms of trade). There is not much evidence here of the supposed

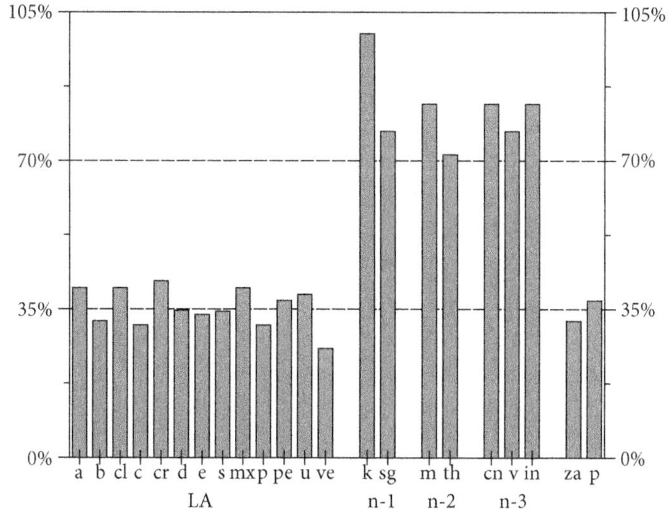


**Figure 13.4** Private Investment as a Percentage of the Income Share of the Top Decile, c. 2009.
*Note*: n-3 = third-tier NICs (China, India and Vietnam), and a = Argentina; b = Brazil; cl = Chile; c = Colombia; cr = Costa Rica; d = Dominican Republic; e = Ecuador; s = El Salvador; mx = Mexico; p = Paraguay; pe = Peru; u = Uruguay; ve = Venezuela; k = Korea; sg = Singapore; m = Malaysia; th = Thailand; cn = China; v = Vietnam; in = India; za = South Africa; and p = Philippines.
*Source:* For income distribution, WDI (2010); for private investment IMF (2010).

revitalizing effects of "financial deepening" promised by Ronald McKinnon and Edward Shaw.

In essence, economic reform and financial liberalization have been unable to reproduce even the relatively low investment rates of the state-led industrialization period; instead, it seems to have unleashed more powerfully the predatory and rentier instincts of the region's capitalist elites (the former especially during the privatization period).[12] In many Asian countries, meanwhile, reforms, especially financial liberalization, may have brought complex challenges to the macro, and the inevitable financial fragilities (as well as increased inequalities, labor insecurity, and so on), but at least the rate of accumulation increased significantly *after* their implementation. In LA, meanwhile, the cloud did not even have that silver lining (see figure 13.5).

The contrast between Brazil and India is particularly telling (left-hand panel)—both countries started their economic reforms with a 22 percent investment rate in GDP; however, by 2010 one (India) had brought this rate up to 37 percent, while the other (Brazil) had brought it down to 19 percent (IPEA, 2011; World Bank, 2011).

And the contrast between LA and Asia is even starker when the comparison is drawn with investment *per worker* (right-hand panel). In Brazil, for example, by 2010 (and despite the post-2004 acceleration of growth) investment *per worker* (in real terms) was still well *below its 1980 level*. Most of LA follows a pattern similar to Brazil. An extreme example is Mexico after the NAFTA agreement: despite the highest level of FDI per worker in the world, by 2010 its investment per worker was also still below its 1981 level. By then, and despite 1997, Korea had a level 3.6 times higher, and Malaysia and Thailand 2.2. In turn, China's 2010 level was 12 times higher; India's was 4.5; and Vietnam had more than trebled this statistic since 1994 (the first year that data are available; see Palma, 2011a). Perhaps from this perspective the contrasting productivity growth performance of LA and many in Asia since 1990—and especially the inability of LA *to sustain* productivity growth—may not be so difficult to explain after all.

Furthermore, in the very few cases in LA where investment actually increased after reforms, as in Chile, it is not obvious why it took so long for it to happen (10 years), let alone why it ran out of steam so easily afterwards (Ffrench-Davis, 2010; Palma, 2011a, 2011b). Moreover, what also remains unclear is why LA's capitalist elite—despite its huge share of national income, and the well-defined and enforced property rights, "pro-market" reforms, and tsunami of FDI—starts experiencing feelings of vertigo every time that private investment manages to rise much above 15 percent of GDP.

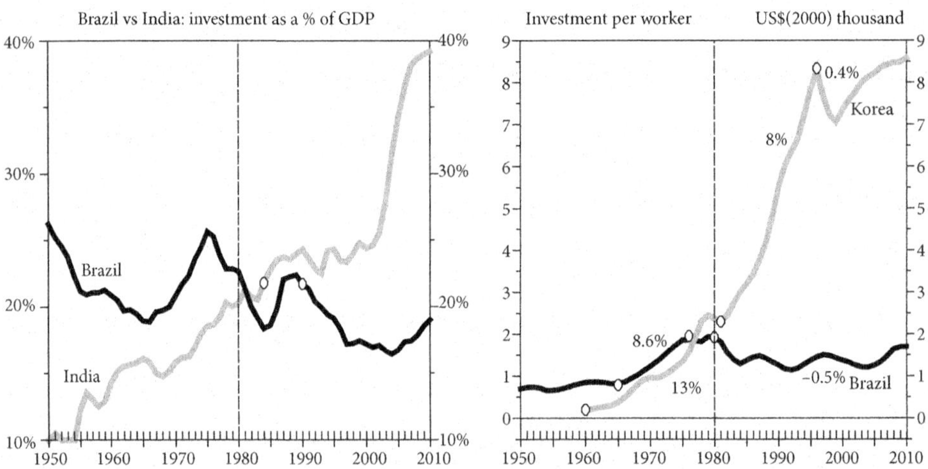


**Figure 13.5** Investment Patterns in Latin America and Asia, 1950–2010
*Note*: In the left-hand panel, white circles indicate the beginning of economic reform (for India, 1980; for Brazil, 1990—Collor's 'New Brazil' Plan). In the right-hand panel, percentages shown in the graph are growth rates in the respective periods (for Brazil, 1965–1976 and 1980–2010; and for Korea, 1960–80, 1981–97 and 1997–2008. 3-year moving averages.
*Sources:* For investment, WDI (2010); for investment in LA before 1960, CEPAL (2010); for India (http://mospi.gov.in/). For employment, GGDC (2009).

## 2.4. The Third Stylized Fact: The Growing Costs of Capital Inflows in Terms of Factor Payment Abroad

As is evident from figure 13.6 the fortunes of LA's factor payments abroad (interest payment, profit repatriation, etc.) took a rather remarkable turn after the appointment of Paul Volcker (with his flamboyant monetarism) to the Fed in 1979, and the election of Reagan a year later—as most of LA's debt was saddled with flexible interest rates. LA's interest payments on foreign debt alone jumped (in 2010 US$) from US$29 billion in 1978 to US$95 billion in 1982 (or nearly half the region's exports). Unsurprisingly, LA ended up with a foreign debt crisis.

Overall factor payments abroad (debits) then fell from US$108 billion in 1982 to US$61 billion in 1992. However, it jumped again (mostly due to increased profit repatriation by FDI) to US$122 billion in 2010 (having reached US$135 billion in 2007—see figure 13.6).

As a result, in LA, in the two decades after financial liberalization *US$1.5 trillion* of net inflows (in 2010 US$, 1989–2010) got wiped out in terms of "net transfer of resources" due to a net factor payment abroad of US$1.6 trillion (US$2.3 trillion in terms of debits). The figures for the 2000s were net inflows of US$672 billion and negative net transfers of US$321 billions—due to net factor payments of almost US$1 trillion (US$1.4 trillion in debits). In fact, if "net" transfer of resources also excludes increases in reserves (as some have argued that it should), the net transfer of resources reaches a *negative* figure of US$810 billion just in the 2000s. Large inflows, even when they have a strong FDI component, are certainly not a free lunch.

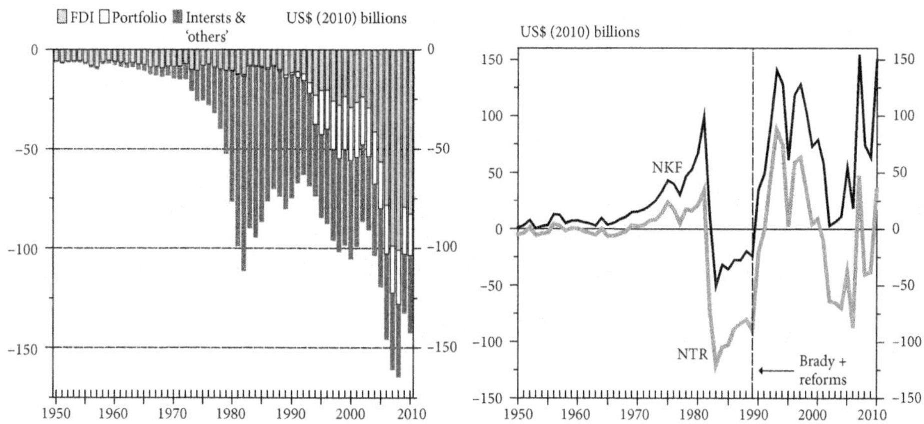


**Figure 13.6** Latin America: Factor payments abroad, 1950–2010. Net private capital flows and net transfer of resources, 1950–2010.

*Note*: NFK = net private capital inflows; and NTR = net transfer of resources (NKF–net factor payments). In left-hand panel, payments are gross.

*Source*: ECLAC (2011).

In Chile, for example, toward the end of the 2010s, profit repatriation by (mostly copper) FDI was equivalent to two-thirds of all public expenditures, as well as twice the overall level of public expenditures in education, health, and housing combined. Furthermore, it was equivalent to about 1.6 times Bolivia's GDP, and twice Paraguay's GDP. In fact, Chile is one of the few countries in the world with no royalty on mineral extraction—the tax it euphemistically calls "royalty" is a specific tax, not a "royalty". Furthermore, as this was not enough, the Concertación government that created this meager specific tax gave FDI an additional "magical-realist" concession: foreign corporations can account for this specific tax as *a cost of production*. With such a "lightly-touched" fiscal attitude, no wonder LA's "new" left is so welcome at Davos.

## 3. The "Three Routes" to Financial Crisis

Figure 13.7 shows the crucial issue at stake, common to all these crisis countries, but especially to LA: the remarkable surge in inflows on the heels of financial liberalization. In LA, the turnaround following the opening up of the capital account is remarkable. In 2010 US$, the difference between the two periods (pre- and post-liberalization) amounts to US$277 billion in Brazil, US$194 billion in Argentina, and US$125 billion in Mexico. In fact, the turnaround in Brazil or in Argentina alone was larger than in the three East Asian economies combined (US$153 billion). These surges are even more impressive in relative terms to exports and savings (particularly in Chile). In fact, some of these countries even began to be important players in the newly developed derivatives markets (IMF, 2011a).

Foreign capital swamped these countries due to several "push" and "pull" factors. The main "push" factor consisted of excess liquidity in international financial markets—from this perspective, DCs continued to play their historical role of being a "financial market of last resort" (Palma, 1998). As mentioned above, this role (of an emergency "liquidity outlet") is not that different from the one played by the subprime mortgages during the financial cycle that followed 9/11. Other "push" factors common to both regions included business-cycle conditions, interest-rate changes, the rise of institutional investors (such as mutual funds, pension funds, hedge funds) always in search of new high-yield financial assets (hopefully with low-correlation in returns with their existing portfolio), and demographic forces in industrial countries. There was, however, a crucial difference between LA and EA in terms of the "pull factors." In EA there was an urgent need for foreign finance to help sustain high levels of corporate investment in the face of falling profitability; in LA, instead, the key "pull factor" was the combination of radical economic reforms (in particular, wholesale privatizations,

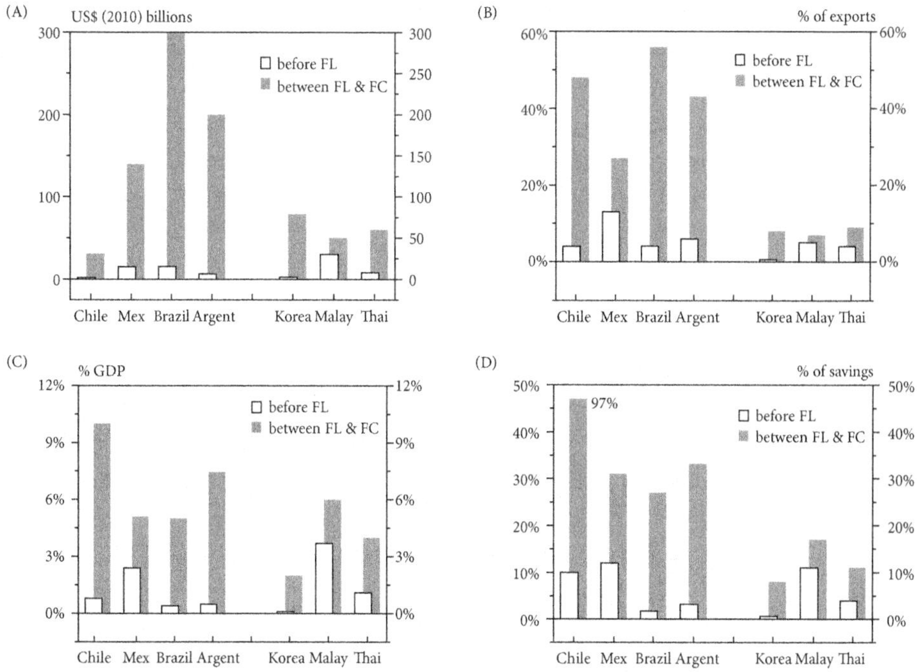


**Figure 13.7** A: Latin America and East Asia: aggregate net private inflows. B: Aggregate net private inflows as % of exports. C: Aggregate net private inflows as % of GDP. D: Aggregate net private inflows as % of savings.
*Note*: FL = financial liberalization; FC = financial crisis; Mex = Mexico; Argent = Argentina; Malay = Malaysia; and Thai = Thailand. The period "between" covers the years between financial liberalization and financial crisis. The period "before" covers a similar number of years before financial liberalization.
*Source:* World Bank (2011).

and the speed and intensity of trade liberalization) and the opening up of the capital account in a context of undervalued asset markets (and when many domestic corporations were eager to join the stock market just to attract foreign buyers), high interest-rate spreads, and expectations of exchange-rate appreciation. Optimism regarding the success of economic reforms was in excess supply, partly as a result of the massive "spin" put on them by those to be found circling around the Washington Consensus.

That is, there was a major difference regarding "pull" factors, as in LA a significant proportion of inflows had practically to "invent" a need for themselves (i.e., it was a supply in search of a demand, as it takes two to tango). The key characteristic of LA's "pull" factors is that they fed into themselves: inflows were attracted by newly created domestic "magnetisms"; these inflows generated pro-cyclical dynamics, which attracted more inflows. Finally, a crucial "pull" factor in all routes was the "moral hazard" created by the near-certainty in international financial markets (particularly after

1994 in Mexico) that, as in every good old Western, the cavalry, in the form of a vast international rescue operation, could be counted on to arrive in the nick of time, should the "natives" threaten to default or close their capital accounts.

One way of testing, which was the *causa causans* of the surge in inflows ("exogenous push" in LA vs. "endogenous pull" in EA), is by looking at the time sequence between changes in the current and in the capital accounts. The question here is, what is the driving force behind the balance-of-payments cycle? Does the current account "lead" the capital account (endogenous pull), or is it the other way around (exogenous push)? This issue can be tested with the help of the Granger time-precedence or predictability test (often misleadingly called the Granger causality test). The results of this test show a major difference between LA and EA in this "chicken-and-egg" problem: in LA changes in the capital account tend to *precede*—and are useful for the *prediction* of—changes in the current account, while in EA the time dynamic is the opposite (see Palma, 2003, Ocampo and Palma, 2008).

This is also an important finding from the point of view of the role of capital controls: if the primary source of the LA financial cycle is an externally induced (i.e., "exogenous push") change in the capital account, controls on inflows are more likely to be a "first-best" countercyclical policy option if one wants to deal with the excesses of the financial cycle at their *source*. In EA, meanwhile, the results of the test indicate a more macroeconomic textbook time sequence: changes in the current account—the result of developments *in the domestic real economy*—proceed, and are useful to predict, changes in the capital account. It therefore seems less clear that in this region capital controls should be the dominant component of a "first-best" policy to deal with the inflow problems at the source. This does not mean that capital controls cannot help; it means that they are a "second-best" policy, because the "first-best" one would be to deal with the domestic problems leading the changes in the current account (e.g., the amount of finance needed to sustain high levels of corporate investment).

## 3.1. The Latin American Story: To Sterilize or Not to Sterilize a Mainly "Exogenous Push" of Foreign Capital—"Route 1" versus "Route 2"

Figure 13.8 shows some of the major differences in LA between Brazil ("route 2"), which decided for sterilization, and Chile, Mexico, and Argentina ("route 1"), which decided instead to trust the traditional beliefs of the first law of welfare economics: let markets solve private imbalances by themselves.

In "route 1", the response to the surge in private inflows was to ride them out by unloading them into the domestic economy via a credit boom (panel A), and asset bubbles (panel C).[13] The other (Brazil) was precisely the reverse: try to stop the resulting pro-cyclical dynamics by placing an "iron curtain" around them in the Central Bank (via sterilization).

The crucial factor in understanding the different behavior of Brazil is the timing of its financial liberalization (second half of 1994); this coincided with the unfolding of the growing Mexican financial fragilities that led to the December 1994 crisis. Therefore, high degrees of sterilization and high interest rates were continued *after* the successes of the "real plan" in conquering inflation in order to avoid following a Mexican "route 1" crisis path.

Regarding routes 1 and 3, even though there was a similarity in the speed of credit expansion, there also was a crucial difference: the use made of this additional credit. As mentioned above, while "route 1" directed it toward increased consumption and asset speculation (panels B and C), Korea did so mostly toward corporate investment (see figure 13.10). Furthermore, in "route 1," a bubble similar to that of stocks took place in real estate; in Mexico, for example, the relevant price index jumped 16-fold between financial

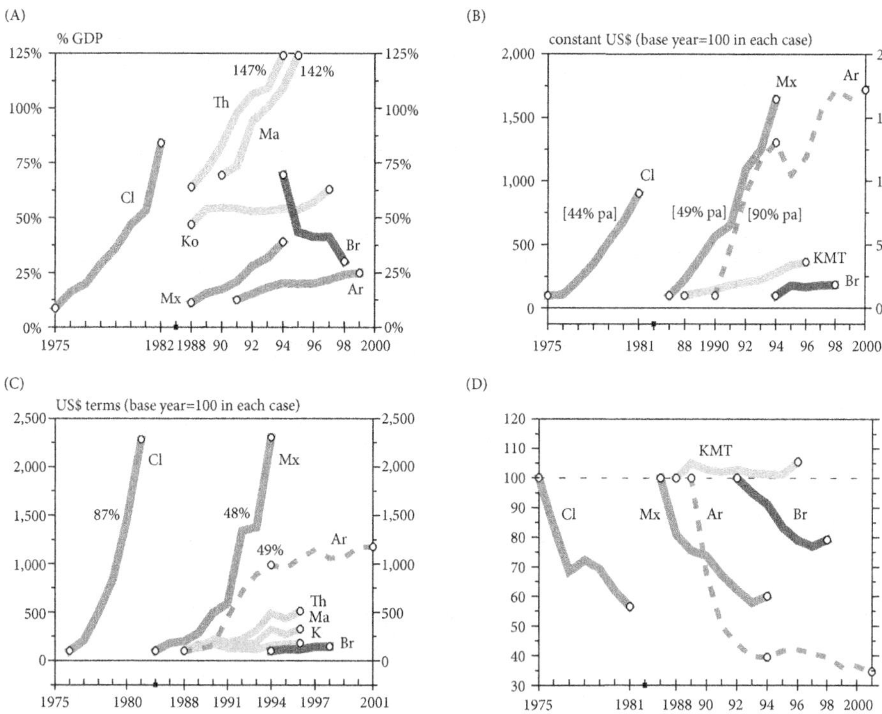


**Figure 13.8** A: East Asia and Latin America: credit to the private sector. B: Imports of consumer goods. C: Annual stock market indices. D: Real effective exchange rates. *Note*: [Cl] = Chile; [Mx] = Mexico; [Ar] = Argentina; [Br] = Brazil; [Ko] = Korea; [Ma] = Malaysia; [Th] = Thailand; and [KMT] = average of Korea, Malaysia, and Thailand. Percentages in panels B and C are average *annual* rates of growth. The percentages for Argentina correspond to 1990–1994.

*Sources:* Credit to the private sector, World Bank (2011); imports of consumer goods, UN (2011); stock markets, DataStream (2011); and exchange rates, IMF (2011a).

liberalization and financial crisis, while there was little increase in the indices of Korea or Brazil (see Palma, 2002a, 2003). Finally, the cases of Malaysia and Thailand are characterized by having one foot in each camp. Their surges in inflows were initially necessary to sustain their ambitious private investment programs—both Malaysia and Thailand tried to sustain a share of private investment in GDP above 30 percent. But, contrary to Korea, there was still plenty of "spare cash" after that to follow at least one element of "route 1" too—the spare liquidity fueled a (near) Latin-style asset bubble in their stock markets and real estate.[14]

However, remarkably, in these two East Asian countries massive credit expansion was associated with a *drop* in the share of consumption in GDP—in Malaysia this share declined by nearly 10 percentage points of GDP (to 56.1 percent); in Thailand there was a drop by 3 percentage points (to 64.9 percent). No similarity with "route 1" here! Therefore, no other macroeconomic variable so transparently demonstrates the different "routes" to financial crises than the behavior of private consumption (panel B), and asset prices (panel C). In terms of the former, for example, while in "route 2" Brazil sales of new cars grew by only 39 percent between 1994 and 1997 (to fall again by 23 percent in the months before the 1998 crisis), in "route 1" Argentina they grew *five-fold* between 1991 and the 1995 "Tequila crisis" (McKinsey, 2004). And in terms of the stock market, "efficient capital market" theorists were probably not very well acquainted with LA when they stated that stock prices are supposed to be a "random walk." That is, particularly under risk neutrality, in stock markets there is supposed to be no scope for profitable speculation (i.e., a rational stock market cannot be beaten on any *consistent* basis). The key point here is that if financial markets get misaligned, they are always supposed to "self-correct." And although in LA they surely got misaligned, they certainly failed to self-correct. In Chile (1975–1981), for example, the dollar-denominated value of stocks grew at 87 percent p.a., or 12 times faster than real GDP; in Mexico (1988–1994), meanwhile, it grew 13 times faster than GDP, and in Argentina (1990–1994) 6 times faster.

Therefore, when students are taught these days that smart market players are bound to force stock prices to become rational, LA is probably not in the syllabus. The irony is that "utility-maximizing" agents are supposed to do that by doing exactly the opposite of what they do in real life: take the other side of trades if prices begin to develop a pattern—as this is bound to have no substance, because share prices are supposed to exhibit no serial dependencies (meaning that there can be no "patterns" to asset prices). In other words, for the efficient market theology a "rational" surfer (proficient in rational expectations) is not the one that has fun riding waves but is the one that gets drowned trying to create undertows...

And in the years preceding these financial crises, stock prices took on a pattern and they did so in "tulip mania" style—see panel C for clear examples in which market participants, instead of dutifully following "nontrending random walks," were quite happy to systematically profit from market failures. As mentioned above, the key point here is that these are clear examples of markets that are driven by buyers who took little notice of underlying values (fundamentals)—i.e., markets in which investors have powerful incentives to interpret information in a biased fashion *in a systematic way*. Here, in order to have a financial crisis, there is no need for traumatic real-world events—"fat tails" occur mostly because under these circumstances there is a higher than normal likelihood of entirely self-made catastrophic events.

Finally, particularly in "route 1" countries, the surge of inflows also distorted "fundamentals"; panel D shows the case of the remarkable revaluation of real exchange rates—in Chile, for example, at a time when the current account deficit was reaching a level equal to all exports, and in Mexico, Brazil, and pre-Tequila-crisis Argentina one equivalent to about half their exports (or more), their exchange rates were in freefall *revaluations*. What a contrast with EA, where a fundamental component of their Keynesian "pro-growth macro" was to keep the exchange rate competitive *and* stable despite huge inflows and booming exports.

It is really difficult to fit LA's real effective exchange-rate picture with the basic postulate of the neoliberal creed regarding the need to liberalize, lift "artificial" market distortions, and stop governments' "discretionary" policies in order to allow the economy to get "its prices right." Massive inflows into LA, particularly in relation to exports, and the use of exchange-rate-based stabilization policies (based on the oldest macroeconomic law of them all: one can only solve a macroeconomic imbalance by creating another one) brought this crucial price (the exchange rate) to a level that would be rather hard to brand as "right."

Moreover, the current account was not the only casualty of the exchange rate overvaluation; the latter was also (not surprisingly) distorting the composition of what little investment there was toward the nontradable sector. In Mexico, for example, while investment in residential construction doubled between 1981 and 1994, investment in machinery fell by half (and at a time in which trade liberalization had already rendered a significant amount of the stock of capital in manufacturing obsolete; see Palma, 2005). Easy access to credit, the distortion in relative prices between tradables and nontradables, and the asset bubble in real estate set in motion a huge Kuznets cycle—not surprisingly, the best performing sector in the Mexican stock market was construction.

This is a rather odd picture: in fact, "route 1" economies ended up switching the engine of growth away from their supposedly desired aim—domestically financed private investment in (increasingly sophisticated) tradable production—toward a more laid-back (postmodernist?) one of externally financed private consumption, and private investment in nontradable activities and unprocessed commodities. That is, a growth model with a clear bias for "low-hanging-fruit"-type activities.

Finally, the collapse of savings in LA is also definitely not the "Promised Land" of McKinnon and Shaw—who (misinterpreting Joseph Schumpeter) famously declared in 1973 that in DCs the main constraint on savings was financial "repression": in their respective periods between financial liberalization and financial crises, gross domestic savings as a share of GDP fell in Chile by no less than 13 percentage points, in Brazil by 9, in Mexico by 8, and in Argentina by 6 (World Bank, 2011). The flip side was booming consumption—in Chile, the share of consumption in GDP grew by 10 percentage points (to no less than 91 percent); in Mexico by 7 points (to 83 percent); in Brazil by 6 points (to 85 percent); and in Argentina by 5 points (to 85 percent; World Bank, 2011). The irony, of course, is that in mainstream macroeconomic textbooks it is still taught today that one of the main benefits of opening up the capital account is to smooth consumption over time!

Given this evidence, it is difficult to understand how, as late as 1996, the World Bank (1996) was still preaching to DCs to continue implementing "route 1"-type policies—that is, preaching DCs to follow the credo of the (strongest version of the) "efficient-capital-market" theory and the first law of welfare economics. As mentioned above, the recipe was simple, as recipes from the Washington Consensus usually are (in fact, this simplicity is probably their main analytical attraction): try to keep public finances in balance, and allow markets to resolve the resulting private imbalances by themselves. All what was required for this was market discipline, self-regulation, and civilized governance.

It is also particularly difficult to understand the mainstream insistence on the supposed countercyclical nature of inflows, as well as its aversion to countercyclical macro and capital controls. Let alone its persistence in portraying "complete markets" as Paradise Lost. Even in the very unlikely scenario that for finance complete markets could do the trick, there is not much chance of this utopia taking shape this side of eternity.

Turning to "route 2", the crucial vulnerability of Brazil lies mainly in high interest rates leading straight into a public-sector "Ponzi" finance system (see figure 13.9).

First, the Brazilian Central Bank overreacted to external shocks (an attitude I have elsewhere called "macho-monetarism"; see Palma, 2006). In fact, at times—and even when there was no fear of devaluation—the Brazilian Central Bank set deposit rates as much as 20 percentage points above international rates plus country risk. The crucial ideological point to understand here is that these were post "UK-ERM-crisis" times, when "collective memories" (and second-generation models) were directing all the blame for financial crises toward central banks' trepidation of interest-rate hikes. That is, financial crises were supposed to be the exclusive territory of feeble central bankers/finance ministers—in the case of the United Kingdom, for example, Norman Lamont's imperfect commitment to a currency peg. The uniqueness of the Brazilian political economy scenario is that the post-1992 "macho-monetarism" macro that emerged came from this understanding of 'second-generation' crises ("one should not be afraid to do what it takes")

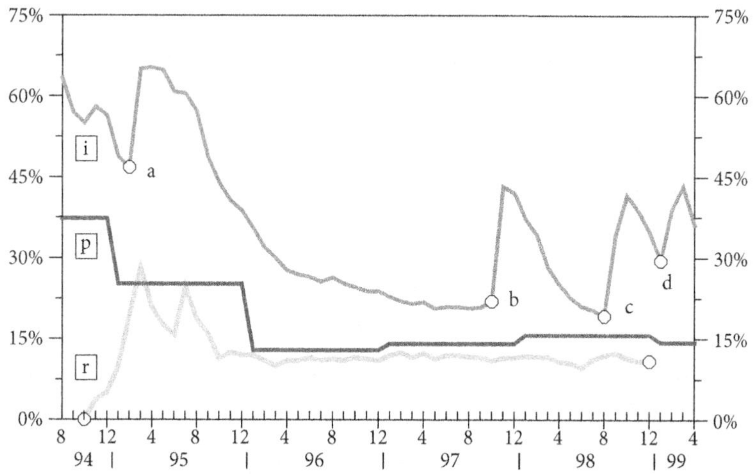


**Figure 13.9** Brazil: How to walk into a public sector Ponzi by overreacting to external shocks, by the unnecessary high cost of sterilization (i – r), and by the violation of a "golden rule" (i > p).

*Note*: [i] = annualized nominal interest rate paid for public debt; [p] = annual growth rates of public revenues; and [r] = income received for foreign-exchange reserves (assumed to be the domestic-currency-equivalent to returns on US Treasury Bills). Domestic currency, nominal terms (inflation between 1995 and 1998 was relatively low: the wholesale price index increased by 6.4%, 8.1%, 7.8%, and only 1.5%, respectively). [a] = Mexican crisis; [b] = East Asian crisis; [c] = Russian default; and [d] = domestic default by the State of Minas Gerais.

*Sources:* BCB (2011); Palma (2002b, 2006).

left a much longer-lasting effect—in fact, with other factors, it generated a path-dependent dynamic that still occurs today (leading Brazil to the highest real interest rates in the world).[15] Not surprisingly, in its last financial report Banco Santander indicates that one-quarter of all its worldwide profits came from its Brazilian operations despite this country having only half that share in its overall assets; meanwhile, in both Spain and the United Kingdom the relationship is exactly the other way around. In other words, Santander's profit margins in Brazil are about three times higher than those in Spain and in the United Kingdom—32 percent in Brazil (as of September 30, 2011, trailing 12 months [ttm]), while in its operations in Spain it only managed 12.6 percent. In fact, Santander's "operating margin" in Brazil reached no less than 48 percent (ttm, same period).[16] And these asymmetries are not the result of current European difficulties, as they have been going on for a long time. These asymmetries form a crucial part of the already mentioned Latin American "two-times-half-style-capitalism," in which (compared with other parts of the world) institutional arrangements and political settlements are such that the domestic elite and foreign corporations are able, grosso modo, to get twice as much from half the effort.

Second, the resulting high cost of sterilization becomes evident in the difference between what was paid for the paper sold to sterilize and what was recuperated from the return on their holding of foreign-exchange reserves (i.e., between lines "**i**" and "**r**"). Finally, Brazil systematically violated a fiscal "golden rule" by paying a much higher rate for its public debt than the rate at which it managed to increase public revenues (let alone its income per capita; on these issues, see Lopes, 2009; Palma, 2006).

Furthermore, the levels of lending rates that followed were remarkable: the annualized *real* interest rate paid for working capital peaked at 60 percent, while that for consumer credit did so at 115 percent. With these rates, of course, hardly any financial asset of the banking system (mostly made of household and corporate debt) could perform; as discussed elsewhere, nonperforming loans—as well as a remarkable lack of "transparency" in the banking sector, weak regulatory public institutions, and the end of "inflation income" by the banking system—led to a succession of banking crises, each adding a significant amount to the stock of the public-sector debt due to a populist policy of indiscriminate bailouts of both private and public banks.

In fact, the ease with which the Brazilian government could finance its domestic debt was due primarily to private banks falling over themselves to buy public paper, as this was just about the only financial asset that could perform at such rates. Regarding the rest of their portfolio, private banks (not having read—or, more likely, having read but not understood—Stiglitz) tried to increase profitability by the self-defeating policy of ever-increasing spreads, leading to nonperforming debt increasing even faster (see Lopes, 2009; Palma, 2002b, 2006). Therefore, no prizes for guessing in which country (in both regions) the crisis of the domestic banking system came *well before* the overall financial crisis (and was a major component that led up to it)—as opposed to countries in which the banking crisis came either immediately before the crash, or only *after* the crash, when sharp devaluations hit both sides of bank-balance sheets (leading to exploding foreign exchange liabilities and bank portfolios becoming nonperforming due to falling incomes and asset-price deflation).

The case of Brazil is also very important for the critique of "moral-hazard-type" mainstream crisis analysis. For example, according to McKinnon and Pill (1997), the main cause of agents losing their capacity to assess and price their risk properly is that internal and external moral hazards led to "artificially" low interest rates; these, in turn, gave a false incentive to accumulate excessive amounts of private (let alone public) risk. However, in Brazil, although high interest rates did help to avoid a "route 1" financial crisis, they did so by creating a different (but equally damaging) type of financial crisis ("route 2"). So, the magical realism of Brazil's "route 2" is that it created a financial crisis by trying to avoid one.

## 3.2. The East Asia Story of an "Endogenous Pull" of Foreign Capital: The Cost of Maintaining High Levels of Investment in the Face of Rapidly Falling Profit Rates

In a sense, EA's story is less transparent than LA's. Inflows were not as remarkably large and their composition was more stable; real effective exchange rates remained stable; current account deficits, when looked at as share of exports, were small; interest rates were low and stable, and there was no consumption boom, no collapse of savings, and no deficits in the public sector. So, what about the often-mentioned moral-hazard-led investment boom?

As mentioned above, the left-hand panel of figure 13.10 shows that in LA (despite the tsunami of FDI) private investment seems to find a "natural ceiling" at about 15 percent of GDP, while in "Schumpeterian" EA it seems to be twice as high.[17] Furthermore, the graph (using IMF data) also shows that in Korea, Malaysia, and Thailand there is little evidence of a pre-1997 "moral-hazard-led" investment boom (as third-generation models and the IMF would like us to believe; see IMF, 1998; Krugman, 2001). Therefore, the key question that still needs to be answered is why the Korean corporate sector needed such large capital inflows to finance an ambitious but relatively *stable* investment effort. The right-hand panel provides the answer.

As discussed in detail elsewhere (Palma, 2003, 2006), and mainly due to declining profitability (a decline that had little to do with the Krugman's total factor productivity (TFP)-type critique of Korea, and a lot to do with a

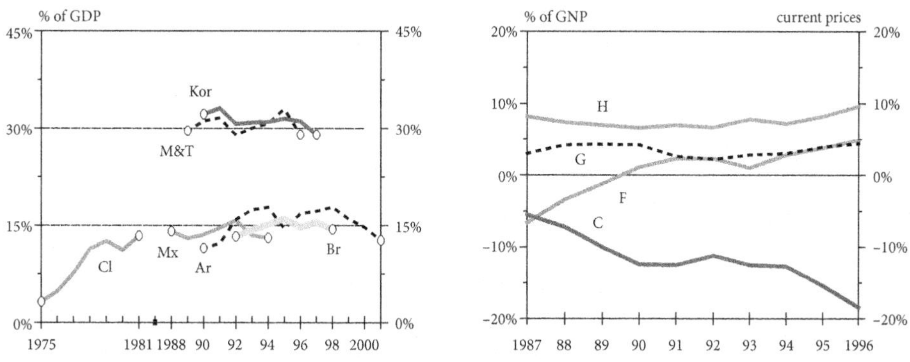


**Figure 13.10** East Asia and Latin America: Private investment between the beginning of financial liberalization and respective financial crisis. South Korea: Sectoral surpluses of the household, government, foreign, and corporate sectors, 1987–1996. *Note*: [M&T] = average of Malaysia and Thailand. [H] = households; [G] = government; [F] = balance of the financial account of the balance of payments; and [C] = corporate sector. Sectoral surpluses are the differences between sectoral savings and investment. *Sources:* For private investment, IMF (2011b); and for Korea's sectoral surpluses, KCB (2011).

"technology-led" collapse of micro-electronic prices),[18] the corporate sector had to finance its high, but relatively *stable*, levels of investment by switching from retained profits to debt. This process caused the sectoral deficit of the corporate sector to increase from about 5 percent to nearly 20 percent of GNP, absorbing in the process not only all the increase in the surplus of the "foreign sector," but also that of the household and government sectors as well.[19]

Consequently, is the IMF (1998) right (as well as other critics of the "East Asian model") when it blames all on moral-hazard-led 'over' investment? Again, the answer is (as is so often the case) more complex than a typical Washington Consensus one. The crucial issue that leads to misunderstandings in the East Asian crisis is forgetting that once you have gone into the type of high-tech exports characteristic of the region, you can only be competitive if able to produce at the cutting edge of (a rapidly changing) technology. And to be able to remain at that level, there seems to be little option but to invest at East Asian heights. Therefore, when profitability collapsed, the choice for Korea was whether to stay in the micro-electronics business altogether, or to look for a new type of development pattern elsewhere (and in doing so, allowing in the process for a significant amount of its accumulated physical, human, institutional, and social capital to depreciate). In the memory-chip business, for example, this meant that Korea had to invest what it took to catch up with Taiwan's breakthrough into a 16-megabyte D-Ram chip, or to leave the industry—as nobody wanted to buy Korea's obsolete 4-megabyte chip anymore. That is, it had to decide between investing in what it took to keep exporting micro-chips or switching to exporting potato chips (as it were). Even better, instead of exporting D-Ram memory chips, why not follow the LA example—with its above-mentioned "low-hanging-fruit-type" export style—and return to the less capital-intensive (and less technologically challenging) silk and seaweed, Korea's two main exports before its massive industrialization drive?

In fact, what might have been an effective solution for EA as a whole was a Keynesian-style program of regional investment coordination, because what triggered the collapse of the price of the D-Ram memory in 1995 was massive new Taiwanese investment coming on stream at the wrong time (i.e., when prices were already weakening due to a rapidly growing supply).

## 4. The Day of Reckoning

Unsurprisingly, given the size and instability of inflows and macroeconomic imbalances, Minskyan financial fragilities—fragilities that were specific to each route—quickly began to emerge. Furthermore, countries in all three routes also had to face three common problems: (1) shortening of the term structure of their foreign debt (in Thailand, for example, the share of short-term debt in total debt grew from 15 percent to 52 percent between the beginning of financial liberalization and the 1997 crisis; IMF, 2011b); (2) a rapid decline in the ratio of reserves to short-term debt (in Mexico this ratio fell from 1.6 in 1993 to 0.6 in 1994, while in Brazil it did so from 1.2 in 1995 to 0.6 in 1998; Ibid.); and (3) the constant danger that, in a financially liberalized economy, the attack could also come from "within" (particularly when the ratio of "reserves to M2" became particularly low—in Mexico, for example, this ratio fell from 23 percent in 1993 to just 5 percent in 1994; Ibid.).

In sum, "route 1" countries, after massive surges in inflows, tried to keep public finances in balance and hoped (in vain) that markets would resolve the resulting private imbalances. As it happened, the result was rather different from that predicted by mainstream thinking: it was a path to financial crisis led by an explosion of credit to the private sector, declining levels of interest rates after price stabilization, and a rapid real-exchange revaluation. All of these produced consumption booms (with a rapidly growing import content), asset bubbles (both in stocks and in real estate), a collapse of savings, deteriorating current accounts, a bias in the already low levels of investment toward residential construction, and growing nonperforming bank assets.[20] The imbalances created by the liberalization of capital accounts, instead of being tamed by "automatic stabilizers," were amplified by automatic "destabilizers" (Stiglitz 2003). In the meantime, foreign and domestic debts exploded, while the term structure of the foreign debt deteriorated, and the growing currency mismatch in the balance sheets of the corporate and banking sector made them ever more vulnerable to currency depreciation. This route generated so many financial fragilities that it did not take much for it to face a sudden collapse of confidence and an abrupt withdrawal of finance, leading to major financial crises.

Because in LA events helping to precipitate such collapses are never in short supply, financial crises did follow. In 1994 in Mexico, for example, within the 12 months prior to the December crisis, there was a massive indigenous uprising in Chiapas; the assassination of the presidential candidate of the ruling party (the PRI); a not-very-transparent presidential election; the assassination of the Secretary General of the PRI (with the widespread belief that the president had been involved in both assassinations); and a central bank that would only release information on foreign reserves every four months giving "insiders" a huge advantage allowing them to sell their "Tesobonos" to "information-challenged" foreign investors. (The share of the latter in "Tesobonos" increased from 6% in February to 60% in August; see Armendáriz, 2003). The speed of Clinton's reaction to the Mexican crisis was related to this.) All of these events, of course, provided plenty of political thrills in an increasingly financially fragile economy (Palma, 2006). Basically, in DCs "utility maximizing cum rational expectations" agents operating in "free" markets are a little bit more complex (and original) phenomena than the idealized fictional constructions of mainstream models. In fact, at the end of 1994 it only took a relatively small external shock (a tiny increase in US interest rates in November, which produced a minor bond crisis) for the debacle to take place (Kregel, 1998; Palma, 2003a).

All these crises represented huge costs for the respective economies; in Chile, for example, the "Chicago boys" experiment ended up with a 20 percent drop in GDP ( between the third quarters of 1981 and 1983), with unemployment reaching over 30 percent, and with the share of the population in absolute poverty doubling to 55 percent. Furthermore, the cumulative cost of the rescue of the banking system was equivalent to 43 percent of GDP; in addition, the "administrative" cost of this rescue reached an extra 9 percent of GDP (Barandiarán and Hernández, 1999; see also Díaz-Alejandro, 1984; Palma, 1998).

The path to financial crisis for "route 2" Brazil also started with a surge in inflows, but the scene was soon dominated by Brazil's effort to avoid becoming "another Mexico." High interest rates and sterilization were successful in avoiding a repeat of "route 1," and in consolidating price stabilization; however, soon, they also created massive domestic financial fragilities in the banking sector and in state-government finances, leading to an increase in public debt through continuous (often indiscriminate and sometimes politically corrupt) private and public banking and state-government rescue activities (one of these was the huge amount of subsidies to state governments and state banks paid by the government to get through parliament the necessary institutional reforms needed for Cardoso's re-election—see Lopes, 2009, and Palma, 2006). Moreover, this public debt exploded due to high interest rates (i.e., a public-sector Ponzi finance system had ballooned out of control) while the real economy imploded because of these rates. But high interest rates became ever more necessary in order to sustain the "peg" and avoid further domestic banking crises due to both high foreign-exchange liabilities in the financial sector, and a possible stampede by edgy fund managers. Again, it did not take much (just one of many of Yeltsin's follies in 1998 and a minor internal political crisis—a state governor declaring a moratorium on its state debt with the central bank) for this route to end up in a major financial crisis.

Finally, in "route 3" countries, there was another massive surge in inflows leading to an increase of private credit at low interest rates. However, this did not lead to consumption booms, or collapses of saving—and in Korea there were not even asset bubbles in the stock market or real estate. Rather, in the context of declining profitability (particularly the sphere of microelectronics due to collapsing prices), there was a high (though stable) level of investment, in a "high-tech" world where there was competitiveness only at the cutting edge of a very rapidly changing technology. This ended up producing corporate debt/equity ratios that even in this part of the world should have caused dizziness. Added to this, Korea had same bizarre regulation that gave the corporate sector a strong incentive to borrow abroad "short" (long-term borrowing had to face significantly more red tape), as well as a central bank that seemed to have enjoyed the thrill of living dangerously (and omnipotently) with low levels of reserves. The resulting rapid decline in the ratio of reserves to short-term debt made Korea particularly vulnerable to events in Thailand and Malaysia (at the time of the Thai devaluation, Korean reserves could only cover half its short-term liabilities; in fact, they were not even enough to cover debt with 90 days' maturity or less).

Again—and despite a stunning growth record, and fundamentals that although not perfect were the envy of most DCs—it did not take much for this route to also encounter a major financial crisis. Basically, voracious fund managers—eager to profit from long-standing but only precipitately acknowledged "peccadilloes" (the precarious balance-sheet structure of the Thai banking system)—had a much-delayed collapse of confidence that led to bank runs and a major financial crisis.

## 5. How Can One Explain That Most of the Economic Profession, Financial Markets, and the Financial Press Still Insist That These Crises Were "Undeserved" and "Unpredictable"?

It is difficult to understand the mainstream insistence that most of the blame for these crises should lie on very specific—and perfectly avoidable—'exogenous' issues; i.e., external to the spontaneous working of highly liquid and 'light-touch' regulated financial markets. "Missing markets" are often part of this story. Ultimately, there is always "chance." In this mainstream narrative, financial markets are supposed to play only the essentially *passive* role of having the intrinsic ability to supply effectively the credit intermediation and payment services that are needed for the real economy to work, and of discounting a future that is predictable (in a probabilistic sense). Furthermore, they are supposed to be able to do so with amazing accuracy no matter how over-liquid and under regulated they are. So if unmanageable financial instability occurs, one of two things has to be the excuse: either a missing market is creating a "market failure," or something "foreign" is meddling in these markets (e.g., a government behaving irresponsibly by monetising a large fiscal deficit). If none of these two can be identified, it must be "chance." On the whole, something interfering in the market tends to be favored in the position of the culprit. In the case of Mexico, for example, most of the attention in mainstream literature has been diverted toward a relatively expansionary macro-policy in an election year; in Brazil, toward the political stalemate that delayed endlessly a necessary fiscal reform (a *Waiting for Godot*-type story); in Korea, toward a supposedly "moral-hazard-driven over-investment-cum-corporate-debt" story; and in Thailand, toward a "crony-capitalist-driven unbalanced-balance-sheet" story. In a way, this mainstream attitude (of barking up the wrong tree) is no different from what happened after the 2008 financial crisis, when the usual suspects blamed everything on China or Greenspan, or they pointed at "liberals" for introducing the 1977 law that helped low-income people get mortgages. Anything would do (including the fall of the Berlin Wall, excessive testosterone in trading rooms, or even sunspots!—see Palma, 2009a for the "blame list"), except the possibility that the *autonomous* outcome of the free interaction of supposedly utility-maximizing agents, interacting in friendly regulated and over-liquid financial markets, could be an *endogenous* financial crisis (rather than some sort of "equilibrium").

So, how can one explain this attitude from most of the economic profession, financial markets, and the financial press? The answer to this complex question has at least three components. The *Wall Street Journal* provides a good insight into the first one. In an editorial soon after the beginning of the subprime crisis it stated that "the recent market turmoil is [...] raising the stock of one person: a little-known economist whose views have suddenly become very popular [...] Hyman Minsky" (August 18, 2007). Perhaps had they read (and, more importantly, had they read and understood) such obscure economists as Keynes, Minsky, Kindleberger, and so many others (including Stiglitz and Krugman) the *Wall Street Journal* (otherwise known as the *Pravda* of Wall Street) could have become more effective at predicting financial crises—and at realizing how "deserved" they usually are. The journal might even have learned how avoidable they could become under a revamp set of FDR/Keynesian-Bretton-Woods-type arrangements.[21]

This also applies to the "new" left which, when in government, often follows extreme versions of the mainstream orthodoxy (both in developing and developed countries). In terms of friendly regulation of financial markets, for example, nothing beats the "purity of belief" of New Labour in the form of Gordon Brown's Financial Service Authority (FSA). When in 1997 he created a new regulatory body for the financial industry (the FSA), he set it up not only as an "independent nongovernmental body" (i.e., a company limited by guarantee), but also as one that was actually financed by the financial services industry. Furthermore, he appointed ex-bankers as the chairman, chief executive officer, and nonexecutive directors. That is, he set the FSA up as operationally independent of the government, funded entirely by the financial corporations it was supposed to regulate, and led by financial-industry insiders. Thus, New Labour found a rather ingenious solution to the problem of "regulatory capture"; if, supposedly, lobbyists inevitably succeed in capturing the regulators, why not make them the regulators in the first place.

With Brown's "limited-touch" attitude toward financial regulation (so 'limited' that no one ever felt it), perhaps it is not surprising that at the beginning of the current financial crisis the first bank failure (Northern Rock) took place in the United Kingdom (one year before Lehman's Brothers). In fact, this bank became the first UK bank in 150 years to suffer a traditional bank run—a bank that had become famous for its 125% mortgages, and for its high-risk business model which involved borrowing short in wholesale credit markets (75% of its funds coming from this source, with the majority of interbank loans maturing overnight), to issue long-term mortgages based on this funding (to then re-sell—or securitize—these mortgages). Not surprisingly, with this type of balance sheet, Northern Rock was particularly vulnerable to a "credit crunch." In other words (and not surprisingly), with this type of "limited-touch" regulation, over-liquid financial markets became self-destructive. In fact, it would not be an exaggeration to say that Northern Rock is a good example of how "self-regulation-cum-excess-liquidity" led to the self-destructive "bananization" of financial markets!

Indeed, in the UK the regulatory failings in the lead up to the current financial crisis were such—and the degree to which the FSA has been discredited as a result—that for many observers it came as no surprise that its new Chair tried to regain 'the moral high ground' with its speech at the 2011 annual Mansion House banquet hosted by the Lord Mayor of London (see epigraph at the beginning of the paper).

I sometimes wonder whether mainstream economics today is just shorthand for "nothing left to decide"—and, of course, "nothing left to think about *critically*" (Palma, 2009b). In fact, the attitude of many mainstream economists toward policy making (before and after the current crisis) resembles Lord Kelvin's attitude toward physics at the end of the nineteenth century, when he famously declared that in physics "there is nothing new to be discovered now. All that remains is more and more precise measurement" (Kelvin, 1900). From this perspective, the incapacity of mainstream economists to consider alternative points of view is such that even the "New Keynesians" still work within a "complete markets" paradigm and with the strongest version of the efficient-markets hypothesis (Buiter, 2009).

Along this line, perhaps the most amusing definition by a mainstream economist of what "heterodox economics" is all about is found in a Working Paper of the Chilean Central Bank (that analyzes the post-1982 banking crisis in Chile). According to the authors, "The Chilean solution to the crisis was heterodox in the sense that many policies appear to have been arbitrary, and policy mistakes were made…along the way" (Barandiarán and Hernández, 1999). This attitude toward alternative points of view can only be explained by the usual dynamics of idealization: when there is an unremitting need to sustain the idealization of something (in this case, that of the "purity of markets" in the face of so much evidence against it in the form of recurring 'endogenous' financial crises), what is needed is simultaneously to demonize something else (in this case, anything to do with alternative points of view). In fact, the more evident the flaws are of what is being idealized, the stronger the demonization of the alternative view has to be.[22]

That is, in LA, as in most of the Anglo-American world, economic reforms were carried out with a peculiar political ideology—what I like to call the "Anglo-Iberian" neoliberal fundamentalism—where "toxic ideas" were as damaging as "toxic assets" in the leadup to the many financial crises discussed here.[23] A case in point is Gustavo Franco, the president of the Brazilian Central Bank who led Brazil into the 1999 financial crisis: for him, "[the alternative for Brazilians today] is to be neo-liberal or neo-idiotic [neo-burros]" (*Veja*, November 15, 1996). And, of course, "burros" (and "obscure" economists, such as Minsky) belong in intellectual gulags. In fact, for Franco, his main task in government was to help "undo forty years of stupidity."[24] With this "reverse-gear" attitude, LA's experiment in economic reform and financial liberalization almost inevitably ended up as an exercise in "not-very-creative" destruction.

This reminds me of what Keynes once said (discussing Say's Law) about Ricardo conquering England as completely as the Holy Inquisition conquered Spain. Something similar has happened in LA, where its special brand of neoliberalism has conquered the region, including many in its left-wing intelligentsia, just as fiercely as the Holy Inquisition conquered Spain. In fact, this process has been so successful that it has actually had the effect of "closing the imagination" to conceptualizing alternatives.

Second, another part of the answer to the above question is the way in which many within mainstream economics, international financial markets, and the financial press have interpreted economic news before, during and after the financial crash. Following Steiner's (1993) psychoanalytical understanding of the difficulty the human mind has in recognizing reality when faced with particularly complex and emotionally charged problems—and of its usual failure to live with them and adjust accordingly—I distinguish three stages in what could be called the "financial-realities-awareness" cycle: first, there is a "lack-of-awareness" phase, characterized by a growing detachment from reality (the manic/euphoria/irrational exuberance phase); then, at the time of the crash, there is a (more truthful, but short-lived) "sudden-awareness" window (e.g., Greenspan's "shock disbelief"); but this is soon transformed into a new form of (omnipotent) "lack-of-awareness" scenario, characterized by the need to cover up, evade, and distort (e.g., it is all the fault of governments, anyway!).

In the first (mania) phase of each financial cycle, which could be called the initial "turning-a-blind-eye" stage, good news is often overstated and bad news simply ignored. Eventually, when some bad news can no longer be ignored (e.g., in the current crisis, when in August 2007 HSBC announced increased provisions for nonperforming subprime mortgages), this is reluctantly acknowledged but with the clear understanding that "everything is still under control" despite the fact that most of the pieces of the financial fragilities puzzle are already evident (see, for example, figure 13.1).

The second stage of the "awareness" cycle comes to the fore when a catastrophic event suddenly reveals what so far has been denied (e.g., Lehman's demise, in the current cycle) and then reality sets in. Now there is an abrupt turn toward total panic and dismay. Suddenly, bad news is felt as devastating (and sometimes is even exaggerated), and everybody seems completely overwhelmed by the catastrophe. According to Greenspan, for example, this happened to him after Lehman's, and his reaction was one of "shocked disbelief"; he then famously acknowledged to a congressional committee that what he found was nothing short of "a flaw in my economic ideology—in the conceptual framework with which I have dealt with reality." And he was "very distressed by that fact." And when he was asked, "In other words, you found that your view of the world, your ideology, was not right, it was not working?" He replied, "Yes—precisely. That's precisely the reason I was shocked, because I had been going for 40 years or more... [with the idea that my view of the world] was working exceptionally well."[25]

However, this second stage in the "awareness cycle" seems to be short-lived because it is often followed by a further twist. Basically, soon after the "sudden-awareness" stage there is a turn toward a new form of a "lack of awareness"—a retreat from the (unbearable) shock into a new form of omnipotence. In a nutshell, the extent of the crash and its (ideological and analytical) repercussions are so devastating that they cannot any longer be acknowledged. When in the second stage "truth" is recognized, it is found to be unbearable. Its sustainable recognition would involve a loss of what kept us going, and the mourning of this loss is too difficult. So the "shocked disbelief" begins to fizzle out, and reality begins to be evaded, misrepresented, distorted, and covered up in a new "lack-of-awareness" scenario. The most important issue here is that (very conveniently) it is as if nothing needs to be properly mourned—especially the economic ideology responsible for the crisis (the "toxic ideas" that led to the financial crises). After all, the current global financial crisis is (or should be) to the grandiose Reagan and Thatcher neoliberal counterreformation what the fall of the Berlin Wall was to the Communist paradigm. Only a new form of "lack of awareness" can help avoid this unbearable scenario. Therefore, in order to sustain the status quo after the crash there is a new need to cover up, evade, and distort. So, the focus of attention quickly (and conveniently) switched from the distressing idea of the self-destructive nature of unregulated and over-liquid financial markets, to the more familiar terrain of the 'usual (and ideologically less threatening) suspects', such as problems relating to China (how could it not be China!), labor rigidities, uncontrolled immigration, excessive regulation, and (for sure) big governments. And in the United Kingdom, of course, the European Union had to be a cause. Shocked disbelief? What shocked disbelief?

In other words, if until the crash those involved (politicians, mainstream academics, financial markets, and financial press) are initiqlly unable to acknowledge the existence of a fundamental problem, why would anybody fix it? And if *after* the shock the new urgency is about moving away from the unbearable awareness, and into a new phase in which the main concern is not the further revelation of truth, but the cover-up of truth, what is the hope for a proper understanding? The key issue here seems to be the difficulty for those involved in creating the economic environment that led to the crisis of *sustaining* their full awareness of what has happened. For example, although many things have already been said regarding the speed, the size, and the nature of the rescue operations after each financial crisis (including the urgent need to stop the rot, as well as old boys' networks at work, corruption, and so on), perhaps an *additional* component of these rescue operations (particularly their urgency) is that they are *a fundamental component of the "cover-up."* When Clinton quickly intervened after the Mexican crisis with his more than $70 billion rescue package (in 2010 US$), he was not just saving his mates from Wall Street (who had been caught badly exposed in Mexico); most probably, he was *also* trying to turn the page as quickly as possible—so that one could turn a blind eye to the evidence emerging from that crisis regarding the risks associated with full opening of the capital account in middle-income countries. The same happened with the massive IMF intervention in Brazil and East Asia. And in the case of Chile, when the government was happy to spend more than 50 percent of GDP rescuing the banking system after the 1982 crisis, and when most governments in industrialized countries were all too happy to shower financial markets with trillions of dollars following Lehman's downfall—bringing the concept of a "soft budget constraint" to a totally new dimension—perhaps they were *also* trying to cover up quickly their unbearable "shocked disbelief." And, inevitably, some eternally optimistic Keynesians were bound to mistake the soft budget constraint for a "vast, Keynesian, fiscal stimuli."[26] That is, instead of being part of a cover-up, keeping financial dinosaurs on life support was definite evidence that "we are all Keynesian again"!

Also, often the cover-up extends to personal responsibility. A clear example is that of Larry Summers who, as Clinton's Secretary of the Treasury, led the financial deregulation brigade that created the conditions under which financial sanity was left to depend entirely on "self-regulation" and "market discipline." Summers, for example, led the repeal of the 1933 Glass-Steagall Act, and he also vehemently opposed the regulation of derivative contracts. Then, nearly a decade later, as Obama's Director of the National Economic Council, Summers had the task to undo a mess that to a great extent was his creation. So it should probably come as no surprise that when he devised Obama's (so-called) fiscal stimulus plan, almost all funds were diverted to keep financial relics afloat (and save his own tarnished reputation) rather than to create a proper fiscal stimulus to encourage output and employment.[27] Furthermore, when he was asked about the collapse of AIG, Summers's response was typical of this third stage in the "awareness/lack-of-awareness" cycle. He answered, "There are a lot of terrible things that have happened in the last eighteen months, but what's happened at A.I.G…the way it was not regulated, the way no one was watching…is outrageous."[28]

Could it be that this is the same Summers who in 1998, in his testimony before Congress, had argued against the regulation of all types of derivative contracts (including AIG's credit default swaps—even of their "naked" counterparts), because "the parties to these kinds of contract are largely sophisticated financial institutions that would appear to be eminently capable of protecting themselves from fraud and counterparty insolvencies. [...] To date there has been no clear evidence of a need for additional regulation of the institutional OTC derivatives market, and we would submit that proponents of such regulation [i.e., Brooksley Born, the chairperson of the Commodity Futures Trading Commission, who became strongly in favor of regulation in derivative markets after the LTCM debacle] must bear the burden of demonstrating that need."[29] Some would argue that Summers' "outrage" at the lack of regulation in derivative markets was just sheer hypocrisy, but I would not be at all surprised if by then he had basically lost touch with his own past, and he actually believed what he was saying.

However, in this new 'lack-of-awareness' scenario, characterized (as mentioned above) by a retreat from the (unbearable) shock into a new form of omnipotence, in which the main concern is not the further revelation of truth, but the cover up of truth, the current British Chancellor, George Osborne, should take pride of place. In a recent address to the EBRD (18/5/12), he proclaimed that "[a]s the storms of the Eurozone crisis gather, there is a risk that the good work [we have done in Britain during] the last 20 years in building a stable financial sector and creating jobs and prosperity is unwound." (http://www.ebrd.com/pages/homepage.shtml#&panel1-1). And close behind comes Niall Ferguson, when he argued that the current banking crisis is not the result of too little but of too much regulation: "Banks are on the receiving end of a raft of financial regulation that is killing their business model."[30] That is, we are now supposed to believe that financial regulation is not the cure but the disease itself!

This type of cover-up makes it possible for the "purity of belief" not have to come into conflict with the intricacies of the real world. But, inevitably, this ideological status quo ex-post crash is ever more in need of further cover-ups! Also, in the post-crash narrative, "chance" is often also used as a (convenient) validation of the new turning of a blind eye. Again, Greenspan provides an example; after having acknowledged the dreadfulness of his initial "shocked disbelief," and his dismay of finding a major flaw in his economic ideology, he soon began to argue that, after all, the 2008 crisis might well have been a "one-in-a-hundred-year" event. That is, it was still possible that the crisis was *undeserved* and *unpredictable* after all! In the same spirit, in most analyses of the 1997 East Asian crisis (especially in third-generation models), the fundamental ex post assumption is that this crisis started with a bank run that occurred in Thailand *by chance*—the outcome of financial markets turning their attention to Southeast Asia (with some trepidation) due to the British transfer of Hong Kong to China (Chang and Velasco, 2001—the Thai government was forced to float the baht on July 2, 1997, one day after this transfer). In turn, second-generation models want us to believe that the Exchange Rate Mechanism (ERM) crisis in the United Kingdom was just a "self-fulfilling" shock in an economy that was fundamentally sound: speculators who believe that other speculators were about to attack were encouraged to do so themselves. The same happened in the 1998 Brazilian crisis: it was all supposed to be bad luck: "contagion" from unrelated events far away—literally, at the other end of the world (in Asia and Russia). And in the case of Korea, the crises supposedly occurred due to another random event: a sudden flight of capital from another economy that was also fundamentally sound following the crisis in Thailand.

And so on. (see appendix). After all, as Sophocles had already warned us a long time ago (via one of his characters), "our mortal life is ruled by chance. There is no such thing as foreknowledge" (quoted in Steiner, 1993).

However, as Žižek explains,

> Repetition, according to Hegel, plays a crucial role in history: when something happens just once, it may be dismissed as an accident, something that might have been avoided if the situation had been handled differently; but when the same event repeats itself, it is a sign that a deeper historical process is unfolding.... The same holds for... financial crises. (2011, 1)

Therefore, the convenient use of the idea of "chance" helps preserve the ideological status quo. The key point here is that if after the shock (and the unbearable awareness) the new urgency is not about the further revelation of truth, but the cover-up of truth, there is little hope for a proper understanding. Furthermore, the crash, instead of helping reveal the self-destructive nature of unregulated and over-liquid financial markets (a particularly distressing idea for mainstream thinking), is transformed into a further confirmation of traditional beliefs—and governments, financial regulation, labor rigidities, uncontrolled immigration, China, the Euro, and so on can be further demonized.

And third, particularly as far as LA is concerned, there is a specific element to the genesis of recent financial crises: the peculiar politico-institutional framework in which financial liberalization and economic reform were carried out in the region, as opposed to the way in which they were implemented in Asia (see Palma, 2011a). Part of this framework is the "original sin" of LA's economic reforms: the bizarre collection of "first-generation" heads of state that initiated these reforms. Although not unfamiliar to Latin American political history, Pinochet, Salinas, Collor, Menem, Fujimori, Alemán, Bucaram, and many others certainly deserve several entries in *The Guinness Book of Records*, particularly under the headings of cynicism, corruption, human rights abuses, electoral fraud, and petit bourgeois parvenu-populism. Almost invariably, after having initially got into power by using an anti-neoliberal discourse (even Pinochet's initial discourse was closer to that of 1930s Franco than to 1970s Friedman), their sudden eagerness to switch to the neoliberal camp was in part related to the opportunity to create a new structure of property rights from which massive new rents could be extracted. And, of course, the more successful they were in selling the neoliberal dream, the more extravagant the predatory capitalism that followed could be. And in their eagerness to support the process of economic reform and financial liberalization in LA, those associated with the Washington Consensus somehow succeeded in turning a blind eye to the Russian-style predatory nature taken by these reforms, especially during the process of privatization. In fact, it is quite remarkable how in these circles what was going on in this respect was basically ignored: from the corruption of some of the "Chicago boys" in Chile, who were dismantling the huge state apparatus for their own benefit (Mönckeberg 2001), to Salinas's privatization extravaganza, where one privatization alone (a telephone company) made one individual (practically overnight) the fourth largest billionaire in the world (he then began his rapid ascent to become the world's number one).[31] In fact, probably never in the history of the region has success or failure in business depended so much on political connections as during the first stages of the neoliberal era. All this gives Marx's concept of "primitive accumulation" a new meaning. And despite Menem having run a privatization circus no different from Salinas's, as late as 1998, in the annual meeting of the IMF and the World Bank, Michel Camdessu (then the head of the IMF) still introduced Menem as "the president with the best economic policies in the world"—which is rather like praising Al Capone for having the best business model in the beverages industry.

And by opting for such a blatant "turning a blind eye" to corruption and mismanagement, all that mainstream academics and the financial press could do in their respective "lack-of-awareness phase" was to come up with such uncontroversial recommendations as the need for "optimal sequences" or the need for good governance. That is, after each financial crisis mainstream economists slowly began to recommend supposedly optimal policies for closing the stable gates well after all the horses had bolted.

## Conclusion

The moral of the story of the "three routes" during the second cycle of capital inflows (from "Brady bonds" to the Argentinian 2001–2002 crisis) is that no matter how middle-income DCs that have opened up their capital account fully have tried to handle the absorption of the sudden surges of inflows that usually follow, they have ended up in a major financial crisis. And regarding the current third cycle, the jury is still out in terms of both how long the current unprecedented amount of inflows and favorable terms of trade would last, and on the nature of the (inevitable) "correction"—no prizes for guessing where my money would be (Palma, 2011a).

To indicate the extent of the likely "correction" ahead, although LA's current account deficits in 2010 stood at only 1.1 percent of GDP, had the terms of trade been those of 2003 (the year before the commodity-price boom), this deficit would have jumped to 4.9 percent (Ocampo, 2011). Furthermore, this figure is particularly high for those countries that benefited most from the commodity boom. Corresponding figures for Chile in 2010 were a surplus of 1.9 percent versus a deficit of 15.5 percent. In other words, at the time of this writing LA not only had already adjusted fully to its new terms of trade and abundance of inflows (as if these were a permanent state of affairs), but also has done so almost entirely via increased consumption. Therefore, if its terms of trade were to return to its pre-commodity-boom levels, or if the current levels of inflows were to reverse drastically (both events entirely likely), the domestic adjustment needed in many countries would be no different (or worse) than that of the 1982 debt crisis. And if both adjustments were to take place simultaneously, it could be like Greece but without German taxpayers. In other words, the post-2008 (commodity-price and inflow) recovery is so fragile that candles should be lit for speculators continuing to believe that commodities will remain the sole one-way bet and that China and India will continue their (forced) march toward their rightful place under the sun.

Of course, with hindsight, one can always think of hypothetical ways in which the worst excesses in each route could have been avoided, but the fact is that surges in inflows into economies with newly open capital accounts have created such pro-cyclical dynamics and risk accumulation that they have proved extraordinarily difficult to absorb. And as Brazil has shown, desperate attempts to deal with the open-capital account/inflow problem via sterilization and "tough" monetary policies, instead of helping to avoid a financial crisis, it just changes the nature of the crisis. In all probability, "first-best" capital controls (i.e., an attempt to deal with the problem at source) could have been a much more effective way forward.[32]

All of the above makes it difficult to understand the direction followed by mainstream literature on financial crises. From this perspective, one of the main points of this chapter is to show that what these countries had were truly *deserved* and fairly *predictable* financial crises.[33] The financial fragilities of route 3 were more intricate, but only Malaysia could possibly argue that its crisis was, to a certain extent, "undeserved."

The end result of all of the above (and in particular the three issues discussed in section 5) is that mainstream literature has ended up paying little attention to (what I believe are) the four main issues surrounding financial crises in DCs with open-capital accounts. First, why is it that the incentive mechanisms and resource allocation dynamics of "friendly regulated" domestic financial and asset markets have failed so badly under the pressure of surges in inflows (and the resulting injection of liquidity) by purely *endogenous* reasons? As a result, otherwise "utility-maximising" agents operating in "lightly touched" regulated markets have ended up accumulating more risk than was privately, let alone socially, efficient. This excessive amount of risk has become evident in the alternate phase of the cycle, that of the sudden stop in external financing.[34] Second, why is it that some basic self-adjustment mechanisms—such as relative price adjustments (e.g., real exchange rates)—have also failed badly when faced with such sharp changes in external and domestic liquidity? Instead of helping to bring these economies back to a sustainable growth path, these adjustment mechanisms have tended to augment the cycle (no "self-adjusting" equilibria here—just pro-cyclical dynamics). As mentioned above, the imbalances created by the liberalization of capital accounts and inflow booms, instead of being tamed by automatic stabilizers have been amplified by automatic destabilizers. Third, why is it that in financially liberalized economies market forces have also often pushed governments and central banks into further *pro-cyclical* policies (and politics) rather than into countercyclical ones? Fourth, as the successful Chilean and Colombian experiences with capital controls in the 1990s show (see Ocampo and Palma, 2008), there is a clear role for pro-active "agency" (e.g., public policy and regulation) in order to counteract the pro-cyclical dynamics of open-capital accounts—and of financial liberalization in general. In fact, mainstream economics' aversion to them (the "any intervention would simply make things worse" mechanical response from a typical "Stepford economist") resembles what a Chilean president famously said at the beginning of the twentieth century: "In life there are two types of problems, those that will get solved by themselves, and those that have no solution" (see Palma, 2009b). The contemporary mainstream economics version of this worldview is that now in financial markets there are only two types of problems: those that can be solved by themselves if markets are allowed to operate more freely, and those that have no solution.

My main argument is that the fundamental explanation of these crises points not just to a set of "market failures," but to a *systemic market failure*: evidence suggests that some financial crises, as with those studied here, are basically the *spontaneous* outcome of actions by supposedly utility-maximizing cum rational expectations agents, freely operating in "lightlytouched" regulated, *over-liquid* financial markets.

A crucial issue here is that financial markets (as opposed to many other markets) invariably have had the capacity to clear *regardless of their amount of liquidity*. And they do so only partially by reducing transaction costs, margins, and spreads to traditional customers; they also do so by opening up new (and increasingly risky) "outlets" for that liquidity, in which they often do the opposite regarding spreads. That is, they did not only open up a new subprime "outlet" with practically no transaction costs (a signature would do), but after a short "teaser" period, subprime mortgages usually became two to three times more expensive than normal mortgages. And finally, an increasing amount of fraud can become another particularly helpful (and widely used) "outlet" for excess liquidity.

The issue here is that only when financial markets operate as "seller markets" (i.e., relative shortage of liquidity) are they able to unload their liquidity without having to accumulate an amount of risk that is privately—let alone socially—inefficient. But when excess liquidity turns them into "buyer markets," the process of "clearing" invariably leads to the opposite environment, because they then have to attract (and often literally invent) a sufficient level of demand for that liquidity (no matter what). In extreme cases, any new demand would do—even people with "no income, no job, and no assets," as with the famous "ninja" mortgage in the recent subprime debacle, when financial markets under the pressure of having to clear excess liquidity (and after having exhausted every possible alternative, and independently from the 1977 Community Reinvestment Act), change their business motto to "redlining is no more"! That is, when financial markets began a process known as 'reverse redlining'—i.e., when lenders and insurers begin to target specifically those consumers that had been previously denied those services altogether (consumers that had been previously part of redliners' blacklists).

And in order to create new "outlets" for their liquidity, financial markets usually follow an age-old device: they progressively lower their operational standards, and they reduce the transaction costs of this liquidity. Also, as the current chair of the FSA recently stated at the annual Mansion House banquet, financial engineering can be an ingenious instrument to disguise the declining quality of new financial assets: "swollen financial markets tend to produce socially useless products and innovations, including a number of derivatives and hedging products, and aspects of the asset management industry and equity trading. [So] markets are not always wise."[35] And yet another traditional clearing mechanism by "swollen" financial markets (especially relevant here) is the rediscovery of emerging markets—as mentioned above, for international financial markets DCs have traditionally played the "customer of last resort" role (e.g., in the 1820s, 1860s, 1920s, 1970s, and 2000s).[36]

A crucial component in the dynamics leading to the creation of the necessary clearing levels of demand has been emphasized by Kindleberger (2000): a sudden access to easy credit invariably leads to a surge in expectations and animal spirits. This process then reinforces itself, becoming yet another self-fulfilling prophecy. Easy access to cheap credit fuels the expectations of future performance—a performance that is enhanced by the additional expenditure brought about by the extra borrowing. "Overlending" and "overborrowing" became, therefore, the result of a closely interrelated process, as well as one that had a clear *direction of causality*: the propensity to overlend led to the propensity to overborrow.

Basically, markets as a whole are not always right—indeed, in the case of financial markets they can be seriously wrong *as a whole*. For example, in the financial crises analyzed here there is plenty of evidence that over-liquid and "lightly touched" regulated financial markets can be driven by buyers who take little notice of underlying values (i.e., when investors have incentives to interpret information in a biased fashion *in a systematic way*). At the same time, as Long-Term Capital Management learned the hard way (soon after two of its directors had won the Nobel Memorial Prize in Economics), high liquidity can easily make assets that appeared to belong to independent clusters in the past become correlated—so diversification against those clusters cannot provide sufficient "staying power" anymore. Also, as the recent collapse of MF Global (and its "missing" customer funds) indicates—a collapse brought about by an overreliance on short-term funding, which dried up as revelations of its leveraged bets on European sovereign debt came to light—the capacity of agents operating in unregulated financial markets to learn from previous mistakes seems rather limited. For Keynes, perhaps, this would not come as a surprise. According to Deane, "The iconoclastic conclusion of [Keynes's] analysis was that there was no invisible hand translating private self-interests into social benefit. This was the nub of the Keynesian heresy" (1980, 182).

In reality, in over-liquid financial markets there seems to be no invisible hand able to translate private self-interests into *private* benefits in a sustainable way either! From this point of view, maybe the invisible hand is so invisible simply because it does not really exist—or, if it does, there is plenty of evidence that indicates that it becomes overwhelmed by the dynamics of over-liquid financial markets. Or, perhaps, under these circumstances it just prefers to take a sabbatical leave.

The essential point here is that mainstream economists will continue to find it difficult to get anywhere near a proper understanding of financial crises until they give up their "idolatry" of the market—idolatry in the sense of a "worship of a thing" (see Britton, 2002). As Stiglitz has said, this crisis is not just the outcome of a market failure here or there, "but a total failure of financial markets."[37] And the argument that this only happened because we still do not have "complete markets" sounds increasingly hollow—AIG, for example, with its new type of derivatives, had moved precisely into previously "missing" insurance markets (e.g., CDSs and "naked" CDSs)—and by the end of 2007, the outstanding CDS amount was US$62 trillion. Could anyone at the time actually believe that, if there was a financial crisis, those that had issued these CDSs had the capacity to respond?

In fact, over-liquid financial markets are so difficult to tame that one should not idealize the effectiveness of financial regulation either. Paraphrasing Churchill, perhaps the best thing one could say about "regulated" financial markets is that "many forms of resource allocation have been tried and will be tried in this world of sin and woe. No one should pretend that under excess-liquidity conditions the one done by 'regulated markets' is perfect or all-wise. Indeed, it has been said that under these conditions regulated financial markets are the worst form of resource allocation, except for all those other forms that have been tried from time to time."

In other words, there is no substitute for avoiding that financial markets become over-liquid in the first place. That is, the first best option is to keep them "tight," because once they become "swollen," even New Deal or Bretton Woods types of regulations would inevitably struggle.

Excess liquidity is also bound to create conditions that exacerbate problems such as skewed incentives for managers, herding behavior among traders, investment bankers and hedge fund managers who are under constant threat of withdrawals of funds if they underperform in the market, and so on. In DCs, sudden surges of inflows have proved to be a paradigmatic case of this, where stock markets can grow on average at 87 percent, 49 percent, and 48 percent p.a. for many years in a row (as in Chile, Argentina, and Mexico, respectively; see figure 13.8). It would take a very brave investment manager, blessed with infinitely patient investors, to fight trends like these—even if they patently are deviations from fundamental values (Rajan, 2005). And DCs are not alone in this: in Portugal between 9/11 and the 2008 financial crisis, for example, the value of the stock of financial assets grew 17 times faster than GDP; in Spain, 8 times, and in Greece, 6 (in Greece, of all countries, the value of the stock of financial assets *trebled* in the five years before the crisis). Can anybody argue with a straight face that something *real* was actually happening in these economies to justify these financial euphorias? Or that in, say, Greece or Portugal asset prices were rising like this in order to reflect new available information or more solid fundamentals? In the meantime, in Eastern Europe the value of the stock of financial assets also grew far ahead of GDP (eight times faster); in LA, six times faster; and in Africa, five (see figure 13.1). To dismiss these types of experiences as simply "not empirically efficient" (Malkiel, 2007) is what gives economics a bad name.

As Pascal once said (1662), "Man is equally incapable of seeing the nothingness out of which he was drawn and the infinite in which he is engulfed." Despite the insistence of mainstream analysis, many financial crises take place mostly due to factors that are *intrinsic* (or inherent) to the workings of over-liquid and underregulated financial markets rather than to *extrinsic* (or relational) ones. That is, it is unlikely that the same financial markets would have worked much differently had they been operating in different surroundings. From this point of view, the main weakness of the mainstream understandings of financial crises is that they suffer from "extrinsicism," or the tendency to place major emphasis on external matters rather than on more profound realities—an analogy in ethics would be in the difference between emphasizing the external observance of laws and precepts, and emphasizing the ultimate principles underlying moral conduct. By doing so, most mainstream economists miss the point entirely: the tragedy of these financial crises does not lay on the supposed inevitable recurrence of government failures—and certainly not on chance—but in the fact that these crises, more often than not, are fully *deserved* and fairly *predictable*. From this point of view, these crises belong to what Oscar Wilde (1890) called 'the real tragedies of life', those that "occur in such an inartistic manner that they hurt us by their crude violence, their absolute incoherence, their absurd want of meaning, their entire lack of style. They affect us just as vulgarity affects us. They give us an impression of sheer brute force, and we revolt against that." Even new behavioral psychology approaches, no matter how appealing, so far have just highlighted biases in individuals and committees and not in "unregulated and over-liquid" financial markets.

That is, the markets are still idealized in that it is thought that the problems do not lie in them, but in the fact that (unfortunately) they are populated by imperfect individuals.

Perhaps the main lesson of these financial crises is that it is about time to think again (as some are trying—e.g., Bibow, 2009; Davidson, 2009; Harcourt, 2011; Taylor, 2010; as well as Stiglitz, Krugman, Roubini among others) about all the complex theoretical issues that led Minsky to conclude that finance could so easily become fragile; that led Kindleberger to warn us about how excess liquidity leads us to oscillate between manias and panics; and, especially, that led Keynes to conclude that "above all, let finance be primarily national" (1933, 759).

Needless to say, a fundamental part of this task is to turn Lucas's famous "residue of things" upside-down:

> The problem that the new theories, the theories embedded in general equilibrium dynamics of the sort that we know how to use pretty well now—there's a residue of things they don't let us think about. They don't let us think about the U.S. experience in the 1930s, or about financial crises and their real consequences in Asian and Latin America, they don't let us think very well about Japan in the 1990s. (2004, 23)

Part of the task ahead is about transforming these "odd things" that mainstream economics sees as "residue"—including, of course, the current global financial crisis—into the events that form part of the cornerstone of our analytical thinking on how financial markets actually work in the real world.

However, given the current political and economic environment, to be able to think again about these complex theoretical "things" one has to deal with at least two main risks. One is that unless the above "rethinking" is done with a purpose, heterodox economics runs the risk that its discourse could be overcome by "the narcissism of lost causes." That is, sometimes it's just too easy to admire the sublime beauty of critical reason doomed to be marginalized. The other risk, of course, is (in a sense) the opposite: it is also too easy to avoid marginalization by quitting *critical* thinking, and absorbing the fundamentals of the alternative hegemonic (mainstream) paradigm—ending up with a "prudent" discourse made of *skepticism* cum social conscience (although with the latter in the area of "diminishing returns").

The problem with critical thinking, of course, is that it is a distancing, even debilitating, activity. It distances us from conventions, from established assumptions, and from settled beliefs. It takes what we know from familiar, unquestioned settings and makes it strange. And it does so not necessarily by supplying new information, but by inviting and provoking a new way of seeing. Therefore, a key challenge ahead for heterodox economics is how to steer a course that avoids both types of evasion: that of the false beauty of the "lost cause," and that of prudent "uncritical" thinking—not least because (as argued above) when reality is evaded, it is also bound to be distorted and misrepresented.

# Appendix

The main issue behind the existence of 'generation-models' of financial crises is that mainstream economics cannot accept the possibility that the *autonomous* outcome of the free interaction of utility-maximising cum 'rational' expectations agents, interacting in friendly-regulated financial markets, could be an *endogenous* financial crisis. The outcome of the above could only be some sort of 'equilibrium'; this may well be a 'sub-optimal' one, but it has to be a self-adjusting equilibrium of sorts. From this point of view, a financial 'crisis' proper can only take place if there is some kind of interference in the incentive mechanisms and/or resource allocation dynamics of financial markets. Examples of the latter are lax fiscal discipline, fixed exchange rates with a wrong peg, central bankers unwilling to take tough action when necessary, self-fulfilling loops (e.g., bank runs), and so on.[38] As these 'interferences' vary from one crisis to another, their models can only be developed *after the event*.

The so-called 'first generation' models tried to explain the currency crises in the US in the early 1970s. Presidents Johnson and Nixon followed inconsistent macroeconomic policies: persistent deficits with a fixed exchange rate peg. So, the US got the crisis it deserved—Nixon run out of reserves. This was an inevitable outcome (given the policies); and its timing was fairly predictable. Finally, 'first-generation' crises seem to do no harm, as they only reveal an economic problem that was there in the first place.

The inspiration for second-generation modelling was the speculative attack on the European fixed-exchange currency system (ERM), which started with the run on the Pound Sterling in 1992. The UK had entered the ERM in October 1990, but was forced to exit in 1992 when its currency came under major pressure from speculators. There were several obvious differences between the UK 1992-crisis and the assumptions of 'first-generation' models. Seignorage was not the issue, but the willingness of the British government to defend the peg; as many considered that the pound sterling had entered the ERM at an overvalued rate, the British government had to show that it would do what it took to defend that peg. Therefore, the crisis took place not because the government run out of reserves (as in the US); the abandonment of the peg was a matter of policy choice: in 1992 the British Chancellor chose not to pay the price for defending the peg (higher interest rates), while French officials made the opposite decision a year later (when it was the turn of the Franc to come under attack). So, 'second generation' models are about an imperfect commitment to a currency peg. When the peg ceases to be credible, investors will demand higher interest rates in order to hold assets denominated in the country's currency. As macroeconomic polices before the crisis are not irresponsible, crises are not 'deserved'; neither are they 'predictable', as their nature is mostly about chance—i.e., 'self-fulfilling' crises of confidence in which speculators who believe that other speculators are about to attack are themselves encouraged to do so. As everything is about forcing a currency off its peg, there is no reason for a negative shock on output or employment. In fact, as a result of the crisis an artificial policy constraint is removed (the peg); so its impact could well be positive.

Finally, as the latter was clearly not the case in 1997-East Asia, 'third-generation' models try to explain why abandoning a peg could be at times so harmful to output and employment. There are several narratives; the most common one emphasises "moral-hazard-driven" bubbles, which were followed by balance-sheet driven crises when the bubbles burst. Therefore, in 'third-generation' models crises become harmful because they are no longer about problems with monetary policy. Basically, they are mostly about chance: something—as Krugman (2001) says, it could be almost anything—causing a sudden large currency depreciation; and this depreciation creating havoc with balance sheets. On the liability side of balance sheets, if the price of foreign exchange suddenly rises, and firms have substantial foreign currency debts, their net worth falls. On their asset side the story is one of a decline in confidence leading to a fall in asset prices, which leads to a fall in investment that validates both the decline in asset prices and the fall in confidence. The economy thus plunges into a crisis in the real economy on both accounts.

In sum, in first-generation models scenarios crises are supposed to be 'deserved' and predictable, but not harmful to the real economy. In second-generation ones, instead, crises are 'undeserved' and unpredictable, but still not harmful. Finally, in third-generation scenarios financial crises are again 'undeserved' and unpredictable, but this time they are instead harmful (as they are not just about problems with monetary policy).

## ACKNOWLEDGMENTS

This paper builds on previous work (Palma, 2003a, and 2006). I would like to thank Edna Armendáriz, Stephanie Blankenburg, Antonio David, Ashwini Deshpande, Jonathan DiJohn, Jerry Epstein, Samer Frangie, Daniel Hahn, Geoff Harcourt, Jan Kregel, Domna Michailidou, José Antonio Ocampo, Arturo O'Connell, Ernestina Palma Matte, Carlota Pérez, Ignês Sodré, John Steiner, Cornelia Staritz, Lance Taylor and participants at various seminars for helpful comments. Lastly, I am very grateful to my former Ph.D. student Carlos Lopes for the many lively discussions we had on financial crises before his sudden death; I dedicate this paper to him. The usual caveats apply.

## Notes

1. For this first cycle, see Díaz-Alejandro (1984), Ffrench-Davis (2010), Frenkel (1998); Marcel and Palma (1988), and Palma (1998).
2. Some argue that the third cycle finished in 2008, and a fourth cycle began after the downturn in 2009; however, for LA the so-called fourth cycle is nothing else but the resumption of the third after a brief pause in 2008—led by the same type of inflows, and by the same commodity-price boom (see figures 13.2, 13.3, and 13.4). For how these three financial cycles relate to the long-term "technology cycle," see Pérez (2002).
3. Although Chile's 1982 crisis belongs to the first cycle, as Chile opened up its capital account two decades before the rest of the region, its 1982 crisis resembles a "route 1" crisis (for a full account of the process of economic reform in Chile, see Ffrench-Davis, 2010). In terms of Argentina, this country was the only one that, when first in trouble (1995), managed to continue with the same policies for several years thanks to generous IMF help and some skillful—but eventually self-defeating—"financial engineering." Therefore, events between its two crises (1995 and 2001) are unique and do not really fit into any of the routes. However, for reasons of space I cannot discuss in detail the intricacies of these events (1995–2001). For analyses, see Chudnovsky (2002) and O'Connell (2002).
4. For a brief description of these models, see Appendix; see also Krugman (2001).
5. http://finance.yahoo.com/news/bringing-expired -debt-back-to-life.html.
6. While in OECD countries personal income-tax collection reaches on average 9% of GDP, in LA it amasses less than 1%—with income tax evasion fluctuating around 50%, equivalent on average to 4.5% of GDP (ECLAC, 2010). From this perspective, there is little doubt that LA confirms Schumpeter's hypothesis that "the fiscal history of a people is above all an essential part of its general history" (1918).
7. Part of this phenomenon is the fairly unimpressive role of mostly rentier Spanish multinationals. To paraphrase Oscar Wilde, for LA to have been conquered by Spain once may be regarded as a misfortune; twice looks like carelessness.
8. For these ratios, see Palma (2011a).
9. TFP aficionados, however, may well argue that there is a positive twist in this.
10. For example, as discussed below, the share of LA in Banco Santander's worldwide profits is twice that of its assets, while in its European operations it is exactly the other way around.
11. At least easy access to mobile assets helps oligarchies to become democratic (Boix, 2003).
12. See, for example, Mönckeberg (2001), Wolf (2007), and Winter (2007).
13. Argentina's lower domestic-credit ratios throughout (panel A) relate to a long-standing (and well-founded) generalized mistrust of banks. In LA, part of the bubble in the stock market (panel C) was that the opening of the capital account involved the sale of state companies as well as the flotation of private corporations. Both operations produced a large private sector wealth effect that fueled financial speculation but led to little or no new investments. This did not happen in Asia: there were no major privatizations, and corporations were not floated in the stock market just to make them attractive to "gringos."
14. In Malaysia there was a (Latin-style) 12.3-fold increase in real-estate prices, while in Thailand there was an almost 8-fold increase (Palma, 2003). The same

happened in their stock markets (panel C), but these bubbles were dwarfed by those in Chile or Mexico.

15. A recent study by Brazil's "Fecomercio" indicated that "the interest rate on credit cards in Brazil's financial hub of Sao Paulo averages 238 percent." See http://finance.yahoo.com/news/Creditcard-debt-may-threaten-apf-3046211331.html?x=0. That of HSBC reaches 490 per cent per year (*Financial Times*, 27/9/2012). With such "lightly touched" financial regulation (that allows this type of interest rate), no wonder Latin America's "new" left is paraded as an example at the annual meetings of the IMF and the World Bank. According to a Financial Times' analyst, "...the debt service burden [of Brazilian households] has risen to 24 per cent of disposable income....To put this into context, the US consumer "blew up" when the debt service burden hit 14 per cent..." (25/9/2012; see also Palma, 2012).
16. See http://finance.yahoo.com/q/ks?s=BSBR. In fact, no less than 43% of Santander's profits were generated in Latin America, 20 percentage points more than in all its huge Continental Europe operations.
17. Note that in LA the decision to sterilize or not to sterilize—and the corresponding huge interest-rate differentials—made little difference in terms of private investment.
18. The D-Ram price per megabyte, for example, fell from US$26 (1995) to US$10 (1996), US$4 (1997), and less than US$1 (1998). Memory chips were one of Korea's main export items.
19. The conglomerate Daewoo alone, for example, ended up with a corporate debt of US$80 billion—more than the combined foreign debt of Chile and Colombia. Korean corporations preferred to acquire debt than to float equity because they could borrow with less than one percentage point spread over Treasury Bills.
20. Nonperforming loans in Mexico's banks doubled every year, reaching 10% of GDP in 1994 (see Kregel, 1998).
21. See, for example, Epstein and Pollin (2011).
22. For an analysis of the process of idealization, see Sodré (2009).
23. In fact, we now know that Greenspan was even against tightening regulation against financial fraud, because (supposedly) 'rational' markets can expose fraud more effectively than regulators (http://www. dailykos.com/story/2009/3/27/172419/727). Madoff probably disagrees.
24. For Keynes, instead, the opening up of an economy "should not be a matter of tearing up roots but of slowly training a plant to grow in a different direction" (1933, 759).
25. See http://www.pbs.org/newshour/bb/business/july-dec08/crisishearing _10-23.html.
26. See http://www.guardian. co.uk/business/2009/jan/18/economic-depression.
27. Six months into Obama's "stimulus plan," while over a trillion dollars had been spent (or committed) on subsidizing financial markets—together with the defense sector, the leading welfare recipients in the country—less than 1 percent had actually been made available for highway and environmental cleanup projects (http://money.cnn.com/2009/08/04/news/economy/stimulus_spending/index.htm).
28. See http://www.bbc.co.uk/blogs/nickrobinson/2011/04/I_told _you_so.html.
29. Ibid.
30. http://washpost.bloomberg.com/Story? docId=1376-M761211A1I4H01-3S7IT9SMODKH556206DDS QIF3V.

31. See especially Wolf (2007) and Winter (2007). Furthermore, Salinas handed over to Slim exclusivity in Mexico's fixed-line phone market—when, supposedly, privatization was about encouraging competition. According to a recent study (quoted in Winter, 2007), of the top 10 Mexicans on *Forbes*' billionaires list, at least half of them are "creatures of the State." Basically, they got there exploiting what Douglas North's calls "limited access order."
32. Despite its 1998-1999 financial crisis, Brazil has continued with many of its "route 2" policies, with the current cost of sterilization at well over US$50 billion a year—not least because its recent taxes on inflows are so porous that speculators only have to pay them if they have bad accountants.
33. For a prediction of the Mexican crisis, see TDR (1994). For that of Brazil, see Palma (1998). For a pre-crisis warning on East Asia's growing financial fragilities, see BIS (1997), and for one of the current crisis, see Rajan (2005).
34. For Kindleberger, there is one thing that international financial markets can do that is even more damaging for DCs than "overlending": halt that lending abruptly (Kindleberger, 1978).
35. See http://www.ft.com/cms/s/0/ab724158-a7a2-11de-boee-00144feabdco.html#axzz1eU zyS4Yq.
36. For how this connects to the technology cycle, see Pérez (2002).
37. http://www.youtube.com/user/TheFlawMovie?blend=3& ob=5.
38. For a brief summary and bibliography, see Krugman (2001).

## References


Armendáriz, Edna. (2003). *Financial Liberalisation and Financial Crises: The Case of Mexico (1988–1994)*. Unpublished Ph.D. thesis, Cambridge University.

Barandiarán, Edgardo, and Leonardo Hernández. (1999). "Origins and Resolutions of a Banking Crisis: Chile 1982–1986," *Working Papers Central Bank of Chile* 57.

BCB. (2011). Available at http://www.bcb.gov.br/?TIMESERIESEN.

Bibow, Jorg. (2009). *Keynes on Monetary Policy, Finance and Uncertainty. Liquidity Preference Theory and the Global Financial Crisis*. New York: Routledge.

BIS. (1997). *Bank for International Settlements: 67th Annual Report*. Available at http://www.bis.org/publ/ar67f01.htm.

BIS. (2011). "BIS Statistics." Available at http://www.bis.org/statistics/index.htm.

Boix, Carles. (2003). *Democracy and Redistribution*. Cambridge: Cambridge University Press.

Britton, Ronald. (2002). "Fundamentalism and Idolatry." In C, Covington et al., eds., *Terrorism and War*. London: Karnac.

Buffett, Warren E. (1984). "The Superinvestors of Graham-and-Doddsville." Available at http://www.tilsonfunds.com/superinvestors.html.

Buiter, Wilhelm. (2009). "The Unfortunate Uselessness of Most State-of-the-Art Academic Monetary Economics." *Financial Times*, 3 March.

Chang, Roberto, and Andrés Velasco. (2001). "A Model of Currency Crises in Emerging Markets." *Quarterly Journal of Economics* 116(2): 489–517.

Chudnovsky, Daniel. (2002). *La Gestación de la Crisis Argentina*. Buenos Aires: CENIT.

DataStream. (2011). Available at http://online.thomsonreuters.com/datastream/.
Davidson, Paul. (2009). *The Keynes Solution: The Path to Global Economic Prosperity*. New York: Palgrave.
Deane, Phyllis. (1980). *The Evolution of Economic Ideas*. Cambridge: Cambridge University Press.
Díaz-Alejandro, Carlos F. (1984). "Latin American Debt: I Don't Think We Are in Kansas Anymore." *Brookings Papers on Economic Activity* 15(2): 335–403.
ECLAC. (2010). *La Hora de la Igualdad. Brechas por Cerrar, Caminos por Abrir*. Available at http://www.eclac.org/publicaciones.
ECLAC. (2011). "Statistical Division." http//www.eclac.org.
Epstein, Gerald, and Robert Pollin. (2011). "Regulating Wall Street: Exploring the Political Economy of the Possible." *PERI Working Papers Series*, 256, March.
Ffrench-Davis, Ricardo. 2010. *Economic Reforms in Chile: From Dictatorship to Democracy*. New York: Palgrave.
Fama, Eugene. (1976). *Foundation of Finance*. New York: Basic Books.
Frenkel, Roberto (1998). "Capital Market Liberalization and Economic Performance in Latin America," CEPA Working Papers, 6.
GGDC. (2011). "Total Economy Database." Available at http://www.conference-board.org/economics/.
Griffin, Keith. (1970). "Foreign Capital, Domestic Savings and Economic Development." *Bulletin of the Oxford University Institute of Economics & Statistics* 32(2): 99–112.
Harcourt, Geoffrey. (2011). "The Crisis in Mainstream Economics." *Real-World Economics Review* 11(53): 47–52.
HFR. (2007). "Hedge Fund Research: Global Hedge Fund Industry Report." https://www. hedgefundresearch.com.
IMF. (1998). *World Economic Outlook*. Washington: IMF.
IMF. (2011a). *Global Financial Stability Report*. Washington: IMF.
IMF. (2011b). "WEO Database." Available at http://www.imf.org/external/pubs/ft/weo/2011/01/weodata/index.aspx.
IPEA. (2011). "Instituto de Pesquisa Econômica Aplicada." Available at http://www.ipeadata.gov.br/.
KCB. (2011). Available at http://ecos.bok.or.kr/EIndex_en.jsp.
Kelvin, Lord (William Thomson). (1900). "Address to the British Association for the Advancement of Science." Available at http://scienceworld.wolfram.com/biography/Kelvin.html
Keynes, John M. (1933). "National Self-sufficiency." *The Yale Review* 22(4): 755–769.
Kindleberger, Charles P. (2000). *Manias, Panics, and Crashes: A History of Financial Crises*. 4th edition. New York: John Wiley and Sons.
Kregel, Jan. (1998). "East Asia Is Not Mexico." Geneva: UNCTAD.
Krugman, Paul. (2001). *Crises: The Next Generation?* Tel Aviv: Razin.
Lewis, Michael. (2009). "Wall Street on the Tundra." *Vanity Fair*, April.
Lopes, Carlos F. L. (2009). *A High Interest Trap: The Making of the Brazilian Crisis*. Rio de Janeiro: BNDS.
Lucas, Robert E. (2004). "Keynote Address to the 2003 Hope Conference: My Keynesian Education." *History of Political Economy* 36(4): 12–24.
Malkiel, Burton. (2007). "Investment Opportunities in China." Available at http://www.youtube.com/watch?gl=CA&hl=en&v=uVcVoH4qtgw.
Marcel, Mario, and José Gabriel Palma. (1988). "Third World Debt and Its Effects on the British Economy." *Cambridge Journal of Economics* 12(3): 361–400.

McKinnon, Ronald, and Huw Pill. (1997). "Credible Economic Liberalizations and Overborrowing." *American Economic Review* 87(2): 189–193.

McKinsey. (2004). Available at http://www.mckinsey.com/mgi/reports/pdfs/newhorizons/auto.pdf.

Mönckeberg, María Olivia. (2001). *El Saqueo de los grupos económicos al Estado de Chile.* Santiago: Ediciones B.

Ocampo, José Antonio. (2009). "Latin America and the Global Financial Crisis." *Cambridge Journal of Economics* 33(4): 703–724.

Ocampo, José Antonio. (2011). "Macroeconomic Policy for Development: Countercyclical Policies and Production Sector Transformation." *CEPAL Review* 36(104): 7–35.

Ocampo, José Antonio, and José Gabriel Palma. (2008). "Dealing with Volatile External Finances at Source: The Role of Preventive Capital Account Regulations." In José Antonio Ocampo and Joseph E. Stiglitz, eds., *Capital Market Liberalization and Development*, 170–204. Oxford: Oxford University Press. Available at http://www.imf.org/external/np/seminars/eng/2011/res/pdf/jao.pdf.

O'Connell, Arturo. (2002). "The Recent Crisis of the Argentine Economy." Ankara: METU.

Palma, José Gabriel. (1998). "Three and a Half Cycles of 'Mania, Panic and [Asymmetric] Crash': East Asia and Latin America Compared." *Cambridge Journal of Economics* 22(6): 789–808. Reprinted (with a postscript) in Ha-Joon Chang, José Gabriel Palma and Hugh Whittaker, *Financial Liberalisation and the East Asian Crisis*, New York: Palgrave, 2001.

Palma, José Gabriel. (2002a). "The Three Routes to Financial Crises: The Need for Capital Controls." In John Eatwell and Lance Taylor, eds., *International Capital Markets—Systems in Transition*, 297–338. Oxford: Oxford University Press.

Palma, José Gabriel. (2002b). "The Magical Realism of Brazilian Economics: How to Create a Financial Crisis by Trying to Avoid One." In John Eatwell and Lance Taylor, eds., *International Capital Markets—Systems in Transition*, 391–432. Oxford: Oxford University Press.

Palma, José Gabriel. (2003). "The 'Three Routes' to Financial Crises." In Ha-Joon Chang, ed., *Rethinking Development Economics*, 347–378. London: Anthem Press.

Palma, José Gabriel. (2005). "The Six Main Stylised Facts of the Mexican Economy since Trade Liberalisation and NAFTA." *Industrial and Corporate Change* 14(6): 941–991.

Palma, José Gabriel. (2006). "The 1999 Financial Crisis in Brazil: 'Macho-monetarism' in Action." *Economic and Political Weekly* 41(9): 727–737.

Palma, José Gabriel. (2009a). "The Revenge of the Market on the Rentiers: Why Neo-liberal Reports of the End of History Turned Out to Be Premature." *Cambridge Journal of Economics* 33(4): a829–a869. For an extended version, see http://www.econ.cam.ac.uk/dae/repec/cam/pdf/cwpe 0927.pdf.

Palma, José Gabriel. (2009b). "Why Did the Latin American Critical Tradition in the Social Sciences Become Practically Extinct?" In Mark Blyth, ed., *The Handbook of International Political Economy*, 243–265. New York: Routledge.

Palma, José Gabriel. (2011a). "Why Has Productivity Growth Stagnated in Most Latin American Countries since the Neo-liberal Reforms?" In José Antonio Ocampo and Jaime Ros, eds., *The Oxford Handbook of Latin American Economics*, 568–607. Oxford: Oxford University Press. For an extended version, see http://www.econ.cam.ac.uk/dae/repec/cam/pdf/cwpe1030.pdf.

Palma, José Gabriel. (2011b). "Homogeneous Middles vs. Heterogeneous Tails, and the End of the 'Inverted-U': The Share of the Rich Is What It's All About." *Development and Change* 42(1): 87–153. For an extended version, see http://www.econ.cam.ac.uk/dae/repec/cam/pdf/cwpe 1111.pdf.

Palma, José Gabriel. (2012). "Was Brazil's recent growth acceleration the world's most overrated boom?" In C. Pitelis (ed.), *The BRICs and Beyond*, Cambridge University Press. Forthcoming.

Pascal, Blaise. (1662). *Pensées*. Available at http://www.ccel.org/ccel/pascal/pensees.toc.html.

Pérez, Carlota. (2002). *Technological Revolutions and Financial Capital*. Cheltenham, UK: Elgar.

Rajan, Raghuram G. (2005). "Has Financial Development Made the World Riskier?" *NBER Working Paper* No. 11728.

Schumpeter, Joseph. (1918). "The Crisis of the Tax State." *International Economic Papers* 2(4): 5–38.

Smith, Adam. (1776). *An Inquiry into the Nature and Causes of the Wealth of Nations*. Available at http://metalibri.wikidot.com/title:an-inquiry-into-the-nature-an d-causes-of-the-wealth-of.

Sodré, Ignês. (2009). "Imparadised in Hell." Forthcoming.

Steiner, John. (1993). " Two Types of Pathological Organizations in Oedipus the King and in Oedipus at Colonus." In *Psychic Retreats: Pathological Organizations in Psychotic, Neurotic and Borderline Patients*, 116–130. New York: Routledge.

Stiglitz, Joseph E. (2000). "Capital Market Liberalization, Economic Growth and Instability." *World Development* 28(6): 1075–1086.

Stiglitz, Joseph E. (2003). "Whither Reform? Toward a New Agenda for Latin America." *CEPAL Review* 28(80): 7–37.

Taylor, Lance. (2010). *Maynard's Revenge: The Collapse of Free Market Macroeconomics*. Cambridge: Harvard University Press.

TDR. (1994). *Trade and Development Report*. Geneva: UNCTAD.

United Nations. (2011). UN-COMTRADE. Available at http://comtrade.un.org/.

Wade, Robert and Silla Sigurgeirsdottir. 2010. 'Lessons from Iceland.' *New Left Review*, 65, September. Wilde, Oscar. 1890. The Picture of Dorian Gray. Philadelphia: James Sullivan Publisher.

Winter, Brian. (2007). "How Slim Got Huge." Available at http://www.foreignpolicy.com/articles/2007/10/11/how_slim_got_huge.

Wolf, Martin. (2007). "Why Plutocracy Endangers Emerging Market Economies.". *Financial Times*, 6 November.

World Bank. (1996). *World Development Report*. Washington: World Bank.

World Bank. (2011). *World Development Indicators*. Washington: World Bank.

Žižek, Slavoj. (2011). "Shoplifters of the World Unite." *London Review of Books*, 19 August.

# CHAPTER 14

# FINANCIAL AND CURRENCY CRISES IN LATIN AMERICA

MARIO DAMILL, ROBERTO FRENKEL, AND MARTIN RAPETTI

## 1. Introduction

This chapter analyzes the experiences of financial crises in Latin America (LA) between the 1970s and the 2000s. During this period the region went through two waves of financial crises. The first one, which spread virtually all over the region, occurred during the early 1980s and its effects extended almost throughout the decade. This is the reason why the 1980s in LA were labeled as the "lost decade." The second wave began with the Mexican crisis in 1995 and continued with those in Brazil in 1998–1999 and in Argentina in 2001–2002. These two waves of financial crises share a common feature: they were preceded by booms of capital inflows.

Each financial crisis has its own particularities. However, at a certain level of abstraction, crises in developing countries have shared several important elements. In this regard, analyzing financial crises in Latin America has no added value compared with studying those in Asia, Russia, or Turkey. For this reason, our analysis in this paper can easily be extended to financial crises in other developing countries. There is something, however, that makes Latin America special. This is related to the fact that the region started to participate earlier in the international capital markets and was a pioneer in experiencing financial crises. Latin America suffered a higher number of crises than any other region, and its major countries experienced more than one crisis in the last third of the twentieth century. This gives a unique opportunity to draw lessons from the comparative analysis between countries in the same period but also from the analysis of the same country in different periods. Or, using the econometric jargon of panel data, the experience in LA provides "experiments" to control for both time-specific and country-specific effects. The analysis of crises in LA is the topic of the first part of this chapter.

Between the Argentine crisis in 2001–2002 and the financial disruption in the United States in 2008–2009, developing countries went through a prosperous period without suffering crises. LA countries were part of this process. Attempting to identify the cause of something that does not happen may not seem an attractive analytical strategy at first sight. However, after three decades in which financial crises occurred almost sequentially in the developing world, it seems relevant to raise the question of why no relevant financial crisis occurred during this time. This seems especially relevant because in this period capital inflow to emerging markets intensified while no major change in the international financial architecture and institutions occurred. The assessment of this issue is the topic of the second part of the chapter.

## 2. Latin America during the First Three Decades of Financial Globalization

### 2.1. The Financial Context Leading to Crises

All financial crises in developing countries have been associated with preceding booms of capital inflows. The first modern wave of foreign capital inflows to Latin America started in the late 1960s simultaneously with the process of deregulation and development of financial markets in developed countries. Major LA economies integrated to this process right from the beginning. Brazil started to tap the Eurodollar market in the late 1960s, whereas Argentina, Chile, Colombia, Mexico, Peru, and Venezuela did it at different moments of the 1970s.

The motivations and instruments to absorb capital from abroad varied among countries. Brazil initially attracted foreign resources to finance moderate current account deficits caused by the high rates of economic growth that the country was experiencing during those years. Later on, after the oil shock in 1973, external finance requirements increased to sustain higher current account imbalances that resulted from the maintenance of rapid growth in a context of substantially higher oil prices. During this process, capital inflows were mostly intermediated by the government and targeted to support its centralized development strategy. The accumulation of external debt was mostly public because authorities applied severe controls on private-capital inflows.

In the early 1970s, Argentina, Chile, and Uruguay followed an extremely different approach. They opened private access to external finance as a part of a set of market-friendly reforms that were meant to change the economic structure. Together with an almost complete opening of the capital account for the private sector, they liberalized the domestic financial systems, reduced taxes on trade, tackled fiscal imbalances, and carried out with different intensities the privatization of some public enterprises. In a way, the so-called Southern Cone experiments anticipated the reforms carried out in LA and other developing countries in the late 1980s and early 1990s under the Washington Consensus paradigm.

In between the Brazilian and the Southern Cone poles, other countries, such as Colombia, Mexico, Peru, and Venezuela, also opened their capital accounts and allowed the private sector to engage to some extent in external finance.

This first wave of capital inflows to Latin America ended abruptly in 1981–1982, causing severe financial and currency crises. A common response to the crises was to nationalize private-sector external debts through different idiosyncratic mechanisms and to establish institutional arrangements in which debt payments and renegotiations were intermediated by international commercial banks, the International Monetary Fund (IMF), and other international financial institutions. During most of the 1980s, LA countries operated under a regime characterized by two main elements: (1) foreign finance was severely rationed and (2) negotiations with creditors and international financial institutions imposed significant net transfers of resources abroad. Under these constraints, most countries in the region experienced a combination of low growth and high and rising inflation throughout the decade.[1]

The region began to face more favorable conditions to stabilize their economies and provide environments more conducive to growth only when the access to international finance was reestablished in the late 1980s. The Mexican default in 1982 is usually used as the date in which the first wave of capital inflows to LA came to an end. Similarly, the starting date of the second wave of capital inflows to the region can be set in 1989, when Mexican authorities signed the Brady agreement to restructure its external debt.[2] Thus, the region entered the new decade with comfortable access to the international financial markets. This process coincided with the implementation of Washington Consensus reforms, which made LA countries more attractive to investors within the international financial community. An important difference between the beginning of the first and second waves of capital inflows is worth noting; namely that the second one found LA countries with a heavy burden of the financial obligations inherited from the first one.

With the development of this second wave of capital inflows to emerging markets, the faith in global financial integration gradually started to gain supporters. The predominant view held that the world was witnessing a new phase in which capital inflows to emerging market economies were meant to last for a long time. It was seen as the realization of a sustained process toward complete financial integration at a global scale. This was certainly the view of the international financial institutions and market participants (IMF, 1997). It was also the view of LA policy makers. The possibility of a financial crisis, herding behavior, and contagion effects was widely undermined. The extension and magnitude of the capital-inflow boom to emerging markets during the first half of the 1990s was certainly related to this underestimation of risks.

Contradicting these beliefs, the boom was interrupted in the end of 1994, when (again) Mexico faced a sudden stop of capital inflows. The Mexican crisis spread to other economies in the region, most notably to Argentina. It revealed the risks and volatility that emerging markets were exposed to, but it also showed that a rapid and effective international intervention could operate as a shield against financial disruption. Thanks to a generous assistance package with contributions from the IMF and the US Treasury, Mexico met all its financial commitments in time. This helped rebuild investors' confidence and by late 1995 capital inflows were booming again.

A new sudden stop of capital inflows to the region was triggered by the Asian and Russian financial crises in 1997–1998. The financial and real negative effects caused by these crises were severe and led to a domino effect in South America. In late 1997, Chile began to experience a substantial reversion of capital flows but because of the higher degree of exchange-rate flexibility and capital controls, it managed to cope with the adverse external conditions. In 1998, capital inflows gradually began to revert in Brazil, a process that finally led to a currency crisis in early 1999. Colombia followed a similar pattern, exacerbated by the occurrence of a severe financial crisis in 1999. The devaluation in Brazil put deflationary pressures to an already stagnant Argentina that in 2001 declared a massive default of its external debt and in early 2002 was forced to abandon its currency board and devalue its currency. The Argentine crisis in turn hit Uruguay, which also experienced a financial and currency crisis in 2002.

The sequence of crises during the 1990s had negative impacts in LA economies, especially in Argentina where the social cost of the crisis was extreme. But it also induced changes in the macroeconomic policies of the countries, especially in terms of their exchange-rate policies. We analyze these issues in section 3.

## 2.2. The Crises

During the first half of the 1970s, Argentina, Chile, and Uruguay had suffered severe economic and political crises that derived in persistently high inflation rates. The military coups that took power immediately afterward tried to take advantage of the international financial conditions to induce radical changes in the economic structures and to fight inflation at the same time. As mentioned above, the Southern Cone programs include the liberalization of the domestic financial systems, the reduction of taxes on trade and of fiscal imbalances and opening of the capital account of the balance of payments. In the second half of the 1970s, all three countries also oriented their exchange-rate policies toward stabilizing prices, adopting active crawling peg regimes. The so-called *tablitas* were schedules of preannounced rates of devaluation, which were meant to function as nominal anchors for inflation. In all three cases, the private sector was the main recipient of external credits. The experiences led to substantial real exchange-rate (RER) appreciation and a rapid increase in current account deficits and foreign debts. In all three cases, the experiences ended up with massive financial and currency crises.

Mexico also opened its capital accounts and borrowed from the international capital markets, but it did not abandon its traditional pegged exchange-rates regime no introduce any other significant policy change as in the Southern Cone cases. Due to an excessively expansive fiscal policy during the early 1970s, Mexico suffered a balance-of-payment crisis in 1976, forcing the authorities to devalue for the first time in more than 20 years. After a year of sequential adjustments, the exchange rate was fixed again in early 1977. About that time, the discovery of voluminous oil reserves changed economic perspectives about the country. The perception that the change in oil prices represented a permanent change encouraged the government to initiate an ambitious industrialization program borrowing from the international capital markets. The economy expanded at rates of 8–9 percent between 1978 and 1981, inducing an acceleration of the inflation rate, which remained at about 20 percent yearly. Given the fixed exchange rate, the RER appreciated and current account deficit soared. This dynamic finally led to a severe financial and external debt crisis in 1982.

The main crises in the 1990s were those of Mexico (1994–1995), Argentina (1995), Brazil (1998–1999), Argentina again (2001–2002), and Uruguay (2002). A common feature of these crises—similar to the Southern Cone cases—is that they were preceded by stabilization programs in which the fixing of the exchange rate was used as the main nominal anchor.

In 1988, Mexico launched a stabilization program that combined fiscal adjustment and fixed exchange-rate and income policies.[3] Since the stabilization program was launched, the RER tended to appreciate and the economy started to register increasing current account deficits. The change in the international financial conditions during the late 1980s helped the country maintain the macroeconomic policies thanks to the increasing capital inflows. This configuration persisted until 1994, when the fear of foreign investors concerning the sustainability of the (virtually) fixed exchange rate triggered a reversal of capital flows and a balance-of-payments crisis.

In 1994, Brazil launched the Real Plan, a stabilization program that included a comprehensive adjustment of fiscal accounts, an opened capital account, a monetary reform—in which a new currency, the "Real," was introduced—and an almost fixed exchange-rate regime. The effects of the Real Plan on the real exchange rate, the external accounts and debt accumulation were similar to those observed in Mexico and Argentina. The process finally led to an exchange-rate crisis in early 1999.

Argentina launched the "convertibility" regime in early 1991, which was characterized by the fixing of the domestic currency against the US dollar and the establishment of a currency board system by law. The convertibility was implemented concurrently with liberalizing measures, including an almost complete liberalization of trade flows and full deregulation of the capital account of the balance of payments. The program was very successful at curbing high inflation. However, as occurred in Mexico, stabilization came together with the appreciation of the RER, large current account deficits, and a growing external debt. In 1995, the contagion of the Mexican crisis led to massive capital outflows. Granted a voluminous financial assistance package carried by the IMF, the Argentine authorities managed to preserve the currency board but they could not prevent the financial crisis that led many domestic banks to bankruptcy. As mentioned above, another reversal of capital inflows started in 1998 after the Asian and Russian crisis and accelerated after the Brazilian crisis in 1999. This time, the massive run against the domestic currency and bank deposits led to an extremely severe financial and external debt crisis in 2001 and the devaluation of the peso in 2002. The crisis spread to Uruguay, which presented similar features: a virtually fixed exchange rate, overvalued RER, and large current account deficits. In 2002, the country experienced a severe banking and currency crisis.

A more detailed analysis of the crises reviewed above indicates that certain features in the institutional and macroeconomic policy configuration were common to all: (1) the exchange rate was fixed or semifixed; (2) the RER was overvalued and the current accounts were in deficits; (3) capital accounts were virtually fully convertible (i.e., free capital movements); (4) capital inflows in the preceding boom had been large in relation to the size of existing local money and capital markets; and (5) the regulation of national financial systems during the boom phase was weak and permissive.[4] Such an analysis also reveals that the combination of these ingredients led in all these cases to a cyclical macroeconomic dynamic, with an initial expansionary phase followed by a period of stagnation or recession and growing financial and external weakness that culminated in financial and currency crises.

## 2.3. The Cyclical Dynamics Leading to a Crisis

The prototypical boom-and-bust cycle resulting from the above set ingredients and experienced by several LA countries can be described as follows.[5]

The rapid deregulation of previously "repressed" capital markets raises domestic interest rates.[6] In such a context, the combination of credibly fixed (or predetermined) exchange rates and capital account liberalization leads to significant spreads between the yields of foreign and domestic assets. Initially, a few local players take advantage of the arbitrage opportunities, issuing foreign debt to do so. Their exposure to risk essentially depends on the probability that the exchange-rate rule is altered (i.e., the exchange-rate risk). From the viewpoint of the individual investor, engaging in external borrowing to exploit an arbitrage opportunity has no significant effect on the sustainability of the exchange-rate rule. However, since the first movers are exploiting significant benefits, other players have strong incentives to jump in, even when by doing so their combined actions may have negative macroeconomic consequences.

Capital inflows expand liquidity and credit in the economy. As a result, domestic interest rates and spreads fall, and output and employment grow. The expansion of aggregate demand leads to price increases (particularly in nontradable sectors), which under fixed (or predetermined) exchange-rate regimes generates an appreciation of the RER. The real appreciation reinforces the inflow of capital that is seeking capital gains by holding domestic assets and, therefore, further fuels the expansion of credit and output growth. The combined effect of RER appreciation and economic growth stimulates the demand for imports, while exports weaken. The worsening of the trade balance along with the increase in interest and dividend payments resulting from the reduction of the net foreign assets lead to a current account deficit.

Given the progressive worsening of the external balance, the credibility of the exchange-rate rule weakens. As the probability of exchange-rate devaluation increases, the balance sheet of the domestic financial system—which is short on foreign currency and long in local assets—becomes increasingly fragile. Some players, possibly the most risk-averse or the best-informed, begin undoing their positions in domestic assets, leading to a slowdown in the capital inflows. Authorities increase interest rates in order to retain capital. However, there eventually comes a point at which no interest rate can attract new external financing. Foreign exchange reserves at the central bank, which grew during the booming phase of the cycle, begin falling as the monetary authority intervenes to sustain the exchange-rate regime. However, the run against the central bank's foreign exchange reserves cannot be stopped and the exchange-rate rule is finally abandoned. A sequential or simultaneous twin (currency and financial) crisis is the final outcome.

## 2.4. Financial Crises in Developing and Developed Countries

Those who are familiar with the work of Hyman Minsky would find the cyclical dynamics that led to financial and currency crises in Latin America (and other developing countries) very intuitive.[7] This should not be a shocker. The boom-and-bust cyclical dynamics described above was actually inspired by Minsky's theory of financial crises.[8]

In Minsky's model, crises are always preceded by a period of economic and financial boom. During the booming phase, there are widespread optimistic expectations about the future. Confidence increases and risk perception reduces. In this environment, agents take risky positions and the system becomes increasingly fragile. At some point, some event calls agents' attention about the high degree of exposure to risk in the system. A phase of distress begins. The emerging perception of higher risk makes most agents switch their portfolios in favor of safer and liquid assets. The excess demand for liquidity and low-risk assets ends up pricking the bubble, which results in a massive loss of wealth. In this contractive phase, pessimistic expectations are rampant. The deflationary developments in the financial markets turn most agents either liquidity-constrained or bankrupt, affecting in either case their spending decisions negatively. Private consumption falls, and investment collapses. What started as a contraction in the financial sector will eventually spread out to the whole economy. The financial crisis then leads to a systemic economic crisis.

Recent financial crises in the United States, Europe, and other developed countries induced a revalorization of Minsky's work. It is not surprising why analysts and observers of the financial markets in the United States have brought Minsky's ideas back from an almost total intellectual exile. The conditions that caused and then helped develop recent crises correspond very neatly to Minsky's model.

In this regards, crises in Latin American (and other developing) countries shared a similar cyclical dynamics with those observed in developed countries and therefore are not singular. There is, however, a key difference between them. The difference lies on the factors that kicked off the booming phase of the cycles. In the case of Latin America, the financial bubbles and innovations that emerge and develop in the booming phase resulted from the implementation of new macroeconomic policy rules that provide a profitable environment for financial arbitrage between domestic and foreign assets. As described in section 2.2, the beginning of the booming period coincided with the implementation of a new macroeconomic configuration including fixed or semifixed exchange-rate arrangements, the liberalization of the capital account, and the domestic financial systems and a poor or lax regulation of them.

In sum, the trigger of the Minskyan cycle observed in Latin American crises has an important exogenous component. Foreign capital inflows and outflows then play a key role by multiplying the forces driving the cycle. On the other hand, the factors that trigger the cycle in the US financial crisis were essentially endogenous. This is, in fact, a key insight of Minsky's theory of financial systems: the bubbles and the innovations that emerge and develop in the booming phases are the natural and spontaneous result of the evolution of financial systems. The real state bubble and the financial innovations that started with the securitization of mortgages (and other debts) were key ingredients of the booming phase of the Minskyan cycle in the subprime crisis. Both the bubble in real-estate prices and the financial innovations were processes that developed in the real-estate and financial markets, which nurtured each other during a long period. The comparison thus makes clear the difference between the exogenous nature of the elements triggering the booming phase in Latin American crises and the endogenous dynamics of the cycle in the subprime crisis.

## 3. A Virtuous Phase during the 2000s

In the last three decades of the twentieth century, financial and currency crises in developing countries were frequent and severe. On the contrary, since 2002 and up to the eruption of the subprime crisis in 2008, developing countries experienced a period of unusual stability. This change was associated with a new set of macroeconomic policies followed by many of these countries that contributed to shape a new international financial scenario.

Two main changes within the macroeconomic policy framework in developing countries started to operate since the Asian crises (Frenkel and Rapetti, 2010). First, developing countries gradually switched their exchange-rate arrangements from pegs to more flexible regimes. Exchange-rate flexibility has traditionally been understood as the lack of official intervention in the domestic foreign exchange (FX) market. Flexibility in the current context, on the contrary, means that the monetary authority preserves the ability to intervene in the FX market whenever it finds it necessary to do so. In this sense, a pure floating regime does not have a minimum commitment because it implies the commitment of not intervening. Manage floating represents the most flexible regime instead, because it allows monetary authorities to intervene discretionally.

Similarly to pure floating, an advantage of manage floating is its preventive role. A country adopting such an arrangement cannot fall victim of a speculative attack. A key advantage compared to pure floating is that managed floating allows intervening in the market so as to give guidance to the evolution of the RER in the short and medium run. In this regard, manage floating combines the advantages of a pure floating with the discretion to use FX interventions to react to changes in the domestic and international context, adjusting the level of the exchange rate to the requirements of economic policy. If not de jure, many developing countries have switched to de facto manage floating arrangements during this period.

The other major innovation in the macroeconomic policy framework followed by many developing countries has been that in the more recent period they have engaged in financial globalization as net suppliers of capital flows. Contrary to previous decades, capital has recently moved from developing countries to developed countries.[9] Many of the emerging market economies, which had initially entered the system as recipients of capital inflows that are financing current account deficits, have in recent years started to generate current account surpluses—or to reduce significantly the previous deficits—and to persistently accumulate FX reserves.

In a set of 29 emerging market economies,[10] only four showed current account surpluses in 1997. In the same set, the number of countries with current account surpluses was 14 in 2001, 18 in 2004, and 14 in 2006. In the same set of countries, the ratio between the aggregate amount of the surpluses and the absolute value of the aggregate deficits was 0.35 in 1997, 1.40 in 2001, 3.93 in 2004, and 4.64 in 2006. Excluding China, the ratio was 0.04 in 1997, 1.13 in 2001, 2.73 in 2004, and 2.15 in 2006.

Current account surpluses and the availability of large amounts of FX reserves are indicators of external robustness because—as was emphasized in section 2—they indicate a low probability that the country will face difficulties in meeting its external commitments. These indicators are used by international investors in their portfolio decisions. Research has also shown that they perform well at predicting the probability of balance-of-payment crises (Kaminsky, Lizondo, and Reinhart, 1998). Moreover, an increase in the number of surplus countries can also diminish the risk of deficit countries because it reduces the chances of herd behavior and contagion. Overall, as the number of developing countries running current account surpluses increases, the risk premium in developing countries *as a whole* should go down.

This is what effectively has happened since late 2002. The risk premia of developing countries declined and by mid-2005 they had fallen below the minimum registered in the pre-Asian crisis period. In mid-2007, country risk premia reached a historical low, significantly lower than the minimum level of the pre-Asian crisis period and also significantly lower than the spread of US high-yield bonds. They only started to rise in July 2007, once the concerns about the subprime crisis emerged. However, since that moment up until the Lehman Brothers bankruptcy in mid-September 2008, developing countries' risk premia remained at levels comparable to the low records of the pre-Asian crisis period, showing a fairly robust relative performance of emerging markets' financial assets. The financial contagion following the collapse of Lehman Brothers was short and by 2009 many developing countries had recovered access to the international financial system at low interest rates.

These tendencies were clearly observed in Latin America.[11] LA countries both switch to more flexible managed floating regimes and actively accumulate foreign exchange reserves, benefiting from a systematic reduction in their risk premia and experiencing a period of rapid growth without suffering any financial or currency crises.

After the crisis in 1994–1995, Mexico let the peso float while using a policy of monetary aggregates to control inflation. In 1999, the country switched to a regime combining a floating exchange rate and inflation targeting (FIT). Also in 1999, Brazil, Colombia, and Chile joined the club of Latin American countries using a FIT regime. Brazil did so as a result of the currency crisis it suffered at the beginning of that year. Peru had been using managed floating jointly with a monetary regime based on quantitative monetary targets since the early 1990s. In 2002, the central bank formally adopted a FIT regime.

Despite their public statements about their exchange-rate regime choice, none of these Latin American countries have let their currencies float the way they would be assumed to do under a conventional pure floating regime. The central banks of these countries have not had a passive role in the determination of the exchange rate and therefore their regimes can be better classified as managed floating. Intervention in the FX market has been common practice among the countries. Moreover, central banks in these countries have explicitly claimed a right to intervene in the FX market. The process of reserve accumulation, however, was not homogenous across countries. Between 2004 and 2008, Brazil quadrupled its stock of FX reserves, Peru more than tripled it, and Colombia doubled it. Mexico, although increasing the stock of FX reserves during this period (an increase of 50 percent), had a less systematic strategy. The Central Bank of Chile had a more passive role in the FX market: it only began to accumulate reserves persistently in mid-2007, increasing its stock of FX reserves by 50 percent between that period and Lehman Brothers' collapse.

In search of greater flexibility, Argentina followed a somewhat different path than that of the FIT countries. After the 2001–2002 crisis, the central bank adopted a pragmatic managed floating arrangement, which implicitly aimed to combine a certain degree of short-run exchange-rate volatility with the preservation of a competitive RER in the medium run. The exchange-rate policy has also had an explicit goal of FX reserve accumulation meant to protect against volatility in international financial flows. A competitive RER combined with fiscal discipline (to which the public debt restructuring in 2005 contributed substantially) provided the economy a sound macroeconomic configuration. It was the first time in its modern history that Argentina maintained current account and fiscal surpluses for such a long period (2002–2010). This macroeconomic configuration was undoubtedly a key factor in explaining the sharp acceleration of growth. Since the second half of 2002, the economy grew steadily at annual rates of 8–9 percent, maintaining a relatively dynamic export performance. Although since 2007 the inflation rate accelerated substantially and the macroeconomic configuration started to show signs of deterioration, the economy remained robust against financial contagion.

## 4. Conclusions

The history of crises in Latin America has revealed the weaknesses and inadequacy of loosely regulated domestic financial systems. Comprehensive regulation is essential to avoid instability and crises. However, the conclusion that follows from the study and analysis of the crisis episodes in LA economies suggests that the prevention of financial instability and crises in countries like these may involve elements that go beyond the regulation of domestic financial systems. Preventing crises in developing countries requires not only the regulation of domestic financial systems, but also a consistent macroeconomic configuration, which includes the exchange-rate policy and the policies related to the management of the balance of payments and the stock of FX reserves. Crisis episodes in Latin America (and other emerging markets) have shown, in particular, that developing countries should aim for (1) exchange-rate systems that provide flexibility and reduce the space for speculation, (2) preventive measures to manage capital movements, and (3) policies that secure robust external accounts, including the accumulation of FX reserves and the avoidance of overvalued RERs. Latin American and other developing countries have adopted these policy orientations in the first decade of the 2000s and this explains why there were not any financial crises during this period.

## Further Readings

The literature on analyzing financial and currency crises in LA is vast. For a detailed description of the Southern Cone programs and crises, see: Canitrot (1981), Damill and Frenkel (1987), Fernández (1985), and Frenkel (1983a, 1983b) for the Argentina case; Corbo (1985), Diaz-Alejandro (1985), and Ffrench-Davis (1983) for the Chilean case; and Hanson and de Melo (1985) for the Uruguayan case. The Mexican crisis in 1994–1995 and the "Tequila effect" have been analyzed by Sachs et al. (1996) and Ros (2002). For the Brazilian crisis in 1999, see De Paula and Alves (2000) and Kregel (1999). Argentina's convertibility crisis generated an extensive discussion: see Damill, Frenkel, and Juvenal (2003); Damill, Frenkel, and Rapetti (2010); Galiani, Heymann, and Tomassi (2003); Mussa (2002); and Perry and Servén (2002). Palma (1998) compares the East Asian crises of 1997–1998 with those of Mexico in 1994–1995 and the Southern Cone of the early 1980s. He also anticipated somewhat the Brazilian crisis of 1998–1999.

## Notes

The authors are researchers at CEDES, Argentina.

1. The notable exception was Chile and, to a lesser extent, Colombia. Chile managed to recover growth and stabilize the inflation rate since the mid-1980s. Chile's exceptional performance was partly due to its ability to restructure its foreign debt and to get more generous funding from the international financial institutions.

2. The Brady Plan was a program launched by the US government in 1989, which aimed to help highly indebted countries relieve their debt burdens with international banks. Debt was converted into bonds called Par and Discount, collateralized with US Treasury bills. Following Mexico, Costa Rica (1989), Venezuela (1990), Uruguay (1991), Argentina (1992), and Brazil (1992) signed debt-restructuring agreements within this framework.
3. The exchange-rate regime was later replaced with a slightly more flexible arrangement.
4. See Frenkel (2003).
5. The following narrative was originally formalized by Frenkel (1983b). The model was inspired by the Southern Cone experiences and later on synthesized and presented in English in Williamson (1983) and Taylor (1991). Taylor (1998) labeled the dynamics as the "Frenkel-Neftci" cycle and found that it helps explain other developing-country crises, such as those in Asia in 1997–1998 and in Russia in 1998.
6. In a high-inflation context, as observed in the LA countries where this set of policies was implemented in the form of stabilization programs, the likelihood of finding attractive domestic interest rates is even higher.
7. This section draws on Frenkel and Rapetti (2009).
8. A synthetic presentation of his model of financial crises can be found in Minsky (1977) and the most polished and mature exposition of his thought is in Minsky (1986). Charles Kindleberger (1978) provides an exhaustive historical account of financial crises analyzed under Minsky's framework.
9. In the 1980s, there was also a trend of net capital flows moving from low-income to high-income countries. But this was a transitory consequence of the external sector adjustments of Latin American economies after their crises. In the course of renegotiations of Latin America's defaulted external debts, which lasted from 1982 to 1990, there was no voluntary lending from private sources and most of these countries went through current account adjustments in order to pay some proportion of the interest dues.
10. The data set comprises 24 out of 25 countries included in the Emerging Markets index, elaborated by MSCI Barra: Argentina, Brazil, Chile, China, Colombia, Czech Republic, Egypt, Hungary, India, Indonesia, Israel, Jordan, Korea, Malaysia, Mexico, Morocco, Pakistan, Peru, Philippines, Poland, Russia, South Africa, Thailand and Turkey, in addition to Bulgaria, Ecuador, Panama, Ukraine, and Venezuela.
11. See Frenkel and Rapetti (2011) for details.

## References

Canitrot, Adolfo. (1981). "Teoría y práctica del liberalismo: política anti-inflacionaria y apertura económica en la Argentina, 1976–81." *Desarrollo Económico* 21(82): 131–189.

Corbo, Vittorio. (1985). "Reforms and Macroeconomic Adjustments in Chile during 1974–1984." *World Development* 13(8): 893–916.

Damill, Mario, and Roberto Frenkel. (1987). "De la apertura a la crisis financiera. Un análisis de la experiencia argentina de 1977 a 1982." *Ensayos Económicos* 37, Banco Central de Argentina.

Damill, Mario, Roberto Frenkel, and Luciana Juvenal. (2003). "Las cuentas públicas y la crisis de la convertibilidad en la Argentina." *Desarrollo Económico* 43(170): 203–230.

Damill, Mario, Roberto Frenkel, and Martin Rapetti. (2010). "The Argentinean Debt: History, Default and Restructuring." In Barry Herman, José Antonio Ocampo, and Shari Spiegel, eds., *Overcoming Developing Country Debt Crises*, 179–230. Oxford: Oxford University Press.

De Paula Luiz Fernando, Antonio José Alves. (2000). "External Financial Fragility and the 1998–1999 Brazilian Currency Crisis." *Journal of Post Keynesian Economics* 22(4) (Summer): 589–617.

Diaz Alejandro, Carlos. (1985). "Good-bye Financial Repression, Hello Financial Crash." *Journal of Development Economics* 19(1–2): 1–24.

Fernández, Roque. (1985). "The Expectation Management Approach to Stabilization in Argentina during 1976–82." *World Development* 13(8): 871–892.

Ffrench-Davis, Rircardo (1983). "The Monetarist Experiment in Chile: A Critical Survey." *World Development* 11: 905–926.

Frenkel, Roberto. (1983a). "La apertura financiera externa: el caso argentino." In Rircardo French-Davis, ed., *Relaciones financieras externas y su efecto en la economía latinoamericana*. Mexico: Fondo de Cultura Económica.

Frenkel, Roberto. (1983b). "Mercado financiero, expectativas cambiarias y movimientos de capital." *El Trimestre Económico* L(200), October-December.

Frenkel, Roberto. (2003). "Globalization and Financial Crises in Latin America." *CEPAL Review* 80: 41–54.

Frenkel, Roberto, and Martin Rapetti. (2009). "A Developing Country View of the Current Global Crisis: What Should Not Be Forgotten and What Should Be Done." *Cambridge Journal of Economics* 33(4): 685–702.

Frenkel, Roberto, and Martin Rapetti. (2010). "Economic Development and the International Financial System." In Stephany Griffitth-Jones, José Antonio Ocampo, and Joseph Stiglitz, eds., Time for a Visible Hand. Oxford: Oxford University Press.

Frenkel, Roberto, and Martin Rapetti. (2011). "Exchange Rate Regimes in Latin America." In José Antonio Ocampo and Jaime Ros, eds., *Handbook of Latin American Economics*. Oxford: Oxford University Press.

Galiani, Sebastián, Daniel Heymann, and Mariano Tomassi. (2003). "Great Expectations and Hard Times: The Argentine Convertibility Plan." *Economía* 3(2): 109–160.

Hanson, James, and Jaime de Melo. (1985). "External Shocks, Financial Reforms, and Stabilization Attempts in Uruguay during 1974–83." *World Development* 13(8): 917–939.

IMF (International Monetary Fund). (1997). "International Capital Markets. Development, Prospects, and Key Policy Issues, World Economic and Financial Surveys." Washington, DC, September.

Kaminsky, Graciela, Sergio Lizondo, and Carmen Reinhart. (1998). "Leading Indicators of Currency Crisis." IMF Staff Papers, 45(1): 1–48.

Kindleberger, Charles. (1978). *Manias, Panics, and Crashes: A History of Financial Crisis*. New York: John Wiley and Sons.

Kregel, Jan. (1999). "Was There an Alternative to the Brazilian Crisis?" *Brazilian Journal of Political Economy* 19(3): 23–38.

Minsky, Hyman. (1977). "A Theory of Systemic Fragility." In Edward I. Altman and Arnold W. Sametz, eds., *Financial Crises: Institutions and Markets in a Fragile Environment*. New York: John Wiley and Sons.

Minsky, Hyman. (1986). *Stabilizing an Unstable Economy*. New Haven: Yale University Press.

Mussa, Michael. (2002). "Argentina and the Fund: From Triumph to Tragedy." Institute for International Economics, Washington, DC.

Palma, Gabriel. (1998). "Three and a Half Cycles of 'Mania, Panic, and [Asymmetric] Crash": East Asia and Latin America Compared." *Cambridge Journal of Economics* 22: 789–808.

Perry, Guillermo, and Luis Sérven. (2002). "The Anatomy and Psychology of a Multiple Crisis: Why Was Argentina Special and What Can We Learn from It?" World Bank, Office of the Chief Economist for Latin America, Washington, DC.

Ros, Jaime. (2002). "From the Capital Surge to the Financial Crisis and Beyond: Mexico in the 1990s." In Ricardo Ffrench-Davis, ed., *Financial Crises in "Successful" Emerging Economies*. Washington, DC: Brookings Institution Press.

Sachs, Jeffrey, Aron Tornell, and Andrés Velasco. (1996). "Financial Crises in Emerging Markets: The Lessons from 1995." *Brookings Papers on Economic Activity* 1996 (1): 147–215.

Taylor, Lance. 1991. *Income Distribution, Inflation, and Growth. Lectures on Structuralist Macroeconomic Theory*. Cambridge, MA: MIT Press.

Taylor, Lance. (1998). "Capital Market Crises: Liberalisation, Fixed Exchange Rates and Market-driven Destabilization." *Cambridge Journal of Economics* 22: 663–676.

Williamson, John. (1983). *Open Economy and the World Economy: A Textbook in International Economics*. New York: Basic Books.

CHAPTER 15

# THE ASIAN FINANCIAL CRISIS, FINANCIAL RESTRUCTURING, AND THE PROBLEM OF CONTAGION

C. P. CHANDRASEKHAR AND JAYATI GHOSH

THE Asian crisis of 1997–1998 focused attention on the dangers for developing countries within a world dominated by fluid finance. It brought home the fact that financial liberalization can result in crises even in "miracle economies." The crisis marked a major setback to the "East Asian miracle": more than a decade after that crisis, the affected economies have not really been able to recover their pre-crisis dynamism. And the more successful Asian economies in the subsequent period (such as China and, to a lesser extent, India) have since been much more cautious about extensive financial liberalization.

It is now quite obvious that currency and financial crises have devastating effects on the real economy. Even when crises are essentially financial in origin and in their unfolding, their effects unfortunately do not remain confined to the realm of finance. The ensuing liquidity crunch and wave of bankruptcies result in severe deflation, with attendant consequences for employment and the standard of living. The post-crisis adoption of conventional International Monetary Fund (IMF) stabilization strategies tends to worsen the situation. Thereafter, governments become so sensitive to the possibility of future crises that they continue to adopt very restrictive macroeconomic policies and restrain public expenditure even in crucial social sectors. Finally, asset-price deflation and devaluation pave the way for foreign capital inflows that finance a transfer of ownership of assets from domestic to foreign investors, thereby enabling a conquest by international capital of important domestic assets and resources.

In some ways all the economies that were deeply involved in the Asian crisis (Thailand, South Korea, Indonesia, Malaysia, and the Philippines) have recovered, at least in terms of the eventual resumption of output growth. But the recovery has not meant a return to "miracle" status. Instead, it has been accompanied by significant acquisition, at deflated prices, of productive assets in these economies by foreign firms. It has involved a substantial restructuring of the financial sector. It has altered the nature of engagement with the world system of these economies. And it has involved a setback to achievements on the human development front.

A key insight that emerges from an analysis of the Asian crisis is how market-oriented strategies to cope with the crisis created further financial fragility in many post-crisis economies, thereby rendering them extremely vulnerable to future contagion and volatility, exactly in the manner that has been experienced in 2008 and 2009. To that extent, the Asian crisis effectively predicted the severe impact on both the financial variables and the real economy that the global crisis of 2007–2008 had upon developing countries in particular.

This is important for not only understanding the post-crisis trajectory of the affected Asian economies, but also because it is now more than evident, more than a decade after the crisis, that the international financial system has still not evolved effective ways of preventing such crises among emerging economies and reducing their damaging effects. In this chapter, we examine the trajectory of the Asian crisis and consider how it has triggered changes in the financial structures of developing countries that in turn create new fragilities and exacerbate existing ones.

In the next section, we briefly summarize the main elements of the crisis and its trajectory. In the third section we consider post-crisis economic patterns and changes in financial structure in these economies. In the final section we outline the implications for financial fragility and real economic processes that continue to be relevant in the evolving global economy.

## The Trajectory of the Asian Crisis

The pre-crisis development trajectories differed substantially across the countries that were most affected by the East Asian crisis. South Korea pursued a state-directed and highly regulated export-led growth strategy (Amsden, 1992; Wade, 2004), which gave way to a more liberalized regime much later. Malaysia and Thailand had much more recent histories of rapid economic growth, within relatively open economic regimes relying on foreign investment to deliver both export and output growth. In Indonesia, oil revenues and a strong state relying on internal and external clientelist relations (between the state and private capital internally, and between the American and Indonesian governments internationally) played an important role in the development path. The Philippines was never really much of a "tiger" except in the matter of export growth, and that did not translate into any major transformation of domestic productive structures.

The literature on the East Asian crisis (Chang, Palma, and Whittaker, 2001; Radelet and Sachs, 2000) usually dates it as starting on July 2, 1997, when the Thai currency, the *baht,* was allowed to float and promptly depreciated in value by around 40 percent relative to the US dollar. Signs of impending problems had been evident in several economies for some months previously: in Thailand speculative attacks on the currency from around August 1996 were warded off only with great difficulty by the Thai government; in South Korea several *chaebols* faced difficulties in servicing their loans from January 1997. But the sharp and sudden currency depreciations in the five "crisis" countries were the most obvious symptoms of the crisis. They were triggered by three factors. First, a collapse in investor confidence resulted in a panicked withdrawal of funds invested in equities and also prevented the rollover of short-term debt by multinational banks that had lent in the region. Second, there was a scramble for dollars on the part of domestic banks and corporations with imminent dollar commitments, the domestic currency costs of which were rising in the wake of depreciation. And finally, there was an increase in speculative operations by domestic and international traders cashing in on currency volatility.

While all of these factors operated in most Southeast Asian economies, their ability to withstand the crisis, by intervening in currency markets and combating speculation, was substantially different. Thailand, which faced speculative attacks on the *baht* in August 1996 and May 1997, was the first to succumb. Unable to prevent the flight of capital and denuded of foreign currency reserves, the country had to turn to the IMF for stand-by credit and for help in working out a debt-rescheduling package. As the contagion, mediated by the "confidence" of foreign investors and lenders, spread to other economies,

Indonesia caved quickly, whereas the South Korean government battled for months to stabilize the *won* without IMF assistance but failed. Others, notably Malaysia (and, of course, Taiwan, which is rarely discussed even though it faced an equivalent decline in exports without experiencing a financial crisis), chose to go it alone and eventually achieved at least a basic stability of their currencies without recourse to IMF assistance or policy direction.

The real economic crisis appeared after this financial collapse, especially after the IMF was called in, but once it began the real economic crunch soon threatened to outpace the financial crash. With a combination of a liquidity crunch, bankruptcies, and IMF-sponsored deflation playing a role, not only did domestic manufacturing output and GDP contract massively in these countries, but unemployment rose sharply and standards of living fell dramatically in societies long accustomed to stability and high growth. Given the close integration through trade and investment of the economies of the region, this contraction affected even those that did not opt for the IMF route to stabilization.

The crisis spawned a large variety of theories on the crisis's origins and extent. One argument heard frequently is that it was a crisis of "overaccumulation," such that markets could not absorb the output of additional investment (Erturk, 2002). It is clear that capacity creation was in excess of demand growth, especially when assessed in the post-crisis context. But this was a symptom rather than a cause of the problem, which was that a very rapid rate of growth through high investment rates in these economies was based on substantial export penetration, such that international market shares in exports would have to continuously increase. Obviously, such a trajectory is not sustainable over long periods, and so the problems that emerged were inherent in the trade and industrialization strategies that these countries were following. The region's excessive focus on exports as the engine of growth became more difficult, because competing developing-country exporters (such as China) entered the scene, exemplified by the impact of the devaluation of the Chinese renminbi in 1994.

This was a more significant problem than the policy of maintaining fixed exchange rates, which has also been blamed for the crisis. In fact, real exchange rates were likely to have appreciated even more with large capital inflows if nominal rates were flexible. The existence of "crony capitalism" and opaque financial systems have also been cited as causes (Hughes, 1999), although these were always more controversial as explanations and have been rendered much less convincing after the outbreak of the US financial crisis in 2008.

Rather than these factors, it is now widely accepted that the most crucial proximate factor for the crisis was financial liberalization, specifically external or capital-account liberalization. During the early 1990s, almost all East Asian countries liberalized their financial sectors and allowed local corporations, banks, and nonbank financial institutions to freely access international capital markets with little commitment to earn the foreign exchange needed to service the costs of such access. This allowed inflows of capital that enabled short-term borrowing for long-term projects, and this arrangement broke the link between domestic agents' ability to access foreign exchange and their need to earn it. This was associated with the use of new instruments, specifically derivatives contracts that were enabled by deregulation. As Kregel (1998, p. 67) has noted, the role of derivatives contracts can explain the existence of a number of puzzles associated with the Asian financial crisis. "The shift to short-term commercial bank lending in a region that traditionally relied on direct investment, the allocation of resources to low return uses in an area considered to be highly profitable, lax prudential supervision in systems that had introduced financial reforms early, and the co-movement of asset prices and exchange rates, which was to have been eliminated by direct equity investments, are all linked to the characteristics of derivative contracts used to provide lending to Asia."

The capital inflows into the region that increased as a result of the capital account liberalization and investor bullishness about export growth caused appreciation of the real exchange rate. This occurred irrespective of the exchange-rate pegs that many economies in the region maintained with respect to the US dollar, as the capital inflows were associated not only with higher asset market values, but also with increased domestic activity that increased demand for domestic goods and services.[1] This shifted incentives for investment within the economy from tradables to nontradables (especially real-estate and domestic asset markets), and it caused current account deficits to occur as exports effectively became more expensive and imports were cheaper. As a result, the capital inflows were associated with current account deficits and deceleration of exports that laid the seed for the eventual reversal of investor confidence. Thus, it was no accident that all these economies experienced property and real-estate booms, as well as stock-market booms, at some time in the years between 1993 and 1996. These booms in turn generated the incomes to keep domestic demand and growth growing at relatively high rates. This soon resulted in signs of macroeconomic imbalance, not in the form of the government's rising fiscal deficits but as a current account deficit reflecting the consequences of debt-financed private profligacy.

It was inevitable that this would eventually result in a collapse of investor confidence. When that did occur, capital was pulled out and currencies depreciated; those with dollar commitments in the offing rushed into the market to purchase dollars early and cut their losses. The spiral continued, generating a liquidity crunch and a wave of bankruptcy. Therefore, financial liberalization was associated with excessive dependence on foreign capital inflows, especially short-term debt. This was probably the single most important explanatory factor for the nature and the severity of the crisis in East Asia.

The specific role of financial liberalization was further underlined by the fact that other economies in the region that also experienced export slowdowns in 1996 and 1997 but had not liberalized finance and capital accounts to the same extent (such as Taiwan and Vietnam) did not experience a financial crisis. Mobile capital allowed for faster and more extreme appreciation of exchange rates and also more rapid reversals of capital flows in the crisis-hit economies than in other less financially exposed economies within the region.

One conclusion that has been constantly repeated since the start of the Asian crisis in mid-1997 is the importance of "sound" macroeconomic policies, once financial flows had been liberalized. It has been suggested that countries like Thailand, South Korea, and Indonesia faced such problems because they allowed their current account deficits to become too large, reflecting too great an excess of private domestic investments over private savings. However, with completely unbridled capital flows, it is no longer possible for a country to control the amount of capital inflow or outflow, and both types of movements can create consequences that are undesirable. If, for example, a country is suddenly chosen as a preferred site for foreign portfolio investment, it can lead to huge inflows that in turn cause the currency to appreciate, thus encouraging investment in nontradables rather than tradables, and altering domestic relative prices and therefore incentives. Simultaneously, unless the inflows of capital are simply (and wastefully) stored up in the form of accumulated foreign exchange reserves, they must necessarily be associated with current account deficits.

This means that any country that does not exercise some sort of control or moderation over private capital inflows can be subject to very similar pressures. These then create the conditions for their own eventual reversal, when the current account deficits are suddenly perceived to be too large or unsustainable. In other words, what all this means is that once there are completely free capital flows and completely open access to external borrowing by private domestic agents, there can be no "prudent" macroeconomic policy; the overall domestic balances or imbalances will change according to the behavior of capital flows, which will themselves respond to the economic dynamics that they have set into motion.

## Adjustment, Recovery, and Aftermath

The initial adjustment to the crisis varied significantly across countries, with an acceleration of liberalization in some (South Korea and Thailand) and greater intervention in others (Malaysia). The immediate response tended to be significantly affected by the extent of IMF intervention; indeed, the IMF has been strongly criticized (Chandrasekhar and Ghosh, 1999; Stiglitz, 2004) for its role because it responded in ways that may have intensified the crisis. In situations of asset deflation and associated collapse in economic activity in the crisis-hit countries, it imposed further deflationary pressure by demanding tight monetary policy and high interest rates (in order to reduce the capital outflows) and reductions in public expenditures (to generate more fiscal surpluses or reduce fiscal deficits). As a result, Thailand, Indonesia, and South Korea experienced exceptionally sharp reductions in economic activity, and the subsequent recovery was essentially facilitated by a combination of devaluation-induced export increases and some fiscal expansion, including what was enabled by the Miyazawa Initiative.[2] By contrast, Malaysia, which did not go to the IMF and had also imposed temporary capital controls in order to prevent further capital flight during its fiscal stimulus, also recovered relatively quickly. In the event, while exports recovered quickly, it is also likely that the financial bailouts to domestic companies and banks along with the fiscal stimulus responses that were initiated in 1998 against IMF advice and in the teeth of criticism from the United States and some European countries also played positive roles in generating the recovery.

Over the subsequent decade, all these economies have recovered, albeit in different ways and to different degrees determined by the nature of the policy response in individual countries. But the recovery has not meant a return to "miracle" status. This is because the crisis did not lead to real changes in the export-led strategy of growth or to greater financial regulation that would have reduced financial fragility and enabled more inclusive growth (Ghosh and Chandrasekhar, 2009a).

Export growth, which was seen as the key to the success of these five economies in the late 1980s and the first half of the 1990s, is often cited as the best indication of the recovery as well. Pre-crisis export growth in the region was very high, between 10 and 20 percent per year in US dollar terms. The deceleration of export growth in 1996 is widely recognized as one of the proximate causes of the crisis. The export recovery occurred within a couple of years: by 2000 all five countries were showing sharp increases in rates of export growth. Subsequently, however, export growth has been very volatile in all five countries and has been strongly influenced by global developments. GDP growth also recovered, but in general this involved growth rates that have been slightly lower, and definitely more volatile, than the growth rates of the previous period. But the most startling change was the broad macroeconomic shift in terms of a large divergence between savings and investment rates. The East and Southeast Asian region generally had very high savings rates—between 30 and 45 percent. But the period subsequent to the financial crisis saw an increase in these already high rates, especially in the "crisis" countries. However, investment rates (that is, the share of investment in GDP) plummeted in all these countries, with the sole exception of Thailand where it first fell and then rose again, albeit not reaching its earlier peak.

Therefore in all five countries, 1997 and 1998 marked a clear break from the earlier trend, when typically domestic investment rates were higher than savings rates, and the balance was met by an inflow of foreign capital. The latter is in fact what one would expect in a developing country, because it is generally supposed that developing countries are characterized by a shortage of investible resources. Therefore, economic openness, especially to foreign investment, is designed to allow foreign resources to add to domestic savings in order to generate a higher rate of investment than would be possible using only domestic resources. After the crisis, from 1998 onward, these five economies actually became *more* "open" in policy terms, especially with respect to rules regarding foreign investment. Nevertheless, after 1998 the five countries stopped being net recipients of foreign savings and instead showed the opposite tendency of net resource outflow, as domestic savings were higher than investment. This meant that there was a process of squeezing out savings from the population as a whole but not investing it within the economy to ensure future growth. Instead, these savings were effectively exported, either through capital outflows or by adding to the external reserves of the central banks, which were typically held in very safe assets abroad (such as US Treasury Bills). This occurred despite the continuing need for more investment within these countries, because the development project is still not complete in these countries and especially in Indonesia, Thailand, and the Philippines, where poverty and backwardness are still prevalent.

This rather paradoxical situation, which is reflective of a broader international tendency whereby developing countries have been providing their resources to the developed world, and in particular to the United States, has been described by some as a "savings glut" (Bernanke, 2005). Weak or inadequate financial intermediation and undeveloped financial institutions have been blamed for this outcome. But the evidence shows that as financial institutions became more sophisticated, and imitated the North Atlantic model, the divergence between domestic savings and investment actually grew (and was indeed the largest within economies with the most developed and sophisticated financial systems, such as Malaysia and Indonesia). In any case, it is apparent that the problem in these countries was not the rise in savings so much as it was the collapse in investment, suggesting not a savings glut so much as *an investment famine*. True, savings rates increased, affected also by crisis-induced shifts in income distribution that reduced workers' consumption and transferred more income to those in a better position to save. But the sharp collapse in investment rates came about because of other factors that then led to the emergence of this "savings surplus."

The growing savings surplus was partly—but only partly—the result of the decisions of private agents in these countries, and even these private decisions were strongly affected by official economic policies. For example, stringent monetary conditions, increasing real interest rates, and an excess of very rigid and inflexible forms of prudential regulation caused bank credit to be less easily available for investment. A range of other post-crisis measures dampened private investment by directly and indirectly raising the costs of finance and reducing access to them. This obviously reduced investment by large corporate entities, and it had even stronger detrimental effects on small enterprises, which found it more difficult to access credit. It is worth noting that the only economy that showed a different pattern in savings and investment—Thailand—is one where the government of Thaksin Shinawatra systematically made greater access to institutional credit to small enterprises and farmers composed a major plank of the post-crisis reconstruction strategy (Pasuk and Baker, 2009). But monetary and financial policies are only one part of the story. A very large role in the reduction of aggregate investment was played by fiscal policies of governments in these countries, who increased their own savings and cut down on fiscal deficits or increased fiscal surpluses. Even though the financial crisis in these countries was essentially brought on by private profligacy in a financially liberalized environment, the aftermath of the financial crises created an environment of excessive caution on the part of governments. The pressure was on governments to keep budget deficits under control by reducing spending. As a result, governments in these countries did not spend as much as could be easily sustained by the economy, to ensure better conditions for the people, or to encourage more sustainable growth and generate more employment.

So the major cause for this apparent excess of capital, which was then exported to the United States and other developed countries, was deflationary policies on the part of these governments, which suppressed domestic consumption and investment. One obvious reason for this was the fear of a repeat of the large and destabilizing movements of speculative capital that were such a strong feature of the financial crisis of 1997–1998. The idea was to guard against the possibility of such potentially damaging capital flight by building up substantial foreign exchange reserves, even when they could involve large fiscal losses. The other reason was that the economic strategy in these countries was still centered on the obsession with exports as the engine of growth, which, combined with deflationary domestic policies, kept levels of aggregate domestic investment lower than savings. This caused an "excess supply" of foreign exchange in the currency market, which would in turn involve an appreciation of currencies, thereby adversely affecting exports.

In a world of liberalized trade where exchange rates cannot be easily controlled, this meant that currencies had to be kept at "competitive" levels through market-based means. And this in turn meant that foreign currency inflows—whether through more exports or remittances or through capital flows—had to be counteracted by central bank market intervention to purchase foreign currency and to prevent undesired appreciation of the currency. The macroeconomic counterpart—and cause—of the rising foreign exchange reserves held by the central banks of all these countries was therefore the excess of domestic savings over investment, which was actually a huge potential waste for these economies. Financial liberalization effectively resulted in the choice of deflationary strategies by governments. This then contributed to the excess of domestic savings over investment, thereby threatening currency appreciation. This is what led to the accumulation of unutilized foreign exchange in the form of growing foreign exchange reserves that were invested in "safe" assets abroad such as US Treasury Bills.

## Changes in Financial Structure

After a brief intermission in the immediate aftermath of the 1997 crisis, there was a revival of capital flows to developing countries. Triggered by the intensification of financial liberalization during and after the financial crisis, that revival turned into a veritable surge after 2003. Although the crisis of 2008 dampened flows briefly, subsequently the infusion of cheap liquidity into developed country markets has resulted in a new surge in capital flows. In sum, developing countries have continued to be recipients of foreign capital flows that in most cases are also far in excess of their current account deficits, if any (Ghosh and Chandrasekhar, 2009a).

This long-term surge in capital flows to developing countries has also been associated with a transformation of their domestic financial structures. Over the years, when developing countries, including developing countries in Asia, were attracting large financial flows from developed countries, they were also attracting and accommodating in their financial systems the carriers of those flows, namely foreign financial firms. This required reforming their financial rules and reshaping their regulatory frameworks to create an environment conducive to the mode of functioning of these firms (Fornari and Levy, 2000). The idea appears to have been that if you want to attract capital, you need to attract the carriers of capital. And if you want to attract the carriers of capital, you have to create for them an environment that they would find conducive. That environment is seen as defined by the model that was shaped in the United States, not in 1934 by the Glass-Steagall Act, but by developments after the 1980s, which culminated in the Financial Services Modernization Act. Thus, what financial liberalization and reform do is to reposition financial structures and regulatory frameworks in developing countries to resemble those in the Anglo-Saxon world; to replicate, despite the lower levels of per capita income or levels of development otherwise measured in these countries, the Anglo Saxon model of finance within their own borders (Chandrasekhar, 2008). This phenomenon of "structural contagion" has been inadequately discussed in the literature on finance and development.

The resulting structural changes and the entry of new institutions and instruments have been substantial. For example, despite the notoriety of hedge funds, gained from the role they are alleged to have played in the currency speculation that precipitated the 1997 crisis, hedge fund activity in developing countries has increased substantially in recent years. Encouraged by liberalization that ensures not only the entry but also the proliferation of instruments, the growth of derivatives markets, the emergence of futures, and the increase in shorting possibilities, firms have devoted much attention to these markets. Portfolio diversification by financial investors in developed countries seeking new targets, higher returns, and/or a hedge fund has also resulted in the entry of private equity firms. Private equity involves investment in equity linked to an asset that is not listed and therefore not publicly traded in stock markets. This broad definition includes a range of transactions or assets, such as venture capital investments, leveraged buyouts, and mezzanine debt financing, where the creditor expects to gain from the appreciation in equity value by exploiting conversion features such as rights, warrants, or options.

Given this tendency for Asian financial systems to increasingly resemble those in the Anglo-Saxon world, the question arises as to whether the financial sectors in Asian countries are characterized by vulnerabilities of the kind we saw in developed countries in 2008 and after. This question remains valid even if the crisis in Asia has not taken the form it has in most developed countries. There has been no financial implosion in these countries. Asian banks are well capitalized. They are not overexposed to toxic assets such as collateralized debt obligations linked to the housing market in developed countries. Nor are they engaged in risky profit seeking to the same degree. Even in terms of capital adequacy ratios, most banking systems in developing Asia are relatively sound.

But this does not mean that there has been no fallout of the restructuring of financial systems in Asia. In fact, the process has been associated with similar tendencies of the socialization of risk, which are already evident in the United States and Europe (Chandrasekhar, 2004).

Consider, for example, the case of India. One consequence of financial liberalization is that there has been a rapid expansion of bank credit, which grew at more than double the rate of increase of nominal GDP in the five years before mid-2008. As a result, the ratio of outstanding bank credit to GDP (which had declined in the initial post-liberalization years from 30.2 percent at the end of March 1991 to 27.3 percent at the end of March 1997) doubled over the next decade to reach about 60 percent by the end of March 2008. Thus, one consequence of financial liberalization was an increase in credit dependence in the Indian economy, a characteristic imported from developed countries. The growth in credit outperformed the growth in deposits, resulting in an increase in the overall credit-deposit ratio from 56 percent at the end of March 2004 to 73 percent at the end of March 2008. This increase was accompanied by a corresponding drop in the investment-deposit ratio, from 51.7 percent to 36.2 percent, which indicates that banks were shifting away from their earlier conservative preference to invest in safe government securities in excess of what was required under the statutory liquidity ratio norm.[3]

These changes were not primarily driven by an increase in the commercial banking sector's lending to the productive sectors of the economy. Instead, retail loans became the prime drivers of credit growth. The result was a sharp increase in the retail exposure of the banking system, with personal loans increasing from slightly more than 8 percent of total bank credit in 1992–1993 to more than 23 percent by 2005–2006. Within retail credit, the growth in housing loans was the highest in most years. The share of housing finance in total credit rose from 5 percent in 2001–2002 to 12 percent in 2006–2007 and was still at 10 percent in 2009–2010. The credit-financed boom in the housing market triggered a spiral in housing prices, which in turn fueled the boom further. Indeed, much of the recent rapid expansion of the Indian economy can be traced to such credit-fueled demand for housing and consumer durables, even as mass consumption stagnated. Because of the leverage that these practices of finance permitted, debt-financed private expenditure became a substitute for debt-financed public expenditure, and this helped to sustain and raise real economy growth during the years of fiscal contraction (Ghosh and Chandrasekhar, 2009b).

Even those at the Indian central bank took notice of this process:

> Demand for housing finance has emerged as a key driver of bank credit in the past few years. As incomes grow further and the pace of urbanisation picks up, and, in view of the substantial backlog, demand for housing and housing finance can be expected to record continuous high growth over the next few years. In view of the expected high demand, pressure on real-estate prices may continue. Moreover, real-estate markets are characterised by opacity and other imperfections in developing countries, and certainly in India. Such developments can easily generate bubbles in the real-estate market, because of problems in the elasticity of supply, and information asymmetries. Strong demand for housing and buoyancy in real-estate prices in an environment of non-transparency, thus, could potentially pose risks to the banking system. In conjunction with interest rate cycles, the banking system as well as the regulator would need to be vigilant to future NPAs (non-performing assets) and the US-like sub-prime woes. (Mohan, 2007, 2222)

This implies recognition of the possibility that the rapid increase in credit and retail exposure would have brought more tenuous borrowers into the bank credit universe in India as well. A significant (but as yet unknown) proportion of this could be "subprime" lending. To attract such borrowers, banks have been offering attractive interest rates below the benchmark prime lending rate. More recently, banks, including public-sector banks, have been opting for the scheme of initial "teaser rates" on housing loans, which tend to attract borrowers of doubtful repayment capacity into the housing market. These are all tendencies reflective of the fragility that precipitated the 2008 crisis in many developed countries.

So, even though the conventional indicators of banking sector performance in India and other Asian countries suggest that they are safe, there are tendencies that indicate potential fragility. If these intensify and lead to financial failure, it could result in inadequate liquidity and credit stringency, especially if foreign capital exits these economies because of the uncertainties that arise.

It is in this context that we need to assess the "positive," recovery-inducing effects of the return of capital flows to Asia. The region has once again become the main attractor of equity capital from abroad, with flows far exceeding those to transition economies in Europe and to Latin America. Bank credit in Asia, which did not decline much even during the global recession, also seems to be turning around and regaining the rapid growth it recorded in the period since 2003. Thus, underlying the much-celebrated V-shaped growth trajectory, with its sharp recovery, is a return to precisely those tendencies that were temporarily stalled by the reversal of capital flows that magnified the effects of trade dependence on growth. In fact, it is not a substantial recovery in global trade flows that underlies the return to growth in these countries; rather it is their ability to combine a fiscal stimulus with a return to a debt-financed, consumption- and housing-investment-led growth path. The idea seems to be that when required to exit from a fiscal stimulus, to whatever degree, credit-financed demand will continue to sustain growth in these countries.

We are witnessing trends that imply an increase in financial fragility and can lead to further financial crises, with extremely adverse implications for growth, stability, employment, and social welfare. This is the element of continuity in a world that is seen as having changed substantially. In this context, self-regulation clearly does not help. New measures to govern finance and financial flows are a necessity.

## Notes

1. The recent experience of some eurozone countries like Ireland and Greece shows how such a process can occur not just with fixed exchange rates but even within a common currency area.
2. The Miyazawa Initiative launched in October 1998 aimed to create, in the context of the crisis, a short-term fund financed by countries in the region holding excess foreign reserves. The fund was to provide loans at low interest rates to Asian countries facing balance-of-payment difficulties, a run on their reserves, and a depreciation of their currencies. The initiative was seen by some as an attempt to set up the equivalent of an Asian Monetary Fund that would provide balance-of-payment financing at low interest rates and without the conditions associated with IMF lending. US objections are partly seen as responsible for

an early end to the initiative, which provided less financing than it was initially expected to deliver.

3. Data in this and the subsequent paragraphs are from CFSA (2009).

## References


Amsden, Alice. (1992). *Asia's Next Giant: South Korea and Late Industrialization*. New York: Oxford University Press.

Bernanke, Ben. (2005). "The Global Savings Glut and the US Trade Deficit." Sandridge Lecture, Virginia Association of Economics, Richmond, Virginia. http://www.federalreserve.gov/boarddocs/speeches/2005/200503102/.

Chandrasekhar, C. P. (2004). "Financial Liberalization, Fragility and the Socialization of Risk: Can Capital Controls Work?" G24 Discussion Paper. http://www.g24.org/TGM/002gva04.pdf.

Chandrasekhar, C. P. (2008). "Global Liquidity and Financial Flows to Developing Countries: New Trends in Emerging Markets and Their Implications." G24 Discussion Paper. http://www.networkideas.org/featart/jul2008/G24.pdf.

Chandrasekhar, C. P., and Jayati Ghosh. (1999). *Crisis and Conquest: Learning from East Asia*. New Delhi: Orient Longman.

Chang, Ha-Joon, Gabriel Palma, and Hugh Whittaker. (2001). Financial liberalisation and the Asian Crisis, London: Palgrave.

Committee on Financial Sector Assessment (CFSA). (2009). *India's Financial Sector Assessment: Overview Report*. March. Mumbai: Government of India and Reserve Bank of India.

Erturk, Korkut. (2002). "Overcapacity and the East Asian Crisis." *Journal of Post Keynesian Economics* 24(2): 253–275.

Fornari, Fabio, and Aviram Levy. (2000). "Global Liquidity in the 1990s: Geographical Allocation and Long-run Determinants, BIS Conference on International Financial Markets and the Implications for Monetary and Financial Stability." *BIS Conference Papers* No. 8. http://www.bis.org/publ/confer08a.pdf.

Ghosh, Jayati, and C. P. Chandrasekhar. (2009a). *After Crisis: Adjustment, Recovery and Fragility in East Asia*. New Delhi: Tulika.

Ghosh, Jayati, and C. P. Chandrasekhar. (2009b). "The Costs of 'Coupling': The Global Crisis and the Indian Economy." *Cambridge Journal of Economics* 33: 725–739.

Group of 10. (2001, January 25). *Report on Consolidation in the Financial Sector*. http://www.imf.org/external/np/g10/2001/01/Eng/index.htm.

Hughes, Helen. (1999). "Crony Capitalism." *Policy* (Spring): 1–9.

Ip, G. (2007, October 12). "Income Inequality Widens." *Wall Street Journal*.

Kregel, Jan. (1998). "Derivatives and Capital Flows: Applications to Asia." *Cambridge Journal of Economics Special Issue on Asian Financial Crisis* 22(6): 677–692.

Mohan, Rakesh. (2007). "India's Financial Sector Reforms: Fostering Growth While Containing Risk." *Reserve Bank of India Bulletin*, December, http://rbidocs.rbi.org.in/rdocs/Speeches/PDFs/81616.pdf

Organisation for Economic Cooperation and Development. (2003). *Institutional Investors Statistical Year Book 1992–2001*. Paris: OECD.

Pasuk Phonpaichit and Christopher Baker (2009) "Thai capital after the Asian crisis", in Jayati Ghosh and C. P. Chandrasekhar (eds) *After Crisis: Adjustment, Recovery and Fragility in East Asia*, 89–107. New Delhi: Tulika.

Radelet, Steven, and Jeffrey Sachs. (2000). "The Onset of the East Asian Financial Crisis." In Paul Krugman, ed., *Currency Crises*, 105–147. Chicago: University of Chicago Press.

Stiglitz, Joseph E. (2004). "Capital Market Liberalization, Globalization and the IMF." *Oxford Review of Economic Policy* 20(1): 57–71.

Wade, Robert. (2004). *Governing the Market: Economic Theory and the Role of the Market in East Asian Industrialization*. Princeton: Princeton University Press.

CHAPTER 16

# SPECULATION AND SOVEREIGN DEBT

## AN INSIDIOUS INTERACTION

GERALD A. EPSTEIN AND

PIERRE HABBARD

FOUR years after the financial crisis and near financial collapse of 2008, the world economy again faces the prospect of a deepening economic crisis. The precipitating event is the spreading financial contagion from the sovereign debt and banking crisis in Europe over the summer. "For the first time since October 2008"—the IMF wrote in September 2011—"risks to global financial stability have increased" (IMF, 2011a).

As the sovereign debt crisis in Europe intensifies and threatens to engulf the economies and banking systems of many European countries—Greece, Ireland, Portugal, Italy, Spain, and now France—and beyond, the issue of financial gambling and speculation and its impact on stability, growth, and employment in the real economy once again takes center stage. Why are interest rates on some forms of European sovereign debt so high and volatile? Why are equity prices in private banks so sensitive to rumors and so variable from day to day? Why are funding interest-rate spreads that European banks face so high and variable? What role do the credit-ratings agencies play in promoting volatility and contagion? And, last but not least, are global financial conglomerates that have become too big to fail a symptom or a cause of the current crisis?

In OECD countries 50 percent more people were unemployed in 2010 than in 2007 while globally 84 million more people now live in extreme poverty than before the crisis, most of them in developing countries. For G20 countries alone, OECD and ILO estimates suggest that 110 million jobs must be created by 2015 to return to pre-crisis employment rates—22 million jobs per year.

It would be simplistic to blame financial speculators alone for the global crisis. Free capital flows, low interest rates—the "great moderation"—and surplus liquidity contributed to global imbalances within and between regions. And financial speculators took advantage of that. In the broad sense of the term, financial speculation led to a speculative bubble in the United States, it led to the creation of dangerous leverage and interconnections among financial firms, and it diverted investment from real productive investment and itself contributed to massive inequality within societies. But the root causes also relate to broader problems in the underlying real economies.

The crisis exposed the unsustainability of the model of growth that has prevailed. Growing inequality in the United States and many countries has been linked by the 2009 UN Commission of Experts, chaired by Joseph Stiglitz, to the deficiencies in global aggregate demand that in turn were and are at the center of the current crisis (ETUI, ITUC, and TUAC, 2011). As in the 1920s and the Great Depression, rising inequality combined with financial deregulation and the erosion of bargaining power of the middle- and lower-income classes across industrialized economies (Kumhof and Rancière 2010).

If the global economy is today on the edge of a double-dip recession it is also because of the failure of the global governance system and the way governments, and the G20 in particular, have managed the crisis. The coordinated and inclusive approach to economic recovery measures that prevailed in 2009 was replaced by competitive and premature exit as governments, under pressure from bond markets, moved to fiscal consolidation, through cuts in public expenditures, wages, pensions, and social programs. In June 2010, Global Unions warned the G20 that "this risks tipping the global economy back into recession with catastrophic results." (Global Unions, 2010).

Financial speculation was a cause of the crisis. It triggered the initial shock in April 2007 through derivatives markets—what was then the "subprime" credit crunch—and has been an accelerant ever since, with the continuing large-scale presence of shadow banking and large financial conglomerates, both of which, this paper argues, are the main agents of financial speculation today.

The purpose of this paper is to provide a definition of financial speculation, identify the main sources of speculation—the markets, forms of trading, and financial institutions that foster speculative behavior—and to assess how the sovereign bond markets and the state of the public finances are being affected, notably in the light of the current Euro debt crisis. The overarching question is what kinds of policies and regulatory reforms would be needed to reduce speculation and its impact and to limit the financial forces that are pushing our economies into destructive crises.

## The Rise of Financial Speculation

Providing a stable definition of financial speculation is a complex task. And measuring the size and impact of financial speculation is even more challenging, partly due to the lack of data, which is itself a corollary of the lack of regulation and supervision of the financial market. But what is clear is that the scale of global financial trading cannot be explained by the needs of the productive real sector:

- Global foreign exchange transactions are many times greater than GDP or international trade and were 20 percent higher in April 2010 (4 trillion US dollars in daily turnover) than in April 2007 (3.3 trillion), as seen in figure 16.1. This 20 percent growth in transactions post-crisis cannot be explained by the state of global international trade during that period.
- Similarly there is a growing disconnect between trading flows in derivatives and flows in the underlying assets that derivatives are supposed to be tied to. In notional amounts, the total value of over-the-counter (OTC) derivatives was equivalent to 2.6 times world GDP in 1998 and rose to 9 times world GDP in 2010. As a point of comparison, global primary financial assets (listed equity, debt securities, and bank assets) have remained in the range of 1.5–2 times world GDP throughout the period 1998–2010.
- The number of derivatives contracts on commodity exchanges used to grow modestly, from 10 to 15 million contracts between 1993 and 2004. But since 2005 it has exploded, including post-crisis, reaching 65 million in 2010. That, too, cannot be explained by the growth of the underlying commodities markets.

**Derivative Securities:** Financial contracts such as forwards, futures, options, and swaps whose values depend on the values of other asset prices, such as exchange rates, interest rates, or stock prices.

**Forward contracts:** Forward contracts represent agreements for delayed delivery of financial instruments or commodities in which the buyer agrees to purchase and the seller agrees to deliver, at a future date, a specific instrument or commodity at a specified price or yield. Forward contracts are generally not traded on organized exchanges and their contractual terms are not standardized.

**Options:** Option contracts convey either the right or the obligation, depending on whether the reporting institution is the purchaser or the writer, respectively, to buy or sell a financial instrument or commodity at a certain price up to a specified future date.

**Swaps:** Swaps are transactions in which two parties agree to exchange payment streams based on a specified notional amount for a specified period.

| In USD Bn, 2010 (*and % change since 2007*) | "*Traditional" foreign exchange markets* | | *OTC derivatives* | | | | | | | | |
|---|---|---|---|---|---|---|---|---|---|---|---|
| | | a | b | c | d | | | | | | |
| | **Foreign exchange transactions** (a+b) | Spot transactions | Forex Derivatives | Interest Rate | Other OTCs (equity, commodity and credit) | *of which CDS* | *of which CDS on sovereign bonds* | **All OTC derivatives** (b+c+d) | **Exchange -traded derivatives** | **Exchange traded equity** | **World GDP (current USD)** |
| **Daily average trading** (*April*) | 3981 (*+19.8%*) | 1490 (*+48.3%*) | | | | | | | | 252 (*−37.6%*) | |
| **Notional amounts outstanding** (*June*) | | | 62933 (*+9.3%*) | 478093 (*+25.4%*) | 41629 (*−39.6%*) | 31057 (*−31.3%*) | 2392 (*+60.5%*) | 582655 (*+14.7*) | 75941 (*−20.1%*) | | |
| **Gross market values** (*June*) | | | 3158 (*+95.8%*) | 18508 (*+175%*) | 3007 (*+8.4%*) | 1694 (*+120.6%*) | | 24673 (*+121.9%*) | | | |
| | | | | | | | | | | | 63049 (*+13%*) |

**Figure 16.1** Foreign exchange markets, OTC and exchange-traded derivatives, traded equity, and GDP worldwide in 2007.
*Source*: BIS, 2010a, 2010b; World Federation of Exchange, World Bank

## Short-term "Directional" and Leveraged Bets That Are Guided by Noise Trading

According to the narrow, most common, definition, speculation is the placement of a bet on the short-term changes in prices of a commodity or a financial asset. The bet can be that the price will rise (taking a long position) or fall (taking a short position) in the short term. The amount of money to be gained (or lost) can increase through the means of taking out more borrowing (leverage) to make the bet. Financial speculation is closely associated with arbitrage trading strategies. Arbitrage exploits short-term pricing inefficiencies by simultaneously buying and selling a security at two different prices in two different markets. To the extent that this arbitrage involves bets, even in the short run, it is a form of speculation.

The key point about making a bet on short-term changes in prices is that a speculator will rely on the expectations and bets that *others* are making in the marketplace, much more than on an assessment of the underlying long-term value of the asset. Some economists refer to this as "noise trading." Keynes likened it to a gamble on a beauty contest in which people win, not by guessing which contestant is more beautiful, but by guessing who the others will guess is more beautiful, who in turn are guessing the guesses of others.

## Driving Asset Prices (and Risk) Away from the (Real Economy's) Fundamentals

Speculation is self-feeding, leading to more speculation and making hedging and risk management for real economy purposes more difficult by creating more uncertainty. Asset prices are driven by fear and rumor rather than by rational assessment of underlying factors. By moving asset prices away from their likely real values, either through short-term volatility or long-term swings ("bubbles"), speculation increases the probability that risk will be shifted to taxpayers and workers—the ones to bear the burden should a new crisis be precipitated.

Speculation of this type can be destructive because of the levels of systemic risks and interconnectedness of the financial sector. If speculation is connected with long chains of bets and interconnections among financial institutions, then the financial impacts of the bets "gone wrong" made by one institution can spread through many institutions. If very large, this can lead to economywide disruptions and to pressure for taxpayer bailout. As noted by Blundell-Wignall and Paul Atkinson (2011) of the OECD,

> When one party to a derivatives transaction makes a huge gain, another institution is making a huge loss—and that loss (if marked to market

> transparently) may cause a financial firm to fail. Systemic financial stability risk rises, because derivatives both raise leverage and require each participant in the chain of counterparties to be able to perform their obligations in order for others to be able to perform their own. In this way derivatives raise systemic risk, without adding any new equity or debt capital for the economy.

Similar speculation is now exacerbating the sovereign debt crisis in Europe from Greece to Spain, Italy, and other countries, the risk being spread through interconnected banking and shadow banking systems.

## A Broader Approach to Speculation: Any Financial Activity That Does Not Contribute to Increases in Income or Sustainable Wealth of the Real Economy

Speculation can also be defined more broadly as any socially unproductive financial activity. Substantial resources devoted to the financial sector and the high incomes and profits generated divert wealth away from other sectors of the economy, or they even destroy wealth in other sectors in the process. Under such a broad definition, speculation encompasses all activities for which the social utility to the real economy is close to zero—it is not limited to nor necessarily involves speculating on short-term changes in asset prices. And as Keynes emphasized, when speculation of this type is widespread and dominates entrepreneurship, then society's resources are not likely to be well invested. Keynes (1936, 159) noted that this type of investing can make asset prices highly variable, can lead to asset bubbles that are self-reinforcing, and can lead to financial crashes when sentiment changes:

> Speculators may do no harm as bubbles on a steady stream of enterprise. But the position is serious when enterprise becomes the bubble on a whirlpool of speculation. When the capital development of a country becomes a by-product of the activities of a casino, the job is likely to be ill-done. The measure of success attained by Wall Street, regarded as an institution of which the proper social purpose is to direct new investment into the most profitable channels in terms of future yield, cannot be claimed as one of the outstanding triumphs of laissez-faire capitalism.

The term "financial innovation" is central to the broader definition of speculation. Financially "innovative" transactions that are motivated by regulatory arbitrage or by tax arbitrage do not necessarily qualify as purely speculative trading individually, but would do so on an aggregate level. An investor lending to a company that engages in real-estate speculation might not himself be taking a speculative bet (if, for example, his return is guaranteed) but the overall financial project lacks social benefit. To take a powerful contemporary example, packaging highly risky subprime mortgages into collateralized debt obligations (CDOs) and selling them for a fee is not speculative—because the fee is guaranteed—but the activity is not socially useful if it leads to a real-estate bubble that crashes.

From an institutional perspective, financial speculation is associated with the rise of global financial conglomerates and the associated shadow banking system. Credit-rating agencies also played a destructive role, especially when making their incomes on fees. Rating mortgages AAA for a fee when they are clearly highly risky is not socially useful, even if it is not speculative in the narrow sense of placing a price-directional bet.

## Financial Innovation and Derivatives

Certain financiers and economists justify the large incomes accruing to financial institutions and object to financial regulation on the grounds that financial innovation is highly socially productive. They argue that structured products—CDOs and asset-back securities—and derivatives—futures, forwards, options, and swaps—rank among those innovative products that aim to manage risks or to stabilize incomes associated with an underlying financial asset—bank credit, listed bond and equity, currency, commodity, and so on.

But derivatives simply shift risk; they do not eliminate aggregate risk. Examples include a bank or a hedge fund exploiting differences of tax treatment of debt and equity or a bank trading a derivative to reduce artificially the "riskiness" of securities and thereby bypass prudential regulatory requirements. Some economists, including Paul Volcker, have questioned the social value of many financial innovations. Crotty and Epstein (2009) use previous studies to calculate the number and percentage of innovations that are at least partly motivated by tax and accounting arbitrage or regulatory arbitrage. Their estimates reveal that—at a minimum—roughly one-third of these financial "innovations" are motivated by these factors, rather than by efficiency improvements.

## The Rise of Global Complex Financial Conglomerates

So far we have approached financial speculation through a market, product, and transaction perspective. But who sits behind the trading desk? Who sells derivatives and structured products with the intent or knowledge that they will be traded for purely speculative purposes? In short what are the institutional foundations that underpin speculation? A brief overview of how financial markets are structured leaves no doubt about who pulls the levers: large financial conglomerates, which by their size, international coverage and complexity have become systemically important—those that are, from the taxpayer point of view, "too big to fail" (TBTF): AIG, Merrill Lynch, Lehman Brothers in 2008, Bear Stearns in 2007.

In all major OECD economies, assets held by the three largest banks as a share of GDP rose significantly in the run-up to the crisis and have continued to do so post-crisis (see figure 16.2). On the whole, this is specific to OECD economies (large emerging economy members of the G20 do not show a similar pattern with the notable exception of South Africa). The number of banks controlling three-quarters of foreign exchange turnover decreased both before and after 2007 in most OECD economies. A similar process of concentration is taking place in all segments of the derivatives markets. For example while in 1998 30 banks dominated the foreign exchange forward rate market and 14 dominated the options market; in 2001 these markets were dominated by 14 and 10 firms, respectively. In the fast growing market for exchange-traded funds (ETFs; see section below), early movers such as State Street and Black Rock are now being overshadowed by the global financial conglomerates.

The rise of TBTF groups and their move to more speculative behavior is closely associated with the changing business model of banks. Historically, commercial retail banking—financing the real economy through deposits and loans to households and nonfinancial companies—was separated from investment banking, which is composed of speculative, volatile, but highly remunerating financial services including corporate finance, brokerage and trading, research, and analysis. Following waves of deregulation—in the United States the gradual removal of the Glass-Steagall Act—large banks have amalgamated both retail and investment banking activities and also in some cases were expanded to include insurance activities.

During the 1990s, the corporate governance and business model of large OECD banks shifted from a "creditor culture"—that of traditional loans-and-deposits activities—to an "equity culture" led by shareholder-value maximization. The shift was not neutral in the ways banks would manage risk (Blundell-Wignall et al., 2009). Banks diversified their activities and moved into high-risk, but also highly rewarding, investment banking and trading activities. This concentration of wealth created a concentration of power and also made governments and economies more vulnerable to their risky and speculative behavior. And this is what happened with Lehman Brothers, Merrill Lynch, Bear Stearns, Northern Rock, and AIG in 2008. According to the former IMF chief economist Simon Johnson, "The big banks at the heart of our financial system blew themselves up. [...] No one forced the banks to take on so much risk" (Johnson, 2011). According to the IMF the frequency of distress (defined as a full year of negative return, reception of government support through capital injection, or transfer of assets) in 2007–2009 was 67 percent higher for investment banks and for banks cumulating investment and retail banking than for retail banks alone (IMF, 2011b). For the OECD (2011a), "It can be argued on competition grounds that the oligopolistic structure of banking likely contributed to the financial crisis."

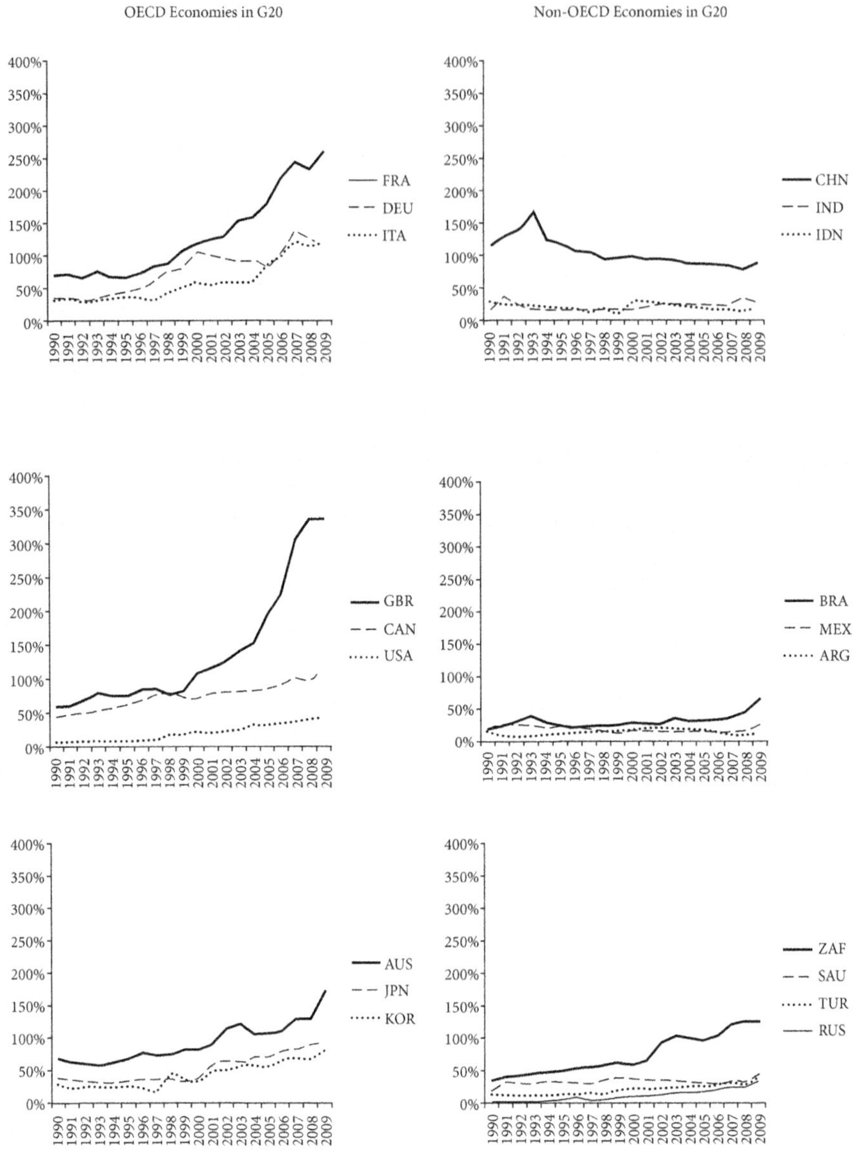


**Figure 16.2** Total assets of the largest three banks as a share of GDP.
*Source*: OECD, 2011a.

## The Rise of Shadow Banking and Pools of Capital

There has been increased attention to the role of the shadow banking system in the generation of speculative, and more broadly unproductive, financial activity (Pozsar et al., 2010; Pozsar, 2011). The size of the resources available to the shadow banking system is not known with any precision—they include the set of relatively unregulated financial institutions such as hedge funds, private equity firms, and related financial pools of funds, as well as off-balance-sheet banking activities, including structured products, such as asset-backed commercial papers that are sold using special investment vehicles. Pozsar has estimated these funds to be nearly US $4 trillion. They are provided by pension funds, insurance funds, nonfinancial corporations, wealthy individuals, and others. Some of these funds are held off balance sheets or in investment vehicles by commercial and investment banks and brokers themselves. These are the pools of capital available for financial investment, including speculative investment.

Shadow banking is of concern because it includes activities that would normally fall under banking supervision such as maturity/liquidity transformation and credit intermediation, but it itself is not subject to proper regulation and supervision. For the Financial Stability Board (FSB) (2011a) shadow banking raises "systemic risk concerns, in particular, by leverage and flawed credit risk transfer." Because it is outside the regular banking system, shadow banking is an open door to all forms of regulatory arbitrage. It undermines bank, insurance, asset management, and securities regulation and leads to a build-up of additional leverage and risks in the system. The use by large banks of off-balance-sheet transactions and derivatives trading to evade international banking prudential regulation—the "Basel II" and in the future "Basel III" regulatory regimes—are raised as key concerns both by the FSB (2011a) and the OECD (2011a).

Unlike TBTF groups, the rise of shadow banking is not limited to OECD economies. Emerging countries are also affected. In China, for example, there is an increasing gap in the statistics between credit flows on one hand and the balance sheet of regulated banks on the other, which points to significant growth in shadow banking, hard to measure by official statistics.

## The Complicity of Rating Agencies in the 2008 Crisis

The three credit-rating agencies (CRAs) that currently form a global oligopoly—Moody's, Standard & Poor's, and Fitch—are widely understood to have played a controversial role in the run-up to the crisis. Their ratings are pro-cyclical—they are over-optimistic during growth cycles and over-pessimistic during downturns—and are used as a basis for speculation. Until the 1970s, the business model was investor-based: ratings were paid for by investors for a fee. Being remunerated by investors, not by issuers, the agencies were protected from any undue influence from the issuer. That changed in the 1970s when CRAs shifted to the issuer-pays model to boost their profits. But this model came at the cost of much greater exposure to conflicts of interest: financial institutions pay for their own ratings.

The ratings inflation that took place prior to the crisis—and hence the procyclicality of the CRA business models—is well documented (see White, 2010). The OECD (2011a) sees evidence of "significant ratings grade inflation" that took place prior to the crisis through "systematic departures" from technical

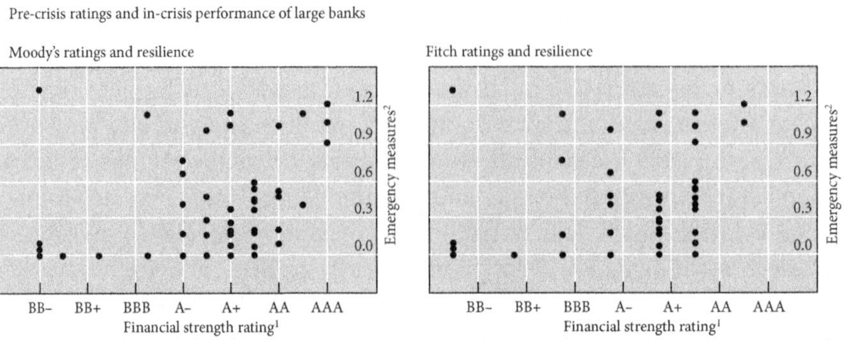


¹ Referred to as "individual rating" by Fitch and "bank financial strength rating" by Moody's.² Sum of the values of fixed income, capital and hybrid instruments issued and assets sold from mid-2007 to end-2009, divided by total equity in 2006.

**Figure 16.3** Comparison between rating grades of 60 large banks pre-crisis and scale of emergency measures taken post-crisis
*Source*: BIS, 2011a.

valuation models as agencies made "discretionary upward adjustments in ratings in efforts to retain or capture business." Comparing the rating grades attributed in mid-2007 to large banks by Moody's and Fitch with the scale of the banks' reliance on "emergency measures" taken post-crisis (including sales of assets and government-sponsored support), the BIS (2011a) finds a positive relationship. As shown in figure 16.3, the higher the rating grade pre-crisis, the bigger was the level of government support and emergency sales post-crisis! The BIS analysis also reveals important inconsistencies pre- and post-crisis between the three leading rating agencies. Only 8 percent of the banks were rated similarly by the agencies mid-2007. For 33 percent of these banks, the three ratings differed by two notches or more.

## New Forms of Financial Speculation Post-crisis

In sum, in its narrow sense, financial speculation is a short-term directional bet on the price movement of an asset that is leveraged through borrowing (so the gains can be potentially huge as with the losses) and guided by "noise trading" (guessing what other traders are guessing, not by objectively verifiable economic indicators, or "market fundamentals"). Financial speculation raises the systemic risks because it is often associated with high degrees of borrowing, often leads to interconnections among multiple financial institutions, often in different jurisdictions, and leads to the mispricing of risks and hence the misallocation of assets through short-term volatility or long-term swings in asset prices (i.e., speculative bubbles). Accordingly, it diverts valuable resources—financial, political, and human resources—away from productive investment in the real economy and wealth creation in society. It is fueled by deregulation, financial "innovation," and the growing concentration of assets and financial power—as seen in the rise of large financial conglomerates—and rating agencies with significant conflicts of interest.

In its broader sense, speculation is financial activity that does not contribute to income or sustainable wealth in the real economy and thus uses up resources in socially unproductive financial activities. At its worst, it is financial activity that actually destroys income and wealth.

There is no definitive "blacklist" of markets, institutions, or trading strategies that together would capture the concept of financial speculation. This is because financial speculation is a moving target. It reinvents itself. Being short-term driven and over-inclined to exploit any form of arbitrage, speculative behavior can take multiple forms and adjust almost instantly to market movements and changes in taxation and regulation. The following four examples are typical: three forms relate to trading strategies (carry trade, high-frequency trading and naked short selling) and one to a fast-growing set of products, ETFs.

## Carry Trade

Carry trade involves borrowing low-cost currencies and investing in currencies carrying high interest rates with low exchange-rate volatility between the two—for example, borrowing in Japanese yen and investing in Brazilian reais. If the standard theories of efficient markets were true, then this type of investment would not be profitable because the impact of the higher interest rate on expected profits would be offset by the expectation that the currency would depreciate. But this does not seem to happen: large amounts of speculative investments flow into high interest-rate currencies and then flow out again when the currency is expected to decline. These carry-trade flows can create major macroeconomic management problems for ministries of finance and central banks and thus lead to mispriced exchange rates.

Measuring the impact of carry trade is difficult to achieve. There are no direct data on the size because for the most part they take place off balance sheets and hence fuel the shadow banking sector.

The carry trade lost much of its attraction, however, following the 2008 crisis and the rise in exchange-rate volatility. But carry trades have once again become important as interest-rate differentials have grown and as the liquidity available to speculators has increased. Many countries, especially in the developing world, are now adopting capital management techniques—including restrictions on capital flows—to try to discourage the carry trade.

## Exchange-Traded Funds

Four years after the 2007 "subprime" crisis, the market for securitization of debt—asset-backed securities (ABSs), including residential and commercial mortgage-backed securities (RMBs and CMBs), and collateralized debt obligations (CDOs)—has still not recovered. The volume of issuance in the European Union and the United States fell considerably after 2008 and what is left is almost entirely reliant on government-backed purchase programs—Freddie Mac, Fannie Mae, and Ginnie Mae in the United States and the European Central Bank in Europe (Blommestein et al., 2011).

While private structured products that are not backed by government have completely disappeared from the market, trading in ETFs has exploded post-crisis. In a low interest-rate environment, institutional investors, not least workers' pension funds, are now more than ever in the "search for yields," and ETFs prima facie offer the ideal risk profile and return.

Like collateralized debt, ETFs are lightly regulated investment vehicles that pool a diverse range of asset classes into one fund. As such, it allows investors to access illiquid markets—such as real estate—that otherwise would not be possible because of prudential regulation of liquidity and market risks (Basel II, Solvency II, pension funding rules, etc.). According to the FSB (2011b), ETFs have grown at an average of 40 percent a year over the past decade. The assets under the management of ETFs were valued at US $1.2 trillion. And just like CDOs, the market for ETFs started with relatively simple products (funds pooling different listed equities) but has gradually moved into more complex and opaque synthetic ETFs ("ETFs of ETFs," which are reminiscent of the subprime era "CDOs of CDOs" or "$CDO^2$"). In Europe in particular, synthetic ETFs represent close to half of the market. The recent "rogue trader" at UBS was making bets using ETFs. For the *Financial Times* commentator Gillian Tett, "ETF growth in the past three years [looks] extraordinarily similar to the CDOs charts back in 2005."[1] For OECD experts (2011a), "The equity derivatives business generally, and ETFs in particular, have all the early requirements for a bubble to develop."

## High-Frequency Trading

Automatic electronic trading and brokering—or computer-generated "algorithmic trading"—have become widespread across organized exchanges, in foreign exchange transactions and listed equity among others. Much algorithmic trading is benign, insofar as it is limited to routine low-impact transactions. That is not the case, however, for the fastest growing form of algorithmic trading, high-frequency trading (HFT). HFT consists of executing frequent but small trades in milliseconds to make profits from incremental price movements in a given listed security (market making) or exploiting differences in pricing between two separate trading venues (arbitrage). Trading decisions are not taken by human beings but by computer-generated algorithms. Positions (effective ownership of the security) are held for just seconds or fractions of a second. The daily portfolio turnover is exceptionally high. HFT is thus the most extreme form of "short-term" investment: not only is effective ownership held for just a fraction of a second, but the overall "investment" in the market is flat by the end of the trading day (see figure 16.4 for an illustration of HFT). As with all lightly regulated financial activities, data on HFT are scarce and incomplete. It is estimated that HFT accounted for circa 25 percent of spot foreign exchange transactions worldwide in 2010 (Kim and Rime, 2010), 56 percent of US equity trading (up from 21 percent in 2005), and 38 percent of European equity trading (up from 9 percent in 2007) (IOSCO, 2011).

Proponents of HFT argue that it adds liquidity to the market and that some of its trading strategies—such as arbitrage—help improve price transparency and reduce market imperfections. That view is not, however, shared by the experts at the International Organization of Securities Commissions (IOSCO, representing stock exchange authorities worldwide) for whom HFT poses a number of risks to the efficiency of markets, their "fairness and integrity," and financial stability. The "very short term nature [...] coupled with the risk of high speed, high volume trading algorithms might move the market prices away from fundamental values" and "impair the price discovery process" (IOSCO, 2011). HFT may also amplify transmission of shocks across markets and asset classes, which, according to the IOSCO could potentially increase "the speed at which a systemic crisis could develop." These risks materialized when HFT algorithms contributed to the May 2010 "Flash Crash," which saw the Dow Jones index lose 5 percent of its value in less than 5 minutes. Following a human error in a single large selling order on the S&P500, HFT computers started panicking and in turn started aggressively selling.

Importantly, regulators are concerned that the confidence of institutional investors, including pension funds, is being undermined as a result of the fear of being "gamed" by the "low-latency" trading of HFT (i.e., high-speed execution of orders). Given the importance of "low latency" trading, computers need to be located inside the trading venues where they operate, so that they receive market information before others (including orders and executions), so making a profit: "shaving" one millisecond off every trade could be worth $100 million a year to a large HFT firm.[2] The IOSCO also questions whether HFT offers a new opportunity for "engaging in abusive practices on a larger scale than would have previously been possible," citing various forms of trading abuses: "momentum ignition," "quote stuffing," "spoofing," and "layering." This could push traditional investors to "withdraw" from the regulated trading venues and place their orders in nonregulated venues and trading platforms housed within financial groups, hence creating "dark pools" of liquidity outside the scrutiny of supervisory authorities (IOSCO, 2011).

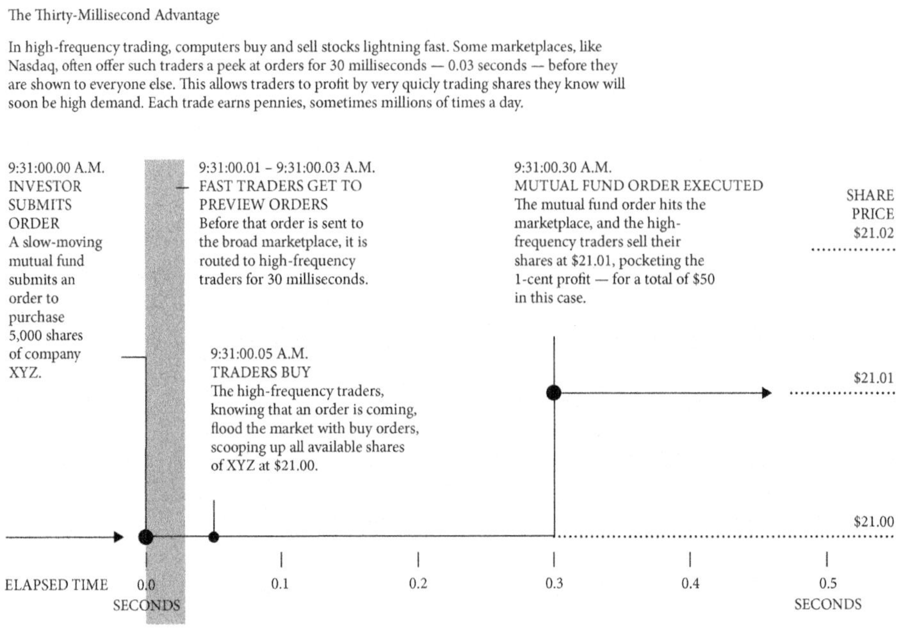


**Figure 16.4** High-frequency trading (HFT)—the "millisecond advantage" over traditional investors.
*Sources*: Schulmeister, 2011; http://www.nytimes.com/2009/07/24/business/24trading.html.

## Short Selling and Naked Credit Default Swaps

Similar to credit-rating agencies, the credit default swaps (CDS) markets have been shown to misprice risk in a pro-cyclical fashion and to have contributed to speculative financial behavior that amplifies the up and down swings of financial asset prices.

In essence a CDS is a type of insurance: a buyer of CDS is taking out insurance against the risk of default of a given loan, and the seller is taking on the risk in exchange for a fee. Yet the CDS markets performed very poorly in measuring risks of large banks prior to the crisis. BIS (2011a) research shows that the 60 large banks' CDS spreads in 2007 were negatively correlated with the scale of emergency support that was received post-crisis. The lower the price of the CDS insurance was pre-crisis, the higher the emergency support was post-crisis.

The problem with such market-based credit default-rating systems is that CDS markets (for example, the CDS on Greek 10-year government bonds) do not necessarily reflect the actual risk of default of the underlying asset (the risk of default of the Greek government). They can either overestimate or underestimate the risk of default. Various market forces are at play. At the outset, CDS markets, as is the case for any other market, demand a "risk premium" (or an "excess return") above the objectively determined risk level of the underlying asset. This means that, by definition, CDS overestimate credit default risk, although such overestimation is difficult to measure.

More fundamentally, however, CDS markets are subject to external market forces that have no connection with the underlying asset. An example would be a sudden "risk aversion" or a "rush to safety" by markets that follows a particular triggering event. For the IMF (2010a) the prices of insuring against sovereign default via CDS markets "depend on the global level of risk aversion in addition to the actual probability of default of the sovereign." Global risk aversion, the IMF argues, "has likely weighed on the price of sovereign protection, without implying any relation to higher default probabilities."

A case in point is the sudden downgrading of US sovereign debt by Standard & Poor's in August 2011. In theory the downgrading would have increased the risk default of the US government as perceived by the market, thereby increasing the yield on the US government bonds, which in turn would have raised US debt servicing. But that is not what happened. It is in fact the opposite that had happened: following the downgrading, the 10-year US Treasury bond actually fell to a record low 2 percent in mid-August. This is because the US downgrading triggered market turmoil, which prompted a global rush to safety assets, to which category US bonds belong. Accordingly the immediate impact of the downgrading of the US government bonds was a decrease in its cost of borrowing.

The flip side of the coin is that market "risk aversion"—while benefiting some sovereign currencies (the United States in the above case)—can destabilize the debt market of other sovereign currencies, as seen in the case of the Mediterranean European countries. For OECD and IMF experts (Blommestein et al., 2010) the "uninformed or irrational" behavior of CDS markets can have a "self-feeding" function in the deterioration of the crisis, leading to "a self-fulfilling negative outcome." The OECD and the IMF do not elaborate, however, on the causes of such irrational behavior.

Other observers have linked such a "self-fulfilling negative outcome" to the highly speculative trading strategy of selling short on naked CDS. Naked CDS is when a trader takes out insurance (the CDS) on an underlying asset that they do not own. Selling short happens when a trader borrows (for a fee) a given security, sells it with the expectation that its price will fall, buys it back at a lower price, and returns it to the lender. The combination of the two—naked CDS and short selling—has nothing to do with insurance. It is a bet—pure speculation:

- Traders buy "long" CDS of a given bond, say, Greek government bonds.
- At the same time traders sell short the underlying asset; traders "borrow" Greek government bonds, say, from pension funds that earn a fee in return and then "sell" the Greek bonds.
- The short selling pushes the prices of the Greek bonds down, which in turn increases the risk of default as perceived by the CDS market.
- Accordingly the value of the CDS on the Greek bonds increases.

- Traders complete the short selling: they buy back the Greek bonds they had borrowed and then sold, then return them to their original owners (in this case, a group of pension funds).

Traders then make a double profit: one on the rise of the CDS (buying long), and the other on the decrease of the Greek bonds (selling short).

The downward spiral is amplified by the credit-rating agencies, which follow rather than lead. There is clearly an incentive for coordinated manipulation. The probability of default is not independent of the cost of borrowing—hence there may be self-fulfilling expectations driving the price of the asset down lower and lower. This is one of the processes affecting sovereign debt and bank equity in Europe currently.

## The Sovereign Bond Markets

Government debt across OECD economies has been soaring since 2008. By the end of 2011, total OECD central government debt is expected to reach US$ 33.4 trillion (EUR 22.2 trillion, or 71.7 percent of GDP), while general government debt (i.e., central, local, and other public liabilities) should reach 100 percent of GDP. Compared with 2007, total OECD government debt will rise by 30 percentage points by 2012. The number of OECD countries with over 100 percentage points debt levels will increase from 3 before the crisis to 8 in the coming decade, while the number of countries with debt levels above 80 percent GDP is expected to more than double (OECD, 2010a).

Under pressure to finance the bailout of banks that were nearly insolvent, as well as the stimulus packages that followed, issuance conditions worsened for government treasuries in 2009. Governments issued more short-term debt than usual (i.e., Treasury Bills, or "T-bills" whose maturity is below 12 months, typically 3 months) as compared to long-term debt ("T-bonds" whose maturity often is 10 years). The share of foreign holdings in total government debt has also been increasing.

Increasing reliance on short-term borrowing or on foreign capital is typically viewed by the markets as resulting in increased vulnerability, because it exposes governments to higher levels of market risks, be it risks regarding interest rates or foreign exchange. This creates incentives and opportunities for more speculation by the market that are related to sovereign debt issues.

### Intertwining between Government and Banks' Liabilities

The 2008 crisis and the taxpayer-financed government interventions in the banking and insurance sector that followed exposed the extent to which risks and liabilities of government finance and the banking sector have become greatly intertwined. Governments delivered various forms of direct support to bankers and guarantees on financial assets and transactions. According to the IMF (2011c), of the US$ 1.72 trillion in direct government support to banks (capital injections and asset purchases), just US$ 0.45 trillion have been recovered, with US$ 1.27 trillion still outstanding. Between October 2008 and December 2010, government guarantees have been provided to more than 200 banks headquartered in 20 OECD economies, issuing close to €1 trillion in bonds—circa 5 percent of GDP of the countries concerned. There are no plans to phase out these government-sponsored support schemes any time soon.

In addition to these explicit guarantees on bonds, governments also provide "implicit" guarantees in the form of the belief of the market that governments will bail out the banking sector if needed in the future, just as they did in 2008-2009. A proxy measurement of this implicit government support to the large banks is the gap between their "stand-alone rating" by credit agencies, which accounts for the bank's specific credit risk, and their "all-in-rating," which adds the likelihood of government support to the stand-alone rating. While even all-in-ratings of large banks have declined since 2007, BIS analysis (2011a) finds that the decline would have been much larger had it not been for the increase in implicit government support post-crisis: as shown in figure 16.5, stand-alone ratings decreased in bigger proportions than all-in ratings. In the case of the United States and United Kingdom, implicit government guarantees

Stand-alone ratings and the importance of external support[1]

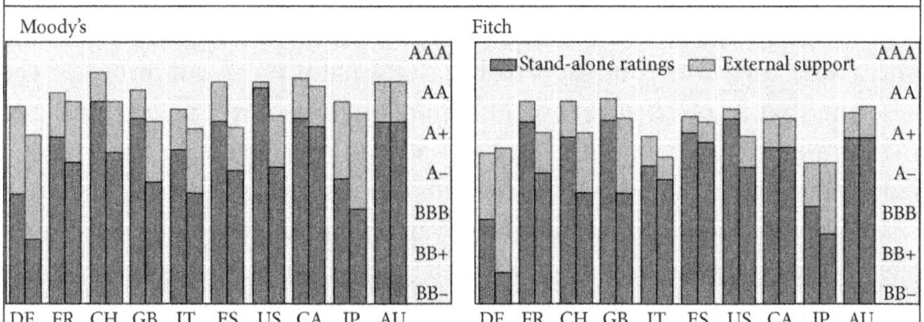


DE = German banks (8; 8); FR = French banks (4; 2); CH = Swiss banks (2; 2); GB = UK banks (5: 5); IT = Italian banks (3; 3); ES = Spanish banks (4; 3); US = US banks (7; 6); CA = Canadian banks (5; 5); P = Japanese banks (5; 3); AU = Australian banks (4; 4). The first figure in parentheses refers to the number of banks rated by Moody's, and the scond to the number rated by Fitch.

[1] For each country, the first bar plots average ratings in mid-2007, and the second those in April 2011. The stand-alone rating plus the rise due to external support equals the all-in rating.

**Figure 16.5** Stand-alone ratings of large banks and external support by governments, 2007-2010.
*Source*: BIS, 2011a.

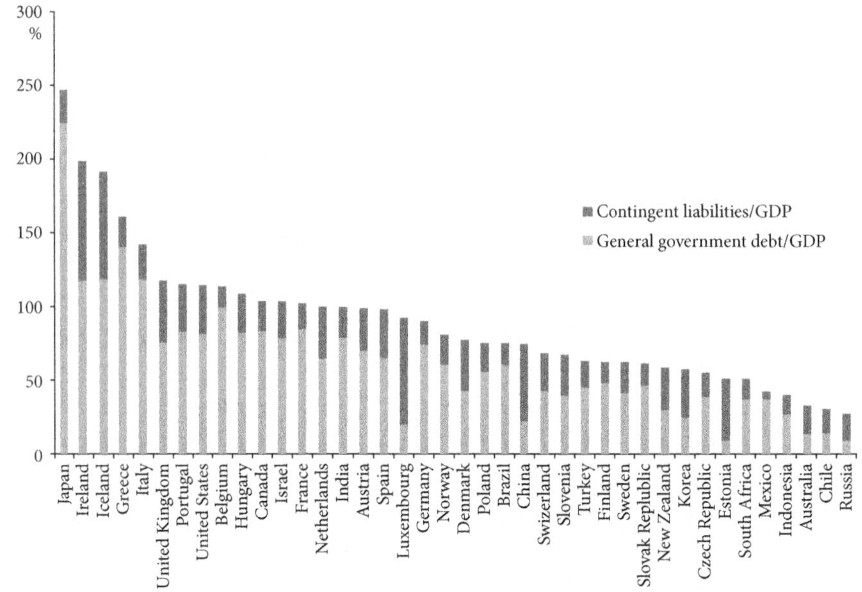


**Figure 16.6** Contingent liabilities and general government debt in GDP % in OECD and emerging economies in 2010.
*Source*: Kim and Schich, 2011.

lifted the rating grades of the US and UK banks by one to two notches in 2010. In the same vein, the currently A+-rated German banks would fall to the BB+ "junk bonds" category, were it not for the implicit backing of the German government.

If anything, this shows that not only has implicit government, and hence taxpayer, support for banks increased post-crisis, but it has in fact become a sine qua non condition to the sustainability of a number of them. Considering that implicit government support has also expanded significantly for medium-sized and smaller banks, one can legitimately claim that the banking sector as a whole is heavily subsidized by taxpayers. This impression is supported when one looks at governments' balance sheets. On average the contingent liabilities (e.g., explicit and implicit guarantees) to which governments are exposed and which are factored into their sovereign ratings are equivalent to 20–30 percent GDP for OECD economies. In Luxembourg, China, Ireland, and Iceland they account for more than 50 percent of GDP, as seen in figure 16.6.

## The Vicious Circle

Clearly the situation becomes exacerbated for governments that are tied by a monetary union, as is the case of the Euro countries, and are subject to the speculative attacks of the financial markets. Governments lose their capacity to issue debt because they no longer have a currency they control alone, and they become hostage to sudden changes in market "sentiments," "risk appetite," rumors, with knock-on effects on government access to external finance. This is especially problematic because these debts are being held by large, concentrated banking institutions so that the sovereign debt crisis also leads to a banking crisis. Destructive speculation is exacerbated by CDS—including naked swaps—that allow bets against sovereign debt and banks, and have been worsened by opaque instruments such as ETFs that are lightly regulated and poorly understood. These instruments and sources of speculation are creating contagion and pushing countries and banks into liquidity crises that could become solvency crises (De Grauwe, 2011).

What results from the above developments—speculative behavior as a moving target that adapts and adjusts instantly to market and regulatory change, the rise of global financial conglomerates that coexist with shadow banking, and the increasing intertwining between government and banking finance—is a chain reaction in the sequencing of the crisis and the interaction between financial speculation and sovereign debt:

- *Step 1*: Pre-crisis and as a result of years of deregulation and lax supervision, governments let large banks grow and diversify their activities to the point where they had become too big to fail or to be adequately governed or supervised. Governments also let shadow banks, market infrastructure, and trading grow without proper supervision.
- *Step 2*: The combination of the two—the creation of large financial conglomerates and the deregulation of markets and trading venues—fed new forms of speculative behavior, pre- and post-crisis.
- *Step 3:* The financial crisis in 2008 prompted a global economic and social recession. In response governments needed to implement an economic stimulus program, which was financed by unprecedented increases in public debt. A massive transfer of debt, and hence of risk and liabilities from creditors to governments and taxpayers then occurred: the losses generated by the banking sector and global financial conglomerates in particular were taken over through various channels by governments and taxpayers—and ultimately citizens.
- *Step 4:* Because that transfer was not conditioned to any proper degree on reregulation or restructuring of the financial sector—there were "no strings attached" to the bailing out of the bankers—the cost of financial speculation in effect is being internalized on the governments' balance sheets. That cost can be measured by the size of government "contingent liabilities," which is calculated by agencies as an addition to their public debt and negatively affects their sovereign ratings.
- *Step 5*: Government and private banking finance has become closely intertwined. As government policy turns to austerity measures, the recovery

has become ever more fragile and uncertain. Speculative attacks continue due to governments' failure to eliminate through regulation the vehicles of financial speculation that caused the 2007-2008 crisis in the first place. As sovereign ratings are downgraded country by country, the crisis has been transformed into a sovereign debt crisis and the highly interconnected banking sector is subject to renewed stress. This adds further pressure on the government balance sheet through inflated contingent liabilities.

## What Regulatory Policy Response?

In a world ruled by robust and efficient international governance systems, collective intelligence would have led governments to cooperate in response to the above sequencing of the crisis since 2007. They would have collectivized the risks each of them is facing individually, and they would have accelerated financial reforms to choke off the sources of financial speculation.

But that is not what happened.

### The G20 (In-)Action Plan

In response to the financial crisis in 2008, governments created the G20 forum at the head-of-state level, which first met in November 2008. G20 "Recommendations for Strengthening Financial Stability" were adopted in London in April 2009 and it is they that drive the regulatory reform agenda. In the United States, the crisis led to a parallel though connected regulatory reform process, which culminated with the adoption of the Dodd-Frank Act in July 2010.

Much has been learned about the causes of the recent financial crisis and the role of speculation, narrowly and broadly defined, in causing it. And indeed with the G20 and through the Dodd-Frank process a detailed and in some areas robust financial reform agenda has been developed. While the reform process (if implemented) might well stabilize and keep afloat the current financial system—at least for the time being—there is no ambition to tackle the speculative forces that triggered the crisis in 2007 and in 2008.

Part of the problem is that the G20 agenda and the Dodd-Frank implementation have become bogged down by extremely strong lobbying efforts on the part of financial actors and their allies in politics, or they have come second to the immediate management of the economic crisis by governments. Actual reforms have been implemented very slowly, or they have been pushed aside altogether. Divisions between regulators in Europe and the United States have also contributed to the slow implementation of reform. The financial crisis itself has been used as an argument to delay reform, on the grounds that it will push an already vulnerable financial system over the edge.

As the G20 process evolved, the level of ambition decreased. The London Summit in April 2009 may be remembered as a historic moment with great potential that was wasted subsequently when, meeting in Toronto in June 2010, G20 leaders turned to austerity measures and at the same time rejected any bold reform of the financial sector. As a result, there is very little emerging from official bodies that is likely to stem speculation anytime soon unless policies markedly change.

The main regulatory reform initiatives that were taken in the United States and in Europe, the regions most affected by the financial crisis, in response to the G20 Action Plan were as follows:

- In the United States, financial reforms were passed in a single legislative act, the Dodd-Frank Act in July 2010. But the passage of the act itself left key aspects of rule making and implementation open, to be determined by a complex rule-making process over several years. Overall, on paper, the Dodd-Frank goes beyond what is being proposed in Europe in many respects, but currently the implementation of its provisions is being stalled and undermined by political forces and financial lobbying in the United States.
- Europe does not have any equivalent to Dodd-Frank. Here the reform process is taking place through separate channels.[3] And unlike in the United States, several of the EU regulatory reform initiatives are still pending. On the positive side, many of them are to be passed as "regulations," not as "directives," which means that, once agreed, their implementation should be swifter and leave less room for national exception.

## Regulation of OTC Derivatives

In September 2009, the G20 Leaders meeting in Pittsburgh made three fundamental commitments regarding the OTC derivatives markets:

- All standardized OTC derivative contracts should be traded on exchanges or electronic trading platforms and cleared through "central counterparties" (CCPs) by the end of 2012 at the latest. CCPs are supposed to increase security against counterparty default risk (the risk that the party on the opposite side of the trade does not fulfill its obligations).
- OTC derivative contracts should be reported to trade repositories.
- Nonstandardized, non-centrally cleared contracts should be subject to higher capital requirements.

Dodd-Frank and the above EU directives and regulations are broadly similar in their requirements. However, and as noted above, the act has yet to be implemented by the regulatory authorities. In a stock-taking report on OTC markets issued in April 2011 the FSB concluded that "many jurisdictions have yet to make key decisions" regarding OTC derivatives regulations, and among those that had take action, "difference in approaches are emerging." And indeed divergence exists between the EU and the United States regarding CCP clearing and capital requirements.

The G20 Action Plan does not go much beyond registration and clearing of OTC derivatives. In particular, restricting trading through position limits and bans on short selling is not part of the G20 program. In Europe, however, the European Commission has circulated a proposal of regulation to restrict naked short selling on CDS, including restriction on sovereign CDS in times of market stress. Currently in the EU, each national authority has its own rules and powers in connection with short selling. In August 2011 several continental European authorities enforced a ban on short selling—measures that were symbolic to a large extent, as they could not extend to cross-border trading from jurisdictions that did not ban such practices. While the European Parliament has adopted a welcome aggressive stance against short selling, the European Council is currently supporting a much watered-down version of the commission's proposal.

## Taxing Financial Transactions

Taxing financial transactions is a direct way to reduce speculative trading (and raise revenue). Despite the support of a growing number of G20 countries and of UN agencies and the late change of position by the IMF, the proposal of creating a financial transaction tax (FTT) has never been addressed by the G20 or the FSB. But at the European level, there is a strong likelihood that an FTT will move forward, and this may have some impact on overall speculation in the market.

The recent shift of position by the European Commission on the FTT—now ranking among its strongest supporters—is welcome. The EC would suggest, for the Eurozone, a 0.1 percent tax on equity and bond trading and 0.01 percent on derivatives. The low percentage on derivatives would suggest that the EC is set for a revenue-generating approach with minimal impact on trading volumes.

## Credit-Rating Agencies

The Dodd-Frank Act strengthens the accountability and transparency requirements for the ten currently registered Nationally Recognized Statistical Rating Organizations (NRSROs). Provisions include rules to prevent conflicts of interest and issuers of structured products from choosing the rating agencies, including through a random process. Transparency of the methodologies used for the rating and reporting requirements are also strengthened under the SEC jurisdictions. In addition, in principle, the act makes it easier for some lawsuits to be brought against CRAs. The Dodd-Frank provision calls on the Securities and Exchange Commission to create a ratings oversight board with investor representatives in the majority. This board will choose a rating agency to conduct the initial evaluation of each new set of structured finance products. Securities issuers would not be allowed to participate in the assignment of raters, and the assignments would be based on an evaluation of accuracy of ratings over time. In addition, under this approach, the SEC will have an Office of Credit Ratings with the authority to write rules and levy fines. Investors will now be able to recover damages in private antifraud actions brought against rating agencies for gross negligence in the rating (see Epstein and Pollin, 2011). However, it is not clear that this provision of the Dodd-Frank Act will be implemented because, in an attempt to bury it, financial lobbyists were able to subject it first to a study and possible alteration before implementation.

In Europe, a new EU regulation on CRA came into force in 2011 and is broadly in line with Dodd-Frank although there is divergence on some aspects such as reducing reliance on CRAs. As welcome as they may be, there is little doubt that the oligopoly created by the three largest CRAs, controlling 90 percent of the global market, will only be partially affected by these reforms.

## Dealing with Global Financial Conglomerates

What to do about global financial conglomerates that are too big to fail has been a central policy issue of the G20 process ever since the first crisis summit in November 2008. Work is under way to reinforce "resolution authority," which would allow government-appointed authorities to preemptively take control of a global systemically important financial institution (G-SIFI) that has become no longer viable in order to prevent costly bailout and contagion effects in the financial system. However, the more central question of whether the very existence of TBTF groups is at all desirable has gradually been eliminated from the FSB and G20 process.

In April 2010, the FSB recommended that members consider imposing limits on the complexity and size of financial groups. But these limits have not been implemented. In Basel III and similar capital regulation in the United States, provisions require higher capital requirements for large complex financial organizations, but critics question whether even these higher capital standards will be enough to discourage dangerous activity.

## Limits to Size and Complexity

In addition to capital standards, there is a patchwork of other regulations, particularly within Dodd-Frank, to deal with risky and speculative behavior: these include the Volcker Rule, to limit proprietary trading and bank investment in hedge and private equity funds; limits on crossholdings of debt among financial institutions; and the designation of financially significant institutions that would subject institutions to closer regulation and possible limitations on speculative and risky activities (D'Arista and Epstein, 2011; Epstein and Pollin, 2011).

There is no equivalent to the Volcker rule in Europe. In fact, at the EU level there is no regulation that would require or even encourage segregation of investment banking from retail banking, and there are not any plans to adopt "swaps push-out" rules whereby resolution and government assistance would specifically exclude or be highly restricted with respect to derivatives trading. Some member-states are moving ahead, however. In the United Kingdom, the "Vickers Commission" has released proposals to "ringfence" investment banking operations through separate boards of directors and higher capital ratios than those foreseen by the FSB for TBTF groups. But both types of activities could exist within the same financial conglomerate, so it is not at all clear that this ringfencing addresses the too-big-to-fail problem. Would the government really be less likely to bail out an investment bank if it were closely tied into the foreign exchange markets and derivatives markets—with all the systemic risks involved—even if it were not closely tied to its own retail bank?

## Taxing Banks' Balance Sheets

Another area that has not seen much progress since the early stage of the G20 process is that of specific taxation on the balance sheets of TBTF groups. In April 2010 the IMF proposed the creation of a financial stability contribution (FSC), which would apply to the balance-sheet liabilities of large financial institutions (at least large banks, perhaps insurance groups as well) and would be calibrated to the degree of riskiness of their liabilities. Such an FSC, the IMF argued, could help reduce groupwide leverage and risk profile. But this has now been dropped. President Obama's proposal of a financial crisis responsibility fee (FCR) was made in January 2010, but it was dropped from the Dodd- Frank Bill.

## Corporate Governance of Banks

Despite the fact that the crisis exposed major failures in the governance of large banks, not least the incompetence and irresponsibility of many boards of directors in monitoring and assessing groupwide risk management (OECD, 2010b), nothing or very little has been acted at national levels. The European Commission has launched a broad consultation on the role of institutional investors and on risk management by banks, but to date no tangible regulatory reform is foreseen. Dodd-Frank, however, sets new requirements on the disclosure of CEO pay (as a ratio of average workers' pay) and the SEC is considering facilitating shareholders' access to the annual general meeting of shareholders, a long-overdue reform to promote responsible shareholder activism within the United States.

## Concluding Remarks and Recommendations

Financial speculation, especially in its broader sense, contributed to the economic crisis by encouraging massive asset bubbles and by creating a massive network of leverage and complex, opaque interconnections among financial institutions that unraveled in unpredictable ways when the bubble burst. Moreover, speculation has been an accelerant to the crisis ever since, with the persistence of shadow banking and large financial conglomerates. Financial speculation is a moving target. It reinvents itself. It takes multiple forms and adjusts instantly to market movements and changes in regulations.

Clearly the way out of the crisis will require much broader policies, and a shift in the paradigm of the way economic policy and financial regulation are to be conceived. It will require more robust and efficient international governance systems that help collectivize and effectively mitigate systemic risks than those that are currently in place, not least within Europe. In that context this chapter is concerned with the kinds of policies and regulatory reforms that would be needed to reduce speculation and its impact and to limit the financial forces that are pushing our economies into destructive crises. For financial reform to address the problem of speculation in both its narrow and broader forms, a three-tier response is suggested to limit destabilizing short-term bets by financial traders that disrupt the efficient functioning of financial markets and that threaten to drive financial actors and institutions into liquidity or solvency crisis.

Key regulatory reforms would include the following:

- The creation of a financial transaction tax would go a long way in curbing short-term speculative trading, including high-frequency trading.
- All forms of derivatives trading should shift to organized exchanges, while taxation and prudential rules applying to the remaining over-the-counter trading should be set at prohibitive levels.
- Trading strategies would have restrictions, including a ban on naked short selling.

Large financial firms have a high degree of leverage and are interconnected to other sectors and institutions in the economy. Failure to limit destructive risk-taking by these large financial firms places the whole economy at risk.

This leads to destructive situations in which taxpayers are either forced to bail out the banks or to risk bank insolvencies, leading to a broader economic crisis that costs them their jobs and their savings. Key regulatory reforms to solve this issue would include the following:

- Splitting large financial conglomerates through mandatory separation of commercial and investment banking activities—a return to a modernized version of the Glass-Steagall Act regime—through strict competition rules so that no financial firms can create oligopolistic situations. As a transitory measure, outright nationalization of large financial conglomerates could be an efficient way to restructure the financial sector.
- The corporate governance of banks can be reformed so that risk management and remuneration are aligned with long-term financial stability interests and so that stakeholders' interests can be rebalanced in favor of better protection of creditors and of workers in the company.
- Regulation of the shadow banking systems could include (i) prohibitive prudential rules and taxation regimes on off-balance-sheet trading of asset-backed securities (such as CDOs), (ii) alignment of hedge funds, ETFs, and other private pools of capital with standard asset-management regulation, and (iii) extending the current international cooperation on offshore financial centers beyond tax evasion concerns to include tax and regulatory arbitrage.
- All government guarantees that currently benefit the banking sector could be gradually phased out by creating—or expanding—industry-funded insurance schemes that could be financed by the IMF-proposed FSC and a financial activity tax (FAT).
- Credit-rating agencies could shift their business model back to an investor-pay model, which could be done by pooling investors' fees into a single fund per industry and increasing their legal liability, developing competition through the creation of public agencies, and reducing reliance on CRAs in banking and public finance prudential regimes.

And, perhaps, most difficult of all, the following actions must be taken re-orient financial institutions and markets away from risky and destructive activities toward those that contribute to investment in productivity-enhancing technologies; provide good, well-paying, and meaningful jobs; and provide capital and insurance facilities to improve the operations of the economy for people.

Clearly no single list of specific regulatory reforms would satisfy this broader objective because it entails no less than reversing the balance of power between democratically elected governments and the financial markets. Areas for policy action would include these:

- Diversifying the financial sector through a larger array of public and cooperative financial institutions can provide socially productive financial activities, including public banks, cooperative banks, and insurance companies.

A challenging component of this revival will be an institutional framework to prevent such financial institutions from engaging in the same kinds of speculative investments and, in some cases, corrupt practices that have been so destructive in the private financial sector. Regarding cross-border flows, introducing or reinforcing existing capital control measures could be considered.

- Designing mechanisms, including through progressive taxation, to better align the pay of financiers with their contribution to society: in the United States especially, and in other countries as well, the compensation of financial actors is much higher than that in many other professions and is not aligned with the social risks and costs that finance imposes on the rest of society (Crotty, 2011).
- Protecting financial reform processes from regulatory capture. Financial regulatory reforms must involve citizens and should not be left in the hands of technicians or given political elites, themselves under the influence of bankers and their traders. There is a need across G20 economies to reform the way political parties are financed so as to protect democratic systems against vested interests of the financial sector. Giving the civil society more of a voice in the policies of the private financial institutions would increase the weight of the interests of the public in financial behavior.
- Changing the measurement of growth. Away from traditional GDP measuring we need a new growth indicator that takes better account of social and inequality factors. For Stiglitz, Sen, and Fitoussi, "part of the reason why the crisis took many by such surprise is that the 'measurement' systems [used] to assess and monitor economic performance failed" (Fitoussi et al., 2009).

The reform agenda being debated and, to some extent implemented in the United States and Europe partly address the first two issues: limiting destructive speculation and reducing the risks associated with TBTF banks. As we have seen, however, the reform agenda on these fronts is moving very slowly if not actually stalling. But even worse, there has been no attempt to confront the broader problem: to what extent is the financial sector really serving the needs of democracies, of working families, of productive businesses, and of governments; and how does the financial sector have to be restructured? It is time to get the financial governance and restructuring debate back at the center of the political agenda. At the same time efforts must be redoubled to achieve rigorous implementation of Dodd-Frank and the G20 financial reform agenda.

## Notes

1. "This $2bn Mess Has Uncanny Historical Echoes," FT.com, September 15, 2011.
2. "Wall Street's Secret Advantage: High-speed Trading," *The Week*, June 28, 2010, http://theweek.com/article/index/204396/wall-streets-secret-advantage-high-speed-trading.

3. EU initiatives include the following:- The ongoing review of the Markets in Financial Instruments Directive (MiFID), including transparency and reporting to regulators of derivatives trading, which are incentives for trading on organized exchanges. A proposal of European market infrastructures regulation (EMIR), covering OTC derivatives trading through CCPs and registration with trade repositories. A proposal for a regulation on short selling and certain aspects of credit default swaps. The review of the market abuse directive (MAD) empowering national regulators to fix position limits and create categories of traders in the commodity derivatives market. The fourth review of the capital requirement directive (CRD IV) including new capital requirements for non-CCP-cleared OTC transactions.

## References


BIS. (2010a). "Triennial and Semiannual Surveys—Positions in Global Over-the-Counter (OTC) Derivatives Markets at End-June 2010." Monetary and Economic Department, BIS, November 2010. http://www.bis.org/publ/otc_hy1011.pdf.

BIS. (2010b). "Triennial Central Bank Survey—Report on Global Foreign Exchange Market Activity in 2010." Monetary and Economic Department, BIS, December 2010. http://www.bis.org/publ/rpfxf10t.pdf.

BIS. (2011a). "International Banking and Financial Market Developments." *BIS Quarterly Review*. June 2011. http://www.bis.org/publ/qtrpdf/r_qt1106.pdf.

Blommestein, Hans, et al. (2010). "Debt Markets: Policy Challenges in the Post-Crisis Landscape." *OECD Journal: Financial Market Trends* 2010(1). http://www.oecd.org/dataoecd/10/41/45988118.pdf.

Blommestein, Hans ,et al. (2011). "Outlook of the Securitisation Market." *OECD Journal: Financial Market Trends* 2010(1). http://www.oecd.org/dataoecd/36/44/48620405.pdf.

Blundell-Wignall, Adrian, and Paul Atkinson. (2011). "Global SIFIs, Derivatives and Financial Stability." *OECD Journal—Financial Market Trends* 2011(1). http://www.oecd.org/dataoecd/62/10/48299884.pdf.

Blundell-Wignall, Adrian, et al. (2009). "The Elephant in the Room: The Need to Deal with What Banks Do." *OECD Journal: Financial Market Trends* 2009(2). http://www.oecd.org/dataoecd/13/8/44357464.pdf.

Crotty, James. (2011). The Bonus-Driven "Rainmaker" Financial Firm: How These Firms Enrich Top Employees, Destroy Shareholder Value and Create Systemic Financial Instability (Revised)." Political Economy Research Institute (PERI). http://www.peri.umass.edu/fileadmin/pdf/working_papers/working_papers_201-250/WP209_revised3.pdf.

Crotty, James, and Gerald Epstein. (2009). "A Financial Precautionary Principle: New Rules for Financial Product Safety." http://www.wallstreetwatch.org/working_papers/workingpaper1.pdf.

D'Arista, Jane, and Gerald Epstein. (2011). "Dodd-Frank and the Regulation of Dangerous Interconnectedness." In *The Future of Financial Reform; Will It Work? How Will We Know?* New York: Roosevelt Institute. http://www.rooseveltinstitute.org/sites/all/files/Will_It_Work_Financial_Interconnection.pdf.

De Grauwe, Paul. (2011). "The Governance of a Fragile Eurozone." Working Paper, University of Leuven and CEPS, April 2011. http://www.econ.kuleuven.

be/ew/academic/intecon/Degrauwe/PDG-papers/Discussion_papers/Governance-fragile-eurozone_s.pdf.

Epstein, Gerald, and Robert Pollin. (2011). "Regulating Wall Street: Exploring the Political Economy of the Possible." Political Economy Research Institute (PERI). http://www.peri.umass.edu/fileadmin/pdf/working_papers/working_papers_251–300/WP256.pdf.

ETUI, ITUC, and TUAC. (2011). "Exiting from the Crisis: Towards a Model of More Equitable and Sustainable Growth." http://exitingthecrisis.org.

Fitoussi, Jean-Paul, et al. (2009). "Report by the Commission on the Measurement of Economic Performance and Social Progress." September 2009. http://www.stiglitz-sen-fitoussi.fr/documents/rapport_anglais.pdf.

FSB. (2011a). "Shadow Banking: Scoping the Issues." April 12, 2011. http://www.financialstabilityboard.org/publications/r_110412a.pdf.

FSB. (2011b). "Potential Financial Stability Issues Arising from Recent Trends in Exchange-Traded Funds (ETFs)." April 2011. http://www.financialstabilityboard.org/publications/r_110412b.pdf.

Global Unions. (2010). "Take Action on Jobs to Sustain the Recovery—Global Unions' Statement to the G8/G20 Ontario Summits Canada." June 2010. http://www.tuac.org/en/public/e-docs/00/00/07/25/document_doc.phtml.

IMF. (2010). "Fiscal Exit: From Strategy to Implementation." November 2010. http://www.imf.org/external/pubs/ft/fm/2010/fm1002.pdf.

IMF. (2011a). Global Financial Stability Report. September 2011. http://www.imf.org/External/Pubs/FT/GFSR/2011/02/index.htm.

IMF. (2011b). "The Too-Important-to-Fail Conundrum: Impossible to Ignore and Difficult to Resolve." IMF Staff Discussion Note, May 27, 2011. http://www.imf.org/external/pubs/ft/sdn/2011/sdn1112.pdf.

IMF. (2011c). "Addressing Fiscal Challenges to Reduce Economic Risks." http://www.imf.org/external/pubs/ft/fm/2011/02/pdf/fm1102.pdf.

IOSCO. (2011). "Regulatory Issues Raised by the Impact of Technological Changes on Market Integrity and Efficiency." Consultation Report, IOSCO, July 2011. http://www.iosco.org/library/pubdocs/pdf/IOSCOPD354.pdf.

Johnson, Simon. (2011). "The Ruinous Fiscal Impact of Big Banks." Baseline Scenario, February 3, 2011. http://baselinescenario.com/2011/02/03/the-ruinous-fiscal-impact-of-big-banks/.

Keynes, John Maynard. (1936). *The General Theory of Employment, Interest and Money*. London: Macmillan.

Kim, Byoung-Hwan, and Dagfinn Rime. (2010). "The $4 Trillion Question: What Explains FX Growth since the 2007 Survey?" BIS Quarterly Review, December 2010. http://www.bis.org/publ/qtrpdf/r_qt1012e.pdf.

Kim, Byoung-Hwan, and Sebastian Schich. (2011). "Guarantee Arrangements for Financial Promises: How Widely Should the Safety Net Be Cast?" OECD Journal: Financial Market Trends. January 2011. http://www.oecd.org/dataoecd/42/49/48297609.pdf.

Kumhof, Michael Romain Rancière. (2010). "Inequality, Leverage and Crises." IMF Working Paper WP/10/268, November 2010. http://www.imf.org/external/pubs/ft/wp/2010/wp10268.pdf.

OECD. (2010a). "Economic Outlook n°88." November 2010. http://www.oecd.org/dataoecd/63/57/46435606.pdf.

OECD. (2010b). "Corporate Governance and the Financial Crisis—Conclusions and Emerging Good Practices to Enhance Implementation of the

Principles." Directorate for Financial and Enterprise Affairs, OECD Steering Group on Corporate Governance, February 2010. http://www.oecd.org/dataoecd/53/62/44679170.pdf.

OECD. (2011a). "Bank Competition and Financial Stability." August 2011, http://www.oecd.org/dataoecd/14/49/48501035.pdf.

Pozsar, Zoltan. (2011). "Institutional Cash Pools and the Triffin Dilemma of the U.S. Banking System." IMF Working Paper, WP/11/90. http://www.imf.org/external/pubs/ft/wp/2011/wp1190.pdf.

Pozsar, Zoltan. Tobias Adrian, Adam Ashcraft, and Hayley Boesky. (2010). "Shadow Banking." Staff Report no. 458, Federal Reserve Bank of New York, July 2010. http://www.newyorkfed.org/research/staff_reports/sr458.pdf.

Schulmeister, Stephan. (2011). "Implementation of a General Financial Transactions Tax." Austrian Institute of Economic Research (WIFO), June 2011, http://www.wifo.ac.at/wwa/jsp/index.jsp?fid=23923&id=41992&typeid=8&display_mode=2.

White, Lawrence. (2010). "The Credit Rating Agencies." *Journal of Economic Perspectives* 24(2): 211–226.

CHAPTER 17

# WHITHER THE EURO?

## HISTORY AND CRISIS OF EUROPE'S SINGLE-CURRENCY PROJECT

ROBERT GUTTMANN AND
DOMINIQUE PLIHON

When looking at the historic background of European integration, it becomes clear that the process has for over half a century been subject to a stop-go pattern in which financial crises have played a crucial role. Such crises have been recurrent, each time resetting the course of the integration process. Perhaps that pattern is inevitable in light of systemic contradictions that block progress, thereby let imbalances fester to the point of rupture, and only find (at least temporary) resolution in the aftermath of such shake-ups. A post-crisis period of movement eventually gives way to atrophy again as the old contradictions resurface. Those manifest themselves most durably around the age-old question of how far to push integration, a question made more complicated to deal with by the simultaneous deepening of the European Union (pushing in the direction of a United States of Europe) and its widening (in consecutive steps from 6 to 27 countries). These debates around the nature of Europe's federalism have been driven by a long-standing struggle between those pushing for a more market-oriented approach and those favoring a strong public-policy role for the government. While that struggle is largely political in nature, it is also rooted in the reality that since its inception the European Union has been composed of two very different groups of countries. In the face of these complications, stalemates arise recurrently, which only major financial crises seem able to shake up.

In this contribution we trace that recurrent pattern of financial crisis and institutional reform shaping the European integration project through its key chapters to arrive at today's sovereign debt crisis of the eurozone, which has already seen huge bailout packages for three countries (Greece, Ireland, Portugal) as well as the introduction of several new crisis-management mechanisms. By taking a historical approach we can identify the structural flaws besetting the single-currency project from its inception, and we illustrate how they morphed into the different facets of a systemic crisis in the face of an asymmetric shock from the US-centered "subprime" crisis in 2007–2008.

## 1. From Customs Union to a Single Currency

The origins of European integration date from the end of World War II when a consensus emerged among leading politicians that only closer political and economic integration among long-hostile neighbors could ensure the peace and prosperity that a century of warfare had rendered impossible for so long. Key among those were the respective leaders of France and Germany, Charles de Gaulle and Konrad Adenauer, both of whom were sympathetic to the ideals of the great European integrationists Jean Monnet and Robert Schumann while also pragmatically inclined to bury long-standing conflict between these two powers at the heart of Europe. That pragmatism was, of course, not least fueled by the reality of a Cold War taking root across Europe and dividing the continent into two irreconcilable ideological blocs along an Iron Curtain. Be that as it may, it did not take long for the integration idea to take root in the Western half of Europe, around a new alliance between the two old enemies, France and (West) Germany.

Following the successful experiment of the European Coal and Steel Community that was started in 1950, six European countries (Germany, France, Italy, Belgium, Netherlands, and Luxembourg) signed the Treaty of Rome in 1957 to launch, among other provisions, a customs union known as the European Economic Community (EEC). As is always the case with a customs union, such an arrangement was seen from its inception as the first step in a much more ambitious political project. Centered around a common trade policy that combined systematic removal of internal trade barriers with a collectively shared set of trade barriers vis-à-vis the rest of the world (in this case, a common external tariff), the EEC provided for an early example of shared policy making in a crucial area. This was soon followed by other initiatives for policy cooperation, notably a common agricultural policy and provision of structural funds for infrastructure projects in lesser developed regions. While the EEC was thus from the very beginning more than just a customs union and even referred to itself already then as a "common market," it took a while before it actually took that very step in the Single European Act of 1987. From then on it followed the classic trajectory of integration, continuing shortly thereafter with an economic and monetary union (in the Maastricht Treaty of 1992) and so putting itself at the threshold of the final step, political union, which after much bitter debate only managed to inch foward with the Lisbon Treaty of 2009.

This logic of continuously deeper integration embodied in the launch of a customs union pushes member nations more or less inevitably toward adoption of a single currency as tends to happen in the wake of a monetary union—a step already envisaged in the EEC as early as 1970 with publication of the Werner Plan.[1] But there was, parallel to this integration process, a second sequence of events nudging Europe early on in the direction of a single currency. That push came from the collapse of the postwar international monetary system known as Bretton Woods in 1971, the first of three systemic financial crises fundamentally shaping the evolution of the European integration project. Once Bretton Woods' dollar-gold link had been broken by Nixon's suspension of automatic convertibility between the two on August 15, 1971, the stage had been set for a major devaluation of the US dollar. The danger here was that such a devaluation, if allowed to reflect long-standing changes in relative degrees of competitiveness, would end up being much more pronounced vis-à-vis Germany's deutsche mark than, say, the French franc or the Italian lira, and so price German products out of export markets. The common agricultural policy and structural funds for poorer regions would also have been severely disrupted if there had been strong divergences in intra-EU exchange-rate adjustments following the breakdown of Bretton Woods. The only way to avoid such internal differentiation tearing apart the community was to maintain collectively fixed exchange rates among its members, an undertaking made much easier by the Smithsonian Agreement of December 1971, which reset fixed exchange rates between the EC, Japan, and the United States at more realistic levels. The agreement, while setting a new band of +/- 2.25 percent for currencies to fluctuate relative to their central rate against the US dollar, implied a possible 9 percent-width for intra-EEC adjustments in extreme cases—a range of currency-price fluctuations soon considered excessive by European leaders who agreed in the Basel Agreement of April 1972 to limit this intra-EEC band to half that width at 4.5 percent. Thus was formed among the (now nine) members of the EEC the so-called "snake in the tunnel."

This new arrangement had barely lasted a year when it was subjected to a brutal shock due to sustained speculative pressure on the US dollar, forcing the Americans in March 1973 to abandon the Smithsonian Agreement in favor of letting the dollar float freely. The collapse of the tunnel split the Europeans right down the middle. On the one side were the Germans and their (mostly smaller) neighbors who insisted on floating collectively against the dollar by maintaining fixed exchange rates among themselves. On the other side were the other large economies of Western Europe, notably France, Italy, and Britain, whose leaders found it difficult, if not impossible, to maintain the anti-inflationary discipline needed for any fixed-rate arrangement with low-inflation Germany. These countries ended up opting instead for flexible exchange rates, thinking that currency depreciations would let them maintain or regain industrial competitiveness. In reality, however, their respective currency depreciations canceled each other out while at the same time feeding speculator expectations of further declines. In the end all three countries ended up with excessive currency-price adjustments fueling inflationary pressures and requiring major interest-rate hikes that slowed growth, thus seeing their initial depreciation strategy clearly fail. Amidst another dollar crisis, unfolding in late 1978 and early 1979, France, Britain, and Italy were ready to join with Germany.

The new reform, known as the European Monetary System (EMS) and launched in March 1979, had three important features. It established a grid of fixed exchange rates with tight fluctuation bands (the so-called Exchange Rate Mechanism), put a monetary reference unit at the center of that grid (the European Currency Unit), and empowered an intra-EMS mechanism to manage the system (European Monetary Cooperation Fund). The ECU, a basket of member currencies initially introduced with the launch of the snake in 1972 as a value anchor, gave the deutsche mark such a large weight that Germany ended up exerting strong anti-inflationary discipline on the other EMS members. The ECUs, which were issued by the EMCF and used in its exchange-stabilization interventions, also served as reserves and for official settlements among EMS members. If prevailing exchange rates proved unsustainable and had to be changed, the needed adjustments would have to be symmetrical, thus combining both devaluations and revaluations. Between 1979 and 1983 there were several such adjustments, as members had to find realistic and sustainable exchange-rate levels among an asymmetric shock induced by US-led disinflation and global recession. After the spectacular policy reversal by the socialist Mitterand government amid a crisis of the French franc in March 1983, ending the penultimate attempt to decouple from the German anti-inflation stance, the EMS became substantially more stable to the point where it saw no exchange-rate adjustments after 1987. At that time EMS members could keep their respective currencies pretty stable within the ERM grid through appropriate changes in national interest policies while gradually seeing their (mostly nominal) macroeconomic performance criteria converge. That success of the EMS laid the institutional foundation for the leap into a single currency.

The two vectors driving toward a single currency—the integration dynamic of a customs union and the successful monetary-cooperation experience around the EMS—fused together when the EC took the leap into a common market with the Single European Act of 1987 (SEA). This crucial step in the integration dynamic involves typically, among other liberalization steps, abolition of controls pertaining to the cross-border movements of capital. As noted by Robert Mundell (1960), there exists an "impossible triangle" between free cross-border movements of capital, fixed exchange rates, and autonomous monetary policy, which cannot coexist at the same time. One of those conditions would have to cease. Since the EU had just introduced liberalization of capital movements after making fixed exchange rates stick in the EMS, it was the national autonomy of monetary policy that had to give. With the double success of the EMS and then the SEA, the leap into a single currency became not only necessary (to resolve Mundell's dilemma), but also possible.

As the five-year period of implementation of the common market came to a close, the Maastricht Treaty of 1992 put into motion a three-stage plan for adoption of a single currency over a ten-year period. That decade-long transition was to foster above all nominal convergence of the EU economies pertaining to exchange rates, interest rates, inflation rates, budget deficits, and public debt. But the single-currency project was almost immediately threatened when the EMS, the institutional platform for the launch of the single-currency project, came under intense speculative pressure in the summer of 1992. The system had already come under a great deal of stress after Germany's mishandled unification in 1990–1991 had pushed up interest rates in the midst of an economic slowdown.[2] When the Danes rejected the single-currency plan in a June 1992 referendum, political tensions arose to add to economic woes. Against this background of growing uncertainty currency traders began to wonder to what extent prevailing exchange rates within the ERM, after not having changed at all for five years, had become out of balance with relative changes in international competitiveness among EU members. There were also growing doubts as to the ability or willingness of those members to satisfy the rather ambitious convergence criteria set forth in the Maastricht Treaty in time, especially when considering possibly high social and economic costs arising from the pursuit of these. When the gradually intensifying attacks on presumably overvalued currencies finally had grown into a full-blown storm by mid-August, speculators forced strong devaluations of the Irish punt, Italian lira, Spanish peseta, and Portuguese escudo, while—most spectacularly—pushing the British pound out of the ERM altogether. The crisis was only contained when the Germans intervened in support of the French franc. That currency came, however, under renewed attack nearly a year later, and this time the market pressure was such that no bailout operation among fellow central banks was viable. By September 1993 the persistent currency crisis had forced EU governments to abandon the tight grid of the ERM and let their currencies instead float within a much wider band of +/- 15 percent from their target levels.[3]

The currency crisis of 1992–1993 was not only inevitable, but also a necessary adjustment that in the end strengthened the single-currency project. It set in motion a transition period during which exchange rates within the ERM were allowed to find more realistic levels in accordance with market sentiments. And this resetting of currency prices made the subsequent phases and steps of the single-currency project easier to implement. By January 1999 the euro came into being as the single currency shared by 12 (of the then-15) nations of the EU.

One additional legacy of the 1992–1993 crisis worth noting is that Britain, upon being pushed out of the ERM, has managed since then to achieve higher growth and lower unemployment than its counterparts in the eurozone. This is a reminder that the EMS, with its bias toward rather restrictive monetary and fiscal policies discussed in greater detail in section 2 below, does carry considerable social and economic costs, which have manifested themselves above all in terms of perennially slow growth and structurally high unemployment across much of the eurozone.

## 2. Policy Biases in the Eurozone

In this section, dealing with the launch of the euro, we explore a direct connection between the institutional choices made in the wake of the EU's economic and monetary union and the ideological preferences rooted in economic theory; this connection has shaped the modus operandi of the eurozone ever since. That link is of crucial importance in understanding why and how the eurozone works (or does not), especially its management of a major crisis hitting the zone in late 2009.

The adoption of a single currency among several countries has important theoretical roots in Mundell's notion of an "optimal currency area" (OCA) (Mundell, 1961). This concept, for which the Columbia University economist won the Nobel Prize in Economics in 1999, explores the conditions under which a single currency would work optimally for a region combining different nation-states (or, as in the case of the United States, for a nation-state with distinctly different regions). The question of a single currency arises in the first place when a region has reached a high level of economic integration thanks to free trade and unrestricted flow of capital across its borders. Apart from these necessary prerequisites Mundell identified four more conditions that would help a single-currency area work better: a high degree of labor mobility across borders; wage and price flexibility; a mechanism for automatic fiscal transfers from stronger to weaker states; and sufficiently synchronized business cycles among OCA members. All of these conditions are needed to facilitate necessary market adjustments while allowing macroeconomic stabilization policies to work effectively. The latter objective applies with particular urgency to the "one-size-fits-all" monetary policy of a single-currency zone, which would be greatly helped if national business cycles were reasonably synchronized.

Even though Mundell's OCA concept is itself rooted in the (mostly ideological) conviction of mainstream economic theory that markets adjust automatically to durable equilibrium between supply and demand, it highlights usefully the real need for alternative adjustment mechanisms once a monetary union has deprived national policy makers of using either exchange rates or interest rates, normally the easiest and most effective policy tools. That problem of adjustment becomes, as Mundell himself pointed out, a truly challenging one in the face of shocks affecting diverse parts of the system differently. The viability of an OCA will thus be tested most thoroughly in the face of such an asymmetric shock—a hypothesis borne out recently when the fallout of the US-centered "subprime" crisis morphed into the most serious global financial crisis since the Great Depression of the 1930s, which hit the members of the eurozone from very different angles (see section 4 below).

That crisis confirmed what has been clear from the very beginning, namely that the eurozone does not meet Mundell's criteria for an OCA:

- For one, the EU obviously lacks the kind of wage and price flexibility that neoclassical economists consider essential for rapid and effective market adjustments to temporary disequilibria. While most contemporary capitalist economies show downwardly rigid prices, including the price of labor, this is probably even more the case within the EU where traditions of strong labor movements and of active industrial policies in favor of national champions still prevail. Even though trade unions in Europe are a lot weaker than they used to be a generation or two ago, collective bargaining agreements and labor protection laws still have a comparatively strong presence in many EU countries as does monopolistic price behavior of leading industrial firms.
- Moreover, the EU is characterized by powerful linguistic, cultural, and even policy-based barriers to labor mobility across borders despite efforts, such as the Schengen Agreement, to facilitate the movement of people from one country to another within the union. Many European nation-states have very deep regional cultures that are highly differentiated from each other, with populations that are rather resistant to change and locally grounded. Nor is the social climate very welcoming for immigrants unless they adopt very rapidly local customs and language skills.
- Finally, the EU is also found lacking with regard to Mundell's emphasis on sizable and automatic fiscal transfers. Those simply are not adequate in the EU context. With EU members providing only a small fraction of their tax revenues to the European Commission at the center of the union's federal policy apparatus, the EC's annual budget amounts to just 1 percent of the EU's GDP and is thus far smaller than the budgets of its respective national counterparts. So-called structural and regional policies, which have obviously become more important over the years in the EU context as a means of transferring funds from richer to poorer countries, have been quite successful in facilitating the catching-up

> processes of the latter. Still, a general lack of intra-EU solidarity has kept those funds relatively limited, especially when considering new and additional needs arising from the recent inclusion of so many relatively poor Central and East European countries into the union. Hence it is fair to say that fiscal federalism is still in its infancy within the European Union, with fiscal policy mostly a matter of national policy making.

Notwithstanding Mundell's subsequent argument that creation of a single currency gives its members advantageous protections even under less-than-ideal conditions (see Mundell, 1973), the fact remains that the eurozone has lacked some key criteria needed for an OCA and continues to lack them a decade later. The absence of true OCA conditions has lent greater urgency to creation of a federal policy framework along Keynesian lines with which to compensate for the eurozone's shortcomings as a suboptimal currency zone. With regard to fiscal policy, it would have been useful, for example, to have a strongly progressive tax system capable of redistributing income toward greater equality. Large cross-border infrastructure projects in transportation, energy, and communication have strongly redistributive effects as well, while at the same time modernizing the industrial apparatus and creating much-needed jobs with high value added (e.g., "green" jobs). And an EU-wide industrial policy of "picking winners" aimed at promoting the growth industries of tomorrow would also help improve the internal cohesion of the EU. At the same time it would have been helpful for Europe's growth prospects to have had both a relatively lax monetary policy and a competitive (i.e., relatively low) valuation of the euro.

Unfortunately, such a compensatory pro-growth policy mix was not realistically in the cards due to two major biases at the center of the EU's modus operandi. The first of these relates to a strong and persistent preference for *monetarist* policy prescriptions.[4] Regarding inflation as the primary evil to be avoided, monetarism stresses both a "hard money" policy by the central bank as well as balanced budgets on the fiscal-policy side. It also favors an overvalued currency that, by making imports relatively cheap, helps to keep inflation in check. Apart from the general rise of monetarism in the wake of the conservative counterrevolution launched by Margaret Thatcher and Ronald Reagan in the early 1980s, following a period of high and frightfully accelerating inflation (between 1969 and 1982), there are also internal reasons for that anti-Keynesian philosophy's influence within the EU. The key here is to appreciate modern Germany's profound obsession with price stability, rooted in its disastrous experience with hyperinflation during the 1920s and in the success of a strong deutsche mark as the symbol of postwar renaissance, which turned the Bundesbank into one of the most beloved institutions of a reborn society. As the largest and most powerful member of the EU, Germany's influence has weighed heavily on the others. No single currency would have been possible without it reflecting the policy structures and preferences of Germany, notably its hostility to anything encouraging inflationary pressures.

This bias in favor of monetarist policy prescriptions was already evident in the founding document of the economic and monetary union (see European Commission, 1990). And that same bias also shaped many of the subsequent institutional choices made during the implementation of EMU, especially those enshrined in the Maastricht Treaty two years later. Specifically, we are talking here about the intense push for "political independence" of the newly created European Central Bank, its emphasis on price stability as the ECB's sole and exclusive policy objective, the prohibition against the central bank's monetization of debt (i.e., purchases of government securities by the central bank which the monetarists regard as highly inflationary), and the stress put on a "no bailout" clause according to which countries in trouble because of excessive (budget and/or trade) deficits cannot expected to be helped by other member nations of the eurozone.

At the same time the eurozone has also been subjected to a *mercantilist* bias, emanating from a relentless German strategy of export-led growth. This push pervades all aspects of German society and runs through the entire spectrum of its highly competitive economy. We can see that clearly when looking at Germany's other macro-drivers underpinning its chronically large trade surpluses, specifically its high savings rate (compared to investments) and its fiscal discipline aimed at keeping budget deficits in check. As a matter of fact, postwar Germany has had a distinctly anti-Keynesian bias of largely forgoing the use of fiscal stimuli in the form of deficit spending, perhaps a legacy of associating Keynesian policies with the kind of militarist Keynesianism promoted by Hitler and his finance minister Hjalmar Schacht during the 1930s. Be that as it may, Germany's strong integration with its smaller, similarly anti-inflation and export-oriented neighbors (e.g., Netherlands, Denmark, Austria, Switzerland), first institutionalized in the aforementioned "snake" experiment of a deutsche mark zone during the 1970s, makes that power center even stronger. The eventual full integration of East Germany and rapidly developing ties to its Eastern neighbors, notably Poland, the Czech Republic, Slovakia, and Hungary, will, if anything, only enhance Germany's status as a trading superpower.

The trouble with this relentless push for trade surpluses emanating from Germany and its neighbors at the core of the eurozone is that it puts a lot of pressure on deficit-prone countries at the periphery of that region, notably Ireland, Portugal, Spain, Italy, and Greece, all of whom are characterized by propensities for excess consumption, large budget deficits, higher built-in inflation, and frequent trade deficits. The only thing that saves France and Britain, two countries with similarly pro-inflationary constellations of policy and habit, from being as vulnerable as that group on the periphery is that they are much larger and have very competitive sets of industries. But even those two countries find it hard to live with the asymmetry dividing the eurozone so sharply into two camps of surplus and deficit countries.

# 3. Implementation Dynamics

At first, the introduction of the euro in 1999 appeared to have been a success. Not only was the new currency accepted by the public, but the euro system also eliminated (nominal) exchange-rate fluctuations and thereby the possibility of exchange-rate crises. It also substantially decreased inflation and (real) interest rates in the former soft-currency countries. As the euro rapidly became a globally traded currency, it offered smaller and most vulnerable countries an added shock absorber. And during the first years of its existence there were several countervailing forces at work, which reduced the tension between two fundamentally different groups of countries as well as the potential for regional intra-zone imbalances. For one, the currency crisis of 1992–1993 had left the more inflation-prone bloc of southern countries with more competitive exchange rates. At the same time pressure from Germany had lessened in the wake of its decade-long absorption of unification, which caused significant post-unification shifts toward larger budget deficits and a shrinking export surplus. Finally, the euro started quite weakly, falling from its initial level of 1€ = $1.18 in early 1999 to just €1 = $0.84 in April 2002 and so staying below its presumed purchasing-power-parity level for several years. The competitive exchange rate combined with a generally favorable global growth environment, only temporarily disrupted by a fairly mild recession in 2000–2001, to boost the trade performance of even the weaker members of the eurozone. Those initially favorable conditions for rebalancing eroded with the gradual strengthening of the euro after 2003.

Mainstream economic doctrine had assumed that the EMU framework would lead to nominal and real convergence among its countries, and the initially favorable environment in the eurozone should have made it easier to achieve this important objective.[5] This, however, did not happen. EMU countries experienced divergent evolutions following the launch of the euro. Much of this divergence was driven by the aforementioned confluence of monetarist and mercantilist biases at the center of the eurozone. At the crux of the eurozone's growth dynamic during its first decade was the very strong pressure exerted on labor by a combination of government policy and industrial restructuring, resulting in relatively spectacular declines in wage shares as indicated in table 17.1. The wage share in GDP decreased in the eurozone on average by 2.3 percent from 1999 to 2007. This decline was especially pronounced in Spain (–4.3 percent), Germany (–3.9 percent), and the Netherlands (–2.7 percent). Increasing business profitability and price competitiveness through downward pressure on wages became a major strategy in mercantilist countries. This strategy boosted exports but put a brake on private consumption in these countries, thereby dampening overall demand in the eurozone. No attempt was made by the EU members or by the EU Commission to harmonize wage evolution. Through this noncooperative game Germany, Austria, the Netherlands, and Sweden succeeded in supporting their growth with a positive contribution of net

**Table 17.1** Major macroeconomic indicators

| | GDP growth rate | Domestic demand growth rate | Inflation rate (GDP deflator) | Real interest rate (long term) | Wage share in GDP change in perc. point | Public balance % GDP | Gross public debt % GDP | Current account balance % GDP |
|---|---|---|---|---|---|---|---|---|
| | 1999–2007 | 1999–2007 | 1999–2007 | 1999–2007 | 1998–2007 | 2010 (1) | 2010 (1) | 2010 (1) |
| France | 2.2 | 2.7 | 1.8 | 2.4 | −0.2 | −7.7 | 83.0 | −3.3 |
| Germany | 1.6 | 0.7 | 0.8 | 3.1 | −3.9 | −3.7 | 75.7 | 4.8 |
| Netherlands | 2.5 | 2.0 | 2.6 | 1.5 | −2.7 | −5.8 | 64.8 | 5.2 |
| Austria | 2.5 | 1.6 | 1.5 | 3.0 | −4.4 | −4.3 | 70.4 | 3.0 |
| Ireland | 6.6 | 6.2 | 3.5 | 1.4 | −2.1 | −32.2* | 97.4 | −1.1 |
| Italy | 1.5 | 1.7 | 2.4 | 2.2 | −0.5 | −5.0 | 118.9 | −3.2 |
| Spain | 3.7 | 4.6 | 3.9 | 0.8 | −4.3 | −9.3 | 64.6 | −4.8 |
| Greece | 4.1 | 4.2 | 3.2 | 1.0 | −2.1 | −9.6 | 140.2 | −10.6 |
| Eurozone | 2.1 | 1.7 | 2.0 | 2.1 | −2.3 | −6.3 | 84.1 | −0,5 |
| UK | 2.8 | 3.5 | 2.4 | 2.3 | 0.6 | −10.5 | 77.8 | −2.2 |
| USA | 3.0 | 3.1 | 2.4 | 2.5 | −1.9 | −11.3 | 92.2 | −3.4 |

*Notes*: (1) European Commission, Autumn Forecast 2010. * Including one-off costs related to banking sector support measures amounting to 19.9 percent of GDP.
*Source*: Mathieu and Sterdyniak (2010).

exports. These mercantilist countries of Northern Europe ran substantial current account surpluses, while Southern countries experienced widening external deficits. As a result the factors of growth, notably the balance between domestic demand versus exports, have been quite divergent among European countries, feeding large macroeconomic and external imbalances (see table 17.1).

With a single monetary policy setting a unique nominal interest rate for the entire eurozone, its members ended up having very different real interest rates. The single monetary policy was contractionary for Germany, Austria, and Italy, where real interest rates had been high relative to growth rates, while it ended up being expansionary for Ireland, Greece, and Spain, where real interest had been low compared to growth rates. In the latter countries, companies and households had a strong incentive to borrow and invest, which boosted their GDP growth and inflation. Those catching-up countries thus ended up having structurally higher output growth and inflation rates than the more "mature" countries, as shown in table 17.1.

Fiscal policies also differed greatly among the members of the eurozone in the run-up to the major crisis at the end of the 2000s. Notwithstanding the attempt with the so-called Stability and Growth Pact (SGP) of 1997 to impose uniform limits for budget deficits and public-debt levels (of 3 percent and 60 percent of GDP, respectively) in the face of still-decentralized policy making, the eurozone members ended up with fairly divergent levels of either in the course of the euro's first decade. In 2007, just before the onset of the crisis, Germany and the Netherlands had a public balance close to zero (0.2 percent of GDP), with a correspondingly low level of net public debt, whereas Italy, Greece, and Portugal ran high deficits and public debts although their fiscal situation was at that point still not dramatic. Tellingly, only Greece ran budget deficits that were considerably higher than the SGP limit of 3 percent per year.

Underpinning this growing heterogeneity of economic indicators among eurozone members is a systemic inertia of macroeconomic policy, a point strongly made by many Keynesian economists focusing on Europe (e.g., Fitoussi and Saraceno, 2009). This weakness can be traced to the institutions of economic governance in Europe, notably the statute of the ECB obliging it to focus exclusively on inflation, the program of structural reforms consisting essentially of liberalizing markets for goods, labor, and capital, and the limits on discretionary fiscal policy imposed by the aforementioned SGP. The SGP ceilings on annual budgets and public debt ignore cyclical factors and fail to take account of the specific situations of EMU members with respect to their external balance, competitiveness, or private debt. These rules do not allow corrective action against countries that carry out too-restrictive policies or that accumulate excessive imbalances in terms of external surpluses and deficits, or financial and real-estate bubbles. Moreover, the process of coordination of economic policies (under Articles 121 and 136 of the Maastricht Treaty) is purely formal. In fact, there are no concerted macroeconomic strategies within the EU for the short and the long run. In this context it was not a surprise that there was no European strategy adapted to the circumstances and specificities of each country during the eurozone crisis of 2009–2010.

## 4. The Systemic Crisis of the Eurozone

The summer of 2007 saw the onset of a major financial crisis, which eventually turned into the worst economic crisis since the Great Depression of the 1930s. Its initial causes related to the malfunctioning of the financial sector. Widespread securitization of mortgages nourished fast growth of credit and lowered credit standards, as banks believed they had passed on credit risk. Well-paid rating agencies decorated the new assets with triple-A ratings even though they were obviously far riskier than that. Banks shifted credit off balance sheets into structured investment vehicles to escape regulatory requirements on capital. All this combined to fuel a massive property bubble, which eventually overshot and burst. Although the crisis originated in the United States, it spread quickly to Europe due to the exposure of the European banks to the toxic assets.

In the early stages of the crisis it was expected that Europe would be hit less than the United States, whose "subprime crisis" could be traced to its excessive deregulation of financial markets and monetary policy accommodation. Over the preceding 25 years, the dollar-based international monetary system had turned the United States into the center of a relentless financial globalization process, which directed a large chunk of the world's excess savings towards US-issued liabilities that automatically funded a large amount of America's (debt-financed) excess spending. That process spread America's toxic assets across the world. Hence, even if the number of spectacular bankruptcies in Europe was limited, the EU banking sector proved to be as fragile. The sequencing of disruptions in Europe has been similar to that of the United States. Bank failures would trigger a crisis of confidence, which paralyzed interbank markets and forced massive asset sales into declining markets. The asset depreciation in turn deepened the ensuing credit crunch to the point of forcing drastic spending declines in the private sector.

The argument that the EU's prudent macroeconomic management would be the winning strategy turned out to be wrong. The exact opposite was true, explaining in large part why the financial crisis has hit the eurozone hardest (Fitoussi and Saraceno, 2009). During the crisis the European Central Bank remained faithful to its core beliefs that inflation is mainly a monetary phenomenon and price stability the priority, if not the sole objective. Using its control over certain short-term interest rates as the key instrument for controlling inflation, the ECB kept key eurozone interest rates unchanged at a level of 4 percent from June 2007 to June 2008! It then saw fit to raise them in July 2008 because of the increase in energy prices, an error that cast doubt about the ECB's understanding of the real extent of the crisis. Only in the fall of 2008, when it became clear that the main threat had become deflation rather than inflation, did the ECB begin a series of interest-rate cuts. In contrast, US policy responses to the crisis were much stronger. The Fed rapidly curbed short-term interest rates close to zero and then launched massive liquidity-injection programs in support of the banking system. And, as shown in table 17.2, the fiscal stimulus adopted by the European countries from 2008 to 2010 was significantly smaller, at only 1.4 percent of GDP for the EU-27 (or 1.6 percent in the eurozone), when compared with the 5.6 percent stimulus in the United States over the same three-year period.

The weak policy reaction of the eurozone countries to the crisis is not least linked to the EU's peculiar ideological (political) and institutional characteristics of economic governance, which, as discussed already in the preceding two

**Table 17.2** Stimulus plans: Stimulation impact (as percentage of GDP)

| | Total | 2008 | 2009 | 2010 |
|---|---|---|---|---|
| EU-27 | 1.4 | 0.1 | 0.8 | 0.5 |
| Eurozone | 1.6 | 0.2 | 0.8 | 0.6 |
| United States | 5.6 | 1.0 | 2.1 | 2.4 |

*Source*: Fitoussi and Saraceno, 2009.

sections, resulted in a rule-based system aimed at preventing discretionary interventions and pursuing price stability. The Stability and Growth Pact and the strict inflation targeting by the ECB have led to restrictive macroeconomic policies and to two decades of slow growth coupled with high unemployment. The objective of more rapid growth was to have been attained through structural reforms alone, meaning the systematic deregulation of labor, product, and capital markets. But this heavy emphasis on structural reforms constrained European governments to engage in noncooperative policies through fiscal and social competition.

Apart from excessively restrictive macroeconomic policies, there is another major reason why the crisis has been deeper in Europe than in the United States. It is the fact that this crisis has been fundamentally an asymmetric shock within the eurozone. Even before the crisis erupted, the eurozone was marked by swelling imbalances between two groups of countries engaged in unstable macroeconomic strategies. On one side, the neomercantilist strategies of a group of northern "virtuous" countries (Germany, Austria, Netherlands) reaped competitiveness gains and huge external surpluses. On the other side, a group of southern countries experienced rapid yet unbalanced growth, driven by negative real interest rates and accumulating large external deficits (Mathieu and Sterdyniak, 2007). The economic policy framework created by the Maastricht Treaty, specifically the SGP constraints on discretionary fiscal policy and the anti-inflation bias of the ECB, failed to contain these imbalances. The Stability and Growth Pact, together with new limits on state aid, sharply curtailed the scope for national industrial policies with which to boost productivity in the deficit countries. Nor have there been sufficiently large EU budgets and/or significant fiscal transfers targeting productive investments in the poorer regions to help those become more competitive. In the absence of exchange-rate realignments within the zone, strategies for increased competitiveness have come to be based mainly on wage moderation and increased deregulation of labor markets.

Such an adjustment strategy is, however, difficult to put into practice successfully. For one, labor markets are not as flexible as economic textbooks and EU treaties would like them to be. In addition, the adjustment via labor markets has a clear deflationary bias, because any country with a current account deficit will have to adjust through wage restraint and disinflation—pressure that the deficit countries on the eurozone's periphery could not easily cope with (Stockhammer, 2010). Nor has it helped those countries on the periphery that the core (northern) countries did manage to engage in more aggressive wage-moderation policies and labor-market policies. Between 2000 and 2007 unit labor costs declined by 0.2 percent per year in Germany while rising by 2 percent in France, 2.3 percent in Britain, and between 3.2 percent and 3.7 percent in Italy, Spain, and Ireland. Apart from persistent productivity differentials, you have also higher inflation rates in the periphery countries pushing up nominal wages there faster than in Germany (Onaram, 2007). As inflation differentials persist across European countries, there have been creeping changes in real exchange rates that have accumulated over the years. Real exchange rates have strongly diverged since the introduction of the euro. Germany has devalued by more than 20 percent in real terms vis-à-vis Portugal, Spain, Ireland, and Greece since 1999. All this helped turn the periphery of Europe into markets for the core (northern) countries without any prospect of catching up. When the subprime crisis emanating from the United States morphed into a global cataclysm, it was bound to hit the core and the periphery of the eurozone therefore very differently. While the shock impact of this crisis threw the entire EU into deep recession and pushed budget deficits rapidly higher, its asymmetric nature manifested itself by exposing much greater structural vulnerabilities in the peripheral countries, notably Greece, Spain, Portugal, and Ireland.

It is in this context that we have to understand how a revision of budget-deficit data by the newly elected Papandreou government in Greece in December 2009 could grow into a full-fledged crisis rocking the entire eurozone. That announcement of much worse deficits than had been admitted until then by the preceding (Karamanlis) government sent shockwaves through global markets as investors began to doubt the ability of Greece to manage its public finances. Soon this crisis of confidence extended to other countries in the periphery (Ireland, Spain, Portugal, even Italy) whose budget deficits and public debt levels were seen as unsustainably large. New financial instruments, in particular credit default swaps, greatly facilitated massive speculative attacks on European sovereign bonds as large numbers of investors realized that the euro system was flawed and incapable of rebalancing. That systemic crisis of the eurozone, best viewed as stage II of a global financial crisis originating in the United States in late 2007, was allowed to intensify rapidly in the face of inadequate crisis-management mechanisms. Political and ideological differences among eurozone members, always latently present, broke into the open in the face of relentless financial-market turmoil. A lack of cooperation and consensus made effective crisis management more difficult.

Pushed to the brink, eurozone authorities finally came up with a more coherent response in May 2010, which consisted of three important elements. The first was a bailout package for Greece in return for major structural reforms in that country. A total of €750 billion, funded by contributions from member nations, the European Commission, and the International Monetary

Fund, provided a large back-stop mechanism with which to contain contagion. And, lastly, the eurozone members agreed to retool their crisis-management powers favoring greater convergence, fiscal discipline, and aid transfers. Apart from representing abandonment of the hitherto sacrosanct "no bailout" clause, this three-pronged package contained several additional institutional changes of significance, notably a commitment by the European Central Bank to buy the sovereign debt of troubled members and a new economic-governance framework for macroeconomic surveillance of member nations' budgets, debt, and growth trends.

The Greek crisis was, however, only the first stage of a relentless crisis-contagion process, which has hit a growing number of countries in the eurozone. In November 2010 Ireland was the second country succumbing to this crisis. The deeper underlying reason for the Irish crisis was the failure of the country's leading banks in the wake of the bursting of that country's real-estate bubble (with the real-estate sector amounting to 25 percent of GDP at the peak of the boom). Forced to come to the rescue of its top four banks in the face of their near-certain default, the Irish government saw its budget deficit explode to an unprecedented 32 percent of GDP. The costs of bailing out Anglo-Irish Bank, Ireland's largest bank, are currently estimated to amount to €34 billion (or $45.5 billion). But what ultimately triggered the loss of market confidence was the decision of the European Council on October 29, 2010, under German pressure, to stop fully guaranteeing sovereign debt of the European states after 2013, which implied inevitable losses for the creditors.

The €85 billion worth of emergency assistance measures given to Ireland on November 28, 2010, did not reassure markets with regard to the eurozone's capacity to face its unfolding systemic crisis effectively. The markets immediately attacked Portugal and Spain as the next countries on the rescue list. On May 17, 2011, Portugal—Europe's oldest nation-state—joined Greece and Ireland in the eurozone's intensive-care ward, obtaining a €78 billion rescue package from the European Union and the IMF. Soon thereafter, with global bondholders wondering which domino might come next, Belgium and Italy began to feel the pressure of steadily rising risk premia (measured against German bund yields representing the default-free rate).

During the EU summit of March 23 and 24, 2011, European leaders decided, in the face of relentless pressure from the financial markets, to make urgent changes in the Lisbon Treaty and thereby open the way for a new competitiveness pact that came to be known as the "pact for the euro." That accord extended the wage and budget austerity policies imposed on Greece, Ireland, and, to a lesser extent, Portugal to much of the rest of the EU. It included abolition of wage indexation, creation of a common corporate tax base, raising the retirement age, and constitutional "debt brakes" for both budget deficits and public debt. These measures, proposed by Germany with the active support of France, had the objective of turning the entire eurozone into one "large well-managed Germany." Such a vision strikes us as troubling, considering Germany's comparatively poor job-creation record since the inception of the euro in 1999 (even though Germany has admittedly done better in that regard over the last year and a half). European governments committed themselves at that point to strengthen solidarity among the members of the eurozone by reinforcing the SGP and by turning the European Financial Stability Facility into a more permanent €500 billion bailout mechanism known as the European Stability Mechanism (ESM). By institutionalizing austerity across a large swath of the eurozone, this reform risked pushing the deficit countries of the eurozone into a debt trap where fiscal restraint would be undone continuously by economic slowdown. Far from giving governments greater room to maneuver against pressure from the financial markets, it may well have pushed the eurozone further into a longer-lasting social, economic, and political crisis.

The next stage in the battle between eurozone governments and increasingly nervous financial markets came during the second half of 2011 when it became abundantly clear that the initial bailout package for Greece was failing and needed to be followed up with further assistance amid recession-induced pressure on its budget deficit. The difficult negotiations surrounding a second bailout package centered on convincing bondholders to accept limited losses ("haircuts") in order to reduce Greece's debt burden modestly. This prospect of a restructuring of Greece's debt, even though kept limited and "voluntary" so as not to constitute a "credit event" triggering credit default swaps and a possibly chaotic default, only unnerved the bond markets further. At that point bank shares also came under enormous pressure across the entire EU, in anticipation of now seemingly inevitable losses on their large bondholdings. Slowly but surely, yields on Spanish, Italian, and even French bonds were pushed toward unsustainable levels as market pessimism called for higher-risk premia. Facing rapidly escalating pressure, eurozone leaders finally came to a three-pronged agreement in late October 2011. A new bailout package, which would be coupled with more significant restructuring of Greece's bonds to reduce its debt burden by 50 percent, was coupled with an expansion in intervention capacity of the European Financial Stability Facility and measures to strengthen the loss-absorption capacity of European banks in the face of mounting losses on their sovereign bondholdings. The untidy collapse of the Papandreou government in the wake of this agreement undid any market-calming effects it may have had, putting more pressure above all on Italy where political paralysis had soured prospects for effective policy reforms needed to deal with that country's heavy public-debt levels.

After two years of unrelenting contagion, the euro crisis has now morphed into a public-sector, banking, and political crisis of the first order, one that will undoubtedly engulf the entire world economy as liquidity gets drained out of the global financial system and losses mount. An optimistic scenario, in which EU leaders manage to stop the crisis and resume faster growth, has become highly unlikely. This would require a much lower euro, a large-scale EU-wide stimulus package (e.g., of infrastructure investments), and much-strengthened lender-of-last-resort mechanisms at the least—all measures very difficult to pull off in the face of public anger, political divisions, and financial panic.

Alternatively, the Europeans may simply muddle through if they can somehow avoid having to bail out Spain and/or Italy. Assuming further that their bailouts help Greece, Ireland, and Portugal stabilize their debt burdens sufficiently while European banks manage to absorb relatively modest losses without too much turmoil, then European leaders may have a chance to implement several needed structural reforms which would have never come about (or much later!) without such an existential crisis. These reforms would all push in the direction of further European integration, involving greater fiscal transfers from rich to poorer countries, issue of federal eurobonds in lieu of national sovereign debt, substantial domestic pro-growth reforms, and much strengthened eurozone institutions. Were these reforms not to come about, the eurozone risks a lost decade of stagnation and globally shrinking influence.

Unfortunately, however, the crisis has deepened sufficiently to oblige us to think the unthinkable—the disintegration of the single-currency area. Such a scenario risks a truly catastrophic chain of defaults, capital flight, and recessionary pressures for which the Europeans better start getting prepared. We do not know how this crisis will play out, but we know that it might spell the end of the euro as we know it.

## 5. The International Key-Currency Status of the Euro

The crisis of the eurozone certainly raises the question of the long-term viability of the European currency. Its course so far has revealed that the institutional architecture of the euro's construction is incomplete and needs further extension, as happened in the May 2010 or October 2011 responses. In light of the continued deepening of the crisis, it is far from clear that the worst has been averted by these improvements in its crisis-management capacity. The eurozone needs to find ways to achieve faster and better balanced growth. It would then be able to posit a more effective challenge to the world-money status of the US dollar. As shown in table 17.3, the share of the euro is far behind that of the dollar for international trade. But its share has already grown to approach that of the dollar with respect to financial and banking transactions.

The international role of the euro is bound to increase in the future to the extent that its zone, whose gross domestic product, population size, and trade

Table 17.3 Global market shares of key currencies

| Market Shares (%) | Dollar | Euro | Yen |
|---|---|---|---|
| Invoicing of international trade (a) | 40–45 | 15–20 | – |
| Payments for energy and other raw materials (a) | 85–90 | 10–15 | – |
| Denominations of international bonds (b)* | 37.1 | 46.6 | 2.9 |
| Cross-border bank assets (b)* | 39.9 | 38.3 | 3.6 |
| Currency transactions (c)* | 86.3 | 37 | 16.5 |
| Foreign exchange reserves (b)** | 64.2 | 26.5 | 3.1 |

(a) in 2007; (b) % of worldwide total; (c) total 200 percent. *In 2007. **In 2008.
*Sources*: ECB; Bank for International Settlements; International Monetary Fund.

volume match that of the United States (see table 17.4), can realize its full economic potential. But that role may be lagging to the extent that the political biases and institutional constraints of the eurozone condemn it to suffer slow growth and unsustainable imbalances. The current crisis has shown the costs and benefits of this dilemma quite starkly.

Notwithstanding its internal imbalances and policy biases, the introduction of the euro has put into play for the first time a currency whose scale may well one day rival that of the US dollar. As its growing international presence and, more slowly, that of the yuan presage a movement from a dollar standard to a tripolar international monetary system, the EU's struggles with policy coordination and convergence will serve as a useful model for the imperatives of global governance in the future. It remains to be seen whether the eurozone will let its monetarist and mercantilist biases crowd out the EU's social-democratic traditions of a mixed economy and welfare state, which portend a capitalism with a humanistic face as a model for the rest of the world.

Table 17.4 Scale of world's leading economies in 2008

| | United States | Eurozone | Japan | China | Russia |
|---|---|---|---|---|---|
| GDP ($ bn, PPP)[a] | 13 108,8 | 10 011,6 | 4 022,3 | 7 262,7 | 2 081,1 |
| Population (in millions)[a] | 304,2 | 324,2 | 127,3 | 1 330 | 140,7 |
| Openness ratio (% of GDP)[b] | 10,4 | 16,2 | 14,7 | 30,2 | 23,4 |
| Stock market ($ tr)[c] | 10,8 | 2,6* | 3,4 | 4,6** | 1,3 |
| Exports ($ bn)[a] | 1 046,2 | 4 051,9 | 714,3 | 1 231,5 | 381,7 |

*Sources*: [a]CEPII (CHELEM database); [b]Authors' own calculations on basis of CHELEM database of CEPII (Paris) for 2007; openness ratio for eurozone excludes intrazone trade; [c]World Federation of Exchange, 2009. Stock markets: *Euronext; **Shanghai + Shenzen + Hong Kong.

## Notes

1. We use three different names—European Economic Community (EEC), European Community (EC), and European Union (EU)—to denote the European integration project. These denominations correspond chronologically to the different stages of European integration, with European Union the latest adopted after 1992.
2. When Germany started its unification in late 1990, it picked an exchange rate between Deutsche marks and Ostmarks that largely overvalued the latter. This benefited long-deprived East Germans but created very large budget deficits, inflationary pressures, and high interest rates in Germany.
3. The EMS crisis of 1992–1993 reinforced so-called second-generation currency-crisis models (Obstfeld, 1986, 1994) which stressed the intertemporal unsustainability of a given policy mix and credibility problems arising from that. See also Buiter, Corsetti, and Pesenti (1998) for a thorough assessment of that crisis.
4. Monetarism, a modern version of the age-old Quantity Theory of Money (see Friedman, 1956, 1968), stresses price stability as the overriding policy objective and moderate, steady, money-supply growth as the best way to achieve this goal.
5. A good summary of that doctrine can be found in De Grauwe (1996).

## References

Buiter, W., G. Corsetti, and P. Pesanti. (1998). *Financial Markets and European Monetary Cooperation: The Lessons of the 1992–93 Exchange Rate Mechanism Crisis*. Cambridge: Cambridge University Press.

De Grauwe, P. (1996). "The Economics of Convergence: Towards a Monetary Union in Europe." *Review of World Economics* 132(1): 1–27.

European Commission. (1990). *One Market, One Money: An Evaluation of the Potential Benefits and Costs of Forming an Economic and Monetary Union*. Brussels: European Economy-44, October, 351 pages, available at http://ec.europa.eu/economy_finance/publications/publication7454_en.pdf.

Fitoussi, J. P., and F. Saraceno. (2009). "How Deep Is a Crisis? Policy Responses and Structural Factors behind Diverging Performances." *Observatoire Français des Conjonctures Economiques (OFCE)*. Working Paper No. 2009–31 (November).

Friedman, M. (1956). "The Quantity Theory of Money: A Restatement." In M. Friedman, ed., *Studies in the Quantity Theory of Money*, 64–75. Chicago: University of Chicago Press.

Friedman, M. (1968). "The Role of Monetary Policy." *American Economic Review* 58(1): 1–17.

Mathieu, C., and H. Sterdyniak. (2007). "How To Deal With Economic Divergences Within EMU?" *Observatoire Français des Conjonctures Economiques (OFCE)*. Working Paper No. 2007–14 (May).

Mathieu, C., and H. Sterdyniak. (2010). "European Debt Crisis and the Fiscal Exit Strategies." *Observatoire Français des Conjonctures Economiques (OFCE)*. Working Paper No. 2010–11 (June).

Mundell, R. (1960). "The Monetary Dynamics of International Adjustment under Fixed and Flexible Exchange Rates." *Quarterly Journal of Economics* 74(2): 227–257.

Mundell, R. (1961). "A Theory of Optimum Currency Area." *American Economic Review* 51(4): 657–665.

Mundell, R. (1973). "Uncommon Arguments for Common Currencies." In H. Johnson and A. Swoboda, eds., *The Economics of Common Currencies*, 114–132. London: George Allen & Unwin.

Obstfeld, M. (1986). "Rational and Self-Fulfilling Balance-of-Payments Crises." *American Economic Review* 76(1): 72–81.

Obstfeld, M. (1994). "The Logic of Currency Crises." NBER Working Paper #4640, Cambridge, MA: National Bureau of Economic Research.

Onaram, O. (2007). "International Financial Markets and Fragility in Eastern Europe: Can It Happen Here?" In J. Becker and R. Weissenbacher, eds., *Dollarization, Euroization and Financial Instability*, 129–148. Marburg: Metropolis Verlag.

Stockhammer, E. (2010). "Income Distribution, the Finance-Dominated Accumulation Regime and the Present Crisis." In S. Dullien, E. Hein, A. Trüger, and T. van Treeck, eds., *The World Economy in Crisis—The Return of Keynesianism?* Marburg: Metropolis Verlag.

## CHAPTER 18

# THE EUROZONE CRISIS THROUGH THE PRISM OF WORLD MONEY

COSTAS LAPAVITSAS

## 1. A World Crisis Deflected through World Money

The world crisis that began in 2007 is an event of historic significance that will mark the future development of capitalism. The crisis has had several dimensions, including financial, banking, commercial, and industrial. Perhaps its most notable aspect, however, has been that a real-estate collapse in the United States eventually turned into a monetary crisis in Europe. Or, to put it differently, a financial crisis eventually became a crisis of sovereign debt and consequently a crisis of the euro, the novel form of world money that European powers have collectively created.

World money is a characteristic concept of Marxist monetary theory that can shed fresh light on the eurozone crisis. World money pertains to the world market, which is qualitatively different from national markets with regard to the integral institutional, legal, and financial mechanisms that support market operations. World money is also qualitatively different from national monies with regard to the room that it leaves for state intervention in the monetary realm. No state can exercise control over world money similar to that exercised over national money. Consequently, the functioning of world money crystallizes the tensions among competing capitalist economies in the world market. Furthermore, the form taken by world money—silver, gold, or a national currency—critically affects its operations in the world market, including the power that world money can itself lend to states.

The euro is an unusual form of world money, jointly created by a coterie of European states that differ dramatically in economic and political power. This peculiarity of the euro lies at the heart of the eurozone crisis, and it helps explain the form that the world crisis has taken in Europe as well as the policies adopted to confront it. To use traditional Marxist terms, the euro as world money has acted as the mediator of the world crisis in Europe. The institutional and economic mechanisms that were put in place to support it as world money have created fault lines within the eurozone along which the crisis has emerged in full. These fault lines relate, fundamentally, to the appearance of core and periphery within the eurozone and to the corresponding hierarchical and political relations within the monetary union. The crisis has, in turn, demonstrated the precarious character of the euro as a form of world money that has been created by an alliance of disparate states.

Section 2 of this chapter discusses the Marxist theory of world money and identifies key features of contemporary world money. Section 3 briefly recaps the current world crisis in terms of the systemic transformation of the world economy in recent decades. The world economy has been characterized by financialization, a set of processes that has been at the root of the crisis. Section 4 considers the euro as an attempt by European states, primarily Germany, to create a new world money that is appropriate to conditions of financialization. The euro is peculiar insofar as it has been created through a monetary union, rather than by a unitary or federal state. Section 5 subsequently examines the role of the euro in mediating the world crisis in Europe. Section 6 concludes by considering the implications for policy, particularly in the periphery of the eurozone.

## 2. World Money in Marxist Monetary Theory

The concept of world money is one of the least developed but most penetrating contributions made by Marx to monetary theory. In a few pages, Marx (1867, 240–244) defined world money as part of "money as money." The latter is a composite function of money, made up of money as hoard (reserve), money as means of payment (settlement of obligations), and money as world money. For Marx (1867, 242), "World money serves as the universal means of payment, as the universal means of purchase, and as the absolute social materialisation of wealth as such (universal wealth). Its predominant function is as means of payment in the settling of international balances."

The common element among the three subfunctions of "money as money" is that, while performing them, money stands aside from the simple circulation of commodities and appears as the sole adequate form of value. On those occasions it is the only form of value capable of meeting the purposes of market participants. There are two dimensions to money acting in this way. First, capitalists and others are obliged to possess it, that is, its use involves an element of external compulsion and is not merely a choice on the part of economic agents. Put differently, lack of money could lead to a capitalist failure, even when value production had remained essentially unimpaired. Second, "money as money" confers an element of power to its holder. Given that only money can adequately represent value, its holder is able to intervene in markets when others cannot, even if they possess plentiful value in other forms. The holder of "money as money" could thus exercise a determining influence over the process of value creation and circulation.

The characteristics of compulsion and power jointly reaffirm the "moneyness" of the universal equivalent, that is, its ability to dominate commodities by being the independent form of value. This ability is masked when money functions as the measure of value or means of circulation; for, in performing these functions, money is either abstract or a fleeting presence that could be replaced by other means, such as credit. The function of "money as money," in contrast, reaffirms the irreplaceable presence of money at key junctures of capitalist circulation. This is perhaps why Marx referred to this function by the term "as money."

"Money as money" sets Marx apart from classical political economy. The hoarding function, for instance, inherently contains the possibility of crisis, because money stops buying commodities and then lies idle. Ricardo, for one, had considerable difficulty with this notion; his debate with Malthus on this issue, including the international role of money, is well known in economic theory.[1] The paying function, on the other hand, contains an element of compulsion on the economic agent, who could go bankrupt even due to temporary lack of money, if there were obligations to be met. The element of compulsion was emphasized by the Banking School in the middle of the nineteenth century. The Banking School argued against constraining the ability of the Bank of England to provide means of payment in a crisis, as had happened under the Bank Act of 1844, passed due to the influence of the Currency School.[2] For the Banking School, the Bank of England had to provide a generally acceptable means of payment to ease the external compulsion felt by otherwise sound market participants.

With regard to both hoarding and means of payment, Marx's monetary theory breaks with the notion of spontaneous market equilibrium. In this respect Marx's theory (and other monetary theorists who share a similar approach) reveals the continuing influence of the mercantilists, for whom money is not simply a "veil" on harmonious markets but an independent factor determining the performance of markets. The perseverance of mercantilist ideas in this area of monetary theory is not a quirk of the history of economic thought but a result of the behavior of the capitalist economy itself. Above all, crises, disruptions of circulation, and corresponding state interventions in the monetary sphere are instances in which money sums up and dominates capitalist economic activity in practice. Keynes (1936, ch. 23) also discovered the continuing validity of elements of mercantilist monetary thought when he examined the phenomenon of the interwar crisis. Keynesian liquidity preference and state management of the supply of money belong to a current of monetary theory that has a mercantilist strain to it.

The mercantilist pedigree of "money as money" is at its clearest in connection with world money, a subfunction that is specific to Marx's monetary theory. World money arises in the world market, which differs from national markets in two vital respects. First, the world market lacks the organization of national markets because it is underpinned by legal, conventional, practical, and customary mechanisms that are not as homogeneous as those used by national markets. Relative lack of homogeneity reflects the absence of a world state that could have imposed on the world market conditions analogous to those of national markets. In practice, the world market contains international private capitals that have to navigate a sea of legal, customary, practical, and even cultural specificities. But it also contains several nation-states that facilitate settlement of the aggregate accounts created by private capitals as well as transferring value for state purposes of borrowing, subsidies, and payments. In short, the world market is the terrain over which international private capital meets the system of nation states.

Second, the world market lacks the backbone of an integrated credit system analogous to that of national markets. To be sure, credit and finance permeate the world market, facilitating transactions among private capitals and among states. But that is not the same as possessing a structured credit system that comprises ordered layers of credit, typically including commercial, banking, and money-market relations.[3] For the same reason, there is no world central bank that could act as a lender of last resort and as issuer of legal tender. The flows of global credit might be vast, but they are anarchic and do not amount to a world credit system.

World money is thus called upon to play an even more vital organizing role in the world market than national money in domestic markets. Namely, world money has to be a generally accepted means of hoarding (reserve) and means of payment for both international capitals and nation states. The lack of spontaneous equilibrium in the world market takes the form of gigantic crises that require the intervention of world money as reserve and means of payment. In order to deliver its tasks, world money must also be a commonly agreed measure of value that could reliably commensurate the values of commodities and of past obligations. It must provide a common language for both private capitals and nation states in the world market, thus transcending national peculiarities.

Matters are further complicated because world money also mediates relations among states. World money is necessarily an instrument of state policy, including the exercise of interstate political and military power. Consequently, its functioning in the world market does not solely reflect spontaneous relations but also the conscious intervention of states in the field of economy. World money can act as the reserve and means of payment in the world market in good part because states choose to deploy it in their own transactions.

The actual functioning of world money, therefore, contains an element of deliberate intervention by the state that operates in parallel with the lack of spontaneous equilibrium in the world market. Money as reserve and money as means of payment in the world market become instruments of interstate power, particularly in times of crisis. This dimension of money as money is clear in Marx's analysis of the concrete functioning of world money under conditions of his era, found across several chapters of part V of the third volume of *Capital*.[4] His discussion lacks theoretical coherence because it is essentially a set of notes, but there is no doubt about the thrust of his approach. The world market does not have a tendency to adjust itself spontaneously; disequilibria in the balance of trade require violent readjustments through crises and involve the forced flows of world money; the ability of a state to access reserves of world money is an element of global power. The mercantilist dimension of Marx's approach is apparent in this connection, particularly in relation to the monetary theory of Sir James Steuart. It does not take long, for instance, to detect in Marx's analysis the imprint of Steuart's view that that there is no automatic equilibration of trade balances through flows of money.[5] After all, Marx (1867, 243) had explicitly approved of Steuart's term "money of the world" in his own brief discussion of "world money."

The last important issue to mention in this connection is the form actually taken by world money. Marx (1867, 240–241) explicitly stated that world money reverts to the commodity form, in particular gold, though silver has for centuries also acted as world money. For Marx, reversal to the commodity form was another way of reasserting the essential "moneyness" of world money. However, this view has not fared well in the course of history. The gold standard, which dictated the form of world money for most of the nineteenth century, came to an end at the outbreak of World War I in 1914. Since then, world money has taken a variety of forms, all of which have contained elements of explicit state management. The conscious, or state-driven, elements of world money have come to the fore, compared to its spontaneous, or market-driven, elements.

World money in the period following World War II has taken the form of national currencies (above all, the dollar). Its functions have been performed by credit money that is domestically created and rests on the fiat of national governments. During the Bretton Woods period this form of world money retained a degree of convertibility with gold, but since the mid-1970s the link with commodity money has been snapped. Delivering the functions of reserve formation and means of payment in the world market—underpinned by the capacity to make values commensurate across the world—has come to depend on state authority in ways that are unprecedented in the history of capitalism. By the same token, world money has become even more clearly an instrument of state power, in particular, of hierarchical, imperial power in the world market. For these reasons, modern world money has been called "quasi-world-money" in Marxist literature.[6]

In the contemporary world market the functioning of world money has become contested terrain among the national currencies of the major capitalist powers. The dollar has dominated the field for decades, resting on the overwhelming economic, political, and military power of the United States. But the Japanese yen and the deutsche mark have challenged the dollar's supremacy for much of the postwar period. This is the appropriate context within which to analyze the rise of the euro, as is discussed in section 4. However, before discussing the euro as world money, it is necessary briefly to recap the causes of the current world crisis.

## 3. A Crisis of Financialization

The crisis that broke out in the eurozone is manifestly part of the global upheaval that commenced in 2007, the broad outline of which is by now well understood. There was a gigantic bubble in the US real-estate sector during 2001–2006, which burst in 2007 and became an international financial crisis, involving commercial banks, investment banks, insurance companies, and other financial institutions. Lehman Brothers failed in 2008, transforming the financial crisis into a global recession as exports and investments collapsed and consumption retracted. Massive state intervention followed across much of the world, which ameliorated the recession and rescued financial institutions. But rising expenditures together with falling tax revenues due to recession led to a crisis of public finance in 2009–2010; Europe was hit especially hard. Problematic public finance, in turn, threatened to plunge banks back into crisis. To sum up, the global crisis started in finance, moved to production, invaded the public sector, and threatened to return to finance.

This complex crisis reflects three decades of financialization.[7] Since the 1970s, productive capital has gone truly global, and multinational corporations have come to dominate the world economy as they never have before. Dynamic industrial capitalism has emerged in several countries in what used to be called the "Third World," and much capitalist production has shifted to the East. During the same period, neoliberal economic theory and policy have been on the ascendant: markets have been freed and real wages have been kept stagnant across advanced capitalist countries; income inequality has meanwhile become pronounced.

Against this background, finance has thoroughly permeated capitalist economies and societies. Large multinationals have become financialized, that is, they are regularly active in financial markets and draw financial profits. Banks have been transformed and now make large profits from financial transactions in the form of fees, commissions, and own-trading as well as from lending to households. The livelihood of workers has also become financialized, relying increasingly on private finance. Stagnant real wages and retreating public provisions have meant that workers have to borrow for housing, health, education, and regular consumption. Workers also rely on private finance for pensions, insurance, and other forms of saving.

The financialization of capitalism has entailed dramatic economic and social changes. The relative weight of finance has increased across a range of developed and developing countries. The demands and the operations of the financial system have come increasingly to shape economic policy and to affect the performance of entire economies. New social layers have emerged that draw profits and rents from financial transactions. These layers include elements of industrial capital, which also derive profits from financial transactions. The most effective mechanisms for the fabulous enrichment of the bourgeoisie in recent decades have been, first, access to financial assets, such as share options, and second, low taxation facilitated by neoliberal policies.

The global crisis that burst forth in 2007 has resulted from contradictions, tensions, and imbalances that are inherent to financialized capitalism. It has originated in the realm of mortgage lending to workers—often to the poorest and most marginal workers in the United States—an unprecedented phenomenon in the history of capitalism. It was exacerbated by the relative weakness of productive capital in countries where financialization has progressed most, namely in the United States and United Kingdom. It has revealed important differences among the countries of advanced financialization, particularly as Germany and Japan have retained substantial industrial capacity on a global scale.[8] And it has affected the newly industrializing countries less, mostly because they have been protected by huge—and very costly—foreign exchange reserves. In its early phase, at least, the crisis has reshaped the world economy in favor of the dynamic industrial capitalism of the East, especially of China.

The light that the crisis has cast on the pathology of contemporary capitalism is most vivid for world money. The current crisis has revealed that, under conditions of financialized capitalism, all forms of world money are diseased. The dollar, by far the dominant form, is issued by a state that faces huge and systemic budget deficits in an economy with persistent current account deficits. The yen is issued by another state that has enormous debts relative to GDP and is based on an economy that has practically stagnated for two decades. Finally, the euro, the most plausible competitor of the dollar, is issued by a group of states that differ profoundly in competitiveness, have weak cross-border labor mobility, and lack fiscal transfer mechanisms among them.

The global crisis has become a eurozone crisis because the euro has crystallized tensions and imbalances that are inherent to European capitalism. The mechanisms that were put in place to support the euro in its role as world money have mediated the emergence of the crisis in Europe. In turn, the global crisis, as it has moved from the financial, to the productive, to the public sphere, it has become a crisis of the particular form of world money that has been collectively created by European powers.

## 4. The Travails of Creating a New World Money

The euro is an unprecedented form of world money. It does not represent an already existing domestic money that has been catapulted into the role of world money through the strength of its national economy and state. Rather, it has been created ex nihilo through the monetary union of several states of vastly different economic and political power. This is, at once, a source of both strength and weakness for the euro. Above all, however, the euro has been created in order to serve the interests of large European multinationals and financial institutions. It is a response of large European capital to the conditions of financialization; it represents an attempt to secure better terms for European capitals in the evolving world market.

To operate as world money, the euro must be a reliable means of hoarding (reserve) and a means of payment in the world market, as was shown in section 2. To act in these two roles, it must also be a reliable unit of account for market prices and contractual agreements. The creators of the euro have constantly tried to ensure its ability adequately to deliver these functions. In this regard there is no comparison between the euro and the dollar, which is the dominant form of world money. The dollar is already sustained by a global institutional framework and by various practices that tie it in a myriad of ways to its users. It draws acceptability, for instance, from its accounting role in key commodity markets, such as oil, as well as from its role as the main means of reserve and payment in global finance. Not least, the dollar is supported by the political and military might of the most powerful imperial state, the United States.

In contrast, the euro has had to establish global relations of trust and acceptability from scratch through its newly devised institutional framework as well as by creating a record of reliable delivery of the measuring, hoarding, and paying functions. The institutional mechanisms of the eurozone were designed with this overriding purpose, as is briefly shown below. To a significant extent they have succeeded, thus delivering benefits to European capital that have been far from negligible. The growing acceptability of the euro has allowed European banks to expand globally; it has helped European industrial capital to impose tough discipline on workers at home as well as make acquisitions abroad. Moreover, the task of creating global acceptability for the euro has been made easier because the euro has inherited some of the mantle of the old deutsche mark. Yet the euro is not the currency of a unitary or federal state but of an alliance of disparate states. This has been its key weakness and the source of much of the current trouble.

A glance at the institutional framework of the euro confirms that the purpose of the institutions is to buttress the functioning of the euro as world money. A European Central Bank (ECB) was created to have complete command over monetary policy and independence from national governments. The ECB is obliged by its statutes to ensure the stability of the euro as a unit of account by keeping inflation below 2 percent, thus ensuring the euro's acceptability as an international means of payment and means of reserves. A homogeneous market for bank borrowing was also created, which has the ECB at its core. European banks can therefore obtain liquidity denominated in units of account that are acceptable across the world. The resulting ability to pay and to form reserves has given to European banks the strength to expand globally.[9]

To ensure the acceptability of the euro as a global reserve it was also necessary to have mechanisms of fiscal discipline. In this respect, however, there can be no comparison with the dollar. In spite of the large deficits of the US government, the dollar has continued to operate as world money due to its long track record and the existing norms of actually using the dollar in the world market. In contrast, the euro would find it hard to compete against the dollar as a reserve, particularly among financial institutions, if the issuing states could not demonstrate fiscal discipline, at least over a lengthy initial period. The solution has been to impose the institutional framework of the Stability and Growth Pact on member states, which brought fiscal stringency through the arbitrary limits of 3 percent of GDP for budget deficits and 60 percent for aggregate public debt. Unfortunately, responsibility for compliance was left to each sovereign state. Even more decisively, responsibility to honor public debt has also resided with each sovereign state, although this aspect of the euro was not clear to financial markets for several years. Individual state responsibility for fiscal discipline has been the immediate catalyst of the eurozone crisis.

With monetary policy determined by the ECB and fiscal policy placed in the straitjacket of the Stability and Growth Pact, the pressures of economic adjustment within the eurozone were necessarily directed to the labor market. Competitiveness in the internal market—by far the prevalent field of trade for member states—was left to be decided by productivity growth and labor costs. There are, however, major historical, institutional, and cultural differences among European labor markets as well as tremendous divergences in real wages and welfare provisions. Labor mobility is restricted, though far from negligible. The result was to create a "race to the bottom" for wages and conditions among eurozone members. The main beneficiary was industrial capital.[10]

Since the eurozone crisis broke out, much has been made of the apparent contradiction between homogeneous monetary policy and nonhomogeneous fiscal policy across the eurozone. There is nothing novel about this observation, which had in essence been made by conservative Anglo-Saxon economists in the 1990s.[11] The point is that this "technical" weakness of the euro is directly related to the political and social difficulties of creating a new world money jointly by several European states. A new world money cannot be created by technical processes alone but must involve complex social relations domestically as well as relations among nations globally. Ultimately, it is these relations that have led to the eurozone crisis, not the "technical" faults of the euro.

Access to world money is a mark of bourgeois power on a world scale—economically, politically, and even militarily, because money remains "the sinews of war." To be more precise, command over world money is an integral element of imperial power. In the context of Europe this means primarily German power, because France appears to have reconciled itself to a subordinate position in the eurozone. From the very beginning the euro was intended as a means of securing the global interests of German capital but also of projecting German power, which might not be military but certainly is economic and political. The problem for Germany was, and remains, that its economy is not large enough to allow the deutsche mark to become a world money capable of competing against the dollar. Hence, the German ruling class was compelled to participate in a monetary union that included involving lesser states over which Germany would attempt to exercise disciplining power. At the same time, the concern of the German ruling class was to avoid incurring more fiscal costs than were absolutely necessary in managing the monetary union.

Of necessity, therefore, the euro had to be a fluid compromise with regard to the states that were drawn into it. Equally necessarily, its support mechanisms have reflected the partial control exercised by Germany over the rest of the participants. Extended membership was essential in order to create a large-enough internal market that would give to the new currency sufficient scope to act as a means of reserve and payment globally. Consequently, all member states had to be able to draw some benefits from the monetary union, but under no circumstances were they to impose major fiscal costs on the collective purse of the German ruling class. This cold calculation has been masked by the ideological verbiage of Europeanism, particularly as the German ruling class has been unable openly to declare its national interest since the end of World War II. In short, the lack of a homogeneous fiscal policy in the eurozone reflects the limited power of Germany together with its desire to minimize fiscal costs. The German ruling class has been obliged to create a world money out of unwieldy materials.

## 5. The Euro Mediates the World Crisis in Europe

The world crisis that commenced in 2007 has been mediated in Europe by the mechanisms of the euro. By the same token, the crisis has brought into sharp relief the social and imperial relations underpinning the euro as world money. Given its construction and underlying purpose, the eurozone has created a sharp internal division between a core and periphery. The "race to the bottom" that was forced onto member states by the mechanisms of the euro was won by Germany in the 2000s. The reason was, purely and exclusively, that German employers have been ruthless at keeping wages down since the early 1990s. As a result, a periphery has emerged within the eurozone, made up of countries that have progressively lost competitiveness and have recorded persistent current account deficits. These deficits were mirrored by surpluses of countries of the core, above all, of Germany.[12]

To finance its deficits the periphery has inevitably had to borrow abroad. For much of the 2000s borrowing abroad was cheap because the ECB had kept interest rates low. The lenders were naturally the banks of core countries, mostly those of France and Germany. Furthermore, peripheral banks were able to expand their domestic lending because they had access to cheap funds internationally. Financialization proceeded apace in the periphery, providing the wherewithal for real-estate speculation and growth of consumption.[13] For a brief period it appeared as if the periphery had been able to make significant gains from eurozone membership, recording relatively high rates of growth. The social layers most closely associated with financialization benefited accordingly. The precarious nature of this success became apparent when the world crisis broke out in 2007. Borrowing from abroad to finance current account deficits, together with debt created through domestic financialization, had resulted in enormous peripheral indebtedness, mostly of the private sector (typically banks and households) and to a lesser extent of the public sector. Consequently, the periphery found itself under German economic and political domination as never before in its history.

The process through which the weakness of the periphery has manifested itself is plain. The financial storm that broke out after the collapse of Lehman Brothers in 2008 hit mostly German banks in Europe, because they had invested in US subprime paper. But the recession that followed affected both Germany and the periphery through falling exports and reduced investments. Peripheral states were confronted with declining tax revenues, while attempting to support aggregate demand and to rescue banks; budget deficits escalated. Given their already vast indebtedness, it became apparent in 2009–2010 that peripheral countries faced a debt crisis, primarily of public but also of private debt.

The crisis of the periphery has cast an unforgiving light on the eurozone. For one thing, it has shaken the ideology of Europeanism that has buttressed the social acceptability of the euro within Europe. It has become clear that the eurozone is not a cooperative association of "Europeans" but a hierarchical monetary union aiming to establish a new money that can operate globally. Within this union, the core does not accept the obligation to honor the debts of the periphery. Bond markets eventually realized that they were mistaken when they lent freely to Greece, Ireland, Portugal, and Spain on the assumption that there could be no national default within the eurozone. Thus, in 2009, the danger of peripheral default emerged sharply because of the extent of peripheral indebtedness. If peripheral default occurred, there would be a major risk of bank failure at the core, and that might have reignited the international banking crisis that had been pacified in 2009. The core of the eurozone, therefore, found itself obliged to deal with the problem of peripheral debt out of self-interest. The way it has done so has cast further light on the euro as world money.

## 6. Instead of a Conclusion: The Costs of Rescuing a New World Money

Led by Germany, the core has been primarily concerned with rescuing the banks and the rest of the financial system from the burden of peripheral debt. Thus, the ECB has provided liquidity to banks, accepting as guarantees the problematic public debt of the peripheral nations. The ECB has even been allowed to ignore its own statutes—including previously solemn undertakings never to buy public debt—with the aim of stabilizing the secondary markets in peripheral public debt. In addition, the core has put together rescue packages in order to lend money to peripheral states that were cut off from the bond markets. The price of the emergency lending—apart from high interest rates—has been severe austerity. Together with the IMF, the core has forced the periphery to undertake deep cuts in social spending, public investment, wages, pensions, and so on, with the aim of cutting budget deficits. It has also enforced further deregulation of labor and other markets, and it has also encouraged privatization. The aim has been to deal with the problem of peripheral insolvency through austerity and liberalization, that is, by transferring the potential losses to the incomes of workers across the periphery. On the other hand, austerity might lead to deep recession and thus make default more likely.

The underlying reasons for the policy response of the eurozone have to do with the nature of the euro as a peculiar form of world money. The crisis has posed a tough dilemma for Germany, the leading imperial country within the union. On the one hand, Germany has been concerned to preserve the euro, which means avoiding a major banking crisis. On the other, it has been reluctant to take upon itself the cost of peripheral default, which could prove to be very large. And it has not been prepared to bear any additional costs of borrowing on behalf of peripheral countries in the future. Furthermore, the German ruling class has also had to reckon with the difficulty of imposing further sacrifices on the German people, given the severe wage restraint that has prevailed in the country for two decades. Such are the awkward choices of imperial power.

Quite rationally, the German ruling class initially opted to impose austerity on peripheral countries in order to shift the cost of problematic debt onto peripheral workers' income, while continuing to provide liquidity to banks. The unfortunate by-product of its rationality, however, has been that it has intensified the danger of recession and hence of peripheral default. While the banks of the core remain heavily exposed to public debt of both peripheral and core countries, this poses a deadly risk for the eurozone as a whole. Consequently, Germany has been obliged continually to rebalance its approach, calibrating the pressure on peripheral countries in order to avoid default. In this vein, Germany has been prepared even to tolerate some losses from a managed restructuring of peripheral debt, or a lengthening of the duration of the debt, in order to prevent core banks from collapsing.

German choices have been largely conditioned by the heavy exposure of the banks of the core to the periphery. If the danger of bank collapse was successfully lifted, the German ruling class would be able to rebalance its relation to peripheral countries as a whole. Needless to say, austerity would continue to be imposed on the periphery at every turn, seeking to minimize any losses that Germany might have to take itself. Wage restraint would also continue to be applied to German workers in order to protect the competitiveness of German capital. If it succeeded, the German ruling class would probably emerge as the undisputed master of the euro and of the European economy more generally.

For peripheral countries, in contrast, future prospects are far from rosy. Their economies have failed to integrate successfully in the monetary union. To remain in the eurozone they have to engage in tough austerity, exacerbating unemployment and undermining their productive base. The provision of social welfare is likely to suffer, while wages and conditions for labor will become worse. Growth rates are likely to be low and variable. The conditions of cheap borrowing that prevailed in the 2000s are unlikely to return in the future. Inequality and social tensions will rise as a thin layer of the domestic ruling classes—typically connected to the financial system but also containing elements of industrial capital—will probably continue to profit from the current policies. The price of German imperial ascendancy sustained by the euro will be economic, social, and national decline for the periphery. It remains to be seen whether the periphery will accept these bleak prospects in order to continue using a new world money that operates mostly for the benefit of others.

## Notes

1. See, for instance, Ricardo (1810, 64–65).
2. This view was clearly, and sharply, articulated by Tooke (1844).
3. The logical ordering of credit relations is examined in Itoh and Lapavitsas (1999, ch. 4).
4. See, for instance, Marx (1894, chs. 30, 31, 32).
5. See, for instance, Steuart (1767, vol. III, bk. IV, pt. II, ch. VIII; vol. III, bk. II, ch. XXVIII).
6. See, for instance, Lapavitsas (2006). The term was originally coined by Makoto Itoh.
7. The view of financialization that is summed up in this section has been developed in several publications and discussion papers of Research on Money and Finance, see www.researchonmoneyandfinance.org.
8. This is shown with clarity, though from a different theoretical perspective on financialization, by Stockhammer (2010).
9. See RMF (2009a, 2009b).
10. See RMF (2010a).
11. See, for instance, Feldstein (1997). See also "An Interview with Milton Friedman," in Samuelson and Barnett (2007, ch. 6).
12. See RMF (2010a).
13. The processes resulting in peripheral indebtedness are discussed in detail in RMF (2010b).

## References

Feldstein, M. 1997. "The Political Economy of the European Economic and Monetary Union: Political Sources of an Economic Liability." *National Bureau of Economic Research Working Paper Series* no. 6150.

Itoh, M., and C. Lapavitsas. 1999. *Political Economy of Money and Finance*. London: Macmillan.

Keynes, J. M. 1936 (1973). *The General Theory of Employment, Interest and Money*. London: Macmillan.

Lapavitsas, C. 2006. "Power and Trust as Constituents of Money and Credit." *Historical Materialism* 14(1): 129–154.

Marx, K. 1867 (1976). *Capital*. Vol. 1. London: Penguin.

Marx, K. 1894 (1981). *Capital*. Vol. 3. London: Penguin.

Research on Money and Finance (RMF). 2010a. *Eurozone Crisis: Beggar Thyself and Thy Neighbour*. Occasional Report 1, March. www.researchonmoneyandfinance.org.

Research on Money and Finance (RMF). 2010b. *The Eurozone between Austerity and Default.* Occasional Report 2, September. www.researchonmoneyandfinance.org.

Ricardo, D. 1810 (1951). *Letters.* In P. Sraffa and M. Dobb, eds., *The Works and Correspondence of David Ricardo*, Vol. VI. Cambridge: Cambridge University Press.

Samuelson, P., and W. Barnett, eds. 2007. *Inside the Economist's Mind: Conversations with Eminent Economists.* Oxford: Blackwell.

Steuart, J. 1767 (1995). *An Inquiry into the Principles of Political Economy, Vols. I, II, III, IV, in Works, Political, Metaphysical, and Chronological, of the Late Sir James Steuart.* London: Routledge.

Stockhammer, E. 2010. "Neoliberalism, Income Distribution and the Causes of the Crisis." Research on Money and Finance, Discussion Paper no. 19. www.researchonmoneyandfinance.org.

Tooke, T. 1844 (1959). *An Inquiry into the Currency Principle.* London: LSE Reprint Series.

# PART IV

# THE ROLE OF INSTITUTIONAL AND STRUCTURAL CHANGE IN THE DEVELOPMENT OF FINANCIAL CRISES

CHAPTER 19

# CHANGES IN THE POSTWAR GLOBAL ECONOMY AND THE ROOTS OF THE FINANCIAL CRISIS

DAVID M. KOTZ

## 1. Introduction

The financial and economic crisis that arose in 2008 originated in the United States and then immediately spread to much of the global economy. Examining the specific features of the economic system from which the crisis emerged is a key step in developing an understanding of the factors that produced this crisis. It may also shed light on the causal factors of financial crises in general. This chapter presents an analysis of the institutional features of both the global and the US political economies in the decades preceding the crisis.

As the dominant power among capitalist countries over the entire postwar period, the United States has played a unique role in the global system, symbolized by the US dollar's status as the world's dominant reserve and trading currency. When global capitalism underwent a major restructuring starting in the late 1970s, the United States, along with the United Kingdom, played a leading role in promoting that process. To understand the roots of the current crisis, it is essential to examine the new institutions that emerged in the late 1970s and early 1980s both in the US and the global economies.

While a capitalist economic system is defined by certain invariant features, the specific institutional form of capitalism periodically has changed significantly.[1] Not every historically existing institutional form of capitalism has produced serious financial crises, as will be noted below. Identifying the roots of a severe financial and economic crisis requires attention to the specific institutional form of capitalism that prevailed in the period preceding the outbreak of the crisis. The institutional form of capitalism in the decades leading up to the current crisis is often called neoliberalism, a term that will be defined in section 3 below.

Section 2 presents a brief overview of the postwar system of regulated capitalism, which prevailed for some 25 years after World War II. Section 3 introduces neoliberal capitalism, which replaced regulated capitalism by the early 1980s. Section 4 examines the features of neoliberal capitalism that existed at the global level. Section 5 considers the country-level features of neoliberal capitalism for the country from which the crisis emerged, the United States. Section 6 explains how neoliberal capitalism, despite promoting a series of long economic expansions over several decades, produced unsustainable long-run trends that set the stage for the severe financial and economic crisis that broke out in 2008. It also draws some lessons about the conditions that lead to financial crises in general.

## 2. Overview of the Postwar System of Regulated Capitalism

The capitalism that emerged from the Great Depression of the 1930s and World War II was significantly changed from its pre-Depression form. In the developed capitalist countries the state both grew larger relative to the economy and took on a more active, interventionist role. This assumed somewhat different forms in different countries, reflecting the particular history of each region and country. In Western Europe it took the form of social democracy and in Japan a corporatist form, while in the United States a kind of military Keynesianism developed.

However, they all shared certain common features. The sharp capital-labor struggles of the prewar period were replaced by a more peaceful, rule-based collective-bargaining relation. Governments established more or less comprehensive social welfare programs. Governments sought to tame the business cycle through active use of fiscal and monetary policies. In addition, governments actively intervened in the private sector in various ways through regulation, taxation, and subsidies, including significant state control over the financial sector. In many countries state-owned enterprises played an important role in some industries, although not in the United States. Large corporations in key industries established a system of price leadership that stabilized both prices and profits. The term "regulated capitalism" seems an apt one for that period.

New capitalist institutions also arose at the global level. The most important of these was the Bretton Woods system, which originated at a conference held in Bretton Woods, New Hampshire, in 1944. This system involved fixed exchange rates among the major trading currencies, with the US dollar, backed by gold at a fixed rate, serving as the major trading and reserve currency. The International Monetary Fund (IMF) was established to manage the new system, which allowed nation-states the right to exercise significant control over cross-border capital movements and, to a limited extent under certain circumstances, over trade in goods and services.

The dominant economic ideas in the postwar decades also differed sharply from the pre-Depression orthodoxy. The old ideas had assigned to government few economic responsibilities other than the protection of private property, enforcement of contracts, maintenance of public order, issuance of money backed by precious metals, and the protection of economic interests abroad. Unregulated market forces were supposed to take care of the rest. Trade unions were viewed as would-be monopolists in the sale of labor-power.

In the postwar period a new Keynesian-regulationist orthodoxy arose. While this included the strictly Keynesian idea that a market economy could not avoid serious depressions unless the state stood ready to compensate for fluctuations in private investment, it went beyond that view. Market failures were also seen at the micro level. The new orthodoxy endorsed state regulation of certain sectors of the economy, collective bargaining to overcome employers' advantage in wage setting, regulation of product and job safety, environmental protection measures, and progressive income taxes. In the United States, Paul Samuelson's famous textbook *Economics* (1948) embodied the new Keynesian-regulationist economic paradigm.[2]

By the 1960s regulated capitalism appeared to be a big success. While the business cycle had not been eliminated, no major depression had occurred. In the United States the degree of income inequality actually declined somewhat from 1948 to 1973, with the income share of the bottom 20 percent of families rising from 4.9 percent to 5.5 percent while the share of the richest 5 percent declined from 17.1 percent to 15.5 percent (US Census Bureau, 2010). The developed capitalist countries as a whole showed the fastest economic growth in 1948–1973 of any long period for which data are available (Madisson, 1995). This period came to be called the "Golden Age of capitalism" (Marglin and Schor, 1990). The free-market theorists' warnings of economic disaster should government interfere in the market seemed misplaced, and the old free-market theory appeared to be permanently consigned to the proverbial dustbin of outmoded ideas.

During this so-called Golden Age, the banks were closely regulated by the state in most developed capitalist countries, including the United States. There was relatively little financial speculation in those decades. Banks and other financial institutions mainly engaged in the traditional activities of lending funds to industry, making long-term fixed-rate commercial and home mortgage loans and holding them to maturity, floating new stock and bond issues, and selling conventional insurance. There were no big US bank failures in this period and no significant financial panic or crisis in the developed capitalist countries.

However, at the very moment of the seeming triumph of regulated capitalism, problems of growing severity were welling up under the surface. After the mid-1960s capital-labor conflict sharpened, straining the compromise between the two sides. The average profit rate began a long decline in the major capitalist countries (Kotz and McDonough, 2010, 110, figure 4.1). By the early 1970s inflation was accelerating. Starting in 1967 severe stresses emerged in the previously successful Bretton Woods monetary system, and during 1971 to 1973 it collapsed.

The business cycle peak year of 1973 marked the end of the Golden Age. There followed a period that many analysts regard as the crisis phase of the postwar system of regulated capitalism (Bowles, Gordon, and Weisskopf, 1990). A relatively severe recession hit the US economy in 1974–1975, followed by years of accelerating inflation and instability in the international monetary system. A general sense emerged that things were spinning out of control, while efforts to reestablish economic stability using the Keynesian tools did not succeed. In response to this crisis of postwar-regulated capitalism, the institutional form of capitalism, along with the dominant economic ideas, changed with surprising rapidity.

## 3. The Rise of Neoliberal Capitalism

By the early 1980s a new form of capitalism had replaced regulated capitalism. In the 1990s the term neoliberalism arose to describe this new form of capitalism. Neoliberalism refers to the new institutions, policies, and ideas that came to predominate first in the United States and United Kingdom, from which they spread to many other countries as well as defining a new global-level form of capitalism. Neoliberalism is traditionally associated with the trilogy of liberalization, privatization, and stabilization. Liberalization refers to freeing of markets and firms from state regulation. Privatization refers not only to selling off state-owned enterprises but also to contracting out public services to private enterprises. Stabilization refers to cuts in government social programs, tight monetary policy, and efforts to achieve budget balance, justified by the aim of stabilizing the price level.[3] As will be explained below, neoliberal capitalism has involved a broader set of institutional changes than is suggested by the above three terms.

What came to be called neoliberal capitalism began to emerge in the second half of the 1970s in the United States and the United Kingdom. While many identify this shift in the United States with President Ronald Reagan, it actually began before he took office in January 1981. A program of deregulation of regulated industries was launched during the administration of President Jimmy Carter, starting with the Airline Deregulation Act of 1978. President Carter also introduced efforts to deregulate trucking and oil prices, and he pushed the antitrust suit against AT&T, which led to the breakup of that regulated monopoly. The Carter administration also called for cutbacks in social programs and tax cuts for business. President Carter appointed Paul Volcker to the Federal Reserve Chairmanship in 1979, who promptly initiated a policy of very tight monetary policy that eventually drove the unemployment rate up to double digits, undermining the bargaining power of organized labor. In the United Kingdom, the 1979 election of Margaret Thatcher launched a similar direction of economic change. In 1981 the Reagan administration deepened the commitment to a new direction in economic policy, adding a direct assault on the trade unions signaled by the breaking of an air traffic controllers' strike in that year.

During 1979-1981 a new set of economic and political ideas rapidly gained influence in the public-policy arena, which justified and promoted the developing institutional shifts. At the time, these ideas had a variety of names: free-market theory, monetarism, supply-side economics, and conservative economics. Among academic economists these ideas had been percolating even earlier, with the rise of rational expectations theory (Lucas and Rapping, 1969) and a renewed interest in the writings of Frederick Hayek.

The initial shifts away from regulated capitalism—in the realms of government policy and economic ideas—can be understood as a groping for some solution to the seemingly intractable problems that had emerged in the 1970s. There were sharp political and ideological battles in that decade over whether the system of regulated capitalism needed more than modest revisions, and if it did, what kinds of changes would resolve the problems. However, in the United States and United Kingdom, the outcome of this complex battle was a rapid plunge toward the renunciation of regulated capitalism and an effort to dismantle it. The revived free-market economic ideas provided the rationale for a program of liberalization, privatization, and so-called stabilization. The term neoliberalism eventually arose to describe this program and set of ideas, based on the meaning of "liberalism" denoting limited government intervention in markets, and the recognition that the old pre-Depression free-market ideas had returned in new forms (hence the "neo" prefix).[4]

The reasons why neoliberal capitalism arose at this time are complex and cannot be considered here (see Kotz, 2002; Wolfson and Kotz, 2010). It may be that more than one possible response to the 1970s crisis of regulated capitalism could have succeeded, based on some definition of "success." In any event, it was neoliberal capitalism that actually supplanted regulated capitalism, and it will be argued here that the neoliberal transformation of capitalism did resolve the problems that had undermined regulated capitalism. Neoliberalism ushered in a period of long economic expansions and high profits, while simultaneously planting the seeds of the financial and economic crisis that broke out in 2008.

The neoliberal version of capitalism has a peculiarity, in that, unlike in the preceding period of regulated capitalism, the new dominant institutions did not equally take root in every part of the capitalist world. Capitalism in the US and UK were relatively thoroughly restructured based on neoliberal precepts, as was the case in many parts of Latin America and Africa. The transition countries in Europe and central Asia incorporated the neoliberal model even more thoroughly in their newly developed capitalist systems. On the other hand, the Western European countries adopted only some neoliberal institutions while retaining many features of regulated capitalism. Japanese capitalism changed little toward the neoliberal direction. Several Asian countries, including China, developed new types of state-directed mixed economies in this period. The neoliberal model was perhaps most fully incorporated at the global level of cross-country trade and capital movements, where the role of the IMF and the World Bank changed and new neoliberal global institutions were constructed.[5]

In light of the above considerations, neoliberalism can be best understood by separately analyzing its global dimension and its features in the dominant capitalist power, the United States. These are explored in the following two sections.

## 4. Global-Level Features of Neoliberal Capitalism

The new system that replaced Bretton Woods permitted relatively free movement of goods, services, and capital across national boundaries. This new system of international trade and investment was embodied in a series of treaties and agreements that have been enforced by various institutions, including the IMF, the World Trade Organization, and various regional organizations (Kotz and McDonough, 2010). Fixed exchange rates gave way to the managed float of the major trading currencies.

The elimination of these barriers encouraged significant cross-border integration of the production process. Many goods came to be produced, not in a single country, but as the product of many countries' value added, as components and parts moved around the world for assembly of the final product. In some sectors a truly global production system emerged. At the same time, the financial system became increasingly integrated globally. This was never fully achieved, as some countries, including China and India, held back from joining a single global financial market. Nevertheless, a major part of the world's financial system became very interdependent and intermeshed. This globalization of the real and financial aspects of capitalism was promoted by technological changes in transportation, communication, and data processing, but it could not have developed without the change in the global institutions that regulate cross-border economic transactions.

As national markets gave way to much larger global markets, the nature of competition among large corporations changed. The major corporations in each industry invaded one another's markets, causing the old system of price leadership among a few long-time and familiar rivals to break down. In place of co-respective competition among rivals, there arose a tendency toward unrestrained competition. Price cutting and price wars, which had largely disappeared in much of the economy in the regulated capitalist era, returned with a vengeance. Big corporations in the leading capitalist countries, which had previously made positive profits in good years and bad, now faced a much more threatening competitive environment, which included not just the possibility of one year's negative profit but the previously unthinkable danger of being driven into bankruptcy.

One more feature of neoliberal capitalism is best understood as a global-level feature: the newly dominant neoliberal ideas. Although the rebirth of the old liberal ideas originated mainly in the United States and United Kingdom, these ideas rapidly spread around the world. They even became dominant among intellectuals and academics in countries whose governments did not fully adopt neoliberal policies, such as China and India. Neoliberal ideas are described in Kotz and McDonough (2010, 94) as follows: "Neoliberal ideology is marked by a glorification of individual choice, market relations, and private property; a view of the state as inherently an enemy of individual freedom and economic efficiency; and an extreme individualist conception of society." Neoliberal economists asserted that an unregulated market system is optimal and that government efforts to correct any problems that may arise from the private sector will only worsen the final result. It would be difficult to underestimate the importance of the role played by neoliberal ideas in promoting and justifying the policies and institutional changes that took place in this period, both at the global and nation-state levels.

## 5. Neoliberal Capitalism in the United States

The neoliberal restructuring of the US economy can be best understood under three headings: the capital-labor relation, the state-economy relation, and internal relations within capital. All three were transformed. Each will be considered in turn.

I have argued elsewhere that the central feature of neoliberalism is the change it brings about in the relation between capital and labor (Wolfson and

Kotz, 2010). Regulated capitalism had at its core a compromise between capital and labor, in the sense that the two sides informally agreed to bargain over wages, working conditions, and other related matters. In the United States, this compromise enabled labor to share in the increases in output that flowed from productivity growth. From 1948 to 1973 the real wages of nonsupervisory workers rose at the average rate of 2.2 percent per year, nearly as fast as the 2.4 percent per year growth rate in output per worker over that period (*Economic Report of the President*, 1988, 298, 300). This indicates an almost equal sharing between capital and labor of the benefits of productivity growth. In that period, a significant proportion of the working class found stable jobs at a living wage. As was noted above, the degree of income inequality declined somewhat over that period.

These conditions changed sharply as a result of neoliberal restructuring. Big business, most of which had accepted collective bargaining since the late 1940s, turned against trade unions. With support from the state, the newly hostile employer stance succeeded in rapidly undermining labor's bargaining power. From 1979 to 2007 the real hourly wage of nonsupervisory workers actually declined slightly, by 1.0 percent, although output per worker continued to rise in that period, by 72.7 percent, or 2.0 percent per year, indicating that none of the benefit of rising productivity went to the workers (US Bureau of Labor Statistics, 2009).[6] Even in the late 1990s, when the unemployment rate fell to 4 percent, real wage growth barely kept up with productivity growth, rather than spurting to a rate well above the productivity growth rate as had occurred at times of low unemployment rates in the regulated capitalist era (Kotz, 2009a, 184, table 13.4).

The share of family income received by the top 5 percent jumped from 15.3 percent in 1979 to a high of 21.5 percent in 2006, before declining slightly in 2007, while the shares of each of the lower four quintiles declined (US Census Bureau, 2010). The income share of the richest hundredth of 1 percent rose from 1 percent to 1.5 percent of total income in the 1950s to 5 percent in 2000 and again in 2005, a level not seen previously since the late 1920s (Piketty and Saez, 2007).

The character of private-sector employment also changed in the neoliberal era. In place of long-term stable jobs with prospects for periodic advancement, a growing share of employment came to consist of part-time and temporary jobs as employers demanded "flexible labor markets."[7] This trend even affected some professional jobs, as colleges and universities, particularly in the public sector, replaced tenured and tenure-track professors with part-time and temporary instructors. This created an underclass of low-paid, overworked college instructors, many of them with doctorates in their field.

Employers made use of the reduced barriers to capital movement to batter down workers' wages by threatening to shift production to low-wage countries. In many cases unionized workers accepted large pay cuts, only to have their jobs outsourced a few years later anyway.

Second, the state role in the economy changed. The US government did not actually shrink in size relative to GDP, a fact that has misled some analysts into thinking the neoliberal call for a "free-market" economy was only words. The active attempt to regulate, guide, and stabilize the economy of the regulated capitalist era was replaced by a hands-off approach. Believing that a capitalist economy performed best if left unregulated, both macro-level and micro-level interventions were renounced. At the macro level, countercyclical fiscal policy was given up as unnecessary. Because money is ultimately a creation of the state (along with the banking system), the Federal Reserve cannot avoid having some impact on money and credit. However, the Fed's role shifted from pursuing some balance of low inflation and low unemployment to single-mindedly aiming for price stability.

Even bigger changes occurred at the micro level. Virtually all of the previously state-regulated sectors, in transportation, power, and communication, were deregulated, apart from local regulation of some local natural monopolies. Most significant was the gradual deregulation of the financial sector, a process that began in earnest in the early 1980s and continued through the end of the 1990s (see chapter 21 about deregulation in this volume). The federal government also backed away from enforcement of environmental and occupational and consumer-product safety regulations.

While privatization of state-owned enterprises occurred in other developed capitalist countries, the United States had few government-owned enterprises at the start of the neoliberal era. Privatization in the United States took the form of contracting out public services from state agencies to private companies, in such areas as welfare programs, military services, and prisons. As the state was hollowed out, it lost the capability to effectively oversee such contracting arrangements, creating opportunities for contracting companies to gain huge profits at the public's expense. At one point the Bush II administration, despite the existence of a comparatively effective tax-collection system in the United States, even proposed contracting out the collection of federal taxes. This proposal was buried under charges of reviving the medieval practice of tax farming.

Despite a few setbacks to the neoliberal agenda, there were significant cuts in social programs in the neoliberal era. While state social welfare programs did not shrink to their levels in the pre-Depression era, the social wage that had arisen under regulated capitalism was chipped away. In the previous era, there had been a steady expansion in collectively provided goods and services, such as education, and in such social provisions as public pensions and health-care programs. All of these had complemented the rising private incomes of working people. In the neoliberal era, declining private incomes for the majority were joined with shrinking public services. The public schools were increasingly starved of funds. The retirement age for a full Social Security pension was raised. The main welfare system for the poor was discontinued, replaced by a temporary aid system in the 1990s during the Clinton administration. The unemployment compensation system covered a shrinking proportion of the unemployed. The legal minimum wage fell further and further behind the rising cost of living.

The tax system grew less progressive. Tax rates under the relatively progressive federal income tax system were reduced, particularly for high-income earners, while the regressive payroll taxes were increased. At the same time, taxes on corporate profits and property income were reduced. As a result, the total tax burden on the rich declined while that on middle-income families rose. This enabled the same neoliberal politicians who had promoted these changes to demand further cuts in public programs, ostensibly to help the tax-burdened middle class.

The third area of change was in the internal relations within capital. One change—the replacement of co-respective competition by unrestrained rivalry among large corporations—occurred at the global level and was discussed above. This development was quite pronounced in the United States, as large companies in many industries sought to drive their rivals out of the market.

A second development was a change in the relation between financial and nonfinancial capital. The relation between financial and nonfinancial capital has changed several times since the rise of big business in the United States in the late nineteenth century (Kotz, 2011). In the period of regulated capitalism, financial institutions operated under a system of close regulation by state agencies, which included controls over what financial products and services could be offered and even allowable interest rates for some types of institutions. This regulatory system made the financial sector serve capital accumulation in the real sector. Financial deregulation in the neoliberal era turned the banks and other financial institutions loose, freeing them to engage in whatever activities were most profitable, with little if any oversight from the state. The result was a gradual separation of financial from nonfinancial capital, as the major financial institutions shifted their activities from loan-based financing of nonfinancial corporations toward purely financial and often speculative activities. This transformation was profitable for the financial sector, as the share of financial-sector profits in total corporate profits more than doubled from 20.4 percent in 1979 to 41.1 percent in 2003 (US Bureau of Economic Analysis, 2010).[8] The expansion of financial activities and the changes in their character in this period have often been called "financialization" (Epstein, 2005; Orhangazi, 2008; and chapter 25 on financialization in this volume).[9]

During the neoliberal era changes occurred within large corporations. Under regulated capitalism the CEO was traditionally promoted from within, from among high-level managers who had spent their careers with the company. Attaining the CEO position was normally the last step before retirement, and CEOs strongly identified with the interests of their companies. In the neoliberal era, a market arose for CEOs, which involved hiring them from outside the company. As this became the new norm, the relation between a CEO and the company changed. Now the typical CEO would expect to spend only a few years at a company before arranging a move to a bigger one. Instead of the long-run interests of the company, the CEO now had an incentive to burnish the company's short-term performance indicators (such as the stock price) to compile the most impressive résumé. The heightened competition of neoliberal capitalism reinforced the tendency to focus on short-term results, because the ever-present threat of near-term bankruptcy causes long-term considerations to fade into the background.

Many analysts, including Marx (1967, chap. 14), have observed that a large capitalist enterprise resembles a planned economy in its internal relations. A plan is established and each employee is expected to contribute to carrying it out effectively. However, under neoliberal capitalism, market principles and relations began to penetrate inside enterprises. In some sectors company officials' pay was tied to what they could demonstrate in the way of individually generated profit. Instead of a cooperative team of high-level officials, company officials began to resemble a competing group of individuals, each striving to maximize his or her own income, without regard for the effects on the long-term performance of the company.

## 6. Neoliberal Capitalism and Financial Crisis

Neoliberal capitalism is a coherent system, in which the key institutions are mutually consistent and reinforce one another. Neoliberal ideology supports and justifies the whole set of institutional changes that constitutes neoliberal restructuring. It can be argued that neoliberal restructuring was accurately directed at the central feature of regulated capitalism that had led it into a crisis in the 1970s, namely the high degree of bargaining power of labor in that form of capitalism. Some analysts argue that it was the loss of capital's ability to effectively control labor and other popular groups that produced the crisis of the 1970s, with a declining rate of profit, spiraling inflation, and international monetary instability (Bowles, Gordon, and Weisskopf, 1990). Neoliberal restructuring took aim at all of the institutions that had bolstered the bargaining power of labor and other popular groups. By so doing, it restored effective control to capital. The result was the reversal of the declining profit rate, which began a long-term rise in the early 1980s in the United States and Western Europe (Kotz and McDonough, 2010, 110, figure 4.1). Neoliberal capitalism produced three long economic expansions, which in the United States lasted from 1982 to 1990, 1991 to 2000, and 2001 to 2007. The 1990s expansion was the longest of the entire postwar period. After the mid-1980s inflation was never a problem.

By the early 2000s neoliberal capitalism had reached maturity. It had survived eight years of a Democratic Party administration in the United States and a Labour government in the United Kingdom since 1997. Indeed, neoliberalism was extended and deepened under the Democrats and Labour.[10] This has a parallel in the survival and expansion of regulated capitalism in the United States under the Republican administrations of Dwight D. Eisenhower and Richard M. Nixon. History suggests that a coherent institutional form of capitalism, once established, has great staying power, as long as it delivers high profits and economic expansion (Kotz and McDonough, 2010).

The term "Great Moderation" arose among mainstream economists in the early 2000s to describe the perceived success of neoliberalism at stabilizing capitalism. Unbeknownst to such thinkers, the stabilization was far from permanent. The very means by which neoliberal capitalism promoted long expansions produced long-run trends that were unsustainable and bound to eventually bring a financial and economic crash.

Because neoliberalism made capital fully dominant over labor, each time the economy began a period of expansion the profit rate rose rapidly, encouraging growing investment by business. However, with real wages stagnating, in each expansion there was a problem of who would buy the growing volume of goods produced by an expanding economy. In regulated capitalism, real wages had risen at approximately the same rate as output during expansions, so this particular problem did not arise. Rising investment is itself a source of demand, and it can sustain an expansion for a time, but eventually the result would be production of excess capacity.

Thus, the very success of neoliberal capitalism at raising profits by suppressing wage growth created an incipient problem of overproduction relative to demand during economic expansions. A long expansion under such conditions is possible only if some group consumes more than its income. The first half of the 1990s expansion was sluggish, but after 1995 growth averaged 4.1 percent per year and lasted another five years. The reason for this was the bubble that started in 1995 on the New York Stock Exchange. First, investment growth shot upward in 1995, and then consumer spending growth suddenly accelerated to 4.9 percent per year in the last three years of the expansion, as upper-middle and upper-income households, believing they were growing rich through stock appreciation, went on a spending binge (Kotz, 2003). The 1990s expansion ended abruptly when the stock-market bubble burst in 2000.

The expansion of the 2000s was not nearly as vigorous as that of the 1990s. Nevertheless, the US economy was able to expand for six years as a huge housing bubble enabled a large segment of the population to maintain and even increase spending by borrowing against home values. Gross withdrawals by homeowners from home equity reached 9–10 percent of disposable personal income in 2004–2006 (Greenspan and Kennedy, 2007).[11]

Economic expansion under neoliberal capitalism depended on debt-financed household consumer spending. Asset bubbles provided the security against which households were able to borrow. To complete the circle, the institutions of neoliberal capitalism promoted the growth of large asset bubbles, as well as providing a transformed financial system that was ready to make risky loans to the owners of bubble-inflated assets. Asset bubbles tended to arise in neoliberal capitalism because, with profits rising rapidly and household wealth concentrating at the very top, there tended to be a greater volume of funds seeking investment than the available productive investment opportunities. As a result, some of those funds found their way into purchasing assets, which starts an asset bubble. However, an asset bubble cannot grow very large unless financial institutions are ready to lend to those who speculate in the asset—and the deregulated financial institutions, freed to pursue maximum profits, were eager to make highly profitable but risky loans to support such speculation (see chapters 3 on speculation and 23 on derivatives in this volume).

Finally, for an asset bubble to translate into rising consumer spending, financial institutions must lend to households that hold the appreciating assets. If households had to sell the assets to finance their spending, the bubble would collapse. In the 2000s the deregulated financial institutions were ready to make second mortgage loans even to families with low or no income. While such lending may seem irrational, it was widely believed during the housing bubble that housing prices would never stop rising. If that were true, loans based on homes would be safe, regardless of the income of the homeowner (see chapter 20 regarding bank lending and the subprime crisis in this volume). Furthermore, even for financial operators who doubted the permanence of rising real-estate prices, the penetration of an individualistic market orientation inside financial firms encouraged enthusiastic participation in such lending practices, because they generated big commissions for those involved, which need not be given back if the loans turned bad—the firm would then bear the loss.

However, this process caused a secular rise in household debt in the neoliberal era. Prior to the early 1980s, the ratio of household debt to disposable income had been relatively stable, rising somewhat in expansions and falling in recessions. Starting in the early 1980s, that ratio rose rapidly, more than doubling from 59.0 percent in 1982 to 128.8 percent in 2007 (Kotz, 2009, 314). This was an unsustainable trajectory. Once the last great bubble of the neoliberal era burst—as all bubbles eventually do—a financial crisis was bound to result.

The deregulated financial institutions own financing policies in the 2000s worsened the eventual crash. As the profits of financial institutions grew rapidly from their speculative activities, the urge to increase their rate of profit via increased leverage proved irresistible. While household debt relative to income doubled over the neoliberal era, the financial sector itself took on debt at an astonishing rate. Between 1980 and 2008, the ratio of financial-sector debt to GDP rose from 20 percent to 120 percent of GDP (US Federal Reserve System, 2009). As a result, when the housing bubble burst starting in 2006–07, it soon rendered many highly leveraged financial institutions insolvent.

Historical evidence suggests that a severe financial crisis tends to bring a relatively severe and long-lasting economic recession or period of stagnation. To this should be added the direct effect of an asset bubble collapse on the real sector. By 2007 about 40 percent of the $20 trillion market value of US housing was bubble-inflated fictitious wealth, according to one estimate (Baker, 2007, 8). The disappearance of some $8 trillion in housing wealth not only tends to bring a financial crisis but also tends to directly cause a real sector recession through the wealth effect on consumer spending.

## 7. Conclusions

The preceding analysis suggests several conclusions about financial crises. The neoliberal form of capitalism can promote economic expansion for a time, but it gives rise to unsustainable long-term trends that eventually set the stage for a severe financial crisis. The tendency of neoliberal capitalism to promote large asset bubbles also contains the direct seeds of a severe real-sector recession due to the effects on the real sector from the eventual bursting of large asset bubbles. Also, the history of past severe crises and their aftermath suggests that, once the neoliberal form of capitalism gives rise to a severe financial and economic crisis, the resolution of that crisis is likely to require major institutional restructuring, rather than just some policy adjustments within the framework of the existing form of capitalism.

There are also implications for the regulated form of capitalism. That form of capitalism may now appear as an attractive alternative to neoliberal capitalism. Regulated capitalism does not give rise to financial crises, and it also provides a wider sharing of the gains of economic growth. However, based on the historical experience of postwar-regulated capitalism, it appears that regulated capitalism, like neoliberal capitalism, has its own internal problems that prevent it from being indefinitely sustainable.

## Notes

1. In brief, the defining features of capitalism are the wage-labor relation and production for profit through exchange.
2. The new orthodoxy did not entirely shed the old reverence for market forces. The textbooks advocated taxes and subsidies over direct regulation wherever feasible to correct market failures, viewing taxes and subsidies as devices that worked through market forces rather than supplanting them.
3. The third part of the trilogy, stabilization, is based on the theory that inflation ultimately results from an excessive growth in the money supply that in turn is due to government budget deficits.

4. The prefix *neo* means new or new and different. In most of the world, the term "liberalism" had long referred to a policy or ideology of limited government intervention in markets. However, the United States is an exception—there, liberalism has the opposite meaning, causing much confusion in response to the term "neoliberalism" in the United States.
5. For an analysis of the varying degree of neoliberal restructuring and its implications, see Kotz and McDonough (2010).
6. The rate of change in such variables as wages and productivity over a long period are best measured from one business-cycle peak to another. Viewing neoliberal capitalism as established by the early 1980s, the year 1979 is the closest peak year (the next is 1990). The year 2007 was also a business-cycle peak year.
7. The often-heard calls for more flexible labor markets actually means more flexibility for only one side of the market—the employers—while workers are required to give up hard-won job rights.
8. Financial-sector profits continued to rise during 2003-2006, but nonfinancial-sector profits rose faster during that period.
9. Financialization is not the same as the finance capital relation that arose in the late nineteenth century. Finance capital involved a merger of financial and nonfinancial capital, with the former in the dominant position. Financialization entailed the separation of financial from nonfinancial capital. See Kotz (2011).
10. The so-called Financial Services Modernization Act of 1999, the last major financial deregulation bill, which banned the regulation of derivatives, was actively promoted by the Clinton administration's Secretary of the Treasury, Lawrence Summers, and was signed into law by President Bill Clinton.
11. For a detailed analysis of the effects of the housing bubble on consumer spending, see Kotz (2008, 2009b).

## References

Baker, Dean. (2007). *Midsummer Meltdown: Prospects for the Stock and Housing Markets.* Washington, DC: Center for Economic and Policy Research. www.cepr.net.

Bowles, Samuel, David M. Gordon, and Thomas E. Weisskopf. (1990). *After the Wasteland: A Democratic Economics for the Year 2000.* Armonk, NY: M. E. Sharpe.

*Economic Report of the President.* (1988). Washington, DC: US Government Printing Office.

Epstein, Gerald, ed. (2005). *Financialization and the World Economy.* Cheltenham, UK: Edward Elgar.

Greenspan, Alan, and James Kennedy. (2007). "Sources and Uses of Equity Extracted from Homes." Federal Reserve Board Finance and Economics Discussion Series No. 2007–20. http://www.federalreserve.gov/pubs/feds/2007/200720/200720pap.pdf.

Kotz, David M. (2002). "Globalization and Neoliberalism." *Rethinking Marxism* 14(2): 64–79.

Kotz, David M. (2003). "Neoliberalism and the U.S. Economic Expansion of the 1990s." *Monthly Review* 54(3): 15–33.

Kotz, David M. (2008). "Contradictions of Economic Growth in the Neoliberal Era: Accumulation and Crisis in the Contemporary U.S. Economy." *Review of Radical Political Economics* 40(2): 174–188.

Kotz, David M. (2009a). "Economic Crises and Institutional Structures: A Comparison of Regulated and Neoliberal Capitalism in the U.S." In Jonathan Goldstein and Michael Hillard, eds., *Heterodox Macroeconomics: Keynes, Marx and Globalization*, 176–188. London: Routledge.

Kotz, David M. (2009b). "The Financial and Economic Crisis of 2008: A Systemic Crisis of Neoliberal Capitalism." *Review of Radical Political Economics* 41(3): 305–317.

Kotz, David M. (2011). "Financialization and Neoliberalism." In Gary Teeple and Stephen McBride, eds., *Relations of Global Power: Neoliberal Order and Disorder*, 1–11. Toronto: University of Toronto Press.

Kotz, David M., and Terrence McDonough. (2010). "Global Neoliberalism and the Contemporary Social Structure of Accumulation." In Terrence McDonough, Michael Reich, and David M. Kotz, eds., *Contemporary Capitalism and Its Crises: Social Structure of Accumulation Theory for the Twenty First Century*, 93–120. Cambridge: Cambridge University Press.

Lucas, Robert E. Jr., and Leonard Rapping. (1969). "Real Wages, Employment, and Inflation." *Journal of Political Economy* 77(5): 721–754.

Madisson, Angus. (1995). *Monitoring the World Economy, 1820–1992*. Paris and Washington, DC: Development Center of the Organisation for Economic Cooperation and Development.

Marglin, Stephen, and Juliet Schor, eds. (1990). *The Golden Age of Capitalism: Reinterpreting the Postwar Experience*. Oxford: Clarendon Press.

Marx, Karl. (1967). *Capital: A Critical Analysis of Capitalist Production*. Volume I. New York: International Publishers.

Orhangazi, Ozgur. (2008). *Financialization and the U.S. Economy*. Cheltenham, UK: Edward Elgar.

Piketty, Thomas, and Emmanuel Saez. (2007). "Income Inequality in the United States, 1913–1998." Updated table A3. http://elsa.berkeley.edu/~saez/.

Samuelson, Paul M. (1948). *Economics: An Introductory Analysis*. New York: McGraw-Hill.

US Bureau of Economic Analysis. (2010). "National Income and Product Account Table 1.14." http://www.bea.gov.

US Bureau of Labor Statistics. (2009). "Series for Average Hourly Earnings of Non-supervisory Workers in 1982 Dollars and Series for Output per Hour in the Nonfarm Business Sector." http://www.bls.gov/.

US Census Bureau. (2010). "Current Population Survey, Annual Social and Economic Supplements." http://www.census.gov/hhes/www/income/data/historical/families/index.html.

US Federal Reserve System. (2009). "Flow of Funds Accounts, Z-1 Statistical Release." http://www.federalreserve.gov/.

Wolfson, Martin H., and David M. Kotz. (2010). "A Reconsideration of Social Structure of Accumulation Theory." In Terrence McDonough, Michael Reich, and David M. Kotz, eds., *Contemporary Capitalism and Its Crises: Social Structure of Accumulation Theory for the Twenty First Century*, 72–90. Cambridge: Cambridge University Press.

CHAPTER 20

# BANK LENDING AND THE SUBPRIME CRISIS

GARY DYMSKI

From the 30,000-foot level, the US subprime crisis resulted from some very elemental mistakes by banks. The 2007–2009 ruptures in the US financial system occurred because banks began making excessively risky subprime loans on housing in the 2000s. When these ruptures caused a stop to virtually all housing-related credit flows, the housing market slumped. This slump was initially triggered by widespread defaults on subprime mortgages; as overall housing prices declined, many households holding prime mortgage loans also went into foreclosure. This sharp decline ended a housing bubble in some parts of the country, and it led the US macroeconomy into a deep and prolonged recession.

When the causes of the subprime crisis are unfolded in this way, it seems a simple matter to assign blame. Fault can be divided among several suspects: myopic and/or greedy borrowers, mortgage brokers, and bank loan departments; inattentive regulators and ratings agencies; and ill-advised governmental supports for housing. In this retrospective view, it is no surprise that loans made on overvalued assets, with inadequate (or even zero) collateral to borrowers who often lacked the income to make payments, went bad. So the lessons to be learned are apparently very simple, even timeless: precautions against undue risk should guide loan making; well-informed regulators, bank owners, and liability holders should punish banks whose risk taking becomes excessive; and governmental intervention in the housing market should be minimized or eliminated. As John Gapper put it in the *Financial Times*, "If the president wants another Sputnik moment,...he should dare to dream of a free market in mortgages" (Gapper, 2011).

Most economists' reactions to and analyses of the subprime crisis have used this approach, treating this episode as another staging of a Greek tragedy. *This Time Is Different: Eight Centuries of Financial Folly*, the ironically titled and widely applauded study by Reinhart and Rogoff (2009), captured the primary sentiment: people episodically make huge errors involving asset bubbles, with disastrous financial consequences; it was ever thus, and so it ever will be.

The only difficulty with this oddly soothing conclusion is that this 30,000-foot view of the role of bank lending in the subprime crisis smoothes away institutional developments that precipitated an unprecedented sequence of bailouts and supports—with untold consequences for the future economic functionality of the financial system. Further, this view eliminates the historical context of the origination of subprime lending: the fact that its creation resulted from the triple intersection of the strategic transformation of US banking in the 1980s and 1990s, the financial exclusion experienced by racial/ethnic minorities, and the structure of global imbalances that emerged in the neoliberal era. There was nothing timeless about the subprime crisis: it emerged because a novel conjuncture of contradictory forces and stresses led first to the boom and then to the bust. And the consequences for the United States—the immense loss of wealth by households, especially racial/ethnic minorities, and the dysfunctionality of the financial system—will be felt for decades.

This chapter unfolds this largely overlooked story of how and why the transformation of bank lending led to the subprime crisis. To set up this story, the next section explains why many economists' analyses of the subprime crisis obviates the need for an institutional and historical approach to this subject. Then, in order, I examine the crisis of the US banking industry in the 1980s, the transformation of banks' strategies and of financial structure in the 1980s and 1990s, the shift from financial exclusion to exploitative inclusion for racial/ethnic minorities, risk shifting and the explosion of securitized debt, and finally the crisis itself.

## Why Economists Have Overlooked the Institutional Roots of the Subprime Crisis

At the risk of mischaracterizing the explosively growing economics literature on the subprime crisis, some central themes can be identified. A good starting point is the volume by Reinhart and Rogoff (2009); for these authors, what matters most about this crisis is not its individual determinants, but that it is one of a sequence of crises stretching back into the past. Each of these—the

Latin American debt crisis in the 1980s, the East Asian crisis of the 1990s, the debt buildup of US corporations in the 1980s, and so on—had its peculiarities, but ultimately each involves one common element: the conviction that "this time is different." In effect, human fallibility is the ultimate root. This fallibility, in turn, involves two interacting elements: the breakdown of optimistic assessments of future returns for the assets on which loans are based, and the inability of financial authorities to either prevent unwise lending or to compel borrowers to repay.[1] The breakdown of expectations can be due to the rise and then bursting of an asset bubble (Kindleberger, 1978), or in turn to a breakdown in confidence, generating a crash as one form of self-fulfilling prophecy (Farmer, 2010). And even in the absence of expectational errors or corrections, borrowing-lending relations can end in crisis when regulatory flaws reward (instead of preclude) perverse incentives.

Moral hazard is viewed as the problem most likely to emerge when regulation errs: agents will attempt to take too many risks—betting on success, against the odds—if they are insufficiently fearful of the consequences of an adverse outcome; or, agents whose bets went wrong may attempt to avoid paying. Most analysts (for example, Republican Commissioners, 2010) see moral hazard as an ever-present tendency in financial systems, because these systems use, in Louis Brandeis's (1914) term, "other people's money." Those whose money is being used, so to speak, may not be sufficiently vigilant; those "using" the money may have suspect motives or simply be willing to gamble.[2]

The specific mixture of factors that is active in any particular episode of financial crisis depends on circumstances that vary in time, by place, and by analytical perspective. Elliott and Baily (2009) note that three narratives have been constructed regarding who is to blame for the 2007-2009 financial crisis. One view blames government housing policies, a second view blames Wall Street for its "reckless behavior, greed, and arrogant belief in its own ability to understand and manage excessively complex investments" (page 3); a third view sees the crisis as "a very broad-based event with a wide range of people and institutions bearing responsibility, including many outside the United States" (page 4), including regulators and individual consumers and investors.

Why has economists' writing about subprime lending and its crisis largely overlooked its historical and institutional roots in banks' strategic shifts, racial inequality in financial (and housing) markets, and global imbalances? For one thing, the long and tangled US history of racial/ethnic discrimination in financial and housing markets is viewed by many economists as involving social factors not reducible to preferences, which are outside the boundaries of their discipline.[3] For example, the book-length analyses of the subprime crisis by Morris (2008) and Shiller (2008) make virtually no mention of the links between subprime lending and racial inequality.[4] Similarly, the discussions of the historical background of the subprime crisis in this and other economists' texts focus narrowly on the development of the market mechanisms involved, not of the broader tableau of social forces within which subprime lending (and predatory lending, more broadly) emerged.

In effect, many economists view their proper realm of investigation as "the economy," which reflects and is modified by the evolving social structure of human relations, but which is analytically separable. The Elliott-Baily depiction of the causes of the financial crisis has been widely accepted,[5] in part because it captures the emphasis of economists and policy makers on "mistakes and bad actions" (page 4) within the institutional structure that now exists for housing finance. By now, many accounts by economists and economic journalists have described what is known about the market mechanisms of subprime finance and how they failed.[6]

## The 1980s US Banking Crisis

After the Great Depression, the U.S. banking system was rebuilt in the 1930s on the principle of segmented markets.[7] Deposit and savings rates were controlled by governments, and only the richest households could move any funds outside the formal banking system. Different depository institutions provided for different financing and transaction needs: commercial banks provided transaction accounts and met business working-capital demand; savings and loan institutions provided time deposits and funded long-term, low-interest home mortgages. Because price competition was disallowed, competition took the form of customer-base maximization (within government-determined geographic market areas). This encouraged cross-subsidies: between rich and poor households in banks' deposit markets; and between larger, prosperous businesses and smaller "mom and pop" businesses in their loan portfolios.

The United States' segmented-market, administered-pricing, nowhere-to-exit banking approach led to bank-based credit flows. Commercial banks specialized in short-term loans for firms' working capital and in longer-term loans for business expansion; consumer credit was relatively rare. At the hub of the economy's growth process were the "thrifts"- savings-and-loan associations and mutual savings banks. Thrifts captured households' savings deposits and then used them to support mortgage lending for housing purchase and rehabilitation. Immediately after World War II, the federal Veterans Administration and Federal Housing Administration programs provided half of all housing finance; but over time, local thrifts' financing of local home purchases became part and parcel of the "American dream."

Banks in the 1960s held most household savings. But high and unstable interest rates in the 1970s led to disintermediation: banks lost funds to nonbank intermediaries that could pay market interest rates far exceeding banks' ceiling rates under Regulation Q. Money market mutual funds and a wide range of equity- and non-equity-based mutual funds were created, absorbing large portions of the savings of upper-income customers. This in turn encouraged the large firms who were traditionally banks' most profitable and creditworthy loan customers to borrow funds directly in credit markets. By the late 1970s, firms that had previously relied on banks for short-term credit largely borrowed in commercial credit markets. These firms also aggressively expanded corporate bond markets.

Banks compensated for the loss of their blue-chip loan customers by cutting costs and reshaping their strategies. The banks' first strategic reaction occurred in the late 1970s and early 1980s: they made many loans abroad, especially to Latin America. These loans were made in an increasingly stressed macroeconomic environment. The US economy slowed substantially at the end of the 1970s, even while price inflation and energy costs skyrocketed. The Federal Reserve intervened aggressively, and nominal interest rates rose to unprecedented nominal levels. This brought on even more profound micro and macroeconomic chaos, and it worsened disintermediation. Banks defended themselves in this unsettled environment by moving toward short-term and floating-rate loans. Debt payments for overseas debtors climbed into the stratosphere. The resulting recession, together with the discovery of new global sources of oil, led to the collapse of commodity prices.

Caught in the pincers of high interest rates, economic slowdown, and falling energy prices, Mexico—once Latin America's best hope for a commodity-led boom—defaulted on its debt obligations in August 1982. Other nations followed, pushed by lenders' reluctance to roll over their outstanding overseas credits. A debt crisis swept across Latin America. In the United States, high interest rates together with a deep recession undercut the viability of the US savings and loan industry. When fixed-rate deposits were replaced by market-rate borrowing, the thrifts' very long-term, fixed-interest rate loan commitments began to generate negative cash flows. The US government stepped in and orchestrated sales of both distressed thrifts and distressed commercial banks in hard-hit US oil-producing states.

## Bank Mergers and the Emergence of Upscale Retail Banking

The Latin American debt crisis devastated the balance sheets of most of the US money-center banks. These institutions had been so aggressive in making loans to Latin America that in some cases their net worth turned negative. Manufacturers Hanovers and Chemical ultimately disappeared; Citibank barely survived. The question was, what to do with a banking system with so many insolvent or nearly insolvent participants?

Wall Street helped the stronger money-center banks return to financial health. Much of the unpaid sovereign debt was securitized and taken off lenders' balance sheets (especially via Brady bonds). For insolvent savings and loans and oil-patch commercial banks, distress acquisitions by stronger domestic partners provided a way out. Permitting strong banks to merge with weak thrifts and commercial banks required changes in the legal framework governing banking. Laws prohibiting interstate banking were suspended and eventually repealed. Antitrust laws forbidding excessive concentration in bank deposit markets were also set aside. "Overbanking" could, in the eyes of bank regulators, be reduced without introducing market power as long as market "contestability" was maintained.

The distress mergers of the 1980s triggered a more general bank-merger wave, which has shrunk the number of US banks by more than half since 1980 (Dymski, 1999).[8] Superregional banks such as NationsBank and Bank America (which themselves merged in 1999) were created through merger strategies; over time, banks that spanned a region began to seek a nationwide reach. The banks that sought to take leading positions in the US banking industry made heavy investments in centralized databases and data-processing facilities. These investments facilitated a decisive strategic shift in both traditional banking practices and other financial services. In the credit market, the informational basis of loan making shifted from personal knowledge and character assessments to standardized assessments based on household assets, debts, and income levels.

This reshaped commercial banking and consumer lending. Banks turned away from cross-border loans, and instead, aggressively marketed domestic loan products such as credit cards and lines of credit, especially to prosperous middle-market customers. The same trend happened with innovative lower-cost or interest-plus deposit accounts, as well as money market and other mutual funds. Banks and nonbanks alike sought customers with secure income streams and substantial equity, who could be sold multiple financial instruments. In effect, upscale financial customers could access services and assets—such as mutual and hedge funds—previously only available to the wealthy. The growth of individualized retirement (401k) plans further boosted this strategic shift.

Facilitating this strategic shift was the explosive growth of markets for loan securitization. More and more categories and risk classifications of loans could be offloaded onto nonbank portfolios after being originated by bank or nonbank lenders. From the mid-1980s until the mid-2000s, the US complex of nonbank financial markets, funds, and instruments—Wall Street—far outpaced other global financial centers in size and sophistication. It offered globally privileged advantages of liquidity and underwriting.

The expansion of bank-supplied financial services and the growth of securitization led to a shift in the locus of bank income earning. For all banks, non-interest income grew from less than 30 percent of interest income to 75 percent by the 2000s; for large banks, fee-based and trading income typically vastly exceeds interest income. So for large banks, profits from their loan making were increasingly being generated not by interest earned over time but by fees earned on securitization. When these loans were provided to stable, multiproduct customers, banks' incentives were to ensure repayment capability. Because growing large banks like BankAmerica and Citi were creating standardized instruments suited for large customer bases, optimizing on the potential return from their investments meant finding more loyal, stable, multiproduct customers. This meant both competing to install new branches in areas where desirable customers could be found, and undertaking mergers and acquisitions. The end result of these competitive dynamics was a steady growth in the market share of a small set of mega-commercial banks: Chase, Citicorp, Bank of America, and Wells Fargo. Two of these four—Chase and Citi—were among the survivors of the group of money-center banks; they continued to compete in money-center operations even while building diversified consumer-banking operations.

What explains these strategic shifts? Dow and Smithin (1999, 87) argue that the increased uncertainty associated with globalization leads banks to put an increasing premium on "the need to establish trust and confidence in an uncertain environment." The increasing geographic scope of transactions makes it more and more difficult to find and identify zones of trust and confidence; consequently, most banks have turned toward proxies for trust/confidence. Standardized information provided a means of characterizing the reliability ("trust and confidence") of the economic units that ask them for credit or other financial services.

In the wake of the savings and loan crisis of the 1980s, the standardized assessments used to make loan decisions involved market-based assessments of assets used as collateral, as well as borrowers' income, other debt obligations, and credit history. Until the mid-1990s, the dividing line between economic units that qualified for "trust" and those that did not defined the point of bifurcation between those who were given ready access to upscale financial services and loans and those who were excluded from such access.[9] Standard units with standard homes in standard neighborhoods defined the front-line in banks' efforts to reduce uncertainty and compensate for the erosion of personalized trust relations. The best example of this use of standardized criteria was provided by the secondary-market facility provided by the Federal National Mortgage Association (FNMA). In the 1980s, the FNMA increased its capacity and accepted "plain vanilla" mortgages—mortgage loans that met certain requirements, involving loan-income ratios, 20 percent down payments, and so on. Initially, the only other mortgages that were sold onto secondary markets were "jumbo" loans exceeding the FNMA maxima; these mortgages were insured privately by a small number of specialized insurers.

The adoption of centralized information-processing technologies implementing these standardized assessment techniques permitted banks to expand the spatial market area in which their financial products could be marketed and sold. Because many banks developed such techniques, robust competition for standardized units' business emerged: margins in lending to or conducting transactions with these units were driven down.

The space for other forms of financial intermediation was not completely squeezed by the emergence of this new consumer banking. Indeed, between 1999 and 2007, one new bank charter was issued in the United States for every two banks that disappeared in unassisted mergers. The most important niche markets for newcomer banks involved converting localized knowledge about local businesses into loans (including, in some cities, ethnic banks).

## From Financial Exclusion to Exploitative Financial Inclusion

How were households and businesses outside the upscale retail category treated in this changed financial world? Economic units falling outside "standard" categories, who don't meet the test for super-inclusion—those with low or unstable incomes, those living in "substandard" areas or structures, and so on—were obliged to pay their own way. Whatever cross-subsidies existed previously were eliminated. They were charged high prices for financial services; these prices included both premia for risks that could not be readily assessed and offloaded and premia imposed because of monopolistic pricing policies. Banks have often offered services to these nonstandard customers indirectly—through subsidiaries, through the provision of finance to firms operating subprime financial services, and so on.

Banking systems have always been unevenly distributed over space and across customer classes. While restrictions on price competition provided banks with competitive incentives to maximize their customer bases, racial and other forms of discrimination still led them to ignore and underserve some areas. Many lower-income households maintained whatever cash they have "under the mattress" and are unbanked. For these units, payment transactions were accomplished by utilizing cash, money-order services, and check cashers. Borrowing was done by bringing durable goods to pawnshops or obtaining high-cost credit from finance companies. These households were subject to *financial exclusion* in that they do not have access to the same financial services that the average household can obtain, at the prices the average household pays; they had the use of fewer services, and they paid more for the ones received.

The strategic shifts undertaken by large banks in the 1980s had several implications for banking in lower-income areas. While branches were opened in upscale areas, they were closed in lower-income areas. Because lower-income customers purchase fewer high-end financial products than upper-income customers, so bank branches remaining in lower-income areas functioned less as mechanisms for pooling savings and more as vehicles for generating fee-based revenues (Dymski and Veitch, 1996).

Paralleling bank-branch closures in lower-income communities were growing tiers of nonbank suppliers of financial services, offering high-price substitutes for services that formal-sector banks provide more cheaply elsewhere, in areas that formal-sector banks had abandoned. Credit flows, which elsewhere facilitate the accumulation of new human or physical assets in the primary sector, instead led to asset deaccumulation. These institutional gaps reflect long-standing patterns of racial and ethnic inequality and discrimination.

Until the 1990s, financial infrastructure in lower-income areas largely operated independently of the structures of formal-sector banking. The check cashers and loan stores in areas without bank branches were all locally funded and operated. But in the 1990s, things changed (Barr, 2004). Advances in securitization technology, and new procedures for pricing and off-loading risk—the same factors that supported the explosive growth of upscale retail banking—transformed informal finance. Increasingly, the fees collected in the informal sector, and the loans made there, were collected directly or indirectly by megabanks, generating fees for Wall Street firms.

Technological change and business consolidation transformed the landscape of cash management and payments by lower-income households. The markets for cash cards grew explosively, and mobile banking grew as well (though more slowly than in Africa and Latin America). Large banks and ethnic banks began to compete for the remittance business of the many US migrant workers, a market they had previously ignored.

Check-cashing stores were increasingly operated as franchises; they developed routinized links with parent corporations, which in turn were often subsidiaries of large banks. These upstream connections routinized their access to funds. As these stores moved from a cash basis to a funding basis, they began extending credit to their customers, especially via payday and tax-refund anticipation loans. These loans were, by the mid-1990s, classified by activists as "predatory lending": loans whose high interest rates, high fees, onerous nonpayment penalties, and short maturities make them both substantially more expensive than primary-market loans and also far more likely to end in default (or punitive rollover). While lenders viewed these harsh terms as justified by borrowers' riskiness, community activists were alarmed that their many years of advocacy for equal access to credit had succeeded only in opening the way to exploitative financial inclusion.

By the 1990s, subprime mortgage loans already emerged as the most well-known form of predatory lending. Initially, subprime loans were marketed in minority neighborhoods, whose residents had often been denied access to mortgage financing. In some cases, these loans were sold as second mortgages to cash-poor, house-rich homebuyers. In other cases, minority loan applicants who previously would have been denied a home-purchase loan were provided with one—though this loan might have higher carrying costs, higher fees, and create more risk of loss than a conventional mortgage loan. In the United States, subprime loans grew by 900 percent between 1993 and 1999 (HUD, 2000). They were made disproportionately in minority neighborhoods. A nationwide study of 2000 HMDA data by Bradford (2002) found that African Americans were, on average, twice as likely as whites to receive subprime loans, and Latinos were nearly twice as likely.[10]

It should be noted that what has facilitated the growth of predatory and subprime lending is the continued growth of secondary markets for these instruments. Banks and the other lenders who make these loans did not hold them; they were combined, repackaged, and sold off, often with guarantees provided by a third party. This reflected the expansion of what is now commonly known as the "originate-to-distribute" model of loan making, which relied on a "chain" of financial-market participants that minimally included "originators, arrangers, distributors and managers" (Financial Stability Forum, 2008, 8). This model was already accounting for most "plain vanilla" home-mortgage loans by the late 1980s. The next jump was from low-risk to high-risk securitization. "Plain vanilla" securities were virtually risk-free due to the tight restrictions on debt-payment-to-income and loan-to-value ratios: borrowers' incomes could decline without precipitating default, and the 20 percent down-payment requirement provided a large collateral cushion for absorbing shocks to home prices. Further, it was understood by market participants—though never put on paper—that the government-sponsored enterprises (GSEs) that underwrote a large share of the securities were operating under an implicit government guarantee. But now securitization moved into risk. The key was the creation of the structured investment vehicle (SIV). This instrument, invented in 1988 for Citibank, permitted banks to fund higher-yield paper using commercial paper, off-balance sheet (Mollenkamp et al., 2007).

And it was not only large commercial banks were interested in this paper. New investment vehicles, especially hedge and private-equity funds, were growing quickly into sizable players. The long period of US current-account deficits led to systematic capital-account surpluses; while foreign investors typically steered toward safety, the financial markets were awash with liquidity. Meanwhile, the lax regulatory philosophy of Congress and the Federal Reserve encouraged this innovation with little or no oversight. The Gramm-Leach-Bliley Act repealed the Glass-Steagall Act's firewalls between investment and commercial banking, and it also eliminated the BHC prohibition of combinations among banks, securities companies, and insurance companies. This not only cleared the way for a $70 billion deal that created the world's largest financial services firm (*Wall Street Journal*, April 13, 1998), but also created many more possibilities for large financial firms to participate in this market.

Another critical move was the passage of the Commodity Futures Modernization Act of 2000; this act clarified that most over-the-counter derivatives transactions would be overseen under general federal "safety and soundness" guidelines and would not be subject to either the CFTC or to laws governing financial securities. This act permitted the expansion of over-the-counter derivatives, including derivatives written on the securities created from risky paper (such as subprime mortgages).

The regulatory attitude of the Federal Reserve toward subprime credit was made eminently clear through its passivity. Concerned about the spread of predatory lending—especially subprime loans whose trigger mechanisms often resulted in dispossession—Congress passed the Homeownership Equity Protection Act in 1994. However, the Federal Reserve, which was charged with writing regulations to implement the act, dragged its feet. Alan Greenspan, who was Federal Reserve Chairman in the 1990s, asserted in 2010 under testimony (Greenspan, 2010, 13–14) that the Federal Reserve had been unclear about which portions of the market were covered under the legislation; however, he also noted that the Federal Reserve regarded this act as inappropriately throttling the emerging subprime market, which promised to extend credit to new classes of borrowers.

So borrowers in predatory and subprime loan markets participated indirectly in all the machinations of Wall Street's cash-flow-bundling and risk-redistribution apparatus. The financial exploitation that in the past would have involved localized oppression was now conducted via the routinized extraction of excess interest and fees by megabanks and mutual funds.

## Booming Housing Prices, Stagnating Incomes, Subprime Crisis

The institutional plumbing required for securitizing predatory credit was not created for the sole purpose of extracting fees and wealth from lower-income neighborhoods and people of color. These institutional mechanisms were used to offload many other kinds of debt, including credit-card debt, automobile loans, student loans, and manufactured housing loans. By the end of the 1990s, nearly $1 trillion of asset-backed securities were outstanding (FCIC, 2011, 45). So originate-to-distribute lending took off.

The stage was then set for the creation of a global financial crisis—at the root of which, as we have seen, is the bifurcation between upscale and low-end customers that emerged in the past two decades. The first step in this crisis occurred when US housing prices began an ascent to unprecedented levels relative to income, in the early 2000s. The housing-price bubble in a number of US submarkets—California, Nevada, Arizona, and Florida especially prominent among them—created a challenge for lenders. The incomes of prospective homebuyers grew far more slowly than did housing prices. Conventional, "plain vanilla" loans—which required strict ratios of down payments to loans, and of debt burden to income—would not permit these prospects to get into the housing market.

Fortuitously, the subprime loan mechanism that had been developed for minority areas provided the solution: that is, loans whose higher risks were due to low down payments and which carried high prospective rates could be originated and sold, just as higher-risk loans had been for homes in declining urban neighborhoods. The character of this exceptional risk simply had to be reframed. In making subprime loans to existing and prospective homeowners in lower-income and minority areas, lenders offset the insecurity of borrowers' incomes with the security offered by a home whose value far exceeded the loan on that home.

As the housing boom proceeded in some areas, even less weight could be put on borrowers' incomes (famously, many loans were made without borrowers even declaring their incomes); the current and future expected value of the home that represented lenders' collateral bore ever more weight. Indeed, so certain did lenders—or more accurately, the loan brokers acting as their representatives—in some markets become that they would arrange loan-payment terms for an introductory period that would not cover the longer-term carrying cost of the amount borrowed. This anticipation that the entire loan could be refinanced in two years—at which point the home (collateral) would have jumped appreciably in value. Loan contracts of this type became especially prevalent in areas with skyrocketing housing prices—in California, for example, half of all mortgage loans made in 2005 and 2006 were made with no down payments and with low introductory rates. These subprime loans failed the "plain vanilla" test in several ways and thus were made with high fees, large penalties for nonpayment, and so on.

The term "lender" here requires explanation. As with any loan, the creation of a loan contract generates a set of borrower repayment obligations that an entity that has resources to commit is willing to take on. In the old banking architecture, this lender was local and had ongoing contact with the borrower. In the securitization architecture, this lender had no contact with the borrower. The relationship was intermediated by a mortgage broker, and certified, bundled, and sold off to a third party that knew nothing about the borrower. So the megabank that orchestrated the transaction was not the lender; in some sense, the "lender" disappears from view in the originate-to-distribute model. This is one thing when well-collateralized, government-underwritten mortgages are involved, as in the mortgage-backed securities market that grew into a global giant in the 1980s. It is another thing when the loans involved are high-risk.

Risk was indeed a concern not only because of default, but also because the underlying mortgages could be paid off early, retired due to home sales, and so on. Risk was handled in two ways. First, securities bundlers and buyers relied on credit-rating agencies' certification of the security's default-risk level. The sterling reputation of Wall Street credit-rating agencies made this a nearly automatic prospect.[11] Second, risk was also insured against via the derivatives market. As noted, the 2000 Commodity Futures Modernization Act of 2000 gave the green light to the expanded use of derivatives, especially over-the-counter derivatives. Strides in computability and the increasing volume in the asset-backed securities markets led a number of underwriters to develop insurance mechanisms. Most famously, AIG used derivatives known as credit default swaps to "insure" the paper written by its megabank customers. While they worked like insurance for the sellers, credit default swaps had the advantage of requiring no good-faith money; as long as housing prices rose, AIG could treat its swaps as money-for-nothing. The creation of credit default swaps meant a new field of play for the zero-sum derivatives-market games that hedge funds, megabanks, and other players play in modern financial markets. These players soon made bets on "synthetic" subprime securities—that is, not on securities that really existed, but on notional securities with the characteristics of "real" securities. This, of course, permitted players in this arena to become hugely leveraged.

While California, Florida, Nevada, and other locales with exploding home prices attracted most of the media attention, a large share of mortgage lending in other areas also involved subprime contracts. In US rust-belt cities like Cleveland and Detroit, many households borrowed against their homes—sometimes more than once—to offset declining incomes. Not only were union-wage jobs being lost in these cities, but family emergencies and more costly health-care-generated cash-flow needs often could be met only by remortgaging the household's primary source of net worth, its home. In many other areas home prices did not explode, but rose steadily, without incomes keeping pace. In California, for example, housing prices steadily climbed in "affordable" areas, faster than the modest incomes of the households trying to buy homes there. Housing developers accommodated, turning dusty small cities in the San Joaquin Valley, Inland Empire, and Coachella Valley into ready-made suburban-tract expanses.

When rising housing prices and strained household incomes in the 2000s made "plain vanilla" mortgage loans unobtainable for many potential homebuyers, the numbers of people applying for subprime lending rose; at its peak in 2006, it accounted for 23.5 percent of the market (FCIC, 2011, 70). Households in minority areas were disproportionately targeted for subprime loans, even when they could have qualified for prime loans. The extensive residential racial/ethnic segregation of US cities had the effect of multiplying the impact of subprime lending in minority neighborhoods: these loans were concentrated there, and residents in segregated neighborhoods were more likely to receive subprime loans (Rugh and Massey, 2010).

Two *Wall Street Journal* reporters (Brooks and Simon, 2007) showed that loan brokers pushed subprime loans onto borrowers who qualified for plain vanilla loans. Behind this "subprime" pushing, in at least some cases, were incentive systems that paid brokers higher fees for subprime than for prime loans (Hudson, 2010).

In 2007, housing prices stopped growing and started falling. At that point, speculative position taking by market insiders versus the uninformed overwhelmed the housing-financing activities. Some of the megabanks at the heart of the subprime securitization markets, in the words of *New York Times* reporters (Morgenson and Story, 2009), "bundled bad debt, bet against it, and won"—that is, banks such as Goldman Sachs continued to earn fees from new subprime securitizations even as they "shorted" the credit default swap market.

As refinancing unpayably high mortgages became nonviable, the subprime market crashed. This triggered margin calls on hundreds of billions of dollars of derivatives contracts whose interlaced contingent payments (to and from counterparties elsewhere in the financial markets) depended on the market valuation of securities containing subprime mortgages. The unchecked position taking in derivatives markets on "synthetic" as well as "real" subprime securities meant that realized risk often far exceeded these funds' capital.[12] This risk skyrocketed as secondary markets for subprime securities disappeared. As megabanks were forced to take this paper back onto their books—at hugely discounted prices—megabanks' balance sheets and stock prices also swooned. Virtually every large Wall Street institution became at least technically insolvent at some point during the resulting debacle that played out in late 2008 and early 2009 (Lohr, 2009).

## Why Did Subprime Lending Become "Mainstream" in the Mid-2000s?

Leaving aside the excessive speculation due to Wall Street firms' position taking in derivatives markets, it is worth considering why subprime lending spread beyond the boundaries of the minority and lower-income communities in which it—and other forms of predatory lending—originated. For a period of time—the mid-2000s—subprime mortgage loans were not reserved for the desperate and the uninformed, but instead they became virtually a new "normal." Why did this happen?

Four characteristics of the emerging world of globalized finance facilitated subprime loan making in both types of areas—and encouraged the spread of subprime loans throughout far more of the US housing market than was warranted. One was the housing boom itself; uncertainty about housing values, and the growing desperation of those not yet "in the market," accelerated demand for these loans. Second, the proliferation of financial wealth managers seeking to exceed the market rate of return, together with plentiful short-term liquidity, ensured the supply of credit to support these loans. Indeed, so attractive were these securitized funds as investment outlets that banks, hedge funds, and private-equity funds created a variety of innovative, opaque financial instruments—such as SIVs (structured investment vehicles) and CDOs (collateralized debt obligations)—as vehicles for boosting their cash flow.

A third characteristic encouraging the proliferation of loan making that disregarded tried-and-true risk assessments was the institutional fragmentation of credit processes. Loan making once involved assessing risk, lending funds, and holding those funds until loans were retired. This process became disarticulated: the assessment of risk, the lending of funds, the servicing of loans, and the holding of loans all are done by different financial-market players. Accentuating this trend is the fragmentation of the housing-market process: different players assess home values, sell the homes, repossess them, and resell them. While much of the media commentary on the subprime crisis has focused on "people who shouldn't have bought homes," a number of the industry players involved in the housing/mortgage nexus have perverse incentives; to cite the most egregious example, credit-rating agencies and assessors are paid by lenders and thus have incentives to minimize risk and maximize the home values built into loans.

The fourth and final characteristic that fueled the subprime bubble was the process identified above as the banks' key response to their 1980s crisis: standardization. Standardization evolved in the 1990s and early 2000s: once it had been a means of guaranteeing that the payment obligations bundled together in mortgage-backed securities were relatively homogeneous. Standardization then emerged as a strategy for constructing heterogeneous portfolios whose aggregate risk-and-return characteristics could be sold as unitary commodities to financial wealth holders (including, of course, SIVs and CDOs). The success of widespread mortgage-market securitization in the 1980s—including, crucially, not just FNMA-backed paper but also securities based on "jumbo loans"—led to ready market acceptance of securities of diverse types. Wealth holders seeking a higher return than FNMA-backed securities came to disregard the underlying risk of buying privately guaranteed portfolios of subprime loans.

These four factors accentuated the strategic shifts of banking described above. Not only were banks engaged in pursuing distinct deposit and financial-service customer bases with customized financial services; they increasingly sought to augment their earnings by purchasing and financing packages of SIVs and CDOs, either on their own account or through subsidiaries. Just as the success of megabanks such as Citi and Bank of America in pursuing upscale retail customers forced banks worldwide to make strategic adjustments, the success of some banks in boosting their earnings from SIV/CDO investments created an imitation effect that was also itself global, as the experiences of Iceland's banks, Ireland's banks, and the British bank Northern Rock indicate. That explains why some of the first signs that US subprime lending might generate a global financial crisis appeared in funds operated by European banks.

## Conclusion

This chapter has focused attention on some of the overlooked causes of the subprime crisis. We have shown how strategic shifts initiated by US megabanks in the 1980s led to the transformation of consumer banking and to the nature of bank lending itself; these changes in turn gave rise to subprime lending and finally to the subprime crisis.

In the 1980s, disintermediation, the Latin American debt crisis, and the savings-and-loan crisis forced basic shifts in the US financial system. The basis of housing finance was transformed from intermediaries' savings deposits to securities markets. Large banks developed models of financial-service delivery based on the use of standardized information in centralized databases to make customer-segment-specific decisions regarding the terms and conditions of credit, savings, and transaction accounts, and on the increasing use of loan securitization as a means of offloading risk and maintaining predictable cash flows. Banks' returns from this approach were enhanced by acquisitions of bank and nonbank financial firms to extend their customer bases.

The existence of sophisticated securitization mechanisms, customer databases, and wealth owners (largely funds) willing to hold higher-risk/higher-return securities then facilitated the megabanks' entry into serving markets they had previously shunned, especially racial/ethnic minorities and lower-income areas. Further innovations in securitization, combined with shifts in potential customer markets, gave rise to several forms of "predatory lending," one of which was subprime lending. As securitization took off, a housing-market boom led to the wider use of subprime loans to finance housing in the broader market. The mechanisms used to offset risk in this market backfired and instead gave rise to an unregulated speculative market in derivatives whose implosion was one reason that the resulting financial crisis proved so severe.

Arguably, each of these three causes has had (and continues to have) profound consequences for the economic and social efficiency of bank lending in the United States. Lawmakers in Washington treated the breakdown of the securitization-based system for supplying credit as the equivalent of the breakdown of all bank-lending capacity. This was demonstrably not the case, but this framing had important consequences for the distribution of federal assistance, including the de facto awarding of too-big-to-fail status on a small number of privileged intermediaries. Because such a disproportionate share of subprime loans were made to racial/ethnic minorities, who are subject even today to substantial racial/ethnic segregation, the systematic failures of subprime loans—leading, often, to foreclosures, repossession, and/or short sales—will have a profound impact on the racial/ethnic distribution of net worth and thus on the economic prospects of the next generation of racial/ethnic minority residents. In turn, during and after the crisis, huge public subsidies have been provided to large banks, directly and indirectly, in exchange for only marginal changes in their activities. This ensures that the dysfunctional financial architecture, which so quickly emerged in the 2000s as a complement to the growth of subprime lending, built on overleveraging and immense levels of liquidity risk, will not be reformed. Bank lending is now the equivalent of a dog that is wagged by its tail—in this case, by megabanks' zero-sum position taking in derivatives markets. Megabanks' use of their positional power to protect their privileges detracts from efforts to restore the economic and social efficiency of their core banking operations.

In the end, for all the sophistication of the financial machinery that underlay it, the fact remains that the subprime credit market was a social construction, whose fragilities led to its breakdown and failure. In effect, the creation of a new set of technical apparatuses for transforming credit instruments—and making fees along the way—required a series of profound interventions into particularly fragile layers of the US social system, layers in which having access to employment and education and security is already problematic.

## Notes

1. Reinhart and Rogoff (2009, chap. 4).
2. Ironically, Chief Justice Brandeis used this term to point to a historically specific problem in early twentieth-century United States—"our financial oligarchy." The literature on moral hazard assumes that the impulse to cheat arises preinstitutionally, as a consequence of the interaction of human motivation and risk-reward structures.
3. On why economists missed the social dimensions of the financial crisis, see Dymski (2010a). The caveat "not reducible to preferences" is necessary because even economists most committed to the market model have been quite willing to analyze social phenomena (such as discrimination) in the context of preference orderings. The classic example is Becker (1971).
4. These two sources were chosen because in late 2008—after this chapter was in a final form—a number of analysts, such as Calomiris (2008), began to assert that the Community Reinvestment Act (CRA) and governmental insistence that banks make socially responsive loans injected these issues into economists' discussions. In any case, racial inequality was mentioned by economists only in passing, in the context of whether the CRA had forced banks to lend to risky borrowers (and thus forced them to create subprime loans). See Dymski (2010b).
5. See Wallison (2010); Thomas, Hennessey, and Holtz-Eakin (2011).
6. See, among many others, Rajan (2010) and Lewis (2010). A book whose approach is closer to the approach taken here is Johnson and Kwak (2010).
7. The material in this section draws heavily on Dymski (1999).
8. After 1987, unassisted mergers have never fallen below the annual level of 3 percent of all existing banks; at the peak of the merger wave, over 6 percent of all commercial banks disappeared both in 1997 and 1998.
9. Dow and Smithin predicted this bifurcation as well, on the basis of the banks' need to protect their basic monetary assets: "The fragility of the credit system calls into question the reliability of one or another substitute exchange media; so the development of a hierarchical financial system is likely...continued activity in the economy implies a need to judge the quality of individual promises to pay on an ongoing basis. This is what determines the need for a basic monetary asset" (1999, 87–88).

10. This likelihood remained stable until the market crashed in late 2007; see, for example, Avery, Brevoort, and Canner (2007) on the racial/ethnic distribution of prime and subprime lending in 2006.
11. In retrospect, it came out that this system was deeply flawed: megabanks could "shop" for ratings, or overrule agencies' rejections, and even subject them to fraud (FCIC, chap. 9).
12. Lewis (2010) provides detail on behavior in the derivatives markets associated with subprime lending.

## References


Avery, Robert B., Kenneth P. Brevoort, and Glenn B. Canner. (2007). "The 2006 HMDA Data." *Federal Reserve Bulletin* 93 (December 2007): A107-A136.

Barr, Michael. (2004). "Banking the Poor." *Yale Journal on Regulation* 21(121): 121–239.

Becker, Gary. (1971). *The Economics of Discrimination*. 2nd ed. Chicago: University of Chicago Press.

Bradford, Calvin. (2002). *Risk or Race? Racial Disparities and the Subprime Refinance Market*. Washington, DC: Center for Community Change.

Brandeis, Louis D. (1914). *Other People's Money: And How the Bankers Use It*. New York: F. A. Stokes.

Brooks, Rick, and Ruth Simon. (2007). "Subprime Debacle Traps Even Very Credit-Worthy: As Housing Boomed, Industry Pushed Loans to a Broader Market." *Wall Street Journal*, December 3, A1.

Calomiris, Charles W. (2008). "The Subprime Turmoil: What's Old, What's New, and What's Next." Working Paper, American Enterprise Institute, October.

Dow, Sheila, and Neil Smithin. (1999). "The Structure of Financial Markets and the 'First Principles' of Monetary Policy." *Scottish Journal of Political Economy* 46(1): 72–90.

Dymski, Gary A. (1999). *The Bank Merger Wave*. Armonk, NY: M. E. Sharpe.

Dymski, Gary A. (2010a). "Development as Social Inclusion: Reflections on the US Subprime Crisis." *Development* 53(3): 368–75.

Dymski, Gary A. (2010b). "Understanding the Subprime Crisis: Institutional Evolution and Theoretical Views." Kirwan Institute for the Study of Race and Ethnicity, Ohio State University, March.

Dymski, Gary A., and John M. Veitch. (1996). "Financial Transformation and the Metropolis: Booms, Busts, and Banking in Los Angeles." *Environment and Planning A* 28(7): 1233–1260.

Elliott, Douglas J., and Martin Neil Baily. (2009). "Telling the Narrative of the Financial Crisis: Not Just a Housing Bubble." Brookings Institution, November 23. www.brookings.edu/papers/2009/1123_narrative_elliott_baily.aspx.

Farmer, Roger. (2010). *Expectations, Employment, and Prices*. Oxford: Oxford University Press.

Financial Crisis Inquiry Commission (FCIC). (2011). *The Financial Crisis Inquiry Report*. Washington, DC: US Government Printing Office.

Financial Stability Forum. (2008). *Report of the Financial Stability Forum on Enhancing Market and Institutional Resilience*. Basel, Switzerland, April 7. http://www.financialstabilityboard.org/publications/r_0804.pdf.

Gapper, John. (2011). "Take Fannie and Freddie Off the Road." *Financial Times*, January 27.

Greenspan, Alan. (2010). "Testimony of Alan Greenspan—Financial Crisis Inquiry Commission." Financial Crisis Inquiry Commission Hearing on Subprime Lending and Securitization and Government-Sponsored Enterprises (GSEs), Day 1, April 7. http://cybercemetery.unt.edu/archive/fcic/20110310173928/http://c0182412.cdn1.cloudfiles.rackspacecloud.com/2010-0407-Greenspan.pdf.

Housing and Urban Development (HUD). (2000). *Unequal Burden: Income and Racial Disparities in Subprime Lending in America*. Washington, DC: Department of Housing and Urban Development.

Hudson, Michael W. (2010). *The Monster: How a Gang of Predatory Lenders and Wall Street Bankers Fleeced America—and Spawned a Global Crisis*. New York: Times Books, 2010.

Johnson, Simon, and James Kwak. (2010). *13 Bankers: The Wall Street Takeover and the Next Financial Meltdown*. New York: Pantheon, 2010.

Kindleberger, Charles P. (1978). *Manias, Panics, and Crashes: A History of Financial Crises*. New York: Basic Books, 1978.

Lewis, Michael. (2010). *The Big Short: Inside the Doomsday Machine*. New York: W. W. Norton, 2010.

Lohr, Steve. (2009). "Ailing Banks May Require More Aid to Keep Solvent." *New York Times*, February 13.

Mollenkamp, Carrick, Deborah Solomon, Robin Sidel, and Valerie Bauerlein. (2007). "Gordian Knot: How London Created a Snarl in Global Markets: SIVs Fueled Debt Boom, but Now Banks Scramble to Prop Up the Funds." *Wall Street Journal*, October 18, A1.

Morgenson, Gretchen, and Louise Story. (2009). "Banks Bundled Bad Debt, Bet against It and Won." *New York Times*, December 24, A1.

Morris, Charles R. (2008). *The Trillion Dollar Meltdown: Easy Money, High Rollers, and the Great Credit Crash*. New York: PublicAffairs.

Rajan, Raghuram G. (2010). *Fault Lines: How Hidden Fractures Still Threaten the World Economy*. Princeton: Princeton University Press.

Reinhart, Carmen, and Kenneth Rogoff. (2009). *This Time Is Different: Eight Centuries of Financial Folly*. Princeton: Princeton University Press.

Republican Commissioners on the Financial Crisis Inquiry Commission. (2010). *Financial Crisis Primer: Questions and Answers on the Causes of the Financial Crisis*. Washington, DC,: American Enterprise Institute, December 15. http://www.aei.org/papers/economics/fiscal-policy/financial-crisis-primer-questions-and-answers-on-the-causes-of-the-financial-crisis/

Rugh, Jacob S., and Douglas S. Massey. (2010). "Racial Segregation and the American Foreclosure Crisis." *American Sociological Review* 75(5): 629–651.

Shiller, Robert J. (2008). *The Subprime Solution*. Princeton: Princeton University Press.

Thomas, Bill, Keith Hennessey, and Douglas Holtz-Eakin. (2011). "What Caused the Financial Crisis?" *Wall Street Journal*, January 27, A21.

Wallison, Peter J. (2010). "Slaughter of the Innocents: Who Was Taking the Risks That Caused the Financial Crisis?" *AEI Financial Services Outlook* November–December: 1–9.

CHAPTER 21

# DEREGULATION AND THE NEW FINANCIAL ARCHITECTURE

DAMON SILVERS

THE global financial crisis that began in 2007 had its roots in a global financial landscape that was significantly different from that which had existed during the postwar years. Technology and innovation were significant contributors to the transformation of the global financial architecture. But regulatory change in the form of deregulation was at the heart of the particular shape that the world's financial markets took in the post-cold war era. The United States, home to the world's largest capital markets and the world's largest pools of savings, was the trendsetter in financial deregulation. This chapter looks at the role of deregulation in the financial crisis through the prism of the US experience. The United States had the most developed regulatory structure in the postwar era, and it led the way in dismantling that structure, though in a sense the first move was the collapse of the postwar currency regulation system in 1971. Other countries undertook similar efforts, ranging from the privatization of financial institutions in a range of countries, to establishment of equity markets in former Communist countries, to the liberalization of securities markets in the United Kingdom's Big Bang in the 1980s. But the United States set the tone, and ultimately, the consequences in the United States triggered the global financial and economic crisis.

There is a larger story of policy change that is beyond the scope of this chapter but is central to understanding the financial crisis. That is the story of how, following 1970 global labor-market deregulation, "structural adjustment," the global trading regime, and national tax policies combined to repress workers' incomes and to increase economic insecurity and economic inequality. The mirage that finance could create income was a response to the lack of income itself among the working majorities of the world, particularly in the United States. But that story is too large for this chapter.

## The Postwar Regulatory Scheme and the Resulting Financial Architecture

Following the Crash of 1929 and the Great Depression, the United States adopted a comprehensive financial regulatory scheme. The intellectual roots of this regime lay in diverse sources—some as old as the American Republic itself. The New Deal regulatory system owed something to Thomas Jefferson's fundamental skepticism of the power of finance. There was also something about the core ideas of the New Deal that reflected in the financial space the fundamental political insight of the Federalist Papers—that dividing powerful institutions is critical to maintaining liberty. More direct intellectual contributors to the New Deal system included Justice Louis Brandeis, Ferdinand Pecora, Adolph Berle and Gardiner Means, and John Maynard Keynes. Brandeis's concepts of regulation through transparency and decentralization in finance—best remembered through his maxim that "sunlight is the strongest disinfectant"—were central concepts of New Deal securities and banking regulation. Pecora's hearings built the case for dividing investment and commercial banking and punishing speculators. Finally, Berle and Means's analysis of that new thing the public corporation demonstrated that private investors on their own were unlikely to be effective overseers of public corporations' increasingly powerful management.

Among the lessons policy makers took from the combination of these intellectual influences and their experience of the Crash of 1929 and its aftermath were (1) that deposit insurance was necessary for a stable banking system; (2) that insured deposits should not be lent out to traders in securities markets; (3) that overall leverage and short selling needed to be limited to ensure stable securities markets, and that unsophisticated investors investing in pooled accounts should not pursue strategies requiring either buying on margin or short selling; (4) that housing finance should be predominantly long-term fixed-rate loans, which could be made only by banks with government assistance in the form of government-sponsored mortgage intermediaries; (5) that government should encourage savings to be invested through insured banks in loans to operating businesses and homeowners, rather than in the capital markets or in uninsured financial institutions like brokerages; (6) that securities markets should be transparent and fair to small investors; and (7) that markets for both currencies and gold should be limited.

These insights were embodied in a series of landmark pieces of financial legislation in the 1930s—including the Glass-Steagall Act, the Federal Deposit Insurance Corporation Act, the Securities Act, the Securities Exchange Act, the Investment Company Act, and a series of statutes that created the Federal National Mortgage Corporation, the Federal Home Loan Banks, and the federal system of savings banks with the purpose of channeling household savings into the housing market. The international currency system was regulated through the Bretton Woods Treaty system, administered in substantial part by the International Monetary Fund (IMF).

The New Deal regulatory system was explicitly designed both to lower the risk of financial crises and to direct savings toward productive investment and away from speculative activity. It was a system that involved mandated transparency, prudential regulation, explicit subsidies and guarantees for certain types of institutions—particularly banks, outright bans on certain types of transactions—naked insurance contracts, securities transactions with margins over 50 percent, short selling by mutual funds—and the separation of what had been relatively homogeneous financial markets into clear silos: distinct capital markets with distinct purposes and regulatory systems.

## The Intellectual Roots of Deregulation

At one level, the intellectual roots of deregulation were simply old ideas returned to fashion—the economic philosophy of the mid-nineteenth century resurrected with political passion by philosophers like Hayek and economists like Milton Friedman. As memories of the Depression faded, Friedman in particular, through his *Monetary History of the United States*, profoundly affected economists' understanding of what had caused the Great Depression, shifting the debate from one about Wall Street booms and busts and Keynesian aggregate demand to one about simple and obvious mistakes in managing the money supply by the Board of Governors of the Federal Reserve.

At a more technical level, the development of financial economics undermined the logic behind the efforts of the New Deal regulatory regime to create separate, siloed capital markets. Two key papers in financial economics, Franco Modigliani and Merton Miller's paper on the equivalency of debt and equity, and Fischer Black and Myron Scholes's paper on valuing options, together with the equation that allowed puts—or options to sell securities, calls—options to buy securities, and risk-free debt to be related to each other, together had the effect of encouraging the idea that all capital markets, and all capital-market instruments, were intimately connected to each other. It became increasingly difficult as this work grew in influence to explain why investors should not be able to move seamlessly from positions in puts, and calls, to positions in risk-free debt, and then back again.

By the 1970s, few people who lived through the Crash of 1929 and its aftermath were left in active public life. Fears of financial panic, rampant deflation, and mass unemployment were replaced in the minds of policy makers by a sense of frustration with the postwar regulatory environment—a sense that financial regulation had become a straitjacket—preventing value-enhancing transactions and leaving public companies in the control of managers who focused on building conglomerate empires rather than making money for their investors. Stagflation was the major macroeconomic problem—a combination of weak growth and high inflation that seemed connected to strong regulation and high taxes and siloed capital markets.

## The Collapse of Bretton Woods, the End of the Gold Standard, and the Deregulation of Currencies

Financial-market deregulation in the late twentieth century began with currency-market deregulation in the context of the collapse of the Bretton Woods accord.

After World War II, the victorious Allies created a global system of relatively fixed exchange rates, the Bretton Woods system, named after the New Hampshire resort hotel where the initial meetings took place in 1944 that set up the system. This system pegged various countries' exchange rates to the dollar, which in turn was fixed to the price of gold at $35 an ounce. Countries suffering from structural trade imbalances could petition the IMF to change their exchange rate with the dollar. The Bretton Woods regime effectively eliminated private markets in currencies as a means by which exchange rates were set. Currency markets were price takers, not price setters.

In the late 1960s, inflationary pressures grew in the United States as a result of the Vietnam War and a gradual shift in the US balance-of-payments position from being a net exporter to being a net importer. Under these pressures, currency traders sought to convert dollars to gold, draining the gold reserves of the United States. Eventually, in 1971, the Nixon administration "closed the gold window," allowing the dollar to float against the price of gold and against other currencies.

In the years that followed, floating exchange rates and floating gold prices replaced the Bretton Woods–era currency price bands. This new world of market-based exchange rates was the backdrop to the deregulation of national capital markets and the rise of a global market in currency derivatives dwarfing in notional amounts any financial market the world had ever seen.

In particular two features of deregulated currency markets ultimately were important contributors to the financial crisis of 2008. The first was the incentive that countries like China that were pursuing export-led growth strategies had to stockpile the currencies of their trading partners, rather than convert those currencies into their own domestic currency. Absent stockpiling, the value of their domestic currency would have increased, and hurt the competitiveness of their exports. The second was the practical need, in a world where any country's currency was vulnerable to raids by financial actors, for all countries to hold significant amounts of reserves in dollars, so as to be able to use those dollars to manage the value of their own currency. Together these two structural features of a deregulated global currency regime were to help fuel a glut of dollar-denominated credit in the context of both global trade imbalances and US economic policy in the first decade of the twenty-first century.

## Deregulating Equities Markets—the 1970s

Securities markets in the 1970s in the United States were not just regulated by the Securities and Exchange Commission (SEC). Most trading took place on stock exchanges that were not just exchanges but were regulatory bodies, referred to as self-regulatory organizations, which set rules for both traders and listed companies, subject to SEC approval. While this system survives today in weakened and fragmented form—with the former power of the exchanges now divided between the remaining exchanges and the Financial Industry Regulatory Authority (FINRA), in the postwar years the exchanges were far more powerful. In addition to a variety of limitations on investors' ability to borrow money to buy securities—the margin rules, and limitations on short selling—there was a very basic regulation in place at the exchanges that acted as a damper on trading and profoundly shaped the economics of stock brokerages. That was the simple rule that there was a minimum fee for trading securities on the exchanges, which is called the fixed commission rule.

Today, this seems like a strange idea, that regulators would prevent market actors in an arena as profoundly market-driven as a securities exchange from competing based on price. But in the postwar era price regulation in the name of price and industry stability was common. The Interstate Commerce Commission regulated the prices railroads and over-the-road trucking firms could charge. The Federal Communications Commission did the same for AT&T, the national monopoly phone company. The Federal Aviation Administration did the same for airline fares. While in some cases rate regulation was a product of the Progressive Era belief that monopolies like AT&T had to be regulated, the widespread regulation of prices by government bodies had its real roots in the depths of the Depression, when falling prices bankrupted sound businesses across industry after industry. Regulation was not motivated by fear of monopoly power; it was protection against what was termed at the time as "destructive competition."

In securities markets, fixed commissions meant that old-fashioned stockbrokers could be profitable under the Glass-Steagall rules, with very limited margin businesses, no ties to commercial banks, and in general levels of capital low enough that major brokers could be operated as private partnerships. Fixed commissions also meant that investors both large and small had to incur meaningful costs to trade—in essence placing a regulatory obstacle in the way of high-frequency trading strategies and incentivizing longer-term investing.

On May 1, 1975, the SEC banned fixed minimum commissions. The commission at the time saw this as a pro-investor initiative, allowing brokers to compete for business by lowering commissions, to the benefit of investors both in simple cost terms and by creating more liquid markets. While the consequences were not immediate, the ban on fixed commissions and the rise of information technology led to dramatic increases in trading volumes, a steep decline in the profitability of traditional brokerage businesses, and a resulting crisis for the business model of broker research. One of the long-term consequences was the conversion of the major brokerages from partnerships to public corporations, and/or, following the weakening of Glass-Steagall in the 1990s, their acquisition by commercial banks or insurance companies—deep pools of capital looking for higher returns. In the new deregulated securities markets, it was not enough to be a middleman, you needed to deploy capital of your own.

An unanticipated consequence of the conversion from partnerships to public companies was that the management of securities firms no longer had their own personal net worth exposed in case of firm bankruptcy. Stockbrokers and investment bankers now enjoyed the same shield of limited liability that commercial bankers and railroad and auto executives had long enjoyed. Along with that went a profound asymmetry of risk and reward—infinite upside, capped downside. These developments were to contribute greatly to the mix of incentives and corporate governance structures that fed the bubble after 2003 and wrought further destruction in the collapse that followed.

## Housing—The Origin of the Thirty-Year Fixed-Rate Mortgage and Why The American Dream Requires Government Support

Prior to the Great Depression, farmers and homeowners could borrow money to buy and improve property from banks. But banks with short-term deposits generally were not willing to lend for more than five years—leaving households and farms exposed to changes in both real-estate prices and credit-market conditions. Housing values fell in advance of the Great Crash, and they fell faster as the Depression deepened. Because of short-term mortgages. properties were foreclosed en masse even when the borrowers could pay the principal and interest because bankers would not refinance as prices fell. In response, the federal government created through the Federal Home Loan Bank Act of 1932 and the National Housing Act of 1934 the Federal Housing Authority, the Federal National Mortgage Corporation (FNMA, later "Fannie Mae,") and the Home Loan Bank Boards to provide both credit insurance and protection against what would be called later "tail risk" inherent in interest-rate and housing markets. Without such a system, homeowners are exposed to frequent refinancing risk many cannot bear, destabilizing communities and the broader middle class.

The New Deal housing finance system was made of the Federal Housing Authority with secondary market support from a government-owned FNMA, oriented toward less affluent homebuyers, significantly supplemented after World War II by the Veterans Administration, and the growing regulated savings and loan industry, backed up by regional Federal Home Loan Banks, for more affluent homebuyers.

All the components of the New Deal housing finance system were designed to encourage the spread of long-term housing finance vehicles in the form of the 30-year fixed-rate nonrecourse home mortgage. It was key to the viability of this form of housing finance that savings and loans (S&Ls) paid regulated interest rates, so there was no chance that savings and loans would have to pay interest rates on deposits that exceeded their cost of attracting depositors. In order for mortgage lenders to be assured of depositors, there were rules barring commercial banks from paying interest on checking accounts. In effect, if you wanted to invest in a government-insured deposit institution that paid interest, you had to do so through a savings and loan that paid a fixed interest rate and was largely limited to investing your funds in mortgages.

## Deregulation and the Collapse of Savings and Loans

In the late 1970s, the SEC allowed mutual funds to be established that invested in short-term debt instruments ("commercial paper") and paid a variable rate of interest to their investors while more or less promising that the invested principle was not at risk and would not vary in value from day to day. These money market funds were quickly formidable competition for savings and loans in a time of high inflation.

As savings and loan institutions saw their deposits fleeing to money market funds, Congress responded to their pleas for help with the Garn-St. Germain

Act and the Depository Institutions Deregulation and Monetary Control Act (DIDMCA), which lifted the cap on the interest rates that savings and loans could pay depositors. At the same time, they lifted restrictions on the types of assets that savings and loans could invest in. Savings and loans went from highly regulated, housing finance-focused institutions to institutions competing with money markets and commercial banks on the basis of yield, free to seek returns in a wide variety of credit markets. But of course the federal guarantee of deposits in the S&Ls were kept in place, even as both interest rates and investment assets were deregulated.

The immediate result was the shift in savings and loans away from housing finance and toward commercial real estate, leading to the S&L crisis. In response to the collapse of hundreds of savings and loans, in 1989 Congress passed the Financial Institutions Reform, Recovery and Enforcement Act (FIRREA), which created the Resolution Trust Corporation of the early 1990s. But the longer-term impact was to require that policy makers had to replace the S&Ls and their captive funding structure with major new sources of housing finance capital, a process that led policy makers to the Federal National Mortgage Corporation and its counterpart and competitor, the Federal Home Loan Mortgage Corporation. And here begins one part of the story of the rise of shadow banking and its role in the new financial architecture in the bubble years.

## Mortgage Securitization—How the World's Biggest Financial Market Went from Being One of the Most Tightly Regulated to Being Essentially Unregulated

When the heavily regulated New Deal housing finance system unraveled in the inflationary environment of the late 1970s, it left in its wake a profound challenge. Homeowners expected 30-year fixed-rate mortgages, but banks and the remaining savings and loans could not bear the risk involved in the timing mismatch of short-term deposits and commercial paper on the one hand, and 30-year mortgages on the other. In addition there was an issue of geographic concentration. Mortgage securitization seemed to offer an answer to both questions, initially within a framework that seemed to offer regulatory protections from the dynamics that led to the S&L fiasco.

The Federal National Mortgage Association was originally a federally controlled entity created to provide a secondary market for FHA loans. In 1968, Congress converted the FNMA into a for-profit corporation with a broader mandate to raise funds by issuing debt to use to purchase loans from issuing banks and savings and loans. In 1970, Congress created a competing organization, the Federal Home Loan Mortgage Corporation (FHLMC, known as "Freddie Mac"), also charged with selling debt to finance the purchases of low- to moderate-income families' mortgages. Together, Fannie Mae and Freddie Mac came to be known as the government-sponsored enterprises (GSEs).

But the growth of Fannie Mae and Freddie Mac required buyers of mortgage-backed securities. Banks and other regulated private financial institutions were not allowed to buy mortgage-backed securities until the passage of the Secondary Mortgage Market Enhancement Act of 1984. In parallel, the SEC exempted asset-backed securitization vehicles from most provisions of the Investment Company Act, which would otherwise have covered the trusts that bought up mortgages and had issued securities against them to the public.

By 1993, 60 percent of all those newly entered into mortgages were securitized. But they continued to be securitized almost entirely through GSEs that only purchased conforming mortgage loans—loans that were 30-year fixed terms, with a 20 percent down payment. The GSEs' conforming loan standard, backed up by the Office of Federal Housing Enterprise Oversight (OFHEO), ensured that the GSEs in this period were essentially regulated institutions—subject to substantive limitations on their manner of doing business.

But at the same time, starting in the 1980s in the environment described in Michael Lewis book *Liars' Poker*, we begin to see the emergence of a fully deregulated mortgage market. This market came into existence to finance nonconforming mortgages, usually mortgages whose principal amount was larger than the GSE's statutory limit or whose structure is not 30-year fixed interest rates. This market allows mortgage initiators that are increasingly outside the regulatory system entirely—storefront operations that are not subject to the general jurisdiction of bank regulators either at the state or the federal level—but who are, it turns out, being financed by large regulated institutions. This is the beginning of a world of subprime loans and unregulated originators, capitalized by the biggest names in finance.

In the aftermath of the S&L crisis, Congress took several re-regulatory steps of the kind that followed each financial crisis of the deregulatory era. One of these measures created a common regulator, OHFEO, for Fannie, Freddie, and the Federal Home Loan Banks. A second, the Home Ownership and Equity Protection Act of 1994, gave the Board of Governors of the Federal Reserve the power to regulate all mortgage issuers to prevent abuses of the very type that were at the heart of the subprime crisis 10 years later. Critically this act gave the Federal Reserve Board comprehensive jurisdiction over all mortgage originators, including both bank and nonbank market participants. While much of the story of deregulation is about the undoing of laws and regulation, a key part of the story in mortgages is the refusal of the Federal Reserve Board under then Chairman Alan Greenspan to use the comprehensive power it had to regulate mortgage markets.

By the mid-1990s, the pieces were in place in a deregulated mortgage market for a wholesale shift from 30-year fixed mortgages to short-term mortgages. Securitization, largely unregulated mortgage companies driven by executive pay linked to their stock prices, and regulators who did not believe in regulating at the Federal Reserve were all in place. But the wholesale shift did not occur until 10 years later, when the larger capital-market conditions existed to support it—most particularly the creation of universal banks and an unregulated market in credit insurance.

It is critical to note here that, contrary to what many have said, in the end the GSEs were secondary actors in the financial crisis and came relatively late to the party in 2004 and 2005. Private-label subprime securities, backed up by the balance sheets of too-big-to-fail banks and securitized by their brokerage arms, were the drivers of the bubble. Ultimately, when the GSEs got into the game, they did so by buying junk securities issued by the large banks.

## Banks, the End of Glass-Steagall, and the Rise of Too Big to Fail

One of the key New Deal regulatory reforms was the separation of the business of taking insured deposits and making loans from the business of underwriting and trading securities. This meant that banks could not themselves underwrite mortgage securities. In 1987, the Federal Reserve Board and the federal courts began to allow bank holding companies to set up affiliates to deal in commercial paper—short-term debt securities, including mortgage-backed securities. But securities dealings could contribute no more than 5 percent of a bank holding company's gross revenues. This was a very important limit on the growth of the private-label mortgage securitization business. The private-label securitization business is where, rather than Fannie Mae or Freddie Mac running the securitization process, private financial institutions like Salomon Brothers and Goldman Sachs buy up mortgages and sell interests in the resulting pools. The 5 percent rule limited bank involvement in mortgage securitizations to a small fraction of the market. The result was that the only firms that could underwrite private-label mortgage securities at scale were the relatively thinly capitalized broker dealers like Salomon Brothers, which had pioneered this market. It also meant that the business of funding mortgage origination and the business of mortgage securitization remained largely separate, which was a check on the spread of bad underwriting standards.

But in 1997, amid a general enthusiasm for financial deregulation bred by the high-tech stock bubble, the Federal Reserve lifted the gross revenue limitation from 5 percent to 25 percent. The next step in destroying Glass-Steagall was the Federal Reserve's approval of the Citicorp-Travelers merger. Citi had already acquired Salomon Brothers Smith Barney, the brokerage house that had pioneered private-label mortgage-backed securities. Citigroup was of course later at the center of the financial crisis of 2008 and was the single largest bank recipient of TARP funds. Congress completed the deregulatory project by passing the Gramm-Leach-Bliley Act, removing all barriers to the combination within a bank holding company of banking, securities dealing, insurance, and investment-management businesses, including proprietary trading across all markets.

But Glass-Steagall repeal was not the only profound deregulatory change in the banking system in the 1990s. The United States has a dual bank regulatory system, where banks are regulated both by the federal government and by state governments. All banks are subject to state banking laws as well as federal ones. Many states had bank regulatory statutes that limited the number of branches a single bank could own. In 1994 Congress passed and President Clinton signed the Riegle-Neal Interstate Banking and Branching Efficiency Act of 1994, repealing barriers in federal law to interstate banking. By the end of the 1990s most states had eliminated these barriers to banking consolidation. At the same time barriers to ownership of banks across state lines, which had been in place since the Depression had fallen.

The result was that, by 2000, all the deregulatory steps had been taken to allow the reappearance of universal national megabanks in the United States. Some said that the key move made in the New Deal was the breakup of the House of Morgan. By 2003, the House of Morgan was back, in the form of the megabank JP Morgan Chase. It took the financial crisis itself to determine who the real survivors would be. They have turned out to be four giant commercial banks—in addition to JP Morgan Chase, they are Citigroup, Bank of America, and Wells Fargo. Together these institutions control 62 percent of the assets of all US bank holding companies. Together with the two surviving independent broker dealers—Goldman Sachs and Morgan Stanley, nominally now chartered as bank holding companies—these institutions dominate US financial markets across the broken-down silos of New Deal bank regulation.

Most important, for the story of the financial crisis, these developments lifted the regulatory barriers to the metastasization of private-label mortgage finance. Universal banks could originate mortgages, capitalize nominally independent mortgage companies to originate the really embarrassing ones, underwrite the securitizations of those mortgages, and then do the servicing of the same. They could pick and choose where to commit their capital in the process, laying off the riskier steps on less well informed parties. They could make money on dubious transactions without taking the risk, or so they thought.

This chapter is not in an expansive-enough stage to get into the role played in these issues by the Basel Committee on Bank Supervision. However, it is worth noting that the Basel process was another area where the banking crises of the late 1980s and the early 1990s appeared to give rise to a more serious regulatory framework, only to give way before concepts of self-regulation and notions that the new financial architecture had ended risk as we know it by spreading it around. This approach culminated in Basel II, analyzed by the Federal Reserve Governor Daniel Tarullo in his book *Banking on Basel*, where bank regulators looked to bank management themselves to assess through computer models that they themselves designed the safety and soundness of their own institutions.

Finally, a point about funding sources and systemic risk. Regulated banks in the New Deal era largely had three sources of capital: insured deposits, long-term debt, and long-term equity. They were carefully regulated to ensure that none of their capital was susceptible to bank runs. But the new deregulated megabanks had additional, significant sources of capital that were quite susceptible to runs. These sources included commercial paper and the uninsured money market funds that invested in it, overnight lending from other financial institutions, largely organized in the London Interbank Market (LIBOR), and asset-backed short-term credit deals with a wide variety of financial actors called repos. These new, unregulated sources of capital were key to the ability of megabanks to grow and to finance new businesses such as derivatives dealing and mortgage securitization, and they were key sources of instability when trouble came.

It is important to note here that up until this point the story of deregulation is the story of financial activity being liberated from substantive constraints within a general framework of regulatory oversight. For example, throughout the 1980s, savings and loans were regulated by state and federal bank regulators. As commissions were deregulated, the overall business of both exchanges and broker dealers remained subject to the oversight of the SEC. We had yet to see the phenomenon of regulatory holes, or true shadow markets. The process by which financial activity escapes regulatory oversight entirely or almost entirely is really a story of the 1990s.

## Derivatives—Creating an Unregulated Financial Market to Creating Unregulated Credit Insurance

A financial derivative is nothing but a contract between two parties that references some third thing—a stock, a bond, a loan, the price of a commodity, an interest rate or a currency exchange rate, or, more exotically, weather conditions, or truthfully—anything the mind of a financial engineer can come up with. Because derivatives are plastic instruments, what they really are is a means for creating in a deregulated legal space something familiar—a loan or a stock, or more commonly, insurance. An important parallel phenomenon was the development in the area of investment management of the hedge fund, another legal construct whose purpose was to escape the regulatory strictures constraining investment companies. It is no accident that hedge funds rapidly became the second largest class of participants in the derivatives market.

A large-scale financial derivatives market was impossible when banks were limited to certain types of assets in their portfolios. As the limits were removed in the 1980s, entrepreneurial figures at institutions like Bankers Trust realized that the lifting of investment limitations for banks meant that banks could not just invest in long-standing instruments like mortgage-backed securities, they could create new products and new markets through the instrument of the over-the-counter derivative. Initially, derivatives were sold to operating companies as a way, for example, to convert high-coupon fixed-rate debt into relatively low-coupon floating debt, or to manage currency-price or energy-price risks. In the course of the 1990s, over-the-counter derivatives markets exploded, growing at a rate that dramatically outpaced the growth of economies, of financial institutions, and of other financial markets.

However, during this period derivatives were subject to two layers of regulation. First, to the extent that the parties to derivative transactions were themselves regulated entities like public companies, banks, and insurance companies, those parties were subject to disclosure requirements and to safety and soundness regulation in their dealings with derivatives. Unfortunately, regulators had a pattern of underestimating the potential impact of derivatives dealings on the entities they regulated until it was too late.

At the same time, in the 1990s derivatives markets were subject to regulation by the Commodities Futures Trading Commission (CFTC), like other financial instruments. The CFTC had the authority to police market conduct and to require that participants in derivatives transactions post capital to support their positions, limiting the leverage and risk associated with the derivatives market.

This may sound like derivatives were relatively well regulated for a new financial product during the 1990s. But the truth was that derivatives were not really new—they were a new type of vehicle for doing very old-fashioned things like buying insurance or options. And if you compared the regulation of the derivatives markets in the 1990s to the regulation of insurance markets, it was clear that derivatives themselves were a form of deregulation.

But even the light regulation represented by the combination of the CFTC and the regulation of transacting firms were onerous for the derivatives lobby. And so, over the strenuous objections of the Clinton Administration CFTC Chairman Brooksley Born, the Clinton Administration, led by soon-to-be-Citigroup-executive Robert Rubin joined in a bipartisan effort with the then Republican chair of the Senate Banking Committee, Phil Gramm, to take jurisdiction over derivatives away from the CFTC and leave the market entirely unregulated. This was accomplished at the end of 2000 through the passage of the Commodities Futures Modernization Act.

But before deregulated derivatives could have their full destructive effect on our financial system, there was first the somewhat smaller-scale fiasco of derivatives and Enron. Enron and its banks used financial derivatives disguised as energy derivatives and the flaws in the accounting system's approach to derivatives to hide billions of dollars of debt from Enron's investors and the general public. Senator Gramm's wife, Wendy Gramm, helped preside over this activity from her position on Enron's board following her departure from a seat on the Commodities Futures Trading Commission.

For a brief time after Enron's collapse at the end of 2001, it seemed there might be some political momentum to reregulate derivatives. However, once derivatives regulation failed to make it into the Sarbanes-Oxley Act that momentum dissipated, and the derivatives market remained without regulation, without transparency or capital requirements, free to operate under the same accounting rules that Enron had successfully manipulated.

The way was now paved for bond insurance in the form of credit default swaps to be sold without the capital to back it up.

## The Weakening Power of the Securities Laws

A final aspect of the deregulatory story that has gotten relatively little attention is the weakening of private rights of action by investors against capital-market intermediaries like underwriters, lawyers, and accountants, and in particular underwriters. During the height of New Deal financial regulation, investors had the right under Rule 10-b-5 of the Securities and Exchange Act to bring claims for aiding and abetting securities fraud against broker dealers who underwrote fraudulent securities offerings or otherwise assisted issuers in defrauding investors. The likelihood that fraudulent conduct would be met with expensive and burdensome private litigation was an important factor encouraging a certain amount of care by capital-market intermediaries.

But in 1994, the Supreme Court found in *Central Bank of Denver* that there was no private right of action under the securities laws for aiding and abetting liability. This case was followed by Congress's passage of the Private Securities Litigation Reform Act of 1995 (PSLRA), which raised the evidentiary burden a plaintiff in a private securities case had to meet before a court would allow the plaintiff to get discovery.

It appeared as a result of these changes that it would be difficult for investors to recover damages in major securities fraud cases involving financial institutions. But then the Enron case arrived, which involved a bankrupt company, Enron, that had colluded with deep-pocketed banks to defraud investors and employees of tens of billions of dollars. It was the largest and most egregious case of securities fraud since the Depression. Early in the securities fraud case, while most of the 5,000 laid-off Enron employees were still out of a job, a federal district judge in Houston found that while there was no aiding and abetting liability under the federal securities laws in private rights of action, there was scheme liability—and she allowed multibillion-dollar claims against several large banks to proceed on that basis.

By the time the Enron case reached the Supreme Court, in tandem with a case raising similar issues called *Broadridge*, memories of Enron had faded. In *Broadridge* the Supreme Court found that there was no scheme liability either under the federal securities laws.

During this same period, in the Dura and Tellabs cases, the Supreme Court interpreted the PSLRA to further raise the level of evidence needed of the defendant's intent and the theory of loss causation before the plaintiff would be allowed to use the powers of the court to gather evidence.

The net result was to make it dramatically less likely that public investors in mortgage-backed securities or the stocks or bonds of banks, insurance companies, and investment banks would ever be in a position to sue over losses resulting at least in part from financial institution conduct. Together with such structural changes as the shift from partnership to public company, and from a stand-alone broker dealer to a universal bank with at least indirect access to insured deposits as a source of capital, the defanging of private litigants gave risk-tolerant bankers much less to fear from the legal system.

## Deregulation and the New Capital-Markets Architecture

By the first years of the new millennium, deregulation, technology, and globalization had produced a new capital-markets architecture, one where banks were increasingly the organizer of transactions and the servicer of customers, not the provider of capital. To the extent that banks needed capital, they no longer sought to grow their deposit base, which was expensive and time-consuming. Instead, they sought funding in the commercial paper, interbank lending, and repo markets. Bank mortgage lending was no longer confined by bank capital but was instead a function of the availability of liquidity in a global market in mortgage-backed securities. Investors who wanted bond insurance now could choose between traditional providers of credit insurance and the credit default swap market.

This was an architecture where dramatically greater volumes of financial transactions were under way than had been the case mere years earlier. Yet it was a financial system that was vulnerable to problems of the pre-Depression era—like crises of credit confidence and volatility in asset prices or interest rates. Structures and markets that had been heralded as bulwarks of stability turned out to be sources of contagion.

The consequences of deregulation were free-floating currency markets, the dominance of securitization, the originate to distribute model of mortgage finance, the ability of banks to capitalize the originate to distribute model and derive revenue from the capital market side while convincing themselves they were not bearing the risk, the consolidation of commercial banking, the existence of mortgage insurance without the cost of capital to support it, and the lack of accountability for financial intermediaries or their highly paid employees. These all set the stage for the economic devastation to come.

## Note

The views expressed within this chapter are my own and are not necessarily those of the AFL-CIO, the Congressional Oversight Panel, its staff, or its chair.

## Selected Sources on Deregulation and the Financial Crisis

Berle, Adolph, and Gardiner Means. (1967). *The Modern Corporation and Private Property*. New York: Harcourt.

Black, Fischer and Myron Scholes. (1973). "The Pricing of Options and Corporate Liabilities." *Journal of Political Economy* 81(3): 637–654.

Brandeis, Louis. (1914). *Other People's Money and How the Bankers Use It*. New York: Stokes.

Congressional Oversight Panel, Special Report on Regulatory Reform. (2009). http://cybercemetery.unt.edu/archive/cop/20110401223225/http://cop.senate.gov/reports/library/report-012909-cop.cfm.

The Financial Crisis Inquiry Commission. (2011). *The Financial Crisis Inquiry Report*. US Government Printing Office, January.

Friedman, Milton, and Anna Schwartz. (1963). *A Monetary History of the United States, 1867–1960*. New York: Princeton University Press.

Hirsh, Michael. (2010). *Capital Offense: How Washington's Wise Men Turned America's Future over to Wall Street*. Hoboken, NJ: John Wiley.

Keynes, John Maynard. (1936). *The General Theory of Employment, Interest and Money*. London: Macmillan.

Madrick, Jeffrey. (2011). *The Age of Greed: The Triumph of Finance and the Decline of America, 1970 to the Present*. New York: Knopf.

Modigliani, Franco, and Merton Miller. (1958). "The Cost of Capital, Corporation Finance and the Theory of Investment." American Economic Review 48(3): 261–297.

Morgenson, Gretchen. (2011). *Reckless Endangerment: How Outsized Ambition, Greed and Corruption Led to Economic Armageddon*. New York: Henry Holt.

Moss, David A. (2004). *When All Else Fails: Government as the Ultimate Risk Manager*. Cambridge, Harvard University Press.

Pecora, Ferdinand. (1939). *Wall Street under Oath: The Story of Our Modern Money Changers*. New York: A. M. Kelley.

Russell, Ellen. (2007). *New Deal Banking Reforms and Keynesian Welfare State Capitalism*. New York: Routledge.

Scheer, Robert. (2010). *The Great American Stickup: How Reagan Republicans and Clinton Democrats Enriched Wall Street While Mugging Main Street*. New York: Nation Books.

Senate Permanent Subcommittee on Investigations. (2011). *Wall Street and the Financial Crisis: Anatomy of a Financial Collapse, Majority and Minority Staff Report*. April 11. http://levin.senate.gov/imo/media/doc/supporting/2011/PSI_WallStreetCrisis_041311.pdf.

Stiglitz, Joseph. (2003). *The Roaring Nineties: A New History of the World's Most Prosperous Decade*. New York: W. W. Norton.

Stiglitz, Joseph. (2010). *Freefall: America, Free Markets and the Sinking of the World Economy*. New York: W. W. Norton.

Tarullo, Daniel. (2008). *Banking on Basel: The Future of International Financial Regulation*. Washington: Peterson Institute.

CHAPTER 22

# WHAT WE DON'T TALK ABOUT WHEN WE TALK ABOUT BANKING

JENNIFER S. TAUB

SHADOW banking has surpassed traditional banking in terms of size and systemic importance. With approximately $16 trillion in liabilities, compared to $13 trillion for traditional banking (Pozsar, Adrian, Ashcraft, and Boesky, 2010, 65), this shadow sector is a significant savings allocator. And it plays a crucial role in the availability and pricing of consumer and commercial loans. Based upon scale alone, monitoring this system is important. However, in addition to size, this sector is also associated with instability. Shadow banking links together the largest financial-system participants and provides a source of extreme leverage Additionally, this sector is prone to runs; it sources unstable short-term funding for financial firms (Ricks, 2010, 1) that can drive up asset prices during booms and then quickly dry up upon asset reversals, furthering the deleveraging cycle (Hsu and Moroz, 2010, 1);. Indeed, it was the run on the shadow banking system in 2008 that transformed the nonprime mortgage securities meltdown into a full-blown Global Financial Crisis (D'Arista and Epstein, 2010, 13). Extensive government support in the form of Federal Reserve liquidity facilities and government guarantees was deployed, to rescue this parallel banking sector and to protect traditional banks from exposure. However, after these bailouts of the shadow system, its components have not been brought into the light, let alone under adequate prudential supervision by government regulators.

The government-initiated reform measures enacted to date lack consistency and cohesion. Too little attention has been paid to how the varied links in this system interconnect with each other and with "traditional" banking and the broader economy. For example, investment banks used massive amounts of very short-term funding to load up on risky, overvalued mortgage-linked securities. When the value of those securities came into question, the funding was abruptly pulled away. Much of this fragile funding was sourced from the shadow banking sector's multitrillion-dollar repurchase agreement ("repo") market. Additionally, repo transactions can be used to mask debt. These transactions were used by Lehman Brothers to hide roughly $50 billion in borrowing off balance sheets (Taub, 2010a). Lehman had used a strained interpretation of the legal and accounting rules to treat cash it borrowed (for which it pledged collateral) as if it were proceeds of sales (Taub, 2010b). And strategically timed repos were deployed by approximately 18 other large banks, resulting in the appearance of 42 percent less borrowing (Kelly et al., 2010). Yet little has been done to address the dependence on the repo market.

Conversely, some shadow players like money market mutual funds (MMFs) that were already subject to heavy controls in the United States have been further regulated. While these new rules were designed to strengthen the MMFs, making them less prone to runs by their own investors, these same changes may create even more instability and risk for bank and shadow bank counterparties who depend on them for short-term financing. Additionally, with regard to some of the most risky "nonbank" financial firms, such as hedge funds, the regulatory reform measures to date have been flimsy at best (Taub, 2009). Accordingly, this chapter first will describe what is meant by "shadow banking" and the role that it played in the financial crisis. Next, it will highlight two key components of the shadow banking system: MMFs and the repo market. Finally, I will analyze certain regulatory efforts as of early 2011 and make further recommendations for reform.

## What Is the Shadow Banking System?

It was first identified in 1993 as "the parallel banking system" by the economists and financial-market experts Jane D'Arista and Tom Schlesinger; later labeled in 2006 by Paul Tucker at the Bank of England as "Russian doll" finance; in 2007 (Tett, 2011), it was named the "shadow banking system" by PIMCO's managing director, Paul McCulley. And that name stuck.

But what is shadow banking? In the most general sense, the shadow banking sector includes those financial intermediaries, *other than* traditional depository institutions, including thrifts and banks (hereinafter referred to as banks), that stand between savers at one end and borrowers at the other. As estimated by a Federal Reserve Bank of New York (FRBNY) staff report in 2010, shadow banks had liabilities of $16 trillion as compared to traditional banks that had $13 trillion. Leading into the "panic" portion of the financial crisis, in March 2008, at its peak, borrowing through the shadow system stood at $20 trillion (Pozsar, Adrian, Ashcraft, and Boesky, 2010, 65). In comparison, the Financial Crisis Inquiry Commission (FCIC) Report, using Federal Reserve Flow of Funds data, calculated traditional bank funding to be $13 trillion in 2010 (up from around $9.5 trillion in 2008) and shadow banking $8.5 trillion in 2010 (down from around $13 trillion in 2008) (FCIC Report 2011, 32). This variance between the New York Fed and FCIC data perhaps stems from a lack of consensus as to which firms should be classified as shadow banks or what activities should be considered shadow banking.

A simple list of examples provided by Phil Angelides, the chairman of the FCIC, would include "investment banks, off-balance-sheet entities, money market funds, and hedge funds, as well as some affiliates of traditional banks" (Angelides 2011, 2). The former SEC commissioner Christopher Cox would also add insurance companies and the government-sponsored enterprises (GSEs) Fannie Mae and Freddie Mac to this grouping (Cox, 2010). However, as detailed below, there is not consensus yet on what constitutes this definition. There are some elements central to most descriptions. This includes a financial institution that is not subject to bank regulatory supervision engaging in activities typically considered "banking." Traditional banking activities involve intermediation—channeling deposited savings into investments, and providing a system for transferring payments from one entity or person to another. This is how consumers and businesses saved or borrowed money throughout much of the twentieth century. The savers placed deposits at banks or thrifts, and then these institutions loaned money out to individuals to buy homes or businesses to purchase inventory, for instance.

Banking is inherently unstable in that it involves both lending out most of what is borrowed from depositors (and keeping only a fraction on reserve, for example, 10 percent). What makes banking profitable is also what makes it hazardous, namely that banks borrow from depositors for the short term and loan out those deposits for a longer term at higher interest rates. In other words, the maturity of such loans (assets) often exceeds the very short maturity of deposits (liabilities). Thus, the assets held by traditional commercial banks, such as consumer and commercial loans, are less liquid than the deposits, which can be redeemed by bank customers on demand. Accordingly, in such a system, even the slightest hint that a bank may have made some bad loans or be facing trouble can lead to a run on the bank by those afraid they will not be able to get their money out if others get there first.

As a result, since the Great Depression era, traditional banks (and their depositors) have been protected from bank runs through the creation of deposit insurance as well as the safety net of lender-of-last-resort protection from the Federal Reserve. However, in order to avoid the moral hazard of the bank externalizing risks onto the deposit fund and Fed, regulators look at, among other factors, the quality and valuation of assets (including loans) on the bank's balance sheet and the ratio of assets to liabilities (leverage) to ensure that the bank has sufficient internal resources to absorb losses.

Unlike traditional banking, with shadow banking the funding side of "bank" activities is not supplied by customer deposits. In place of deposits, there are many intermediary institutions that aggregate savings. One of those intermediaries is the MMF. Because shadow banking does not rely on customer deposits, shadow financing is performed without the backstop of deposit insurance or central bank lender-of-last-resort protection, without reserve requirements, and without supervision by a regulator monitoring the safety and soundness of the institution. While traditional banks are subject to a government-based regulatory framework, shadow banks historically have not been. Instead, the "policing" or "regulating" mechanism is provided through the private sector, typically by credit-rating agencies or trading counterparties.

The line between what is "traditional" and what is "shadow" banking seems to hinge on whether there is microprudential supervision tied to liquidity backstops. However, those who discovered this parallel system and those who revived concerns about it also emphasize its systemic impact and thus the need to have shadow banks subject to microprudential supervision, but also to have all banks subject to *macro*prudential regulation. As discussed below, in particular there is still a need to regulate the amounts of short-term debt and not just leverage, taken on both by traditional banks with publicly supplied liquidity backstops and by other shadow "nonbank" financial entities.

When they discovered the "parallel banking system," D'Arista and Schlesinger predicted that the deregulation afoot would leave "deep-seated structural forces that continue to weaken banks and destabilize the nation's credit markets" (1993, 2). They also pointed to "profound changes in the U.S. financial system" as the root cause of the banks' problems. They wrote:

> Over the last two decades, the U.S. system has been reshaped by the spread of multifunctional financial conglomerates and the emergence of an unregulated parallel banking system. Along with other powerful trends like securitization, these events have broken down the carefully compartmentalized credit and capital marketplace established in New Deal legislation. (D'Arista and Schlesinger, 1993, 2)

At the heart of D'Arista and Schlesinger's definition of parallel banking is the growth of nondeposit liabilities to fund banking-type activities emerging in concert with the creation and growth of MMFs. They expressed concern about the disparate regulatory treatment for traditional banks as compared to these parallel institutions.

> Any serious effort to reconstitute the U.S. financial system, must begin by defining its current structure—not the structure outlined in law and regulation,

> but the actual framework in practice in the marketplace. All indicators confirm that banks no longer maintain a dominant place in that system. Others, obviously, have assumed their functions. Since soundness regulation clearly is needed for banks, it should be extended as well to institutions that have assumed many of the functions of banks. (5)

In addition, they recommended that

> the financial playing field must be leveled by raising, not lowering, standards of prudential supervision and public obligation. In other words, all financial institutions should be treated the same way. (5)

They recommended uniform licensing of any entity that "directly accepts funds from the public for investment; makes loans to the public or buys loans or securities using funds other than its own equity capital and retained earnings; or, sells loans or third party securities to financial institutions or investors." In addition to MMFs, at the time, the parallel banks they identified included finance companies (like General Electric Capital Corporation and General Motors Acceptance Corporation).

When McCulley used the "shadow banking system" term, it was in the midst of the subprime meltdown in late August 2007, during a talk at the Federal Reserve summit in Jackson Hole, Wyoming. He suggested that they were already witnessing a "run on the shadow banking system." Included on his list of shadow banks were investment banks, conduits, structured investment vehicles, and hedge funds. More generally, he later explained that

> unlike conventional, regulated banks, unregulated shadow banks fund themselves with uninsured short-term funding, which may or may not be backstopped by liquidity lines from real banks. Since they fly below the radar of traditional banking regulation, these levered-up intermediaries operated in the shadows without backstopping from the Federal Reserve's discount window or access to FDIC deposit insurance. (McCulley 2009, 1)

The term "shadow banking" has a pejorative connotation, given its previous association with pawn shops and check-cashing centers and by others to characterize money laundering associated with drug trafficking, arms trading, and terrorism (United Nations, 2000). In terms of the concept, McCulley's formulation echoes that of D'Arista and Schlesinger, with the emphasis on the rise of nondeposit liabilities. Evidence of a common source can be seen in McCulley's likening his formulation to Hyman Minsky's observations of "fringe banks and other financial institutions" (1986, 281). Similarly, D'Arista presented early versions of the Parallel Banking System paper at the Levy Institute at workshops conducted by Minsky.

McCulley blamed this system for the bubble and the bust. In 2009 he wrote that "the rise of this system drove one of the biggest lending booms in history and collapsed into one of the most crushing financial crises we have ever seen" (McCulley, 2009, 1). Others have joined the chorus. In 2010, he explained to the FCIC that the crisis within the shadow banking system occurred on

September 15, 2008, when Lehman Brothers filed for bankruptcy protection. This transformed the run into a chaotic process, leading to the run on the MMFs (described below) and a variety of US and other government interventions to end the run.

In the words of Angelides,

> During this crisis, we have seen the shadow banking system upended, first by a liquidity crisis in 2007 as mortgages went bad at an accelerating rate, and building to a crescendo in the fall of 2008 when there was a 19th Century style panic, a run on the short-term, often overnight loans that fund so much business financing in America and around the world. The market froze. Interest rates soared on the short-term loans. (2010, 5)

As a result of the proven frailty of this parallel system, there are many recommendations about what should be done. McCulley suggested to the FCIC that "a key guidepost for reform of our financial regulatory structure is simple: what an institution does, not what it is called, should determine how it is regulated" (2010, 10–11). This claim is similar to D'Arista and Schlesinger, who, as noted above, argued that "in other words, all financial institutions should be treated the same way"(1993, 5).

## Regulating the Shadow Banking System: Moving from Resistance to Readiness

Historically, there has been resistance to regulating the parallel banking system. Instead, the approach was to loosen up on both traditional banking and shadow banking, under the theory that sophisticated counterparties had the proper incentives and skills to police the market (Taub, 2011). This was the justification, for example, offered by former Federal Reserve Chairman, Alan Greenspan, and others for the deregulation of derivatives (President's Working Group, 1999). One can look at the five largest independent US (former) investment banks as another instructive example.

Until 2004, US investment banks had no consolidated regulator at the parent level to oversee their operations. However, their broker-dealer subsidiaries were regulated by the Securities and Exchange Commission (SEC). In order to continue to do business in Europe, they were required to choose a domestic regulator. The five largest investment banks chose the SEC and took on the designation of "consolidated supervised entities" or CSEs. This was a voluntary arrangement. The SEC did not have the statutory authority to impose capital requirements on investment bank holding companies. However, in theory, this voluntary arrangement gave the SEC the ability to oversee capital, liquidity, and risk at the new CSEs. In exchange for being supervised on a consolidated basis, the investment banks were allowed to change the net capital calculations for their broker-dealer subsidiaries. According to some experts, this resulted in lower net capital at the broker-dealer level and more leverage (Pozen, 2010). In addition, though the SEC took on this obligation, it did not have the mind-set or could commit the staffing necessary to do the job.

As the SEC chairman who took her position after the crisis explained, there were 24 people assigned to monitor the five banks. Yet none of these examiners worked on-site at the investment banks, according to the FCIC report. The two dozen staff members were up against armies. For example, a former Lehman CEO, Richard Fuld, described while testifying before the House Financial Services Committee in 2010, that of the 28,000 employees at Lehman, more than 100 staff in legal, audit, and other departments were responsible for financial statements. At the same hearing, SEC Chairman Mary Schapiro, who was not in charge of the agency when Lehman failed, acknowledged that the "SEC did not have the... mindset to be the prudential regulator of the largest financial institutions in the world" (Schapiro, 2010).

Looking back, regulators admit that the CSE program was a failure. Ultimately, one investment bank went bankrupt, two had to be rescued by traditional bank conglomerates, but with government support, and the remaining two, Goldman and Morgan Stanley, surrendered their shadow statuses and came into the light to gain access to Federal Reserve lending facilities and survive the crisis. They became bank holding companies, which are now subject to the Federal Reserve for prudential supervision.

In the United States and on the international front, a desire to bring shadow banking activities under prudential regulatory oversight has been expressed. This sentiment was set out in a report published in November 2010 by the Financial Stability Board (FSB), the entity established by the Group of 20 in 2009 to coordinate international reforms:

> With regulatory requirements on the banking system tightening, the need intensifies for more systematic attention to activities in the shadow banking sector. This sector continues to play an important role in credit intermediation and liquidity transformation outside the rigorous capital and liquidity regulatory framework that applies to banks. Addressing the issues that this raises, and putting in place the needed safeguards, are one of the priorities of the FSB's forward agenda. (Financial Stability Board, 2010, 1)

Notwithstanding that agenda, nearly three years after the crisis, there was still not an international consensus as to what would be considered a part of the shadow banking system. As of early 2011, the FSB continued to work toward a mapping of shadow banks. The expectation was that the FSB would at some point produce recommendations so that these entities will not become larger havens to hide from oversight or enforcement (Main, 2011).

As the FSB and member country regulators began this job of mapping of classifying, there appeared to be resistance. When Gary Cohn, the Chief Operating Officer of Goldman Sachs, dared at the World Economic Forum in Davos in 2011 to suggest that with inconsistent regulation, business would travel to the "less regulated, more opaque sector" if only banks faced additional regulation, he angered many (Samuel, 2011). Beyond Davos, in some other quarters, it is taboo to discuss the shadow banking system. For example, the FCIC, tasked by the US Congress with investigating the causes of the crisis was unable to produce a bipartisan report partly due to a dispute over this parallel system. This was an odd result, as 9 out of the 10 commissioners appeared to agree in large part on many issues. Indeed the primary dissenting statement authored by three of the four Republican appointees was in accord with many of the key findings provided in the report endorsed by the six Democratic appointees. As confirmed by a Democratic appointee, and former chairman of the CFTC, Brooksley Born, "All four Republicans [appointees to the Financial Crisis Inquiry Commission] voted in favor of banning the phrases 'Wall Street' and 'shadow banking' and the words 'interconnection' and 'deregulation' from the panel's final report" (Nasiripour, 2010).

Ultimately, however, the report, the primary dissenting statement and Peter Wallison's separate dissenting statements do use the term "shadow banking" but with great skepticism. The primary dissenting statement rejected the argument that "insufficient regulation of an ambiguously defined shadow banking sector" was "the single cause of the crisis" (FCIC Report, 2011, 414). It is not clear that anyone claimed it was the sole cause. Nevertheless, what is telling in this statement is the qualifying words "ambiguously defined." Additionally, in his dissenting statement, Wallison, a fellow at the conservative American Institute and a longtime proponent of deregulation, dismissed the majority report, including the allegation that the financial-system "deficiencies included a lack of adequate regulation of the so-called 'shadow banking system'" (469). This was odd, given that a parade of regulators testified before the FCIC about shadow banking. The FDIC Chairman Sheila Bair, SEC Chairman Mary Schapiro, Treasury Secretary Timothy Geithner, and former Treasury Secretary Paulson, among others, testified to its existence and provided similar descriptions of its scope.

## Money Market Mutual Funds

Before discussing the run on MMFs, it's important to understand how they function in the shadow banking system. Money market mutual funds are collective investment vehicles that were first offered in the early 1970s. Regulated by the SEC, these funds are limited to investing in high-quality assets with short maturities. These include, for example, US Treasury Bills, repurchase agreements, and commercial paper. Commercial paper is an unsecured promissory note (an IOU) with a maturity of no more than 270 days, but often 30 days, that is issued by a corporation. There are more than 750 MMFs registered with the SEC. which have around $3.8 trillion in assets. Because they typically maintain a stable net asset value (NAV) of at least $1.00 and offer higher returns than bank accounts and check-writing privileges, savers think of them as more attractive but equally as safe as an insured bank deposit account. Roughly 20 percent of household cash balances in the United States are held in MMFs. This perception of safety has enabled MMFs to attract trillions of dollars away from depository institutions. However, the expectation of absolute safety proved to be an illusion during the crisis when there was a "run" on MMFs, largely by institutional investors.

While MMFs look like bank accounts, they are not. MMFs do not pay into the FDIC deposit insurance fund, they do not have access to the Federal Reserve discount window, and they are not subject to safety and soundness supervision by a banking regulator. And they were not restricted as to the return they can pay (whereas bank accounts used to be subject to interest rate caps). As such, when they were launched, the regulated banking industry was concerned about perceived unequal treatment. While they are subject to detailed restrictions in terms of the instruments in which they can invest (such as in terms of diversity, maturity, liquidity, and quality), bank competitors considered this regulatory framework to be less onerous.

This uneven playing field was defended as justifiable regulatory accommodation for innovation. This new type of investment grew from managing about $1 billion in 1973 to a peak in 2008 of roughly $4 trillion in the United States and $5.8 trillion worldwide. While under the Riegle-Neal Interstate Banking and Branching Efficiency Act of 1994, no depository institution may hold more than 10 percent of total US deposits (subject to organic growth and a few other exceptions), the same cannot be said of MMFs. For example, in 2010, one fund family, Fidelity Investments, claimed to manage approximately $450 billion in MMF assets, that, if composed exclusively of US funds, could represent about 16 percent of the then total of approximately $2.8 trillion.

MMFs are an essential, sizeable link in the shadow market intermediation chain. They compete with banks for customer savings, but, instead of using this funding to lend money directly to borrowers, they invest it in tradable instruments with short maturities. Given that MMFs are highly regulated by the SEC, it is a bit incongruous to think of them in this category, grouped together with the nearly unregulated shadow banks like hedge funds. However, even SEC Chairman Mary Schapiro at an FCIC hearing suggested that they might fit in this bucket. Chair Schapiro offered, "For example, are money market funds part of the shadow banking system? They're highly regulated entities, but they're—they're not part of banks, although they are important parts of the financial system" (Schapiro, 2010, 98). Yet they are at the heart of shadow banking. According to a report by the staff of the FRBNY:

> The traditional banking system relies on deposits gathered through bank branches for funding. The shadow banking system relies on the issuance of money market instruments (such as CP, ABCP and repo) to money market investors (such as money market mutual funds) for funding, as well as the

> issuance of longer-term medium-term notes (MTNs) and public bonds to medium- to longer-term debt investors such as securities lenders, pension funds and insurance companies. (Pozsar, Adrian, Ashcraft, and Boesky, 2010, 46)

This deserves some unpacking. At the beginning of the shadow banking intermediation chain are the MMFs. Stated more plainly, MMFs connect the individuals and institutions that for traditional banks act as depositors with those individuals and institutions who need to borrow money. The MMF does not directly loan money. It is merely one of the middlemen. By comparison, in the traditional banking system, the chain is shorter. For most of the twentieth century, banks were the main intermediary between depositors and borrowers. With shadow banking, however, savers began to invest in MMFs, which then paid higher yields than the interest on traditional bank accounts. The cash would then need to be invested, indirectly making its way to borrowers. The path was not direct because MMFs are limited in the types of securities they can hold in terms of maturity.

For example, historically, no individual security held by an MMF could have a maturity longer than 13 months and the dollar-weighted average maturity of the fund could be no longer than 90 days. (As noted below, this has been shortened to 60 days.) So, instead of using savings to make a home or car loan, the MMF must find another middleman. The MMF can purchase asset-backed commercial paper from a conduit sponsored by a bank or sponsored by a finance company. This conduit issues what is called asset-backed commercial paper (ABCP). These ABCP conduits thus are shadow banks. They perform maturity, liquidity, and quality transformation. Even though the underlying mortgage maturity may be 30 years or a car loan 5 years, the paper issued by the conduit is much shorter, perhaps redeemable in 30 days and considered an appropriate short-term investment.

## The Repo Market

The repo market is a significant link between shadow banking and the broader economy. Yet it remains relatively obscure. Some investment banks funded up to 50 percent of their assets in the repo markets prior to the crisis. In addition to Lehman Brothers using repo transactions to hide $50 billion of debt off balance sheets, other banks used similar window-dressing strategies to lower debt levels at the end of fiscal quarters by 42 percent on average (Taub, 2010b). In terms of size, it is estimated that there were roughly $4.3 trillion US repurchase agreements outstanding in March 2008, before the collapse of Bear Stearns. This has been considered the peak of the repo market. In March 2011, the size of the market was approximately $2.7 trillion. If reverse repurchase agreements are also included, the figures are $7 trillion for March 2008 and more than $4.9 trillion for March 2011 (SIFMA, 2011).

In the clearest terms, a repo is a collateralized loan. Structurally, it is a two-part arrangement. The seller (borrower of cash) agrees to sell securities at a discount to a buyer (lender of cash). This discount is known as the "haircut." Under that same agreement, that original seller agrees to buy them back at a future date plus interest. For example, a repo seller might provide $100 million worth of securities to the buyer. In exchange the buyer applying a 1 percent haircut would provide only $99 million in cash. The next day, the seller would pay back the $99 million plus interest and the buyer would return the securities. The securities are known as "collateral." Collateral types range from US Treasuries to riskier asset classes including, for example, mortgage-backed securities, equities, and sovereign debt. Buyers (lenders) in the repo market are cash-rich institutional investors like pension funds and mutual funds that need a liquid but relatively safe place to invest cash, often overnight. Buyers may also be broker dealers and banks that need the collateral securities to cover short positions. Sellers (borrowers) in the repo market are often broker dealers and banks that use these arrangements to finance asset purchases and to leverage.

Repos provide shadow financing with the assistance of another shadow player, the MMF. For example, MMFs supply cash to repo sellers, including large investment banks, so they can purchase assets (including securities, such as residential mortgage-backed securities, and collateralized debt obligations). One might describe the chain between consumer savers and consumer borrowers through these shadows as follows. A saver, instead of depositing money in a traditional bank, invests in an MMF. The fund then takes a portion of the cash it collects from these savers and loans it to an investment bank through the repo market. The securities that the investment bank might purchase are asset-backed securities, bonds backed by the cash flows from consumer loans that it purchased from a finance company and put into a conduit it sponsored off the balance sheet. It is then the loan originator, who completes the chain by providing access to funds to the borrower. Whereas with "traditional" banking, there was just one link, the bank or thrift between the depositor and the borrower, with this shadow banking example, there are at least five: the money market fund, the repo seller (borrower), the securitization conduit, the investment-bank sponsor of the conduit, and the loan originator.

## Money Market Funds and Repos in the Financial Crisis

During the crisis, on September 15, 2008, when Lehman Brothers filed for bankruptcy protection, Reserve Primary fund, an MMF that had substantial investments in commercial paper issued by Lehman, had to reprice its shares—it "broke the buck." The investment adviser (the money management firm) that operated Reserve Primary did not have the resources to prop up the fund. In contrast, all other MMFs that suffered losses either due to Lehman's failure or earlier in 2007, due to problems with ABCP issued by structured investment vehicles that were heavily exposed to subprime mortgages, received financial support from their investment advisers. Without that financial support to help absorb these losses, they would have had to break the buck. The week Lehman failed, according to the SEC, MMF shareholders redeemed 14 percent of outstanding assets from taxable MMFs, for a total of approximately $300 billion. The run was largely on funds open to institutional investors. In comparison, net outflows for prime retail funds were only 4.6 percent. As a result of the run on the institutional taxable funds, the fund managers had to hold large cash positions instead of continuing to invest in commercial paper and repo. This resulted in liquidity being pulled from those firms that borrow in the commercial paper markets; at the end of September, MMFs reduced holdings in top-rated commercial paper by 29 percent, or approximately $200 billion. This was tremendously painful for large industrial firms that depended on investors "rolling" the paper when it matured. The ability to make payroll, and keep the lights on at some large businesses, was at stake.

In response to a concern about a run on MMFs, and thus a subsequent drying up of the commercial paper market representing liquidity to a wide range of corporate borrowers, on September 19th, the Treasury took an unprecedented step. For participating funds, to help end the run, it insured MMF investors up to the amount of the value of their shares, as of that date. In a separate move, the Fed created the Asset-Backed Commercial Paper Money Market Mutual Fund Liquidity Facility (or AMLF). Through AMLF, banks and bank holding companies were given credit to purchase commercial paper from MMFs. There were many lessons in this experience. While aggregating institutional cash might be considered efficient, the FRBNY staff report found that this concentration of such cash in "wholesale funding markets" led to instability because "institutional cash balances are well-informed, herd-like and fickle, and as such, any entity, vehicle or activity that relies on them for funding and lacks contagion-free, alternative sources of liquidity, is an inherently fragile structure" (Pozsar, Adrian, Ashcraft, and Boesky, 2010, 69).

The repo market was also a source of weakness during the crisis. After Lehman failed, counterparties lost confidence in each other. Unable to roll over the repo loans, firms were forced to sell assets at whatever price they could. As Professor Gary Gorton explained, "The current panic centered on the repo market, which suffered a run when 'depositors' required increasing haircuts, due to concerns about the value and liquidity of the collateral should the counterparty 'bank' fail" (2009, 4). These repo lenders also refused to roll over existing repos. Both actions created "massive deleveraging...resulting in the banking system being insolvent" (Gorton, 2009, abstract).

Repo contributed heavily to the maturity mismatch and interconnectedness at the center of the crisis and should remain a focus of prudential regulators. For example, the Goldman Sachs CEO Lloyd Blankfein noted that

> certainly, enhanced capital requirements in general will reduce systemic risk. But we should not overlook liquidity. If a significant portion of an institution's assets are impaired and illiquid and its funding is relying on short-term borrowing, low leverage will not be much comfort. (2010, 9)

## Money Market Mutual Fund Reform

Using existing statutory authority, in 2010, the SEC announced amendments to Rule 2a-7 of the Investment Company Act. These included shortening the weighted average maturity for an entire MMF portfolio of holdings from 90 to 60 days, improving credit quality, and reducing the amount of illiquid securities from 10 percent to 5 percent. In addition, taxable MMFs are now required to hold 10 percent of assets in instruments with daily liquidity. This means cash or cash equivalents. In addition, as a result of this new rule, all MMFs are required to hold 30 percent with weekly liquidity. This means, for example, cash, US Treasury securities, certain other types of government securities, and securities that can be converted to cash in five business days. The general purpose of these changes was to deal with liquidity—where MMF shareholders can create sudden outflows. As stated in the Final Rule, "[W]e have adopted the higher liquidity thresholds, under which we estimate that approximately 90 percent of retail and institutional funds would have been able to satisfy the level of redemption demands during individual days as well as the week of greatest redemption pressure in the fall of 2008 (September 15–19)" (US Securities and Exchange Commission, 2010, 10078). In addition, SEC rule making now permits MMFs to suspend redemptions in the event of a crisis when the NAV falls below $1 in value. The purpose of the rule is to avoid a race to the exit and allow the fund to sell the assets and evenly distribute the proceeds to the fund investors.

There are some experts who believe this is sufficient reform for money funds and others who believe more must be done. The most important question is whether these measures to make MMFs a stronger link will weaken the whole chain. In other words, whether or not funds are reformed further in such a way to make them even less susceptible to runs by their own investors, we will not have solved the main problem that stronger funds, more capable of pulling financing from those entities and instruments in which they invest, will make those dependent on the funds more fragile unless those entities are required to retain both more capital and also mitigate their own maturity mismatch problems.

Professor William Birdthistle contends that this rule making "*increases* rather than decreases the likelihood of future runs on money market funds and consequential failures of the credit markets" (2010, 1186). Birdthistle has faulted the SEC approach for subsidizing MMFs at the expense of other types of investments. He has questioned the failure to consider the systemic risk associated with these and recommended the following: "By either replacing fixed NAVs with floating ones or, instead, requiring the industry to adopt insurance to cover their fixed obligations, the SEC might increase the transparency and long-term well-being of a cornerstone of the U.S. economy" (Birdthistle, 2010, 1200) A floating-rate NAV would presumably show investors in money market funds that they do fluctuate in value. The idea then is that perhaps those who might have invested in a money market fund would move to a bank account or would better select among money market funds, moving from those that decline in value.

In contrast, Professor Jonathan Macey appears to approve of the changes that MMFs have undergone as a result of the SEC rule making and cautions against further meddling. Macey has identified the benefits of money funds. For individuals and institutions they have for 40 years been "a commercially attractive alternative to bank deposits." He points to the fact that money funds historically are "less susceptible to collapse" (2011, abstract). In addition, he contends that the entire system benefits from their existence as they provide liquidity to capital markets through purchases of commercial paper, municipal securities, and repos. As one example, they hold approximately 40 percent of outstanding commercial paper. In addition, he argues that their existence takes pressure off of the FDIC as a backstop to banks. Without these funds, he notes, roughly $2 trillion would move into the depository institutions. He argues that because there is less of a maturity mismatch with money funds than banks, they are inherently less prone to runs.

In addition to scholars, regulators question whether the SEC has gone far enough. Secretary Paulson considered this question in testimony before the FCIC. He praised these vehicles but also wrote that "the expectation that these funds can provide better yields than Treasury Bills or insured deposits, and at the same time provide complete liquidity and no loss of principal, is unrealistic" (2010, 6). Yet his leading suggestion is more disclosure to customers. His secondary recommendation was to explore the floating NAV. It is surprising that barring checking accounts and other similar features that savers associate with banks was not on the list.

In an October 2010 report by the President's Working Group on Financial Markets (PWG), the Treasury expressed the view that recent rule changes were not sufficient. While they "should enhance investor protection and mitigate the risk of runs," they "could not, by themselves be expected to prevent a run on MMFs of the scale experienced in September 2008" (PWG, 2010, 1). Accordingly, the PWG report includes eight additional policy proposals. They are (1) requiring MMFs to have a floating NAV, (2) providing an external liquidity facility or backstop for MMFs that would help handle liquidity issues when redemptions outpace the ability to sell assets, (3) requiring institutional investors who make large redemption requests to take their redemptions in kind and not in cash, (4) creating an insurance program (similar to the Treasury Temporary Guarantee Program that was set up during the crisis), though the PWG was not clear whether this would be funded privately or publicly, (5) authorizing two tiers of MMFs, one with stable values and some with floating, (6) authorizing two tiers, but having retain investors invest in the stable value funds and institutional in the floating value, (7) regulating MMFs as "special purpose banks" with prudential oversight and regulation, and (8) regulating imitations, such as offshore stable value funds, so as to avoid investors shifting into shadow versions of MMFs.

Thereafter, the SEC sought public comment on the PWG report, with a deadline of early 2011. The strongest support from the MMF industry was for a privately funded liquidity facility. The Investment Company Institute, the trade association for mutual fund advisory firms, rejected nearly all of the PWG suggestions and supported only "creating a private emergency facility to serve as a back-up source of liquidity for prime money market funds in the event of unusual market stress" (Investment Company Institute, 2010, 58). The Mutual Fund Directors Forum, a membership organization that represents the independent directors of mutual funds and other investment companies, also expressed concern about the PWG report. The only two suggestions it thought should be studied were the private liquidity facility and possibly insurance (Mutual Fund Directors Forum, 2011).

One of the most innovative suggestions came from Fidelity Investments. In a letter to the SEC the firm first noted that "MMFs provide critical low-cost, short-term, stable funding for federal government (including Government-Sponsored Enterprises), corporations, financial institutions as well as state and local governments and not-profits, including universities and hospitals" (Goebel, 2011, 1). In addition to this social utility, the letter expressed the view that implementation of many of the PWG alternatives would result in "massive disruption to the short-term capital markets" (Goebel, 2011, 13). It rejected the private liquidity facility as not likely to be worth the costs and complications. As an alternative, Fidelity suggested creating a reserve within each MMF composed of a portion of the MMF's income. Once built up over a number of years, the holdback of shareholder income could stop. While a reserve has some appeal as it rings of internalizing losses, in fact, it would be more sensible if the fund adviser, the entity that collects fees out of the fund assets, set aside that reserve by contributing to the reserve by either forgoing management fees or making direct contributions for a period and leaving those inside of the fund. It was these advisers who benefited from the government intervention, and the pain of having to invest their own funds will help prevent the moral hazard that might be associated with having a shareholder-funded cushion at their disposal.

## Repo Reform

As for dependency on the repo market, more must be done to address the maturity mismatch associated with the use of short-term (often overnight) repo funding by banks to finance longer-term assets. While investment banks have financed up to 50 percent of their assets in the repo markets, the treatment of this financing for regulatory capital and leverage purposes does not fully take into account its significance. Moreover, the recently announced SEC rules affecting mutual funds will only send more cash into repurchase agreements. This will likely increase now that the SEC is requiring taxable MMFs to hold 10 percent of total assets in instruments that the fund has the right to receive cash with one day's notice and 30 percent that give the fund the right to receive cash in five business days.

Some suggestions on reforming the repo market include rolling back the 2005 changes to the US Bankruptcy Code, which expanded the classification of collateral that would receive special treatment during bankruptcy proceedings (Lubben, 2010). Upon filing for bankruptcy, a debtor has the benefit of the "automatic stay." This provides breathing room for the debtor and is supposed to avoid a rush to the courthouse to force debtors into bankruptcy, a form of a run on a struggling firm. Once the stay is in effect, parties to agreements with the debtor have to wait to see how much they will receive out of the estate. Additionally, under the code, avoidance powers permit the canceling of contracts and clawback rights permit bringing back to the debtor preferential payments made during a short window of time before the bankruptcy filing. The purpose of the stay, the avoidance powers, and the clawback abilities are to help maximize the value of the estate to fairly distribute it to all creditors. Unlike other creditors, lenders of cash against protected types of repo collateral are not subject to the stay, avoidance powers, or preferential payment clawbacks (Anker et al., 2008; Burroughs et al., 2008). Some argue that special protection for repo counterparties undermines these values and creates systemic risk. For example, Professor Stephen Lubben has explained that, due to this special treatment, there are

> risks created by the rush to close out positions and demand collateral from the firms. Not only does this contribute to the failure of an already weakened firm, by fostering a run on the firm, but it also has consequent effects on the markets generally as parties rush to sell trades with the debtor and buy corresponding positions with new counterparties. (2010, 10)

With these concerns in mind, some have recommended that the special treatment only apply to those repo "lenders" who loan against more transparent and relatively safer collateral types such as US Treasuries.

While Henry Paulson said he had ideas for how to fix the "regulatory flaws" in the shadow banking system, his concept for the repo markets as expressed in his prepared written testimony for the FCIC, resembled more of a technology tune-up than meaningful reform. Paulson suggested "policies, procedures, and systems" improvements in the infrastructure of the triparty repo market. However, what needs to be addressed is the problem on the other side, that of repo borrowers bringing on short-term, unstable debt to finance longer-term, illiquid assets. Secretary of the Treasury Timothy Geithner suggested that the then-pending financial reform legislation would help resolve this inherent problem. However, the final Dodd-Frank Wall Street Reform and Consumer Protection Act does not provide a solution.

## Conclusions

When D'Arista and Schlesinger identified the parallel banking system in 1993, they recommended that all financial institutions be treated the same. Similarly, when McCulley rediscovered and renamed these nonbank financial intermediaries the "shadow banking system," he suggested that "what an institution does, not what it is called, should determine how it is regulated." As Gorton attests, "The reality is that the 'shadow banking system' is, in fact, banking" (2009, 5). Inconsistent regulation of the traditional banks and shadow banks has presented problems. In addition, inconsistent regulation of various links in the financial intermediation chain also creates vulnerabilities. As explained by the FRBNY staff report,

> Along the chain of specialist intermediaries in the shadow banking system, the weakest link in the chain is the pinch-point that can destabilize the entire chain. Over the course of the financial crisis, the main pinch-points were the providers of wholesale funding (money market investors, such as MMFs, for example), which withdrew funding at the end of the chain and lead to funding problems further up the chain, all the way to the ultimate borrowers. (Pozsar, Adrian, Ashcraft, and Boesky, 2010, 70)

In the crisis, shadow banking was been given the safety nets of lender-of-last-resort privileges (including the various Fed liquidity programs to support the triparty repo market) and access to insurance, for example when Treasury stepped in to insure MMF "deposits." Yet, at the same time, shadow banks were not and are not subject to prudential supervision. Such a combination can encourage excessive risk taking. Yet fixing this problem with just one link in the chain is not sufficient. While it is clear that the weakest link in the chain can be destabilizing, the strongest link can be as well. Inconsistency creates instability. Only with consistent macroprudential regulation that is updated to meet innovation with consistent standards can we move from naming and blaming to taming the parallel banking system.

## References


Angelides, Phil. (2010). Comments in the Official Transcript of Financial Crisis Inquiry Commission Hearing on the "Shadow Banking System," Day 1, May 5, available at http://fcic-static.law.stanford.edu/cdn_media/fcic-testimony/2010-0505-Transcript.pdf

Anker, Philip D, Andrew N. Goldman, and James H. Miller. (2008). "Safe Harbor or Adrift in Bankruptcy: Treatment of Mortgage 'Repurchase Agreements' and Servicing Rights in Bankruptcy Court." Wilmer Hale, February 22.

Birdthistle, William A. (2010). "Breaking Bucks in Money Market Funds." *Wisconsin Law Review*, 5: 1155–1201.

Blankfein, Lloyd. (2010). The Official Transcript of the First Public Hearing of the Financial Crisis Inquiry Commission Hearing, January 13, Day 1.

Burroughs, Katherine A., and Jonathan F. Tross, Dechert LLP. (2008). "The Treatment of Mortgage Loan Repurchase Agreements in Chapter 11 Bankruptcy." available at http://www.dechert.com/The_treatment_of_mortgage_loan_repurchase_agreements_in_Chapter_11_Bankruptcy_03-01-2008/ http://www.dechert.com/The_treatment_of_mortgage_loan_repurchase_agreements_in_Chapter_11_Bankruptcy_03-01-2008/

Cox, Christopher. (2010). Written Testimony at the Financial Crisis Inquiry Commission Shadow Banking Hearing, May 5, Day 1.

D'Arista, Jane, and Gerald Epstein. (2010). "Dodd-Frank and the Regulation of Dangerous Financial Interconnectedness: Will It Work? How Will We Know?" The Future of Financial Reform, The Roosevelt Institute, October 4.

D'Arista, Jane, and Tom Schlesinger. (1993). "The Parallel Banking System." In Gary Dymski, Gerald Epstein, and Robert Pollin, eds., *Transforming the U.S. Financial System: Equity and Efficiency for the 21st Century*. Armonk, NY: M. E. Sharpe.

Financial Crisis Inquiry Report: Final Report of the National Commission on the Causes of the Financial and Economic Crisis in the United States. (2011). Official Government Edition, January (the FCIC Report). http://www.fcic.gov.

Financial Stability Board. (2010). "Progress since the Washington Summit in the Implementation of the G20 Recommendations for Strengthening Financial Stability." Report to G20 Leaders.

Geithner, Timothy. (2010). Prepared Testimony before the Financial Crisis Inquiry Commission, Hearing on the "Shadow Banking System," Day 2, May 6.

Goebel, Scott C. (2011). Letter to Elizabeth Murphy, Secretary, Securities and Exchange Commission, Regarding President's Working Group on Money Market Fund Reform, January 10.

Gordon, Jeffrey N. (2009). Columbia Law School Letter to Elizabeth M. Murphy, Secretary, SEC (September 9), p. 3, cited by Birdthistle.

Gorton, Gary B. (2009). "Slapped in the Face by the Invisible Hand: Banking and the Panic of 2007." Yale and NBER, Prepared for the Federal Reserve Bank of Atlanta's 2009 Financial Markets Conference: Financial Innovation and the Crisis, May 11–13, p. 4.

Hsu, Jason, and Max Moroz. (2010). "Shadow Banks and the Financial Crisis of 2007–2008." March 19, available at http://papers.ssrn.com/sol3/papers.cfm?abstract_id=1574970

Investment Company Act of 1940. 15 U.S.C. Section 80a-et seq.

Investment Company Institute. "Frequently Asked Questions about the Treasury's Temporary Guarantee Plan for Money Market Mutual Funds," available at http://www.ici.org/faqs/ci.faqs_guaranty_plan.print

Investment Company Institute. (2010). Letter to Elizabeth Murphy, Secretary, Securities and Exchange Commission, Regarding President's Working Group Report on Money Market Fund Reform Options, January 10.

Kelly, Kate, Tom McGinty, and Dan Fitzpatrick. (2010). "Big Banks Mask Risk Levels: Quarter-End Loan Figures Sit 42% Below Peak, Then Rise as New Period Progresses; SEC Review." *Wall Street Journal*, April 9.

Lubben, Stephen J. (2010). "The Bankruptcy Code Without Safe Harbors." *American Bankruptcy Law Journal* 84.

Macey, Jonathan. (2011). "Reducing Systemic Risk: The Role of Money Market Funds as Substitutes for Federally Insured Bank Deposits." *Yale Law and Economics Research Paper* 422, January 4. http://papers.ssrn.com/sol3/papers.cfm?abstract_id=1735008

Main, Carla. (2011). "Shadow Banks, Dodd-Frank, UBS Notice: Compliance." *Bloomberg*, February 7.

McCulley, Paul. (2009). "The Shadow Banking System and Hyman Minsky's Economic Journey." PIMCO Global Central Banks Focus, May.

McCulley, Paul. (2010). Written Testimony at the Financial Crisis Inquiry Commission Shadow Banking Hearing, May 6, Day 2.

Minsky, Hyman. (1986). *Stabilizing an Unstable Economy*. New Haven: Yale University Press.

Mutual Fund Directors Forum. (2011). Letter to Elizabeth Murphy, Secretary, Securities Exchange Commission, Regarding President's Working Group on Money Market Fund Reform, January 10.

Nasiripour, Shahien. (2010). "Financial Crisis Panel in Turmoil as Republicans Defect; Plan to Blame Government for the Crisis." *Huffington Post*, December 15.

Paulson, Henry. (2010). Testimony in Official Transcript of Financial Crisis Inquiry Commission Hearing on the "Shadow Banking System," Day 2, May 6, pp. 1, 6, and 11.

Pozen, Robert. (2010). *Too Big to Save: How to Fix the U.S. Financial System*. New York: Wiley.

Pozsar, Zoltan, Tobias Adrian, Adam B. Ashcraft, and Hayley Boesky. (2010). "Shadow Banking." Federal Reserve Board of New York Staff Report No. 458 (July 1).

President's Working Group on Financial Markets. (1999). Report on Over-the-Counter Derivatives Markets and the Commodity Exchange Act, November.

President's Working Group on Financial Markets. (2010). Report on Money Market Reform Options, October.

Ricks, Morgan. (2010). "Shadow Banking and Financial Regulation." Columbia Law and Economics Working Paper No. 370 (August 31).

Samuel, Juliet. (2011). "Goldman's Cohn's Warning Makes Hedge Funds Furious." *City A.M.*, January 28.

Schapiro, Mary. (2010). Testimony, Official Transcript of the First Public Hearing of the Financial Crisis Inquiry Commission, January 14, Day 2.

Schapiro, Mary. (2010). Testimony during the Question-and-Answer Session after Prepared Remarks before the House Committee on Financial Services Hearing, "Public Policy Issues Raised by the Report of the Lehman Bankruptcy Examiner" ("Lehman Hearing"), April 20, archived webcast (author notes on file).

Securities Industry and Financial Markets Association. "US Primary Dealer Financing," published quarterly. http://www.sifma.org/

Taub, Jennifer S. (2009). "Recommendations for Reality-Based Regulation of Hedge Funds and Other Private Pools of Capital." S.A.F.E.R. Policy Brief #9, October 21. http://papers.ssrn.com/sol3/papers.cfm?abstract_id=1543862.

Taub, Jennifer S. (2010a). "A Whiff of Repo 105." The Baseline Scenario, March 16. http://baselinescenario.com/2010/03/16/a-whiff-of-repo-105/.

Taub, Jennifer S. (2010b). "Lehman Brothers and Repo 105: A Powerful Case of Addiction." *Journal of Regulation and Risk*, North Asia, 2 (Summer/Autumn).

Taub, Jennifer S. (2011). "The Sophisticated Investor and the Global Financial Crisis." In James P. Hawley, Shyam J. Kamath, and Andrew T. Williams, eds., *Corporate Governance Failures: The Role of Institutional Investors in the Global Financial Crisis*. Philadelphia: University of Pennsylvania Press.

Tett, Gillian. (2011). "Branding a Billion-Dollar Business: How the Sector Got Its Name—and Why It Would Prefer a Different One." *Financial Times*, February 3.

"United Nations Treaty Targets the Funding of Terrorism." (2000). Press Release L/T/4342, PI/1216, January 12.

US Securities and Exchange Commission. (2010). Money Market Fund Reform, Release No. IC–29132; File Nos. S7–11– 09, S7–20–09, Federal Register Vol. 75, No. 42, March 4, p. 10076 ("Mutual Fund Rule Amendment").

CHAPTER 23

# DERIVATIVES IN THE CRISIS AND FINANCIAL REFORM

MICHAEL GREENBERGER

In the fall of 2008, nontransparent, poorly capitalized, and almost wholly unregulated over-the-counter (OTC) derivatives prompted the collapse of the world's highly vulnerable economic markets. Tens of trillions of dollars worth of these financial products were pegged to the economic performance of a highly inflated housing market. The sudden collapse of this market triggered unfunded, often synthetic, OTC derivative guarantees (e.g., naked credit default swaps) of subprime mortgages that were worth many trillions of dollars. Additionally, the interconnectedness of the OTC derivatives market—an immense, global market that consists of thousands of counterparties trading interest rate, currency, foreign exchange, and energy derivatives—required taxpayers to subsidize guarantors that could not satisfy their counterparty obligations (worth trillions of dollars) or risk a total meltdown of the world economy. Today, the world is still struggling to recover from the worst financial crisis since the Depression and global economic growth is likely to remain slow for some time to come.

This chapter explains how the deregulated derivatives market facilitated the 2008 financial crisis. First, it provides an overview of the development of derivative instruments and the history of market regulation. It discusses the highly charged political events surrounding the deregulation of a rapidly expanding derivatives market at the end of the twentieth century and explains how deregulation occurred despite mounting evidence that unregulated markets posed significant risks to the US and world financial systems. It also discusses how the creation of increasingly sophisticated synthetic derivatives products created a casino culture among Wall Street banks, large financial institutions, and affluent investors. Second, the chapter shows that derivative instruments like naked credit default swaps destabilized the subprime mortgage market and thereby facilitated the crisis. Third, it documents how the interconnectedness of the swaps market created "too big to fail" financial institutions that posed systemic risk to the US economy and how the opacity of the swaps market prevented regulators from managing that risk. Fourth, and finally, the chapter examines how the Dodd-Frank Wall Street Reform and Consumer Protection Act (Dodd-Frank) aims to mitigate the documented risks associated with unregulated derivatives trading and how government regulators are working to implement the provisions of the act.

# The History of Derivatives and Derivatives Market Regulation

## The Early Derivatives Market

In 1865, farmers and grain merchants coalesced in Chicago to hedge price risk in corn, wheat, and other grains using what are thought to be the earliest sustained derivatives transactions in the United States (Levy, 2006, 307–309). Historically, these kinds of derivatives are referred to as futures contracts. As Johnson and Hazen observe, "[t]he traditional futures contract is an agreement between a seller and a buyer that the seller (called a short) will deliver to the buyer (called a long), at a price agreed to when the contract is first entered, and the buyer will accept and pay for a specified quantity and grade of an identified commodity in the future" (Johnson and Hazen, 2004, 25). While first developed for the agriculture sector, futures contracts later expanded into metals and energy products, particularly in the 1980s and 1990s.

Since their creation, futures markets have been subject to price distortion (i.e., rather than providing hedging, these markets can cause payments of unnecessary and unexpected higher or lower spot prices) through excessive speculation, fraud, and/or manipulation. As one disgruntled farmer told the House Agriculture Committee in 1892, "the man who managed or sold or owned those immense wheat fields has not as much to say with the regard to the price of the wheat than some young fellow who stands howling around the Chicago wheat pit could actually sell in a day" (Levy, 2006, 307).

After low farm prices wreaked financial havoc on America's agriculture sector during the Depression, President Roosevelt recommended legislation to Congress that became the Commodity Exchange Act (CEA) of 1936. The legislation was one of President Roosevelt's earliest market reform proposals (Roosevelt, 1938). The CEA followed in the wake of the Securities Acts of 1933 and 1934 and it largely aligns with that regulation of the equities markets (i.e., futures contracts were required to be traded on publicly transparent and fully regulated exchanges supported by clearing mechanisms that would ensure that contractual commitments were backed by adequate capital).

Under the CEA, regulated exchanges ensured that futures contracts were subject to: (1) public and transparent pricing based on market demand; (2) disclosure of the actual traders to the federal government; (3) regulation of intermediaries (i.e., brokers and their employers); (4) stringent rules for customer protection; (5) self-regulation by exchanges directly supervised by a federal regulator to detect unlawful trading activity; (6) prohibitions against fraud, market manipulation, and excessive speculation; and (7) enforcement of all these requirements by the federal regulator, private individuals, and the states through government-sponsored law suits, private rights of action, and *parens patriae* suits brought by appropriate state officials, respectively (Greenberger, 2011).

Further, the requirement that futures contracts be cleared was integral to the CEA's regulatory format. In other words, the CEA required that a well-capitalized and regulated intermediary institution stand between the counterparties of a futures contract to ensure that the commitments undertaken pursuant to those contracts are adequately capitalized through the collection of margin (Greenberger, 2011). Because clearing facilities guarantee against any contractual failure, they have a significant incentive to strictly enforce the capital adequacy of traders. To this end, clearing facilities produce highly disciplined assessments of the market price of a futures position, collect initial margin immediately after the futures trade is executed, and collect variation margin when the contract price moves against the counterparty to the trade (Johnson and Hazen, 2004, 189–190).

## The Standardization of Swaps and Their Exemption from Exchange-Trading Requirements

By the 1980s, a variant of futures contracts was developed, which was commonly referred to as a "swap" (Das, 2006, 26, 34–37; Johnson and Hazen, 2004, 6). When it first addressed "swaps" contracts, the Commodity Futures Trading Commission (CFTC) defined them as "an agreement between two parties to exchange a series of cash flows measured by different interest rates, exchange rates, or prices with payment calculated by reference to a principal base (notional amount)" (CFTC, 1989, 30, 695). Swaps contracts were customized agreements that reflected the parties' unique financial interests.

In a classic interest-rate swap transaction, one party to the agreement exchanges a floating interest-rate obligation on an existing loan for a fixed-rate obligation to be paid by a swap dealer or by another counterparty to which the swap has been assigned by the swap dealer. Usually, the person swapping the floating rate for a fixed rate is expecting (or hedging against the fact) that the fixed rate will be lower than the floating rate (Greenberger, 2011).

After the banks (or swap dealers) developed swaps contracts in the 1980s, the acute similarities between futures contracts and swaps prompted market participants and regulators to ask whether swaps should be subject to the mandatory exchange-trading requirement of the CEA. In 1989, the CFTC exempted swaps from the CEA exchange-trading requirement. The agency explained that a swap is not subject to regulation if it is "negotiated by the parties as to their material terms, based upon individualized credit determinations, and documented by the parties in an agreement or series of agreements that is not fully standardized" (CFTC, 1989, 30, 694). The CFTC also explained that "the swap must not be marketed to the public" in order to qualify for the exchange-trading exemption (Johnson and Hazen, 2004, 43).

Swap dealers and banks contended that there was "uncertainty" as to the legal effect of the CFTC's exemption for swaps because the CEA did not explicitly authorize the CFTC to grant such an exemption. In 1992, Congress addressed this uncertainty by authorizing the CFTC to create exemptions from the CEA's mandatory exchange-trading requirement for, inter alia, "swaps agreements," which "are not part of a fungible class of agreements that are standardized as to their material economic terms" (CEA, 2010, sec. 4[c][5][b]).

In 1993, the CFTC adopted a rule that provided a clear exemption from the CEA's exchange-trading requirement for those swaps that were "not part of a fungible class of" standard economic agreements (CFTC, 2009, sec. 35.2[b]). Moreover, exempt swaps agreements were not to be "traded on or through a multilateral transaction execution facility" (CFTC, 2009, sec. 35.2[d]). A "multilateral transaction execution facility" allows one party to offer a swaps agreement electronically to many other parties, rather than offering agreements merely on a bilateral, or one-to-one basis (Greenberger, 2011).

Even before the CFTC exempted swaps from the CEA's requirements in 1993, the International Swaps and Derivatives Association (ISDA)—known at the time as the International Swaps Dealers Association—created a Master Agreement in an attempt to standardize the execution of a swap (Greenberger, 2011). The ISDA Master Agreement is 18 pages long and includes boilerplate language on the essential aspects of a swaps transaction. A 13-page "schedule" accompanies the Master Agreement and includes the ISDA Credit Support Annex; the latter is 16 pages long and outlines how swap counterparties should post and transfer collateral. These documents helped to ensure that OTC swaps exhibited all of the trading characteristics of traditional exchange-traded standardized futures contracts and could easily be traded electronically on a multilateral basis (CFTC, 1998, 26, 114).

## The Growth of the Swaps Market, the Mounting Risks Associated with Swaps Trading, and Resistance to Swaps Regulation

By 1998, demand for OTC derivatives—instruments that the ISDA Master Agreement had mostly standardized—was growing at a rapid pace. As the CFTC reported: "The notional value of outstanding contracts in these instruments was $28.733 trillion [in 1997], up 12.9% from year-end 1996, 62.2% from year-end 1995, and 154.2% from year-end 1994." The CFTC also reported that: "ISDA's 1996 market survey noted that there were 633,316 outstanding contracts in these [derivatives] instruments as of year-end 1996, up 47% from year-end 1995, which in turn represented a 40.7% increase over year-end 1994" (CFTC, 1998, 26, 115).

On May 7, 1998, the CFTC promulgated a "concept release" on OTC derivatives that found that these now-standardized derivatives products were almost certainly subject to the CEA's mandatory exchange-trading requirement (and therefore were being traded in violation of the law). The release called for public comment on the development of various alternative regulatory features that would exempt swaps from the mandatory exchange-trading requirement (CFTC, 1998, 26, 114).

According to the CFTC's release, any regulatory system for swaps would be applied "prospectively" only and the existing market would be sanctioned retroactively under the CEA (CFTC, 1998, 26, 114). The CFTC asked the public to answer a series of questions pertaining to what, *if any*, of the features of a fully regulated exchange-trading requirement should be applied to the swaps market (e.g., reporting and disclosure, capital adequacy, clearing, exchange trading, regulation of intermediaries, self-regulation, or application of antifraud and antimanipulation principles). The CFTC expressly stated that it had no preconceived notion of the answers to these questions.

The CFTC issued its May 1998 release and inquiry on swap regulation because unregulated swaps had caused several financial calamities. In footnote 6 of the concept release, the CFTC cited Jerry A. Markham's *Commodities Regulation: Fraud, Manipulation & Other Claims*, which listed "22 examples of significant losses in financial derivatives transactions" (CFTC, 1998, 26, fn. 6; Markham, 1997). In the same footnote, the CFTC cited a 1997 report by the Government Accountability Office that "identified 360 substantial end-user losses" (CFTC, 1998, 26, fn. 6).

Prior to 1998, one of the most prominent swaps-based scandals was the 1994 bankruptcy of Orange County—at that time the largest municipal default in the nation's history. Orange County was one of the country's wealthiest counties and the fifth most populous county in the United States. The county executed many poorly understood interest-rate swaps and suddenly found itself facing massive debt when interest rates quickly rose. Overall, the county lost approximately $1.6 billion. Eventually, Merrill Lynch agreed to pay $400 million to

Orange County to settle claims involving the derivatives trades that had caused the County to go bankrupt (Baldassare, 1998, 172).

The CFTC's sister agencies within the President's Working Group (the Treasury, Federal Reserve [the Fed], and Securities and Exchange Commission [SEC]) strongly opposed the CFTC's concept release inquiry (*Frontline*, 2009). They issued a statement on the same day that the CFTC published its release, which asked Congress to enact a statutory moratorium to the same release. Congress enacted a six-month moratorium in 1999, a year after the CFTC had issued the concept release (US Congress, *Congressional Record*, 2000, 10079).

Despite strong opposition to swaps regulation by prominent financial regulators, the collapse of Long-Term Capital Management (LTCM) in September 1998 revived support for swaps regulation. Prior to its collapse, LTCM was the country's largest and most successful hedge fund. Notwithstanding its size, LTCM collapsed after it sustained $4.6 billion (or about 90 percent of its capital) in losses over several weeks from its OTC derivatives positions. Banks and government regulators feared that LTCM's failure would cause many of its OTC derivative counterparties and creditors to fail and, subsequently, put some of the world's largest financial institutions at risk. Concern about the systemic effect of LTCM's failure was so great that, on September 23, 1998—about 48 hours after receiving notice about LTCM's potential collapse—14 of LTCM's major creditors contributed a total of $3.6 billion to buy out the fund in order to keep it from failing. This private buyout and rescue was conducted under the auspices of the New York Federal Reserve (President's Working Group on Financial Markets, 1999a, 10–17).

After a full day of hearings before the House Financial Services Committee on October 1, 1998, Congress asked the President's Working Group (PWG) to prepare a report on the failure of LTCM and to recommend actions for preventing similar systemic failure from occurring in the future. In April 1999, the PWG issued the requested report. The report noted that "[t]he near collapse of [LTCM] highlighted the possibility that problems at one financial institution could be transmitted to other institutions, and potentially pose risks to the financial system" (PWG, 1999a, viii).

The PWG report recommended that the SEC, CFTC, and Treasury receive expanded authority to require OTC derivative counterparties to provide credit-risk information, and to keep records and reports on market concentrations, trading strategies, and risk models. The report also recommended that the three agencies have authority to inspect counterparties' risk-management models (PWG, 1999a, 39–40). Fed Chairman Alan Greenspan declined to endorse these recommendations; however, he deferred judgment to those regulators with supervisory authority (PWG, 1999a, 39).

Shortly after the LTCM episode, 12 of the world's largest banks formed the Counterparty Risk Management Policy Group (CRMPG) to study the practices that led to the LTCM crisis and to recommend self-regulatory practices that would prevent such an episode from reoccurring. In June 1999, CRMPG issued a detailed 57-page report, which acknowledged faulty supervision of OTC swaps desks within its institutions and proposed a broad array of management practices, including improved supervision and reporting requirements for OTC derivatives trades. Also, CRMPG recommended that its members commit to meet informally and periodically with their primary regulator to discuss OTC "market trends and conditions" and provide reports "detailing certain large exposure information on a consolidated basis group" (CRMPG, 1999, 10–11).

Although PWG and CRMPG recommended implementing some standards for swaps trading, both organizations ultimately opposed government regulation of swaps. The CRMPG report opposed "new regulation" and concluded that "[i] t would be a mistake to attempt to codify risk management practices in that fashion" (CRMPG, 1999, 10–11). Consequently, the new rules and the informal meetings with regulators that CRMPG proposed never materialized. Moreover, by November 1999, the PWG after a significant turnover of personnel and in a reversal of the position it took in its April 1999 report, recommended to Congress that financial OTC derivatives be affirmatively and expressly deregulated. The PWG argued that even the mere threat of regulation (as previously advanced by the CFTC) would discourage the growth of swaps markets and drive swaps trading from the United States. At that time, the PWG lobbied for "an exclusion from the CEA['s regulatory requirements] for bilateral transactions between sophisticated counterparties (other than transactions that involve non-financial commodities with finite supplies)" (PWG, 1999b, 2).

## The Deregulation of the Futures and Swaps Markets

On December 21, 2000, President Clinton signed into law the Commodity Futures Modernization Act of 2000 (CFMA). The CFMA removed OTC derivatives transactions from the exchange-trading and clearing requirements established under the CEA as long as the counterparties to the swap were "eligible contract participants." An "eligible contract participant" was a counterparty that had over $10 million in total assets; however, some limited exceptions allowed lesser amounts of assets for individuals using swaps for risk-management purposes (Johnson and Hazen, 2004, 328–329). The SEC was similarly barred from OTC derivatives oversight except for the very limited fraud jurisdiction it maintained over securities-based swaps.

In passing the CFMA, Congress ensured that speculative activity in swaps and certain traditional energy futures products, which were also deregulated under the CFMA, would remain unchecked by federal and/or state regulators. The CFMA removed the CEA's bar against excessive speculation (i.e., speculation that exceeds the market's need for liquidity) in newly deregulated energy futures, which could now legally trade OTC. Also, the CFMA prevented the CFTC from taking action to stop excessive speculation either in swaps or in those deregulated energy futures, which had previously been required to trade on exchanges. Specifically, the CFMA expressly preempted state gaming and anti-bucket shop laws that would have been a check on speculative activity authorized by the CFMA (CEA, 2009, sec. 16[e][2]).

Congress also ensured that the CFMA itself could not be used as a basis to challenge the legality of a swap. The statute provided that "no agreement, contract, or transaction between eligible contract participants…shall be void, voidable, or unenforceable…based *solely on the failure…to comply with…this Act*" (CEA, 2009, sec. 25[a][4], emphasis added).

In sum, despite the obvious risks associated with swaps, the CFMA removed a multitrillion-dollar OTC derivatives market from nearly all the pertinent federal and state regulations that had applied to trading markets since the New Deal. The CFMA also removed the derivatives market from a central premise of the common law of contracts: illegal contracts—contracts that violate a statute—are unenforceable. Thus, almost no law applied to the swaps market.

## The Growth of Collateralized Debt Obligations, Credit Default Swaps, and a Casino Culture in the Subprime Mortgage Market

In the years leading up to the crisis, banks began to embed simple mortgage-backed securities (MBSs) within highly complex collateralized debt obligations (CDOs). These CDOs consisted of huge numbers of MBSs that had been separated and then reconfigured into "tranches" (i.e., tiers of similar mortgages that persons could invest in). Also, banks created credit default swaps (CDSs) that allowed investors in CDOs to protect against the risk of default if they paid a fee. Banks quickly developed CDSs to allow investors to speculate on the mortgage market.

The different tranches within CDOs offered gradations of risk to persons who wished to invest in subprime mortgages and diversify their investment portfolio; however, investors came to view CDO tranches as relatively risk-free investments. The continuous reframing of the form of risk—for example, as subprime mortgages were organized into MBSs and then into CDOs—unmoored investors from the essential risk underlying loans to non-creditworthy individuals. Additionally, the false assurances given by credit-rating agencies about the safety of CDO tranches meant that CDOs received misleadingly high credit ratings. Most importantly, the "insurance" offered on CDOs in the form of CDSs appeared to shield investors from the risks associated with even the most precarious subprime loans (Greenberger, 2010, 100–101).

In the context of the subprime mortgage market, a CDS involved an exchange between two counterparties: one counterparty agreed to pay a "premium" in return for the other counterparty's "guarantee" of the financial viability of a particular CDO or certain of the tranches therein. In other words, CDSs placed a floor under bets made on the success of mortgages to non-creditworthy lenders; they seemingly protected investors in CDOs against major loses. Thus, CDSs facilitated investment in the subprime securitization process. They fueled demand for the subprime mortgages and MBSs that made-up the CDOs; they encouraged lax mortgage lending practices as lenders struggled to satisfy demand.

For their part, the issuers of CDSs were almost certainly beguiled by the utopian view (supported by ill-considered mathematical algorithms) that housing prices would always rise. They believed that even a borrower who could not afford a mortgage at initial closing would soon be able to extract value out of his or her home because the value of the home was constantly appreciating; the extracted value would allow the borrower to refinance and pay his or her mortgage obligations. Consequently, writing a CDS was deemed to be "risk free" and many investors wrote as many CDSs as possible in order to secure a huge and supposedly guaranteed cash flow from CDS "premia" (Greenberger, 2010, 102).

The supposedly risk-free nature of CDSs generated so much demand for these financial instruments that financial institutions began to create synthetic CDOs. Synthetic CDOs comprised of a series of "naked" CDSs, which provided investors who had *no* risk in any underlying mortgage-backed instruments or CDOs with a guarantee against default against CDOs they selected for "insurance" (Kimball-Stanley, 2008, 251–252). Synthetic CDOs and naked CDSs allowed investors to "short" the mortgage-lending market without actually owning any mortgage risk either from MBSs or real CDOs. The holders of synthetic CDOs selected what they believed to be the weakest tranches in "real" CDOs and bet that those weak tranches would fail. Purchasers of synthetic CDOs paid little consideration (i.e., the relatively small premium) to place a perfectly logical bet that persons who could not afford mortgages would not pay their mortgages. State insurance law banned similar guarantees in the "real" insurance market because the guarantees insured someone else's risk. This ban had existed for over two centuries in the insurance markets; however, investors in the derivatives market routinely used naked CDSs to bet on the stability of select subprime mortgages that they did not own. CDSs existed outside of the prohibitions of the regulated insurance industry merely because of the semantics of being labeled a "swap," rather than insurance.

The 2010 suit by the SEC against Goldman Sachs for fraud related to the bank's marketing of a subprime mortgage product reveals how synthetic CDS instruments facilitated near unlimited bets on subprime mortgages. Leaving aside the fraud allegation made by the SEC, the SEC's lawsuit revealed that hedge fund manager John Paulson worked with Goldman Sachs to select tranches from a series of CDOs that he deemed most likely to fail. Paulson also worked with Goldman to locate institutions that believed that the tranches Paulson had selected—and that neither party to the bet owned—would survive and, subsequently, were willing to bet against Paulson and his prediction that the tranches would lose value. In other words, Goldman located institutions that would insure Paulson against the failure of the tranches that he had selected, but did not own (Field, 2010). The bets were executed as synthetic CDOs, which comprised of a series of naked CDSs each of which "insured" a tranche within a given CDO against default. According to the SEC, Goldman charged Paulson a $15 million fee to review tranches that he did not own and to help him bet against the success of those mortgage instruments.

Paulson won about $1 billion for betting that homeowners would default on their mortgages. Despite Paulson's huge financial gain—a gain that had an equally huge inverse impact on his losing counterparties—his trades presented a moral hazard. Again, leaving aside the question of fraud—specifically, whether Goldman defrauded Paulson's counterparties when it arranged for them to take the opposite side of the Paulson bet—Paulson was merely gambling that subprime mortgages would fail. He used naked CDS instruments to place a lawful bet worth billions of dollars on homeowners' potential defaults on mortgages that neither Paulson nor his counterparty owned. In turn, the naked CDS instruments that Paulson traded created a perverse incentive to ensure that homeowners did not pay their mortgages. In fact, many investors who bet that mortgages would fail fiercely opposed congressional attempts to "rescue" subprime borrowers by adjusting mortgages to keep homeowners from defaulting and thereby losing their homes (Grim, 2009). Thus, CDS instruments created a casino culture that rewarded investors for shorting the subprime mortgage market and, by extension, betting against the health of the US economy.

Synthetic CDOs and naked CDSs proved so popular that there were three to four times as many synthetic instruments betting on the viability of subprime mortgages at the time of the meltdown than CDSs guaranteeing actual risk (Kopecki and Harrington, 2009; US Congress, Senate, 2008). Consequently, to the extent that the guarantors of CDSs (e.g., AIG) had to be rescued by the US taxpayer, the chances were very high that the "bailout" was of failed naked CDS bets that mortgages would be paid. The bailout of the subprime mortgage market used US taxpayer money to make winning bettors whole.

The fact that "synthetic" CDOs and "naked" CDSs were nothing more than "bets" on the viability of the subprime market emphasizes the importance of the CFMA and Congress's express preemption of state gaming and anti-bucket shop laws (Johnson and Hazen, 2004, 975). Had those laws not been preempted, at least some states would surely have banned these investments as unlicensed gambling or illegal bucket shops. An action of this sort by even a single state would have disrupted the "naked" CDS market throughout the country.

# Credit Default Swaps Destabilized the Subprime Mortgage Market and Facilitated the Economic Meltdown

The unregulated multi-trillion dollar CDO-CDS swaps market substantially heightened the risks posed by the securitization of subprime mortgage loans. The near insatiable demand for synthetic "bets" on the subprime mortgage market prior to the 2008 crisis created a huge financial market that was undercapitalized, opaque, and immune from state and federal regulation. This overheated and highly speculative betting on the subprime mortgage market fomented a mortgage crisis, then a credit crisis, and finally a "once-in-a-century" systemic financial crisis that, but for huge interventions by US taxpayers, would have led to a devastating Second Great Depression.

The enormity of this under-capitalized and opaque market cannot be overstated. In October 2008, the notional value of the unregulated OTC derivatives market was estimated to be in excess of $600 trillion (Sheridan, 2008). Real and "naked" CDSs accounted for between $35 and $65 trillion of the $600 trillion figure (Bank for International Settlements, 2008, A108).

Even by conservative estimates, CDSs presented a sizeable part of the economy prior to the 2008 financial crisis. The Fed has estimated that the amount at risk in swaps transactions is about 3 percent of the notional amount of a swap; however, because CDSs function much like insurance, the entire amount of the sum guaranteed by the CDS is at risk when a default is triggered. Combining the *lower* figure for the value of outstanding CDSs in September 2008 ($35 trillion) with 3 percent (the Fed's conservative estimate of the amount at risk in a swaps transaction) of the notional value of the unregulated OTC market exclusive of CDSs (3 percent of $565 trillion or $16.95 trillion) indicates that the amount at risk at the time of the meltdown was at least $52 trillion or close to the equivalent of the world's GDP (Sirri, 2008).

Absent the strict regulations outlined in the CEA—regulations that were largely repealed by the CFMA—the immense size of the market in subprime mortgages threatened the stability of US derivatives and securities markets as well as the US and world economies. The lack of capitalization in the OTC subprime mortgage swaps market meant that many of the losing counterparties did not have the resources to pay the winning counterparties. In fact, had these losing parties not received a bailout from US taxpayers many of them would have collapsed under the strain of paying losing bets that were not properly capitalized. Also, the lack of transparency prevented regulators from realizing that the high demand for synthetic CDO investment tools was sparked by insurance in the form of synthetic and real CDSs that were not properly capitalized (Greenberger, 2010, 101–102).

Additionally, the interconnectedness of financial institutions (discussed in detail in the succeeding section) meant that the collapse of a single major financial institution would likely have destabilized the worldwide economy. In this sense, the intervention by US taxpayers as the lender of last resort stemmed the onset of a worldwide depression.

At the time of the crisis, even former proponents of the CFMA acknowledged that the statute removed important safeguards from the OTC swaps market. In September 2008, then SEC Chairman Christopher Cox—who as a Congressman had voted for the CFMA—testified before the Senate Banking Committee regarding the need for market reform as Congress considered bank bailout (TARP) legislation. In his testimony, Chairman Cox called the CDS market a "regulatory black hole" in need of "immediate legislative action" (O'Harrow and Dennis, 2008).[1] Additionally, former SEC Chairman Arthur Levitt and even former Fed Chair Alan Greenspan—both of whom supported the CFMA in 2000—acknowledged in 2008 that the deregulation of the CDS market contributed to the financial crisis (Goodman, 2008).

## Interconnectedness and Opacity: Systemic Risk Derived from All Types of Swaps

Although CDSs and synthetic CDOs almost certainly facilitated the rapid destabilization of the financial markets, the interconnectedness and opacity of the OTC market triggered destabilizing economic events even prior to the 2008 crisis. These events include the 2005–2008 energy and food commodity bubble, the near-failure of LTCM in 1998, the Orange County bankruptcy of 1994, and now, through cross-currency swaps that masked the full extent of sovereign debt, the European sovereign debt crisis (Greenberger, 2008, 2–3; Greenberger, 2009, 4–5; Story, Thomas, and Schwartz, 2010).

The financial crisis and its immediate aftermath revealed that the remainder of the unregulated OTC derivatives market was central to the crisis's causation. In the years immediately prior to the financial crisis, the OTC derivatives market interconnected banks to such an extent that large financial institutions became "too big to fail." In other words, banks became so big that their collapse would have facilitated a cascading collapse of the financial system. Thus, "too big to fail" financial institutions could rely on US taxpayer bailouts to protect them against failure because the US government feared that the failure of a major financial institution would undermine the entire financial system (Greenberger, 2008).

As the Lehman bankruptcy proceedings revealed, Lehman at the time of its collapse was a counterparty or guarantor of over 930,000 OTC derivatives (Charles,

2009, 16). To the extent that these contracts did not involve CDSs, they involved unregulated interest-rate, currency, foreign exchange, and energy swaps. The Lehman liquidators engaged in a huge battle with Lehman's OTC derivative counterparties over the value of amounts owed by Lehman pursuant to those derivatives. The liquidators argued that Lehman's counterparties greatly exaggerated the amount of money Lehman owes (Murphy and Sakoui, 2010; Sandler, 2012).

Of course, it was the failure of Lehman, and the cascading adverse and substantial impacts caused by its bankruptcy, that, on the day after Lehman's failure, led the Fed and the Treasury to alter course and intervene in the market in order to prevent AIG's bankruptcy and, later, to recommend the TARP bailout. These novel actions by the Fed and Treasury established the correlation between the interconnectedness of unregulated OTC swaps transactions and the "too-big-to-fail" doctrine (Congressional Oversight Panel, 2010, 9).

Additionally, the fact that swaps were never properly accounted for on balance sheets meant that all derivatives—not just credit derivatives—played an important role in facilitating the 2008 financial crisis. As a direct result of intensive lobbying by ISDA, swaps regulators adopted policies that allowed companies to obscure the vast majority of their swaps-related debt:

> banks and corporations that trade swaps do not play by the same rules as other individuals and businesses. Banks are permitted to exclude their full exposure to swaps from their financial statements and instead report only the "fair value" changes in those swaps over time. Such reporting is like an individual reporting only the change in their debt balances, instead of reporting the debts themselves. (Partnoy and Turner, 2010, 88)

Prior to the financial meltdown, a double barrier of opacity masked the risks associated with swaps of all kinds. First, since swaps were private and bilateral, the risks associated with these instruments were not apparent to financial regulators. Second, these swaps-based risks were hidden on the balance sheets of the institutions that were most likely to suffer from the adverse impact of a swaps trade. This balance-sheet opacity blinded regulators and market observers to the volatile and toxic nature of the contractual obligations embedded in swaps. Also, when the crisis became full-blown in September 2008, the opacity of the swaps market prompted creditors and policy makers to fear the worst. As a result, bank lending froze up and the credit crisis resulted.

## Recent Financial Reform

### The Dodd-Frank Act

On July 21, 2010, President Obama signed the Dodd-Frank Wall Street Reform and Consumer Protection Act into law (Dennis, 2010). Title VII of that act transforms the regulation of OTC derivatives by subjecting standardized swaps to clearing and exchange-trading or exchange-trading-like requirements, capital and margin requirements, and increased record keeping and reporting. The legislation addresses the key problems described above in connection with the largely unregulated swaps market, including the lack of market transparency for regulators and counterparties and the absence of sufficient capital resources to protect against risk.

The act defines "swap" in broad terms. According to the act, swaps include any transaction that provides for the exchange of payments based on the value of one or more underlying financial interest(s) of any kind, or dependent on the occurrence, nonoccurrence, or extent of occurrence of an event or contingency associated with a potential financial consequence (Dodd-Frank Act, 2010, sec. 721[a][21]). The act specifies, however, that swaps do not include "any sale of a nonfinancial commodity or security for deferred shipment or delivery, *so long as the transaction is intended to be physically settled*" (Dodd-Frank Act, 2010, sec. 721[a][21], emphasis added).

The act requires all swap dealers and major swap participants to register with banking regulators, the CFTC, and/or the SEC (Dodd-Frank Act, 2010, sec. 731). A swap dealer is a person who (1) holds itself out as such, (2) makes a market in swaps, (3) regularly enters into swaps for its own account in the ordinary course of business, or (4) engages in activity generally recognized in the trade as dealing in swaps. (Dodd-Frank Act, 2010, sec. 721[a][21]). A major swap participant is an entity that (1) maintains a substantial position in swaps, excluding transactions used to hedge commercial risk, (2) creates substantial counterparty exposure that could undermine the banking system or financial markets, or (3) is highly leveraged, not subject to capital requirements, and maintains a substantial position in swaps (Dodd-Frank Act, 2010, sec. 721[a][13]).

Registered swap dealers and major swap participants must disclose material risks, material incentives, and/or conflicts of interests that are related to swaps. (Dodd-Frank Act, 2010, secs. 731, 764). They must meet capital and margin requirements and conform to business conduct rules, including rules related to fraud and market manipulation, that are set by financial regulators (clearing organizations and exchanges can supplement those requirements) (Dodd-Frank Act, 2010, secs. 731, 764). In addition, these financial entities must conform to position limits that are set for commodity futures derivatives by exchanges in accordance with minimum standards set by financial regulators (Dodd-Frank Act, 2010, secs. 737, 763[h]).

The act imposes clearing and exchange-trading or exchange-trading-like requirements on standardized swaps transactions (Dodd-Frank Act, 2010, secs. 723, 763). As noted previously, because clearing facilities stand between the buyer and seller of a contract to guarantee each party against the failure of the other, the facilities have a strong incentive to establish and enforce the capital adequacy of traders, including the collection of margin. Under the act, the regulatory agencies decide what types of swaps must be cleared and designated clearing organizations (DCOs) inform their regulatory agencies if they plan to clear additional types of swaps (Dodd-Frank Act, 2010, secs. 723, 763). DCOs must give their members and other parties nondiscriminatory access to clearing (Dodd-Frank Act, 2010, secs. 723[a][3], 763[a]).

Further, swaps that must be cleared must be traded on a designated contract market, securities exchange, or swap execution facility (Dodd-Frank Act, 2010, secs. 723[a][3], 763[a]). Importantly, swaps that are so nonstandard that no exchange will accept them do not have to be exchange traded; however, those that are appropriately standardized must still be cleared and are subject, where appropriate, to capital and margin requirements (Dodd-Frank Act, 2010, secs. 723[a][3], 731, 763[a], 764[a]).

The Dodd-Frank Act contains a narrow "end-user" exception from clearing and exchange-trading requirements. End users are businesses that "rely on derivatives to hedge commodity price fluctuations and to insulate their businesses and consumers from risk" (Commodity Markets Oversight Coalition, 2010). These businesses include, for example, airlines using swaps to hedge the purchase of fuel. During the legislative process that led to the act, end users argued for this exception to the clearing and exchange-trading requirements. End users claimed that adhering to these requirements would increase their costs by requiring, inter alia, the payment of margin, which was often not required in the unregulated OTC derivatives markets. End users also claimed that clearing requirements—and the costs the requirements imposed—were unnecessary because end users do not pose systemic risk (American Gas Association et al., 2010; Coalition of Derivatives End Users, 2009).

The narrow "end-user" exemption from Dodd-Frank's clearing and exchange-trading requirements is only available to parties that are not financial entities and use swaps to hedge or mitigate commercial risk. A party that intends to use the exemption must notify the CFTC or SEC of its intent and must explain in general terms how it will meet its financial obligations with respect to the non-cleared swaps (Baker Botts, 2012). Small businesses such as credit unions and savings associations that have total assets of $10 billion or less are deemed non-financial entities and so can take advantage of the "end-user" exemption (Dodd-Frank Act, 2010, secs. 723[a][3], 763[a]). The "end-user" exception does not cover swaps in which both parties are major swap participants, swap dealers, or other specified financial entities (Dodd-Frank Act, 2010, secs. 723[a][3], 763[a]).

Senators Dodd and Lincoln reinforced the importance of Dodd-Frank's "end-user" exemption when they stated explicitly in the legislative history of the act that regulators should not impose margin requirements on end users: "The legislation does not authorize the regulators to impose margin on end users... If regulators raise the cost of end user transactions, they may create more risk" (Dodd and Lincoln, 2010).

Dodd-Frank imposes a real-time reporting requirement for all standardized swaps. Thus, real-time reporting applies both to swaps that are subject to mandatory clearing and to swaps and security-based swaps that are not cleared

(Dodd-Frank Act, 2010, secs. 727, 729; CFTC, 2012 Swap Data Recordkeeping and Reporting Requirements). As relevant, DCOs (or, if the swap is not cleared, the designated reporting counterparty) must report the execution of standardized swaps to a registered swap data repository (CFTC, 2012 Swap Data Recordkeeping and Reporting Requirements). Alternatively, if no swap data repository will accept the report, the swap execution must be reported to regulators "in a manner that does not disclose the business transactions and market positions of any person" (Dodd-Frank Act, 2010, sec. 727). The act defines "real-time public reporting" as public dissemination of data relating to a transaction, including price and volume, as soon as technologically practicable after the time at which the swap transaction has been executed (Dodd-Frank Act, 2010, secs. 727, 763[i]).

Sections 727 and 763 of Dodd-Frank authorize federal regulators to make swap transaction and pricing data available to the public in such a form and at such times as are deemed appropriate to enhance price discovery. As CFTC Chairman Gensler has stated, data reporting allows "swap data repositories to perform their core function of collecting and maintaining swaps data and making it directly and electronically available to regulators... swaps data [must] be collected not only when the transaction occurs, but also for each lifecycle event and valuation over its duration" (Gensler, 2010). Under Dodd-Frank's reporting requirements, prudential and market regulators will receive all relevant and necessary data in a timely manner. In turn, receipt of this data will allow regulators to effectively exercise their enforcement authorities by properly monitoring, supervising, and regulating entities that could pose systemic risk to the US financial system.

In addition to imposing reporting requirements, Dodd-Frank requires that all registered swap dealers and major swap participants maintain daily trading records of swaps and all related records and recorded communications—electronic mail, instant messages, recordings of telephone calls—for a time period set by the CFTC and SEC (Dodd-Frank Act, 2010, secs. 731, 764[a]). Each registered swap dealer and major swap participant is required to maintain a complete audit trail for conducting comprehensive and accurate trade reconstructions (Dodd-Frank Act, 2010, secs. 731, 764[a]).

One of the more controversial provisions in the Dodd-Frank Act is the Lincoln, or "Push-Out," rule, which prohibits federal assistance to swaps entities (i.e., swap dealers and major swap participants) with respect to certain credit derivatives, most commodity derivatives, and all equity derivatives (Dodd-Frank Act, 2010, sec. 716; Fitch, 2012). Federal assistance is defined broadly to include federal deposit insurance or access to the Federal Reserve's discount window (Dodd-Frank Act, 2010, sec. 716[b]). The rule permits swaps entities that deal in "interest rate, currency, gold/silver, credit derivatives referencing investment-grade securities, and hedges" to still have access to federal assistance (Fitch 2012). Also, the Push-Out rule applies to swaps activity that occurs only after the rule takes effect in July 2013 (Simpson Thacher Memorandum, 2012).

The logical consequence of the Push-Out rule will be to encourage the largest US bank holding companies to "push out," or divest, their risky swaps trades, so that they retain access to federal banking assistance.

Similarly, the Volcker rule prohibits any specified banking entity (i.e., an insured depository institution, a company that controls an insured depository institution, a bank holding company, or any affiliate or subsidiary of the foregoing) from engaging in proprietary trading (that is, trading that is on a bank's own behalf and not for a customer) unless certain exceptions are found applicable (Dodd-Frank Act, 2010, sec. 619; Davis Polk, 2010). The rule also prohibits the banking entity from acquiring or retaining an interest that exceeds 3 percent in a hedge fund or private equity fund (collectively referred to as "covered funds") (Orrick, 2011; CFTC, 2012, Prohibitions and Restrictions on Proprietary Trading). Although the regulations implementing the Volcker rule have yet to be finalized, the Federal Reserve anticipates that the rule will be finalized within the next two years and has stated that banking entities must comply with the Volcker Rule "by no later than the end of the conformance period," which is July 21, 2014 (Davis Polk, 2012, Volcker Rule Conformance Period Guidelines; Eisert, 2012). However, the Fed has reserved the right to postpone the compliance date (Davis Polk, 2012, Volcker Rule Conformance Period Guidelines). Despite the fact that the Volcker rule will not be implemented for at least two years, the activities prohibited by the rule have already begun to move from banking entities covered by the rule to other financial entities (Craig, 2012).

The Push-Out and Volcker rules aim to reduce the size and the integration of "too big to fail" institutions by moving risky swaps transactions from federally insured institutions and bank holding companies to more diverse areas of the market such as hedge funds and/or other financial entities not considered "too big to fail." The rules "will reduce the scale, complexity, and interconnectedness [of] banks [and] reduce the possibility that banks will be too big or too complex to resolve in an orderly manner should they fail" (US Congress, Senate, 2010, 9).

Further, Dodd-Frank's elimination of the preemption of state gaming and bucket-shop laws for nonsecurity-based swaps may allow state regulators to act under these laws for the first time in many years and thus serve as another regulatory check on highly speculative and systemically risky "bets" by large US financial institutions (Sidley, 2011). The gaming and bucket-shop preemption remains, however, in effect for security-based swaps (Dodd-Frank Act, 2010, sec. 767).

Dodd-Frank explicitly preempts application of state insurance laws to "insurance-like" products, such as CDSs. The act states that swaps and security-based swaps "shall not be considered to be insurance" and "may not be regulated as an insurance contract under the law of any State" (Dodd-Frank Act, 2010, secs. 722[b], 767). As applied to swaps, the Dodd-Frank provision preempting state insurance laws was almost certainly included in the statute because Eric Dinallo, in his then-capacity as New York Insurance Superintendent, seriously considered regulating CDSs as insurance and because the National Council of Insurance Legislators was working on a model code to regulate CDSs as insurance while Dodd-Frank was being drafted (National Conference of Insurance Legislators, 2009; New York State Insurance Department, 2008).

Importantly, the act narrows but does not eliminate the CFMA provision that prohibited swaps contracts from being voided based only on their violation of the CEA. The act states that swaps and hybrid instruments between eligible contract participants are not "void, voidable, or unenforceable, and no party...shall be entitled to rescind, or recover any payment...under this section or any other provision of Federal or State law, based solely on the failure of the agreement, contract, or transaction (i) to meet the definition of a swap...or (ii) to be cleared" (Dodd-Frank Act, 2010, sec. 739). Thus, a contract could be voidable for violating provisions of the act that are not related to the definition of a swap or to clearing.

Finally, Title II of Dodd-Frank creates a resolution authority, known as the "Orderly Liquidation Authority," which allows the orderly unwinding of a "too-big-to-fail" institution to be handled administratively rather than in a bankruptcy proceeding (Dodd-Frank Act, 2010, sec. 204). That said, the unwinding of the obligations of OTC counterparties would almost certainly have been—in the absence of the Title VII reforms—too complex to be undertaken either by banking regulators or by a court. As Robert Johnson has observed:

> When a ["too-big-to-fail" institution] is in trouble—and there are substantial holdings of complex and opaque derivatives on the balance sheets of all [such] firms—resolution authorities have difficulty unraveling the spider web of exposures and valuing them properly...Unfortunately, it is easy to understand why resolution authorities could be induced to forebear rather than resolve [the unwinding of a too-big-to-fail institution] when they have no clarity about its structure and patterns of exposures. In such a circumstance, it may be easier to incur the risk that the insolvent [firm's] balance sheet should continue to deteriorate. (Johnson 2010, 123)

## Final Rules for Derivatives

As of this writing, the CFTC and SEC (and other federal regulators) are finalizing regulations to satisfy the statutory requirements of Title VII and other portions of Dodd-Frank discussed in this chapter. The principal regulator under Title VII—the CFTC—has completed over two thirds of its 60 rulemakings under Dodd-Frank and is scheduled to complete the rulemaking process by early 2013 (Davis Polk, 2012, Two Year Anniversary Report, 9; Scheid, 2012). The SEC has finalized only about one third of its required Dodd-Frank rulemakings (Davis Polk, 2012, Two Year Anniversary Report, 9). As has been previously mentioned, financial regulators anticipate implementing the Volcker rule by July 2014 (Eisert, 2012).

The proposed and final rules promulgated under Title VII and other provisions discussed herein will clarify and elaborate upon the general provisions in the statute; however, until *all* Dodd-Frank rules are final, it is not possible to elaborate fully on how they will impact the statutory scheme and on how that statutory scheme will be implemented in detail. Space restrictions herein prevent a full discussion of even those CFTC and SEC rules that are final. However, these administrative actions must be consulted carefully in order to gain a full understanding of how financial regulators will implement the statutory provisions in Dodd-Frank that relate to OTC derivatives (CFTC, 2012).

## Conclusion

Had the norms of market regulation been applicable to the pre-Dodd-Frank OTC derivatives market, clearing requirements would have ensured that swaps transactions were adequately capitalized. Moreover, the transparency and price discipline facilitated by the Dodd-Frank reforms would have allowed regulators to have observed and monitored the mounting risks and therefore might have prevented the financial chaos that ultimately ensued.

Dodd-Frank aims to place OTC derivatives under a regulatory framework that is similar to the regulatory regimes that for decades have successfully governed other financial investments, such as securities and traditional commodity futures trading. These markets demand clearing and exchange trading, record keeping and reporting, and margin and capital requirements for standardized swaps. By reviving traditional investor protections, Dodd-Frank has the potential to prevent a future financial collapse similar to that which occurred in the 2008 financial crisis.

## Note

1. "The regulatory black hole for credit default swaps is one of the most significant issues we are confronting on the current credit crisis," Cox said. "It requires immediate legislative action" (O'Harrow and Dennis, 2008).

## References

American Gas Association et al. (2010). Letter to Sen. Harry Reid and Sen. Mitch McConnell, May 3. http://www.ngsa.org/Assets/docs/filings%20testimony/congressional/otc%20letter%20from%20energy%20coalition%20on%20end-user%20exemption.pdf.

Baker Botts. (2012). "CFTC Publishes Final Rule Governing the End-User Exception to the Swap Clearing Requirement." *Energy Regulatory Update*, July 17. http://www.bakerbotts.com/file_upload/Update201207EnergyReg-CFTCPublishesFinalRulesGoverningtheEnd-UserException2.htm.

Baldassare, Mark. (1998). *When Government Fails: The Orange County Bankruptcy*. Berkeley: University of California Press.

Bank for International Settlements. (2008). "Table 23A: Derivative Financial Instruments Traded on Organised Exchanges." *BIS Quarterly Review: Statistical Annex* (September). http://www.bis.org/publ/qtrpdf/r_qa0809.pdf.

Charles, GuyLaine. (2009). "OTC Derivative Contracts in Bankruptcy: The Lehman Experience." *New York Business Law Journal* 13(1): 14–17.

Coalition of Derivatives End Users. (2009). Letter to Sen. Mike Crapo, October 29. http://www.uschamber.com/sites/default/files/hill-letters/091029_derivatives.pdf.

*Commodity Exchange Act, US Code Annotated* 7 (2009 & 2010), §§1–26.

*Commodity Futures Modernization Act, US Code Annotated* 7 (2000), §§5–9, 27; *US Code Annotated* 11 (2000), §§781–784; *US Code Annotated* 15 (2000), §§77–78.

Commodity Futures Trading Commission. (1989). "Policy Statement Concerning Swap Transactions." *Federal Register* 54, no. 139 (July 21): 30,694–30,697.

Commodity Futures Trading Commission. (1998). "Over-the-Counter Derivatives." *Federal Register* 63, no. 91 (May 12): 26,114–26,127.

Commodity Futures Trading Commission. (2009). "Exemption of Swap Agreements." *Code of Federal Regulations*, title 17, sec. 35.2.

Commodity Futures Trading Commission. (2011). "Position Limits for Futures and Swaps." *Federal Register* 76, no. 223 (November 8): 71626, 71685–71699.

Commodity Futures Trading Commission. (2012). "Business Conduct Standards for Swap Dealers and Major Swap Participants With Counterparties." *Federal Register* 77, no. 33 (February 17): 9735–9736, 9822–9829.

Commodity Futures Trading Commission. (2012). "Further Definition of 'Swap Dealer,' 'Security-Based Swap Dealer,' 'Major Swap Participant,' 'Major Security-Based Swap Participant' and 'Eligible Contract Participant.'" *Federal Register* 77, no. 100 (May 23): 30596–30597, 30743–30757.

Commodity Futures Trading Commission. (2012). "Prohibitions and Restrictions on Proprietary Trading and Certain Interests in, and Relationships With, Hedge Funds and Covered Funds." *Federal Register* 77, no. 30 (February 14): 8430.

Commodity Futures Trading Commission. (2012). "Swap Data Recordkeeping and Reporting Requirements." *Federal Register* 77, no. 9 (January 13): 2137–9.

Commodity Futures Trading Commission. (2012). "Dodd Frank Act."http://www.cftc.gov/LawRegulation/DoddFrankAct/index.htm.

Commodity Markets Oversight Coalition. (2010). Open Letter to Congress on House-Senate Conference Priorities for Derivatives Reform Legislation, June 8. http://www.airlines.org/PublicPolicy/Coalition/Documents/CMOC_2010JUNE_ConfCommitteeFINAL.pdf.

Congressional Oversight Panel. (2010). *June Oversight Report: The AIG Rescue, Its Impact on Markets, and the Government's Exit Strategy*. http://cop.senate.gov/documents/cop-061010-report.pdf.

Counterparty Risk Management Policy Group. (1999). *Improving Counterparty Risk Management Practices*. New York: Counterparty Risk Management Policy Group. http://www.isda.org/educat/pdf/CRMPG-Report6-99.pdf.

Craig, Susanne. (2012). "Goldman Moves to Comply With Volcker Rule." *New York Times*, May 10. http://dealbook.nytimes.com/2012/05/10/goldman-moves-to-comply-with-volcker-rule/.

Das, Satyajit. (2006). *Traders, Guns & Money: Knowns and Unknowns in the Dazzling World of Derivatives*. London: FT Prentice Hall Press.

Davis Polk. (2010). "Senate-House Conference Agrees on Final Volcker Rule." *Davis Polk Regulatory Tracker*, July 18. *Client Memorandum*, June 25. http://www.davispolk.com/files/Publication/fc554a6c-8944-445c-bf78-067d27dfd107/Presentation/PublicationAttachment/c05dc6b1-c895-4aac-aafc-919e31d24b78/062510_volcker_final.pdf.

Davis Polk. (2012). "Two Year Anniversary Report." *Davis Polk Regulatory Tracker*, July 18. http://www.davispolk.com/files/Publication/15a76992-d82a-4d15-a2db-fcde9effc3d0/Presentation/PublicationAttachment/b82f9d23-0edc-49eb-af02-ff97ff34bd56/071812_Dodd.Frank.Progress.Report.pdf.

Davis Polk. (2012). "CFTC Adopts Historical Swaps Recording and Reporting Requirements." *Client Memorandum*, June 5. http://www.davispolk.com/files/Publication/1733b81b-1716-4685-b477-ff10b09abe18/Presentation/PublicationAttachment/a5a9a914-e6c2-4d29-948b-00e87bf74433/060512_Historical_Swaps_Rule.pdf.

Davis Polk, (2012). "Volcker Rule Conformance Period Guidelines." *Client Memorandum*, April 20. http://www.davispolk.com/files/Publication/7cdedd1a-8b50-48ec-a862-022932610473/Presentation/PublicationAttachment/310bd06f-3d1d-4012-bf2e-0285650aa2de/042012_volcker.pdf.

Dennis, Brady. (2010). "Obama Signs Financial Overhaul into Law." *Washington Post*, July 22.

Dodd, Christopher, and Blanche Lincoln. (2010). Letter to Rep. Barney Frank and Rep. Colin Peterson, June 30. http://online.wsj.com/public/resources/documents/dodd-lincoln-letter070110.pdf.

*Dodd-Frank Wall Street Reform and Consumer Protection Act, US Code Annotated* 7 (2010), §§1–26; *US Code Annotated* 15 (2010), §§78, 8301–8344.

Eisert, Edward. (2012). "As Volcker Rule implementation lumbers on, some practical considerations." *Thomson Reuters*, May 4. http://newsandinsight.thomsonreuters.com/Securities/Insight/2012/05_-_May/As_Volcker_Rule_implementation_lumbers_on,_some_practical_considerations/.

Federal Deposit Insurance Corporation. (2012). "FDIC Initiatives under the Dodd-Frank Wall Street Reform and Consumer Protection Act. http://www.fdic.gov/regulations/reform/initiatives.html.

Field, Abigail. (2010). "Inside the SEC's Legal Claim against Goldman Sachs." *Daily Finance*, April 16. http://www.dailyfinance.com/story/investing/inside-the-secs-legal-case-against-goldman-sachs/19443106.

Fitch Ratings. (2012). "Swaps Push-Out Rule Effects Limited for Major Banks." *Fitch Wire*, June 5. http://www.fitchratings.com/web/en/dynamic/articles/Swaps-Push-Out-Rule-Effects-Limited-for-Major-Banks.jsp.

*Frontline*. (2009). "The Warning." Broadcast October 20 by PBS. http://www.pbs.org/wgbh/pages/frontline/warning/etc/script.html.

Gensler, Gary. (2010). "The New Environment for OTC Derivatives." Remarks at the International Swaps and Derivatives Association Regional Conference, New York, NY, September 16. http://www.cftc.gov/PressRoom/SpeechesTestimony/ChairmanGaryGensler/opagensler-50.html.

Goodman, Peter S. (2008). "Taking a Hard New Look at a Greenspan Legacy." *New York Times*, October 8. http://www.nytimes.com/2008/10/09/business/economy/09greenspan.html?pagewanted=all.

Greenberger, Michael. (2008). Testimony before the House Energy and Commerce Subcommittee on Oversight and Investigations Regarding Energy Speculation: Is Greater Regulation Necessary to Stop Price Manipulation? Part II, June 23. http://michaelgreenberger.com/files/June_23_2008_testimony.pdf.

Greenberger, Michael. (2009). Testimony before the Commodity Futures Trading Commission on Excessive Speculation: Position Limits and Exemptions, August 3. http://michaelgreenberger.com/files/CFTC_AFR_Sign_On_Testimony_August_3.pdf.

Greenberger, Michael. (2010). "Out of the Black Hole: Regulatory Reform of the Over-the-Counter Derivative Market." In Robert Johnson and Erica Payne, eds., *Make Markets Be Markets*, 99–116. New York: Roosevelt Institute.

Greenberger, Michael. (2011). "Overwhelming a Financial Regulatory Black Hole with Legislative Sunlight: Dodd-Frank's Attack on Systemic Economic Destabilization Caused by an Unregulated Multi-Trillion Dollar Derivatives Market." 6 *Journal of Business & Technology Law* 127. http://digitalcommons.law.umaryland.edu/cgi/viewcontent.cgi?article=2060&context=fac_pubs.

Grim, Ryan. (2009). "Dick Durbin: Banks 'Frankly Own the Place.'" *Huffington Post*, April 29. http://www.huffingtonpost.com/2009/04/29/dick-durbin-banks-frankly_n_193010.html.

Gustini, Raymond J., Lloyd H. Spencer, William E. Kelly, Keith L. Krasney, Paulette J. Morgan, Barry M. Rothchild, and Tiana Butcher. (2010). "Dodd-Frank Wall Street Reform and Consumer Protection Act Signed." *Nixon Peabody LLP Global Finance Alert*, July 23. http://www.nixonpeabody.com/linked_media/publications/Global_Finance_Alert_7_23_2010.pdf.

Johnson, Phillip McBride, and Thomas Lee Hazen. (2004). *Derivatives Regulation*. New York: Aspen.

Johnson, Robert. (2010). "Credible Resolution: What It Takes to End Too Big to Fail." In Robert Johnson and Erica Payne, eds., *Make Markets Be Markets*, 117–34. New York: Roosevelt Institute.

Kimball-Stanley, Arthur. (2008). "Insurance and Credit Default Swaps: Should Like Things Be Treated Alike?" *Connecticut Insurance Law Journal* 15: 241–266.

Kopecki, Dawn, and Shannon D. Harrington. (2009). "Banning 'Naked' Default Swaps May Raise Corporate Funding Costs." *New York Times*, July 24. http://www.nytimes.com/2010/04/19/opinion/19krugman.html?dbk.

Levy, Jonathan Ira. (2006). "Contemplating Delivery: Futures Trading and the Problem of Commodity Exchange in the United States, 1875–1905." *American Historical Review* 111(2): 307–335.

Markham, Jerry A. (1997). *Commodities Regulation: Fraud, Manipulation and Other Claims*. Deerfield, IL: Clark Boardman Callaghan.

Murphy, Megan, and Anousha Sakoui. (2010). "Lehman Sues Nomura over Derivatives' Claims." *Financial Times*, April 23.

National Conference of Insurance Legislators. (2009). *Credit Default Insurance Model Legislation*. http://www.ncoil.org/HomePage/2010/03212010CDIModel.pdf.

New York State Insurance Department. (2008). "Recognizing Progress by Federal Government in Developing Oversight Framework for Credit Default Swaps, New York Will Stay Plan to Regulate Some Credit Default Swaps." Press release, November 20. http://www.dfs.ny.gov/insurance/press/2008/p0811201.htm.

O'Harrow, Robert, Jr., and Brady Dennis. (2008). "Downgrades and Downfall." *Washington Post*, December 31. http://www.washingtonpost.com/wp-dyn/content/article/2008/12/30/AR2008123003431.html.

Orrick, Herrington & Sutcliffe. (2011). "The Impact of the Volcker Rule on the Sponsorship and Ownership of Private Funds by Banking Entities." October. http://www.orrick.com/fileupload/4165.pdf.

Partnoy, Frank, and Lynn E. Turner. (2010). "Bring Transparency to Off-Balance Sheet Accounting." In Robert Johnson and Erica Payne, eds., *Make Markets Be Markets*, 85–94. New York: Roosevelt Institute.

President's Working Group on Financial Markets. (1999a). *Hedge Funds, Leverage, and the Lessons of Long-Term Capital Management*. Washington, DC: Department of the Treasury.

President's Working Group on Financial Markets. (1999b). *Over-the-Counter Derivatives Market and the Commodities Exchange Act*. Washington, DC: Department of the Treasury.

Roosevelt, Franklin D. (1938). Public Papers and Addresses of Franklin D. Roosevelt, 3 Pub. Papers 81.

Sandler, Linda. (2012). "Lehman Unloads Uranium and Real Estate to Pay Creditors." *Bloomberg Businessweek*, July 12. http://www.businessweek.com/news/2012-07-12/lehman-unloads-uranium-and-real-estate-to-pay-creditors.

Scheid, Brian. (2012). "CFTC Surprises No One By Delaying Dodd-Frank Rules Some More." *Platts: The Barrel*, May 11. http://www.platts.com/weblog/oilblog/2012/05/11/cftc_surprises.html.

Sheridan, Barrett. (2008). "600,000,000,000,000? It's a Number No One Questions, but the Size of the Derivatives Market Is Not as Shocking as It Looks." *Newsweek*, October 18. http://www.newsweek.com/2008/10/17/600-000-000-000-000.html.

Sidley Austin. (2011). "CFTC and SEC Finalize Key Dodd-Frank "Entity Definitions," *Sidley Updates*, May 11. http://m.sidley.com/cftc-and-sec-finalize-key-dodd-frank-entity-definitions-05-11-2012/.

Simpson Thacher. (2012). "Memorandum: Federal Banking Regulators Clarify Effective Date for the Swaps 'Push-Out' Rule Under Dodd-Frank." April 2. http://www.simpsonthacher.com/google_file.cfm?TrackedFile=4B46116604D6EDD896B179&TrackedFolder=585C1D235281AED996A07D5F9F9478AB5A90188899.

Sirri, Erik. (2008). Testimony before the House Committee on Agriculture on Credit Default Swaps, October 15. http://www.sec.gov/news/testimony/2008/ts101508ers.htm.

Skadden, Arps, Slate, Meagher & Flom. (2011). "Dodd-Frank Rulemaking: Volcker Rule and SIFI Proposals." *Commentary and Insights*. November 17. http://www.skadden.com/evites/NY/Dodd_Frank_Rule_Making_Volcker_Rule_and_SIFI_Proposals_111711.pdf.

Story, Louise, Landon Thomas Jr., and Nelson D. Schwartz. (2010). "Wall St. Helped to Mask Debt Fueling Europe's Crisis." *New York Times*, February 13. http://www.nytimes.com/2010/02/14/business/global/14debt.html.

US Congress. Senate. Committee on Agriculture. (2008). *The Role of Financial Derivatives in the Current Financial Crisis: Hearing before the Senate Agricultural Committee*. 110th Cong. http://www.gpo.gov/fdsys/pkg/CHRG-110shrg838/html/CHRG-110shrg838.htm.

US Congress. Senate. Committee on Banking, Housing, and Urban Affairs. (2010). *Restoring American Financial Stability Act of 2010*. 111th Cong. Senate Report 111–176.

US Congress. Senate. Committee on Homeland Security and Governmental Affairs, Permanent Subcommittee on Investigations. (2009). *Excessive Speculation in the Wheat Market.* 111th Cong. http://hsgac.senate.gov/public/index.cfm?FuseAction=Files.View&FileStore_id=fb439667-dcd3-4025-b95b-1b91f8ea29d1.

US Congress. Senate. *Congressional Record.* (2000). 106th Cong., 2d sess. Vol. 146, pt. 7, 10079.

US Congress. Senate. Permanent Subcommittee on Investigations. (2007). *Excessive Speculation in the Natural Gas Market.* 110th Cong. http://hsgac.senate.gov/public/_files/REPORTExcessiveSpeculationintheNaturalGasMarket.pdf.

CHAPTER 24

# FROM INNOVATION TO FINANCIALIZATION

## HOW SHAREHOLDER VALUE IDEOLOGY IS DESTROYING THE US ECONOMY

WILLIAM LAZONICK

## Maximizing Shareholder Value

The United States is the richest economy in the world. Yet in the 2000s the United States has been unable to deliver equitable and stable economic growth to its own population (Lazonick, 2009a, ch. 1; 2009b; 2012). The national unemployment rate, which was over 6 percent in the "jobless recovery" of 2003, exceeded 10 percent in the "jobless recovery" of 2009, and in July 2012 was still over 8 percent. The distribution of income has become increasingly unequal over the past three decades, with a disappearance of middle-income jobs. In the 1990s and 2000s even the jobs of well-educated and experienced members of the labor force have been vulnerable to downsizing and offshoring. Meanwhile, there has been a growing concentration of income among the richest households. The share of total income (including capital gains) going to the top 1 percent of households in the income distribution rose from about 9 percent in the mid-1970s to over 22 percent on average in 2005–2008 (Alvaredo et al., 2011).

A prime reason for the decline of employment opportunities and the growth in income inequality in the last three decades in the United States is the way in which US business corporations are governed, and in particular the way in which the stock-based remuneration of corporate executives influences their resource-allocation decisions. In the 1980s and 1990s agency theorists advocated stock-based compensation so that corporate executives would have the incentive to "maximize shareholder value" (MSV), which would supposedly improve the performance of the economy as a whole (Jensen, 1986; Jensen and Murphy, 1990). In this chapter I argue that, on the contrary, MSV is an ideology that has been destructive for the performance of the US economy.

In the next section, I show that agency theory makes false assumptions about those participants in the economy who make risky investments, and hence about who should therefore be rewarded if and when those investments generate returns. Innovation theory, which can comprehend the roles of governments and of workers in making risky investments in productive capabilities, is far more powerful than agency theory in explaining the relation between risky investments and superior economic performance (see Lazonick and O'Sullivan, 2000; Lazonick, 2010b, 2011; Lazonick and Mazzucato, 2012). Then I show that in the corporate economy of the United States over the past three decades, the implementation of the incentives advocated by agency theory for the sake of MSV have resulted in an explosion of top executive pay. I go on to document the importance of stock buybacks in the United States as an instrument for MSV that, by manipulating a company's stock price, helps to boost executive pay. I contend that in the United States the use of stock-based compensation, and in particular stock options, to motivate corporate executives to have a strong personal interest in the performance of their company's stock prices has resulted in not only an inequitable distribution of income but also unstable economic performance and reduced investment in innovation. I conclude with a brief discussion of the types of public policies that would be needed to correct these corporate governance problems.

## Critique of MSV Theory

It was only in the early 1980s that corporate executives began to embrace the ideology that, for the sake of superior economic performance, companies should maximize shareholder value (Rappaport, 1981, 1983). Among academic economists, agency theorists supported this ideology by propounding a shareholder-value perspective on corporate governance that is consistent with the neoclassical theory of the market economy (Fama and Jensen, 1983a, 1983b). Especially in the United States, some three decades later MSV remains the dominant ideology of corporate governance in business schools, economics departments, executive suites, and corporate boardrooms.

The argument put forward by agency theorists is that among all the stakeholders in the business corporation only shareholders are "residual claimants." The amount of returns that shareholders receive depends on what is left over after other stakeholders, all of whom it is argued have guaranteed contractual claims, have been paid for their productive contributions to the firm. If the firm incurs a loss, the return to shareholders is negative, and vice versa.

By this argument, shareholders are the only stakeholders who have an incentive to bear the risk of investing in productive resources that may result in superior economic performance. As residual claimants, moreover, shareholders are the only stakeholders who have an interest in monitoring managers to ensure that they allocate resources efficiently. Furthermore, by selling and buying corporate shares on the stock market, public shareholders, it is argued, are the participants in the economy who are best situated to reallocate resources to more efficient uses.

The fundamental problem with the agency perspective on MSV is that it simply is not the case that shareholders are the only participants in the business enterprise who make investments in productive resources without a guaranteed return (see Lazonick, 2011). Taxpayers through government agencies and workers through the firms that employ them also make such risky investments on a regular basis. From this perspective, both the state and labor have "residual claimant" status.

Any realistic account of economic development must take into account the role of the state in (a) making infrastructural investments that, given the required levels of financial commitment and inherent uncertainty of economic outcomes, business enterprises would not have made on their own; and (b) providing business enterprises with subsidies that encourage investment in innovation. Indeed, in terms of investment in new knowledge with applications to industry, the United States was the world's foremost developmental state over the course of the twentieth century (see Block, 2009; Block and Keller, 2011; Lazonick, 2008). As one prime example, it is impossible to explain US dominance in computers, microelectronics, software, and data communications without recognizing the role of government in making seminal investments that developed new knowledge and infrastructural investments that facilitated the diffusion of that knowledge (see, for example, Abbate, 2000; National Research Council, 1999). As another prime example, the 2011 budget of the National Institutes of Health (NIH) for life sciences research was $30.6 billion, almost double in real terms the budget of 1993 and triple in real terms the budget of 1985. Since the founding of the first national institute in 1938 through 2011, NIH spending totaled $796 billion in 2011 dollars (Lazonick and Tulum, 2011).

More generally, the US government has made investments to augment the productive power of the nation through federal, corporate, and university research labs that have generated new knowledge as well as through educational institutions that have developed the capabilities of the future labor force. Business enterprises have made ample use of this knowledge and capability. In effect, in funding these investments, the state (or more correctly, its body of taxpayers) has borne the risk that the nation's business enterprises would further develop and utilize these productive capabilities in ways that would ultimately redound to the benefit of the nation, *but with the return to the nation in no way contractually guaranteed.*

In addition, the US government has often provided cash subsidies to business enterprises to develop new products and processes, or even to start new firms. The public has funded these subsidies through current taxes, borrowing against the future, or by making consumers pay higher product prices for current goods and services than would have otherwise prevailed. Multitudes of business enterprises have benefited from subsidies without having to enter into contracts with the public bodies that have granted them in order to remit a guaranteed return from the productive investments that the subsidies help to finance.

Like taxpayers, workers can also find themselves in the position of having made investments without a contractually guaranteed return. In an important contribution to the corporate governance debate, Margaret Blair (1995) argued that, alongside a firm's shareholders, workers should be accorded residual-claimant status because they make investments in "firm-specific" human capital at one point in time with the expectation—but without a contractual guarantee—of reaping returns on those investments over the course of their careers. Moreover, insofar as their human capital is indeed firm-specific, these workers depend on their current employers for generating returns on their investments. A lack of interfirm labor mobility means that the worker bears some of the risk of the return on the firm's productive investments and hence can be considered a residual claimant. Blair goes on to argue that if one assumes, as shareholder-value proponents do, that only shareholders bear risk and residual-claimant status, there will be an underinvestment in human capital to the detriment of not only workers but also the economy as a whole.

I concur with Blair's argument that workers often have residual-claimant status. From the perspective of innovation theory, however, I look at the relation between the risks that workers bear and rewards that workers may or may not receive differently. Quite apart from whether nor not their skills are "firm-specific," workers often contribute their time and effort over and above the levels required by their current level of pay to a collective and cumulative innovation process. By definition, this innovation process can only generate returns in the future; indeed, because the innovation process is uncertain, it may not in fact generate returns. As members of the firm, therefore, workers bear the risk that the extra expenditures of time and effort will not yield the gains from innovative enterprises from which they can be rewarded. If, however, the innovation process does generate returns, workers, as risk-bearers, have a claim to a share (Lazonick, 1990, 2010a).

Therefore MSV ideology, as put forth by agency theorists, provides a flawed rationale for denying taxpayers and workers residual-claimant status, and thereby excluding them from sharing in the gains of innovative enterprise. But, to turn agency theory on its head, on what grounds do *public shareholders* have residual-claimant status? Put differently, what risk-bearing role do public shareholders play in the innovation process? Do they confront uncertainty by strategically allocating resources to innovative investments? No. As portfolio investors, they diversify their financial holdings across the outstanding shares of existing firms to minimize risk. They do so, moreover, with limited liability, which means that they are under no legal obligation to make further investments of "good" money to support previous investments that have gone bad. Indeed, even for these previous investments, the existence of a highly liquid stock market enables public shareholders to cut their losses instantaneously by selling their shares—what has long been called the "Wall Street walk."

Without this ability to exit an investment easily, public shareholders would not be willing to hold shares of companies when they cannot exercise direct allocative control over assets. It is the liquidity of a public shareholder's portfolio investment that differentiates it from a direct investment, and indeed that distinguishes the public shareholder from a private shareholder who, for lack of liquidity of his or her shares, must remain committed to his or her direct investment until it generates financial returns. The modern corporation entails a fundamental transformation in the character of private property, as Berle and Means recognized almost 80 years ago in *The Modern Corporation and Private Property*. As property owners, public shareholders own tradable shares in a company that has invested in productive assets. In an innovative enterprise, however, the most important productive assets are human assets—assets that, in a free society, cannot be owned by others.

Given the central role of the development and utilization of human assets in the growth of the firm, the fundamental role of the US stock market has been to transform illiquid claims into liquid claims on the basis of investments that have already been made, thereby separating shareownership from managerial control. Business corporations sometimes do use the stock market as a source of finance for new investments, although the cash function has been most common in periods of stock-market speculation when the lure for public shareholders to absorb new issues has been the prospect of quickly "flipping" their shares to make a rapid speculative return. Public shareholders want financial liquidity; investments in innovation require financial commitment. It is only by ignoring the role of innovation in the economy, and the necessary role of insider control in the strategic allocation of corporate resources to innovation, that agency theory can argue that superior economic performance can be achieved by maximizing the value of those actors in the corporate economy who are the ultimate outsiders to the innovation process.

## The Impact of MSV

My book *Sustainable Prosperity in the New Economy? Business Organization and High-Tech Employment in the United States* (Lazonick 2009a) focused on employment opportunities in information and communication technology (ICT), an industrial sector that has been central to economic growth in recent decades. Especially in the 1980s and 1990s ICT created a strong demand for college-educated white-collar workers even as good jobs for high school-educated blue-collar workers disappeared in the face of manufacturing challenges from East Asian nations. In the 1990s, however, the character of employment opportunities for college-educated white-collar workers also changed dramatically as leading corporations such as IBM and Hewlett-Packard that had previously offered employees the realistic expectation of a career with one company now opted to employ a flexible labor force, even laying off older, more experienced (and more expensive) workers in the Internet boom of the late 1990s as they hired younger, less experienced (and less expensive) workers. In the 2000s these new workers were likely to be employed by US multinational corporations in lower-wage developing economies such as India and China. The changed employment situation for college-educated workers in the United States is apparent in the decline in the 2000s in job tenure and the wage premium to a college education (Farber, 2008).

I summarize these structural changes in employment conditions that have permanently eliminated "middle-class" jobs in the US economy as *rationalization*, *marketization*, and *globalization*. From the beginning of the 1980s rationalization, characterized by plant closings, eliminated the jobs of unionized blue-collar workers (Lazonick, 2012). From the beginning of the 1990s marketization, characterized by the end of a career with one company as an employment norm, placed the job security of middle-aged and older white-collar workers in jeopardy. From the 2000s globalization, characterized by the offshoring of employment, left all types of members of the US labor force, even those with advanced educational credentials and substantial work experience, vulnerable to displacement.

In each case the structural change in employment took root in a cyclical downturn: rationalization in the double-dip "blue-collar" recession of 1980–1982, marketization in the "white-collar" recession of 1990–1991, and globalization in the "Internet" recession of 2001. In historical retrospect we now know that the recoveries that followed the recessions of 1990–1991 and 2001 were "jobless" as, respectively, marketization and globalization continued after gross domestic product had begun to increase. Indeed, in terms of blue-collar employment, the recovery from the recessionary conditions of 1980–1982 was also jobless, but the continuation of plant closings in 1983 and beyond was offset for the economy as a whole by new employment opportunities for white-collar workers created by the microelectronics boom.

Initially, each of these structural changes in employment could be justified in terms of changes in industrial conditions related to technologies, markets, and competition. The plant closings that characterized rationalization were a response to the superior productive capabilities of Japanese competitors in consumer durable and related capital goods industries that employed significant numbers of unionized blue-collar workers. The erosion of the one-company-career norm among white-collar workers that characterized marketization was a response to the dramatic technological shift from proprietary technology systems to open technology systems that was integral to the microelectronics revolution. The offshoring of the jobs of well-educated and highly experienced US members of the labor force that characterized globalization was a response to the emergence of large supplies of highly capable labor in nations such as China and India.

Once US corporations adopted these structural changes in employment, however, corporate executives often pursued these employment strategies purely for greater financial gain. Some companies closed manufacturing plants, terminated experienced workers, and offshored production to low-wage areas of the world to increase profits, often at the expense of the company's long-term competitive capabilities. Moreover, as these changes became embedded in the structure of US employment, financialized business corporations declined to invest in new, higher-value-added job creation on a scale that could at least offset the job losses from rationalization, marketization, and globalization.

Legitimized by shareholder value ideology, over the past three decades trillions of dollars that could have been spent on innovation and job creation in the US economy have instead been used to manipulate corporate stock prices. With superior corporate performance defined as meeting Wall Street's expectations of steadily rising quarterly earnings-per-share targets, companies turned to massive stock repurchases to boost their stock prices. From 2001 through 2010 S&P 500 companies—which account for about 75 percent of the market capitalization of all US publicly listed corporations—spent about $3 trillion on stock buybacks, equal to in excess of 50 percent of their net income. In addition, these companies distributed dividends equal to about 40 percent of net income over the decade, bringing the total payout ratio (buybacks plus dividends) to well over 90 percent. The average buybacks per company more than quadrupled from less than $300 million in 2003 to more than $1.2 billion in 2007, before falling to around $700 million in 2008 and $300 million in 2009. Average buybacks rebounded to $600 million in 2010, and about $800 million in 2011, or about $400 billion for the S&P 500 as a whole (Lazonick, 2010b, 2011).

What was unique about the recession that began in December 2007 and ended in June 2009 was that it was primarily the result of financialization, especially in the subprime mortgage market and emanating from the financial sector. In my view, that recession and the prolonged joblessness of the subsequent recovery represent culminations of rationalization, marketization, and globalization in the presence of the financialized business corporation. The primary cause of the current jobless recovery is neither a mismatch in the labor market nor a lack of business confidence—the two main contenders among conventional economists for explaining the sluggishness of reemployment. Rather, the most potent explanation for the current dearth of employment opportunities in the United States is the financialized business corporation characterized by massive stock buybacks and outsized executive pay.

The prime reason why the US economy gets a "match" between the capabilities of labor supplied and labor demanded is because major business corporations invest in the capabilities of the types of workers whom they require. From this perspective, a so-called mismatch results from a failure of business corporations to make these investments in the training—both formal and on-the-job—of the US labor force. Indeed when educated and experienced workers suffer permanent job losses in their areas of specialization, valuable human capital quickly atrophies.

I contend, furthermore, that the financialization of the corporation has exacerbated permanent job losses from rationalization, marketization, and globalization while undermining investment in innovation and new high-value-added job creation in the United States. In 2011 US corporations were sitting on more than $1 trillion in cash, even after the sharp rebound in stock repurchases in 2010 and 2011 from recession-induced declines in 2008 and 2009. Much of this cash is held abroad by US multinational corporations that are exploiting a tax loophole that permits them to avoid paying corporate taxes in the United States until they repatriate the profits. Indeed, some corporate executives are pushing for a tax holiday on repatriated profits so that they can use the untaxed funds to, among other things, perform stock buybacks (see Chambers and Catz, 2010; Lazonick, 2011; see also Dharmapala et al., 2010). Rather than manifesting a lack of business confidence, these cash hoards also reflect a desire by corporate executives to have cash available for stock repurchases as, in the years ahead, companies use an escalation of repurchases to compete to boost their stock prices, as was the case from 2003 to 2007. The globalization of the labor force for educated and experienced workers is here to stay. In the absence of a change in corporate financial behavior, the future of the US economy is more booms, busts, and jobless recoveries, with each boom more speculative, each bust more devastating, and each recovery more jobless than the one before.

Why do corporations repurchase stock? Executives often claim that buybacks are financial investments that signal confidence in the future of the company and its stock-price performance (Louis and White, 2007; Vermaelen, 2005, ch. 3). In fact, however, companies that do buybacks never sell the shares at higher prices in order to cash in on these investments. To do so would be to signal to the market that its stock price had peaked. According to the "signaling" argument, we should have seen massive sales of corporate stock in the speculative boom of the late 1990s, as was in fact the case of US industrial corporations in the speculative boom of the late 1920s when corporations took advantage of the speculative stock market to pay off corporate debt or bolster their corporate treasuries (O'Sullivan, 2004). Instead, in the boom of the late

1990s corporate executives as *personal investors* sold their own stock to reap speculative gains (often to the tune of tens of millions). Yet, if anything, these same corporate executives as *corporate decisionmakers* used corporate funds to repurchase their companies' shares in the attempt to bolster their stock prices—to their own personal gain.

Those gains have been enormous. According to the AFL-CIO (2009), the ratio of the average pay of CEOs of 200 large US corporations to the pay of the average full-time US worker was 42:1 in 1980, 107:1 in 1990, 525:1 in 2000, and 380:1 in 2011. Based on proxy statement data in Compustat, table 24.1 shows the average compensation of the highest-paid corporate executives in the United States, and the percentage of that compensation derived from exercising stock options (the difference between the stock-option exercise price and the market price of the stock on the exercise date).

Also included in table 24.1 are the S&P 500 Index (with over 80 percent of its component stocks being traded on the NYSE) and the NASDAQ Composite Index to illustrate the positive correlation of stock-price performance with both the level of executive pay and the proportion of that pay derived from stock-option exercises. The impact of NASDAQ on executive pay was especially strong in the late 1990s when speculation drove stock prices, whereas companies listed on the NYSE as well as NASDAQ were engaged in large-scale stock repurchases that helped to push up the S&P 500 from 2003 to 2007.

As shown in table 24.1, the average annual real compensation in 2010 dollars of the 100 highest-paid corporate executives named in company proxy statements was $20.9 million in 1992–1995, $78.0 million in 1998–2001, and $65.3 million in 2004–2007. As can also be seen in table 24.1, large proportions of these enormous incomes of top executives have come from gains from cashing in on the ample stock-option awards that their boards of directors have bestowed on them.[1] The higher the "top pay" group, the greater the proportion of the pay of that group that was derived from gains from exercising stock options. For the top 100 group in the years 1992–2010, this proportion ranged from a low of 49 percent in 2010 to 87 percent in 2000, when the mean pay was at its highest. In 2000 the mean pay of the top 3,000 was, at $10.8 million in 2010 dollars, only 10 percent of the mean pay of the top 100. Nevertheless, gains from exercising stock options accounted for 67 percent of the total pay of the top 3,000 group (Lazonick, 2010b).

Note in table 24.1 how the average pay of the highest-paid corporate executives has risen and fallen with the fluctuations of major stock-market indices. In the 1980s and 1990s, as shown in table 24.2, high real stock yields characterized the US corporate economy. These high yields came mainly from stock-price appreciation as distinct from dividend yields, which were low in the 1990s despite high dividend payout ratios.[2] With the S&P 500 rising almost 1,400 percent from March 1982 to August 2000, the availability of gains from exercising stock options became almost automatic. Given the extent to which the explosion in US top executive pay over the past three decades has depended on gains

**Table 24.1** Total compensation of top executives of US-based corporations, average for 100, 500, 1,500, and 3,000 highest-paid "named" executives on proxy statements, and the proportion of total compensation derived from gains from exercising stocks options, 1992–2009

| | S&P 500 Index | NAS-DAQ Index | NAS-DAQ/ S&P | Top 100 | | Top 500 | | Top 1,500 | | Top 3,000 | |
|---|---|---|---|---|---|---|---|---|---|---|---|
| | | | | Mean $m. | % SO | Mean $m. | % SO | Mean $m. | % SO | Mean $m. | % SO |
| **1992** | 100 | 100 | **1.00** | 23.1 | *71* | 9.3 | *59* | 4.7 | *48* | 2.9 | *42* |
| **1993** | 109 | 119 | **1.10** | 21.1 | *63* | 9.1 | *51* | 4.8 | *42* | 3.1 | *36* |
| **1994** | 111 | 125 | **1.13** | 18.5 | *57* | 8.1 | *45* | 4.4 | *35* | 2.9 | *29* |
| **1995** | 131 | 155 | **1.18** | 21.0 | *59* | 9.7 | *48* | 5.3 | *40* | 3.5 | *34* |
| **1996** | 162 | 195 | **1.20** | 32.4 | *64* | 13.9 | *54* | 7.2 | *47* | 4.6 | *41* |
| **1997** | 210 | 243 | **1.16** | 44.2 | *72* | 18.6 | *61* | 9.5 | *55* | 5.9 | *49* |
| **1998** | 261 | 300 | **1.15** | 76.0 | *66* | 26.7 | *64* | 12.5 | *58* | 7.5 | *53* |
| **1999** | 319 | 462 | **1.45** | 68.9 | *82* | 27.4 | *71* | 13.2 | *63* | 7.8 | *57* |
| **2000** | 341 | 614 | **1.80** | 104.0 | *87* | 40.5 | *80* | 18.7 | *72* | 10.8 | *67* |
| **2001** | 284 | 332 | **1.17** | 62.9 | *77* | 23.9 | *66* | 11.5 | *58* | 6.9 | *53* |
| **2002** | 237 | 252 | **1.06** | 38.1 | *57* | 17.1 | *49* | 8.8 | *43* | 5.5 | *38* |
| **2003** | 232 | 275 | **1.18** | 48.7 | *64* | 21.2 | *55* | 10.8 | *48* | 6.7 | *44* |
| **2004** | 272 | 330 | **1.21** | 55.4 | *75* | 25.0 | *62* | 12.9 | *55* | 8.1 | *50* |
| **2005** | 290 | 348 | **1.20** | 67.5 | *78* | 28.7 | *63* | 14.5 | *56* | 9.0 | *51* |
| **2006** | 316 | 463 | **1.47** | 68.9 | *69* | 29.6 | *598* | 15.4 | *52* | 9.7 | *47* |
| **2007** | 354 | 428 | **1.21** | 69.3 | *73* | 30.2 | *60* | 15.8 | *52* | 9.7 | *47* |
| **2008** | 291 | 356 | **1.22** | 47.5 | *58* | 20.7 | *55* | 10.9 | *45* | 7.0 | *47* |

| | | | | | | | | | | | |
|---|---|---|---|---|---|---|---|---|---|---|---|
| **2009** | 227 | 307 | **1.35** | 30.4 | *52* | 14.8 | *37* | 8.3 | *28* | 5.5 | *23* |
| **2010** | 271 | 386 | **1.43** | 35.9 | *49* | 18.3 | *40* | 10.4 | *32* | 5.0 | *28* |

Mean compensation in millions of 2010 US dollars.

"Named" executives are the CEO and other four highest-paid executives in a given year reported by listed companies in their annual proxy statements to shareholders.

S&P 500 Index and the NASDAQ Composite Index set to 100 in 1992 for purposes of comparison.

Total compensation (TDC2 in the Compustat database) is defined as "total compensation for the individual year comprised of the following: Salary, Bonus, Other Annual, Total Value of Restricted Stock Granted, Net Value of Stock Options Exercised, Long-Term Incentive Payouts, and All Other Total."

%SO means the percent of total compensation that the whole set (100, 500, 1,500, or 3,000) of highest-paid executives derived from gains from exercising stock options.

Note that company proxy statements (DEF 14A SEC filings) report the compensation of the company's CEO and four other highest-paid executives. It is therefore possible that some of the highest-paid executives who should be included in each of the "top" categories are excluded. The mean compensation calculations are therefore lower bounds of actual average compensation of the highest-paid corporate executives in the United States.

*Sources*: Standard and Poor's Compustat database (Executive Compensation, Annual); Yahoo! Finance at http://finance.yahoo.com (Historical Prices, Monthly Data).

**Table 24.2** Average annual US corporate stock and bond yields (%), 1960–2009

| | 1960–1969 | 1970–1979 | 1980–1989 | 1990–1999 | 2000–2009 |
|---|---|---|---|---|---|
| Real stock yield | 6.63 | −1.66 | 11.67 | 15.01 | −3.08 |
| *Price yield* | 5.80 | 1.35 | 12.91 | 15.54 | −2.30 |
| *Dividend yield* | 3.19 | 4.08 | 4.32 | 2.47 | 1.79 |
| *Change in CPI* | 2.36 | 7.09 | 5.55 | 3.00 | 2.57 |
| Real bond yield | 2.65 | 1.14 | 5.79 | 4.72 | 3.41 |

Stock yields are for Standard and Poor's composite index of 500 US corporate stocks. Bond yields are for Moody's Aaa-rated US corporate bonds.
*Sources*: Updated from Lazonick and O'Sullivan, 2000, 27, using US Congress, 2010, tables B-62, B-73, B-95, and B-96.

from exercising stock options, there is a need to understand the drivers of the stock-price increases that generate these gains. In the 2000s the stock-option gains of these executives have come primarily through manipulation, with the stock buyback as the key instrument of stock-market manipulation.

Figure 24.1 shows how the escalating stock repurchases from 2003 through 2007 helped to boost the stock market, driving the S&P 500 even higher in 2007 than its previous peak in 2000 before the 2008 financial debacle. In 2008 repurchases fell substantially for these 438 companies, constrained by a dramatic decline in combined net income from $583 billion in 2007 to $132 billion in 2008. Nevertheless, their combined repurchases only declined from $523 billion to $369 billion. In addition, these companies paid out $5 billion more in dividends in 2008 than in 2007. Allocated differently, the billions spent on buybacks could have helped stabilize the economy. Instead, collectively, these companies spent 108 percent of their net profits on repurchases in 2008.

In work reported elsewhere, I have examined how buybacks have adversely affected the delivery of higher-quality, lower-cost products in a range of industries from oil refining to health insurance (Lazonick, 2009b, 2010, 2011; Lazonick and Tulum, 2011). Some brief examples:

- Exxon Mobil, the world's largest petroleum refiner, did $174.5 billion in buybacks during 2001–2010—the most of any company—even though there is a need for large-scale investments in alternative energy. Among the top 50 stock repurchasers in 2001–2010 were two other petroleum refiners: Chevron at #21 with $26.0 billion and ConocoPhillips at #25 with $22.0 billion.
- Leading ICT companies do massive buybacks even as they shift high-tech jobs from the United States to low-wage countries and as they pressure the US government to make larger investments in the high-tech

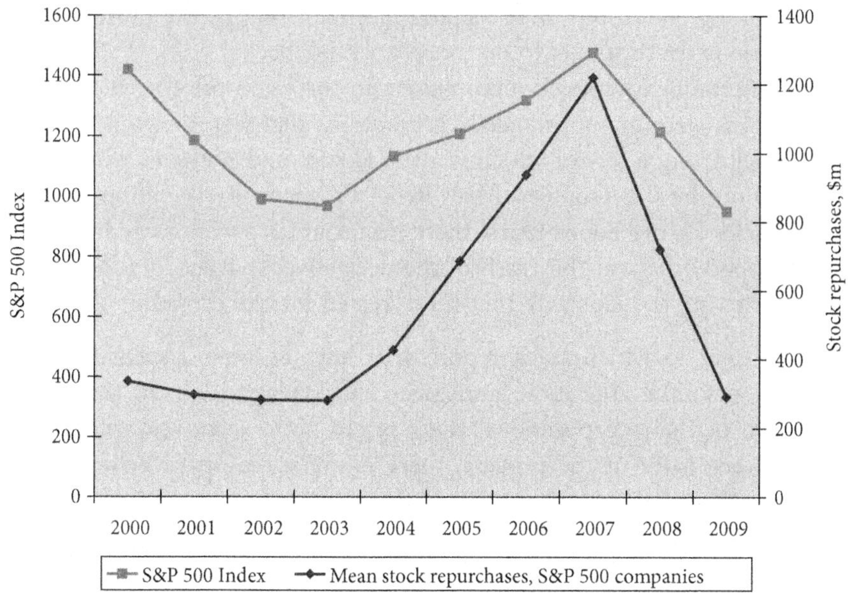


**Figure 24.1** Stock repurchases by the S&P 500 (456 companies) and the movement of the S&P 500 Index, 2000–2009.
*Sources:* Standard and Poor's Compustat database (North America, Fundamentals Annual); Yahoo! Finance at http://finance.yahoo.com (Historical Prices, Monthly Data).

knowledge base. Yet the $48.3 billion that Intel spent on buybacks in 2001–2010 was four times the total of $12.0 billion that, over the same period, the US government allocated to the National Nanotechnology Initiative.

- Pharmaceutical drug prices cost twice as much in the United States when compared with other countries. The industry benefits from government-funded life sciences research under the National Institutes of Health (NIH). The total annual budget of the NIH averaged $30.9 billion from 2009 through 2012. In opposing congressional regulation of drug prices, the industry argues that high prices fund R&D expenditures in the United States. Yet among leading biopharma companies, in 2001–2010 Amgen did repurchases equal to 100 percent of R&D expenditures; Pfizer, 62 percent; Johnson & Johnson, 59 percent; and Merck, 35 percent.
- Among the top 50 repurchasers in the United States for the period 2001–2010 were three of the largest corporate health insurers: UnitedHealth Group at #20 with $26.5 billion in buybacks (88 percent of net income), Wellpoint at #27 with $21.9 billion (101 percent), and Aetna at #46 with $12.0 billion (102 percent). When these health insurers increase their profits by raising premia, excluding people with

preexisting conditions, and capping lifetime benefits, the most likely use of those extra profits is to do more stock buybacks.

- Among the biggest stock repurchasers in the years prior to the financial crisis were many financial corporations that were responsible for the meltdown, a few of which went bankrupt and many of which were bailed out by the Troubled Asset Relief Program. By spending money on buybacks during boom years, these financial corporations reduced their ability to withstand the crash of the derivatives market in 2008, thus exacerbating the jeopardy that they created for the economy as a whole.

Given the extent to which stock repurchases have become a systematic mode of corporate resource allocation, and given the extent to which, through this manipulation of their corporations' stock prices, top executives have enriched themselves personally in the process, there is every reason to believe that, in the absence of legislation that restricts both stock repurchases as well as speculative and manipulative gains from stock options, executive behavior that places personal interests ahead of corporate, and national, interests in innovation and job creation will continue in the future.

## Policy Responses to MSV

A fundamental problem with US-style stock options is that they are unindexed; that is, they rarely carry performance criteria that would only permit gains from the exercise of stock options that are warranted by productive performance (Bebchuk and Fried, 2004). When the gains from exercising stock options depend simply on stock-price movements, an executive, or any other employee with stock options, can gain from stock-price increases that result from speculation or manipulation as well as from improvements in the company's productive performance. Indeed, as we have seen, top executives can augment their stock-option gains by allocating corporate resources to do buybacks, the sole purpose of which is to manipulate a company's stock price. Some of the stock-based compensation of US executives is undoubtedly attributable to innovation—that is, real productivity gains from generating higher-quality, lower-cost products—although even then there is the question of whether the amounts of stock-based compensation that executives secure from their boards of directors are equitable relative to other contributors to the innovation process. Be that as it may, there is strong evidence that since the last half of the 1990s it has been speculation and manipulation that have been the main drivers of the explosion in the pay of US corporate executives.

Under legislation known as "Say-on-Pay," the Dodd-Frank Wall Street Reform and Consumer Protection Act of 2010 gave public shareholders the right to express their opinions to corporate management on issues related to executive compensation. A case in point is the announcement in April 2011 of the Say-on-Pay modification of the conditions under which Jeffrey Immelt, the CEO of General Electric (GE), could receive stock options awarded to him in 2010. Acting on the advice of Institutional Investor Services, Immelt will now get 50 percent of his 2010 option awards if GE's total shareholder return (dividend yield plus stock-price yield) is equal to or better than the return of the S&P 500 for the years 2011–2014. Under the modification, Immelt will receive the other 50 percent of those options if GE's industrial businesses generate operating cash totaling at least $55 billion in 2011–2014 (Crooks and McCrum, 2011).

The total shareholder-return requirement effectively says that Immelt can get the options if GE is just an average performer among the S&P 500 companies. The larger question, however, is what will drive the S&P 500 Index average upward over the period 2011–2015. If the quadrupling of stock repurchases by S&P 500 companies from 2003 to 2007 is a guide, we can expect that the years 2011–2015 will also witness a massive manipulation of the market through an escalation of buyback activity. GE participated fully in the 2003–2007 buyback mania, increasing its repurchases from $1.2 billion in 2003 to $14.9 billion in 2007. From 2001 to 2010, GE expended $48.5 billion on stock buybacks—placing it at #10 among all US corporations—equal to 29 percent of its net income and 1.7 times its R&D spending. The Say-on-Pay shareholder-return performance criterion is a license to Immelt to manipulate GE's stock price to gain his stock-option awards. Indeed, across the board, a proliferation of Say-on-Pay proposals, advocated by the consulting firm Institutional Shareholder Services, will encourage US business corporations to compete to support high stock prices, using buybacks as their main competitive weapons.

The Say-on-Pay performance condition for the other half of Immelt's options to be exercisable is that GE must generate at least $55 billion in cash from its industrial businesses, as distinct from GE Capital Services (GECS), in 2011–2014. This performance condition creates the impression that shareholders want Immelt to invest in real productive assets to expand GE's industrial businesses. Indeed, at GE's annual general meeting in April 2010, with the company just recovering from GECS's losses in the financial crisis of 2008–2009, Immelt told shareholders, "We're an industrial company first" (Sechler, 2010). Meanwhile Immelt gave speeches around the country about the need to create more manufacturing jobs in the United States; upon being named chair of President Obama's new Council on Jobs and Competitiveness in January 2011, he declared in a *Washington Post* op-ed piece that "there is nothing inevitable about America's declining manufacturing competitiveness if we work together to reverse it" (Immelt, 2011).

But does the Say-on-Pay target of $55 billion in cash from operations of GE's industrial businesses over 2011–2014 imply an expansion of GE's investments in its nonfinancial businesses? To the contrary. *The fact is that over the previous four years, 2007–2010, GE's cash from industrial operating activities was* *almost $74 billion.* In reality, the Say-on-Pay performance condition expects Immelt to bring about *a 25 percent reduction in GE's industrial businesses.* So much for working together to reverse the nation's declining manufacturing competitiveness.

If the Dodd-Frank reform legislation had understood what drives executive pay in the United States, it would have recognized that Say-on-Pay is part of the problem, not the solution. Through a combination of stock options and stock buybacks, Say-on-Pay reinforces an alignment between the incentives of top executives and the interests of public shareholders that has been undermining investment in America's future. The result over the coming years will be an escalation of stock buybacks to manipulate stock prices until the next financial crisis once gain temporarily slows the practice.

Looking back, the US Securities and Exchange Commission (SEC) has also played a role in encouraging the destructive combination of stock buybacks and stock options. The relaxation of SEC rules against stock-price manipulation has enabled US corporations to do large-scale stock repurchases. Under the Securities Exchange Act of 1934, stock repurchases can be construed as an attempt to manipulate a company's stock price. In 1982, however, with the promulgation of Rule 10b-18, the SEC provided companies with a "safe harbor" in which manipulation charges would not be filed if each day's open-market repurchases were not greater than 25 percent of the stock's average daily trading volume and if the company refrained from doing buybacks at the beginning and end of the trading day.[3]

According to a contemporary news report, Rule 10b-18 "made it easier for companies to buy back their shares on the open market without fear of stock-manipulation charges" (Hudson, 1982). SEC Chairman John Shad was an advocate of the rule change, arguing that large-scale open-market purchases would fuel an increase in stock prices that would be beneficial to shareholders. One of the SEC commissioners, John Evans, argued that, as a result of Rule 10b-18, some manipulation would go unprosecuted, but he then agreed to make the commission's vote for the rule change unanimous.

As a complement to Rule 10b-18, in 1991 the SEC made a rule change that enabled top executives to make quick gains by exercising their stock options and immediately selling their shares. Under Section 16(b) of the Securities Exchange Act, corporate directors and officers as well as shareholders with more than 10 percent of the corporation's shares are prohibited from making "short-swing" profits through the purchase and the subsequent sale of corporate securities within a six-month period. As a result, top executives who exercised stock options had to hold the acquired shares for at least six months before selling them. Treating a stock option as a derivative, in 1991 the SEC deemed that the six-month holding period required under Section 16(b) was from the grant date, not the exercise date (Rosen, 1991). The new rule eliminated the risk of loss between the exercise date and the sale date, and it gave top executives flexibility in their timing of option exercises and immediate stock sales so that they could personally benefit from, among other things, price boosts from buybacks.

Legitimized by MSV ideology, the transition of the US business corporation from innovation to financialization has left the US economy vulnerable to financial crises. By enabling speculation and manipulation of securities markets, this transition played a major role in permitting the double-digit annual growth rates in stock-price yields in the 1980s and 1990s, as shown in table 24.2. This sustained, but ultimately unsustainable, increase in stock prices gave Wall Street the credibility that, in command of "other people's money," it could generate persistently high yields on investment portfolios. With the stock market stagnating in the 2000s, however, portfolio investors looked to the subprime mortgage market as a new source of high yields.

Yet the very existence of a large body of subprime borrowers came about in large part from the failure of US industrial corporations since the 1980s to invest in innovation and value-added job creation while middle-class jobs were permanently lost through rationalization, marketization, and globalization. Through subprime lending, Wall Street in effect sought to exploit the vulnerability of a working-class population to which the financialized business corporation no longer delivered middle-class jobs. In the process, US business executives in general, and not just those on Wall Street, saw their personal fortunes balloon through speculation in and manipulation of financial markets and particularly the stock market. Armed with MSV ideology, they equated their own good fortune with the health of the economy as a whole. The recent financial crisis exposed this false belief, but unfortunately in the second decade of the twenty-first century, executives and politicians have yet to learn the lessons of the destructiveness of the financialized corporation. Meanwhile the base of middle-class jobs continues to erode.

Any government policy agenda that seeks to recreate the middle class in the United States needs to begin with an attack on the financialized business corporation. This policy agenda then needs to engage in constructive programs in collaboration with a nonfinancialized business community to rebuild the capabilities of the US labor force to engage in innovative enterprise. The policy agenda for sustainable prosperity includes, in brief,[4] five major reforms:

- Ban stock repurchases by established US corporations so that corporate financial resources that could be allocated to innovation and job creation are not wasted for the purpose of manipulating a company's stock price.
- Index employee stock options to an indicator of innovative performance such as market share, employment, or innovative activity rather than stock-price movements so that executives cannot gain from speculation in and manipulation of their companies' stock prices.
- Regulate the employment contract to ensure that workers who contribute to the innovation process share in the gains that are created by innovation.

- Create work programs that make productive use of and enhance the productive capabilities of educated and experienced workers whose human capital would otherwise deteriorate through the lack of other relevant employment.
- Implement taxes on the gains from innovation to fund those government agencies that need to invest in the public knowledge base required for the next round of innovation.

It will be very difficult to justify these reforms if Americans do not question the ideology that companies should be run to maximize shareholder value. It is an ideology that results in inequity and instability and that ultimately undermines the productive foundations of economic growth. While shareholder-value ideology has currency throughout the world, its pervasive and unquestioned acceptance has become an almost uniquely American phenomenon. The United States is engaged in global competition with highly innovative national economies in which shareholder-value ideology does not hold sway. As long as US-based corporations are permitted to be governed by this ideology, the US economy will remain incapable of generating middle-class jobs on the scale that is needed to restore sustainable prosperity. Indeed, judging from the changes in employment that have occurred in the US economy over the past three decades, the achievement of equitable and stable growth will become more and more out of reach.

## Acknowledgment

The research in this paper has been funded by the Ford Foundation project on Financial Institutions for Innovation and Development, the Institute for New Economic Thinking project on the Stock Market and Innovative Enterprise, and the European Commission project on Finance, Innovation, and Growth. Martin Wolfson provided very useful comments.

## Notes

1. A stock option award gives an employee the nontransferable right to purchase a certain number of shares of the company for which he or she works at a preset "exercise" price between the date the option "vests" and the date it "expires." Typically in US option grants, the exercise price is the market price of the stock at the date that the option is granted; vesting of the option occurs in 25 percent installments at each of the first four anniversaries from the grant date; and the

expiration date of the option is 10 years from the grant date. Unvested options usually lapse 90 days after termination of employment with the company.

2. In the 1980s dividends paid out by US corporations increased by an annual average of 10.8 percent while after-tax corporate profits increased by an annual average of 8.7 percent. In the 1990s these figures were 8.0 percent for dividends (including an absolute decline in dividends of 4.0 percent in 1999, the first decline since 1975) and 8.1 percent for profits. The dividend payout ratio—the amount of dividends as a proportion of after-tax corporate profits (with inventory evaluation and capital consumption adjustments)—was 48.9 percent in the 1980s and 55.0 percent in the 1990s compared with 39.5 percent in the 1960s and 41.6 percent in the 1970s. From 2000 to 2009 the dividend payout ratio was 61.5 percent, including a record 70.4 percent in 2007.
3. In 2003 the SEC amended Rule 10b-18 "to simplify and update the safe harbor provisions in light of market developments since the Rule's adoption." The amendments also required that, in their 10-Q filings with the SEC, companies report the number and value of shares repurchased in the previous quarter and the average price paid per share. See http://www.sec.gov/rules/final/33–8335.htm.
4. Details of these reforms are available in Lazonick (2012).

## References


Abbate, Janet. (2000). *Inventing the Internet*. Cambridge, MA: MIT Press.

AFL-CIO. (2010). "Executive PayWatch." http://www.aflcio.org/corporatewatch/paywatch/pay/index.cfm

Alvaredo, Facundo, Tony Atkinson, Thomas Piketty, and Emanuel Saez. (2011). "Top Incomes Database." January. http://g-mond.parisschoolofeconomics.eu/topincomes/

Bebchuk, Lucian, and Jesse Fried. (2004). *Pay without Performance: The Unfulfilled Promise of Executive Compensation*. Cambridge, MA: Harvard University Press.

Berle, Adolf A., and Gardiner C. Means. (1932). *The Modern Corporation and Private Property*. New York: Macmillan.

Blair, Margaret M. (1995). *Ownership and Control: Rethinking Corporate Governance for the Twenty-First Century*. Washington, DC: Brookings Institution.

Block, Fred. (2009). "Swimming against the Current: The Rise of a Hidden Developmental State in the United States." *Politics & Society* 36(2): 169–206.

Block, Fred, and Matthew Keller, eds. (2011). *State of Innovation: The US Government's Role in Technology Development*. Boulder CO: Paradigm.

Chambers, John, and Safra Catz. (2010). "The Overseas Profits Elephant in the Room; There's a Trillion Dollars Waiting to Be Repatriated If Tax Policy Is Right." *Wall Street Journal*, October 20.

Crooks, Ed, and Dan McCrum. (2011). "GE Changes Share Option Plan for Immelt." *Financial Times*, April 20.

Dharmapala, Dhammika, C. Fritz Foley, and Kristin J. Forbes. (2010). "Watch What I Do, Not What I Say: The Unintended Consequences of the Homeland Investment Act." April 27, MIT Sloan Research Paper No. 4741–09.http://ssrn.com/abstract=1337206

Fama, Eugene F., and Michael C. Jensen. (1983a). "Agency Problems and Residual Claims." *Journal of Law and Economics* 26(2): 327–349.

Fama, Eugene F., and Michael C. Jensen. (1983b). "Separation of Ownership and Control." *Journal of Law and Economics* 26(2): 301–325.

Farber, Henry. (2008). "Job Loss and the Decline of Job Security in the United States." Princeton University Industrial Relations Section Working Paper no. 520, Princeton University, June 4.http://dataspace.princeton.edu/jspui/handle/88435/dsp01xk81jk38d.

Hudson, Richard L. (1982). "SEC Eases Way for Repurchase of Firms' Stock: Agency Assures It Won't File Charges of Manipulation If Certain Rules Are Met." *Wall Street Journal*, November 10, 2.

Immelt, Jeffrey R. (2011). "A Blueprint for Keeping America Competitive." *Washington Post*, January 21.

Jensen, Michael C. (1986). "Agency Costs of Free Cash Flow, Corporate Finance, and Takeovers." *American Economic Review* 76(2): 323–329.

Jensen, Michael C., and Kevin J. Murphy. (1990). "Performance Pay and Top Management Incentives." *Journal of Political Economy* 98(2): 225–264.

Lazonick, William. (1990). *Competitive Advantage on the Shop Floor*. Cambridge, MA: Harvard University Press.

Lazonick, William. (2008). "Entrepreneurial Ventures and the Developmental State: Lessons from the Advanced Economies." World Institute of Development Economics Research Discussion Paper dp2008-01.http://www.wider.unu.edu/publications/working-papers/discussion-papers/2008/en_GB/dp2008-01/_files/78805634425684379/default/dp2008-01.pdf.

Lazonick, William. (2009a). *Sustainable Prosperity in the New Economy? Business Organization and High-Tech Employment in the United States*. Upjohn Institute for Employment Research.

Lazonick, William. (2009b). "The New Economy Business Model and the Crisis of US Capitalism." *Capitalism and Society* 4(2): Article 4.

Lazonick, William. (2010a). "The Chandlerian Corporation and the Theory of Innovative Enterprise." *Industrial and Corporate Change* 19(2): 317–349.

Lazonick, William. (2010b). "The Explosion of Executive Pay and the Erosion of American Prosperity." *Entreprises et Histoire* 57: 141–164.

Lazonick, William. (2011). "The Innovative Enterprise and the Developmental State: Toward an Economics of 'Organizational Success.'" Paper presented at the conference of the Institute for New Economic Thinking, Bretton Woods, NH, April 10.

Lazonick, William. (2012). "The Fragility of the US Economy: The Financialized Corporation and the Disappearing Middle Class." In Dan Breznitz and John Zysman, eds., *National Adjustments to a Changing Global Economy*, New York: Oxford University Press.

Lazonick, William, and Mariana Mazzucato (2012), "The Risk-Reward Nexus in the Innovation-Inequality Relationship: Who Takes the Risks? Who Gets the Rewards?, Paper presented at the annual conference of the International Schumpeter Society, University of Queesland, Brisbane, Australia, July 2.

Lazonick, William, and Mary O'Sullivan. (2000). "Maximizing Shareholder Value: A New Ideology for Corporate Governance." *Economy and Society* 29(1): 13–35.

Lazonick, William, and Öner Tulum. (2011). "US Biopharmaceutical Finance and the Sustainability of the US Biotech Business Model." *Research Policy*. 40(9): 1170–1187.

Louis, Henock, and Hal White. (2007). "Do Managers Intentionally Use Repurchase Tender Offers to Signal Private Information? Evidence from Firm Financial Reporting Behavior." *Journal of Financial Economics* 85(1): 205–233.

National Research Council. (1999). *Funding a Revolution: Government Support for Computing Research*. Washington, DC: National Academies Press.

O'Sullivan, Mary. (2004). "What Drove the US Stock Market in the Last Century?" INSEAD Working Paper, Fontainebleau, France.

Rappaport, Alfred. (1981). "Selecting Strategies That Create Shareholder Value." *Harvard Business Review* 59(3): 139–149.

Rappaport, Alfred. (1983). "Corporate Performance Standards and Shareholder Value." *Journal of Business Strategy* 3(4): 28–38.

Rosen, Jan M. (1991). "New Regulations on Stock Options." *New York Times*, April 27.

Sechler, Bob. (2010). "GE's Immelt Says 'We're an Industrial Company First." *Dow Jones News Service*, April 28.

US Congress. (2010). *Economic Report of the President*. Washington, DC: US Government Printing Office.

Vermaelen, Theo. (2005). *Share Repurchases: Foundations and Trends in Finance*. Hanover, MA: Now Publishers.

CHAPTER 25

# FINANCIALIZATION AND THE GLOBAL ECONOMY

ENGELBERT STOCKHAMMER

ONE of the hallmarks of economic development since the early 1980s has been the increasing role of finance, often summarily referred to as financialization. The processes involved have had domestic as well as international dimensions. The task of this chapter is to summarize debates about both of them. In doing so we will ask what changes financialization has brought to the macroeconomic regime, in particular what its effects have been on the growth trajectory, on the stability of the system, in income distribution and, if countries have been affected, whether in the same way or in different ways.

The chapter will first discuss "financialization," that is, changes in the role of the financial sector. I will highlight (1) changes in household behavior, in particular with regards to household debt; (2) changes in the behavior of nonfinancial businesses, such as shareholder value orientation and increased financial activity; and (3) changes in the financial sector, in particular the emergence of the (hardly regulated) shadow banking sector, a shift toward household credit (rather than business credit) and a shift to investment banking/fee-generating business. Second, I will discuss the international dimension of financialization. Here the liberalization of capital flows and its consequences, the determination of exchange rates by capital flows (rather than by current account disequilibria), will be discussed. International financial liberalization has not fulfilled the neoliberal promise of generating investment-based growth; instead, it has given rise to a series of financial crises that were typically driven by a swing of capital inflows (a "capital-flow bonanza") followed by capital-flow reversals. Third,

I offer an interpretation of the finance-dominated accumulation regime as having given rise to two distinct growth models (based on Stockhammer, 2010a, 2010b): a credit-financed consumption-driven growth model (mostly in Anglo-Saxon countries) and an export-driven growth model (in Germany, Japan, and, possibly, China). Both growth models suffer from a structural demand deficiency, which is due to wage suppression, but each tries to overcome this by different means (credit-financed consumption or export orientation). I thus will highlight how financialization with its domestic and international effects has interacted with a polarization of income distribution to generate the structural imbalances that led to the crisis of 2007–2009.

## Financialization

Financialization is the term used to summarize a broad set of changes in the relation between the "financial" and "real" sector; these changes give greater weight than before to financial actors or motives. The term has encompassed phenomena as diverse as shareholder value orientation, increasing household debt, changes in attitudes of individuals, increasing incomes from financial activities, increasing frequency of financial crises, and increasing international capital mobility (see Ertürk et al., 2008 for a useful collection of seminal contributions).[1] Most authors regard financialization as one of the key components of a broader societal shift in social and economic relations from a Fordist accumulation regime to a new "neoliberal" regime (e.g., Glyn, 2006; Harvey, 2005).

The debate on financialization is fueled by the popular perception that finance is increasingly dominating real activity. While the exact meaning of this statement is hard to pin down, there is ample evidence that financial activity has grown faster than real activity (as measured for example by GDP). To illustrate this, figures 25.1 to 25.3 present data for the United States. Figure 25.1 gives the stock-market capitalization and stock-market turnover. From 1997 stock-market capitalization exceeds GDP, rising from 58 percent of GDP in 1988 to 163 percent in 1999 (and flattening out thereafter). The rise of stock-market turnover is even more spectacular in the period from 33 percent in 1988 to 383 percent in 2008. Figure 25.2 gives the share of financial profits and profits from abroad to total corporate profits. This share has risen from just above 12 percent in 1948 to a peak at 53 percent in 2001. Finally, financialization has come with a dramatic increase in debt levels across different sectors. Figure 25.3 shows the debt of households, businesses, and the financial sector (as a ratio to GDP). While the business sector has increased its debt from 52 percent of GDP (in 1976) to 77 percent (2009), household debt has increased from 45 percent (1976) to 96 percent (2009), with a clear acceleration in the early 2000s. Most spectacularly, the debt of the financial sector

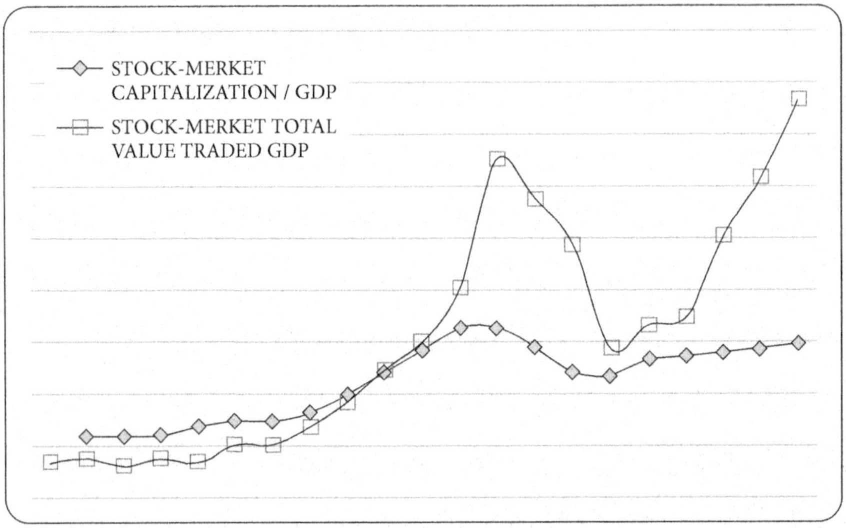


**Figure 25.1** Stock market capitalization and value traded as a ratio to US GDP.
*Source*: World Bank Financial Structure data set (Beck, Demirgüç-Kunt, and Levine, 2010).

has increased from 16 percent to 111 percent (in 2009).[2] The popular perception of the increasing role of finance is clearly substantiated by economic data: activity on financial markets has increased faster than real activity; financial profits make up an increasing share of total profits; and households as well as the financial sector are taking on a lot more debt. The following shall explore some of the changes financialization has brought to these economic sectors.

Financialization was made possible by a series of measures to deregulate the financial sector and to liberalize international capital flows. Many of these

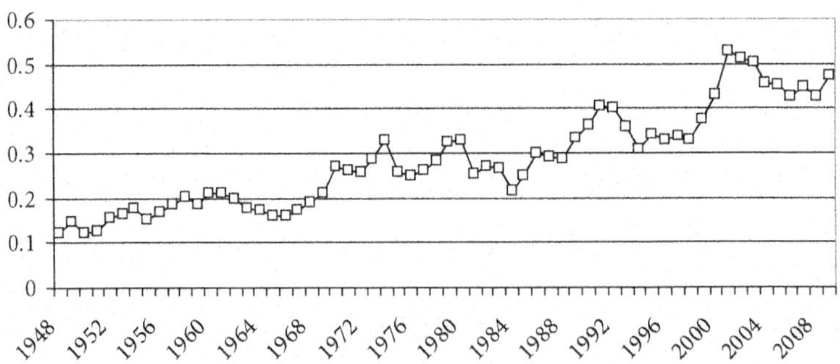


**Figure 25.2** Financial and international profits as share of corporate profits.
*Note*: Financial and international profits include domestic financial profits and (net) profits from abroad as share of corporate profits (with inventory valuation and capital consumption adjustments). There is a (minor) break in the series in 2001.
*Source*: Bureau of Economic Analysis, National Income and Product Accounts, table 6.16B-D

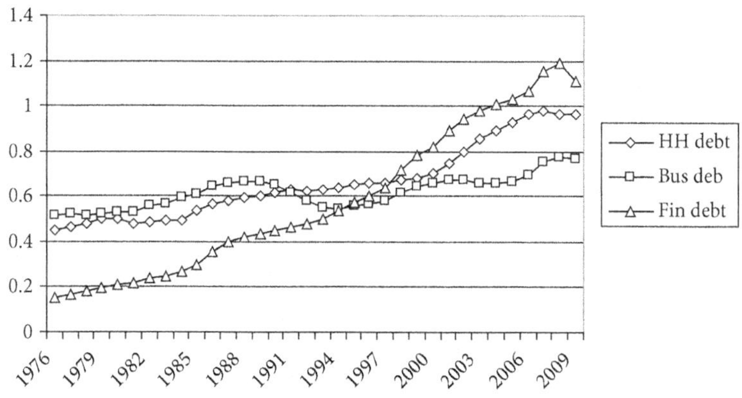


**Figure 25.3** Debt of households, businesses, and financial sectors (as ratio to GDP), in United States.

*Source*: FED Flow of Funds, table D.3: Credit Market Debt Outstanding by Sector. Household, business, and financial debts are the total debt outstanding by households, businesses, and domestic financial sectors, respectively, all divided by GDP.

measures were themselves reactions to increasing activities on the part of private agents to circumvent financial regulation. These measures include the phasing out of controls on international capital flows, a deregulation of the types of transactions that banks are allowed to engage in, and the lifting of the interest-rate ceiling (on deposits as well as on credit). The new financial landscape that arose was populated by new financial institutions ranging from money market funds to private equity and hedge funds and by a seemingly untiring wave of financial innovation that led to ever newer financial instruments.

A first important area of debate has been the financialization of *nonfinancial businesses*. A reassertion of the shareholder in the form of activist institutional investors and a wave of mergers and acquisitions often in the form of hostile takeovers have led to what has become known as "shareholder value orientation." Ideologically this was backed by theories of corporate governance that analyzed firms in terms of principal agent problems and that advocated shareholder value orientation as the appropriate goal of the firm (e.g., Jensen and Meckling, 1976). Firms' goals now prominently feature the rate of return on equity. This is done by means of increasing payouts in the form of dividends and via share buybacks. Remarkably, these developments have come with lower rates of investment by firms and, at the same time, with higher debt ratios of firms. In other words, firms often have taken out loans to buy back shares to increase shareholder value.

Political economy approaches highlight the social costs of such strategies that often involved downsizing of employment and pressure on wages. Lazonick and O'Sullivan (2000) argue that there has been a shift from what they call "retain and reinvest" to "downsize and distribute." Fligstein (1990) argues that financial control is a particular model of controlling an organization, thus locating the source of financialization of nonfinancial firms in management. In the meantime a growing empirical literature has aimed to demonstrate that increasing financial activity of nonfinancial firms has had a negative effect on (real) investment of these firms (Demir, 2009; Orhangazi, 2008; Stockhammer, 2004). Shareholder value orientation seems to be most pronounced in Anglo-Saxon countries, with continental European countries moving in the same direction.

The effects of financialization on *households* have been as profound as those on businesses. Individuals and households have become used to relying on credit.[3] This has involved changes in attitudes as well as changes in financial institutions and instruments, among which the widespread use of credit cards is the most obvious. Household debt levels have increased sharply since the mid-1970s. In terms of volumes, mortgage credit is the most important form of credit for households in all countries. Some authors have argued that consumption expenditures in the Anglo-Saxon countries seem to be determined by changes in asset prices or in credit rather than by income (Guttmann and Plihon, 2010). Faced with falling savings rates (in particular in the United States), mainstream economic institutions have investigated to what extent consumption expenditures react to asset prices. The falling saving rates were first explained by a wealth effect due to the rise in the value of financial assets because of the stock-market boom.[4] In the late 1990s a 5 percent marginal propensity to consume out of financial wealth was often quoted (with some more qualification for European countries; e.g., Boone et al., 1998). The stock-market crash in 2000, however, did not result in a slowdown in consumption growth. The unabated US consumption boom was then explained by booming house prices. Residential property was now identified as the key source of the wealth effect because it is more frequently accepted as collateral. Case (2001), Catte(2004), Girouard(2006), and their coauthors all found a substantially higher marginal propensity to consume out of property wealth than out of financial assets.[5]

However, the more fundamental issue is whether the increase in household debt should be regarded as part of a rational decision process or as the outcome of broader social and cultural processes. Much of the mainstream literature assumes that households rationally increased their debt ratios as their wealth increased. From a political economy point of view, increasing household debt is the result of increasing consumption norms in the face of stagnating mass incomes (Barba and Pivetti, 2009; Cynamon and Fazzari, 2009). A substantial part of the accumulated debt is due to households maintaining consumption levels that are unsustainable (and thus could be considered irrational). Or it could be due to a different strategy on the part of banks. From this perspective it is misleading to speak of a wealth effect; rather, it should be called a *credit access effect*.

While household debt consists overwhelmingly of mortgages everywhere, the dynamics of consumption expenditures and household debt have differed substantially across countries. In the United States the consumption share in GDP had been increasing since about 1980. The trend is similar in the United Kingdom. Notably, in many countries the strong increases in household debt ratios coincided with property bubbles. However, in Germany and France debt ratios have increased much less and consumption ratios have declined since 1980. There has been a remarkable divergence between countries.

Financialization has had important ramifications for the *financial sector* itself. First, as a shadow banking system emerged, a substantial and growing part of the financial sector does not take the form of (traditional) banking (or insurance), but of other, typically much less regulated, institutions such as investment funds, money market funds, hedge funds, private equity funds, and special purpose vehicles. This shadow banking system has also served as a motor for financialization (for an early account, see D'Arista and Schlesinger, 1993). One important aspect of the emergence of the shadow banking sector is financial innovation, that is, the development of new financial instruments that often helped to circumvent traditional banking regulation. Adrian and Shin (2010) estimate that in the United States the shadow banking system is now as large as the regular banking sector (measured in terms of assets). Second, within banking this development has led to a shift toward fee-generating business rather than traditional banking, which generates income as a result of the interest differential between rates on deposits and on loans. Part of this has been the emergence of what has been called the originate-and-distribute model of banking (in particular in the United States), where mortgages were quickly sold in the form of asset-backed securities. Third, within banking there has been a shift to lending to households rather than to firms. In particular mortgages are now by far the largest loan positions (Ertürk and Solari, 2007; Lapavitsas, 2009).

Supporters of financial deregulation have argued that financialization will provide a superior way of dealing with risk; for example, securitization was supposed to slice risk into different parts (by means of different securities) and allocate it to those who were best equipped to hold it. The financial system would thus be more stable (e.g., IMF 2006, 51) and society would be better off. In contrast Keynesians have long argued that financial markets are intrinsically unstable and tend to generate endogenous boom-bust cycles (Minsky, 1986). More recently, they have highlighted conflicts of interest and the dangers of the belief that risk could easily be sliced by means of looking at past correlations (Aglietta and Rebérioux, 2005;Crotty, 2009). The crisis of 2008-2009 has shaken the optimistic liberal outlook somewhat, but its impact on economic debates is not yet clear.

## Financial Globalization

Financialization has also had important effects along the international dimension. The liberalization of international capital flows has led to increased volatility of exchange rates, often culminating in a violent exchange-rate crisis. This has led to a rich debate on the effects of capital-flow liberalization or, more broadly, of financial globalization.

The argument in favor of financial globalization is based on standard neoclassical economics and argues that financial globalization would allow capital to be allocated to its most efficient use. In particular it would benefit developing countries. Two important implications of this argument are (1) that one would expect capital flows from rich to poor countries and (2) that there would be a positive correlation between indicators of financial globalization and growth. This approach had been advocated by McKinnon and Shaw and recently by Mishkin(2006). It has informed economic policy around the globe, in particular in the form of International Monetary Fund (IMF) programs imposed on developing countries. However, financial globalization has clearly not lived up to expectations. On average, capital has been flowing "uphill," that is, from poor to rich countries. And even within the mainstream it is now accepted that "the majority of studies are unable to find robust evidence in support of the growth benefits of capital account liberalization"(Kose et al., 2009). While true believers still defend financial globalization on the grounds that the benefits do materialize indirectly (Kose et al., 2006) and would show up in the future (Mishkin, 2006) or if only more sophisticated methods were used (Henry, 2007), the empirical evidence for lack of positive growth effects is rather solid (Rodrik and Suramanian, 2009; earlier: Stiglitz, 2000).

In contrast to the liberal vision, financial globalization and liberalization seem to have led, first, to frequent exchange-rate crises driven by volatile capital flows and, second, to long-lasting international imbalances. As a consequence of financial globalization, exchange-rate movements are increasingly determined by capital flows rather than by economic fundamentals such as current account positions. Indeed, episodes of massive capital inflows followed by sudden and sharp capital-flow reversals, resulting in exchange-rate crises, have been a common feature in particular for emerging and developing countries (Epstein, 2005; Reinhart and Reinhart, 2008). The macroeconomic dangers of volatile capital flows have so far been felt most acutely in emerging economies. Mexico in 1994, Turkey in 1994 and 2001, several countries in the course of the Southeast Asian crisis in 1997–1998, and Argentina in 2001 are all examples of such crises that are related to capital flows. All of them have led to severe recessions (at times with double-digit declines in real GDP), some of them long-lasting, others more short-lived.[6] However, the European Monetary System (EMS) crisis in 1992–1993 also shook developed economies.

The reason why changes in the exchange rate have such a devastating effect is that in liberalized international markets it is usually profitable to engage in interest arbitrage, that is, borrow in one currency and invest or lend in another (often called carry trade). If, say, interest rates in Turkish lira are higher than those in euros (with exchange rates expected to be stable), it is tempting to take out a euro credit and lend in Turkish lira. By implication, assets and liabilities will then be denominated in different currencies.

Abrupt exchange-rate realignments may then have disastrous effects on firms' or banks' balance sheets.

Second, the liberalization of capital flows has also allowed countries to sustain current account deficits (or surpluses) at higher levels and for a longer time than during the Bretton Woods system.[7] The flip side of the current account is net capital flows: abstracting from changes in Central Bank reserves, net exports have to equal (net) capital outflows. Financialization has thus allowed countries to run larger current account deficits, provided that they can attract the corresponding capital inflows. Financial liberalization and globalization have, ironically, increased the potential for different developments across countries—as long as international financial markets remain calm. Typically the revaluation on financial markets has come abruptly with capital-flow reversals and exchange-rate crises.

In the run-up to the financial crisis in 2008-2009 the United States, the United Kingdom, Ireland, and Greece ran large current account deficits, whereas Germany, Japan, and China had large surpluses. International imbalances have played a prominent role in the debate on the causes of the 2008-2009 crisis, but they can be associated with quite different theoretical interpretations. Bernanke (2005) coined the term "savings glut," which argued that forces outside the United States have been the main driving force behind the US current account deficit. Politically this has served to shift the blame on to China.[8] Indeed, there were massive capital inflows to the United States, mostly from (Asian and OPEC) developing countries. After the Southeast Asian financial crisis, several Asian countries (notably China) pursued a strategy of undervaluation, which has proven quite effective from a development perspective (UNCTAD, 2008). The question of whether these inflows have been forced onto the United States or whether they have been sucked in by the US financial sector is difficult to establish. But the savings glut hypothesis certainly downplays the dominant role of US institutions in the world economy, in particular the massive financial engineering that had been going on.

## A Finance-Dominated Accumulation Regime?—Financialization and Economic Performance: Growth, Distribution, and Stability

Financialization and financial globalization have changed economic actors, their goals, and their constraints. There is an ongoing theoretical debate on the characteristics of a "finance-led" or "finance-dominated" accumulation regime (e.g., Boyer, 2000; Hein, 2011; van Treeck, 2009). To conclude, I assess the impact of financialization on economic performance, income distribution, and stability. The finance-dominated accumulation regime has been characterized by a sluggish overall economic performance with increasing financial fragility due to rising debt levels. But due to persistent international imbalances the specific effects have been quite different across countries.

I (2010a, 2010b) have argued that financialization has given rise to *two different growth models*: a consumption-driven growth model (mostly in Anglo-Saxon countries) and an export-oriented growth regime in other countries (such as Germany and Japan), both of which are explained as the results of the interaction of trends in the polarization of income distribution and of financialization. In Anglo-Saxon countries the shortfall of disposable income has been compensated by credit and increasing debt levels. The property boom allowed households to take out loans that they could not afford, but the arrangements seemed reasonable to banks, which assumed that property prices would continue to increase. These countries developed a *credit-financed consumption boom* that came with current account deficits. The resulting capital inflows again fueled the property bubble and bubbles in other financial markets. In the second group of countries median working-class households faced a similar stagnation in wages. In these countries private consumption expenditures remained weak. Here net exports played the key component of demand growth. Thus these countries developed an *export-led growth model.*

Financialization also has had profound effects on *income distribution.* At least three channels have been discussed in the literature. First, there has been the rise of what is often called "rentiers income," which is interest and dividend income as well as capital gains and has been well documented (Duménil and Lévy, 2001; Powers et al., 2003). Second, the rise of incomes in the financial sector, most notably in the form of bonuses, has widened income disparity. Third, financialization seems to have shifted the power balance between capital and labor in various ways ranging from changes in corporate governance to the increased range of possibilities opened to firms by financial globalization (ILO, 2008). Several studies have found econometric evidence that financial globalization has led to a decline in wage shares (Jayadev, 2007; Stockhammer, 2009).

The debate on the effects on financialization on *economic (and financial) stability* is characterized by a strange schizophrenia. On the one hand, there has been a series of major crises since financialization began that have obviously been related to the financial sector: the debt crisis in 1982, the savings and loans crisis in the United States in the 1980s, the EMS crisis in 1992–1993, the peso crisis in 1994, the Asian crisis, the dot.com bubble, and finally the crisis of 2008–2009. On the other hand, a mainstream literature has declared this period one of increased stability, often referred to as the Great Moderation, which has given rise to substantial and technically sophisticated literature. The Great Moderation hypothesis, of course, has been called into question by the 2008–2009 crisis.

To illustrate how this literature has missed the elephant in the room, the IMF 2007c) has presented evidence that business cycles have become more *moderate* since the 1970s: "output volatility (...) has been significantly lower than during the 1960s" (85). Naturally, one would assume that this means that crises have become milder and less frequent. However, according to the IMF (2002, table 3.1) recessions have become *deeper* in the post-Bretton Woods era. How is this possible? As output growth (and expansions) was much higher in the Fordist era than in the post-Fordist era, volatility has indeed decreased while crises become harsher.[9] But this does not mean that recessions have become less severe! Indeed, financial crises have become more frequent and more severe (Eichengreen and Bordo, 2003; Reinhart and Rogoff, 2009).

The crisis of 2008-2009 has been the deepest crisis for capitalist economies since the Great Depression. It should be obvious that its causes are deeply connected with the processes of financialization and financial globalization. Whether the brutal return of financial instability to the capitalist centers marks the beginning of the end of financialization or the return to an unstable financialized normality of liberal capitalism will be the subject of future political struggles.

## Acknowledgments

This chapter builds closely on previous work by the author (Stockhammer, 2010a, 2012) and has benefited from comments by Iren Levina and Fidelma Murphy.

## Notes

1. The debate on financialization is one where theories lag behind societal and economic changes. It draws on different theoretical and methodological approaches. Cultural economists have highlighted the incompleteness and contradictions of the discursive strategies of financialization (Froud et al., 2006), while macroeconomists have tried to identify the conditions for viable growth regimes; economic sociologists have argued that (financial) markets have to be constructed by specific actors with specific interest (MacKenzie and Millo, 2003), while post-Keynesian economists have highlighted the fragile nature of finance-led growth. One of the first prominent authors to use the term financialization was Arrighi, (1994) who identified long waves of economic development in global capitalism that involve hegemonic and geographic shifts. While the upswings of these long waves are characterized by increased manufacturing and trade activity, in the downturns a process of financialization occurs: the leading power had initially established

a competitive advantage in terms of production, but it shifts toward financial activities as its growth model gets exhausted and other players catch up. In contrast to Arrighi most of the recent debate uses the term more narrowly to refer to the period since the 1970s.

2. These figures refer to *gross* debt. Typically debt will be used to acquire assets. The difference between the value of the assets and gross debt is net debt. It is useful to look at gross debt as the valuation of assets that may at times change dramatically as happened in 2008–2009, whereas the nominal value of debt is fixed.
3. A second important area where households have become financialized is with respect to the provision of old-age retirement. Many countries have shifted from a state-provided Social Security scheme to an increased prominence of private, market-based provision of pensions (Blackburn, 2007; Langley, 2004). More generally, financialization is part of a process by which various kinds of provisions against risks and the uncertainties of the future are organized via private capital market arrangements rather than through institutional arrangements. Prime examples include the shift from publicly provided pay-as-you-go pension systems to capital-based systems. Health insurance and the financing of education are other examples.
4. The distribution of household debt (and of its growth) is an important if underresearched issue. Brenner (2003, 191) argues that most of the fall in the savings rate (in the late 1990s) occurred in the top income groups, who also benefited most from the increase in financial wealth. Evidence for the early 2000s, however, suggests that the debt burden has grown fastest for middle-class households (Wolff, 2009).
5. While there is substantial evidence for the United States (albeit based on a short period of observations!) to back up this story, the evidence on European economies was always much thinner. Typically the wealth effects estimated for continental European economies were not statistically significant or much smaller.
6. The fact that some countries recover quickly after a deep recession does not imply that everything returns to the way they before the crisis. Onaran (2009) argues that financial crises often lead to lasting changes in functional income distribution.
7. Financialization is part of the globalization of production. International production networks require international financial transactions and, in a setting with market-determined exchange rates, have given rise to various instruments to hedge against exchange-rate variations. Direct foreign investment and its associated income flows will show up within financial income (e.g., in the form of dividends paid by a foreign subsidiary; Milberg and Winkler, 2009).
8. While the imbalances argument has politically supported pressure on China to change its *exchange-rate policy*, there has been surprisingly little pressure on Germany, the other big surplus country, to alter its *wage policy*. Arguably, Germany's wage suppression is one of the roots of the 2010 European crisis (Lapavitsas et al., 2010).
9. In discussing the question of stability it is important to note that by historical standards all developed economies are still characterized by big government: automatic stabilizers are in place and government consumption forms a sizable part of value added. The resilience of a sizable government sector and (by historical standards) a functional welfare state combined with active monetary policy may be a reason for why financial crises have so far not had a devastating effect on (advanced) economies (Stockhammer, 2008).

## References


Adrian, Tobias, and Hyun Song Shin. (2010). "The Changing Nature of Financial Intermediation and the Financial Crisis of 2007–09." Federal Reserve Bank of New York Staff Reports 439.

Aglietta Michel, and Andre Rebérioux. (2005). *Corporate Governance Adrift: A Critique of Shareholder Value*. Cheltenham, UK: Edward Elgar.

Arrighi, Giovanni. (1994). *The Long Twentieth Century*. London: Verso.

Barba, Aldo, and Massimo Pivetti. (2009). "Rising Household Debt: Its Causes and Macroeconomic Implications—A Long-Period Analysis." *Cambridge Journal of Economics* 33: 113–137.

Beck, Thorsten, AsliDemirgüç-Kunt, and Ross Levine. (2010). "A New Database on Financial Development and Structure." Updated November 2010. http://econ.worldbank.org/WBSITE/EXTERNAL/EXTDEC/EXTRESEARCH/0,,contentMDK:20696167~pagePK:64214825~piPK:64214943~theSitePK:469382,00.html.

Bernanke, Ben. (2005). "The Global Saving Glut and the US Current Account Deficit." Sandridge Lecture, Virginia Association of Economics, Richmond, Virginia, March 2005. http://www.federalreserve.gov/boarddocs/speeches/2005/200503102/default.htm.

Blackburn, Robin. (2007). *Age Shock: How Finance Is Failing Us*. London: Verso.

Boone, Laurence, Claude Giorno, and Pete Richardson. (1998). "Stock Market Fluctuations and Consumption Behaviour: Some Recent Evidence." OECD Economics Department Working Papers No. 208. Paris: Organisation of Economic Cooperation and Development.

Boyer, Robert. (2000). "Is a Finance-led Growth Regime a Viable Alternative to Fordism? A Preliminary Analysis." *Economy and Society* 29(1): 111–145.

Brenner, Robert. (2003). *The Boom and the Bubble*. London: Verso.

Case, Karl, Robert Shiller, and John Quigley. (2001). "Comparing Wealth Effects: The Stock Market Versus the Housing Market." NBER Working Paper No. w8606, November.

Catte, P., N. Girouard, R. Price, and C. André. (2004). "Housing Markets, Wealth and the Business Cycle."OECD Economics Working Paper 394. Paris: Organisation of Economic Cooperation and Development.

Crotty, James. (2009). "Structural Causes of the Global Financial Crisis: A Critical Assessment of the 'New Financial Architecture.'" *Cambridge Journal of Economics* 33:563–580.

Cynamon, Barry, and Steven Fazzari. (2009). "Household Debt in the Consumer Age: Source of Growth—Risk of Collapse. *Capitalism and Society* 3(2): art. 1.

D'Arista, Jane, and T. Schlesinger. (1993). "The Parallel Banking System." In G. Dymski, G. Epstein, and R. Pollin, eds., *Transforming the US Financial System: Equity and Efficiency for the 21st Century*. Armonk, NY: M.E. Sharpe.

Demir, Firat. (2009). "Financial Liberalization, Private Investment and Portfolio Choice: Financialization of Real Sectors in Emerging Markets." *Journal of Development Economics* 88: 314–324.

Duménil, Gerard, and Dominique Lévy. (2001). "Costs and Benefits of Neoliberalism: A Class Analysis." *Review of International Political Economy* 8(4): 578–607.

Eichengreen, Barry, and Michael Bordo. (2003). "Crises Now and Then: What Lessons for the Last Era of Financial Globalization?" In P. Mizen, ed., *Monetary History,*

*Exchange Rates and Financial Markets: Essays in Honour of Charles Goodhart*. Vol.2. Cheltenham, UK: Edward Elgar.

Epstein, Gerald, ed. (2005). *Financialization and the World Economy*. Cheltenham, UK: Edward Elgar.

Ertürk, Ismail, Julie Froud, Sukhdev Johal, Adam Leaver, and Karel Williams, eds. (2008). *Financialization at Work. Key Texts and Commentary*. London: Routledge.

Ertürk, Ismail, and Stefano Solari. (2007). "Banks as Continuous Reinvention." *New Political Economy* 12(3): 369–388.

Fligstein, Neil. (1990). *The Transformation of Corporate Control*. Cambridge, MA: Harvard University Press.

Froud, Julie, Sukhdev Johal, Adam Leaver, and Karel Williams. (2006). *Financialization and Strategy: Narrative and Numbers*. London: Routledge.

Girouard, N., M. Kennedy, and C. André. (2006). "Has the Rise in Debt Made Households More Vulnerable?" OECD Economics Working Paper 535.

Glyn, Andrew. (2006). *Capitalism Unleashed: Finance, Globalization and Welfare*. New York: Oxford University Press.

Guttmann, Robert, and Dominique Plihon. (2010). "Consumer Debt and Financial Fragility." *International Review of Applied Economics* 24(3): 269–283.

Harvey, David. (2005). *A Short History of Neoliberalism*. Oxford: Oxford University Press.

Hein, Eckhard. (2011). "Financialisation, Distribution and Growth." In E. Hein and E. Stockhammer, eds., *A New Guide to Keynesian Economics and Economic Policies*. Cheltenham, UK: Edward Elgar.

Henry, Peter. (2007). "Capital Account Liberalization: Theory, Evidence, and Speculation." Brookings Global Economy and Development Paper No. 4, January.

ILO. (2008). *World of Work Report 2008. Income Inequalities in the Age of Financial Globalization*. Geneva: ILO.

IMF. (2002). "Recessions and Recoveries." Chapter 3 of World Economic Outlook 2002/1.

IMF. (2006). *Global Financial Stability Report April 2006*. Washington: IMF, 2006.

IMF. (2007). "The Changing Dynamics of the Global Business Cycle." Chapter 5 of: World Economic Outlook 2007/2.

Jayadev, Arjun. (2007). "Capital Account Openness and the Labour Share of Income." *Cambridge Journal of Economics* 31: 423–443.

Jensen, M., and W. Meckling. (1976). "Theory of the Firm: Managerial Behavior, Agency Costs, and Ownership Structure." *Journal of Financial Economics* 3: 305–360.

Kose, M. Ayhan, Eswar Prasad, Kenneth Rogoff, and Shang-Jin Wei. (2009). "Financial Globalization: A Reappraisal." *IMF Staff Papers* 56: 8–62.

Langley, Paul. (2004). "In the Eye of the 'Perfect Storm': The Final Salary Pensions Crisis and the Financialization of Anglo-American Capitalism." *New Political Economy* 9(4): 539–558.

Lapavitsas, Costas. (2009). "Financialised Capitalism: Crisis and Financial Expropriation." *Historical Materialism* 17: 114–148.

Lapavitsas, C., A. Kaltenbrunner, D. Lindo, J. Michell,J. P. Painceira, E. Pires, J. Powell, A. Stenfors, and N. Teles. (2010). "Eurozone Crisis: Beggar Thyself and Thy Neighbour." RMF Occasional Report, March 2010. http://researchonmoneyandfinance.org/media/reports/eurocrisis/fullreport.pdf.

Lazonick, William, and Mary O'Sullivan. (2000). "Maximising Shareholder Value: A New Ideology for Corporate Governance." *Economy and Society* 29(1): 13–35.

MacKenzie, Donald, and Yuval Millo. (2003). "Constructing a Market, Performing Theory: The Historical Sociology of a Financial Derivatives Exchange." *American Journal of Sociology* 109: 107–145.
Milberg, William, and Deborah Winkler. (2009). "Financialisation and the Dynamics of Offshoring in the USA." *Cambridge Journal of Economics* 34: 275–293.
Minsky, Hyman. (1986). *Stabilizing an Unstable Economy*. New Haven: Yale University Press.
Mishkin, Frederic S. (2006). *The Next Great Globalization: How Disadvantaged Nations Can Harness Their Financial Systems to Get Rich*. Princeton: Princeton University Press.
Onaran, Özlem. (2009). "Wage Share, Globalization, and Crisis: The Case of Manufacturing Industry in Korea, Mexico, and Turkey." *International Review of Applied Economics* 23(2): 113–134.
Orhangazi, Özgür. (2008). "Financialisation and Capital Accumulation in the Non-financial Corporate Sector: A Theoretical and Empirical Investigation on the US Economy: 1973–2003." *Cambridge Journal of Economics* 32: 863–886.
Power, D., G. Epstein, and M. Abrena. (2003). "Trends in the Rentier Income Share in OECD Countries 1960–2000." PERI Working Paper 58a.
Reinhart, Carmen, and Vincent Reinhart. (2008). "Capital Flow Bonanzas: An Encompassing View of the Past and Present." NBER Working Paper No. W14321.
Reinhart, Carmen, and Kenneth Rogoff. (2009). *This Time Is Different: Eight Centuries of Financial Folly*. Princeton: Princeton University Press.
Rodrik, Dani, and Arvind Suramanian. (2009). "Why Did Financial Globalization Disappoint?" *IMF Staff Papers* 56(1): 112–138.
Stiglitz, Joseph. (2000). "Capital Market Liberalization, Economic Growth and Instability." *World Development* 28(6): 1075–1086.
Stockhammer, Engelbert. (2004). "Financialization and the Slowdown of Accumulation." *Cambridge Journal of Economics* 28(5): 719–741.
Stockhammer, Engelbert. (2008). "Some Stylized Facts on the Finance-Dominated Accumulation Regime." *Competition and Change* 12(2): 189–207.
Stockhammer, Engelbert. (2009). "Determinants of Functional Income Distribution in OECD Countries." IMK Studies, No. 5/2009. Düsseldorf.
Stockhammer, Engelbert. (2010a). "Income Distribution, the Finance-Dominated Accumulation Regime and the Present Crisis." In S. Dullien, E. Hein, A. Truger, and T. van Treeck, eds., *The World Economy in Crisis—The Return of Keynesianism?* Metropolis Verlag.
Stockhammer, Engelbert. (2010b). "Neoliberalism, Income Distribution and the Causes of the Crisis." Research on Money and Finance Discussion Papers 19.
Stockhammer, Engelbert. (2012). "Financialization." In J. Toporovski and J. Mitchell, eds., *Handbook of Critical Issues in Finance*. Cheltenham, UK: Edward Elgar.
UNCTAD. (2008). *Trade and Development Report 2008*. New York: United Nations.
Van Treeck, Till. (2009). "The Political Economy Debate on 'Financialisation'-a Macroeconomic Perspective." *Review of International Political Economy* 16(5): 907–944.
Wolff, Edward. (2009). "Recent Trends in Household Wealth in the United States. Rising Debt and the Middle-Class Squeeze—An Update to 2007." Levy Economics Institute Working Paper 589.

CHAPTER 26

# THE INTERNATIONAL SPREAD OF FINANCIALIZATION

WILLIAM K. TABB

THIS chapter suggests the usefulness of financialization as an overarching conception of the ways in which national economies and economic relations between and among countries have developed, and not only in ways that contributed to the current crisis and are likely to induce future global crises unless the current financialized structure of accumulation is replaced. Theorizing how globalization and financialization interact in terms of tensions and uneven development in the world system is in its early stage of scholarly research. The suggestions here can only be suggestive of a larger collective inquiry. This chapter assembles pieces of such an analysis, reviews salient literature, and comments on how such developments in the world system can be understood. The first part discusses definitions and interpretations of financialization primarily in the context of the US economy; a second section looks at experiences of other countries; a third examines global imbalances, which as phenomena are hardly new but represent a global pattern that is part of financialization's impact in the present neoliberal era in a far more encompassing way. The contention underlying the chapter is that, as a construct, financialization provides important insight into financial crises and the trajectory of contemporary capitalism. A conclusion raises further issues related to longer-run developments at the level of the world system.

# MEANINGS OF FINANCIALIZATION

Financialization denotes the dominance of the financial sector in the totality of economic activity such that financial markets dictate nonfinancial company behaviors and significantly shape the overall economy. Finance capital, footloose and flexible, interposes itself whenever arbitrage opportunities present themselves anywhere on the planet. It represents the increased power of abstract capital as opposed to productive capital. Within even presumably non-financial corporations, therefore, it is the finance people, not those involved in production or sales, that set company strategies. When the financial sector moves beyond lubricating the wheels of commerce to dominate the "real" economy, problems develop. Companies are seen as portfolios of financial assets to be bought and sold, reorganized, merged, spun off, or closed down for short-term profits and tax benefits. On another level, financialization is a policy choice of governments in alliance with internationally oriented financial institutions. It is a tool of accumulation pushed powerfully by the American state and other money-centered governments.

Ours is an epoch in which financialization has become the dynamic center of accumulation enlarging the sphere in which fortunes are made by speculating on and manipulating the future values of financial assets. There are consequences for citizens, who can rely less on employers and the state and who must themselves take on greater uncertainty and higher levels of debt in order to finance consumer purchases, homes, education, retirement, and other quality-of-life decisions. While many of its characteristics are unique to the contemporary conjuncture, there have been other periods of intense financialization, rapid creation of debt, and excessive leverage, for example, the 1920s. Taking the perspective of the longue durée, as this term is used by the French Annales School, the present period resembles earlier turning points in which global hegemons, the British and before them the Dutch, came to depend more on their financial sectors as their capacity to command world markets in production declined (Arrighi and Silver, 1999).

If the United States is facing such a turning point, its territorial economy and most workers can be seen in conflict with US-based international finance and transnational corporations. In the globalized world of the twenty-first century, as the share of national income going to capital has grown at the expense of labor, continued financialization in the world system may represent a major long-term transition. The direction and new institutional arrangements and corresponding public philosophy of an emergent hegemonic bloc is, of course, open to contestation at both the national and global levels.

Internationally, the rapid increase in financial flows from creditor nations (now in the Global South rather than as formerly in the Global North) and from surplus accruing to capital in rich countries that cannot be profitably invested productively and so seeks speculative outlets promotes overextension of national governments in the same manner that easy credit can destabilize households and businesses. In terms of the economics of financialization and crisis, the pro-cyclicality of the transmission mechanism from the financial sector with its growing funding creates asset-price bubbles, pumping money into new "hot" asset classes. Most recently there has been the growth in the extent of food and energy as investment categories for portfolio diversification using derivatives (Wray, 2008), creating a situation in which collateralized security markets drive the prices of underlying commodities.

While in the 1990s private investment was an important contributor to economic growth in the United States it was much reduced in the first decade of the new century. Corporate behavior changed from the "retain and invest" model of corporate behavior in the earlier period to "downsize and distribute" (Lazonick and O'Sullivan, 2000), creating "the financialized corporation" in which the incentives of executives were to extract rents for themselves. The imperative to maximize shareholder value combined with the generous use of stock options as the dominant factor in executive compensation. Stock buybacks became an important factor in raising equity prices and to a significant degree became necessary to offset the scale of issuance of stock options. Banks have been among the biggest stock repurchasers. From 2000 to 2007 Citigroup bought almost $42 billion of its own stock; Lehman Brothers, $17 billion worth, including more than $5 billion in 2006–2007; and Washington Mutual, which, like Lehman, went bankrupt in 2008, $13 billion. The records of these and other financial firms lead to the conclusion that buying their own stocks had reduced their capacity to cope with cash-flow problems when the derivatives market collapsed with consequences for the entire economy (Lazonick, 2010, 696–697). The combination of such behavior and the inability of policy makers and mainstream financial economists to understand the central elements of financialization, the behavioral consequences of enshrining maximizing shareholder value above other goals, the debt on balance sheets, and the use of speculative instruments led to a gigantic misallocation of resources, to instability, and to the worst crisis since the Great Depression.

Von Treeck (2009), using Bureau of Economic Analysis figures on investment, profits, and share prices, graphically shows that while net operating profits for US nonfinancial corporations have grown since 1960 even faster than the S&P 500 index, net nonfinancial private investments lagged. Buybacks exceeded new stock issuance in the American economy and dividend payments have also contributed to a falling trend in retained earnings. The emergence first of Japan and later other developing-country competitors, many in East Asia, and then of China squeezed profits from domestic operations and encouraged outsourcing by large US-based corporations. There was therefore less need to invest domestically, freeing earnings to buy back company stock (and to raise the value of options exercised by executives).

In epochal terms the wage-led growth of the national Keynesian social structure of accumulation was replaced by debt-fueled consumption spending as labor's compensation stagnated and tasks were offshored (McDonough, Reich, and Kotz, 2010). The impacts of such contradictory moments of financialization impose on traditional Keynesian components of aggregate demand. The rate of real domestic investment falls while financial assets grow. On one hand, financialization slows consumption through the channel of wage moderation, while on the other, it increases spending through debt-fueled consumption that cannot be continued indefinitely and makes crisis inevitable. The effect of short-term maximization of shareholder value reduces real investment compared to past periods with similar macro circumstances. Speculative currency movements impact net exports in ways that were less prominent in the past and so on.

These trends were a response to global excess capacity and the loss of competitiveness of US plants. The source of profitability shifted from domestic to foreign production, kept profit rates up even as American workers' wages fell, and led to an increase in the ratio of capital to labor incomes. Milberg (2008, 3) suggests that the globalization of production "helped sustain higher levels of financialization of the U.S. non-financial corporate sector and financialization created greater incentives for cost-reducing and flexibility enhancing globalized production by U.S. lead firms." The deterioration of the US trade balance coincides with the increased profitability observed for US companies operating in the global market (Kregel, 2008).

Financial-sector profits as a percentage of GDP increased substantially—from 1 percent at the end of World War II, going above 2 percent in the late 1990s, and exceeding 3 percent in the opening years of the new century. Significantly, return on revenues did not rise but return on assets did, thanks to higher leverage and greater risk taking. To some extent the new financial instruments requiring high-speed computers and sophisticated programming meant that, in a number of trading areas, large firms had a strong advantage. Derivatives were sold overwhelmingly by the largest five banks, which sold 95 percent of over-the-counter derivative products and made profits of 30 percent or so selling these complex and opaque instruments globally to both unsuspecting investors and those whose use of them obscured what should have been more transparent dealings.

## Financialization and the World Economy

For those who wished to hide the extent of their financial difficulties, derivatives sold by major banks enabled them to move liabilities off balance sheets to obscure the extent of debt. Companies and wealthy individuals found they could use financial instruments to avoid taxation. European banks proved adept at using derivatives, buying triple A-rated structured products that could be counted against Basil II capital requirements, foiling the intent of regulators. These opaque and finally dangerous products were widely funded through repurchase agreements with US money market mutual funds. Such regulatory arbitrage came back to haunt many large European financial institutions, which needed government bailouts in the wake of the collapse of the value of these securitized obligations. European banks in both current account surplus and deficit countries created large amounts of asset-backed commercial paper and used off-balance-sheet vehicles funded with short-term debt to purchase long-term assets. Like the American banks engaging in these practices, they retained the credit risks associated with these assets. The first banks to collapse and be bailed out by their governments were not in the United States but in Germany. IKB Deutsche Industriebank and Sachsen Landesbank provided credit guarantees of more than three times their equity capital (Acharya and Schnabl, 2009). What economists were slow to grasp was that financial risk generated by international transfers of savings can accumulate even in a region that does not have an external trade imbalance. This was the case for European creditors holding US-issued financial products, which turned out to be toxic. It was not the countries that had higher trade with the United States (either in finance or in real product markets) that had the most intense crises but those that had followed its financialization products example (Rose and Spiegel, 2009).

The effect of financialization in Europe has been "slow and fragile accumulation" and a substantial decline in wage shares in national income (Stockhammer, 2008). This was so even in the homeland of the "coordinated market economy" (Hall and Gingerich, 2004), Germany, where share buybacks had been completely banned before 1998 due to the memory of the country's financial crisis of 1931. In 1991 the tax on stock-exchange dealings was removed. In 2002 capital gains taxation changed to favor investors and shareholders. Hedge funds were legalized in 2003. Overall, value orientation grew at the expense of physical investment in a process that looked very much like convergence to the Anglo-American model and away from the traditional German one (von Treeck, 2009). Deregulation of labor markets and partial privatization of pension funds in Germany are other indications of this trajectory. Weak domestic consumer and industrial demand for loans from the late 1990s led Germany's financial sector to look for opportunities abroad, which were found in, among other places, American-originated securitized loans, much to the investors' later regret.

In France the ratio of dividend payments to net operating surplus rose dramatically from the end of the 1980s to the end of the 1990s (Dallery, 2009, 501). Duménil and Lévy (2005, 38) find that while in the early 1980s the profit rate for financial corporations was well below that for nonfinancial corporations, by the late 1990s financial profit for the financial corporations greatly exceeded those for the nonfinancial corporations. Even in Japan, Monk (2009, 59) tells us that Japanese corporate managers are today primarily concerned with their stock prices as a measure of performance and pension fund provisions; defined benefit plans are undergoing changes similar to those found in the United States.

Epstein and Jayadev (2005, table 3.1) report a higher rate of labor exploitation and transfer to rentier income for most of the OECD countries. Similar patterns could be observed in middle-income countries with strong foreign bank entry and growing financialization. In Latin America financial liberalization was one of the outcomes of the response to the debt crisis of the early 1980s and led to a large increase in foreign ownership of banks and expanded consumer lending (Malinowitz, 2009). By the early 1990s Korea had responded to political pressure that came not only from foreign interests but also from its own large companies wishing to escape state control and borrow abroad for financial liberalization (Epstein, 2005, 14). The levels of borrowing grew and proved costly in the wake of the Asian financial crisis later in that decade.

Yilmaz Akyüz and Korkut Boratav (2005) show how Turkey's experience in the financial crisis from 2001 was very much like that of other emerging market economies that relied on capital inflows to finance a growing external deficit and to fund domestic investments only to watch capital abandon the economy on fears of exchange-rate deterioration, which became a self-fulfilling process. This crisis did not discourage reliance on foreign capital inflows, which, in Turkey as in many other emerging markets, led to growing foreign control of the local financial sector. Finance absorbed almost 60 percent of the incoming foreign direct investment in 2007 as foreign bank presence in the economy grew. In Mexico 80 percent of bank assets came into foreign ownership (Lapavitsas, 2009, 123). This was a global trend. Governments succumbing to the pressure for financial liberalization ended up financializing their domestic economies' growth with debt, often with significant control of the process in the hands of foreign-owned institutions.

The countries of Europe's peripheries, which had grown impressively before this crisis, owed their success to large foreign borrowing at low interest rates and on easy credit terms that fostered a boom in consumer spending and construction but not investment in assets capable of generating a surplus for repayment. Resulting difficulties were most visible in Eastern Europe and the group of countries disparagingly called the PIGS (Portugal, Ireland, Greece, and Spain), but also in other economies that were part of the eurozone and were worsened as regional austerity kicked in. Financial integration and a common currency without fiscal union were to prove unsustainable.

German voters expressed outrage at bailing out feckless Greeks and others: assistance from the German banks, which were the largest holders of much eurozone sovereign debt, had put the euro at stake. Ireland guaranteed the debt of its national banks; it was to address the huge, unpayable loans of property developers who were cozy with the bankers and government leaders. These banks had issued loans based on their access to foreign lenders. It was the citizenry that would pay for this political choice to bail out the banks for the foreseeable future.

National differences exist along with shared patterns. For example, Gregory Connor, Thomas Flavin, and Brian O'Kelly (2010) find almost all the factors that were believed to have caused the US financial crisis were missing in the Irish case and vice versa. Yet the crises looked very much alike. They credit "the knock-on effects of the U.S. liquidity-credit crisis, particularly its effect on the interbank borrowing market" but suggest that the credit environment was so precarious that the Irish crisis would likely have occurred even in the absence of this effect. National differences in institutions and the varying stories of blame and conclusions reached in different countries as to desirable policy reform have produced clashes among regulatory authorities and regulators as to what steps should be taken to make international financial markets safer from now on.

Structural inadequacies exposed members of the eurozone that were unable to devalue their way out of their perilous situations alarmed investors, and drove the cost of credit default swaps to insure against sovereign default going skyward. When borrowing costs for Greece rose on fears of sovereign default, so, too, did those for the Portuguese, Spanish, and Irish governments and the stock of banks with large exposures came under pressure. Because so much of the debt was unpayable despite the harshest austerity, workouts were inevitable. The taxpayer rescues and austerity measures imposed as private debt were socialized, and this left the bankers free to return to dangerous practices once again.

Sorting through who was liable for what, given the extensive globalization of finance, would not be easy, whether dealing with claims of creditors to Lehman Brothers with its thousands of foreign subsidiaries or with lenders to Greece whose banks had themselves made unwise loans to Bulgaria, Romania, and Serbia. Without agreed-upon workout procedures, the only people who could look forward to guaranteed employment growth were bankruptcy lawyers.

Mainstream theory's core of efficient markets and rational expectations has lost its standing as the main result of the global financial crisis. The inflow and outflow of foreign capital have not followed patterns that mainstream theory predicts but rather result in highly volatile exchange rates, violations of purchasing power parity, trade imbalances, and more internationally correlated business cycles generated by repeated financial crises (Blecker, 2005). Much conventional thinking about international finance, optimal currency areas and exchange rates, home country regulation, and efficient cross-border allocation of capital areas needs to be revised in the light of the widespread crises impacting the centers of global capitalism. The financialization view is helpful not only in understanding what happens with national economies but also in tracing the interrelations of finance in the world system. The growth of financial assets relative to global output accentuates the assets' role in destabilizing markets. The capacity of huge amounts of capital to flood in and out of markets can now destabilize major economies. Matters are relatively worse for smaller states.

The more financially integrated a country is and the more extensive its financialization, the greater its need for foreign reserves. Once reserves are taken into account the usual measures of potential difficulty—current account balances and short-term debt levels—are not statistically significant predictors of the coming depreciation of its currency (Obstfelt, Shambaugh, and Taylor, 2009). Findings that financial integration is essentially uncorrelated with investment rates in this context suggest the unproductive nature of advancing financialization. As Schularick (2010, 2 and 4) concludes, "Globalization during the past decade was diversification finance, not development finance in the form of net transfer of capital," leading him to write that "it could finally be time to ask how we can make financial globalization safe for the world instead of trying to make the world safe for financial globalization."

Such a reconsideration is overdue. From 1980 to 2008 the world's financial assets nearly quadrupled relative to the size of global GDP. In 2007 the total value of financial assets peaked at $194 trillion (Roxburgh et al., 2009, 8). The Global Financial Crisis interrupted this trajectory, raising the question of what would happen when a new normal is established. One would think that in the slower growing core of the capitalist world system private debt is likely to slow and public debt to increase substantially in relation to GDP. This produces worry about the growth of public debt and a demand is felt almost everywhere to cut government spending. But this has a growth-inhibiting impact if aggregate demand is not buoyed by other sources. Assets grow in emerging markets where economic growth is considerably more rapid than in the older centers of the world economy. There is divergence both within and between the regions of the traditional core and periphery of the world system. Most of the global borrowing (which rose by 70 percent between 2000 and 2009) was done by the United States, the United Kingdom, and the eurozone. Its increase was significantly more rapid than its rate of growth. Borrowing in these years also increased in the developing world but more in line with their better economic performance. As growth slowed and debt grew in emerging market economies there was less demand to offset slower growth in the traditional core of the world system. If more robust financialization spreads to these economies they may face similar bubble prospects.

## Financialization and Global Imbalances

Between January 1999 and July 2008 the world's official reserves rose from $1.6 billion to $7.5 billion, an amazing growth rate. These reserves were held heavily in the form of US government or government agency securities by underwriting the low interest rates in the United States; this increased borrowing and imports, adding to unemployment in the United States. On the other side emerging markets ran surpluses and built up reserves. China as of June 2010 held 30 percent of the world's total reserves (which came to half of its own GDP). Looking for ways to benefit, many investors turned to currency speculation, which has grown considerably. The average daily trading volume in 2010 reached $4 trillion a day, up 20 percent from the previous Bank for International survey in 2007. For many countries, rapid movement of speculative capital in and out of their economies represents a clear and present danger. Not long ago, the International Monetary Fund (IMF) would have urged total financial liberalization of capital markets and forbidding capital controls, but there has been a rethinking of this position given the potential destructiveness of such flows. There is greater sympathy with the view of the chair of the UK Financial Services Authority, Adair Turner, that "foreign exchange carry trades are as far as I can see, of zero value and potentially destabilizing" (Tett and Garnham, 2010) Central bankers are cautious in announcing exit strategies and interest-rate changes well in advance; this is not unrelated to fears that a sudden need to unwind positions can be disastrous for the macroeconomy. The estimated carry trade-related deals account for 15 to 20 percent of market activity in the global foreign exchange market, a market in which London alone turns over more than a trillion and a half dollars a day. Haruhiko Kurdoda, the president of the Asian Development Bank, estimates the size of the yen carry trade at its peak was around $1 trillion and Zhu Min, the deputy governor of the People's Bank of China, put the 2010 dollar carry trade at a trillion and a half dollars.

The most significant bilateral integration of America and China in terms of capital flows raises questions about the future of financialization and the world economy. It represents an extreme version of factors present more widely. China's pegging its exchange rate with the US dollar gives the Sino-American relation a similar caste to that between Germany and its euro neighbors. And as the Germans want the rest to copy their thrifty ways, the rest of the region wishes Germans would spend and import more, so it is with China and the United States. Both China and Germany are involved essentially in vendor finance, lending money to their customers so they can buy more of their exports. Each recycles its surplus. It is unlikely these debtors will quickly become more competitive even as they seek loans from wealthier European countries and the IMF. Such lending inevitably is political as conditionality is required. Without the option of devaluation it is not clear that repayment will be possible. Structural adjustment demands may simply be too much politically in debtor countries. Citizens in countries from whom new loans are asked, the Germans above others, resent such burdens. It is not so simple for the German voter to just insist the Greeks fend for themselves, because Germany's banks are Greece's largest creditor. In 2010 Hypo Real Estate Holdings, the major German financial player whose failure led it to be taken over by the German taxpayers, held more than $10 billion worth of Greek debt.

Ben Bernanke, the Federal Reserve chairman, had developed an analysis of the US balance-of-payments problem dating from the late 1990s, which saw America as the passive recipient of the world's surplus savings, or a savings glut as he characterized it (Bernanke, 2005). The Chinese have been singled out in this regard. However, from 1997 to 2004 China's surplus doubled but the US deficit increased by four and a half times. China's surplus was $29 billion in these years. The US deficit rose by $490 billion. While after that China's surplus rose at a rate comparable to the US deficit the initial imbalance was caused by the rapid rise of borrowing in the United States accompanying rampant financialization. The United States has been running a trade deficit since 1976; until 2000, the largest was with Japan. Since then China has been the major exporter although to a significant extent it finished its products by using Japanese and other East Asian parts. By 2006 the United States ran a $235 billion deficit with China (exports to China amounted to $52 billion while imports were $287 billion). These were goods that Wal-Mart, Mattel, and others once produced within the United States. There has been a mutually self-reinforcing interaction between the global value chain and financialization.

Even those emerging markets that resisted financial liberalization experienced a rapid growth of financial assets. The compound growth rate of financial assets in India was 19 percent and in China 24 percent between 1990 and 2008; "financial depth" is expected to increase significantly faster in emerging markets than the core countries for the foreseeable future (Roxburgh et al., 2009). The ratio of financial assets to GDP is significantly lower than the core countries and growth rates are significantly faster. Financiers based in New York and London have moved to position themselves to gain from such prospects.

Imbalances built up in the years preceding the Global Financial Crisis were caused on the deficit side by low savings rates, asset-price booms, and large financial investment speculation drawing in foreign capital and on the surplus side from countries with savings rates exceeding domestic investment. These are long-standing patterns, but the dramatic and rapid capital inflows from 2005 to 2008 reflected "financial excesses" (Blanchard and Milesi-Ferretti, 2009) hardly reducible to blame from a single cause. In the long list of factors a number of critics pointed not only to the use of high leverage and derivative transactions that obscured the debt levels of banks and national governments but short-term capital flows that had not long before been celebrated as contributing to the efficiency of financial markets. Speaking in Davos, Adair Turner denounced the extensive carry trade as "economically valueless." Turner noted that, while lucrative returns were available from short-term positions held using currencies borrowed at low interest and invested in other currencies in speculative punting, if he could "wave a wand" and greatly reduce the carry trade he was "pretty certain the world would be a better place" (Sorkin, 2010).

Justin Lin (2009, 76), the World Bank's chief economist, argues that the sorts of financial markets and institutions in the developed world are inappropriate for low-income countries and that if the goal is providing services to enterprises and households small local banks are best. Lin cites the examples of the successful development trajectories of Japan, South Korea, and China, which adhered to simple banking systems, did not integrate their finances with global markets, and did not even build stock markets until late in the development process. Many developing nations hold large foreign reserves, overwhelmingly in US dollar-denominated government securities as a buffer against foreign exchange crises and speculator attacks on their currencies. This is not a benign process because investment funds continue to flow into financial markets, requiring these governments to hold more low-interest foreign reserves while foreign speculators earn high short-term profits from currency appreciation as funds flood into their markets.

Core-based institutions give increased weight to the emerging market economies for opportunity because these economies are expected to account for three-quarters of growth in global output in coming years. Peripheral financialization grows as emerging economies attract hedge funds and private equity fund money even as locals who have grown wealthy are drawn to speculative investments. In 2009 the Shanghai, Shenzen, and Hong Kong stock exchanges attracted $60 billion from initial public offerings, more than twice the amount raised by IPOs in the United States. High-risk corporate bonds are not currently permitted in China but the pressure toward allowing more financial risk taking is growing. China is being urged by, among others, Guo Shuqing, the chairman of the state-controlled China Reconstruction Bank, to introduce junk bonds in order to provide companies with growth capital. Shanghai's financial center, Pudong, began trading stock index futures in 2010 and has become a popular venue for speculators. Despite government efforts to see that the exchange used for hedging by those who actually produce and sell commodities to final users 90 percent of trades are opened and closed the same day, suggesting that "Chinese investors love new financial products. Their passion, at times bordering on mania, explains why Shanghai stocks rocket in price on their trading debuts and why local equity funds can raise billions of renminbi on the day they are launched" (Cookson, 2010, 26). It is possible that China's economy, which was driving force-propelling global growth, might be the scene of the next great crisis. George Soros warned that "China is now trying to rein in the rate of growth and exercising very strong restraints on its banking system. But because of that constraint and because of the big demand for money, a shadow banking system has arisen that is growing out of control" (*Bloomberg Businessweek*, 2011, 16).

## Conclusion

Approaching an understanding of the Global Financial Crisis through a view of financialization allows a counternarrative to the dominant orthodoxy and better explains the sources, nature, and trajectory of global financial flows. Extensive financialization modeled on Anglo-American practices has spread widely. The Global Financial Crisis and the manner in which it has been addressed raises questions not only of the sustainability of financialization-led growth in the core economies and the extent to which emerging market economies will resist or embrace a financialization path. It would be presumptuous to speculate overly on the shape of financialization, but it is difficult to envision new regulation at national and global levels, which will make more than a dent in crisis-prone financialization of the world economy despite new regulatory initiatives such as Basel III and, in the United States, the Dodd-Frank Wall Street Reform and Consumer Protection Act (Tabb, 2012, chapter 6).

The financial crisis had been "solved" in a way that increased concentration. One can easily envision capacity to avoid social control in further allowing a tightening of the oligopolistic grip of the firms atop global finance so that the bailouts necessitated the last time will be inevitable the next time around, despite steps taken to specify mechanisms needed to wind down failed, systemically significant financial institutions. At the end of 2009 the 10 biggest banks accounted for 70 percent of global banking assets, up from 59 percent three years earlier. While regulatory reform would influence the nature of future growth of financialization, and tougher regulatory restrictions could destroy the value of banking franchises as funding costs rose and banks need more capital, it is likely that the performance of players in the industry will continue to diverge, increasing concentration further. Asian banks and those in emerging markets can be expected to grow more rapidly (Bowers, Hamoir, and Marrs, 2010), as will the number and riches of East Asians, oil and other commodity exporters, and sovereign wealth funds, further complicating the complexity of crises and the resolution mechanisms following major defaults. Regulators and legislators who do not take the cost of ever-expanding financialization and the logic of short-term financial speculation seriously enough in designing assertive policies to more substantially limit the freedom of the speculator herd may come to rue their decision.

The implications of the dramatic increase in financialization with its creation of extreme leveraged debt positions has been to increase system fragility and economic instability. The punishing austerity and forced internal devaluation (through falling wages, public spending, and widespread working class suffering) forced on the euro debtor countries and others cannot be sustained and will in any event hardly lead to the growth necessary for debt repayment. What is seen as a financial and fiscal crisis is best understood as an intensification of class struggle over who shall bear the cost of the crisis the banks and other financial speculators have caused with the acquiescence and often encouragement of politicians and regulators who have promoted a social structure of accumulation premised on corporate-led globalization and financialization that cannot be sustained. The current global depression signals the need for a new regulatory regime for the world system. There is no technical fix to what is a political struggle with enormous consequences.

## References


Acharya, Viral, and Philipp Schnabl. (2009). "Do Banks Spread Global Imbalances? The Case of Asset-Backed Commercial Paper during the Financial Crisis of 2007–09." International Monetary Fund (November): 1–59. http://www.imf.org/external/np/res/seminars/2009/arc/pdf/acharya.pdf.

Akyüz,Yilmaz, and Korkut Boratav. (2005). "The Making of the Turkish Financial Crisis." In Gerald A. Epstein, ed., *Financialization and the World Economy*, 260–288. Northampton, MA: Edward Elgar.

Arrighi, Giovanni and Beverly J. Silver (1999). *Chaos and Governance in the Modern World System*. Minneapolis: University of Minnesota Press.

Ben S. Bernanke, "The Global Saving Glut and the U.S. Current Account Deficit," Remarks At the Sandridge Lecture, Virginia Association of Economists, Richmond, Virginia, March 10, 2005. http://www.federalreserve.gov/boarddocs/speeches/2005/200503102.

Blanchard, Olivier, and Gian Maria Milesi-Ferretti. (2009). "Global Imbalances: In Midstream?" Research Department, International Monetary Fund (December): 1–31. www.imf.org/external/pubs/ft/spn/2009/spn0929.pdf.

Blecker, Robert A. (2005). "Financial Globalization, Exchange Rates and International Trade." In Gerald A. Epstein, ed., *Financialization and the World Economy*. Northampton, MA: Edward Elgar. 183–209.

*Bloomberg Businessweek*. (2011). "Quoted." April 25-May1.

Bowers, Tab, Olivier Hamoir, and Anna Marrs. (2010). "What's Next for Global Banking," *McKinsey Quarterly*, March.

Connor, Gregory, Thomas Flavin, and Brian O'Kelly. (2010). "The U.S. and Irish Credit Crises: Their Distinctive Differences and Common Features." March. http://www.irisheconomy.ie/Notes/IrishEconomyNote10.pdf.

Cookson, Robert. (2010). "Wealthy Traders Fuel Mania for Chinese Financial Futures." *Financial Times*, April 29.

Dallery, Thomas. (2009). "Post-Keynesian Theories of the Firm under Financialization." *Review of Radical Political Economics* 41(4): 492–515.

Duménil, Gerard, and Dominique Lévy. 2005. "Costs and Benefits of Neoliberalism: A Class Analysis." In Gerald A. Epstein, ed., *Financialization and the World Economy*. Northampton, MA: Edward Elgar. 17–45.

Epstein, Gerald. 2005. "Introduction: Financialization and the World Economy." In Gerald A. Epstein, ed., *Financialization and the World Economy*, 3–16. Northampton, MA: Edward Elgar.

Epstein, Gerald A., and Arjun Jayadev. (2005). "The Rise of Rentier Income in OECD Countries: Financialization, Central Bank Policy and Labor Solidarity." In Gerald A. Epstein, ed., *Financialization and the World Economy*, 46–74. Northampton, MA: Edward Elgar.

Hall, Peter A., and Daniel W. Gingerich. (2004). "Varieties of Capitalism and Institutional Complementarities in the Macroeconomy: An Empirical Analysis." MPIfG Discussion Paper 04/5. http://www-management.wharton.upenn.edu/guillen/Hall/Hall.MPIfGSpaper.pdf.

Kaufman, Frederick. (2011). "How Goldman Sachs Created the Food Crisis." Council on Foreign Relations, http://www.cfr.org/united-states/fp-goldman-sachs-created-food-crisis/p24904.

Kregel, Jan. (2008). "Using Minsky's Cushions of Safety to Analyze the Crisis in the US Subprime Mortgage Market." *Levy Institute, Public Policy Brief, No. 93*. http://www.levyinstitute.org/pubs/ppb_93.pdf.

Lapavitsas, Costas. (2009). "Financialisation Embroils Developing Countries." Papeles de Europa 19. http://revistas.ucm.es/cee/00000000/articulos/PADE0909220108A.PDF.

Lazonick, William. (2010). "Innovative Business Models and Varieties of Capitalism: Financialization of the U.S. Corporation," *Business History Review* 84 (Winter): 675–702.

Lazonick, William, and Mary O'Sullivan. (2000). "Maximizing Shareholder Value: A New Ideology for Corporate Governance." *Economy and Society* 29(1): 13–35.

Lin, Justin. (2009). "Walk, Don't Run." *The Economist*, July 11.

Malinowitz, Stanley. (2009). "Financialization and the Latin American Economies." http://lasa.international.pitt.edu/members/congress-papers/lasa2009/files/MalinowitzStanley.pdf.

McDonough, Terrence, Michael Reich, and David M. Kotz, eds. (2010). *Understanding Contemporary Capitalism and Its Crises: Social Structure of Accumulation Theory for the Twenty-First Century*. New York: Cambridge University Press.

Milberg, William. (2008). "Shifting Sources and Uses of Profits: Sustaining US Financialization with Global Value Chains." *Economy and Society* 37(3): 420–451.

Monk, Ashby H. B. (2009). "The Financial Thesis: Reconceptualizing Globalisation's Effect on Firms and Institutions." *Competition and Change* 13(1): 51–74.

Obstfelt, Maurice, Jay C. Shambaugh, and Alan M. Taylor. (2009). "Financial Instability, Reserves, and Central Bank Swap Lines in the Panic of 2008." NBER Working Paper 14826.

Rose, Andrew K., and Mark M. Spiegel. (2009). "Cross-Country Causes and Consequences of the 2008 Crisis: Early Warning." FRBSF Working Paper 2009–17. http://www.frbsf.org/publications/economics/papers/2009/wp09-17bk.pdf.

Roxburgh, Charles, Susan Lund, Charles Atkins, Stanislas Belot, Wayne W. Hu, and Moira S. Pierce. (2009). *Global Capital Markets: Entering a New Era*. McKinsey Global Institute. http://www.mckinsey.com/mgi/reports/pdfs/gcm_sixth_annual_report/gcm_sixth_annual_report_full_report.pdf.

Schularick, Moritz. (2010). "The End of Financial Globalization 3.0." *The Economists' Voice* 7(1): 1–5.

Sorkin, Andrew Ross. (2010). "Regulators Tackle 'Carry Trades.'" *New York Times*, February 11.

Stockhammer, Engelbert. (2008). "Some Stylized Facts on the Finance-Dominated Accumulation Regime." *Competition and Change* 12(2): 184–202.

Tabb, William K. (2012). *The Restructuring of Capitalism in Our Time*. New York: Columbia University Press.

Tett, Gillian, and Peter Garnham. (2010). "Carried Away." *Financial Times*, April 30.

van Treeck, Till. (2009). "The Macroeconomics of 'Financialisation' and the Deeper Origins of the World Economic Crisis." Working Paper 9/2009, Hans Böckler Foundation. http://www.boeckler.de/pdf/p_imk_wp_9_2009.pdf.

Wray, L. Randall. (2008). "The Commodities Market Bubble: Money Manager Capitalism and the Financialization of Commodities." http://www.levyinstitute.org/pubs/ppb_96.pdf.

PART V

# POLICY AND INSTITUTIONAL CHANGE TO LIMIT FINANCIAL CRISES

CHAPTER 27

# INTERNATIONAL AND REGIONAL COOPERATION FOR DEALING WITH FINANCIAL CRISES

JOSÉ ANTONIO OCAMPO

FINANCIAL crises have important international dimensions, indeed dramatic ones. This is associated with contagion, an essential feature of financial-sector dynamics. These international dimensions are particularly important when crises originate in the major industrial centers and spread to the rest of the world, with the Great Depression of the 1930s and the 2007–2008 Global Financial Crisis as remarkable examples. Others have strongly affected the "periphery" of the system, such as the debt crisis of Latin America and large parts of the developing world in the 1980s and the crisis that erupted in East Asia in 1997 and then spread to other emerging and developing economies. During global crises, there might also be special regional dimensions, as in the cases of Central and Eastern Europe during the initial years of the recent global crisis and peripheral Western Europe in 2010–2012.

International cooperation should therefore be built up to manage these international dimensions. However, there is a significant dearth of international cooperation in this area. In some cases, mechanisms have a partial scope or involve only a limited number of members. An important case in the area of crisis prevention is the Basel Committee on Banking Supervision, created in 1974 to harmonize standards of banking regulation among major industrial countries, which are then adopted by other countries. An additional case is the Financial Stability Forum, created after the Asian crisis by the Group of 20 (G20) to prevent a major financial crisis from occurring. Although it miserably failed in that task, this forum was upgraded into the Financial Stability Board, which was given the task of coordinating the efforts to reregulate the financial sector among the G20 countries. As we will see, a major gap in this effort has been the lack of attention to regulating cross-border financial flows.

In the area of crisis management, a broader set of institutions has been put in place in the past, particularly emergency balance-of-payments financing, some ad hoc debt-relief initiatives, and a few regional institutions. The IMF has also been given the responsibility of coordinating global monetary cooperation, but it has not fully exercised this function and has not contributed to correcting global payments imbalances, a major source of uncertainty to the global financial system and of exchange-rate volatility. Furthermore, the existing international monetary system has been criticized by actually contributing to building up such imbalances.

This chapter will analyze several dimensions of this cooperation, dealing in variable ways with crisis prevention and management. The first two sections analyze cooperation aimed at correcting global payments imbalances and associated debates on the global monetary system. The issues discussed in these sections include the "self-insurance" mechanism put in place by emerging and developing countries to deal with global financial crises: the large accumulation of foreign exchange reserves. The third section looks at the regulation of cross-border capital flows. The fourth considers IMF financing, the poor global counterpart of the function of central banks as lenders of last resort, and a missing institution: an international debt workout mechanism. The last is regional cooperation.

## Global Payments Imbalances and Macroeconomic Policy Cooperation

Global monetary cooperation was incorporated at Bretton Woods in the Articles of Agreement of the IMF, which states that the first objective of this institution is to provide "the machinery for consultation and collaboration on international monetary problems." This objective has clearly not been met in the past. In fact, one of the essential features of the current international arrangements has been the tendency of major economies to sidetrack the Fund in its effort at macroeconomic policy coordination and to use alternative informal mechanisms among major countries ("Gs" of different character) for that task.

Macroeconomic policy cooperation has to deal with major spillovers that national decisions have on other countries. Several agreements have dealt in the past with exchange rates (e.g., the 1971 Smithsonian Agreement and the Plaza and Louvre Accords of the mid-1980s) and coordinated monetary expansion during financial crises (notably after the US subprime crisis of August 2007 and the collapse of Lehman Brothers in mid-September 2008) or critical conjunctures (after the September 11, 2001, terrorist attacks). The rarest has been fiscal cooperation. The Maastricht agreement among European countries is perhaps the best example, but it is also one that has been characterized by frequent deviation from commitments. Since the international monetary system is based on the use of multiple currencies, lack of fiscal cooperation and the fact that national authorities (regional in the case of the European Union) may have different perspectives on monetary policies, some level of exchange-rate flexibility is essential to adjust for different national (regional) decisions.

Because of this, and the fact that since its creation it was agreed that the IMF should focus its attention on exchange rates, this is perhaps the area in which the international community should look for better forms of cooperation. This is important not only for exchange rates as such, which can generate major externalities, but, more importantly and as already pointed out, because exchange-rate movements reflect divergence in other macroeconomic policies. The 2010 debate on the "currency wars" was, for example, associated with the effects that monetary expansion in the United States was having on capital flows toward emerging economies.

The way these adjustments operate is determined in large part by the design of the international monetary system. In this regard, it is useful to recall that the IMF was created at Bretton Woods in 1944 on the basis of the dual gold-dollar system; other countries fixed their exchange rates vis-à-vis the dollar but could modify them if they faced imbalances.[1]

This arrangement collapsed in the early 1970s and was replaced by a system based on fiduciary dollars—that is, on the use of the *national* currency of the major world power as a global currency. It is secondarily a system of competing fiduciary reserve currencies, but the dollar continues to be dominant (see below). Other countries are free to choose any exchange-rate regime. So the exchange-rate system became in fact a "nonsystem," which is only subject to the constraint that, as Article IV of the IMF Agreement reads, countries should "avoid manipulating exchange rates or the international monetary system in order to prevent effective balance of payments adjustment or to gain an unfair competitive advantage over other members." This is also stated in the June 2007 decision on IMF surveillance. However, both the Fund and the G20 have failed to determine so far what "manipulation" means.

The current exchange-rate (non)system has failed to meet two additional objectives set in the first IMF Article of Agreement: to "lessen the degree of disequilibrium in the international balance of payments" and "to promote exchange stability." The issue of global payments imbalances is illustrated in figure 27.1. These imbalances grew dramatically during the world economic boom of 2003-2007. The major trend was a rising deficit in the United States and, at the end of the boom, in Europe, counterbalanced by surpluses in China, Japan, and several developing countries, mainly East Asian and commodity exporters. Within these groups, there were also major surpluses and deficits, particularly in Europe (a major surplus in Germany but also large deficits in some peripheral countries) and in the developing countries (many countries ran deficits). The dramatic recession that followed after September 2008 led a sharp reduction in the imbalances, to about half of previous levels, with the United States and Europe cutting their deficits and with developing countries, excluding China, reducing their surpluses.[2]

The incapacity of the system to provide exchange-rate stability is illustrated in figure 27.2 in terms of the major bilateral exchange rate: that between the euro and the US dollar. This rate experienced a significant level of "excess volatility" during the recent Global Financial Crisis, as it did in the early 1990s, during the European monetary crisis that followed the adoption of full capital account convertibility by European countries in 1990, and in the early 2000s, during the burst of the technology bubble in the United States.

The system could therefore be improved by introducing, through international cooperation, elements that provide some level of stability to exchange rates. One way would be to evolve into a system of reference rates among major currencies, as has been suggested by Williamson (2007), among others. This implies that major countries would follow some form of managed floating—the

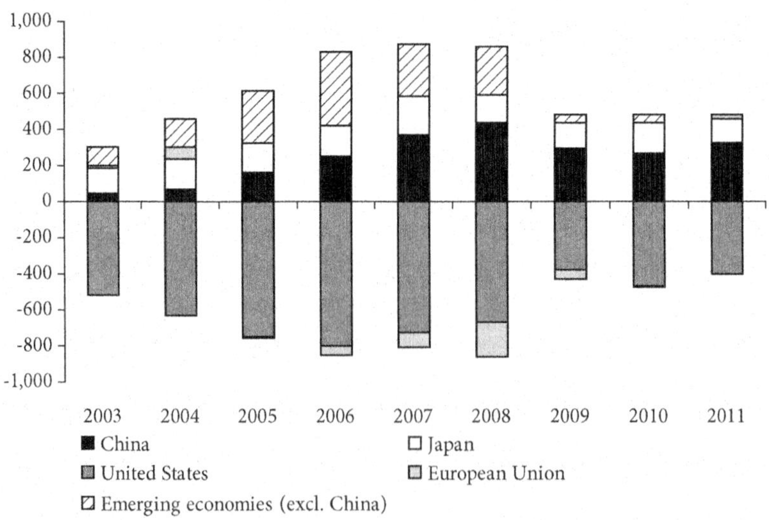


**Figure 27.1** Current account deficit (billion dollars).
*Source*: International Monetary Fund, *World Economic Outlook Database*, 2010–2012.

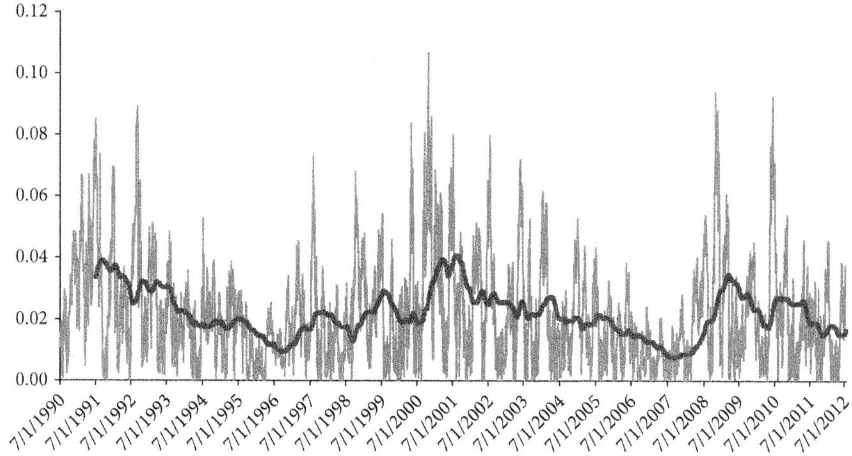


**Figure 27.2** Volatility of the euro/US dollar exchange rate: Deviation with respect to the 12 months MA in absolute value.
*Source*: Bloomberg.

system that most emerging economies have actually chosen over the past decade. Multilaterally agreed parities or bands would be the cornerstone of such a system, and this would help give some level of stability to the way markets operate, which in the past have been characterized by extended periods of deviation from equilibrium. Guidelines would indicate that interventions in foreign exchange markets and other macroeconomic policies would have to support the movement of exchange rates toward the agreed parities or bands (i.e., reinforce depreciation if the currency is perceived to be overvalued and appreciation if it is undervalued). Such rules would also adopt an implicit definition of what "manipulating" the exchange rate means.

In this framework, the process leading to deciding on exchange-rate parities would have to take into account other determinants of the exchange rate, and in this sense the parities would summarize a significant amount of macroeconomic information. But a complementary—or perhaps alternative—approach would be to look directly at payments imbalances, and particularly at *current* account imbalances, which are equivalent in macroeconomic terms to looking at saving-investment imbalances and to those between aggregate spending and production. Indeed, as Dervis (2010) has pointed out, the definition of current account target zones that the United States proposed in 2010 was a recognition that the focus should be on the effects of overall economic policies on national savings and investment, not just on exchange rates.[3]

Even better, of course, would be to look at payments imbalances together with measures of the global output (including employment) gaps and associated inflationary pressures. Furthermore, they could include indicators of public- and private-sector debt ratios, to analyze both debt sustainability issues as well as the policy space for expansionary macroeconomic policies. This seems the approach chosen by the G20's Mutual Assessment Process (MAP) (G20, 2011). But a simpler set of indicators may be better. This is why the reference exchange-rate proposal is a good idea, or alternatively a focus on current account deficits and global output gaps.

There are also major institutional challenges to building these forms of cooperation. History shows that there is a strong demand for cooperation only during crises, but it is equally essential to have cooperation during periods of prosperity, when crises are incubated. An additional issue is representation in the decision-making process. For both reasons, it would be better to fulfill the expectation that the IMF should be "the machinery for consultation and collaboration on international monetary problems." A basic advantage of the G7 is, nonetheless, that small groups help build up confidence and thus a broader exchange among a small set of relevant policy actors. But this does not contradict the objective of representativeness if the regular and intensive dialogue among the countries that are systemically important is embedded into a global institution. This is why the G20's MAP should be done within the IMF framework, possibly involving a smaller number of systemically important countries. One important innovation introduced by the IMF in 2010 that partly captures this proposal is the spillover reports, though they strictly belong to its surveillance activities.

## Global Imbalances and the Global Reserve System

Global payments imbalances are closely linked with the inequities and instabilities of the global reserve system (Ocampo, 2010a, 2010b). One of the major sources of instabilities is derived from the use of the US national currency as a global currency, a point underscored by the Belgian economy Robert Triffin (1961, 1968) in the debates of the 1960s. Under the fiduciary dollar standard, these instabilities are associated with strong cycles in the real dollar exchange rate and US current account deficits (see figure 27.3). During the expansionary phase, the United States swamps the world with liquidity, leading to rising current account deficits and a depreciation of the dollar—indicating, in fact, that the system does not impose macroeconomic discipline on the reserve-issuing country. In turn, almost invariably, corrections of US current account deficits take place amid and indeed contribute to global recessions or strong slowdowns. During both phases of these cycles, the world becomes hostage to the macroeconomic conditions and policies of the reserve currency country, with the latter generally adopted without any consideration as to their international impact.

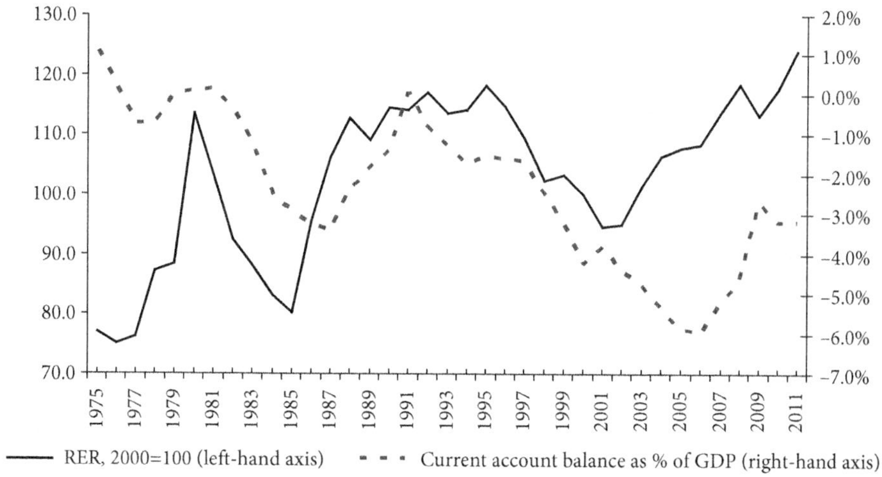


**Figure 27.3** US current account balance and real exchange rate.
*Source*: IMF, *International Financial Statistics*. The real exchange rate is depicted here to show an increase when there is a real depreciation (the opposite convention to that used by the IMF). It is calculated as the inverse of the real exchange rate estimated by the Fund.

In turn, the major inequities of the system are derived from the need that developing countries face to accumulate foreign exchange reserves to manage the strong procyclical swings of capital flows, but such reserves are nothing else than transfers of resources to the reserve-issuing countries. This inequity became very visible since the 1990s and, particularly, in the aftermath of the sequence of emerging country crises that started in East Asia in the late twentieth century. As figure 27.4 indicates, until the 1980s the foreign exchange reserves of low- and middle-income countries were not unlike those of high-income countries: around 3 percent of GDP. Since then, they started to diverge, and sharply so since the Asian crisis. Prior to the current financial crisis (toward the end of 2007), middle-income countries, excluding China, held on average reserves equivalent to slightly over 20 percent of GDP, and low-income countries over 13 percent. With the exception of Japan, high-income countries continued to hold reserves equivalent to around 3 percent of GDP.

This phenomenon, which came to be called "self-insurance," involves not only accumulating reserves to face an eventual "sudden stop" in external financing but also absorbing through reserve accumulation a large part of what countries consider excess capital inflows. The basic rationale for this policy is avoiding appreciation pressures and growing current account deficits during periods of booming capital inflows which, as past experience indicates, are strong predictors of crises. There is increasing evidence that strong reserve positions and avoidance of overvaluation and current account deficits significantly contributed to relatively good performance of developing countries during the recent Global Financial Crisis.[4] So, in a broad sense, self-insurance is nothing

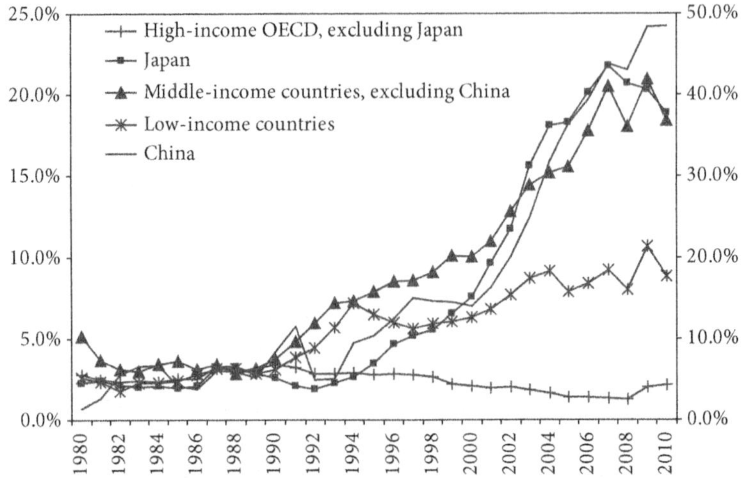


**Figure 27.4** International reserves by level of development (% of GDP; all country groupings according to left-hand axis, China according to right-hand axis).
*Source*: World Bank, *World Development Indicators*, based on information from IMF.

else than a prudential or countercyclical macroeconomic policy aimed at moderating the domestic effects of procyclical capital flows. Despite this positive effect, it must be emphasized that this policy generates a "fallacy of composition": if many countries adopt a policy aimed at generating surplus or small current account deficits, they contribute to the generation of global imbalances and, through them, to the potential instability of the system.

Although the global reserve system may naturally evolve into one more clearly based on competing reserve currencies (Eichengreen, 2011), such an alternative would not solve the inequities and instability of current arrangements. It could actually add another problem: the instability of exchange rates among major reserve currencies—a problem that, as already pointed out, is already partly present in the current arrangement. In any case, it is unclear whether the system would evolve in that direction, due both to the "network externalities" associated with the use of a common currency, and the limitations of alternative currencies. Particularly, the euro, backed by a heterogeneous group of countries and lacking a unified eurobond market, has proved to be an imperfect substitute of the dollar, and the renminbi is still an inconvertible currency that operates in a country with a largely closed capital account.

The inequities and instability of current arrangements are why the world monetary system should be based on a truly global reserve currency: a fiduciary currency backed by the central banks of the world. This is what was hoped for when special drawing rights (SDRs) were created in the 1960s. An important step during the Global Financial Crisis was, therefore, the G20 decision, adopted in London in April 2009, to revive this dormant mechanism of international cooperation, by issuing SDRs equivalent to $250 billion, along with the US decision to complete the congressional approval process for the smaller 1997 allocation.

These areas constitute, however, only the beginning of a debate concerning reform of the global monetary system. The major proposals in this area were made by the central bank governor of China in March 2009 (Zhou, 2009) and by the Commission of Experts convened in 2009 by the president of the UN General Assembly on Reforms of the International Monetary and Financial System, chaired by Joseph Stiglitz (United Nations, 2009).[5] This process must therefore be completed by transforming the SDRs into the major global reserve asset, as the IMF Articles of Agreement already state. Among other advantages, this system would provide a mechanism for the IMF to play a more active role during crises, by issuing SDRs in a countercyclical way and using them to finance its countercyclical lending. This would be the global equivalent of how central banks operate, and this was evident on a massive scale during the recent crisis. I will return to this issue below.

## Capital Account Regulations

"Excessive" exchange-rate volatility associated with capital flows points toward an additional area for international cooperation: capital account regulations. It is useful in this regard to recall that a major agreement during the recent crisis was that deregulated financial activities can be a source of major macroeconomic disruptions. The G20 thus led a major effort to reregulate finance, mainly at the national level. However, *cross-border* finance was left almost entirely out of the agenda, as it did not require any regulation—or indeed as it was not part of finance. A particular twist of terminology is also involved in discussing this issue: domestic financial regulations are called by that name, but if they involve cross-border flows, they are called "controls." They should be referred to by their appropriate name: capital account *regulations*.[6]

The essential problem here is that capital flows, as finance in general, are highly procyclical. Agents that are perceived to be risky borrowers are subject to the strongest swings in the availability and costs of financing. These riskier agents include emerging economies and, more generally, developing country borrowers in global markets. There is overwhelming evidence that capital flows to developing countries are strongly procyclical and have become one of the major determinants (and perhaps *the* major determinant) of business cycles in emerging economies (Ocampo, Spiegel, and Stiglitz 2008; Prasad et al., 2003). Furthermore, the cyclical supply of finance is increasingly driven by portfolio decisions in industrial countries, which may be entirely delinked from demand for capital by emerging and developing countries. These countries face further problems: their domestic financial markets are significantly more "incomplete" and are plagued by variable mixes of currency and maturity mismatches, and their capital markets are shallower and small relative to the magnitude of the speculative pressures they face.

The cyclical behavior that characterizes capital flows goes beyond the volatility of short-term flows. Even more important are the *medium-term* cycles in the availability and costs of financing. Since the mid-1970s, we have experienced three full medium-term cycles—from the mid-1970s to the end of the 1980s, from 1990 to 2002, from 2003 to 2009—and we are in the beginning of a fourth one. The major problem with these cyclical swings is their strong effect on major macroeconomic variables in recipient countries: that is, on exchange rates, interest rates, domestic credit, and asset prices. As a result of this, procyclical capital flows exacerbate major macroeconomic policy trade-offs, significantly limiting the space to undertake countercyclical macroeconomic policies. For example, during a boom, countries may float the exchange rate to maintain some degree of monetary policy autonomy, but this merely displaces the effects of procyclical capital flows to the exchange rate. If this happens, the resulting deterioration in the current account allows these countries to "absorb" the increasing flows but experience indicates that it also increases the probability and costs of crises.

Authorities may try to stabilize the exchange rate by accumulating the excess supply of capital as foreign exchange reserves while sterilizing their domestic monetary effects. But such sterilized accumulation generates quasi-fiscal losses that are particularly costly in countries with high domestic interest rates. During boom periods, capital account regulations can therefore be justified as a way to help authorities manage booms while avoiding exchange-rate appreciation, the risks associated with rising current account deficits or costly foreign exchange reserve accumulation. During crises, they may also be used as a way to avoid or mitigate capital flight, which has the opposite macroeconomic effects.

More generally, these regulations can play a dual role: they are a complementary macroeconomic policy tool and help reduce the risks associated with liability structures tilted toward volatile capital flows. As a macroeconomic policy tool, they provide some room for countercyclical monetary policies. During booms, they increase the policy space to undertake contractionary monetary policy while reducing exchange-rate appreciation pressures. In turn, during crises, they can create some room for expansionary monetary policies. Viewed as a liability policy, capital account regulations recognize the fact that procyclical behavior and, particularly, reversibility varies significantly according to the nature of capital flows: foreign direct investment is more stable than portfolio and debt flows and, among the latter, short-term debt flows are particularly volatile.[7]

Capital market regulations obviously segment domestic from international markets, but this recognizes the fact that markets are already segmented. Indeed, the basic flaw of capital account liberalization is that it does not recognize the implications of this basic fact. As with prudential regulations, capital account regulations can be either quantitative (or administrative) or price-based, but there are more complex typologies (see, for example, IMF, 2011). The former include, among others, prohibitions or ceilings on certain capital flows, derivative operation or net exposure in foreign currencies; minimum stay periods; and restrictions on foreign investors taking positions in domestic securities or rules on what types of agents can undertake some capital transactions (residents versus nonresidents, and corporate versus noncorporate). In turn, price-based regulations include unremunerated reserve requirements on capital inflows, taxes on inflows or outflows, and larger reserve requirements for external liabilities or net exposure in foreign currencies. Furthermore, they can be partly substituted by domestic prudential regulations when they involve domestic financial intermediation, though not when they entail access to external capital markets by nonfinancial domestic agents.[8] They thus belong to the family of what have come to be called "macroprudential regulations," including particularly countercyclical prudential regulations (for an early analysis of this link, see Ocampo, 2003).

Overall, the evidence indicates that capital account regulations help generate a mix of increased monetary autonomy, reduced exchange-rate pressures, and smaller flows, with some skepticism by several authors on the latter effect.[9] Some of these effects may be temporary, indicating that further reinforcement may be required to maintain their effectiveness. They also help improve debt profiles and thus act as an effective liability policy that reduces external vulnerability. There is also evidence that countries using regulations on capital inflows fared better during the Global Financial Crisis (Ostry et al., 2010) and that the new regulations put in place by some countries since 2010 have been at least partly effective (Gallagher, 2011; IMF, 2011).

Debates on this issue since 2010 have emphasized some *global* dimensions of these regulations. The first and essential problem is the asymmetry generated between the strength of several emerging economies and the continuing weakness of most industrial countries. This situation, which is likely to continue, implies that the latter have to maintain expansionary policies, but the former are gradually moving toward more restrictive policies, though they are partially constrained for doing so by massive capital inflows. In short, the "multispeed" character of the recovery creates a need for a mirror asymmetry in monetary policies, which would be very difficult to manage without some restrictions on capital flows. This is particularly troublesome when the major reserve currency-issuing country, the United States, maintains an expansionary monetary policy. An additional problem is that unilateral actions by countries also have negative externalities on other countries: that is, regulations by some may generate even stronger flows toward those not doing so. This is also true, of course, of interventions in foreign exchange markets.

Therefore, capital account regulations should be an essential part of international cooperation. The IMF (2011) has recognized that they can play a positive role, as part of the broader family of macroprudential regulations, and it has taken the step to openly discuss this issue and suggest a possible "policy framework" for discussion. Furthermore, this has been the first step taken to include cross-border capital flows within ongoing efforts at strengthening prudential regulation worldwide.

Such a policy framework should start, however, by designing a mechanism to cooperate with countries that use these policies. In fact this may require eliminating provisions in several free trade agreements (particularly those signed by the United States) that restrict the use of such regulations. And, in any case, any guidelines or identification of "best practices" in this area should recognize the fact that there is no obligation to capital account convertibility under the IMF Articles of Agreement; therefore, countries should continue to have full freedom to manage their capital accounts. This is implicitly recognized by indicating that they do not imply any new obligations under IMF surveillance.

## Emergency Balance-of-Payments Financing and Debt Workouts

Since World War II, the international community has been able to count on emergency financing from the IMF during balance-of-payment crises. As figure 27.5 indicates, this mechanism provided increasing countercyclical financing, especially during the debt crisis of the 1980s and the succession of crises that began in 1994 –Mexico, East Asia, Russia, South America, and Turkey. Following this pattern, the IMF increased its loans significantly during the Global Financial Crisis.

After the Mexican crisis, the need to create new credit lines to mitigate the effects of capital account volatility and, more generally, to expand the magnitude of programs for individual countries began to be recognized. So, in the face of the Asian crisis, the IMF created two new credit facilities: the supplemental reserve facility, which served as a framework for the large loans made during the crises of the late twentieth and early twenty-first centuries, and the contingent credit line, which had a more preventive aim. The latter was never tapped and was suspended in 2003. For the poorest countries, the structural adjustment lines created in the mid-1980s were transformed in 1999 into the poverty reduction and growth facility (PRGF). In January 2006, a credit line was added for those countries aimed at facilitating recovery after negative shocks—from trade and natural disasters—and conflicts with neighboring countries.

The Global Financial Crisis led to further reforms in all of these areas. In October 2008, the IMF created a new precautionary facility, the short-term liquidity facility (SLF), which could be disbursed without the traditional IMF ex-post conditionality. Yet, as the global crisis deepened, no country called on it. Interestingly, the same day that the IMF announced the creation of the SLF, the US Federal Reserve finalized reciprocal currency arrangements with Mexico, the Republic of Korea, Singapore, and Brazil, which were extensively used. This implied that, despite their shorter maturities, the Fed swap lines (and others that arouse later on around the world) were clearly superior to IMF loans in terms of scale, flexibility, and lack of conditionality.

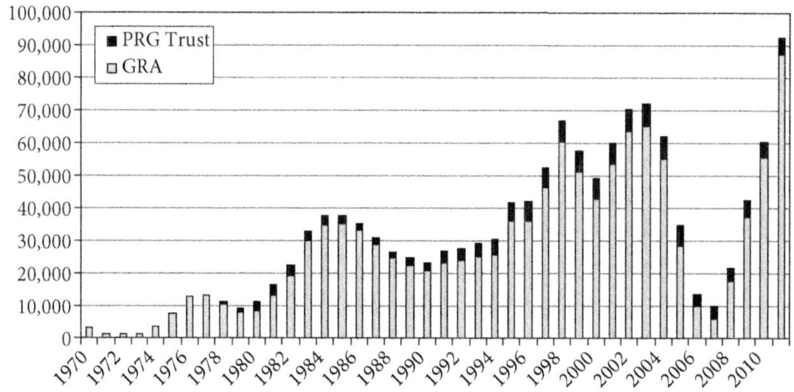


**Figure 27.5** Use of IMF resources (million SDRs)

*Notes*: PRG Trust: Facilities for low-income countries; GRA: General Resource Account.

*Source*: International Monetary Fund (http://www.imf.org/external/np/fin/tad/extcred1.aspx).

As a result of strong pressure to adopt stronger measures, in March 2009 the IMF approved an overhaul of its lending framework. First of all, it created a new preventive facility, the flexible credit line (FCL), for countries with solid fundamentals; the scale of the resources and the period for which it can be used were improved in August 2010. Second, the March 2009 package doubled the other credit lines and allowed a wider use of stand-by agreements for preventive purposes (termed "high-access precautionary arrangements"). In August 2010, a new precautionary credit line (PCL) was created for countries that the IMF deems to have good policies but that do not meet the criteria of the FCL. The other significant reform introduced in March 2009 was to eliminate the relationship between IMF disbursements and structural conditionality. These reforms were accompanied by the elimination of several existing credit lines. This process was accompanied in December 2009 by a major reform of facilities for low-income countries, which involved the redesign of concessional loan lines as a menu of options, which takes into account the debt vulnerability of countries and their macroeconomic and public finance management capacity.

Aside from continuing to improve this menu, the major pending issue relates to how IMF lending is financed. The typical mechanisms used in the past are quotas and "arrangements to borrow"—a network of loans from central banks or governments to the Fund. The disadvantages of the first are that quota adjustments have tended to lag in relation to the size of the world economy, and the Fund is forced to manage a multiplicity of currencies, most of which cannot be used to finance its programs. This is why arrangements to borrow are a necessary complement to quotas under the current system. Their basic disadvantage is that, despite the expansion of the number of countries that contribute to these arrangements, they are not a truly multilateral mechanism.

This is why it makes sense to have a fully SDR-funded IMF, which would blend the creation of international money with its lending functions, in a similar way to how central banks' money creation and financing operate at the national level. Aside from the basic advantage of making IMF lending self-financed, it would actually make SDRs a more useful international monetary instrument, by allowing unutilized SDRs kept as international reserves by countries to be used to lend to countries that need them for liquidity purposes. This would thus match the countercyclical *allocations* of SDRs (if they are essentially issued during crises) with countercyclical *financing.*

There are two alternative ways to design fully SDR-funded IMF lending. The first was suggested by Jacques Polak three decades ago: IMF lending during crises would create new SDRs (similar to the way lending by central banks creates domestic money), but such SDRs would be automatically destroyed once such loans are paid (Polak, 1979). The other mechanism would be to treat the SDRs not used by countries as deposits in (or lending to) the IMF that could then be used by the institution to lend to countries in need (Ocampo, 2010a, 2010b). These proposals would imply a change in the meaning of the "quotas" of member states, which would not involve actual transfers of resources to the IMF but would in any case be essential to determine borrowing limits and SDR allocations (Polak, 2005, part II).

For any of these solutions to work, it is, of course, essential that IMF credit lines should continue to improve in terms of their size, timeliness, and conditionality. Recent reforms seem to have been unable to overcome the stigma associated with borrowing from this institution and thus have not corrected the demand for self-insurance. This is why a more ambitious reform is required, perhaps by adopting at least partially one part of Keynes's original plan for a postwar arrangement: the creation of an overdraft (drawing) facility that can be used *unconditionally* by *all* IMF members up to a certain limit and for a preestablished time period. Such a facility would be more similar to swap arrangements and would contribute to making the system more symmetric between surplus and deficit countries, thus partially correcting a major problem of all international monetary systems (Keynes, 1942–1943).

In any case, the system cannot rely exclusively on emergency financing, as the availability of such financing could raise moral hazard issues. Emergency financing serves to correct the problems of access to liquidity during crises from turning into insolvency but are not adequate to manage problems of overindebtedness. This is why a regular institutional framework to manage debt overhangs at the international level must be created: a debt court for sovereign debts similar to those created to manage bankruptcies in national economies, the decisions of which are legally binding.[10]

The only regular institutional mechanism of this type in place is the Paris Club, which deals exclusively with official financing. The system has also relied in the past on ad hoc mechanisms, such as the Baker and Brady Plans of the 1980s and the Heavily Indebted Poor Countries Initiative since the mid-1990s, and its successor, the 2005 Multilateral Debt Relief Initiative. But it has depended heavily on traumatic individual debt renegotiations, including those with banks under the so-called London Clubs. The problem with all these mechanisms, and therefore with the existing (again) nonsystem, is that relief generally comes too late, after high indebtedness has had devastating effects on countries. This is also true of the Paris Club, due to its traditional reliance on sequential debt rescheduling, which again means that countries are left with debt overhangs for excessively long periods. The system is also horizontally inequitable, as it does not treat all debtors or all creditors with uniform rules.

The discussion of the new international financial architecture should solve this problem by creating an international debt court, which would serve both as the mediator and eventual arbitrator of both public- and private-sector international loans. Privately run restructuring mechanisms, based on the active use of collective action clauses, are clearly insufficient in this regard. Debtors may in fact delay using the mechanism in order to avoid antagonizing creditors. It is also unlikely to generate a uniform treatment of creditors and fails to treat official and private lending with a unique set of rules, therefore maintaining the horizontal inequalities of the current system.

Any debt workout mechanism that is developed at the global level would have to start with defaults by debtor countries, which would then trigger off the negotiations. The system must be based on the principle that, after renegotiations, the debt ratio is sustainable, thus allowing borrowers a "fresh start" and even a (relatively) swift return to private capital markets. Furthermore, active support by multilateral development bank lending during and after renegotiations is essential, and these institutions should also support countries' return to markets.

The major initiative to design a multilateral mechanism of this sort was the 2001 IMF proposal to create a sovereign debt-restructuring mechanism (SDRM), which failed due to opposition from the United States and some major developing countries. No global initiative has been launched in this area during the current crisis, but the Greek debt restructuring and the deeper one that would have to come to manage this country's debt overhang may serve as the basis to reignite this debate.

## Regional Financial Cooperation

Four major arguments can be made for a more active use of regional monetary arrangements.[11] First, the current globalization process is characterized by deeper intraregional trade and investment flows. This calls for a world institutional architecture that takes into account such "open regionalism," as well as the heterogeneity of the international community. Second, regional arrangements could not only provide most of the exceptional financing for smaller countries but also help deter would-be speculators from attacking individual countries within a region. Third, they can help increase the supply of services to small and medium-sized countries. Finally, regional institutions generally enjoy a greater sense of ownership by member states, particularly by smaller countries. Of course, regional cooperation also faces significant challenges. Particularly, some groups of developing (particularly low-income) countries may not be able to supply the relevant services, and there is a need to build strong institutions to manage such cooperation.

The best-known case of regional monetary and, more broadly, macroeconomic policy cooperation is, of course, that of Western Europe. This process has been closely linked to trade and broader economic integration and has been accompanied by a strong emphasis on institution building, albeit in a gradual and pragmatic way. The major objective of macroeconomic cooperation was historically real exchange-rate stability, which was seen as the only way to create a level playing field for intraregional trade. Since the breakdown of the Bretton Woods parities, this generated a sequence of regional exchange-rate arrangements, which eventually led to the European Monetary Union (EMU) and the adoption of the euro. The commitment to exchange-rate stability implied that capital mobility was subordinated to that objective for a long time. This meant that capital account regulations were in place for decades, being reestablished when necessary. They were multilaterally removed only in 1990. This step was followed by a major crisis in 1992 and the subsequent decision to move to a common currency. This was combined with the Stability and Growth Pact, which established explicit fiscal rules, a far less successful arrangement. Although tougher European fiscal rules were agreed on in 2011, it remains to be seen how they will perform in practice. In turn, the 2010–2012 crisis in several euro members led to the creation, as an emergency measure, of the European Financial Stability Facility, which would be succeeded in 2012 by the European Stability Mechanism. However, there is a consensus that the initial size of these facilities was clearly insufficient to stem the deep crisis of the euro area in 2010–2012.

Contrary to the European history and to the equally rich experience in the area of regional cooperation in development financing—particularly regional, subregional, and interregional (Islamic Development Bank) development banks—there is a dearth of experiences in the area of monetary cooperation in the developing world. This is despite the fact that, aside from the reasons that justified European monetary cooperation, two additional rationales are present in the developing world: building stronger walls of defense against global financial shocks, and avoiding distorting competition among export-oriented economies. There is also recognition that stronger fiscal rules (with an equally strong countercyclical component) and a true banking union (common prudential regulation, supervision and deposit insurance) are essential counterparts of the monetary union.

Experiences with monetary unions have not been abundant and they have not always been successful. The Eastern Caribbean Currency Union and the Rand Monetary Area have been relative successes, whereas similar arrangements in Western Africa have had a checkered history. Other arrangements have been in place for some time, particularly regional payments agreements, which reduce the need for foreign exchange to settle intraregional transactions and are thus particularly useful to mitigate the effects of foreign exchange scarcity on intraregional trade during crises. Initiatives have been abundant in recent years, involving macroeconomic dialogue and balance-of-payments financing. The most ambitious is the Chiang Mai Initiative launched in 2000 by ASEAN, China, Japan, and the Republic of Korea. Preexisting arrangements in this area are the Latin American Reserve Fund (FLAR is its Spanish-language acronym) and the ASEAN Swap Arrangement.

The experience of FLAR, made up of the five Andean countries plus Costa Rica and Uruguay, demonstrates that even a modest fund (with a subscribed capital of slightly over $2 billion) can make essential contributions to the balance-of-payments financing of developing countries. Since 1978 FLAR has provided such financing to member states, which has exceeded that of the IMF for its smallest members throughout its history, and for the members as a whole at critical times (1982–1988 and 1998–2002). Its financing was clearly countercyclical, speedier than that of the IMF, and its preferred-creditor status has been reflected in its healthy portfolio, even in the face of major crises in the region. It also shows that the fear that "soft conditionality" would result in major losses by an institution providing emergency liquidity financing is exaggerated.

The agreed mechanism under the Chiang Mai Initiative was originally the negotiation of bilateral swap arrangements among the central banks of member countries. Aside from liquidity financing during crisis, the mechanism has provided an instrument of policy dialogue. The decision to fully multilateralize this arrangement, put in place a surveillance process, and increase its size in 2009 was a major step forward. However, this mechanism was not tapped during the recent financial crisis, a fact that reflects some problems (see below).

One way to understand these initiatives is that they break up monetary cooperation into its basic components: macroeconomic policy dialogue and eventual policy surveillance, liquidity support during crises, and exchange-rate coordination. Given the frequency of shocks faced by developing countries, they generally eliminate (or, at least, significantly postpone in time) the desirability of the third component—which, as we have seen, was the major objective of European cooperation.

The strong complementarity of global and regional arrangements implies that the IMF of the future should be better viewed as the apex of a *network* of regional and subregional reserve funds and swap arrangements. This model could be extended to the provision of macroeconomic surveillance and dialogue. However, careful consideration should be given to the links between global and regional arrangements. In this regard, during the recent crisis, Europeans chose rescue packages that mixed resources from the IMF and the European Financial Facility. In contrast, as access to Chiang Mai swap lines beyond a certain limit (20 percent of the agreed swap lines) required an IMF program, countries that may have used the initiative during the crisis (Indonesia and the Republic of Korea) did not do so, because they were unwilling to agree on any such program with the Fund. In turn, the use of the Latin American Reserve Fund has traditionally been delinked from any program with the global institution. The links between the IMF and regional arrangements must be subject, therefore, to flexible designs that reflect each region's preferences.

## Notes

This chapter draws from the 14th annual UNU-WIDER Lecture delivered by the author (Ocampo, 2011).

1. It is interesting to remember that, in its original design, this included the principle that modifications of the exchange-rate parities should be subject to consultation, a principle that, nonetheless, never worked in practice.
2. There is an extensive literature on this issue. One of the best-known papers, by Obstfeld and Rogoff (2010), underlines the links between the global imbalance and the financial crisis.
3. It is also interesting to recall that, in the discussions of the early 1970s, the United States backed a "reserve indicator" system, under which each IMF member would have been assigned a target level of reserves and forced to adjust to keep reserves around that target.
4. See, among many others, Llaudes, Salman, and Chivakul (2010).
5. See also a broader debate on this issue in *Journal of Globalization and Development* (2010), volume 1, issue 2.
6. Epstein, Grabel, and Jomo (2003) have also suggested the term "capital management techniques," and the IMF (2011) refers to them as "capital-flow management measures."
7. The classic treatment about the riskiness of short-term capital is Rodrik and Velasco (2000).
8. In the latter case, price-based regulations can also be substituted by tax provisions applying to foreign currency liabilities (see, for example, Stiglitz and Bhattacharya, 2000).
9. See, among others, three papers by the IMF and IMF experts (Ariyoshi et al., 2000; IMF, 2011; Ostry et al., 2010), as well as work by Magud and Reinhart (2007), Kawai and Lamberte (2010), and Ocampo (2003, 2008).
10. See the contributions to Herman, Ocampo, and Spiegel (2010) and United Nations (2009, ch. 5).
11. For an analysis of these issues, see the contributions to Ocampo (2006) and McKay, Volz, and Wölfinger (2011).

## References

Ariyoshi, Akira, Karl Habermeier, Bernard Laurens, Inci Ötker-Robe, Jorge Iván Canales-Kriljenko, and Andrei Kirilenko. (2000). "Capital Controls: Country Experiences with Their Use and Liberalization." Occasional Paper 190. Washington, DC: International Monetary Fund.

Dervis, Kemal. (2010). "The G-20 and Macroeconomic Policy Coordination at the Crossroads: A Macroeconomic Agenda for the G-20." In Colin Bradford et al., eds., *The G-20 Seoul G-20 Summit: Strengthening the Global Recovery*, 3–8. Washington, DC: Brookings Institution.

Eichengreen, Barry. (2011). *Exorbitant Privilege: The Rise and Fall of the Dollar and the Future of the International Monetary System*. New York: Oxford University Press.

Epstein, Gerald, Ilene Grabel, and K. S. Jomo. (2003). "Capital Management Techniques in Developing Countries." In Ariel Buira, ed., *Challenges to the World Bank and the IMF: Developing Country Perspectives*, 141–174. London: Anthem Press.

G20 (Group of 20). (2011). Communiqué, Meeting of Finance Ministers and Central Bank Governors, Washington, DC, April 14–15.

Gallagher, Kevin. (2011). "Regaining Control? Capital Controls and the Global Financial Crisis." PERI Working Paper No. 250, February. Political Economy Research Institute, University of Massachusetts at Amherst.

Herman, Barry, José Antonio Ocampo, and Shari Spiegel, eds. (2010). *Overcoming Developing Country Debt Crises*. New York: Oxford University Press.

IMF (International Monetary Fund). (2011). "Recent Experiences in Managing Capital Inflows: Cross-Cutting Themes and Possible Policy Framework." *IMF Policy Paper*, February 14.

Kawai, Mashiro, and Mario B. Lamberte, eds. (2010). *Managing Capital Flows: The Search for a Framework*. Cheltenham, UK: Edward Elgar and Asian Development Bank Institute.

Keynes, John M. 1942–1943. "The Keynes Plan." In J. Keith Horsefield, ed., *The International Monetary Fund 1945–1965: Twenty Years of International Monetary Cooperation*, Vol. III: Documents, 3–36. Washington, DC: International Monetary Fund, 1969.

Llaudes, Ricardo, Ferhan Salman, and Mali Chivakul. (2010). "The Impact of the Great Recession on Emerging Markets." IMF Working Paper WP/10/237, October.

Magud, Nicolas, and Carmen Reinhart. (2007). "Capital Controls: An Evaluation." In Sebastian Edwards, ed., *Capital Controls and Capital Flows in Emerging Economies: Policies, Practices and Consequences*, 645–674. Chicago: University of Chicago Press.

McKay, Julie, Ulrich Volz, and Regine Wölfinger. (2011). "Regional Financing Arrangements and the Stability of the International Monetary System." *Journal of Globalization and Development*, 1(2), Article 5.

Obstfeld, Maurice, and Kenneth Rogoff. (2010). "Global Imbalances and the Financial Crisis: Products of Common Causes." In Reuven Glick and Mark M. Spiegel, eds., *Asia and the Global Financial Crisis*, 131–172. San Francisco: Federal Reserve Bank of San Francisco.

Ocampo, José Antonio. (2003). "Capital Account and Counter-Cyclical Prudential Regulation in Developing Countries." In Ricardo Ffrench-Davis and Stephany Griffith-Jones, eds., *From Capital Surges to Drought: Seeking Stability for Emerging Markets*, 217–244. London: Palgrave Macmillan.

Ocampo, José Antonio, ed. (2006). *Regional Financial Cooperation*. Washington, DC: Brookings Institution and ECLAC.

Ocampo, José Antonio (2008). "A Broad View of Macroeconomic Stability." In Narcis Serra and Joseph E. Stiglitz, eds., *The Washington Consensus Reconsidered*, 63–94. New York: Oxford University Press.

Ocampo, José Antonio. (2010a). "Reforming the Global Reserve System." In Stephany Griffith-Jones, José Antonio Ocampo and Joseph E. Stiglitz, eds., *Time for a Visible*

*Hand: Lessons from the 2008 World Financial Crisis*, 289–313. New York: Oxford University Press.

Ocampo, José Antonio. (2010b). "Special Drawing Rights and the Reform of the Global Reserve System." In Jomo Kwame Sundaram, ed., *Reforming the International Financial System for Development*, 314–342. New York: Columbia University Press.

Ocampo, José Antonio. (2011). *Reforming the International Monetary System*. WIDER Annual Lecture 14. Helsinki: United Nations, University World Institute for Development Economics Research (UNU-WIDER).

Ocampo, José Antonio, Shari Spiegel, and Joseph E. Stiglitz. (2008). "Capital Market Liberalization and Development." In José Antonio Ocampo and Joseph E. Stiglitz, eds., *Capital Market Liberalization and Development*, 1–47. New York: Oxford University Press.

Ostry, Jonathan D., Atish R. Ghosh, Karl Habermeier, Marcos Chamon, Mahvash S. Qureshi, and Dennis B. S. Reinhardt. (2010). "Capital Inflows: The Role of Controls." IMF Staff Position Note, SPN/10/04, February 19. Available at www.imf.org.

Polak, Jacques J. (1979). "Thoughts on an International Monetary Fund Based Fully on SDR." Pamphlet Series No. 28. Washington, DC: International Monetary Fund.

Polak, Jacques J. (2005). *Economic Theory and Financial Policy: Selected Essays of Jacques J. Polak 1994–2004*. Edited by James M. Boughton. Armonk, NY: M. E. Sharpe.

Prasad, Eswar S., Kenneth Rogoff, Shang-Jin Wei, and M. Ayhan Rose. (2003). "Effects of Financial Globalization on Developing Countries: Some Empirical Evidence." Occasional Paper 220. Washington, DC: International Monetary Fund.

Rodrik, Dani, and Andrés Velasco. (2000). "Short-Term Capital Flows." In *Proceedings of the Annual World Bank Conference on Development Economics 1999*, 59–90. Washington, DC: World Bank.

Stiglitz, Joseph E., and Amar Bhattacharya. (2000). "The Underpinnings of a Stable and Equitable Global Financial System: From Old Debates to a New Paradigm." In *Proceedings of the Annual World Bank Conference on Development Economics 1999*, 91–130. Washington, DC: World Bank.

Triffin, Robert. (1961). *Gold and the Dollar Crisis*. Rev. ed. New Haven: Yale University Press.

Triffin, Robert. (1968). *Our International Monetary System: Yesterday, Today and Tomorrow*. New York: Random House.

United Nations. (2009). *Report of the Commission of Experts Convened of the President of the UN General Assembly on Reforms of the International Monetary and Financial System* (Stiglitz Commission), September. New York: United Nations. http://www.un.org/ga/econcrisissummit/docs/FinalReport_CoE.pdf.

Williamson, John. (2007). *Reference Rates and the International Monetary System*. Policy Analysis 82, January. Washington, DC: Peter G. Peterson Institute for International Economics.

Zhou Xiaochuan. (2009). "Reform the International Monetary System." People's Bank of China, Beijing. http://news.xinhuanet.com/english/2009-03/26/content_11074507.htm

CHAPTER 28

# PRODUCTIVE INCOHERENCE IN A TIME OF APERTURE

## THE IMF AND THE RESURRECTION OF CAPITAL CONTROLS

ILENE GRABEL

THE Global Financial Crisis of 2008 raises many important questions for students of development, not least of which is what are the likely effects of the crisis on the policy choices available to developing countries in the coming years. This question is critically important because the last several decades of neoliberalism have had extraordinarily pernicious effects on policy space for development. This narrowing of policy space took place through various institutional, political, and ideational mechanisms (Chang and Grabel, 2004; Gallagher, 2005; Shadlen, 2005; Wade, 2003). The pressure to deepen the move to neoliberal reform in the developing world intensified after the East Asian crisis of 1997–1998 (Grabel, 2003; Wade, 2007).

As of this writing, it appears that the ongoing Global Financial Crisis is having important (though uneven) effects on policy space. In particular, the financial crisis has normalized the use of capital controls in developing countries. The resurrection of capital controls as a legitimate part of the policy toolkit may constitute the most significant expansion of policy space in the developing world of the past three decades. However, this expansion of policy space is not occurring across all geographic areas or policy domains. In the mixed and even contradictory responses to the financial crisis we find a historic moment of what I term "productive incoherence" (Grabel, 2011). This incoherence has displaced the constraining "neoliberal coherence" that marked the neoliberal era.

By productive incoherence I refer to the many responses to the crisis by national governments, multilateral institutions (particularly the IMF), and the economics profession that to date have not congealed into any sort of consistent strategy or regime. The term is intended to signal the absence of a unified, consistent, universally applicable response to the crisis—either in the domain of rhetoric or policy making. This incoherence is radically different from the response to the Asian crisis, which was remarkably coherent in the sense of cementing the neoliberal regime. The responses to the current crisis range from those that reflect substantial continuity with neoliberalism to those that represent pronounced discontinuity. In this sense, the present incoherence is productive, signaling as it does not the death of neoliberalism, certainly, but the erosion of the stifling consensus that has secured and deepened neoliberalism across the developing world over the past several decades.

## The Resurrection of a Diminished IMF in a World of Relatively Autonomous Developing Countries

The current financial crisis has resurrected the IMF and ushered in a substantial change in the sources of IMF funding. But we are also seeing an equally dramatic change in the geography of IMF activity. In fact, even if the crisis has served to restore the IMF's influence in certain domains, this has occurred against the backdrop of a substantial diminution in the geography of the institution's influence.

Policy makers across the developing world sought to insulate themselves from the hardships and humiliations suffered by East Asian policy makers at the hands of the IMF after that region's economic crisis of the late 1990s. The explicit goal was to escape the IMF's orbit. The Fund did this by relying on a diverse array of strategies: self-insuring against future crises through the over-accumulation of reserves; the attraction of international private capital inflows; the establishment of swap arrangements among central banks; and a new reliance on trade finance, private investment, and official development assistance from fast-growing developing countries such as China and Brazil (Ketkar and Ratha, 2008).

The dramatic decline in the IMF's loan portfolio after the Asian crisis indicates the degree to which these escapist strategies proved to be successful. Even in the context of the current crisis, countries did their best to stay clear of IMF oversight. Indeed, during the current crisis, South Korea would have been a good candidate for a (precautionary) Flexible Credit Line with the Fund. But it did not apply for the credit line, presumably because of its prior experience with the Fund and to avoid the stigma of being one of its clients (Wade, 2010, fn. 10). Instead, it negotiated a reserve swap with the US Federal Reserve.

Those developing countries that have been able to maintain their autonomy during the crisis have used the resulting policy space to pursue a variety of countercyclical macroeconomic policies and, lately, various types of capital controls (see the following section). Their ability to do so indicates the degree to which the IMF's geographic reach has been compromised in the years following the Asian crisis. Equally important for the matter at hand, the behavior of these autonomous states has served as an example for less powerful states that, in turn, have reacted to the crisis in ways that were considered unimaginable in previous crises.

## Capital Controls: The "New Normal"

The current crisis has quickly achieved something that heterodox economists had been unable to do for a quarter of a century. It has provoked policy makers around the world to deploy capital controls as a means to protect domestic economies from the financial instability and trade dislocation associated with uncontrolled international capital flows. What is perhaps more surprising and hopeful is that the IMF has responded to these controls in a way that makes clear that they are necessary and/or prudent. The credit-rating agencies fail to flinch these days when new controls are announced, and private investors continue to flood these same markets.

This reception contrasts sharply with the IMF and investor condemnation that was provoked when Malaysia imposed stringent capital controls during the Asian crisis. At the time the IMF called these controls on capital outflows a "step back" (*Bloomberg*, 2010), and a representative article in the international business press stated that "foreign investors in Malaysia have been expropriated, and the Malaysians will bear the cost of their distrust for years" (cited in Kaplan and Rodrik, 2001, 11). More recently, capital controls in Thailand were reversed by the central bank within a few days after their implementation in

December 2006 (following a coup) after they triggered massive capital flight (*Bloomberg*, 2010). The IMF's response to the capital controls imposed during the current crisis makes it easier for other countries to follow suit, and it appears that they are doing so (as we will see below).

Capital controls were the norm in developing and wealthy countries in the decades that followed World War II (Helleiner, 1996). At that time, they were widely understood by academic economists, policy makers, and officials at multilateral institutions to be an essential tool of economic management. Policy makers deployed capital controls in order to enhance macroeconomic policy autonomy, promote financial and currency stability, protect domestic industries and sectors from foreign control or competition, and ensure the provision of adequate credit to favored sectors and firms at the right price (Epstein, Grabel, and Jomo, 2004). In the first several decades of its existence, the IMF supported capital controls, a position that was consistent with and reflected the views of the economics profession (and, notably, the views of John Maynard Keynes) and public figures (such as the US Treasury's Harry Dexter White). The views of the staff at the institution and of the profession more broadly, of course, shifted dramatically during the neoliberal era. Thus, the new shift in thinking and practice on capital controls at the IMF represents an important reversal that takes us back in the direction of the postwar institution.

The reception that greeted Malaysia's capital controls during the Asian crisis was unremarkable inasmuch as it was consistent with the view of neoliberal economists and policy makers at the time. Indeed, up until the Asian crisis the Fund was poised to modify its Articles of Agreement to make the liberalization of all international private capital flows a central purpose of the Fund and to extend its jurisdiction to capital movements. But despite the neoliberal tenor of the times, some developing countries nevertheless maintained capital controls—most famously, Chile and Malaysia, but also China, India, Colombia, Thailand, and a few others.

Then a notable development occurred. In the wake of the Asian crisis, IMF research staff started to change their views on capital controls modestly and cautiously. In the post-Asian crisis context, the center of gravity at the Fund and in the academic wing of the economics profession shifted away from an unequivocal, fundamentalist opposition to any interference with the free flow of capital to a tentative, conditional acceptance of the macroeconomic utility of some types of capital controls. Permissible controls were those that were temporary, market-friendly, focused on capital inflows, and introduced only when the economy's fundamentals were mostly sound and the rest of the economy was liberalized (Prasad et al., 2003). Academic literature on capital controls in the decade that followed the Asian crisis reflected this view: as Gallagher (2010a) points out, cross-country empirical studies (many of which are reviewed in Magud and Reinhart, 2006) offered strong support for the macroeconomic achievements of controls on inflows. Evidence supporting the achievements of outflow controls is less abundant but nontrivial. Research on Malaysia by

Kaplan and Rodrik (2001) is strongly in favor of the achievements of Malaysia's controls on outflows. Magud and Reinhart's review (2006) bears out this view of Malaysia's outflow controls as well. Epstein and colleagues (2004) also survey evidence on the achievements of inflow and outflow controls in seven countries.

Although the seeds of an intellectual evolution had been planted in the post-Asian crisis context, there was push back in this period from ideologues in the academic wing of the profession (Edwards, 1999; Forbes, 2005). In addition, there was a curious disconnect between the research of IMF staff, on the one hand, and, on the other, the creeping tolerance for capital controls by the institution's economists when they worked with particular countries (as a 2005 report by the IMF's internal watchdog, the Independent Evaluation Office, acknowledges) (IMF, 2005, 48; see also Chwieroth, 2010). Hence, despite the modest intellectual progress on capital controls that began after the Asian crisis, capital controls were still largely viewed as an exceptional measure.

But something happened during the current global crisis. Policy makers quietly began to impose various capital controls on both inflows and outflows, often framing them as simply prudential policy tools (akin to what Epstein and colleagues in 2004 termed "capital management techniques"). These controls are now becoming part of the global financial landscape. At the same time, we see that the ideas of economists at the Fund on capital controls have continued to evolve with the consequent effect of now normalizing this policy instrument.

The case of Iceland is particularly interesting for the discontinuity that it demonstrates in connection with the IMF's view of capital controls (see Wade, 2009, on the case more broadly). Iceland was the first country to sign an SBA during the current crisis. (SBAs are the IMF's basic short-term loan agreement.) What is most interesting about the Icelandic SBA is that it includes provisions regarding the need for stringent capital controls, something that we do not find in earlier SBAs that the IMF signed in connection with East Asian countries or in other crises during the neoliberal era. Even more surprising, the SBA provided for controls on outflows.

Iceland's controls were initially imposed prior to the signing of the SBA in October 2008, though the agreement with the Fund made a very strong case for their necessity and maintenance as a means to restore financial stability. These capital controls were designed to protect the Icelandic krona from collapsing due to capital outflows from the country. (As soon as the crisis emerged, the krona depreciated by 70 percent. Because most of Iceland's debt is denominated in foreign currency, the large currency depreciation had severe spillover effects on debt-service abilities.) Not surprisingly, given the IMF's long-held allergy to capital controls, IMF staff were questioned repeatedly in news conferences about what seemed to be an abrupt about-face. Fund staff repeatedly said that the capital controls in the country were crucial to prevent a free fall of the currency, that they were explicitly temporary, and that it was a priority of the Fund to end all restrictions as soon as possible. The country's central bank announced that it would begin a sequenced removal of its capital controls in November 2009, but since that time liberalization has not occurred. Indeed, as of May 2011, the IMF was still cautioning the country's officials that they would need to proceed slowly if they were to loosen capital controls.

Although the IMF's stance with respect to Iceland's capital controls initially appeared anomalous, it soon became clear that it marked a dramatic precedent. For example, the SBA with Latvia of December 2008 allowed for the maintenance of preexisting restrictions arising from a partial deposit freeze at Parex, the largest domestic bank in the country (IMF, 2009a). Soon thereafter, a joint World Bank-IMF report (2009, table 1.4) on the current crisis notes without evaluation that six countries (namely, China, Colombia, Ecuador, Indonesia, the Russian Federation, and Ukraine) all imposed some type of capital control during the crisis.[1] Another Fund report acknowledges that Iceland, Indonesia, the Russian Federation, Argentina, and Ukraine all put capital controls on outflows in order to "stop the bleeding" related to the crisis (IMF, 2009b). These reports neither offer details on the nature of these controls nor commentary on their ultimate efficacy, something that further suggests that capital controls—even on outflows—have a kind of "taken-for-granted" aspect at the Fund these days.

The Brazilian case is also notable because it illustrates the policy space that is increasingly being appropriated by policy makers in developing countries that remain independent of the Fund. In late October 2009, Brazil imposed capital controls via a tax on portfolio investment. The controls were aimed at slowing the appreciation of the currency in the face of significant international capital inflows to the country. Initially they involved a 2 percent tax on money entering the country to invest in equities and fixed-income investments, while leaving foreign direct investment untaxed. The IMF's initial reaction to Brazil's controls on capital inflows was ever so mildly disapproving. A week later the IMF's Dominique Strauss-Kahn reframed the message on Brazil's capital controls. The new message was, in a word, stunning: "I have no ideology on this"; capital controls are "not something that come from hell" (cited in Guha, 2009). Since then, Brazil has continued to strengthen its controls on inflows by raising the tax on inward portfolio investment (in fixed-income bonds) several times and by extending the scope of the controls in efforts to close identified channels of evasion, such as through purchases of American Depository Receipts.

As the crisis continues to grind on, other developing countries have implemented controls on capital outflows and especially on inflows. Some strengthened existing controls while others continue to introduce new measures. Many of these measures have been driven by the challenges associated with high levels of international capital inflows—namely, high levels of foreign investment are fueling asset and price inflation and are also placing currencies under pressure to appreciate. In December 2009 Taiwan imposed new restrictions on inflows that seek to reduce speculative pressures from overseas investors. The controls preclude foreign investors from placing funds in time deposits. About the same time, China added to its existing controls on inflows and outflows.

Then, in June 2010, Indonesia announced what its officials awkwardly term a "quasi-capital control" that governs short-term investment. Indonesia's new inflow controls seek to dampen speculation in the country via a one-month holding period for central bank money market securities, the introduction of longer maturity instruments, and new limits on the sales of central bank paper by investors and on the interest rate on funds deposited at the central bank (Wagstyl, 2010). In the same month, South Korea also announced controls on inflows, which its officials have continued to strengthen since that time. The controls limit the amount of currency forward and derivatives trading in which financial institutions can engage, and they limit the foreign currency loans extended by banks to local companies. Also in June, Argentina and Venezuela implemented controls on outflows: in Argentina they involve stricter limits on US dollar purchases (Webber, 2010), and in Venezuela they involve new restrictions on access to foreign currency (Mander, 2010). In October 2010, Thailand introduced a 15 percent withholding tax on capital gains and interest payments on foreign holdings of government- and state-owned company bonds. Finally, Peru has deployed a variety of inflow controls since early 2008. The country's reserve requirement tax (which is a type of control on capital inflows) has been raised three times between June and August 2010. More recently, we have seen that sterilization and new capital controls are being layered over existing controls in efforts to mitigate the currency appreciation, inflation pressures, and asset bubbles induced by the current flood of foreign investment into rapidly growing developing countries.

The response of investors (and credit-rating agencies) to these initiatives is silence and, in some cases, tacit approval. The response by economists at the IMF has been the same.

This new acceptance of capital controls by the IMF is reflected not just in official statements made by key officials, but also in the numerous research reports issued by the institution's staff and in the Fund's official reports. For example, an IMF report on low-income countries states that the impact of the crisis on banking systems in these countries has been modest insofar as "the existence of capital controls in several countries and structural factors have helped moderate the direct and indirect effects of the financial crisis" (IMF, 2009c, 9 fn. 9). A joint report by the World Bank and the Fund discusses capital controls in the same cautionary vein, though the brief discussion concludes that, "nonetheless, capital controls might need to be imposed as a last resort to help mitigate a financial crisis or stabilize macroeconomic developments" (World Bank-IMF, 2009, 65). In a policy note, IMF economists (Ostry et al., 2010) reached far beyond the Fund's public statements or practice to date in regards to controls on inflows. Ostry and colleagues commend controls on capital inflows for preventing economic contractions in countries that relied on them; reducing financial instability; and reducing financial fragility by lengthening the maturity structure of countries' external liabilities and improving the composition of capital inflows. These findings pertain to capital controls that were in place before and after the Asian crisis, as well as during the current crisis. The report also indicates that "such controls, moreover, can retain their potency even if investors devise strategies to bypass them" (5).

After this policy note was released, several prominent IMF watchers praised the Fund for finally embracing a sensible view of capital controls. For example, Ronald McKinnon stated that he was "delighted that the IMF has recanted" (cited in Rappeport, 2010); a former IMF official, Eswar Prasad, stated that the paper represented a "marked change" in the IMF's advice (cited in Wroughton, 2010), and Dani Rodrik (2010) stated that the "the stigma on capital controls [was] gone" and that the "policy note is a stunning reversal—as close as an institution can come to recanting without saying, 'Sorry, we messed up.'" No less telling is the sharp rebuke to the empirical work by Ostry and colleagues by William Cline (2010), which is illustrative of the discomfort that "true believers" in capital account liberalization have with what they see as the Fund's troubling and wrong-headed new embrace of capital controls.

In the lead-up to the fall 2010 IMF-World Bank meetings, the IMF's Global Financial Stability Report (2010a) also reiterated the basic and very important message that had appeared in the 2010 policy note and elsewhere that "capital controls may have a role in the policy toolkit." Recent statements by top officials at the Fund (and the World Bank) further illustrate a general normalization of capital controls as a policy tool. For example, in a summer 2010 speech, the IMF's Strauss-Kahn stated that "it is just fair that these [developing] countries would try to manage the inflows" as a last resort against a flood of investors pumping up inflation and asset values (cited in Oliver, 2010). Top officials at the World Bank have also gone on record in support of capital controls. For example, the Bank's president, Robert Zoellick, had this to say of the reemergence of capital controls in Asia: "It's not a silver bullet but it doesn't surprise me that people are trying them and they may help at the margin" (cited in Gallagher, 2010b). Seasoned IMF watchers were more than a little surprised when the director of the Fund's Western Hemispheric department failed in October 2010 to convince Colombian officials to deploy capital controls in response to the rapid appreciation of its currency (Crowe, 2010).

Given the inertia at the IMF, its actions during the current crisis mark a minor revolution, at least by its standards. The IMF didn't drive this process of reform, but its economists have adjusted their thinking quickly in response to the exigencies of the crisis and in response to the widespread deployment of capital controls in many countries. This is not to suggest that the normalization of capital controls ends all discussion of the matter at the Fund, of course. Indeed, we should not be surprised to find some evidence of tension and equivocation concerning capital controls at the Fund in the years ahead. We would expect that long-held ideas—especially those that have hardened to the level of ideologies and been codified in institutional practices over many years—have long half-lives (Grabel, 2003). The process of changing these ideas and practices is necessarily uneven; moreover, progress will inevitably generate pushback from within the institution itself. Hence, we should expect to find continuing evidence of tension and equivocation in future IMF reports that preclude a clear and decisive Fund verdict on capital controls.

It is beyond the scope of this chapter to investigate just why the IMF has evolved as I describe here. But it is likely that some combination of several factors is responsible. First, the views of IMF staff on capital controls appear to be continuing the evolution that began after the Asian crisis. Second, IMF leadership and staff may be driven by a pragmatic recognition that the institution has no effective choice but to amend its policy prescriptions, owing to the diminution of its influence in the developing world since the Asian crisis. Relatedly, there may be concern at the IMF about existing and future competition with other institutions (such as the World Bank, the Asian Development Bank, Brazil's National Development Bank) and regional and bilateral financial arrangements (such as the Chiang Mai Multilateralisation agreement involving members of ASEAN, and South Korea, China, and Japan; the Latin American Reserve Fund; the Bank of the South; the Bolivarian Alliance for the Americas, etc.) in the area of crisis management (see extensive discussion of this matter in Grabel, 2012). Third, the plasticity of IMF staff views on capital controls may well reflect the influence of leading academic economists, who themselves have come to question and in some respects reject the traditional neoliberal prescription for development. Fourth, the Global Financial Crisis, coming just a decade after the Asian crisis, may be encouraging those economists at the IMF (and the World Bank) who have long had reservations about the neoliberal model to give voice to their concerns and to assert themselves more effectively. It is important to keep in mind in this connection that like any complex organization, the IMF comprises diverse constituencies that may very well disagree among themselves about some fundamental matters pertaining to the institution's strategies (see Chwieroth, 2010). And, fifth, policy makers in developing countries that are independent of the Fund are utilizing their policy autonomy and are experimenting, among other things, with diverse types of capital controls. As a reflection of their growing confidence, I note here that, for the first time in the institution's history, several developing countries (namely, China, India, Brazil, Russia, and South Korea) became lenders to the IMF in April 2009.

We may find that the patience of economists at the Fund will be severely taxed as other countries test the limits of the policy space to deploy capital controls that have arisen as a consequence of the crisis. What is clear from the foregoing is the tenuous situation in which the IMF now finds itself, as it has begun to acknowledge the reality of its diminished influence across the developing world and the necessity of capital controls in cases of financial disruption and significant currency appreciation, while not wanting to lose control over just when, how, and by whom this policy instrument is employed. In late 2010 and early in 2011 the IMF provided us with an interesting vantage point from which to observe the continuing tension within the institution on capital controls. In several reports, Fund staff note that the institution is seeking to develop standards for the appropriateness of different types of controls (IMF, 2010b, 2011a, 2011b; Ostry et al., 2011). This effort is reminiscent of a project that was stalled by the Asian crisis. The current discussion of developing standards for controls was also given life by the French government, which seemed eager to use its new leadership of the G20 and G8 in early 2011 to give the Fund a role in coordinating capital controls via a code or mandate on the subject. The issue has since fallen off the European agenda. But the fact that the IMF tested the waters on the matter of controlling capital controls is instructive. Far more instructive is the fact that Brazil and numerous developing countries in the G24 (a group of key developing countries that work through the World Bank and the Fund) unequivocally and quite publicly rejected any such role for the Fund (G24, 2011; Wagstyl, 2011). Notably, the Fund has not issued a public response to this rebuke by developing countries.

## Pro-Cyclical Policy Adjustments in Countries under IMF Programs: The "Old Normal"

The above should not be read to suggest that IMF actions during the current crisis have consistently expanded policy space in the developing world. Indeed, once we step away from the issue of capital controls we see that in critical respects the Fund's conditionality programs during the current crisis evidence strong continuity with the pro-cyclical fiscal and monetary policy adjustments that the institution put in place during the Asian and the earlier Mexican crises (see Grabel, 2011).

Indeed, a large number of recent studies of the SBAs (and other assistance programs) negotiated during the current crisis have established that the IMF has promoted pro-cyclical macroeconomic policy adjustments or targets (Eurodad, 2009; Muchhala, 2009; Solidar, 2009; Van Waeyenberge et al., 2010; Weisbrot et al., 2009). For example, a study by Van Waeyenberge and colleagues (2010) of 13 low-income countries with IMF programs in place prior to and during the current crisis concludes that they preclude countries from utilizing countercyclical policies and public investment programs. Similarly, a study by Weisbrot and colleagues (2009) of 41 countries that had Fund programs in 2009 finds that 31 of these agreements involve tightening fiscal or monetary policy or both. Fund programs across the European periphery are also illustrative of the pro-cyclical policy adjustments that we have seen in previous crises. Interestingly, in cases involving European countries, the EU and the German government appear to be going even further than the IMF regarding demands for fiscal austerity (Lütz and Kranke, 2010). The continued and intense pressure for fiscal contraction in Greece is instructive in this regard.

Moreover, despite rhetoric by Fund staff to the contrary, expansive forms of conditionality (that involve, e.g., privatization, market liberalization, and labor-market and pension-system reform) have also returned as a key feature of recent Fund programs. Finally, the greater degree of fiscal flexibility granted by the Fund in some country contexts (particularly on the Eastern side of the European periphery) has little to no practical significance. See Grabel (2011) for discussion of both the continuities and the discontinuities in Fund practice during the current crisis.

## Looking Ahead

We have seen that the crisis has at once resurrected the IMF as a central actor in crisis management at the same time that it has revealed its diminished influence as a consequence of the successful escapist strategies of large developing countries from the IMF's orbit. For the first time in recent memory, the IMF finds itself forced to respond after the fact to developing country economic strategies that flout the neoliberal prescription. In this context, the institution has demonstrated a new flexibility concerning capital controls that should be striking to long-term IMF watchers. Associated with these changes, the "what is to be done?" question is being answered today more inconsistently and pragmatically than in the recent past. At the very same time, the IMF has continued to press for the kinds of damaging pro-cyclical macroeconomic adjustments that have long marked its SBAs with countries in distress. Second, and equally important, the incoherence of the responses to the current crisis is productive in that it has inaurated an expanding policy space for development.

It is not yet clear what the ultimate outcome of this uneven, recent expansion of policy space will be. It might be that the center of the battle over policy space will shift, especially if the IMF's new interest in coordinating capital controls turns out to constrain national policy autonomy. Or perhaps the battle over policy space will shift altogether from the IMF to other arenas, such as negotiations over bilateral trade agreements (Gallagher, 2010a, 2010b). Even under the best of circumstances, capital control reform may not reach smaller, struggling developing economies that lack the resources, geopolitical power, and/or inclination to pursue a truly developmentalist path. In reading the tea leaves we should also bear in mind that the new thinking on capital controls is occurring at the same time that there are important steps toward major structural transformation in the global financial architecture. This broader transformation involves, among other things, the emergence of a more decentralized, pluralistic, and heterogeneous financial architecture that is marked by a variety of regional and bilateral financial institutions and arrangements in the developing world (see Grabel, 2012). It could be that this transformation complements and secures the expansion of policy space for development that has resulted from the normalization of capital controls. And in that case, the incoherence of the present conjuncture might prove to be very productive, indeed.

## ACKNOWLEDGMENTS

I am grateful for the very useful reactions to this research offered by the books' editors and by George DeMartino and participants at conferences or seminars at the Central Bank of the Argentine Republic, Federal University of Rio de Janeiro, the Political Economy Research Institute of the University of Massachusetts at Amherst, the New School for Social Research, the IDEAs conference in Muttukadu, India, Cornell University, and at a session of AFFE at ASSA. I benefited immensely from the research assistance of Stu Thomas.

## NOTES

1. An IMF report (2009a) notes in passing that in Ukraine and Pakistan it "encouraged timely elimination of exchange restrictions on current payments." If this is code for stronger opposition, it would suggest the existence of a greater degree of continuity between the IMF's current view of capital controls and the view that it held during the Asian crisis. Weisbrot and colleagues (2009) mention that there was conflict between Pakistan and the IMF over capital controls, but information on the content of these discussions is unavailable at this time.

## REFERENCES

*Bloomberg*. (2010). "Asia Should Consider Capital Controls to Stem Asset-Bubble Risks." May 6. http://www.bloomberg.com/news/2010-05-06/asia-should-consider-capital-controls-to-stem-asset-bubble-risks-un-says.html.

Chang, Ha-Joon, and Ilene Grabel. (2004). *Reclaiming Development: An Alternative Economic Policy Manual*. London: Zed Books.

Chwieroth, Jeff. (2010). *Capital Ideas: The IMF and the Rise of Financial Liberalization*. Princeton: Princeton University Press.

Cline, William. (2010). "The IMF Staff's Misleading New Evidence on Capital Controls." *Peterson Institute for International Economics*. www.piie.com/realtime/?p=1351.

Crowe, Darcy. (2010). "Colombia Rules Out Capital Controls." Dow Jones, October 19. http://colombiareports.com/colombia-news/economy/12457-colombia-central-bank-rules-out-capital-controls.html.

Edwards, Sebastian. (1999). "How Effective Are Capital Controls?" *Journal of Economic Perspectives* 13(4): 65–84.

Epstein, Gerard, Ilene Grabel, and K. S. Jomo. (2004). "Capital Management Techniques in Developing Countries: An Assessment of Experiences from the 1990s and Lessons for the Future." G24 Discussion Paper No. 27. prepared for the XVIIIth Technical Group Meeting of the G-24 in Geneva, Switzerland, March 8–9, 2004, United Nations: NY and Geneva.

Eurodad. 2009. "Bail-out or Blow-out? IMF Policy Advice and Conditions for Low-Income Countries at a Time of Crisis. http://www.eurodad.org/uploadedFiles/Whats_New/Reports/Bail-out%20or%20blow-out.pdf

Forbes, Kristin. (2005). "Capital Controls: Mud in the Wheels of Market Efficiency." *Cato Journal* 25(1): 153–166.

G24. (2011). "Communique." Washington DC, 14 April. http://siteresources.worldbank.org/DEVCOMMINT/Documentation/22889617/DC2011-0008(E)G24Communique.pdf.

Gallagher, Kevin, ed. (2005). *Putting Development First: The Importance of Policy Space in the WTO and International Financial Institutions.* London: Zed Books.

Gallagher, Kevin. (2010a). "Policy Space to Prevent and Mitigate Financial Crises in Trade and Investment Agreements." G-24 Discussion Paper No. 58. New York: United Nations.

Gallagher, Kevin. (2010b). "Obama Must Ditch Bush-era Trade Deals." *Guardian*, June 30. http://www.guardian.co.uk/commentisfree/cifamerica/2010/jun/30/obama-bush-us-trade.

Grabel, Ilene . (2011. "Not Your Grandfather's IMF: Global Crisis, 'Productive Incoherence,' and Developmental Policy Space." *Cambridge Journal of Economics* 35: 805–830

Grabel, Ilene. (2012). "Financial Architectures and Development: Resilience, Policy space, and Human Development in the Global South." Political Economy Research Institute Working Paper Number 281, University of Massachusetts-Amherst.

Grabel, Ilene. (2003). "Ideology, Power and the Rise of Independent Monetary Institutions in Emerging Economies." In Jonathan Kirshner, ed., *Monetary Orders: Ambiguous Economics, Ubiquitous Politics*. Ithaca, NY: Cornell University Press.

Guha, Krishna. (2009). "IMF Refuses to Rule Out Use of Capital Controls." *Financial Times*. http://www.ft.com/cms/s/0/e3fd1610-c818-11de-8ba8-00144feab49a.html.

Helleiner, Eric. (1996). *States and the Reemergence of Global Finance*. Ithaca, NY: Cornell University Press.

International Monetary Fund (IMF). (2005). "Evaluation Report: The IMF's Approach to Capital Account Liberalization." Independent Evaluation Office. Washington, DC: IMF.

International Monetary Fund (IMF). (2009a). "Review of Recent Crisis Programs. Strategy, Policy and Review Department." http://www.imf.org/external/np/pp/eng/2009/091409.pdf.

International Monetary Fund (IMF). (2009b). *Annual Report on Exchange Rate Arrangements and Exchange Restrictions*. Washington, DC: IMF.

International Monetary Fund (IMF). (2009c). *The Implications of the Global Financial Crisis for Low-Income Countries*. Washington, DC: IMF. https://www.imf.org/external/pubs/ft/books/2009/globalfin/globalfin.pdf.

International Monetary Fund (IMF). (2010a). *Global Financial Stability Report*. Washington, DC: IMF.

International Monetary Fund (IMF). (2010b). "The Fund's Role Regarding Cross-Border Capital Flows." Policy, Strategy and Review and Legal Departments. http://www.imf.org/external/np/pp/eng/2010/111510.pdf.

International Monetary Fund (IMF). (2011a). "Policy Responses to Capital Flows in Emerging Markets, Asia and Pacific Department." http://www.imf.org/external/pubs/ft/sdn/2011/sdn1110.pdf.

International Monetary Fund (IMF). (2011b). "Recent Experiences in Managing Capital Inflows-Cross-Cutting Themes and Possible Policy Framework." Strategy, Policy, and Review Department. http://www.imf.org/external/np/pp/eng/2011/021411a.pdf.

Kaplan, Ethan, and Dani Rodrik. (2001). "Did the Malaysian Capital Controls Work?" NBER Working Paper No.8142. Cambridge: National Bureau of Economic Research.

Ketkar, Suhas, and Dilip Ratha, eds. (2008). *Innovative Financing for Development*. Washington, DC: World Bank. http://siteresources.worldbank.org/INTPROSPECTS/Resources/334934-1110315015165/%5Be-book%5DInnovative_Financing_for_Development.pdf.

Lütz, Susanne, and Matthias Kranke. (2010). "The European Rescue of the Washington Consensus? EU and IMF Lending to Central and Eastern European Countries." LEQS Paper No.22. London: London School of Economics.

Magud, Nicolas, and Carmen Reinhart. (2006). "Capital Controls: An Evaluation." NBER Working Paper No.11973. Cambridge: National Bureau of Economic Research.

Mander, Benedict. (2010). "Venezuela Begins Anti-inflation Plan." *Financial Times*, June 8. http://www.ft.com/cms/s/0/ff0eeb3c-7294-11df-9f82-00144feabdc0.html.

Molina-Gallart, Nuria. (2009). "Bail-out or Blow-out? IMF Policy Advice and Conditions for Low-Income Countries at a Time of Crisis." *Eurodad*. http://www.eurodad.org/uploadedFiles/Whats_New/Reports/Bail-out%20or%20blow-out.pdf.

Muchhala, Bhumika. (2009). "The IMF's Financial Crisis Loans: No Change in Conditionalities." *Third World Network*. http://www.twnside.org.sg/title2/par/IMF.Crisis.Loans-Overview.TWN.March.2009.doc.

Oliver, Christian. (2010). "IMF Warns on Emerging Market Currency Controls." *Financial Times*, July 11. http://www.ft.com/cms/s/0/5ba241aa-8ce9-11df-bad7-00144feab49a.html.

Ostry, Jonathan, Atish Ghosh, Karl Habermeier, Marcos Chamon, Mahvash Qureshi, and Dennis Reinhardt. (2010). "Capital Inflows: The Role of Controls." IMF Staff Position Note No. 4. http://www.imf.org/external/pubs/ft/spn/2010/spn1004.pdf.

Ostry, Jonathan, Atish Ghosh, Karl Habermeier, Luc Laeven, Marcos Chamon, Mahvash Qureshi, and Annamaria Kokenyne. (2011). "Managing Capital Inflows: What Tools to Use?" IMF Staff Position Note No. 11.

Prasad, Eswar, Kenneth Rogoff, S. J. Wei, and M. A. Kose. (2003). "Effects of Financial Globalization on Developing Countries: Some Empirical Evidence." http://www.imf.org/external/np/res/docs/2003/031703.htm.

Rappeport, Alan. (2010). "IMF Reconsiders Capital Controls Opposition." *Financial Times*, February 22. www.ft.com/cms/s/0/ec484786-1fcf-11df-8deb-00144feab49a.html.

Rodrik, Dani. (2010). "The End of an Era in Finance." *Project Syndicate*. http://www.project-syndicate.org/commentary/rodrik41/English.

Shadlen, Kenneth. (2005). "Exchanging Development for Market Access? Deep Integration and Industrial Policy under Multilateral and Regional-Bilateral Trade Agreements." *Review of International Political Economy* 12(5): 750–775.
Solidar. (2009). "Doing a Decent Job? IMF Policies and Decent Work in Times of Crisis." http://www.eurodad.org/uploadedFiles/Whats_New/Reports/Doing%20a%20decent%20job.pdf.
Van Waeyenberge, Elisa, Hannah Bargawi, and Terry McKinley. (2010). "Standing in the Way of Development? A Critical Survey of the IMF's Crisis Response in Low-Income Countries, Eurodad and Third World Network." http://www.eurodad.org/whatsnew/reports.aspx?id=4083.
Wade, Robert. (2003). "What Strategies Are Viable for Developing Countries Today? The WTO and the Shrinking of 'Development Space.'" *Review of International Political Economy* 10(4): 627–644.
Wade, Robert. (2007). "The Aftermath of the Asian Financial Crisis: From 'Liberalize the Market' to 'Standardize the Market' and Create a 'Level Playing Field.'" In Bhumika Muchhala, ed., *Ten Years After: Revisiting the Asian Financial Crisis*, 173–194. Washington, DC: Wilson Center Press.
Wade, Robert. (2009). "Iceland as Icarus: From 'Miracle' to Crash, and Beyond." *Challenge* 52(3) (May–June): 5–33.
Wade, Robert. (2010). "The State of the World Bank." *Challenge* 53(4) (July–August): 1–25.
Wagstyl. Stefan (2011). "IMF and Capital Controls: Sauce for the Goose Should Be Sauce for the Gander." *Financial Times*, April 6. http://www.ft.com/beyond-brics.
Wagstyl, Stefan. (2010). "Indonesia: Controls or Quasi-controls on Capital Inflows?" *Financial Times*, June 16. http://blogs.ft.com/beyond-brics/2010/06/16/indonesia-controls-or-quasi-controls-on-capital-inflows/.
Webber, Jude. (2010). "Argentina Unveils Tighter Controls on US Dollar Buys." *Financial Times*, June 8. http://blogs.ft.com/money-supply/2010/06/08/argentina-unveils-tighter-controls-on-dollar-buys/.
Weisbrot, Mark, Rebecca Ray, Jake Johnston, Jose Antonio Cordero, and Juan Antonio Montecino. (2009). "IMF-Supported Macroeconomic Policies and the World Recession: A Look at Forty-One Borrowing Countries." October. Washington, DC: Center for Economic and Policy Research.
World Bank-IMF. (2009). "Global Monitoring Report 2009." http://siteresources.worldbank.org/INTGLOMONREP2009/Resources/5924349-1239742507025/GMR09_book.pdf.
Wroughton, Lesley. (2010). "IMF Endorses Capital Controls as Temporary Measure." *Reuters.com*, February 19. http://www.reuters.com/article/idUSN1912428020100219.

CHAPTER 29

# THE JAPANESE BOOM AND BUST

## "LEAN" AND "CLEAN" LESSONS

ROBERT N. McCAULEY

ONE of the lessons drawn from the financial crisis of 2007–2009 is that the tools of banking supervision should be employed with a macroeconomic perspective in order to work against overly rapid credit growth amid buoyant asset prices; this settled a debate between those who had argued for this point of view and those who believed that monetary policy should only clean up after a crisis (White, 2009). Yet in retrospect, the apparent lack of effect of the introduction of Basel I at the late stages of the Japanese bubble of the 1980s raises questions as to the efficacy of such a policy, as well as that of the more focused policies of the Japanese authorities to constrain the growth of bank loans. This chapter seeks to review the lessons of the Japanese bubble for attempts to "lean" against the wind of rapid credit growth.

Even as policy makers in the United States and United Kingdom struggle with policy challenges in the aftermath of the bursting of the real-estate bubbles, it is also timely to draw anew on the lessons of Japan's "clean," that is, its range of policies adopted in the wake of the collapse of equity and real-estate prices in the early 1990s. Advice offered to the Japanese authorities in the 1990s and 2000s is due for fresh reflection (Wolf, 2012). Banking supervision, fiscal policy, monetary policy, debt management, and foreign exchange policy all deserve a review.

This chapter looks at why the Japanese boom was so large and then asks the related question of why macroprudential policies that were applied did not work better. In the summary, lessons are drawn regarding the policy responses but not necessarily the ones that were drawn before the recent US experience.

# Why Was the Japanese Boom and Bust among the Worst in Modern History?

Nowadays, observers draw parallels between the recent US real-estate bubble and the Japanese bubble of the 1980s (Ueda, 2011). However, it is important to recognize how big the Japanese bubble really was and to identify the specific factors that inflated it to such dimensions.

A thorough comparison of the cleaning up after the bust in Japan with recent crises is perhaps premature. Nakaso (2001, 59–60) draws comparisons to the leading industrial country contenders as of 10 years ago. He shows higher peak nonperforming loans as a ratio of GDP in Sweden (13.2 percent versus 7.8 percent in Japan) but worse accumulated loan losses in Japan (13 years of bank operating profits in Japan versus 6 years in Sweden) and a larger use of public funds (14 percent of GDP in Japan versus 4 percent in Sweden or 7 percent in Finland).[1]

The Japanese enjoyed their bubble in every possible way. Households borrowed to buy overpriced homes, famously taking on multigenerational mortgages and accumulating financial assets. Industrial and commercial firms borrowed to invest at home and abroad, to buy each other's shares, and to turn their treasuries into profit centers through so-called *zaitech*. Real-estate firms leveraged up their holdings at home and then acquired Rockefeller Center and other properties abroad.

While lopsided financial deregulation, monetary policy, and supervisory weakness all deserve emphasis (Hoshi and Kashyap, 2000; Okina et al., 2001; Ueda, 2000), two overlooked but long-standing structural factors helped to aggravate the Japanese financial imbalances. First, the financial structure of Japan made for an especially strong mutual reinforcement between rising asset prices and the liberal extension of bank credit. Second, high levels of social homogeneity and trust in Japanese society interacted with a rare lack of dependence on foreign investors to produce a boom-and-bust cycle with an unusually local character. This character extended to both the boom and the period of denial in the early to mid-1990s.

## Japanese Banks as Equity Holders

The initial conditions in Japanese finances could hardly have been more propitious for inflating a bubble. Japanese banks, the economy's beating heart, entered the 1980s owning a substantial share of all Japanese-listed equity. The "main bank" typically was among the top five shareholders of a given firm, with a holding limited after 1987 to 5 percent of a given firm's equity (Aoki, Patrick, and Sheard, 1994, 13–14). The bank's borrowers in turn owned bank shares in a system of cross-holdings.

This cross-holding system shielded corporate governance from outside investors and also served an insurance function (Sheard, 1991). The cross-holding ratio increased sharply around the time that Japan joined the Organisation for Economic Co-operation and Development (OECD), lowered controls on capital inflows, and amended its securities laws to allow takeover bids (Miyajima and Kuroki, 2007, 85). This timing points to the importance that Japanese managers put on restricting governance to stable shareholders.

Regarding the insurance function, cross-holdings of shares served to spread risks across firms while making for systemic instability across time at the macro level. If one firm's profitability declined for some reason, it could realize gains from its cross-holdings. These were accounted for in a very conservative fashion (lower of cost or market), meaning that capital gains would not be regularly distributed but could be realized in an hour of need. At the aggregate level, however, higher land prices and anticipated profits would blow up the value of cross-held shares, leaving firms richer. This wealth effect for banks in particular carried the potential for hugely powerful pro-cyclical feedback from asset prices to lending.

### *Banks held 100–140 percent of their own equity in customers' listed equities.*

Banks' single-digit percentage holdings in their customers added up to a big equity price exposure. In the mid-1980s, such holdings amounted to more than 100 percent of the *city bank's own equity*, and more in the case of the long-term credit banks and the trust banks. While the unrealized gains on cross-held shares were not disclosed to shareholders, they were known in the market[2] and to the international rating agencies. One can think of the Japanese bank as being a pile of assets and liabilities sitting on top of an equity mutual fund.

### *As equity prices rose, banks became richer and lent more.*

Despite its providing insurance against losses at particular firms, this financial structure created a direct link between equity prices and the (mark-to-market) capital of Japan's main credit institutions. When land prices and the stock market rose sharply in the 1980s, the market-price-based capital-asset ratio went up. Japanese banks became disproportionately richer: Kane and colleagues (1991) find that the stock-market beta for large Japanese banks was two. In other words, a 10 percent rise in the Topix saw a 20 percent rise in the big banks' shares. Conservative accounting aside, bank managers, counterparties, and rating agencies all accepted greater risk taking on the basis of higher (market-based) wealth.

In particular, Japanese banks could lend more. The return on assets became less important to growth and the Japanese banks won market share by cutting lending margins. Armed with triple-A ratings, the major Japanese banks found easy access to the global funding markets. Domestic customers could borrow dollars and swap them into yen so that loans (credit) could expand faster than deposits (money). In short, the rise in equity prices in Tokyo represented a gusher of equity to Japanese banks, which supported a strong flow of credit to borrowers in Japan and the rest of the world.

Stepping back, the reader may wonder whether the connection between asset prices and credit availability is not ubiquitous in modern financial systems. The usual story is that firms or households have assets like land that can be used as security for bank loans. As the land price rises, the borrower enjoys access to more credit or to the same credit on better terms.

In Japan, the usual story played out. Big banks that had lost their major corporate borrowers, owing to the decline of investment relative to cash flows and bond market development, turned to lending to small firms against the security of land (Ueda, 2000a). As a result, land became easier to borrow against at collateral values that presumed further price rises. In addition to this familiar mechanism, higher land prices and easy credit had raised share prices and thereby directly fed bank capital. Banks could take more risk and expand their balance sheets without the need to earn and to retain cash flow. Thus, higher asset prices not only made the borrower more creditworthy, it armed the banks to take on more risk and to extend more credit. The cross-holdings that served an insurance function at the micro, cross-sectional level became over time a runaway engine of macroeconomic instability.

Sometimes the story of the connection between Japanese bank capital and equity holdings starts and ends with the treatment of unrealized gains on such equities in Basel I. Faced with the prospect of Japanese banks' shortfall of capital under the international rules, the Japanese banking supervisors argued in the Basel Committee on Banking Supervision (BCBS) for a provision to allow unrealized gains to count toward equity. In the event, Basel I permitted 45 percent of such unrealized gains to count toward the lower-quality capital ("tier 2") that made up the second 4 percent of the 8 percent required capital buffer.[3] To be sure, this provision meant that Japanese banks' regulatory capital rose and fell with the Nikkei.

However, it would be a misapprehension to imagine that this regulation introduced the cyclicality into Japanese bank equity. Instead, it should be seen as no more than partially recognizing it. The 55 percent haircut reflected the taxes payable on realization of the gains. Moreover, the 45 percent of gains counted toward lower-quality capital (not higher-quality tier 1 equity). McCauley and Zimmer (1991) found that tier 2 capital in the form of subordinated debt barely affected the cost of capital for a bank—it was only the spread over interbank rates that added to costs, and this was modest for well-rated banks. Indeed, when the Japanese banks sold subordinated debt in the early 1990s to replace lost stock-market wealth (Ito and Sasaki, 2002), it was done at very narrow spreads.

But the compelling argument against assigning a key role to this regulation was the fact that Japanese banks realized gains massively in the late 1980s as part of their efforts to meet the tier 1 requirements, as described below. Banks could have mobilized the mark-to-market wealth in shares even without regulatory recognition of unrealized gains.[4]

## Social Homogeneity, Trust, and Lack of Dependence on Foreign Investment

A conjecture that may be worth consideration is that certain societies are more subject to asset-price bubbles than others. Kindleberger and Aliber's (2005) propagation mechanism leans strongly on social comparison (Sabini, 1992, 37–43): "There is nothing so disturbing to one's well-being and judgement as to see a friend get rich." If others of similar means are getting ahead fast and one is not, one may pay more attention to this negative contrast than to one's own material progress (Baumeister et al., 2001; Rozin and Royzman, 2001). Might it not be that in more homogeneous and trusting societies that the force of such comparisons and the sting of negative contrast are both stronger? Ethnic homogeneity leads to higher levels of trust (Alesina and Ferrara, 2002). And higher levels of trust lead to higher stock-market participation (Giannetti and Koskinen, 2010; Guiso, Sapienza, and Zingales, 2008).

The problem is the way that the Japanese answer the World Value Survey question, "Generally speaking, would you say that most people can be trusted or that you have to be very careful in dealing with people?" They are not particularly on the trusting side: Japan registers near the mean, just between the United States and Germany. If this measure matters, the Nordic countries and Iceland, rather than Japan, were culturally susceptible to their bubbles in the late 1980s and 2000s, respectively. However, Japanese interviewees express world-beating trust in their judiciary, which may be the kind of trust that matters.[5] Certainly, a high fraction of the Japanese population buys shares, 30 percent, just below Australia (40 percent) and New Zealand (31 percent).

Social homogeneity and trust at home, however, may count for little if a bubble depends on flows from foreign investors. Here, Japan stands out. At the outset, in the mid-1980s, some 7 percent of Japanese shares were held by nonresidents. By the peak of the bubble, foreign investment had fallen to some 3 percent of the shareholdings. Global equity investors headed for the exits as Tokyo shares showed price-earnings ratios between 60 and 80 in the late 1980s.

If foreign investors were skeptical, foreign intellectuals were often encouraging. Ezra Vogel's *Japan as Number One* set the tone as early as 1979. Harvard Business School followed with encomia to Japanese industrial relations, bank-firm relations, and general management prowess (Porter, 1992). This intellectual support buttressed the projections of rapid growth that high equity prices required. Paradoxically, a combination of little support from foreign investors but much support from foreign intellecturals may have helped propel the Japanese boom.

It remains a question whether the level of trust, or particular kinds of trust, contributes to the formation of bubbles. The idea that the unusually small stake of global investors in Japanese equity and real estate allowed the boom to last unusually long seems at least prima facie plausible. This idea returns below with the suggestion that the cleanup after the Japanese bust was prolonged not only for various Japanese reasons but also because credit developments in Japan depended unusually little on the risk perceptions of foreign investors.

## Why Didn't Macroprudential Policy Protect Japanese Banks?

Basel III, crafted since the Global Financial Crisis, includes a new countercyclical buffer that is intended to make financial systems more robust in the face of credit booms of the kind experienced by Japan in the late 1980s (BCBS, 2009). The commitment by regulators to this approach makes it important to learn what one can from experiments in the past with such policies. Caruana (2010a, 2010b) has posed the counterfactual question, "Could it have been different this time?" with this tool, examining the recent cases of the US, UK, and Spanish economies, and venturing back into the 1990s to consider the Mexican case as well.

The Japanese case poses a related question: why did the macroprudential policies adopted *not* work to make the financial system more robust? After all, the international agreement on Basel I in part responded to the international expansion of Japanese banks with a requirement that Japanese banks raise equity. With much the same effect, the new countercyclical buffer would have required higher levels of capital. In brief, the tightening of capital for the Japanese banks did not work because of the above-described effect on their equity of the high Tokyo share prices. Another macroprudential measure that the Japanese authorities adopted harkened back to the days of window guidance over banks. Banks were told to reduce their loan growth in the late 1980s.[6] The effect of this measure was also limited, in this case by both domestic evasion (dollar loans booked in Japan were not covered) and international evasion (loans booked at foreign branches) by banks.

Both modern (higher required equity) and old-fashioned (window guidance) approaches to restraining lending amid a credit boom did not seem to work as the banking system eventually plunged into a systemic crisis needing widespread government intervention. What are the lessons?

## Basel I and the Japanese Credit Boom

As Kapstein (1991) tells the tale, the US Congress insisted on tighter capital requirements for banks as a price for increasing the size of the IMF to deal with the Latin American debt crisis. Before the crisis, the Federal Reserve had held that the large multinational US banks were more diversified than their regional competitors and so could operate on narrower capital cushions. The International Lending and Supervision Act of 1983 led the Federal Reserve to look for an international agreement to ensure that tighter capital requirements not put US banks at a competitive disadvantage. This led to an embrace of the Bank of England's risk-based capital requirements as a better mousetrap. The Federal Reserve and the Bank of England thereby presented to the rest of the world a united front representing the two major financial centers, London and New York.

President Corrigan of the Federal Reserve Bank of New York then enlisted the support of the Japanese authorities for this package. It must be remembered that at that time the Japanese banks were expanding rapidly around the globe (figure 29.1). In the United States, they moved beyond lending to Japanese firms' US affiliates to becoming important participants in the syndicated loans to large firms (Seth and Quijano, 1991).[7] According to Kapstein (1991), the Japanese authorities acceded because it would be "painless" for the Japanese banks to raise the equity from about 2 percent to 4 percent. No doubt, this is not the whole story.

With the number three financial center of Tokyo on board, the effort turned to continental Europe. The BCBS published a consultative paper in December 1987, and the Basel Capital Accord (or the 1988 Accord) setting out minimum capital against risk-weighted assets was approved by the G10 Governors and released to banks in July 1988. In principle, the agreement called for implementation by the end of 1992 of the minimum ratio of capital to risk-weighted assets of 8 percent. In practice, internationally active banks sought to demonstrate to counterparties and rating agencies their full implementation well before then. The outline agreement was broadly known by mid-1987, so one can consider that the policy of tightening the capital requirements for the Japanese banks

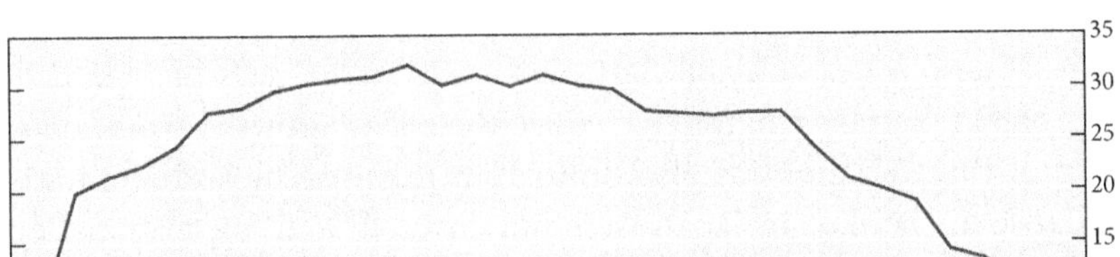


**Figure 29.1** Japanese bank share of BIS bank foreign claims.
*Source*: BIS.

occurred well before the formal implementation. If the tightening occurred in 1987–1989, it occurred before the peak of the bubble (the end of 1989 for large-cap shares and a year later for small-cap shares).[8]

## *Bound by Basel I, the Japanese banks raised huge amounts of equity.*

Japanese banks stepped up their equity issuance by a factor of 10 in the year to March 1988 and went to new highs in the following two years (figure 29.2). Pettway and colleagues (1991) interpret this as a response to the Basel Accord. The scale of the equity rise, at more than $10 billion at the peak in the year to March 1990, was very large, especially for banks reporting good profits in the midst of rapidly growing credit. In addition, the Japanese banks sold convertible bonds in large amounts. Carrying rock-bottom interest rates, these would lead to greater profits and retained earnings even if they never converted and would add equity if they did convert.

In addition, the Japanese banks realized gains on cross-held shares. This latter behavior is at first blush very puzzling on several grounds. Usually firms that are in difficulty, not profitable firms in the midst of a boom, would sell cross-held shares (Sheard, 1991). And it was very expensive to realize the gains—as noted above, some 55 percent of the gain would be payable in income taxes, whereas realizing such gains when a firm is in difficulty would usually mean it would offset losses. Moreover, Pettway and colleagues (1991) report that Japanese bank share prices did not suffer from new equity issuance, in contrast to the usual finding for US banks. So if the issuance of new shares did not injure shareholder wealth, while a realization of capital gains cost half the gain, why not just sell more shares?

In retrospect, it appears that the Japanese banks used the realization of capital gains to provide them with profits at a time when their breakneck expansion was not producing much in the way of operating earnings. This inference can

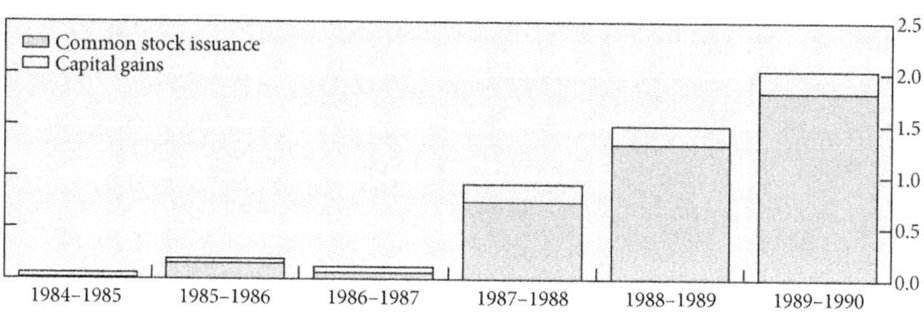


**Figure 29.2** Japanese banks common stock issuance and cross-hold shares capital gains.

*Note*: Common stock issues for 77 commercial banks; capital gains on cross-held shares for six city banks and two long-term capital banks.

*Sources*: Pettway et al. (1991, 564) and McCauley and Zimmer (1991, 40).

be drawn from the decomposition of the pre-tax profit of the Japanese banks (McCauley and Zimmer, 1991, 40). In the fiscal years ending in March 1988 through March 1990, something like two-thirds of Japanese bank profits arose from the realization of gains on cross-held shares. The Japanese banks realized enough capital gains to show sufficient profits to sell their common shares and convertible bonds. This was like a perpetual motion machine.

It should be understood that the Japanese banks did not dispose of the shares. The well-understood drill was to send a sell order to the Osaka exchange, allow the broker to purchase it, and then promptly buy back the share from the broker. Therefore, latent reserves became high-grade equity—albeit after a 55 percent tax payment on the capital gain.[9]

It is beyond the scope of this chapter to strike the balance between the weakening of the capital of the Japanese banks from the tax payment on the realized gains against the strengthening of their capital from the equity and convertible bond sales. From figure 29.2 it appears that the latter must have predominated, but the equity sales are for 77 commercial banks while the realized gains are for a narrower group of big-city and long-term-credit banks. It is likely that on balance the Japanese banks strengthened their capital bases in the late 1980s very considerably, even as their rapid loan growth exposed them more and more to the risk of a decline in equity and land values.[10]

### *Basel I was similar to macroprudential policy in Basel III.*

The equity issuance by Japanese banks that Basel I induced lagged the timing of a hypothetical countercyclical capital buffer as envisioned by Basel III. This buffer responds to an acceleration of private credit in relation to its trend. In Japan, this began in the early 1980s (figure 29.3).[11]

As a result, the credit gap (Drehmann et al., 2010), the excess of private credit to GDP over its previous trend, turned positive in the early 1980s (figure 29.4).

The countercyclical buffer kicks in when the gap hits 2 percent of GDP and ranges up to a 2.5 percent addition to the ratio of required capital to weighted

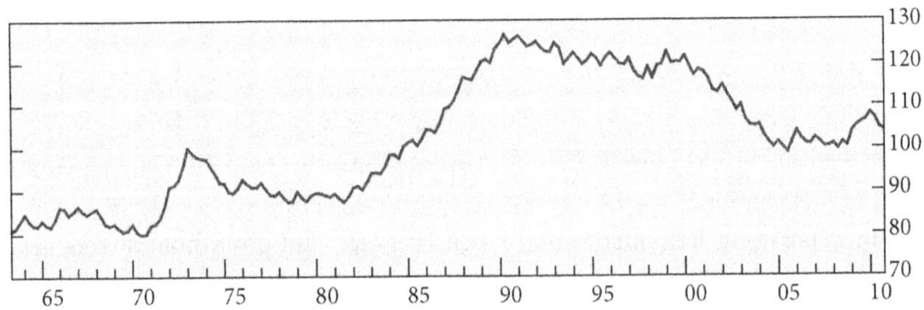


**Figure 29.3** Private credit/GDP ratio in Japan.
*Source*: National data; OECD; BIS calculations.

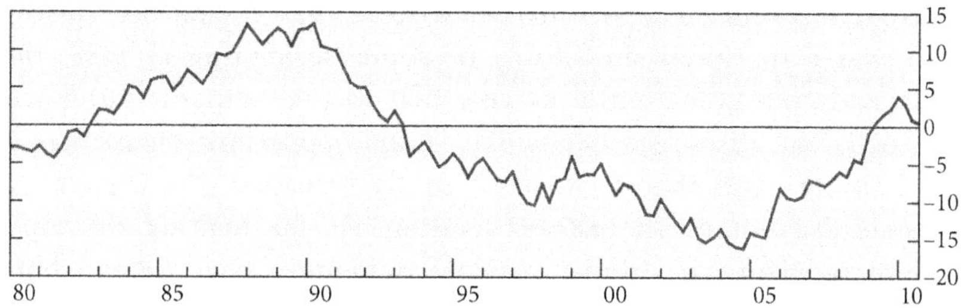


**Figure 29.4** Credit gap in Japan.

Deviation of credit/GDP from its one-sided long-term trend (i.e., a trend determined only from information available at the time assessments are made) in percentage points.
*Source*: National data; OECD; BIS calculations.

assets in the respective economy. Accordingly, the buffer would have started to rise in 1983 to reach 2.5 percent of risk-weighted exposure to Japanese borrowers by 1987 (figure 29.5).

In sum, the countercyclical capital buffer as called for in Basel III would have been similar in size but a year or two earlier than the increased capital raised in preparation for Basel I. The first international capital agreement thus serves as a natural experiment for the effect of a hypothetical countercyclical buffer in response to rapid growth of credit to the private sector in Japan in the 1980s.

## *Why didn't Basel I capital tightening do more good?*

The higher capital requirements could serve two purposes: to slow down the rate of loan expansion by the Japanese banks or to make them more

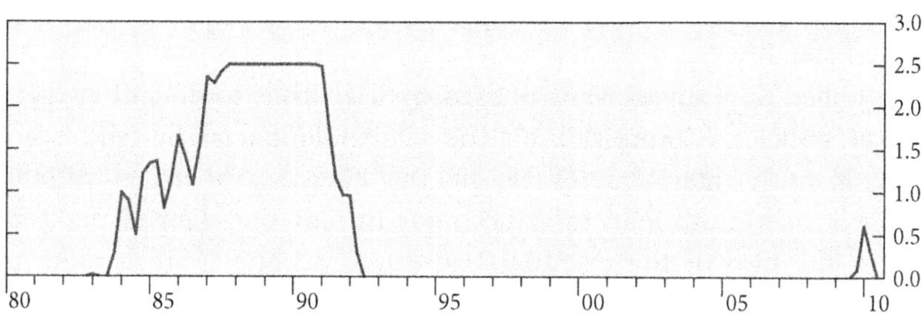


**Figure 29.5** Countercyclical capital buffer: Japan.

The countercyclical buffer is 0 when the value of the credit/GDP gap is below 2, and 2.5 when it is above 10 percent; for gaps between 2 and 10 percent the buffer is calculated as 0.25 times the value of the credit/GDP gap exceeding 2 percent.
*Source*: BIS calculations.

resilient to the eventual downturn in asset prices. What we observe is that there was a marginal slow-down in domestic lending in 1988, though Fukumoto and colleagues (2010) ascribe that to the "window guidance" by the Bank of Japan, discussed below. Given the opportunity to realize gains on cross-holdings and thereby to ease equity issuance, the higher capital requirements did not much restrain lending. As for making the Japanese banks more resilient, the higher capital could only have helped but evidently not enough to prevent a systemic crisis. Without the late 1980s capital raising, more big banks might well have suffered the nationalization experienced by Long Term Credit Bank of Japan and Nippon Credit Bank (Nakaso, 2001).

Again, some accounts highlight as a big mistake the Japanese authorities' successful push for Basel I to recognize as tier 2 capital 45 percent of the unrealized gains on Japanese banks' shareholdings. Clearly, in retrospect, it is systemically dangerous to have stock-market gains feeding regulatory bank capital directly. However, it is not clear that the Japanese banks would have been better off without this measure. They might, after all, have realized more gains on cross-held shares (while retaining the shares and the risk exposure to the Nikkei)—leaving them even weaker after the tax payment.

To say that the countercyclical buffer probably would not have done the job in Japan in the late 1980s is not a criticism of the tool.[12] Rather it is a recognition that only a more powerful policy could address the systemic instability inherent in the system of share cross-holdings. Subsequent policies point in the direction of more powerful policies. Japan's Shareholdings Restriction Law of 2001 required banks to reduce shareholdings below their own (tier 1) capital. As shares hit a 19-year low in 2002, the Bank of Japan decided to buy shares from banks to promote financial stability (Bank of Japan, 2005, 5–7), that is, to reduce the linkage between the Topix and Japanese banks' capital (figure 29.6). This drastic measure, taking the central bank some distance from conventional policy, highlighted the challenge that Japan's financial structure posed to financial stability.[13]

Clearly, banking supervision needed to use other tools and to get help from other policies (Committee on the Global Financial System, 2010). In Hong Kong, with interest rates set by the currency board, a progressive tightening of maximum loan-to-value ratios in 1991–1997 helped make banks resilient in the face of the eventual two-thirds decline in real-estate prices (McCauley et al., 1999, chap. 10). In the case of Japan, interest rates could play a role. Despite low consumer-price inflation, Ueda (2000) and Okina and colleagues (2001) judge that interest rates were left too low for too long. The next section discusses the central bank's attempt to restrain lending through quantitative means. Cross-border lending frustrated this effort and so it is worth considering how Basel III's countercyclical buffer interacts with such regulatory arbitrage.

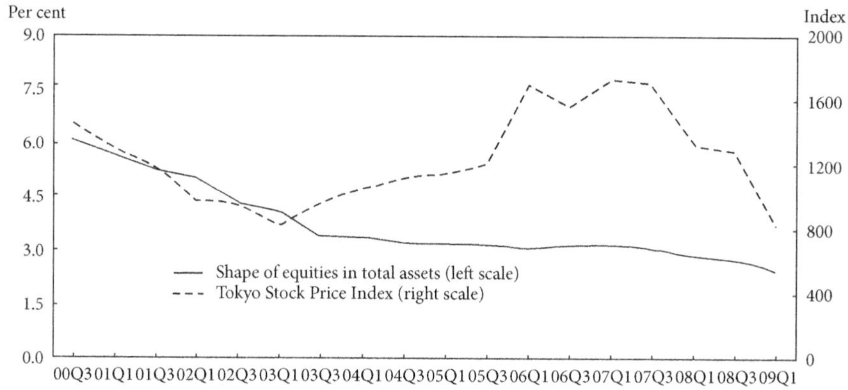


**Figure 29.6** Banks' equity holdings have declined but remain high.
*Source*: Bank of Japan and Datastream in OECD (2009).

## Restrictions on Lending: "Window Guidance"

If the early adoption of Basel I by Japanese banks anticipated the countercyclical buffer in Basel III, another measure by the Japanese authorities in the late 1980s looked back to older practices. As Fukumoto and colleagues (2010) recall, window guidance had been in the Bank of Japan's repertoire since the mid-1950s. Originally applied to city banks that dominated corporate lending and depended on refinancing from the Bank of Japan, quantitative controls had been extended in subsequent periods of stringency to other banks. The opening of the corporate bond market to big firms in the early 1980s led the big banks to enter the market for loans to small and medium-sized enterprises, relying on real-estate collateral. Thus, when the Bank of Japan resorted once again to window guidance in 1987 (Okina et al., 2001), the potential distributional implications had changed from previous occasions (Hoshi et al., 1993). The big banks no longer lent heavily to big companies with share cross-holdings, so tighter window guidance did not necessarily mean that firms with strong bank ties enjoyed preferential access to credit.

Other liberalization moves, however, left the window guidance very partial in its effects. The Foreign Exchange Law of 1980 had removed the vestiges of capital controls. As a result, window guidance that was limited to loans denominated in yen that were booked at domestic offices left a loophole through which a Kubota tractor could fit. To get around the window guidance, Japanese banks booked *dollar* loans at their domestic offices, and they also round-tripped funds from Tokyo to foreign branches, which in turn extended loans to domestic borrowers, mostly in dollars (figure 29.7). Such loans rose from less than $100 billion in the mid-1980s to $400 billion by the end of the decade. Offshore loans by foreign banks present a challenge, given an open capital account, but it is not clear why the Bank of Japan did not try to broaden its window guidance to dollar loans at home or those extended by branches of Japanese banks (e.g., in Hong Kong).

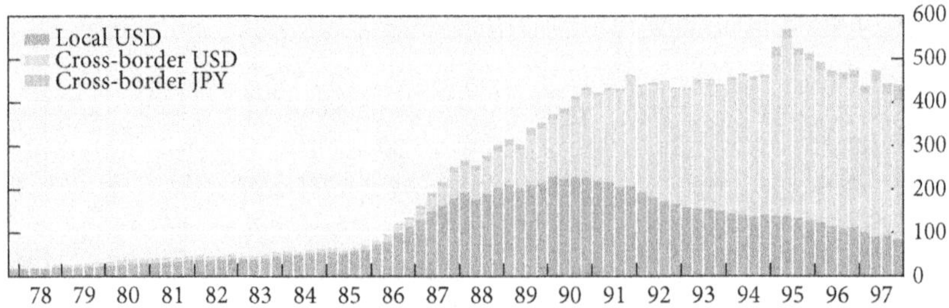


**Figure 29.7** Cross-border and local dollar claims on Japanese nonbanks.
*Source*: BIS.

As noted, window guidance is a throwback to monetary policy in the 1950s through the 1970s, as practiced not only by the Bank of Japan but also by the Bank of England and the Banque de France. The possibility of extending credit from offshore, however, is a problem not only for these old-fashioned tools but also for the new macroprudential tools.

The countercyclical capital buffer, in principle, represents a breakthrough in international cooperation. It will not only apply to home banks' exposures to domestic borrowers. In addition, supervisors in other jurisdictions will apply it to their own (foreign) banks with exposures to host-country borrowers. A form of mutual recognition is called for. If, for instance, the Japanese authorities had required an extra 2.5 percent capital against risk-weighted claims on Japanese obligors, US or European supervisors would have required the same from their own banks that were competing to lend to Japanese borrowers as well.

## What Are the Lessons to Be Drawn from Japan's Post-Bubble Policies?

The following subsections look at bank supervisory policy, fiscal policy, monetary policy, and debt management. Space constraints imply a telegraphic treatment of these issues.

### Bank Supervisory Policy—Why So Long to Clean?

The gap between the peak of the bubble in Japan and widespread capital injections by the government into Japanese banks lasted about 10 years. The policy response to the Nordic banking crisis stands in striking contrast (Borio et al., 2010): fairly early recognition of the problem of widespread distress among bank borrowers, rigorous supervisory challenge of bank valuations, removal of bad loans from banks, and parliamentary appropriation of public funds to recapitalize the banks, including nationalization where necessary and the restructuring of banks to reduce capacity. The Korean authorities adopted something like this set of measures in 1997–1998; the Japanese authorities only then began to get a grip on the required measures (Nakaso, 2001).

If an outside observer asks (OECD, 2009) why Japan took so long to deal with the problem, then answers range widely. Surely the financial system had been managed on a convoy basis and a tiny bank supervision bureaucracy subject to short rotation assignments had not established proper standards for nonperforming loans or disclosure of capital positions. More generally, the Micawber syndrome was evident, as it was hoped that "something [the Nikkei and property prices] would turn up." Recently, Koo and Sasaki (2010) have argued that, while Japanese banks may have held on to their bad loans, they set aside provisions against them starting early in the 1990s; so by the late 1990s they had largely come to grips with their bad credits.

However, an important permissive factor in the gradualist approach was Japan's unusually low reliance on foreign funding to finance its credit boom.[14] When the Nordic or Korean banks' domestic loan books soured, they lost access to the international interbank market on which they had relied for funding. True, Japanese banks were subject to a slow international run in the late 1990s in the so-called Japan premium period in which Japanese banks paid rates above the going rates on dollar loans. But this came quite late in the story in part because of the conviction of external creditors that the Japanese government, having its dollar reserves, were standing behind the banks. Japan's strength as a creditor nation permitted long and costly delay.

And the social standing of bankers in Japan's society must be given its due as a positive internal reason for Japan's delay. Parents sought young bankers as mates for their daughters. The share cross-holdings were more symmetric than the underlying power relationship: main banks sent in managers to firms in distress, but there are no reports of industrial firms sending mangers into distressed banks. Powerful bureaucrats (themselves also prized mates) were supposed to be in a position to resolve problems in big banks. However, "The increasing awareness of ordinary Japanese citizens of widespread connections and informal networks between the political, government and business spheres would become one of the most important impediments to large-scale injections of public funds in the banking industry" (Rixtel, 2002, 190). The Japanese public had to scare itself with domestic runs on the banks before legislators would vote for public bank recapitalization.

The effects of the delay were not confined to the financial sector. As Japanese banks played for time, they kept borrowers without much prospects alive by rolling over loans and in effect paying themselves interest on their loans (so-called evergreening). As a result, the restructuring of the economy away from sectors dependent on leverage was slowed.[15]

## Fiscal Policy—A Reassessment?

A gradual reassessment is taking place regarding Japan's fiscal policy in the so-called lost decade of the 1990s. The fact that the United States has widened its fiscal deficit out to 10 percent is one reason for this. It has done so in response to a recession accompanied by a rise in the household savings rate by about 5 percent of income. This experience affords new perspective on the deterioration of the general government deficit in Japan to the 5–10 percent range in the late 1990s against the backdrop of the 14 percent of GDP swing of Japanese nonfinancial corporations from financial deficit to surplus (Koo, 2003, 7).

The composition of Japan's extraordinary public spending programs in the 1990s may yet come up for a reassessment as well. Observers have derided Japan's bridges to nowhere as misplaced concrete pathways with little contribution to long-term growth. Again, the composition of fiscal stimulus elsewhere may offer a new perspective.

## Monetary Policy—Achievements

Japanese monetary policy also attracted much attention, not all of it favorable, from economists outside of Japan. Reflection on Japanese monetary policy prepared policy makers elsewhere for the challenges of the past several years.[16] Two contributions to monetary practice stand out, while two other policies have a more uncertain legacy.

Japanese monetary policy taught the world that short-term policy rates can go to zero (Shirakawa, 2001). This is no small accomplishment, because banks normally derive much profit from the difference between yields paid to depositors and the wholesale interbank yields. Bankers are never keen on a zero interest-rate policy and a central bank must be free from capture to implement such a policy (Epstein and Ferguson, 1984). Ironically, in the Global Financial Crisis, central banks tended to stop short of zero in setting their policy rates, not in the interest of bank profitability, but to keep the money market alive.

The Bank of Japan demonstrated the "policy duration effect," or the power of a commitment to maintain zero policy rates for some period (Bernanke et al., 2004; Krugman, 1998; Okina and Shiratsuka, 2004; Oda and Ueda, 2007; Ueda, 2005). Through such a commitment the Bank of Japan pushed yields down well out to intermediate maturity bonds. The yield on the 10-year Japanese government bond reached ½ percent, a level that Keynes regarded as impossible owing to fears (well justified in the event) that yields could only go up. Japan's experience taught us that a central bank promising to maintain its policy rate at a very low level for a very long time can drive bond yields to previously unimagineable lows.

So-called quantitative easing, in which bank reserves were pushed up to five times their normal level by the central bank, may count as less an innovation than the above two. In the end, replacing the interbank market with holdings of excess bank reserves at the central bank may have contributed more to financial stability than to monetary policy per se.[17]

Purchases of government bonds by the Bank of Japan seem not to have played a major role. They helped to reach the quantitative easing targets but empirical analysis did not generally find that they lowered bond yields beyond the policy duration effect.[18] This is in contrast to analyses of the Federal Reserve bond buying (Gagnon et al., 2010). Proponents of bond buying hold that the central bank should try harder (Gagnon, 2009, 7). Another view is that the debt managers took the opportunity of central bank bond buying to extend the maturity of the debt, a policy with an echo in the United States today (Turner, 2010).

## Debt Management—The Missed Opportunity

Such observations lead to a question of whether the management of the duration of the government debt for macroeconomic purposes properly belongs with the central bank or the debt manager. Clearly, in using this tool the central bank does not enjoy the monopoly that it has over setting the short-term policy rate (Borio and Disyatat, 2009, 8). The conventional wisdom, after years of increasingly "professional" management of government debt, is that it would confuse the mission of the debt manager to give him what might be considered a monetary assignment (affecting interest rates). Economists writing on the subject often do not pose the question (Auerbach and Obstfeld, 2005; Kuttner, 2006).

However, several considerations suggest that the debt manager is in the better position to change the duration of outstanding government debt (McCauley and Ueda, 2009; Turner, 2010). First, the Treasury's balance sheet is generally substantially larger than that of the central bank. This means that, if the central bank and the debt manager row in different directions, the boat is likely to move in the direction of the debt manager. Second, if the debt manager issues a short-duration obligation instead of, or in exchange for, a long-duration obligation, any subsequent "loss" is only an opportunity loss (interest payments could have been lower with the bond). In contrast, a central bank might register realized losses on its holdings of government bonds, in the extreme leading to a recapitalization of the central bank, possibly at some cost in terms of independence. Finally, a purely debt-management operation avoids the issue of monetization—the financing of the government through money, with all its historical baggage.

In Japan, there were discussions in the Ministry of Finance about helping to reduce long-term yields by depending more heavily on short-term debt. This could have been done without increasing rollover risk with floating-rate notes (a form of which the Ministry actually introduced). There was some public discussion as well (Shirakawa 2001, 479). In the event, it was left to the Bank of Japan, with its relatively small balance sheet, to buy government bonds even as the debt managers lengthened maturities.

### Foreign Exchange Policy—Is It Really Foolproof?

Svennson (2003) argues that the monetary policy can always fend off deflation by forcing a depreciation of the currency. This argument was published in a year in which the Japanese authorities bought hundreds of billions of dollars against a backdrop of economic weakness and deflation. This experience raises two questions regarding Svennson's claim.

First, at a zero interest rate, is sterilized versus unsterilized intervention a distinction without a difference (Ueda, 2000, 2001)? A purchase of foreign exchange can be indifferently financed by a Treasury bill with practically a zero yield or by central bank liabilities at a zero yield. There is evidence of no more than temporary and opportunistic non-sterilization of the Japanese intervention of 2003–2004 (Gerlach et al (2012b). Gerlach and colleagues (2012a) argue that, whatever its effect on the yen's exchange rate, this intervention eased monetary conditions globally: the Japanese investment of the dollars purchased against yen led to a decline in US bond yields that was transmitted to other major bond markets, including Japan's.[19]

Second, this advice may be foolproof for a small economy like that of Sweden, but what about for a larger economy? Taylor (2007) reports that he argued within the US administration to accept the Japanese intervention in 2003 because it was required to ensure the growth of the money supply in Japan. Other interpretations highlight the importance of international political cooperation between Japan and the United States as the quid pro quo. In any case, in the absence of capital controls, depreciation may not be foolproof if the major trading partner does not accept it.

## Conclusions

The main point of this chapter is that one cannot safely conclude too much from the natural experiment of a sharp rise in the required capital of Japanese banks amid the boom of the late 1980s. Japanese banks' huge shareholdings meant that asset prices pumped up the lending capacity of the banking system directly. Under these circumstances, Basel I's fortuitously timed requirements, like Basel III's countercyclical buffer, could not reasonably be expected to restrain credit or to keep the banks sound in the event of lower asset prices. Japan's particular financial structure at the time rendered Japanese banks' mark-to-market capital extraordinarily pro-cyclical and required stronger counter-measures than either Basel I or Basel III.

The short messages are that the expensive delay in cleaning up after the bust may have reflected both the political constraints arising from the industrial and social preeminence of Japanese banks and the lack of dependence of the boom on foreign participation. Japan's fiscal policy in response to the bust may undergo a reappraisal, even though the unsustainability of its current fiscal trajectory is manifest (Cecchetti et al., 2010). Controversy over whether Japan's monetary policy went far enough in unconventional directions should not obscure its acknowledged accomplishments: practical demonstration of a zero interest-rate policy and the efficacy of a commitment to maintain it for some time. It remains a matter of debate whether recommendations that the authorities shorten the duration of the public debt should have been addressed to the fiscal authorities rather than to the central bank. Finally, whether currency depreciation is a foolproof means to ward off deflation remains to be seen.

## Acknowledgments

I have benefited from discussions with Robert Aliber, Claudio Borio, Stephen Cecchetti, Karl Cordewener, Mathias Drehmann, Edward J. Frydl, Clark McCauley, Patrick McGuire, Frank Packer, and Kazuo Ueda. Thanks to Jakub Demski and Michela Scatigna for research assistance. The views expressed here are mine alone and are not necessarily those of the BIS.

## Notes

1. Shirakawa (2001, 471) shows losses on land of twice GDP and losses on equities of up to a half of GDP in the 1990s. See also Okina and colleagues (2001, 401). Koo (2008, 16–17) contrasts Japanese losses on land and equities of three times GDP versus Goldsmith's estimate of one times GDP for the United States after 1929. See also Honohan and Laeven (2005).
2. McCauley and Zimmer (1991) relied on the *Nikkei Money and Bond Newsletter.*
3. "Revaluations can arise…from a notional addition to capital of hidden values which arise from the practice of holding securities in the balance sheet valued at historic costs….[This] is relevant to those banks whose balance sheets traditionally include very substantial amounts of equities held in their portfolio at historic cost but which can be, and on occasions are, realised at current prices and used to offset losses. The Committee considers these 'latent' revaluation reserves can be included among supplementary elements of capital since they can be used to absorb losses on a going-concern basis, provided they are subject to a substantial discount in order to reflect concerns both about market volatility and

about the tax charge which would arise were such cases to be realised. A discount of 55 percent on the difference between the historic cost book value and market value is agreed to be appropriate" (BCBS, 2006, 15).

4. Indeed, without the 45 percent of such gains counting toward tier 2, the incentives to realize the gains to add to tier 1 capital would have been all the stronger. Because realizations were costly to the banks' underlying equity insofar as the 55 percent tax became due, if the tier 2 recognition of the unrealized gains inhibited realization, it may have actually contributed to the capital strength of Japanese banks. See below.
5. Guiso and colleagues (2008, 2590) find that a legal enforcement proxy as well as the World Value Survey trust response had predicted the percentage of the population that participated directly in the stock market.
6. There was also a more directed policy attempting to reduce the growth of lending against real-estate collateral. Domestically, banks extended credit to real-estate through nonbank financial firms (e.g., *jusen*)—a shadow banking system story.
7. According to McCauley and Seth (1992), the foreign bank share of commercial and industrial loans to US firms rose from one-fifth to one-third between 1984 and 1987, with the Japanese banks in the lead. See Sullivan (1992).
8. Okina and colleagues (2001, 414) show that the big Japanese banks almost doubled their tier 1 capital between March 1988 and March 1990, while their risk assets rose by less than a half.
9. Miyajima and Kuroki (2007, 81) publish Nippon Life data that show that banks' holdings of listed firms' equity actually rose from 14.9 percent at the end of the fiscal year in 1987 to 15.7 percent at the end of the fiscal year in 1990. Only from 1997 on, when the recognition of loan losses bit, did Japanese banks actually consistently sell off cross-held shares. See also McGuire (2009):
10. The Ministry of Finance tightened the carry-back rules in the 1990s, preventing banks from reaching back to recover those tax payments when the Japanese banks began recognizing their losses.
11. The figure is based on only the gross claims of the monetary system on the private nonfinancial sector from the Bank of Japan's monetary survey. A broader measure from the flow of funds, with a higher ratio of private debt to GDP, shows a similar pattern.
12. There is a question about whether Japanese banks' capital in the late 1980s, given full realization of capital gains on shareholdings, would have met the stringent standards of Basel III (BCBS, 2010a, 2010b). Kane and colleagues (1991) imply a positive answer.
13. Under Basel II (BCBS, 2006), there are several possibilities (paragraphs 340–355). One, based on simple risk weights, attaches a 300 percent risk weight to publicly traded equities. Another, based on internal models, sets a floor of a 200 percent risk weight for traded equities. Yet another, based on the probability of default/loss given default, sets a floor of 100 percent for certain equities (paragraph 352). The phase-in period for existing equity holdings ends in 2014.
14. See Aliber and Zoega (2011) for a bubble economy very dependent on foreign credit.
15. See Ahearne and Shinada (2005), Hoshi et al. (2004), Peek and Rosengren (2005), and Sekine et al. (2003).
16. See Ahearne et al. (2002), Bernanke (2002, 2003), Bernanke et al. (2004), Clouse et al. (2000), and Congdon (2010). For an updated review, see Ueda (2012).

17. Baba and colleagues (2005) find that the dispersion of certificate of deposit rates across banks was low during the quantitative easing period.
18. See Oda and Ueda (2007); however, Bernanke and colleagues (2004) find that Bank of Japan purchases of government bonds had lowered bond yields.
19. On the effectiveness of the intervention in holding down the yen's exchange rate, see Ito's (2004, 2005) and Fatum's (2010) findings for the effectiveness of the intervention and Fatum and Hutchison's (2005, 2010) findings against. See also Galati et al. (2005).

## References

Ahearne, A., G. Gagnon, J. Haltimaier, and J. Kamin. (2002). "Preventing Deflation: Lessons from Japan's Experience in the 1990s." International Finance Discussion Papers No. 729. Board of Governors of the Federal Reserve System.

Ahearne, A. G., and Naoki Shinada. (2005). "Zombie Firms and Economic Stagnation in Japan." *International Economics and Economic Policy* 2: 363–381.

Alesina, A., and E. La Ferrara. (2002). "Who Trusts Others?" *Journal of Public Economics* 85: 207–234.

Aliber, R. Z., and G. Zoega. (2011). *Preludes to the Icelandic Financial Crisis.* Basingstoke: Palgrave Macmillan.

Aoki, M., H. Patrick, and P. Sheard. (1994). "Introductory Overview." In M. Aoki and H. Patrick, eds., *The Japanese Main Bank System*, 3–50. Oxford: Clarendon Press.

Auerbach, A. J., and M. Obstfeld. (2005). "The Case for Open-Market Purchases in a Liquidity Trap." *American Economic Review* 95(1): 110–137.

Baba, N., S. Nishioka, N. Oda, M. Shirakawa, K. Ueda, and H. Ugai. (2005). "Japan's Deflation, Problems in the Banking System and Monetary Policy." BIS Working Papers No. 188.

Bank of Japan. (2005). *Financial Stability Report: Measures Taken by the Bank of Japan for Financial System Stability.* August. Tokyo: Bank of Japan.

Basel Committee on Banking Supervision (BCBS). (2006). "Basel II: International Convergence of Capital Measurement and Capital Standards: A Revised Framework—Comprehensive Version." June.

Basel Committee on Banking Supervision (BCBS). (2009). "Consultative Proposals to Strengthen the Resilience of the Banking Sector Announced by the Basel Committee." December.

Basel Committee on Banking Supervision (BCBS). (2010a). "Group of Governors and Heads of Supervision Announces Higher Global Minimum Capital Standards." September 12.

Basel Committee on Banking Supervision (BCBS). (2010b). "The Basel Committee's Response to the Financial Crisis: Report to the G20." October.

Baumeister, R., E. Bratslavsky, C. Finkenauer, and K. Vohs. (2001). "Bad Is Stronger Than Good." *Review of General Psychology* 5(4): 323–370.

Bernanke, B. (2002). "Deflation: Making Sure 'It' Doesn't Happen Here." Speech given before the National Economists Club in Washington, DC, November 21.

Bernanke, B. (2003). "Some Thoughts on Monetary Policy in Japan." Remarks to the Japan Society for Monetary Economics, May 31.

Bernanke, B., V. Reinhart, and B. Sack. (2004). "Monetary Policy Alternatives at the Zero Bound: An Empirical Assessment." *Brookings Papers on Economic Activity* 94(2): 1–78.

Borio, C., and P. Disyatat. (2009). "Unconventional Monetary Policies: An Appraisal." BIS Working Papers No. 292, November.

Borio., C, B. Vale, and G. von Peter. (2010). "Resolving the Financial Crisis: Are the Lessons from the Nordics Being Heeded?" BIS Working Papers No. 311, June.

Caruana, J. (2010a). "Macroprudential Policy: Could It Have Been Different This Time?" Speech to the People's Bank of China Seminar on Macroprudential Policy, in cooperation with the International Monetary Fund, Shanghai, October 18.

Caruana, J. (2010b). "Why Basel III Matters for Latin American and Caribbean Financial Markets." Speech to the ASBA-FSI High-Level Meeting on "The Emerging Framework to Strengthen Financial Stability and Regulatory Priorities in the Americas," Antigua, November 19.

Cecchetti, S., M. Mohanty, and F. Zampolli. (2010). "The Future of Public Debt: Prospects and Implications." BIS Working Papers No. 300, March.

Clouse, J., et al. (2003). "Monetary Policy When the Nominal Short-Term Interest Rate Is Zero." *Topics in Macroeconomics* Pages 1–63, ISSN (Online) 1534–5998, DOI: 10.2202/1534-5998.1088, September3(1).

Committee on the Global Financial System. (2010). "Macroprudential Instruments and Frameworks: A Stocktaking of Issues and Experiences." CGFS Papers No. 38, May.

Congdon, T. (2010). "Monetary Policy at the Zero Bound." *World Economics* 11(1) (January–March): 11–46.

Drehmann, M., C. Borio, L. Gambacorta, G. Jimenez, and C. Trucharte. (2010). "Countercyclical Capital Buffers: Exploring Options." BIS Working Papers No. 317, July.

Epstein, G., and T. Ferguson. (1984). "Monetary Policy, Loan Liquidation, and Industrial Conflict: The Federal Reserve and the Open Market Operations of 1932." *Journal of Economic History* 44(4) (December): 957–983.

Fatum, R. (2010). "Foreign Exchange Intervention When Interest Rates Are Zero: Does the Portfolio Balance Channel Matter After All?" Federal Reserve Bank of Dallas, Globalization and Monetary Policy Institute Working Paper No. 57, July.

Fatum, R., and M. Hutchison. (2005). "Foreign Exchange Intervention and Monetary Policy in Japan, 2003–04." *International Economics and Economic Policy*, 2: 250–259.

Fatum, R., and M. Hutchison. (2010). "Evaluating Foreign Exchange Market Intervention: Self-Selection, Counterfactuals and Average Treatment Effects." *Journal of International Money and Finance* 29: 570–584.

Fukumoto, T., M. Higashi, Y. Inamura, and T. Kimura. (2010). "Effectiveness of Window Guidance and Financial Environment—In Light of Japan's Experience of Financial Liberalization and a Bubble Economy." *Bank of Japan Review*, 2010-E-4, August.

Gagnon, J. (2009). "The World Needs Further Monetary Ease, Not an Early Exit." Peterson Institute for International Economics Policy Brief 09–22, December.

Gagnon, J., M. Raskin, J. Remaché, and B. Sack. (2010). "Large-Scale Asset Purchases by the Federal Reserve: Did They Work?" Federal Reserve Bank of New York Staff Reports No. 441, March.

Galati, G., W. Melick, and M. Micu. (2005). "Foreign Exchange Market Intervention and Expectations: An Empirical Study of the Yen/Dollar Exchange Rate." *Journal of International Money and Finance* 24: 982–1011.

Gerlach-Kristen, P., R. McCauley, and K. Ueda. (2012a). "Currency Intervention and the Global Portfolio Balance Effect," BIS Working Papers no 389, October.

Gerlach-Kristen, P., R. McCauley, and K. Ueda. (2012b). "Did the Bank of Japan Sterilise the Ministry of Finance Currency Intervention in 2003–2004?" Manuscript.

Giannetti, M., and Y. Koskinen. (2010). "Investor Protection, Equity Returns and Financial Globalization." *Journal of Financial and Quantitative Analysis* 45(1) (February): 135–168.

Guiso, L., P. Sapienza, and L. Zingales. (2008). "Trusting the Stock Market." *Journal of Finance* 58(6) (December): 2557–2600.

Honohan, P., and L. Laeven, eds. (2005). *Systemic Financial Crises: Containment and Resolution*. Cambridge: Cambridge University Press.

Hoshi, T., and A. K. Kashyap. (2000). "The Japanese Banking Crisis: Where Did It Come From and How Will It End?" In B. Bernanke and J. Rotemberg, eds., *NBER Macroeconomics Annual 1999* 14: 129–201.

Hoshi, T., D. Scharfstein, and K. J. Singleton. (1993). "Japanese Corporate Investment and Bank of Japan Guidance of Commercial Bank Lending." In K. J. Singleton, ed., *Japanese Monetary Policy*. Chicago: University of Chicago Press.

Hoshi, T., D. Scharfstein, and K. J. Singleton. (2004). "Japan's Financial Crisis and Economic Stagnation." *Journal of Economic Perspectives* 18(1): 3–26.

Ito, T. (2004). "The Yen and the Japanese Economy, 2004." In C. F. Bergsten and J. Williamson, eds., *Dollar Adjustment: How Far? Against What?*, 171–196. Washington, DC: Institute for International Economics, 2004.

Ito, T. (2005). "Interventions and Japanese Economic Recovery." *International Economics and Economic Policy* 2: 219–239.

Ito, T., and Yuri N. Sasaki. (2002). "Impacts of the Basel Capital Standard on Japanese Banks' Behaviour." *Journal of the Japanese and International Economies* 16: 372–397.

Kane, E. J., K. Anul, and A. Demiurgic-Kunt. (1991). "The Capital Positions of Japanese Banks." In G. Rhee and R. P. Chang, eds., *Pacific-Basin Capital Markets Research, Volume II*, 125–141. Amsterdam: Elsevier.

Kapstein, E. (1991). *Supervising International Banks, Origins and Implications of the Basel Accord, Princeton Essays in International Finance*. Department of Economics. International Finance Section. Princeton, NJ: Princeton University.

Kindleberger, C. P., and R. Z. Aliber. (2005). *Manias, Panics and Crashes*. 6th ed. Basingstoke: Palgrave Macmillen.

Koo, R. (2003). *Balance Sheet Recession*. Singapore: Wiley.

Koo, R. (2008). *The Holy Grail of Macroeconomics: Lessons from Japan's Great Recession*. Singapore: Wiley.

Koo, R., and M. Sasaki. (2010). "Japan's Disposal of Bad Loans: Failure or Success?" Nomura Research Institute NRI Papers No. 151, March 1.

Krugman, P. (1998). "It's Back: Japan's Slump and the Return of the Liquidity Trap." *Brookings Papers on Economic Activity* 2: 137–205.

Kuttner, K. (2006). "Can Central Banks Target Bond Prices?" NBER Working Paper 12454, August.

McCauley, R., J. Ruud, and F. Iacono. (1999). *Dodging Bullets: Changing US Corporate Capital Structures in the 1980s and 1990s*. Cambridge, MA: MIT Press.

McCauley, R., and R. Seth. (1992). "Foreign Bank Credit to US Corporations: The Implications of Offshore Loans." *Federal Reserve Bank of New York Quarterly Review* 17 (Spring): 52–65.

McCauley, Robert N., and Kazuo Ueda. (2009). "Government Debt Management at Low Interest Rates." *BIS Quarterly Review* June: 35–51.

McCauley, Robert N., and Steven A. Zimmer. (1991). "Bank Cost of Capital and International Competition." *Federal Reserve Bank of New York Quarterly Review* 15: 33–59.

McGuire, P. (2009). "Bank Ties and Firm Performance in Japan: Some Evidence Since Fiscal 2002." *Bank of Japan Monetary and Economic Studies* 27 (November): 99–141.

Miyajima, H., and F. Kuroki. (2007). "The Unwinding of Cross-Shareholding: Causes, Effects and Implications." In M. Aoki, G. Jackson, and H. Miyajima, eds., *Corporate Governance in Japan*. Oxford: Oxford University Press.

Nakaso, H. (2001). "The Financial Crisis in Japan during the 1990s: How the Bank of Japan Responded and the Lessons Learnt." BIS Papers No. 6.

Oda, N., and K. Ueda (2007). "The Effects of the Bank of Japan's Zero Interest Rate Commitment and Quantitative Monetary Easing on the Yield Curve: A Macro-Finance Approach." *Japanese Economic Review* 58(3): 303–328.

OECD. (2009). "Financial Stability: Overcoming the Crisis and Improving the Efficiency of the Banking Sector." *Economic Survey of Japan 2009* 18 (September): 47–73.

Okina, K., M. Shirakawa, and S. Shiratsuka. (2001). "The Asset Price Bubble and Monetary Policy: Japan's Experience in the late 1980s and the Lessons." *Bank of Japan Monetary and Economic Studies* 19 (February): 395–450 .

Okina, K., and S. Shiratsuka. (2004). "Policy Commitment and Expectation Formation: Japan's Experience under Zero Interest Rates." *North American Journal of Economics and Finance* 15: 75–100.

Peek, Joe, and Eric S. Rosengren. (2005). "Unnatural Selection: Perverse Incentives and the Misallocation of Credit in Japan." *American Economic Review* 95(4): 1144–1166.

Pettway, R., T. Kaneko, and M. T. Young. (1991). "International Bank Capital Standards and the Costs of Issuing Capital Securities by Japanese Banks." *Journal of Banking and Finance* 15(3): 559–580.

Porter, M. E. (1992). "Capital Disadvantage: America's Failing Capital Investment System." *Harvard Business Review* 70: 65–82.

Rixtel, A. van (2002). *Informality and Monetary Policy in Japan: The Political Economy of Bank Performance*. Cambridge: Cambridge University Press.

Rozin, P., and E. B. Royzman. (2001). "Negativity Bias, Negativity Dominance, and Contagion." *Personality and Social Psychology Review* 5: 296–320.

Sabini, J. (1992). *Social Psychology*. New York: W. W. Norton.

Sekine, T., K. Kobayashi, and Y. Saita. (2003). "Forbearance Lending: The Case of Japanese Firms." *Monetary and Economic Studies* 21(2): 69–91.

Seth, R., and A. Quijano. (1991). "Japanese Banks' Customers in the United States." *Federal Reserve Bank of New York Quarterly Review* 16(1): 79–82.

Sheard, P. (1991). "The Economics of Interlocking Shareholding in Japan." *Ricerche Economiche* 45(2–3): 421–448.

Shirakawa, M. (2001). "Monetary Policy under the Zero Interest Rate Constraint and Balance Sheet Adjustment." *International Finance* 4: 463–489.

Sullivan, J. (1992). *Invasion of the Salarymen: The Japanese Business Presence in America*. Westport, CT: Praeger.

Svennson, L. (2003). "Escaping from a Liquidity Trap and Deflation: The Foolproof Way and Others." *Journal of Economic Perspectives* 17(4): 145–166.

Taylor, J. B. (2007). *Global Financial Warriors: The Untold Story of International Finance in the Post-9/11 World*. New York: W. W. Norton.

Turner, P. (2010). "Fiscal Dominance, the Long-Term Interest Rate and Central Banks." Paper presented to a Bank of Norway conference, "What Is a Useful Central Bank?" Oslo, November 18.

Ueda, K. (2000a). "Causes of Japan's Banking Problems." In T. Hoshi and H. Patrick, eds., *Crisis and Change in the Japanese Financial System*, 59–81. Boston: Kluwer Academic.

Ueda, K. (2000b). "Japan's Experience with Zero Interest Rates." *Journal of Money Credit and Banking* 32(4): 1107–1109.

Ueda, K. (2001). "Japan's Liquidity Trap and Monetary Policy." Speech to the Japan Society of Monetary Economics, Fukushima University, September 29.

Ueda, K. (2005). "The Bank of Japan's Struggle with the Zero Lower Bound on Nominal Interest Rates: Exercises in Expectations Management." *International Finance* 8(2): 329–350.

Ueda, K. (2011). "Japan's Bubble, the USA's Bubble and China's Bubble." *China and the World Economy* 19(1): 47–62.

Ueda, K (2012). "Deleveraging and Monetary Policy: Japan Since the 1990s and the United States Since 2007." *Journal of Economic Perspectives* 26 (4): 1–27.

Vogel, E. (1979). *Japan as Number One: Lessons for America*. Cambridge, MA: Harvard University Press.

White, William R. (2009). "Should Monetary Policy 'Lean or Clean' "? Federal Reserve Bank of Dallas, Globalization and Monetary Policy Institute, Working Paper No. 34, August.

Wolf, M. (2012). "Lunch with the FT: Paul Krugman" *Financial Times*, 26 May.

CHAPTER 30

# THE ROLE OF THE FEDERAL RESERVE

## LENDER OF LAST RESORT

CHRISTOPHER RUDE

THE US banking crisis linked mortgages and money by way of securitization and credit derivatives. It originated in the US housing and related mortgage markets, which came under pressure in 2006, but it soon spread to the rest of the US economy and then to the rest of the world. It began in earnest in August 2007, when the turmoil moved from the securitized US mortgage markets to the interbank dollar funding market, causing it to freeze up on August 9 (FRBNY, 2008c, 28). Worries about the extent and distribution of the mortgage-related losses had become so extensive that market participants no longer had faith in one another's creditworthiness, and the market that provides US banks and other dollar-based financial institutions with their liquidity became illiquid as a result. An already very troubled financial system was imploding because the large commercial banks, investment houses, and insurance companies that were at the heart of the US financial system could not borrow short-term from one another, and this was happening just when a loss of confidence was sending liquidity preferences soaring. Asset-backed commercial paper (ABCP), much of it built on now-questionable mortgage credit derivatives, was the vehicle. No one knew how to value it. No one knew which mortgages were involved. Then, in September 2008, the entire US banking and financial system collapsed as a social financial system in a period of acute turmoil as violent and decisive as that of the banking crisis of 1931. From this point forward, what at first appeared as a US-based "subprime mortgage market crisis" revealed itself to be a financial crisis of major proportions.

Under the impact of these developments, the profits of US banks, insurance companies, and securities firms fell from $380 billion in the second quarter of 2007 to $243 billion in the second quarter of 2008, then to *minus* $53 billion in the fourth quarter: the first quarterly loss since the 1930s (BEA, 2010). Financial firms continued to make dividend payments. The losses were taken from retained earnings. Financial-sector profits had been $468 billion in 2006 at the height of the construction boom.

What happened between August 2007 and September 2008 that caused matters to come to a head in this way? The US financial system was wounded by the time the dollar funding market froze up in the third quarter of 2007. In the interim, however, the general macroeconomy weakened, and this pulled asset prices down. A classic debt deflation was under way, with falling financial and real-estate prices feeding on one another in a downward spiral. The crisis, accordingly, spread from the interbank market outward while it simultaneously exploded globally. Investors everywhere were scrambling to reduce their leverage, meet rising margin calls, raise capital, and otherwise reduce their losses and exposures. But it was already difficult if not impossible for the major US financial institutions to flee their risky and losing investments to the safety of "money" because a safe, private-sector money had ceased to exist. Credit derivatives amplified the turmoil. Many investors discovered that the credit insurance they thought they had bought in the form of derivatives was illusionary. Others used naked credit default swaps to bet in favor of a competitor's downgrade or bankruptcy. The explosion came in September 2008 when the turmoil leaped from the interbank dollar funding market to the commercial paper market, precipitating a run on money market mutual funds with devastating effects on the broader economy. For a time, the US financial system stopped "intermediating between savers and investors," and this disruption of the circulation of US interest-bearing capital disrupted the circulation of productive capital across the globe, making US financial capital politically responsible for a world economic crisis.

The blockage did not last long, however. Financial markets stabilized, investors regained their confidence, stock prices rebounded, and, beginning in early 2009, US banks, insurance companies, and securities firms became profitable again. Domestic financial profits increased to $142 billion in the first quarter of 2009, then to $247 billion in the fourth quarter of 2009 and then $359 billion in the second quarter of 2010 (BEA, 2010). Sometime in 2009, US financial capital began to reassert itself again, and as it did so, the US economy stopped weakening and the profits of US nonfinancial corporations rebounded and layoffs abated. As measured by GDP, the US economy began growing again. By the end of the year, a weak, "jobless" recovery was under way.

What happened to turn matters around? The US state in the form of the Federal Reserve intervened to stabilize its financial system. The US monetary authority lowered its emergency lending interest rate to zero. Beginning in December 2007, it established a system of credit facilities designed to stabilize the interbank market under which it advanced its credit against increasingly bad collateral. In September 2008, it used these emergency lending programs to flood the US financial system with vast quantities of its own zero-interest rate, but essentially riskless security. Finally and equally important, as the US financial system recovered and gained strength in 2009, the Federal Reserve withdrew its emergency lending support from the US financial system, choosing instead to underwrite it through the purchase of US Treasury, government-sponsored enterprise (GSE), and GSE mortgage-backed securities (MBS).

The Federal Reserve did not and probably could not prevent the crisis from worsening over time, but it did bring order to the US financial system as it was failing. During the emergency, it lent freely against collateral, some of it questionable, thereby taking on its financial system's credit and liquidity risks. When money market conditions improved, it gave its support to the mortgage market, underwriting its securitization, taking on additional credit and liquidity risks. In exchange, it provided the US banking system with a costless "riskless" security, into which it could collapse, and in sufficient quantities to make its collapse orderly. Not a private-sector security, this was a politically riskless security and economically riskless because it was sanctioned by the Federal Reserve as an institution of the capitalist state. The policy necessarily involved a disciplining of US interest-bearing capital. For its policies to work, the Federal Reserve had to make certain that its credit was impeccable: there would be no default on a Federal Reserve loan or any other asset in its portfolio. By asserting its autonomy vis-á-vis private capital in this way, it re-established the political power of US financial capital. It acted as US financial capital's political center, enabling US financial capital to resume the role it had previously played since at least the early 1980s in the circulation and control of a large part of the United States and the world's aggregate social capital. US financial capital came out of the crisis temporarily weakened but not out of power.

In August 2007, the US financial system began to unravel; in September 2008, the circuit of US financial capital came to a halt, precipitating a major economic downturn; in early 2009, the circuit of US financial capital resumed its course. Assuming that the crisis unfolded in this way, this paper reviews the Federal Reserve's response to the crisis from its inception in August 2007 to April 2010, when one of its more important emergency lending facilities, the Term Auction Facility (TAF), was finally retired. It explores three questions: (1) What specifically did the Federal Reserve do to end the financial crisis? (2) How did its policies work economically and politically? And (3) What were the effects of the US state's emergency response to the crisis on its banking and financial-market regulations?

## The Response of the US State to the Financial Crisis

The Federal Reserve's response to the crisis was not superstructural but material. The US central bank changed how it interacted economically with its financial system, and by changing its material connection with US interest-bearing capital in this way, it changed the US financial system, giving US interest-bearing capital a new and different, fundamentally political, unity embodied in its new operating procedures. Prior to the emergency, open-market operations (OMOs) in the US Treasury market were the Fed's principal policy tools. Only banks maintained reserve accounts at the Fed, and only US banks could borrow from the Fed's primary discount window. The Federal Reserve held US Treasury securities on the asset side of its balance sheet (its portfolio of loans, foreign exchange, and other assets was tiny by comparison). And the Federal Reserve used its OMOs in the US Treasury market to target the overnight federal funds rate, the assumption being that monetary policy affects the economy through its effects on financial institutions' cost of funds. After August 2007, the Fed began to behave differently.[1]

US monetary authorities responded to the crisis in a traditional manner with a swift and large reduction in their official interest rates, and by the end of 2008, the Federal Reserve's overnight federal funds target rate, at just above 0.0 percent, would be close to what Federal Reserve Chairman Ben Bernanke has called its "zero lower bound," meaning, because nominal interest rates can only be positive, further interest-rate reductions were impossible.[2] But the Fed took three other steps that together implied an abandonment of the central bank's traditional monetary-policy practices, including the targeting of the federal funds rate. First, and beginning in December 2007, the Federal Reserve reorganized itself as a financial institution, that is, it changed the way in which it provided credit to the financial system, to whom and on what terms. Recognizing that US interest rates were already low ahead of the crisis and that the breakdown of the interbank market could not be solved by a simple reduction in interest rates, it became a direct lender to a wide variety of financial institutions and not just to commercial banks or within the United States, thereby taking on the active management of the United States' global credit and liquidity risks. Second, after holding the total size of its balance sheet roughly constant since August 2007, in September 2008, to counter the contractionary shock that the events of that month were sending through the world economy, the Federal Reserve used the ability to lend that it had developed in the interim to engineer the largest increases in bank reserves in US history, increases in reserves more than necessary to push the federal funds rate to zero and which US banks absorbed as excess reserves. Third, beginning in early 2009 and as liquidity returned to the funding markets, the Federal Reserve gradually reduced the amount of reserves that it supplied through its emergency lending programs, but as it did so it replaced them with reserves supplied through the open-market purchase of long-dated US Treasury, GSE, and agency MBS, thus keeping its asset total roughly constant at its new historically high level. OMOs were once again the preferred policy tool but these were operations in the agency debt or agency MBS market, not just the Treasury market, and interest rates remained at their zero lower bound.

## The Federal Reserve's Response to the Crisis: The Details

On December 17, 2007, the Federal Reserve established two new lending facilities: a TAF, under which it lent US banks federal funds for one month (rather than overnight) through regularly scheduled auctions, and a system of foreign exchange swap lines with foreign central banks, under which it gave its partner central banks access to the dollars that they then lent to their own troubled banks (Armantier, Krieger, and McAndrews 2008; Board, 2010c, 2010d; FRBNY, 2008a, 2008b, 2008c; Fleming and Klagge, 2010; McAndrews, Sarker, and Wang, 2008). These two facilities quickly became the principal means by which the US central bank created new credit. Meanwhile, behind the scenes, the Fed adjusted its portfolio of US Treasury securities to accommodate its new reliance on lending (FRBNY, 2008c, 2009). As the Fed increased the amount of credit created through the TAF and swap lines, it reduced its holdings of US Treasuries by a similar amount, thus keeping the total size of the Federal Reserve's portfolio of loans and securities as well as the size of its liabilities to depository institutions in the form of bank reserves roughly constant. In response to acute instability that overtook the US financial markets in March 2008, it established a Term Securities Lending Program (TSLP) under which it began lending primary dealers US Treasury securities against a wide variety of collateral, including private-label MBS, seized $30 billion in nonperforming mortgage-related credit securities from Bear Stearns on the 14th, facilitating its forced purchase by JPMorgan Chase two days later, and this gave primary dealers and thus investment banks access to its discount window (Board, 2010c, 2010d; FRBNY, 2008a, 2008b, 2009; Fleming, Hrung, and Keane, 2008). All the while, it was careful to sterilize any effects that these actions might have on the supply of central bank credit through reverse OMOs in the US Treasury market.

The Federal Reserve's initial response to the crisis was thus a radical one. Between December 2007 and March 2008, the Federal Reserve transformed itself from being a participant in the US Treasury market into a direct lender, replacing US Treasuries with less liquid and creditworthy loans on the asset side of its balance sheet. It extended term and overnight Federal Reserve credit to US banks and nonbanks alike (in keeping with the 1998 repeal of Glass-Steagall) and it provided dollar credit to foreign central banks, not for exchange-rate purposes but to maintain the liquidity of the offshore as well as the domestic dollar funding markets. And it absorbed a large quantity of distressed assets, increasing its risks incalculably. But it did not supply new monies, engaging in a swap of its good and liquid credit for the private sector's bad and frozen credit instead. The policy was simple: the Federal Reserve took measures to bring the US money market back to life, assuming that the US financial system as a whole had enough if not the right kind of liquidity in the right places, and as it was increasing its lending, it accepted increasingly less creditworthy securities as collateral, all the while reducing its holdings of "safe" US Treasuries to keep the money supply constant. This was not an interest-rate policy. The Fed was assuming responsibility for US interest-bearing capital's liquidity and credit risks in policies that have since then come to be called "toxic waste-removal" policies.

The increase in the stock of high-powered state money that came in September 2008 was an emergency measure, driven by events that were occurring on the ground in a confused, rapidly changing, and fluid situation that included the US Treasury's takeover of Fannie Mae and Freddie Mac, Lehman Brothers' bankruptcy on the 15th, the transformation of the two remaining "bulge bracket" US investment banks (Goldman Sachs and Morgan Stanley) into bank holding companies, and the creation (at least on paper) of the US Treasury's $700 billion Troubled Assets Relief Program (TARP) as well as a rapid weakening of the underlying real economy both in the United States and elsewhere. The increase was also not operationally neutral. As it was increasing the money supply, the Fed was organizing itself again in a second wave of reform that did not alter as much as it consolidated and built on the steps taken earlier. It took over the multinational insurance company American International Group (AIG) on the16th, launched a series of programs designed to support the commercial paper market, including a Commercial Paper Funding Facility (CPFF), under which it began purchasing ABCP from issuers, and started paying interest on bank reserves (Board, 2010c, 2010d; FRBNY, 2008a, 2008b, 2008c, 2009; Tobi, Kimbrough, and Marchioni, 2009). More than necessary to bring the federal funds rate to zero, the increase meant a change in the Fed's response to the crisis from a simple asset swap to a policy that Bernanke has called a "quantitative easing." But here, too, the process was one of consolidation rather than repudiation. The increase was accomplished using the TAF, dollar swap lines with foreign central bankers, newly created CPFF, and an expanded discount window—all products of the crisis—and its effects on the Federal Reserve's credit and liquidity risks were as immense as its sheer size. One also has to keep in mind that the Federal Reserve, even then fearful of the inflationary implications of its policies, took measures to drain reserves from the banking system, working together with the US Treasury, using a Supplemental Financing Program (SFP) created two days after Lehman Brothers' demise, for this purpose.[3]

US and foreign financial markets entered a very troubled period following the September events. Lehman's bankruptcy was particularly damaging. Commercial paper had been one of its specialties, and when it was suddenly absent, the turmoil leaped from the interbank to the broader money markets. The explosion came when one money market fund that had extensive dealings with Lehman could not keep the value of its currency on par with the US dollar. It "broke the buck," precipitating a run on money market mutual funds. A panic went through the US financial system, causing it, and not just its financial markets, to freeze up. An international banking and financial system based on the hegemony of the major US investment banks, commercial banks, securities firms, and insurance companies fell apart.

It soon became apparent, however, that the Fed's massive lending program was having its intended effect. In early 2009, the financial system came to life: confidence improved; prices for US banks, insurance companies, and securities firms rose in the equity markets (raising capital adequacy ratios); and banking and finance became profitable again. As US financial capital began to circulate again, the broader economy stabilized.

Under these circumstances, the Federal Reserve undertook a new set of policy initiatives. Most important, it launched a Large-Scale Asset Purchase (LSAP) program under which it purchased large quantities of Treasury, agency debt, and agency mortgage-backed securities in the open market and for its own account, and it gradually reduced the amount of credit extended through its various emergency lending programs—all the while holding its portfolio of loans and securities roughly constant at its new historically high level (FRBNY, 2009, 2010a). Under the LSAP, the US monetary authority purchased $300 billion of long-dated Treasury securities, $172 billion of agency debt securities, and an astonishing $1.25 trillion of agency MBS by the end of 2009, thereby acknowledging without openly saying so that all three types of securities had government guarantee. It simultaneously let the amount of credit it had extended under the TAF, the dollar swap lines, the CPFF, and various other emergency lending programs decline. These were temporary credit facilities. To end them, it let them mature without renewing them, in actions coordinated concretely with the asset purchases. To keep total assets constant, maturing credits were rolled over into asset purchases. The Federal Reserve completed all its purchases under the LSAP in March 2010. Most of the Fed's emergency credit facilities, including the foreign central bank dollar swap line, were closed that February. The TAF was closed on April 8, 2010.

## Effect on the Fed's Balance Sheet and the Money Supply

The effects of all these developments on the composition and size of the Federal Reserve's portfolio of assets and thus on its risk exposures and bank reserves are astonishing (see table 30.1). On August 15, 2007, at the onset of the crisis, 96 percent

**Table 30.1** Size and composition of Federal Reserve assets on selected dates, August 2007–April 2010 (millions of US dollars or percentage of total Federal Bank credit

| | Reserve Bank Credit | Treasuries Held Outright, Net of Those Lent Term | Federal Agency Debt | Federal Agency MBS | Treasuries Lent Term | Repurchase Agreements | Discount Borrowing | Term Auction Credit | Central bank FX Swaps | CPFF | Assets seized from Bear-Stearns and AIG | Float and Other Federal Reserve assets |
|---|---|---|---|---|---|---|---|---|---|---|---|---|
| 08/15/07 | 850,981 | 789,601 | – | – | – | 24,000 | 264 | – | – | – | – | 37,115 |
| 12/19/07 | 872,709 | 769,755 | – | – | – | 57,750 | 4,765 | – | – | – | – | 40,438 |
| 03/12/08 | 881,876 | 703,436 | – | – | – | 77,000 | 28 | 60,000 | – | – | – | 41,412 |
| 09/10/08 | 910,817 | 363,883 | – | – | 115,899 | 126,750 | 23,556 | 150,000 | 62,000 | – | 29,327 | 39,401 |
| 12/17/08 | 2,239,399 | 293,792 | 17,621 | – | 182,346 | 80,000 | 206,544 | 447,959 | 583,135 | 318,843 | 66,597 | 42,564 |
| 04/14/10 | 2,321,445 | 776,711 | 168,903 | 1,101,874 | – | – | 79,325 | – | – | 7,809 | 90,569 | 96,255 |
| 08/15/07 | 100.0% | 92.8% | 0.0% | 0.0% | 0.0% | 2.8% | 0.0% | 0.0% | 0.0% | 0.0% | 0.0% | 4.4% |
| 12/19/07 | 100.0% | 88.2% | 0.0% | 0.0% | 0.0% | 6.6% | 0.5% | 0.0% | 0.0% | 0.0% | 0.0% | 4.6% |
| 03/12/08 | 100.0% | 79.8% | 0.0% | 0.0% | 0.0% | 8.7% | 0.0% | 6.8% | 0.0% | 0.0% | 0.0% | 4.7% |
| 09/10/08 | 100.0% | 40.0% | 0.0% | 0.0% | 12.7% | 13.9% | 2.6% | 16.5% | 6.8% | 0.0% | 3.2% | 4.3% |
| 12/17/08 | 100.0% | 13.1% | 0.8% | 0.0% | 8.1% | 3.6% | 9.2% | 20.0% | 26.0% | 14.2% | 3.0% | 1.9% |
| 04/14/10 | 100.0% | 33.5% | 7.3% | 47.5% | 0.0% | 0.0% | 3.4% | 0.0% | 0.0% | 0.3% | 3.9% | 4.1% |

*Source:* Board of Govenors of the Federal Reserve System (2010b).

of the Federal Reserve's $851 billion portfolio of loans and securities existed in the form of US Treasury securities held outright or through repurchase agreements (see table 30.1). Its credit and liquidity risks were minimal. On December 19, 2007, two days before the implementation of the TAF and dollar swap lines on the 21st, it held more Treasuries through repurchase agreements and less was held outright, but otherwise there was little change in the size and composition of its portfolio. Matters changed significantly from this point forward.

By March 12, 2008, just ahead of the forced purchase of Bear Stearns by JPMorgan Chase on the 16th, the Federal Reserve's credit supply was $882 billion, of which $60 billion, or 7 percent, was term auction credit. By September 10, 2008, just ahead of Lehman Brothers' bankruptcy on the 15th, only 40 percent of its portfolio of $911 billion consisted of US Treasury securities held outright (net of those lent term under the TSLP). Of these, 14 percent was repurchase agreements; 13 percent, 3 percent, 17 percent, and 7 percent existed, respectively, as lent Treasuries, emergency discount borrowing, term auction credit, and drawings on the foreign exchange swap lines—all forms of lending. Another 3 percent was the "toxic waste" the central bank had seized from Bear Stearns to make its purchase by JPMorgan acceptable. On the eve of the September 2008 banking crisis, therefore, the Fed's credit and liquidity risks were considerable. As a matter of policy, it had become a lender to a number of troubled, clearly undercapitalized, and possibly insolvent financial institutions, lending a total of $352 billion to US interest-bearing capital through its various emergency lending facilities, assumed legal ownership of $29 billion worth of the worst of the "toxic waste" the US financial system had produced, and it would face a significant "embarrassment" should a financial institution fail with a large advance from the Federal Reserve on its books.

Between September 10 and December 17, 2008, the Federal Reserve's portfolio of loans and securities more than doubled to $2.2 billion. The expansion was accomplished with massive increases in securities lending, discount window borrowing, term auction credit, swap line drawings, and credit advanced through the newly created CPFF. The Federal Reserve's net holdings of Treasuries and its repurchase agreements declined. On December 17, 2008, just 13 percent of its portfolio was US Treasuries held outright (net of those lent under the TSLP). Within the rest of the portfolio, 4 percent was repurchase agreements; 78 percent of its money-creating assets were loans that hitherto might have been supplied by the private sector but which the Fed chose to make for emergency reasons. Of that 78 percent, 8 percent, 9 percent, 20 percent, 26 percent, and 14 percent were in the form of lent Treasuries, discount borrowing, borrowing through the TAF, drawings on the foreign exchange swap lines, and credit created through the CPFF, respectively. Another 3 percent of the portfolio was the mortgage securities and credit derivatives it seized from Bear Stearns and AIG, assets that no one in the private sector would willingly hold.

The composition of the Federal Reserve's portfolio on April 14, 2010, shows the effects of the unwinding of the various emergency lending programs and the LSAP. On that date, there was little or no emergency lending: the balances on the TAF, swap lines, and TSLP were all zero; the balance for the CPFF was nearly zero; discount window borrowing was a modest 3 percent. There were no outstanding repurchase agreements. The Bear Stearns and AIG toxic-waste residuals were 4 percent. Of the Fed's portfolio in 2010, 88 percent consisted of securities held outright: 33 percent, 7 percent, and a remarkable 48 percent in the form of outright holdings of US Treasury, agency, and agency MBS, respectively. At the start of the crisis, the Fed owned no mortgage-backed securities. At the end of the period under review, it owned $1.1 trillion.

The effects of these developments on the reserves of the US private banking system are equally remarkable (FRBNY, 2010a). On August 15, 2007, at the start of the crisis, bank reserves were $6 billion. By September 10, 2008, they were $26 billion. On December 17, 2008, bank reserves were an astonishing $797 billion, $771 billion higher than just three months earlier. Between September 10 and December 17, 2008, for reasons having to do with its TARP spending and the policy of draining bank reserves under the SFP, the US Treasury increased its deposits at the Fed by $479 billion, preventing this amount from going to the private banking system. Bank reserves would have been $1.3 billion then, had the US Treasury not done this. US Treasury deposits at the Fed declined significantly between December 17, 2008, and April 14, 2010, and largely because of this, the supply of reserves actually available to banks increased from $797 million to $1 billion.

Banks' excess reserves were $1.3, $1.3, $1.4, and $2.3 billion on August 15, 2007; December 19, 2007; March 12, 2008; and August 10, 2008, respectively (FRBNY, 2010a). They were $774 billion on December 17, 2008, and $1.1 billion on April 14, 2010. Banks' excess reserves had averaged $817 *million* from January 1959 to August 2008. US interest-bearing capital ended its 2007–2008 crisis awash in idle state money.

## The Political Economy of the Federal Reserve's Response to the Crisis

Judged in terms of its success in preventing what at first appeared as a US "subprime mortgage market" crisis from intensifying and then exploding into a global economic slowdown, the Federal Reserve's response to the crisis was a clear failure. Conditions in the interbank market only worsened over time. When the Fed flooded the US banking system with unprecedented quantities of reserves in September 2008, banks held them as idle funds at the Fed rather than investing them. The Fed's entry into the mortgage market in 2009 did nothing to slow the pace of foreclosures, which, by then, had falling incomes and unemployment, not subprime mortgages, as its cause. But it is wrong to conclude from this that the Federal Reserve failed completely or that it failed in every way. The Federal Reserve is an institution of the US state with immense political as well as economic powers. Its decisive intervention into the US financial system affected the crisis in significant ways, creating order out of what would have otherwise been chaos. The policy was not to prevent the US financial system from failing—that proved to be impossible—but rather to make it fail in a particular way. For a year, the Fed's efforts focused on trying to get the interbank market going again, holding the quantity of its total credit constant. In September 2008, after failing in these efforts, the Fed flooded the economy with massive amounts of its own liquidity, finally allowing the US financial system to dissolve into its monetary base, but into a monetary base made up almost entirely of unused state money. It then used the LSAP program to underwrite the financial sector's recovery.

For such a policy to work as a stabilizing, order-creating strategy, the Federal Reserve had to accomplish another goal, which the very same policy seems at first to make impossible: it had to maintain the soundness of its money not just against every other kind of money but absolutely. The Federal Reserve took responsibility for US money capital's liquidity and credit risks in the only way possible: by taking on these risks itself. Having assumed responsibility for the US financial system in this way, the problem was to manage its own risks in such a way as to bring order and stability to the US economy as a whole. Private-sector risk-free money no longer existed and the mortgage market was in disarray. The Federal Reserve gave the US financial system a risk-free state security as an alternative security into which it could collapse, assuming responsibility for the private sector's risks in exchange, and to do this, it had to manage its risks not just carefully but in a particular way.

Hence, one should not confuse the Fed's success in giving the US banking system a solid monetary base into which it could safely dissolve with generosity. Any borrowing from the Fed came with its set of imposing conditions, including but not limited to those pertaining to which kind of collateral to accept and at what price. The discipline over US interest-bearing capital that the Federal Reserve's switch to lending allowed it to exercise also expressed itself as an unwillingness to lend, as when it refused to make an emergency loan to Lehman Brothers because it did not have the necessary collateral, allowing the firm to fail in a disorderly manner. The Federal Reserve may well keep large amounts of the toxic funds that it took from Bear Stearns and AIG on its books for years, but as a minimal principle, its lending policies assumed that its loans would be paid back with interest and on its own essentially political terms. Not subject to the law of value in the same way that private capital is, the Fed—as an institution of the capitalist state with the coercive powers of the law behind—necessarily imposed a capitalist logic on its individual capitalist borrowers to protect their general, collective interests, even draining reserves from the banking system at the height of the crisis to maintain discipline.

Central banks are peculiar institutions, caught up as they are in a very specific set of contradictions. As institutions of the state, they exhibit a characteristic relative autonomy vis-à-vis the individual private financial capital they supervise and regulate, an autonomy that expresses itself in the first instance in central banks' well-known secrecy and "independence." But as financial institutions, central banks participate in the financial markets alongside these same individual interest-bearing capitals as financial capitals themselves, and for this reason, in each and every central bank a necessary economic unity is established between the state and the individual capitals with which it conducts its operations.[4] Monetary policy codifies and shapes this mixture of political relative autonomy and unmediated economic unity between the private sector and the state, and any change in money policy necessarily involves a change in this autonomy and unity and thus in the central bank's regulations and operating procedures.

Because central banks are in fact state institutions with their own independence and autonomy vis-à-vis the private sector, monetary policy is always articulated with the state's overall political role in maintaining social cohesion, ultimately in the maintenance of simple "law and order." This is what states "do." It is their function to act as the cohesive factor in society. In a society that is divided into classes, this means that monetary policy cannot be understood apart from the state's more general political role to organize the dominant classes politically and to disorganize the dominated classes politically. This means, further, that monetary policy is always articulated structurally with the state's overarching political, ideological, and repressive roles in the field of class struggle, and thus in the class struggle not only between the dominant and dominated classes but also between the various factions within the dominant classes. Monetary policy thus plays an essential role in maintaining class exploitation and domination and in organizing the balance of power within the ruling class itself, but it does so through the immediate economic unity that it establishes between the state, whose monetary policy it sets, and interest-bearing capital. This is why central banks are concerned with the value of their currency not just against the currency of other central banks or relative to the credit of the private sector, but absolutely. Political class interests are at stake. This is also why central banks necessarily exercise a disciplining function vis-à-vis the individual capitals they regulate and whose political interests they organize. The political unity of these disparate individual capitals exists in their states and thus as an autonomous, independent factor. In the case of US interest-bearing capital during its time of crisis, its political unity existed, not in itself, but in the Federal Reserve's risk-free credit.

Here, then, is how the Federal Reserve's political economic alchemy worked. As a central bank it was both "inside" and "outside" the financial system that it was reorganizing, materially united with US interest-bearing capital through its operations as a financial capital itself, on the one hand, subject not to the logic of individual capitalist competition but to the political organizing logic of an autonomous capitalist state, on the other. The Federal Reserve was successful in giving its (and hence the world's thoroughly dollarized) financial system a risk-free security into which it could collapse, but not because of the quality of the loans that it made to the private sector. These were intentionally "bad" loans. The Fed had this capacity because of the "faith" that US and foreign capital continued to have in the global political power of US financial capital. This faith was not subjective. It lay in the objective political power of US financial capital as it existed materially in the Federal Reserve as an institution of the state, and as Poulantzas (1975, 70) put it, state "institutions and apparatuses do not 'possess' their own 'powers,' but simply express and crystallize class powers." The Federal Reserve gave the US and the international financial system a political center, reorganizing US financial capital's hegemony within the US and world economies and restoring neoliberalism as a class-based social system under which financial capital is hegemonic, as it did so.

## The "New" Federal Reserve and the Regulation of US Interest-Bearing Capital

It is tempting to say that the Federal Reserve nationalized a large part of the US banking and financial system—if not the system as a whole, then certainly its short-term money markets. But it is wrong to characterize what happened in this way, at least in a politically meaningful sense of the term "nationalization." It did play a crucial role in shaping and reshaping the US financial system, engineering JPMorgan Chase's purchase of Bear Stearns, for example. But concerning matters of capital ownership, its role was limited to that of engineering mergers and acquisitions. In no instances did it seek to allocate capital, and in no instances did it take over the control of capital.[5] As an autonomous financial institution of great economic power and as an autonomous institution of a state with the force of law behind it, it held itself equally distant from every individual capital, paying attention to each only to the degree that systemic issues were involved.

The unity that the US state in the form of a "new" Federal Reserve has with interest-bearing capital is nonetheless different from the unity that existed just prior to the crisis, shaped as it was by an ideological commitment to "deregulation"—to the "freeing" of financial markets from the state. That unity was deliberately loose, scattered, and disorganized, the assumption being that this way of regulating the financial system would make it more "efficient," that is, more profitable. Thus, while Bank of America and Citigroup came under the jurisdiction of the Fed, Bear Stearns and Lehman Brothers reported to the Securities and Exchange Commission, and the Comptroller of the Currency had regulated AIG. And while some financial products and markets, such as mortgages and loans for small businesses, were regulated legally, other products and markets, credit default swaps, for example, were not.

The principles of neoliberal financial-market regulation were outlined most clearly in the Basel capital accord with its associated "Three Pillars" of minimal capital requirements, supervisory review of capital adequacy, and public disclosure (Basel Committee, 2003). Banks were understood financially as speculative "risk takers" and were required to set a certain amount of capital aside as self-insurance, their regulation (form of unity with the state) strangely privatized. In this regime, banks and bank holding companies were allowed, even encouraged, to use their own risk models and management systems to determine their own appropriate levels of risk capital; the regulators, including those at the Federal Reserve, discharged their responsibilities once they determined that the private sector's risk models and management systems were "state of the art," and any enforcement was left to the private sector, which punished banks with low capital ratios by refusing to fund them. The market discipline that this system has produced since the onset of the crisis was severe: banks in trouble, that is, banks with falling capital and risky and losing investments, were capital-starved, forcing central banks everywhere to "intervene" to rescue them. The failure of this regime was also complete. The crisis began when the private sector's risk models and hence its risk-management systems broke down, that is, when market participants realized they could not price the credit derivatives that Basel had encouraged them to use. It came to a head, in part, because investors used credit default swaps to bet against one another.

A crisis in a monetary policy regime does not mean its end, however. In a financial crisis, macroeconomic banking and financial-market stability is something that a regulator must impose, which is why the US authorities stepped into the breach to assume direct responsibility for the US financial system's aggregate credit and liquidity risks, violating and therefore changing the rules of the regulatory system they had worked so hard to create as they did so. But one must be careful not to conclude more than this. Not only do the Basel capital requirements remain legally in force in the United States, but the scope of their application has in fact been strengthened as a consequence of the crisis. Because all internationally active US banks and bank holding companies are subject by US law to the Basel regulations, a greater share of US financial capital than before is now subject to the Basel rules due to the demise of the major US investment banks and their transformation into or purchase by banks and bank holding companies. The end of US investment banking as it existed prior to the crisis has another implication: the Federal Reserve, working with the US Treasury and the FDIC, has assumed de facto responsibility for every aspect and dimension of the US banking and financial system. Today, US interest-bearing capital has essentially one regulator: its central bank.[6]

The Federal Reserve's new operating procedures do not mark an end to the regulatory regime of neoliberalism, therefore, but rather they have transformed the Fed from a classical to a neoclassical phase, where the term "neoclassical" indicates that the new regime can be understood only as an imitation and refinement of its immediate predecessor with its faith in markets, privatization, mathematical finance, and "independent" central banks. First, the Fed's emergency lending facilities were auctions. Under the TAF, for example, the authorities set the maturity and quantity of credit to be auctioned off, and the private sector, through a competitive bidding process, set the interest rate. Second, throughout the crisis, the Federal Reserve followed a practice characteristic of the Basel accords in which its own operations are privatized. It took Bear Stearns' and AIG's toxic waste off the hands of US capital by transferring this waste to itself, then it immediately returned the management of these assets to the private sector. It used private investment managers as its agents when it purchased mortgage-backed securities under the LSAP program. Third, the obvious failures of the credit derivatives revolution notwithstanding, mathematical models still play a role in US monetary policy. The value of the bad assets that the Federal Reserve holds is not determined by any market but by the solutions in its private-sector money managers' asset-pricing models. And, fourth, the Federal Reserve increased its institutional capacity to lend over the course of the crisis, and by increasing its "instrumental independence" in this way, it increased its ability to influence, regulate, and control private capital. Lending against collateral is something that a central bank can do entirely on its own. Its lending programs are retired now, but it can always reactivate them.

The autonomy of the Federal Reserve as an institution of the state vis-à-vis other institutions of the US state, especially with regard to its more representative institutions, is immense. Everything that it did in response to the crisis was legal under existing legislation except for the decision to pay interest on bank reserves. It did not have to ask for new legislation to do what it did in every other detail, and in this one instance, new legislation was needed only to speed up the policy changes. In many cases, the US monetary authorities simply had to change certain operational rules that they had imposed on themselves. This was how the TAF and LSAP were created. In other instances, including in particular its seizures of the worst of the private sector's bad assets and the measures taken to support the commercial paper market, the Federal Reserve acted under emergency powers given to it by the legislation that created it.

Its emergency powers under section 13(3) of the 1913 Federal Reserve Act are sweeping.[7] In an emergency, a Federal Reserve bank can advance its own credit to *any* individual or legal entity in the United States should the US monetary authorities determine that that individual or legal entity is unable to obtain "adequate" funding from *any* bank. The only other requirement is that the loan is secured to the "satisfaction" of the Federal Reserve bank involved, implying that it and it alone can determine the terms of its advances, including in particular what kind of collateral it will accept and at what price. Not only are these emergency powers completely flexible, but nothing that a Federal Reserve bank does under section 13(3) is subject to outside review. Standing at the intersection of the private and the state, during an emergency, monetary policy also stands at a zone of indistinction between the law and lawless force. What is particularly important about the Fed's exercise of its emergency measures in this regard is who did and did not obtain assistance: Bear Stearns and AIG would be assisted, but Lehman Brothers or a homeowner in default on his or her mortgage would have to sink or swim. The Federal Reserve's disciplinary "misdeeds" are sins of omission.

Another aspect of the Federal Reserve's independence helps explain why nothing that it did while the crisis was unfolding received the attention given to the US Treasury Department when, in the initial draft of the legislation that created the TARP, the Treasury Secretary attempted to give himself powers similar to those that the Federal Reserve Board chairman was exercising daily. The offending paragraph of the initial draft was this, offensive only because of its candor (*New York Times*, 2008): "Decisions by the Secretary pursuant under the authority of this Act are non-reviewable and committed to agency discretion, and may not be reviewed by any court of law or any administrative agency."

The aspect of the Fed's independence and autonomy in question is not just its secrecy but its long-standing political invisibility, too: monetary policy is normally not a matter for open public discussion, deemed to be the domain of the technical expert instead, if not a priesthood. During the crisis, the financial press duly reported what the experts had done, but that was largely the end of the public discussion. Beyond that, there was almost an organized consensus to be silent about what the Fed was doing. Its secrecy did not matter, making it and its emergency actions beyond reproach. Far from constituting a nationalization of the US banking system, therefore, the Federal Reserve's assumption of certain activities that had hitherto been handled privately was in fact nationalization's opposite: it was further privatization of the US state in the sense that its activities were not subject to democratic scrutiny, not even the very limited public scrutiny of a liberal republic. The Federal Reserve used its emergency powers to restore the neoliberal order when it bought US financial capital back to life. The United States is less democratic as a result. The Fed did its work secretly, behind closed doors, hardly noticed by anyone.

## Conclusion: The Federal Reserve's Response to the Crisis in Perspective

Liberal criticism of the Federal Reserve's behavior focuses on its failure to prevent the crisis from getting worse. In the least, it is argued, the Federal Reserve should have engaged in quantitative easing earlier on. But central banks are very conservative institutions, and when they exercise their lender-of-last-resort responsibilities, they are not necessarily generous. The Federal Reserve gave shelter to US interest-bearing capital by providing it with ample quantities of order-creating liquidity, thereby avoiding an acute political crisis in which the hegemony of American capitalism would be thrown into doubt. Having accomplished this, its one primary goal, it did little more.

In the midst of the Great Depression of the 1930s, Keynes famously asked (2007, 115–116): "Why would anyone outside a lunatic asylum wish to use money as a store of wealth," for "it is a recognized characteristic of money as a store of wealth that it is barren; whereas practically every other form of wealth yields some interest or profit"? His answer was this (Keynes, 2007, 116):

> Because, partly on reasonable and partly on instinctive grounds, our desire to hold money as a store of wealth is a barometer of the degree of our distrust of our own calculations and conventions concerning the future. Even tho[ugh] this feeling about Money is itself conventional or instinctive, it operates, so to speak, at a deeper level of our motivation. It takes charge at the moments when the higher, more precarious conventions have weakened. The possession of actual money lulls our disquietude; and the premium which we require to make us part with money is the measure of the degree of our disquietude.

Central bankers have the same "feeling" about money as the bankers, industrialists, and financiers who similarly participate in the circulation of interest-bearing capital, but this common feeling causes them to respond to the crisis in very different ways. The bankers, industrialists, and financiers, caring for their individual interests, scramble in search of "liquidity." The central bankers, concerned about the stability of the financial system as a whole and the value of their currency, act according to other principles, which operate "at a deeper level of [their] motivation" at moments when their "higher, more precarious conventions have weakened." What are these principles?

Public statements by Federal Reserve officials about their policies must be read closely, given the care they take in making them. Hence, it is noteworthy when, in a speech on Federal Reserve policies during the crisis, the chairman made the following candid statement about why he was not able to save Lehman Brothers (Bernanke, 2008, 3):

> To avoid the failure of Bear Stearns, we facilitated the purchase of Bear Stearns by JPMorgan Chase by means of a Federal Reserve loan, backed by assets of Bear Stearns and a partial guarantee from JPMorgan. In the case of AIG, we judged that emergency Federal Reserve credit would be adequately secured by AIG's assets. However, neither route proved feasible in the case of the investment bank Lehman Brothers. No buyer for the firm was forthcoming, and the available collateral fell well short of the amount needed to secure a Federal Reserve loan sufficient to pay off the firm's counterparties and continue operations.

In the absence of a buyer, Lehman Brothers failed because it could not obtain a loan from the Fed, a loan denied because it did not have the necessary collateral. During the crisis, the Federal Reserve stepped in to actively manage the US financial system's credit and liquidity risks, but it did so in a capitalist manner, as a defense of property.

Bernanke may have had certain personal feelings about the suffering the crisis may have caused, and in his public statements, he has referred to people's suffering in order to deflect any criticism that might be forthcoming. But as a central banker he has not recognized that social relations are involved. There is not even the recognition of use values, only the abstraction of the commodity form in its most reified, alienated form of interest-bearing capital. During the crisis, the Federal Reserve stepped in to fill certain gaps that had appeared in the abstract commodity space of financial capital, but once this space had been spanned, it let the circulation of US interest-bearing capital resume its abstract and empty course—on the condition that the value of its risk-free state money was preserved. As institutions of the state, central banks have capacities that give them nearly sovereign powers. But the immediate unity that they have with interest-bearing capital constrains them to exercise this sovereignty in a particular way: as a defense of interest-bearing capital. The Federal Reserve had the capacity to assist others, to lend for the purpose of ending foreclosures, for example, but it did not. The consequences of its one-sided defense of interest-bearing capital on society and society's lesser members are, well, collateral damage.

How then should one characterize the Federal Reserve's response to the crisis? It responded to the crisis as a lender of last resort precisely in the way that Walter Bagehot, the man who coined this description of a central bank's proper behavior, argued it should when he said (1999, 64–65):

> What is wanted and what is necessary to stop a panic is to diffuse the impression, that though money may be dear, still money is to be had. If people could be really convinced that they could have money if they wait a day or two, and that utter ruin is not coming, most likely they would cease to run in such a mad way for money. Either shut the [central] Bank at once, and say it will not lend more than it commonly lends, or lend freely, boldly, and so that the public may feel you mean to go on lending. To lend a great deal, and yet not give the public confidence that you will lend sufficiently and effectually, is the worst of all policies.

For the first full year of the crisis, the Fed did not lend as it had "commonly" lent prior to the crisis, but it did not follow the "worst of all policies" either, which is to "lend a great deal, and yet not give the public confidence that you will lend sufficiently and effectually." Then, beginning in September 2008, it lent "freely, boldly," all the while assuring the public that it would go on lending, broadening its support under the LSAP. The Federal Reserve, from the point of view of capital, exercised its lender-of-last-resort duties sensibly and responsibly. The Federal Reserve diffused the impression that money was dear and could not be had—but only if one was a systematically important financial capital in trouble.

# Notes

1. The Federal Reserve is a financial institution with its own assets and liabilities, and like any financial institution, its assets must equal its liabilities. One can depict the central bank's balance sheet as follows:

| Assets: factors supplying reserve funds | Liabilities: factors absorbing reserve funds |
|---|---|
| US Treasury, federal agency and agency MBS securities held outright | Currency in circulation |
| Repurchase agreements | Reverse repurchase agreements |
| Loans to US banks | US Treasury balances at reserve banks |
| Drawings on foreign exchange swap lines with foreign central banks | Other nonreserve deposits |
| Seized assets | Other liabilities and capital |
| Other assets | Bank reserves |

   The Federal Reserve creates reserve funds when it purchases an asset from or makes a loan to a financial institution, using the reserve account that the institution involved has at the Federal Reserve as the means of payment: reserves expand when the Fed deposits the required funds in the institution's reserve account. An asset sale or the maturation of a loan destroys reserves. The bank-reserve liabilities of the Federal Reserve are assets of the banks that hold them. By law, US banks must hold a certain amount of their assets at a reserve bank in the form of bank reserves (or cash) to "back up" their demand deposits. These are "required" reserves. Banks can hold more reserves at a reserve bank than necessary to meet their reserve requirements. These are "excess" reserves. Primary dealers are those financial institutions that have a direct dealing relationship with the open market desk of the FRBNY. One does not have to be a bank to be a primary dealer; most are securities firms.
2. Around the turn of the century, there was policy debate about whether it is possible and desirable to provide stimulus to an economy when short-term nominal interest rates are just above zero and there is concern about deflation. These conditions existed in Japan at the time, and the Bank of Japan was finding it difficult to stimulate its depressed economy as a result. In his contribution to the debate, then Governor Bernanke, writing together with several other US monetary researchers, explored the effectiveness of an alternative set of policy tools to complement the Fed's continued use of the federal funds rate as its operational target should it find itself constrained, like the Bank of Japan, by its "zero lower bound" (Bernanke and Reinhart, 2004; Bernanke, Reinhart, and Sack, 2004). Bernanke suggested, in particular, that policy makers consider three different policies: (1) supplying more reserves than is necessary to push short-term nominal interest rates to zero ("quantitative easing"), (2) adjusting the maturity and composition of a central bank's assets to affect the term structure of interest rates if not the relative prices of broad asset classes (money, bonds, mortgages), holding the total supply of central

bank credit constant, and (3) clear and repeated public statements of its intention to continue easing. Useful background information on the instruments that the Federal Reserve used to implement theses policies, including the use of autions to supply credit, can be found in Federal Reserve System Study Group on Alterative Instruments for System Open Market Operations (2002).

3. Under the SFP, the US Treasury sold Treasury Bills to primary dealers in special auctions and then deposited the proceeds in a special Treasury SFP account at the Fed, absorbing a large part of the Fed's monetary expansion as it did so.
4. Harvey (1999, 322) describes this unity in the following way:

> A part of the state apparatus is entirely caught up in the circulation process of interest-bearing capital. There is an aspect, and only *an* aspect, of the state which cannot be considered even *relatively* autonomous of capital because it is necessarily constructed in the image of the motion of capital itself. The administrators of this aspect of the state apparatus manage the circulation of interest-bearing capital and function as "the executive committee of bourgeoisie" no matter what their political allegiance. A necessary unity is thereby established between a part of the state apparatus and the money capitalists, industrialists and financiers who similarly participate in the circulation of interest-bearing capital. From the outside it appears as if a section of the state colludes directly with industrial and financial interests. A new definition of finance capital comes to the fore: one in which all three interests are unified.

5. The Federal Reserve assumed legal ownership of the assets that it seized from Bear Stearns and AIG but not economic control. These assets functioned as collateral to secure the emergency loans that it made to these two firms, and these assets are managed, and therefore controlled, by the private sector. A limited liability corporation (LLC) that has the FRBNY as its sole benefactor holds the toxic waste that the Federal Reserve seized from Bear Stearns. Black Rock Financial Management manages these assets. The toxic funds that the Federal Reserve seized from AIG and the ABCP that it has purchased from money market mutual funds are also held by LLCs that have the FRBNY as a sole benefactor. AIG manages the assets of its related LLC; PIMCO manages the portfolio of ABCP.
6. Goldman Sachs, for example, continues to exist as an independent capital firm but it is no longer an investment bank. It is rather a bank holding company and, as such, is subject to the Basel rules and no longer regulated by the SEC but by the Fed. The same is true of Merrill-Lynch because of its purchase by Bank of America.
7. Section 13(3) of the Federal Reserve Act was subsequently amended as a result of the Dodd-Frank Wall Street Reform and Consumer Protection Act of 2010. During the emergency, Section 13(3) read as follows (FRBNY, 2009a):

> In unusual and exigent circumstances, the Board of Governors of the Federal Reserve System, by the affirmative vote of not less than five members, may authorize any Federal [R]eserve [B]ank, during such periods as the said board may determine, at rates established in accordance with the provisions of section 14, subdivision (d), of this Act, to discount for any individual, partnership, or corporation, notes, drafts, and bills of exchange when such notes, drafts, and bills of exchange are endorsed or otherwise secured to the satisfaction of the Federal [R]eserve [B]ank: Provided, That before discounting any such note, draft, or bill of exchange for an individual, partnership, or corporation the Federal [R]eserve [B]ank shall obtain evidence that such individual, partnership, or corporation

is unable to secure adequate credit accommodations from other banking institutions. All such discounts for individuals, partnerships, or corporations shall be subject to such limitations, restrictions, and regulations as the Board of Governors of the Federal Reserve System may prescribe.

## References


Armantier, O, S. Krieger, and J. McAndrews. (2008). "The Federal Reserve's Term Auction Facility." *FRBNY Current Issues in Economics and Finance* 14(5). New York: Federal Reserve Bank of New York.

Bagehot, W. 1999. *Lombard Street: A Description of the Money Market.* New York: Wiley.

Basel Committee on Banking Supervision. (2003). *Overview of the new Basel Capital Accord.* Basel: Bank for International Settlements.

Bernanke, B. (2008). "Federal Reserve Policies in the Financial Crisis." Speech, Greater Austin Chamber of Commerce, Austin, Texas, December 1. Washington, DC: Federal Reserve Board.

Bernanke, B., and V. Reinhart. (2004). "Conducting Monetary Policy at Very Low Interest Rates." *American Economic Review* 94(2): 85–90.

Bernanke, B., V. Reinhart, and B. Sack. (2004). "Monetary Policy Alternatives at the Zero Bound: An Empirical Assessment." *Brookings Papers on Economic Activity* 2: 1–100. Washington, DC: Brookings Institute.

Board of Governors of the Federal Reserve System. (2009a). "Federal Reserve Act, Section 13: Powers of Federal Reserve Banks, (3) Discounts for Individuals, Partnerships and Corporations." Washington, DC: Federal Reserve Board.

Board of Governors of the Federal Reserve System. (2010a). "Statistical Release H.3: Aggregate Reserves of Depository Institutions and the Monetary Base, 2002–2010." Washington, DC: Federal Reserve Board.

Board of Governors of the Federal Reserve System. (20 10b). "Statistical Release H.4.1: Factors Affecting Reserve Balances of Depository Institutions and Condition Statement of Federal Reserve Banks, 2002–2010." Washington, DC: Federal Reserve Board.

Board of Governors of the Federal Reserve System. (2010c). "Regulatory Reform: Usage of Federal Reserve Credit and Liquidity Facilities." Washington, DC: Federal Reserve Board.

Board of Governors of the Federal Reserve System. (2010d). "Credit and Liquidity Programs and the Balance Sheet." Washington, DC: Federal Reserve Board.

Bureau of Economic Analysis. (2010). "Corporate Profits, 2006–2010." Washington, DC: Bureau of Economic Analysis.

Federal Reserve Bank of New York (FRBNY). (2008a). "Forms of Federal Reserve Lending to Financial Institutions." New York: FRBNY.

Federal Reserve Bank of New York (FRBNY). (2008b). "Understanding the Recent Changes to Federal Reserve Liquidity Provision." New York: FRBNY.

Federal Reserve Bank of New York (FRBNY). (2008c). "Domestic Open Market Operations for 2007." New York: FRBNY.

Federal Reserve Bank of New York (FRBNY). (2009). "Domestic Open Market Operations for 2008." New York: FRBNY.

Federal Reserve Bank of New York (FRBNY). (2010a). "Domestic Open Market Operations for 2009." New York: FRBNY.

Federal Reserve System Study Group on Alternative Instruments for System Open Market Operations. (2002). *Alternative Instruments for Open Market and Discount Window Operations*. Washington, DC: Federal Reserve Board.

Fleming, M., W. Hrung, and F. Keane. (2008). "Repo Market Effects of the Term Securities Lending Facility." FRBNY Staff Reports No. 426. New York: FRBNY.

Fleming, M., and N. Klagge. (2010). "The Federal Reserve's Foreign Exchange Swap Lines." *FRBNY Current Issues in Economics and Finance* 16(4).

Harvey, D. (1999). *Limits to Capital*. New York: Verso.

Keynes, J. M. (2007). "The General Theory of Employment." In D. Moggridge, ed., *The General Theory and After: Part II: Defence and Development*, 109–123. New York: Cambridge University Press.

McAndrews, J., A. Sarkar, and Z. Wang. (2008). "The Effects of the Term Auction Credit Facility on the London Inter-Bank Offered Rate." FRBNY Staff Reports, No. 335. New York: FRBNY.

*New York Times*. (2008). Text of draft proposal for bailout plan. September 21.

Poulantzas, N. (1975). *Political Power and Social Classes*. New York: New Left Books.

Tobi, K., K. Kimbrough, and D. Marchioni. (2009). "The Federal Reserve's Commercial Paper Funding Facility." *FRBNY Policy Review*, August. New York: FRBNY.

CHAPTER 31

# MONETARY POLICY AND CENTRAL BANKING AFTER THE CRISIS

## THE IMPLICATIONS OF RETHINKING MACROECONOMIC THEORY

THOMAS I. PALLEY

## Competing Visions of Reform

The Global Financial Crisis of 2008 and the Great Recession have prompted a retrospective on the conduct of monetary policy and central banking (Bernanke, 2010).Before the crisis economists and central bankers were in a celebratory mode, with talk about the "Great Moderation" and praise for advances in monetary economics that had helped stabilize the economy (Bernanke, 2004; Blanchard, 2008; Goodfriend, 2007): now there is talk among policy insiders of the need to rethink monetary policy.

The status quote that insiders wish to rethink includes changing the role of monetary policy in dealing with asset bubbles; making the central bank the banking system supervisor; and dealing with the problem of the zero lower bound to nominal interest rates.

This chapter presents an outsider reform program that instead focuses on central bank governance and independence; reshaping the economic philosophy of central banks to be more intellectually open-minded; major monetary policy reform to include adoption of an inflation target equal to the minimum unemployment rate of inflation (MURI) and implementation of asset-based reserve requirements (ABRR); and regulatory reform to address problems of flawed incentives, excessive leverage, and maturity mismatch.

The proposed outsider reform program is rooted in a rethinking of macroeconomic theory, which the crisis compelled. There are some overlaps between the insider and outsider reform programs but they are more form than substance. That is dangerous because it can confuse debate if similarity of form is mistaken for similarity of substance.

The insider program makes no changes to macroeconomic theory and is uncritical of the Federal Reserve's past actions. From its perspective, any failings of the Federal Reserve have been unwitting sins of omission. The outsider program fundamentally challenges existing macroeconomic theory and is also highly critical of the Federal Reserve. From its perspective the failings of the Federal Reserve have included significant sins of commission rooted in political capture, cognitive capture, and intellectual hubris.

The outsider critique can be taken even further. The Federal Reserve is already legally mandated to pursue maximum employment with price stability. However, it needs institutional transformation that makes it think of itself as an agent for helping realize the "American Dream." That means it should have a duty to shape the allocation of credit and the financial system in ways that ensure growth, a high employment rate, and a fair shake for all.

Finally, I critique existing monetary policy and central bank practice and its recommended reforms by focusing on the US Federal Reserve. However, the principles that are articulated and many of the proposed reforms carry over to monetary policy and central banking everywhere, including the Bank of England and the European Central Bank.

## Insider Rethinking of Policy

The starting point for the discussion is the current rethinking of monetary policy and central banking by policy insiders. This discussion is reflected in a series of papers by Blinder (2010a, 2010b, 2010c)that look at three principal areas: monetary policy and asset-price bubbles; the role of regulation in monetary policy; and the policy implications of the zero lower bound to the nominal interest rate.

With regard to governance, Blinder (2010a) frames the issue in terms of "central bank independence," which he strongly supports. He is essentially content with the current structure and rejects change, particularly regarding the Federal Open Market Committee (FOMC) and the private corporation status of the 12 district Federal Reserve banks. The argument is that the existing structure has worked well, so why change it now?

With regard to the role of monetary policy in dealing with asset bubbles, Blinder (2010b) frames the issue as whether monetary policy should "lean against" bubbles or "mop up afterwards." The consensus has been "mop up afterward." Now, there is an emerging argument for distinguishing between credit-led bubbles and equity-type bubbles, in which credit plays only a minor role (Blinder, 2008; Mishkin, 2008), and toward leaning against credit bubbles and mopping up afterward equity bubbles.

The new approach to bubbles in turn motivates new thinking about regulatory supervision. Blinder (2010b) defends a generic tendency to caution about bubble activism on the grounds that central banks have no information advantage, and they also lack targeted instruments so costs of collateral damage from intervention may outweigh benefits. However, a central bank might have the information and instruments to deal with bank-based credit bubbles if it is also the banking system supervisor. That argument therefore recommends making the central bank the banking system supervisor, and the argument is further supported by adding a third goal for monetary policy of financial stability (in addition to the existing goals of low inflation and high employment).

The third issue is the zero lower bound (ZLB) to nominal interest rates that limits the Federal Reserve's ability to lower interest rates. In a presentation at the Federal Reserve Bank of Boston conference of October 16, 2010, Blinder (2010c) argues for more safeguards against bumping up against the ZLB. Principal among these is a higher inflation target, a policy proposal that has also been floated by the IMF chief economist Olivier Blanchard and his coauthors (2010).

## The Outsider Case for More Profound Reform

Blinder's (2010a, 2010b, 2010c, 2008), Mishkin's (2008), and Blanchard and colleagues' (2010) proposals represent the "insider" view of the reform of monetary policy and central banking. Blinder is a former vice president of the Federal Reserve; Mishkin is a former governor of the Federal Reserve; Blanchard is chief economist at the IMF; and all three are leading academic economists holding positions at Princeton, Columbia, and MIT, respectively. Their proposals leave both the institutional structures of central banking (the Federal Reserve) and the theory justifying policy essentially unchanged.[1]

This insider program can be contrasted with an outsider program that argues for more substantive reform. The starting point is the recognition that central banks are critically important institutions in today's system of financial capitalism. Without the Federal Reserve, the US government would have been unable to stop the financial crisis of 2008. And without it, the US government would likely now be having considerable difficulty in financing its huge budget deficit.

Central banks' power is rooted in their ability to issue money and set interest rates. This is a constructive and vital power, which means the Federal Reserve must be part of the policy solution. But it is also a power that can be abused, which means the Federal Reserve can be part of the problem. The challenge is to see that central bank powers are deployed properly on behalf of the public interest; are not abused via arbitrary or excessive use; and its powers cannot be used by others on their own behalf.

Right now, that is not the case. The Federal Reserve failed to deploy its powers properly as evidenced by the policy failures that led up to the crisis. Its powers are also too much in the service of financial-market interests, in part to save the economy from destructive speculative activities. The clearest evidence of this is the new concern about the "too-big-to-fail (TBTF)" problem whereby megabanks are too big to fail and are therefore subsidized in credit markets because lenders know the central bank will not let big banks fail for fear of the collateral damage the failure will inflict. The TBTF problem surfaced during the crisis but a similar problem has been evident for a while in the form of the "Greenspan put," which protected the stock market against declines, again for fear of collateral macroeconomic damage.[2]

An outsider reform program involves four parts, as illustrated in figure 31.1. Those parts are governance reform; change of economic philosophy; monetary policy reform; and regulatory reform. This outsider framing of the reform question is substantially different from the insider framing in two critical respects. First, insider reformers frame the problem of how to improve the Fed's performance within the existing institutional and theoretical frame. There is no mention or indication of the possibility that the Federal Reserve may have contributed to the making of the crisis. For insiders there have been no sins of commission on the part of the Federal Reserve, only unwitting sins of omission.

Second, insider reformers see no problem regarding the political capture of the Federal Reserve by financial-market interests. The theory of regulatory capture, whereby regulated interests capture their regulators, is well known among economists. However, from an insider perspective the theory is germane to other agencies but not the Federal Reserve, which explains the uncritical discussion about central bank independence (which will be discussed below).

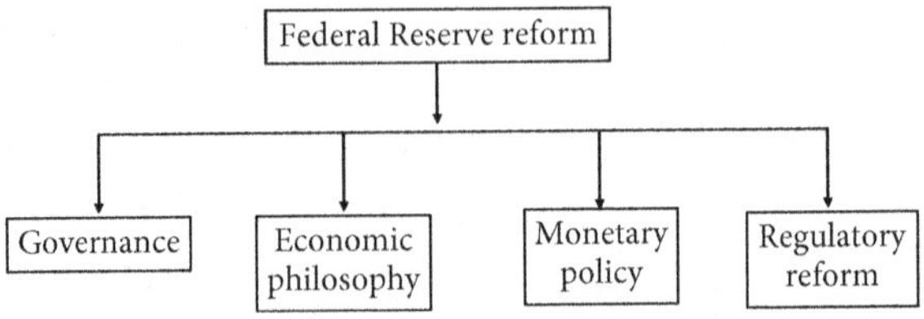


**Figure 31.1** A program to reform the Federal Reserve.

## Governance and Central Bank Independence

The Global Financial Crisis and the subsequent government rescues of banking systems have led to a rediscovery of political economy and its relevance for understanding monetary policy, regulatory policy, and the Federal Reserve. The argument is that in the 1990s and 2000s financial interests were able to capture the regulatory system and used this capture to their advantage to push unsound deregulation and to block needed regulation. That capture was evident in the financial deregulation and lack of reregulation that characterized the period 1980–2008. The Glass-Steagall Act (1933), an iconic piece of New Deal legislation that had barred firms from undertaking both investment and commercial banking activities and had barred banks from owning insurance companies, was repealed in 1999. Citigroup went so far as to buy Travelers Insurance a year in advance of Glass-Steagall's repeal.

Another example of capture is from 1998 when Treasury Secretary Robert Rubin and Federal Reserve Chairman Alan Greenspan successfully blocked attempts by Brooksley Born, head of the Commodity Futures Trading Commission, to regulate the derivatives market. The Commodities Futures Modernization Act of 2000 exempted derivatives from regulation and allowed them to be traded almost entirely free of regulation in "over-the-counter" markets. In 2004 the Securities and Exchange Commission passed its net capital exemption rule that reduced the amount of capital that Wall Street's largest brokerage houses had to hold, and it also allowed investment banks to adopt self-regulation with regard to assessing the value of their capital at risk. An immediate consequence of the rule was a surge in investment bank leverage and debt-to-equity ratios rose from around 15 to 1 in 2004 to over 30 to 1 by 2008.

This process of regulatory and political capture is documented by Johnson and Kwak (2010) in their best-seller *13 Bankers: The Wall Street Takeover and the Next Financial Meltdown*. Their thesis is that bankers remain firmly in control of the political-regulatory process and have successfully blocked any needed postcrisis reform and regulation.

The traditional focus of capture theory is microeconomic regulation. However, the logic of capture theory also applies to macroeconomic policy, something that is entirely missing from the little mainstream discussion about capture. Macroeconomic policy capture is particularly important for monetary policy and central banking because it can affect the relative policy emphasis given to inflation versus unemployment. It will also affect the willingness to use regulatory tools (i.e., balance-sheet restrictions, margin requirements, and reserve requirements) for purposes of enhancing macroeconomic policy. That is particularly germane to the issue of asset-price bubbles and their macroeconomic impacts.

Epstein (1992) distinguishes between financial capital, industrial capital, and labor. I(1996)have argued that financial capital is likely to have a strong preference for low inflation to protect financial wealth; industrial capital will have a preference for a stronger real economy and lower unemployment to boost demand and profits; and workers will want full employment to boost real wages. In that case, if financial interests dominate the Federal Reserve it will tend to produce macroeconomic outcomes characterized by higher unemployment and lower inflation (i.e., a point further down the Phillips curve, which is the trade-off between inflation and unemployment).

The issue of policy preferences is also germane to the question of central bank independence. Insider economists argue that central bank independence is a mechanism for helping address politicians' incentive to push inflation too high. For instance, using a game-theoretic natural rate of unemployment model, Barro and Gordon (1983) show that policymakers will push inflation too high in an attempt to secure temporary real output gains. There are three features to note. First, the model assumes a vertical Phillips curve, which offers only temporary output gains. Second, even those gains come from "fooling" private-sector agents into making suboptimal supply decisions. Third, the public is assumed to have a unified set of preferences that differs from politicians' preferences, and it is this that causes politicians to impose suboptimal outcomes on the public. Thus, politicians are effectively represented as the public enemy.

For insider economists, central bank independence is viewed as a way to solve this preference conflict issue. The problem is that such assumptions are false and central bank independence does not solve the preference conflict. The reality is that the public's preferences are divided according to economic interests. Consequently, central bank independence may simply entrench one set of interests—probably those of financial capital.

In a model like that of Barro and Gordon (1983) a financially dominated central bank will choose suboptimally low inflation if the economy has a negatively sloped long-run Phillips curve that causes permanent output losses and continual higher unemployment (Palley, 1996).

In a sense, the frame of central bank independence is wrong. Instead, the frame should be establishing institutions that deliver best outcomes within the context of constitutional democracy. That is an enormously difficult challenge that mainstream economists evade de facto via two assumptions. First, they assume the public's preferences are unified. Second, they assume they have the "true" model of the economy as described by the theory of the natural rate of unemployment. These assumptions remove conflict about policy goals and conflict about how the economy works and what is economically feasible.

Neither of these two assumptions is true. The public's preferences are clearly divided, as evidenced by contested politics. Second, there are lots of views about how the economy works, of which the mainstream view is but one—albeit it is a view that dominates economics because mainstream economists suppress alternative views by denying them space. These considerations mean that poorly designed central bank independence may worsen the real-world policy problem by giving dominance to particular interests. For instance, by entrenching financial interests it may lead to suboptimal inflation and unemployment. Furthermore, it may also cause political damage by undermining principles of constitutional democracy.

That said, there may still be a place for central bank independence as a means of restraining populist political pressures on monetary policy. However, any independence must always be granted subject to self-conscious awareness of the problem of conflicting preferences, the problem of conflicting views about the economy, and with absolute deference to constitutional democracy. That means central banks must be accountable to elected officials, fully represent competing interests, and avoid capture.

With regard to the Federal Reserve, I suggest the following institutional reforms.

*Reform #1: Nationalize the Federal Reserve system so that it is fully owned by the federal government.* The presidents of the district Federal Reserve banks are currently appointed by the boards of directors of those banks, which are 50 percent owned by private member banks. Instead, these district banks should be nationalized and their presidents appointed by the US president, subject to Senate confirmation. The rationale is to diminish the possibility for private influence within the system.

*Reform #2: Change the Federal Reserve appointment structure so that every four years the incoming president gets to appoint his Federal Reserve Chairman, subject to Senate confirmation.* Voters hold the president responsible for the economy and the president should therefore have full opportunity to pursue his policy. This would strengthen democratic accountability of the Federal Reserve.

*Reform #3: The Federal Reserve should issue an annual social report that explicitly addresses the question of institutional capture.* The report would be presented to Congress and would address the social, commercial, and political backgrounds of appointees and senior management with an eye to ensuring wide representation of points of view. The very requirement of a report would constitute a public acknowledgment of the potential for capture and the report itself would be a focal point for annually considering the problem.

*Reform #4: Rationalize the Federal Reserve system and reduce the number of district banks to four (New York, plus three others) plus the Board of Governors.* The existing structure of 12 district banks is costly and outdated, reflecting the railroad economy of the nineteenth century. The current time of budget austerity provides an opportune and justified moment to prune and modernize the Federal Reserve system.

## Economic Philosophy Reform

The Global Financial Crisis revealed a catastrophic failure of thought at the Federal Reserve. Despite employing hundreds of economists, the entire Federal Reserve system was taken aback by the crisis; failed to understand it as it was happening; and has been repeatedly surprised by the depth and duration of the Great Recession.

One explanation is that the Federal Reserve succumbed to "groupthink," which was also part of a larger groupthink in the economics profession. That groupthink pushed an "intellectual cleansing" of all who disagreed with the new economic consensus.

It also created the conditions for the "black swan" event that blindsided the Federal Reserve. Such a black swan event is not a statistical phenomenon concerning low probability, distant tail outcomes. Instead, it is a sociological phenomenon produced by closed mindedness that blinded the Federal Reserve to the reality of economic developments.

Viewed in this light, the Federal Reserve's failure reflects a lack of pluralism rooted in a fundamentally wrongheaded belief that it has access to truth and that its model is the true model. As the philosopher Karl Popper (1959) showed, that is epistemologically impossible. The best that is possible is to have a model that is not rejected by the facts. However, because of the coarseness of tests in economics, that means having to live with several theories and models.

It can be argued that the Federal Reserve's intellectual failure is the root cause of its policy failure, and Buiter (2008) argues that the Federal Reserve was subject to cognitive capture. Buiter represents this phenomenon as a purely intellectual failure, but the ideas that dominated policy supported the interests of finance. Viewed in that light, cognitive capture is simply the intellectual extension of conventional regulatory capture. That speaks to the need for reform that protects against any future intellectual failure.

*Reform #5: The Federal Reserve should be legally mandated to promote a pluralistic open-minded approach to economics and economic policy that self-consciously avoids the pitfalls of ideology and groupthink.* There is value in Congress debating intellectual pluralism and passing legislation both to provide instruction to the Federal Reserve and to change its intellectual frame, as happened with the Employment Act of 1946. As a first step in this direction, the Federal Reserve should commission an investigation into its failure to foresee the crisis and its failed predictions about recovery.[3] Delivering on such a law requires ultimately having the right people in charge, which is why personnel change at the Federal Reserve is so important, but the first step is mandating action.

An example of the type of thinking that must make it into the Federal Reserve system is Hyman Minsky's (1992 [1993])"financial instability hypothesis." The crisis has boosted Minsky's standing, and economists are increasingly mentioning him. However, that mention is a token signal and the fundamental analytical framework remains unchanged. From a Minsky perspective, "success breeds excess breeds failure," and finance has a genetic proclivity to instability. I have (2009a)argued that a Minskyan perspective implies the following policy propositions.

*Policy proposition #1:* Policymakers must exercise self-conscious skepticism toward euphoria (i.e., no more policy-maker chatter of "great moderations" and "new economies").

*Policy proposition #2:* Capitalist economies always need significant regulation to contain financial speculation and financial excess. Milton Friedman is the philosophical advocate of a deregulated economy and the justification is provided by the first welfare theorem of competitive general equilibrium theory. Hyman Minsky is the philosophical advocate of a regulated economy, and the justification is provided by his financial instability hypothesis. That is fundamentally different from, though also compatible with, the conventional market failure justification for regulation, which is rooted in competitive general equilibrium theory. The policy implication is that it undoes the presumption that regulation is guilty until proven innocent. Instead, some form of regulation is always needed.

*Policy proposition #3:* Discretion dominates rules. Models, numbers, and rules are always insufficient for policymaking, and there is always a need for judgment because the economy is subject to an evolutionary dynamic that cannot be foreseen. That said, policy should still be credible and clear. As Keynes (1936) emphasized, uncertainty is costly in market economies. It can paralyze economic action, and it can also induce costly defensive actions. Policymakers should therefore reduce policy-induced uncertainty by ensuring that policy is credible and clear. This is a valuable policy lesson provided by new classical macroeconomics, and it is one that carries over to Keynesian and Minskyan macroeconomics.

## Monetary Policy Reform

A third area of reform is the conduct of monetary policy, and here rethinking of macroeconomics prompts four reforms as illustrated in figure 31.2.[4]

*Reform #6: Central banks should target inflation so as to hit the minimum sustainable rate of unemployment.* The Phillips curve is backward-bending and central banks should aim for the inflation rate that minimizes the unemployment rate. In the United States, that rate of inflation is probably between 3 and 5 percent and it can be termed the minimum unemployment rate of inflation (MURI, which is an acronym that can be contrasted with Milton

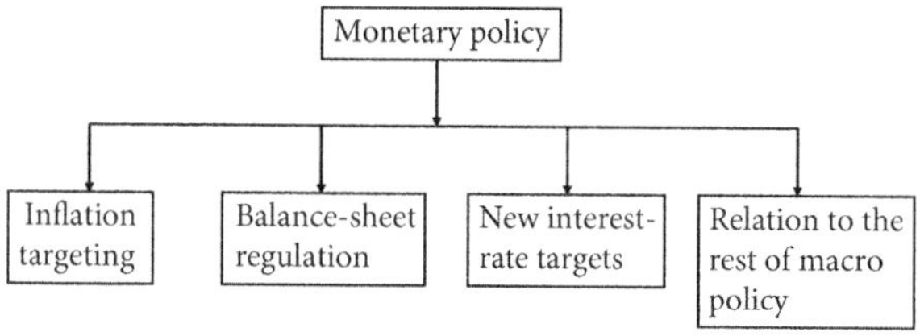


**Figure 31.2** Monetary policy reform.

Friedman's NAIRU, the non-accelerating inflation rate of unemployment).The backward-bending Phillips curve and the MURI are illustrated in figure 31.3.

Blanchard and colleagues (2010) and Blinder (2010c) have also suggested raising the inflation target but their reasoning is to push up nominal interest rates to avoid getting caught in the ZLB trap, as has happened in the Great Recession. That reasoning leaves unchallenged the theory of a natural rate of unemployment and its claim of a vertical Phillips curve. It also implies sticking with the flexible labor-market agenda that is the implicit policy recommendation of Friedman's natural-rate theory and that has contributed so much to the worsening of income distribution.

According to that theory, the natural rate of unemployment is determined by labor-market frictions including unions, high minimum wages, fringe benefits that raise labor costs, and employee protections. If policymakers want to bring down the natural rate, they should eliminate these features. The Blanchard-Blinder insider justification for a higher inflation target sticks with this thinking.

It is therefore important to get right the justification for a higher inflation target. The theory of the backward-bending Phillips curve provides a justification, but here too it is important to get the right theory. Justifications for a backward-bending Phillips curve have been provided by both Akerlof and colleagues (2000) and Palley (2003a).Akerlof and colleagues (2000) identify near-rational expectations and the process of expectation formation as the cause of the backward bend. They argue that as inflation increases, agents'

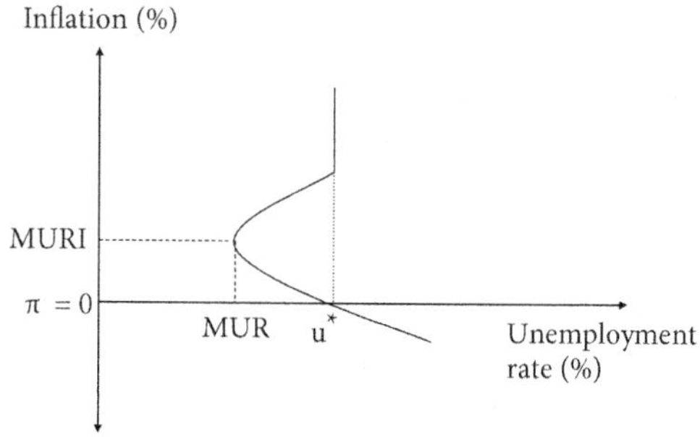


**Figure 31.3** The backward-bending Phillips curve.

expectations become fully rational, causing the Phillips curve to bend backward. I have previously (2003a) identified incomplete incorporation of inflation expectations into nominal wage settlements as the cause of the backward bend. The argument is that workers in sectors with unemployment are willing to accept some modest real wage reduction via inflation at low rates of inflation. However, they resist too-rapid reductions by too-high inflation and this resistance causes the Phillips curve to bend backward once inflation passes a critical threshold.

As I have argued (2009b, 2011), there is an important distinction between these two approaches. One approach (Akerlof et al., 2000) generates a Phillips trade-off by fooling workers into misperceiving inflation at low rates. It therefore lacks a welfare justification for nonzero inflation. Another approach (Palley 2003a) emphasizes the role of inflation in greasing the wheels of wage adjustment in labor markets. It therefore has a welfare justification for nonzero inflation.

Furthermore, the extent of incorporation of inflation expectations into wage settlements reflects conditions of job-market security and labor militancy. These conditions can change, in which case the backward-bending Phillips curve will shift and the MURI will shift. Policy that fails to change in response to such shifts will be suboptimal, but policymakers need the right theory if they are to recognize and respond to shifts. The bottom line is that it is important to have the right economic theory to arrive at the right policies and provide them with appropriate reasoning and justification.

Lastly, the rationale for targeting inflation should be absolutely clear. Here, the old distinction (Friedman, 1975) between "intermediate" and "ultimate" targets can help. Inflation is both an intermediate and ultimate target that is selected to help reach the other ultimate target, which is the unemployment rate. At very low rates, inflation is of minimal utility concern, and instead employment and unemployment are the real concerns. Given this, it is critical that inflation targeting (including MURI targeting) be lodged in a policy framework that explicitly states that the monetary authority has a responsibility for real economic performance. Absent that, it is easy for policy to slip into thinking inflation is the only ultimate target. Once that happens, the natural tendency is to push for a lower inflation target so that policy ends up producing suboptimal outcomes with regard to the real economy.

*Reform #7: Central banks should adopt a system of asset-based reserve requirements that enables targeted discretionary countercyclical balance-sheet controls on the financial sector. This system should apply to shadow banks and hedge funds.* A central lesson of the financial crisis and the last decade is that monetary authorities cannot manage the economy with just interest rates and an inflation target. Doing so leaves the economy exposed to buildups of financial excess. These buildups do not necessarily cause inflation, and therefore they fly under the radar of an inflation-targeting regime. However, they generate financial fragility that can undermine the economy and also leave a large "debt" footprint that retards economic activity and is difficult to escape.

That suggests that inflation targeting should be supplemented by quantitative balance-sheet controls that limit such buildups. One such system of control that is both general and flexible is the ABRR (Palley, 2000, 2003b, 2004, 2006, 2010a). ABRRs extend margin requirements to a wide array of assets held by financial institutions. Financial firms have to hold reserves against different classes of assets, and the regulatory authority sets adjustable reserve requirements on the basis of its concerns with each asset class.

ABRRs provide a new set of policy instruments that can target specific financial-market excess, leaving interest rates policy-free in order to manage the overall macroeconomic situation. They can also help prevent asset bubbles by targeting overheated asset categories, and they are particularly good for targeting house-price bubbles because they can target the issue of new mortgages. By requiring financial firms to retain some of their funds as noninterest-bearing deposits with the central bank, policymakers can affect relative returns on different categories of financial assets.[5] If policymakers want to deflate a particular asset category, they can impose higher reserve requirements on that category, thereby reducing its returns and prompting financial investors and firms to shift funds out of that asset into other relatively more profitable asset categories.

ABRRs also increase the efficacy of monetary policy, especially by enabling central banks to target sector imbalances without recourse to the blunderbuss of higher interest rates. If a monetary authority is concerned about a particular type of asset bubble generating excessive risk exposure, it can impose reserve requirements on that specific asset without damaging the rest of the economy. Furthermore, an ABRR system also acts as an automatic stabilizer. When asset values rise or when the financial sector creates new assets, ABRRs generate an automatic monetary restraint by requiring the financial sector to hold more reserves.

Another benefit is that they provide a policy tool that can encourage public purpose investments such as inner-city revitalization or environmental protection by setting low (or no) reserve requirements on such investments (Pollin, 1993; Thurow, 1972).

ABRRs increase the demand for reserves, which will allow the Fed to exit the current period of quantitative easing and avoid future inflation. In a sense, they provide an alternative to the quantitative easing exit strategy proposed by Chairman Bernanke that involves paying interest on reserves. The latter is costly to the government, and it effectively rewards banks for the crisis they caused because they now gain a new revenue stream (Palley, 2010b). In contrast, ABRRs increase seigniorage revenue for governments at a time of fiscal squeeze.

ABRRs work best when applied uniformly to all financial firms and when linked to geographically specific assets that cannot evade the regulatory net. They are also consistent with the application of other balance-sheet controls. For instance, an ABRR is a form of liquidity requirement, except it requires that liquidity be held against a specified asset class.

They are also consistent with capital standards that aim to discourage excessive risk taking. However, capital requirements can be destabilizing because they are pro-cyclical (capital is eroded in recessions, therefore potentially forcing lending cutbacks that amplify the downturn). Capital standards are also less flexible in the sense of being more difficult to adjust because firms need time to raise capital.

ABRRs can also stabilize exchange rates. For instance, a country suffering undesirable exchange-rate depreciation could impose ABRR requirements on foreign currency deposits of domestic financial institutions. That can complement Chilean-style reserve requirements, designed to fight undesirable currency appreciation by imposing unremunerated reserve requirements on capital inflows.

Lastly, ABRRs can help members of currency unions (e.g., countries using the euro) to fill the policy instrument gap that arises from giving up their domestic currency and ability to determine local interest rates. Because ABRR can be implemented on a geographic basis by national central banks, domestic policy can be better set in accordance with local conditions.

Philosophically, there is a significant difference between ABRRs and insider chatter surrounding the possible need to deal with asset-price bubbles. An ABRR system is designed to be part of a normal standard everyday operation of monetary control, and it is consistent with Minsky's financial instability hypothesis, which emphasizes tendencies to instability. Just as interest-rate control is an ordinary policy measure, so too should be quantitative balance-sheet controls. That ABRRs are good at targeting asset-price bubbles is a supplementary benefit. This contrasts with insider thinking, which appears to frame the issue of balance-sheet controls in terms of special and unusual circumstances of asset-price bubbles rather than everyday management of the financial system. When it comes to everyday management of the economy the insider perspective is still stuck on interest-rate control. This is reflected in the Federal Reserve's new focus on payment of interest on reserves that is designed to strengthen the Fed's control of short-term interest rates, but there is still nothing about quantitative measures aimed at controlling credit and financial asset creation.

*Reform #8: Target more than just the overnight interest rate.* Over the past three decades monetary authorities have used interest-rate policy to target the overnight rate. In the United States, this rate is the federal funds rate. In the eurozone it is the European Central Bank's Lombard rate. There are both narrow technical reasons and broader reasons of macroeconomic theory for targeting additional interest rates.

To the extent that policy aims to affect long-term rates, current policy does so by shifting the entire term structure of interest rates up or down. It may also affect the term structure of interest rates via the expectations of future short-term rates. Thus, according to the expectations theory of the term structure, the current two-period interest rate is the product of the current short-term rate and the current expected two-period short-term rate. This can be expressed as follows:

$$i_{2,t} = [1 + i_{1,t}][1 + E_t[i_{1,t+1}]]-1, \quad (1)$$

where $i_{2,t}$ is the current two-period rate, $i_{1,t}$ is the current one-period rate and, $E_t[i_{1,t+1}]$ is the current expectation of the next period short rate. The term structure and longer period rates are therefore managed indirectly by affecting expectations of future short-period rates.

This indirect management is weak and rests on markets having the correct expectations about future short-period rates. Yet, despite this weakness, monetary authorities have until recently resisted targeting longer-term rates. The reasoning for this is not clear but it seems to be related to some belief that they cannot.

The Federal Reserve's policy of quantitative easing adopted after the crisis has shattered that fiction. It is now clear that monetary authorities can target longer-term rates and they should. Moreover, not only should they target longer-term government bond rates with an eye to managing the risk-free term structure, but they should also target some private-sector interest rates. In particular, the Federal Reserve should consider targeting mortgage-backed security (MBS) interest rates because mortgage rates are so critical for the economy. These rates should be targeted if the central bank feels the spread between MBS rates and government bond rates is inappropriate. A second reason is if the housing market is weak and threatens the economy, in which case intervention that lowers MBS rates can be a form of stabilization policy.

More generally, a Keynesian approach to monetary policy would justify going far beyond targeting just the overnight interest rate. A central message of Keynes's general theory is that financial markets do not set interest rates (of which there are many) in a manner that ensures full employment. That is the Keynesian macroeconomic justification for interest rate–based monetary policy, but there is no reason to restrict policy to targeting just the overnight rate.

*Reform#9: Use the bully pulpit to speak out on behalf of better overall economic policy.* Blinder (2010a) also recommends using the bully pulpit and he proposes enlisting it as an antibubble weapon. What he terms "howling and scowling" can discourage behaviors by banks. Such use of the bully pulpit is entirely appropriate, but the insider take on the issue again casts it narrowly as if the Federal Reserve's failure to use the bully pulpit was exclusively a sin of omission.

The reality is that the Federal Reserve has used the bully pulpit but has used it asymmetrically. Chairmen Greenspan and Bernanke have in the past talked about the benefits of globalization; the need for budget austerity; the case for tax cuts, the case for Social Security cuts; and the damage done by the minimum wage. This is a one-sided use of the bully pulpit that reflects the dominance of a particular economic ideology at the Federal Reserve.

That proves the need for intellectual balance, which in turn speaks for appointing some progressive Federal Reserve governors and district bank presidents who will use the bully pulpit to advocate a different economic agenda. A renewed agenda would stabilize the economy, increase growth, and help the Fed meet its mandate.

For instance, the bully pulpit could be and should have been used to talk about the exchange rate, how an overvalued dollar makes the Fed's job more difficult, and how China exchange-rate manipulation has harmed the American economy. Similarly, the bully pulpit should have been used to talk about the macroeconomic problems that come from worsening income distribution.

## Regulatory Reform

The final set of reforms concerns regulation. This is an enormous area and impossible to cover in detail, but the architecture of needed reform can be easily understood. Regulatory reform overlaps with the ABRR piece of monetary policy reform, revealing how ABRRs play two roles. First, they are a part of monetary policy that manages the level of economic activity; second, they are a part of the regulatory system that ensures financial stability.

The financial crisis revealed unambiguously that the financial system is currently unstable. Regulatory reform is needed. Figure 31.4 identifies the three major causes of the crisis. The first was flawed incentives, which promoted loan pushing and unsound lending. This was particularly true of mortgage lending and mortgage-related products. The second was excessive leverage, which created balance-sheet vulnerability to small losses that wiped out equity, which in turn undermined willingness to lend to weakened firms. Excessive leverage was particularly extreme among Wall Street investment banks. The third was financing mismatch, whereby long-term assets were funded with short-term liabilities. This exposed the system to the equivalent of a bank run when the commercial paper (CP) market froze and lenders were unwilling to rollover CP market loans. This problem was particularly acute among shadow banks and Wall Street investment banks. The combination of all three factors created a disastrously fragile system. Flawed incentives produced toxic loans that caused equity losses; these wiped out equity owing to high leverage. Lenders were unwilling to rollover CP market loans, which triggered insolvency and started

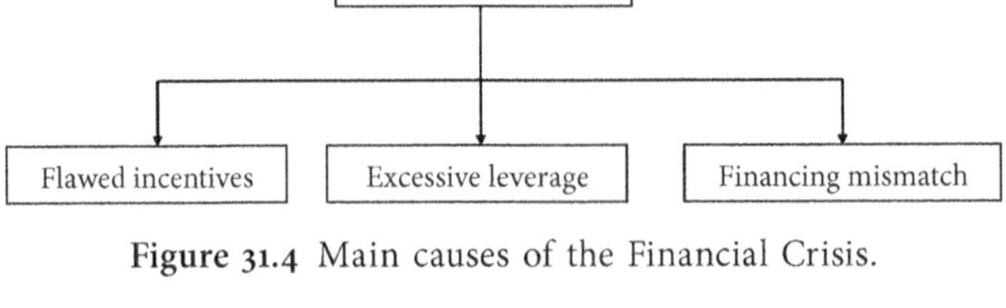


**Figure 31.4** Main causes of the Financial Crisis.

a downward liquidation spiral that worsened equity losses and further reduced willingness to rollover CP loans.

These structural failings can be significantly addressed by the following 10-point plan (some parts of which have been implemented in the Dodd-Frank Wall Street Reform and Consumer Protection Act of 2010):

1. Financial-market regulation should be comprehensive, covering all financial institutions on the basis of function (what they do) rather than form (what they call themselves). This would create a level playing field in which the shadow banking system, Wall Street investment banks, and the structured investment vehicles (SIVs) of commercial banks would all be subject to regulation. Regulatory avoidance should not be tolerated as a means of gaining a competitive advantage.
2. To remedy incentives to loan push, lenders should be required to hold a "stub" ownership interest in all loans they originate. This would leave lenders exposed to future loan losses, thereby diminishing the "loan pushing" incentive that comes with the "originate to distribute" lending model, which has lenders selling loans they make in the secondary market.
3. Additionally, a significant share of top management bonus pay should be in the form of long-dated stock options. This would also help remedy the "originate to distribute" model's incentive to loan push because managers would bear some of the costs if loans subsequently went bad.
4. To remedy the excessive leverage problem, financial firms should be subject to strict leverage limits based on sharply higher equity capital requirements. This will help diminish insolvency risk by giving banks the capacity to withstand losses.
5. To remedy the problem of bank runs, like those that occurred in the CP market, lenders should be subject to reasonable liquidity requirements.
6. It should be illegal for investors to purchase credit default swap insurance coverage on bonds they do not own. This would help prevent assassination of companies' credit standings by speculators hoping to profit from a bankruptcy.
7. The credit default swap market should be regulated and all transactions should pass through market-clearing arrangements. This would help prevent a repeat of the AIG situation, in which the market was unaware of the extent of risk taken on by AIG and that eventually rendered AIG's insurance of no value.
8. To reduce the financing mismatch problem, financial companies should be required to issue contingent convertible bonds (COCOs) as part of their capital structures. Such bonds automatically convert into equity when existing equity is eroded beyond a threshold by losses. The price of these bonds would also act as a "canary in the coal mine" by signaling in advance the riskiness of companies.

9. As discussed earlier, monetary authorities should introduce a system of ABRRs that supplements and reinforces interest-rate policy. ABRRs can be useful for both macroeconomic stabilization and stabilizing the financial system.
10. Political reform should limit political contributions from financial firms. Those contributions buy political influence and they helped drive the policies of flawed deregulation and light-touch regulation of the past 30 years. That influence is also now blocking reregulation (Johnson and Kwak, 2010).

# Conclusion: Political Economy and the Difficulty of Change

The Global Financial Crisis and Great Recession have prompted a rethinking of monetary policy and central banking among insider policymakers. The impulse to rethink is welcome, but it can also mislead because the suggested changes are small, relative to the scale of monetary policy failure. In all important respects, the insider approach to reform leaves essentially unchanged both the theoretical paradigm guiding monetary policy and thoughts about the institutional structures of central banking.

This lack of deep change reflects the entrenched nature of thinking that surrounds monetary policy and central banking, which in turn can be viewed as part of a larger political economy that blocks change. Politicians are disinterested in pushing for change because monetary policy and regulatory policy raise technical issues that have little resonance with the public. Voters do not lobby Congress about the Federal Reserve, and they do not decide how to vote on the basis of Federal Reserve policy, despite its critical impact on their lives.

The Federal Reserve is also protected by Wall Street and the banking and financial community, whose interests it often identifies with because of institutional capture, a tendency to a shared intellectual outlook among those working in finance and banking, and a revolving employment door between Wall Street and the Federal Reserve. Lastly, the Federal Reserve is also protected by its patronage of academia, which includes its own revolving door with university economics departments. That buys the Federal Reserve intellectual cover and legitimacy.

These political and sociological structures make it very difficult to change monetary policy and central banking, but the scale of the policy failure in connection with the financial crisis creates a historic opportunity. Not only should we alter technical policy, but we should transform the identity of the Federal Reserve. The Employment Act of 1946 and the Full Employment and Balanced Growth Act of 1978 charged the federal government with securing maximum employment with price stability. However, since the appointment of Paul Volcker as the Federal Reserve chairman in 1979, the Federal Reserve has retreated from these obligations. From an outsider perspective, not only does the Federal Reserve need to recover a commitment to full employment, but it also needs a transformation that makes it think of itself as an agent for realizing the "American Dream." It is entrusted with monetary policy and regulatory responsibilities, but it should also shape the allocation of credit and the financial system in ways that ensure growth, a high employment rate, and a fair shake for all.

## Notes

1. Having the Federal Reserve become the banking system regulator actually expands its powers, though, balanced against this, the Federal Reserve has surrendered its consumer protection role to the new Consumer Financial Protection Bureau established by the Dodd-Frank Act (2010).
2. The "Greenspan put" was the belief that under Chairman Greenspan the Federal Reserve would sharply lower interest rates to prevent large stock-market declines.
3. The International Monetary Fund (2011) commissioned a similar report, which was prepared by its Independent Evaluation Office, on its failure to foresee the crisis.
4. Many of the arguments presented in this subsection were developed earlier in Palley (2006).
5. The Federal Reserve has recently started paying interest on reserves of banks. A system of ABRR would require ending that, because paying interest on reserves undermines ABRR by removing the penalty that ABRR seeks to impose on particular asset classes.

## References

Akerlof, G.A., Dickens, W.T., and Perry, G.L. (2000). "Near-Rational Wage and Price Setting and the Long Run Phillips Curve," *Brookings Papers on Economic* 1 (2000): 1–60.

Barro, R.J., and D. B. Gordon. (1983). "A Positive Theory of Monetary Policy in a Natural Rate Model." *Journal of Political Economy* 91:589–610.

Bernanke, B.S. (2004). "The Great Moderation." Remarks at the Meetings of the Eastern Economic Association, Washington, DC, February 20.http://www.federalreserve.gov/boarddocs/speeches/2004/20040220/default.htm.

Bernanke, B.S. (2010). "Monetary Policy and the Housing Bubble." Speech presented at the annual meeting of the American Economic Association, Atlanta, Georgia, January 3.http://www.federalreserve.gov/newsevents/speech/bernanke20100103a.htm.

Blanchard, O.J. (2008). "The State of Macro." MIT Department of Economics Working Paper, August 12. http://papers.ssrn.com/sol3/papers.cfm?abstract_id=1235536.

Blanchard, O., G. Dell'Arica, and P. Mauro. (2010). "Rethinking Macroeconomic Policy." Research Department, IMF, Washington, DC, February.http://www.imf.org/external/pubs/ft/spn/2010/spn1003.pdf.

Blinder, A. (2008). "Two Bubbles, Two Paths." *New York Times*, June 15.http://www.nytimes.com/2008/06/15/business/15view.html

Blinder, A. (2010a). "How Central Should the Central Bank Be?" *Journal of Economic Literature* 48(1): 123–133.

Blinder, A. (2010b). "Commentary: Rethinking Monetary Policy in Light of the Crisis." Comments at a symposium sponsored by the Kansas City Federal Reserve Bank, August.http://www.kansascityfed.org/publicat/sympos/2010/blinder-remarks.pdf.

Blinder, A. (2010c). "Revisiting Monetary Policy in a Low Inflation and Low Utilization Environment." PowerPoint presentation at a conference sponsored by the Boston Federal Reserve Bank, October 16.http://www.bos.frb.org/RevisitingMP/presentations/Blinder.pdf.

Buiter, W. (2008). "Lessons from the North Atlantic Financial Crisis." Paper presented at a conference on "The Role of Money Markets," jointly organized by Columbia Business School and the Federal Reserve Bank of New York, May 29–30. http://www.nber.org/~wbuiter/NAcrisis.pdf.

Epstein, G. (1992). "A Political Economy Model of Comparative Central Banking." *Review of Radical Political Economics* 24: 1–30.

Friedman, B.M. (1975). "Targets, Instruments, and Indicators of Monetary Policy." *Journal of Monetary Economics* 1: 443–473.

Goodfriend, M. (2007). "How the World Achieved Consensus on Monetary Policy." *Journal of Economic Perspectives* 21(4): 47–68.

International Monetary Fund. (2011). "IMF Performance in the Run-up to the Financial and Economic Crisis: IMF Surveillance in 2004–07." Prepared by the Independent Evaluation Office of the IMF, Washington, DC, February.http://www.ieo-imf.org/eval/complete/eval_01102011.html.

Johnson, S., and J. Kwak (2010). *13 Bankers: The Wall Street Takeover and the Next Financial Meltdown*. New York: Random House.

Keynes, J.M. (1936). *The General Theory of Employment, Interest, and Money*. London: Macmillan.

Minsky, H.P. (1992). "The Financial Instability Hypothesis." Working Paper No. 74, The Jerome Levy Economics Institute of Bard College, New York.

Mishkin, F. (2008). "How Should We Respond to Asset Price Bubbles?" Speech at the Wharton Financial Institutions Center and Oliver Wyman Institute's Annual Financial Risk Roundtable, Philadelphia, PA, May 15.http://www.federalreserve.gov/newsevents/speech/mishkin20080515a.htm.

Palley, T.I. (1996). "The Institutionalization of Deflationary Policy Bias." *Monnaie et Production*, Vol. X of *Economies et Societes*, 247–268.

Palley, T.I. (2000). "Stabilizing Finance: The Case for Asset-Based Reserve Requirements." Report issued by the Financial Markets Center, Philomont, VA, August. http://www.thomaspalley.com/docs/articles/macro_policy/stabilizing_finance.pdf.

Palley, T.I. (2003a). "The Backward Bending Phillips Curve: Wage Adjustment with Opportunistic Firms." *Manchester School of Economic and Social Studies* 71(1): 35–50.

Palley, T.I. (2003b). "Asset Price Bubbles and the Case for Asset Based Reserve Requirements." *Challenge* 46 (May-June): 53–72.

Palley, T.I. (2004). "Asset Based Reserve Requirements: Reasserting Domestic Monetary Control in an Era of Financial Innovation and Instability." *Review of Political Economy* 16 (January): 43–58.

Palley, T.I. (2006). "Monetary Policy in an Endogenous Money Economy." In Arestis and Sawyer, eds., *A Handbook of Alternative Monetary Economics*, 242–257. Cheltenham, UK: Edward Elgar.

Palley, T.I. (2009a). "A Theory of Minsky Super-cycles and Financial Crises." IMK Working Paper 2/2009, Institute for Macroeconomics, Dusseldorf, Germany.

Palley, T.I. (2009b). "The Backward Bending Phillips Curve: Competing Micro-foundations and the Role of Conflict." *Investigacion Economica* LXVII (20): 13–36.

Palley, T.I. (2010a). "Asset Price Bubbles and Monetary Policy: Why Central Banks Have Been Wrong and What Should Be Done." *Intervention* 7(1): 91–107.

Palley, T.I. (2010b). "The Politics of Paying Interest on Bank Reserves: A Criticism of Bernanke's Exit Strategy." *Challenge* 53 (May/June): 49–65.

Palley, T.I. (2011b). "The Economics of the Phillips Curve: Formation of Inflation Expectations versus Incorporation of Inflation Expectations." IMK Working paper 4/2011, Institute for Macroeconomics, Dusseldorf, Germany.http://www.boeckler.de/pdf/p_imk_wp_4_2011.pdf.

Pollin, R. (1993). "Public Credit Allocation through the Federal Reserve: Why It Is Needed; How It Should be Done." In G. A. Dymski, G. Epstein, and R. Pollin, eds., *Transforming the U.S. Financial System: Equity and Efficiency for the 21st Century*. Armonk, NY: M.E.Sharpe.

Popper, K.R. (1959). *The Logic of Scientific Discovery*. New York: Basic Books.

Thurow, L. (1972). "Proposals for Rechanneling Funds to Meet Social Priorities." In Federal Reserve Bank of Boston, *Policies for a More Competitive Financial System*, 179–189.

# CHAPTER 32

# THE BAILOUT OF THE "TOO-BIG-TO-FAIL" BANKS

## NEVER AGAIN

FRED MOSELEY

The banking sector of the US economy underwent very significant changes in the three decades prior to the recent crisis, all of which increased the instability of this crucial sector and contributed greatly to the crisis. These changes have been described in detail elsewhere in this book, and I will just briefly summarize here the main changes that affected the stability of the banking sector.

First, the banking sector became much more highly concentrated and dominated by a handful of very large banks. In 1990, the 10 largest banks owned about 25 percent of total US bank assets; by 2007, these 10 largest banks owned 60 percent of total bank assets (Fisher, 2010). These megabanks became "too big to fail" because their failure would wreak havoc on the financial system and the economy as a whole. Second, the Glass-Steagall Act (which became a law during the Great Depression) was progressively weakened and finally repealed in 1999, which eliminated the safety firewall between commercial banking and investment banking; it also was the main factor in the rapid concentration of assets in the largest banks. Third, debt replaced deposits as the main source of bank funds (in order to increase the rate of return on bank equity) and especially short-term debt (much of it overnight, i.e., *very* short-term debt). This increasing reliance on borrowed funds is destabilizing because bank deposits are guaranteed by the government (up to some maximum limit), but bank debt is not guaranteed; therefore, bank debt is vulnerable to "runs" by the creditors who refuse to "roll over" the short-term debt. Fourth, the large banks increasingly operated their most risky activities through wholly or partially owned subsidiaries (hedge funds, private equity funds, etc.) known as the "shadow banking system," which was completely unregulated and which allowed these banks to keep a good portion of their debt liabilities off their own balance sheets. And finally, new "innovative" financial products (such as derivatives, mortgage-based securities, etc.) were created, which were supposed to spread risks and stabilize the system but which turned out to do the opposite (the repeal of Glass-Steagall allowed the banks to own and trade these risky products).

Because of these destabilizing structural changes, when the subprime mortgage crisis emerged in 2007–2008, it quickly turned into a very severe general financial crisis, which threatened to bankrupt the banking sector as a whole, especially the largest banks. When the mortgage market crashed, and the quality of the banks' assets was called into serious question, the banks' creditors (including other banks) were no longer willing to continue to lend and there was a new-style "run on the banks" (runs by creditors, rather than by depositors). Fears mounted of a collapse of the banking system and of the economy as a whole. These banks were considered to be "too big to let fail." Bernanke testified before the Financial Crisis Inquiry Commission that 9 of the 10 largest banks in the United States were on the verge of bankruptcy (the lone exception was apparently JPMorgan Chase) (Bernanke, 2010).

## Bailouts

In this state of panic, Treasury Secretary Paulson asked Congress for a blank check of $700 billion in order to bail out the banks (without congressional oversight and review!). Paulson justified this outrageous request by arguing that, if the banks were not bailed out, then the whole financial system would collapse and take the US economy with it. In the memorable words of then President Bush, "this sucker could go down." Even the dreaded "d-word" was heard. It was presented as a kind of economic *Sophie's Choice*—either bail out the banks with taxpayer money or suffer a deep recession or depression.

The public response to the bailout was justifiably outraged, and Congress initially balked but eventually submitted to the intense pressure to "save the economy." A more fully elaborated TARP (Troubled Asset Relief Program) was passed in the fall of 2008 (see Johnson and Kwak, 2010, chapter 6, for a detailed description of the banking crisis and the government bailout of the banks).

The original idea was for the Treasury to purchase the "toxic assets" of the banks at inflated prices so that the eventual losses on these assets would be transferred from the banks to the general public (i.e., to taxpayers). However, this plan turned out to be unworkable because the Treasury and the banks could not agree on an appropriate price for the assets. The banks demanded little or no discount from the original full value of these toxic assets, in spite of the fact that most estimates of the current value of those assets were less than half of their face value. The Treasury was willing to subsidize the banks to some extent, but not to that extent, especially in full view of the public.

As a result of this impasse, the outgoing Bush administration modified the TARP. Instead of buying the banks' toxic assets, the TARP money was used to inject capital into banks by buying preferred shares of stock (essentially like a loan with a fixed rate of interest), which receive a 5 percent rate of return (Warren Buffett was receiving 10 percent on his preferred shares at this same time) and which have no voting rights. Managers of the banks were not replaced, and there were cosmetic limits on executive pay, which were not strictly enforced. The banks' stockowners also benefited because, although the value of existing stock was greatly reduced in value, the stock would have been worth nothing without the bailout. The bondholders of the banks benefited even more, because they were effectively guaranteed that they would be paid in full in the event of future losses.

The most egregious of the bailouts were those of Citigroup and Bank of America. Even the *Financial Times* called the terms of these bailouts "generous." The government "invested"$45 billion in Citi and BofA and, most important, agreed to provide "insurance" for (i.e., to guarantee) about $300 billion of Citi's toxic mortgage-based securities and similar insurance for about $120 billion of BofA's toxic securities.

The incoming Obama administration attempted a new variation of the original Paulson plan (to purchase the banks' toxic assets at inflated prices), which was called the Public-Private Investment Plan (PPIP). PPIP tried to accomplish this goal in a more hidden and deceptive way. Instead of the government spending money to purchase the toxic assets directly, the government would guarantee loans to private investors (e.g., hedge funds), who would also invest some of their own money in order to purchase the banks' assets. The advantage of this strategy (from the administration's point of view) was that they did not have to go before Congress and ask for more money to bail out the banks, which would have been politically impossible. The losses that would occur in the future from the government guarantees would not be included in the current year's budget but instead would show up in future budgets and would have to be paid for by taxpayers down the line.

As it turned out, the price that the hedge funds were willing to pay for the banks' toxic assets, even under these favorable terms, was lower than what the banks were willing to accept. Hedge funds generally required at least a 15 percent discount on face value, and the banks, still clinging to the hope that the economy or the government would eventually restore these toxic assets to their full values, would not accept even this small discount. So the PPIP accomplished very little.

Banks also benefited from other government policies that were enacted by the Federal Reserve, the FDIC, and from the government takeover of Fannie Mae and Freddie Mac. The Fed's policies helped the banks in a variety of ways. The main way was its zero-interest-rate policy, which enabled the banks to borrow from the Fed at zero interest and to buy Treasury bonds at 3 percent or lend out at 5 percent. In effect, the Fed essentially gave money to the banks, so they could lend this money for a sure profit. In addition, the Fed also purchased $1.2 trillion of mortgage-based securities from Fannie Mae and Freddie Mac, which increased the value of mortgage-based securities generally, including the mortgage-based securities owned by banks, which enabled banks to continue to value these securities at their full values (or close to them) and to avoid reported losses.

Banks also benefited from the FDIC policy of guaranteeing all newly issued debt by the banks, in unlimited amounts (the Temporary Lending Guarantee Program). The FDIC guarantee has made it possible for the banks to borrow money at a lower rate of interest than without this guarantee (1/2 to 3/4 percentage points lower). The FDIC claims that this guarantee program will not be funded by taxpayers but will instead be funded by insurance premia paid by the banks. However, if the losses turn out to be greater than the FDIC estimates, then taxpayers will have to make up the difference. As of December 2010, the amount of debt guaranteed under this plan was $267 billion. So far, there have been no significant losses.

Finally, banks have also gained from the policies of the government-sponsored agencies Fannie Mae and Freddie Mac in two main ways. First, Fannie and Freddie have purchased almost 100 percent of the new mortgages issued since the crisis began. Without the support of Fannie and Freddie, the mortgage market would have completely collapsed, and with it the values of the banks' mortgages and mortgage-backed securities would have plummeted.

In addition, in January 2011, Fannie Mae came to an agreement with Bank of America, which settled a dispute between the two banks on terms that were extremely generous to BofA. Fannie Mae had claimed that BofA should have to "buy back" $127 billion worth of mortgages that were sold to Fannie, because the quality of those mortgages was misrepresented by BofA when it sold them to Fannie. The generous settlement required BofA to pay only $1.5 billion—about one cent on the dollar! Any losses greater than this on these mortgages—and they are likely to be much greater—will be borne by Fannie, which means they will eventually be borne by taxpayers. This settlement has been called a "backdoor bailout" of the banks. Fannie and Freddie also have similar claims on other banks (although in smaller amounts), and it appears likely that there will be more backdoor bailouts.

## Effects

As it turned out, this massive government aid enabled the banking system to avoid a collapse, and the financial condition of the banks has improved, especially for the largest banks. Bank losses have been turned into profits (except for Bank of America, which still lost money in 2010), and bank stock prices have risen. (Total bank profits were $82 billion in 2010, after losses in 2008 and 2009 [FDIC, 2011].) This increase in bank profits is in part real and in part fantasy. The real part is due in part to the banks' trading activities (buying and selling securities), rather than to new lending to businesses and households (this point will be discussed further below). The improved profits were due also to the Fed's zero-interest-rate policy, which (as discussed above) enabled the banks to borrow from the Fed at zero interest and to lend at 3–5 percent. However, this zero-interest-rate policy also has caused losses for savers, who earn 2–3 percent less interest on their savings. Thus, the Fed's policy has resulted in a huge transfer of income from savers to the banks, which amounts to around $250 billion a year ($10 trillion in Treasury bonds multiplied by a 2.5-percentage-point interest-rate differential due to the Fed's policy).

The imaginary part of the improved bank profits is due to various accounting tricks. The main such trick was made possible by a hastily enacted change in the accounting rules in the summer of 2009, which no longer required banks to value their assets at current market values ("mark to market"). Instead banks were allowed to determine the values of their assets according to their own "internal models" ("mark to model" or, as some say, "mark to make-believe"), if they plan to continue to own these assets until maturation. This change of accounting rules was opposed by the professional association of accountants (FASB) but lobbied hard by the banks, and the banks prevailed in Congress (once again). This new accounting rule applies especially to mortgages owned by banks. Under this rule, banks have been able to continue to value the mortgages they own at face value or close to face value, in spite of independent estimates that these mortgages are worth much less than that. Therefore, this rule has enabled the banks to avoid losses that would have wiped out a good portion of their reported profits.

Other accounting tricks have included insufficient provisions for future losses (these provisions count against current profits) and counting a reduction in the price of the bonds they owe as "income," on the grounds that they could sell these bonds and buy them back at a lower price (?!). The business press has greeted such accounting tricks with comments such as: "phantom profits," "bank profits appearing out of thin air," "amateur hour for magicians," and "efforts to put lipstick on a very fat pig."

Therefore, it seems likely that there will be more losses for US banks in the future, due to continued losses on home mortgages (made worse by very high rates of unemployment for years to come), as well as further losses on home-equity loans and commercial real-estate loans. And when the losses come, they could cause another banking crisis, because the banks have not made adequate provisions for these future losses.

The banks took advantage of their apparent improved financial conditions and paid back the government bailout money as soon as they could. All the big banks paid back the government within a year (Citi and Bank of America were the last to do so). Banks were eager to repay the capital in order to remove the minor restrictions on executive compensation and to get out from under the stigma of the government bailout.

All in all, the TARP disbursed almost $475 billion (the Dodd-Frank Act in July 2010 reduced the TARP funds to this amount). Of that $475 billion, around $275 billion went to the banks; the rest went to GM and Chrysler ($82 billion), AIG ($70 billion), and housing bailouts ($30 billion). Of the $275 billion that went to banks, about $200 billion has been returned to the government as of December 2010, for a loss of about $75 billion at this point. The Congressional Budget Office (CBO, 2011) estimates that eventually all of this $275 billion will be repaid, and the government will even make a small profit ($16 billion). Many analysts believe that these estimates are too optimistic (e.g., ProPublica, 2011) and do not include estimated losses of $14 billion from the AIG bailout and a $14 billion loss from the auto bailout. In addition, the CBO estimates also do not include losses from Fannie and Freddie, which have indirectly benefited the banks, and also do not include the money that savers have lost because of the Fed's zero interest policy, which (as mentioned above) is estimated to be as much as $250 billion a year. Lastly, the CBO estimates also do not include the increased economic and political power of the big banks, which can be used in the future to gain further access to taxpayer funds.

## Success?

Was the government bailout of the banks a success? It undoubtedly succeeded in averting a more serious financial crisis (at least for the time being), perhaps at a small direct cost. However, the indirect costs have been much greater, as just mentioned. Furthermore, and most important, the bailout has not led to an increase of bank lending to businesses and households. Obama and Bernanke have repeatedly implored the banks to increase their lending, but so far with little success.

Banks were rescued by the government because they perform a vital economic function to provide credit for the economy. However, the banks are still not performing the vital function for which they were rescued. Instead, the bailout has resulted primarily in continued multimillion-dollar salaries for bank executives and in hundreds of billions of dollars of benefits for banks' shareholders and bondholders. Therefore, the bailout not only was grossly unfair, but also has not succeeded in achieving its most important goal of providing credit for the economy. A fairer and more effective way to provide more credit for the economy would have been for the government to take over the banks that had to be rescued, and then these public banks could have provided credit directly to the economy, rather than begging the banks to resume lending (more on this "public option" in banking will be discussed below).

## The Dodd-Frank Financial Reform Act

Everyone now agrees that the government should never again bail out the banks, or the banks should never again be in such a desperate situation in which a bailout seems to be the only alternative to economic catastrophe. That was the stated objective of the Dodd-Frank Act (the Wall Street Reform and Consumer Protection Act), which was passed in July 2010. However, even though this act is of a monstrous size (2,300 pages), it does not go very far in making final decisions about the reforms of the financial sector. There are very few hard-and-fast rules. Instead, the act sets up a framework and a process in which decisions will be made later by a new umbrella regulatory agency called the Financial Stability Oversight Council. It mandates 67 studies to be conducted by the newly created Office of Financial Research.

The main strategy of the Dodd-Frank Act to avoid future bank crises and bank bailouts is *stricter and more comprehensive regulations* (more rules, more reporting, more transparency, greater diligence by regulators, etc.) in order to prohibit banks from engaging in excessive risk taking. However, in my view, better regulation is not likely to be a sufficient solution to the "too-big-to-fail" problem. Better regulation might stabilize the banking system somewhat, but history (including recent history) suggests that banks will figure out ways to circumvent the regulations (including "capturing" the regulators) so that they can engage in greater risk taking in search of greater returns, which will eventually lead to another crisis.

The Dodd-Frank Act also calls for a tax on the biggest banks in order to have an "*orderly liquidation fund*" in the event that a crisis did occur and one or more of the big banks were in danger of failure and had to be rescued. This policy seems both to encourage risk taking by the big banks (because of the knowledge that the bailout fund is available) and at the same time seems not to be nearly enough money in case there were another crisis.

The separation between commercial banking and investment banking was partially restored by a weak form of the Volcker Rule. The original

Volcker Rule prohibited banks from engaging in "proprietary trading" (i.e., trading stocks, bonds, etc., with the bank's own capital as opposed to its customers' money) and also prohibited banks from owning or investing in a hedge fund or private equity fund. The weakened form, which eventually became law, allows proprietary trading for certain low-risk types of trades (e.g., simple hedges on its assets) but prohibits high-risk types of trades (e.g., credit default swaps for which the bank does not own the asset that is being "insured"). The act also allows banks to invest up to 3 percent of tier 1 capital in hedge funds and private equity funds. Critics argue that the line between trading for one's own account and trading for a client is often very murky, and banks are likely to classify all sorts of activities as "servicing clients," even if they are mainly to the banks' own benefit. For this reason, Gerald Epstein and colleagues at the Political Economy Research Institute have presented detailed suggestions for how the Volcker Rule should be implemented in order to maximize its effectiveness—such as clear definitions and prohibitions on proprietary trading, capital charges on exempted trading activities, explicit public transparency requirements, and so on (see Epstein, 2010).

The Dodd-Frank Act also provides for limited reform for *derivatives*. Simple standard "plain vanilla" derivatives (like interest-rate swaps) must be traded on an open exchange (in which prices are public and well publicized). But specifically tailored "customized" derivatives do not have to be traded on an open exchange and will continue to be private "over-the-counter" bilateral trades (in which prices are opaque and unknown by regulators). Because non-standard derivatives are the most lucrative, that is where the banks are likely to concentrate their activities in the years ahead. Therefore, exotic derivatives, with unacknowledged liabilities, are likely to be a continuing source of instability in the US financial system.

The Dodd-Frank Act also allows for, but does not mandate, the creation of a predetermined *accelerated bankruptcy process* (called in the act an "orderly liquidation authority" and often called a "resolution authority") for banks that are "too big to fail" (or "systematically significant"). The objective would be to settle all the claims of creditors and counterparties involved in a bankruptcy process as quickly as possible, in order to minimize disruption of the financial system. This resolution process would be similar to what the FDIC does for smaller banks, but at an accelerated pace.

An accelerated bankruptcy process, with creditors taking losses, is a worthy objective. However, these megabanks are very complicated and operate on a global scale (as do many of their creditors and counterparties). Therefore, it seems unlikely that all the competing claims can be sorted out and settled within a short period of time. And the longer it takes, the longer the disruption in the credit markets will be, which would likely worsen a banking crisis. The final decision about the resolution authority will be made by the Financial Stability Oversight Council.

Critics argue that, without the effective regulation of derivatives, a resolution authority for the big banks will not work. Without full disclosure and the regulation of derivatives on open exchanges, when a crisis occurs, the regulators will not know the nature of all the complex, interlocking derivatives in the system, which would make it very difficult to decide whether or not a resolution process is necessary or even to know what the likely effects of this process will be. Because Dodd-Frank does not do enough to regulate opaque derivatives, this would be another reason for the likely ineffectiveness of a resolution authority.

## Other Proposals

Many economists and analysts think that the Dodd-Frank Act is a weak law that does not really solve the "too-big-to-fail" problem. It relies mainly on better regulation, and that does not seem to be sufficient. Many have suggested that more fundamental reforms are necessary in order to better ensure that taxpayers will never again have to bail out these big banks. The main proposals that have been suggested are the following:

### Limit Size

One widespread proposal is that the "too-big-to-fail" problem should be attacked at its core—the banks are too big, and therefore they should be *broken up* or *reduced in size*, so that their failures would not threaten the entire financial system. Proponents of this strategy include Simon Johnson of MIT, the Nobel Prize winner Joseph Stiglitz, Richard Fisher of the Dallas Fed, and the Vermont Socialist senator Bernie Sanders (and even on occasion Alan Greenspan, whose monetary policies helped to create these "too-big-to-fail" banks). Proponents note that the largest banks are even bigger today than they were before the crisis, due to government-arranged acquisitions (Bank of America acquired Merrill Lynch, Wells Fargo acquired Wachovia, and JPMorgan Chase acquired Washington Mutual and Bear Stearns), and therefore the problem is potentially even worse than before. Some proponents suggest that there should be an explicit maximum size for a bank, defined either in terms of the percentage of a bank's assets in relation to US GDP or to the total assets of the banking sector. Others suggest that, rather than absolutely prohibiting any size beyond a maximum size, banks that exceed a recommended maximum size should be taxed (at a progressive rate). This tax would both give the banks an incentive not to exceed the recommended maximum size and would also provide the government with bailout funds in case one of more of these "too-big-to-fail" banks had to be rescued.

During the debate over the Dodd-Frank bill, an amendment was proposed in the Senate (by Senators Brown and Kaufman), which would have set a maximum size for a bank's assets of 4 percent of GDP for commercial banks and 2 percent of GDP for investment banks. Only the six largest banks would have been affected. The assets of these six largest banks today are 64 percent of GDP(!), and they would have been reduced to 24 percent of GDP if this amendment had passed (their assets were 17 percent of GDP as recently as 1995). However, the amendment failed by a wide margin, with 23 Democrats joining the Republicans to defeat it.

## Limit Leverage

Others argue that size is not the main problem; the main problem is the very high levels of leverage of both the largest and other banks, especially short-term debt, which is vulnerable to a run. Therefore, the solution to this problem is to limit the leverage (debt liabilities) that banks are allowed to take on. Proponents of some version of this proposal include the Nobel Prize winner Paul Krugman, Anat Admati of Stanford Business School, and Roger Lowenstein of *Business Week* (and the author of *The End of Wall Street*). The original House bill had a leverage limit of 15:1 (debt:equity) for the largest banks (with no distinction between short-term debt and longer-term debt), but this limit was not included in the final act. Instead, the act allows the Financial Stability Oversight Council to require the Fed to set up a 15:1 limit on a bank, but only if it considered that bank to pose a "grave threat" to the stability of the financial system.

Critics argue that it would be easy for the large banks to evade a statutory leverage cap, because it can hide debt liabilities in creative ways in off-balance-sheet units. Other critics argue that by the time the Council and the Fed decides that a bank poses a systemic threat, it may be too late to stop a crisis. Other critics argue that there should be even stricter limits on short-term debt.

One way to limit leverage is with higher capital requirements. Dodd-Frank leaves this issue to Basel III and the Financial Stability Oversight Council to determine capital requirements in the future (capital requirements are hardly mentioned in the act). It is not expected that capital requirements will be increased significantly.

## Convertible Contingent Bonds

An innovative proposal to reduce the damage of bank leverage is to create a new kind of bond called a convertible contingent bond (or a COCO bond) that would automatically be converted into equity in case a bank was in danger of failure, with a predetermined "trigger point" for the conversion. The conversion from debt to equity would reduce the bank's debt obligations and recapitalize the bank at the expense of shareholders and the owners of the contingent bonds. Bernanke and other Fed officials have spoken favorably of this option, as has ex-Fed governor Alan Blinder of Princeton University, and it is being promoted by Goldman Sachs. This idea was included in the original Dodd-Frank bill but was removed from the final act.

This proposal would be an improvement over a resolution authority because it is much simpler and predetermined, and it could probably be done in a short period of time. However, there are two main difficulties involved in the implementation of this proposal. In the first place, the precise "trigger point" must be determined. The trigger point is usually defined in terms of a capital ratio (e.g., 6 percent of risk-weighted assets [RWA]). However, in the last crisis, the banks' capital ratios were not a good indicator of the financial condition of the banks. Had COCO bonds been in place, the conversion to equity (at 6 percent of RWA) would have come too late. On the other hand, if the trigger point is set too high, then the conversion would come too early and may turn out to be unnecessary. The most reasonable policy would seem to be "better safe than sorry."

The second difficulty is that the percentage of a bank's capital that should be in COCO bonds has to be determined. The percentage should be high enough so that the bank can be recapitalized and made solvent through the conversion of the COCO bonds, without the need of a government bailout. COCO bonds would have a higher rate of interest than standard bonds (because the risk is greater), and thus they would increase funding costs for banks and also increase interest rates for the banks' customers. Therefore, one would not want the percentage of COCO bonds to be too high. On the other hand, one would also not want the percentage of COCO bonds to be too low, because these bonds are the safety margin and the protection against a crisis and the necessity of a government bailout. Critics argue that COCO bonds might actually increase the instability of the banking system, because approaching the trigger point of a particular bank in trouble could itself cause a run on that bank. This type of bond is called a "death-spiral bond" in Japan.

## Public Banks

The policies discussed in the previous section would be an improvement over Dodd-Frank. However, at the present time, it does not appear likely that these policies will be adopted. The opposition to these policies and the lobbying power of the big banks are too strong to allow passage. If these policies are not put in place and another banking crisis does occur, or if these policies are put in place but a banking crisis occurs anyway, then the government absolutely should not bail out any banks, as everyone now agrees. Instead, the government should take over any bank that is "too big to fail" and is failing and needs to be rescued, and it will need to operate these banks as public banks (i.e., a "public option" in banking).

Such a government takeover would immediately stabilize the crisis situation and restore liquidity in credit markets, because public banks would be backed by the full faith and credit of the federal government. Public banks could also help solve the mortgage crisis by writing down the mortgages in their portfolios that are "underwater" to the current value of the houses that were bought with these mortgages. On the liabilities side of their balance sheets, public banks would be able to work out a fair resolution of the outstanding debt of the failed private banks, based on the current value of their assets. Public banks could determine on the basis of social criteria which creditors would suffer losses and how to settle with foreign creditors (e.g., pension funds could suffer fewer losses).

After the balance sheet has been adjusted to current values, public banks could resume lending to creditworthy businesses and consumers, and in that way they would contribute to an economic recovery. Rather than give money to banks, and begging them to lend this money to businesses and households, public banks could lend directly to these customers and help to revive the economy. Stiglitz (2010, 319) has also suggested that a solution to the banks' unwillingness to increase lending would be to create public banks that would do the lending.

Public banks would also make the economy more stable. Public banks would take fewer risks during an expansion, in order to avoid debt-induced bubbles that inevitably burst and cause so much hardship. For example, there would be no more housing bubbles; instead, the overall housing policy objective would be to make decent affordable housing available for all. With housing more affordable, mortgages would be more affordable and less risky. Public banks could also be used to allocate credit to high-priority social-economic policy objectives, such as affordable housing, green energy, health care, and so on. (For a more complete discussion of the operations and benefits of public banks, see Lapavitsas [2009].) In this way, banking could be made to serve the public for the greater good, rather than to serve the private interests of bankers, which is often at the expense of the greater good, especially in times of crisis.

In this way also we would never again have to bail out the banks. We do not have to accept the economic *Sophie's Choice* presented to us by our "leaders" of a bailout of the banks or economic catastrophe. There is another option for banking—a public option, for the greater good.

## References

Bernanke Ben. (2010). "Causes of the Recent Financial and Economic Crisis." http://www.federalreserve.gov/newsevents/testimony/bernanke20100902a.htm.

Epstein, Gerald. (2010). "The Volcker Rule: Rule Implementation Issues and Study Guide." http://www.peri.umass.edu/fileadmin/pdf/other_publication_types/SAFERbriefs/SAFER_issue_brief24.pdf.

FDIC. (2011). "Quarterly Banking Profile." *FDIC Quarterly* 5(1).

Fisher, Richard. (2010). "Lessons Learned, Convictions Confirmed." Federal Reserve Bank of Dallas. http://www.dallasfed.org/news/speeches/fisher/2010/fs100303.cfm.

Johnson, Simon, and James Kwak. (2010). *13 Bankers: The Wall Street Takeover and the Next Financial Meltdown*. New York: Pantheon.

Lapavitsas, Costas. (2009). "Systematic Failure of Private Banking: A Case for Public Banks." http://www.researchonmoneyandfinance.org/media/papers/RMF-13-Lapavitsas.pdf.

Lowenstein, Roger. (2010). *The End of Wall Street*. New York: Penguin.

ProPublica. (2011). "Eye on the Bailout." http://www.propublica.org/ion/bailout.

Stiglitz, Joseph. (2010). *Freefall: America, Free Markets, and the Sinking of the World Economy*. New York: W. W. Norton.

United States Congressional Budget Office. (2011). *Report on the Troubled Asset Relief Program—March 2011*. http://www.cbo.gov/ftpdocs/121xx/doc12118/03-29-TARP.pdf.

CHAPTER 33

# THE SAVINGS AND LOAN CRISIS AND BAILOUT

## LESSONS FOR POLICY

DORENE ISENBERG

By the end of the 1980s the savings and loan (S&L) industry had been decimated. Yet for decades prior to that it had been a robust industry. It was the core of the process that recycled the savings of Americans into homeownership, which was at the center of the American Dream. The changes that are responsible for the effective demise of the S&Ls are the same phenomena that have been instrumental in constructing the large national and international financial institutions whose speculative actions induced the US housing bubble of 2005–2007, which ended in the Great Recession of 2007–2009. The S&L crisis and bailout took 15 years to resolve. Hopefully, the current crisis will find a faster resolution.

To understand the sources of the S&L crisis, it's necessary to begin with its regulatory history in the era of the New Deal. The forces that produced the long-lived crisis emerged as a confluence of regulatory structures, tight monetary policies, ideological transformations, and the always attractive pull of a real-estate boom.

## The New Deal and Financial Regulation

In the 1930s, New Deal legislation regulated and revitalized the US financial sector after its near destruction in the Great Depression. The massive failures of financial institutions produced a cascading effect that exacerbated the declines in consumption and investment activity as well as the uncertainty that underpinned these economic decisions. In rebuilding the financial sector, both financial stability and economic growth were the foci of the architects. Functional and prudential regulations formed the foundation of the new financial system. Prudential regulation took the form of deposit insurance and a set of regulators for each type of depository institution. Functional regulations reduced competition among the different types of financial institutions by regulating their deposit rates, by deciding the types of assets that each could issue and hold, and by inserting firewalls between the capital markets and depository institutions (Isenberg, 2000, 249). Clear lines were drawn to connect borrowers to the financial institutions that would be their appropriate lenders. As D'Arista (1994, 240) notes, "The ultimate purpose of the framework for financial structure and regulation is to assist financial institutions and markets in performing their economic functions."

Functional regulation split the financial sector into three tranches: capital markets—debt and equity—organized by investment bankers to finance long-term capital needs; commercial banking, which was responsible for short-term loans primarily to the business community; and the thrifts, which were responsible for long-term mortgage loans that financed the homes of middle-class and working-class households. The loans these institutions originated composed the bulk of their assets. The depository institutions relied on the transactions and saving funds of local businesses and residents to finance their loan originations. To keep the depositories from using price competition to attract their depositors, commercial banks were mandated to accept noninterest-bearing transaction deposits and the S&Ls were allowed to accept interest-bearing time deposits. These regulations carved up the available funds in a manner that dampened the intradepository competition, which promoted institutional stability. To further stabilize the sector, the separation of depository institutions from investment banks was accomplished by the Glass-Steagall Act (Isenberg, 2002, 43–45). It constructed a firewall so that there was "no undue diversion of funds into speculative operations" (US Congress, 1933).

On the regulatory side of the S&Ls were the Federal Home Loan Bank Board (FHLBB) and the Federal Savings and Loan Insurance Corporation (FSLIC). Like the Federal Reserve Bank System, the FHLBB was created in 1932 to provide liquidity and supervision for the S&Ls. In 1934, as a component of the National Housing Act, the FSLIC was organized to insure the S&Ls'

deposits. The commercial banks' deposit insurance program had been legislated as part of the Glass-Steagall Act in 1933. The creation of these liquidity facilities and deposit insurance program showed that the full faith and credit of the US government was standing behind the depository institutions. This unique combination of prudential and functional regulation produced a financial structure that relied primarily on market actors to determine the allocation of financial flows. Given that sustained capital development relied on financial institutions operating in a safe and secure manner, regulatory constraints and oversight were integral to the financial sector's stable operation.

These regulatory structures addressed some of the destabilizing tendencies that Hyman Minsky has noted are inherent in capitalism's unregulated financial troubles and were experienced in the Great Depression. Minsky's financial instability hypothesis (addressed in more detail in Minsky [1982]) details how periods of financial calm can evolve into explosive financial bubbles that burst and destroy asset values and, in the worst of times, the real economy. In his financial instability hypothesis, Minsky focuses on the increasing optimism that develops as economic successes multiply and economic activity expands. As optimism increases, real and financial investors tend to take riskier positions which, in the extreme and when unregulated, produce results like the 2000 dot-com bubble or the 2007 subprime mortgage meltdown. Minsky (1986) argues that financial regulation is a must: "If the authorities constrain banks and are aware of the activities of fringe banks and other financial institutions, they are in a better position to attenuate the disruptive expansionary tendencies of our economy" (252).

## How the Savings and Loan Crisis Got Its Start

### Financial Innovations: The 1960s

The years after World War II were initially saturated with fears that a Great Depression could occur from merely the slightest strain on credit markets. In the early 1950s many bankers thought that the decline in Treasury bond prices induced by just the slightest rise in government securities' interest rates would start a deposit-withdrawal stampede. The bankers soon saw that the depositing public was far more trusting of the revitalized financial system than expected. When Treasury bond prices fluctuated, as new bonds with higher interest rates were sold, bank depositors remained calm and their deposits remained in place (Wojnilower, 1980, 279–282).

The bankers gained confidence in the stability of the financial system as the years passed and minor innovations in lending activities were able to produce the credit expansions needed to accommodate the financial needs of the economic expansions. While a brief bout of disintermediation hit the banks' and thrifts' time deposits in 1959 as depositors withdrew their interest-sensitive funds to invest them in US Treasury bonds that bore interest rates that exceeded the deposit rates, in general, the state of confidence in the stability of the financial system continued into the expansion of the 1960s (Wojnilower, 1980, 284–287).

The credit needs of the expanding economy of the 1960s, particularly those of the large corporations, continued unabated, so banks found ways to circumvent their deposit-based lending constraints. Financial innovation introduced liability management in the form of large denomination negotiable certificates of deposit (CD) and Eurodollars. CDs were short-term bank liabilities with market interest rates (Wojnilower, 1980, 285). Eurodollars were loans made from a bank's foreign branches' dollar deposits. Both of these liabilities circumvented banks' dependence on their own deposits and the Fed's tight monetary policies. In time the banks expanded their use of CDs by selling small denomination CDs to individuals who then received interest on these time deposits. Of course, these deposits were attractive: they were interest-bearing and were FDIC-insured. The use of these short-term bank-issued debts to fund loans signaled a move away from the asset-management techniques that banks and thrifts had been utilizing, and this was a breach of a key element in the New Deal's functional regulation: no price competition between depository institutions (Wolfson, 1994, 36).

In 1966 the combination of liability management, fear of inflation, and the Fed's tight monetary policy produced the first postwar credit crunch. The violation of functional regulation in combination with the Fed's tight monetary policy resulted in a major disintermediation of time deposits from the S&Ls. Unlike the banks' CDs, their deposit rates were not market-based. The credit crunch of 1966 showed the banks and S&Ls that the time of Federal Reserve accommodative monetary policy had ended and that financial innovation did, indeed, have a downside (Isenberg, 2000, 253; Wolfson, 1994, 36).

Prior to the introduction of liability-side financial innovations, the S&Ls' profit performance was equal to that of the commercial banks. In the 1950s the S&Ls' rate of return on assets peaked at 0.81 percent and troughed at 0.6 percent while the commercial banks' rate peaked at 0.9 and troughed at 0.6 percent. For most of that decade the S&Ls' rate was higher than the commercial banks. As the expansive 1960s extend through time, the positions of these institutions switched. By 1967 the S&Ls' rate of return troughed at 0.46 percent for its decade low, while the commercial banks' rate moved from its high of 0.82 percent in 1962 to its low of 0.73 percent in 1967 (Isenberg, 2000, 255).

Financial innovation was in part responsible for the profit-rate reversals and eroding prudential regulation. The Federal Reserve at best ignored the commercial banks' innovative regulation transgressions and at worst it was a coconspirator in their actions (Dickens, 1990; Helleiner, 1994). Regardless of the view one takes, the commercial banks' regulators did nothing to rein in their transgressive behavior, and many would argue that their monetary policy decisions were made with the health of the large commercial banks in mind (Helleiner, 1994; Isenberg, 2000). The S&Ls' regulators, on the other hand, did not set monetary policy or allow the S&Ls to participate in these transgressive innovations. This disparity in adherence to the New Deal rules in a period of high credit demand, strong economic growth, and inflation-fighting monetary policy set the stage for future problems and changes.

## Economic Activity, Economic Policy, and Financial Innovation: The 1970s

To start the new decade, President Nixon convened a commission formed of industrialists and financiers to study the problems of the financial sector and introduce a path to change. Soon after this group issued its findings, some members of the House of Representatives commissioned their own study of these troubles. The findings in each of these studies, the Report of the President's Commission on Financial Structure and Regulation (more commonly known as the Hunt Report) and the Financial Institutions in the Nation's Economy study (the FINE study), proposed policies that would deregulate the financial sector and alter depository institutions' asset and liability mix (Isenberg, 2000, 258). The S&L industry's response to these proposals was not supportive, and their political power was still sufficient to keep these particular proposals from being enacted into law immediately (Mason, 2004, 209–211).

Once the 1960s turned into the 1970s, the macroeconomic conditions turned bad. The 1970s opened with a recession and then, in 1973 the deepest recession (to that point) since the Great Depression hit. On top of these economic stresses, inflationary pressures brewed: the never popular Vietnam War would only grind to a halt in 1975; the troubles with oil dependence and their volatile price increases took center stage from 1973 to 1979; and the Bretton Woods agreement was voided with President Nixon's 1971 decision to suspend the dollar's convertibility to gold. This economic environment meant that the fiscal and monetary policies that had been able to support the functional regulation and heretofore the success of the depository institutions was not going to reemerge. The economic problems inducing disintermediation were not going away. The depository institutions and their regulators were presented with a challenge: economic change.

This economic and policy environment pervaded the 1970s. The Federal Reserve tightened its monetary policy in the second half of 1969 and then, again, in 1973 (Isenberg, 2000, 257; Wolfson, 1994, 45–46). At each of these tightenings, the S&Ls experienced disintermediation as the short-term market interest rates surpassed the Regulation Q deposit cap. These periods of deposit outflows were not accompanied by insolvency or earnings problems; they were merely short-term liquidity problems. Even so, they were disruptive to the ongoing business of the financial institutions. In addition to the problems produced by the Fed's tight monetary policies, competition for depository dollars increased because the first of the market-based financial instruments available to small depositors, the money market mutual fund, was created in 1972. Initially, money did not flow heavily into these funds, but once the Fed's tight monetary policy drove short-term interest rates above Regulation Q's caps, they exploded. In 1977 there were only 50 funds with 150,000 customer accounts and net assets of only $4 billion. By mid-1979 they had 1,000,000 accounts worth $25 billion in assets; by mid-1980, the funds had $80 billion in aggregate assets (Dymski, 1990, 15).

To combat these disruptions and market innovations, various new liabilities were introduced in the 1970s for the depository institutions: negotiable order of withdrawals (NOW); automatic-transfer-from-savings (ATS); and money market certificates (MMC). These NOW and ATS accounts did not make a major change in the way that depositors held their money in an S&L, but the MMC was different. Authorized in June 1978, the "MMC was a six-month instrument sold in a minimum denomination of $10,000, with a ceiling rate tied to the average return on the weekly auction of six-month Treasury bills...by the end of December 1978, thrifts had about $47 billion in MMCs, equal to 8 percent of their deposit base" (Dymski, 1990, 16).

The adoption of these interest-bearing deposit liabilities, which were tied to market interest rates, ended functional regulation and the firewalls that dampened interdepository competition. The S&Ls that had been able to lock-in long-term asset prices along with a Regulation Q capped shorter-term deposit rates had been enabled for much of the post-New Deal period to operate with a 2 percent spread. This spread allowed them to maintain their traditional profit rates (Isenberg, 2000, 255). The balance-sheet transformation introduced through financial innovation meant that the Fed's tight monetary policies would no longer produce a short-term liquidity problem, disintermediation, for the S&Ls. It also meant that higher costs for liabilities would be locked in: interest-rate spikes would be translated into higher-cost funds, which would be locked in for the entire term to maturity of the liability. Profits would, therefore, shrink because the price of the long-term assets on their balance sheets would not change. By the end of the 1970s, the financial structure in which the S&Ls could successfully originate and hold 30-year fixed-rate mortgages until maturity had been set up to fail. This change also meant the dedicated financial conduit for home sales had been punctured.

## The Crisis Begins

The S&Ls entered the 1980s with their functional regulation in tatters and wondering about the viability of their prudential regulation. Many researchers who have labored over the S&L crisis have situated the reasons for this disaster in their regulation (Barth, 1991; Brumbaugh, 1988; Kane, 1992) while others have

Table 33.1 Savings and loans failures and net income.

| Year | Failures[1] | Net Income ($m)[2] |
|---|---|---|
| 1980 | 11 | 781 |
| 1981 | 34 | (4,631) |
| 1982 | 73 | (4,142) |
| 1983 | 51 | 1,945 |
| 1984 | 26 | 1,022 |
| 1985 | 54 | 3,728 |
| 1986 | 65 | 131 |
| 1987 | 59 | (7,779) |
| 1988 | 190 | (12,057) |
| 1989 | | (19,172) |

[1]Taken from FDIC (1997), 169.

[2]Taken from Barth (1991), 25.

focused on the period's tight monetary policy or deregulation and its effects (Eichler, 1989; FDIC, 1997; Mason, 2004; White, 1991). As the data covered in table 33.1 indicate, the S&Ls were in a very healthy and successful position throughout the 1960s and had ridden out the turbulent stagflationary years of the 1970s as well as possible. There's no doubt that they emerged from the 1970s more scarred than when they went in, but the reason for most S&Ls' failure before 1980 was fraud, not economic failure. Even though they entered the new decade scarred from their previous bouts with market tumult, they were ill prepared for the challenges of the early 1980s.

Several crucial calls for economic change came together at the start of the 1980s: the international call to stem the export of US inflation; a neoliberal call to reduce government's economic role; a call to deregulate the depository financial institutions; and a call to reestablish the Fed's control over the money supply. Additionally, a transition in economic ideology was occurring. Monetarism was gaining theoretical credibility as Keynesian theory's applicability was being challenged. This transition to new ideology, theory, and policies helped to roil the 1980s.

## Monetarist Monetary Policy

The inflation that had plagued the 1970s had been responsible for several periods of tight monetary policy, but they were child's play compared to the stringent policy put in place in Federal Reserve Chair Paul Volcker's first year in office. Volcker received Senate confirmation as the Federal Reserve chair in August 1979 and in October 1979 he initiated what has been called the "Saturday night massacre" in order to stem inflation. As part of his inflation-fighting policy, Chairman Volcker shifted from targeting the federal funds rate (FFR) to using the bank reserves and money supply variables as a policy tool and target:

> According to the Record of Policy Actions (p. 202), at the October 6 meeting, "the members agreed that the current situation called for additional measures to restrain growth of the monetary aggregates" and "most members strongly supported a shift in the conduct of open market operations to an approach placing emphasis on supplying the volume of bank reserves estimated to be consistent with the desired rates of growth in the monetary aggregates." (Federal Reserve Bank of San Francisco, 2004, 2)

By using bank reserves to tighten the monetary aggregates, the Fed knew that the FFR and other interest rates would be severely impacted. "At the meeting in September, a range of 50 basis points, from 111/4 to 113/4 percent, was set for the funds rate; at the October meeting, this range was increased to 400 basis points, from 111/2 to 151/2 percent" (Federal Reserve Bank of San Francisco, 2004, 2). And, by year's end the FFR was close to 14 percent. In April 1980, it reached its 1980 peak of 17.6 percent. Interest rates fell back to 10 percent but then shot up again before the end of 1980 (Federal Reserve Bank of San Francisco, 2004, 2).

Even the Federal Reserve Bank of San Francisco (FRBSF) agrees that this dramatic increase in interest rates was responsible for the recessions that began in January 1980 and July 1981. While the NBER ends the first recession in July 1980 and shows another one beginning in July 1981, given the continuing high unemployment rates, few other Americans would have believed that there was a six-month expansion in between these recessions. The FRBSF notes, "Late in 1980, interest rates were pushed back up, and the funds rate averaged over 19 percent in June 1981. A new recession began in July, one that saw the unemployment rate reach almost 11 percent by the end of 1982" (2004, 3).

This combination of high interest rates, high inflation, slow to negative economic growth, and high unabating unemployment rates between 1980 and 1983 indicates the whiplashed nature of the US economy. The Fed's shift to targeting monetary aggregates and letting interest rates be determined by the market had induced two destructive recessions and had also created problems of solvency for the S&Ls. Given that most of their liabilities were still governed by Regulation Q, the high market interest rates induced yet another outflow of funds. Additionally, the cost of liabilities with market rates rose. Now the S&Ls had a smaller pool of deposits that cost more. At the same time, their major assets, long-term mortgages, had low fixed interest rates that had been contracted in an earlier period. S&Ls' profits and asset values were slashed. As table 33.1 shows, S&Ls registered negative net income in 1981 and 1982 (Barth, 1991, 38; FDIC, 1997, 168; Mason, 2004, 214). Given the domination of a pro-market ideology, Congress moved to deregulate the financial sector.

## Deregulation

As noted earlier, proposals for depository institutions' deregulation had been introduced with the FINE study and the Hunt Report. The political backing from powerful industry and governmental actors necessary to effect such changes was missing at that time, so the besieged New Deal regulatory structure remained in place. By the end of the 1970s, however, the zeitgeist had changed, as had the financial institutions' lobbying power and the urgency of the S&Ls' problems. In the interim, the ideology of competitive markets had come to dominate the economic and political landscape. Market decision making was seen as better than regulators and as the best method for producing efficient outcomes. On April 1, 1980, the Depository Institutions Deregulation and Monetary Control Act (DIDMCA) became law. It aimed to solve two separate problems: (1) reassert the Federal Reserve's control over the money supply and (2) fix the troubles of the depository institutions by introducing competition.

While the financial innovation of the 1970s had primarily affected the S&Ls' liability side, DIDMCA's reforms affected S&Ls' assets and liabilities. Its deregulatory aspects, however, focused primarily on their asset side. The asset mix available to S&Ls was expanded: they could originate consumer loans, commercial paper, and corporate debt securities, which could account for up to 20 percent of their assets. They could originate acquisition, development, and construction loans, which took them into the risky realm of real-estate development. They were allowed to offer credit-card services. These changes would also shorten the average term to maturity of the assets on their balance sheets. Additionally, all federally insured depository institutions could offer NOW accounts and all their deposits would be insured up to $100,000. Finally, Regulation Q would be phased out over a six-year period (Cargill and Garcia, 1985, 57–61).

The actual impact of DIDMCA on the S&Ls was far different from the salutary effects envisioned by the supporters of deregulation. Instead of returning them to financial health and an engagement in robust activities, it pushed them into insolvency. In 1980 the percentage of assets that mortgages represented dropped from 69.3 to 67.5 (see table 33.2). The S&Ls expanded their consumer, commercial, and real-estate loans, but their net income dropped from $3.6 billion to $0.8 billion (table 33.1). The next year, 1981, was even worse. Mortgages as a percentage of assets fell another 1.5 percent. They continued to expand lending on shorter-term loans, but they were still a very small percentage of the total portfolio. The lifting of all the restrictions on the MMC deposits, which accounted for 40 percent of their total deposits, made S&Ls' interest costs soar (Mason, 2004, 218). By the end of 1981, the S&Ls had net losses of $4.6 billion (table 33.1). In 1982, the next brick in the deregulation edifice, the Garn-St. Germain Depository Institutions Act (Garn-St. Germain), was put in place.

As far as affecting depository health, DIDMCA had lowered net worth requirements from 5 percent of insured accounts to a range between 3 and 6

Table 33.2 Savings and loans assets and rate of return.

| Year | ROA (%) | 1–4 Family Mortgages (%) | Multifamily (%) | Construction Loans (%) | Land Loans (%) | Nonresidential Loans (%) | Commercial Loans (%) | Real-Estate Owned (%) |
|---|---|---|---|---|---|---|---|---|
| 1961 | 0.98 | 84.02 | | | | | | |
| 1962 | 0.98 | 84.37 | | | | | | |
| 1963 | 0.7 | 84.78 | | | | | | |
| 1964 | 0.72 | 85.12 | | | | | | |
| 1965 | 0.67 | 85.36 | | | | | | |
| 1966 | 0.5 | 85.64 | | | | | | |
| 1967 | 0.46 | 85.08 | | | | | | |
| 1968 | 0.6 | 85 | | | | | | |
| 1969 | 0.68 | 86.76 | | | | | | |
| 1970 | 0.57 | 85.58 | | | | | | 0.42 |
| 1971 | 0.71 | 84.79 | | | | | | 0.37 |
| 1972 | 0.77 | 84.99 | | | | | | 0.32 |
| 1973 | 0.76 | 85.71 | | | | | | 0.33 |
| 1974 | 0.54 | 84.5 | | | | | | 0.41 |
| 1975 | 0.47 | 82.5 | | | 0.59 | | | 0.49 |
| 1976 | 0.63 | 78.95 | | 3.61 | 0.86 | | | 0.49 |
| 1977 | 0.77 | 79.04 | | 4.09 | 0.86 | | | 0.39 |

| | | | | | | | | |
|---|---|---|---|---|---|---|---|---|
| 1978 | 0.83 | 69.6 | 7.97 | 4.3 | 0.87 | 2.17 | 1.56 | 0.34 |
| 1979 | 0.69 | 69.27 | 6.62 | 3.85 | 0.93 | 2.77 | 1.76 | 0.32 |
| 1980 | 0.14 | 67.55 | 6.16 | 2.76 | 0.89 | 3.04 | 1.94 | 0.37 |
| 1981 | −0.74 | 65.97 | 5.75 | 2.5 | 0.93 | 2.85 | 2.08 | 0.51 |
| 1982 | −0.63 | 58.02 | 5.77 | 3.26 | 0.99 | 2.9 | 2.34 | 0.79 |
| 1983 | 0.26 | 51.86 | 6.3 | 5.32 | 1.57 | 3.39 | 2.82 | 0.45 |
| 1984 | 0.12 | 46.55 | 6.75 | 5.92 | 2.32 | 8.93 | 1.31 | 0.54 |
| 1985 | 0.38 | 43.91 | 7.22 | 2.7 | 2.88 | 6.97 | 1.77 | 0.88 |
| 1986 | 0.05 | 38.54 | 5.81 | 4.96 | 2.64 | 7.16 | 2.15 | 1.33 |
| 1987 | −0.6 | 37.58 | 5.95 | 4.21 | 2.15 | 7.21 | 1.92 | 1.96 |
| 1988 | −1 | 38.5 | 5.72 | 3.81 | 1.88 | 6.85 | 2.53 | 2.04 |
| 1989 | −0.54 | 41.22 | 5.83 | 3.37 | 1.35 | 6.76 | 2.56 | 1.84 |
| 1990 | −0.35 | 43.04 | 6.14 | 2.55 | 1.06 | 6.31 | 2.19 | 2.17 |
| 1991 | 0.13 | 45.61 | 6.4 | 1.75 | 0.72 | 5.88 | 1.89 | 1.91 |
| 1992 | 0.61 | 45.71 | 6.59 | 1.49 | 0.52 | 5.3 | 0.9 | 1.57 |
| 1993 | 0.63 | 45.79 | 6.88 | 1.64 | 0.48 | 4.99 | 0.66 | 0.88 |
| 1994 | 0.56 | 47.03 | 6.62 | 1.76 | 0.43 | 4.46 | 0.67 | 0.49 |
| 1995 | 0.7 | 47.38 | 6.32 | 1.91 | 0.45 | 4.26 | 0.93 | 0.36 |

Source: Office of Thrift Supervision, 2002 *Fact Book*, table 2.2.1 and table 3.1.

percent, which made more institutions look solvent. Garn-St. Germain allowed S&Ls to issue money market deposit accounts (MMDAs). Given the draw of money market mutual funds (MMMFs) to small investors, many depositors had opted to withdraw their savings to purchase equity positions in these funds, which were invested in short-term liabilities. The MMDAs directly competed with the MMMFs, but they also were FSLIC-insured. Garn-St. Germain also added to the healthier look of the S&Ls by initiating a net worth certificate program for S&Ls that supplied temporary capital and by leaving the definition of adequate reserves and their form strictly up to the FSLIC (FDIC, 1997, 173–174). It also allowed the S&Ls to use the more liberal regulatory accounting rules (RAP). These accounting rule changes made losses look smaller and assets look larger. The overall effect of this deregulation was to extend the FSLIC's forbearance. While the rule-changing motivations focused on allowing the S&Ls to grow out of their problems, these changes actually resulted in covering up the extent of the S&Ls' insolvency and, ultimately, increasing the costs of resolving their troubles.

The accounting changes succeeded in reducing the number of S&Ls requiring immediate resolution: there were 169 failures between 1980 and 1983 (FDIC, 1997, 169). In addition to these failures, the FSLIC had far more cases that it resolved through supervisory mergers or acquisitions. Kane (1989, 26–27) tabulates that over this same time period an additional 262 institutions were resolved by these actions.[1] Even with these additions, Kane notes that 489 additional institutions remained GAAP-insolvent.

When the market interest rates rapidly declined in 1983, the number of actual failures and FSLIC resolutions subsided; by 1985, the S&L crisis had been reignited but by different forces.

## Competitive S&Ls, Another Crisis, and a Bailout

The new freedom that sprang from deregulation refashioned the thrift industry. Banks and S&Ls now competed with each other as well as market-based institutions for assets and liabilities. This alteration meant one of the fundamental aspects of the New Deal regulatory structure, functional regulation, had been abandoned. S&Ls were no longer limited to originating conventional residential mortgages, which were long-lived low-risk assets. They could now originate short-term higher-risk assets such as commercial real-estate loans, which promised higher yields and new ways to grow their assets. In addition to reducing their commitment to residential housing, many S&Ls also reduced their engagement with traditional savers. Rather than continuing to rely on nonmarket-based time deposits, many leaped into the "hot money" markets operated with brokered deposits. To further refashion their new operational profiles, many S&Ls changed their federal charters into state charters. The limits on asset structure were far fewer for state-chartered institutions. This transformation held particularly true for S&Ls in Texas, Florida, and California.[2] And, finally, many of them converted from their traditional mutual ownership to stock ownership (Barth, 1991: 24–29; White, 1991, 102–105). These changes provided the basis for the rapid growth-oriented behaviors characterizing a large portion of the thrift industry.

Along with the erosion of functional regulation in the thrift industry, prudential regulation also declined. Given the change in assets and liabilities held on S&Ls' balance sheets, greater oversight might be warranted because these were new areas of investment for loan officers. Regardless, fewer S&Ls were examined and fewer examiners were employed by the FHLBB. Between 1981 and 1984, 26 percent fewer examinations occurred. While the number of S&Ls had declined during this time period, the size of total assets had risen. This "let-the-market-rule" approach of the FLHBB chair, Edwin Gray, continued until 1984 when Empire Savings and Loan of Mesquite, Texas, was liquidated by examiners. This closure was the largest FSLIC payout in its history to that point (Mason, 2004, 224–226).

Empire Savings and Loans' failure and closure signaled the beginning of a new S&L crisis. This industrial meltdown, unlike the previous one, resulted from an unbridled belief in the efficient and effective decision making of markets. The growth of the thrift industry in the era of deregulation had not been supervised by its regulators or constrained by risk-sensitive investment rules. Their growth had depended on riding a wild real-estate boom to its peak and fostering the use of financial innovation in assets and liability structures. Their bust was just the equally wild ride down the other side of the cycle. This crisis was not an interest-rate problem; it was all about asset quality.

## Real-Estate Bust

The second S&L crisis is rooted in the regional boom-and-bust cycles of real estate but was exacerbated by the "grow big and grow fast" deregulationist 1980s mentality. The 1970s had been the period of go-go banking in the United States, leading to the cataclysmic downfall of Penn Square Bank, Continental Illinois, Seafirst, and others. In the 1980s the deregulationist environment was ripe for go-go thrifts.

The shift into state charters was induced as noted earlier by the lenient regulatory rules of states like California, Texas, and Florida. This leniency worked with regional real-estate bubbles to expand activities in risky lending. While many of the S&Ls that did not jump on the rapid growth wagon continued to concentrate on mortgage lending, the go-go thrifts moved into innovative mortgages and construction lending. Acquisition, development, and construction loans (ADC) were high-risk loans to developers that financed the building of infrastructure required in new housing and commercial developments. For the fastest-growing S&Ls, the fee income from these loans accounted for effectively all net income in 1983 and 1984 (Lowy, 1991, 77). The movement into "nontraditional" assets nearly tripled—from $78.9 billion to $216.1 billion—between 1982 and 1985. Thrifts with annual rates of growth greater than 50 percent booked more than 16 percent of their assets in commercial mortgages and land loans (White, 1991, 102–103). While the percentage of California's S&L assets in these loans never surpassed 25 percent, in Florida and Texas they reached just below 40 percent by 1983. Texas S&Ls' construction lending had risen from $1.8 billion in 1978 to $10.3 billion in 1983, almost six times in 5 years (Eichler, 1989, 98–99).

Because all real-estate bubbles burst, it was merely a question of how long this one would be sustained. The rise in domestic crude oil prices had been responsible for pumping up the Texas economy and real-estate market into the early 1980s. By the end of 1984, oil prices were declining; by 1986, they were down by 60 percent. The Texas real-estate bubble popped. "In Houston, nearly a third of all its office space was unoccupied, and 17 percent of all homes and apartments were vacant" (Mason, 2004, 228–229). In the United States, across the South and Southwest, there had been dependence on rising real-estate prices to validate commercial mortgages and construction loans. White notes that commercial real-estate prices in the South and the Southwest peaked in 1985. Prices for office buildings peaked even earlier in 1984 and fell precipitously thereafter (White, 1991, 111).

Along with the regional troubles, a change in federal tax laws helped to press the air out of the national real-estate market. The Tax Act of 1981 had decreased depreciation periods, thereby stimulating the real-estate market. The Tax Reform Act of 1986, which lengthened depreciation periods and reduced the tax "shelter" provided by real-estate investors, acted to depress real-estate prices, especially in the South and Southwest (White, 1991, 109–111).

Finally, the new competition between S&Ls and commercial banks (CBs) spurred by deregulation fostered a "race to the bottom" in the real-estate lending markets. Borrowers were able to set up "bidding wars" between the banks and S&Ls as each vied for their business. While S&Ls lent to lower-qualified borrowers, they were also known to be utilizing lax underwriting standards to attract customers away from CBs. Given the competition, the CBs adopted many of the S&L practices, which produced higher-risk loans on all depository institutions' balance sheets (FDIC, 1997, 185).

The real-estate boom of the early 1980s was motivated like every other bubble: herd activity pushed up asset prices. The trouble, unfortunately, with this particular bubble was that it occurred at the same time and was fueled in part by all the deregulatory changes that produced the go-go thrifts. This interaction of the revamped deregulated financial structure with the real-estate boom generated a quite toxic concoction. As table 33.1 shows, net income soon was back in negative territory.

## The Failure to Resolve the Crisis

The failure of Empire Savings and Loan was, as noted, just the first signal, albeit an explosive one, that change had arrived. While the impact of the first S&L crisis had peaked and passed by 1983, the methods employed to reduce the impact of that crisis on regulators ensured that thrifts would continue to fail throughout the 1980s. As table 33.1 shows, the number decreased after 1982 as did the total value of their assets, but the number of failures never returned to the single digits of the pre-deregulation era. In 1984, 26 S&Ls failed and 22 of them were resolved through the FSLIC. These numbers stand in contrast to the 71 S&Ls that White notes were RAP-insolvent and the 616 that were RAP-solvent but insolvent when calculated by tangible net worth. Clearly, only the neediest of S&Ls had been resolved in the first S&L crisis and the increase in the number of RAP-insolvent thrifts after 1984 indicates that the deregulated financial and the economic environment had not fostered healthier thrifts.

Given the methods used to resolve the earlier S&L crisis, the FSLIC had been able to cover the necessary payouts with its reserves. In 1980 and 1981, there was no reason to include the assets of vulnerable S&Ls on the edge of insolvency as a contingent liability. White argues that this omission is due to a generalized acknowledgment that the earlier crisis was a high-interest-rate problem, not an asset-quality problem. He continues to say that, in 1985, the GAO, the FSLIC's auditor, decided that their financial statement should reflect as contingent liabilities a projection of the costs of resolving near-term insolvencies. It was this accounting change, reflecting the future need for FSLIC reserves, that in 1986 showed that the FSLIC was incapable of resolving the crisis (White, 1991, 133).

The dawning awareness of the size of this second S&L crisis and the possibility of having to use taxpayers' money to resolve it spawned many attempts to allay such a move. Between 1985 and 1988, several programs were implemented to facilitate the operation of FSLIC: the Management Consignment Program warehoused failed thrifts and replaced their officers; the Federal Asset Disposition Association facilitated the speedy disposal of failed assets; the Competitive Equality Banking Act tightened S&L operations and assets and recapitalized the FSLIC with $10.8 billion of "off-balance-sheet" financing; and the "Southwest Plan" was the aggressive selling of S&Ls based on their significant tax savings to the purchaser. These programs were unable to change the fate of the overburdened FSLIC.

In 1989, Congress passed the Financial Institutions Reform, Recovery, and Enforcement Act (FIRREA). The FSLIC was declared dead and replaced by the FDIC and its new subsidiary, Savings Association Insurance Fund (SAIF);

the new Office of Thrift Supervision supplanted the FHLBB; and the new Reconstruction Trust Corporation (RTC) was to resolve all the insolvent thrifts in two years with $50 billion. Along with the new set of institutions responsible for thrift oversight, FIRREA implemented new rules raising net-worth requirements, changing asset requirements, and redistributing the burden of paying for the resolution of the insolvent S&Ls.

## The Resolution Trust Corporation: The Bailout

The passage of FIRREA indicated that the highest political circles acknowledged that the S&L crisis had to be resolved. The realization that these thrifts were technically dead but, due to the inadequacies of the resolution process, could never actually die earned them the name "zombies." The politicians understood that a financial system heavily populated with the undead was a constant reminder of the crisis and not good for economic growth. The RTC's motto, "Resolving the Crisis, Restoring the Confidence," reflected its goals.

While the FSLIC had resolved 205 thrifts by the end of 1988, there were still 243 with assets of $74.3 billion that were technically RAP insolvent. The number of tangible asset insolvencies was double and their assets valued at four times the values of the RAP insolvents (White, 1991, 175). Because the RTC was created solely to resolve the crisis, it did not have the same operational strictures as the FSLIC who had to maintain confidentiality about the financial position of the insured. RTC was a disposal unit, so it could operate in the open. This openness and the agency's limited life span provided the foundation for new methods of asset disposal. FIRREA mandated them to use private contractors, but the disposal methods were unspecified.

While the FDIC provided most of the RTC staffing, when the RTC disposed of assets it followed its own drummer. RTC insolvents were placed into conservatorship, which generally lasted about 13 months. During this period they controlled the institution and tried to reduce its assets by offering them to bidders in pieces rather than selling them in toto to the acquirer like the FDIC had. These piecemeal sales offered in the public domain resulted in smaller asset sales to the final acquirer at resolution (FDIC, 1998, 119). Another innovative aspect of the resolution process was the use of mortgage-backed securities. Because 96 percent of its residential mortgages were performing assets, they could be bundled and sold much as Fannie Mae had done. These bonds acquired a following and "by 1992 the RTC was selling between $1.5 and $2.1 billion each month of what Wall Street dubbed 'Ritzy Maes.' When the RTC ended operations, more than 21 percent of all mortgages it held were sold under this securitization program" (Mason, 2004, 252).

Given the public funds that financed the RTC operations, one of its programs was to redistribute some of those funds in the form of affordable housing. "Affordable housing was considered an area in which the nation could glean social benefit from the financial crisis by providing an opportunity for low- to moderate-income households to realize their dream of home ownership or to improve their standard of living at affordable rent levels" (FDIC, 1998, 373). While the RTC still had to operate within a framework of least cost resolutions, they were able to resell 81,000 units of multifamily housing and 28,000 units of single-family units to low- and moderate-income families (373).

Another socially conscious aspect of the program was its progress in determining the responsibility for fraudulent and irresponsible financial behavior that produced the S&L crisis. "Between 1992 and 1995, the gross recovery of fines from accounting firms, lawyers, and thrift executives totaled $2.4 billion" (Mason, 2004, 253). In addition, the Justice Department increased its criminal prosecutions with the help of the RTC. More than 1,800 former thrift and bank executives were convicted (253).

The RTC was able to finally resolve the S&L crisis in 1995. It took longer than expected and cost $87.5 billion rather than the $50 billion it was initially seeded, but it completed the job. In the six years of its existence, it successfully resolved 747 S&Ls and disposed of $402.6 billion in assets. In this process of asset disposal, the RTC was able to recover more than 78 percent of book value on all the assets it sold (Mason, 2004, 254–255). Upon its own dissolution, it left a thrift industry that was again solvent, which was its job. It also signaled the beginning of a new era in which light regulation would allow US economic activity to be dominated by bubbles.

## The Connection to Our Current Crisis

Financial crises are always a potential. As Minsky noted, effective financial regulation is necessary to keep the speculative tendencies in financial-market activities from emerging. In other words, expansionary periods have the tendency to produce bubbles. Most often these bubbles have manifested themselves in real-estate and financial-asset markets. In the United States from the 1970s through the 2000s, crises were experienced in numerous financial markets, including commercial paper, real-estate investment trusts, silver, commercial and residential real estate, the stock market, and mortgages and their innovative derivatives. The combination of demand for a particular financial asset (or herd behavior), innovative financial-asset design, and light to no regulation can be toxic as our current economic situation clearly shows. In the S&L crisis, initially, it was the devastatingly tight monetary policy that broke the savings institutions. When the interest rates fell into a more normal range, the S&Ls' financial positions recovered but were still weak as was their insurer. The

FSLIC had singlehandedly resolved the massive failures, which meant government funds were not used but FSLIC reserves were low. It was in the second phase of the crisis that the combination of deregulation, financial innovation, and the regional real-estate booms destroyed the savings and loan industry. Luckily, their weakened state and the government's multitude of programs starting in 1985 to salvage the industry, even before the FSLIC was bankrupted, kept the financial crisis from becoming an economic crisis.

There were many criticisms of the way the S&L industry was eventually bailed out and reconstituted as a slimmed-down version of its old self, but its role as an industrial cleaner is not challenged. Some thought the industrial cleaning was not handled quickly enough; others thought there was too much governmental involvement; many thought it was handled too slowly. However, the thrift sector was stabilized and this kept the residential real-estate market and the US economy out of crisis. It's clear that the RTC's absorption of the failed S&Ls' assets—mostly houses and mortgages—cleared the real-estate market of foreclosed homes. The Case/Shiller Home Price Index (Standard & Poor's, 2011) showed a positive change in housing prices until the beginning of the 1990–1991 recession. Home prices fell briefly in the contraction but had stabilized by 1992. Many homeowners were "underwater" but the market itself was not.

In our current crisis, where the crumbling investment and commercial banks have held on to their toxic assets and foreclosed homes, the financial crisis has been allowed to invade the real economy and create disarray in the housing market. The hands-off nature of the government's involvement in this financial crisis has led to home-price declines, which commenced in 2006 and have not yet hit bottom (Standard & Poor's, 2011). The foreclosed homes continue to sit on the market, swelling supply (Dash, 2011, 1). New construction of homes has stopped, which means that regions in the United States, whose growth depended on the residential construction and commercial activity that followed it, are still in the throes of high unemployment. The reduction in home prices has meant that even homeowners who did not participate in the financial casino have lost net worth and, given the domino effect of declines in demand, many innocent bystanders have lost their jobs. The current handling of our financial crisis failed to contain it. It was allowed to leak into the real sector and to produce the Great Recession.

The ideological transformation between 1989 and 2009 has been vast. The creation of the RTC as the "bad" bank may not have been the first program US policy makers constructed, but even their earlier programs' structures made it clear that the failed assets had to be cleared from the markets or they would pollute them. The policy makers knew the market, if left to its own motivations, would not cordon off the bad assets. It took consciously constructed institutions to cordon them off and make new conduits for their redistribution or resolution. By 2008 this type of governmental intervention to resolve a financial crisis was politically impossible even though it was still an economically sound idea.

The US Treasury's 2008 Troubled Asset Relief Program, while initially aimed at clearing bad assets from banks' balance sheets, ultimately only injected them with new capital and left the bad assets with the banks. There was no relief from the troubled assets, neither for the banks nor for the public. Our previous success had faded from sight when it should have been the beacon for our actions.

## Notes

1. Researchers differ on the exact number of institutions that failed and the number that found a resolution through the market or regulators' aid. Definitions of failure and resolution lie at the bottom of these differences. See in addition to Kane and the FDIC, Barth (1991), Barth and Brumbaugh (1992), and Brumbaugh (1988).
2. Mason (2004) notes that the passage of the 1982 Nolan Bill in California "removed nearly all lending restrictions on state-chartered thrifts and allowed them to invest up to 100 percent of their deposits in virtually any kind of venture" (224). This bill was effectively copied in Florida and Texas, leading to a tripling of these three states' S&L assets between 1982 and 1985 to $214 million. These assets represented almost 20 percent of total industry assets.

## References

Barth, James. (1991). *The Great Savings and Loan Debacle*. Washington, DC: AEI Press.

Barth, James, and R. Dan Brumbaugh, eds. (1992). *The Reform of Federal Deposit Insurance: Disciplining the Government and Protecting Taxpayers*. New York: HarperBusiness.

Brumbaugh, R. Dan. (1988). *Thrifts under Siege*. Cambridge, MA: Ballinger.

Cargill, Thomas E., and Gillian Garcia. (1985). *Financial Reform in the 1980s*. Stanford, CA: Hoover Institution Press.

D'Arista, Jane. (1994). *The Evolution of US Finance, Vol. II*. Armonk, NY: M. E. Sharpe.

Dash, Eric. (2011). "Banks Amass Glut of Homes, Chilling Sales." *New York Times*, May 23.

Dickens, Edwin. (1990). "Financial Crises, Innovations and Federal Reserve Control of the Stock of Money." *Contributions to Political Economy* 9: 1–23.

Dymski, Gary. (1990). "The Structure and Regulation of the US Banking System from the Great Depression to the Present Day." Mimeo. University of Southern California, Los Angeles.

Eichler, Ned. (1989). *The Thrift Debacle*. Berkeley: University of California Press.

FDIC. (1997). *History of the Eighties: Lessons for the Future*. Vol. 1. Washington, DC: FDIC.

FDIC. (1998). *Managing the Crisis: The FDIC and RTC Experience.* Vol. 1. Washington, DC: FDIC.

Federal Reserve Bank of San Francisco. (2004). *FRBSF Economic Letter* 35 (December 3). http://www.frbsf.org/publications/economics/letter/2004/el2004-35.html.

Helleiner, Eric. (1994). *States and the Reemergence of Global Finance: From Bretton Woods to the 1990s.* Ithaca, NY: Cornell University Press.

Isenberg, Dorene. (2000). "The Political Economy of Financial Reform." In Robert Pollin, ed., *Capitalism, Socialism, and Radical Political Economy: Essays in Honor of Howard J. Sherman*, 247–269. Cheltenham, UK: Edward Elgar.

Isenberg, Dorene. (2002). "US Housing Policy Transformation: The Challenge of the Market." In Gary Dymski and Dorene Isenberg, eds., *Seeking Shelter on the Pacific Rim: Financial Globalization, Social Change, and the Housing Market*, 42–62. Armonk, NY: M.E. Sharpe.

Kane, Edward. (1989). *The S&L Insurance Mess: How Did It Happen?* Washington, DC: Urban Institute Press.

Kane, Edward. (1992). "The Incentive Incompatibility of Government-Sponsored Deposit-Insurance Funds." In James Barth and R. Dan Brumbaugh Jr., eds., *The Reform of Federal Deposit Insurance: Disciplining the Government and Protecting Taxpayers*, 144–165. New York: HarperBusiness.

Lowy, Martin. (1991). *High Rollers: Inside the Savings and Loan Debacle.* New York: Praeger.

Mason, David. (2004). *From Buildings and Loans to Bail-Outs.* Cambridge: Cambridge University Press.

Minsky, Hyman. (1982). *Can "It" Happen Again?* Armonk, NY: M. E. Sharpe.

Minsky, Hyman. (1986). *Stabilizing an Unstable Economy.* New Haven, CT: Yale University Press.

Office of Thrift Supervision. (2002). *2002 Fact Book.* http://www.ots.treas.gov/_files/2002FactBook.pdf.

Standard & Poor's. (2011). "S&P/Case-Shiller Home Price Indices: 2010, A Year in Review." In *S&P Indices.* New York: Standard & Poor's.

US Congress. http://www.archive.org/stream/FullTextTheGlass-steagallActA.k.a.TheBankingActOf1933/1933_01248#page/no/mode/1up.

White, Lawrence. (1991). *The Savings and Loan Debacle.* Oxford: Oxford University Press.

Wojnilower, Albert. (1980). "The Central Role of Credit Crunches in Recent Financial History." *Brookings Papers on Economic Activity* 2: 278–339.

Wolfson, Martin. (1994). *Financial Crises: Understanding the Postwar US Experience.* Armonk, NY: M. E. Sharpe.

CHAPTER 34

# PENSION POLICIES TO MINIMIZE FUTURE ECONOMIC CRISES

TERESA GHILARDUCCI

## 1. Overview: Pension Funds in the Greater Context

Changes in the American pension system made the recession that had started in 2007 worse. Pension funds are a large part of the financial landscape but their investment behavior is not the primary way in which the system affects economic growth and stability. The "financialization" of the system—the 30-year shift from a defined benefit (DB) plan to the more dominant defined-contribution (DC) structure—contributed to the 2008–2009 financial crises, and the changing structure will make future business cycles more volatile. In this regard, certain pension reforms could help minimize future financial crises.

In addition to expecting governments to nurture institutions that stabilize the economy (and dismantle those that do not), the public at large has an even more direct stake in the behavior of the pension system and should demand more from it. Without billions of dollars of tax subsidies, it is unlikely that the pension system we see in place today would exist and yet, despite pension funds growing at twice the rate of total financial assets from 1966 to 2008, over the last 42 years (see section 2), pension coverage rates have stagnated at 50 percent of the workforce. Moreover, American employee retirement income security was severely eroded by the drop in financial-asset values starting in

2008,[1] in part because of the transformative process of said "financialization." Overall, the retirement security for the next generation of retirees is getting worse—coverage rates have not improved in 30 years and the replacement rate, the ratio of pensions to preretirement income, is dropping.

Section 2 will concentrate on the unacknowledged macroeconomic, destabilizing aspects of the American pension system. Some analysts have speculated for more than 20 years that pension funds' proclivity, their high level of trading and investment in hedge funds and other derivatives, was a major cause of the rise of the supply of exotic financial instruments (see Kevin Phillips's *Bad Money* [2008] and reports from Michael Porter and the Twentieth Century Fund in 1992), such as swap instruments and securitized assets, which were subsequently a major cause of the financial crises.

Despite the general suspicion that pension funds may have contributed to the financial crises by being a major source of demand for exotic financial instruments, the 2011 Financial Crisis Inquiry Report mentions pension funds only nine times in its 633-page document, with most references being made to the economic fallout of the crises, wherein pensions are cast as victims of intrabank holdings of swaps and other instruments, along with the collective exaggeration of asset values (aided and abetted by the rating agencies) and the consequential increased amount of leveraging, were above and beyond the prime instigators of the crises.

Though, to be sure, the US pension system affects the demand for exotic financial assets, the current employer pension system has a much more subtle and corrosive effect on economic stabilization. The 30-year process of financialization that has taken place, shifting from annuity- based defined-benefit pension plans to financial asset-based 401(k)-type pension plans, has caused people to spend more and work less during periods of economic expansion and spend less and work more during recessions. These pro-cyclical effects, which exaggerate expansions and exacerbate recessions, reduce the effects of automatic stabilizing institutions. Section 3 describes these large and, until now, underestimated destabilizing effects.

Section 4 proposes guaranteed retirement accounts (GRAs) to compete with 401(k) plans and individual retirement accounts (IRAs) as a "public option." GRAs allow employer and worker retirement contributions to smooth out across business cycles. The GRA stands in stark contrast to the Obama administration's proposal to put workers without pension coverage into IRAs at 2 percent of their pay with no contribution from the employer and allowing the worker to opt out. Both of these plans are described in further detail in the 2009 Government Accountability Office report, and strong evidence suggests that Obama's opt-out IRA plan would be a mistake and make things worse. Pension reform must slow down growth in 401(k) and IRA-type plans because, besides the danger to retirement income security, an unappreciated reason for slowing their growth is that the individual, voluntary, commercial pension structure has a negative effect on macroeconomic stability.

Section 5 proposes a way in which to stabilize state and local pension funds. The financial crises have caused assets to drop in value and large increases in contributions to be necessitated from strapped governments, all of which will cause real hardship as states and localities defund ordinary state and local functions in order to pay pension contributions. Some public pension systems will attempt to lower pension contributions.

Overall, I propose a way to attach federal financial assistance to state and local pension reform that will yield two vital outcomes. First, it will induce a positive structural change in the plan design—in particular, one that smoothes out pension funding and yields sensible benefits. Second, federal aid will be attached to programs that give all residents and taxpayers access to the efficient, transparent, and expert pension-fund management services of the public-sector pension fund.

The conclusion describes a proposal for a universal system of supplemental retirement accounts that are consumed as an annuity will go far to achieve the three long-term goals of solvency, stabilization, and security.

## 2. Size of Pension Funds in the Economy

No serious approach to financial reform can ignore the fact that the pension system owns more than a third of corporate equities and that it constitutes the largest source of household and government savings. Pension funds have gained rapidly on banks and other financial institutions in their share of retirement assets and should be encouraged to invest in longer-term instruments such as infrastructure.

The pension system is heavily subsidized by federal and state governments. The subsidies to 401(k) plans come in the form of indirect tax expenditures, which are uncollected revenue due to favorable tax treatment (further explained in the supplement to the federal budget called the Analytical Perspectives), and 401(k) pension plans remain the dominant form of defined contribution plans in the private sector (403[b] plans in the not-for-profit sectors are similarly designed). Because Section (k) of the 401 code of the IRS was implemented in 1978, allowing employers to set aside workers' pay in pretax accounts, employers have increasingly shifted pension coverage from defined benefit plans to a 401(k)-style defined contribution structure for all employees. The share of covered private-sector workers with defined benefit coverage has decreased from 88 percent in 1983 to 36 percent in 2009, while 401(k)-type retirement-plan coverage has increased from 12 percent to more than 63 percent in the same period.

The contributions and earnings on retirement account funds are not taxed until they are withdrawn upon retirement. The tax expenditure or revenue not collected on 401(k)-type plans was, in present value terms, equal to $140 billion for 2010,[2] which is a quarter of the size of benefits paid out of the Social Security system, and it is often overlooked that states also forgo revenue from tax favoritism. Many states implement the federal rules and regulations pertaining to pension plans and so New York, New Jersey, and Connecticut alone did not collect $3 billion of revenue for that year—or about 1 percent of their total revenue and 5 percent of their budget shortfalls in 2011, as the economists Schmitz, Hiltonsmith, Fisher, and Ghilarducci estimated in 2011.

In 2009, the assets of the entire pension system were equal to $11.8 trillion, which is nearly the same size as the national income (in 2009, US national income was over $12 billion). Pension funds slid in terms of their share of financial assets, to 25.7 percent of the financial sector, after having grown to nearly a third of its assets in the 1990s, which was much larger than its 14.7 percent share in 1966 (the commercial bank share grew in 2008, no doubt because some large investment banks specifically took on the designation of commercial banks).

Over half of the workforce participates in voluntary supplemental plans to Social Security and fall in two categories: defined-benefit plans and/or defined-contribution plans. DB plans provide a steady monthly pension benefit until the death of a retiree. The monthly pension amount is derived from a formula that provides monetary credit for each year of service and salary level. In contrast, DC plans are individual pension accounts whereby workers (and often employers) contribute to the account, and the balance upon retirement depends on the levels of contributions and on the investment performance of the portfolio chosen by the worker from financial vehicles chosen, in turn, by the employer.

Many retirement assets—mostly 401(k)-type plans—are also managed by mutual funds, which is where the real action is. The size of the mutual fund sector grew to almost a quarter of all assets in 2009 from 3.6 percent in 1966. Please see Table 1.

There is much to improve in the world of DB pension management. The funding rules need to make funding of DBs more constant over business cycles. Also since DB assets fund long-term liabilities, they are ideal for long-term investments (e.g., infrastructure investments) and, until the Pension Protection Act of 2005, corporations took pension contribution holidays, which inflated stock values and added fuel and air to the financial asset bubble. As Julia Coronado and colleagues observed in 2008, pension consultants often raised interest-rate assumptions based on more risky asset allocations in upturns. These actions reduced the required contributions for every dollar of in-the-future-promise made, which meant that profits artificially soared when profits were already increasing. And yet the Financial Crisis Inquiry Report of 2011 does not cite institutional investor (DB pension funds and endowments) behavior and their large demand for alternative investments as key to the financial crises.

**Table 34.1** Share of assets by financial sector, 1966–2008

| Sector | 1966 | 1978 | 1989 | 1993 | 1999 | 2003 | 2009 |
|---|---|---|---|---|---|---|---|
| Pension Funds | 14.7% | 20.2% | 27.0% | 32.0% | 33.8% | 29.5% | 25.7% |
| • *Pension reserves (of life insurance companies)* | 3.0% | 3.7% | 6.4% | 5.4% | 5.5% | 5.5% | 5.1% |
| • *Private pensions (includes federal pensions) (4)* | 7.8% | 11.8% | 13.9% | 19.3% | 19.8% | 16.8% | 14.8% |
| • *State and local pension funds (5)* | 3.9% | 4.7% | 6.7% | 7.3% | 8.6% | 7.2% | 5.8% |
| Mutual funds (7) | 3.6% | 1.7% | 9.0% | 13.5% | 22.6% | 20.4% | 22.3% |
| Commercial banks (1) | 37.3% | 37.4% | 32.9% | 27.3% | 22.1% | 25.2% | 30.8% |
| Savings institutions (2) | 20.9% | 2.2% | 15.6% | 9.1% | 5.8% | 6.4% | 4.7% |
| Insurance (net of pension reserves) (3) | 17.6% | 1.2% | 10.3% | 10.2% | 8.0% | 7.9% | 7.8% |
| Finance companies (6) | 4.8% | 4.9% | 6.5% | 4.3% | 3.8% | 5.1% | 3.6% |
| Real-estate investment (8) | 0.1% | 0.1% | 0.1% | 0.2% | 0.3% | 0.4% | 0.6% |
| Security brokers (9) | 1.1% | 1.0% | 2.1% | 3.4% | 3.7% | 4.9% | 4.5% |
| Assets by financial sector, 1993–2008 (in trillions $) | 0.974 | 3.262 | 11.031 | 14.28305 | 27.10013 | 32.6351 | 45.91329 |

*Sources*:
(1) US chartered banks—FOF Accounts L.110; foreign banking offices in the US—FOF Accounts L.111; bank holding companies—FOF Accounts L.112; and banks in US possessions—FOF Accounts L.113
(2) Savings institutions—FOF Accounts F.114; and credit unions—FOF Accounts F.115
(3) Life insurance companies—FOF Accounts F.117; property casualty insurance companies—FOF Accounts L.116
(4) Private pension companies—FOF Accounts L.118; federal retirement pension funds—FOF Accounts L.120
(5) State and local pension funds—FOF Accounts L.119
(6) Financial companies—FOF Accounts L.127
(7) Mutual fund companies—FOF Accounts L.121 and L.122
(8) Real-estate investment trusts—FOF Accounts L.128
(9) Security brokers—FOF Accounts L.129
http://www.federalreserve.gov/RELEASES/z1/.

Although the practice of raising actuarial assumptions and taking on more risk is a characteristic of DB plans during periods of expansion—which has a destabilizing effect—the overall design of the DB system is stabilizing because of the in-built payout features, which serve as counterweights to the destabilizing effects of the contribution behavior and are stabilizing because DB pension benefits are paid in the form of a level guarantee of annuities, regardless of the asset values underlying the DB pension promise. The DB structure allows employees to take early retirement during periods of recession, something that greatly helps boost the macroeconomy and is invaluable in stabilizing regional economies, such as the auto and steel industries.

Thus, pension systems are stabilizing if contributions are countercyclical, payouts are not subject to short-run fluctuations in the finance markets, and if the pension system does not encourage pro-cyclical labor supply behavior. In other words, systems should not act to reduce pensions, require more contributions, and encourage people to work or look for work during periods of downturn.

The next section describes the destabilizing features of individual, commercial, financial-based retirement accounts.

## 3. The Destabilizing Macroeconomic Effects of DC Pension Plans

Individual, financial-market-based pension plans like 401(k) plans have destabilizing, pro-cyclical effects, while Social Security has countercyclical, positive effects on macroeconomic stabilization. As this section shows, fiscal or monetary mechanisms that automatically reduce the flow of income or money to individuals and corporations during periods of expansion and that increase such flows (relative to what they would have been in the mechanisms' absence) in times of recession are automatic stabilizers (Davis, 2010; Dolls, Clemens, and Peichi, 2010; Blanchard, Ariccia, and Mauro, 2010; Blanchard, 2006; Fatas and Mihov, 2001; Folette and Cohen, 2000; Eilbott, 1966; Engle, 1952).

Though not a traditional stabilizer, Social Security, perhaps surprisingly, moderates the business cycle in the way that unemployment insurance and the progressive federal income-tax system do. In contrast, 401(k) plans reduce the automatic stabilization properties of these government programs up to an alarming 20 percent.

The Social Security Act was implemented in 1935, with payroll taxes of 1 percent collected in 1938 and the first benefit paid in 1940. The program grew by raising the payroll tax rate, expanding the base, and increasing benefits until 1983. Today, the Social Security system is a DB system without full advance funding (in 2011, the Social Security Trust Fund is substantial, but it will not be redeeming bonds before 2020) and is essentially a pay-as-you-go system.

There are three channels by which retirement plans affect the business cycle: (1) the direct income effect on consumption, (2) the indirect wealth effect on consumption, and (3) the labor supply effect.

When the economy contracts, unemployment rates rise while stock prices and interest rates fall. These changes reduce consumption directly because household income from employment and accumulated assets is reduced.

The wealth effect, on the other hand, reduces consumption indirectly because household wealth is reduced and any perceived future income from wealth and security drops. In other words, when employees and retirees relying on financial-market-based retirement accounts, like 401(k) plans, experience falling stock prices and reduced interest rates, they will be induced to save more and consume less while income and net wealth fall, as the Federal Reserve economist Laurie Pounder discussed in 2009. These effects worsen the impact of the economic contraction. In contrast, if employees have guaranteed pension plans, like Social Security or DB plans, falling asset values do not reduce their retirement wealth or income and, therefore, consumption does not fall as much in periods of contraction (or increase as much during expansion).

The third effect is that of labor supply. The loss of financial asset values in retirement plans may induce older workers to delay retirement, and it may encourage retirees to reenter the labor force, thus further aggravating high unemployment rates. Alternatively, workers may find it more difficult to find work in a bad labor market and may retire early. In good times on the other hand, workers are likely to retire early due to flush asset values, which reduces the size of the labor force when unemployment rates are already low and increases inflationary forces in an expansive cycle.[3]

To test the automatic stabilizing effect of an institution, we measured how the changes in these inflows and outflows of each program react to changes in the GDP output gap by using a multivariable statistical analysis.

The regressions (available from the author) supported the expectations that the net flow of funds in the Social Security system increase in economic contractions because Social Security contributions fall as workers work less, while benefits paid will increase as more senior employees take early retirement. Social Security thus helps keep consumption relatively stable throughout the business cycle.

On the other hand, we found that net flows of 401(k) plans are negative in economic contractions because outflows are likely to drop concurrently with the value of these plans falling with the stock market and older workers staying in the labor market longer because they cannot afford to retire. Meanwhile, contributions to 401(k) accounts drop because households have less money to contribute, not usually because consumers are scrambling to save more in the face of severe losses.

We benchmarked the effect of Social Security inflows and outflows and 401(k) plan inflows and outflows to unemployment insurance, federal disability insurance, Medicare, and federal income taxes. Interestingly, economists paid little attention to automatic stabilizers as real business-cycle theory dominated academia and policy making until the early 2000s. However, attention to automatic stabilization has increased substantially as a result of the 2008–2009 financial crises. In fact, the IMF has taken on vigorous attitude, arguing that automatic spending programs were crucial in tempering the effects of the deep global recession of 2008 because, fortunately, developed nations had in place government-sponsored income maintenance programs that quickly boosted household consumption even when workers lost their jobs, wages stagnated, and other sources of income dried up. In 2010 the former IMF chief economist Raghuram Rajan's (2010) book (see page 100) calls for less fiscal discretionary stimulus and more automatic stabilizers. The lack of an automatic safety net in the United States, Rajan argues, is an economic "fault line" in the world economy.[4]

In their expansive 2009 survey of automatic stabilizers, the OECD economists Julia Darby and Jaques Melitz (2008) concluded that a $1 increase in actual output relative to "full employment" leads to 13.5 cents less social spending, with retirement income programs contributing a third to social spending. In 2010, Ghilarducci, Lessler, and Fisher (2012) expanded their methodology by separating out the effect of each institution on types of pension institutions because pension institutions are different in the United States and behave differently over the business cycle than they do in the OECD.

The program's impact on the economy depends on how outflows and inflows work together. The net effect on the economy is the impact on outflows minus the impact on inflows. If the net impact of the program is positive, an increase in the output gap leads to a net increase in income and wealth to households, which implies that the program contributes to the further expansion of the economy when the economy is already growing, thereby amplifying the cyclical swings in the economy and acting as a destabilizer.

On the other hand, if the net impact of the program is negative, then an increase in the output gap results in the relevant program to reduce household income and wealth, which counteracts and reduces the effect of the shift in the output gap. In the latter case, we consider the program to be an automatic stabilizer. Therefore, the results from this analysis inform us about the automatic stabilization properties of the various pension institutions as well as the government programs that are currently in place. Moreover, the size of the automatic stabilization impacts of the government programs we look at provides a benchmark against which we may compare the impacts of 401(k) and Social Security and Medicare on the economy. This allows us to deduce whether the impacts of the 401(k) and Social Security and Medicare are macroeconomically significant.

All data are annual and national, and the data range starts in 1971 and ends in 2009 for the Old Age and Insurance Program (OASI), disability insurance (DI), and taxes. The data range for 401(k) plans is 1984–2007, and the data range for unemployment insurance (UI) and Medicare is 1971–2008.

Federal income taxes are by far the largest of the programs listed, with tax collections making up an average of 8 percent of GDP over the time periods. The next largest program is Social Security, making up about 4 percent of GDP. Most US workers and employers are required to participate in the Social Security system, whereby coverage rates are more than 93 percent of the workforce (in this, it is no wonder that the system packs a punch). The second largest is Medicare at 2 percent of GDP; 401(k) plans are about 1 percent

**Table 34.2** Net impact on government programs from a 1 percent increase in the ratio of actual to potential GDP from 1971 to 2009

| Program | In Shares of GDP | In Absolute Levels |
|---|---|---|
| OASI (stabilizing because flows are countercyclical) | −0.032 | −0.048 |
| 401(k) | 0.083 | 0.047 |
| UI | −0.076 | −0.037 |
| DI | −0.011 | −0.004 |
| Medicare | −0.038 | 0 |
| Federal Income-Tax Collections | 0.254 | 0.218 |

of GDP, disability insurance about 0.55 percent, and unemployment compensation a small three-tenths of 1 percent of GDP. The very size of Medicare, Social Security, and 401(k) plans makes them important to the macroeconomy (see table 34.2). In 2007, 401(k) inflows (contributions) were $271 billion, which amounted to 1.9 percent of nominal GDP (defined-benefit plan contributions are falling and constitute only 0.4 percent of GDP in 2007, and unlike UI which is just as small, they do not have a built-in countercyclical effect and are therefore not included in this analysis).[5]

Regression results are available upon request; however, the summary of the impact is displayed in table 34.2. When the ratio of actual to potential GDP increases by 1 percent, the economy is expanding, with the Social Security system (OASI) dragging it down a bit by decreasing its share of GDP by 3.2 percent. On the other hand, 401(k) net spending increases as the economy expands and this by a whopping 8.3 percent. This effect is very destabilizing.

The results show that the Social Security program acts as an automatic stabilizer, as do the disability program, the unemployment compensation program, Medicare, and the income tax (for as the economy grows, tax collections grow). Among these government programs, the strongest impact comes from taxes (Auerbach and Feenberg, 2000), followed by unemployment compensation, Social Security, and disability, respectively. The analysis in shares indicates that Medicare has a strong stabilizing impact that trumps that of Social Security, but this result does not hold up in the levels regression.

On the other hand, 401(k) plans are found to be significantly destabilizing. In fact, their impact alone is greater than that of unemployment compensation. If we add up the total impacts of all automatic, governmental stabilizers, we see that for every 1 percentage point increase in the output gap—indicating the economy is expanding—net flows of the various government programs *decrease* by 0.41 percentage points, while, on the other hand, net flows of 401(k) plans *increase* by 0.08 percentage points. Despite the pro-cyclical and exacerbating effect from 401(k) plans, the impact of the programs in terms of absolute levels is stabilizing. For every $1 increase in real GDP, net flows from the various government programs that automatically adjust over the business cycle *shrink* by 31 cents, which temper the expansion.

In all this, it is important to know that, of all these institutions, *only* 401(k) plans are destabilizing, for example, the net outflows from 401(k) plans into consumption *increase* by 4.7 cents in an expansion. In other words, 401(k) plans reduce the automatic stabilization impact of government programs by 15 to 20 percent.[6]

If we add up the total impacts of all the automatic stabilizers due to the government, we see that for every one percentage point increase in the output gap, net flows from the various government programs *shrink* by 0.41 percentage points. On the other hand, net flows from 401(k) plans *increase* by 0.08 percentage points. Looking at levels, for every $1 increase in real GDP, net flows from the various government programs *shrink* by 31 cents. On the other hand, net flows from 401(k) plans *increase* by 4.7 cents.

In other words, 401(k) plans reduce the automatic stabilization impacts of all government programs by a staggering 15–20 percent! This is very significant economically and should be considered by proponents of the Obama administration's plan for automatic GRAs. Our results highlight a significant problem with 401(k) pension plans and, in fact, with any pension plan that is financial market-based. This drawback must be taken into account before any attempts to increase the coverage of 401(k) plans are undertaken.

## 4. Proposal for a Guaranteed Retirement Account (GRA)

As described above, the current financialized pension system makes recessions worse. We need pension reforms that make the three pieces of a pension system—the accumulation piece, investment piece, and the payout or disbursement piece—more stable, efficient, and adequate (guiding principles come from the Government Accounting Office's 2009 report on pension reform). However, as I stress in this chapter, we cannot forget the macroeconomic segment because a nation's pension system should have stabilizing effects on the macroeconomy in order to promote productivity and economic growth.

In light of the evidence contained in this paper and the research conducted, I propose a pension-reform structure called a guaranteed retirement account (GRA) option, which would ensure every worker is covered by a retirement plan that adequately supplements Social Security and helps stabilize the macroeconomy (Ghilarducci, 2007). Similar to President Obama's automatic IRA plans, with the GRA option, a worker (if not already adhering to a DB or

401[k]-type plan that met federal standards) would be automatically enrolled in a GRA option pension plan (which, unlike the Obama administration's plan and more like Social Security, a worker could not opt-out on), which employers and employees would be required to contribute to on a consistent basis in order to ensure that asset accumulation is adequate.

Unlike IRA and 401(k) plans, professional managers would invest GRA contributions at low fees in order to earn the guaranteed rate of return, set at roughly 3 percent real rate of return—pegged to the long-run real growth rate. Every worker would have a $600 pension-contribution tax credit (in order to guarantee that, not just taxpayers at high marginal tax rates would get significant help from the government to save for retirement). These funds would be converted to life annuities upon retirement, whereby a full-time worker who works 40 years and retires at age 65 can expect a benefit equal to roughly 25 percent of preretirement income, adjusted for inflation, assuming a 3 percent real rate of return. Because Social Security provides the average employee with inflation-adjusted benefits equal to roughly 45 percent of preretirement income, the total replacement rate for this prototypical worker would be approximately 70 percent. In this regard, under a GRA plan, funds cannot be accessed before retirement for any reason other than death or disability, however, individuals could take a partial lump sum equal to 10 percent of their account balance or $10,000 (whichever is higher) or opt for survivor benefits in exchange for a lower monthly check. The GRA option is thus similar to the pension vehicles available to university professors (the GRA resembles the TIAA guaranteed rate of return annuity option in the American university and the nonprofit-sector-defined contribution plan called Teachers Insurance Annuity Association-College Retirement Equities Fund [TIAA-CREF]).

Having a GRA option that competes with private-sector retail and brokerage retirement products would increase efficient use of retirement savings. The management of 401(k) and IRA plans presents some of the most business available to the financial sector and is one that is most inefficient and costly for workers across the country. Despite vigorous legislative efforts to make retirement account-management fees transparent, the fees workers pay are effectively hidden and at the same time so large that the fees erode the value of the fund, typically by about 30 percent.

The Guaranteed Retirement Account plan might help reverse the erosion of good employer-provided pension plans. Instead of competing against employers who set the bar low by providing an inferior 401(k) plan, an employer would keep their defined-benefit plans or decent 401(k) without fear of being undercut by employers without good plans, as Arias and Ghilarducci (2011) describe in as a "race to the bottom."

The guaranteed rate of return will not put the government at risk; in fact, a government is the only large and enduring institution that can invest and manage pooled savings and guarantee a rate of return without risk. As Alicia Munnell and colleagues successfully argued in 2008, a government is much better at taking on investment risks than individuals and private institutes are.

The conversion of the tax deduction to a tax credit would also fix one of the most inefficient and unfair aspects of the current pension system wherein the top fifth of all households get over 70 percent of all the tax expenditures for retirement plans, the rectifying of which will help flatten the destabilizing effects of lopsided wealth and income inequality.

The investment structure will not contribute to financial-asset volatility; indeed, it could help it. The pooled funds would be conservatively invested in financial markets because the guaranteed return will be set at something closely projected by the growth rate of real GDP. In this scenario there is a powerful incentive for managers to diversify risk to hit at, say, a 3 percent real target, but there is no incentive to take large bets. Participants are guaranteed close to a 3 percent rate of return adjusted for inflation, a factor that would discourage a highly leveraged asset allocation and risky alternative investments. (If the trustees determine that actual investment returns have been consistently more than 3 percent over a number of years, the surplus will be distributed to participants, though a balancing fund will be maintained to ride out periods of low returns.)

Participants in a GRA scheme begin collecting retirement benefits at the same time as in Social Security, and therefore no earlier than the Social Security Early Retirement Age, which will help promote stabilizing labor-supply effects as people will not have to wait until a financial crisis is over before they can draw on their retirement accounts.

Besides requiring a steady contribution, as is also the case with Social Security, the payout feature helps stabilize the economy. Under a GRA, credited account balances are converted to inflation-indexed annuities upon retirement in order to ensure that workers do not outlive their savings or that their payouts vary with the financial market.

In sum, a GRA-type plan—steady contributions, guaranteed return, annuity payout—meets the criteria of good pension reform. At a steady 5 percent contribution rate, workers accumulate enough assets to supplement their Social Security income to achieve adequate retirement-income replacement rates. The GRA option also eliminates the individual's concerns about investment risk, the risk of making bad choices, and investing in volatile markets. The risk of outliving one's retirement account is also eliminated with the annuity payout. This structure thus helps smooth out consumption across business cycles, thereby making the macroeconomic stabilizing effect an additional bonus of the GRA option.

## 5. State and Local Pension Plans

In 2010, the state and local pension-fund systems were prominently at center stage in the debates about how pension plans help or detract from economic stabilization going forward.

Some state and local pension funds were and are requiring large increases in contributions from very stressed and a financially strapped government, which could cause significant hardship in the long run as state and localities face falling tax revenues in the worst recession since the Great Depression move to defund ordinary state and local functions to pay pension contributions. I propose a way to attach federal financial assistance to state and local pension reform that will yield two vital outcomes: induce positive structural change in the plan design—in particular, one that smoothes out pension funding and yields sensible benefits—and attach federal aid to programs that provide for efficient funds management. As we have argued before, what we need are pension plans and systems that provide economic stabilization, which means a pension system that operates by way of steady consumption during upswings and economic downturns, saving in good times and spending in bad. Taxpayers—many who have no hope of getting a decent retirement account or pension plan and are often pitched as adversaries of the public plans—need access to the excellent financial-management infrastructure that already exists in order to properly manage state and local pension funds for their own precious retirement savings.

As briefly noted, the second effect of this reform is that federal aid will be attached to programs that give the public access to the efficient, transparent, and expert pension-fund management services of the public-sector pension fund. Public-sector plans, as well as private DB plans on average, obtain more returns for less money than 401(k) and IRA plans. The reasons are intuitive: the scale of the investments is larger, the fees are lower, and professional managers don't time markets so they can get the upside of taking on more investment risk, as the economists Beth Almeida and William Fiorina argued in 2008.

Political and economic pressures on public-sector funds preclude political exploration about federal legislation to facilitate states and localities to file for bankruptcy and thus escape pension liabilities, whereby pressure for bankruptcy options is abetted by the fear that pensions are eroding credit ratings. In 2009 and 2010 President Obama conducted a "Race to the Top" contest that offered grants to school districts based on competitive proposals. The contest is not a federal mandate: it is a monetary incentive designed to put in place best practices in schools. Even when it is too early to assess the benefits of the contest, the process definitely encouraged bold solutions for a pressing policy problem. Contests are newish forms of public policy that are coordinated by a central agent, in this case the federal government, to get reluctant and noncommunicative partners together to make changes that serve all interests.

In this regard, the contest is basically a way of bringing parties together within a bargaining environment and it is precisely this bargaining environmental approach that has been suggested for public pension reform. In September 2010, a *New York Times* op-ed by Richard Riordan who is the former Republican mayor of Los Angeles and Alexander Rubalcava, the head of an investment advisory firm, proposed a "Race to the Top" program for state pensions. Sadly, their plan falls short of what is required, counting, as it does, on benefit cuts only and federally directed requirements, instead of running a contest where creativity and innovation are rewarded along basic principles, chief among them a steadying of employer contributions to DB plans so that they are not pro-cyclical.

In light of this, the five principles that would earn points in a contest for federal aid to states and municipal pension funds can be outlined as follows.

*Principle No. 1:* Actuarial assumptions for pension plans must reflect reasonable and responsible rates of return. Under the oversight of credible and recognized accounting boards and standards, they should encourage entry age, standard methods to factor pension costs, and, with this, prevent deceptive accounting practices.

In this regard, to advocate that pension funds should use a "risk-free" rate as a baseline cost for all plans fails to acknowledge the fundamental differences between private-sector and public-sector plans. Private-pension plans are backed by corporations that may go bankrupt and whose liabilities may be ultimately backstopped by the federal Pension Benefit Guarantee Corporation (PBGC). However, state and local governments cannot file bankruptcy proceedings as private businesses: their obligations to interested parties must be unwound through protracted, complex, and expensive legal proceedings, much to the detriment of taxpayers, civil employees, and pensioners alike. Under these circumstances, risk-free rates are useless for the valuation of minimum benefits for claimants.

All sides agree that pension plans should gradually lower their assumed rates of return and many have done so already. Indeed, to win this race, they will have to. However, to call for such a sudden and drastic change in this rate incites the subliminal goal of making it impossible to ensure a smooth transition toward better, more sustainable pension plans, and that should definitely not be the intent.

*Principle No. 2:* Public employers must shoulder their share of the responsibility, pay their pension contributions, and take no financial holidays from these contributions, no exceptions. Payments should cover normal plan costs so that if there are surplus funds, these should be amortized over 30 years past service liabilities and pay over 20 years after rollbacks. In fact, some plans facing the most significant challenges, like those of the states of New Jersey and Illinois, are where public employers failed to contribute over an extended period of time.

*Principle No. 3:* There should be GRAs for all. All residents must be allowed access to state or local pension-fund management facilities to get a guaranteed rate (which could be the TIPS rate or the baseline treasury return, plus the inflation protection rate) on their 401(k) or IRAs.

For this reason and to prevent spillover effects to other localities as stated above, the federal contest must be flexible. For example, it can help facilitate a voluntary individual system of guaranteed accounts where private citizens can opt into public employee pension funds. This will increase compliance because stakeholders will be more diverse and therefore not as subject to targeted political action (see Weller and Helburn, 2010, for various options).

The most persuasive reason to let individuals have access to state and local pension funds is that the fund can guarantee a range of returns on their assets—say 2.7 to 4 percent—without taking on risk. Individuals being averse to financial risk and lacking the skills, time, and resources do poorly when left in charge of managing their own individual financial accounts. We know this at the very latest after more than 30 years of the 401(k) system being in place. Having individuals manage their own accounts yields the insensible result that two otherwise similar individuals, who have contributed identical amounts to their pension funds over their lifetimes, end up with different incomes because they activated their pensions in different environments. We, therefore, propose federal aid to public-sector plans if they allow for the voluntary participation of individuals who would prefer efficient and transparent investment-management services that are not available in the commercial retail markets for 401(k)s and IRAs as Laidler and Robson discuss (2007).

*Principle No. 4:* Benefits that were based on projected earnings in boom times should be rolled back according to principles established in locally arranged negotiations between all stakeholders, whereby unilateral top-down decision arrangements will be discouraged.

For example, most public pension benefits are paid for, but some benefits expanded too fast based on unrealistic assumptions. In this light, small pockets of public-sector workers have already seen their benefits rolled back. For example, in 2006, Colorado's Public Employee Retirement Agency (PERA) determined that it could not reverse the downward trend without major benefit changes and so, based on this harsh reality, it took decisive action. It is thus clear that every situation needs to be evaluated based on its own merits and only stakeholders at the local and municipal levels are in a position to correctly assess these circumstances. In Colorado, the pension cuts were determined to be legal.

*Principle No. 5:* No pensioner can replace more than 100 percent of his or her salary and all pension-spiking provisions and loopholes must be eliminated. In fact, there are very few retired public employees who earn significant pensions and, of those that do, at least half have a career of significant income, with no significant increases in salaries at the end of their working lives. Many good pension reformers, both on the union and management sides, have fought against pension spiking (increasing wages with overtime and other exaggerated base salary increases in order to spike up the final pension benefits), which is a problem that needs to be resolved without question, but it is not a fundamental flaw in public pension arrangements.

These five principles will help state and local governments garner the necessary strength to run the race toward pension security. This will get rid of the magical fairy dust surrounding current high actuarial assumptions, provide only for funded benefit improvements, and channel steady contributions from taxpayers and employers, with no excessive benefits or spiking. Finally, by having access to state pensions, Californians, for instance, might be able to get access to CalPERS, a well-managed, reliable, and incredibly successful pension fund, which will, without a doubt, help to mitigate what some in the media have termed "pension envy" from those taxpayers who lack adequate pensions and who resent public-sector workers who do.

## 6. Conclusion

The 30-year experiment with 401(k)-type retirement plans has failed to bring retirement-income security to the vast majority of American workers (Burtless, 2009). Only half of the workforce has access to a retirement account or pension plan, making retirement assets too low, risky, and leaving their supposed beneficiaries paying account-management fees that are too high. The situation is such that people cash out their accounts to meet immediate needs, and lopsided tax breaks go mainly to the richest taxpayers. Individuals bear too much risk of underaccumulation, volatile returns, and the absence of a steady stream of lifelong retirement income.

The Obama administration's pension-reform proposal of automatically enrolling noncovered workers in IRAs could make things worse. Left to their own devices, workers may not accumulate enough assets to adequately supplement Social Security income because, under the Obama proposal, workers could opt out of the system and employers are not required to contribute. Also, investment mistakes will still occur, because workers would still direct investments in IRAs. Lastly, the payout from IRAs is rarely in the form of an annuity. Moreover and most significantly, the impact on the macroeconomy will be exactly backward from what we want it to be. IRAs and 401(k) plans reduce the automatic stabilization impacts of current social insurance programs by a significant amount and we can estimate this dampening effect of 401(k) plans at a disheartening 15–20 percent. This drawback must under all costs be taken into account before any attempts to increase the coverage of 401(k) plans are undertaken.

GRA options and reforming the state and local pension-funding issues will go a long way in developing a pension system that does not exacerbate expansions and make recessions worse.

## Notes

1. Documentation of the drop in the retirement income and projected retirement income since 2008 can be found in Eisenbrey's 2010 testimony to the Senate and in Alicia Munnell's Retirement Risk Index, at the Center for Retirement Research at Boston College, the Employee Benefit Retirement Research Institute.

2. The calculations on tax expenditures vary. I used the present-value calculation found in the Analytical Perspectives on the Federal Budget (2010).
3. These scholars have discussed the labor-supply effects of asset-based retirement funds thoroughly and recently (Coile and Levine, 2009; Hermes, 2006; Maestas, 2004).
4. Other economists recognize that "social transfers, in particular the rather generous systems of unemployment insurance in Europe, play a key role in the stabilization of disposable incomes and explain a large part of the difference in automatic stabilizers between Europe and the US" (Dolls, Fuest, and Peichl, 2010).
5. One of the earliest definitions of automatic stabilizers is in Eilbott (1966, 450). The unemployment insurance system and the federal tax system are the traditional automatic stabilizers, and we expect them to have strong balancing effects on the economy. Social Security Disability Insurance should not be particularly sensitive to the business cycle because it takes two years of demonstrated disability for a person to qualify. However, because administrator law judges consider job-market prospects as a factor in an award, Social Security disability awards are somewhat countercyclical. State-level disability programs certainly have a more profound effect on the business cycle, because the period of time needed to qualify for benefits is much shorter than that for the federal DI program. However, we do not have state-level disability information to test this prediction. Many economists once believed that Medicare benefits should not be related to the business cycle because expenditures depend on the number of eligible participants and the cost of medical services. However, because people use more medical services in recessions, spending in this program is also countercyclical.
6. We tested the robustness of the estimations with a number of other instruments and found that the change in the share of real gross business investment in real GDP is the best instrument. Gross business investment is insensitive to changes in Social Security (OASI) and Social Security Disability Insurance, 401(k) plans, unemployment insurance, Medicare, and the federal income taxes. First-stage R-squared numbers range from 0.51 to 0.60 for the shares regressions and from 0.54 to 0.87 for the levels regressions, and regression of the fitted residuals from the 2SLS estimation on the exogenous variables, including the instrument, yield an R-squared of approximately zero every time. Thus, we may conclude that the instrument performs well.

## References


Almeida, Beth, and William Fornia. (2008). *A Better Bang for the Buck: The Economic Efficiencies of Defined Benefit Pension Plans*. Washington, DC: National Institute on Retirement Security. http://www.nirsonline.org/storage/nirs/documents/Bang%20for%20the%20Buck%20Report.pdf.

Arias, Daniela, and Teresa Ghilarducci. (2011). "Pension Reform's Stake in Employers." Schwartz Center for Economic Policy Analysis Working Paper, SCEPA, The New School. http://www.economicpolicyresearch.org/guaranteeing-retirement-income/299-pension-reforms-stake-in-employers.html.

Auerbach, Alan, and Daniel Feenberg. (2000). "The Significance of Federal Taxes as Automatic Stabilizers." *Journal of Economic Perspectives* 14(3): 37–56.

Blanchard, Olivier. (2006). "Comments on 'The Case against the Case against Discretionary Policy.'" In Richard Kopcke, Geoffrey Tootell, and Robert Triest, eds., *The Macroeconomics of Fiscal Policy*, 62–67. Cambridge, MA: MIT Press.

Blanchard, Olivier, Giovanni Dell' Ariccia, and Paolo Mauro. (2010). "Rethinking Macroeconomic Policy." International Monetary Fund Staff Position Note SPN/10/03. http://www.imf.org/external/pubs/ft/spn/2010/spn1003.pdf.

Burtless, Gary. (2009). "Financial Market Turbulence and Social Security Reform." In Mitchell Orenstein, ed., *Pensions, Social Security and the Privatization of Risk*. New York: Columbia University Press.

Coile, Courtney, and Phillip B. Levine. (2009)."The Market Crash and Mass Layoffs: How the Current Crisis May Affect Retirement." National Bureau of Economic Research Working Paper No. 15395. http://www.nber.org/papers/w15395.

Coronado, Julia, Olivia Mitchell, Steven A. Sharpe, and S. Blake Nesbitt. (2008). "Footnotes Aren't Enough: The Impact of Pension Accounting on Stock Values." National Bureau of Economic Research Working Paper No. 13726. http://www.nber.org/papers/w13726.

Darby, Julia, and Jacques Melitz. (2008). "Social Spending and Automatic Stabilizers in the OECD." *Economic Policy* 23(56): 716–756.

Davis, Bob. (2010). "QandA: IMF's Blanchard Thinks the Unthinkable." *Wall Street Journal*, February 10. http://blogs.wsj.com/economics/2010/02/11/qa-imfs-blanchard-thinks-the-unthinkable/.

Dolls, Mathias, Clemens Fuest, and Andreas Peichl. (2010). "Automatic Stabilizers and the Economic Crisis in Europe and the U.S." VoxEu.org. http://www.voxeu.org/index.php?q=node/5529.

Egle, W. G. (1952). *Economic Stabilization*. Cinncinati: University of Cincinnati Press.

Eilbott, Peter. (1966). "The Effectiveness of Automatic Stabilizers." *American Economic Review* 56(3): 450–465.

Eisenbrey, Ross. (2010). Testimony to the US Senate Health, Education, Labor and Pensions Committee. http://help.senate.gov/imo/media/doc/Eisenbrey.pdf.

Fatas, Antonio, and Ilan Mihov. (2001). "Government Size and Automatic Stabilizers: International and Intranational Evidence." *Journal of International Economics* 55(1): 3–28.

Folette, Glenn, and Darrell Cohen. (2000). "The Automatic Fiscal Stabilizers: Quietly Doing Their Thing." Working Paper, Federal Reserve Bank of New York. http://www.ny.frb.org/research/epr/00v06n1/0004cohe.pdf.

Ghilarducci, Teresa. (2007). "Guaranteed Retirement Accounts." Economic Policy Institute Briefing Paper No. 204. http://www.sharedprosperity.org/bp204.html.

Ghilarducci Teresa, Joelle Saad-Lessler, Eloy Fisher, 2012. "The Macroeconomic Stabilisation Effects of Social Security and 401(k) plans," Cambridge Journal of Economics, Oxford University Press, vol. 36(1), pages 237–251.

Government Accountability Office. (2009). "Alternative Approaches Could Address Retirement Risks Faced by Workers but Pose Trade-Offs." http://www.gao.gov/new.items/d09642.pdf.

Hermes, Sharon. (2006). "What Role Do Financial and Health Constraints Play in Partial Retirement?" In *Labor and Employment Relations Association Series, Proceedings of the 58th Annual Meeting*. Madison, Wisconsin.

Laidler, David, and William B. P. Robson. (2007). "Ill-Defined Benefits: The Uncertain Present and Brighter Future of Employee Pensions in Canada." C. D. Howe Institute Working Paper. http://www.cdhowe.org/pdf/commentary_250.pdf.

Maestas, Nicole. (2004). "Back to Work: Expectations and Realizations of Work after Retirement." Michigan Retirement Research Center, Working Paper No. 2004-085. http://deepblue.lib.umich.edu/handle/2027.42/50534.

Office of Management and Budget. (2010). *Analytical Perspectives on the Federal Budget.* http://www.whitehouse.gov/sites/default/files/omb/budget/fy2010/assets/spec.pdf.

Phillips, Kevin. (2008). *Bad Money: Reckless Finance, Failed Politics, and the Global Crisis of American Capitalism.* New York: Viking.

Porter, Michael. (1992). "Capital Choices: Changing the Way American Invests in Its Industry." Washington, DC: Council on Competitiveness.

Pounder, Laurie. (2009). "Consumption Response to Expected Future Income." Federal Reserve Board of the United States, International Finance Discussion Papers No. 2009-971. http://www.federalreserve.gov/Pubs/Ifdp/2009/971/default.htm.

Rajan, Raghuram. (2010). *Fault Lines: How Hidden Fractures Still Threaten the World Economy.* Princeton: Princeton University Press.

Riordan, Richard, and Alexander Rubalcava. (2010). "How Pensions Can Get Out of the Red." *New York Times*, September 15. http://www.nytimes.com/2010/09/16/opinion/16riordan.html?.

Schmitz, Lauren, Robert Hiltonsmith, Eloy Fisher, and Teresa Ghilarducci. (2011). "Tax Expenditures for DC Pension Plans for Three States." Schwartz Center for Economic Policy Analysis Working Paper, SCEPA, The New School.

Twentieth Century Fund. (1992). "The Report of Twentieth Century Fund Task Force on Market Speculation and Corporate Governance." New York, New York: Century Foundation Press.

Weller, Christian E., and Amy Helburn. (2010). "States to the Rescue: Policy Options for State Government to Promote Private Sector Retirement Savings." McCormack Graduate School of Policy Studies, University of Massachusetts, Boston Working Paper.http://www.umb.edu/editor_uploads/images/centers_institutes/center_pension_action/StatestoResPolicyOptionsStateGovt_gi_6.1.10_cw.ah.pdf.

Data for the Reported Regressions401(k) Data—Yearly, 1984–2007. Form 5500 Data, Department of Labor, Table E20, http://www.dol.gov/ebsa/publications/form5500dataresearch.html.

Federal Income Taxes, Nominal and Real Gross Domestic Product and Gross Business Investment—Yearly, 1971–2009. National Income Accounts of the United States, Bureau of Economic Analysis. http://www.bea.gov/national/.

Old Age and Insurance Program (OASI), Disability Insurance (DI) and Medicare Data—Yearly, 1971–2009. Social Security and Medicare Boards of Trustees Administration (2010). http://www.ssa.gov/cgi-bin/ops_series.cgi

Unemployment Insurance Data—Yearly, 1971–2009. *Department of Labor Unemployment Insurance Chartbook.* http://www.doleta.gov/unemploy/chartbook.cfm.

CHAPTER 35

# A MINSKYAN ROAD TO FINANCIAL REFORM

L. RANDALL WRAY

THE outlines of Basel 3 have been announced. Some have already dismissed them as too little (and too late!)—even if they had been in place they would have proved no more than a nuisance, a minor little speed bump, on the way to the Global Financial Crisis. The problem is that the architects of reform are working around the edges, taking current bank activities as somehow appropriate. They appear to believe that a simple nip-and-tuck will be sufficient to restrain the excesses of the 2000s. Hyman Minsky would not be impressed. Most of what the financial sector is now doing is actually harmful. Before we can reform the financial system, we need to understand what the financial system does, or, better, what it *should* do. To put it as simply as possible, Minsky always insisted that the proper role of the financial system is to promote the "capital development" of the economy. By this he did not simply mean that banks should finance investment in physical capital. Rather, he was concerned with creating a financial structure that would be conducive to economic development to improve living standards, broadly defined.

I will first examine Minsky's general proposals for reform of the economy—how to restore stable growth that promotes job creation and rising living standards. I then turn to his proposals for financial reform and focus on his writing in the early 1990s when he was engaged in a project at the Levy Economics Institute on reconstituting the financial system (Minsky, 1992a, 1992b, 1993, 1996). As part of that project, he offered his insights on the fundamental functions of a financial system. These thoughts lead quite naturally to a critique of the financial practices that led to the Global Financial Crisis, in order to offer a path toward thorough-going reform.

## General Policies for Reform in Light of the Global Crisis

Minsky (1986) argued that the Great Depression represented a failure of the small-government, laissez-faire economic model, while the New Deal promoted a highly successful Big Government/Big Bank model for financial capitalism. The current crisis represents a failure of the Big Government/Neoconservative model that promoted deregulation, reduced supervision and oversight, privatized earnings, and consolidated market power. It replaced the New Deal reforms with self-supervision of markets, with greater reliance on "personal responsibility" as safety nets were gutted, and with monetary and fiscal policy that is biased against maintenance of full employment and adequate growth to generate rising living standards for most Americans (see Kelton and Wray, 2004; Wray, 2005). Even amid the worst economic calamity since the Great Depression, policy makers are paralyzed by the supposed risks of running budget deficits and "unfunded entitlements" resulting from Social Security shortfalls that might appear 30 or more years in the future. And government officials have confused the well-being of Wall Street's "fat cat" bankers with the well-being of Main Street's households and firms.

We must return to a more sensible model, with enhanced oversight of financial institutions and with a financial structure that promotes stability rather than speculation. We need policy that promotes rising wages for the bottom half so that borrowing is less necessary to achieve middle-class living standards. We need policy that promotes employment, rather than transfers payments—or worse, incarceration—for those left behind. Monetary policy must be turned away from using rate hikes to preempt inflation and toward a proper role: stabilizing interest rates, using direct credit controls to prevent runaway speculation, and providing supervision. And rather than trillions of bailouts and guarantees for the bloated financial sector, we need a combination of a short-term economic stimulus plus long-term commitments by the federal government to repair and improve infrastructure, create jobs, and reduce inequality (see Tymoigne and Wray, 2009; Wray, 2008a, 2008b, 2010).

Minsky insisted that "the creation of new economic institutions which constrain the impact of uncertainty is necessary," arguing that the "aim of policy is to ensure that the economic prerequisites for sustaining the civil and civilized standards of an open liberal society exist. If amplified uncertainty and extremes in income maldistribution and social inequalities attenuate the economic underpinnings of democracy, then the market behavior that creates these conditions has to be constrained" (Minsky, 1996, 14–15). It is time to take finance back from the clutches of Wall Street's casino.

Minsky had long argued that a private sector-led expansion would increase financial fragility, foreseeing the sectoral balance approach later promoted by Wynne Godley. At the aggregate level, the sum of the government balance, the domestic private balance, and the foreign balance must equal zero. In an expansion led by private-sector spending, tax revenues would tend to rise, reducing the government sector's deficit (even moving it to a surplus, as was the case during the Clinton years). At the same time, a country with a high propensity to import (like the United States) would incur a current account deficit. By accounting identity, the private-sector's balance would deteriorate—moving toward a deficit.

What is remarkable is that Minsky (1963) foresaw the implications thirty-three years before it became a reality. The US private sector ran an almost continuous deficit in the decade after Minsky's death in 1996—leading to a massive accumulation of debt. The reasons for this are complex: fiscal policy that was chronically too tight (biased to run surpluses before full employment), mercantilist policies of trading partners that generated a US current account deficit, changing views of debt (households and firms were more willing and able to increase debt loads as memories of the great debt deflation of the 1930s faded), and stagnant real wages since the early 1970s (so that once growth of labor-force participation by women had reached a peak, family living standards could continue to rise only by borrowing). In any case, debt loads eventually became too great to service—reaching five times GDP (compared to "only" three times GDP in 1929 on the precipice of the Great Crash and the Great Depression).

Minsky's general policies to promote financial stability focused on encouraging growth of wages (at a pace consistent with productivity growth) so that consumption would not require debt. Further, he wanted to promote a high-consumption society rather than an economy that grew by encouraging investment (Minsky, 1964, 1968, 1986). In that he deviated from most "Keynesian" policy of the postwar period, which usually sided with neoclassical supply-siders in favoring policy to promote more investment (through business-tax cuts, for example). According to Minsky, investment is destabilizing because it must rely to some degree on external finance; a sustained investment boom actually increases indebtedness and greater fragility. Minsky was well aware that investment would create aggregate profits (as in the Kalecki equation), but as discussed above there would be leakages to the government and foreign sectors in an expansion. Further, an investment boom can create euphoria and rising asset prices—leading to a wave of takeovers and leveraged buyouts, financed by even more debt.

Minsky also took an aggregate mark-up approach to prices: prices are a mark-up over the wage bill in the consumption sector, which ensures that some of the consumption output is available to workers in the investment sector, to capitalists, to government employees, and to foreigners (Minsky, 1986). Hence, all else equal, if investment is a rising share of GDP, this will lend an inflationary bias through a rising mark-up. In addition, because the investment sector tends to be more highly unionized, oligopolized, and technologically advanced, policies that favor it will also tend to generate inflation before full employment is reached. Policy makers would thus move to attenuate an expansion long before it generated full employment in order to fight inflation pressures.

In Minsky's view, growth promoted by government consumption and public infrastructure investment would actually improve private-sector balance sheets—hence this would be financially stabilizing. Still, it would also promote higher mark-ups (relieved to the extent that public infrastructure investment increased potential output). Unlike most progressive Keynesians, Minsky was not a strong supporter of welfare, at least for those who can work. Instead, he always pushed for employment programs as a preferred antipoverty strategy. From the early 1960s he advocated an employer-of-last-resort program—a universal job guarantee funded by the federal government (Minsky, 1965). He argued that this would not be as inflationary as welfare because it could be used to increase aggregate supply even as it increased demand. Further, he believed that offering jobs rather than handouts was more consistent with participatory democracy and with promotion of social inclusion. He argued that by setting a basic living standard and offering an infinitely elastic supply of jobs, the employer-of-last-resort program would achieve full employment without generating inflation pressures (see Harvey, 1989; Kelton and Wray, 2004; Minsky, 1965).

The Global Financial Crisis offers both grave risks as well as opportunities. Global employment and output are collapsing faster than at any time since the Great Depression. Hunger and violence are growing—even in developed nations. The 1930s offer examples of possible responses: on the one hand, nationalism and repression; on the other, a New Deal and progressive policy. Minsky's proposals for reform are in the spirit of the New Deal, although he argued that we cannot simply restore the New Deal reforms—in many ways they are outdated. Still, we should be thinking of reform on a similar scale. Government must play a bigger role, which in turn requires a new economic paradigm that recognizes the possibility of simultaneously achieving social justice, full employment, and price and currency stability through appropriate policy.

There is no question that finance has played an outsized role over the past two decades, both in the developed nations where policy promoted managed money and in the developing nations that were encouraged to open to international capital. Households and firms in developed nations were buried under mountains of debt even as incomes for wage earners stagnated. Developing nations were similarly swamped with external debt-service commitments, while the promised benefits of neoliberal policies usually never arrived. It is time to finally put global finance back in its proper place as a tool to achieving sustainable development. This means substantial downsizing and careful re-regulation. In the next section I examine Minsky's views on the proper role to be played by the financial system.

## Reform of the Financial Sector

In his writings over the last half of the twentieth century, Minsky emphasized six main points:

1. A capitalist economy is a financial system.
2. Neoclassical/mainstream economics is not useful because it denies that the financial system matters.
3. The financial structure has become much more fragile.
4. This fragility makes it likely that stagnation or even a deep depression is possible.
5. A stagnant capitalist economy will not promote capital development.
6. However, stagnation can be avoided by apt reform of the financial structure with apt use of fiscal powers of the government.

With that in mind, let us see what he identified as the essential functions of a financial system (see Minsky, 1992a, 1992b, 1993). These include provision for the following:

1. A safe and sound payments system;
2. Short-term loans to households and firms, and, possibly, to state and local governments;
3. A safe and sound housing finance system;
4. A range of financial services, including insurance, brokerage, and retirement savings services; and
5. Long-term funding of positions in expensive capital assets.

Obviously there is no reason why any single institution should provide all of these services, although the long-run trend has been to consolidate a wide range of services within the affiliates of a bank holding company. The New Deal reforms had separated institutions by function (and state laws against branching provided geographic constraints). Minsky recognized that Glass-Steagall had already become anachronistic by the early 1990s. He insisted that any reforms must take account of the accelerated innovations in both financial intermediation and the payments mechanism. He believed these changes were largely market-driven and not due to deregulation. However, economies of scale in banking are exhausted at a relatively small size. And large "too-big-to-fail" banks are systemically dangerous and are too large and complex to regulate, supervise, or manage. Hence, reforms ought to aim for downsizing. This does not necessarily mean a return to Glass-Steagall separation by function but it does mean that any future policy should favor small institutions over large ones.

Space constraints permit me to comment only briefly on each of the five functions identified as essential by Minsky. In each case, the current arrangements fall short of what is needed.

First, the payments system. Clearing checks at par requires access to the Fed—only the Fed can guarantee that bank liabilities used in payment always maintain parity against cash. And if we are to use bank deposits as the basis of payments, we must have deposit insurance to prevent bank runs at the first hint of crisis. Nothing less than 100 percent coverage will do—as the United Kingdom found out when the crisis hit because its insurance covered only 90 percent of a depositor's funds (it was forced to increase coverage to 100 percent to stop bank runs). What this means is that if we use "private" banks to run our payments system, we must "backstop" them with government guarantees. Effectively, then, they are playing with "house money"—issuing claims on the government to make loans and to purchase risky assets. They are not really private; rather, they are public-private partnerships. If they lose their gambles, Uncle Sam pays (bank owners absorb 5 to 8 percent of the losses, and deposit insurance covers the rest). So the other side of the coin must be close regulation and supervision of the kinds of assets they are permitted to buy.

The alternative is a public payments system—based on the old "postal savings bank" model. This is an extremely cost-efficient and safe way of providing payment services (still used in many countries, including Japan and Italy): wages are deposited directly in the post office, utilities bills are deducted from accounts, and checks can be written for other payments. The postal savings bank would hold only the safest assets—recall the Milton Friedman-Irving Fisher "100 percent reserves" model—such as cash and federal government debt (see Phillips, 1995). Direct access to the central bank ensures par clearing. Government policy would determine the interest rate paid on safe and secure savings.

Turning to short-term lending, when banks are backstopped by government, market incentives are weak because holders of insured deposits do not care if the banks take risky bets. And owners are putting up only 5–10 cents on every dollar bet—with government taking the rest of the risk. (I will bring up the obvious barriers to owners exerting control over well-compensated management, who may well choose to run what my colleague Bill Black calls control frauds.) Because most of the funds used to make loans or buy risky assets are effectively provided by the government, the only justification for using the banks as intermediaries is if they do proper underwriting and can do a better job than the government can. In the case of commercial loans, I think that is highly probable but only if the banks hold the loans to maturity and develop relations with their customers. In other words, securitization is inimical to proper underwriting.

This statement can no longer be controversial in the wake of the scams perpetrated on the argument that "efficient markets" would provide all the incentives needed. Securitization failed spectacularly, mostly because none of those involved in the process ever assessed the creditworthiness of borrowers. The originate to distribute model eliminated underwriting, to be replaced by a combination of brokers who were paid to make liar loans with no chance of repayment, property valuation by assessors who were paid to overvalue real estate, credit-ratings agencies who were paid to overrate securities, accountants who were paid to ignore problems, and monoline insurers whose promises were not backed by sufficient loss reserves (see Kregel, 2008; Wray, 2008a, 2010). Reform must get the assets back onto the banks' books, reviving relationship banking. Financial institutions should be given a choice: either surrender their bank charters that give them access to insured deposits, or do proper underwriting and retain the loans they originate (while financing their positions in the loans by issuing insured deposits). It is also important to prevent chartered banks from shifting risks through derivatives and "insurance"—the incentive to do good underwriting is diminished if others bear the risk.

Obviously, this reverses the trends of the past three decades, during which financial institutions have done everything they could do to shift risks. As we now know, all these efforts failed: for various reasons, all the risks came right back to the banks. Further, the belief that someone else would bear the risks had changed behavior in a way that greatly increased systemic risks. For these reasons, chartered banks should be forced to bear the risks they create. There is still room for institutions and practices outside the realm of chartered banks—but these would not have access to deposit insurance or to par clearing at the Fed. In the past the problem has been that "shadow banks" had lower costs that gave them a competitive advantage over chartered banks that were subject to more constraints and that had to operate a costly payments system. This can be rectified in two ways: compensating chartered banks for operating the payments system, and charging shadow banks for access to it. Alternatively, as discussed above, the payments system could be taken away from banks and operated directly by government savings banks.

The third function is housing finance, particularly important in a nation in which a large majority of households are homeowners. Here, simplest is best: the 30-year fixed-rate mortgages originated and held by thrifts operating as mutuals worked exceedingly well. The incentives for shareholders (technically, the liabilities were not deposits) and borrowing homeowners were well aligned. The thrifts were killed by a combination of change of ownership (gradually, rules were relaxed until an individual could own a thrift—opening the floodgates of control fraud) and Chairman Volcker's experiment in monetarism (raising short-term rates above 20 percent, resulting in insolvency of most thrifts). It may not be possible to bring back the mutuals, but it is relatively easy to promote safe practices. Government insurance of mortgages should be restricted to those originated and held by financial institutions that conform to approved practices. Only fixed-rate mortgages subject to proper underwriting would be included, and only mortgages held by the originator would retain government insurance.

Note, however, that where government takes most of the risk for lending that is seen to be in the public interest (mortgage loans, student loans), the social value of underwriting might be low. Default rates of 5 percent or 10 percent on such loans might be seen to be acceptable so long as there are strong public benefits of financing an activity like homeownership or college education. In that case, it may not be desirable to use financial intermediaries. It might make more sense for the government to cut out the middleman and to make the loans directly. The higher default rates that might result from lower-quality underwriting done by the government could be more than offset by the reduced costs of intermediation. This seems to be the situation in the case of student loans, where policy is moving away from reliance on intermediaries. The other thing to note is that if we are to promote long-term fixed-rate mortgages there must be a promise that the central bank will not embark on any Volcker-esque experiments that drive short-term borrowing rates to 20 percent. Because mortgage lenders will be stuck with long-term fixed-rate assets, there must be a social compact to keep the Fed's overnight-rate target within reasonable bounds.

Moving on to a range of financial services, including brokerage, retirement, and insurance, the argument to consolidate these in "big box" financial superstores was always based on "synergies." In reality, as Minsky and many others have argued, economies of scale in banking are reached at a very small size. Supposed economies of scope have proven to be mostly the ability to dupe customers with "bait-and-switch" schemes. Charles Keating's Lincoln Savings used its FSLIC seal of approval to sell risky and ultimately worthless assets to its elderly widows who thought they were buying insured CDs. More recently, Goldman Sachs allowed one of its hedge fund managers, John Paulson, to design sure-to-fail synthetic collateralized debt obligations that Goldman sold to its own customers, allowing both Goldman and Paulson to use credit default swaps (CDS) to bet on failure. In other words, the "synergy" allows the institution to screw its customers. Worse, large invariably becomes too complex to manage, regulate, or supervise. This allows top management to run the institution as a control fraud, screwing owners. And, finally, because the institution is "too big to fail," Uncle Sam will also get screwed when it is called in for the inevitable bailout.

Hence, following Minsky, all large chartered banks should be prohibited from diversifying across the range of financial services. Instead, they should be narrowly focused in their activities, forced to spin off any business not closely related to making short-term commercial loans and commercial and residential real-estate mortgages. By contrast, Minsky proposed to create a network of local community development banks (CDBs) that would be permitted to engage in a wide range of services, targeted to their communities (Minsky, Papadimitriou,

Phillips, and Wray, 1993). Minsky wanted to include payments services, small business and consumer loans, mortgages, retirement savings, and financial advice within each CDB. The CDBs would be public-private partnerships, with the federal government providing some of the capital base. They would be run by a community board of directors, with government representatives sitting on the boards. Banking would be "intensified"—rather than the megabank holding company with affiliates and branching, each CDB would be local but loosely linked to the network through its relation to a government-owned federal bank for CDBs.

Finally, the financial system needs to help fund long-term positions in complex and expensive capital assets. Historically there are three main approaches to investment banking. In the first, the investment bank either places stocks and bonds issued by firms to finance their capital stock, or it actually takes positions in the stocks and bonds, financing its holding by issuing shorter-term and more liquid liabilities. In the second, a universal bank combines commercial banking and investment banking. In the third, a bank holding company owns various types of financial firms, with firewalls between its investment bank and commercial bank affiliates. Minsky (1992a, 1992b, 1993) argued that the move to money manager capitalism essentially merged these forms. The crisis revealed two related problems. First, underwriting standards deteriorated when investment banks were transformed from partnerships to publicly held firms. (See Galbraith [2009] for a discussion of similar problems in the late 1920s, when investment banks created subsidiary trusts that issued stocks.) The investment banks got caught up in the same "maximization of shareholder value" delusion that gripped all publicly traded firms in the stock-market euphoria. Because top management was rewarded with stock and options, "pump and dump" schemes dominated strategy as short-term trading profits triumphed over longer-run returns. A "trader mentality" was promoted, and traders like Bob Rubin actually rose to the top ranks of many of the investment banks. Second, complex—and opaque—linkages among firms were created because of financial dependency (for example, positions in securities were financed in the commercial paper market) and counterparty risks (for example, risks were supposedly hedged through use of CDS). When problems arose in mortgages, the securities were downgraded, affiliates such as special-purpose vehicles were denied access to the commercial paper market, and CDS "insurance" became worthless when counterparties could not pay. The entire financial system froze because the linkages were broken.

How can we get investment banking back on track? Again, a big part of the problem is underwriting and incentives. An investment bank that plans to sell the debt it helps to originate has less of an incentive to do good underwriting (Mayer, 2010). And when the capital development of the economy becomes a "casino" (where speculation dominates—as Keynes said), it will not be handled well. It will be very difficult to reorient investment banking toward a long-term horizon with proper underwriting when debt is securitized and subject to lax oversight from the Securities and Exchange Commission (SEC), and when the average stock is held less than a year (and the stock market taken as a whole is a negative source of funding of capital assets—because firms are caught up in the casino, purchasing their own equity to share in the gains of a speculative bubble). Minsky emphasized that the capital development of the economy can be mishandled in two ways: the Smithian way and the Keynesian way. It can be misallocated—Smithian—for example, with too much residential real-estate investment. And the aggregate level of investment can be too low, which is Keynesian insufficient investment. Keynes called for socialization of investment—with government determining the aggregate scale. John Kenneth Galbraith also endorsed the socialization of investment to resolve the Smithian problem, with much more investment flowing into public infrastructure. We might pose a new "TINA" to Margaret Thatcher's TINA ("there is no alternative" to free-market capitalism): there is no alternative to socialization of investment—to resolve the Smithian and Keynesian problems.

In any event, what is needed is to change the incentive structure at investment banks so that good underwriting is rewarded. Compensation of top management and traders must be linked to longer-term results. Neither higher-capital ratios (as mandated in Basel III) nor requirements that banks put some "skin in the game" will help. When investment banks originate to distribute, capital ratios are irrelevant (they do not hold the assets on their books). And in a speculative boom, investment bankers are happy to take positions in the dodgy assets that are booming—on the theory they can offload them at the peak. Hence, compensation must be tied to longer-term returns—say, five-year income flows (debt service). To be sure, investment bankers will always pursue a strategy of separating "fools" from their money. It will not be possible to keep up with their innovations of means of doing so. Instead, what is necessary is to reduce the pool of "fools" that will be screwed by investment bankers. To put it as simply as possible, no institution whose mandate is to serve the public interest (pension funds, state and local governments, insurance funds) should be allowed to do business with Wall Street's investment banks. There is ample evidence that they will always lose when dealing with Wall Street. It will be far easier to restrict the pool of "fools" that Wall Street banks are able to dupe than it will be to try to restrict the methods used by Wall Street to screw its customers. Hence, no institutions that are given preferential tax treatment, no public entities, and no individuals with wealth below a mandated minimum (say, $5 million) should be permitted to serve as patsies for Wall Street's investment banks.

This does leave retirement savings up in the air. Like almost all other nations, the United States is an aging society, with a relative decline in its working-age population and a rise of the proportion of seniors. The conventional wisdom has been that if baby boomers accumulate more financial wealth today, they will be able to draw upon that in the future when they retire. To be sure, pension funds have accumulated a huge quantity of financial wealth, and, indeed, they have become so large that they are literally able to "move markets" with their allocations. The commodities price bubble of the mid-2000s was caused by pension funds. The problem is that there is far too much money chasing far too few asset classes that can be expected to generate good returns. And every pension fund manager must beat the average to retain her position. This has led to risky bets in speculative markets, and must lead to disappointment (Nersisyan and Wray, 2010).

Another strategy is required. At the aggregate level, accumulation of financial wealth in pension funds cannot help provide for tomorrow's seniors. The only way to take care of tomorrow's retirees is to increase investments in those areas that will increase tomorrow's real productivity—of the goods and services that seniors and everyone else will want. More thrift today can actually be counterproductive if it reduces today's aggregate demand, leaving plants, equipment, and labor idle—reducing the incentive to invest. Since a for-profit business cannot look very far into the future for profits, there is very little capital investment that can be made today on the prospect that seniors in 2050 will demand output. In other words, almost all the preparation for seniors in the distant future must be made by government—mostly in the form of education and public infrastructure investment. Pension funds make no contribution to that. We must wean society from reliance on private pension plans and accumulations of private pension funds and retirement savings. Instead, the Social Security leg of the retirement stool must be enhanced, and government support for private savings (in the form of tax advantages) should be reduced. At the same time, government should increase its investment in those areas that really will help to take care of future retirees.

## Conclusions

Minsky accepted Keynes's argument that the two outstanding faults of capitalism are its arbitrary and inequitable distribution of income and unemployment. According to Minsky, better economic performance since World War II has not resolved these problems. In his view, poverty can be resolved only through a combination of policies that would achieve three conditions: euthanasia of the rentier; a modest bias of taxes and transfers in favor of the poor; and tight, full employment. Minsky was convinced that the focus of any antipoverty program would have to be tilted toward jobs, not toward transfers and welfare. He defined tight, full employment as a condition such that over a broad range of occupations and industries, employers would like to employ more workers than they do. Tight, full employment helps the poor in several important ways, according to Minsky. Some of the poor move from a condition of unemployment to employment as involuntary unemployment falls. Minsky argued that the evidence shows that periods with higher employment tend to be associated with rising relative wages for the poor. Further, tight, full employment would help to reduce poverty by increasing the number of workers per family; thus, poor families benefit as the total hours worked rises and as wages rise.

More generally, Minsky believed that policy should encourage faster wage growth for low-paying jobs relative to growth of wages for highly paid work. This means that at the low end, wage growth will exceed productivity growth, while, at the high end, productivity growth will exceed wage growth. Similarly, prices will grow in low-wage sectors as costs rise; to prevent inflation overall will require some kind of constraint on prices and wages in high-wage sectors. Minsky argued that such policy can be justified: previously the low-wage workers "subsidized" high-wage workers because wages in the lagging sectors were depressed by unemployment—an argument consistent with the segmented labor markets hypothesis.

Minsky's employer-of-last-resort (ELR) policy, a universal job guarantee program in which the national government offers to pay wages and benefits (and possibly materials costs) for all who are willing to work at the program's compensation level, was designed to simultaneously remedy both of these faults. First, it would ensure tight, full employment by offering a job to anyone willing to work. Second, it would hire off the bottom—setting a base compensation package. Unlike a pump-priming demand stimulus, which puts pressure on wages at the top in the hope that jobs will trickle down, ELR puts pressure on wages at the bottom. Hence, it can achieve full employment while reducing inequality—and without generating inflation pressures. Over time, wages at the bottom would rise faster than productivity. It is possible that government policy might be necessary to restrain wage increases at the top. This would be much more acceptable so long as ELR were in place to ensure no downward wage pressure at the bottom. Otherwise, "wage controls" are likely to put most pressure on the weakest workers.

To Keynes's "two outstanding faults," Minsky added a third: a financially complex capitalist economy will tend to generate instability—a robust financial system is naturally transformed to a fragile system through the normal profit-seeking behavior of entrepreneurs. The success of the New Deal policies and of the postwar "Keynesian" policies actually created conditions that made instability more virulent. According to Minsky, these policies lent an inflationary bias to the economy, encouraged debt, and increased income inequality. As a result, deeper recessions and more frequent and severe financial crises would reappear in the 1970s. Minsky was famous for asking "can it happen again?"—that is, could another debt deflation and Great Depression occur? His answer was that the combination of a Big Bank (Federal Reserve) and Big Government (a federal budget that had grown from less than 3 percent of the economy in 1929 to more than a fifth of the economy in the postwar period) would *probably* be able to prevent "it" from happening again. As he would say, "stability is destabilizing," and while there is no final solution to this fundamental flaw of the capitalist economy, the instability could be constrained by appropriate institutions and interventions. Unfortunately, the set of policies adopted by the neoclassical synthesis Keynesians made matters worse. It is doubly unfortunate that these policies were identified as Keynesian, helped to discredit Keynes's General Theory, and led to a resurrection of neoclassical economics.

According to Minsky, even as the General Theory was abandoned, it became more relevant than ever when instability returned at the end of the 1960s. The run of good times, such as those experienced in the early postwar period, promoted greater leverage and reduction of margins of safety as the value of liquidity declined in the context of postwar optimism and government safety nets. Financial relations become more complex, with more layers of debt interposed between income generation and income receipt. As Minsky argued, to the extent that the institutional structure and swift interventions can constrain crises, risky financial practices are validated and still riskier innovations are encouraged. Fragility rose on a long-term trend, with increasingly severe financial crises. But because deep recessions were avoided, the system was never cleansed of excessive debt—what Minsky termed "financial simplification" that used to occur in depressions, when all debt is wiped out and only equity ownership remains. To make matters worse, over past decades the belief that "markets work to promote the public interest" gained in popularity. All of this put in place conditions that made "it" possible. By denying the possibility of another debt deflation, policy as well as the behavior of the private sector promoted an evolution that led to the inevitable collapse of 2007.

Hence, it is time for fundamental reform of the financial sector. Minsky believed that we need to make "industry" dominate over "speculation" (recalling Keynes's famous dichotomy), and not vice versa, or the capital development of the economy will be mismanaged in two ways: the Smithian/neoclassical way or the Keynes/aggregate demand way. If investment is misdirected, we not only waste resources but also get boom and bust. If investment is too low, we suffer from unemployment and also profits are too low to support commitments—leading to default. Further, when profits are low in "industry" then problems arise in the financial sector because commitments cannot be met. In that case, individual profit-seeking behavior leads to incoherent results as financial markets, labor markets, and goods markets all react in a manner that causes wages and prices to fall, generating a debt deflation. Unfortunately, things are not better when investment is too high: it generates high profits that reward innovation, generating greater risk taking and eventually producing a financial structure that is too fragile. As Minsky always argued, the really dangerous instability in the capitalist economy is in the upward direction toward a euphoric boom. That is what makes the debt deflation possible, because asset prices become overvalued and too much unserviceable debt is issued.

The Smithian ideal is that debt deflations are not endogenous; rather, they must result from exogenous factors, including too much government regulation and intervention. So the solution is deregulation, downsizing government, tax cuts, and making markets more flexible. The Keynesian view is that the financial structure is transformed over a run of good times from a robust to a fragile state as a result of the natural reaction of agents to the successful operation of the economy. If policy makers understood this, they could formulate policy to attenuate the transformation—and then to deal with a crisis when it occurs.

## References


Galbraith, J. K. (2009 [1954]). *The Great Crash, 1929*. New York: Houghton Mifflin Harcourt.

Harvey, Phillip. (1989). *Securing the Right to Employment*. Princeton: Princeton University Press.

Kelton, Stephanie, and L. Randall Wray. (2004). "The War on Poverty after 40 Years: A Minskyan Assessment." *Public Policy Brief*, Levy Economics Institute of Bard College, No. 78.

Kregel, J. (2008). *Minsky's Cushions of Safety: Systemic Risk and the Crisis in the U.S. Subprime Mortgage Market*. Public Policy Brief No. 93. January. Annandale-on-Hudson, NY: Levy Economics Institute of Bard College.

Mayer, M. (2010). *"The Spectre of Banking."* One-Pager No. 3. May 20. Annandale-on-Hudson, NY: Levy Economics Institute of Bard College.

Minsky, H. P. (1963). "Discussion." *American Economic Review* 53(2): 401–412.

Minsky, H. P. (1964). "Longer Waves in Financial Relations: Financial Factors in the More Severe Depressions." *AEA Papers and Proceedings* 54: 324–332.

Minsky, H. P. (1965). "The Role of Employment Policy." In Margaret S. Gordon, ed., *Poverty in* America, 175–200. San Francisco: Chandler.

Minsky, H. P. (1968). "Effects of Shifts of Aggregate Demand upon Income Distribution." *American Journal of Agricultural Economics* 50(2): 328–339.

Minsky, H. P. (1986). *Stabilizing an Unstable Economy*. New Haven, CT: Yale University Press.

Minsky, H. P. (1992a). "Reconstituting the United States' Financial Structure: Some Fundamental Issues." Working Paper No. 69. January. Annandale-on-Hudson, NY: Levy Economics Institute of Bard College. Minsky, H. P. (1992b). "The Capital Development of the Economy and the Structure of Financial Institutions." Working Paper No. 72. January. Annandale-on-Hudson, NY: Levy Economics Institute of Bard College.

Minsky, H. P. (1993). "Financial Structure and the Financing of the Capital Development of the Economy." The Jerome Levy Institute Presents Proposals for Reform of the Financial System, April 23. Manuscript. Minsky Archive. Corpus Christie, TX: Levy Economics Institute.

Minsky, H. P. (1996). "Uncertainty and the Institutional Structure of Capitalist Economies." Working Paper No. 155. April. Annandale-on-Hudson, NY: Levy Economics Institute of Bard College.

Minsky, H. P., D. B. Papadimitriou, R. J. Phillips, and L. R. Wray. (1993). *Community Development Banking: A Proposal to Establish a Nationwide System of Community Development Banks*. Public Policy Brief No. 3. January. Annandale-on-Hudson, NY: Levy Economics Institute of Bard College.

Nersisyan, Y., and L. R. Wray. (2010). *The Trouble with Pensions*. Public Policy Brief No. 109. March. Annandale-on-Hudson, NY: Levy Economics Institute of Bard College.

Phillips, R. J. (1995). *The Chicago Plan & New Deal Banking Reform*. Foreword by H. P. Minsky. Armonk, NY: M. E. Sharpe.

Tymoigne, É., and L. R. Wray. (2009). *It Isn't Working: Time for More Radical Policies*. Public Policy Brief No. 105. October. Annandale-on-Hudson, NY: Levy Economics Institute of Bard College.

Wray, L. Randall. (2005). "The Ownership Society: Social Security Is Only the Beginning..." Levy Economics Institute Public Policy Brief No. 82, August.

Wray, L. Randall. (2008a). *Financial Markets Meltdown: What Can We Learn from Minsky?* Public Policy Brief No. 94. April. Annandale-on-Hudson, NY: Levy Economics Institute of Bard College.

Wray, L. Randall. (2008b). *The Commodities Market Bubble: Money Manager Capitalism and the Financialization of Commodities*. Public Policy Brief No. 96. October. Annandale-on-Hudson, NY: Levy Economics Institute of Bard College.

Wray, L. Randall. (2010). "Minsky's Money Manager Capitalism and the Global Financial Crisis." Unpublished manuscript.

CHAPTER 36

# THE GLOBAL FINANCIAL CRISIS AND AFRICA

## THE EFFECTS AND POLICY RESPONSES

ZUZANA BRIXIOVÁ AND LÉONCE NDIKUMANA

AFRICA has by and large weathered the Global Financial Crisis well. Having posted a relatively fast recovery in sync with other developing and emerging market countries, in 2012 Africa is projected to remain one of the fastest growing regions in the world. Unlike during past crises, in late 2000s African economies were much better positioned against external shocks, with more stable macroeconomic balances, especially lower fiscal and current account deficits, lower inflation rates, and higher foreign exchange reserves. Where fiscal space permitted, African governments also proactively initiated policy responses to support domestic demand and boost key sectors (Kasekende, Brixiova, and Ndikumana, 2010).

Going forward, the continent faces substantial challenges in its attempt to tackle key structural constraints to reach and exceed pre-crisis growth rates. Macroeconomic and financial policies will play a critical role in the post-crisis growth agenda. This chapter documents the performance of African economies during the global financial crisis and discusses the policy responses implemented by governments to cushion the impact of the crisis using selected country illustrations. It concludes with a discussion of the continent's policy challenges and options at the global, regional, and national levels, by underlining the political economy dimensions of these policy challenges.

# 1. Key Characteristics of African Economies Prior to the Crisis

## 1.1. Growth, Inflation, and Credit

With an almost 6 percent annual rate, Africa was among the fastest growing world regions during 2001–2008. A favorable external environment, increased political stability, and improved macroeconomic frameworks underpinned this performance. In some countries (e.g., Rwanda, Ethiopia, Ghana), structural reforms, including a strengthened business climate and financial systems, have played a role. The high growth was accompanied by rising private-capital flows. In addition to high growth, many African countries, including low-income countries (LICs), reached low inflation rates. Moreover, both growth and inflation were less volatile than in the 1990s.

Lower pre-crisis inflation was an improvement from the 1990s, when only less than half of African low-income countries had inflation below 10 percent. In contrast, during the 2000s about two-thirds of this group of countries had inflation below 10 percent. At the same time, the pre-crisis growth was not sufficient to markedly reduce poverty and reach Millennium Development Goals (MDGs)—only 25 percent of the low-income countries grew by 7 percent or more a year on average. Some of the low income countries that posted very low inflation may thus have reached it at the expense to their growth.[1]

African economies at the end of 2008 were characterized by low financial depths. In all Africa's LICs, the stock of private-sector credit in GDP was below the average of this category of countries in other regions, raising the question of whether excessively tight monetary policies have constrained private-sector credit, a key driver of growth.[2] Moreover, sectors critical for generating employment and inclusive growth, such as agriculture, received particularly low shares of total credit.

Performance varied across countries. In fragile states (e.g., Central African Republic, Sierra Leone) private-sector credit growth has remained subdued. In others (e.g., South Africa, Nigeria, Mauritius) private-sector credit grew rapidly, albeit not as fast as in some European emerging markets (table 36.1).

Table 36.1 Private-sector credit in 2004 and 2008 (percentage of GDP)

| | 2004 | 2008 | Change |
|---|---|---|---|
| Sub-Saharan Africa | 26.7 | 37.5 | 10.8 |
| Central Afr. Rep. | 7.2 | 7.0 | −0.2 |
| Chad | 4.0 | 4.8 | 0.8 |
| Sierra Leone | 4.7 | 7.1 | 2.4 |
| South Africa | 67.4 | 86.7 | 19.3 |
| Nigeria | 12.8 | 31.3 | 18.5 |
| Mauritius | 73.1 | 87.8 | 14.8 |
| Estonia | 59.8 | 97.0 | 37.2 |
| Latvia | 54.1 | 90.1 | 36.0 |

*Source:* Authors' calculations based on the African Economic Outlook database and IMF Regional Outlooks for Sub-Saharan Africa.

## 1.2. Savings and Capital Flows

Prior to the crisis, many African countries, especially oil importers, continued to have low savings rates.[3] The aggregate numbers hide important differences among countries though, with higher savings rates in North Africa and among oil exporters. The investment rates of oil exporters, however, were only marginally higher than those of oil importers, suggesting that export proceeds were not fully used for enhancing productive capacity. Instead, they contributed to the oil exporters' rapid accumulation of foreign exchange reserves (Elhiraika and Ndikumana, 2009).

With low savings rates, African countries relied increasingly on capital flows to reduce their resource gaps. As in other developing regions, capital flows to Africa surged, amounting to about 8 percent of total flows and 10 percent of foreign direct investment (FDI) to developing countries during 2001–2008. Reaching almost US$76 billion in 2007, net capital inflows were about 5 percent of Africa's GDP. The increased private-capital flows were driven by better investment climates and increased political and macroeconomic stability. They reflected also the business cycle upswing in advanced economies and heightened investor appetite.[4]

## 1.3. Limited Financial Integration to the Global Economy

Before the crisis, Africa had only limited links with the global financial system, with the bulk of private-capital flows going to a handful of countries.

**Table 36.2** Selected indicators of the size of capital markets in 2008, by region (percentage of GDP)

| | Stock-market capitalization (1) | Total debt (2) | Private debt (3) | Bank assets (4) | Bonds, equities (5) = (1) + (2) |
|---|---|---|---|---|---|
| World, average | 55.0 | 137.1 | 85.1 | 159.9 | 192.1 |
| Advanced economies | 61.3 | 192.1 | 121.9 | 193.6 | 253.4 |
| Newly industrialized Asia | 268.6 | 111.4 | 66.3 | 222.5 | 380.1 |
| EMDEs | 41.5 | 37.9 | 15.1 | 87.5 | 79.4 |
| **Africa** | **34.7** | **12.1** | **6.4** | **54.0** | **46.8** |
| Developing Asia | 59.8 | 54.3 | 23.6 | 131.5 | 114.2 |
| Latin America | 34.6 | 43.0 | 15.5 | 52.0 | 77.6 |
| Middle East | 33.0 | 5.8 | 3.7 | 65.3 | 38.9 |

*Note:* EMDEs stands for emerging market and developing countries.
*Source:* Authors' calculations based on the IMF Global Financial Stability Report (2010).
*Note:* Debt issued at domestic capital markets.

In many countries, prudent macroeconomic policies and the debt relief reduced external vulnerability. The small sizes of African capital markets (table 36.2) together with regulatory and prudential reforms undertaken in the 2000s have lowered further the continent's exposure to global financial shocks.

Even countries with high shares of foreign ownership in the banking sectors (e.g., Ghana) had not accumulated large private external debts in foreign currency and thus avoided currency mismatch pressures when their currencies depreciated. Because the housing finance and real-estate markets—key transmission channels in advanced economies—remain underdeveloped in most of Africa, the continent was also less exposed to negative spillovers from the financial system to the real sector.

Still, high capital inflows have deepened integration of some African emerging and frontier markets[5] (e.g., South Africa, Nigeria, Ghana) into the global financial markets, raising their vulnerability to sudden stops of short-term capital flows, albeit less than in emerging Europe.[6] A few countries (e.g., Mauritius and Morocco) have recorded some asset and housing booms.

# 2. How Did the Global Financial Crisis Affect Africa?

## 2.1. Growth Outcomes

In 2009, export and growth across Africa rapidly decelerated because of the collapse of import demand among the main trading partners and declining commodity prices. Consequently, fiscal and current account balances were negatively affected, while poverty and unemployment increased. Africa's 2009 real GDP growth reached only 2.8 percent, well below the 5.7 percent average over 2001–2008. On a positive note, the continent exhibited surprising resilience as a whole, and most of its countries avoided recession, while output fell in most OECD countries. In 2010 and 2011, sub-Saharan Africa's growth bounced back to 5.3 and 5.1 percent, respectively, and is projected to reach e 5.5 percent in 2014, despite the uneven global recovery (IMF World Economic Outlook database, April 2012).

Growth prospects for Africa as a whole have been dampened by political changes in North Africa, with the growth rate having declined from 5 percent in 2010 to 3.4 percent in 2011. The growth rate is projected to gradually increase to 4.5 and 4.8 percent in 2012 and 2013, respectively (AfDB, OECD, UNECA, and UNDP 2012). Africa's deepening trade and financial ties with East Asia have helped offset the negative impact of the recession in advanced economies.

### *2.1.1. What Drove Africa's Growth Performance in 2009?*

Growth performance in 2009 varied substantially across African countries in the wake of the Global Financial Crisis. This section identifies the initial conditions that may help explain these differences, with an emphasis on macroeconomic and financial factors.[7]

The main results are as follows (see box 36.1). First, there are exchange-rate volatility, higher share of credit in GDP, and greater trade openness associated with growth in 2009. Second, there was a change in growth between 2008 and 2009 that was negatively related to greater exchange-rate volatility, higher trend growth, and larger trade openness. The results reflect the substantial growth contraction among oil-exporting African countries, as well as the growth collapse in financially developed and integrated countries, especially South Africa.

### *2.1.2. Experiences of Emerging and Frontier Markets in Southern and East Africa*

Even past successful performers, middle-income countries in southern Africa such as Botswana, Namibia, and South Africa, have not been spared the impact

## Box 36.1 Drivers of Africa's 2009 Growth Performance

To better understand reasons behind varied growth performance of African countries, year-on-year real GDP growth and change in real GDP growth in 2009 relative to 2008 for a sample of 48 African economies were analyzed. Real GDP growth and the change in real GDP growth were regressed on (log of) GDP per capita in 2008, the share of private-sector credit in GDP in 2008 (percent), the exchange-rate volatility during 2001-2008 (measured by the relative standard deviation), the current account balance during 2001-2008 (in percentage of GDP), and trade openness (share of exports and imports in GDP) in 2008. In addition, pre-crisis trend growth (average during 2001-2007, in percent), the change in credit as a share of GDP during the 2004-2008 years of "credit boom", and the change in terms of trade in 2008 (measured in percentages) were included. The results are summarized in the table below.

Drivers of real GDP growth level and change in 2009

| | Real GDP Growth | Change in Real GDP Growth |
|---|---|---|
| GDP per capita (2008, log) | −0.521 (0.666) | 2.293** (0.043) |
| Trade openness (2008) | −0.0153* (0.054) | −0.0176** (0.017) |
| Exchange-rate variability (2001–2008) | −0.177*** (0.005) | −0.149** (0.01) |
| Credit/GDP (2008) | −0.0349* (0.088) | 0.02767 (0.138) |
| Terms of trade change (2008) | 0.0184 (0.488) | −0.0243 (0.320) |
| Current account balance (2001–2008) | −0.0188 (0.771) | −0.114* (0.059) |
| Trend growth (average of 2001–2007) | −0.0144 (0.921) | −0.521*** (0.000) |
| Change in credit (2004–2008, percentage of GDP) | 0.092 (0.187) | 0.0476 (0.450) |
| Constant | 8.585** (0.018) | -3.019 (0.35) |
| Observations | 48 | 48 |
| R square (adjusted) | 0.127 | 0.315 |

*Source:* Authors' calculations based on the African Economic Outlook database. The results are obtained using OLS estimation; they are robust to alternative specifications. The figures in brackets are p-values. * denotes significance at 10 percent, ** at 5 percent, and *** at 1 percent level.

of the global slump. In fact, the crisis has affected some of these countries particularly severely because of their relatively deeper integration into the global economy and dependence on commodity exports. Some of the countries that grew the fastest in 2008 (Botswana, Namibia, and South Africa) experienced the largest falls in 2009. In 2010, they were recovering due to improved global demand, domestic stimulus policies (e.g., South Africa), and timely assistance from multilateral institutions (e.g., Botswana).

- Besides its financial integration into the global economy, South Africa's production structure made it vulnerable to shocks. The fastest-growing sectors such as construction, finance, real estate, business services, and transport were also hit most severely by the crisis. With real GDP contracting by 1.8 percent, South Africa experienced its first recession in 17 years and was one of the few African countries in recession in 2009.
- The global crisis severely affected Botswana as the demand for diamonds collapsed; subsequently, output contracted by 4 percent in 2009. Because Botswana accumulated significant policy buffers before the crisis, it could implement effective countercyclical policies. The crisis was also mitigated by timely financial assistance from international organizations, including a $1.5 billion loan from the African Development Bank.
- Output in Namibia also contracted in real terms in 2009 by 1.8 percent due to collapsed demand for diamonds, reflected in a decline in output of primary industries by about 24 percent. Appropriately prudent macroeconomic policies adopted prior to the crisis and the accumulated fiscal space (2 percent of GDP budget surplus in the fiscal year for 2008–2009) allowed the government to adopt countercyclical measures in 2009. These supported growth in secondary sectors, especially construction, which grew by 46 percent in the same year.

In contrast to southern African commodity exporters, countries in East Africa such as Ethiopia, Rwanda, Tanzania, and Uganda were among the fastest growing in the world in 2009 and 2010. Less developed domestic capital markets shielded them from the direct impact of the crisis. For example, while the Nairobi stock-market index fell more than the one in South Africa, the impact on the Kenyan economy was limited because of low market capitalization. The shock through the trade channel was also limited due to East Africa's greater product and market diversification and deeper regional integration. In fact, in 2009 the trade balance improved in all the East African Community countries, except for Rwanda where it stagnated. Foreign direct investment inflows into the subregion slightly increased in 2009, while they dropped substantially in Southern Africa. Moreover, most East African countries improved the soundness of their banking sectors in the early to the mid-2000s, which helped maintain public confidence during the crisis.[8]

## 2.2. Channels of Transmission

Africa was protected from the immediate consequences of the Global Financial Crisis by underdeveloped financial markets and limited international linkages. Instead, it was impacted by the crisis more gradually and through somewhat different channels than developed and emerging market economies. The continent was less affected by the liquidity constraints and more by the global recession than emerging Europe, Asia, and Latin America. Besides falling trade, economic activity suffered from declining remittances, reduced FDI, and fewer tourism proceeds. The sections below discuss briefly these channels, with a focus on financial flows.

### 2.2.1. *Decline in Exports*

In 2009, global trade declined by 11 percent. While the impact varied across countries, Africa's commodity exporters (e.g., Angola, Botswana) took a particularly heavy hit. The trade channel worked through both the declining demand in advanced economies and worsening terms of trade. For example, the volume of sub-Saharan Africa's exports declined by 3 percent in 2009 from 2008 levels, while terms of trade deteriorated by 11 percent. Moreover, the access to trade credit was also curtailed with the total trade finance gap rising, as the experience of Nigeria at the end of 2008 showed, when its credit lines with banks in advanced economies dried up. Given that most African countries fund bank loans from deposits, declining export proceeds that lowered deposits also constrained the growth of private-sector credit and money supply, especially for oil exporters.

### 2.2.2. *Remittances*

During this global recession, remittances were no longer the countercyclical buffer they used to be, as the crisis hit hard the main sending sources: developed economies and oil-exporting countries. Estimates by Barajas and colleagues (2010) indicate that in 2009 remittances declined by 7–14 percent in Tunisia, Morocco, and Egypt, and by about 3–7 percent in a number of other African countries. The authors also posited that in most African countries the fall in remittances in 2009 translated into a decline of about 0.1–0.2 percentage points in GDP growth. In several cases, the impact was more severe: Tunisia may have lost between 0.4–0.7 percentage points of real GDP growth, while Morocco lost between 1.1–2.0 percentage points of real GDP growth.

### 2.2.3. *Tightened Credit Conditions and Reduced Capital Flows*

While this channel has played a less prominent role in Africa than in other regions, for countries such as South Africa the tightened global credit conditions meant markedly reduced external finance through bond and equity issuance in 2009. Several frontier markets (e.g., Kenya, Zambia) postponed issuance of their first sovereign bonds on international capital markets until 2012 or beyond. Consequently, as much as $4 billion in sovereign debt issuance was deferred by African countries in 2009 due to tight credit-market conditions. Senegal was an exception, issuing a sovereign bond of $200 million in December 2009.

Due to limited financial integration, Africa on the whole experienced relatively contained decline in private-capital flows, but the impact again varied. There were no major shortfalls in official flows. Moreover, as the evidence in box 36.1 indicates, the impact on growth was felt more in countries and regions with greater depth of financial systems. With official aid projected to stay at the current (relatively low) levels or even to decline, African countries need to enhance efforts to attract more FDI and other private flows in order to reduce the savings-investment gap.

### 2.2.4. *Foreign Direct Investment*

As in other developing regions, FDI flows to Africa increased markedly prior to the crisis, and stocks more than tripled during 2001–2008. They were also less volatile than portfolio flows. The crisis only reinforced this trend, as portfolio flows to several African emerging and frontier markets (e.g., South Africa, Nigeria) reversed abruptly in 2009 but returned in 2010.[9] Because private investment decisions are based on longer-term factors (political and macroeconomic stability, trade openness, human capital stock, liberal investment policies, institutions), the fall in FDI inflows was more gradual and subdued than that of portfolio flows in the first half of 2009.

Despite a 20 percent decline in FDI between 2008 and 2009, these flows were more resilient than other financial flows to Africa. Africa fared better than other world regions except Asia; its share in global FDI rose from 3 percent in 2007 to 5.2 percent in 2009. However, FDI to Africa declined by 14 percent in 2010, lowering the continent's share in total to 4.5 percent.[10]

Vast differences in FDI inflows emerged across Africa's subgroups during the crisis. For example, the Economic Community of Central African States and East African Community trade blocks received more FDI in 2009 than in 2008. Several oil exporters such as Egypt, Nigeria, Angola, and Sudan attracted substantial FDI inflows (above US$3 billion) in 2009. Some frontier markets (e.g., Ghana, Mozambique, Zambia) received more FDI in 2009 than in 2008 due to continued high growth and strong prospects. In the case of Ghana, the 2005 oil discovery helped attract more foreign long-term capital flows. In contrast, FDI to less dynamic low-income countries markedly declined, underscoring the role of fundamentals in offsetting short-term shocks.

The overall resilience of foreign direct investment to Africa during the crisis showed that the pre-crisis growth of private-capital flows was not only commodity-driven but reflected also improved policies and longer-term prospects of African economies. On the policy side, in addition to opening up their investment regimes, a number of African countries shifted from targeting FDI into specific sectors to establishing broad enabling investment climates. Many countries also strengthened their business environments.[11]

## 2.3. Policy Responses

Due to improved macroeconomic frameworks, many African countries were in much stronger positions to counter the 2009 crisis than before the previous global recessions. Nevertheless, substantial differences existed across subgroups. During the five years prior to the crisis, African oil exporters recorded large current account surpluses while other countries, including emerging markets, continued to post deficits. These surpluses allowed oil exporters such as Angola and Nigeria to use the reserves to cushion the impact of the crisis. Differences existed also in pre-crisis growth rates, with fragile states growing by three percentage points less than oil exporters, widening the income gap relative to other countries on the continent.

African countries have adopted a variety of measures in response to the crisis, including bailouts of distressed banks and new regulations in the banking sector (e.g., Nigeria during the banking crisis), fiscal stimulus packages (e.g., Tanzania, Uganda, Kenya, Mauritius), targeted sector assistance (e.g., Nigeria, with credit extension to agriculture), and expansionary monetary policies (e.g., Ghana, Tanzania, Kenya). Even though some countries (e.g., Nigeria) adopted temporary exchange and capital controls, most African countries resisted the protectionist measures that were prevalent in advanced economies.

Except for a few emerging markets such as South Africa, monetary policies in Africa were mostly ineffective in stimulating aggregate demand. Transmission mechanisms of monetary policy are hampered by structural rigidities (e.g., high collateral requirements, the lack of bankable projects, and the lack of competition) and by imperfect information. These factors prevented cuts in policy rates by the central banks into reduced lending rates and increased lending by domestic commercial banks. Often, the conservative lending strategies of commercial banks reflected their concerns about the ability of key sectors to repay loans. The example of Kenya illustrates this point.

To stimulate recovery, the Central Bank of Kenya cut its policy rate from 9 percent in November 2008 to 6 percent in June 2010, while reducing the cash reserve ratio. Despite the decline in both interbank rates and T-bill rates in 2009 and 2010, the commercial banks' lending rates slightly increased. With high lending rates and growth deceleration, private-sector credit started to increase only at the end of 2009, fueled by ample liquidity and increased confidence stemming from recovery in Africa and the global economy. Still, real private-sector credit growth stayed subdued—below 20 percent —for most of 2010. In contrast, net borrowing by the government took off in 2010 so much that it may have crowded out private-sector credit.

Where adopted in Africa (e.g., East Africa), the sometimes heatedly debated countercyclical *fiscal measures* were more effective, as they were overall timely, well targeted, and often accompanied by improvements in the business environment. Moreover, governments kept an overall prudent fiscal stance, convinced by positive results achieved before the crisis. The adopted stimulus measures are thus unlikely to jeopardize debt sustainability. Finally, by focusing mostly on infrastructure outlays, these expenditures not only stimulated aggregate demand but also helped alleviate long-term structural bottlenecks (Kasekende, Brixiova, and Ndikumana, 2010).

To finance countercyclical spending, Kenya used innovative methods such as issuing infrastructure bonds in local currency.[12] The government thus took steps to develop local financial markets by setting a benchmark for pricing corporate bonds. The first infrastructure bond (US$232 million) was sold in February 2009 and was oversubscribed by 45 percent. The second and third bonds, issued later in 2009, were twice oversubscribed. One of the incentives offered, which increased the bonds' attractiveness, was allowing holders to use the bonds as collateral for bank loans while the banks were allowed to pledge the bonds as collateral for their repos. The Gulf African Bank—a fully fledged Islamic bank operating in Kenya—participated in the *sukuk* (Islamic finance adhering) portion of one of the government infrastructure bonds issued.

## 3. Country Experiences in the Wake of the Crisis: The Cases of Nigeria and Ghana

### 3.1. Nigeria

Nigeria was the only country in Africa that experienced major financial sector difficulties during the Global Financial Crisis. The swift action and wide range of measures implemented by the central bank in 2009 and 2010 prevented a full-fledged banking crisis. However, private-sector credit needs to increase to sustain the recovery.

#### *3.1.1. How Did the Global Financial Crisis Impact Nigeria?*

With a 3 percent growth rate in 2009, Nigeria weathered the crisis better than the continent as a whole and than most other African oil exporters. It was also one of the few countries that posted a current account surplus in 2009, even though it sharply deteriorated from 2008 due to falling oil prices. Still, the crisis hit the country's banking sector. The banking crisis of 2008–2009 was domestically driven, but the Global Financial Crisis further amplified it.

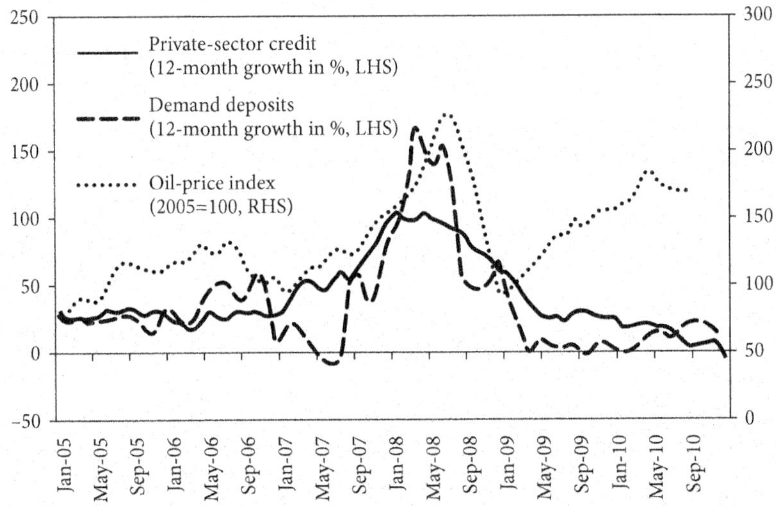


**Figure 36.1** Nigeria: Oil prices, demand deposits, and private-sector credit, percentage change (January 2005–December 2010). Source: Authors' calculations based on the data of the Central Bank of Nigeria (CBN) and IMF IFS database.

On the domestic side, rapid credit growth reflecting excessive risk taking was the main structural weakness in the Nigerian banking sector. Before the crisis, private-sector credit rose by almost 100 percent between March 2007 and the end of 2008 (figure 36.1), fueled by high deposits reflecting high oil prices. Monetary policy contributed by taking a passive stance and inadequately sterilizing the liquidity arising from oil revenues. The supervision authority overlooked some questionable lending practices, especially high loan concentration in the oil sector.[13]

In sum, the Global Financial Crisis impacted the Nigerian banking sector through several channels. First, the plummeting oil prices reduced demand deposits. Given that most loans extended by Nigerian banks are deposit-funded, credit declined accordingly (figure 36.1). Second, plummeting oil and stock-market prices reduced loan repayment rates and increased the share of nonperforming loans.[14] The concerns about rising nonperforming loans were exacerbated by the banks' substantial share of "margin" loans in their portfolios, that is, loans that were secured by oil revenues and stocks. Third, Nigeria's portfolio outflows (2 percent of GDP) together with declining oil revenues reduced foreign exchange reserves. Fourth, a depreciating exchange rate heightened risks related to currency mismatches in banks' balance sheets. Finally, Nigeria's trade credit lines dried up when the crisis hit at the end of 2008.

### 3.1.2. *Structural Reforms to Address the Banking Crisis*

The crisis hit hard Nigerian banks that were heavily exposed to the oil sector and/or the stock market and that depended on foreign credit. In 2009, the banking sector review by the Central Bank of Nigeria (CBN) identified high nonperforming loans, weak corporate governance, inadequate capital buffers, and the lack of liquidity as the main weaknesses.[15] To address these problems, the central bank undertook bank recapitalization, established an asset management company to take over the impaired assets, changed banking regulations and supervision, and replaced management in weak banks. The central bank extended liquidity to five systematically important ailing banks (Naira 420 million, 2.5 percent of GDP) to enable them to meet the capital adequacy requirement.[16] The bailout was financed from the government budget (Central Bank of Nigeria, 2010).

### 3.1.3. *Monetary and Exchange-Rate Policies*

While the central bank's measures prevented a banking crisis and complete crash of the capital market, they partly contributed to the banks' reluctance to lend. Since the central bank's review and reforms in 2009, Nigerian banks have become much more risk-averse. The central bank adopted measures to boost liquidity and stabilize foreign reserves, to lower commercial banks' interest rates and stimulate private-sector credit. Reviving private-sector credit and containing the fall of foreign exchange reserves have thus become a key policy challenge.

The Nigerian central bank's policies aimed at the credit market included (1) a cut of the monetary policy rate from 10.3 percent in September 2008 to 6 percent in December 2009; (2) a cut of the cash reserve requirement from 4 to 1 percent and of the liquidity ratio from 40 to 25 percent; (3) support to banks in difficulties through the discount window and guaranteed interbank lending; (4) ceilings on commercial banks' lending and deposit rates; and (5) a limit on banks' lending to the public sector.[17]

In parallel, the central bank adopted temporary measures to mitigate the decline in foreign exchange reserves, such as (1) replacing wholesale the Dutch auction by the retail version for about six months; (2) cutting the limit on banks' net open foreign exchange position; (3) requesting that oil companies and government agencies temporarily sell foreign exchange to the central bank rather than at the interbank market; (4) requesting that banks temporarily transact forex within +/- 1 percent of the official exchange rate; and (5) managing the official rate within +/- 3 percent around the central rate (Central Bank of Nigeria, 2010).[18]

### 3.1.4. *Sector Measures by the Central Bank of Nigeria*

In addition to the economywide measures, the central bank targeted specific sectors where limited access to credit has been a long-standing challenge. For example, at the end of 2010, the central bank established funds to support manufacturers (Naira 500 billion) and small and medium enterprises in the industrial sector (Naira 200 billion) and infrastructural developments (Naira 300 billion).[19] The central bank also provided a Naira 150 billion credit facility to the manufacturers at a fixed rate of 7 percent through the Bank of Industry and depository institutions. To support further loans to the targeted sectors, the central bank established a Credit Guarantee Scheme for small and medium enterprises (Naira 200 billion) and a Commercial Agricultural Fund (Naira 200 billion). Despite these measures, private-sector credit has not recovered as of early 2011; reviving it constitutes a key challenge.

## 3.2. Ghana

### 3.2.1. *Performance Before the Crisis*

At 6.4 percent annual growth during 2005–2008, Ghana recorded its fastest growth during the past 30 years. Most of the improved performance in the 2000s was due more to stronger policies and institutions than to external conditions (IMF, 2007). At the end of 2007, having achieved a sufficient degree of macroeconomic stability, Ghana successfully issued a $750 million sovereign eurobond.[20] With this oversubscribed bond issuance, it became the second country in sub-Saharan Africa (after South Africa) to access international capital markets. The bond issuance set the benchmark for other frontier markets in Africa seeking sovereign and private-sector borrowing on international capital markets. Ghana's partial liberalization of the capital account since the mid-2000s contributed to increased private-capital inflows.[21]

### 3.2.2. *Resilience during the Crisis: Good Luck or Good Policies?*

Overall, Ghana weathered the crisis well: at 4.7 percent GDP growth rate, it was among the 15 fastest-growing countries in Africa in 2009. However, inflation in 2009 was close to 20 percent due to high domestic demand, food and fuel prices, and exchange-rate pass-through, before falling to 12.2 percent in 2010. The fiscal deficit stayed in double digits and the current account deficit widened. Of concern is also the country's reaccumulation of public debt so quickly after the debt relief: total public debt increased from 51 percent of GDP in 2007 to 65 percent in 2009.

The overall solid economic performance was achieved even though macroeconomic policies were pro-cyclical. Ghana's resilience during the crisis thus rested to a large extent on high prices of gold and cocoa, which accounted for more than 70 percent of export revenues in 2009. The limited integration of Ghana into global financial markets shielded the domestic financial sector. At the same time, Ghana benefited from financial support from donors, which helped sustain reserves that had dropped to precarious levels in 2009 (to two months of imports).

Ghana's macroeconomic outcomes remained good in 2009 and 2010, but its financial sector weakened because of accumulation of government arrears to private contractors who then defaulted on their loans (total nonperforming loans in the banking sector rose from 7 percent in mid-2006 to almost 20 percent in 2009); because several banks had their portfolios concentrated in a few sectors; and because a small development bank experienced financial difficulties.

### 3.2.3. *Policies in Response to the Crisis*

Ghana's macroeconomic policies continued to be pro-cyclical during the crisis years, trying to make up for past slippages, consolidating the fiscal stance, and restoring investors' confidence.

On the fiscal side, the government cut the budget to reverse debt accumulation and reduce the large budget deficits. Outlays seem to follow political cycles, rising during or around the elections (except in 1996). Accordingly, the budget deficit ballooned to 14.5 percent of GDP in 2008, the year of presidential elections.[22] The government thus lacked sufficient fiscal space to implement countercyclical policies when the crisis hit. In fact, real expenditures were cut in 2009, which contributed to a decline of the deficit to 9 percent of GDP.

On the monetary side, the Bank of Ghana was raising its policy rate throughout 2009 to contain inflation. It cut the policy rate in the last quarter of 2009, but the lending rates and the interest-rate spread stayed high.[23] The real growth of the private-credit sector collapsed in 2009 and was subdued in 2010 due to tightened credit conditions and the loss of confidence in the economy by households and businesses.

Unlike many other sub-Saharan Africa countries that lack social assistance programs, Ghana's social program included protection for the most vulnerable, including subsidized electricity tariffs; cash transfers to qualifying households; free maternal health care; grants and subsidies for basic education; and a national youth employment program. The program, which expanded during the crisis, played a somewhat stabilizing role for the low-income segments of the population.

Finally, de facto exchange-rate policy became more flexible, to counter the falling foreign reserves. The exchange rate depreciated by 50 percent against the dollar during 2008 and in the first half of 2009 but strenghtened afterward. Even with these changes, the real exchange rate remained close to its equilibrium value and hence has not jeopardized export competitiveness.

### 3.2.4. *Policies for Post-Crisis Growth*

For Ghana, returning to a high pre-crisis growth path and achieving middle-income status will hinge on adopting appropriate policies and reforms, including (1) fiscal and institutional reforms to improve public financial management; (2) judicious management of oil revenues; (3) raising financing for infrastructure in innovative but sustainable ways; (4) reducing domestic debt and in general keeping the debt sustainable; and (5) increasing access to credit for small and medium enterprises (SMEs) and underserved sectors.[24]

# 4. Africa in the Aftermath of the Crisis: Policy Challenges Ahead

In the aftermath of the Global Financial Crisis, the continent's outlook is promising and probably more optimistic than it has ever been. Africa has defied the stereotypical views of a continent doomed for failure. It has not only demonstrated the ability to post high growth rates and implement costly reforms, but it has done so during such challenging circumstances as was the case during the crisis. Thus, Africa is seen as a next potential driver of global growth, following the footsteps of the Asian tigers. It has the opportunity to capitalize on its immense resource potential, a young population, an emerging middle-class as a source of demand-led growth, and technological innovation. The continent can also leapfrog into the technological revolution as illustrated in its innovative application of mobile technologies (e.g., m-banking, m-agriculture, and, not too far ahead, also m-government).

At the same time, Africa faces substantial policy challenges ahead, which have critical political economy dimensions. The ability of African countries to confront these challenges, individually and collectively, will determine whether or not the continent will indeed capitalize on its reform momentum and seize the opportunities of the twenty-first century. The challenges are at the global, regional, and national levels.

## 4.1. Global Policy Challenges: Global Financial Regulation

The Global Financial Crisis has been accompanied by two major developments with critical implications for Africa. First, the crisis has galvanized attention to the importance of financial stability for countries, regions and the global economy. It has resurrected the traditional debate over the relative roles of the state versus markets in regulating economies. With the debacle of the free-market-based view of regulation, there have been increased calls for a more active role of the state in regulating the financial system and the economy more generally. As many observers suggested, the crisis revealed that it was "time for a visible hand" (Griffith-Jones, Ocampo, and Stiglitz, 2010). A key weakness of the pre-crisis regulatory frameworks was that they were based on incentive systems that were "universal constants" (lacked dynamism), allowing market players to develop innovations to circumvent those same (static) rules (Caprio, 2010).

African countries need to seize the opportunity of this policy shift and reinvigorate the role of the state not only in regulating financial markets but also in providing a framework for high and inclusive growth. Finding the right balance between the role of markets and the role of the state, which will differ across countries and over time, is crucial. In practical terms, the key question is whether African governments are ready and capable to play this developmental role. Clearly, most African low-income countries face severe capacity constraints in the design and implementation of policies.[25]

A related issue is the risk of backtracking on market-oriented reforms, notably privatization of financial institutions. In a few African countries, the state still controls most of the banking sector, undermining competition and efficiency of resource allocations. For example, in Ethiopia the state controls nearly all the commercial banking sector. The government thus exercises substantial control over credit allocation, which opens avenues for corruption and rent seeking and discourages financial reforms. In such circumstances, governments may ride on the pro-regulation tide to consolidate their hold on the economy in the interest of preserving undemocratic regimes. The call for an increased role of the state may then be a double-edged sword for African countries at a time when the continent is pushing for a political opening and a move toward more development-oriented states.

The second development arising from the crisis has been the increased and predominant role of special global bodies in designing the policy reform agenda at the global level and in pushing for compliance with it at the national level. The crisis strengthened institutions such as the G20 and associated specialized bodies such as the Financial Stability Board and the Basel Committee. While these institutions have been mandated with measures to stem the impact of the crisis, they have focused on the issues of financial regulation both at the national and global levels. At times, they have taken the limelight away from conventional and more representative global bodies such as the United Nations and its specialized agencies, the International Monetary Fund, the World Trade Organization, and regional institutions.[26]

The increased prominence of special global bodies has raised important political economy questions for Africa and other developing regions. The first question is that of representation and ownership of policy decisions taken by these global bodies. Given that representation and membership to these bodies is typically based on economic weight, Africa is severely underrepresented. Only few African countries are seen as "systemically important," given the limited size of most economies in the continent, underdeveloped financial markets, and little integration in the global financial markets. Yet African policy makers are expected to subscribe to the decisions of these bodies, even though often these decisions have substantial adverse consequences on African economies. A clear example discussed below is the case of global banking regulations and the continuous move to higher prudential standards under the consecutive generations of Basel banking regulations.

The global banking regulation agenda aims at financial stability at national and global levels by setting standards that govern financial institutions. A key feature of these standards is credit-risk management through capital requirements. The choice of a particular capital regime is at the discretion of national authorities, and Basel II requirements are not mandatory for countries that are not members of the Basel Committee on Banking Supervision.

African banking systems have proven to be well regulated, adequately capitalized, and sufficiently (if not too) liquid. Therefore, capital adequacy is not a primary concern for the majority of African countries. Nigerian banks were the exception, as some had been excessively exposed to the oil sector and the stock market. Commercial bank management had indulged or tolerated speculative behavior that drove the institutions to near collapse. In this case, the central bank intervened and bailed out the banks while overhauling the management, as discussed earlier in the chapter.

So, by and large, capital adequacy is not a critical concern for African banking systems. Yet African authorities have systematically expressed a high commitment to adopting Basel standards, moving up to Basel II, although this is voluntary for countries that are not members of the Basel Committee on Banking Supervision (Gottschalk, 2007).[27] African regulators are concerned that, unless they are clearly seen as adhering or at least moving to adhere to higher Basel standards, they may be penalized by international investors. Specifically, concerns emerged that African banks may be denied access to foreign capital markets if regulators choose not to comply with or at least send clear signals of commitment to high Basel standards (Ward, 2002).

Clearly, rapidly moving up the ladder of banking regulation and supervision standards carries costs for African countries, which may arise directly from the behavior of their banks or from the behavior of banks outside Africa in response to more stringent banking regulations. If African banks adopt higher capital requirements, credit flows to their economies could decline. Moreover, increased capital regulation standards can induce concentration of credit into sectors and activities that banks perceive as least risky. However, this may undermine sectors and activities such as agriculture and small- and medium-sized enterprises, which are most valuable to the majority of African economies in terms of employment and people's livelihoods. Should African regulators choose less stringent capital requirements, they may put their banks at a competitive disadvantage relative to foreign banks operating in Africa that are held to higher standards in their home countries. Higher capital requirements also increase the pro-cyclicality of bank credit, amplifying the impacts of financial and real shocks on the economy (Goodhart and Segoviano, 2004). These implications are of serious concern for African countries as they strive to ease access to finance and encourage private-sector development, employment, growth, and poverty reduction.

African countries, therefore, need to make strategic choices by striking a balance between fostering access to finance on the one hand and financial stability on the other hand. Today, fewer than 20 percent of Africans have access to formal financial services. Private firms in Africa constantly cite inadequate access to credit as one of the top constraints to entrepreneurship, investment and growth. The continent's success in developing the private sector and reducing poverty hinges on increasing access to finance. Hence, innovations in the regulatory framework must be consistent with national agendas of promoting access to finance for households and firms. While attempting to adapt to innovations in financial sector regulation at the global level, African countries need to ensure that this is consistent with their national development goals.

## 4.2. Regional Policy Challenges: Regional Financial Integration and Cross-Border Banking Supervision

With few exceptions (e.g., Mauritius, South Africa), African national financial markets are too small to serve as viable and efficient sources of capital for building vibrant private sectors. The scope for economies of scale is limited and the savings base too narrow to mobilize adequate resources. Financial market integration and cross-border banking thus offer great potential for mobilization of funds to meet the continent's investment demands. Continentalization of banking is increasing, with major banks from emerging markets spreading their reach in low-income countries. Several banks from South Africa and Nigeria and from North African countries have become true regional banks.[28]

Overall, the increasing trend of cross-border banking in Africa is good news for the continent's financial development. It is a channel of technology transfer as well as a vehicle of regulatory discipline transmitted downward on the financial development ladder across countries. However, cross-border banking also poses important challenges. Typically, banking regulations lag behind financial innovations, especially in the African context where human capacity in this sector is particularly low. Harmonization of national regulatory frameworks has also been a critical challenge in the continent's regional integration agenda, even though it is a critical prerequisite for its success. Going forward, it should feature prominently on Africa's regional integration agenda.

## 4.3. Domestic Policy Challenges: The Political Economy of Financial Sector Reform

The relatively good performance of the banking sectors in Africa during the crisis was partly due to the series of financial sector reforms undertaken before the crisis. Low integration into the global financial markets, low exposure to toxic assets, high liquidity and capitalization, and high risk-aversion helped African banks weather the financial storm. Still, African financial sectors exhibit serious structural weaknesses and pervasive inefficiencies, sometimes the same ones that reforms were supposed to alleviate. In particular, banking sectors are characterized by severe inefficiencies in resource allocation across sectors, in economic activities, and by term structure.

These inefficiencies include concentration of credit in high turnover and speculative activities, away from productive and growth-driving activities such as industry, agriculture, and SMEs. Barriers to competition and price distortions prevail, despite the easing of interest-rate repression in most countries. In Burundi, for example, credit to agriculture represented less than 1 percent of total credit during 2003-2008, while the sector accounted for 42 percent of GDP and employed over 80 percent of the population. Industry received less than 2 percent of total credit while contributing 18–20 percent of GDP. The setting of interest rates is often segmented whereby "insiders" (bank employees and shareholders) enjoy subsidized loans while "outsiders" pay exorbitant rates. Detailed microdata indicate that one of the major commercial banks in Burundi charged up to 19 percent to external borrowers while its employees paid less than 4 percent (Nkurunziza, Ndikumana, and Nyamoya, 2012).

So why are financial sector reforms unable to alleviate these structural constraints? Part of the reason is that, in many countries, the financial sector—as other economic sectors—is viewed as a source of rent extraction and a means of consolidation of power by the ruling elite and their associates. Financial policy is, as Mkandawire (1999) puts it, "an appendage to the larger policy orientations or strategies, which in their turn are embedded in the larger political economy of the country" (321). Moreover, as with other reforms, substantial uncertainty prevails about the gains and losses from financial reforms and their distribution among classes of residual claimants. This results in what is referred to as a status quo bias or "obstinacy" of the status quo (Fernandez and Rodrik, 1991). Gains from financial sector reforms include increased efficiency and attracting private investment, including FDI. Losses are in terms of foregone or reduced rents from financial repression and the reduced rewards from monopoly capture of the banking sector (rents from political lending). In the absence of clear transfer schemes or "bribing mechanisms" to solve the status quo bias, key financial reforms are likely to be derailed.

The status quo bias yields a stable equilibrium of rent seeking and inefficient financial intermediation, explaining the resistance to privatization of the banking sector in countries like Ethiopia. It also helps explain the persistent inefficiencies in banking sectors from a social perspective while banks are privately efficient from a profit-maximization perspective. The example of the Burundian banking sector is documented in detail in a study by Nkurunziza, Ndikumana, and Nyamoya (2012), which underscores the links between the concentration of political power and the monopolization of the financial sector. The study also highlights the costly implications of the status quo bias, notably preventable bank failures. Some banks in Burundi were driven to bankruptcy under the watch of the central bank; unfortunately, the costs of these failures were socialized although they were caused by private actions. The public lost its savings, and the culprits of poor management enjoyed impunity while their associates who benefited from politically motivated lending enjoyed the free lunch (the loans are typically not recovered after bankruptcy).

Africa also offers positive experiences of effective financial sector reform and interventions of the authorities to prevent banking crises. One of the most recent cases is that of Nigeria where, as discussed earlier, the central bank stepped in to bail out banks that had suffered from speculative and irresponsible management.

## 4.4. Domestic Policy Challenges: Balancing Long-Term and Short-Term Pay-Offs from Reforms

While the crisis has lowered the immediate pay-offs from reforms, it is encouraging to see that most African countries have maintained macroeconomic stability and continued to implement reforms aimed at improving the business climate. Two key challenges face African policy makers in the coming years. First, they need to strike a balance between long-term growth-oriented policies and short-term strategies aimed at cushioning the impact of exogenous shocks as in the case of an economic and financial crisis. The demand stimulus typically used for this purpose must be carefully managed to prevent macroeconomic instability arising from potential inflation spiral and twin deficits.

Second, the policy makers need to build popular support for reforms, where a precondition for success is addressing distributional issues: reforms will be sustained only when there are clear systematic mechanisms for sharing the gains across society. This means that macroeconomic outcomes alone, in particular high real GDP growth rates, are not enough. Equitable distribution of the gains at the microeconomic (household) level is key, which is best achieved through creating decent employment and increasing access to social services and credit, especially for low-income households.

The recent experience of Tunisia is telling in this respect. Tunisia was long praised for being a good reformer, sustaining solid growth rates over time, transforming its modern sector and systematically topping the competitiveness ratings in Africa. Still, the country (or rather its government) failed on other margins, including job creation, transparency, and public participation in the political domain. With the end of the Zine El Abidine Ben Ali regime, the challenge of the successor governments will not be so much how to achieve similar high rates of growth but how to achieve inclusive growth with job creation and more generally how to establish mechanisms that redistribute wealth and social benefits more equitably. Focusing on employment creation and mainstreaming it in macroeconomic and sectoral policy frameworks would help spare the successor regimes from being toppled by an unemployed educated youth or other disenfranchised groups.

# 5. Summary and Conclusions

On balance, Africa has weathered the Global Financial Crisis well, due to its limited integration into global financial markets as well as appropriately prudent macroeconomic policies and financial sector reforms adopted in the run-up to the crisis. Nevertheless, differences emerged across countries, with some emerging and frontier markets (e.g., Nigeria, South Africa) experiencing temporary portfolio capital outflows. In Nigeria, the crisis has amplified the existing weaknesses of the banking sector, leading to a full-fledged banking sector crisis that was contained by an effective bailout and restructuring of troubled commercial banks by the central bank.

Looking ahead, African policy makers face several challenges in their efforts to develop financial sectors that would support private-sector development and inclusive growth. Key among them is finding a balance between complying with more stringent banking regulation requirements and increasing access to finance for underserved parts of the population to encourage job creation and poverty reduction. To succeed, some countries will need to adopt difficult financial sector reforms, such as gradual privatization of the banking sector, increasing competition, and opening up to foreign investors. Political support for such reforms will hinge on the ability of governments to address distributional issues and establish clear and credible mechanisms for sharing the gains from reforms across the society, and in particular with its discontent groups, such as the unemployed youth.

## Notes

The views and opinions expressed in this paper are those of the authors alone and do not represent the views, opinions, or policies of their institutions of affiliation.

1. Only one African LIC grew above 7 percent and had inflation below 5 percent in 2001–2008; others with inflation below 5 percent grew at a lower rate (Brixiova and Ndikumana, 2010). IMF (2005) and others have documented that LICs that aim at very low inflation may hamper growth in the process.
2. In some countries (Ghana), excessive government borrowing may have crowded out private-sector credit. In many African countries, structural impediments constrain bank lending to the private sector.
3. African countries recorded an increase in savings before the crisis, but they were still about five percentage points of GDP below the average of emerging market and developing economies, especially developing Asia.
4. At the same time, the extent of capital outflows from Africa (amounting to more than $700 billion in the past four decases), remains unacceptably high (Ndikumana and Boyce, 2011).
5. African low-income countries exhibit substantial heterogeneity in terms of the structure of their economies, linkages with the global economy, and fundamentals that determine future growth prospects. Brixiova and Ndikumana (2011) propose a categorization where the resource-poor, nonfragile countries are grouped into (1) emerging markets; (2) frontier markets; (3) transition countries; and (4) pretransition countries. Resource-rich countries and fragile states form separate groups to reflect their specific structural features and challenges. The following criteria are used in the classification: level of income, growth performance (acceleration and resilience), robustness of the macroeconomic framework and stability, the business environment, and financial market development.

6. Quantity-based indicators such as share of the foreign debt and equity assets and liabilities in GDP show that their degree of integration was close to that of emerging markets in other regions, such as Latin America.
7. The approach follows Lane and Milesi-Ferretti (2010), who undertook a similar exercise for 162 countries.
8. Relatively strong growth performance in West Africa's *Nigeria* has benefited from the non-oil sector, stimulated by expansionary fiscal and monetary policies.
9. For example, the portfolio capital outflow amounted to 3 percent of GDP in South Africa in 2008.
10. The 2010 decline of FDI to Africa contrasts with the increases of FDI to Latin America (21 percent) and Asia (10 percent). Specifically, the overall FDI to developing countries increased by 10 percent that year. Subsequently, for the first time developing countries accounted for more than half of the world's FDI.
11. The low initial share of FDI in manufacturing made Africa immune to declining FDI flows. All over the world, the primary sector (agriculture) and services (telecommunications, health services) were less sensitive to the business cycle and less affected by the crisis than manufacturing had been.
12. In 2008 and 2009, Kenya postponed the issuance of its first sovereign external bond. At the same time, with stagnating private-sector credit, the government had to play an active role in stimulating the economy.
13. The 2006 banking-sector reform—aimed at recapitalizing the banking sector—had several unintended negative consequences. As the higher capital buffers required made achieving high returns on assets and profitability challenging, commercial banks expanded their activities and took on excessive risks without adequate risk management. The banking industry's return on average equity nevertheless declined from 25 percent in 2004 to 5 percent in 2008, before collapsing to -162 percent in 2009 due to significant provisioning for bad loans (BGL, 2010).
14. The All Share Index fell by 70 percent between February 2008 and March 2009 and has not shown signs of recovery.
15. The crisis has had a substantial impact on the banking sector: (1) the industry's non-performing loans (NPLs) increased from Naira 303.5 billion in 2008 to Naira 2.82 trillion at the end of 2009; provisioning increased from Naira 270.39 billion in 2008 to Naira 1.89 trillion in 2008. Ten banks that failed the Central Bank of Nigeria (CBN) stress tests amounted for the bulk of the provisioning, which ranged from as little as Naira 323.6 million by Citibank to Naira 74 billion by the Intercontinental Bank (BGL, 2010). As a result of large provisioning, several banks became undercapitalized.
16. The five banks were Afribank, Finbank, Intercontinental Bank, Oceanic International Bank, and Union Bank of Nigeria. Equity market lending of these banks accounted for 16 percent of their portfolios and oil-related lending accounted for 17 percent. The five banks also accounted for a large share of the banking system's NPLs (Institute for International Finance, 2009).
17. Monetary policy rate is the midpoint between the CBN's lending and deposit rate. The discount window was temporarily expanded, and lending extended from overnight up to 360 days. A wide range of collaterals was allowed.
18. On the fiscal side, crisis-response measures included postponing plans to issue $500 million in eurobonds until 2011 or 2012, adjusting budget oil prices (to raise savings) and seeking financing from multilateral institutions.

19. The portion for SMEs and manufacturers aims at refinancing and restructuring banks' existing loans to manufacturers and small and medium enterprises.
20. In Ghana, HIPC (heavily indebted poor countries) and MDRI (Millenium debt relief initiative) debt relief led to a marked reduction in its external debt—from about $80 to $2.7 billion between 2003 and 2007. Domestic public debt fell from 24 percent in 2000 to 13.6 percent in June 2007. The overall fiscal deficit fell from 9 percent in 2000 to 2.5 percent by the end of June 2007.
21. Services gained a disproportionate share in total credit while credit to agriculture and manufacturing declined.
22. Presidential elections in Ghana were held in 1992, 1996, 2000, 2004, and 2008.
23. The interbank and the TB-rates fell in 2009, in part due to capital inflows that raised liquidity.
24. The recent establishing of the collateral registration bureau, well noted and highlighted in the 2010 Doing Business Report, is a step in the right direction.
25. In the area of financial regulation, this has been documented in the various reviews, including the joint World Bank–IMF financial-sector assessment programs.
26. IMF stands for International Monetary Fund, WTO for World Trade Organization, and OECD is the Organisation for Economic Co-operation and Development.
27. In a 2006 survey by the Financial Stability Institute, 12 out of the 17 African countries surveyed reported a commitment to adopt Basel II; that is 71 percent of the respondents. Other regions show higher commitment rates: 100 percent of the respondents for Asia and Middle East, 86 percent for Latin America, and 83 percent for non-BCBS in Europe. Note: BCBS stands for 'Basel Committee for Banking Supervision'.
28. For example, Ecobank, headquartered in Lomé, Togo, operates in 30 countries, including in Europe, has a network of more than 600 branches, and serves a depositor base of more than two million customers.

## References


AfDB, OECD, UNECA, and UNDP. (2012). *African Economic Outlook 2011*. Tunis: AfDB, Paris: OECD, Addis Ababa: UNECA and New York: UNDP.

Barajas, A., R. Chami, C. Fullenkamp, and A. Garg. (2010). "The Global Financial Crisis and Workers' Remittances to Africa: What Is the Damage?' IMF Working Paper No. WP/10/24.

BGL. (2010). "Getting Banks to Lend Again." *BGL Banking Report*. Abuja: BGL.

Brixiova, Z., and L. Ndikumana. (2010). "Supporting Africa's Post-Crisis Growth: The Role of Macroeconomic Policies." African Development Bank Working Paper No. 117.

Brixiova, Z., and L. Ndikumana. (2011). "Characterizing Africa's Economic Dynamism." *African Development Bank Policy Brief*, 2 (8) (June).

Caprio, G. Jr. (2010). "Subprime Finance: Yes We Are Still in Kansas." In Stephany Griffith-Jones, José Antonio Ocampo, and Joseph E. Stiglitz, eds.,

*Time for a Visible Hand: Lessons from the 2008 World Financial Crisis*, 50–61. New York: Oxford University Press.

Central Bank of Nigeria. (2010). *Annual Report* Abuja: CBN.

Elhiraika, A., and L. Ndikumana. (2009). "Reserves Accumulation in African Countries: Sources, Motivations, and Effects." In AfDB and UNECA, *Africa's Development Challenges and Opportunities in the Global Arena: Proceedings of the 2007 African Economic Conference*, 285–315. Paris: ECONOMICA.

Fernandez, R., and D. Rodrik. (1991). "Resistance to Reform: Status Quo Bias in the Presence of Individual-Specific Uncertainty." *American Economic Review* 81(5): 1146–1155.

Goodhart, C., and M. A. Segoviano. (2004). "Basel and Procyclicality: A Comparison of the Standardised and IRB Approaches to an Improved Credit Risk Method." Financial Markets Group, London School of Economics and Political Science, Discussion Paper No. 524.

Gottschalk, R. (2007). "Basel II Implementation in Developing Countries and Effects on SME Development." Institute of Development Institute, University of Sussex; Issues Paper for the ICRIER-InWent Conference on "Financial Globalization and Domestic Financial Sector Development," New Delhi, November 22–23, 2007.

Griffith-Jones, S., J. A. Ocampo, and J. E. Stiglitz, eds. (2010). *Time for a Visible Hand: Lessons from the 2008 World Financial Crisis*. New York: Oxford University Press.

Institute for International Finance. (2009). "Nigeria: Banking Sector Developments and Economic Outlook." *IIF research note* (September).

International Monetary Fund (2007). "Ghana: Ex Post Assessment of the Longer Term Program Engagement," *IMF Country Report No. 07/211.*

International Monetary Fund. (2005). "Monetary and Fiscal Policy Design Issues in Low-Income Countries." *IMF Policy Paper* (August).

Kasekende, L., Z. Brixiova, and L. Ndikumana. (2010). "Africa: Africa's Countercyclical Response to the Crisis." *Journal of Globalization and Development* 1(1): Art. 16.

Lane, P. R., and G. M. Milesi-Ferretti. (2010). "The Cross-Country Incidence of the Global Crisis." IMF Working Paper No. WP/10/171.

Mkandawire, T. (1999). "The Political Economy of Financial Reform in Africa." *Journal of International Development* 11: 321–342.

Ndikumana, L. and J. K. Boyce. (2011). *Africa's Odious Debts: How Foreign Loans and Capital Flight Bled a Continent*. London: Zed Books.

Nkurunziza, J. D., L. Ndikumana, and P. Nyamoya. (2012). "The Financial Sector in Burundi: An Investigation of its Efficiency in Resource Mobilization and Allocation," forthcoming NBER Working Paper.

Ward, J. (2002). "The New Basel Accord and Developing Countries: Problems and Alternatives." Cambridge Endowment for Research in Finance, Working Paper No. 4.

CHAPTER 37

# BEYOND CAPITALISM?

MINQI LI

THE inquiry into the question "beyond capitalism?" presupposes capitalism to be a historical system, that is, a social system that has a finite life and can remain viable only over a certain historical period.

All natural or social systems are ultimately historical systems. For a system to exist and operate, it requires certain basic conditions. Partly because of the changing environment and partly because of the system's own operations, the underlying basic conditions inevitably tend to change over time. Within certain limits, the system can adapt to the changing conditions without altering its basic properties. However, sooner or later a point will be reached when the underlying conditions have changed so much that they are no longer compatible with the normal operation of the existing system. When this point is reached, the existing system would either disintegrate or have to be replaced by a certain new system or systems.

The following questions may be raised. What have been the basic historical conditions required for capitalism to exist and operate? How have these conditions evolved and changed over time? Are we approaching the point where capitalism can no longer operate as a viable historical system? If yes, what will happen to humanity in the historical era beyond capitalism? How can the human civilization be preserved and developed under some new social system? These are the questions that this chapter will discuss.

## THE ENDLESS ACCUMULATION OF CAPITAL

Advocates and opponents of capitalism alike would agree that the capitalist historical era has been characterized by sustained, explosive growth of material production and consumption. According to Angus Maddison (2003), gross world product barely changed from AD 1 to 1000, approximately doubled from 1000 to 1500, tripled from 1500 to 1820, and had expanded by 50 times over the 180 years from 1820 to 2000. Any meaningful conceptualization of capitalism must account for the basic tendency of capitalism to generate seemingly infinite economic growth.

If a society's total product is greater than what is needed to cover the population's basic consumption and to replace the means of production used up in the previous production process, then the remaining part is known as the surplus product. Human civilization emerged when the surplus product became sufficiently large so that a minority group of the population could be freed from direct productive labor and specialize in religious, cultural, and political affairs.

Until now, surplus product has always been owned by a small group of elites, and all "civilized societies" have been characterized by dramatic economic and social inequalities. Throughout the precapitalist era, the surplus product was used by the ruling elites primarily for nonproductive purposes such as the elites' luxury consumption, war, imperial buildings, or other wasteful activities. The precapitalist elites were primarily interested in the direct uses of the surplus product and had little interest in using the surplus product to expand the society's productive capacity. By contrast, under capitalism, a large portion of the surplus product (which appears as profits for individual capitalists) has been used to "accumulate capital," to expand the size of production and develop new technologies that help to increase productivity (Stavrianos, 1981, 33–43). What could explain the fundamental difference in behavior between the capitalist elites and the precapitalist elites?

Unlike all precapitalist societies, capitalism is an economic and social system characterized by the universal dominance of market relations. While market relations have existed for a long time in many different human societies, for much of human history and in most human societies the market had played no more than a marginal role in the overall economic life. It is only under capitalism that nearly every aspect of economic and social life has been dominated by the market, and virtually all processes of material production and consumption are mediated through the market.

In a market, goods and services are produced and sold as commodities. As there are many different producers of commodities, the producers inevitably compete against one another for market share and for the ability to influence market prices. With the dominance of market relations, the capitalists in all areas of the economy engage in constant and intense competition against one another. Those who prevail in the competition will be able to secure their existing profits and possibly make more profits. Those who fail will suffer from shrinking profits, losses, or even bankruptcies (ceasing to be capitalists).

To survive and prevail in competition, all capitalists are under powerful pressure to lower costs and expand production as rapidly as possible. This in turn requires the capitalists to use a large portion of their profits for capital accumulation (buying new machines and new materials, developing new technologies). For the capitalist economy as a whole, this leads to an overwhelming tendency toward seemingly unlimited expansion of material production and consumption or a tendency toward "endless accumulation of capital" (Marx, 1967 [1867], 543–573; Wallerstein, 1979, 1–36).

What has made this universal dominance of market relations possible? Why was this condition absent over thousands of years of history in the precapitalist era? For market relations to become dominant, the purpose of production for most of the producers must be "exchange value" rather than "use value," that is, the purpose of production needs to be "to make money" rather than "to make something for use."

This may be illustrated by Marx's famous formula of "circuit of capital":

$$M - C - M' \ldots M''$$

To start a circuit of capital, a capitalist has to "invest" a certain amount of money (M) with the expectation to get more money (M'). To accomplish this objective, the capitalist needs to use the money to buy certain commodities (C), such as labor power, raw materials, tools, and land. Through the production process, some new commodities with a value greater than the original commodities will be produced. If the capitalist sells the new commodities successfully, they can be exchanged for an amount of money that is greater than the original amount, and the first round of the circuit of capital will be successfully completed.

If this capitalist chooses to use the new money (M') to start another round of circuit of capital, then potentially the capitalist can expect to get an even greater amount of money (M"). If this capitalist keeps engaging in this kind of activity and many other commodity producers engage in similar activities, both the production and exchange of commodities would keep expanding, taking over an increasingly larger part of the economy until the market relations eventually dominate the whole economy (Marx, 1967 [1885], 25–123).

However, in precapitalist societies, this kind of circuit of capital was usually limited to a few nonessential areas (such as long-distance trade) and frequently interrupted. Some essential production inputs (such as labor power and land) were often not commodities, making it impossible to start the circuit of capital. Even when these were commodities, the costs of production could very well be too high relative to the limited and uncertain profit opportunities.

Moreover, most of the great precapitalist civilizations were centralized empires with powerful states reigning over large territories. Under a centralized empire, the state was overwhelmingly more powerful than individual capitalists. Capitalist profits were under the constant threat of heavy taxation and confiscation. Sustained expansion of capitalist activities thus became impossible (Wallerstein, 1983, 11–44).

It required a whole set of more or less fortuitous historical conditions for capitalism to first emerge in Western Europe and later become the dominant system over the entire globe.

# The Rise of Capitalism: Historical Conditions

From the third to the sixth century, all the great classical civilizations on the Eurasian continent were overrun and devastated by the Nomads. Great empires were later rebuilt in the Middle East, India, and China, but not in Western Europe, where the fall of the Roman Empire was followed by a millennium of feudalism with highly decentralized and fluid political structures.

By the sixteenth century, several nation-states of approximately equal size and power had emerged and consolidated in Western Europe. These states engaged in more or less permanent competition in both peace and war. The political competition between nation-states provided a favorable environment for the expansion of capitalist activities. To prevail in interstate competition, the nation-states needed the financial support of capitalists. This made it possible for the capitalists to play the states against one another, forcing the states to protect capitalist property rights and to use lower taxes to attract capital. On the other hand, to increase fiscal revenue, the states were motivated to provide active support to promote capital accumulation.

While the European interstate competition prepared one of the necessary conditions for the rise of capitalism, by itself it was insufficient. Western Europe at the time remained a peripheral part of the global economy, lagging far behind Asia in population, wealth, technology, and the overall size of the market. Moreover, the European economic expansion was approaching the internal ecological limits. Without some other favorable historical developments, the emerging European capitalist "world economy" would have met the constraints of land, biomass energy, and mineral resources and would have ceased to expand. Without the system's overall expansion, the unrestrained competition between the European states would have led to the system's self-destruction.

Luckily for the Europeans, as they desperately looked for alternative trade routes to Asia, they "discovered" the American continent. The American Indians were easily conquered, and the "New World" provided the Europeans with abundant mineral and agricultural resources, more than enough to cover their trade deficits with Asia. Through the infamous slave trade, Africa supplied a massive cheap labor force required for the European exploitation of American resources. It was the conquest of the Americas and the slave trade that allowed the Europeans to overtake Asia and rise to the center of the global economy (Arrighi et al., 2003).

By the time of the industrial revolution, coal started to be used on a large scale. The massive exploitation of fossil fuels freed capitalism from the energy limit that had constrained the expansion of all previous great civilizations. By the nineteenth century, capitalism had become the first global system in human history.

Thus, historically, the rise and expansion of capitalism had depended on a combination of historical conditions: the nation-state system and interstate competition, the abundant supply of cheap labor, and the abundant supply of cheap energy and other resources.

However, the historical development of capitalism has led to several long-term tendencies that have either undermined or transformed these underlying conditions so that by the early twenty-first century, there is evidence suggesting that the existing system may cease to be historically viable in the not-very-distant future.

The following sections consider these long-term historical tendencies and evaluate the argument that capitalism is approaching its own historical limit.

## The Grave Diggers of Capitalism?

In *The Communist Manifesto*, Karl Marx famously predicted that as capitalism developed, a growing proportion of the society's labor force would become wage workers (or the proletarians). As the proletarianized working class grew in strength and learned to get organized, sooner or later it would become so powerful that it would prove to be the "grave diggers" of capitalism (Marx and Engels, 1978 [1848]).

What has happened since *The Communist Manifesto*? From the mid-nineteenth century to the mid-twentieth century, working-class organizations had grown throughout the advanced capitalist countries. In Western Europe, socialist and communist parties became powerful political forces. In response to the growing working-class challenge, the capitalist classes made some major concessions. After World War II, the capitalist institutions were restructured to be based on a new scheme of social compromise (the "New Deal"), which provided the Western working classes with a package of social welfare as well as the promise of rising living standards over time, in exchange for their political loyalty to the capitalist system.

The New Deal compromise did not secure social peace forever. The postwar rapid economic expansion led to the depletion of the remaining rural surplus labor force in the advanced capitalist countries. The working-class bargaining power was further strengthened by the welfare state institutions. By the 1960s, the Western working classes had become strong enough to demand wage rises that started to undermine capitalist profitability. From the mid-1960s to the early 1980s, the profit rate fell in all the advanced capitalist countries, leading to a prolonged period of economic and political instability (Armstrong, Glyn, and Harrison, 1991).

In response to the crisis, the capitalist classes organized a counteroffensive that has been known as "neoliberalism." The neoliberal policies attempted to roll back some of the economic and social gains won by the Western working classes over the previous decades. Much of industrial capital was relocated from the advanced capitalist countries to areas with a large cheap labor force, especially China. The massive expansion of the global cheap labor force helped to undermine working-class bargaining power, and the capitalists enjoyed rising profit rates from the 1980s to the 1990s.

However, the neoliberal "success" had some serious side effects. As the working classes in much of the world suffered from declining living standards, global effective demand was constrained. Many economies attempted to get around this problem by pursuing export-led growth. But it was impossible for all countries to do so. From the 1990s to the early 2000s, the United States had sustained global economic expansion through debt-financed consumption. The large US trade deficits allowed the rest of the world to pursue export-led growth. The growth model was unsustainable and eventually led to the "Great Recession" of 2009 (Li, 2008, 67–92). As global capitalism enters into another prolonged period of economic and political instability, what is likely to happen in the next few decades? Will global capitalism be successfully restructured to reestablish favorable conditions for capital accumulation?

All the advanced capitalist countries are now confronted with serious fiscal crises. Despite the attacks on the working classes in the neoliberal era, the social contract established in the mid-twentieth century has remained mostly intact in the Western countries. The historically entitled working-class rights, in combination with the aging of the population, imply a long-term tendency for pension and health-care costs to rise.

According to the Bank of International Settlements, under the existing government promises, public debt to GDP ratio is set to rise to 400 percent in France, 300 percent in Germany, 250 percent in Italy, 600 percent in Japan, 500 percent in Britain, and 400 percent in the United States by the mid-twenty-first century (Cecchetti, Mohanty, and Zampolli, 2010). Most likely, these astronomical debt levels will not actually materialize. Some time before this time frame, some form of dramatic change will have to take place.

Under the first possibility, if the existing trends are allowed to continue, one or several major capitalist countries will suffer from fiscal bankruptcy, followed by an economic and political collapse. Under the second possibility, some states may attempt to raise taxes on the capitalists. But this will reduce the capitalist profit rate and lead to an accumulation crisis.

Under the third possibility, the states could try to renounce the historically established social contract, undertaking further attacks on working-class living standards. The question is how long the Western working classes will endure declines of living standards before fighting back with a general rebellion against the capitalist system.

One thing is clear in all the advanced capitalist countries: the historical space for social compromise has been exhausted. How about the rest of the world?

Over the neoliberal era, there have been large formations of industrial working classes in the non-Western world. Until now, the large cheap labor force has been functioning as a global reserve army that helps to undermine working-class bargaining power. But this is about to change.

In the coming decades, one would expect that as the non-Western working classes continue to grow in size and learn to get organized, workers will demand higher wages as well as a growing range of political and social rights.

Historically, the Western capitalist classes had managed to accommodate the working-class challenge by providing a package of social reform. However, if the capitalist world system can no longer afford the social reform package for the comparatively small Western working classes, what is the chance for it to offer and afford a similar package to the much larger non-Western working classes?

## Stabilizing the Unstable Capitalism?

In addition to the proletarianization argument, Marx pursued another line of argument in *The Communist Manifesto.* Marx argued that the periodic "commercial crises" were the evidence that the "conditions of bourgeois society" had become "too narrow to comprise the wealth created by them" and the methods employed by the bourgeoisie to get over the crises would simply pave the way for "more extensive and more destructive crises" (Marx and Engels, 1978 [1848], 478).

In *Socialism: Utopian and Scientific*, Engels (1978 [1880]) argued that the basic contradiction of capitalism had to do with the conflict between the objective tendencies toward socialization of production and the capitalist system of private appropriation. According to Engels, this contradiction would lead to increasingly more destructive economic crises and would force capitalism to adopt increasingly socialized forms of economic organizations, such as modern corporations and state regulations. However, Engels believed that ultimately the contradiction could only be resolved through fundamental changes that would bring about the social ownership of the basic means of production.

In *The General Theory*, John Maynard Keynes argued that capitalist investment was fundamentally unstable and, moreover, the development of capitalist financial markets was likely to have further intensified investment instability (Keynes, 1964 [1936], 147–164). Keynes doubted the effectiveness of the monetary policy in stabilizing the capitalist economy. Toward the end of *The General Theory*, Keynes proposed that "a somewhat comprehensive socialisation of investment will prove the only means of securing an approximation of full employment" (1964 [1936], 378). However, Keynes insisted that the proposed socialization of investment would not require social ownership of the means of production.

Hyman Minsky argued that "big government" institutions were indispensable for stabilizing the fundamentally unstable capitalist economy. In a modern capitalist economy, the big government helps to sustain capitalist profits during recessions, and the central bank helps to stabilize asset prices during financial crises. These institutions help to prevent the declines of capitalist profits and investment from developing into a self-sustained downward spiral that had often plunged the free-market capitalist economy into devastating depressions (Minsky 2008 [1986]).

However, big government institutions have strong side effects. Big government deficits in effect help to socialize business losses, and the central bank's lender-of-last-resort actions in effect help to socialize risks of private financial markets. Despite the partial socialization of risks and losses, under big government capitalism, investment decisions continue to be made by private businesses for the purpose of making private profits. Big government capitalism thus encourages excessive risk taking in finance and investment and tends to increase the potential of financial instability.

Thus, on the one hand, big government institutions are indispensable for preventing depressions. On the other hand, big government capitalism does not abolish the inherent tendency under capitalism toward financial instability. On the contrary, with the effective socialization of risks and losses, the excessive risk taking in private investment and finance has led to frequent financial crises with increasingly destabilizing consequences. Pollin and Dymski (1994) referred to this contradiction as the "Minsky paradox."

In the 1970s, the destabilizing consequences mainly found expression in the threat of rampant inflation. Since the 1990s, the advanced capitalist economies have suffered from increasingly more destructive asset bubbles.

The financial crises necessitate government interventions, forcing the government to run large deficits during recessions. However, Li (2009) observes that these deficits have not been offset by surpluses during expansions. As a result, there has been a tendency for the government debt to rise in relation to GDP. The tendency is intensified under neoliberalism because interest rates tend to be relatively high in relation to economic growth rates. The government debt-GDP ratios cannot keep rising indefinitely. Beyond a certain point, the debt-GDP ratio could be so high that the government's ability to intervene with and stabilize the economy would be severely undermined.

From the Marxist perspective, this contradiction of big government capitalism or the so-called Minsky paradox exactly reflects the underlying contradiction between the capitalist system of private appropriation and the objective processes of socialization of production. While the development of the capitalist economy requires growing social regulations through institutions such as big government and the central bank, the basic means of production continue to be owned by private capitalists and used by private capitalists to make private profits.

Thus, on the one hand, a high level of socialization of investment risks and losses has become indispensable for the normal operations of modern capitalism. On the other hand, the lack of social control over investment had led to growing financial instability and increasingly larger government debts. This underlying contradiction will inevitably find its expressions through changing forms of, and perhaps progressively more destructive, economic crises. It seems to be rather difficult, if not impossible, to develop a reasonable mechanism of socialization of investment without compromising the basic framework of capitalism. Contrary to what Keynes argued, the eventual resolution of this structural contradiction may require nothing short of a comprehensive socialization of the basic means of production.

## The Limits to Growth

There is another, more fundamental limit to global capitalist accumulation. Historically, Western capitalism has benefited from the abundant supply of energy and resources as well as a virtually unlimited exploitation of environment. However, after two centuries of relentless capital accumulation, the global ecological system is now approaching the point of total collapse and the ecological space for accumulation has been exhausted.

All human societies depend on the earth's ecological system for survival and development. Human societies use renewable and nonrenewable resources for material production and consumption. The human production processes, in addition to producing useful goods and services, generate material wastes or pollution. To sustain the normal functioning of the ecological systems, the human consumption of nonrenewable resources should be minimized, the human consumption of renewable resources should stay within the ecological system's natural regenerative capacity, and the material wastes generated by human activities need to stay within the ecological system's natural absorptive capacity.

Thus, to maintain ecological sustainability, the human environmental impact (resources consumption and pollution) must stabilize at a level that is within the ecological system's natural limit. However, the capitalist economic system is based on production for profit and endless accumulation of capital. The normal operation of capitalism tends to lead to unlimited expansion of material production and consumption. The basic law of the motion of capitalism is therefore in fundamental conflict with the requirements of ecological sustainability.

The "IPAT" formula is often used to describe the condition required for ecological sustainability:

$$I = P * A * T$$

The formula says that environmental impact (I) depends on population (P), "affluence" or per capital economic output (A), and "technology" or environmental impact per unit of economic output (T). Ecological sustainability requires that environmental impact is stabilized at or falls toward a sustainable level. Under capitalism, there is a tendency for economic output (P * A) to grow indefinitely. Unless this tendency is more than offset by falling environmental impact per unit of economic output, environmental impact inevitably tends to rise, violating the requirement for ecological sustainability (Meadows, Renders, and Meadows, 2005, 124–127).

After centuries of relentless capital accumulation, many aspects of the global ecological system are now on the verge of total collapse. In particular, climate change, caused by greenhouse gases emitted by human consumption of fossil fuels, is now threatening the very survival of the human civilization. The global average temperature is now about 0.8 degree Celsius higher than it was in preindustrial times and rising at a rate of 0.2 degree per decade. There is a growing consensus among scientists that if global warming rises above 2 degrees Celsius, dangerous climate feedbacks may be triggered, leading to the release of more greenhouse gases from the ocean and terrestrial ecological systems. In the event of runaway global warming, much of the world would cease to be inhabitable and catastrophic declines of global population may ensue (Spratt and Sutton, 2009).

Is it possible for the global ecological crisis to be resolved within the historical framework of capitalism? According to the defenders of the existing system, capitalism is an exceptionally innovative system. With proper incentives, capitalists would be motivated to develop "eco-friendly" technologies that help to reduce environmental impact per unit of economic output. If "T" falls sufficiently rapidly, then it can more than offset economic growth to deliver stable or falling environmental impact.

However, in reality, the economic growth rate is almost always higher than the reduction rate of environmental impact per unit of output, so that the global consumption of most natural resources and the global generation of most pollutants continue to grow exponentially. Why has capitalist technological progress failed to deliver ecological sustainability?

To begin with, the pace of technological progress is limited by the pace of infrastructure transformation. Each year only a fraction of the existing capital equipment and buildings may be replaced. Suppose an economy each year replaces 5 percent of its capital infrastructure. Making the heroic assumption that the new capital is twice as efficient as the old capital so that the environmental impact per unit of output falls by 50 percent for the new capital, for the economy as a whole, this represents a reduction of environmental impact per unit of output by 2.5 percent. But a modern advanced capitalist economy often needs a 3 percent economic growth rate to prevent the unemployment rate from rising. Thus, even with this very optimistic assumption about technological progress, the rate of technological progress is smaller than the economic growth rate, implying rising environmental impact.

From a physical science point of view, human economic activities inevitably involve either physical or chemical transformation of the physical world. For the physical or chemical transformations to take place, human activities have to consume some material resources and will inevitably generate some environmental impact. Therefore, the environmental impact per unit of output can never fall to zero. On the other hand, under capitalism, the economic output tends to grow toward infinity. The environmental impact thus inevitably tends to grow in the long run.

In addition to the technical-physical limits, there are fundamental political-economic limits to capitalist solutions of the ecological crisis. Under capitalism, the environment is treated as an "externality" that is free from the point of view of individual capitalists. In a free capitalist market, environmental degradation does not cost individual capitalists anything. There is every incentive for an individual capitalist to maximize environmental degradation for the purpose of profit maximization.

The standard solution to this problem of "externality" is to have the nation-state intervene in the capitalist market. The state may influence the behavior of individual capitalists by using taxes, subsidies, or regulations to get the prices "right" (that is, to modify the market prices so that they take into account the social costs of environmental degradation).

This solution may work under certain conditions, if the environmental problem is relatively small so that the correction of the problem does not cost a significant amount to capitalist accumulation, and if the environmental problem's impact is mostly limited to within the boundary of a nation-state.

However, different aspects of the global ecological system are inherently interrelated. Today, virtually all of the important aspects of the ecological crisis (such as climate change, ocean acidification, deforestation, desertification, soil erosion, water shortage and pollution, and peak oil) are taking place on global scales, and many of them would require a significant amount of financial resources to be addressed. It is beyond the capacity of any nation-state to address the global ecological crisis.

Capitalism has evolved as a system of nation-states. In the capitalist world system, states compete with each other constantly and intensely, in both economic and military terms. To prevail in competition, each state is compelled to promote capital accumulation and pursue maximum economic growth. The states that fail to achieve rapid economic growth tend to suffer from economic and political instability, and they then turn into "failed states."

In this context, any state that engages in environmental regulation that tends to raise the cost of accumulation puts itself at a disadvantage in the interstate competition. The system of interstate competition thus discourages capitalist states from undertaking effective environmental regulations, especially those required to address global environmental problems.

It may be argued that the problem of global ecological crisis could be solved through international cooperation. All capitalist states, or at least all of the major states, may arrive at an international agreement to take simultaneous actions required to deal with the ecological crisis. There are several problems with this solution.

First, an international agreement on global environmental regulations would affect different states differently. Some states may suffer a greater loss of economic growth than some other states, or the implied reduction of economic growth may affect political and social stability in some states. Those states that would be seriously affected would refuse to cooperate, making it impossible for the international agreement to be reached.

Second, the capitalist world system is highly unequal, divided between advanced capitalist countries and peripheral countries. To some extent, peripheral countries need rapid economic growth more than advanced capitalist countries to maintain internal stability and keep up with the interstate competition. Thus, any meaningful international agreement on global environmental regulations would have to arrange to have the advanced capitalist countries compensate the peripheral countries for the loss of economic growth. In reality, the advanced capitalist countries most likely would not be willing to pay or would only pay an insufficient amount.

Third, even if an international agreement may be reached, under the interstate system, there are always incentives for some states to "cheat" on the international agreement, to pursue maximum economic growth themselves while shifting the costs of environmental regulations onto other states.

The inability of the capitalist system to address the global ecological crisis is only one example of the system's general failure to find system-level solutions to system-level problems.

## System-Level Solutions to System-Level Problems?

The nation-state system is essential for the normal operation of capitalism. Interstate competition compels the states to protect capitalist property rights and motivates the states to promote capital accumulation. However, excessive interstate competition could lead to the system's self-destruction. Moreover, as each state pursues only its self-interest, there is the question of how the system's long-term, collective interests may be promoted.

For the capitalist world system to function well, there are some long-term, collective interests that cannot be effectively provided at the nation-state level. For example, how to provide "peace" or prevent major wars between the states? How to coordinate different states' economic policies and secure stable expansion of effective demand at the system level? How to regulate the global environment? All of these are system-level problems that require system-level solutions.

On the other hand, the capitalist world system cannot operate with a world government. If there is indeed a world government with sufficient political power to impose its will on the entire system, then the state (the world government) could prove to be too powerful relative to the individual capitalists. Under certain political conditions, the state may be pressured or motivated to take over much of the surplus product, leading to an end of the capitalist system.

In reality, capitalism has managed to balance the requirement of interstate competition with the need for system-level solutions through successive cycles of hegemonic power. The United Provinces of Holland, the United Kingdom, and the United States have been successive hegemonic powers.

To function as an effective hegemonic power, it is necessary for the hegemonic state to be sufficiently large and to enjoy overwhelming superiority in industrial, financial, and military power relative to other states. Historically, as capitalism expands and grows in complexity, there has been a tendency for the hegemonic state to expand accordingly. Each hegemonic state was much larger than the previous one in term of territorial size and organizational capacity.

As the United States is a continent-sized state, the historical process of hegemonic expansion seems to have reached the limit. As the US hegemonic power is in decline, none of the other continent-sized big states (such as China, India, Russia, Brazil, and the European Union) has a realistic chance to replace the United States to become the next hegemony (Arrighi, 1994).

China may soon overtake the United States to become the world's largest economy. But China could never hope to acquire the overwhelming superiority that the United States enjoyed shortly after World War II. China continues to lag behind the United States in almost all technological frontiers, the Chinese military remains a regional rather than a global power, and China suffers from insurmountable limits set by its internal natural resources and ecological space. The other big states have even smaller chances to replace the United States.

In the foreseeable future, the United States will remain one of the world's largest economies and definitely the world's most formidable military power. But it has lost the overwhelming superiority so that today it is neither willing nor able to provide the necessary system-level solutions to the important system-level problems (Arrighi, 2009).

On the question of maintaining global "peace" or systemwide geopolitical stability, a vital issue has to do with preventing nuclear proliferation. The reality is that a range of middle-sized states have by now developed or nearly developed the capacity to make nuclear bombs. The US strategic failures in Iraq and Afghanistan will probably accelerate nuclear proliferation and potentially could destabilize entire regions from the Middle East to South Asia.

On the question of securing the expansion of global effective demand, over the past one or two decades the world has relied on debt-financed US consumption to lead the global economic expansion. But the process has been inherently unsustainable. In response to the Great Recession of 2009, the US government attempted to keep the economy afloat through massive deficit spending. While in the short run the US government deficit has succeeded in preventing another Great Depression, in the medium and long run, it (along with the structural tendency of rising pension and health-care costs) has set the United States on the path of fiscal bankruptcy.

With respect to the global ecological crisis and especially the impending catastrophe of climate change, the United States has clearly failed to provide any lead in reducing greenhouse gas emissions. Even if the United States were to play a "leading" role in greenhouse gas emission reduction, it would do little good to stabilize the climate unless countries such as China and India would take active steps to reduce emissions. In reality, global negotiations on climate stabilization have so far failed to produce any meaningful results, and global greenhouse gas emissions continue to rise on a catastrophic path.

## The Political Economy beyond Capitalism

There has been a long-term tendency for wage and taxation costs to rise in the advanced capitalist countries. As the non-Western working classes grow in size and learn to get organized, this tendency may start to operate in much of the non-Western world. The rise of global wage and taxation costs would reduce the global profit rate, depriving capitalism of its historical space for social compromise.

After centuries of relentless accumulation, global capitalism has also exhausted the environmental space and the global ecological system is now on the verge of collapse.

As the US hegemonic power is in decline, none of the other big states is in a position to replace the United States to provide system-level solutions to system-level problems. Thus, exactly when the capitalist world system is suffering from a structural crisis, it is also deprived of the effective leadership that would be required if the system were to overcome the crisis.

The combination of these historical factors suggests that the existing social system (capitalism based on production for profit and endless accumulation of capital) is likely to have reached its own historical limit. As the existing system struggles with the structural crisis, there will be intense conflicts among different states, classes, and social groups in the coming decades. The outcome of these conflicts will determine the fate of humanity for centuries to come.

It is conceivable that capitalism may survive the immediate crisis and undertake certain institutional restructurings that would reestablish conditions favoring rapid capital accumulation in the short run. However, in that case, the world is almost certainly heading toward unprecedented ecological catastrophes and the human civilization may not survive.

Under another possible scenario, the ruling class of the existing system may realize that the current system is no longer sustainable. Given this understanding, the ruling elites may choose to transform both the system and themselves so that they will continue to function as a ruling class under a different systemic arrangement. The world may return to some form of precapitalist society with a high degree of inequality. The ruling class exercises monopolistic control over the surplus product. But because the surplus product is mostly consumed or wasted, the global ecological crisis may be alleviated.

Under the third possible scenario, the coming global conflicts will eventually be resolved in a way that is favorable for the world's great majority that have lived under capitalist exploitation. The world will be transformed into a more democratic and more egalitarian system. What is the chance for such an outcome to materialize?

Under capitalism, much of the world's population has been transformed into proletarianized working classes that have learned to get organized for economic and political struggles. Capitalism has also helped to popularize basic education, and "liberal democracy" has become the established political norm. Thus, the collective political consciousness and organizational capacity of the global working population have reached a level that is perhaps higher than in all previous historical periods.

The key question is whether these trends will be sustained in the coming decades and whether the non-Western working classes will join the Western working classes to demand and secure a broad range of economic, social, and political rights. If yes, then the joint forces of the global working classes may be sufficient to turn the global balance of power to their own favor and decide how the world will be transformed in the twenty-first century.

The overwhelming challenge for humanity is to take urgent actions to address the coming ecological crisis and rebuild the global economy in accordance with principles of ecological sustainability. The global environmental impact has to be stabilized at a sustainable level. This in turn requires that the future economic system has to operate as a steady-state economy (that is, an economy with zero economic growth).

To have a steady-state economy, society's surplus product must not be used for capital accumulation. Instead, it has to be subject to society's democratic control and used for public consumption (such as education, health care, environmental cleaning, or general reduction of working time). It follows that the future economic system must not be one that is based on market relations. As is argued above, the dominance of market relations leads to relentless completion, forcing producers to pursue endless accumulation of capital.

According to the classical Marxist conception, the future postcapitalist economy should be based on public ownership of the means of production and societywide planning (Engels, 1978 [1880]). After the collapse of the Soviet Union, this conception has been widely criticized on the ground that the Soviet-style socialist economy was less efficient than capitalism (for an example of this argument, see Roemer, 1994).

In the light of the overwhelming global problems confronting humanity today, this criticism of socialism is no longer relevant. In term of the IPAT formula, a less "efficient" (that is, with a higher "T" or environmental impact per unit of output) but steady-state economy could achieve ecological sustainability by choosing a lower "P" (population) or lower "A" (per capita output). On the other hand, a more "efficient" economy (with a lower "T") would nevertheless be ecologically unsustainable if it keeps growing, leading to increasingly larger "I" (the overall environmental impact).

The future socialist system based on economic and political democracy may or may not be more "efficient" than capitalism as the concept is conventionally defined. But it is quite obvious that a system of socialist planning would allow the society to directly decide the size, the composition, and the uses of the surplus product. Thus, with socialist planning, the society can collectively choose to have a steady-state economy. With capitalism, the society cannot.

To effectively deal with the global ecological crisis, the postcapitalist society will have to find ways to go beyond the capitalist system of nation-states and develop a new global system based on global cooperation. Ideally, a system of global democracy will eventually emerge and replace the current system of nation-states. Short of a global democracy, the postcapitalist states will need to at least find ways to reach global democratic consensus on all important global issues.

If the postcapitalist society fails to achieve this, it may be a matter of time before the competition between different states takes the world back onto the path of capitalist-style accumulation and global ecological destruction.

This will be the ultimate test of humanity's collective wisdom. The hope is that when the great majority of the people in the world do have the opportunity to free themselves from exploitation and collectively decide their own fate in democratic ways, they will realize where their essential interests lie and act accordingly.

## References

Armstrong, Philip, Andrew Glyn, and John Harrison. (1991). *Capitalism since 1945*. Oxford: Basil Blackwell.

Arrighi, Giovanni. (1994). *The Long Twentieth Century: Money, Power, and the Origins of Our Times*. London: Verso.

Arrighi, Giovanni. (2009). *Adam Smith in Beijing: Lineages of the 21st Century*. London: Verso.

Arrighi, Giovanni, Po-keung Hui, Ho-fung Hung, and Mark Selden. (2003). "Historical Capitalism, East and West." In Giovanni Arrighi, Takeshi Hamashita, and Mark Selden, eds., *The Resurgence of East Asia: 500, 150 and 50 Year Perspective*, 259–333. London: Routledge.

Cecchetti, Stephen G., M. S. Mohanty, and Fabrizio Sampolli. (2010). "The Future of Public Debt: Prospects and Implications." Bank of International Settlement Working Papers, Number 300. http://www.bis.org/publ/work300.pdf.

Engels, Friedrich. (1978 [1880]). "Socialism: Utopian and Scientific." In Robert C. Tucker, ed., *The Marx-Engels Reader*, 683–717. New York: W. W. Norton.

Keynes, John Maynard. (1964 [1936]). *The General Theory of Employment, Interest and Money*. New York: First Harvest/Harcourt.

Li, Minqi. (2008). *The Rise of China and the Demise of the Capitalist World-Economy*. London: Pluto Press.

Li, Minqi. (2009). "Socialization of Risks without Socialization of Investment: the Minsky Paradox and the Structural Contradiction of Big Government Capitalism." The Political Economy Research Institute of University of Massachusetts at Amherst, Working Paper 205. http://www.peri.umass.edu/fileadmin/pdf/working_papers/working_papers_201-250/WP205.pdf.

Maddison, Angus. (2003). *The World Economy: Historical Statistics*. Paris: Organisation for Economic Co-operation and Development.

Marx, Karl. (1967 [1867]). *Capital*. Vol. 1. New York: International Publishers.

Marx, Karl. (1967 [1885]). *Capital*. Vol. 2. New York: International Publishers.

Marx, Karl, and Friedrich Engels. (1978 [1848]). "The Manifesto of the Communist Party." In Robert C. Tucker, ed., *The Marx-Engels Reader*, 469–500. New York: W. W. Norton.

Meadows, Donnella, Jorgen Randers, and Dennis Meadows. (2005). *Limits to Growth: The 30-Year Update*. London: Earthscan.

Minsky, Hyman P. (2008 [1986]). *Stabilizing an Unstable Economy*. New York: McGraw-Hill.

Pollin, Robert, and Gary Dymski. (1994). "The Costs and Benefits of Financial Instability: Big Government Capitalism and the Minsky Paradox." In Gary Dymski and Robert Pollin, eds., *New Perspectives in Monetary Macroeconomics: Explorations in the Tradition of Hyman P. Minsky*. Ann Arbor: University of Michigan Press.

Roemer, John E. (1994). *A Future for Socialism*. Cambridge, MA: Harvard University Press.

Spratt, David, and Philip Sutton. (2009). *Climate Code Red: The Case for Emergency Action*. Carlton North, Australia: Scribe.

Stavrianos, Leften Stavros. (1981). *Global Rift: The Third World Comes of Age*. New York: William Morrow.

Wallerstein, Immanuel. (1979). *The Capitalist World-Economy*. Cambridge: Cambridge University Press.

Wallerstein, Immanuel. (1983). *Historical Capitalism*. London: Verso.

# Index

Tables, figures, and boxes are indicated by an italic *t*, *f*, or *b* following the page number.